EVIDENCE

How to use your Connected Casebook

Step 1: Go to **www.CasebookConnect.com** and redeem your access code to get started.

Access Code: SSKEVD5969688111

Step 2: Go to your **BOOKSHELF** and select your Connected Casebook to start reading, highlighting, and taking notes in the margins of your e-book.

Step 3: Select the **STUDY** tab in your toolbar to access a variety of practice materials designed to help you master the course material. These materials may include explanations, videos, multiple-choice questions, flashcards, short answer, essays, and issue spotting.

Step 4: Select the **OUTLINE** tab in your toolbar to access chapter outlines that automatically incorporate your highlights and annotations from the e-book. Use the My Notes area for copying, pasting, and editing your book notes or creating new notes.

Step 5: If your professor has enrolled your class, you can select the **CLASS INSIGHTS** tab and compare your own study center results against the average of your classmates.

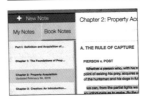

ASPEN CASEBOOK SERIES

Evidence
CASES, COMMENTARY, AND PROBLEMS

Fifth Edition

David A. Sklansky
Stanford University

Andrea L. Roth
University of California, Berkeley

Published by Wolters Kluwer in New York.

Wolters Kluwer Legal & Regulatory U.S. serves customers worldwide with CCH, Aspen Publishers, and Kluwer Law International products. (www.WKLegaledu.com)

To contact Customer Service, e-mail customer.service@wolterskluwer.com, call 1-800-234-1660, fax 1-800-901-9075, or mail correspondence to:

Wolters Kluwer
Attn: Order Department
PO Box 990
Frederick, MD 21705

Printed in the United States of America.

1 2 3 4 5 6 7 8 9 0

ISBN 978-1-5438-0457-7

Library of Congress Cataloging-in-Publication Data

Names: Sklansky, David A., 1959- author. | Roth, Andrea, author.
Title: Evidence : cases, commentary, and problems / David Alan Sklansky,
    Stanley Morrison Professor of Law, Stanford Law School, Faculty
    Co-Director, Stanford Criminal Justice Center; Andrea Roth, Professor of
    Law, UC Berkeley School of Law, Faculty Director, Berkeley Center for
    Law and Technology.
Description: Fifth edition. | New York : Wolters Kluwer, [2020] | Series:
    Aspen casebook series | Includes bibliographical references and index. |
    Summary: "A highly flexible, case-based set of materials focusing on
    core concepts and central controversies in evidence law"—Provided by
    publisher.
Identifiers: LCCN 2019055437 (print) | LCCN 2019055438 (ebook) | ISBN
    9781543804577 (hardcover) | ISBN 9781543819649 (ebook)
Subjects: LCSH: Evidence (Law)—United States. | LCGFT: Casebooks (Law)
Classification: LCC KF8935 .S54 2020 (print) | LCC KF8935 (ebook) | DDC
    347.73/6—dc23
LC record available at https://lccn.loc.gov/2019055437
LC ebook record available at https://lccn.loc.gov/2019055438

About Wolters Kluwer Legal & Regulatory U.S.

Wolters Kluwer Legal & Regulatory U.S. delivers expert content and solutions in the areas of law, corporate compliance, health compliance, reimbursement, and legal education. Its practical solutions help customers successfully navigate the demands of a changing environment to drive their daily activities, enhance decision quality, and inspire confident outcomes.

Serving customers worldwide, its legal and regulatory portfolio includes products under the Aspen Publishers, CCH Incorporated, Kluwer Law International, ftwilliam.com, and MediRegs names. They are regarded as exceptional and trusted resources for general legal and practice-specific knowledge, compliance and risk management, dynamic workflow solutions, and expert commentary.

To Andrea's parents,
Tom and Yvonne Roth,
and to David's brothers,
Mark and Jeff Sklansky

Summary of Contents

CONTENTS

5   OTHER FORBIDDEN INFERENCES

10 PRIVILEGES

11   PHYSICAL EVIDENCE

12   BURDENS, PRESUMPTIONS, AND JUDICIAL NOTICE   757

PREFACE

Evidence law is steeped in the drama of trials. It is critically important for any lawyer who might ever set foot in a courtroom. And it is just plain fascinating. For all these reasons, we love teaching the subject, and most students seem to enjoy learning it.

But students also tend to find evidence law difficult. The rules of evidence are notoriously complicated and confusing. Much of evidence law makes sense only against the backdrop of Anglo-American trial procedure, with which law students typically have only limited familiarity. And students, along with lawyers and judges, often are puzzled by the very nature of evidence law. Is it statutory, judge-made, or a matter of applied logic?

We have tried in this book to capitalize on the inherent attractions of evidence law and to minimize its difficulty. Because actual cases are more interesting and more memorable than made-up problems, the book has more cases than problems. The cases have been selected to illustrate the central concepts and controversies of evidence law, not to provide encyclopedic coverage of the subject, and they have been edited tightly. Problems have been used selectively, sometimes to test students' understanding of the rules, sometimes to highlight ambiguities, and sometimes to encourage reflection on what the rules are trying to accomplish and how well they succeed. Many of the problems are drawn from real cases. Because the Federal Rules of Evidence provide a convenient and now pervasive framework for thinking about evidence law, the structure of the book tracks, wherever possible, the structure of the federal rules. The major exceptions to the ban on hearsay, for example, are addressed in the same order here as in the Federal Rules of Evidence. Because the legislative history of the federal rules, particularly the Advisory Committee's Notes, have proved so highly influential, the cases are accompanied by edited excerpts from the Advisory Committee Notes and, where relevant, congressional reports and floor debates. Because academic commentary has played such a large role in the development of evidence law—and because much of that commentary is so interesting—we have added excerpts from the writings of a wide range of scholars. Wigmore and Morgan are here, but so are Mirjan Damaška and Jennifer Mnookin. These excerpts, too, have been edited tightly, in part to allow room for multiple perspectives.

The book is designed so that it can be presented cover to cover in a four-unit course. The topics are arranged in the order that we address them, but other instructors may choose to vary the sequence. In view of the steadily increasing importance of scientific evidence, probabilistic proof, expert testimony, and demonstrative exhibits, we have included more materials on these topics than evidence casebooks typically contain. We also have included readings on certain other topics traditionally slighted in evidence courses, such as questioning by the judge and by the jury. We have found that students enjoy studying all of these issues, and we think they are sufficiently important to warrant the space we have given them. But instructors who disagree can easily skip those portions of the book or assign readings from them selectively.

This edition, the fifth, is the first that Andrea has co-authored, and it contains a good deal of new material. We have added new cases, new commentary, and new problems throughout the book. There are three entirely new sections: one on hearsay and machine-generated evidence, one on digital forensics, and one on authentication of digital evidence. The materials on scientific proof, judicial notice, and character evidence in sexual assault cases have been updated and substantially revised. We have also added a significant amount of new material in the chapters on hearsay and on privileges. To keep the book a manageable length, we have dropped some older material made redundant by the additions.

We owe thanks to many people. Hundreds of law students at UCLA, Berkeley, Harvard and Stanford have sharpened our understanding of evidence law and made teaching the subject a joy. Several students, in particular, gave countless hours of their time to improving this book and its supporting materials: on the first edition, Carolyn Hoff, Christina Johnson, Hien Nguyn, Meghan Habersack, Robert Horton, and Jonathan Phillips; on the second edition, Katie Wozencroft; on the fourth edition, Brandon Martinez; and on the fifth edition, Ryan Shelley and Safa Ansari-Bayegan. Our editors at Aspen, Wolters Kluwer, and the Froebe Group have been a pleasure to work with. Steven Clymer, Daniel Richman, and several anonymous reviewers criticized early drafts of the first edition of this book perceptively and constructively. Michael Beach graciously helped with the "probability primer" in Chapter 9. A number of instructors who used earlier editions of the book have offered sound and valuable advice for revising it; we are particularly grateful in this regard to George Bach, David Eggert, Tamara Lave, Erin Murphy, Anna Roberts, Avani Mehta Sood, Shanin Specter, James Tomkovicz, and the late Welsh White. Conversations over the years with Paul Bergman, Scott Brewer, Samia Fam, George Fisher, Jeff Fisher, Bob Gordon, Ken Graham, Jimmy Klein, Sandy Levick, Eleanor Swift, Jan Vetter, Alex Whiting, and John Wiley have deepened our understanding of evidence law and made this a better book. We have been blessed at UCLA, at Berkeley, at Harvard, and at Stanford with terrific librarians and strong clerical support. And we never could have finished this book, or even started it, without the support and forbearance of our spouses, Deborah Lambe and John Paul Reichmuth.

David Sklansky
Andrea Roth

November 2019

ACKNOWLEDGMENTS

Mirko Bagaric & Kumar Amarasekara, The Prejudice Against Similar Fact Evidence, 5 Int'l J. Evid. & Proof 71 (2001). Reprinted with permission of Vathek Publishing.

Vaughn C. Ball, The Myth of Conditional Relevance, 14 Ga. L. Rev. 435 (1980). Reprinted with permission of the Georgia Law Review.

Benjamin H. Barton, Do Judges Systematically Favor the Interests of the Legal Profession?, 59 Alabama L. Rev. (2008). Reprinted with permission of the author and the Alabama Law Review.

Jeffrey Bellin and Andrew Guthrie Ferguson, Trial By Google: Judicial Notice in The Information Age 108 Nw. U.L. Rev. 1137, 1159-68, 1174, 1181 (2014).

Kenneth S. Broun, ed., McCormick on Evidence (6th ed. 2006), published by West Group. Copyright © 1954, 1972, 1984, 1987, 1999 by West Publishing Co.; copyright © 2006 by West Group. Reprinted with permission of Thomson Reuters.

Daniel J. Capra & Liesa L. Richter, Character Assassination: Amending Federal Rule of Evidence 404 (B) to Protect Criminal Defendants. 118 Colum. L. Rev. 769 (2018). Reprinted with permission of Columbia Law Review via Copyright Clearance Center.

Mirjan Damaška, Evidence Law Adrift (1997), published by Yale University Press. Copyright © 1997 by Yale University.

James J. Duane, The New Federal Rules of Evidence on Prior Acts of Accused Sex Offenders, published by Carolina University Press.

Robert A. Dykstra, Sallie Hillmon and the Bizarre Origins of the Hillmon Rule 97 Judicature 297 (2014).

David L. Faigman, David H. Kaye, Michael J. Saks & Joseph Sanders, How Good Is Good Enough? Expert Evidence Under *Daubert* and *Kumho*, 50 Case W. Res. L. Rev. 645 (2000).

G. Michael Fenner, The Residual Exception to the Hearsay Rule, 33 Creighton L. Rev. 265 (2000). Reprinted with permission of the author.

Richard D. Friedman, Character Impeachment Evidence: The Asymmetrical Interaction Between Personality and Situation, 43 Duke L. J. 826 (1994).

Richard D. Friedman, "E" Is for Eclectic: Multiple Perspectives on Evidence, 87 Va. L. Rev. 2029 (2001).

Brandon Garrett, The Reliable Application of Fingerprint Evidence. 66 UCLA L. Rev 64, 68 (2018).

Victor Gold, Do the Federal Rules of Evidence Matter?, 25 Loyola L.A. L. Rev. 909 (1992). Reprinted with permission of the author and Loyola of Los Angeles Law Review.

Robert H. Hutchins & Donald Slesinger, Some Observations on the Law of Evidence. This article originally appeared at 28 Colum. L. Rev. 432, 437-439 (1928).

Jonathan J. Koehler, Forensics Or Fauxrensics? Ascertaining Accuracy in Forensic Sciences, 49 Ariz. St. L. J. 1369, 1378-1381 (2017).

John H. Langbein, Historical Foundations of the Law of Evidence: A View from the Ryder Sources. This article originally appeared at 96 Colum. L. Rev. 1168 (1996).

Joseph H. Levie, Hearsay and Conspiracy, 52 Mich. L. Rev. 1159 (1954). Reprinted with permission of the author and Michigan Law Review.

Graham C. Lilly, An Introduction to the Law of Evidence (3d ed. 1996), published by West Publishing Co. Copyright © 1996 by West Publishing Co. Reprinted with permission of West Academic.

Kevin C. McMunigal & Calvin William Sharpe, Reforming Extrinsic Impeachment, 33 Conn. L. Rev. 363, 385-388 (2001). Reprinted with permission of the authors and Connecticut Law Review.

Thomas M. Mengler, The Theory of Discretion in the Federal Rules of Evidence, 74 Iowa L. Rev. 413, 417, 423-424 (1989). Reprinted with permission of the author and Iowa Law Review.

Jennifer Mnookin, The Image of Truth: Photographic Evidence and the Power of Analogy, 10 Yale J. L. & Human. 1, 5, 43-44, 64-65, 70 (1998). Reprinted with permission of the author.

Christopher B. Mueller & Laird C. Kirkpatrick, Evidence, §5.6, at 309-311 (5th ed. 2012) Reprinted with permission of Wolters Kluwer.

Erin Murphy, The New Forensics: Criminal Justice, False Certainty, and the Second Generation of Scientific Evidence, 95 Cal. L. Rev. 721 (2007). Reprinted with permission of the author and California Law Review.

Dale A. Nance, The Best Evidence Principle, 73 Iowa L. Rev. 227 (1998). Reprinted with permission of the author and Iowa Law Review.

Roger C. Park, Evidence Scholarship, Old and New, 75 Minn. L. Rev. 849 (1991). Reprinted with permission of the author and Minnesota Law Review.

Barbara Pfeffer Billauer, Daubert Debunked: A History of Legal Retrogression and the Need to Reassess "Scientific Admissibility" 21 Suffolk J. Trial & App. Advoc. 1, 46-47 (2015-2016).

Daniel C. Richman, Old Chief v. United States: Stipulating Away Prosecutorial Accountability? 83 Va. L. Rev. 939 (1997). Reprinted with permission of the author.

D. Michael Risinger, Navigating Expert Reliability: Are Criminal Standards of Certainty Being Left on the Dock?, 64 Alb. L. Rev. 99 (2000).

Anna Roberts, Reclaiming the Importance of the Defendant's Testimony: Prior Conviction Impeachment and the Fight Against Implicit Stereotyping, 83 U. Chi. L. Rev. 835, 836-838 (2016).

Stephen A. Saltzburg, Michael M. Martin & Daniel J. Capra, Federal Rules of Evidence Manual (7th ed. 1998), published by Lexis Law Publishing. §413.01[1], at 2:413-2 to 413-3 (11th ed. 2015).

Stephen A. Saltzburg, Michael M. Martin & Daniel J. Capra, Federal Rules of Evidence Manual, published by Lexis Law Publishing. §106.02[5], at 1:106-9 to 106–110 (10th ed. 2015).

David A. Sklansky & Stephen C. Yeazell, Comparative Law Without Leaving Home: What Civil Procedure Can Teach Criminal Procedure and Vice Versa, 94 Geo. L. J. 683 (2006). Reprinted with permission of the authors and Georgetown Law Review.

Christopher Slobogin, Doubts About Daubert: Psychiatric Anecdata as a Case Study, 57 Wash. & Lee L. Rev. 919 (2000). Reprinted with permission of the author and Washington & Lee Law Review.

Eleanor Swift, One Hundred Years of Evidence Law Reform: Thayer's Triumph, 88 Cal. L. Rev. 2437 (2000). Copyright © 2000 by the California Law Review. Reprinted by permission of the author and the University of California, Berkeley.

Laurence H. Tribe, Triangulating Hearsay, 87 Harv. L. Rev. 957, 958–961 (1974). Copyright © 1974 by the Harvard Law Review Association. Reprinted with permission of the author and the Harvard Law Review Association.

Jon R. Waltz, The Present-Sense Impression Exception to the Rule Against Hearsay: Origins and Attributes, 66 Iowa L. Rev. 869 (1981). Reprinted with permission of the author and Iowa Law Review.

Glen Weissenberger, The Former Testimony Exception: A Study in Rulemaking, Judicial Revisionism, and the Separation of Powers, 67 N.C. L. Rev. 295 (1989). Reprinted with permission of the author.

Glen Weissenberger & James J. Duane, Federal Rules of Evidence (7th ed. 2011). Carolina Academic Press. Reprinted with permission.

John Shepard Wiley Jr., Taming Patent: Six Steps for Surviving Scary Patent Cases, UCLA L. Rev. 1413 (2002). Reprinted with permission of the author.

Charles Alan Wright & Kenneth W. Graham Jr., Federal Practice and Procedure: Evidence (1980), published by West Publishing Co. Copyright © 1980 by West Publishing Co. Reprinted with permission of Thomson Reuters.

INTRODUCTION TO EVIDENCE LAW

"I took aim, pulled the trigger, and then, suddenly, shots rang out."

A. GOOD NEWS AND BAD NEWS

The Law of Evidence, which I now propose to investigate, is also one of the landmarks of civilization which it is impossible for the philosophical inquirer to overlook.

> John George Phillimore, *The History and Principles of the Law of Evidence as Illustrating Our Social Progress* (1850)

[T]he system, taken in the aggregate, is repugnant to the ends of justice; and . . . this is true of almost every rule that has ever been laid down on the subject of evidence.

> Jeremy Bentham, *Rationale of Judicial Evidence* (1827)

Nobody can fairly pretend to make the Anglo-American law of evidence easy, because it is essentially very difficult.

> John MacArthur Maguire, *Evidence: Common Sense and Common Law* (1947)

[F]oreigners complain that its doctrines and practices are arcane and that they deviate too far from ordinary modes of investigating facts. But even in these laments there is a soupçon of uneasy respect for the exotic charms of the common law.

> Mirjan R. Damaška, *Evidence Law Adrift* (1997)

Foreigners are not the only ones intrigued by the Anglo-American law of evidence. Americans are transfixed, too. Countless movies and television shows feature lawyers squabbling over arcane rules of proof, captivating viewers who may never have dreamed of attending law school. Contributory negligence and implied warranties rarely surface in on-screen dramas, but hearsay doctrine and testimonial privileges come up regularly. Evidence law is a fixture of popular culture.

And for excellent reason. The rules of evidence dictate how and when facts may be proved or disproved at a trial. They regulate, that is to say, our most dramatic and most heavily ritualized process for untangling human affairs gone wrong—a process to which many lawyers happily devote much of their careers. Evidence law constitutes the end product of centuries of effort to make that process as fair, as accurate, and as conclusive as possible. Opinions differ regarding the success of those efforts. But as social artifacts alone, the rules of evidence hold a lasting fascination.

For lawyers, of course, the interest is more than academic. The rules of evidence are the nuts and bolts of courtroom work. Mastering them hardly turns you into a skilled trial lawyer. That takes a good deal more. But without a basic knowledge of evidence law, you cannot even begin to find your way around a courtroom.

Not all lawyers try cases. But all lawyers need familiarity with the rules of evidence, and not just to pass the bar exam. Litigators, even if they are not trial lawyers, need to understand what happens if a case goes to trial. And every lawyer, even one who never litigates, works in the shadow of litigation. All effective legal work is informed in part by the contingency of litigation;

the contingency of litigation is in part the contingency of trial, and the contingency of trial is strongly shaped by evidence law.

Then, too, careers in the law often take unexpected turns. It always pays to be prepared. Trial work is undeniably exciting, and even lawyers who plan never to see the inside of a courtroom can wind up trying cases and enjoying it. Both co-authors of this book tried cases, one as a prosecutor and one as a public defender.

The rules of evidence are thus critically important, particularly for lawyers, and of extraordinary intellectual interest. They may not be "impossible for the philosophical inquirer to overlook," but they amply reward study. And evidence cases can be entertaining, too. They are rooted, after all, in the drama of the courtroom. For all these reasons, few students find evidence law boring, and many greatly enjoy learning it.

That is the good news.

Now for the bad news. Evidence has a reputation as a particularly challenging subject, and the reputation is not entirely undeserved. Several features of evidence law can make it difficult to study. You might as well know about them from the start.

First, evidence law often operates in technical and counterintuitive ways. Some evidence doctrines do take the mushy form familiar to you from other law school courses: "Do X when it is sensible." But many other rules of evidence are considerably more complicated, and they often produce surprising results. The hearsay rule, in particular, can make even treacherous doctrines like the rule against perpetuities look commonsensical by comparison. (That is one reason the hearsay chapter is by far the longest chapter in this book.) Moreover, most evidence rules rely on assumptions about human behavior and psychology that—to put it mildly—have not been subject to rigorous empirical testing.

Second, the rules of evidence frequently cannot be applied without reference to the substantive law governing a particular dispute—the law of contracts, torts, property, or crimes. You have probably already studied these areas of the law, but your knowledge may be rusty or incomplete. This can make it difficult to follow the application of evidence law to specific fact patterns, either real or hypothetical.

Third, there is the terminology. All fields of law employ specialized vocabularies. Evidence law is not unusual in this respect. But the specialized vocabulary of evidence law is particularly large, and the same word or phrase often has two or three completely different meanings. Even the most basic terms of evidence law—terms like "relevant," "competent," "collateral," or "in issue"—sometimes show a maddening slipperiness. Lawyers and judges talking about evidence law sometimes use these terms in their ordinary, everyday senses, and sometimes use them in narrower, more technical ways. It can be hard to keep the definitions straight.

Fourth, beyond matters of terminology, the nature of evidence law itself can seem slippery. At times it can be hard to know exactly what you are studying. What exactly *is* evidence law? Is it a set of common law doctrines? Statutory rules? Constitutional dictates? Applied logic?

A few decades ago this kind of confusion was less likely. Evidence law was almost entirely judge-made and operated within few constitutional constraints. Since then the constitutional constraints have increased, but not by much. The larger change has been the advent of modern codes of evidence. Following years of study, California enacted a comprehensive and influential code of evidence rules in 1965. That same year, an Advisory Committee of judges, lawyers, and law professors appointed by the Supreme Court began drafting federal rules of evidence, much as similar committees earlier had worked out the Federal Rules of Civil Procedure and the Federal Rules of Criminal Procedure. The result was the Federal Rules of Evidence, which were endorsed by the Supreme Court in 1972, enacted by Congress (with significant amendments) in 1974, and signed into law in 1975. Most states now have evidence codes modeled closely on the federal rules. California has retained its own code, though, and in a few other jurisdictions—New York and Washington, D.C., for example—evidence law remains uncodified.

When studying evidence law, you can therefore be at sea regarding what you should be learning, particularly if you plan to practice in a state, like California or New York, that does not have an evidence code tracking the Federal Rules of Evidence. Should you concentrate on the federal rules, which have become so widely influential? Should you focus on the common law doctrines those rules codify? Should you pay greatest attention to the rules in your own state?

Nor is this all. Most questions regarding the admissibility of evidence are resolved by trial judges without written opinions, and appellate reversals of these decisions are relatively rare. Many evidence rules expressly vest broad discretion in trial judges to admit or exclude evidence, and even when appellate judges conclude that a trial judge erred, they frequently deem the error harmless. Therefore, the law on the books often matters less than the law as trial judges apply it. As Professor Maguire put it, "evidence is essentially a matter to be threshed out between counsel and judge in the trial court. The wheat stays there; what goes up in the appellate record seems pretty much chaff." What, then, should you care about: what appellate courts say, or how trial courts act?

There is a fifth and final reason evidence law can be particularly hard to learn. The rules of evidence operate against the backdrop of a more basic set of rules regarding the structure of the Anglo-American trial: rules about the sequence of proof, when and how the lawyers may address the jury, and so on. These rules are matters more of convention than of law, and they have remained largely uncodified. The rules of evidence, and cases applying those rules, often assume familiarity with these conventions without explaining them. This is fine for the principal users of evidence law: trial judges and trial lawyers. They know how trials are conducted. But you may not have had a separate course in trial procedure. You probably have a rough acquaintance with trials. You have read about them and have seen them dramatized. But without a somewhat firmer grasp of Anglo-American trial conventions, the rules of evidence can be hard to decipher.

Now for more good news. The special difficulties surrounding the study of evidence are surmountable, particularly when they are recognized from the outset. Evidence law is easier to learn if you expect it sometimes to operate in technical and counterintuitive ways; if you understand that evidence rules often cannot be applied without reference to the substantive law of contracts, torts, property, and crimes; and if you keep on the lookout for terms with multiple definitions. This is why these sources of confusion have been described at the very beginning of this book. Forewarned is forearmed.

Some additional background will also help. Evidence instructors generally provide their own guidance regarding where students should focus their attention, but following that guidance—or making one's way without it—requires a certain basic comprehension of the nature and development of evidence law. And it helps also to understand, at the outset, the rudimentary conventions of Anglo-American trials, as well as certain implications of those conventions. The remainder of this chapter takes up each of these matters.

B. THE NATURE AND DEVELOPMENT OF EVIDENCE LAW

Evidence law today is overwhelmingly statutory. Evidentiary questions in federal court are governed by the Federal Rules of Evidence, adopted in 1975 and since periodically amended. The vast majority of states have enacted codes of evidence rules closely modeled on the federal rules; typically even the numbering of the rules is the same. The influence of the Federal Rules of Evidence, like that of the Federal Rules of Civil Procedure, therefore extends far beyond the world of federal litigation. They are also on the Multistate Bar Examination. So, any sensible study of evidence law today must focus first and foremost on the Federal Rules of Evidence.

Those rules, however, do not come out of a vacuum. To study the Federal Rules of Evidence intelligently and to make full sense of them, it helps to understand their complicated origin.

Until a few decades ago, American rules of evidence were almost entirely a matter of common law, hammered out by generations of judges and lawyers. Efforts to organize and systematize this mass of rulings began in the early twentieth century with the writings of James Bradley Thayer, who taught evidence and constitutional law at Harvard Law School. Those efforts picked up steam with the work of Thayer's student, John Henry Wigmore, who was for many years Dean of Northwestern University Law School. Wigmore's mammoth treatise on the law of evidence, first published in 1904, is not only the most famous work ever written in the field, it is widely thought to be the most influential treatise ever written on *any* branch of American law. Wigmore also tried his hand at codifying the rules of evidence, but the long, detailed result attracted little attention.

In 1942 the American Law Institute—the same group that later produced the Model Penal Code—published a Model Code of Evidence. The drafter, Edmund Morgan, taught evidence at Harvard along with John Maguire, the scholar who memorably described evidence law as "essentially very difficult." Professor Morgan's Model Code was heavily reformist. Like the Model Penal Code, it sought not to restate the law but to rationalize it. It largely eliminated, for example, the hearsay rule. But the Model Code of Evidence was never adopted anywhere. Nor did it leave any lingering mark on evidence law.

In 1953 the National Commissioners on Uniform State Laws—the organization that had collaborated with the American Law Institute on the Uniform Commercial Code—proposed Uniform Rules of Evidence, which largely codified existing law without seeking to reform it. The Uniform Rules were endorsed by the American Bar Association and, more significantly, they inspired and served as the model for comprehensive evidence codes actually adopted in a few states—among them, eventually, California. The California Code of Evidence, enacted by the legislature in 1965, followed a decade of study by the state's Law Revision Commission. It stuck even closer to prior law than the Uniform Rules and proved even more influential.

Meanwhile, the Judicial Conference of the United States—a nationwide group of federal judges that meets annually by congressional command—began in 1961 to urge the promulgation of Federal Rules of Evidence, to supplement the Federal Rules of Civil Procedure and the Federal Rules of Criminal Procedure. The Supreme Court had issued each of these earlier sets of rules pursuant to the Rules Enabling Act of 1934 after each had been drafted by an Advisory Committee appointed by the Court. In 1965 the Court, acting through Chief Justice Earl Warren, likewise appointed an Advisory Committee of judges, lawyers, and law professors to draft Federal Rules of Evidence.

The principal task of drafting both the rules and the official commentary fell to the Committee's Reporter, Professor Edward Cleary of the University of Illinois College of Law. Learning from earlier efforts at codification, Cleary and the Advisory Committee sought to simplify and to clarify existing law but not to alter it dramatically. Following several preliminary drafts, two rounds of public comments, and approval by the Judicial Conference, the Committee gave its final product to the Supreme Court in 1972, and early the following year the Court forwarded the rules to Congress.

Under the Rules Enabling Act, the rules were to become effective 90 days after their transmittal by the Court, barring objection from both Houses of Congress. This is how the Federal Rules of Civil Procedure and the Federal Rules of Criminal Procedure had become law. But Congress was uneasy about the proposed rules of evidence, particularly those concerning privileges—a controversial topic in early 1973, with the Watergate scandal unfolding and President Nixon aggressively asserting executive privilege. Congress therefore declared that the evidence rules would not take effect unless and until Congress expressly approved them. Both Houses then held hearings on the rules and amended them substantially and in different ways. Both Houses dropped most of the privilege rules. A Conference Committee reconciled the two bills, and the resulting rules were approved by both Houses in December 1974 and signed into law by President Ford in January 1975. They became effective July 1, 1975.

Since 1975, the Federal Rules of Evidence have been amended repeatedly. In some instances Congress has amended the rules on its own, acting through new federal legislation. In other cases amendments have been proposed by a new Advisory Committee on the Federal Rules of Evidence, created in 1993 and appointed by the Judicial Conference rather than the Supreme Court. By statute, amendments proposed by the Advisory Committee must be approved by the Judicial Conference and the Supreme Court. And the Rules Enabling Act now contains a permanent exception, codified at 28 U.S.C. §2074(b), to the general principle that procedural rules proposed by the Supreme Court take effect unless Congress objects: Rules regarding evidentiary privilege "have no force or effect unless approved by Act of Congress."

This story has been told in detail here to make several important points. First, although modern evidence law is overwhelmingly statutory, the most influential statute—the Federal Rules of Evidence—largely codifies preexisting common law. So understanding evidence law under the federal rules and their state counterparts often will require examination of common law materials predating codification. Second, these materials will include both judicial decisions and scholarly commentary, because law professors—especially Wigmore—have played an unusually prominent role in the development of evidence law. Third, the recent history of evidence law is littered with unsuccessful attempts at codification, including the privilege provisions that Congress dropped from the Federal Rules of Evidence. These rejected rules play an ambiguous role in evidence law. Sometimes they are consulted as thoughtful and persuasive statements of what the law is or should be, and sometimes just the opposite—because the rules ultimately did not find favor, they are taken as good indications of what the law is not and should not be.

How then is a topic of evidence law best studied? Start, obviously, with the pertinent provisions of the Federal Rules of Evidence. Your instructor may also ask you to examine the corresponding sections of the California Evidence Code, to highlight what is distinctive in the federal rules. Most sections of this book therefore begin with citations to the applicable provisions of the Federal Rules of Evidence (abbreviated "F.R.E.") and the California Evidence Code ("C.E.C."). The citations are typically followed by excerpts from the legislative history of the federal rule: the official commentary of the Advisory Committee, or pertinent portions of the congressional reports, or both. These materials are important both because they often clarify the thinking behind the rule, and because courts often treat them as authoritative—although that practice recently has grown more controversial.

Like most rules, though, evidence rules cannot be grasped in the abstract, even with the guidance of their legislative history. To understand a rule one must see it in application, and preferably in several applications. With evidence law, this means seeing both how trial courts use the rule and how appellate courts review those uses. This book therefore includes excerpts from lots of cases. Generally the excerpts are short, on the theory that it is more helpful to see the rough outline of three applications than one application in detail. Partly this is because different fact patterns can raise different problems, and partly it is because different judges can see the rule in different ways.

The book also includes frequent excerpts from scholarly commentary on the rules of evidence, both treatises and law review articles. Sometimes this material is included because it summarizes the cases or explains a principle better than any single judicial opinion can do, or even a series of judicial opinions. Sometimes it is included because it sets forth a viewpoint that has been particularly influential in the development of evidence law, even if the current rules reject it. And sometimes it is included simply to provide food for thought regarding the wisdom of the rules of evidence in their current form.

Many of the sections in this book conclude with problems. The problems range in difficulty. Some simply test understanding of the rules and ability to apply them in straightforward situations. Others highlight ambiguities in the rules and seek to provoke reflection on how they should best be applied.

All of the materials in this book—the legislative history, the cases, the scholarly commentary, and the problems—aim to help you understand the origins of the modern rules, the manner in which the rules are applied, and the continuing controversies surrounding the rules. The materials are best studied with a copy of the applicable rules always at the side. This is one reason why the rules themselves, despite their centrality, are not reprinted here; another reason is that the rules are frequently amended, and you should consult the most recent versions.

C.   THE ANGLO-AMERICAN TRIAL

Many of the doctrines now codified in federal and state rules of evidence are intelligible only by reference to the distinctive features of the Anglo-American trial. The rules of evidence were crafted largely by generations of trial judges and trial lawyers, who were hammering out basic conventions of trial practice at the same time. It is often difficult to understand one without knowing something about the other.

The basic rules of trial practice—who asks questions when, and so on—generally have remained matters of custom rather than law. For the most part the law lets trial judges conduct trials the way they see fit. The Federal Rules of Evidence, in particular, say very little about the stages of a trial beyond instructing, in Rule 611, that trial judges should "exercise reasonable control over the mode and order of interrogating witnesses." Chapter 6 of this book examines in detail the few requirements that the Federal Rules of Evidence *do* impose on the overall conduct of trials. At the outset, though, it will help to have a more general sense of what traditionally happens at a trial.

Before the trial actually begins, the judge often hears motions pertaining to how it will proceed. Often these are requests to rule certain evidence admissible or inadmissible. Evidentiary motions heard before trial are called motions *in limine*, to distinguish them from objections raised during the trial, when the evidence is actually presented. (*In limine* is Latin for "at the threshold.") Not all motions *in limine* are actually resolved before trial. Sometimes the judge defers decision, because he or she wants to see how the rest of the evidence unfolds. Evidentiary issues might also arise before trial if a party seeks to challenge a discovery request from the other side for certain evidence, or if a third party seeks to challenge the enforcement of a subpoena, a court order requiring the production of certain evidence.

After any pretrial issues have been addressed and either resolved or deferred, jury selection typically starts—if there is to be a jury. If the parties agree not to use a jury, or if neither side has a right to a jury, the judge holds a *bench trial*, rendering the verdict himself or herself. But most trials of serious matters in the United States, whether criminal or civil, involve a jury. The jury usually is picked through a process called *voir dire*, from the old law

French for "to speak the truth." (The same term is used for preliminary questioning of witnesses to see whether they are competent to testify, or of expert witnesses to see whether they are sufficiently qualified.) Potential jurors are questioned about their backgrounds and outlooks, sometimes by the judge and sometimes by the lawyers. Each side then can exercise a certain number of "peremptory challenges" to disqualify jurors without giving any reason, and can ask the judge to disqualify other jurors "for cause"—i.e., because they appear biased or otherwise unfit for service. Once 12 jurors have passed through this screening, the jury takes an oath to carry out its duties faithfully and is deemed "empanelled." At this point the judge may give the jury some preliminary instructions about the law they will be asked to apply. Then the trial proper begins.

The first stage is *opening statements.* The prosecutor or the lawyer for the plaintiff tells the jury what he or she expects the evidence to show, and then the lawyer for the defendant has the opportunity to make a similar statement or to delay it until later. If there is more than one plaintiff or more than one defendant and they have separate counsel, the lawyers for the plaintiffs all give their opening statements first, and then the lawyers for the defendants.

In theory, an opening statement is not evidence. Indeed, juries are routinely instructed that *nothing* the lawyers say during the trial is evidence. The point of an opening statement is just to give the jury a roadmap of the evidence, not to supply evidence itself. And in theory an opening statement must be descriptive rather than argumentative. "The defendant shot him" is permitted. "The defendant shot him in cold blood, like swatting a fly" is not. In practice, of course, the line between description and argument is often indistinct, and different judges draw the line in different ways.

After opening statements, the prosecutor or the plaintiff's lawyer presents his or her *case in chief.* The lawyer does this by calling witnesses to the stand, questioning them under oath, and often also by offering *physical evidence*—documents, photographs, contraband, bloody clothing, etc. The order in which witnesses are called is generally decided by the lawyer. After the lawyer finishes questioning a witness he or she has called, the lawyer or lawyers for the other side have a chance to do the same. The questioning by the lawyer who called the witness is called "direct examination," and the questioning by the other side is called "cross-examination." After cross-examination, the lawyer who called the witness can ask further questions; this is called "redirect examination." Redirect examination is followed by "re-cross-examination," and then, if necessary, by further redirect examination, and so on.

With important exceptions, which will be taken up in Chapter 6, leading questions are allowed on cross-examination and re-cross-examination but not on direct examination or redirect examination. A leading question is a question that suggests the desired answer, like, "Did your father then throw the computer through the window?" or, "She ate her cereal with a fork, didn't she?" The scope of cross-examination, though, is limited to the credibility of the witness and to any matters raised on direct examination. The scope of redirect examination likewise is limited to the scope of cross-examination, and so on. Leading questions and the scope of interrogation are among the few issues of trial procedure that the Federal Rules of Evidence *do* address, albeit quite loosely. The pertinent provisions are in Rule 611 and are discussed in Chapter 6.

When lawyers object to questions posed by opposing lawyers or answers given by witnesses, they often do so in language that only loosely tracks the doctrines of evidence law. Some standard objections, like "leading" or "hearsay," refer directly to particular rules of evidence. But other standard objections, like "argumentative" or "asked and answered," appeal first and foremost to traditions of trial practice, and only indirectly to the codified rules embracing those traditions.

Physical evidence will be discussed in detail in Chapter 11, but a word or two more should be said about it now. A physical object, whether a business letter or a bag of cocaine, is introduced into evidence in two steps. First it is *marked for identification*, for example as "plaintiff's Exhibit 3." This can take place before trial or during trial, but it generally must occur before the item is shown to a witness. Marking the exhibit not only makes reference to it easier; it also makes the exhibit a permanent part of the record in the case, available for inspection by reviewing courts. But it does not entitle the parties to show the exhibit to the jury. That requires *introducing* the exhibit. Once the necessary predicate has been established—what lawyers call "laying the foundation"—the party seeking to use a marked exhibit as proof asks the judge to admit it into evidence. What constitutes the necessary predicate, and the possible grounds for objection to the admission of physical evidence, are matters taken up in Chapter 11. (Judges and trial lawyers often speak of "laying the foundation" for testimony, as well as for physical evidence. In either case, the phrase refers to the process of satisfying whatever requirements the rules set for introduction of the evidence.)

Evidentiary objections raised during trial may be resolved in a variety of ways, depending on the judge and on the complexity of the issues involved. The judge may simply sustain or deny the objection. The judge may ask opposing counsel for a brief response and then make a ruling. The judge may ask the parties to accompany the court reporter to "sidebar"—i.e., the side of the judge's bench opposite the jury, where the judge can confer with the lawyers out of the jury's earshot. Or the judge may defer consideration of the matter until the jury is out of the courtroom.

After the prosecutor or plaintiff's lawyer announces to the judge that the case in chief is concluded, the defendant's lawyer may move to dismiss the case for insufficient evidence. To grant the motion the judge must conclude not just that the evidence is unconvincing, but that no rational jury could find that it satisfies the applicable standard of proof: "beyond a reasonable doubt" in a criminal case, and either "preponderance of the evidence" or "clear and convincing" in a civil case.

If the motion is denied, the defendant then presents his or her case. If the defendant's lawyer did not make an opening statement at the outset of the trial, he or she can do so now. The defendant's case then goes forward much as the plaintiff's or prosecutor's case proceeded: direct examination, cross-examination, redirect examination, etc.

After the defendant's case is concluded, the prosecutor or plaintiff typically presents a *rebuttal case*. In theory the evidence here must respond to evidence presented in the defendant's case, just as redirect examination is limited to the scope of cross-examination. But trial judges sometimes waive these limitations. Judges also sometimes give defendants the opportunity to present a *surrebuttal case*, responding to the rebuttal case, and the plaintiff or prosecutor may then be allowed to present evidence responding to the surrebuttal case.

After all the evidence has been presented, the lawyers make *closing arguments*. Typically the prosecutor or plaintiff's lawyer goes first, then the defendant's lawyer argues, and then the prosecutor or plaintiff's lawyer gives a *rebuttal argument*. Unlike opening statements, closing arguments are not restricted even in theory to factual statements, but they *are* restricted to claims based on the evidence that has been introduced. Following closing statements, the judge typically gives the jury additional instructions. The jury then deliberates in secret and, if it can, agrees on a verdict.

Several distinctive features of the Anglo-American trial have important implications for evidence law. The first is the jury. Although the rules of evidence apply to bench trials as well as to jury trials, many of the rules seem shaped by concern that certain kinds of proof might unduly influence amateur factfinders—and perhaps also by the need to avoid long interruptions in the trial, given that jurors serve only temporarily. The second is a strong preference for *viva voce* proof—i.e., testimony from live, sworn witnesses, who are subject to cross-examination and whose demeanor the jury can observe.

The third is the pervasive control lawyers exercise over the conduct of the trial. Subject only to generally loose supervision by the judge, lawyers decide what witnesses to call, what questions to ask, what physical evidence to introduce, and in what order to proceed. Most evidence rules take this control for granted, and some actually strengthen it. For example, the introduction of evidence forbidden by the rules generally will not be ground for reversal unless the lawyer for the opposing party knows to raise an objection at trial and chooses to do so; trial lawyers can effectively waive rules of evidence they do not wish to enforce. One reason for having a contemporaneous objection requirement is efficiency, to ensure that the parties bring errors to the trial court's attention when the court still has an opportunity to correct those errors and potentially obviate the need for a retrial. Without the contemporaneous objection requirement, a party might have an incentive to "sow error into the record"; that is, to strategically allow errors to go uncorrected, in a case the party thinks they will likely lose anyway, hoping to argue on appeal for a new trial. Ultimately, the system assumes that fair trials and accurate verdicts are best secured by giving trained advocates substantial leeway in assembling the evidence. Of course that leeway also serves the professional interests of trial lawyers, and perhaps also of trial judges—the two groups most responsible for our current rules of evidence and trial practice. So keep a certain skepticism about the extraordinary power and responsibility our system vests in trial lawyers.

D. The Role of the Trial Judge

There is a fourth and final distinctive feature of Anglo-American trials worth noting at the outset of a course in evidence law: the central role of the presiding judge. Anglo-American trial lawyers have wide latitude to craft their cases as they see fit, but there are important constraints on that latitude, and those constraints are imposed by the trial judge. Evidence law, in particular, grants the trial judge both extensive authority and extensive discretion. The rules describing the role of the trial judge are fundamental to the operation of the entire system.

1. The Trial Judge's Authority

[F.R.E. 104(a); C.E.C. §§310, 400, 405]

ADVISORY COMMITTEE NOTE TO F.R.E. 104(A)

The applicability of a particular rule of evidence often depends upon the existence of a condition. Is the alleged expert a qualified physician? Is a witness whose former testimony is offered unavailable? Was a stranger present during a conversation between attorney and client? In each instance the admissibility of evidence will turn upon the answer to the question of the existence of the condition. Accepted practice, incorporated in the rule, places on the judge the responsibility for these determinations. . . .

If the question is factual in nature, the judge will of necessity receive evidence pro and con on the issue. The rule provides that the rules of evidence in general do not apply to this process. McCormick §53, p. 123, n.8, points out that the authorities are "scattered and inconclusive," and observes:

> Should the exclusionary law of evidence, "the child of the jury system" in Thayer's phrase, be applied to this hearing before the judge? Sound sense backs the view that it should not, and that the judge should be empowered to hear any relevant evidence, such as affidavits or other reliable hearsay.

This view is reinforced by practical necessity in certain situations. An item, offered and objected to, may itself be considered in ruling on admissibility, though not yet admitted in evidence. Thus, the content of an asserted declaration against interest must be considered in ruling whether it is against interest. Again, common practice calls for considering the testimony of a witness, particularly a child, in determining competency. . . .

2. The Trial Judge's Discretion

[F.R.E. 103; C.E.C. §§353, 354]

ROGER C. PARK ET AL., EVIDENCE LAW: A STUDENT'S GUIDE TO THE LAW OF EVIDENCE AS APPLIED IN AMERICAN TRIALS

§§3.12, 3.13 & 3.15, at 99, 101-102, 108-109 (4th ed. 2018)

Even if error is preserved [by an objection at trial] . . . success on appeal of an evidentiary issue is a difficult task because appellate courts are reluctant to reverse trial courts' judgments on evidentiary matters. . . . Many of the federal rules are not categorical but instead grant the trial judge the authority—guided by the terms of the rules themselves—to reach an appropriate result in light of the context of the particular trial. . . .

[In addition, t]he Federal Rules of Evidence, Federal Rules of Civil Procedure, and Federal Rules of Criminal Procedure all mandate that courts disregard errors that do not "affect the substantial rights of the parties." Thus, reversible or prejudicial errors are those that do affect the substantial rights of parties. The definition of substantial rights is vague, and prejudice is determined on a case-by-case basis. . . . Courts differ on the degree of certainty required to find an error harmless. . . . For example, the Ninth Circuit uses a "more probably harmless than not" test for nonconstitutional errors. The Third Circuit standard requires reversal unless it is "highly probable" that the verdict would have been the same if the error had not occurred. In the Fifth Circuit, reversal is required unless the court is "sure, after reviewing the entire record, that the error did not influence the jury, or had but very slight effect on its verdict."

Courts generally apply the same standard for harmlessness to nonconstitutional error in civil cases as in criminal cases, although some courts argue that the standards should differ in accordance with the differing standards of proof applicable to civil and criminal cases. . . .

A finding of plain error has the identical effect on a proceeding as a finding of preserved error—the lower court's decision will be reversed . . . provided the error was prejudicial. . . . [P]lain error is not easily defined and allows for substantial judicial discretion. The facts of the case, the gravity of the offense, and the probable effect of the error are factors considered by the court in determining whether substantial rights have been violated. Some courts require that the error be obvious in the record.

STEPHEN A. SALTZBURG, MICHAEL M. MARTIN & DANIEL J. CAPRA, FEDERAL RULES OF EVIDENCE MANUAL

§103.02[5], at 1:103-10–1:103-11 (11th ed. 2015)

Most appellants do not even get the opportunity to test the harmfulness of error because the deferential standard of review employed . . . makes it extremely difficult to prove error on an evidentiary question in the first place. While pure issues of rule construction are reviewed *de novo*, there are very few such issues that arise in practice. Mixed questions of law and fact are also reviewed *de novo*, and they arise with somewhat more frequency than pure questions of law; for example, the question whether a communication is protected by a privilege is usually a mixed question of law and fact. Still, the vast majority of evidentiary rulings are reviewed under the trial-court-friendly abuse of discretion standard, even where the claim of error has been properly preserved. . . . All in all, the chances of reversal on the ground of an evidentiary error are slim indeed.

UNITED STATES v. WALTON

217 F.3d 443 (7th Cir. 2000)

COFFEY, Circuit Judge.

We review a trial judge's determination of the admissibility of evidence under the abuse of discretion standard. "We afford great deference to the trial court's determination of the admissibility of evidence because of the trial judge's first-hand exposure to the witnesses and the evidence as a whole, and because of the judge's familiarity with the case and ability to gauge the impact of the evidence in the context of the entire proceeding." *United States v. Van Dreel*, 155 F.3d 902, 905 (7th Cir. 1998). Indeed, "[a]ppellants who challenge evidentiary rulings of the district court are like rich men who wish to enter the Kingdom: their prospects compare with those of camels who wish to pass through the eye of the needle." [*United States v. Glecier*, 923 F.2d 496, 503 (7th Cir.) (Bauer, J.), *cert. denied*, 502 U.S. 810 (1991).]

BANDERA v. CITY OF QUINCY

344 F.3d 47 (1st Cir. 2003)

BOUDIN, Chief Judge.

This is an appeal by the City of Quincy from a jury verdict against the city in favor of [the former executive director of its Community Policing Commission,] Kathleen Bandera. The jury awarded Bandera $135,000 in punitive damages for sexual harassment. . . .

At trial, Bandera testified in detail as to her experience and . . . also adduced testimony from a number of witnesses including Nancy Coletta, a female police officer in the Quincy Police Department . . . who had filed then-pending sexual harassment claims of her own against the police department. . . .

Prior to trial, when Coletta was identified as a witness for Bandera, defendants anticipated that Coletta among others would be asked to describe her own experiences with the police and thus moved *in limine* for an order limiting or excluding such testimony on the ground that it was irrelevant or, if relevant, unduly prejudicial under Federal Rule of Evidence 403. The district judge denied the motion without discussion.

At trial Coletta gave testimony of two different types. Primarily, she described the harassment to which she herself had been subject. . . . In addition, Coletta was allowed to testify over objections by the defense as to how Coletta felt about, and assessed, Bandera's own allegations. . . .

Coletta's recitation of her own experiences was relevant . . . to show liability on the part of supervisory officers . . . and also on the city for a pattern of knowing toleration of harassment by its subordinates. . . . Coletta's testimony as to her own assessment of Bandera's experience is quite a different matter.

. . . [S]o far as it appears, Coletta had no actual knowledge of what had happened to Bandera, and her assessments of what Bandera reported to have happened and the psychological impact on Bandera were wholly inappropriate opinion testimony. Fed. R. Evid. 701. . . . Coletta was not qualified as an expert on anything and her assessments were not the limited kind of opinion testimony deemed helpful to a jury (*e.g.*, an estimate of car speed or whether a defendant was intoxicated) but simply jury argument offered from the witness stand. The testimony should certainly not have been admitted.

If the basic objection—improper opinion testimony by a lay witness—had been preserved, we might be tempted to reverse. Quite possibly this phase of the testimony had fairly limited impact: Coletta's assessment of Bandera's situation was nothing like so graphic as Coletta's admissible testimony as to her own experience; her opinions as to Bandera's experience were mildly phrased; and the jury was far more likely to base its judgment on Bandera's own detailed recitation of what had happened to her. Still, whether the testimony's admission could be described safely as harmless error is open to doubt.

But the objection was not in our view properly preserved. Admittedly, the newly amended Federal Rules of Evidence sensibly provide that an objection resolved by a definitive *in limine* ruling admitting evidence need not be renewed at trial. Fed. R. Evid. 103(a) (2000). But if the district judge ruled definitively on anything, it was that Coletta and similar witnesses could testify about their own experience and not that they could assess that of Bandera. This is evident from the *in limine* motion itself.

Then at trial when the opinion testimony was offered, defense counsel said "objection" on several occasions; but few of the objections were explained and the ones that were had to do with time frame. Given earlier general attacks on Coletta's testimony based on relevance and prejudice, we do not think that it was at all necessarily obvious to the magistrate judge that the new objections were to impermissible lay witness opinion. . . .

The law is clear that an objection, if its basis is not obvious, is not preserved unless the ground is stated. Fed. R. Evid. 103(a)(1). . . . This case is a perfect illustration of why that rule is a sound one. Coletta's opinion testimony, although clearly inappropriate, was at the tag end of other testimony to which different objections had been litigated pretrial. If counsel had explained why this new testimony differed and was in no way covered by the district court's *in limine* ruling, there is a good chance that the magistrate judge would have excluded it.

This is not a criticism of counsel. Trials are a rough and ready business; snap judgments as to unexpected testimony have to be made all the time. However, the failure to preserve the objection means review is at most for plain error. Fed. R. Evid. 103(d). As we have noted, it is far from clear that the opinion testimony was harmful. This doubt alone is enough to bar reversal under the plain error doctrine: although the error is plain in retrospect, there is no showing that it probably infected the outcome or caused a miscarriage of justice. . . . [Remanded on other grounds.]

PROBLEMS

1.1. The defendant in a civil tort case, which was tried without a jury, appeals the judgment against him on the ground that the judge allowed the plaintiff to introduce evidence that should have been treated as inadmissible hearsay. At trial the defendant objected to the evidence but not on the grounds of hearsay. If the appellate court ultimately agrees that the evidence was in fact inadmissible hearsay, under what circumstances should it reverse the judgment?

1.2. To prove that certain testimony is not barred by privilege rules, the prosecutor in a criminal case seeks to introduce an affidavit setting forth facts that would make the privilege inapplicable to the testimony in question. Defense counsel says the affidavit itself is inadmissible because it is hearsay. The prosecutor says that the rules of evidence do not apply to the affidavit, because it is offered to prove the admissibility of other evidence. Who is right?

E. THE FUTURE OF EVIDENCE LAW

You are entering the legal profession at an exciting and challenging time for evidence law. The past few decades have witnessed what legal scholar Mirjan Damaška has described as the "scientization of proof." Increasingly, parties to litigation build their cases not just on human eyewitnesses and assertions, but also on the conveyances of scientific instruments and sophisticated software-driven expert systems. Lawyers now have to be prepared to authenticate the contents of e-mails and social media web pages. Soon, trial judges may have to try to distinguish between real videos and so-called "deepfakes" offered into evidence. Demonstrative evidence may soon consist not only of diagrams and summary charts, but virtual reality goggles that help witnesses better explain to juries what they heard and saw at an accident scene. The list goes on.

This rapid march of technology may well require the drafting of certain new evidence rules. For example, just as the drafters of the Federal Rules recently added new authentication provisions to deal with electronically stored and electronically generated information, the drafters may decide that the rules governing admissibility of expert testimony must be modified to account for machine "experts." And, of course, technological advances will require lawyers, judges, and juries to continually develop new skills.

As much as technology may change the nature of evidence and litigation, it will not lessen the need for law students to understand the rules and their underlying rationales. Trial judges and rule drafters will still have to decide how to balance competing concerns such as accuracy, fairness, efficiency, and policy considerations. Trial lawyers will still need to persuade judges, factfinders, or policymakers why certain forms of proof should be allowed or disallowed. The arguments you will encounter in the cases, advisory committee notes, and scholarly commentary in this book will continue to be relevant long into the future.

RELEVANCE

"I'm Virgo with the moon in Aries, if that will help you any."

A. RELEVANCE AND IRRELEVANCE

The two most basic principles of modern evidence law are that all irrelevant evidence should be excluded and that relevant evidence should, as a rule, be admitted. The first of these principles has no exceptions, but the second has very many exceptions. The rest of evidence law, in fact, can be understood as a series of qualifications to the broad proposition that relevant evidence is admissible. That is how James Bradley Thayer thought about evidence law, and here, as elsewhere, his thinking remains highly influential.

As Thayer used the terms, the relevance or irrelevance of a piece of evidence is determined by logic and experience, not by legal rules. Evidence is relevant if it is rationally probative in any way and irrelevant if it is not. This means that evidence need have very little probative force to be relevant. Even extremely weak evidence is relevant as long as it rationally can be given *some* probative value. The question is not whether the evidence makes some material fact likely to be true or unlikely to be true, but rather whether the evidence makes that fact *at least slightly more or less likely than it would be without knowing about the evidence.* This low threshold for relevance is part of the explanation for the absence of any exceptions to the prohibition on irrelevant evidence. The other part of the explanation is that, as Thayer pointed out, the prohibition reflects the legal system's fundamental commitment to basing adjudication on reason.

[F.R.E. 401 & 402; C.E.C. §§210, 350, 351]

ADVISORY COMMITTEE NOTE TO F.R.E. 401

Problems of relevancy call for an answer to the question whether an item of evidence, when tested by the processes of legal reasoning, possesses sufficient probative value to justify receiving it in evidence. Thus, assessment of the probative value of evidence that a person purchased a revolver shortly prior to a fatal shooting with which he is charged is a matter of analysis and reasoning. . . .

Relevancy is not an inherent characteristic of any item of evidence but exists only as a relation between an item of evidence and a matter properly provable in the case. Does the item of evidence tend to prove the matter sought to be proved? Whether the relationship exists depends upon principles evolved by experience or science, applied logically to the situation at hand. The rule summarizes this relationship as a "tendency to make the existence" of the fact to be proved "more probable or less probable."

The standard of probability under the rule is "more . . . probable than it would be without the evidence." Any more stringent requirement is unworkable and unrealistic. As McCormick §152, p. 317, says, "A brick is not a wall," or, as Falknor, Extrinsic Policies Affecting Admissibility, 10 Rutgers L. Rev. 574, 576 (1956), quotes Professor McBaine, ". . . [I]t is not to be supposed that every witness can make a home run." Dealing with probability in the language of the rule has the added virtue of avoiding confusion between questions of admissibility and questions of the sufficiency of the evidence.

The rule uses the phrase "fact that is of consequence to the determination of the action" to describe the kind of fact to which proof may properly be directed. The language is that of California Evidence Code §210; it has the advantage of avoiding the loosely used and ambiguous word "material." The fact to be proved may be ultimate, intermediate, or evidentiary; it matters not, so long as it is of consequence in the determination of the action.

The fact to which the evidence is directed need not be in dispute. While situations will arise which call for the exclusion of evidence offered to prove a point conceded by the opponent, the ruling should be made on the basis of such considerations as waste of time and undue prejudice (see Rule 403), rather than under any general requirement that evidence is admissible only if directed to matters in dispute. Evidence which is essentially background in nature can scarcely be said to involve disputed matter, yet it is universally offered and admitted as an aid to understanding. Charts, photographs, views of real estate, murder weapons, and many other items of evidence fall in this category. A rule limiting admissibility to evidence directed to a controversial point would invite the exclusion of this helpful evidence, or at least the raising of endless questions over its admission. Cf. California Evidence Code §210, defining relevant evidence in terms of tendency to prove a disputed fact.

ADVISORY COMMITTEE NOTE TO F.R.E. 402

The provisions that all relevant evidence is admissible, with certain exceptions, and that evidence which is not relevant is not admissible are "a presupposition involved in the very conception of a rational system of evidence." Thayer, Preliminary Treatise on Evidence 264 (1898). They constitute the foundation upon which the structure of admission and exclusion rests....

KNAPP v. STATE

79 N.E. 1076 (Ind. 1907)

GILLET, J.

Appellant appeals from a judgment in the above-entitled cause, under which he stands convicted of murder in the first degree. Error is assigned on the overruling of a motion for new trial.

Appellant as a witness in his own behalf, offered testimony tending to show a killing in self-defense. He afterwards testified, presumably for the purpose of showing that he had reason to fear the deceased, that before the killing he had heard that the deceased, who was the marshal of Hagerstown, had clubbed and seriously injured an old man in arresting him, and that he died a short time afterwards. On appellant being asked, on cross-examination, who told him this, he answered: "Some people around Hagerstown there. I can't say as to who it was now." The state was permitted, on rebuttal, to prove by a physician over the objection and exception of the defense, that the old man died of senility and alcoholism, and that there were no bruises or marks on his person. Counsel for appellant contend that it was error to admit this testimony; that the question was as to whether he had, in fact, heard the story, and not as to its truth or falsity. While it is laid down in the books that there must be an open and visible connection between the fact under inquiry and the evidence by which it is sought to be established, yet the connection thus required is in the logical processes only, for to require an actual connection between the two facts would be to exclude all presumptive evidence. Within settled rules, the competency of testimony depends largely upon its tendency to persuade the judgment. . . .

We are of opinion that the testimony referred to was competent. While appellant's counsel are correct in their assertion that the question was whether appellant had heard a story to the effect that the deceased had offered serious violence to the old man, yet it does not follow that the testimony complained of did not tend to negative the claim of appellant as to what he had heard. One of the first principles of human nature is the impulse to speak the truth. "This principle," says Dr. Reid, whom Professor Greenleaf quotes at length in his work on Evidence (volume 1, §7n), "has a powerful operation, even in the greatest liars; for where they lie once they speak truth 100 times." Truth speaking preponderating, it follows that to show that there was no basis in fact for the statement appellant claims to have heard had a tendency to make it less probable that his testimony on this point was true. . . . [W]e do not perceive how, without the possibility of a gross perversion of right, the state could be denied the opportunity to meet in the manner indicated the evidence of the defendant as to what he had heard, where he, cunningly perhaps, denies that he can remember who gave him the information. The fact proved by the state tended to discredit appellant, since it showed that somewhere between the fact and the testimony there was a person who was not a truth speaker, and, appellant being unable to point to his informant, it must at least be said that the testimony complained of had a tendency to render his claim as to what he had heard less probable. . . . Judgment affirmed.

UNITED STATES v. DOMINGUEZ

907 F.2d 216 (1st Cir. 1990)
(sub nom. United States v. Maravilla)

BREYER, Circuit Judge.

[Rafael Dominguez was a U.S. Customs officer. A jury found Dominguez and a fellow officer guilty of kidnapping, robbing, and murdering Yamil Mitri when Mitri attempted to carry $700,000 into the United States.]

After presenting evidence that a gunshot killed Mitri, the government introduced evidence showing (a) that Dominguez owned a gun, (b) that a week after Mitri's death, he asked a friend to bring his gun to a Miami gun shop to have the barrel replaced, (c) that the shopowner saw scratches on the barrel, which could have been left by an attempt to remove it, and (d) that the shopowner repaired the barrel but did not replace it. The defendants point out that Dominguez, as a customs officer, had to own a gun. They argue, in light of that fact, that the evidence presented of ownership and about barrel replacement was irrelevant and prejudicial.

We do not see how one could say the evidence is irrelevant. Relevant evidence is evidence "having any tendency to make the existence of any fact that is of consequence . . . more probable or less probable than it would be without the evidence." Fed. R. Evid. 401. Obviously, the fact that Dominguez owned a gun makes his guilt somewhat more probable than if he did not own a gun. The fact that he might have had a good reason, consistent with innocence, for owning a gun, makes the evidence less probative, not irrelevant. Regardless, the government had to show that Dominguez owned a gun in order to show that he tried to have the barrel replaced. The effort to replace, in turn, suggests an effort to eliminate features of the gun that might have linked it with a bullet eventually found in, or near, Mitri's body. And any such effort suggests consciousness of guilt. Given this set of logical connections, the replacement effort makes guilt more probable than had there been no replacement effort; and the evidence, consequently, is relevant.

The defendants point out that the chain of inferences is far weaker than if the government had introduced the gun itself into evidence, for then experts could have tested it to see if it matched the bullet that killed Mitri. The record provides no basis, however, for concluding that the government ever found the bullet. . . . Regardless, the government is perfectly free to introduce weak, as well as strong, evidence. *See, e.g.*, Fed. R. Evid. 401 advisory committee's note ("The standard of probability under the rule is 'more . . . probable than it would be without the evidence.' Any more stringent requirement is unworkable and unrealistic."); Cleary, *McCormick on Evidence* §185, at 542-43 (3rd ed. 1984) ("Under our system, molded by the tradition of jury trial and predominantly oral proof, a party offers his evidence not *en masse*, but item by item. An item of evidence . . . need not prove conclusively the proposition for which it is offered. . . . A brick is not a wall.") (citations omitted). No one claimed that this particular piece of evidence *proved* guilt. It was merely one piece of evidence among many. . . . Affirmed in part and reversed in part [on other grounds].

STATE v. LARSON

843 P.2d 777 (Mont. 1992)

McDonough, Justice.

This is an appeal from a judgment of the First Judicial District Court, Lewis and Clark County, convicting Larson of negligent endangerment. . . . On July 21, 1991, five-year-old Brenda Perry suffered fatal injuries when a horse she and Myron Larson were riding reared and fell backward, crushing Brenda. . . . She died a short time later of internal bleeding. . . .

The accident occurred during a barbecue at a rural home near Helena. [Larson had borrowed the horse from its owner and had then allowed Perry to ride seated behind him. The owner of the horse had warned Larson that the horse was "inexperienced" and "hot-blooded." Three hours after the accident, armed law enforcement officers took a blood sample from Larson.] . . . Lynn Kurtz, a forensic scientist for the State Crime Lab, measured Larson's blood alcohol content at .17 grams of alcohol per 100 milliliters of blood. Kurtz estimated that Larson had a blood alcohol content between .20 and .27 at the time of the accident.

At trial, . . . [the court] permitted Kurtz to compare Larson's blood alcohol level with the level that the scientific community has determined will impair a person's ability to drive a motor vehicle. Kurtz testified that the scientific community has determined that a blood alcohol level of .08 grams of alcohol per 100 milliliters of blood will impair a person's ability to safely operate a motor vehicle. . . .

The prosecution argued that Larson made mistakes in judgment due to his alcohol consumption. In closing, the prosecution mentioned to the jury that Larson's blood alcohol level at the time of the accident was three times the level that will impair a person's ability to drive an automobile. The prosecution also argued that a person who is too impaired to drive an automobile safely is too impaired to ride a horse safely, and certainly is too impaired to allow a five-year-old child on a high-spirited horse with him. . . .

Larson . . . contends that the level of blood alcohol which will impair a person's ability to drive is irrelevant to his conduct relative to a high-spirited young horse. On the contrary, "[r]elevant evidence means evidence having any tendency to make the existence of any fact that is of consequence to the determination of the action more probable or less probable than it would be without the evidence." Rule 401, M.R. Evid.

> The test of relevance is whether an item of evidence will have any value, as determined by logic and experience, in proving the proposition for which it is offered. The standard used to measure this acceptable probative value is "any tendency to make the existence of any fact . . . more probable or less probable than it would be without the evidence."

State v. Fitzpatrick (1980), 186 Mont. 187, 207 (quoting M.R. Evid. Commission Comments).

At Larson's trial, the prosecution offered his blood alcohol level to show that alcohol had impaired his reactions and judgment when he chose to ride double on a high-spirited horse with a young girl. Larson's blood alcohol level on the day of the accident is relevant.

The comparison of Larson's blood alcohol level with that which the scientific community has determined will impair a person's ability to drive a motor vehicle is also relevant. The comparison aided the jury in evaluating Larson's level of intoxication. It allowed the jurors to apply their experience and logic to determine whether Larson's level of intoxication clouded his judgment and impaired his reactions, and its probative value outweighs any prejudice to the defendant. We hold that the court did not abuse its discretion in admitting the comparison. . . . Affirmed.

EDMUND M. MORGAN, BASIC PROBLEMS OF EVIDENCE

185–188 (1961)

In the following example it is not meant to assert that each proposition is more probably true than not, but that it is more probably true than an identical proposition concerning a man as to whom nothing is known. Assume that X has met his death by violence; the proposition to be proved is that Y killed him; the offered item of evidence is a love letter written by

Y to X's wife. The series of inferences is about as follows: From Y's letter, (A), to Y's love of X's wife, (B), to Y's desire for the exclusive possession of X's wife, (C), to Y's desire to get rid of X, (D), to Y's plan to get rid of X, (E), to Y's execution of the plan by killing X, (F). The unarticulated premise, (M), conjoined with (A) is "A man who writes a love letter to a woman is probably in love with her"; that, (N), conjoined with (B) is, "A man who loves a woman probably desires her for himself alone"; that, (O), conjoined with (C) is, "A man who loves a married woman and desires her for himself alone desires to get rid of her husband"; that, (P), conjoined with (D) is, "A man who desires to get rid of the husband of the woman he loves probably plans to do so"; and that, (Q), conjoined with (E) is, "A man who plans to get rid of the husband of the woman he loves is probably the man who killed him." If an arrow represents the drawing of an inference, the series may be represented thus:

```
A)
+) → B)
M)    +) → C)
   N)    +) → D)
      O)    +) → E)
         P)    +) → F
            Q)
```

Now it must be obvious that the value of item A as probative of F varies with the degree of probability of the existence of each presumed fact and inversely with the number of inferences between A and F. . . . [A] distinction must be drawn between the relevance of A as evidence of F on the one hand and its weight on the other. Obviously A standing by itself would not justify the inference of F; indeed, it might not justify even D or E. But the proponent of A may offer another item or several other items, each of which will begin a series of inferences leading to F. . . . [T]he greater the number of items, the stronger will be the foundation for the ultimate inference. Nevertheless, no matter how numerous the items or how short the series of inferences required for each of them, they will never produce certainty. . . . On the other hand, no matter how great the number of items established, they will never make the existence of the ultimate fact a question for the trier unless the total would justify reasonable men in concluding that the existence of the ultimate fact is more probable than its nonexistence.

GRAHAM C. LILLY, AN INTRODUCTION TO THE LAW OF EVIDENCE

§2.2, at 31–32 (3d ed. 1996)

Note that even if most links were strong, probative force would always be limited by the weakest link. . . . Some of the inferential links [in Professor Morgan's example] are comparatively strong (e.g., from love letters to deep affection), yet others are comparatively weak (e.g., from the desire to possess to a plan to kill). Does the love letter still pass the test of relevance? It does because it increases somewhat the likelihood that [the defendant] committed the murder. Of course, whether the prosecution can establish beyond a reasonable doubt that the accused committed the offense charged is an entirely different matter which depends upon the combined probative effect of all of the inculpatory evidence introduced at trial. . . . At the conclusion of the prosecutor's evidence, the judge must decide if a reasonable trier could conclude from all of the evidence that [the defendant] was the murderer.

B. PROBATIVE VALUE AND PREJUDICE

If, as Thayer thought, the vast bulk of evidence law consists of exceptions to the general proposition that relevant evidence is admissible, none of those exceptions is more important than the rule giving trial judges broad discretion to exclude evidence that is more trouble than it is worth — either because it likely will impair rather than assist the jury's search for the truth, or because it simply will take up too much time. Probably more evidence is excluded under this flexible rule than under the rest of the rules of evidence combined, and the authority the rule gives to trial judges creates in each courtroom a kind of parallel, discretionary law of evidence, working alongside the law set forth in the remaining rules.

[F.R.E. 105, 403; C.E.C. §§352, 355]

ADVISORY COMMITTEE NOTE TO F.R.E. 403

The case law recognizes that certain circumstances call for the exclusion of evidence which is of unquestioned relevance. These circumstances entail risks which range all the way from inducing decision on a purely emotional basis, at one extreme, to nothing more harmful than merely wasting time, at the other extreme. Situations in this area call for balancing the probative value of and need for the evidence against the harm likely to result from its admission. The rules which follow in this Article are concrete applications evolved for particular situations. However, they reflect the policies underlying the present rule, which is designed as a guide for the handling of situations for which no specific rules have been formulated.

Exclusion for risk of unfair prejudice, confusion of issues, misleading the jury, or waste of time, all find ample support in the authorities. "Unfair prejudice" within its context means an undue tendency to suggest decision on an improper basis, commonly, though not necessarily, an emotional one.

The rule does not enumerate surprise as a ground for exclusion, in this respect following Wigmore's view of the common law. 6 Wigmore §1849. Cf. McCormick §152, p. 320, n.29, listing unfair surprise as a ground for exclusion but stating that it is usually "coupled with the danger of prejudice and confusion of issues." . . . While it can scarcely be doubted that claims of unfair surprise may still be justified despite procedural requirements of notice and instrumentalities of discovery, the granting of a continuance is a more appropriate remedy than exclusion of the evidence. . . .

In reaching a decision whether to exclude on grounds of unfair prejudice, consideration should be given to the probable effectiveness or lack of effectiveness of a limiting instruction. . . . The availability of other means of proof may also be an appropriate factor.

ELEANOR SWIFT, ONE HUNDRED YEARS OF EVIDENCE LAW REFORM: THAYER'S TRIUMPH

88 Cal. L. Rev. 2437, 2446–2447 (2000)

There are both benefits and costs to granting discretion to the trial judge to admit or exclude evidence. Some commentators argue that deferential appellate review of trial court discretion promotes judicial economy by reducing appellate expenditure of time and energy. Proponents of discretion also contend that many questions that arise in litigation, including the decision to admit or exclude evidence, require individualized and flexible decision making based on the particular context of the case; "they involve multifarious, fleeting, special, narrow facts that utterly resist generalization. . . ." [Maurice Rosenberg, *Judicial Discretion of the Trial Court, Viewed from Above*, 22 Syr. L. Rev. 635, 662 (1971).] Shoe-horning such decisions into rigid rules would promote error and injustice. And once the need for individualized decision making is acknowledged, trial courts are in a superior position to make decisions that require taking the context and specific facts of a case into account. This serves a truth-seeking function, as "rules allowing room for a trial judge's sensitivity to the complexity and uniqueness of a particular case necessarily should promote truth more than rules providing for only mechanical application of a closed and complete system." [Thomas M. Mengler, *The Theory of Discretion in the Federal Rules of Evidence*, 74 Iowa L. Rev. 413, 460 (1989).]

The costs of discretion and deferential review are also well known. There are fears that discretionary power will be exercised arbitrarily and unfairly; that broad and ambiguous principles make evidentiary rulings unpredictable to parties preparing for trial and result in inconsistent outcomes; and that the perceived unfairness of inconsistent outcomes, or outcomes dependent on the personality of the judge one happens to draw, could lead to a loss of confidence in the judicial system. Even more troubling, perhaps, is the fear that trial judges, although closer to the context and facts of the case, simply are not capable of making the subtle and profound judgments that rules like Federal Rule 403 require.

UNITED STATES v. NORIEGA

117 F.3d 1206 (11th Cir. 1997)

KRAVITCH, Senior Circuit Judge:

On February 4, 1988, a federal grand jury for the Southern District of Florida indicted Manuel Antonio Noriega on drug-related charges. At that time, Noriega served as commander of the Panamanian Defense Forces in the Republic of Panama. [The indictment charged that Noriega had used his position of authority to help Colombian drug traffickers smuggle cocaine through Panama and into the United States.] Shortly thereafter, Panama's president, Eric Arturo Delvalle, formally discharged Noriega from his military post, but Noriega refused to accept the dismissal. Panama's legislature then ousted Delvalle from power. The United States, however, continued to acknowledge Delvalle as the constitutional leader of Panama. Later, after a disputed presidential election in Panama, the United States recognized Guillermo Endara as Panama's legitimate head of state.

On December 15, 1989, Noriega publicly declared that a state of war existed between Panama and the United States. Within days of this announcement by Noriega, President George [H.W.] Bush directed United States armed forces into combat in Panama for the stated purposes of "safeguarding American lives, restoring democracy, preserving the Panama Canal treaties, and seizing Noriega to face federal drug charges in the United States." *United States v. Noriega*, 746 F. Supp. 1506, 1511 (S.D. Fla. 1990). The ensuing military conflagration resulted in significant casualties and property loss among Panamanian civilians. Noriega lost his effective control over Panama during this armed conflict, and he surrendered to United States military officials on January 3, 1990. Noriega then was brought to Miami to face the pending federal charges.

Following extensive pre-trial proceedings and a lengthy trial, a jury found Noriega guilty of eight counts in the indictment and not guilty of the remaining two counts. The district court entered judgments of conviction against Noriega upon the jury's verdict and sentenced him to consecutive imprisonment terms of 20, 15 and five years, respectively....

[Before trial,] Noriega gave notice of his intent to use classified information regarding his intelligence work for the United States to rebut the government's assertion that he had unexplained wealth. The government objected to any disclosure of the purposes for which the United States had paid Noriega. In pre-trial proceedings, the government offered to stipulate that Noriega had received approximately $320,000 from the United States Army and the Central Intelligence Agency. Noriega insisted that the actual figure approached $10,000,000, and that he should be allowed to disclose the tasks he had performed for the United States.

The district court held that information about the content of the discrete operations in which Noriega had engaged in exchange for the alleged payments was irrelevant to his defense. Alternatively, it ruled that the tendency of such evidence to confuse the issues before the jury substantially out-weighed any probative value it might have had. The district court's ... ruling, however, left Noriega free to present evidence of the fact, amounts, time, source and method of conveyance of money he alleged he had received from the United States. At trial, Noriega declined to submit evidence regarding monies he allegedly received from the United States, because, he now contends, it would not have appeared credible to the jury absent the excluded details regarding the actual services he had performed. . . .

Our review leads us to conclude that information regarding the purposes for which the United States previously paid Noriega potentially had some probative value. Specifically, had Noriega testified that he had received $10,000,000 from the United States, and had the government then rebutted that testimony by presenting evidence that it had paid Noriega $320,000, evidence regarding what Noriega did for the United States might have helped the jury determine which of the two payment totals was more credible. To the extent that the proffered evidence on the intelligence operations showed that the United States had engaged Noriega to carry out significant duties, the jury might have inferred that he had received the higher figure, rather than the lower sum. Thus, the district court may have overstated the case when it declared evidence of the purposes for which the United States allegedly paid Noriega wholly irrelevant to his defense.

The potential probative value of this material, however, was relatively marginal. Evidence of the purposes for which monies allegedly are given does not aid significantly in the determination of the fact and amount of such purported payments. Further, and more importantly, the district court correctly recognized that the admission of evidence regarding the nature of Noriega's assistance to the United States would have shifted unduly the focus of the trial from allegations of drug trafficking to matters of geo-political intrigue. Accordingly, we cannot conclude that the district court abused its discretion when it determined that the probative value of the proffered material was outweighed substantially by the confusion of issues its admission would have caused. *See* Fed. R. Evid. 403.

. . . Noriega's convictions are Affirmed, and the district court's order denying Noriega's motion for a new trial is Affirmed.

UNITED STATES v. FLITCRAFT

803 F.2d 184 (5th Cir. 1986)

JOHNSON, Circuit Judge:

Robert W. Flitcraft and his wife Rebecca appeal their convictions for failing to file tax returns and filing false withholding exemption certificates. . . . At trial, the Flitcrafts admitted that their income was high enough to make them liable for tax and that they had in fact signed the false withholding forms and failed to file returns. They contested only the Government's contention that these acts were done willfully. Mrs. Flitcraft stated that she had trusted her husband when he told her that he had researched the question and that they owed no tax. Mr. Flitcraft testified that he had read cases and articles that convinced him that his wages were not income, merely an even exchange of money for time. The trial judge, a United States magistrate, refused to allow Flitcraft to introduce the legal materials on which he claimed to have relied, but did allow him to testify about them orally.... The Flitcrafts now argue that the jury would have been more likely to credit the sincerity of the Flitcrafts' belief that they were not subject to filing a return if it had seen the documents.

The Federal Rules of Evidence provide that evidence, though relevant, "may be excluded if its probative value is substantially outweighed by the danger of ... confusion of the issues, or misleading the jury, or by consideration of undue delay, waste of time, or needless presentation of cumulative evidence." Fed. R. Evid. 403. A district court's ruling under Rule 403 will not be disturbed except for an abuse of discretion.

In the present case the introduction of the cases and documents relied on by Flitcraft would have been cumulative because Flitcraft testified to the documents he relied on and their contents. The introduction of the documents themselves would have had little further probative value. In addition, the documents presented a danger of confusing the jury by suggesting that the law is unsettled and that it should resolve such doubtful questions of law.... [Reversed on other grounds.]

ABERNATHY v. SUPERIOR HARDWOODS, INC.

704 F.2d 963 (7th Cir. 1983)

POSNER, Circuit Judge.

One day in 1978 Robert Abernathy drove a flatbed truck loaded with logs to a sawmill in Indiana owned by Superior Hardwoods. The logs were fastened to the bed of the truck with four chains. Abernathy released each chain but before he could stow them all in the cab of the truck Superior Hardwoods' forklift began unloading the logs and one tumbled off and hit Abernathy in the back. Abernathy and his wife sued Superior Hardwoods for negligence, basing federal jurisdiction on diversity of citizenship, and got a jury verdict....

The president of Superior Hardwoods made a videotape with his home videotape system showing a forklift unloading logs from a truck at the sawmill. The videotape was not a tape of the accident, of course — it was made several years later — or even an attempt to reconstruct the accident. It was an attempt (in the defendant's words) "to fairly and accurately depict the method in which log trucks are routinely unloaded at" its sawmill. The district judge allowed the tape to be shown to the jury but only with the sound turned off. Yet according to the defendant the soundtrack proves that Abernathy should have heard the forklift beginning to unload the logs.

The levels both of background noise and of forklift operating noise were relevant to the defense of contributory negligence, and there is no objection in principle to presenting evidence of noise levels through a sound recording, even one made long after the accident. But to be admissible — at least as a matter of law, rather than in the trial judge's discretion — the recording must, of course, meet minimum standards of reliability. This one did not. The microphone was not placed where Abernathy had been standing when he was hit by the log, though it easily could have been; the recording was made by an amateur, using amateur's equipment; and there is no indication that in the courtroom the video recorder's volume control would have been adjusted to produce the same decibel level as the sounds actually recorded.

Although all of these points could have been brought out on cross-examination if the soundtrack had been played to the jury, a district judge is not required to encumber a trial with evidence of slight probative value merely because effective cross-examination might expose its weakness. Fed. R. Evid. 403. . . . Juries have a tough enough time deciding cases intelligently even when they are not assailed by evidence of tangential relevance, and federal trials already take up enough time without being prolonged to receive such evidence. Nor can a district judge rely on counsel's self-interest not to offer worthless evidence. A lawyer with a weak case may throw in a lot of evidence just to confuse the jury — a tactic sometimes called "serving up a muddle." As the federal courts become ever busier, the need for district judges to manage trials with a firm hand becomes ever greater. The district judge in this case is to be commended rather than criticized for not taking the easy way out, which would have been to let in all the minimally relevant nonprivileged evidence either party cared to offer . . . [Affirmed in relevant part.]

UNITED STATES v. McRAE

593 F.2d 700 (5th Cir. 1979)

GEE, Circuit Judge:

About two years ago, appellant McRae killed his wife Nancy by shooting her through the head with his deer rifle at point-blank range. That he did so is admitted; his sole defense at trial was that the shooting was not malicious but accidental. The offense having occurred on the Fort Bliss military reservation, McRae was indicted for second-degree murder under 18 U.S.C. §1111. A jury trial resulted in his conviction and sentence to life imprisonment. . . .

[On appeal the defendant objects to] the admission of various photographs of the deceased and of the death scene. It is said that these should have been excluded under Rule 403, Federal Rules of Evidence, as relevant matter the probative value of which is substantially outweighed by the danger of unfair prejudice. Two of these color prints are indeed as the trial court characterized them gross, distasteful and disturbing. Exhibit 29 is a view of Mrs. McRae's corpse, clothed in her bloody garments, bent forward so as to display an exit wound in the back of her skull produced by part of McRae's dum-dum bullet, which exploded in her brain. Exhibit 22 shows a front view of her body, seated in the chair where she died, her left eye disfigured by the bullet's entry and her head broken by its force. By comparison with these, the other photographs are mild; but these are not pretty even to the hardened eye. Neither, however, was the crime, and these exhibits are not flagrantly or deliberately gruesome depictions of it. The trial court carefully reviewed the government's photographic exhibits, excluding some of little probative value. It found those admitted important to establishing elements of the offense such as Mrs. McRae's position and that of the rifle when it was fired, as bearing on McRae's defense of accident.

Relevant evidence is inherently prejudicial; but it is only *unfair* prejudice, *substantially* outweighing probative value, which permits exclusion of relevant matter under Rule 403. Unless trials are to be conducted on scenarios, on unreal facts tailored and sanitized for the occasion, the application of Rule 403 must be cautious and sparing. Its major function is limited to excluding matter of scant or cumulative probative force, dragged in by the heels for the sake of its prejudicial effect. As to such, Rule 403 is meant to relax the iron rule of relevance, to permit the trial judge to preserve the fairness of the proceedings by exclusion despite its relevance. It is not designed to permit the court to "even out" the weight of the evidence, to mitigate a crime, or to make a contest where there is little or none. Here was no parade of horrors. We refuse to interfere with the trial court's exercise of its discretion. . . . Affirmed.

UNITED STATES v. MEHANNA

735 F.3d 32 (1st Cir. 2013)

SELYA, Circuit Judge.

[Terek Mehanna, a 21-year-old American citizen living with his parents in Sudbury, Massachusetts, traveled from Boston to the United Arab Emirates and Yemen with two other men in 2004. The following year Mehanna] began to translate Arab-language materials into English and post his translations on a website — at-Tibyan — that comprised an online community for those sympathetic to al-Qa'ida and Salafi–Jihadi perspectives. . . . At least some offerings that the defendant translated constituted al-Qa'ida-generated media and materials supportive of al-Qa'ida and/or jihad. [Following a federal investigation, Mehanna was charged and ultimately convicted of providing material support to terrorists, conspiring and attempting to provide such support, and several related offenses. He was sentenced to 210 months in prison. On appeal, Mehanna challenged] the district court's admission of dozens of terrorism-related pictures, videos, and printed materials. This evidence, the defendant insists, vastly exceeded what was necessary to prove the government's case, inflamed the jury, and contaminated the verdict. Federal Rule of Evidence 403 governs this challenge. . . .

We begin with a frank acknowledgment that the collection of terrorist-related media introduced into evidence was extensive. According to the defendant, the "most disturbing" items referenced beheadings. For example, one witness testified about portions of a video in which Abu Musab al-Zarqawi extolled the decapitation of American businessman Nicholas Berg while images of deceased American soldiers were displayed on screen.[9] Other testimony indicated that the defendant circulated a video depicting the beheading

---

9. While this evidence was terrifying, we think that the district court's handling of it was emblematic of the court's measured approach: the court allowed descriptive testimony but did not permit the video itself to be shown to the jury.

of *Wall Street Journal* reporter Daniel Pearl.... [The defendant] also assails the government's introduction of more than thirty propaganda video clips, such as al-Qa'ida's *State of the Ummah;* statements of Osama bin Laden and Ayman al-Zawahiri in book and interview form; and dozens of images portraying gripping scenes, such as the World Trade Center engulfed in flames and al-Qa'ida leaders exhorting their followers....

The government argues convincingly that the defendant's motive and intent are material facts and that the disputed media have probative value with respect to those facts. Specifically, the government posits that the defendant, inspired by terrorist rants, developed an anti-American animus, which culminated in his decision to travel to Yemen to join in al-Qa'ida's struggle. The pictures, videos, and literature that he absorbed and endorsed during that evolutionary process, as well as the materials that he used to recruit others to follow a similar path, doubtless bear on his motive and intent. *See, e.g., United States v. El-Mezain,* 664 F.3d 467, 509-10 (5th Cir. 2011) (holding that material seized from the defendant, "including images of violence and videos glorifying Hamas and depicting Hamas leaders, was probative of the motive or intent of the [defendant] to support Hamas"), *cert. denied,* 133 S. Ct. 525 (2012); *United States v. Jayyousi,* 657 F.3d 1085, 1108 (11th Cir. 2011) (holding that televised interview with Osama bin Laden was properly admitted as "state of mind evidence"); *United States v. Abu-Jihaad,* 630 F.3d 102, 133-34 (2d Cir. 2010) (affirming conclusion that "pro-jihadist contents of the videos were relevant to understanding [the defendant's] motive and intent"). While no picture, video, book, or tract spoke directly to the defendant's purpose in going to Yemen, evidence need not achieve the conspicuousness of a smoking gun in order to have probative value.

Probative value, however, is only one pan of the scale. For Rule 403 purposes, that value must be juxtaposed with prejudicial effect (or, more precisely, with unfairly prejudicial effect).... There is a line past which the government's introduction of relevant evidence for the legitimate advancement of its case goes too far. When that line is crossed, fair play morphs into piling on. But that line is hard to draw, and there is no mathematically precise way in which to plot it.... Moreover, it is different in every case. A court simply cannot say with any degree of assurance that thirteen images of Osama bin Laden may safely be admitted, but that the fourteenth image ought to be excluded.

In the last analysis, the lack of a scientifically accurate measuring device reinforces both the importance of the trial judge's role and the wisdom of affording substantial deference to his balancing decision. In this case, we think it is plain that the question of whether the quantum of evidence introduced by the government crossed the indistinct boundary that separates the permissible from the impermissible is fairly debatable. The district court gave this fairly debatable question careful attention, and we are reluctant to second-guess its judgment....

We are mindful that terrorism-related evidence is often emotionally charged.... But much of this emotional overlay is directly related to the nature of the crimes that the defendant has set out to commit. It should not surprise a defendant that proof of his participation in conspiracies to provide material support to terrorist organizations and to kill Americans here and abroad will engender the presentation of evidence offensive to the sensibilities of civilized people. Terrorism trials are not to be confused with high tea at Buckingham Palace....

The government's evidence plainly packed an emotional punch, but Rule 403 does not ensure that trials — even criminal trials — will be antiseptic affairs. Litigants invariably introduce particular evidence as part of an effort to sway jurors to their point of view. In that sense, "all evidence is meant to be prejudicial." *United States v. Rodriguez-Estrada*, 877 F.2d 153, 156 (1st Cir. 1989). Rule 403 was never designed to alter that reality. "[I]t is only *unfair* prejudice which must be avoided." *Id.* (emphasis in original). *United States v. Rodriguez-Estrada*, 877 F.2d 153, 156 (1st Cir. 1989). Rule 403.

We cannot say that the district court's Rule 403 determinations offended this principle. For the most part, the evidence of which the defendant complains served to discredit his claim that his purpose in Yemen was innocuous.... The court below carefully superintended the ebb and flow of the evidence, displayed a high degree of sensitivity in regard to Rule 403 concerns, took pains to minimize the impact of potentially inflammatory bits of evidence, and gave the jury suitably prophylactic instructions. There is no reason to believe, on this record, that the verdict was the result of passion or prejudice.... Affirmed.

OLD CHIEF v. UNITED STATES

519 U.S. 172 (1997)

Justice SOUTER delivered the opinion of the Court.

... In 1993, petitioner, Old Chief, was arrested after a fracas involving at least one gunshot. The ensuing federal charges included not only assault with a dangerous weapon and using a firearm in relation to a crime of violence but violation of 18 U.S.C. §922(g)(1). This statute makes it unlawful for anyone "who has been convicted in any court of a crime punishable by imprisonment for a term exceeding one year" to "possess in or affecting commerce, any firearm...." "[A] crime punishable by imprisonment for a term exceeding one year" is defined to exclude "any Federal or State offenses pertaining to antitrust violations, unfair trade practices, restraints of trade, or other similar offenses relating to the regulation of business practices" and "any State offense classified by the laws of the State as a misdemeanor and punishable by a term of imprisonment of two years or less." §921(a)(20).

The earlier crime charged in the indictment against Old Chief was assault causing serious bodily injury. Before trial, he moved for an order requiring the Government "to refrain from mentioning — by reading the Indictment, during jury selection, in opening statement, or closing argument — and to refrain from offering into evidence or soliciting any testimony from any witness regarding the prior criminal convictions of the Defendant, *except* to state that the Defendant has been convicted of a crime punishable by imprisonment exceeding one (1) year." He said that revealing the name and nature of his prior assault conviction would unfairly tax the jury's capacity to hold the Government to its burden of proof beyond a reasonable doubt on current charges of assault, possession, and violence with a firearm, and he offered to "solve the problem here by stipulating, agreeing and requesting the Court to instruct the jury that he has been convicted of a crime punishable by imprisonment exceeding one (1) yea[r]." He argued that the offer to stipulate to the fact of the prior conviction rendered evidence of the name and nature of the offense inadmissible under Rule 403 of the Federal Rules of Evidence, the danger being that unfair prejudice from that evidence would substantially outweigh its probative value. . . .

The Assistant United States Attorney refused to join in a stipulation, insisting on his right to prove his case his own way, and the District Court agreed, ruling orally that, "If he doesn't want to stipulate, he doesn't have to." At trial, over renewed objection, the Government introduced the order of judgment and commitment for Old Chief's prior conviction. This document disclosed that on December 18, 1988, he "did knowingly and unlawfully assault Rory Dean Fenner, said assault resulting in serious bodily injury," for which Old Chief was sentenced to five years' imprisonment. The jury found Old Chief guilty on all counts, and he appealed. [The Ninth Circuit affirmed.] . . .

As a threshold matter, there is Old Chief's erroneous argument that the name of his prior offense as contained in the record of conviction is irrelevant to the prior-conviction element, and for that reason inadmissible under Rule 402 of the Federal Rules of Evidence. Rule 401 defines relevant evidence as having "any tendency to make the existence of any fact that is of consequence to the determination of the action more probable or less probable than it would be without the evidence." To be sure, the fact that Old Chief's prior conviction was for assault resulting in serious bodily injury rather than, say, for theft was not itself an ultimate fact, as if the statute had specifically required proof of injurious assault. But its demonstration was a step on one evidentiary route to the ultimate fact, since it served to place Old Chief within a particular sub-class of offenders for whom firearms possession is outlawed by §922(g)(1). A documentary record of the conviction for that named offense was thus relevant evidence in making Old Chief's §922(g)(1) status more probable than it would have been without the evidence.

Nor was its evidentiary relevance under Rule 401 affected by the availability of alternative proofs of the element to which it went, such as an admission by Old Chief that he had been convicted of a crime "punishable by imprisonment for a term exceeding one year" within the meaning of the statute. The 1972 Advisory Committee Notes to Rule 401 make this point directly:

> "The fact to which the evidence is directed need not be in dispute. While situations will arise which call for the exclusion of evidence offered to prove a point conceded by the opponent, the ruling should be made on the basis of such considerations as waste of time and undue prejudice (see Rule 403), rather than under any general requirement that evidence is admissible only if directed to matters in dispute."

If, then, relevant evidence is inadmissible in the presence of other evidence related to it, its exclusion must rest not on the ground that the other evidence has rendered it "irrelevant," but on its character as unfairly prejudicial, cumulative or the like, its relevance notwithstanding.

The principal issue is the scope of a trial judge's discretion under Rule 403, which authorizes exclusion of relevant evidence when its "probative value is substantially outweighed by the danger of unfair prejudice, confusion of the issues, or misleading the jury, or by considerations of undue delay, waste of time, or needless presentation of cumulative evidence." Old Chief relies on the danger of unfair prejudice.

The term "unfair prejudice," as to a criminal defendant, speaks to the capacity of some concededly relevant evidence to lure the factfinder into declaring guilt on a ground different from proof specific to the offense charged. . . . Such improper grounds certainly include the one that Old Chief points to here: generalizing a defendant's earlier bad act into bad character and taking that as raising the odds that he did the later bad act now charged (or, worse, as calling for preventive conviction even if he should happen to be innocent momentarily). As then-Judge Breyer put it, "Although . . . 'propensity evidence' is relevant, the risk that a jury will convict for crimes other than those charged — or that, uncertain of guilt, it will convict anyway because a bad person deserves punishment — creates a prejudicial effect that outweighs ordinary relevance." *United States v. Moccia*, 681 F.2d 61, 63 (C.A.1 1982). Justice Jackson described how the law has handled this risk:

> "Courts that follow the common-law tradition almost unanimously have come to disallow resort by the prosecution to any kind of evidence of a defendant's evil character to establish a probability of his guilt. Not that the law invests the defendant with a presumption of good character, but it simply closes the whole matter of character, disposition and reputation on the prosecution's case-in-chief. The state may not show defendant's prior trouble with the law, specific criminal acts, or ill name among his neighbors, even though such facts might logically be persuasive that he is by propensity a probable perpetrator of the crime. The inquiry is not rejected because character is irrelevant; on the contrary, it is said to weigh too much with the jury and to so overpersuade them as to prejudge one with a bad general record and deny him a fair opportunity to defend against a particular charge. The overriding policy of excluding such evidence, despite its admitted probative value, is the practical experience that its disallowance tends to prevent confusion of issues, unfair surprise and undue prejudice." *Michelson v. United States*, 335 U.S. 469, 475-476 (1948) (footnotes omitted).

Rule of Evidence 404(b) reflects this common-law tradition by addressing propensity reasoning directly: "Evidence of other crimes, wrongs, or acts is not admissible to prove the character of a person in order to show action in conformity therewith." There is, accordingly, no question that propensity would be an "improper basis" for conviction and that evidence of a prior conviction is subject to analysis under Rule 403 for relative probative value and for prejudicial risk of misuse as propensity evidence. Cf. 1 J. Strong, McCormick on Evidence 780 (4th ed. 1992) (hereinafter McCormick) (Rule 403 prejudice may occur, for example, when "evidence of convictions for prior, unrelated crimes may lead a juror to think that since the defendant already has a criminal record, an erroneous conviction would not be quite as serious as would otherwise be the case"). . . .

[A] reading of the companions to Rule 403, and of the commentaries that went with them to Congress, makes it clear that what counts as the Rule 403 "probative value" of an item of evidence, as distinct from its Rule

401 "relevance," may be calculated by comparing evidentiary alternatives. The Committee Notes to Rule 401 explicitly say that a party's concession is pertinent to the court's discretion to exclude evidence on the point conceded. Such a concession, according to the Notes, will sometimes "call for the exclusion of evidence offered to prove [the] point conceded by the opponent...." As already mentioned, the Notes make it clear that such rulings should be made not on the basis of Rule 401 relevance but on "such considerations as waste of time and undue prejudice (see Rule 403)...." The Notes to Rule 403 then take up the point by stating that when a court considers "whether to exclude on grounds of unfair prejudice," the "availability of other means of proof may ... be an appropriate factor." The point gets a reprise in the Notes to Rule 404(b), dealing with admissibility when a given evidentiary item has the dual nature of legitimate evidence of an element and illegitimate evidence of character: "No mechanical solution is offered. The determination must be made whether the danger of undue prejudice outweighs the probative value of the evidence in view of the availability of other means of proof and other facts appropriate for making a decision of this kind under 403. Thus the notes leave no question that when Rule 403 confers discretion by providing that evidence "may" be excluded, the discretionary judgment may be informed not only by assessing an evidentiary item's twin tendencies, but by placing the result of that assessment alongside similar assessments of evidentiary alternatives. See 1 McCormick 782, and n.41 (suggesting that Rule 403's "probative value" signifies the "marginal probative value" of the evidence relative to the other evidence in the case); 22 C. Wright & K. Graham, Federal Practice and Procedure §5250, pp. 546-547 (1978) ("The probative worth of any particular bit of evidence is obviously affected by the scarcity or abundance of other evidence on the same point").

In dealing with the specific problem raised by §922(g)(1) and its prior conviction element, there can be no question that evidence of the name or nature of the prior offense generally carries a risk of unfair prejudice to the defendant. That risk will vary from case to case, for the reasons already given, but will be substantial whenever the official record offered by the Government would be arresting enough to lure a juror into a sequence of bad character reasoning. Where a prior conviction was for a gun crime or one similar to other charges in a pending case the risk of unfair prejudice would be especially obvious, and Old Chief sensibly worried that the prejudicial effect of his prior assault conviction, significant enough with respect to the current gun charges alone, would take on added weight from the related assault charge against him.[8]

---

8. It is true that a prior offense may be so far removed in time or nature from the current gun charge and any others brought with it that its potential to prejudice the defendant unfairly will be minimal. Some prior offenses, in fact, may even have some potential to prejudice the Government's case unfairly. Thus an extremely old conviction for a relatively minor felony that nevertheless qualifies under the statute might strike many jurors as a foolish basis for convicting an otherwise upstanding member of the community of otherwise legal gun possession. Since the Government could not, of course, compel the defendant to admit formally the existence of the prior conviction, the Government would have to bear the risk of jury nullification, a fact that might properly drive the Government's charging decision.

The District Court was also presented with alternative, relevant, admissible evidence of the prior conviction by Old Chief's offer to stipulate, evidence necessarily subject to the District Court's consideration on the motion to exclude the record offered by the Government. Although Old Chief's formal offer to stipulate was, strictly, to enter a formal agreement with the Government to be given to the jury, even without the Government's acceptance his proposal amounted to an offer to admit that the prior-conviction element was satisfied, and a defendant's admission is, of course, good evidence. See Fed. Rule Evid. 801(d)(2)(A).

Old Chief's proffered admission would, in fact, have been not merely relevant but seemingly conclusive evidence of the element. The statutory language in which the prior-conviction requirement is couched shows no congressional concern with the specific name or nature of the prior offense beyond what is necessary to place it within the broad category of qualifying felonies, and Old Chief clearly meant to admit that his felony did qualify, by stipulating "that the Government has proven one of the essential elements of the offense." As a consequence, although the name of the prior offense may have been technically relevant, it addressed no detail in the definition of the prior-conviction element that would not have been covered by the stipulation or admission. Logic, then, seems to side with Old Chief.

There is, however, one more question to be considered before deciding whether Old Chief's offer was to supply evidentiary value at least equivalent to what the Government's own evidence carried. In arguing that the stipulation or admission would not have carried equivalent value, the Government invokes the familiar, standard rule that the prosecution is entitled to prove its case by evidence of its own choice, or, more exactly, that a criminal defendant may not stipulate or admit his way out of the full evidentiary force of the case as the Government chooses to present it. The authority usually cited for this rule is *Parr v. United States*, 255 F.2d 86 (CA5), cert. denied, 358 U.S. 824 (1958), in which the Fifth Circuit explained that the "reason for the rule is to permit a party 'to present to the jury a picture of the events relied upon. To substitute for such a picture a naked admission might have the effect to rob the evidence of much of its fair and legitimate weight.'" 255 F.2d, at 88 (quoting *Dunning v. Maine Central R. Co.*, 91 Me. 87, 39 A. 352, 256 (1897)).

This is unquestionably true as a general matter. The "fair and legitimate weight" of conventional evidence showing individual thoughts and acts amounting to a crime reflects the fact that making a case with testimony and tangible things not only satisfies the formal definition of an offense, but tells a colorful story with descriptive richness. Unlike an abstract premise, whose force depends on going precisely to a particular step in a course of reasoning, a piece of evidence may address any number of separate elements, striking hard just because it shows so much at once; the account of a shooting that establishes capacity and causation may tell just as much about the trigger-man's motive and intent. Evidence thus has force beyond any linear scheme of reasoning, and as its pieces come together a narrative gains momentum, with power not only to support conclusions but to sustain the willingness of jurors to draw the inferences, whatever they may be, necessary to reach an honest verdict. This persuasive power of the concrete and particular is often essential to the capacity of jurors to satisfy the obligations that the law places on them.

Jury duty is usually unsought and sometimes resisted, and it may be as difficult for one juror suddenly to face the findings that can send another human being to prison, as it is for another to hold out conscientiously for acquittal. When a juror's duty does seem hard, the evidentiary account of what a defendant has thought and done can accomplish what no set of abstract statements ever could, not just to prove a fact but to establish its human significance, and so to implicate the law's moral underpinnings and a juror's obligation to sit in judgment. Thus, the prosecution may fairly seek to place its evidence before the jurors, as much to tell a story of guiltiness as to support an inference of guilt, to convince the jurors that a guilty verdict would be morally reasonable as much as to point to the discrete elements of a defendant's legal fault.

But there is something even more to the prosecution's interest in resisting efforts to replace the evidence of its choice with admissions and stipulations, for beyond the power of conventional evidence to support allegations and give life to the moral underpinnings of law's claims, there lies the need for evidence in all its particularity to satisfy the jurors' expectations about what proper proof should be. Some such demands they bring with them to the courthouse, assuming, for example, that a charge of using a firearm to commit an offense will be proven by introducing a gun in evidence. A prosecutor who fails to produce one, or some good reason for his failure, has something to be concerned about. "If [jurors'] expectations are not satisfied, triers of fact may penalize the party who disappoints them by drawing a negative inference against that party." Saltzburg, A Special Aspect of Relevance: Countering Negative Inferences Associated with the Absence of Evidence, 66 Calif. L. Rev. 1011, 1019 (1978) (footnotes omitted). Expectations may also arise in jurors' minds simply from the experience of a trial itself. The use of witnesses to describe a train of events naturally related can raise the prospect of learning about every ingredient of that natural sequence the same way. If suddenly the prosecution presents some occurrence in the series differently, as by announcing a stipulation or admission, the effect may be like saying, "never mind what's behind the door," and jurors may well wonder what they are being kept from knowing. A party seemingly responsible for cloaking something has reason for apprehension, and the prosecution with its burden of proof may prudently demur at a defense request to interrupt the flow of evidence telling the story in the usual way.

In sum, the accepted rule that the prosecution is entitled to prove its case free from any defendant's option to stipulate the evidence away rests on good sense. A syllogism is not a story, and a naked proposition in a courtroom may be no match for the robust evidence that would be used to prove it. People who hear a story interrupted by gaps of abstraction may be puzzled at the missing chapters, and jurors asked to rest a momentous decision on the story's truth can feel put upon at being asked to take responsibility knowing that more could be said than they have heard. A convincing tale can be told with economy, but when economy becomes a break in the natural sequence of narrative evidence, an assurance that the missing link is really there is never more than second best.

This recognition that the prosecution with its burden of persuasion needs evidentiary depth to tell a continuous story has, however, virtually no application when the point at issue is a defendant's legal status, dependent on some judgment rendered wholly independently of the concrete events of later criminal behavior charged against him. As in this case, the choice of evidence for such an element is usually not between eventful narrative and abstract proposition, but between propositions of slightly varying abstraction, either a record saying that conviction for some crime occurred at a certain time or a statement admitting the same thing without naming the particular offense. . . . Nor can it be argued that the events behind the prior conviction are proper nourishment for the jurors' sense of obligation to vindicate the public interest. The issue is not whether concrete details of the prior crime should come to the jurors' attention but whether the name or general character of that crime is to be disclosed. Congress, however, has made it plain that distinctions among generic felonies do not count for this purpose; the fact of the qualifying conviction is alone what matters under the statute. . . . The most the jury needs to know is that the conviction admitted by the defendant falls within the class of crimes that Congress thought should bar a convict from possessing a gun, and this point may be made readily in a defendant's admission and underscored in the court's jury instructions. Finally, the most obvious reason that the general presumption that the prosecution may choose its evidence is so remote from application here is that proof of the defendant's status goes to an element entirely outside the natural sequence of what the defendant is charged with thinking and doing to commit the current offense. Providing status without telling exactly why that status was imposed leaves no gap in the story of a defendant's subsequent criminality, and its demonstration by stipulation or admission neither displaces a chapter from a continuous sequence of conventional evidence nor comes across as an officious substitution, to confuse or offend or provoke reproach.

Given these peculiarities of the element of felony-convict status and of admissions and the like when used to prove it, there is no cognizable difference between the evidentiary significance of an admission and of the legitimately probative component of the official record the prosecution would prefer to place in evidence. For purposes of the Rule 403 weighing of the probative against the prejudicial, the functions of the competing evidence are distinguishable only by the risk inherent in the one and wholly absent from the other. In this case, as in any other in which the prior conviction is for an offense likely to support conviction on some improper ground, the only reasonable conclusion was that the risk of unfair prejudice did substantially out-weigh the discounted probative value of the record of conviction, and it was an abuse of discretion to admit the record when an admission was available.[10] What we have said shows why this will be the general rule when proof of convict status is at issue, just as the prosecutor's choice will generally

10. There may be yet other means of proof besides a formal admission on the record that, with a proper objection, will obligate a district court to exclude evidence of the name of the offense. A redacted record of conviction is the one most frequently mentioned. Any alternative will; of course, require some jury instruction to explain it (just as it will require some discretion when the indictment is read). A redacted judgment in this case, for example, would presumably have revealed to the jury that Old Chief was previously convicted in federal court and sentenced to more than a year's imprisonment, but it would not have shown whether his previous conviction was for one of the business offenses that do not count, under §921(a)(20). Hence, an instruction, with the defendant's consent, would be necessary to make clear that the redacted judgment was enough to satisfy the status element remaining in the case. The

survive a Rule 403 analysis when a defendant seeks to force the substitution of an admission for evidence creating a coherent narrative of his thoughts and actions in perpetrating the offense for which he is being tried.

The judgment is reversed, and the case is remanded to the Ninth Circuit for further proceedings consistent with this opinion.[11]

Justice O'CONNOR, with whom THE CHIEF JUSTICE, Justice SCALIA, and Justice THOMAS join, dissenting.

. . . Federal Rule of Evidence 105 provides that when evidence is admissible for one purpose, but not another, "the court, upon request, shall restrict the evidence to its proper scope and instruct the jury accordingly." Indeed, on petitioner's own motion in this case, the District Court instructed the jury that it was not to "consider a prior conviction as evidence of guilt of the crime for which the defendant is now on trial." The jury is presumed to have followed this cautionary instruction, see *Shannon v. United States*, 512 U.S. 537, 585 (1994), and the instruction offset whatever prejudice might have arisen from the introduction of petitioner's prior conviction. . . .

A jury is as likely to be puzzled by the "missing chapter" resulting from a defendant's stipulation to his prior felony conviction as it would be by the defendant's conceding any other element of the crime. The jury may wonder why it has not been told the name of the crime, or it may question why the defendant's firearm possession was illegal, given the tradition of lawful gun ownership in this country. . . .

. . . I cannot agree that it "unfairly" prejudices a defendant for the Government to prove his prior conviction with evidence that reveals the name or basic nature of his past crime. Like it or not, Congress chose to make a defendant's prior criminal conviction one of the two elements of the §922(g)(1) offense. Moreover, crimes have names; a defendant is not convicted of some indeterminate, unspecified "crime." Nor do I think that Federal Rule of Evidence 403 can be read to obviate the well accepted principle, grounded in both the Constitution and in our precedent, that the Government may not be forced to accept a defendant's concession to an element of a charged offense as proof of that element. I respectfully dissent.

DANIEL C. RICHMAN, *OLD CHIEF V. UNITED STATES*: STIPULATING AWAY PROSECUTORIAL ACCOUNTABILITY?

83 Va. L. Rev. 939, 952–953 (1997)

Although the Court appears willfully blind to the effects of its rule on the government's prospects at trial, Justice Souter's analysis is far more convincing

---

Government might, indeed, propose such a redacted judgment for the trial court to weigh against a defendant's offer to admit, as indeed the Government might do even if the defendant's admission had been received into evidence.

11. In remanding, we imply no opinion on the possibility of harmless error, an issue not passed upon below.

when read, not as description of jury behavior, but as a determination that prosecutors must accept the consequences of a statute that reaches far too many cases that do not comport with popular notions of criminality. . . . Jurors might indeed take §922(g)(1) prosecutions less seriously, and consequently be less likely to return guilty verdicts, when precluded from learning the particulars of defendants' prior records. But if Congress is going to legislate so broadly, the Court suggests, perhaps §922(g)(1) offenses *ought* to be taken less seriously.

PROBLEM

2.1. A criminal defendant is charged in federal court with three counts of being a felon in possession of a firearm. The defendant claims he is not a "felon" within the meaning of the federal prohibition. The prosecutor seeks to introduce into evidence three high-powered, military-style rifles found in the defendant's basement. Defense counsel objects on grounds of relevance and offers to stipulate that three weapons satisfying the statutory definition of "firearm" were found in the defendant's basement. The prosecutor says she does not want to stipulate to this fact but prefers to prove it, in part by introducing the guns into evidence. Does the judge have discretion to overrule the objection?

C. Conditional Relevance

Many rules of evidence make the admissibility of a particular item of proof depend on the answer to a "preliminary question" of fact. The attorney-client privilege, for example, applies only to "confidential" communications. Most preliminary questions of this kind are answered by the trial judge. To apply the attorney-client privilege, for example, the judge simply decides whether he or she believes the communication in question was "confidential."

But when the rule being applied is the ban on irrelevant evidence, things get more complicated. Suppose a piece of evidence — say, in a reckless driving prosecution, the speed of a certain car — is relevant only if some "preliminary fact" is true — say, that the defendant was driving the car. (As you will see, not everyone believes that situations like this actually arise, given the low threshold for relevance. But suppose for the moment that they do.) It seems wrong for the judge to decide whether he or she *personally* believes the defendant was driving the car; if that fact is in dispute, it seems like something the jury should decide.

So the rules direct the judge to allow the speed of the car to be proved as long as there is sufficient evidence to permit *a reasonable jury* to conclude that the defendant was driving the car. The judge applies a "sufficiency" standard, rather than simply deciding for himself or herself whether the preponderance of the evidence suggests that the defendant was at the wheel. The preliminary question the judge has to answer is whether there is sufficient evidence to allow the jury to find the defendant was the driver.

Situations of this kind are instances of "conditional relevance." Lawyers and judges sometimes say loosely that questions of conditional relevance are for the jury rather than the judge, but that is misleading. The judge still decides on the admissibility of the evidence, and the judge does so by considering a preliminary question of fact. It is just that the preliminary question the judge asks in the case of conditional relevance is not whether the preliminary fact is *actually* true, but whether a reasonable jury could *think* so, given the other evidence in the case.

[F.R.E. 104(b); C.E.C. §403]

EDMUND M. MORGAN, BASIC PROBLEMS OF EVIDENCE

45–46 (1961)

It often happens that upon an issue as to existence of fact C, a combination of facts A and B will be highly relevant but that either without the other will have no relevance. For example, if M is charged with having caused the death of X, the fact that X carried life insurance in favor of M is entirely irrelevant unless M knew of it. Or if P sues D for breach of contract, and offers evidence of an oral offer made to X and acceptance thereof by X in behalf of D, the offer and acceptance are irrelevant unless X's authority to act for D also exists. In each of these situations fact A is irrelevant without fact B. It is impossible to offer evidence through witnesses of both simultaneously.... If the proponent can make the existence of B a question for the judge by first offering evidence of the existence of A, he can make the existence of A determinable by the judge by first offering evidence of the existence of B. Consequently where the only objection is lack of relevance, it seems clear that the function of the judge should be to see to it only that sufficient evidence of each is introduced to justify a finding of its existence and the jury should determine the dispute as to each under proper instructions from the judge.

ADVISORY COMMITTEE NOTE TO F.R.E. 104(b)

In some situations, the relevancy of an item of evidence, in the large sense, depends upon the existence of a particular preliminary fact. Thus when a spoken statement is relied upon to prove notice to X, it is without probative value unless X heard it. Or if a letter purporting to be from Y is relied upon to establish an admission by him, it has no probative value unless Y wrote or authorized it. Relevance in this sense has been labelled "conditional relevancy." Morgan, Basic Problems of Evidence 45–46 (1962). Problems arising in connection with it are to be distinguished from problems of logical relevancy, e.g., evidence in a murder case that accused on the day before purchased a weapon of the kind used in the killing, treated in Rule 401.

If preliminary questions of conditional relevancy were determined solely by the judge, as provided in [Rule 104(a)], the functioning of the jury as a trier of fact would be greatly restricted and in some cases virtually destroyed. These are appropriate questions for juries. Accepted treatment, as provided in the rule, is consistent with that given fact questions generally. The judge makes a preliminary determination whether the foundation evidence is sufficient to support a finding of fulfillment of the condition. If so, the item is admitted. If, after all the evidence on the issue is in, pro and con, the jury could reasonably conclude that fulfillment of the condition is not established, the issue is for them. If the evidence is not such as to allow a finding, the judge withdraws the matter from their consideration.... The order of proof here, as generally, is subject to the control of the judge.

STATE v. McNEELY

8 P.3d 212 (Or. 2000)

VAN HOOMISSEN, J.

[Defendant McNeely was convicted of aggravated murder. A fellow jail inmate, Thompson, testified at trial about statements McNeely had made to him.]

Defendant contends . . . that the trial court erred in denying his motion to exclude Thompson's testimony, because Thompson was unable to identify defendant at trial as the man with whom he had spoken in jail. . . . The state responds that Thompson's testimony was "conditionally relevant," citing OEC 104,[5] and, thus, was properly admitted.

Defendant's assignment of error presents a question of conditional relevancy. . . . When dealing with a matter of conditional relevancy under OEC 104(2), the judge determines whether the foundation evidence is sufficient for the jury reasonably to find that the condition on which relevance depends has been fulfilled. If so, the evidence is admitted; if not, the evidence is not admitted. After the judge decides that the foundation evidence is sufficient for the jury reasonably to find the contested fact under OEC 104(2), either party

---

5. OEC 104 provides in part:

   "(1)   Preliminary questions concerning the qualification of a person to be a witness, the existence of a privilege or the admissibility of evidence shall be determined by the court, subject to the provisions of subsection (2) of this section. In making its determination the court is not bound by the rules of evidence except those with respect to privileges."

   "(2)   When the relevancy of evidence depends upon the fulfillment of a condition of fact, the court shall admit it upon, or subject to, the introduction of evidence sufficient to support a finding of the fulfillment of the condition."

   Conditional relevancy means a situation where one fact is relevant only if another fact is proven. Laird C. Kirkpatrick, *Oregon Evidence* 31 (2d ed. 1989 & Supp. 1999).

may introduce evidence before the jury that is relevant to the weight and credibility of the evidence.

At trial, Thompson testified that he had spoken with a man in jail who had admitted choking and killing the victim. If defendant were that man, then Thompson's testimony was relevant evidence. There also was evidence at trial that Thompson and defendant had met in jail in 1993. Thompson testified:

> "I spoke to somebody that represented himself as being [defendant] or was represented by somebody else as being [defendant]."

Thompson related several incriminating conversations that he had with that man. Moreover, there also was evidence that defendant had gained 25 pounds and had shaved off his moustache since the time when he and Thompson were in jail together.

Despite Thompson's inability to identify defendant at trial, the trial court determined that a reasonable juror could find that defendant was the person with whom Thompson had spoken in jail. The record supports that conclusion. We agree with the trial court. Thompson's inability to identify defendant at trial went to the weight the jury might give to his testimony, not to its admissibility. It follows that the trial court did not err in leaving the matter to the jury. . . . [Affirmed.]

VAUGHN C. BALL, THE MYTH OF CONDITIONAL RELEVANCE

14 Ga. L. Rev. 435, 440–446, 453, 467 (1980)

[L]et us consider one of Professor Morgan's illustrations, the case of the oral contract alleged to have been entered into by P and by X as agent for D. Almost all of the illustrations can be cast into a parallel form. In Morgan's formulation, fact A is: offer by P and acceptance by X on behalf of D, all treated as one fact. Fact B is authorization of X to contract for D. "[T]he offer and acceptance are irrelevant unless X's authority to act for D also exists." . . .

[But] problems of evidence . . . deal with *probabilities*, not with truths or falsehoods. . . . The definition of relevancy adopted in all modern writing on the subject and in the Federal Rules recognizes this. . . . [13]

. . . [Whatever the probability of B,] there [is] some possibility of a contract when A occur[s], but by definition no probability of a contract when A [does] not occur. . . . [Therefore,] the probability of a contract [is] greater if A occur[s] than if it [does] not. And evidence which raise[s] A's probability thus change[s] the probability of a contract . . . and thus [is] relevant to the proposition of contract.

---

13. Rule 401 says "any" tendency to make more probable or less probable than it would be without the evidence; and the Note says: "Any more stringent requirement is unworkable and unrealistic," quoting McCormick, who points out that "a brick is not a wall." Everyone recognizes that a brick is not a wall at some point in these analyses. The difficulties of the current doctrine of conditional relevancy stem from the inability to recognize a brick.

The failure to notice and deal with the obvious relation between no offer and acceptance and no contract is what shows that the received doctrine, after paying lip-service to the definition or relevancy based on probability, slips back into the true-false groove, which is so useful in analyzing the substantive law, and so misleading in analyzing evidence. . . . [T]here does not appear to be any scope for the operation of Rule 104(b) at all.

PROBLEM

2.2. The prosecution in a murder case wishes to demonstrate motive by proving that, a week before his death, the victim assaulted the defendant's cousin. Defense counsel objects on grounds of relevance. How should the judge rule? Does it matter whether the judge believes (a) that the defendant knew about the assault, or (b) that the jury could reasonably conclude the defendant knew about the assault?

HEARSAY

"I heard he came into money and moved to a portobello."

A. THE HEARSAY RULE AND ITS RATIONALE

1. Introduction

Wigmore called the hearsay prohibition "the most characteristic rule of the Anglo-American law of Evidence" and said it was second only to jury trial as "the greatest contribution of that eminently practical legal system to the world's methods of procedures." Few commentators since have been so charitable. The general attitude today is probably best summed up by the English evidence scholar Peter Murphy: "There should probably be an organisation called 'Hearsay Anonymous.' Membership would be open to those judges, practitioners and students (not to mention occasional law teachers) to whom the rule against hearsay has always been an awesome and terrifying mystery. Like its partner in terror, the rule against perpetuities, the rule against hearsay ranks as one of the law's most celebrated nightmares."

For better or worse, the hearsay rule and its exceptions are unrivalled for complexity by any other part of American evidence law — or, probably, by any part of the evidence law of any other nation. Hearsay law is complicated not only because the prohibition against hearsay has many exceptions, but also because the prohibition itself can be difficult to comprehend. At its core, though, the hearsay rule expresses a very simple notion: Factual disputes in criminal and civil cases should be decided based on live, sworn testimony, not secondhand accounts of what other people said outside of court. Opinions differ on the merits of this notion, but no one doubts its importance. It reflects the strong and distinctive preference our system of adjudication has historically had for *viva voce* evidence, and a continuing faith that juries are best able to sort truth from falsehood by hearing directly from sworn witnesses subject to cross-examination.

[F.R.E. 801(a)-(c), 802; C.E.C. §§225, 1200]

TRIAL OF SIR WALTER RALEIGH, KNIGHT, FOR HIGH TREASON, BY A SPECIAL COMMISSION OF OYER AND TERMINER, AT WINCHESTER, 17TH NOVEMBER, 1603, 2 JAMES I

1 Criminal Trials 400, 427, 434–436, 441–442, 449, 451, 511
(David Jardine ed., 1850)

[Raleigh was charged with conspiring with Lord Cobham and others to kill James I and to place Lady Arabella Stuart on the throne. Cobham was interrogated in the Tower of London and signed a sworn confession, which he later recanted. His confession was the chief evidence against Raleigh.]

Sir W. Raleigh. . . . But it is strange to see how you press me still with my Lord Cobham, and yet will not produce him; it is not for gaining of time or prolonging my life that I urge this; he is in the house hard by and may soon be brought hither; let him be produced, and if he will yet accuse me or avow this Confession of his, it shall convict me and ease you of further proof.

Lord Cecil. Sir Walter Raleigh presseth often that my Lord Cobham should be brought face to face; if he ask as a thing of grace or favour, they must come from him only who can give them; but if he ask a matter of law, then, in order that we, who sit here as commissioners, may be satisfied, I desire to hear the opinions of my Lords, the Judges, whether it may be done by law.

The Judges all answered, that in respect it might be a mean to cover many with treasons, and it might be prejudicial to the King, therefore by the law it was not sufferable.

Sir W. Raleigh. Good my Lords, let my accuser come face to face, and be deposed. Were the case but for a small copyhold, you would have witnesses or good proof to lead the jury to a verdict; and I am here for my life!

Popham, C.J. There must not such a gap be opened for the destruction of the King as would be if we should grant this; you plead hard for yourself, but the laws plead as hard for the King. Where no circumstances do concur to make a matter probable, then an accuser may be heard; but so many circumstances agreeing and confirming the accusation in this case, the accuser is not to be produced; for having first confessed against himself voluntarily, and so charged another person, if we shall now hear him again in person, he may for favour or fear retract what formerly he hath said, and the jury may, by that means, be inveigled. . . .

Sir Walter Raleigh. I have already often urged the producing of my Lord Cobham, but it is still denied me. I appeal now once more to your Lordships in this: my Lord Cobham is the only one that hath accused me, for all the treasons urged upon me are by reflection from him. It is now clear that he hath since retracted; therefore since his accusation is recalled by himself, let him now by word of mouth convict or condemn me. Campion, the Jesuit, was not denied to have his accusers face to face. And if that be true which hath been some labored all this day, that I have been the setter-on of my Lord Cobham, his instigator, and have *infused* these treasons upon him, as hath been said, then have I been the efficient cause of his destruction; all his honours, houses, lands, and good, and all he hath, are lost by me; against whom, then, should he seek revenge but upon me? And the world knoweth him as revengeful of nature as any man living. Besides, a dying man is ever presumed to speak truth: now Cobham is absolutely in the King's mercy; to excuse me cannot avail him, by accusing me he may hope for favour. It is you, then, Mr. Attorney, that should press his testimony, and I ought to fear his producing, if all that be true which you have alleged.

Lord Henry Howard. Sir Walter, you have heard that it cannot be granted; pray importune us no longer.

Sir Walter Raleigh. Nay, my Lord, it toucheth my life, which I value at as a high a rate as your Lordship does yours.

Lord Cecil. I am afraid my often speaking may give opinion to the hearers that I have delight to hear myself talk. Sir Walter Raleigh has often urged, and still doth urge, the producing of my Lord Cobham, I would know of my Lords the Judges, if it might not stand with the order of our proceedings to take a further time, and know his Majesty's pleasure in that which is desired.

The Judges resolved that the Proceedings must go on and receive an end. . . .

Attorney-General. I shall now produce a witness *viva voce.*

He then produced one Dyer, a pilot, who being sworn, said, Being at Lisbon, there came to me a Portugal gentleman who asked me how the King of England did, and whether he was crowned? I answered him that I hoped our noble King was well and crowned by this, but the time was not come when I came from the coast for Spain. "Nay," says he, "your King shall never be crowned, for Don Cobham and Don Raleigh will cut his throat before he come to be crowned." And this in time was found to be spoken in mid July.

Sir W. Raleigh. This is the saying of some wild Jesuit or beggarly Priest; but what proof is it against me?

Attorney-General. It must per force arise out of some preceding intelligence, and shows that your treason had wings. . . .

The Evidence now seemed at an end; whereupon Sir Walter Raleigh addressed himself to the Jury, and used a speech to this effect:—

Sir W. Raleigh. You, Gentlemen of the Jury . . . if you yourselves would like to be hazarded in your lives, disabled in your posterities,—your lands, goods, and all you have confiscated,—your wives, children, and servants left crying to the world; if you would be content all this should befall you upon a trial by suspicions and presumptions,—upon an accusation not subscribed by your accuser,—without the open testimony of a single witness, then so judge me as you would yourselves be judged. . . .

This ended, the jury were willed to go together; who departed, and stayed not a quarter of an hour, when they returned, bringing in their verdict of Guilty of Treason. . . . The Lord Chief Justice then delivered the judgment of the Court in the usual form in cases of high treason. . . .

The conduct of the Judges on the trial of Sir Walter Raleigh at Winchester has been warmly censured by his numerous biographers, and by most modern historians who have related the transaction: and, undoubtedly, the injustice of the course of evidence and of the conviction is so flagrant, that unprofessional writers and readers are naturally led into the belief, that the whole proceedings must have been, even at that time, grossly contrary to law. Unfortunately, and in spite of the general assertion of lawyers to the contrary, the rules of law are not, even in the present improved state of society, always founded upon the principles of reason and justice; still less were they so in the reign of James I.

LEAKE v. HAGERT

175 N.W.2d 675 (N.D. 1970)

PAULSON, J.

This is an appeal by the plaintiff, Allen Leake, from a judgment of dismissal of his cause of action entered in the District Court of Grand Forks County, North Dakota, and from an order of the trial court denying his motion for a new trial.

Allen Leake's complaint was predicated upon the alleged negligence of the defendant, Charlotte Hagert, in her operation of a motor vehicle on October 25, 1966, wherein she negligently and carelessly drove her automobile into the rear of the plow being towed by a tractor which Leake was operating, causing injuries to Leake and damages to his plow and tractor. Leake's complaint included allegations of damages for hospital and doctor bills; for permanent injuries to his chest and right arm; for pain and suffering;

and for damages to his plow and tractor; and he prayed for a judgment against Charlotte Hagert in the sum of $27,600. Charlotte Hagert, in her answer, admitted that the collision occurred, but, as a defense, denied that the collision was proximately caused by her negligence in the operation of her motor vehicle, and she alleged that the sole and proximate cause of the collision was the negligence of the plaintiff in the maintenance and operation of his tractor and plow, upon a public highway after sunset, without proper lights, reflectors, or other warnings. Charlotte Hagert counterclaimed for damages caused by the alleged negligence of Allen Leake for permanent injuries, for pain and suffering, for hospitalization and medical expenses, and for damages to her 1966 Plymouth automobile; and she prayed for a judgment against him in the sum of $32,000.

All claims and defenses of both Allen Leake and Charlotte Hagert were submitted to a jury, which returned a verdict dismissing the complaint of Allen Leake as well as dismissing the counterclaim of Charlotte Hagert. . . .

[Leake appealed but Hagert did not.]

Leake's first contention on appeal is that certain errors at law occurred during the course of the trial, at the time that the trial court overruled objections to the admission of certain evidence. The evidence objected to was certain testimony adduced from Edward Gross, an adjuster who investigated the accident. Gross testified that Allen Leake's son told him, with reference to the small rear light on the tractor, that the red lens had been out for some time. Edward Gross's testimony concerning the statement of Allen Leake's son was hearsay.

The hearsay rule prohibits use of a person's assertion, as equivalent to testimony of the fact asserted, unless the assertor is brought to testify in court on the stand, where he may be probed and cross-examined as to the grounds of his assertion and his qualifications to make it. *Grand Forks B. & D. Co. v. Iowa Hardware Mut. Ins. Co.*, 31 N.W.2d 495 (1948). *See* 5 Wigmore on Evidence (3d ed.) §§1361, 1364. . . . Leake's son did not testify in the present action; he was not a party to the action; his statement was not made under oath; his statement was not subject to cross-examination; and he was not available as a witness at the time of trial because he was in the Army and overseas. We find that it was error for the trial court to admit into evidence the testimony concerning what Leake's son said to Edward Gross; the son's statement was hearsay and should have been excluded.

Having found that the trial court erred in admitting the statement of Allen Leake's son into evidence, we must determine on this appeal whether such an erroneous admission was prejudicial and constitutes reversible error. Under Rule 61, N.D.R. Civ. P., error in the admission of evidence is not a ground for a new trial unless such error affects the substantial rights of the parties. . . . Other witnesses testified during the trial as to the condition of the taillight and whether the light had a red lens. Curtis Hagert, Myron Larson, and Edward Gross testified to the fact that the rear light was painted or covered with some reddish substance and that there was nothing which would indicate that the red lens had been shattered by the accident. In addition, a statement taken by Edward Gross, from Allen Leake's summary of circumstances surrounding the accident, included a statement that the lens had been out for some time before the accident. This statement was introduced by Allen Leake.

Reviewing the record concerning the testimony submitted with reference to the condition of the light and the lens at the time of the accident, we find that the hearsay statement of Allen Leake's son was erroneously admitted by the trial court, but that such error was not prejudicial. . . . [The judgment is affirmed.]

McCORMICK ON EVIDENCE

§245, at 2:178-81 (Kenneth S. Broun ed., 7th ed. 2013)

The factors upon which the value of testimony depends are the perception, memory, narration, and sincerity of the witness. (1) *Perception*. Did the witness perceive what is described and perceive it accurately? (2) *Memory*. Has the witness retained an accurate impression of that perception? (3) *Narration*. Does the witness' language convey that impression accurately? (4) *Sincerity*. Is the witness, with varying degrees of intention, testifying falsely?

In order to encourage witnesses to put forth their best efforts and to expose inaccuracies that might be present with respect to any of the foregoing factors, the Anglo-American tradition evolved three conditions under which witnesses ordinarily are required to testify: oath, personal presence at the trial, and cross-examination. The rule against hearsay is designed to insure compliance with these ideal conditions, and when one of them is absent, the hearsay objection becomes pertinent.

In the hearsay situation, two "witnesses" are involved. The first complies with all three of the ideal conditions for the giving of testimony but merely reports what the second "witness" said. The second "witness" is the out-of-court declarant whose statement was not given in compliance with the ideal conditions but contains the critical information.

Oath. Among the earliest of the criticisms of hearsay, and one often repeated in judicial opinions down to the present, is the objection that the out-of-court declarant who made the hearsay statement commonly speaks or writes without the solemnity of the oath administered to witnesses in a court of law. The oath may be important in two aspects. As a ceremonial and religious symbol, it may induce a feeling of special obligation to speak the truth, and it may also impress upon the witness the danger of criminal punishment for perjury, to which the judicial oath of an equivalent solemn affirmation would be a prerequisite condition. . . .

Personal presence at trial. Another long-asserted objection is the lack of opportunity for observation of the out-of-court declarant's demeanor, with the light that this may shed on credibility. In addition, the solemnity of the occasion and possibility of public disgrace can scarcely fail to impress the witness, and testifying falsely becomes more difficult if the person against whom it is directed is present. . . .

Cross-examination. The lack of any opportunity for the adversary to cross-examine the absent declarant whose out-of-court statement is reported is today accepted as the main justification for the exclusion of hearsay. As early as 1668, hearsay was rejected because "the other party could not cross-examine the witness sworn." ... Cross-examination, as Bentham pointed out, was a distinctive feature of the English trial system, and the one that most contributed to the prestige of the institution of jury trial. He called it "a security for the correctness and completeness of testimony." The nature of this safeguard which hearsay lacks is indicated by Chancellor Kent: "Hearsay testimony is from the very nature of it attended with all such doubts and difficulties and it cannot clear them up. 'A person who relates a hearsay is not obliged to enter into any particulars, to answer any questions, to solve any difficulties, to reconcile any contradictions, to explain any obscurities, to remove any ambiguities; he entrenches himself in the simple assertion that he was told so, and leaves the burden entirely on his dead or absent author.'" In perhaps his most famous remark, Wigmore described cross-examination as "beyond any doubt the greatest legal engine ever invented for the discovery of truth."

LAURENCE H. TRIBE, TRIANGULATING HEARSAY

87 Harv. L. Rev. 957, 958–961 (1974)

The basic hearsay problem is that of forging a reliable chain of inferences, from an act or utterance of a person not subject to contemporaneous in-court cross-examination about that act or utterance, to an event that the act or utterance is supposed to reflect. Typically, the first link in the required chain of inferences is the link from the act or utterance to the belief it is thought to express or indicate. It is helpful to think of this link as involving a "trip" into the head of the person responsible for the act or utterance (the declarant) to see what he or she was really thinking when the act occurred. The second link is the one from the declarant's assumed belief to a conclusion about some external event that is supposed to have triggered the belief, or that is linked to the belief in some other way. This link involves a trip out of the head of the declarant, in order to match the declarant's assumed belief with the external reality sought to be demonstrated.

The trier must obviously employ such a chain of inferences whenever a witness testifies in court. But the process has long been regarded as particularly suspect when the act or utterance is not one made in court, under oath, by a person whose demeanor at the time is witnessed by the trier, and under circumstances permitting immediate cross-examination by counsel in order to probe possible inaccuracies in the inferential chain. These inaccuracies are usually attributed to the four testimonial infirmities of ambiguity, insincerity, faulty perception, and erroneous memory. In the absence of special reasons, the perceived untrustworthiness of such an out-of-court act or utterance has led the Anglo-Saxon legal system to exclude it as hearsay despite its potentially probative value.

There exists a rather simple way of schematizing all of this in terms of an elementary geometric construct that serves to structure its several related elements. The construct might be called the Testimonial Triangle. By making graphic the path of inferences, and by functionally grouping the problems encountered along the path, the triangle makes it easier both to identify when

a hearsay problem exists and to structure consideration of the appropriate-
ness of exceptions to the rule that bars hearsay inferences.

The diagram is as follows:

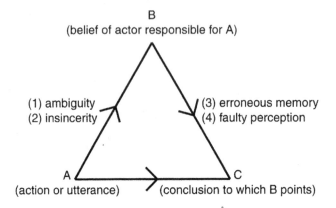

If we use the diagram to trace the inferential path the trier must follow, we
begin at the lower left vertex of the triangle (A), which represents the declarant's (X's) act or assertion. The path first takes us to the upper vertex (B), representing X's belief in what his or her act or assertion suggests, and then takes
us to the lower right vertex (C), representing the external reality suggested
by X's belief. When "A" is used to prove "C" along the path through "B," a traditional hearsay problem exists and the use of the act or assertion as evidence
is disallowed upon proper objection in the absence of some special reason to
permit it.

It is of course a simple matter to locate the four testimonial infirmities
on the triangle to show where and how they might impede the process of
inference. To go from "A" to "B," the declarant's belief, one must remove the
obstacles of (1) ambiguity and (2) insincerity. To go from "B" to "C," the external fact, one must further remove the obstacles of (3) erroneous memory and
(4) faulty perception. . . . By contrast, when the trier's inference can proceed
from "A" directly to "C," the infirmities of hearsay do not arise. For example,
the out-of-court statement "I can speak" would be admissible as nonhearsay to
prove that the declarant was capable of speech, for it is the fact of his speaking
rather than the content of the statement which permits the inference, and that
involves no problems of the statement's ambiguity, or of sincerity, memory, or
perception.

PROBLEM

3.1. In February and March 1857, a Glasgow clerk named Emile
L'Angelier suffered three attacks of internal pain and vomiting. The third
attack killed him. An autopsy found arsenic in his stomach. Several months
later L'Angelier's former lover, Madeleine Smith, was tried before the High
Court of Justiciary in Edinburgh for his murder. The jury returned a verdict of

"not proven," and Smith was set free. The outcome was widely attributed to an evidence ruling by the three presiding judges:

> Amongst L'Angelier's effects was found a little pocket-book. . . . There are various entries of no particular interest, then comes: "Thursday, 19th February. Saw Mimi a few moments. Was very ill during the night. Friday, 20th February. Passed two pleasant hours with Mimi in the drawing room. Saturday, 21st February. Did not feel very well. Sunday, 22nd February. Saw Mimi in drawing room. Promised me French Bible. Taken very ill." These dates cover . . . the dates of the first two illnesses. . . .
>
> The defence, quite rightly, fought hard to obtain the exclusion of this pocket-book from the evidence. The Lord Justice-Clerk, Lord Handyside, and Lord Ivory had to decide this vital question of the pocket-book. The Lord Justice-Clerk and Lord Handyside held that it was not admissible. Lord Ivory disagreed with them. The Lord Justice-Clerk said that he was unable to admit such evidence. "It might relax the sacred laws of evidence to an extent that the mind could hardly contemplate. One could not tell how many documents might exist and be found in the repositories of a deceased person. A man might have threatened another, he might have hatred against him and be determined to revenge himself, and what entries might he not make in a diary for this purpose?" Lord Handyside pointed out that, had the writer of the memoranda still been alive, they could not have been used for evidence. . . . It was generally felt dangerous to admit as evidence memoranda on which no examination could in the nature of things be possible. The pocket-book was therefore ruled out as evidence. . . .

F. Tennyson Jesse, *Trial of Madeleine Smith* 35 (1927). As a result of this ruling, "the prosecution failed to adduce the smallest vestige of evidence that Madeleine met L'Angelier before any of the three occasions on which he was taken ill." *Id.* at 32.

Was the diary hearsay? Were the judges right to exclude it?

2. Nonhearsay Uses of Out-of-Court Statements

The canonical formulation of the hearsay rule bars the use of "out-of-court statements to prove the truth of the matter asserted." The term "out-of-court" is shorthand for any statement other than one made under oath and in front of the factfinder during the same proceeding in which it is being offered in evidence. Testimony in an earlier trial, for example, counts as an out-of-court statement for purposes of the hearsay rule.

The traditional definition of hearsay raises two problems. One is figuring out what constitutes a "statement," and the other is figuring out what it means for a statement to be introduced "for the truth of the matter asserted." Of these two problems, the second causes by far the most trouble and it is the subject of this section. The first problem, the definition of "statement," is taken up in the section following this one.

The easiest way to grasp what it means to introduce a statement "to prove the truth of the matter asserted" is to consider *other* things a statement can be used to prove, *aside* from "the truth of the matter asserted." The cases that follow provide illustrations of such nonhearsay uses of out-of-court statements.

In reading these cases — and the remainder of this chapter — you can avoid a great deal of confusion if you keep in mind several points of terminology.

First, in the definition of hearsay, the "matter asserted" means the matter asserted *in the statement offered into evidence*, not the matter "asserted" by the party offering the evidence. *All* evidence presumably is offered to prove the truth of claims made by the party offering the evidence.

Second, evidence typically is introduced to support not just one proposition but a series of propositions, linked together in a chain of inference. Evidence of an out-of-court statement thus may tend to prove A, which in turn makes B more likely, which in turn suggests C. (Recall the love letter discussed by Professor Morgan in Chapter 2.) If *any one* of the propositions in this chain of inference is "the truth of the matter asserted" in the out-of-court statement, the evidence falls within the traditional definition of hearsay.

Third, the words "witness" and "declarant" have specialized meanings in hearsay law. In everyday parlance, the word "witness" often means someone who sees or observes something, and the word "declarant" is often used for someone who says something under oath. But in hearsay law the term "witness" is reserved for someone who testifies under oath, from the witness stand, and the term "declarant" refers to someone who makes a statement of any kind, whether or not under oath, and whether in or out of court.

Most potential hearsay situations involve two statements. The second one is made under oath in court by a "witness," and it describes the first statement. The person who makes the first statement is called the "declarant." Thus, in *Leake v. Hagert*, Edward Gross was the witness, and Allan Leake's son was the declarant. In *Raleigh's Case*, Dyer was a witness, but the "Portugal gentleman" was just a declarant.

Not all potential hearsay situations involve two statements, because not all out-of-court statements are introduced through the testimony of a live witness. When an out-of-court statement is written — like Cobham's confession in *Raleigh's Case* — the written document itself typically is introduced. When the statement is electronically recorded, the recording is usually offered into evidence. But most out-of-court statements are introduced through the testimony of a witness, so most hearsay situations involve two statements: an in-court statement, by a "witness," about an out-of-court statement, by a "declarant."

ADVISORY COMMITTEE NOTE TO F.R.E. 801(c)

The definition follows along familiar lines in including only statements offered to prove the truth of the matter asserted. McCormick §225; 5 Wigmore §1361, 6 id. §1766. If the significance of an offered statement lies solely in the fact that it was made, no issue is raised as to the truth of anything asserted, and the statement is not hearsay. Emich Motors Corp. v. General Motors Corp., 181 F.2d 70 (7th Cir. 1950), rev'd on other grounds 340 U.S. 558, letters of complaint from customers offered as a reason for cancellation of dealer's franchise, to rebut contention that franchise was revoked for refusal to finance sales through affiliated finance company. The effect is to exclude from hearsay the entire category of "verbal acts" and "verbal parts of an act," in which the statement itself affects the legal rights of the parties or is a circumstance bearing on conduct affecting their rights.

LYONS PARTNERSHIP v. MORRIS COSTUMES, INC.

243 F.3d 789 (4th Cir. 2001)

NIEMEYER, Circuit Judge:

... Lyons Partnership, L.P., ("Lyons"), a Texas limited partnership, owns all of the intellectual property rights to the character "Barney," the well-stuffed Tyrannosaurus Rex with a green chest and stomach, friendly mien, green spots on its back, and yellow "toeballs." Barney is readily recognizable to young children, who repeatedly parrot his song, "I Love You," often testing the patience of nearby adults. . . . [T]he "Barney and Friends" show is viewed weekly by 14 million children, and over 50 million copies of Barney-related videos have been sold. . . . Lyons has registered approximately 25 trademarks and obtained hundreds of copyrights with respect to the name "Barney" and the character's depiction.

... Lyons commenced this action against Morris Costumes, . . . a retail costume-rental establishment in Charlotte, North Carolina. . . . [The complaint alleged, among other things, that Morris Costumes rented a "Duffy the Dragon" costume that infringed Lyons's trademarks in Barney.] After a four-day bench trial, the district court entered judgment in favor of the defendants on all claims. . . .

The district court found . . . that Lyons had not demonstrated a likelihood of confusion between the Duffy costume and the Barney character. It reached its conclusion, however, only after disregarding most of the evidence of actual confusion. . . . Although the court stated that "[t]here is no evidence on which to support a finding concerning actual confusion of children," ample evidence presented at trial would have supported such a finding. . . . [T]he principal at an elementary school testified that when she wore the Duffy costume at a school rally, the children shouted "Barney. Barney. Barney," and parents testified that when they rented the Duffy costume for their children's birthday parties, the children believed that the person dressed as Duffy was in fact Barney. In addition, Lyons offered newspaper clippings that evidenced actual confusion between Duffy and Barney, not only by the children who were the subject of the articles, but by the reporters themselves, who erroneously described Duffy as "Barney."

Despite initially admitting that evidence, the district court's final opinion dismissed it as "unreliable hearsay." If the district court disregarded this evidence because it was hearsay, we believe that this conclusion was erroneous. Lyons did not offer the children's statements or the newspaper articles to prove the truth of the matter asserted—i.e., that the persons wearing the Duffy costume were in fact Barney—but rather merely to prove that the children and the newspaper reporters *expressed their belief* that those persons were Barney. This was direct evidence of the children's and the reporters' reactions and not hearsay.... Because such evidence was highly probative of actual confusion and the existence of actual confusion is often dispositive to a trademark infringement analysis, we ... vacate the district court's judgment as to the Duffy-related trademark claim....

UNITED STATES v. PARRY

649 F.2d 292 (5th Cir. 1981)

LEWIS R. MORGAN, Circuit Judge.

The question in this case is whether the district court erred in excluding certain testimony by the appellant's mother as inadmissible hearsay. We conclude that the evidence should have been admitted and therefore reverse appellant's convictions and remand for a new trial.

Scott Parry was tried before a jury and convicted in consolidated cases of conspiring to distribute phenycyclidine hydrochloride (PCP) and of possessing with intent to distribute PCP and dimethamphetamine hydrochloride.... Parry did not deny that he had participated in the drug transactions described by [two undercover narcotics] agents but argued that, during each of these transactions, he had proceeded upon the good faith belief that he was working for the agents, assisting them in locating drug dealers....

In support of his position that he had known from the outset of the agents' identities, Parry related a conversation he had had with his mother shortly after he met [one of the agents] in October 1974 and well in advance of his arrest in January 1975. Parry testified that, in response to his mother's inquiry, he had stated that the person who had frequently telephoned her home asking to speak to Parry was a narcotics agent with whom he was then working. In an effort to corroborate his story, Parry called his mother as a witness.... Although the government voiced no objection to the proffered testimony, the court ruled that Parry's mother could not testify to "any conversations that she had with her son or that her son had with her."...

The reasons for excluding hearsay are clear: when an out-of-court statement is offered as a testimonial assertion of the truth of the matter stated, we are vitally interested in the credibility of the out-of-court declarant. Because a statement made out of court is not exposed to the normal credibility safeguards of oath, presence at trial, and cross-examination, the jury has no basis for evaluating the declarant's trustworthiness and thus his statement is considered unreliable. Implicit in both the definition and justification for the rule, however, is the recognition that whenever an out-of-court statement is offered for some purpose other than to prove the truth of the matter asserted, the value of the statement does not rest upon the declarant's credibility and, therefore, is not subject to attack as hearsay....

Parry's mother sought to testify that her son had stated that the person who had been telephoning her home was a narcotics agent and that he, Parry, was working with the agent. As Parry explained to the district court, this statement was not offered to prove that the caller was a narcotics agent or that Parry was working with the agent, but to establish that Parry had knowledge of the agent's identity when he spoke. In other words, Parry offered the statement as the basis for a circumstantial inference by the jury that, if this statement was in fact made — a question which the in-court witness could testify to while under oath, before the jury, and subject to cross-examination — then Parry probably knew of the agent's identity. Using an out-of-court utterance as circumstantial evidence of the declarant's knowledge of the existence of some fact, rather than as testimonial evidence of the truth of the matter asserted, does not offend the hearsay rule. . . . Contrary to the government's position, the danger that the jury could improperly use the out-of-court statement as an assertion to be believed does not render the statement inadmissible. Where evidence is admissible for one purpose but not for another, the accepted practice is to admit the evidence with instructions that the jury consider the evidence only for the permissible purpose. A different rule applies only where the probative value of the evidence when used for its allowable purpose is outweighed by the prejudice that would result if the evidence were used for its improper purpose. In this case the dangers associated with the jury's possible misuse of the out-of-court statement are not sufficient to require that the evidence be excluded. The court should admit the statement and give a limiting instruction that the statement is admissible only as circumstantial evidence of Parry's knowledge and not as evidence of the truth of the matter asserted. . . .

Rather than being merely cumulative, the excluded testimony was the only available evidence that could corroborate Parry's story that he had known of the agents' identities, a story the jury may have found self-serving if not farfetched. . . . Moreover, the jury may well have assumed that because Parry did not ask his mother to confirm the existence of the critical conversation, the conversation probably never occurred. Because we are unable to say with fair assurance that the jury was not substantially influenced by the error, we must reverse Parry's conviction and remand for a new trial.

SUBRAMANIAM v. PUBLIC PROSECUTOR

1 W.L.R. 965 (Privy Council 1956)

Their Lordships' reasons for allowing the appeal were delivered by Mr. L. M. D. DE SILVA. This is an appeal, by special leave, from a judgment of the Supreme Court of the Federation of Malaya dismissing an appeal against a conviction in the High Court of Jahore Bahru whereby the appellant was found guilty of being in possession on April 29, 1955, of 20 rounds of ammunition contrary to regulation 4(1)(b) of the Emergency Regulations, 1951, and sentenced to death. . . .

It was common ground that . . . the appellant was found in a wounded condition by certain members of the security forces; that when he was searched there was found around his waist a leather belt with three pouches containing 20 live rounds of ammunition; no weapon of any description was found upon him or in the immediate vicinity.

The defence put forward on behalf of appellant was that he had been captured by terrorists, that at all material times he was acting under duress, and that at the time of his capture by the security forces he had formed the intention to surrender, with which intention he had come to the place where he was found. . . .

The appellant gave evidence in defence. . . . He described how he was forced to accompany the terrorists, one of whom walked in front and two behind, who told him he was being taken to their leader. At this stage an intervention by the trial judge is recorded thus:

> "*Court*: I tell Murugason hearsay evidence is not admissible and all the conversation with the bandits is not admissible unless they are called."

Murugason was counsel assigned to defend the appellant.

In ruling out peremptorily the evidence of conversation between the terrorists and the appellant the trial judge was in error. Evidence of a statement made to a witness by a person who is not himself called as a witness may or may not be hearsay. It is hearsay and inadmissible when the object of the evidence is to establish the truth of what is contained in the statement. It is not hearsay and is admissible when it is proposed to be established by the evidence, not the truth of the statement, but the fact that it was made. The fact that the statement was made, quite apart from its truth, is frequently relevant in considering the mental state and conduct thereafter of the witness or of some other person in whose presence the statement was made. In the case before their Lordships statements could have been made to the appellant by the terrorists, which, whether true or not, if they had been believed by the appellant, might reasonably have induced in him an apprehension of instant death if he failed to conform to their wishes. . . . Their Lordships feel unable to hold with any confidence that had the excluded evidence, which goes to the very root of the defence of duress, been admitted the result of the trial would probably have been the same.

For the reasons which have been given their Lordships have humbly advised Her Majesty that the appeal be allowed.

UNITED STATES v. FELIZ

794 F.3d 123 (1st Cir. 2015)

LYNCH, Circuit Judge.

Victor Feliz, a youth with no prior record, was convicted in December 2012 of possession of a firearm in furtherance of a drug trafficking crime . . . and possession with intent to distribute cocaine base. . . . His conviction was based largely on two written confessions. Before trial, Feliz moved to suppress the confessions as involuntary, being induced by threats made to him as to repercussions to his mother and his young siblings if he did not confess.

The magistrate judge heard testimony from two police officers that the confessions were freely made, and, contrarily, from Feliz and his mother that the government had dictated to him his confessions, which he signed, after officers threatened his mother with deportation and his siblings with being put into state custody. The magistrate judge recommended that the confessions be suppressed as involuntary. . . .

The district court conducted a de novo hearing . . . [and] excluded the defense testimony about the circumstances of the confessions involving police pressure as hearsay. It . . . [subsequently] admitted the confessions into evidence, because, in its view, the record before it contained no evidence of coercion (having excluded that evidence on hearsay grounds). On review, we cannot conclude that the confessions were voluntary, because the district court erroneously excluded from consideration the critical evidence to the contrary. We vacate and remand. . . .

Hearsay is a statement "the declarant does not make while testifying at the current trial or hearing," and "a party offers in evidence to prove the truth of the matter asserted in the statement." Fed. R. Evid. 801(c). Feliz did not attempt to introduce testimony of the officers' threats for the truth of the matter asserted. [His mother Hortencia Feliz] testified, for example, that the officer said "your siblings are all going to the Department of Family." Before the magistrate judge, Hortencia testified that an officer said to Feliz, "We are going to deport your mother." She also testified there that the officers told Feliz that if he did not turn himself in, "they were going to deport me and they were going to call the Department of the Family to take the boy and girls." That testimony would not show that Feliz's siblings would truly be sent to the Department of the Family if he did not turn himself into police custody, or that she would have been deported. Rather, the testimony, if credible, would show the fact that the police officer made the threat to Feliz, a fact within Hortencia's personal knowledge. . . .

The government falls back to its misunderstanding of the hornbook rule of evidence that an out-of-court statement may be offered to "show the effect of the words spoken on the listener." *See United States v. Bailey*, 270 F.3d 83, 87 (1st Cir. 2001) (citing 5 Weinstein's Federal Evidence §801.03[4] (2d ed. 1999)). Since Hortencia was not the intended recipient of the threat, the argument goes, she could not testify to it.

That is incorrect. The testimony here was offered to show the effect of the words spoken on the listener, Feliz. Even though Hortencia was not the target of the threat, she could still testify that the officer made the threatening statement and it was heard by Feliz. The factfinder can then infer the effect on Feliz from that testimony. . . . The government offers no case — and we are aware of none — suggesting that only the listener (and not an independent over-hearer of a conversation) may testify to an out-of-court statement that is relevant to the listener's state of mind. In any event, the formulation "effect of the words on the listener" is not a rigid hearsay exception, but an example of a "more common type[] of nonhearsay utterance[]." 2 McCormick on Evidence §249 (7th ed. 2013). As we have already explained, this statement is a nonhearsay utterance because it is not being used to prove the truth of the matter asserted.[3]

_____

3. There is no safe harbor for the government in the fact that the Federal Rules of Evidence do not generally apply in suppression hearings. . . . If anything, the inapplicability of the Federal Rules of Evidence provide further support for why Hortencia should have been permitted to testify about what she heard, because the evidence was clearly relevant.

UNITED STATES v. JOHNSON

71 F.3d 539 (6th Cir. 1995)

KENNEDY, Circuit Judge.

A jury convicted defendant Keithley Johnson on nine counts of distribution of controlled substances in violation of 21 U.S.C. §841(a)(1), and four counts of mail fraud in violation of 18 U.S.C. §1341. . . . The government's theory at trial was that Drs. Johnson and Uppal, who together ran the Neighborhood Health Clinic ("Clinic"), were engaged in the distribution of controlled substances and illegal medical billing practices. . . .

Defendant . . . argues that the District Court erroneously admitted hearsay evidence. At trial, a former employee of the Clinic, Tina Chapman, testified that pharmacies would telephone the Clinic about prescriptions written by defendant. Chapman testified that she told Dr. Uppal of these phone calls, . . . [and] that on one occasion she heard Dr. Uppal tell defendant over the telephone that "he was going to have to stop writing prescriptions like that." . . .

Hearsay is "a statement, other than one made by the declarant while testifying at the trial or hearing, offered in evidence to prove the truth of the matter asserted." Fed. R. Evid. 801(c). Chapman's testimony of the telephone conversation she overheard is not hearsay because it was not offered to prove the truth of the matter asserted. Rather, as the government argues, this testimony is evidence of defendant's knowledge that he was prescribing medication without a legitimate medical purpose and outside the course of professional practice. As defendant's state of mind is an element of the offense, this evidence is relevant. . . . [Convictions affirmed.]

CAMPBELL v. BOSTON SCIENTIFIC CORP.

882 F.3d 70 (4th Cir. 2018)

WILKINSON, Circuit Judge.

. . . Boston Scientific Corporation (BSC) manufactured a . . . medical device called the Obtryx . . . [which] was designed to be permanently implanted [in women] as a treatment for severe stress urinary incontinence. . . . The Obtryx is made of Marlex polypropylene. While polypropylene mesh has long been used in implantable medical devices, Marlex polypropylene's manufacturer included a caution on its Material Safety Data Sheet (MSDS) stating that it should not be used "in medical applications involving permanent implantation in the human body." J.A. 4355. [Four women who received Obtryx implants sued BSC, alleging that they suffered severe complications. Following a jury trial, they each received multi-million dollar awards.]

. . . BSC objects to the admission of the MSDS Caution evidence. . . . BSC argues that the Caution was inadmissible hearsay.

But the MSDS Caution was not hearsay evidence, because it was not admitted for its truth. . . . [T]he MSDS Caution was offered not to establish that the Caution was accurate, but instead to demonstrate that BSC had "notification ... of the manufacturer's concerns about the safety of its product for permanent implantation" and to address BSC's "knowledge of potential safety concerns in its final product." J.A. 660-61. One need not assume that the Caution is true to find it relevant to BSC's state of mind at various times. . . . Affirmed.

UNITED STATES v. JEFFERSON

650 F.2d 854 (6th Cir. 1981)

NATHANIEL R. JONES, Circuit Judge.

Louis Charles Jefferson appeals from his conviction for possession with intent to distribute heroin and bond jumping. . . . The district court properly admitted a letter and two mailgrams into evidence to show that Jefferson had been sent notice of the hearing he failed to attend. These were not offered to prove the truth of the matter asserted, but only to show that Jefferson had been sent notice of the hearings. [Conviction for bond jumping affirmed.]

UNITED STATES v. SAAVEDRA

684 F.2d 1293 (9th Cir. 1982)

EAST, District Judge.

Saavedra appeals from her judgments of conviction for conspiracy to commit wire fraud in violation of 18 U.S.C. §371, and three substantive counts of wire fraud in violation of 18 U.S.C. §1343. . . . The underlying fraud involved wrongfully charging Western Union money orders to improperly obtained Master Charge numbers. The principal architects of the fraud were inmates in . . . the Los Angeles County Jail. The inmates would telephone individuals whose numbers had been obtained from the city phone book, and would pose as law enforcement or bank security personnel checking on credit card problems. The inmate would have the person read off his or her credit card number to "verify" it, and would then call Western Union and order a money order, charging it to the misappropriated credit card number. The inmate would direct the money order to a specific Western Union office, made out to someone on the outside who would pick it up. . . . Saavedra, using the names Carlotta Santana and Charlotte Carpenter, acted as one of these outside persons. . . .

Saavedra . . . contends that the District Court erred in admitting hearsay evidence against her. She complains of the admission of the testimony of three victims of the credit card fraud scheme. These witnesses testified that in the fall of 1977 they received telephone calls from unknown males who identified themselves as law enforcement officers and elicited the victims' credit card numbers. . . .

The testimony objected to here was not offered to prove that the statements made by the unidentified callers were true; i.e., that they were in fact law enforcement officials investigating credit card "problems." Instead, this testimony was introduced to show how the credit card numbers were fraudulently obtained by persons posing as law enforcement officers, thus providing circumstantial evidence that the later unauthorized use of those numbers to purchase money orders was intentional, and that others besides Saavedra were involved in the scheme to defraud. . . . Affirmed.

HANSON v. JOHNSON

201 N.W. 322 (Minn. 1924)

WILSON, C.J.

Action in conversion. Appeal from judgment by defendants. Case was tried to the court without a jury.

It is claimed that the court erred in the reception of evidence. Plaintiff owned and leased a farm to one Schrik under a written lease, the terms of which gave plaintiff two-fifths of the corn grown. The tenant gave a mortgage to defendant bank on his share of the crops. The tenant's mortgaged property was sold at auction by the bank with his permission. At this sale a crib of corn containing 393 bushels was sold by the bank to defendant Johnson. If plaintiff owned the corn it was converted by defendants.

In an effort to prove that the corn was owned by plaintiff, and that it was a part of his share, he testified over the objection of hearsay . . . that when the tenant was about through husking corn he was on the farm and the tenant pointed out the corn in question (and a double crib of corn) and said: "Mr. Hanson, here is your corn for this year, this double crib here and this single crib here is your share for this year's corn; this belongs to you, Mr. Hanson."

A bystander was called, and against the same objection testified to having heard the talk in substantially the same language.

There is no question but that plaintiff owned some corn. It was necessary to identify it. The division made his share definite. This division and identity was made by the acts of tenant in husking the corn and putting it in separate cribs and then his telling Hanson which was his share, and the latter's acquiescence therein. The language of the tenant was the very fact necessary to be proved. The verbal part of the transaction between plaintiff and the tenant was necessary to prove the fact. The words were the verbal acts. They aid in giving legal significance to the conduct of the parties. They accompanied the conduct. There could be no division without words or gestures identifying the respective shares. This was a fact to be shown in the chain of proof of title. It was competent evidence. It was not hearsay. . . . Affirmed.

CREAGHE v. IOWA HOME MUTUAL CASUALTY CO.

323 F.2d 981 (10th Cir. 1963)

SETH, Circuit Judge.

The plaintiff-appellant has an unsatisfied judgment against Muril J. Osborn obtained in a damage action which arose from a collision between the plaintiff's car and Osborn's truck. In the case at bar, appellant alleges that the appellee insurance company was the insurer of Osborn's truck at the time of the accident, and seeks to collect this judgment from it. The appellee admits that at one time it issued a liability policy to Osborn, but asserts that he cancelled it shortly before the accident. Osborn was not a party to this suit and did not appear as a witness....

Appellant challenges the action of the trial court in admitting the testimony of the agent of appellee and his employee ... that the insured stated he wanted the policy cancelled, also that his check for some of the premiums in addition to those initially made was then returned. Appellant asserts that this testimony was hearsay.

The hearsay rule does not exclude relevant testimony as to what the contracting parties said with respect to the making or the terms of an oral agreement. The presence or absence of such words and statements of themselves are part of the issues in the case. This use of such testimony does not require a reliance by the jury or the judge upon the competency of the person who originally made the statements for the truth of their content. Neither the truth of the statements nor their accuracy are then involved. In the case at bar we are not concerned with whether the insured was truthful or not when he told the agent he wanted the policy cancelled and that he did not need it any more. It is enough for the issues here presented to determine only whether or not he made such statements to the agent. The fact that these statements were made was testified to by the agent, and his competency and truthfulness as to this testimony was subject to testing through cross-examination by counsel for appellant, and this was done at considerable length. The fact that the statements with which we are here concerned related to an oral termination of a written contract does not lead to a rule different from that prevailing for the formation of an oral agreement. The reasons for the rule permitting such testimony are the same in both instances....

[T]he testimony with which we are here concerned is admissible since it is part of, or is the oral agreement to cancel the insurance policy. Oral agreements can only be established by testimony as to the conversation which was had between the parties. This testimony may be given by a witness to such conversation, as was the agent of the appellee in this instance.... Affirmed.

UNITED STATES v. MONTANA

199 F.3d 947 (7th Cir. 1999)

Posner, Chief Judge.

The defendant was convicted of bank robbery and related offenses and given a very long sentence — almost 30 years. James Dodd committed the actual robbery; Montana drove the getaway car. Dodd pleaded guilty, and testified at Montana's trial, as Montana's witness, that Montana had not known that Dodd was planning to rob the bank. Shortly before the end of the trial, Dodd gave Montana's lawyer a note for Montana's mother, who after she read it told the lawyer that the note demanded money in exchange for Dodd's having testified favorably to Montana. The following morning, a deputy U.S. marshal heard Dodd tell Montana to tell Montana's father that "it's going to be $10,000" for the favorable testimony. The district judge allowed the marshal to testify to what he had heard. . . .

[Montana complains the marshal's testimony about Dodd's out-of-court statement was hearsay.] The government argues that it was admissible as a "verbal act," thus echoing the linguist's distinction between performative . . . utterances [and those that] narrate, describe, or otherwise convey information[. The latter] are judged by their truth value (information is useful only if true — indeed is *information* only if it is true); the former — illustrated by a promise, offer, or demand — commit the speaker to a course of action. Performative utterances are not within the scope of the hearsay rule, because they do not make any truth claims. Had the marshal overheard Dodd tell Montana, "your father has promised me $10,000," Dodd's overheard statement would have been hearsay, because its value as evidence would have depended on its being truthful, that is, on such a promise having actually been made. But what in fact was overheard was merely a demand — in effect, "give me $10,000" — and so the only issue of credibility was whether the marshal was reporting the demand correctly, and *his* testimony was not hearsay. Affirmed.

PROBLEMS

3.2. The defendant in a prosecution for assault with a deadly weapon testifies that he shot the victim after the victim pulled out a hunting knife and said, "I'm going to slit your throat." Is the victim's statement hearsay?

3.3. After a gossip magazine describes a soap opera actress as "perpetually intoxicated," the actress sues for libel, and seeks to introduce a copy of the magazine. Is the magazine hearsay?

3.4. To prove falsity, the actress seeks to introduce a newspaper article describing her as "well known for shunning drugs and alcohol." Is the article hearsay?

3.5. To prove absence of malice, the gossip magazine calls one of its reporters, who testifies that a director who worked with the actress told the reporter the actress "always has booze on her breath." Is the director's statement hearsay?

3.6. A patient injured during surgery sues the surgeon and the hospital. To prove negligence by the hospital, the plaintiff seeks to prove that, a year before her surgery, a nurse told the hospital that the surgeon was incompetent. Is the nurse's statement hearsay?

3.7. A developer brings an action to quiet title to a tract of farmland. A farmer intervenes, claiming that she owns the land. To prove adverse possession, the farmer seeks to call witnesses who have heard her refer to the land as hers. Would this testimony recount hearsay?

3.8. The plaintiff in an automobile collision case calls the police officer who investigated the accident. The plaintiff seeks to have the officer testify that an eyewitness, who can no longer be located, told the officer in a tape-recorded interview that the other driver was speeding. The plaintiff also seeks to play the tape for the jury. Does any of this evidence involve hearsay?

3.9. The strength of an alibi offered by a criminal defendant depends on when the defendant arrived at a bar. The prosecution calls a waitress at the bar, who testifies that, shortly before the defendant arrived, the waitress asked the bartender what time it was, and the bartender said, "Nine thirty." Is the bartender's statement hearsay? What if the bartender testifies, in addition to the waitress, and explains that, although he did not see the defendant arrive, he recalls that the waitress asked him for the time at 9:30? Would there be a hearsay problem?

3.10. To prove that a testator was incompetent, his son seeks to prove that the testator claimed to have a summer house on Mars. Is the testator's claim hearsay?

3.11. To prove that a testator was incompetent, his son seeks to prove that the testator's co-workers complained that the testator kept dead fish in his desk. Are the complaints hearsay?

3. Implied Assertions

Sometimes people "communicate" without trying. They put on sweaters, for example, and thereby signal that they are cold. Or they leave a theater and thereby indicate that the play is over. Judges sometimes have treated evidence of this kind of conduct as hearsay when it is offered to prove the truth of what it seems to suggest — i.e., that it was cold, or that the play was over. But the Federal Rules of Evidence and most state codes of evidence have defined hearsay to include only "statements" offered to prove the truth of what they assert. "Statements" are in turn defined to include nonverbal conduct only when it is *intended* as a form of communication.

What about *verbal expressions* that reveal something other than what the speaker intended to communicate? They, too, are generally treated as non-hearsay, either on the ground that they are not offered to prove "the truth of the matter asserted," or — as in the influential opinion in *United States v. Zenni* — on the ground that there *is* no "matter asserted." This result is more controversial, as *State v. Dullard* and the excerpt from Professor Tribe's article illustrate. But *Dullard* represents the minority approach; most courts — both at the federal and the state level — follow *Zenni*.

UNITED STATES v. ZENNI

492 F. Supp. 464 (E.D. Ky. 1980)

BERTELSMAN, District Judge.

This prosecution for illegal bookmaking activities presents a classic problem in the law of evidence, namely, whether implied assertions are hearsay. The problem was a controversial one at common law, the discussion of which has filled many pages in the treatises and learned journals. Although the answer to the problem is clear under the Federal Rules of Evidence, there has been little judicial treatment of the matter, and many members of the bar are unfamiliar with the marked departure from the common law the Federal Rules have effected on this issue.

The relevant facts are simply stated. While conducting a search of the premises of the defendant, Ruby Humphrey, pursuant to a lawful search warrant which authorized a search for evidence of bookmaking activity, government agents answered the telephone several times. The unknown callers stated directions for the placing of bets on various sporting events. The government proposes to introduce this evidence to show that the callers believed that the premises were used in betting operations. The existence of such belief tends to prove that they were so used. The defendants object on the ground of hearsay....

[T]he utterances of the absent declarants are not offered for the truth of the words,[7] and the mere fact that the words were uttered has no relevance of itself.[8] Rather they are offered to show the declarants' belief in a fact sought to be proved. At common law this situation occupied a controversial no-man's land. It was argued on the one hand that the out-of-court utterance was not hearsay, because the evidence was not offered for any truth stated in it, but for the truth of some other proposition inferred from it. On the other hand, it was also argued that the reasons for excluding hearsay applied, in that the evidence was being offered to show declarant's belief in the implied proposition, and he was not available to be cross-examined. Thus, the latter argument was that there existed strong policy reasons for ruling that such utterances were hearsay.

The classic case, which is discussed in virtually every textbook on evidence, is *Wright v. Tatham*, 7 Adolph. & E. 313, 386, 112 Eng. Rep. 488 (Exch. Ch. 1837), and 5 Cl. & F. 670, 739, 47 Rev. Rep. 136 (H.L. 1838). Described as a "celebrated and hard-fought cause,"[10] *Wright v. Tatham* was a will contest, in which the will was sought to be set aside on the grounds of the incompetency of the testator at the time of its execution. The proponents of the will offered to introduce into evidence letters to the testator from certain absent individuals on various business and social matters. The purpose of the offer was to show that the writers of the letters believed the testator was able to make intelligent decisions concerning such matters, and thus was competent.

---

7. That is, the utterance, "Put $2 to win on Paul Revere in the third at Pimlico," is a direction and not an assertion of any kind, and therefore can be neither true nor false.

8. Cf. United States v. McLennan, 593 F.2d 943 (9th Cir. 1977), in a criminal case, the defense was advice of counsel. Statements made by counsel to the defendant were not hearsay, because it was relevant what the advice was. Of a similar nature would be a policeman's statement, "Go through the stop sign," if it were illegal to go through it unless directed by an officer. Other examples of expression admissible as non-hearsay, because they are verbal acts, relevant merely because they occurred, are "I agree" offered to show a contract was made; or "He took a bribe," offered to show a slander was published.

10. McCormick [on Evidence] §250 [(2d ed. 1972)]. This case "entailed no less than four separate trials, hundreds of pages of published transcript, numerous appeals, vast amounts of money, and the participation of most of England's high judiciary, before it was finally concluded in 1838." [Weinstein's Evidence] ¶801(a)(01) at 801-54.

One of the illustrations advanced in the judicial opinions in *Wright v. Tatham* is perhaps even more famous than the case itself. This is Baron Parke's famous sea captain example. Is it hearsay to offer as proof of the seaworthiness of a vessel that its captain, after thoroughly inspecting it, embarked on an ocean voyage upon it with his family?

The court in *Wright v. Tatham* held that implied assertions[11] of this kind were hearsay. The rationale, as stated by Baron Parke, was as follows:

> "The conclusion at which I have arrived is, that proof of a particular fact which is not of itself a matter in issue, but which is relevant only as implying a statement or opinion of a third person on the matter in issue, is inadmissible in all cases where such a statement or opinion not on oath would be of itself inadmissible; and, therefore, in this case the letters which are offered only to prove the competence of the testator, that is the truth of the implied statements therein contained, were properly rejected, as the mere statement or opinion of the writer would certainly have been inadmissible."

This was the prevailing common law view, where the hearsay issue was recognized. But frequently, it was not recognized....

The common law rule that implied assertions were subject to hearsay treatment was criticized by respected commentators.... In a frequently cited article the following analysis appears:

> "But ought the hearsay rule be deemed applicable to evidence of conduct? As McCormick has observed, the problem 'has only once received any adequate discussion in any decided case,' *i.e.*, in *Wright v. Tatham*, already referred to. And even in that case the court did not pursue its inquiry beyond the point of concluding that evidence of an 'implied' assertion must necessarily be excluded wherever evidence of an 'express' assertion would be inadmissible. But as has been pointed out more than once (although I find no *judicial* recognition of the difference), the 'implied' assertion is, from the hearsay standpoint, not nearly as vulnerable as an express assertion of the fact which the evidence is offered to establish.

> "This is on the assumption that the conduct was 'nonassertive' that the passers-by had their umbrellas up for the sake of keeping dry, not for the purpose of telling anyone it was raining; that the truck driver started up for the sake of resuming his journey, not for the purpose of telling anyone that the light had changed; that the vicar wrote the letter to the testator for the purpose of settling the dispute with the latter, rather than with any idea of expressing his opinion of the testator's sanity. And in the typical 'conduct as hearsay' case this assumption will be quite justifiable.

> "On this assumption, it is clear that evidence of conduct must be taken as freed from at least one of the hearsay dangers, i.e., mendacity. A man does not lie to himself. Put otherwise, if in doing what he does a man has no intention of asserting the existence or non-existence of a fact, it would appear that the trustworthiness of evidence of this conduct is the same whether he is an egregious liar or a paragon of veracity. Accordingly, the lack of opportunity for cross-examination in relation to his veracity or lack of it, would seem to be of no

---

11. The problem is the same whether the relevant assertion is implied from verbal expression, such as that of the betters in the instant case or the letter writers in Wright, or from conduct, as in the sea captain example. See F. R. Ev. 801(a)....

substantial importance. Accordingly, the usual judicial disposition to equate the 'implied' to the 'express' assertion is very questionable."[16]

The drafters of the Federal Rules agreed with the criticisms of the common law rule that implied assertions should be treated as hearsay and expressly abolished it. . . . They did this by providing that no oral or written expression was to be considered as hearsay, unless it was an "assertion" concerning the matter sought to be proved and that no nonverbal conduct should be considered as hearsay, unless it was intended to be an "assertion" concerning said matter.[18] . . .

The Advisory Committee note concerning this problem states:

"The definition of 'statement' assumes importance because the term is used in the definition of hearsay in subdivision (c) [of Rule 801]. *The effect of the definition of 'statement' is to exclude from the operation of the hearsay rule all evidence of conduct, verbal or nonverbal, not intended as an assertion. The key to the definition is that nothing is an assertion unless intended to be one.*

"It can scarcely be doubted that an assertion made in words is intended by the declarant to be an assertion. Hence verbal assertions readily fall into the category of 'statement.' Whether nonverbal conduct should be regarded as a statement for purposes of defining hearsay requires further consideration. Some nonverbal conduct, such as the act of pointing to identify a suspect in a lineup, is clearly the equivalent of words, assertive in nature, and to be regarded as a statement. Other nonverbal conduct, however, may be offered as evidence that the person acted as he did because of his belief in the existence of the condition sought to be proved, from which belief the existence of the condition may be inferred. This sequence is, arguably, in effect an assertion of the existence of the condition and hence properly includable within the hearsay concept. . . . Admittedly evidence of this character is untested with respect to the perception, memory, and narration (or their equivalents) of the actor, *but the Advisory Committee is of the view that these dangers are minimal in the absence of an intent to assert and do not justify the loss of the evidence on hearsay grounds.* No class of evidence is free of the possibility of fabrication, but the likelihood is less with nonverbal than with assertive verbal conduct. The situations giving rise to the nonverbal conduct are such as virtually to eliminate questions of sincerity. Motivation, the nature of the conduct, and the presence or absence of reliance will bear heavily upon the weight to be given the evidence. . . . *Similar considerations govern nonassertive verbal conduct and verbal conduct which is assertive but offered as a basis for inferring something other than the matter*

---

16. Falknor, [*The "Hear-say" Rule as a "See-Do" Rule: Evidence of Conduct*, 33 Rocky Mt. L. Rev. 133,] 136 [(1961)]. The context makes clear that the author would apply the same analysis "where the conduct, although 'verbal,' is relevant, not as tending to prove the truth of what was said, but circumstantially, that is, as manifesting a belief in the existence of the fact the evidence is offered to prove." *Id.* at 134.

18. *See* the sea captain illustration discussed, *supra.* In an unpublished ruling this court recently held admissible as non-hearsay the fact that a U.S. mining inspector ate his lunch in an area in a coal mine now alleged to have been unsafe, and that other inspectors who observed operations prior to a disastrous explosion issued no citations, when it would have been their duty to do so, if there had been safety violations. These non-assertive acts would have been hearsay under the rule of *Wright v. Tatham* but are not hearsay under Rule 801 of the Federal Rules of Evidence, because the inspectors did not intend to make assertions under the circumstances. *Boggs v. Blue Diamond Coal Company* (E.D. Ky. No. 77-69, Pikeville Division).

asserted, also excluded from the definition of hearsay by the language of subdivision (c)." (Emphasis added).

This court, therefore, holds that, "Subdivision (a)(2) of Rule 801 removes implied assertions from the definition of statement and consequently from the operation of the hearsay rule."[20]

Applying the principles discussed above to the case at bar, this court holds that the utterances of the betters telephoning in their bets were nonassertive verbal conduct, offered as relevant for an implied assertion to be inferred from them, namely that bets could be placed at the premises being telephoned. The language is not an assertion on its face, and it is obvious these persons did not intend to make an assertion about the fact sought to be proved or anything else.

As an implied assertion, the proffered evidence is expressly excluded from the operation of the hearsay rule by Rule 801 of the Federal Rules of Evidence, and the objection thereto must be overruled. An order to that effect has previously been entered.

STATE v. DULLARD

668 N.W.2d 585 (Iowa 2003)

CADY, Justice.

[Brett Dullard was convicted of possession of ephedrine or pseudoephedrine with intent to use it as a precursor, after a search of his home revealed three unopened boxes of Benadryl (an allergy medicine containing pseudoephedrine) and other materials and equipment commonly used to manufacture methamphetamine.] The police also found a small spiral notebook in a wooden desk located in the garage. It contained a handwritten note from an unidentified person. The note read as follows:

B—
I had to go inside to pee + calm my nerves somewhat down.
When I came out to go get Brian I looked over to the street North of here + there
sat a black + white w/the dude out of his car facing our own direction — no one
else was with him

... The handwritten note was also introduced into evidence over Dullard's hearsay objection. The State argued the note was not offered to prove the truth of the matters it asserted but to connect Dullard to the items in the garage used to manufacture methamphetamine and the Benadryl. The State argued the note was written to Dullard based on the first letter of his first name....

Hearsay "is a statement, other than one made by the declarant while testifying at the trial ... offered in evidence to prove the truth of the matter asserted." Iowa R. Evid. 5.801(c). Hearsay is not admissible unless it is exempt from the rule or falls within one of the exceptions. *See id.* 5.802....

---

20. Weinstein, ¶801(a)(01) at 801-56; McCormick §250 at 599.

A statement is defined under our rules of evidence as "(1) an oral or written assertion or (2) nonverbal conduct of a person, if it is intended by the person as an assertion." Iowa R. Evid. 5.801(a). The term assertion is not similarly defined in the Iowa or federal rules of evidence. Nevertheless, it is generally recognized to be a statement of fact or belief. . . .

Under the State's argument in this case, the author of the note asserts he or she is nervous and that the police are watching the house. The State acknowledges this note constitutes a written assertion under the rule, but claims it was not hearsay because it was not offered to prove the truth of the assertion, but a different proposition inferred from the words of warning. The State maintains it was offered to show the declarant's belief that the recipient of the note needed to be told of the events because he was involved in the drug activity in the garage and was in possession of the drug lab materials. . . .

[T]he resolution of this issue requires us to examine the concept of implied assertions and the extent to which they constitute statements under our definition of hearsay. . . . The issue we confront has been imbedded in debate and controversy throughout the development of the common law, and has continued to be debated to a large degree following the adoption of the federal rules of evidence. *See United States v. Zenni*, 492 F. Supp. 464, 465 (E.D. Ky. 1980). . . . Despite the wealth of legal commentary and some scholarly court decisions on the subject, no clear answer or approach has emerged. In truth, many courts have not engaged in a serious examination of the subject of implied assertions as hearsay, while those who have follow divergent paths. Legal scholars advocate a variety of positions, with a slight preference, perhaps, to favor an approach that would include most implied assertions within the definition of hearsay, at least where the declarant intended to some degree to assert the proposition. The United States Supreme Court has never squarely addressed the issue . . . [and the] federal circuit courts of appeals are fairly evenly divided. . . .

Federal rule of evidence 801(a) appears to support the departure from the common law, evidenced more by the advisory committee note accompanying the rule than the language of the rule itself. . . . The thrust of the advisory committee note is that the same considerations that justify the specific exclusion of nonverbal conduct not intended as an assertion from the definition of a statement under rule 801(a) — the minimal dangers resulting from the inability to cross-examine the declarant — support, by analogy, the similar exclusion of nonassertive verbal conduct, as well as assertive verbal conduct offered as a basis for inferring something other than the asserted matter. . . .

Generally, a position taken by the advisory committee on federal rules is persuasive authority for determining the meaning of our Iowa rules of evidence. This is because the federal definition of hearsay and the defined terms within the definition are nearly identical to the corresponding Iowa rules. Thus, in the same manner, we typically follow federal decisions interpreting rules closely aligned to the Iowa rules and we look for guidance to the United States Supreme Court advisory committees' notes. On the other hand, the persuasiveness of the committee notes on implied assertions is undermined by the clear split of authority among the federal circuit courts, as well as many legal scholars. . . .

The circumstances of this case, as well as other cases, can make it tempting to minimize hearsay dangers when a declaration is assertive but offered as a basis for inferring a belief of the declarant that most likely was not a significant aspect of the communication process at the time the declaration was made. Absent unusual circumstances, the unknown declarant likely would not have thought about communicating the implied belief at issue, and this lack of intent arguably justifies excluding the assertion from the hearsay rule. Nevertheless, we are not convinced that the absence of intent necessarily makes the underlying belief more reliable, especially when the belief is derived from verbal conduct as opposed to nonverbal conduct.

Four dangers are generally identified to justify the exclusion of out-of-court statements under the hearsay rule: erroneous memory, faulty perception, ambiguity, and insincerity or misrepresentation. Yet, the distinction drawn between intended and unintended conduct or speech only implicates the danger of insincerity, based on the assumption that a person who lacks an intent to assert something also lacks an intent to misrepresent. The other "hearsay dangers," however, remain viable, giving rise to the need for cross-examination. Moreover, even the danger of insincerity may continue to be present in those instances where the reliability of the direct assertion may be questioned. If the expressed assertion is insincere, such as a fabricated story, the implied assertion derived from the expressed assertion will similarly be unreliable. Implied assertions can be no more reliable than the predicate expressed assertion. Paul R. Rice, *Should Unintended Implications of Speech be Considered Nonhearsay? The Assertive/Nonassertive Distinction Under Rule 801(a) of the Federal Rules of Evidence*, 65 Temp. L. Rev. 529, 538 (1992).

The consequence of the committee's approach is to admit into evidence a declarant's belief in the existence of a fact the evidence is offered to prove, without cross-examination, just as if the declarant had explicitly stated the belief. Yet, if the declarant of the written note in this case had intended to declare his or her belief that Dullard had knowledge and possession of drug lab materials, the note would unquestionably constitute hearsay. Implied assertions from speech intended as communication clearly come within the definition of a statement under rule 5.801(a)(1). Unlike the committee, however, we do not believe indirect or unintentional assertions in speech are reliable enough to avoid the hearsay rule. We think the best approach is to evaluate the relevant assertion in the context of the purpose for which the evidence is offered.

We recognize this approach will have a tendency to make most implied assertions hearsay. *See* Christopher B. Mueller, *Incoming Drug Calls and Performative Words: They're Not Just Talking About It, Baron Parke!*, 16 Miss. C. L. Rev. 117, 121-22 (1995). However, we view this in a favorable manner because it means the evidence will be judged for its admission at trial based on accepted exceptions or exclusions to the hearsay rule. It also establishes a better, more straightforward rule for litigants and trial courts to understand and apply.

Additionally, we interpret legislative enactments consistent with common law principles when the language used by the legislature does not specifically negate the common law. Clearly, there is no explicit language in our definition of hearsay under rule 5.801(a) and (c), as with the federal rule, that categorizes implied assertions from oral or written words as nonhearsay. The rule only expressly excludes unintended conduct. The characterization arrived at by the committee is achieved by analogy to nonverbal conduct. Yet, the specific exclusion under the rule of nonverbal conduct as nonhearsay, in the absence of the specific exclusion of nonassertive verbal conduct or assertive verbal conduct offered to infer something other than the matter asserted from the definition of a statement, tends to indicate that the legislature may not have intended to exclude such implied assertions from the hearsay rule. *See* [David E. Seidelson, *Implied Assertions and Federal Rule of Evidence 801: A Continuing Quandary for Federal Courts*, 16 Miss. C. L. Rev. 33 (1995)]. Thus, the rule should be read to incorporate our common law approach....

Having determined the note to be hearsay, we next consider whether it would be admissible, as secondarily argued by the State, under the exemption to the hearsay rule applicable to the statements by co-conspirators pursuant to Iowa Rule of Evidence 5.801(d)(2)(E).... Proof of a conspiracy must include evidence independent of the co-conspirator's statement. *State v. Florie*, 411 N.W.2d 689, 696 (Iowa 1987). In addition to the statement, "the circumstances surrounding the statement, such as the identity of the speaker, the context in which the statement was made, or evidence corroborating the content of the statement" must be considered. Fed. R. Evid. 801 advisory committee's note, 1997 amendment. In this case, there was insufficient evidence to establish the speaker's identity, the time and place the expressed or implied assertions were made, and any other circumstances supporting a conspiracy between the unknown declarant and Dullard.

Without elaborating in great detail, we also fail to find any other exception to the hearsay rule that would allow the note to be admitted.... Accordingly, the note was improperly admitted.... [P]rejudice is apparent because the admission of the note played a pivotal role in establishing the possession element of the crime and Dullard was unable to cross-examine the declarant to overcome this prejudice. This is not a case in which there is otherwise overwhelming evidence of guilt.... We conclude the judgment and sentence of the district court must be reversed based on the error in admitting the hearsay evidence. The case shall be remanded for a new trial.

LAURENCE H. TRIBE, TRIANGULATING HEARSAY

87 Harv. L. Rev. 957, 972 (1974)

Rule 801(a), by defining a "statement" as *assertive* verbal or nonverbal conduct, eliminates from the very definition of hearsay in Rule 801(c) any seemingly nonassertive conduct of a party. Even apart from the well-known difficulty that it is question-begging to define conduct as nonassertive when the very issue may be whether or not it was designed to deceive a viewer, the justification for this treatment of apparently nonassertive conduct seems dubious. The best that can be said for it is that, if the conduct is truly nonassertive, there is no possibility of its insincerity. But the problem of ambiguity is, if anything, greater.... And, of course, [the risks of erroneous memory and faulty perception are as significant] here as in any hearsay situation. In terms of both theory and result, it is thus hard to justify the exclusion of such utterances from the very definition of hearsay....

PROBLEMS

3.12. A criminal defendant charged with murder claims that the victim's husband killed her. He seeks to introduce evidence that the victim's husband fled the country after the victim was found dead. Would this evidence involve hearsay under the view expressed by Baron Parke in *Wright v. Tatham?* Would it involve hearsay in federal court today?

3.13. A traveler contracts pneumonia after a three-hour bus trip through upstate New York in January. He sues the bus company for the cost of his hospitalization, claiming that he got sick because the driver failed to keep the bus adequately heated. The bus company seeks to prove that none of the other passengers on the bus complained about the temperature, and that two passengers took off their sweaters midway through the trip. Would any of this evidence involve hearsay under *Wright v. Tatham?* Under the Federal Rules of Evidence?

3.14. A police officer testifies in a murder case that when she asked the victim who shot him, the victim pointed to a picture of his wife. Would Baron Parke treat this evidence as hearsay? Would the Federal Rules of Evidence?

3.15. The prosecution in a burglary case seeks to prove that a bloodhound, after sniffing a pair of gloves left at the crime scene, led the police to the defendant's house, and then barked quietly when the defendant answered the doorbell. The dog's handler offers to testify that the dog is trained to bark quietly when confronted with the source of the scent the dog has been tracking. Would any of this evidence involve hearsay under Baron Parke's view? Under the Federal Rules of Evidence?

3.16. Consider the following remarks by Lord Ackner in *Regina v. Kearley*, 2 App. Cas. 228 (H.L. 1992):

> Following the appellant's arrest and when he was either not at his home nor within earshot, a number of telephone calls were made to his home which were answered by the police, in which the caller inquired whether he could speak to Chippie (the appellant's nickname), and asked to be supplied with drugs. Later, while the police were still on the premises, a number of persons arrived at the house, some with money, also asking to be supplied with drugs. It is these requests that certain police officers were allowed to recount in evidence, none of those who made the inquiries being called by the prosecution.
>
> Each of those requests was, of course, evidence of the state of mind of the person making the request. He wished to be supplied with drugs and thought that the appellant would so supply him. It was not evidence of the fact that the appellant had supplied or could or would supply the person making the request. But the state of mind of the person making the request was not an issue at the trial; accordingly evidence of his request was irrelevant and therefore inadmissible....
>
> It will be apparent from what I have already stated that the application of the hearsay rule does not, on the facts so far recited, fall for consideration. The evidence is not admissible because it is irrelevant. It is as simple as that....

Partly on these grounds and partly on grounds of hearsay — citing *Wright v. Tatham* — the House of Lords held for the defendant in *Kearley*. Was Lord Ackner right that the evidence was inadmissible even if it was not hearsay, because it was irrelevant? If so, was *United States v. Zenni* wrongly decided?

3.17. Britain's Criminal Justice Act 2003 restricts the definition of hearsay to statements that appear to have been intended by the speaker "(a) to cause another person to believe the matter, or (b) to cause another person to act . . . on the basis that the matter is as stated." §115(3). Does this provision effectively overrule *Wright v. Tatham*? Is the definition of hearsay in Britain now the same as under the Federal Rules of Evidence?

3.18. When police officers enter an apartment where a woman has been shot to death, they hear a parrot saying, "Polly wanna cracker . . . Polly wanna cracker . . . Pretty bird . . . HARRY DON'T SHOOT! . . . Pretty bird." Gary Larson, *The Complete Far Side: Volume One, 1980-1986*, at 9 (2003). If the victim's husband, Harry, is prosecuted for murder and the officers testify at trial about what they heard, would their testimony recount hearsay under the Federal Rules of Evidence? Under Baron Parke's view?

B. HEARSAY AND CONFRONTATION

The Sixth Amendment to the United States Constitution gives every criminal defendant the right "to be confronted with the witnesses against him." Like the hearsay rule, the Confrontation Clause was a reaction against the kind of procedures used, infamously, against Sir Walter Raleigh. It is clear that the two rules partly overlap. But the Supreme Court has found it difficult to say exactly *how* the two prohibitions overlap, and in what ways the constitutional right to confrontation diverges from the hearsay rule.

Three limitations on the reach of the Confrontation Clause are uncontroversial, because they flow directly from the constitutional language. The first is that the clause applies only in "criminal prosecutions." The second is that the clause grants a right of confrontation only to "the accused." And the third is that the right is satisfied if the accused is "confronted." There is disagreement about what "confrontation" necessarily entails, but there is broad consensus that the requirement is fully satisfied by in-court testimony, in the presence of the defendant, subject to cross-examination.

These three, straightforward limits on the reach of the Confrontation Clause mean that the clause has no implications for three large categories of hearsay: hearsay in civil cases, hearsay introduced against the prosecution in criminal cases, and hearsay declarations from someone who winds up testifying in open court, subject to cross-examination. The remaining question, which has generated much controversy, is when the Constitution prohibits the introduction, against a criminal defendant, of hearsay from a declarant who does not testify.

In *Ohio v. Roberts*, 448 U.S. 56 (1980), the Supreme Court read the Confrontation Clause to allow hearsay of this kind, so long as the evidence fell within a well-established exception to the hearsay rule or carried comparable "indicia of reliability." The Court stuck with this interpretation for almost a quarter-century. More recently, however, the Court has rejected the *Roberts* approach, and has announced a different test for determining when hearsay violates the Confrontation Clause. What matters, the Court now says, is whether the out-of-court statement was "testimonial." The decision that initially announced this new approach — *Crawford v. Washington* — is excerpted below, along with the most recent decision interpreting and applying the *Crawford* test, *Ohio v. Clark.* As the opinions in *Clark* indicate, the Justices have disagreed about how far to extend *Crawford* and how best to define "testimonial." We will return to these questions later in the book: both later in this chapter, when we address the hearsay exception for public reports, and in Chapter 9, when we discuss expert testimony.

The overruling of *Roberts* means that a good deal of hearsay not excluded by the hearsay rule (because, for example, it falls within one of the exceptions addressed later in this chapter) is now nonetheless inadmissible if offered against a criminal defendant. And even when evidence in a criminal case *is* excluded by the hearsay rule, it can be important to know whether it is also barred by the Confrontation Clause. For one thing, the harmless error rules are less forgiving of evidence admitted in violation of the Constitution. Under *Chapman v. California*, 386 U.S. 18 (1967), a constitutional error generally requires reversal of a defendant's conviction unless the prosecution can show that the error was harmless "beyond a reasonable doubt." As we saw in Chapter 1, courts apply varying criteria for determining whether an ordinary evidentiary error was harmless, but these criteria are almost always easier to satisfy than the *Chapman* standard. Even more important, the Supreme Court has sharply restricted the use of limiting instructions to avoid violations of the Confrontation Clause. That restriction, announced in *Bruton v. United States*, 391 U.S. 123 (1968), is taken up later in this chapter.

CRAWFORD v. WASHINGTON

541 U.S. 36 (2004)

Justice SCALIA delivered the opinion of the Court.

. . . On August 5, 1999, Kenneth Lee was stabbed at his apartment. Police arrested petitioner [Michael Crawford] later that night. After giving petitioner and his wife [Sylvia] *Miranda* warnings, detectives interrogated each of them twice. Petitioner eventually confessed that he and Sylvia had gone in search of Lee because he was upset over an earlier incident in which Lee had tried to rape her. The two had found Lee at his apartment, and a fight ensued. . . . Sylvia generally corroborated petitioner's story about the events leading up to the fight, but her account of the fight itself was arguably different — particularly with respect to whether Lee had drawn a weapon before petitioner assaulted him. . . .

The State charged petitioner with assault and attempted murder. At trial, he claimed self-defense. Sylvia did not testify because of the state marital privilege, which generally bars a spouse from testifying without the other spouse's consent. See Wash. Rev. Code §5.60.060(1) (1994). In Washington, this privilege does not extend to a spouse's out-of-court statements admissible under a hearsay exception, see *State v. Burden*, [841 P.2d 758, 761 (Wash. 1992)], so the State sought to introduce Sylvia's tape-recorded statements to the police as evidence that the stabbing was not in self-defense. Noting that Sylvia had admitted she led petitioner to Lee's apartment and thus had facilitated the assault, the State invoked the hearsay exception for statements against penal interest, Wash. Rule Evid. 804(b)(3) (2003).

Petitioner countered that, state law notwithstanding, admitting the evidence would violate his federal constitutional right to be "confronted with the witnesses against him." Amdt. 6. . . . The trial court here admitted the statement. . . . The prosecution played the tape for the jury and relied on it in closing, arguing that it was "damning evidence" that "completely refutes [petitioner's] claim of self-defense." The jury convicted petitioner of assault. The Washington Court of Appeals reversed . . . [but the] Washington Supreme Court reinstated the conviction. . . .

The Sixth Amendment's Confrontation Clause provides that, "[i]n all criminal prosecutions, the accused shall enjoy the right . . . to be confronted with the witnesses against him." We have held that this bedrock procedural guarantee applies to both federal and state prosecutions. . . . We must . . . turn to the historical background of the Clause to understand its meaning.

The right to confront one's accusers is a concept that dates back to Roman times. The founding generation's immediate source of the concept, however, was the common law. English common law has long differed from continental civil law in regard to the manner in which witnesses give testimony in criminal trials. The common-law tradition is one of live testimony in court subject to adversarial testing, while the civil law condones examination in private by judicial officers. See 3 W. Blackstone, Commentaries on the Laws of England 373-374 (1768).

Nonetheless, England at times adopted elements of the civil-law practice. Justices of the peace or other officials examined suspects and witnesses before trial. These examinations were sometimes read in court in lieu of live testimony, a practice that "occasioned frequent demands by the prisoner to have his 'accusers,' *i.e.*, the witnesses against him, brought before him face to face." 1 J. Stephen, History of the Criminal Law of England 326 (1883). In some cases, these demands were refused. See 9 W. Holdsworth, History of English Law 216-217, 228 (3d ed. 1944); *e.g.*, *Raleigh's Case*, 2 How. St. Tr. 1, 15-16, 24 (1603); *Throckmorton's Case*, 1 How. St. Tr. 869, 875-876 (1554); cf. *Lilburn's Case*, 3 How. St. Tr. 1315, 1318-1322, 1329 (Star Chamber 1637).

Pretrial examinations became routine under two statutes passed during the reign of Queen Mary in the 16th century, 1 & 2 Phil. & M., c. 13 (1554), and 2 & 3 *id.*, c. 10 (1555). These Marian bail and committal statutes required justices of the peace to examine suspects and witnesses in felony cases and to certify the results to the court. It is doubtful that the original purpose of the examinations was to produce evidence admissible at trial. See J. Langbein, Prosecuting Crime in the Renaissance 21-34 (1974). Whatever the original purpose, however, they came to be used as evidence in some cases, see 2 M. Hale, Pleas of the Crown 284 (1736), resulting in an adoption of continental procedure. See 4 Holdsworth, *supra*, at 528-530.

The most notorious instances of civil-law examination occurred in the great political trials of the 16th and 17th centuries. One such was the 1603 trial of Sir Walter Raleigh for treason. Lord Cobham, Raleigh's alleged accomplice, had implicated him in an examination before the Privy Council and in a letter. At Raleigh's trial, these were read to the jury. Raleigh argued that Cobham had lied to save himself: "Cobham is absolutely in the King's mercy; to excuse me cannot avail him; by accusing me he may hope for favour." 1 D. Jardine, Criminal Trials 435 (1832). Suspecting that Cobham would recant, Raleigh demanded that the judges call him to appear, arguing that "[t]he Proof of the Common Law is by witness and jury: let Cobham be here, let him speak it. Call my accuser before my face. . . ." 2 How. St. Tr., at 15–16. The judges refused, and, despite Raleigh's protestations that he was being tried "by the Spanish Inquisition," the jury convicted, and Raleigh was sentenced to death.

One of Raleigh's trial judges later lamented that "'the justice of England has never been so degraded and injured as by the condemnation of Sir Walter Raleigh.'" 1 Jardine, *supra*, at 520. Through a series of statutory and judicial reforms, English law developed a right of confrontation that limited these abuses. For example, treason statutes required witnesses to confront the accused "face to face" at his arraignment. Courts, meanwhile, developed relatively strict rules of unavailability, admitting examinations only if the witness was demonstrably unable to testify in person. Several authorities also stated that a suspect's confession could be admitted only against himself, and not against others he implicated. /

One recurring question was whether the admissibility of an unavailable witness's pretrial examination depended on whether the defendant had had an opportunity to cross-examine him. In 1696, the Court of King's Bench answered this question in the affirmative, in the widely reported misdemeanor libel case of *King v. Paine*, 5 Mod. 163, 87 Eng. Rep. 584. The court ruled that, even though a witness was dead, his examination was not admissible where "the defendant not being present when [it was] taken before the mayor . . . had lost the benefit of a cross-examination." . . . [B]y 1791 (the year the Sixth Amendment was ratified), courts were applying the cross-examination rule even to examinations by justices of the peace in felony cases. . . .

Controversial examination practices were also used in the Colonies. . . . [Partly as a result, many] declarations of rights adopted around the time of the Revolution guaranteed a right of confrontation. The proposed Federal Constitution, however, did not. At the Massachusetts ratifying convention, Abraham Holmes objected to this omission precisely on the ground that it would lead to civil-law practices. . . . Similarly, a prominent Antifederalist writing under the pseudonym Federal Farmer criticized the use of "written evidence." . . . The First Congress responded by including the Confrontation Clause in the proposal that became the Sixth Amendment.

This history supports two inferences about the meaning of the Sixth Amendment.

First, the principal evil at which the Confrontation Clause was directed was the civil-law mode of criminal procedure, and particularly its use of *ex parte* examinations as evidence against the accused. It was these practices that the Crown deployed in notorious treason cases like Raleigh's; that the Marian statutes invited; that English law's assertion of a right to confrontation was meant to prohibit; and that the founding-era rhetoric decried. The Sixth Amendment must be interpreted with this focus in mind.

Accordingly, we once again reject the view that the Confrontation Clause applies of its own force only to in-court testimony, and that its application to out-of-court statements introduced at trial depends upon "the law of Evidence for the time being." 3 Wigmore §1397, at 101; accord, *Dutton v. Evans*, 400 U.S. 74, 94 (1970) (Harlan, J., concurring in result). Leaving the regulation of out-of-court statements to the law of evidence would render the Confrontation Clause powerless to prevent even the most flagrant inquisitorial practices. Raleigh was, after all, perfectly free to confront those who read Cobham's confession in court.

This focus also suggests that not all hearsay implicates the Sixth Amendment's core concerns. An off-hand, overheard remark might be unreliable evidence and thus a good candidate for exclusion under hearsay rules, but it bears little resemblance to the civil-law abuses the Confrontation Clause targeted. On the other hand, *ex parte* examinations might sometimes be admissible under modern hearsay rules, but the Framers certainly would not have condoned them.

The text of the Confrontation Clause reflects this focus. It applies to "witnesses" against the accused — in other words, those who "bear testimony." 2 N. Webster, An American Dictionary of the English Language (1828). "Testimony," in turn, is typically "[a] solemn declaration or affirmation made for the purpose of establishing or proving some fact." *Ibid.* An accuser who makes a formal statement to government officers bears testimony in a sense that a person who makes a casual remark to an acquaintance does not. The constitutional text, like the history underlying the common-law right of confrontation, thus reflects an especially acute concern with a specific type of out-of-court statement.

Various formulations of this core class of "testimonial" statements exist: "*ex parte* in-court testimony or its functional equivalent — that is, material such as affidavits, custodial examinations, prior testimony that the defendant was unable to cross-examine, or similar pretrial statements that declarants would reasonably expect to be used prosecutorially," Brief for Petitioner 23; "extrajudicial statements . . . contained in formalized testimonial materials, such as affidavits, depositions, prior testimony, or confessions," *White v. Illinois*, 503 U.S. 346, 365 (1992) (Thomas, J., joined by Scalia, J., concurring in part and concurring in judgment); "statements that were made under circumstances which would lead an objective witness reasonably to believe that the statement would be available for use at a later trial," Brief for National Association of Criminal Defense Lawyers et al. as *Amici Curiae* 3. These formulations all share a common nucleus and then define the Clause's coverage at various levels of abstraction around it. Regardless of the precise articulation, some statements qualify under any definition — for example, *ex parte* testimony at a preliminary hearing.

Statements taken by police officers in the course of interrogations are also testimonial under even a narrow standard. Police interrogations bear a striking resemblance to examinations by justices of the peace in England. The statements are not *sworn* testimony, but the absence of oath was not dispositive. Cobham's examination was unsworn, see 1 Jardine, Criminal Trials, at 430, yet Raleigh's trial has long been thought a paradigmatic confrontation violation. Under the Marian stat-utes, witnesses were typically put on oath, but suspects were not. See 2 Hale, Pleas of the Crown, at 52. Yet Hawkins and others went out of their way to caution that such unsworn confessions were not admissible against anyone but the confessor.

That interrogators are police officers rather than magistrates does not change the picture either. Justices of the peace conducting examinations under the Marian statutes were not magistrates as we understand that office today, but had an essen-tially investigative and prosecutorial function. See 1 Stephen, Criminal Law of England, at 221; Langbein, Prosecuting Crime in the Renaissance, at 34-45. England did not have a professional police force until the 19th century, see 1 Stephen, *supra*, at 194-200, so it is not surprising that other government officers performed the investigative functions now associated primarily with the police. The involve-ment of government officers in the production of testimonial evidence presents the same risk, whether the officers are police or justices of the peace.

In sum, even if the Sixth Amendment is not solely concerned with testimo-nial hearsay, that is its primary object, and interrogations by law enforcement officers fall squarely within that class. . . .

The historical record also supports a second proposition: that the Framers would not have allowed admission of testimonial statements of a witness who did not appear at trial unless he was unavailable to testify, and the defendant had had a prior opportunity for cross-examination. The text of the Sixth Amendment does not suggest any open-ended exceptions from the confrontation require-ment to be developed by the courts. Rather, the "right . . . to be confronted with the witnesses against him," Amdt. 6, is most naturally read as a reference to the right of confrontation at common law, admitting only those exceptions estab-lished at the time of the founding. As the English authorities above reveal, the common law in 1791 conditioned admissibility of an absent witness's exam-ination on unavailability and a prior opportunity to cross-examine. The Sixth Amendment therefore incorporates those limitations. The numerous early state decisions applying the same test confirm that these principles were received as part of the common law in this country. . . .

We do not read the historical sources to say that a prior opportunity to cross-examine was merely a sufficient, rather than a necessary, condition for admissibility of testimonial statements. They suggest that this requirement was dispositive, and not merely one of several ways to establish reliability. This is not to deny, as THE CHIEF JUSTICE notes, that "[t]here were always exceptions to the general rule of exclusion" of hearsay evidence. Several had become well established by 1791. But there is scant evidence that exceptions were invoked to admit *testimonial* statements against the accused in a *criminal* case.[6] Most

---

6. The one deviation we have found involves dying declarations. The existence of that exception as a general rule of criminal hearsay law cannot be disputed. See, *e.g., Mattox v. United States*, 156 U.S. 237, 243-244 (1895); *King v. Reason*, 16 How. St. Tr. 1, 24-38 (K.B. 1722); 1 D. Jardine, Criminal Trials 435 (1832); . . . 1 G. Gilbert, Evidence 211 (C. Lofft ed. 1791); see also F. Heller, The Sixth Amendment 105 (1951) (asserting that this was the *only* recognized criminal hearsay exception at common law). Although many dying declarations may not be testimonial, there is authority for admitting even those that clearly are. . . . We need not decide in this case whether the Sixth Amendment incorporates an exception for testimonial dying decla-rations. If this exception must be accepted on historical grounds, it is *sui generis*.

of the hearsay exceptions covered statements that by their nature were not testimonial — for example, business records or statements in furtherance of a conspiracy. We do not infer from these that the Framers thought exceptions would apply even to prior testimony. . . .[7]

Our caselaw has been largely consistent with these two principles . . .[8] . . . [but] the same cannot be said of our rationales. [*Ohio v. Roberts*, 448 U.S. 56 (1980),] conditions the admissibility of all hearsay evidence on whether it falls under a "firmly rooted hearsay exception" or bears "particularized guarantees of trustworthiness." This test departs from the historical principles identified above in two respects. First, it is too broad: It applies the same mode of analysis whether or not the hearsay consists of *ex parte* testimony. This often results in close constitutional scrutiny in cases that are far removed from the core concerns of the Clause. At the same time, however, the test is too narrow: It admits statements that *do* consist of *ex parte* testimony upon a mere finding of reliability. This malleable standard often fails to protect against paradigmatic confrontation violations. . . .

Where testimonial statements are involved, we do not think the Framers meant to leave the Sixth Amendment's protection to the vagaries of the rules of evidence, much less to amorphous notions of "reliability." Certainly none of the authorities discussed above acknowledges any general reliability exception to the common-law rule. Admitting statements deemed reliable by a judge is fundamentally at odds with the right of confrontation. To be sure, the Clause's ultimate goal is to ensure reliability of evidence, but it is a procedural rather than a substantive guarantee. It commands, not that evidence be reliable, but that reliability be assessed in a particular manner: by testing in the crucible of cross-examination. The Clause thus reflects a judgment, not only about the desirability of reliable evidence (a point on which there could be little dissent), but about how reliability can best be determined. Cf. 3 Blackstone, Commentaries, at 373 ("This open examination of witnesses . . . is much more conducive to the clearing up of truth"); M. Hale, History and Analysis of the Common Law of England 258 (1713) (adversarial testing "beats and bolts out the Truth much better").

The *Roberts* test allows a jury to hear evidence, untested by the adversary process, based on a mere judicial determination of reliability. It thus replaces the constitutionally prescribed method of assessing reliability with a wholly foreign one. In this respect, it is very different from exceptions to the Confrontation Clause that make no claim to be a surrogate means of assessing

---

7. We cannot agree with THE CHIEF JUSTICE that the fact "[t]hat a statement might be testimonial does nothing to undermine the wisdom of one of these [hearsay] exceptions." Involvement of government officers in the production of testimony with an eye toward trial presents unique potential for prosecutorial abuse — a fact borne out time and again throughout a history with which the Framers were keenly familiar. This consideration does not evaporate when testimony happens to fall within some broad, modern hearsay exception, even if that exception might be justifiable in other circumstances.

8. . . . [W]e reiterate that, when the declarant appears for cross-examination at trial, the Confrontation Clause places no constraints at all on the use of his prior testimonial statements. See *California v. Green*, 399 U.S. 149, 162 (1970). . . . The Clause also does not bar the use of testimonial statements for purposes other than establishing the truth of the matter asserted. See *Tennessee v. Street*, 471 U.S. 409, 414 (1985).

reliability. For example, the rule of forfeiture by wrongdoing (which we accept) extinguishes confrontation claims on essentially equitable grounds; it does not purport to be an alternative means of determining reliability. See *Reynolds v. United States*, 98 U.S. 145, 158–159 (1879).

The *Raleigh* trial itself involved the very sorts of reliability determinations that *Roberts* authorizes. In the face of Raleigh's repeated demands for confrontation, the prosecution responded with many of the arguments a court applying *Roberts* might invoke today: that Cobham's statements were self-inculpatory, 2 How. St. Tr., at 19, that they were not made in the heat of passion, *id.*, at 14, and that they were not "extracted from [him] upon any hopes or promise of Pardon," *id.*, at 29. It is not plausible that the Framers' only objection to the trial was that Raleigh's judges did not properly weigh these factors before sentencing him to death. Rather, the problem was that the judges refused to allow Raleigh to confront Cobham in court, where he could cross-examine him and try to expose his accusation as a lie.

Dispensing with confrontation because testimony is obviously reliable is akin to dispensing with jury trial because a defendant is obviously guilty. This is not what the Sixth Amendment prescribes....

Roberts' failings were on full display in the proceedings below. Sylvia Crawford made her statement while in police custody, herself a potential suspect in the case. Indeed, she had been told that whether she would be released "depend[ed] on how the investigation continues." In response to often leading questions from police detectives, she implicated her husband in Lee's stabbing and at least arguably undermined his self-defense claim. Despite all this, the trial court admitted her statement, listing several reasons why it was reliable. In its opinion reversing, the Court of Appeals listed several *other* reasons why the statement was *not* reliable. Finally, the State Supreme Court relied exclusively on the interlocking character of the statement and disregarded every other factor the lower courts had considered. The case is thus a self-contained demonstration of *Roberts'* unpredictable and inconsistent application.

Each of the courts also made assumptions that cross-examination might well have undermined. The trial court, for example, stated that Sylvia Crawford's statement was reliable because she was an eyewitness with direct knowledge of the events. But Sylvia at one point told the police that she had "shut [her] eyes and ... didn't really watch" part of the fight, and that she was "in shock." The trial court also buttressed its reliability finding by claiming that Sylvia was "being questioned by law enforcement, and, thus, the [questioner] is ... neutral to her and not someone who would be inclined to advance her interests and shade her version of the truth unfavorably toward the defendant." The Framers would be astounded to learn that *ex parte* testimony could be admitted against a criminal defendant because it was elicited by "neutral" government officers. But even if the court's assessment of the officer's motives was accurate, it says nothing about Sylvia's perception of her situation. Only cross-examination could reveal that.

The State Supreme Court gave dispositive weight to the interlocking nature of the two statements — that they were both ambiguous as to when and whether Lee had a weapon. The court's claim that the two statements were *equally* ambiguous is hard to accept. Petitioner's statement is ambiguous only in the sense that he had lingering doubts about his recollection: "A.

I could a swore I seen him goin' for somethin' before, right before everything happened.... [B]ut I'm not positive." Sylvia's statement, on the other hand, is truly inscrutable, since the key timing detail was simply assumed in the leading question she was asked:"Q. Did Kenny do anything to fight back from this assault?" Moreover, Sylvia specifically said Lee had nothing in his hands after he was stabbed, while petitioner was not asked about that.

The prosecutor obviously did not share the court's view that Sylvia's statement was ambiguous — he called it "damning evidence" that "completely refutes [petitioner's] claim of self-defense." We have no way of knowing whether the jury agreed with the prosecutor or the court. Far from obviating the need for cross-examination, the "interlocking" ambiguity of the two statements made it all the more imperative that they be tested to tease out the truth.

We readily concede that we could resolve this case by simply reweighing the "reliability factors" under *Roberts* and finding that Sylvia Crawford's statement falls short. But we view this as one of those rare cases in which the result below is so improbable that it reveals a fundamental failure on our part to interpret the Constitution in a way that secures its intended constraint on judicial discretion. Moreover, to reverse the Washington Supreme Court's decision after conducting our own reliability analysis would perpetuate, not avoid, what the Sixth Amendment condemns. The Constitution prescribes a procedure for determining the reliability of testimony in criminal trials, and we, no less than the state courts, lack authority to replace it with one of our own devising....

Vague standards are manipulable, and, while that might be a small concern in run-of-the-mill assault prosecutions like this one, the Framers had an eye toward politically charged cases like Raleigh's — great state trials where the impartiality of even those at the highest levels of the judiciary might not be so clear. It is difficult to imagine *Roberts* providing any meaningful protection in those circumstances.

Where nontestimonial hearsay is at issue, it is wholly consistent with the Framers' design to afford the States flexibility in their development of hearsay law — as does *Roberts*, and as would an approach that exempted such statements from Confrontation Clause scrutiny altogether. Where testimonial evidence is at issue, however, the Sixth Amendment demands what the common law required: unavailability and a prior opportunity for cross-examination. We leave for another day any effort to spell out a comprehensive definition of "testimonial." Whatever else the term covers, it applies at a minimum to prior testimony at a preliminary hearing, before a grand jury, or at a former trial; and to police interrogations. These are the modern practices with closest kinship to the abuses at which the Confrontation Clause was directed.... Where testimonial statements are at issue, the only indicium of reliability sufficient to satisfy constitutional demands is the one the Constitution actually prescribes: confrontation.

The judgment of the Washington Supreme Court is reversed....

Chief Justice REHNQUIST, with whom Justice O'CONNOR joins, concurring in the judgment.

I dissent from the Court's decision to overrule *Ohio v. Roberts*, 448 U.S. 56 (1980).... Between 1700 and 1800 the rules regarding the admissibility of

out-of-court statements were still being developed. There were always exceptions to the general rule of exclusion, and it is not clear to me that the Framers
categorically wanted to eliminate further ones. . . . It is an odd conclusion
indeed to think that the Framers created a cut-and-dried rule with respect to
the admissibility of testimonial statements when the law during their own
time was not fully settled. . . .

Exceptions to confrontation have always been derived from the experience that some out-of-court statements are just as reliable as cross-examined
in-court testimony due to the circumstances under which they were
made. . . . That a statement might be testimonial does nothing to undermine
the wisdom of one of these exceptions. . . .

"[I]n a given instance [cross-examination may] be superfluous; it may be
sufficiently clear, in that instance, that the statement offered is free enough
from the risk of inaccuracy and untrustworthiness, so that the test of cross-
examination would be a work of supererogation." 5 Wigmore §1420, at 251. In
such a case, as we noted over 100 years ago, "The law in its wisdom declares
that the rights of the public shall not be wholly sacrificed in order that an
incidental benefit may be preserved to the accused." *Mattox*, 156 U.S., at 243.
By creating an immutable category of excluded evidence, the Court adds little
to a trial's truth-finding function and ignores this longstanding guidance. . . .

In *Idaho v. Wright*, 497 U.S. 805 (1990), we held that an out-of-court statement was not admissible simply because the truthfulness of that statement
was corroborated by other evidence at trial. As the Court notes, the Supreme
Court of Washington gave decisive weight to the "interlocking nature of the
two statements." No re-weighing of the "reliability factors," which is hypothesized by the Court, is required to reverse the judgment here. A citation to
Idaho v. Wright would suffice. . . . I believe that this would be a far preferable
course for the Court to take here.

OHIO v. CLARK

576 U.S. _____ (2015)

Justice ALITO delivered the opinion of the Court.

. . . Darius Clark, who went by the nickname "Dee," lived in Cleveland,
Ohio, with his girlfriend, T.T., and her two children: L.P., a 3-year-old boy, and
A.T., an 18-month-old girl. Clark was also T.T.'s pimp, and he would regularly
send her on trips to Washington, D.C., to work as a prostitute. In March 2010,
T.T. went on one such trip, and she left the children in Clark's care.

The next day, Clark took L.P. to preschool. In the lunchroom, one of L.P.'s
teachers, Ramona Whitley, observed that L.P.'s left eye appeared bloodshot.
She asked him "[w]hat happened," and he initially said nothing. Eventually,
however, he told the teacher that he "fell." When they moved into the brighter
lights of a classroom, Whitley noticed "[r]ed marks, like whips of some sort," on
L.P.'s face. She notified the lead teacher, Debra Jones, who asked L.P., "Who did
this? What happened to you?" According to Jones, L.P. "seemed kind of bewil-
dered" and "said something like, Dee, Dee." Jones asked L.P. whether Dee is "big

or little," to which L.P. responded that "Dee is big." Jones then brought L.P. to her supervisor, who lifted the boy's shirt, revealing more injuries. Whitley called a child abuse hotline to alert authorities about the suspected abuse.

When Clark later arrived at the school, he denied responsibility for the injuries and quickly left with L.P. The next day, a social worker found the children at Clark's mother's house and took them to a hospital, where a physician discovered additional injuries suggesting child abuse. L.P. had a black eye, belt marks on his back and stomach, and bruises all over his body. A.T. had two black eyes, a swollen hand, and a large burn on her cheek, and two pigtails had been ripped out at the roots of her hair.

A grand jury indicted Clark on five counts of felonious assault (four related to A.T. and one related to L.P.), two counts of endangering children (one for each child), and two counts of domestic violence (one for each child). At trial, the State introduced L.P.'s statements to his teachers as evidence of Clark's guilt, but L.P. did not testify. Under Ohio law, children younger than 10 years old are incompetent to testify if they "appear incapable of receiving just impressions of the facts and transactions respecting which they are examined, or of relating them truly." Ohio Rule Evid. 601(A). After conducting a hearing, the trial court concluded that L.P. was not competent to testify. But under Ohio Rule of Evidence 807, which allows the admission of reliable hearsay by child abuse victims, the court ruled that L.P.'s statements to his teachers bore sufficient guarantees of trustworthiness to be admitted as evidence.

Clark moved to exclude testimony about L.P.'s out-of-court statements under the Confrontation Clause. The trial court denied the motion, ruling that L.P.'s responses were not testimonial statements covered by the Sixth Amendment. The jury found Clark guilty on all counts except for one assault count related to A.T., and it sentenced him to 28 years' imprisonment. Clark appealed his conviction, and a state appellate court reversed on the ground that the introduction of L.P.'s out-of-court statements violated the Confrontation Clause.

In a 4-to-3 decision, the Supreme Court of Ohio affirmed. It held that, under this Court's Confrontation Clause decisions, L.P.'s statements qualified as testimonial because the primary purpose of the teachers' questioning "was not to deal with an existing emergency but rather to gather evidence potentially relevant to a subsequent criminal prosecution." The court noted that Ohio has a "mandatory reporting" law that requires certain professionals, including preschool teachers, to report suspected child abuse to government authorities. In the court's view, the teachers acted as agents of the State under the mandatory reporting law and "sought facts concerning past criminal activity to identify the person responsible, eliciting statements that 'are functionally identical to live, in-court testimony, doing precisely what a witness does on direct examination.'" (quoting *Melendez-Diaz v. Massachusetts,* 557 U.S. 305 (2009))....[W]e now reverse....

The Sixth Amendment's Confrontation Clause, which is binding on the States through the Fourteenth Amendment, provides: "In all criminal prosecutions, the accused shall enjoy the right . . . to be confronted with the witnesses against him." In *Ohio v. Roberts,* 448 U.S. 56 (1980), we interpreted the Clause to permit the admission of out-of-court statements by an unavailable witness, so long as the statements bore "adequate 'indicia of reliability.'" Such indicia are present, we held, if "the evidence falls within a firmly rooted hearsay exception" or bears "particularized guarantees of trustworthiness."

In *Crawford v. Washington,* 541 U.S. 36 (2004), we adopted a different approach. We explained that "witnesses," under the Confrontation Clause, are those "who bear testimony," and we defined "testimony" as "a solemn declaration or affirmation made for the purpose of establishing or proving some fact." The Sixth Amendment, we concluded, prohibits the introduction of testimonial statements by a nontestifying witness, unless the witness is "unavailable to testify, and the defendant had had a prior opportunity for cross-examination." Applying that definition to the facts in *Crawford,* we held that statements by a witness during police questioning at the station house were testimonial and thus could not be admitted. But our decision in *Crawford* did not offer an exhaustive definition of "testimonial" statements. Instead, *Crawford* stated that the label "applies at a minimum to prior testimony at a preliminary hearing, before a grand jury, or at a former trial; and to police interrogations."

Our more recent cases have labored to flesh out what it means for a statement to be "testimonial." In *Davis v. Washington* and *Hammon v. Indiana,* 547 U.S. 813 (2006), which we decided together, we dealt with statements given to law enforcement officers by the victims of domestic abuse. The victim in *Davis* made statements to a 911 emergency operator during and shortly after her boyfriend's violent attack. In *Hammon,* the victim, after being isolated from her abusive husband, made statements to police that were memorialized in a "battery affidavit."

We held that the statements in *Hammon* were testimonial, while the statements in *Davis* were not. Announcing what has come to be known as the "primary purpose" test, we explained: "Statements are nontestimonial when made in the course of police interrogation under circumstances objectively indicating that the primary purpose of the interrogation is to enable police assistance to meet an ongoing emergency. They are testimonial when the circumstances objectively indicate that there is no such ongoing emergency, and that the primary purpose of the interrogation is to establish or prove past events potentially relevant to later criminal prosecution." Because the cases involved statements to law enforcement officers, we reserved the question whether similar statements to individuals other than law enforcement officers would raise similar issues under the Confrontation Clause.

In *Michigan v. Bryant,* 562 U.S. 344 (2011), we further expounded on the primary purpose test.* The inquiry, we emphasized, must consider "all of

---

* [Bryant was convicted of murder based on the victim's statements to the police after they found him lying on the ground at a gas station with a gunshot wound to his abdomen. The victim, Covington, "appeared to be in great pain, and spoke with difficulty." In response to the officers' questions, he said "that he had a conversation with Bryant, whom he recognized based on his voice, through the back door of Bryant's house. Covington explained that when he turned to leave, he was shot through the door and then drove to the gas station, where police found him." Covington then was transported to the hospital and died within hours. The Supreme Court reasoned, in an opinion written by Justice Sotomayor, that *Crawford* requires examination of the "primary purposes" both of the declarant and the questioner, and that "the circumstances of the encounter as well as the statements and actions of Covington and the police objectively indicate that the 'primary purpose of the interrogation' was 'to enable police assistance to meet an ongoing emergency.'" The majority therefore concluded that Covington's statements were not testimonial and that the Confrontation Clause allowed them to be

the relevant circumstances." And we reiterated our view in *Davis* that, when "the primary purpose of an interrogation is to respond to an 'ongoing emergency,' its purpose is not to create a record for trial and thus is not within the scope of the [Confrontation] Clause." At the same time, we noted that "there may be *other* circumstances, aside from ongoing emergencies, when a statement is not procured with a primary purpose of creating an out-of-court substitute for trial testimony.... [T]he existence *vel non* of an ongoing emergency is not the touchstone of the testimonial inquiry." Instead, "whether an ongoing emergency exists is simply one factor . . . that informs the ultimate inquiry regarding the 'primary purpose' of an interrogation."

One additional factor is "the informality of the situation and the interrogation." A "formal station-house interrogation," like the questioning in *Crawford,* is more likely to provoke testimonial statements, while less formal questioning is less likely to reflect a primary purpose aimed at obtaining testimonial evidence against the accused. And in determining whether a statement is testimonial, "standard rules of hearsay, designed to identify some statements as reliable, will be relevant." In the end, the question is whether, in light of all the circumstances, viewed objectively, the "primary purpose" of the conversation was to "creat[e] an out-of-court substitute for trial testimony." Applying these principles in *Bryant,* we held that the statements made by a dying victim about his assailant were not testimonial because the circumstances objectively indicated that the conversation was primarily aimed at quelling an ongoing emergency, not establishing evidence for the prosecution. Because the relevant statements were made to law enforcement officers, we again declined to decide whether the same analysis applies to statements made to individuals other than the police.

Thus, under our precedents, a statement cannot fall within the Confrontation Clause unless its primary purpose was testimonial. "Where no such primary purpose exists, the admissibility of a statement is the concern of state and federal rules of evidence, not the Confrontation Clause." [*Bryant.*] But that does not mean that the Confrontation Clause bars every statement that satisfies the "primary purpose" test. We have recognized that the Confrontation Clause does not prohibit the introduction of out-of-court statements that would have been admissible in a criminal case at the time of the founding. See *Giles v. California,* 554 U.S. 353 (2008); *Crawford,* 541 U.S., at 56, n.6. Thus, the primary purpose test is a necessary, but not always sufficient, condition for the exclusion of out-of-court statements under the Confrontation Clause. . . .

In this case, we consider statements made to preschool teachers, not the police. We are therefore presented with the question we have repeatedly reserved: whether statements to persons other than law enforcement officers are subject to the Confrontation Clause. Because at least some statements to individuals who are not law enforcement officers could conceivably raise

---

introduced against *Bryant.* In dissent, Justice Scalia argued that the declarant's purpose should be controlling, but that from *either* Covington's perspective or the perspective of the police officers who questioned him, it was obvious that the purpose of the conversation was to establish what had happened for purposes of a later trial, not to respond to an ongoing emergency. Justice Ginsburg also dissented, and Justice Thomas concurred in the judgment. — ED.]

confrontation concerns, we decline to adopt a categorical rule excluding them from the Sixth Amendment's reach. Nevertheless, such statements are much less likely to be testimonial than statements to law enforcement officers. And considering all the relevant circumstances here, L.P.'s statements clearly were not made with the primary purpose of creating evidence for Clark's prosecution. Thus, their introduction at trial did not violate the Confrontation Clause.

L.P.'s statements occurred in the context of an ongoing emergency involving suspected child abuse. When L.P.'s teachers noticed his injuries, they rightly became worried that the 3-year-old was the victim of serious violence. Because the teachers needed to know whether it was safe to release L.P. to his guardian at the end of the day, they needed to determine who might be abusing the child.[1] Thus, the immediate concern was to protect a vulnerable child who needed help. . . . As in *Bryant*, the emergency in this case was ongoing, and the circumstances were not entirely clear. L.P.'s teachers were not sure who had abused him or how best to secure his safety. Nor were they sure whether any other children might be at risk. As a result, their questions and L.P.'s answers were primarily aimed at identifying and ending the threat. Though not as harried, the conversation here was also similar to the 911 call in *Davis*. The teachers' questions were meant to identify the abuser in order to protect the victim from future attacks. Whether the teachers thought that this would be done by apprehending the abuser or by some other means is irrelevant. And the circumstances in this case were unlike the interrogation in *Hammon*, where the police knew the identity of the assailant and questioned the victim after shielding her from potential harm.

There is no indication that the primary purpose of the conversation was to gather evidence for Clark's prosecution. On the contrary, it is clear that the first objective was to protect L.P. At no point did the teachers inform L.P. that his answers would be used to arrest or punish his abuser. L.P. never hinted that he intended his statements to be used by the police or prosecutors. And the conversation between L.P. and his teachers was informal and spontaneous. The teachers asked L.P. about his injuries immediately upon discovering them, in the informal setting of a preschool lunchroom and classroom, and they did so precisely as any concerned citizen would talk to a child who might be the victim of abuse. This was nothing like the formalized station-house questioning in *Crawford* or the police interrogation and battery affidavit in *Hammon*.

L.P.'s age fortifies our conclusion that the statements in question were not testimonial. Statements by very young children will rarely, if ever, implicate the Confrontation Clause. Few preschool students understand the details of our criminal justice system. . . . Thus, it is extremely unlikely that a 3-year-old child in L.P.'s position would intend his statements to be a substitute for trial testimony. On the contrary, a young child in these circumstances would simply want the abuse to end, would want to protect other victims, or would have no discernible purpose at all.

---

1. In fact, the teachers and a social worker who had come to the school *were* reluctant to release L.P. into Clark's care after the boy identified Clark as his abuser. But after a brief "stare-down" with the social worker, Clark bolted out the door with L.P., and social services were not able to locate the children until the next day.

As a historical matter, moreover, there is strong evidence that statements made in circumstances similar to those facing L.P. and his teachers were admissible at common law. See Lyon & LaMagna, The History of Children's Hearsay: From Old Bailey to Post-*Davis,* 82 Ind. L.J. 1029, 1030 (2007); see also *id.,* at 1041–1044 (examining child rape cases from 1687 to 1788); J. Langbein, The Origins of Adversary Criminal Trial 239 (2003) ("The Old Bailey" court in 18th-century London "tolerated flagrant hearsay in rape prosecutions involving a child victim who was not competent to testify because she was too young to appreciate the significance of her oath"). And when 18th-century courts excluded statements of this sort, see, *e.g., King v. Brasier,* 1 Leach 199, 168 Eng. Rep. 202 (K.B. 1779), they appeared to do so because the child should have been ruled competent to testify, not because the statements were otherwise inadmissible.... It is thus highly doubtful that statements like L.P.'s ever would have been understood to raise Confrontation Clause concerns. Neither *Crawford* nor any of the cases that it has produced has mounted evidence that the adoption of the Confrontation Clause was understood to require the exclusion of evidence that was regularly admitted in criminal cases at the time of the founding. Certainly, the statements in this case are nothing like the notorious use of *ex parte* examination in Sir Walter Raleigh's trial for treason, which we have frequently identified as "the principal evil at which the Confrontation Clause was directed." *Crawford*; see also *Bryant.*

Finally, although we decline to adopt a rule that statements to individuals who are not law enforcement officers are categorically outside the Sixth Amendment, the fact that L.P. was speaking to his teachers remains highly relevant. Courts must evaluate challenged statements in context, and part of that context is the questioner's identity. Statements made to someone who is not principally charged with uncovering and prosecuting criminal behavior are significantly less likely to be testimonial than statements given to law enforcement officers. It is common sense that the relationship between a student and his teacher is very different from that between a citizen and the police. We do not ignore that reality. In light of these circumstances, the Sixth Amendment did not prohibit the State from introducing L.P.'s statements at trial....

Clark's efforts to avoid this conclusion are all off-base. He emphasizes Ohio's mandatory reporting obligations, in an attempt to equate L.P.'s teachers with the police and their caring questions with official interrogations. But the comparison is inapt. The teachers' pressing concern was to protect L.P. and remove him from harm's way. Like all good teachers, they undoubtedly would have acted with the same purpose whether or not they had a state-law duty to report abuse. And mandatory reporting statutes alone cannot convert a conversation between a concerned teacher and her student into a law enforcement mission aimed primarily at gathering evidence for a prosecution.

It is irrelevant that the teachers' questions and their duty to report the matter had the natural tendency to result in Clark's prosecution. The statements at issue in *Davis* and *Bryant* supported the defendants' convictions, and the police always have an obligation to ask questions to resolve ongoing emergencies. Yet, we held in those cases that the Confrontation Clause did not prohibit introduction of the statements because they were not primarily intended to be testimonial. Thus, Clark is also wrong to suggest that admitting L.P.'s statements would be fundamentally unfair given that Ohio law does not allow incompetent children to testify. In any Confrontation Clause case, the individual who provided the out-of-court statement is not available as an in-court witness, but the testimony is admissible under an exception to the hearsay rules and is probative of the defendant's guilt. The fact that the witness is unavailable because of a different rule of evidence does not change our analysis.

Finally, Clark asks us to shift our focus from the context of L.P.'s conversation with his teachers to the jury's perception of those statements. Because, in his view, the "jury treated L.P.'s accusation as the functional equivalent of testimony," Clark argues that we must prohibit its introduction. Our Confrontation Clause decisions, however, do not determine whether a statement is testimonial by examining whether a jury would view the statement as the equivalent of in-court testimony. The logic of this argument, moreover, would lead to the conclusion that virtually all out-of-court statements offered by the prosecution are testimonial. The prosecution is unlikely to offer out-of-court statements unless they tend to support the defendant's guilt, and all such statements could be viewed as a substitute for in-court testimony. We have never suggested, however, that the Confrontation Clause bars the introduction of all out-of-court statements that support the prosecution's case. Instead, we ask whether a statement was given with the "primary purpose of creating an out-of-court substitute for trial testimony." *Bryant*. Here, the answer is clear: L.P.'s statements to his teachers were not testimonial. . . . We reverse the judgment of the Supreme Court of Ohio. . . .

Justice SCALIA, with whom Justice GINSBURG joins, concurring in the judgment.

I agree with the Court's holding. . . . L.P.'s primary purpose here was certainly not to invoke the coercive machinery of the State against Clark. . . . Nor did the teachers have the primary purpose of establishing facts for later prosecution. Instead, they sought to ensure that they did not deliver an abused child back into imminent harm. Nor did the conversation have the requisite solemnity necessary for testimonial statements. A 3–year–old was asked questions by his teachers at school. That is far from the surroundings adequate to impress upon a declarant the importance of what he is testifying to. . . .

I write separately, however, to protest the Court's shoveling of fresh dirt upon the Sixth Amendment right of confrontation so recently rescued from the grave in *Crawford v. Washington*. . . . For several decades before that case, we had been allowing hearsay statements to be admitted against a criminal defendant if they bore "indicia of reliability." *Ohio v. Roberts,* 448 U.S. 56, 66 (1980). Prosecutors, past and present, love that flabby test. *Crawford* sought to bring our application of the Confrontation Clause back to its original meaning, which was to exclude unconfronted statements made by *witnesses — i.e.,* statements that were *testimonial.* We defined testimony as a "solemn declaration or affirmation made for the purpose of establishing or proving some fact," — in the context of the Confrontation Clause, a fact "potentially relevant to later criminal prosecution," *Davis v. Washington,* 547 U.S. 813, 822 (2006).

Crawford remains the law. But when else has the categorical overruling, the thorough repudiation, of an earlier line of cases been described as nothing more than "adopt[ing] a different approach" — as though *Crawford* is only a matter of tweedle-dum tweedle-dee preference, and the old, pre-*Crawford* "approach" remains available? . . . But snide detractions do no harm; they are just indications of motive. Dicta on legal points, however, can do harm, because though they are not binding they can mislead. Take, for example, the opinion's statement that the primary-purpose test is merely *one* of several heretofore unmentioned conditions ("necessary, but not always sufficient") that must be satisfied before the Clause's protections apply. That is absolutely false, and has no support in our opinions. The Confrontation Clause categorically entitles a defendant *to be confronted with the witnesses against him*; and the primary-purpose test sorts out, among the many people who interact with the police informally, *who is acting as a witness and who is not*. Those who fall into the former category bear testimony, and are therefore acting as "witnesses," subject to the right of confrontation. There are no other mysterious requirements that the Court declines to name.

The opinion asserts that future defendants, and future Confrontation Clause majorities, must provide "evidence that the adoption of the Confrontation Clause was understood to require the exclusion of evidence that was regularly admitted in criminal cases at the time of the founding." This dictum gets the burden precisely backwards — which is of course precisely the idea. Defendants may invoke their Confrontation Clause rights once they have established that the state seeks to introduce testimonial evidence against them in a criminal case without unavailability of the witness and a previous opportunity to cross-examine. The burden is upon the prosecutor who seeks to introduce evidence *over* this bar to prove a long-established practice of introducing *specific* kinds of evidence, such as dying declarations, for which cross-examination was not typically necessary. A suspicious mind (or even one that is merely not naïve) might regard this distortion as the first step in an attempt to smuggle longstanding hearsay exceptions back into the Confrontation Clause — in other words, an attempt to return to *Ohio v. Roberts*.

But the good news is that there are evidently not the votes to return to that halcyon era for prosecutors; and that dicta, even calculated dicta, are nothing but dicta. They are enough, however, combined with the peculiar phenomenon of a Supreme Court opinion's aggressive hostility to precedent that it purports to be applying, to prevent my joining the writing for the Court. . . .

Justice THOMAS, concurring in the judgment.

. . . I would use the same test for statements to private persons that I have employed for statements to agents of law enforcement, assessing whether those statements bear sufficient indicia of solemnity to qualify as testimonial. . . . This test is grounded in the history of the common-law right to confrontation, which "developed to target particular practices that occurred under the English bail and committal statutes passed during the reign of Queen Mary, namely, the civil-law mode of criminal procedure, and particularly its use of *ex parte* examinations as evidence against the accused." [*Davis v. Washington*, 547 U.S. 813, 835 (Thomas, J., concurring in judgment in part and dissenting in part).]

. . . I have identified several categories of extrajudicial statements that bear sufficient indicia of solemnity to fall within the original meaning of testimony. Statements "contained in formalized testimonial materials, such as affidavits, depositions, prior testimony, or confessions" easily qualify. . . . And statements not contained in such materials may still qualify if they were obtained in "a formalized dialogue"; after the issuance of the warnings required by *Miranda v. Arizona,* 384 U.S. 436 (1966); while in police custody; or in an attempt to evade confrontation. That several of these factors seem inherently inapplicable to statements made to private persons does not mean that the test is unsuitable for analyzing such statements. All it means is that statements made to private persons rarely resemble the historical abuses that the common-law right to confrontation developed to address, and it is those practices that the test is designed to identify.

Here, L.P.'s statements do not bear sufficient indicia of solemnity to qualify as testimonial. They were neither contained in formalized testimonial materials nor obtained as the result of a formalized dialogue initiated by police. Instead, they were elicited during questioning by L.P.'s teachers at his preschool. Nor is there any indication that L.P.'s statements were offered at trial to evade confrontation. To the contrary, the record suggests that the prosecution would have produced L.P. to testify had he been deemed competent to do so. His statements bear no "resemblance to the historical practices that the Confrontation Clause aimed to eliminate." *Ibid.* [*Michigan v. Bryant,* 562 U.S. 344 379 (2011) (opinion of Thomas, J.).] The admission of L.P.'s extrajudicial statements thus does not implicate the Confrontation Clause. . . .

PROBLEMS

3.19. In a prosecution of Richard for bank robbery, the defense seeks to call a private investigator, who will testify about an interview she conducted with a waitress. The waitress told the investigator that Richard was in her restaurant at the time of the robbery. Is this evidence hearsay? Would its introduction violate the Confrontation Clause?

3.20. In a murder prosecution, the prosecutor seeks to introduce the written report of the victim's autopsy, to prove the victim was killed by a bullet that entered through the back of the victim's head. The coroner who conducted the autopsy and prepared the report has since died. Is the report hearsay? Would its introduction violate the Confrontation Clause?

3.21. In a statutory rape prosecution of Devon, the prosecutor seeks to call Warrington, who will testify that he was present when Devon met the victim, and that the victim told Devon that she was underage. Is this evidence hearsay? Would its introduction violate the Confrontation Clause?

C.   EXCEPTIONS TO THE HEARSAY RULE

LAURENCE H. TRIBE, TRIANGULATING HEARSAY

87 Harv. L. Rev. 957, 957 (1974)

As long ago as 1937, Edmund Morgan lamented that "the hearsay rule in its present form is the result of a conglomeration of conflicting considerations modified by historical accident." And Charles McCormick even earlier criticized "the mitigation of a rigid rule by numerous rigid exceptions." But while the British have seen fit to virtually abandon the hearsay rule in civil cases, progress in the United States has been exceedingly slow.

ADVISORY COMMITTEE NOTE TO ARTICLE VIII OF THE F.R.E.

Common sense tells that much evidence which is not given [under oath, in the presence of the trier of fact, and subject to cross-examination] may be inherently superior to much that is. Moreover, when the choice is between evidence which is less than best and no evidence at all, only clear folly would dictate an across-the-board policy of doing without. The problem thus resolves itself into effecting a sensible accommodation between these considerations and the desirability of giving testimony under the ideal conditions.

The solution evolved by the common law has been a general rule excluding hearsay but subject to numerous exceptions under circumstances supposed to furnish guarantees of trustworthiness. Criticisms of this scheme are that it is bulky and complex, fails to screen good from bad hearsay realistically, and inhibits the growth of the law of evidence. . . .

Abandonment of the system of class exceptions in favor of individual treatment in the setting of the particular case, accompanied by procedural safeguards, has been impressively advocated. Admissibility would be determined by weighing the probative force of the evidence against the possibility of prejudice, waste of time, and the availability of more satisfactory evidence. . . . Procedural safeguards would consist of notice of intention to use hearsay, free comment by the judge on the weight of the evidence, and a greater measure of authority in both trial and appellate judges to deal with evidence on the basis of weight. The Advisory Committee has rejected this approach to hearsay as involving too great a measure of judicial discretion, minimizing the predictability of rulings, enhancing the difficulties of preparation for trial, adding a further element to the already over-complicated congeries of pretrial procedures, and requiring substantially different rules for civil and criminal cases. The only way in which the probative force of hearsay differs from the probative force of other testimony is in the absence of oath, demeanor, and cross-examination as aids in determining credibility. For a judge to exclude evidence because he does not believe it has been described as "altogether atypical, extraordinary. . . ." Chadbourn, Bentham and the Hearsay Rule —A Benthamic View of Rule 63(4)(c) of the Uniform Rules of Evidence, 75 Harv. L. Rev. 932, 947 (1962).

The approach to hearsay in these rules is that of the common law, i.e., a general rule excluding hearsay, with exceptions under which evidence is not required to be excluded even though hearsay. The traditional hearsay exceptions are drawn upon . . . [and supplemented with] provision for hearsay statements not within one of the specified exceptions "but having comparable [equivalent] circumstantial guarantees of trustworthiness." This plan is submitted as calculated to encourage growth and development in this area of the law, while conserving the values and experience of the past as a guide to the future.

1. Prior Statements by Witnesses

The Federal Rules of Evidence usefully divide most of the myriad exceptions to the hearsay rule into two categories: exceptions that apply whether or not the declarant is available to testify in court, codified in Rule 803, and exceptions that apply only if the declarant is unavailable, codified in Rule 804. Rule 804 also describes the various ways in which a witness can be "unavailable." Before getting to any of that, though, the federal rules exempt two special classes of statements from the hearsay rule by declaring them "not hearsay"— even though they satisfy the traditional definition of hearsay. (Nothing turns on the fact that the federal rules call these statements "not hearsay" as opposed to "hearsay but nonetheless admissible"; in effect, these are exceptions by another name.) The first of these special classes consists of certain out-of-court statements by declarants who testify as witnesses, in court and under oath, in the very proceedings in which their earlier statements are offered as evidence.

In studying each of the various exceptions to the hearsay rule addressed in this chapter, it is important to ask whether the statements it exempts from the hearsay ban are nonetheless inadmissible against a criminal defendant by virtue of the Confrontation Clause. For prior statements by witnesses, the answer will generally be no, because the declarant's appearance in court as a witness in the trial satisfies the requirement of confrontation. For other exceptions, the answer will often be less clear.

[F.R.E. 801(d)(1); C.E.C. §§1235–1236, 1238]

ALBERT v. McKAY & CO.

174 Cal. 451 (1917)

Sloss, J.

For some years prior to March 10, 1913, Frank H. Albert had been in the employ of the defendant, McKay & Co., a corporation owning and operating a lumber mill at Eureka, in Humboldt county. On the day named, Albert's clothing was caught in an appliance attached to one of the shafts used in the transmission of power for the mill machinery, his body was drawn against the rapidly revolving shaft, and he received injuries which caused his death. He was survived by a widow and a minor child. This action was brought by the widow, as administratrix of his estate, to recover damages for the alleged negligent killing of her intestate. Upon the trial the plaintiff recovered a verdict in the sum of $8,000, and judgment was entered accordingly. The defendant appeals from the judgment, bringing up the evidence by means of a bill of exceptions.

... [The plaintiff alleged] that the machinery was negligently started after Albert had begun to work.... [But t]estimony of numerous witnesses is unanimous to the effect that the machinery, including the shaft in question, was running before Albert went to the lower floor, and that it was not stopped until the discovery of his body on the shaft. There was no competent evidence in contradiction of this.... [The plaintiff points to the testimony of] one Elener, a blacksmith in defendant's employ [who testified on direct examination that the machinery had been running continuously]. The proper foundation having been laid by cross-examination, the plaintiff sought to impeach him by calling in rebuttal a witness who testified that Elener had said, shortly after the accident, that the machinery had not been running, and that somebody must have left the tightener down after Albert had started working. When a witness is impeached by proof of prior inconsistent statements, the effect is merely to discredit him as a witness. The former statements made by him are incompetent for any other purpose. They do not constitute evidence of the truth of the facts so stated by him. 2 Wigmore on Evidence, §1018; *Keyes v. Geary Street, etc., R. R. Co.*, 152 Cal. 437, 441, 93 Pac. 88; *Worley v. Spreckels Bros. Com. Co.*, 163 Cal. 60, 71, 124 Pac. 697.

In the absence of any conflict, the jury had no right to find a verdict based upon the theory that the machinery had been negligently started after Albert had placed himself in close proximity to the shaft. This is not a case in which such negligence can be inferred under the doctrine of *res ipsa loquitur*. The rule has no application to the facts of this case. The plaintiff charged ... that Albert's death was caused by the negligent starting of the machinery. If there had been any evidence to show that the machinery was started after Albert took his position near the shaft, it might be said that the mere occurrence of the accident warranted an inference that the defendant had been negligent in setting the shaft in motion. But such inference cannot, of course, be indulged in face of the undisputed testimony that the machinery had not been started at all and therefore could not have been started negligently.... The judgment is reversed.

ADVISORY COMMITTEE NOTE TO F.R.E. 801(d)(1)

Considerable controversy has attended the question whether a prior out-of-court statement by a person now available for cross-examination concerning it, under oath and in the presence of the trier of fact, should be classed as hearsay. If the witness admits on the stand that he made the statement and that it was true, he adopts the statement and there is no hearsay problem. The hearsay problem arises when the witness on the stand denies having made the statement or admits having made it but denies its truth. The argument in favor of treating these latter statements as hearsay is based upon the ground that the conditions of oath, cross-examination, and demeanor observation did not prevail at the time the statement was made and cannot adequately be supplied by the later examination. The logic of the situation is troublesome. So far as concerns the oath, its mere presence has never been regarded as sufficient to remove a statement from the hearsay category, and it receives much less emphasis than cross-examination as a truth-compelling device.... [T]he fact is that, of the many common law exceptions to the hearsay rule, only that for reported testimony has required the statement to have been made under oath. Nor is it satisfactorily explained why cross-examination cannot be conducted subsequently with success. The decisions contending most vigorously for its inadequacy in fact demonstrate quite thorough exploration of the weaknesses and doubts attending the earlier statement. . . . In respect to demeanor, as Judge Learned Hand observed in DiCarlo v. United States, 6 F.2d 364 (2d Cir. 1925), when the jury decides that the truth is not what the witness says now, but what he said before, they are still deciding from what they see and hear in court. The bulk of the case law nevertheless has been against allowing prior statements of witnesses to be used generally as substantive evidence. Most of the writers and Uniform Rule 63(1) have taken the opposite position.

The position taken by the Advisory Committee in formulating this part of the rule is founded upon an unwillingness to countenance the general use of prior prepared statements as substantive evidence, but with a recognition that particular circumstances call for a contrary result. The judgment is one more of experience than of logic. The rule requires in each instance, as a general safeguard, that the declarant actually testify as a witness, and it then enumerates three situations in which the statement is excepted from the category of hearsay. Compare Uniform Rule 63(1) which allows any out-of-court statement of a declarant who is present at the trial and available for cross-examination.

Prior inconsistent statements traditionally have been admissible to impeach but not as substantive evidence. Under the rule they are substantive evidence. As has been said by the California Law Revision Commission with respect to a similar provision:

"Section 1235 admits inconsistent statements of witnesses because the dangers against which the hearsay rule is designed to protect are largely nonexistent. The declarant is in court and may be examined and cross-examined in regard to his statements and their subject matter. In many cases, the inconsistent statement is more likely to be true than the testimony of the witness at the trial because it was made nearer in time to the matter to which it relates and is less likely to be influenced by the controversy that gave rise to the litigation. The trier of fact has the declarant before it and can observe his demeanor and the nature of his testimony as he denies or tries to explain away the inconsistency. Hence, it is in as good a position to determine the truth or falsity of the prior statement as it is to determine the truth or falsity of the inconsistent testimony given in court. Moreover, Section 1235 will provide a party with desirable protection against the 'turncoat' witness who changes his story on the stand and deprives the party calling him of evidence essential to his case." Comment, California Evidence Code §1235. . . . Moreover, the requirement that the statement be inconsistent with the testimony given assures a thorough exploration of both versions while the witness is on the stand and bars any general and indiscriminate use of previously prepared statements.

Prior consistent statements traditionally have been admissible to rebut charges of recent fabrication or improper influence or motive but not as substantive evidence. Under the rule they are substantive evidence. The prior statement is consistent with the testimony given on the stand, and, if the opposite party wishes to open the door for its admission in evidence, no sound reason is apparent why it should not be received generally.

The admission of evidence of identification finds substantial support, although it falls beyond a doubt in the category of prior out-of-court statements. . . . The basis is the generally unsatisfactory and inconclusive nature of courtroom identifications as compared with those made at an earlier time under less suggestive conditions. . . .

REPORT OF THE SENATE JUDICIARY COMMITTEE

S. Rep. No. 93-1277 (1974)

As submitted by the Supreme Court, subdivision (d)(1)(A) made admissible as substantive evidence the prior statement of a witness inconsistent with his present testimony. The House severely limited the admissibility of prior inconsistent statements by adding a requirement that the prior statement must have been subject to cross-examination, thus precluding even the use of grand jury statements. . . . [W]e think the House amendment should be rejected and the rule as submitted by the Supreme Court reinstated.

REPORT OF THE CONFERENCE COMMITTEE

Conf. Rep. No. 93-1597 (1974)

The House bill provides that a statement is not hearsay if the declarant testifies and is subject to cross-examination concerning the statement and if the statement is inconsistent with his testimony and was given under oath subject to cross-examination and subject to the penalty of perjury at a trial or hearing or in a deposition. The Senate amendment drops the requirement that the prior statement be given under oath subject to cross-examination and subject to the penalty of perjury at a trial or hearing or in a deposition.

The Conference adopts the Senate amendment with an amendment, so that the rule now requires that the prior inconsistent statement be given under oath subject to the penalty of perjury at a trial, hearing, or other proceeding, or in a deposition. The rule as adopted covers statements before a grand jury. Prior inconsistent statements may, of course, be used for impeaching the credibility of a witness. When the prior inconsistent statement is one made by a defendant in a criminal case, it is covered by Rule 801(d)(2).

REPORT OF THE SENATE JUDICIARY COMMITTEE

S. Rep. No. 94-199 (1975)

In . . . Gilbert v. California, 388 U.S. 263, 272 n.3 (1967), the Supreme Court, noting the split of authority in admitting prior out-of-court identifications, stated, "The recent trend, however, is to admit the prior identification under the exception [to the hearsay rule] that admits as substantive evidence a prior communication by a witness who is available for cross-examination at the trial." And the Federal Courts of Appeals have generally admitted these identifications. . . .

In the course of processing the Rules of Evidence in the final weeks of the 93d Congress, the provision excluding such statements of identification from the hearsay category was deleted. . . . Concern was . . . expressed that a conviction could be based upon such unsworn, out-of-court testimony. Upon further reflection . . . it appears the rule is desirable. Since these identifications take place reasonably soon after an offense has been committed, the witness' observations are still fresh in his mind. The identification occurs before his recollection has been dimmed by the passage of time. Equally as important, it also takes place before the defendant or some other party has had the opportunity, through bribe or threat, to influence the witness to change his mind.

Both experience and psychological studies suggest that identifications consisting of nonsuggestive lineups, photographic spreads, or similar identifications, made reasonably soon after the offense, are more reliable than in-court identifications. Admitting these prior identifications therefore provides greater fairness to both the prosecution and defense in a criminal trial.

UNITED STATES v. OWENS

484 U.S. 554 (1988)

Justice SCALIA delivered the opinion of the Court.

On April 12, 1982, John Foster, a correctional counselor at the federal prison in Lompoc, California, was attacked and brutally beaten with a metal pipe. His skull was fractured, and he remained hospitalized for almost a month. As a result of his injuries, Foster's memory was severely impaired. When Thomas Mansfield, an FBI agent investigating the assault, first attempted to interview Foster, on April 19, he found Foster lethargic and unable to remember his attacker's name. On May 5 Mansfield again spoke to Foster, who was much improved and able to describe the attack. Foster named respondent as his attacker and identified respondent from an array of photographs.

Respondent was tried . . . for assault with intent to commit murder. . . . At trial, Foster recounted his activities just before the attack, and described feeling the blows to his head and seeing blood on the floor. He testified that he clearly remembered identifying respondent as his assailant during his May 5th interview with Mansfield. On cross-examination, he admitted that he could not remember seeing his assailant. He also admitted that, although there was evidence that he had received numerous visitors in the hospital, he was unable to remember any of them except Mansfield, and could not remember whether any of these visitors had suggested that respondent was the assailant. Defense counsel unsuccessfully sought to refresh his recollection with hospital records, including one indicating that Foster had attributed the assault to someone other than respondent. Respondent was convicted and sentenced to 20 years' imprisonment to be served consecutively to a previous sentence. . . .

Rule 801(d)(1)(C) defines as not hearsay a prior statement "of identification of a person made after perceiving the person," if the declarant "testifies at the trial or hearing and is subject to cross-examination concerning the statement." . . . It seems to us that the more natural reading of "subject to cross-examination concerning the statement" includes what was available here. Ordinarily a witness is regarded as "subject to cross-examination" when he is placed on the stand, under oath, and responds willingly to questions. . . . [L]imitations on the scope of examination by the trial court or assertions of privilege by the witness may undermine the process to such a degree that meaningful cross-examination within the intent of the Rule no longer exists. But that effect is not produced by the witness' assertion of memory loss — which . . . is often the very result sought to be produced by cross-examination, and can be effective in destroying the force of the prior statement. Rule 801(d)(1)(C), which specifies that the cross-examination need only "concer[n] the statement," does not on its face require more. . . .

The premise for Rule 801(d)(1)(C) was that, given adequate safeguards against suggestiveness, out-of-court identifications were generally preferable to courtroom identifications. Advisory Committee's Notes on Rule 801. Thus, despite the traditional view that such statements were hearsay, the Advisory Committee believed that their use was to be fostered rather than discouraged. Similarly, the House Report on the Rule noted that since, "[a]s time goes by, a witness' memory will fade and his identification will become less reliable," minimizing the barriers to admission of more contemporaneous identification is fairer to defendants and prevents "cases falling through because the witness can no longer recall the identity of the person he saw commit the crime." H.R. Rep. No. 94-355, p. 3 (1975). See also S. Rep. No. 94-199, p. 2 (1975). To judge from the House and Senate Reports, Rule 801(d)(1)(C) was in part directed to the very problem here at issue: a memory loss that makes it impossible for the witness to provide an in-court identification or testify about details of the events underlying an earlier identification. . . .

[For similar reasons, the court found no violation of the Confrontation Clause, which the court reaffirmed requires only "an *opportunity* for effective cross-examination, not cross-examination that is effective in whatever way, and to what extent, the defense might wish." Conviction upheld. Justice Brennan, joined by Justice Marshall, filed a dissenting opinion. Justice Kennedy took no part in deciding the case.]

PROBLEMS

3.22. How would *Albert v. McKay Co.* be decided today under the Federal Rules of Evidence? Under the California Evidence Code?

3.23. In an assault prosecution, the victim testifies and identifies the defendant from the witness stand as her assailant. The prosecution then seeks to have the victim testify that she earlier picked the defendant out of a lineup. Is the victim's testimony about the earlier identification barred by the hearsay rule? By the Confrontation Clause?

3.24. Following a bank robbery, a customer picks a suspect out of a lineup and identifies him as the robber. The customer does not testify at trial, but the government seeks to have a police officer who was present at the lineup testify about the identification. Is this testimony barred by the hearsay rule? By the Confrontation Clause?

3.25. Suppose the customer does testify at trial but no longer recognizes the defendant: When asked whether the robber is present in court, the customer says he is unsure. May a police officer who was present at the lineup testify that the customer identified the defendant as the robber?

3.26. In 2003, prosecutors associated with the International Criminal Tribunal for the former Yugoslavia (ICTY) were investigating allegations, ultimately substantiated, that members of the Kosovo Liberation Army (KLA) had tortured and murdered civilians at a prison camp in the village of Llapushnik. In formal, videotaped interviews, two former members of the KLA said that Fatmir Limaj, another KLA member, had commanded soldiers at the camp. When Limaj was prosecuted at the ICTY in 2005, the witnesses recanted, and the prosecutors moved to introduce the videotaped interviews both for impeachment and as "substantive evidence" of Limaj's role as a commander. The three-judge panel presiding over the trial granted the motion, relying on an ICTY rule that gave trial judges discretion to admit hearsay that was relevant and had sufficient indicia of reliability. Months later, though, the same judges acquitted Limaj, finding insufficient evidence that he exercised authority over the soldiers who carried out the tortures and murders. In their written ruling, the judges noted they were "not persuaded . . . that the prior inconsistent statements of these two witnesses can safely be relied upon as the sole or principal basis for proof of a material fact," especially "because each witness, in oral evidence, disavowed, in very material respects, what previously had been stated in the interview." *Prosecutor v. Limaj et al.*, No. IT-03-66-T (ICTY, Nov. 30, 2005); *see* Pascale Chifflet, *The First Trial of Former Members of the Kosovo Liberation Army: Prosecutor v. Fatmir Limaj, Haradin Bala, and Isak Musliu*, 19 Leiden J. Int'l L. 459, 466-469 (2006). Would this evidence be handled differently under the Federal Rules of Evidence? How *should* it be handled?

2. Admissions by Opposing Parties

Two classes of statements are deemed "not hearsay" under Federal Rule of Evidence 801 even though they satisfy the traditional definition of hearsay. The first, discussed above, consists of certain statements by declarants who also give sworn, in-court testimony in the trial in which their statements are offered into evidence. The second class of statements given this special treatment consists of various kinds of "admissions by party-opponents." When an out-of-court statement is offered into evidence against the person who made it, the statement qualifies as an "admission" and therefore is exempt from the hearsay rule — regardless of whether the statement seems on its face to "admit" anything contrary to the declarant's interest. What matters is not the content of the statement but the identity of the declarant and the party against whom it is introduced.

The admissions doctrine is not limited to statements made directly by the party against whom they are introduced. It also applies when, for any of several other reasons, it seems somehow right to hold the party against whom the evidence is offered at least partially responsible for the out-of-court statement.

Unlike most of the exceptions to the hearsay rule, which find their justification largely in considerations of reliability, the admissions doctrine is rooted, at least nominally, in notions of adversarial fairness. Whether those notions, or any others, can justify the breadth of the admissions doctrine remains controversial.

It is also unclear whether the Supreme Court's reinterpretation of the Confrontation Clause in *Crawford v. Washington* and later cases will require reconsidering the admissibility, in criminal cases, of some statements previously introduced as admissions. Direct admissions will not be affected: the defendant cannot persuasively claim he has had no chance to "confront" himself. And most co-conspirator admissions will probably qualify as nontestimonial, and thus escape Confrontation Clause scrutiny — as the Supreme Court itself pointed out in *Crawford*. This will likely be true also of many if not most adopted admissions, authorized admissions, and employee admissions. Some statements in the latter categories, though, may wind up being deemed "testimonial," throwing into doubt their admissibility against any criminal defendant who has not previously had an opportunity to cross-examine the declarant.

a. Direct Admissions

i. Generally

[F.R.E. 801(d)(2)(A); C.E.C. §1220]

SALVITTI v. THROPPE

23 A.2d 445 (Pa. 1942)

STERN, Justice.

[Joseph Salvitti and his wife were injured when the car Salvitti was driving hit a tree. Salvitti claimed he swerved to avoid a negligently driven truck. He and his wife sued Throppe, the truck driver's employer.]

Plaintiffs testified that defendant and the driver of the truck visited them, admitted that the accident was their fault, and promised that "everything would be taken care of." The acknowledgment by a party that it was he who was at fault is admissible as a declaration against interest. Defendant, while conceding this to be the general rule, urges that in the present case the testimony should have been rejected because he was not present at the time of the accident and could have based his remark only on what his driver told him. Personal knowledge, however, is not required in the case of an admission by a party. It is said in Wigmore on Evidence, 3d Ed., volume 4, pp. 12, 13, sec. 1053: "Since a party may make a claim and file averment of pleadings without regard to personal knowledge of the facts, it would be fallacious to exact, in his contrary admissions, an element of personal knowledge which is not required for the original advancement of his claim. . . . Add to this that, in the psychology of testimony, a person's assertions regarding his own affairs have always some testimonial value regardless of the exactness of his personal observation of the data leading to his belief." Of course, the weight to be attributed by the jury to such an admission would naturally depend upon whether it was made by defendant on the basis of his own knowledge or of information imparted to him by others.

Judgment affirmed.

ADVISORY COMMITTEE NOTE TO F.R.E. 801(d)(2)

Admissions by a party-opponent are excluded from the category of hearsay on the theory that their admissibility in evidence is the result of the adversary system rather than satisfaction of the conditions of the hearsay rule. Strahorn, A Reconsideration of the Hearsay Rule and Admissions, 85 U. Pa. L. Rev. 484, 564 (1937); Morgan, Basic Problems of Evidence 265 (1962); 4 Wigmore §1048. No guarantee of trustworthiness is required in the case of an admission. The freedom which admissions have enjoyed from technical demands of searching for an assurance of truthworthiness in some against-interest circumstance, and from the restrictive influences of the opinion rule and the rule requiring firsthand knowledge, when taken with the apparently prevalent satisfaction with the results, calls for generous treatment of this avenue to admissibility.

EDMUND MORGAN, ADMISSIONS

1 UCLA L. Rev. 18, 19 (1953)

The admissibility of an admission made by the party himself rests not upon any notion that the circumstances in which it was made furnish the trier means of evaluating it fairly, but upon the adversary theory of litigation. A party can hardly object that he had no opportunity to cross-examine himself or that he is unworthy of credence save when speaking under the sanction of an oath. His adversary may use against him anything which he has said or done. Originally he had no chance to make an explanation, but since about the middle of the 1800's, he has been competent as a witness and can furnish the trier with all pertinent information within his knowledge. Consequently the orthodox decisions refuse to apply to evidence of personal admissions restrictions usually applicable to testimonial evidence.

UNITED STATES v. McGEE

189 F.3d 626 (7th Cir. 1999)

RIPPLE, Circuit Judge.

A jury found John Earl McGee guilty of one count of bank robbery.... He claims that ... the district court erred in admitting under Federal Rule of Evidence 801(d)(2)(A) his statement to the police....

The prosecution ... called Detective Carl Buschmann of the Milwaukee Police Department to testify that he interviewed Mr. McGee on August 20, 1997, concerning the July 5 robbery of North Shore Bank. Detective Buschmann testified that, during the interview, Mr. McGee provided three different versions of the events of July 5, 1997. First, Mr. McGee said that he had taken a bus to the North Shore Bank that day to open an account but left the bank when he was told he would need two forms of identification. After Mr. McGee was informed that co-defendants Natasha Williams and Bridget Womack had provided statements implicating him in the robbery, he admitted that he had lied about taking the bus and decided to change his story. [He then said Womack had driven him to the bank. He gave two different accounts of how he had returned home. He continued to deny any involvement in or knowledge of the robbery.]

Mr. McGee contends that his statement to Detective Buschmann is not admissible under Rule 801(d)(2) as an admission by a party-opponent because it was not inculpatory.... We cannot accept this submission.... [No] Seventh Circuit case of which we are aware establishes a requirement that admissions by a party-opponent be inculpatory in order to be admissible as nonhearsay under Rule 801. Nor does the case law from the other circuits indicate that an admission must be inculpatory; the courts that have addressed the issue have held that, in accordance with the language of Rule 801(d)(2) the statement need only be made by the party against whom it is offered.

We agree with the other circuits that Rule 801(d)(2)(A) should be interpreted on its face to require only a party's own statement offered against the party. We therefore reject Mr. McGee's contention that the district court erred in admitting his statement to Detective Buschmann.... [T]he judgment of the district court is affirmed.

McCORMICK ON EVIDENCE

§254, at 2:263–64 (Kenneth S. Broun ed., 7th ed. 2013)

A type of evidence with which admissions may be confused is evidence of declarations against interest. The latter, treated under a separate exception to the hearsay rule, must have been against the declarant's interest when made. Although most admissions are against interest when made, no such requirement is applied to admissions. For example, if a person states that a note is forged and then later acquires the note and sues upon it, the previous statement may be introduced as an admission although the party had no interest when he or she made the statement. Hence the common phrase "admissions against interest" is an invitation to confuse two separate theories of admitting hearsay and erroneously engraft an against-interest requirement on admissions.

UNITED STATES v. PHELPS

572 F. Supp. 262 (E.D. Ky. 1983)

BERTELSMAN, District Judge:

. . . The case arises out of the prosecution of the defendants for willful possession of 169 pounds of marijuana and a pound and-a-half of cocaine with intent to distribute, which conduct is prohibited by 21 U.S.C. §841(a)(1) . . . . At a bench conference, counsel for defendant Phelps advised the court that he was going to seek to introduce through the testimony of one of the officers, that, when the officers discovered the cocaine in the gym bag, Phelps had stated, "That is my gym bag, but Taylor put it in the trunk." The unusual feature concerning the introduction of this statement was that the statement was sought to be introduced by Phelps himself and the objection to the testimony was made, not by the United States, but by the co-defendant Taylor. . . .

Although the proponent of the testimony was the declarant himself, the testimony constituted hearsay under F.R. Ev. 801. . . . Further, it is equally clear that the statement was not excluded from the definition of hearsay by the fact that it was an admission. . . . The statement of a party may be introduced as an admission only when offered *against* that party. This principle is reflected by the standard but often unanalyzed objection that such testimony by a party constitutes a "self-serving declaration." 6 J. Wigmore, *Evidence* §1732 (1976). Some confusion arises by reason of the fact that, to be admissible, a party's out-of-court statement need not have been against his interest when made. But it may not be offered in his *favor*, but only *against* him. . . . Therefore, the court sustained the objection and excluded the testimony.

ii. Admissions and Multiple Hearsay

[F.R.E. 805; C.E.C. §1201]

REED v. McCORD

54 N.E. 737 (N.Y. 1899)

MARTIN, J.

This action was to recover damages for personal injuries to the plaintiff's intestate which occasioned his death, and was based upon the alleged negligence of the defendant. The plaintiff had a verdict, which was not directed by the court. From the judgment entered thereon an appeal was taken. . . .

Upon the trial of this action the official stenographer for the board of coroners was called and permitted, under the defendant's objection and exception, to testify that upon the hearing before the coroner the defendant gave evidence to the effect that all machines of the make of the one in use when the decedent was killed were alike; that at the time of the injury the dog of the machine was not in position, which caused the accident; and that "the man who had charge of it supposed the dog was in position, and he released his hold on the thing, and it commenced to revolve, and then he got down so as to put his foot on it, and it was going so rapidly that it slipped past." It was admitted that the defendant was not present when the accident occurred, and hence, it is obvious that his statement before the coroner was not based upon his personal knowledge, but upon what he had learned as to the situation and how the accident occurred. The contention of the appellant is that, as his admissions were not based upon his personal knowledge, proof of them should have been excluded, and that his exception to their admission was well taken. The defendant being a party to this action, his admissions against his own interest were evidence in favor of his adversary, if of a fact material to the issue. If he had merely admitted that he heard that the accident occurred in the manner stated, it would have been inadmissible, as then it would only have amounted to an admission that he had heard the statement which he repeated, and not to an admission of the facts included in it. That would have been in no sense an admission of any fact pertinent to the issue, but a mere admission of what he had heard, without adoption or indorsement. Such evidence is clearly inadmissible. But the admissions proved in this case were not of that character. They were plain admissions of facts and circumstances which attended the intestate's injury. In a civil action the admissions by a party of any fact material to the issue are always competent evidence against him, wherever, whenever, or to whomsoever made. . . . Judgment affirmed.

FOSTER v. COMMISSIONER OF INTERNAL REVENUE

80 T.C. 34 (1983), vacated in part on other grounds,
756 F.2d 1430 (9th Cir. 1985)

DAWSON, Judge:

Although Fed. R. Evid. 805 does not technically apply because admissions do not constitute hearsay statements under Fed. R. Evid. 801(d)(2), . . . hearsay within an admission is subject to objection, unless, of course, an exception to the hearsay rule applies. However . . . there is a difference between offering as an admission a party's out-of-court statement that "A said that x is a fact" for the purpose of proving that x is a fact, and offering as an admission a party's out-of-court statement that "x is a fact" for that same purpose. . . . [A] party's lack of personal knowledge that x is a fact does not render inadmissible his statement to that effect. Returning to our example, even though a party's out-of-court statement that "x is a fact" is based on A's having told him that fact rather than on his personal knowledge, the statement is still admissible as an admission. Of course, a party is entitled to try to lessen the *weight* of an admission by introducing evidence that it was not based on personal knowledge.

STEPHEN A. SALTZBURG, MICHAEL M. MARTIN & DANIEL J. CAPRA, FEDERAL RULES OF EVIDENCE MANUAL

§805.01[2], at 4:805-2–805-3 (11th ed. 2015)

[P]arty-opponent statements under Rule 801(d)(2) and certain prior statements of available witnesses under Rule 801(d)(1) are defined as not hearsay. So Rule 805 could technically be read to be inapplicable to situations in which these statements are included within another statement that is hearsay. But, courts have held that the technical difference between Rule 801(d) "not hearsay" and Rule 803, 804, and 807 "hearsay subject to exception" cannot control the application of Rule 805's limitation on multiple hearsay. As one court put it: "For the purpose of the hearsay-within-hearsay principle expressed in Rule 805, non-hearsay statements under Rule 801(d) . . . should be considered in analyzing a multiple-hearsay statement as the equivalent of a level of the combined statements that conforms with an exception to the hearsay rule." Thus, the mere fact that one level of a multiple level statement qualifies as exempt from the hearsay rule does not excuse the other levels from satisfying the Rule 805 requirement that each level satisfy the hearsay rule. Conversely, a statement admissible under Rule 801(d) can be admitted when included in another hearsay statement if the other hearsay statement qualifies as an exception. And, of course, Rule 805 will be satisfied if one of the statements is admissible under an exemption or exception and the other is offered for a proper non-hearsay purpose. . . .

iii. Admissions and Completeness

[F.R.E. 106; C.E.C. §356]

BEECH AIRCRAFT CORP. v. RAINEY

488 U.S. 153 (1988)

Justice BRENNAN delivered the opinion of the Court.

In this action we address . . . whether, on the facts of this litigation, the trial court abused its discretion in refusing to admit, on cross-examination, testimony intended to provide a more complete picture of a document about which the witness had testified on direct.

This litigation stems from the crash of a Navy training aircraft at Middleton Field, Alabama, on July 13, 1982, which took the lives of both pilots on board, Lieutenant Commander Barbara Ann Rainey and Ensign Donald

Bruce Knowlton. . . . The two pilots' surviving spouses brought a product liability suit against petitioners Beech Aircraft Corporation, the plane's manufacturer, and Beech Aerospace Services, which serviced the plane under contract
with the Navy. The plaintiffs alleged that the crash had been caused by a loss
of engine power, known as "rollback," due to some defect in the aircraft's fuel
control system. The defendants, on the other hand, advanced the theory of
pilot error, suggesting that the plane had stalled during [an] abrupt avoidance
maneuver. . . .

Five or six months after the accident, plaintiff John Rainey, husband of
the deceased pilot and himself a Navy flight instructor, sent a detailed letter
to Lieutenant Commander Morgan. [Morgan had investigated the accident for
the Navy and had written a report concluding that pilot error probably caused
the collision.] Based on Rainey's own investigation, the letter took issue with
some of [Morgan's] findings and outlined Rainey's theory that "[t]he most
probable primary cause factor of this aircraft mishap is a loss of useful power
(or rollback) caused by some form of pneumatic sensing/fuel flow malfunc-
tion, probably in the fuel control unit."

At trial Rainey did not testify during his side's case in chief, but he was
called by the defense as an adverse witness. On direct examination he was
asked about two statements contained in his letter. The first was to the effect
that his wife had unsuccessfully attempted to cancel the ill-fated training
flight because of a variety of adverse factors including her student's fatigue.
The second question concerned a portion of Rainey's hypothesized scenario
of the accident:

> "Didn't you say, sir, that after Mrs. Rainey's airplane rolled wings level, that
> Lieutenant Colonel Habermacher's plane came into view unexpectedly at its
> closest point of approach, although sufficient separation still existed between the
> aircraft. However, the unexpected proximitely [*sic*] of Colonel Habermacher's
> plane caused one of the aircrew in Mrs. Rainey's plane to react instinctively
> and abruptly by initiating a hard right turn away from Colonel Habermacher's
> airplane?"

Rainey admitted having made both statements. On cross-examination,
Rainey's counsel asked the following question: "In the same letter to which
Mr. Toothman made reference to in his questions, sir, did you also say that the
most probably [*sic*] primary cause of this mishap was rollback?" Before Rainey
answered, the court sustained a defense objection on the ground that the
question asked for Rainey's opinion. Further questioning along this line was
cut off.

Following a 2-week trial, the jury returned a verdict for petitioners. . . . [T]he Eleventh Circuit reversed and remanded for a new trial [in part
based on a violation of Federal Rule of Evidence 106]. . . . We agree with the
unanimous holding of the Court of Appeals en banc that the District Court
erred in refusing to permit Rainey to present a more complete picture of what
he had written to Morgan.

We have no doubt that the jury was given a distorted and prejudicial
impression of Rainey's letter. The theory of Rainey's case was that the accident
was the result of a power failure, and, read in its entirety, his letter to Morgan
was fully consistent with that theory. While Rainey did discuss problems his

wife had encountered the morning of the accident which led her to attempt to cancel the flight, and also agreed that her airplane had violated pattern integrity in turning left prematurely, the thrust of his letter was to challenge Morgan's theory that the crash had been caused by a stall that took place when the pilots turned sharply right and pitched up in attempting to avoid the other plane. Thus Rainey argued that Morgan's hypothesis was inconsistent with the observations of eyewitnesses, the physical findings in the wreckage, and the likely actions of the two pilots. He explained at length his theory of power failure and attempted to demonstrate how the various pieces of evidence supported it. What the jury was told, however, through the defendants' direct examination of Rainey as an adverse witness, was that Rainey had written six months after the accident (1) that his wife had attempted to cancel the flight, partly because her student was tired and emotionally drained, and that "unnecessary pressure" was placed on them to proceed with it; and (2) that she or her student had abruptly initiated a hard right turn when the other aircraft unexpectedly came into view. It is plausible that a jury would have concluded from this information that Rainey did not believe in his theory of power failure and had developed it only later for purposes of litigation. Because the court sustained defense counsel's objection, Rainey's counsel was unable to counteract this prejudicial impression by presenting additional information about the letter on cross-examination.

The common-law "rule of completeness," which underlies Federal Rule of Evidence 106, was designed to prevent exactly the type of prejudice of which Rainey complains. In its aspect relevant to this litigation, the rule of completeness was stated succinctly by Wigmore: "[T]he opponent, against whom a part of an utterance has been put in, may in his turn complement it by putting in the remainder, in order to secure for the tribunal a complete understanding of the total tenor and effect of the utterance." 7 J. Wigmore, Evidence in Trials at Common Law §2113, p. 653 (J. Chadbourn rev. 1978). The Federal Rules of Evidence have partially codified the doctrine of completeness in Rule 106:

> "When a writing or recorded statement or part thereof is introduced by a party, an adverse party may require the introduction at that time of any other part or any other writing or recorded statement which ought in fairness to be considered contemporaneously with it."

In proposing Rule 106, the Advisory Committee stressed that it "does not in any way circumscribe the right of the adversary to develop the matter on cross-examination or as part of his own case." Advisory Committee's Notes on Fed. Rule Evid. 106. We take this to be a reaffirmation of the obvious: that when one party has made use of a portion of a document, such that misunderstanding or distortion can be averted only through presentation of another portion, the material required for completeness is *ipso facto* relevant and therefore admissible under Rule 401 and 402. The District Court's refusal to admit the proffered completion evidence was a clear abuse of discretion.

While much of the controversy in this suit has centered on whether Rule 106 applies, we find it unnecessary to address that issue. Clearly the concerns underlying Rule 106 are relevant here, but, as the general rules of relevancy permit a ready resolution to this litigation, we need go no further in exploring the scope and meaning of Rule 106.... [18] ... [W]e hold that on the facts of this litigation the District Court abused its discretion in restricting the scope of cross-examination of respondent Rainey by his counsel, and to that extent we affirm the Court of Appeals' judgment....

[Chief Justice Rehnquist, joined by Justice O'Connor, filed an opinion dissenting from this part of the Court's opinion.]

PROBLEM

3.27.   In a murder prosecution, a police officer testifies for the government that, when arrested, the defendant said, "I did it. I shot him." On cross-examination of the officer, the defense seeks to elicit that, immediately after making those statements, the defendant said, "It was self-defense. He tried to kill me." The government objects on grounds of hearsay. How should the judge rule?

b. Adoptive Admissions

[F.R.E. 801(d)(2)(B); C.E.C. §1221]

ADVISORY COMMITTEE NOTE TO F.R.E. 801(d)(2)(B)

Under established principles an admission may be made by adopting or acquiescing in the statement of another. While knowledge of contents would ordinarily be essential, this is not inevitably so: "X is a reliable person and knows what he is talking about." Adoption or acquiescence may be manifested in any appropriate manner. When silence is relied upon, the theory is that the person would, under the circumstances, protest the statement made in his presence, if untrue. The decision in each case calls for an evaluation in terms of probable human behavior. In civil cases, the results have generally been satisfactory. In criminal cases, however, troublesome questions have been raised by decisions holding that failure to deny is an admission: the inference is a fairly weak one, to begin with; silence may be motivated by advice of counsel or realization that "anything you say may be used against you"; unusual opportunity is afforded to manufacture evidence; and encroachment upon the privilege against self-incrimination seems inescapably to be involved. However, recent decisions of the Supreme Court relating to custodial interrogation and the right to counsel appear to resolve these difficulties. Hence the rule contains no special provisions concerning failure to deny in criminal cases.

18. Nor would a hearsay objection have been availing. Although the question called for Rainey to testify to an out-of-court statement, that statement was not offered "to prove the truth of the matter asserted." Rule 801(c). Rather, it was offered simply to prove what Rainey had said about the accident six months after it happened, and to contribute to a fuller understanding of the material the defense had already placed in evidence.

UNITED STATES v. FORTES

619 F.2d 108 (1st Cir. 1980)

LEVIN H. CAMPBELL, Circuit Judge.

Following a jury trial in the District Court for the District of Massachusetts appellants Fortes and Jemison were convicted of armed robbery under 18 U.S.C. §2113(d).... In order to link Fortes and Jemison with this robbery, the government relied heavily on the testimony of Anton Ward, who at the time of trial was serving a three-year prison sentence for conspiracy to commit bank robbery imposed by the United States District Court for the District of Connecticut....

Jemison challenges the district court's admission, against her, of certain statements made by Fortes [in a conversation with Ward two days after the robbery].... Ward stated that both Fortes and Jemison were present during the conversation. Ward testified that at this time he asked appellants "if they did a bank robbery," and that Fortes answered affirmatively, providing details of the robbery. Fortes' recitation, according to Ward, contained a description of Jemison's participation, including the information that she had taken the bank's money while Fortes held a shotgun and that she had difficulty separating the "red money" from the "regular money." Jemison objected repeatedly to the admission of Fortes' statements against her....

This testimony was properly received against Jemison under Fed. R. Evid. 801(d)(2)(B), which allows the introduction of so-called adoptive admissions, including admissions by silence or acquiescence. See IV Wigmore §1071 (Chadbourn rev. 1972). The general rule has been stated as follows:

> "'When a statement tending to incriminate one accused of committing a crime is made in his presence and hearing and such statement is not denied, contradicted, or objected to by him, both the statement and the fact of his failure to deny are admissible in a criminal prosecution against him, as evidence of his acquiescence in its truth' ... if made 'under such circumstances as would warrant the inference that he would naturally have contradicted them if he did not assent to their truth.'"

Arpan v. United States, 260 F.2d 649, 655 (8th Cir. 1958) (citations omitted). *See Sparf v. United States*, 156 U.S. 51 (1895).

... [W]e have no difficulty in concluding that an inquiry of two persons as to whether they had "done a bank robbery," followed by an affirmative response by one of them describing his participation with the other in the crime, is the type of exchange to which the silence of the unresponsive accomplice, assuming he is present and conscious of the conversation, "gives consent." IV Wigmore §1071, at 102 (Chadbourn rev. 1972). Further, sufficient facts were introduced preliminarily to show, by way of foundation, that Jemison heard the statements detailing her conduct in the robbery and comprehended them. Ward testified several times that Jemison was present during the conversation and implied that he had directed his questions to both Jemison and Fortes, asking "if they did a bank robbery." We thus do not have the situation which existed in cases cited by Jemison where no evidence was offered to show that the defendant against whom the statements were introduced had any relation to the conversation in issue, although he might have been somewhere present in the room in which the conversation took place. We note also that Jemison failed to object to this line of questioning specifically on the grounds of insufficient foundation, see Fed. R. Evid. 103(a)(1); she likewise did not request that the government elicit fuller preliminary information; and on cross-examination of Ward, Jemison did not attempt to rebut the foundation laid by the government as to her presence at the time of the conversation or her ability to hear or understand Fortes' incriminating comments. In these circumstances, we find that Fortes' inculpatory remarks, recounted by Ward, were properly admitted against Jemison. The ultimate weight given them was, of course, a matter for the jury.... [Convictions affirmed.]

SOUTHERN STONE CO. v. SINGER

665 F.2d 698 (5th Cir. Unit B 1982)

R. LANIER ANDERSON, III, Circuit Judge:

[Southern Stone Co. was never paid for limestone rock it sold to S&M Materials Co., and was unable to collect on a judgment it obtained against S&M. Seeking to pierce the corporate veil,] Southern Stone brought this action against Thomas D. Moore, Sam M. Singer and Susan M. Singer, the officers, directors and shareholders of S&M, and against The Singer Company, a corporation wholly owned by Sam Singer at all times relevant to this action.... The jury returned a verdict in favor of Susan Singer and The Singer Company, but against appellants Sam Singer and Moore. We reverse and remand for a new trial as to Sam Singer's and Moore's liability because of the prejudicial effect of the erroneous admission of a letter written by Southern Stone's counsel to Moore....

After S&M stopped doing business, Moore started his own corporation, TM, Inc. ("TM"), in order to continue in the business of hauling and selling lime purchased from Southern Stone. This new corporation eventually ran up a sizeable account with Southern Stone.... The district court permitted the introduction into evidence of a letter written on December 8, 1977, to Moore by Southern Stone's counsel.[4]

---

4. The body of the letter reads as follows:

This will confirm our conversation this date at which time you told me that Mr. Singer instructed you to buy on account, all the lime that you could from Southern Stone Company's quarry in Lee County, Alabama, and if necessary to even lease other truck [*sic*] if S&M's trucks were otherwise busy and to haul the lime from Lee County quarry of Southern Stone Company to S&M Materials Co. in Russell County and at a place that S&M Materials Co. had leased for the special purposes of stockpiling lime outside of Phenix City, Alabama. At the time the instructions were given to you to buy all the lime that you could on the account of S&M from Southern Stone Company, Inc. Mr. Singer had made the decision on behalf of S&M Materials Company 2 or 3 months before the business closed that S&M Materials Company was going out of business as of December 31, 1976.

I believe this is the same information that you relayed to Mr. Mark C. Gallups sometime ago.

P.S. If any of the above is incorrect, please advise me.

The letter purports to relate several statements made by Moore to Southern Stone's counsel concerning the activities of Moore and Sam Singer in the final months of S&M's operation and concerning the date Singer decided to end S&M's business. . . .

Southern Stone argues that the letter is admissible under Fed. R. Evid. 801(d)(2)(B) as a statement in which Moore manifested his adoption or his belief in its truth. Although Southern Stone's counsel, not Moore, wrote the letter, Southern Stone argues that Moore's failure to respond to the letter, in the face of a postscript requesting a reply if the letter incorrectly recounted Moore's remarks, sufficiently indicates Moore's adoption or belief in the truth of the letter's contents, in effect transforming the letter into Moore's own statement about what he said during the conversation. However, the mere failure to respond to a letter does not indicate an adoption unless it was reasonable under the circumstances for the sender to expect the recipient to respond and to correct erroneous assertions. . . . All the circumstances surrounding this letter do not support a reasonable expectation of any response. The only reason Moore went to the office of Southern Stone's counsel was to sign a personal note for the account that TM owed Southern Stone. Southern Stone introduced no evidence indicating that Moore was there to discuss any matters relating to his former involvement with S&M, which was the entire subject matter of the letter. Indeed, S&M had ceased operations nearly a year prior to the meeting between Moore and Southern Stone's counsel. Moore testified that the reason he never responded to the letter was that at the time, he was no longer involved with S&M, "didn't care what was going on" and considered that "the corporation was gone." Moore also testified that he could remember nothing about the conversation. Because of Southern Stone's failure to lay a foundation for the introduction of the letter more solid than Moore's mere failure to respond, the letter did not meet the requirements of Rule 801(d)(2)(B) and could not be admitted on that basis.

Once stripped of its asserted status as, in effect, Moore's own admission as to what he said in the conversation, the letter can be viewed only as a hearsay declaration of Southern Stone's counsel as to what Moore said. The letter involves two levels of hearsay: the letter says that Southern Stone's counsel said (first level) that Moore made certain admissions (second level). Even if Moore's declarations are not hearsay under Fed. R. Evid. 801(d)(2)(A) (statements of a party offered against the party), the first level of hearsay still exists. In attempting to explain why its counsel did not personally testify as to his conversation with Moore, Southern Stone stated that it might be improper for the attorney representing Southern Stone in the trial of this case also to testify on Southern Stone's behalf. Southern Stone should have engaged other trial counsel if it had any reservations about placing its trial attorney on the witness stand. Southern Stone cannot create its own exception to the hearsay rule by failing to retain such other counsel. Because we perceive no other applicable hearsay exception for which Southern Stone laid an adequate foundation, the letter was inadmissible. . . . Reversed and Remanded.

MOSS v. COMMONWEALTH

531 S.W.3d 479 (Ky. 2017)

Opinion of the Court by Justice VENTERS

Shawn Thompson was shot and killed while he and Sarah Sanders were visiting the Simpson County residence of Appellant [Daniel Lee Moss] and Christina Layle. Appellant informed the 911 operator that he had been attacked in his home and had to shoot his assailant (Thompson). Officers from the Simpson County Sheriffs office ... arrived first to find Thompson lying face up on the porch with his head at the bottom of the front steps. Sanders was kneeling over Thompson, hugging him and screaming. . . .

In order to calm what was described as a chaotic scene, the officers took Appellant, Layle, and Sanders into the residence and seated them in the living room. . . . Appellant was explaining to Jones what had happened when Sanders screamed, "You shot him in the back for no reason." Appellant made no reply; he remained seated with his hands partially covering his face and mouth. . . .

[Appellant was charged with murder, but the trial jury] instead convicted him of the lesser charge of second-degree manslaughter based upon an imperfect self-defense theory. . . . [The Court of Appeals affirmed.]

Appellant argues that the trial court [erred by interpreting Rule 801A(b)(2) of the Kentucky Rules of Evidence to allow testimony about] Sanders' accusation that Appellant "shot [Thompson] in the back for no reason," coupled with Appellant's failure to respond. . . .

Even though Sanders' accusation might otherwise be inadmissible hearsay, KRE 801A(b)(2) would permit its introduction into evidence *if*, under the circumstances, Appellant's conduct including his failure to reply "manifested [his] adoption or belief in its truth." . . . [A] suspect's failure to deny an incriminating accusation is not an admission of guilt under circumstance in which "there is seemingly no natural and proper call" to contradict the accusation. *Griffith* [*v. Commonwealth*, 63 S.W.2d 594, 596 (Ky. 1933).] Appellant would have had no "natural and proper call" to contradict Sanders' outburst when he was then and there in the process of telling his side of the story to the police, especially after his explanation had provoked Sanders' accusation. Engaging Sanders in a debate about the shooting would not be a reasonable option under such circumstances and would not have been helpful to police trying to quiet a chaotic situation. Given those circumstances, it cannot reasonably or fairly be said that Appellant was naturally called to contradict Sanders' accusation ... Appellant's failure to verbally protest Sanders' accusation did not "manifest an adoption or belief in its truth." KRE 801A(b)(2). . . .

[Nonetheless the error was harmless.] As established by the verdict convicting Appellant of second-degree manslaughter, the jury necessarily rejected the inference that Appellant admitted by his silence that he shot Thompson for no reason. The jury was evidently persuaded that Appellant's reason for shooting Thompson was his actual, but mistaken, belief that he needed to use deadly force to protect himself from Thompson. . . . The verdict dispels our concern that the jury was influenced by the error. . . . [Affirmed.]

PROBLEM

3.28. Dryden is prosecuted for sexually abusing his stepdaughter when she was 10 years old. The prosecution wishes to prove that when the girl's mother confronted Dryden with the allegations and asked whether they were true, Dryden replied, "I don't remember doing that, but I can't swear that I haven't blocked it out." Is this interchange admissible against him at trial?

c. Authorized Admissions

[F.R.E. 801(d)(2)(C); C.E.C. §1222]

HANSON v. WALLER

888 F.2d 806 (11th Cir. 1989)

MARCUS, District Judge:

. . . Appellants brought this action on behalf of the deceased, Alfaretta Spina ("Spina") who died of injuries sustained after being struck by a truck driven by Appellee Ralph Waller ("Waller"). . . . Appellants contend that it was error to allow the Defendant at trial to put into evidence, a letter from Appellants' first attorney Mr. Thompson to Defendant's attorney Mr. Dorsey. The letter, as read into the evidence, indicated the following:

> Dear Mr. Dorsey: As per my previous letter to you of June the 29th, 1987, enclosed herewith please find copies of the photographs taken from the scene of the accident along with photographs taken from the same type truck the Defendant Waller was driving, which shows it impossible for him to see Ms. Spina if in crossing the street she had reached a position directly in front of the truck when the traffic light changed. If you care to discuss the matter with me, please feel free to call and with kindest personal regards, I remain, Very truly yours, Thomas L. Thompson, Jr.

. . . Rule 801(d)(2)(C) specifically excludes statements used against a party which were made by another person authorized by the party to make a statement concerning the subject, from the definition of hearsay. This provision has been applied to allow in evidence statements made by attorneys in a representational capacity. *See, e.g., United States v. Ojala*, 544 F.2d 940, 946 (8th Cir. 1976); *Williams v. Union Carbide Co.*, 790 F.2d 552, 555-56 (6th Cir. 1986). Although an attorney does not have authority to make an out-of-court admission for his client in all instances, he does have authority to make admissions which are directly related to the management of litigation. *United States v. Dolleris*, 408 F.2d 918, 921 (6th Cir. 1969), *cert. denied*, 395 U.S. 943 (1968). In the instant case, the letter sent by Mr. Thompson to Mr. Dorsey was clearly related to the management of the Appellants' litigation. Therefore, the contents of the letter fall within the hearsay exclusion provided by Rule 801(d)(2)(C). Finally, we observe that the Appellants have not demonstrated that the revelation of the contents of the letter was harmful to their case at trial. Accordingly, we find no error. . . .

ADVISORY COMMITTEE NOTE TO F.R.E. 801(d)(2)(C)

No authority is required for the general proposition that a statement authorized by a party to be made should have the status of an admission by the party. However, the question arises whether only statements to third persons should be so regarded, to the exclusion of statements by the agent to the principal. The rule is phrased broadly so as to encompass both. While it may be argued that the agent authorized to make statements to his principal does not speak for him, Morgan, Basic Problems of Evidence 273 (1962), communication to an outsider has not generally been thought to be an essential characteristic of an admission. Thus a party's books or records are usable against him, without regard to any intent to disclose to third persons. 5 Wigmore §1557. . . . Cf. Uniform Rule 63(8)(a) and California Evidence Code §1222 which limit status as an admission in this regard to statements authorized by the party to be made "for" him, which is perhaps an ambiguous limitation to statements to third persons.

PROBLEM

3.29. The plaintiffs in a product liability lawsuit against a bicycle manufacturer seek to introduce evidence that a spokesperson for the company admitted that "the design of that particular bike has proven defective." The company claims that it fired the spokesperson hours before she made that statement; the plaintiffs claim the spokesperson was dismissed shortly *after* making the statement. After hearing conflicting testimony on this question, the judge concludes that it is impossible to tell which side is right, but that the evidence slightly favors the company's account. Should the jury be told about the spokesperson's statement?

d. Agent and Employee Admissions

[F.R.E. 801(d)(2)(D); C.E.C. §§1224, 1225]

ADVISORY COMMITTEE NOTE TO F.R.E. 801(d)(2)(D)

The tradition has been to test the admissibility of statements by agents, as admissions, by applying the usual test of agency. Was the admission made by the agent acting in the scope of his employment? Since few principals employ agents for the purpose of making damaging statements, the usual result was exclusion of the statement. Dissatisfaction with this loss of valuable and helpful evidence has been increasing. A substantial trend favors admitting statements related to a matter within the scope of the agency or employment.

MAHLANDT v. WILD CANID SURVIVAL & RESEARCH CENTER, INC.

588 F.2d 626 (8th Cir. 1978)

VAN SICKLE, District Judge [sitting by designation].

This is a civil action for damages arising out of an alleged attack by a wolf on a child. The sole issues on appeal are as to the correctness of three rulings which excluded conclusionary statements against interest. Two of them were made by a defendant, who was also an employee of the corporate defendant; and the third was in the form of a statement appearing in the records of a board meeting of the corporate defendant.

On March 23, 1973, Daniel Mahlandt, then 3 years, 10 months, and 8 days old, was sent by his mother to a neighbor's home on an adjoining street to get his older brother, Donald. Daniel's mother watched him cross the street, and then turned into the house to get her car keys. Daniel's path took him along a walkway adjacent to the Poos' residence. Next to the walkway was a five foot chain link fence to which Sophie had been chained with a six foot chain. In other words, Sophie was free to move in a half circle having a six foot radius on the side of the fence opposite from Daniel.

Sophie was a bitch wolf, 11 months and 28 days old, who had been born at the St. Louis Zoo, and kept there until she reached 6 months of age, at which time she was given to the Wild Canid Survival and Research Center, Inc. It was the policy of the Zoo to remove wolves from the Children's Zoo after they reached the age of 5 or 6 months. Sophie was supposed to be kept at the Tyson Research Center, but Kenneth Poos, as Director of Education for the Wild Canid Survival and Research Center, Inc., had been keeping her at his home because he was taking Sophie to schools and institutions where he showed films and gave programs with respect to the nature of wolves. Sophie was known as a very gentle wolf who had proved herself to be good natured and stable during her contacts with thousands of children, while she was in the St. Louis Children's Zoo.

Sophie was chained because the evening before she had jumped the fence and attacked a beagle who was running along the fence and yapping at her.

A neighbor who was ill in bed in the second floor of his home heard a child's screams and went to his window, where he saw a boy lying on his back within the enclosure, with a wolf straddling him. The wolf's face was near Daniel's face, but the distance was so great that he could not see what the wolf was doing, and did not see any biting. Within about 15 seconds the neighbor saw Clarke Poos, about seventeen, run around the house, get the wolf off of the boy, and disappear with the child in his arms to the back of the house. Clarke took the boy in and laid him on the kitchen floor.

Clarke had been returning from his friend's home immediately west when he heard a child's cries and ran around to the enclosure. He found

Daniel lying within the enclosure, about three feet from the fence, and Sophie standing back from the boy the length of her chain, and wailing. An expert in the behavior of wolves stated that when a wolf's wail is a sign of compassion, and an effort to get attention, not a sign of attack. No witness saw or knew how Daniel was injured.

Clarke and his sister ran over to get Daniel's mother. She says that Clarke told her, "a wolf got Danny and he is dying." Clarke denies that statement. The defendant, Mr. Poos, arrived home while Daniel and his mother were in the kitchen. After Daniel was taken in an ambulance, Mr. Poos talked to everyone present, including a neighbor who came in. Within an hour after he arrived home, Mr. Poos went to Washington University to inform Owen Sexton, President of Wild Canid Survival and Research Center, Inc., of the incident. Mr. Sexton was not in his office so Mr. Poos left the following note on his door:

> Owen, would call me at home, 727-5080? Sophie bit a child that came in our back yard. All has been taken care of. I need to convey what happened to you.

Denial of admission of this note is one of the issues on appeal.

Later that day, Mr. Poos found Mr. Sexton at the Tyson Research Center and told him what had happened. Denial of plaintiff's offer to prove that Mr. Poos told Mr. Sexton that, "Sophie had bit a child that day," is the second issue on appeal.

A meeting of the Directors of the Wild Canid Survival and Research Center, Inc., was held on April 4, 1973. Mr. Poos was not present at that meeting. The minutes of that meeting reflect that there was a "great deal of discussion . . . about the legal aspects of the incident of Sophie biting the child." Plaintiff offered an abstract of the minutes containing that reference. Denial of the offer of that abstract is the third issue on appeal.

Daniel had lacerations of the face, left thigh, left calf, and right thigh, and abrasions and bruises of the abdomen and chest. Mr. Mahlandt was permitted to state that Daniel had indicated that he had gone under the fence. Mr. Mahlandt and Mr. Poos, about a month after the incident, examined the fence to determine what caused Daniel's lacerations. Mr. Mahlandt felt that they did not look like animal bites. The parallel scars on Daniel's thigh appeared to match the configuration of the barbs or tines on the fence. The expert as to the behavior of wolves opined that the lacerations were not wolf bites or wounds caused by wolf claws. Wolves have powerful jaws and a wolf bite will result in massive crushing or severing of a limb. He stated that if Sophie had bitten Daniel there would have been clear apposition of teeth and massive crushing of Daniel's hands and arms which were not injured. Also, if Sophie had pulled Daniel under the fence, tooth marks on the foot or leg would have been present, although Sophie possessed enough strength to pull the boy under the fence.

The jury brought in a verdict for the defense.

The trial judge's rationale for excluding the note, the statement, and the corporate minutes, was the same in each case. He reasoned that Mr. Poos did not have any personal knowledge of the facts, and accordingly, the first two admissions were based on hearsay; and the third admission contained in the minutes of the board meeting was subject to the same objection of hearsay, and unreliability because of lack of personal knowledge.

. . . [T]he statement in the note pinned on the door is not hearsay, and is admissible against Mr. Poos. It was his own statement, and as such was clearly different from the reported statement of another. . . . It was also a statement of which he had manifested his adoption or belief in its truth. And the same observations may be made of the statement made later in the day to Mr. Sexton that, "Sophie had bit a child. . . ."

Are these statements admissible against Wild Canid Survival and Research Center, Inc.? They were made by Mr. Poos when he was an agent or servant of the Wild Canid Survival and Research Center, Inc., and they concerned a matter within the scope of his agency, or employment, i.e., his custody of Sophie, and were made during the existence of that relationship.

Defendant argues that Rule 801(d)(2) does not provide for the admission of "in house" statements; that is, it allows only admissions made to third parties. The notes of the Advisory Committee on the Proposed Rules . . . discuss the problem of "in house" admissions with reference to Rule 801(d)(2)(C) situations. This is not a (C) situation because Mr. Poos was not authorized or directed to make a statement on the matter by anyone. But the rationale developed in that comment does apply to this (D) situation. Mr. Poos had actual physical custody of Sophie. His conclusions, his opinions, were obviously accepted as a basis for action by his principal. . . .

Weinstein states categorically that although an express requirement of personal knowledge on the part of the declarant of the facts underlying his statement is not written into [Rule 801(d)(2)(D)], it should be. He feels that is mandated by Rules 805 and 403. . . . [N]either rule mandates the introduction into Rule 801(d)(2)(D) of an implied requirement that the declarant have personal knowledge of the facts underlying his statement. So we conclude that the two statements made by Mr. Poos were admissible against Wild Canid Survival and Research Center, Inc.

As to the entry in the records of a corporate meeting, the directors as primary officers of the corporation had the authority to include their conclusions in the record of the meeting. So the evidence would fall within 801(d)(2)(C) as to Wild Canid Survival and Research Center, Inc., and be admissible. The "in house" aspect of this admission has already been discussed. . . .

But there was no servant, or agency, relationship which justified admitting the evidence of the board minutes as against Mr. Poos. None of the conditions of 801(d)(2) cover the claim that minutes of a corporate board meeting can be used against a non-attending, non-participating employee of that corporation. The evidence was not admissible as against Mr. Poos.

There is left only the question of whether the trial court's rulings which excluded all three items of evidence are justified under Rule 403. He clearly found that the evidence was not reliable, pointing out that none of the statements were based on the personal knowledge of the declarant.

Again, that problem was faced by the Advisory Committee on Proposed Rules. In its discussion of 801(d)(2) exceptions to the hearsay rule, the Committee said:

> The freedom which admissions have enjoyed from technical demands of searching for an assurance of trustworthiness in some against-interest circumstances, and from the restrictive influences of the opinion rule and the rule requiring

first hand knowledge, when taken with the apparently prevalent satisfaction with the results, calls for generous treatment of this avenue to admissibility.

So here, remembering that relevant evidence is usually prejudicial to the cause of the side against which it is presented, and that the prejudice which concerns us is unreasonable prejudice; and applying the spirit of Rule 801(d)(2), we hold that Rule 403 does not warrant the exclusion of the evidence of Mr. Poos' statements as against himself or Wild Canid Survival and Research Center, Inc. But the limited admissibility of the corporate minutes, coupled with the repetitive nature of the evidence and the low probative value of the minute record, all justify supporting the judgment of the trial court under Rule 403.

The judgment of the District Court is reversed and the matter remanded to the District Court for a new trial consistent with this opinion.

SEA-LAND SERVICE, INC. v. LOZEN INTERNATIONAL, LLC

285 F.3d 808 (9th Cir. 2002)

Graber, Circuit Judge:

Plaintiff Sea-Land Service, Inc. (Sea-Land), brought this action against Defendant Lozen International, LLC (Lozen), to recover money owed under a shipping contract. Lozen counterclaimed for damages resulting from Sea-Land's failure to timely deliver one of the shipments at issue. The parties settled and dismissed Sea-Land's claim, but they were unable to reach an agreement with respect to Lozen's counterclaims. As to those, the district court entered summary judgment in favor of Sea-Land. . . .

Lozen appeals, arguing . . . that the district court improperly excluded Exhibit 4, an internal company e-mail authored by one Sea-Land employee and forwarded to Lozen by a second Sea-Land employee. The district court excluded this evidence on the ground that Lozen "makes no argument, nor does it present any evidence indicating the identity or job title of [the] employee" who authored the forwarded e-mail. Lozen argues that the e-mail is admissible and is not hearsay because it is an admission by a party opponent. Fed. R. Evid. 801(d)(2)(D). . . .

Exhibit 4 is an admission by a party opponent. The original e-mail, an internal company memorandum, closes with an electronic "signature" attesting that the message was authored by "Mike Jacques," Sea-Land's "Rail Reefer Services Coordinator" at the time the e-mail was written. Jacques is listed as one of Sea-Land's employees in Exhibit 9, a letter from Sea-Land to Lozen that the district court *did* admit into evidence. The original e-mail also appears to concern a matter within the scope of Jacques' employment.

More importantly, however, Jacques' original e-mail was forwarded to Lozen by Laurie Martinez, a second Sea-Land employee. She copied the entire body of Jacques' internal memorandum into her e-mail and prefaced it with the statement, "Yikes, Pls note the rail screwed us up. . . ." Martinez thereby incorporated and adopted the contents of Jacques' original message, because her remark "manifested an adoption or belief in [the] truth" of the information contained in the original e-mail. Fed. R. Evid. 801(d)(2)(B); . . . *cf. Alvord-Polk, Inc. v. F. Schumacher & Co.*, 37 F.3d 996, 1005 n.6 (3d Cir. 1994) (holding that statements of company president, which were reprinted in company publications, were not hearsay but were instead admissible as adoptive admissions). Further, there is evidence in the record that Martinez was one of Sea-Land's employees at the time her message was written and that the contents of the e-mail were within the scope of her employment. Her admission (including the incorporated portion) therefore conforms to the requirements of Rule 801(d)(2)(D).

For these reasons, the district court abused its discretion when it excluded the e-mail. . . . Reversed and Remanded for proceedings consistent with this opinion.

PROBLEMS

3.30. The owners of all rights to the animated character "Seymour the Super Spaniel" bring a trademark infringement suit against the manufacturer of a "plush toy" that looks similar to Seymour. To prove that children are likely to confuse the defendant's toy with Seymour, the plaintiffs seek to prove that the defendant has made the following statements to wholesale purchasers: (a) "Kids can't tell this thing apart from Seymour." (b) "I showed the dog to my six-year-old niece, and she said, 'Oh, it's Seymour!'" (c) "My bookkeeper tells me we run out of inventory every time a new Seymour movie comes out." Which, if any, of these statements are barred by the hearsay rule?

3.31. A delivery company fires a driver after his truck collides with a motorcycle. The driver then telephones the motorcyclist and admits that he was speeding. The motorcyclist sues the driver and the delivery company for negligence, proceeding against the delivery company on a theory of *respondeat superior*. Is the driver's statement admissible against the driver? Against the company?

3.32. A newspaper reports that the "old time marinade" advertised by a fast food chain is mayonnaise and food coloring. The chain sues for libel. The newspaper seeks to have its reporter testify that she was told the ingredients by the chain's Vice President for Menus and Recipes. Is the testimony admissible to prove lack of malice? To prove the actual ingredients?

3.33. During a circus performance, a lion escapes and mauls a spectator to death. Hours later the lion tamer tells his supervisor that the latch on the lion's cage was rusty and weak. The circus company, Amazing Inc., is prosecuted in state court for criminally negligent homicide. The state code of evidence is substantially identical to the Federal Rules of Evidence. Assume the lion tamer does not testify at trial. Would the hearsay rule or the Confrontation Clause bar the introduction of his statement against Amazing Inc.?

e. Co-Conspirator Admissions

[F.R.E. 801(d)(2)(E); C.E.C. §1223]

ADVISORY COMMITTEE NOTE TO F.R.E. 801(d)(2)(E)

The limitation upon the admissibility of statements of co-conspirators to those made "during the course and in furtherance of the conspiracy" is in the accepted pattern. While the broadened view of agency taken in [Rule 801(d) (2)(D)] might suggest wider admissibility of statements of co-conspirators, the agency theory of conspiracy is at best a fiction and ought not to serve as a basis for admissibility beyond that already established. See Levie, Hearsay and Conspiracy, 52 Mich. L. Rev. 1159 (1954); Comment, U. Chi. L. Rev. 520 (1958). The rule is consistent with the position of the Supreme Court in denying admissibility to statements made after the objectives of the conspiracy have either failed or been achieved. Krulewitch v. United States, 336 U.S. 440 (1949); Wong Sun v. United States, 371 U.S. 471, 490 (1963).

REPORT OF THE SENATE JUDICIARY COMMITTEE
S. Rep. No. 93-1277 (1974)

While [proposed Rule 801(d)(2)(E)] refers to a coconspirator, it is this committee's understanding that the rule is meant to carry forward the universally accepted doctrine that a joint venturer is considered as a coconspirator for the purposes of this rule even though no conspiracy has been charged. United States v. Rinaldi, 393 F.2d 97, 99 (2d Cir.), cert. denied, 393 U.S. 913 (1968); United States v. Spencer, 415 F.2d 1301, 1304 (7th Cir. 1969).

JOSEPH H. LEVIE, HEARSAY AND CONSPIRACY
52 Mich. L. Rev. 1159, 1161–1166 (1954)

The odd thing about this exception to the hearsay rule is its very existence. Why single out conspiracies for preferential treatment? ... The usual reason given for the co-conspirators' exception is the classical agency rationale that co-conspirators are co-agents and, as such, liable for each other's declarations. . . . [This] begs the question. The rules of agency govern the substantive law of conspiracy; they decide who is a member of the conspiracy. As such they are involved in determining *against whom* the evidence may be admitted. . . . [T]hey are not relevant in determining *why* it should be admitted.

Wigmore's theory that such declarations are admitted because they are trustworthy (and accordingly the need for cross-examination is less acute) fares no better. Wigmore argues that since the interest of all conspirators is identical, an admission of one against his interest is against the interest of each. This fails to distinguish between declarations showing the existence of a conspiracy and declarations concerning the membership or aims. Of course sane men do not falsely admit to conspiracy. Conspirators' declarations are good to prove that some conspiracy exists and less trustworthy to show its aims and membership. The conspirator's interest is likely to lie in misleading the listener into believing the conspiracy stronger with more members (and different members) and other aims than it in fact has. It is no victory for common sense to make a belief that criminals are notorious for their veracity the basis for law.

. . . The true reason for the exception explains both its growth and the parallelism of that expansion to the expansion of the law of conspiracy. That reason is simply: There is great probative need for such testimony. Conspiracy is a hard thing to prove. The substantive law of conspiracy has vastly expanded. This created a tension solved by relaxation in the law of evidence. Conspirators' declarations are admitted out of necessity.

BOURJAILY v. UNITED STATES

483 U.S. 171 (1987)

Chief Justice REHNQUIST delivered the opinion of the Court.

Federal Rule of Evidence 801(d)(2)(E) provides: "A statement is not hearsay if . . . [t]he statement is offered against a party and is . . . a statement by a coconspirator of a party during the course and in furtherance of the conspiracy." We granted certiorari to answer three questions regarding the admission of statements under Rule 801(d)(2)(E): (1) whether the court must determine by independent evidence that the conspiracy existed and that the defendant and the declarant were members of this conspiracy; (2) the quantum of proof on which such determinations must be based; and (3) whether a court must in each case examine the circumstances of such a statement to determine its reliability.

In May 1984, Clarence Greathouse, an informant working for the Federal Bureau of Investigation (FBI), arranged to sell a kilogram of cocaine to Angelo Lonardo. Lonardo agreed that he would find individuals to distribute the drug. When the sale became imminent, Lonardo stated in a tape-recorded telephone conversation that he had a "gentleman friend" who had some questions to ask about the cocaine. In a subsequent telephone call, Greathouse spoke to the "friend" about the quality of the drug and the price. Greathouse then spoke again with Lonardo, and the two arranged the details of the purchase. They agreed that the sale would take place in a designated hotel parking lot, and Lonardo would transfer the drug from Greathouse's car to the "friend," who would be waiting in the parking lot in his own car. Greathouse proceeded with the transaction as planned, and FBI agents arrested Lonardo and petitioner immediately after Lonardo placed a kilogram of cocaine into petitioner's car in the hotel parking lot. In petitioner's car, the agents found over $20,000 in cash.

Petitioner was charged with conspiring to distribute cocaine, in violation of 21 U.S.C. §846, and possession of cocaine with intent to distribute, a violation of 21 U.S.C. §841(a)(1). The Government introduced, over petitioner's objection, Angelo Lonardo's telephone statements regarding the participation of the "friend" in the transaction. The District Court found that, considering the events in the parking lot and Lonardo's statements over the telephone, the Government had established by a preponderance of the evidence that a conspiracy involving Lonardo and petitioner existed, and that Lonardo's statements over the telephone had been made in the course of and in furtherance of the conspiracy. Accordingly, the trial court held that Lonardo's out-of-court statements satisfied Rule 801(d)(2)(E) and were not hearsay. Petitioner was convicted on both counts and sentenced to 15 years. The United States Court of Appeals for the Sixth Circuit affirmed. . . . We affirm.

Before admitting a co-conspirator's statement over an objection that it does not qualify under Rule 801(d)(2)(E), a court must be satisfied that the statement actually falls within the definition of the Rule. There must be evidence that there was a conspiracy involving the declarant and the nonoffering party, and that the statement was made "during the course and in furtherance of the conspiracy." Federal Rule of Evidence 104(a) provides: "Preliminary questions concerning . . . the admissibility of evidence shall be determined by the court." Petitioner and the Government agree that the existence of a conspiracy and petitioner's involvement in it are preliminary questions of fact that, under Rule 104, must be resolved by the court. The Federal Rules, however, nowhere define the standard of proof the court must observe in resolving these questions.

We are therefore guided by our prior decisions regarding admissibility determinations that hinge on preliminary factual questions. We have traditionally required that these matters be established by a preponderance of proof. Evidence is placed before the jury when it satisfies the technical requirements of the evidentiary Rules, which embody certain legal and policy determinations. The inquiry made by a court concerned with these matters is not whether the proponent of the evidence wins or loses his case on the merits, but whether the evidentiary Rules have been satisfied. Thus, the evidentiary standard is unrelated to the burden of proof on the substantive issues, be it a criminal case, see *In re Winship*, 397 U.S. 358 (1970), or a civil case. The preponderance standard ensures that before admitting evidence, the court will have found it more likely than not that the technical issues and policy concerns addressed by the Federal Rules of Evidence have been afforded due consideration. As in *Lego v. Twomey*, 404 U.S. 477, 488 (1972), we find "nothing to suggest that admissibility rulings have been unreliable or otherwise wanting in quality because not based on some higher standard." We think that our previous decisions in this area resolve the matter. See, *e.g., Colorado v. Connelly*, [479 U.S. 157 (1986)] (preliminary fact that custodial confessant waived rights must be proved by preponderance of the evidence); *Nix v. Williams*, 467 U.S. 431, 444 n.5 (1984) (inevitable discovery of illegally seized evidence must be shown to have been more likely than not); *United States v. Matlock*, 415 U.S. 164 (1974) (voluntariness of consent to search must be shown by preponderance of the evidence); *Lego v. Twomey, supra* (voluntariness of confession must be demonstrated by a preponderance of the evidence). Therefore, we hold that when the preliminary facts relevant to Rule 801(d)(2)(E) are disputed, the offering party must prove them by a preponderance of the evidence.[1]

Even though petitioner agrees that the courts below applied the proper standard of proof with regard to the preliminary facts relevant to Rule 801(d)(2)(E), he nevertheless challenges the admission of Lonardo's statements. Petitioner argues that in determining whether a conspiracy exists and whether the defendant was a member of it, the court must look only to independent evidence — that is, evidence other than the statements sought to be admitted. Petitioner relies on *Glasser v. United States*, 315 U.S. 60 (1942), in which this Court first mentioned the so-called "bootstrapping rule." The relevant issue in *Glasser* was whether Glasser's counsel, who also represented another defendant, faced such a conflict of interest that Glasser received ineffective assistance. Glasser contended that conflicting loyalties led his lawyer not to object to statements made by one of Glasser's co-conspirators. The Government argued that any objection would have been fruitless because the statements were admissible. The Court rejected this proposition:

> "[S]uch declarations are admissible over the objection of an alleged coconspirator, who was not present when they were made, only if there is proof *aliunde* that he is connected with the conspiracy. . . . Otherwise, hearsay would lift itself by its own bootstraps to the level of competent evidence."

The Court revisited the bootstrapping rule in *United States v. Nixon*, 418 U.S. 683 (1974), where again, in passing, the Court stated: "Declarations by one defendant may also be admissible against other defendants upon a sufficient showing, *by independent evidence*, of a conspiracy among one or more other defendants and the declarant and if the declarations at issue were in furtherance of that conspiracy" (emphasis added) (footnote omitted). Read in the light most favorable to petitioner, *Glasser* could mean that a court should not consider hearsay statements at all in determining preliminary facts under Rule 801(d)(2)(E). Petitioner, of course, adopts this view of the bootstrapping rule. *Glasser*, however, could also mean that a court must have *some* proof *aliunde*, but may look at the hearsay statements themselves in light of this independent evidence to determine whether a conspiracy has been shown by a preponderance of the evidence. The Courts of Appeals have widely adopted the former view and held that in determining the preliminary facts relevant to co-conspirators' out-of-court statements, a court may not look at the hearsay statements themselves for their evidentiary value.

Both *Glasser* and *Nixon*, however, were decided before Congress enacted the Federal Rules of Evidence in 1975. . . . Petitioner concedes that Rule 104, on its face, appears to allow the court to make the preliminary factual determinations relevant to Rule 801(d)(2)(E) by considering any evidence it wishes, unhindered by considerations of admissibility. That would seem to many to be the end of the matter. Congress has decided that courts may consider hearsay

---

1. We intimate no view on the proper standard of proof for questions falling under Federal Rule of Evidence 104(b) (conditional relevancy). We also decline to address the circumstances in which the burden of coming forward to show that the proffered evidence is inadmissible is appropriately placed on the nonoffering party. . . . Finally, we do not express an opinion on the proper order of proof that trial courts should follow in concluding that the preponderance standard has been satisfied in an ongoing trial.

in making these factual determinations. Out-of-court statements made by anyone, including putative co-conspirators, are often hearsay. Even if they are, they may be considered, *Glasser* and the bootstrapping rule notwithstanding. But petitioner nevertheless argues that the bootstrapping rule, as most Courts of Appeals have construed it, survived this apparently unequivocal change in the law unscathed and that Rule 104, as applied to the admission of co-conspirator's statements, does not mean what it says. We disagree.

Petitioner claims that Congress evidenced no intent to disturb the bootstrapping rule, which was embedded in the previous approach, and we should not find that Congress altered the rule without affirmative evidence so indicating. It would be extraordinary to require legislative history to *confirm* the plain meaning of Rule 104. The Rule on its face allows the trial judge to consider any evidence whatsoever, bound only by the rules of privilege. We think that the Rule is sufficiently clear that to the extent that it is inconsistent with petitioner's interpretation of *Glasser* and *Nixon*, the Rule prevails.[2]

Nor do we agree with petitioner that this construction of Rule 104(a) will allow courts to admit hearsay statements without any credible proof of the conspiracy, thus fundamentally changing the nature of the co-conspirator exception. Petitioner starts with the proposition that co-conspirators' out-of-court statements are deemed unreliable and are inadmissible, at least until a conspiracy is shown. Since these statements are unreliable, petitioner contends that they should not form any part of the basis for establishing a conspiracy, the very antecedent that renders them admissible. . . .

Even if out-of-court declarations by co-conspirators are presumptively unreliable, trial courts must be permitted to evaluate these statements for their evidentiary worth as revealed by the particular circumstances of the case. Courts often act as factfinders, and there is no reason to believe that courts are any less able to properly recognize the probative value of evidence in this particular area. The party opposing admission has an adequate incentive to point out the shortcomings in such evidence before the trial court finds the preliminary facts. If the opposing party is unsuccessful in keeping the evidence from the factfinder, he still has the opportunity to attack the probative value of the

---

2. The Advisory Committee Notes show that the Rule was not adopted in a fit of absent-mindedness. The Note to Rule 104 specifically addresses the process by which a federal court should make the factual determinations requisite to a finding of admissibility:

> "If the question is factual in nature, the judge will of necessity receive evidence pro and con on the issue. The rule provides that the rules of evidence in general do not apply to this process. McCormick §53, p. 123, n.8, points out that the authorities are 'scattered and inconclusive,' and observes:
>
> "'should the exclusionary law of evidence, "the child of the jury system" in Thayer's phrase, be applied to this hearing before the judge? Sound sense backs the view that it should not, and that the judge should be empowered to hear *any relevant evidence*, such as affidavits *or other reliable hearsay*.'" (emphasis added).

The Advisory Committee further noted: "An item, offered and objected to, *may itself be considered in ruling on admissibility*, though not yet admitted in evidence" (emphasis added). We think this language makes plain the drafters' intent to abolish any kind of bootstrapping rule. Silence is at best ambiguous, and we decline the invitation to rely on speculation to import ambiguity into what is otherwise a clear rule.

evidence as it relates to the substantive issue in the case. See, *e.g.*, Fed. R. Evid. 806 (allowing attack on credibility of out-of-court declarant).

We think that there is little doubt that a co-conspirator's statements could themselves be probative of the existence of a conspiracy and the participation of both the defendant and the declarant in the conspiracy. Petitioner's case presents a paradigm. The out-of-court statements of Lonardo indicated that Lonardo was involved in a conspiracy with a "friend." The statements indicated that the friend had agreed with Lonardo to buy a kilogram of cocaine and to distribute it. The statements also revealed that the friend would be at the hotel parking lot, in his car, and would accept the cocaine from Greathouse's car after Greathouse gave Lonardo the keys. Each one of Lonardo's statements may itself be unreliable, but taken as a whole, the entire conversation between Lonardo and Greathouse was corroborated by independent evidence. The friend, who turned out to be petitioner, showed up at the prearranged spot at the prearranged time. He picked up the cocaine, and a significant sum of money was found in his car. On these facts, the trial court concluded, in our view correctly, that the Government had established the existence of a conspiracy and petitioner's participation in it.

We need not decide in this case whether the courts below could have relied solely upon Lonardo's hearsay statements to determine that a conspiracy had been established by a preponderance of the evidence. . . . It is sufficient for today to hold that a court, in making a preliminary factual determination under Rule 801(d)(2)(E), may examine the hearsay statements sought to be admitted. As we have held in other cases concerning admissibility determinations, "the judge should receive the evidence and give it such weight as his judgment and experience counsel." *United States v. Matlock*, 415 U.S. at 175. The courts below properly considered the statements of Lonardo and the subsequent events in finding that the Government had established by a preponderance of the evidence that Lonardo was involved in a conspiracy with petitioner. We have no reason to believe that the District Court's factfinding of this point was clearly erroneous. We hold that Lonardo's out-of-court statements were properly admitted against petitioner. . . . Affirmed.

[Justice Stevens filed a concurring opinion.]

Justice BLACKMUN, with whom Justice BRENNAN and Justice MARSHALL join, dissenting.

. . . By all accounts, the [common law co-conspirator] exemption was based upon agency principles, the underlying concept being that a conspiracy is a common undertaking where the conspirators are all agents of each other and where the acts and statements of one can be attributed to all. As Judge Learned Hand explained this in a frequently quoted remark:

> "When men enter into an agreement for an unlawful end, they become ad hoc agents for one another, and have made a 'partnership in crime.' What one does pursuant to their common purpose, all do, and, as declarations may be such acts, they are competent against all." *Van Riper v. United States*, 13 F.2d 961, 967 (CA2), cert. denied *sub nom. Ackerson v. United States*, 273 U.S. 702 (1926).

. . . [D]espite the recognized need by prosecutors for co-conspirator statements, these statements often have been considered to be somewhat unreliable. It has long been understood that such statements in some cases may constitute, at best, nothing more than the "idle chatter" of a declarant or, at worst, malicious gossip. Moreover, when confronted with such a statement, an innocent defendant would have a difficult time defending himself against it, for, if he were not in the conspiracy, he would have no idea why the conspirator made the statement.... Because of this actual "real world" experience with the possible unreliability of these statements, the Advisory Committee retained the agency rationale for this exemption in Rule 801(d)(2)(E), as well as the safeguards, albeit limited, against unreliability that this rationale provided the defendant. The independent-evidence requirement was one such safeguard. If this requirement is set aside, then one of the exemption's safeguards is lost....

ADVISORY COMMITTEE NOTE TO 1997 AMENDMENT TO F.R.E. 801(d)(2)

Rule 801(d)(2) has been amended in order to respond to three issues raised by *Bourjaily v. United States*, 483 U.S. 171 (1987). First, the amendment codifies the holding in *Bourjaily* by stating expressly that a court shall consider the contents of a coconspirator's statement in determining "the existence of the conspiracy and the participation therein of the declarant and the party against whom the statement is offered." ...

Second, the amendment resolves an issue on which the Court had reserved decision. It provides that the contents of the declarant's statement do not alone suffice to establish a conspiracy in which the declarant and the defendant participated. The court must consider in addition the circumstances surrounding the statement, such as the identity of the speaker, the context in which the statement was made, or evidence corroborating the contents of the statement in making its determination as to each preliminary question. This amendment is in accordance with existing practice. Every court of appeals that has resolved this issue requires some evidence in addition to the contents of the statement.

Third, the amendment extends the reasoning of *Bourjaily* to statements offered under subdivisions (C) and (D) of Rule 801(d)(2)....

PROBLEM

3.34. Following his arrest, a bank robber waives his *Miranda* rights and tells the police that an employee of the bank disabled the security cameras for him. Is this statement admissible against the employee in a prosecution for aiding and abetting bank robbery, or in a civil suit brought against the employee by the bank?

f. Admissions and the *Bruton* Rule

When two or more defendants are tried together, a prior statement by one of the defendants will be admissible against that defendant as an admission, but typically cannot be introduced against the other defendant or defendants without violating both the hearsay rule and the Confrontation Clause. You know by now that the usual way of dealing with situations like this, where evidence is admissible against one party to a case but inadmissible against other parties, is with a limiting instruction. But the Supreme Court has deemed this procedure unacceptable when the evidence in question is an incriminating statement by a codefendant. As you will see, the lines the Court has drawn have been controversial.

BRUTON v. UNITED STATES

391 U.S. 123 (1968)

Mr. Justice BRENNAN delivered the opinion of the Court.

This case presents the question, last considered in *Delli Paoli v. United States*, 352 U.S. 232, whether the conviction of a defendant at a joint trial should be set aside although the jury was instructed that a codefendant's confession inculpating the defendant had to be disregarded in determining his guilt or innocence.

A joint trial of petitioner and one Evans in the District Court for the Eastern District of Missouri resulted in the conviction of both by a jury on a federal charge of armed postal robbery, 18 U.S.C. §2114. A postal inspector testified that Evans orally confessed to him that Evans and petitioner committed the armed robbery. The postal inspector obtained the oral confession, and another in which Evans admitted he had an accomplice whom he would not name, in the course of two interrogations of Evans at the city jail in St. Louis, Missouri, where Evans was held in custody on state criminal charges. Both petitioner and Evans appealed their convictions to the Court of Appeals for the Eighth Circuit. That court set aside Evans' conviction on the ground that [under *Miranda v. Arizona*, 384 U.S. 436 (1966)] his oral confessions to the postal inspector should not have been received in evidence against him. However, the court, relying upon *Delli Paoli*, affirmed petitioner's conviction because the trial judge instructed the jury that although Evans' confession was competent evidence against Evans it was inadmissible hearsay against petitioner and therefore had to be disregarded in determining petitioner's guilt or innocence.[2]

---

2. At the close of the Government's direct case, the trial judge cautioned the jury that Evans' admission implicating petitioner "if used, can only be used against the defendant Evans. It is hearsay insofar as the defendant George William Bruton is concerned, and you are not to consider it in any respect to the defendant Bruton, because insofar as he is concerned it is hearsay."

The instructions to the jury included the following:

"A confession made outside of court by one defendant may not be considered as evidence against the other defendant, who was not present and in no way a party to the confession. Therefore, if you find that a confession was in fact voluntarily and intentionally made by the defendant Evans, you should consider it as evidence in the case against Evans, but you must not consider it, and should disregard it, in considering the evidence in the case against the defendant Bruton. . . .

...We hold that, because of the substantial risk that the jury, despite instructions to the contrary, looked to the incriminating extrajudicial statements in determining petitioner's guilt, admission of Evans' confession in this joint trial violated petitioner's right of cross-examination secured by the Confrontation Clause of the Sixth Amendment. We therefore overrule *Delli Paoli* and reverse.

The basic premise of *Delli Paoli* was that it is "reasonably possible for the jury to follow" sufficiently clear instructions to disregard the confessor's extrajudicial statement that his codefendant participated with him in committing the crime. If it were true that the jury disregarded the reference to the codefendant, no question would arise under the Confrontation Clause, because by hypothesis the case is treated as if the confessor made no statement inculpating the nonconfessor. But since *Delli Paoli* was decided this Court has effectively repudiated its basic premise.[3] . . . True, the repudiation was not in the context of the admission of a confession inculpating a codefendant but in the context of a New York rule which submitted to the jury the question of the voluntariness of the confession itself. *Jackson v. Denno*, 378 U.S. 368. Nonetheless the message of *Jackson* for *Delli Paoli* was clear. We there held that a defendant is constitutionally entitled at least to have the trial judge first determine whether a confession was made voluntarily before submitting it to the jury for an assessment of its credibility. More specifically, we expressly rejected the proposition that a jury, when determining the confessor's guilt, could be relied on to ignore his confession of guilt should it find the confession involuntary. Significantly, we supported that conclusion in part by reliance upon the dissenting opinion of Mr. Justice Frankfurter for the four Justices who dissented in *Delli Paoli.*

That dissent challenged the basic premise of *Delli Paoli* that a properly instructed jury would ignore the confessor's inculpation of the nonconfessor in determining the latter's guilt. "The fact of the matter is that too often such admonition against misuse is intrinsically ineffective in that the effect of such a nonadmissible declaration cannot be wiped from the brains of the jurors. The admonition therefore becomes a futile collocation of words and fails of its purpose as a legal protection to defendants against whom such a declaration should not tell." The dissent went on to say, as quoted . . . in *Jackson*, "The Government should not have the windfall of having the jury be influenced by evidence against a defendant which, as a matter of law, they should not consider but which they cannot put out of their minds." To the same effect, and also cited in the *Jackson* note, is the statement of Mr. Justice Jackson in his concurring opinion in *Krulewitch v. United States*, 336 U.S. 440, 453: "The

---

"It is your duty to give separate, personal consideration to the cause of each individual defendant. When you do so, you should analyze what the evidence shows with respect to that individual, leaving out of consideration entirely any evidence admitted solely against some other defendant. Each defendant is entitled to have his case determined from his own acts and statements and the other evidence in the case which may be applicable to him."

3. We emphasize that the hearsay statement inculpating petitioner was clearly inadmissible against him under traditional rules of evidence. . . . There is not before us, therefore, any recognized exception to the hearsay rule insofar as petitioner is concerned and we intimate no view whatever that such exceptions necessarily raise questions under the Confrontation Clause.

naive assumption that prejudicial effects can be overcome by instructions to the jury ... all practicing lawyers know to be unmitigated fiction. . . ."

The significance of *Jackson* for *Delli Paoli* was suggested by Chief Justice Traynor in *People v. Aranda*, 63 Cal. 2d 518, 528-29, 47 Cal. Rptr. 353, 358-59:

> "Although *Jackson* was directly concerned with obviating any risk that a jury might rely on an unconstitutionally obtained confession in determining the defendant's guilt, its logic extends to obviating the risks that the jury may rely on any inadmissible statements. If it is a denial of due process to rely on a jury's presumed ability to disregard an involuntary confession, it may also be a denial of due process to rely on a jury's presumed ability to disregard a codefendant's confession implicating another defendant when it is determining that defendant's guilt or innocence.
>
> "Indeed, the latter task may be an even more difficult one for the jury to perform than the former. Under the New York procedure, which *Jackson* held violated due process, the jury was only required to disregard a confession it found to be involuntary. If it made such a finding, then the confession was presumably out of the case. In joint trials, however, when the admissible confession of one defendant inculpates another defendant, the confession is never deleted from the case and the jury is expected to perform the overwhelming task of considering it in determining the guilt or innocence of the declarant and then of ignoring it in determining the guilt or innocence of any codefendants of the declarant. A jury cannot 'segregate evidence into separate intellectual boxes.' . . . It cannot determine that a confession is true insofar as it admits that A has committed criminal acts with B and at the same time effectively ignore the inevitable conclusion that B has committed those same criminal acts with A."

. . . Those who have defended reliance on the limiting instruction in this area have cited several reasons in support. Judge Learned Hand, a particularly severe critic of the proposition that juries could be counted on to disregard inadmissible hearsay,[8] wrote the opinion for the Second Circuit which affirmed Delli Paoli's conviction. In Judge Hand's view the limiting instruction, although not really capable of preventing the jury from considering the prejudicial evidence, does as a matter of form provide a way around the exclusionary rules of evidence that is defensible because it "probably furthers, rather than impedes, the search for truth. . . ." *Nash v. United States*, 2 Cir., 54 F.2d 1006, 1007. Insofar as this implies the prosecution ought not to be denied the benefit of the confession to prove the confessor's guilt, however, it overlooks alternative ways of achieving that benefit without at the same time infringing

---

8. Judge Hand addressed the subject several times. The limiting instruction, he said, is a "recommendation to the jury of a mental gymnastic which is beyond, not only their powers, but anybody's else," *Nash v. United States*, 2 Cir., 54 F.2d 1006, 1007; "Nobody can indeed fail to doubt whether the caution is effective, or whether usually the practical result is not to let in hearsay," *United States v. Gottfried*, 2 Cir., 165 F.2d 360, 367; "it is indeed very hard to believe that a jury will, or for that matter can, in practice observe the admonition," *United States v. Delli Paoli*, 2 Cir., 229 F.2d 319, 321. Judge Hand referred to the instruction as a "placebo," medically defined as "a medicinal lie." Judge Jerome Frank suggested that its legal equivalent "is a kind of 'judicial lie': It undermines a moral relationship between the courts, the jurors, and the public; like any other judicial deception, it damages the decent judicial administration of justice." *United States v. Grunewald*, 2 Cir., 233 F.2d 556, 574. . . .

the nonconfessor's right of confrontation.[10] Where viable alternatives do exist, it is deceptive to rely on the pursuit of truth to defend a clearly harmful practice.

Another reason cited in defense of *Delli Paoli* is the justification for joint trials in general, the argument being that the benefits of joint proceedings should not have to be sacrificed by requiring separate trials in order to use the confession against the declarant. Joint trials do conserve state funds, diminish inconvenience to witnesses and public authorities, and avoid delays in bringing those accused of crime to trial. But the answer to this argument was cogently stated by Judge Lehman of the New York Court of Appeals, dissenting in *People v. Fisher*, 249 N.Y. 419, 432, 164 N.E. 336, 341:

> "We still adhere to the rule that an accused is entitled to confrontation of the witnesses against him and the right to cross-examine them. . . . We destroy the age-old rule which in the past has been regarded as a fundamental principle of our jurisprudence by a legalistic formula, required of the judge, that the jury may not consider any admissions against any party who did not join in them. We secure greater speed, economy and convenience in the administration of the law at the price of fundamental principles of constitutional liberty. That price is too high."

Finally, the reason advanced by the majority in *Delli Paoli* was to tie the result to maintenance of the jury system. "Unless we proceed on the basis that the jury will follow the court's instructions where those instructions are clear and the circumstances are such that the jury can reasonably be expected to follow them, the jury system makes little sense." We agree that there are many circumstances in which this reliance is justified. Not every admission of inadmissible hearsay or other evidence can be considered to be reversible error unavoidable through limiting instructions; instances occur in almost every trial where inadmissible evidence creeps in, usually inadvertently. . . . "A defendant is entitled to a fair trial but not a perfect one." *Lutwak v. United States*, 344 U.S. 604, 619. It is not unreasonable to conclude that in many such cases the jury can and will follow the trial judge's instructions to disregard such information. Nevertheless, as was recognized in *Jackson v. Denno, supra*, there are some contexts in which the risk that the jury will not, or cannot, follow instructions is so great, and the consequences of failure so vital to the defendant, that the practical and human limitations of the jury system cannot be ignored. Such a context is presented here, where the powerfully incriminating extrajudicial statements of a codefendant, who stands accused side-by-side with the defendant, are deliberately spread before the jury in a joint trial. Not only are the incriminations devastating to the defendant but their credibility is inevitably suspect, a fact recognized when accomplices do take the stand and the jury is instructed to weigh their testimony carefully given the recognized motivation to shift blame onto others. The unreliability of such evidence is intolerably compounded when the alleged accomplice, as here, does not testify and cannot be tested by cross-examination. It was against such threats to a fair trial that the Confrontation Clause was directed.

---

10. Some courts have required deletion of references to codefendants where practicable. For criticisms suggesting that deletions (redaction) from the confession are ineffective, *see, e.g.*, Note, 72 Harv. L. Rev. 920, 990 (1959); Comment, 24 U. Chi. L. Rev. 710, 713 (1957); Note, 74 Yale L.J. 553, 564 (1965). . . .

. . . Despite the concededly clear instructions to the jury to disregard Evans' inadmissible hearsay evidence inculpating petitioner, in the context of a joint trial we cannot accept limiting instructions as an adequate substitute for petitioner's constitutional right of cross-examination. The effect is the same as if there had been no instruction at all.

Reversed.

Mr. Justice WHITE, dissenting.

. . . Here we deal with a codefendant's confession which is admitted only against the codefendant and with a firm instruction to the jury to disregard it in determining the defendant's guilt or innocence. That confession cannot compare with the defendant's own confession in evidentiary value. As to the defendant, the confession of the codefendant is wholly inadmissible. It is hearsay, subject to all the dangers of inaccuracy which characterize hearsay generally. Furthermore, the codefendant is no more than an eyewitness, the accuracy of whose testimony about the defendant's conduct is open to more doubt than would be the defendant's own account of his actions. More than this, however, the statements of a codefendant have traditionally been viewed with special suspicion. Due to his strong motivation to implicate the defendant and to exonerate himself, a codefendant's statements about what the defendant said or did are less credible than ordinary hearsay evidence. Whereas the defendant's own confession possesses greater reliability and evidentiary value than ordinary hearsay, the codefendant's confession implicating the defendant is intrinsically much less reliable.

The defendant's own confession may not be used against him if coerced, not because it is untrue but to protect other constitutional values. The jury may have great difficulty understanding such a rule and following an instruction to disregard the confession. In contrast, the codefendant's admissions cannot enter into the determination of the defendant's guilt or innocence because they are unreliable. This the jury can be told and can understand. Just as the Court believes that juries can reasonably be expected to disregard ordinary hearsay or other inadmissible evidence when instructed to do so, I believe juries will disregard the portions of a codefendant's confession implicating the defendant when so instructed. Indeed, if we must pick and choose between hearsay as to which limiting instructions will be deemed effective and hearsay the admission of which cannot be cured by instructions, codefendants' admissions belong in the former category rather than the latter, for they are not only hearsay but hearsay which is doubly suspect. If the Court is right in believing that a jury can be counted on to ignore a wide range of hearsay statements which it is told to ignore, it seems very odd to me to question its ability to put aside the codefendant's hearsay statements about what the defendant did. . . .

GRAY v. MARYLAND

523 U.S. 185 (1998)

Justice BREYER delivered the opinion of the Court.

. . . In 1993, Stacy Williams died after a severe beating. Anthony Bell gave a confession, to the Baltimore City police, in which he said that he (Bell), Kevin

Gray, and Jacquin "Tank" Vanlandingham had participated in the beating that resulted in Williams' death. Vanlandingham later died. A Maryland grand jury indicted Bell and Gray for murder. The State of Maryland tried them jointly.

The trial judge, after denying Gray's motion for a separate trial, permitted the State to introduce Bell's confession into evidence at trial. But the judge ordered the confession redacted. Consequently, the police detective who read the confession into evidence said the word "deleted" or "deletion" whenever Gray's name or Vanlandingham's name appeared. Immediately after the police detective read the redacted confession to the jury, the prosecutor asked, "after he gave you that information, you subsequently were able to arrest Mr. Kevin Gray; is that correct?" The officer responded, "That's correct." The State also introduced into evidence a written copy of the confession with those two names omitted, leaving in their place blank white spaces separated by commas. The State produced other witnesses, who said that six persons (including Bell, Gray, and Vanlandingham) participated in the beating. Gray testified and denied his participation. Bell did not testify.

When instructing the jury, the trial judge specified that the confession was evidence only against Bell; the instructions said that the jury should not use the confession as evidence against Gray. The jury convicted both Bell and Gray. Gray appealed.

Maryland's intermediate appellate court accepted Gray's argument that *Bruton* [*v. United States*, 391 U.S. 123 (1968),] prohibited use of the confession and set aside his conviction. Maryland's highest court disagreed and reinstated the conviction. We granted certiorari. . . .

In deciding whether *Bruton*'s protective rule applies to the redacted confession before us, we must consider both *Bruton*, and a later case, *Richardson v. Marsh*, 481 U.S. 200 (1987), which limited *Bruton*'s scope. . . . [*Richardson*] involved a joint murder trial of Marsh and Williams. The State had redacted the confession of one defendant, Williams, so as to "omit all reference" to his codefendant, Marsh — "indeed, to omit all indication that anyone other than . . . Williams" and a third person had "participated in the crime." The trial court also instructed the jury not to consider the confession against Marsh. As redacted, the confession indicated that Williams and the third person had discussed the murder in the front seat of a car while they traveled to the victim's house. The redacted confession contained no indication that Marsh — or any other person — was in the car. Later in the trial, however, Marsh testified that she was in the back seat of the car. For that reason, in context, the confession still could have helped convince the jury that Marsh knew about the murder in advance and therefore had participated knowingly in the crime.

The Court held that this redacted confession fell outside *Bruton*'s scope and was admissible (with appropriate limiting instructions) at the joint trial. The Court distinguished Evans' confession in *Bruton* as a confession that was "incriminating on its face," and which had "expressly implicat[ed]" Bruton. By contrast, Williams' confession amounted to "evidence requiring linkage" in that it "became" incriminating in respect to Marsh "only when linked with evidence introduced later at trial." The Court held "that the Confrontation Clause is not violated by the admission of a nontestifying codefendant's confession with a proper limiting instruction when, as here, the confession is redacted to eliminate not only the defendant's name, but any reference to his or her existence." The Court added: "We express no opinion on the admissibility of a confession in which the defendant's name has been replaced with a symbol or neutral pronoun."

. . . [U]nlike *Richardson*'s redacted confession, [the confession in this case] refers directly to the "existence" of the nonconfessing defendant. The State has simply replaced the nonconfessing defendant's name with a kind of symbol, namely the word "deleted" or a blank space set off by commas. The redacted confession, for example, responded to the question "Who was in the group that beat Stacey," with the phrase, "Me,   and a few other guys." And when the police witness read the confession in court, he said the word "deleted" or "deletion" where the blank spaces appear. We therefore must decide a question that *Richardson* left open, namely whether redaction that replaces a defendant's name with an obvious indication of deletion, such as a blank space, the word "deleted," or a similar symbol, still falls within *Bruton*'s protective rule. We hold that it does.

Bruton, as interpreted by *Richardson*, holds that certain "powerfully incriminating extrajudicial statements of a codefendant" — those naming another defendant — considered as a class, are so prejudicial that limiting instructions cannot work. Unless the prosecutor wishes to hold separate trials or to use separate juries or to abandon use of the confession, he must redact the confession to reduce significantly or to eliminate the special prejudice that the *Bruton* Court found. Redactions that simply replace a name with an obvious blank space or a word such as "deleted" or a symbol or other similarly obvious indications of alteration, however, leave statements that, considered as a class, so closely resemble *Bruton*'s unredacted statements that, in our view, the law must require the same result.

For one thing, a jury will often react similarly to an unredacted confession and a confession redacted in this way, for the jury will often realize that the confession refers specifically to the defendant. This is true even when the State does not blatantly link the defendant to the deleted name, as it did in this case by asking whether Gray was arrested on the basis of information in Bell's confession as soon as the officer had finished reading the redacted statement. Consider a simplified but typical example, a confession that reads "I, Bob Smith, along with Sam Jones, robbed the bank." To replace the words "Sam Jones" with an obvious blank will not likely fool anyone. A juror somewhat familiar with criminal law would know immediately that the blank, in the phrase "I, Bob Smith, along with   , robbed the bank," refers to defendant Jones. A juror who does not know the law and who therefore wonders to whom the blank might refer need only lift his eyes to Jones, sitting at counsel table, to find what will seem the obvious answer, at least if the juror hears the judge's instruction not to consider the confession as evidence against Jones, for that instruction will provide an obvious reason for the blank. A more sophisticated juror, wondering if the blank refers to someone else, might also wonder how, if it did, the prosecutor could argue the confession is reliable, for the prosecutor, after all, has been arguing that Jones, not someone else, helped Smith commit the crime.

For another thing, the obvious deletion may well call the jurors' attention specially to the removed name. By encouraging the jury to speculate about the reference, the redaction may overemphasize the importance of the confession's accusation — once the jurors work out the reference. That is why Judge Learned Hand, many years ago, wrote in a similar instance that blacking out the name of a codefendant not only "would have been futile. . . . [T]here could not have been the slightest doubt as to whose names had been blacked out," but "even if there had been, that blacking out itself would have not only laid the doubt, but underscored the answer." *United States v. Delli Paoli*, 229 F.2d 319, 321 (CA2 1956), *aff'd*, 352 U.S. 232 (1957), *overruled by Bruton v. United States*, 391 U.S. 123 (1968). *See also Malinski v. New York*, 324 U.S. 401, 430 (1945) (Rutledge, J., dissenting) (describing substitution of names in confession with "X" or "Y" and other similar redactions as "devices . . . so obvious as perhaps to emphasize the identity of those they purported to conceal").

Finally, *Bruton*'s protected statements and statements redacted to leave a blank or some other similarly obvious alteration, function the same way grammatically. They are directly accusatory. Evans' statement in *Bruton* used a proper name to point explicitly to an accused defendant. And *Bruton* held that the "powerfully incriminating" effect of what Justice Stewart called "an out-of-court accusation," 391 U.S., at 138 (Stewart, J., concurring), creates a special, and vital, need for cross-examination — a need that would be immediately obvious had the codefendant pointed directly to the defendant in the courtroom itself. The blank space in an obviously redacted confession also points directly to the defendant, and it accuses the defendant in a manner similar to Evans' use of Bruton's name or to a testifying codefendant's accusatory finger. By way of contrast, the factual statement at issue in *Richardson* — a statement about what others said in the front seat of a car — differs from directly accusatory evidence in this respect, for it does not point directly to a defendant at all.

. . . We concede that *Richardson* placed outside the scope of *Bruton*'s rule those statements that incriminate inferentially. We also concede that the jury must use inference to connect the statement in this redacted confession with the defendant. But inference pure and simple cannot make the critical difference, for if it did, then *Richardson* would also place outside *Bruton*'s scope confessions that use shortened first names, nicknames, descriptions as unique as the "red-haired, bearded, one-eyed man-with-a-limp," *United States v. Grinnell Corp.*, 384 U.S. 563, 591 (1966) (FORTAS, J., dissenting), and perhaps even full names of defendants who are always known by a nickname. This Court has assumed, however, that nicknames and specific descriptions fall inside, not outside, *Bruton*'s protection. *See Harrington v. California*, 395 U.S. 250, 253 (1969) (assuming *Bruton* violation where confessions describe codefendant as the "white guy" and give a description of his age, height, weight, and hair color). The Solicitor General, although supporting Maryland in this case, concedes that this is appropriate.

That being so, *Richardson* must depend in significant part upon the kind of, not the simple fact of, inference. *Richardson*'s inferences involved statements that did not refer directly to the defendant himself and which became incriminating "only when linked with evidence introduced later at trial." The inferences at issue here involve statements that, despite redaction, obviously refer directly to someone, often obviously the defendant, and which involve inferences that a jury ordinarily could make immediately, even were the confession the very first item introduced at trial. Moreover, the redacted confession with the blank prominent on its face, in *Richardson*'s words, "facially incriminat[es]" the codefendant. Like the confession in *Bruton* itself, the accusation that the redacted confession makes "is more vivid than inferential incrimination, and hence more difficult to thrust out of mind." 481 U.S., at 208.

Nor are the policy reasons that *Richardson* provided in support of its conclusion applicable here. *Richardson* expressed concern lest application of *Bruton*'s rule apply where "redaction" of confessions, particularly "confessions incriminating by connection," would often "not [be] possible," thereby forcing prosecutors too often to abandon use either of the confession or of a joint trial. Additional redaction of a confession that uses a blank space, the word "delete," or a symbol, however, normally is possible. Consider as an example a portion of the confession before us: The witness who read the confession told the jury that the confession (among other things) said,

> "*Question:* Who was in the group that beat Stacey?
> "*Answer:* Me, deleted, deleted, and a few other guys."

Why could the witness not, instead, have said:

> "*Question:* Who was in the group that beat Stacey?
> "*Answer:* Me and a few other guys."

Richardson itself provides a similar example of this kind of redaction. The confession there at issue had been "redacted to omit all reference to respondent — indeed, to omit all indication that anyone other than Martin and Williams participated in the crime," and it did not indicate that it had been redacted. *But cf. post* (SCALIA, J., dissenting) (suggesting that the Court has "never before endorsed . . . the redaction of a statement by some means other than the deletion of certain words, with the fact of the deletion shown").

The *Richardson* Court also feared that the inclusion, within *Bruton*'s protective rule, of confessions that incriminated "by connection" too often would provoke mistrials, or would unnecessarily lead prosecutors to abandon the confession or joint trial, because neither the prosecutors nor the judge could easily predict, until after the introduction of all the evidence, whether or not *Bruton* had barred use of the confession. To include the use of blanks, the word "delete," symbols, or other indications of redaction, within *Bruton*'s protections, however, runs no such risk. Their use is easily identified prior to trial and does not depend, in any special way, upon the other evidence introduced in the case. We also note that several Circuits have interpreted *Bruton* similarly for many years, yet no one has told us of any significant practical difficulties arising out of their administration of that rule.

. . . The judgment of the Court of Appeals is vacated, and the case is remanded for further proceedings not inconsistent with this opinion. . . .

Justice SCALIA, with whom THE CHIEF JUSTICE, Justice KENNEDY, and Justice THOMAS join, dissenting.

. . . The almost invariable assumption of the law is that jurors follow their instructions. This rule "is a pragmatic one, rooted less in the absolute certitude that the presumption is true than in the belief that it represents a reasonable practical accommodation of the interests of the state and the defendant in the criminal justice process." *Richardson*. We have held, for example, that the state may introduce evidence of a defendant's prior convictions for the purpose of sentencing enhancement, or statements elicited from a defendant in violation of *Miranda v. Arizona*, 384 U.S. 436 (1966), for the purpose of impeachment, so long as the jury is instructed that such evidence may not be considered for the purpose of determining guilt. *Spencer v. Texas*, 385 U.S. 554 (1967); *Harris v. New York*, 401 U.S. 222 (1971). The same applies to code-fendant confessions: "a witness whose testimony is introduced at a joint trial is not considered to be a witness 'against' a defendant if the jury is instructed to consider that testimony only against a codefendant." *Richardson, supra.* In *Bruton*, we recognized a "narrow exception" to this rule: "We held that a defendant is deprived of his Sixth Amendment right of confrontation when the facially incriminating confession of a nontestifying codefendant is introduced at their joint trial, even if the jury is instructed to consider the confession only against the codefendant." 481 U.S., at 207. We declined in *Richardson*, however, to extend *Bruton* to confessions that incriminate only by inference from other evidence. When incrimination is inferential, "it is a less valid generalization that the jury will not likely obey the instruction to disregard the evidence." 481 U.S., at 208. Today the Court struggles to decide whether a confession redacted to omit the defendant's name is incriminating on its face or by inference. On the one hand, the Court "concede[s] that the jury must use inference to connect the statement in this redacted confession with the defendant," but later asserts, on the other hand, that "the redacted confession with the blank prominent on its face . . . 'facially incriminat[es].'" The Court should have stopped with its concession: the statement "Me, deleted, deleted, and a few other guys" does not facially incriminate anyone but the speaker. The Court's analogizing of "deleted" to a physical description that clearly identifies the defendant . . . does not survive scrutiny. By "facially incriminating," we have meant incriminating independent of other evidence introduced at trial. Since the defendant's appearance at counsel table is not evidence, the description "red-haired, bearded, one-eyed man-with-a-limp" would be facially incriminating — unless, of course, the defendant had dyed his hair black and shaved his beard before trial, and the prosecution introduced evidence concerning his former appearance. Similarly, the statement "Me, Kevin Gray, and a few other guys" would be facially incriminating, unless the defendant's name set forth in the indictment was not Kevin Gray, and evidence was introduced to the effect that he sometimes used "Kevin Gray" as an alias. By contrast, the person to whom "deleted" refers in "Me, deleted, deleted, and a few other guys" is not apparent from anything the jury knows independent of the evidence at trial. Though the jury may speculate, the statement expressly implicates no one but the speaker.

Of course the Court is correct that confessions redacted to omit the defendant's name are more likely to incriminate than confessions redacted to omit any reference to his existence. But it is also true — and more relevant here — that confessions redacted to omit the defendant's name are less likely to incriminate than confessions that expressly state it. The latter are "powerfully incriminating" as a class; the former are not so. Here, for instance, there were two names deleted, five or more participants in the crime, and only one other defendant on trial. The jury no doubt may "speculate about the reference," as it speculates when evidence connects a defendant to a confession that does not refer to his existence. The issue, however, is not whether the confession incriminated petitioner, but whether the incrimination is so "powerful" that we must depart from the normal presumption that the jury follows its instructions. I think it is not — and I am certain that drawing the line for departing from the ordinary rule at the facial identification of the defendant makes more sense than drawing it anywhere else.

The Court's extension of *Bruton* to name-redacted confessions "as a class" will seriously compromise "society's compelling interest in finding, convicting, and punishing those who violate the law." *Moran v. Burbine*, 475 U.S. 412, 426 (1986). We explained in *Richardson* that forgoing use of codefendant confessions or joint trials was "too high" a price to insure that juries never disregard their instructions. The Court minimizes the damage that it does by suggesting that "[a]dditional redaction of a confession that uses a blank space, the word 'delete,' or a symbol . . . normally is possible." In the present case, it asks, why could the police officer not have testified that Bell's answer was "Me and a few other guys"? The answer, it seems obvious to me, is because that is not what Bell said. Bell's answer was "Me, Tank, Kevin and a few other guys." Introducing the statement with full disclosure of deletions is one thing; introducing as the complete statement what was in fact only a part is something else. And of course even concealed deletions from the text will often not do the job that the Court demands. For inchoate offenses — conspiracy in particular — redaction to delete all reference to a confederate would often render the confession nonsensical. If the question was "Who agreed to beat Stacey?", and the answer was "Me and Kevin," we might redact the answer to "Me and [deleted]" or perhaps to "Me and somebody else," but surely not to just "Me" — for that would no longer be a confession to the conspiracy charge, but rather the foundation for an insanity defense. To my knowledge we have never before endorsed — and to my strong belief we ought not endorse — the redaction of a statement by some means other than the deletion of certain words, with the fact of the deletion shown. The risk to the integrity of our system (not to mention the increase in its complexity) posed by the approval of such free-lance editing seems to me infinitely greater than the risk posed by the entirely honest reproduction that the Court disapproves.

. . . For these reasons, I would affirm the judgment of the Court of Appeals of Maryland.

3. Spontaneous and Contemporaneous Statements

Unlike the admissions doctrine, most exceptions to the hearsay rule pertain to out-of-court statements that for one reason or another are thought particularly reliable. Most of these exceptions apply regardless of whether the declarant is also available to testify as a witness, and are codified in Federal Rule of Evidence 803. The first two exceptions listed in Rule 803 derive from common law decisions allowing the introduction of statements made contemporaneously with the events they describe; often the events had placed the declarant under some kind of emotional strain. There is a long-standing debate about whether it was chiefly the contemporaneity or the emotional strain that justified an exception to the hearsay rule. The Federal Rules of Evidence sidestep that debate by creating two separate exceptions, one tied to contemporaneity and one requiring emotional stress.

Many statements that fall within these exceptions may nonetheless be inadmissible against a criminal defendant under *Crawford v. Washington*.

[F.R.E. 803(1), (2); C.E.C. §§1240, 1241]

ADVISORY COMMITTEE NOTE TO F.R.E. 803

The exceptions are phrased in terms of nonapplication of the hearsay rule, rather than in positive terms of admissibility, in order to repel any implication that other possible grounds for exclusion are eliminated from consideration.

The present rule proceeds upon the theory that under appropriate circumstances a hearsay statement may possess circumstantial guarantees of trustworthiness sufficient to justify nonproduction of the declarant in person at the trial even though he may be available. The theory finds vast support in the many exceptions to the hearsay rule developed by the common law in which unavailability of the declarant is not a relevant factor. The present rule is a synthesis of them, with revision where modern developments and conditions are believed to make that course appropriate.

In a hearsay situation, the declarant is, of course, a witness, and neither this rule nor Rule 804 dispenses with the requirement of firsthand knowledge. It may appear from his statement or be inferable from circumstances. See Rule 602.

Exceptions (1) and (2). In considerable measure these two examples overlap, though based on somewhat different theories. The most significant practical difference will lie in the time lapse allowable between event and statement.

The underlying theory of Exception (1) is that substantial contemporaneity of event and statement negate the likelihood of deliberate or conscious misrepresentation. Moreover, if the witness is the declarant, he may be examined on the statement. If the witness is not the declarant, he may be examined as to the circumstances as an aid in evaluating the statement.

The theory of Exception (2) is simply that circumstances may produce a condition of excitement which temporarily stills the capacity of reflection and produces utterances free of conscious fabrication. Spontaneity is the key factor in each instance, though arrived at by somewhat different routes. Both are needed in order to avoid needless niggling.

While the theory of Exception (2) has been criticized on the ground that excitement impairs accuracy of observation as well as eliminating conscious fabrication, Hutchins and Slesinger, Some Observations on the Law of Evidence: Spontaneous Exclamations, 28 Colum. L. Rev. 432 (1928), it finds support in cases without number. See cases in 6 Wigmore §1750; Annot. 53 A.L.R.2d 1245 (statements as to cause of or responsibility for motor vehicle accident); Annot., 4 A.L.R.3d 149 (accusatory statements by homicide victims).

Since unexciting events are less likely to evoke comment, decisions involving Exception (1) are far less numerous. . . .

With respect to the *time element*, Exception (1) recognizes that in many, if not most, instances precise contemporaneity is not possible and hence a slight lapse is allowable. Under Exception (2) the standard of measurement is the duration of the state of excitement. "How long can excitement prevail? Obviously there are no pat answers and the character of the transaction or event will largely determine the significance of the time factor." Slough, Spontaneous Statements and State of Mind, 46 Iowa L. Rev. 224, 243 (1961). . . .

Participation by the declarant is not required: a non-participant may be moved to describe what he perceives, and one may be startled by an event in which he is not an actor. . . . Whether *proof of the startling event* may be made by the statement itself is largely an academic question, since in most cases there is present at least circumstantial evidence that something of a startling nature must have occurred . . . [e.g.,] the condition of the declarant (injuries, state of shock). . . . Nevertheless, on occasion the only evidence may be the content of the statement itself, and rulings that it may be sufficient are described as "increasing," Slough, supra at 246, and as the "prevailing practice," McCormick §272, p. 579. . . . Moreover, under Rule 104(a) the judge is not limited by the hearsay rule in passing upon preliminary questions of fact.

Proof of declarant's perception by his statement presents similar considerations when declarant is identified. However, when declarant is an unidentified bystander, the cases indicate hesitancy in upholding the statement alone as sufficient, a result which would under appropriate circumstances be consistent with the rule.

Permissible *subject matter* of the statement is limited under Exception (1) to description or explanation of the event or condition, the assumption being that spontaneity, in the absence of a starting event, may extend no farther. In Exception (2), however, the statement need only "relate" to the startling event or condition, thus affording a broader scope of subject matter coverage. . . . See Sanitary Grocery Co. v. Snead, 67 App. D.C. 129, 90 F.2d 374 (1937), slip-and-fall case sustaining admissibility of clerk's statement. "That has been on the floor for a couple of hours," and Murphy Auto Parts Co., Inc. v. Ball, 101 U.S. App. D.C. 416, 249 F.2d 508 (1957), upholding admission, on issue of driver's agency, of his statement that he had to call on a customer and was in a hurry to get home. . . .

UNITED STATES v. OBAYAGBONA

627 F. Supp. 329 (E.D.N.Y. 1985)

WEINSTEIN, Chief Judge:

[A jury found defendant Florence Obayagbona guilty of conspiring to sell heroin to an undercover FBI agent, Michael Turner. She moved to set aside the verdict, arguing that hearsay had been improperly introduced against her. Equipped with a hidden tape recorder and using the pseudonym "Joe," Turner had negotiated the purchase from another woman,

Clara Onaiwu, in the presence of Obayagbona and an informant who had introduced Turner to Onaiwu. Obayagbona wore a black-and-white dress; "Onaiwu was more colorfully attired." According to Turner's testimony at trial, Obayagbona took a sample of heroin out of her purse and handed it to him. Other agents then arrested both women, as well as Turner and the informant. Obayagbona testified she had nothing to do with the deal, and that Onaiwu gave the sample to Turner. Onaiwu, who pleaded guilty, corroborated Obayagbona's account.]

Agent Turner, "under arrest" for the sake of the scenario, was handcuffed and thus unable to touch the controls of his tape recorder. While the machine continued to record, his fellow agents asked about the heroin. . . . After the testimony of Onaiwu and the defendant, the government sought on rebuttal to introduce the tape of Agent Turner's statement made contemporaneously with the arrest: "The girl in the black and white handed it to me out of her purse." Over objection, the court allowed the tape to be played. According to a stipulation, "14 minutes and 25 seconds" elapsed between the receipt of the sample by Special Agent Turner and his taped statement. . . .

Under Rule 803(2), a statement "relating to a startling event or condition made while the declarant was under the stress of excitement caused by the event or condition" is not excluded by the hearsay rule. When a statement is offered as an excited utterance, the trial court must find two conditions: "First, there must be an occurrence or event sufficiently startling to render inoperative the normal reflective thought processes of an observer. Second, the statement of the declarant must have been a spontaneous reaction to the occurrence or event and not the result of reflective thought." McCormick, Evidence §297, at 85455 (Cleary, 3d ed. 1984). Under Rule 104(a) of the Federal Rules of Evidence, the trial court makes the determination as to the existence of excitement and the applicability of this exception.

Determination of excitement is facilitated by the recording. On tape Agent Turner's voice is exultant — he has just completed his job, a successful arrest has been made, and the pent-up tension of his performance in the role of "Joe" has just come to an abrupt end. Testimony, and Turner's recording, depict a quick and somewhat chaotic arrest that would continue the excitement of receiving and testing the sample. Such a situation engenders excitement. Listening to the tape, the court determined that there were valid psychological guarantees against fabrication. It is not likely that the witness was deliberately fabricating evidence. He was too excited to do so.

The fact that the excited witness was a law enforcement agent does not preclude admissibility under the excited utterance exception. Law officers are subject to strain and excitement, much like people in other walks of life.

Agent Turner's statement is admissible as well under Rule 803(1). It is a statement "describing or explaining an event or condition made while the declarant was perceiving the event or condition, or immediately thereafter." . . .

Illustrative of the Rule's application is *United States v. Andrews*, 765 F.2d 1491, 1500 (11th Cir. 1985). The government there introduced in rebuttal a tape that a police officer made, recording his impressions of what he saw while looking through the defendant's window. Defendant argued on appeal that this was self-serving hearsay recorded out of the presence of the defendant, and was repetition rather than rebuttal. Both the district and the appellate courts found that this recording fell within the exception for present sense impressions.

Although the *Andrews* statement was somewhat more contemporaneous than Turner's, similar circumstances create a similar guarantee of trustworthiness. Rule 803(1) provides that "immediately thereafter" must be close enough to allow an inference of spontaneity. The Advisory Committee's notes recognize that "precise contemporaneity" is often not possible. A few minutes' pause after the moment at which the statement could have been made is within the period contemplated in Rule 803(1).

Where a precisely contemporaneous declaration cannot be made, near contemporaneity fulfills the requirements of 803(1). Agent Turner spoke at his first opportunity. His declaration was as spontaneous as possible: there had elapsed only two minutes and 25 seconds after the arrest and less than 15 minutes after delivery of the sample. By its nature the statement could not have been made in the presence of Onaiwu or the defendant. It was repressed and then exploded almost as a reflex as soon as Agent Turner was free to speak. . . . The motion for a new trial or for a judgment of acquittal is denied.

PEOPLE v. CUMMINGS

31 N.Y.3d 204 (2018)

WILSON, J.

[Three men standing on a corner were shot by a gunman who escaped in a minivan. Several minutes later, one of the victims called 911.] About 20 seconds into the call, someone in the background can be faintly heard saying, "Yo, it was Twanek, man! It was Twanek, man!" . . . [Defendant Twanek Cummings was charged in connection with the shootings. During his] first trial, the People sought to admit the unidentified person's statement on the 911 call under the excited utterance exception to the hearsay rule. The court denied the application. The jury deadlocked, and the court declared a mistrial . . . [On retrial,] the court allowed admission of the statement as an excited utterance [and Cummings was found guilty of assault.]

Although hearsay, excited utterances may be admissible because, "as the impulsive and unreflecting responses of the declarant to the injury or other startling event, they possess a high degree of trustworthiness, and, as thus expressing the real tenor of said declarant's belief as to the facts *just observed by him*, may be received as testimony of those facts" (*People v. Caviness*, 38 N.Y.2d 227, 231 [1975] [emphasis added]). . . . The People are correct that lack of identification of the declarant does not make an excited utterance inadmissible per se, but facts must exist from which a reasonable trier of fact could infer that the declarant personally observed the incident. Here . . . [we cannot tell] whether the declarant personally observed the shooting or was passing on hearsay several times removed. . . . Because there is no evidence from which a reasonable inference can be drawn that the declarant personally observed the incident, admission of the statement heard in the background of the 911 call was error. . . . [Reversed.]

RIVERA, J. (concurring).

. . . [T]he excited utterance exception to the hearsay rule[,] . . . while longstanding, warrants serious reconsideration. . . . Legal scholars and jurists have questioned the continued vitality of this exception, in light of advances in psychology and neuroscience that demonstrate an individual's inability to accurately recall facts when experiencing trauma, and, in turn, to create falsehoods immediately. For example, the Seventh Circuit has stated that, "as with much of the folk psychology of evidence, it is difficult to take this rationale [that immediacy negates the likelihood of fabrication] entirely seriously, since people are entirely capable of spontaneous lies in emotional circumstances. Old and new studies agree that less than one second is required to fabricate a lie." (*Lust v. Sealy, Inc.*, 383 F.3d 580, 588 [7th Cir. 2004] [internal quotation marks and citation omitted]). . . . Science, fact, and common sense suggest that we should cabin, if not outright abandon, the exception. . . .

UNITED STATES v. ELEM

845 F.2d 170 (8th Cir. 1988)

McMILLIAN, Circuit Judge.

Appellant, Jimmy Dean Elem, appeals from the district court's judgment entered on a jury verdict convicting him for possession of a firearm by a convicted felon in violation of Title 18 U.S.C. app §1202(a)(1) (West Supp. 1984). . . . [A]ppellant challenges the district court's ruling upon the government's pre-trial *in limine* motion to exclude certain exculpatory statements made by the appellant to the police at the time he was taken into custody. Appellant, in response to a police question about whether the gun was his, answered, "No," and in response to a police inquiry about the flourishing of a weapon, appellant answered, "You won't be able to make that." Appellant now contends that these statements were admissible as a part of the *res gestae* or as excited utterances under Fed. R. Evid. 803(2). The district court disagreed and excluded both statements as impermissible hearsay.

The doctrine of *res gestae* has an undistinguished past. According to Wigmore, courts in general have reduced the term "*res gestae*" to a useless and misleading shibboleth by embracing within it two separate and distinct categories of verbal statements, one of which is truly an exception to the hearsay rule and the other of which is not, the two being admissible in evidence under different principles. 6 Wigmore, *Evidence* §1767, at 255 (Chadbourn rev. 1976). When the utterance of certain words constitutes or is part of the details of an act, occurrence or transaction which in itself is relevant and provable, the utterance may be proved as a verbal act, just as may be a visual observation of an event. This is not hearsay evidence; it is not admitted for the purpose of proving the truth of what was said, but for the purpose of describing the relevant details of what took place. . . .

The character of utterance that is admissible as a genuine exception to the hearsay rule, also under the customary label of "*res gestae*," is a spontaneous exclamation, which may or may not be exactly contemporaneous with the provable act or event. *Id.* §1745 *et seq.* . . . This type of statement is received in a testimonial capacity as evidence of the truth of the fact asserted.

> This general principle is based on the experience that, under certain external circumstances a physical shock, of stress of nervous excitement may be produced which stills the reflective faculties and removes their control, so that the utterance which then occurs is a spontaneous and sincere response to the actual sensations and perceptions already produced by the external shock. Since this utterance is made under the immediate and uncontrolled domination of the senses, and during the brief period when considerations of self-interest could not have been brought fully to bear by reasoned reflection, the utterance may be taken as particularly trustworthy (or at least as lacking the usual grounds of untrustworthiness), and thus as expressing the real tenor of the speaker's belief as to the facts just observed by him; and may therefore be received as testimony to those facts.

Id. §1747, at 195. . . .

In his brief appellant cites both prongs of what has been defined by courts as coming under the aegis of the *res gestae* doctrine, i.e., the verbal acts doctrine, and the excited utterance doctrine. Appellant seems to rely, however, not on the verbal acts doctrine but on the excited utterance doctrine. . . . [I]t is the excitement and the spontaneity that supply the indicia of trustworthiness and reliability which supports the admission of hearsay under this exception. Here we find nothing in the record to support appellant's contention that he was unduly excited so as to alter any of his conscious reflections. . . . [Conviction affirmed.]

GRAHAM C. LILLY, AN INTRODUCTION TO THE LAW OF EVIDENCE

§7.9, at 279 (3d ed. 1996)

The phrase "res gestae" still appears in judicial opinions despite widespread condemnation. A declaration is said to be admissible despite the hearsay rule if it constitutes a part of the "the thing done." Often, the term is used to signify the admission of a statement having independent legal significance (a "verbal act"), that is, a statement that is consequential simply because it was uttered and regardless of its truth. . . . [S]uch a statement is not hearsay and thus need not be entered under an exception. Unfortunately, the res gestae label is sometimes indiscriminately applied to hearsay declarations that fit within the exceptions of excited utterance, present sense impression, physical condition, or state of mind. . . . The imprecision of the term, coupled with careless usage by the courts, has been a source of perplexity for students and lawyers. Fortunately, the res gestae label continues to lose favor; the term is not included in the Federal Rules of Evidence or their counterpart, the Revised Uniform Rules of Evidence. Some lawyers may lament its omission. "If you wish to tender inadmissible evidence," Lord Blackburn reminds us, "say it is part of the res gestae." Tregarthen, The Law of Hearsay Evidence 21 (1915).

ROBERT M. HUTCHINS & DONALD SLESINGER, SOME OBSERVATIONS ON THE LAW OF EVIDENCE

28 Colum. L. Rev. 432, 437–439 (1928)

One need not be a psychologist to distrust an observation made under emotional stress; everyone accepts such statements with mental reservation. M. Gorphe cites the case of an excited witness to a horrible accident who erroneously declared that the coachman deliberately and vindictively ran down a helpless woman. Fiore tells of an emotionally upset man who testified that hundreds were killed in an accident; that he had seen their heads rolling from their bodies. In reality only one man was killed, and five others injured. . . .

That participants, as well as bystanders, have their perceptions clouded by strong emotions will not be doubted. When a carriage containing the inevitable psychologist upset, that worthy gentleman amused himself and his companions by taking depositions while they awaited assistance. He had no known reality to check their stories against, but it was obvious that if any one was right, all the rest were wrong. That even trained observers are fallible is well brought out in an editorial in the *New York World* in which several accounts of newspaper reports of the striking of Kerensky on his recent visit to America are printed. Though the reporters were all experts, and situated close to the platform, each told a different story of what must have been a fairly simple event.[1]

What emotion gains by way of overcoming the desire to lie, it loses by impairing the declarant's power of observation. . . . [A]ccording to this view, the best evidence of all is a statement made in immediate response to an external stimulus which produces no shock or nervous excitement whatever.

---

1. These are descriptions of the manner in which the young woman struck her blow:

WORLD: "Slashed him viciously across the cheek with her glove."
NEWS: "Struck him on the left cheek with the bouquet."
AMERICAN: "Dropped her flowers and slapped him in the face with her gloves."
TIMES: "Slapped his face vigorously with her gloves three times."
HERALD TRIBUNE: "Beat him on the face and head . . . a half-dozen blows."
EVENING WORLD: Struck him across the face "several times."
MIRROR: Struck him a single time.
POST: "Vigorously and accurately slapped him."

And this is what happened next:

AMERICAN: Kerensky "reeled back."
EVENING WORLD: "He stood unmoved."
NEWS: "He stepped back, maintaining a calm pose."
WORLD: He stood still, but used his arms to "wave back his friends."
HERALD Tribune: He stood still, with his arms "thrown back."
JOURNAL: "He reeled."
POST: "He remained unmoved."
MIRROR: "He reeled from the blow. His supporters were stemmed by a handful of royalists. Fists flew; noses ran red; shirts and collars were torn."

JON R. WALTZ, THE PRESENT-SENSE IMPRESSION EXCEPTION TO THE RULE AGAINST HEARSAY: ORIGINS AND ATTRIBUTES

66 Iowa L. Rev. 869, 875 (1981)

It was Dean Wigmore, in the 1904 edition of his evidence treatise, who argued that contemporaneousness of event and descriptive statement, without more, was an insufficient guarantor of trustworthiness. He substituted as the essential ingredient a spontaneity born of shock or excitement induced by the perceived event or condition. In typically imperial terms, Wigmore ... assert[ed] that "[t]o admit hearsay simply because it was uttered at the time something else was going on is to introduce an arbitrary and unreasoned test and to remove all limits of principle. . . ." Such was the impact of Wigmore's treatise on bench and bar that for most of this century the debatable exception for excited utterances has enjoyed at least grudging acceptance while the arguably more defensible exception for calm, contemporaneous observations languished.

PROBLEMS

3.35. *United States v. Obayagbona* and *United States v. Elem* were decided before the United States Supreme Court reinterpreted the Confrontation Clause in *Crawford v. Washington*. Would *Crawford* and its progeny change the result in either case?

3.36. Pauline sues Devon for damages caused when their cars collided. Devon's wife, Wilma, was a passenger in Devon's car at the time of the accident. Pauline seeks to testify that, immediately following the accident, Wilma told her in a state of great agitation that Devon had "been sleeping terribly all week long." Does the hearsay rule prohibit this testimony?

3.37. Dumbarton is charged with murdering Vasquez. The prosecution seeks to have a witness testify that she spoke with Vasquez by telephone on the night he died, and that he ended the conversation by saying, "Oh, there's the door. It must be Dumbarton. Talk to you later." The defense objects on grounds of hearsay and confrontation. How should the judge rule?

4. State of Mind

[F.R.E. 803(3); C.E.C. §§1250–1252, 1260]

a. Generally

When an out-of-court statement is used as circumstantial proof of the declarant's state of mind, the hearsay rule is not implicated, because the statement is not offered to prove the truth of what it asserts. Think of the children yelling "Barney, Barney, Barney!" in *Lyons Partnership v. Morris Costumes, Inc.* or the defendant in *United States v. Parry* telling his mother that he was working with a narcotics agent. But sometimes a statement *explicitly* describes the speaker's state of mind: "Hey, I think that's Barney!" or "I think she's an undercover cop," or "I hate him." Statements of this kind seem to qualify as hearsay when used to prove what the declarants believed, knew, or felt. But they fall within a longstanding exception for statements describing the declarant's state of mind.

ADVISORY COMMITTEE NOTE TO F.R.E. 803(3)

Exception (3) This is essentially a specialized application of Exception (1), presented separately to enhance its usefulness and accessibility. See McCormick §§265, 268. . . .

UNITED STATES v. HARRIS

733 F.2d 994 (2d Cir. 1984)

GEORGE C. PRATT, Circuit Judge:

George Harris and Angelo Mamone appeal from judgments entered on jury verdicts . . . convicting them of conspiracy to distribute heroin . . . and attempting to possess heroin with the intent to distribute in violation. . . .

The prosecution of Harris and Mamone was largely the product of an arrangement between the government and one Mahlon Steward, a narcotics dealer with a lengthy criminal record, who agreed to act as an informant and undercover operative for the federal Drug Enforcement Administration (DEA) following his most recent arrest in May 1981. Posing as a prospective heroin purchaser, Steward led the DEA to Harris, who, in turn, eventually led the DEA to Mamone. . . . The government built its case around the testimony of Steward and tape recordings of telephone conversations that Steward initiated with Harris. . . . [T]he defense sought to portray Harris's conversations with Steward as "an eventually doomed and misguided attempt to maintain his parole status without jeopardizing his life." The defense thus attempted to establish that Harris knew Steward was an informant and only played along with him out of fear of what would happen to him if he refused. . . .

[C]ounsel for Harris proposed at the completion of the government's case to call Rafael Hernandez, Harris's parole officer from Detroit, as his first defense witness. According to Harris's written offer of proof, submitted at the request of the district judge: [Hernandez would testify that] "during the period of time of the time charged in the Indictment, George Harris expressed to Rafael Hernandez that the Government and people were after him and trying to set him up." . . .

After hearing brief argument, the district judge excluded this proffer, reasoning that "[i]t is plainly blatantly hearsay, unreliable and self-serving." When counsel for Harris then made an oral offer of proof with respect to similar proposed testimony by Ira Auslander, Harris's Detroit counsel, the district judge ruled "I would exclude that on the same ground. . . . If I am wrong, I am sure the Second Circuit knows their cases." . . .

Because of the manner in which these matters were handled, it is not clear precisely how either of these witnesses would have testified. Though both witnesses were present at trial, the district judge made his rulings without first requiring a *voir dire* of either witness. . . . [W]e are left with only the written offer of proof of the parole officer, quoted above, which is susceptible to varying interpretations, particularly as to time, and defense counsel's oral representations that Harris's Detroit attorney would testify "that exactly around the time of the Super Bowl . . . Mr. Harris told him that Mr. Steward had brought an agent to him, that he believed he brought an agent to him."

Taking these offers of proof at face value, as unfortunately we must on this record, we believe the district judge erred in excluding the proffered testimony as hearsay. Depending on the precise phraseology used by each witness, their testimony would have been admissible either as nonhearsay, or under the then existing state of mind hearsay exception. To the extent that Harris told either witness that he had "an encounter with some people who could cause him trouble"; that "the Government and people were after him and trying to set him up"; that "the Government was trying to set him up" (written offer of proof of Rafael Hernandez); and/or that "Mr. Steward had brought an agent to him" (oral offer of proof of attorney Auslander), the district judge erred in characterizing these statements as hearsay under Fed. R. Evid. 801(c). These statements were admissible, not for their truth, but instead as circumstantial evidence of Harris's state of mind — his knowledge of Steward's cooperation. On the other hand, to the extent that Harris told either his parole officer or attorney "that he *believed* [Steward] brought an agent to him" (emphasis added) (oral offer of proof of attorney Auslander), this statement would indeed have been hearsay under Fed. R. Evid. 801(c), since its evidentiary significance depended on the truth of the matter asserted — Harris's belief. However, such a "statement of the declarant's then existing state of mind" should have been admitted as a hearsay exception under Fed. R. Evid. 803(3). *See United States v. DiMaria,* 727 F.2d 265 at 271 (2d Cir. 1984) (citing cases). . . .

The government's attempt to avoid these conclusions is unpersuasive. The government . . . suggests that "[r]ather than focusing on academic analyses intent on rigid classification, it would be more profitable to analyze the probative value of the statement and to examine the dangers stemming from its admission in light of other factors." The "other factor" the government deems most significant is whether "the circumstances indicate plainly a motive to deceive." . . .

As Judge Friendly observed [in *DiMaria*]:

> It is doubtless true that all the hearsay exceptions in Rules 803 and 804 rest on a belief that declarations of the sort there described have "some particular assurance of credibility." . . . But the scheme of the Rules is to determine that issue by categories; if a declaration comes within a category defined as an exception, the declaration is admissible without any preliminary finding of probable credibility by the judge, save for the "catch-all" exceptions of Rules 803(24) and 804(b)(5) and the business records exception of Rule 803(6) ("unless the source of

information or the method or circumstance of preparation indicate lack of trustworthiness"). As Judge Weinstein has stated, "the scheme adopted for the hearsay article in the federal rules is that of a system of class exceptions coupled with an open-ended provision in Rules 803(24) and 804(b)(5), and with the exemption of certain prior statements from the definition of hearsay" . . . , even though this excludes certain hearsay statements with a high degree of trustworthiness and admits certain statements with a low one. This evil was doubtless thought preferable to requiring preliminary determinations of the judge with respect to trustworthiness, with attendant possibilities of delay, prejudgment and encroachment on the province of the jury. (Citations omitted.)

. . . [Reversed.]

b. The *Hillmon* Doctrine

Over a century ago, in the most famous hearsay case in American history, the Supreme Court extended the state-of-mind exception to statements of intent offered to prove that the declarants actually did what they said they would. Modern evidence codes retain this rule, although controversy continues over its justification and proper scope.

MUTUAL LIFE INS. CO. v. HILLMON
145 U.S. 285 (1892)

On July 13, 1880, Sallie E. Hillmon, a citizen of Kansas, brought an action against the Mutual Life Insurance Company, a corporation of New York, on a policy of insurance, dated December 10, 1878, on the life of her husband, John W. Hillmon, in the sum of $10,000, payable to her within 60 days after notice and proof of his death. On the same day the plaintiff brought two other actions,—the one against the New York Life Insurance Company, a corporation of New York, on two similar policies of life insurance, dated, respectively, November 30, 1878, and December 10, 1878, for the sum of $5,000 each; and the other against the Connecticut Mutual Life Insurance Company, a corporation of Connecticut, on a similar policy, dated March 4, 1879, for the sum of $5,000.

In each case the declaration alleged that Hillmon died on March 17, 1879, during the continuance of the policy, but that the defendant, though duly notified of the fact, had refused to pay the amount of the policy, or any part thereof; and the answer denied the death of Hillmon, and alleged that he, together with John H. Brown and divers other persons, on or before November 30, 1878, conspiring to defraud the defendant, procured the issue of all the policies, and afterwards, in March and April, 1879, falsely pretended and represented that Hillmon was dead, and that a dead body which they had procured was his, whereas in reality he was alive and in hiding.

. . . On February 29, 1888, after two trials at which the jury had disagreed, the three cases on for trial, under the [trial court's] order of consolidation. . . . [P]laintiff introduced evidence tending to show that on or about

March 5, 1879, Hillmon and Brown left Wichita, in the state of Kansas, and traveled together through southern Kansas in search of a site for a cattle ranch; that on the night of March 18th, while they were in camp at a place called "Crooked Creek," Hillmon was killed by the accidental discharge of a gun; that Brown at once notified persons living in the neighborhood, and that the body was thereupon taken to a neighboring town, where, after an inquest, it was buried. The defendants introduced evidence tending to show that the body found in the camp at Crooked Creek on the night of March 18th was not the body of Hillmon, but was the body of one Frederick Adolph Walters. Upon the question whose body this was there was much conflicting evidence, including photographs and descriptions of the corpse, and of the marks and scars upon it, and testimony to its likeness to Hillmon and to Walters.

The defendants introduced testimony that Walters left his home at Ft. Madison, in the state of Iowa, in March, 1878, and was afterwards in Kansas in 1878, and in January and February, 1879; that during that time his family frequently received letters from him, the last of which was written from Wichita; and that he had not been heard from since March, 1879. The defendants also offered the following evidence:

Elizabeth Rieffenach testified that she was a sister of Frederick Adolph Walters, and lived at Ft. Madison; and thereupon, as shown by the bill of exceptions, the following proceedings took place:

> "Witness further testified that she had received a letter written from Wichita, Kansas, about the 4th or 5th day of March, 1879, by her brother Frederick Adolph; that the letter was dated at Wichita, and was in the handwriting of her brother; that she had searched for the letter, but could not find the same, it being lost; that she remembered and could state the contents of the letter.
>
> "Thereupon the defendants' counsel asked the question, 'State the contents of that letter;' to which the plaintiff objected, on the ground that the same is incompetent, irrelevant, and hearsay. The objection was sustained, and the defendants duly excepted. The following is the letter as stated by witness:
>
> "Wichita, Kansas, March 4th or 5th or 3d or 4th, — I don't know, — 1879. Dear Sister and All: I now in my usual style drop you a few lines to let you know that I expect to leave Wichita on or about March the 5th with a certain Mr. Hillmon, a sheep trader, for Colorado, or parts unknown to me. I expect to see the country now. News are of no interest to you, as you are not acquainted here. I will close with compliments to all inquiring friends. Love to all. I am truly your brother, FRED ADOLPH WALTERS."

Alvina D. Kasten testified that she was 21 years of age, and resided in Ft. Madison; that she was engaged to be married to Frederick Adolph Walters; that she last saw him on March 24, 1878, at Ft. Madison; that he left there at that time, and had not returned; that she corresponded regularly with him, and received a letter about every two weeks until March 3, 1879, which was the last time she received a letter from him; that this letter was dated at Wichita, March 1, 1879, and was addressed to her at Ft. Madison, and the envelope was postmarked "Wichita, Kansas, March 2, 1879"; and that she had never heard from or seen him since that time.

The defendants put in evidence the envelope with the postmark and address, and thereupon offered to read the letter in evidence. The plaintiff objected to the reading of the letter. The court sustained the objection, and the defendants excepted.

This letter was dated "Wichita, March 1, 1879," was signed by Walters, and began as follows:

"Dearest Alvina: Your kind and ever welcome letter was received yesterday afternoon about an hour before I left Emporia. I will stay here until the fore part of next week, and then will leave here to see a part of the country that I never expected to see when I left home, as I am going with a man by the name of Hillmon, who intends to start a sheep ranch, and, as he promised me more wages than I could make at anything else, I concluded to take it, for a while at least, until I strike something better. There is so many folks in this country that have got the Leadville fever, and if I could not of got the situation that I have now I would have went there myself; but as it is at present I get to see the best portion of Kansas, Indian Territory, Colorado, and Mexico. The route that we intend to take would cost a man to travel from $150 to $200, but it will not cost me a cent; besides, I get good wages. I will drop you a letter occasionally until I get settled down. Then I want you to answer it."

... The jury, being instructed by the court to return a separate verdict in each case, returned verdicts for the plaintiff against the three defendants respectively for the amounts of their policies and interest, upon which separate judgments were rendered. The defendants sued out four writs of error, one jointly in the three cases as consolidated, and one in each case separately.

Mr. Justice GRAY, after stating the case as above, delivered the opinion of the court.

[The judgments are reversed because the trial court allowed each of the three defendants to exercise only one peremptory challenge during jury selection. By statute, each defendant was entitled to three peremptory challenges.]

... There is, however, one question of evidence so important, so fully argued at the bar, and so likely to arise upon another trial, that it is proper to express an opinion upon it.

This question is of the admissibility of the letters written by Walters on the first days of March, 1879, which were offered in evidence by the defendants, and excluded by the court.... The position taken at the bar that the letters were competent evidence ... as memoranda made in the ordinary course of business, cannot be maintained, for they were clearly not such.

But upon another ground suggested they should have been admitted. A man's state of mind or feeling can only be manifested to others by countenance, attitude, or gesture, or by sounds or words, spoken or written. The nature of the fact to be proved is the same, and evidence of its proper tokens is equally competent to prove it, whether expressed by aspect or conduct, by voice or pen....

The existence of a particular intention in a certain person at a certain time being a material fact to be proved, evidence that he expressed that intention at that time is as direct evidence of the fact as his own testimony that he then had that intention would be. After his death there can hardly be any other way of proving it, and while he is still alive his own memory of his state of mind at a former time is no more likely to be clear and true than a bystander's recollection of what he then said, and is less trustworthy than letters written by him at the very time and under circumstances precluding a suspicion of misrepresentation.

The letters in question were competent not as narratives of facts communicated to the writer by others, nor yet as proof that he actually went away from Wichita, but as evidence that, shortly before the time when other evidence tended to show that he went away, he had the intention of going, and of going with Hillmon, which made it more probable both that he did go and that he went with Hillmon than if there had been no proof of such intention. In view of the mass of conflicting testimony introduced upon the question whether it was the body of Walters that was found in Hillmon's camp, this evidence might properly influence the jury in determining that question.

The rule applicable to this case has been thus stated by this court: "Wherever the bodily or mental feelings of an individual are material to be proved, the usual expressions of such feelings are original and competent evidence. Those expressions are the natural reflexes of what it might be impossible to show by other testimony. If there be such other testimony, this may be necessary to set the facts thus developed in their true light, and to give them their proper effect. As independent, explanatory, or corroborative evidence it is often indispensable to the due administration of justice. Such declarations are regarded as verbal acts, and are as competent as any other testimony, when relevant to the issue. Their truth or falsity is an inquiry for the jury." *Insurance Co. v. Mosley*, 8 Wall. 397, 404, 405.

. . . Upon principle and authority, therefore, we are of opinion that the two letters were competent evidence of the intention of Walters at the time of writing them, which was a material fact bearing upon the question in controversy; and that for the exclusion of these letters, as well as for the undue restriction of the defendants' challenges, the verdicts must be set aside, and a new trial had. . . .

Judgment reversed, and case remanded to the circuit court, with directions to set aside the verdict and to order a new trial.

BROOKS W. MacCRACKEN, THE CASE OF THE ANONYMOUS CORPSE

Am. Heritage, June 1968, at 51, 75–77

[T]he insurance-company attorneys apparently presented no sound theory by which the Walters letters could have been held admissible, and we are told that the point was "miserably argued." Nevertheless, the Supreme Court justices voted unanimously to decide in favor of the insurance companies on general principles. . . . The preparation of the Supreme Court's opinion was assigned to Justice Horace Gray, who could be relied upon to find a precedent for the decision if anyone could do so. He was the most learned and resourceful member of the court — a Harvard graduate, former chief justice of Massachusetts, an heir to wealth, and a thorough Bostonian. Typically, his opinions were larded with judicial citations and legal principles. Yet we are reliably told that even he was in "dense darkness" about how to justify the admission of Walters' letters, until a suggestion came from his young legal secretary's father, James Bradley Thayer, professor of evidence at Harvard Law School. Together Justice Gray and Thayer brought forth a new legal theory and adorned it with their authority. . . . [N]o court would have allowed Walters' letter to be admitted in evidence if he had written his sweetheart saying, "I have left Wichita with Hillmon the sheep trader." Such a letter would indisputably have been hearsay. But the learned professor suggested that there was a logical difference between a hearsay account of a past fact and Walters' personal expression of his then present intent; the Supreme Court agreed. . . .

[N]o one ever found Hillmon. Walters never showed up either. . . . Between 1892 and 1897 two more trials were held (the fourth and fifth of the series) and two more juries disagreed. . . . By this time New York Life . . . thought it wise to settle with Sallie Hillmon, but . . . Mutual Life and Connecticut Mutual continued to contest the case. [The sixth trial resulted in a verdict for the plaintiff, but was reversed on evidentiary grounds by the Supreme Court in 1903.] A seventh trial was then too much to contemplate even for the parties themselves; and a settlement with the last of the insurance companies was finally reached. (Counting accumulated interest, the "widow" eventually received a total of $35,700 from the three companies.) She had been for some years happily remarried, with no apparent apprehensions of bigamy. . . . The truth in the Hillmon case is as debatable today as it was when it began.

ROBERT A. DYKSTRA, SALLIE HILLMON AND THE BIZARRE ORIGINS OF THE *HILLMON* RULE

97 Judicature 297 (2014) (reviewing Marianne Wesson, A Death at Crooked Creek: The Case of the Cowboy, the Cigarmaker, and the Love Letter (2013))

[Marianne Wesson, a professor of evidence law at the University of Colorado and also a crime novelist, spent years investigating the *Hillmon* case.] Professor Wesson came to believe that the [Dearest Alvina] letter was a fraud, penned by Frederick Walters, true enough, but dictated by W. H. Buchan, an insurance company attorney. In return, Walters was promised a monthly salary for the rest of his life, so long as he disappeared, never revealed his true identity, and kept Buchan informed of his address. "It could have happened that way," writes Wesson. "The longer I think about it, the more I believe it must have happened that way, more or less."

And what about the body in the grave? . . . Wesson . . . located a Hillmon descendent living in Montana, who agreed to contribute his DNA, and in 2006 she received permission to have the body exhumed by Professor Dennis Van Gerven, an anthropologist from Boulder, aided by a few graduate students. Alas, the bones had been so scoured by ground water over the years that the extraction of useful DNA proved impossible.

But Wesson had one more string to her bow. Three years earlier, at the National Archives branch in Kansas City, she had discovered in the Supreme Court files for Hillmon a trove of seven photographs: two studio portraits of Frederick Walters, three of John Hillmon, and — most importantly — two (front and profile) of the corpse briefly displayed at Lawrence in 1879.

Ingenious photoshop work by Van Gerven, superimposing the corpse's facial profile against the facial frontal view of Walters, then of Hillmon, effectively demonstrated that the corpse could not have been Walters. In the absence of any other candidates, it must have been John Hillmon, just as the determined Sallie had maintained for so many years.

SHEPARD v. UNITED STATES

290 U.S. 96 (1933)

Mr. Justice CARDOZO delivered the opinion of the Court.

The petitioner, Charles A. Shepard, a major in the medical corps of the United States Army, has been convicted of the murder of his wife, Zenana Shepard, at Fort Riley, Kan., a United States military reservation. The jury having qualified their verdict by adding thereto the words "without capital punishment" (18 U.S.C. §567), the defendant was sentenced to imprisonment for life. The judgment of the United States District Court has been affirmed by the Circuit Court of Appeals for the Tenth Circuit, one of the judges of that court dissenting. A writ of certiorari brings the case here.

The crime is charged to have been committed by poisoning the victim with bichloride of mercury. The defendant was in love with another woman, and wished to make her his wife. There is circumstantial evidence to sustain a finding by the jury that to win himself his freedom he turned to poison and murder. Even so, guilt was contested, and conflicting inferences are possible. The defendant asks us to hold that by the acceptance of incompetent evidence the scales were weighted to his prejudice and in the end to his undoing.

The evidence complained of was offered by the government in rebuttal when the trial was nearly over. On May 22, 1929, there was a conversation in the absence of the defendant between Mrs. Shepard, then ill in bed, and Clara Brown, her nurse. The patient asked the nurse to go to the closet in the defendant's room and bring a bottle of whisky that would be found upon a shelf. When the bottle was produced, she said that this was the liquor she had taken just before collapsing. She asked whether enough was left to make a test for the presence of poison, insisting that the smell and taste were strange. And then she added the words, "Dr. Shepard has poisoned me."

The conversation was proved twice. After the first proof of it, the government asked to strike it out, being doubtful of its competence, and this request was granted. A little later, however, the offer was renewed; the nurse having then testified to statements by Mrs. Shepard as to the prospect of recovery. "She said she was not going to get well; she was going to die." With the aid of this new evidence, the conversation already summarized was proved a second time. There was a timely challenge of the ruling.

She said, "Dr. Shepard has poisoned me." The admission of this declaration, if erroneous, was more than unsubstantial error. As to that the parties are agreed. The voice of the dead wife was heard in accusation of her husband, and the accusation was accepted as evidence of guilt. If the evidence was incompetent, the verdict may not stand. . . .

Witnesses for the defendant had testified to declarations by Mrs. Shepard which suggested a mind bent upon suicide, or at any rate were thought by the defendant to carry that suggestion. More than once before her illness she had stated in the hearing of these witnesses that she had no wish to live, and had nothing to live for, and on one occasion she added that she expected some day to make an end to her life.... This testimony opened the door, so it is argued, to declarations in rebuttal that she had been poisoned by her husband. They were admissible, in that view, not as evidence of the truth of what was said, but as betokening a state of mind inconsistent with the presence of suicidal intent.

The testimony was neither offered nor received for the strained and narrow purpose now suggested as legitimate.... Aside, however, from this objection, the accusatory declaration must have been rejected as evidence of a state of mind, though the purpose thus to limit it had been brought to light upon the trial. The defendant had tried to show by Mrs. Shepard's declarations to her friends that she had exhibited a weariness of life and a readiness to end it, the testimony giving plausibility to the hypothesis of suicide. Wigmore, §1726; *Commonwealth v. Trefethen*, 157 Mass. 180, 31 N.E. 961. By the proof of these declarations evincing an unhappy state of mind, the defendant opened the door to the offer by the government of declarations evincing a different state of mind, declarations consistent with the persistence of a will to live. The defendant would have no grievance if the testimony in rebuttal had been narrowed to that point. What the government put in evidence, however, was something very different. It did not use the declarations by Mrs. Shepard to prove her present thoughts and feelings, or even her thoughts and feelings in times past. It used the declarations as proof of an act committed by some one else, as evidence that she was dying of poison given by her husband. This fact, if fact it was, the government was free to prove, but not by hearsay declarations. It will not do to say that the jury might accept the declarations for any light that they cast upon the existence of a vital urge, and reject them to the extent that they charged the death to some one else. Discrimination so subtle is a feat beyond the compass of ordinary minds. The reverberating clang of those accusatory words would drown all weaker sounds. It is for ordinary minds, and not for psychoanalysts, that our rules of evidence are framed. They have their source very often in considerations of administrative convenience, of practical expediency, and not in rules of logic. When the risk of confusion is so great as to upset the balance of advantage, the evidence goes out. Thayer, Preliminary Treatise on the Law of Evidence, 266, 516; Wigmore, Evidence, §§1421, 1422, 1714.

These precepts of caution are a guide to judgment here. There are times when a state of mind, if relevant, may be proved by contemporaneous declarations of feeling or intent. *Mutual Life Ins. Co. v. Hillmon*, 145 U.S. 285, 295; *Shailer v. Bumstead*, 99 Mass. 112; Wigmore, §§1725, 1726, 1730. Thus, in proceedings for the probate of a will, where the issue is undue influence, the declarations of a testator are competent to prove his feelings for his relatives, but are incompetent as evidence of his conduct or of theirs. *Throckmorton v. Holt*, 180 U.S. 552, 571, 572, 573: *Waterman v. Whitney*, 11 N.Y. 157, 62 Am. Dec. 71; *Matter of Kennedy*, 167 N.Y. 163, 172, 60 N.E. 442. In suits for the alienation of affections, letters passing between the spouses are admissible in aid of a like purpose. Wigmore, §1730; *Ash v. Prunier (C.C.A.)*, 105 F. 722; *Mutual Life Ins. Co. v. Hillmon, supra*, page 297; *Jameson v. Tully*, 178 Cal. 380, 173 P. 577; *Cottle v. Johnson*, 179 N.C. 426, 102 S.E. 769; *Curtis v. Miller*, 269 Pa. 509, 512, 112 A. 747. In damage suits for personal injuries, declarations by the patient to bystanders or physicians are evidence of sufferings or symptoms (Wigmore, §§1718, 1719), but are not received to prove the acts, the external circumstances, through which the injuries came about. Wigmore, §1722; *Amys v. Barton*, (1912) 1 K.B. 40; *Chicago & A.R.R. Co. v. Industrial Board*, 274 Ill. 336, 113 N.E. 629; *Peoria Cordage Co. v. Industrial Board*, 284 Ill. 90, 119 N.E. 996; *Larrabee's Case*, 120 Me. 242, 113 A. 268; *Maine v. Maryland Casualty Co.*, 172 Wis. 350, 178 N.W. 749. Even statements of past sufferings or symptoms are generally excluded (Wigmore, §1722(b); *Cashin v. New York, N.H. & H.R.R. Co.*, 185 Mass. 543, 70 N.E. 930), though an exception is at times allowed when they are made to a physician (*Roosa v. Loan Co.*, 132 Mass. 439, 440; *Cleveland, C., C. & I.R. Co. v. Newell*, 104 Ind. 264, 271, 3 N.E. 836; *contra, Davidson v. Cornell*, 132 N.Y. 228, 237, 30 N.E. 573). So also in suits upon insurance policies, declarations by an insured that he intends to go upon a journey with another may be evidence of a state of mind lending probability to the conclusion that the purpose was fulfilled. *Mutual Life Ins. Co. v. Hillmon, supra*. The ruling in that case marks the high-water line beyond which courts have been unwilling to go. It has developed a substantial body of criticism and commentary.[2] Declarations of intention, casting light upon the future, have been sharply distinguished from declarations of memory, pointing backwards to the past. There would be an end, or nearly that, to the rule against hearsay if the distinction were ignored.

The testimony now questioned faced backward and not forward. This at least it did in its most obvious implications. What is even more important, it spoke to a past act, and, more than that, to an act by some one not the speaker. Other tendency, if it had any, was a filament too fine to be disentangled by a jury.

The judgment should be reversed and the cause remanded to the District Court for further proceedings in accordance with this opinion.

ADVISORY COMMITTEE NOTE TO F.R.E. 803(3)

... The exclusion of "statements of memory or belief to prove the fact remembered or believed" is necessary to avoid the virtual destruction of the hearsay rule which would otherwise result from allowing state of mind, provable by a hearsay statement, to serve as the basis for an inference of the happening of the event which produced the state of mind. Shepard v. United States, 290 U.S. 96 (1933); Maguire, The Hillmon Case —Thirty-Three Years After, 38 Harv. L. Rev. 709, 719-731 (1925); Hinton, States of Mind and the Hearsay Rule, 1 U. Chi. L. Rev. 394, 421–423 (1934). The rule of Mutual Life Ins.

---

2. Maguire, *The Hillmon Case*, 38 Harvard Law Review, 709, 721, 727; Seligman, *An Exception to the Hearsay Rule*, 26 Harvard Law Review, 146; Chafee, *Review of Wigmore's Treatise*, 37 Harvard Law Review, 513, 519.

Co. v. Hillmon, 145 U.S. 285 (1892), allowing evidence of intention as tending to prove the doing of the act intended, is, of course, left undisturbed.

The carving out, from the exclusion mentioned in the preceding paragraph, of declarations relating to the execution, revocation, identification, or terms of declarant's will represents an ad hoc judgment which finds ample reinforcement in the decisions, resting on practical grounds of necessity and expediency rather than logic. McCormick §271, pp. 577–578; Annot. 34 A.L.R.2d 588, 62 A.L.R.2d 855. A similar recognition of the need for and practical value of this kind of evidence is found in California Evidence Code §1260.

REPORT OF THE HOUSE JUDICIARY COMMITTEE

Rule 803(3) was approved in the form submitted by the Court to Congress. However, the Committee intends that the Rule be construed to limit the doctrine of Mutual Life Insurance Co. v. Hillmon, 145 U.S. 285, 295–300 (1892), so as to render statements of intent by a declarant admissible only to prove his future conduct, not the future conduct of another person.

UNITED STATES v. HOULIHAN

871 F. Supp. 1495 (D. Mass. 1994)

YOUNG, District Judge.

In the early morning hours of Monday, March 2, 1992, James Boyden Jr. was found dead in the vicinity of Spice Street, Charlestown. He had been shot in the back of the head. . . . As he was leaving [his sister's apartment the previous evening], he allegedly told his sister that he was going out "to meet Billy Herd." [Herd and others were charged with Boyden's murder and related offenses.]

As the trial unfolded, the government . . . [sought] to admit the statement of James Boyden Jr. to his sister that he intended to meet Herd as relevant circumstantial evidence that it was Herd who killed him later that evening. The government argued that this statement is admissible because it constitutes a statement of a then existing mental or emotional condition under Federal Rule of Evidence 803(3). Over objection, the Court admitted the statement and Marie Boyden Connors was allowed so to testify. This memorandum explains the Court's reasoning.

This case presents an issue of first impression in the First Circuit, namely, whether the out-of-court statement of a victim-declarant of an intention to meet with a defendant on the evening of the victim's murder can be admitted at trial as circumstantial evidence of the meeting. . . . Prior to the adoption of the Federal Rules of Evidence, the Supreme Court addressed this issue in the famous case of *Mutual Life Insurance Co. of New York v. Hillmon*, 145 U.S. 285 (1892). In *Hillmon*, an insurance company sought to introduce out-of-court statements by a declarant, Walters, that he intended to travel with the insured, Hillmon. The hearsay statement was used as the principal proof that Hillmon had actually traveled with Walters. . . . Thus, under *Hillmon*, out-of-court statements of a declarant are admissible to prove the subsequent conduct of others. . . . The question for this Court, then, is whether in enacting Rule 803(3) Congress codified in full the reasoning of *Hillmon*, or whether it sought to limit the case's application. . . .

Unfortunately, the legislative history of Rule 803(3) only serves to obfuscate the analysis. While the Advisory Committee's Note to Rule 803(3) states that "the rule of *Mutual Life Insurance Co. v. Hillmon*, allowing evidence of intention as tending to prove the doing of the act intended, is, of course, left undisturbed," the Report of the House Judiciary Committee states that "the committee intends that the rule be construed to limit the doctrine of *Mutual Life Insurance Co. v. Hillmon*, so as to render statements of intent by a declarant admissible only to prove his future conduct, not the future conduct of another person." The Senate Report and the Conference Report are silent on this point.

Courts that have had the opportunity to consider the application of Rule 803(3) are divided. . . . Some courts have held that a declarant's statement of intent may be admitted against a non-declarant only when there is independent evidence connecting the declarant's statement with the non-declarant's conduct. *See United States v. Jenkins*, 579 F.2d 840, 842–43 (4th Cir.), *cert. denied*, 439 U.S. 967 (1978) (declarant's statement of intent is not admissible to prove subsequent conduct of third party, but is admissible to prove why third party acted as he did where there exists independent evidence that third party did in fact engage in the alleged conduct).

Similarly, the Second Circuit has held that "declarations of intentions or future plans are admissible against a nondeclarant when they are linked with independent evidence that corroborates the declaration." *United States v. Nersesian*, 824 F.2d 1294, 1325 (2d Cir.), *cert. denied*, 484 U.S. 958 (1987). . . . A district judge in the Northern District of Illinois has likewise adopted this approach. *See United States v. York*, No. 86 CR 315, 1987 WL 5938, at *7 (N.D. Ill. Jan. 12, 1987) (hearsay testimony held inadmissible where victim-declarant's statement that she intended to meet with the defendant at a particular time could not be corroborated with particularity). *But cf. Johnson v. Chrans*, 844 F.2d 842, 846 n.4 (7th Cir.), *cert. denied*, 488 U.S. 835 (1988) (explaining that in some circumstances the Seventh Circuit has been willing to admit a declarant's out-of-court statements to prove conduct of another person, despite opposite result under Illinois state law). . . .

To the contrary, the Ninth Circuit has held that statements of a declarant's intent are admissible under Rule 803(3) to prove subsequent conduct of a person other than the declarant without corroborating evidence. *See United States v. Pheaster*, 544 F.2d 353, 374–80 (9th Cir. 1976), *cert. denied sub nom. Inciso v. United States*, 429 U.S. 1099 (1977) (in kidnapping prosecution, trial court did not err in admitting testimony of a friend of the victim that shortly before the victim disappeared he told his friend that he was going to meet a person with the same name as the defendant). In holding statements of intent admissible against third parties, the Pheaster court recognized that such testimony could be unreliable, but rejected this as grounds for its exclusion. The Ninth Circuit explained that

> [t]he inference from a statement of present intention that the act intended was in fact performed is nothing more than an inference.... The possible unreliability of the inference to be drawn from the present intention [of the declarant] is a matter going to the weight of the evidence which might be argued to the trier of fact, but it should not be a ground for completely excluding the admittedly relevant evidence.

The court also acknowledged the "theoretical awkwardness" of applying a state of mind exception to prove conduct, but dismissed this objection because of the impressive array of authority favoring such application....

The language of Rule 803(3) clearly says that statements of intent are admissible. Thus, because it does not by its terms limit the class of persons against whom such statements of intent may be admitted, this Court rules that Rule 803(3) codifies *Hillmon* as written and does not disturb its conclusion or its reasoning.... [H]ad Congress intended to limit the admissibility of such statements, it presumably would have done so. This Court will not venture to graft a limitation where none exists.

As Rule 803(3) is unambiguous, this Court is unpersuaded by appeals to legislative history. . . . Even if the Court were properly to engage in an examination of Rule 803(3)'s legislative history, the conflicting nature of that evidence would nevertheless lead us right back to the text. . . . [W]hile the approach adopted by the Second and Fourth Circuits may seem practical and fair, it is really little more than judicial policymaking. . . . For the reasons set forth above, on December 14, 1994, during the twenty-third day of trial, Marie Boyden Connors was permitted to testify, over timely objection, that as her brother James Boyden Jr. left her apartment for the last time, he said, he "was going to meet Billy Herd."

PROBLEMS

3.38. Sam is arrested when he tries to enter the United States from Mexico and cocaine is found underneath his car. At his trial on charges of attempted smuggling, he wishes to elicit testimony from the arresting officer that, when the cocaine was discovered, Sam said, "I don't know where that came from." The prosecutor objects on grounds of hearsay. How should the judge rule?

3.39. In 1800 a carpenter named Levi Weeks was tried in New York City for the murder of a 22-year-old woman named Elma Sands. Weeks and Sands had lived in the same boarding house until Sands went missing; her body was found several days later at the bottom of a well. Two months earlier, Sands had told a cousin that Weeks had proposed marriage but that he insisted on keeping the engagement secret, and just before disappearing Sands told another cousin that she and Weeks were going away to be married. A wealthy brother paid for Weeks to be represented at trial by three prominent lawyers, two of whom were Aaron Burr and Alexander Hamilton. The defense successfully invoked the hearsay rule to keep the jury from learning what Sands had told her cousins about her secret engagement and impending marriage, and Weeks was acquitted. *See* Paul Collins, *Duel with the Devil* 17-28 (2013); Estelle Fox Kleiger, *The Trial of Levi Weeks* 42-43 (1989). Was this an appropriate application of the hearsay rule? Would the same result be reached today? Consider the following commentary on the case: "[T]he cause of justice is not well served by hiding facts from the jury. . . . Without the looming portent of marriage Levi Weeks was without a motive to commit the crime. . . . Denying [the] jury access to the true facts of the case enabled Weeks' extremely clever lawyers to create a kind of shadow play in which the real issues of the case were minimized." Bill James, *Popular Crime: Reflections on the Celebration of Violence* 14 (2012 ed.).

3.40. Henry Jumpertz was acquitted in 1859 of the murder of his mistress, Sophie Werner. The prosecutors argued Jumpertz had killed Werner to rid himself of her, and Jumpertz claimed Werner had committed suicide. To show that Werner was suicidal and to rebut the prosecution's claim of motive, Jumpertz introduced a letter that he said he had received from Werner shortly before she died. In the letter Werner declared she soon would "renounce[] the world" and be "in the grave." Jumpertz also called two witnesses who testified they had discussed the letter with him shortly after he had received it. *See* Jennifer L. Mnookin, *Scripting Expertise: The History of Handwriting Identification Evidence and the Judicial Construction of Reliability*, 87 Va. L. Rev. 1723 (2001). Should this evidence have been admitted?

3.41. Former football star O.J. Simpson was charged in Los Angeles in 1994 with the murders of his former wife, Nicole Brown Simpson, and her friend, Ronald Goldman. The prosecution sought to introduce evidence that shortly before her death Nicole Brown Simpson told relatives and friends that her ex-husband was stalking her and that she was afraid of him. The trial judge excluded the testimony on grounds of hearsay. *See* Gerald F. Uelmen, *The O.J. Files* 102-104 (1998). Following Simpson's acquittal, relatives of the victims won a civil judgment against him for wrongful death. The judge in the civil case admitted, to prove state of mind, the statements excluded in the criminal case. The civil plaintiffs argued (but the prosecutors did not) that Nicole's state of mind was relevant to support the claim that she made a final break with him on the day of the murders, which in turn gave him the motive to kill her. Was the ruling in either the criminal or the civil case erroneous? (The ruling in the civil case was affirmed on appeal. *See Rufo v. Simpson*, 103 Cal. Rptr. 2d 492 (Cal. App. 2001).) If the criminal case were tried today, would the stalking statements be excluded under the Confrontation Clause?

5. Injury Reports

Codifying common law decisions, the Federal Rule of Evidence 803(4) exempts from the hearsay rule a broad range of statements made to physicians or others for the purpose of medical diagnosis. The theory is that self-interest tends to keep a patient honest. But, controversially, the federal rule expands the exception to cover many statements made to physicians hired not for treatment but simply for diagnosis with an eye to litigation. Debate has also surrounded the use of Rule 803(4) and its state-law analogs to allow into evidence out-of-court statements identifying the perpetrators of sexual abuse, particularly of children.

The Supreme Court's revised interpretation of the Confrontation Clause, announced in *Crawford v. Washington*, has created an additional layer of uncertainty about when the Constitution permits out-of-court injury reports to be introduced against a criminal defendant. In many cases, the answer will depend on whether the statement is deemed "testimonial."

[F.R.E. 803(4); C.E.C. §§1251, 1253, 1370]

ADVISORY COMMITTEE NOTE TO F.R.E. 803(4)

Even those few jurisdictions which have shied away from generally admitting statements of present condition have allowed them if made to a physician for purposes of diagnosis and treatment in view of the patient's strong motivation to be truthful. The same guarantee of trustworthiness extends to statements of past conditions and medical history, made for purposes of diagnosis or treatment. It also extends to statements as to causation, reasonably pertinent to the same purposes, in accord with the current trend. Statements as to fault would not ordinarily qualify under this latter language. Thus a patient's statement that he was struck by an automobile would qualify but not his statement that the car was driven through a red light. Under the exception the statement need not have been made to a physician. Statements to hospital attendants, ambulance drivers, or even members of the family might be included.

Conventional doctrine has excluded from the hearsay exception, as not within its guarantee of truthfulness, statements to a physician consulted only for the purpose of enabling him to testify. While these statements were not admissible as substantive evidence, the expert was allowed to state the basis of his opinion, including statements of this kind. The distinction thus called for was one most unlikely to be made by juries. The rule accordingly rejects the limitation. This position is consistent with the provision of Rule 703 that the facts on which expert testimony is based need not be admissible in evidence if of a kind ordinarily relied upon by experts in the field.

ROCK v. HUFFCO GAS & OIL CO.

922 F.2d 272 (5th Cir. 1991)

THORNBERRY, Circuit Judge:

...This litigation stems from two accidents allegedly suffered by Richard D. Rock while employed as a steward/cook for Offshore Food Service, Inc. of Houma, Louisiana. Offshore Food Service provides food catering services to offshore drilling platforms and vessels in the Gulf of Mexico.

On July 13, 1987, Rock was assigned to work on the Huffco Fixed Platform 206A, which was located in the High Island Region off the coast of Galveston,

Texas. On the morning following his arrival, as he was leaving his sleeping quarters, Rock claimed that his foot fell through a rusted part of a step located just outside of his doorway causing him to sprain his ankle. There were no witnesses to the accident. . . . Doctors reported that Rock had a tender and swollen right ankle and described the injury as a moderate sprain. The ankle was placed in a six inch plaster splint, and Rock was instructed not to put any weight on the ankle, to walk with crutches, and to elevate the ankle when possible.

On July 21, 1987, after a few days of rest, Rock returned to work. . . . [O]n August 26, 1987, Rock claimed to have re-injured his ankle by slipping in some grease on the floor of [a jack-up rig owned by the Dual Drilling Company]. The only potential witness to the accident was Barry Breaux, another Offshore Food's employee assigned to work with Rock. During his deposition, Breaux reported that he was in the galley at the time of the accident but did not see Rock fall. In fact, Breaux claims that Rock had previously advised him of a plan to fake such an accident. . . .

Because of his ankle's worsening condition, Rock consulted Dr. A. Delmar Walker on September 17th and 27th of 1987. As part of those examinations, Rock provided the doctor with a history of the injury to his ankle including a description of the two incidents discussed above. On October 1, 1987, Dr. Walker referred Rock to a vascular surgeon, Dr. Fritz J. Rau, who again asked Rock for a history of the injury to his ankle. . . .

Apparently, as a result of the injury to his ankle, Rock was suffering from a condition known as venous insufficiency. This occurs when the veins in the lower legs fail to return blood to the torso. Several surgeries were performed on Rock in an attempt to restore normal blood flow, but his condition deteriorated. In addition to his vascular condition, Rock developed infections, possibly resulting from the surgical procedures themselves. Rock died from a heart attack on December 12, 1988. . . .

After Rock's death, surviving members of his family . . . pursued negligence claims against the defendants. . . . [The district court granted summary judgment to the defendants, on the ground that there was no admissible evidence that Rock had injured himself on the rig.] Specifically, the court concluded that the evidence offered by plaintiffs constituted hearsay, which did not fall within any of the recognized exceptions to the hearsay rule. . . .

Appellants . . . suggest that written and testimonial evidence concerning the history of Rock's alleged accidents, which were given by Rock to the doctors treating his ankle, should be admissible under Federal Rule of Evidence 803(4). This rule provides that otherwise inadmissible hearsay should not be excluded if the statement was initially "made for purposes of medical diagnosis or treatment and describ[es] medical history, or past or present symptoms, pain, or sensations, or the inception or general character of the cause or external source thereof insofar as *reasonably pertinent to diagnosis or treatment.*" Fed. R. Evid. 803(4) (emphasis added).

Admissibility of a statement made to one's physician turns on the guarantee of the absent declarant's trustworthiness. *See* Fed. R. Evid. 803(4) advisory committee's note. Therefore, before admitting such hearsay statements, the court should determine whether the statements were reasonably considered by the declarant as being pertinent to the diagnosis or treatment sought.

Details of the injury not necessary for treatment but serving only to suggest fault "would not ordinarily qualify" as an exception to the hearsay rule under Rule 803(4). *See id.* A case cited by plaintiffs, *Ramrattan v. Burger King Corp.*, 656 F. Supp. 522 (D. Md. 1987), illustrates the application of this rule. In *Ramrattan*, the district court held that a statement made to a physician that the defendant's car struck his vehicle was admissible under Rule 803(4), but that "statements concerning who ran the red light or the fault of the parties are not pertinent to diagnosis or treatment."

The plaintiffs argue that Drs. Walker and Rau considered the cause of Rock's injury pertinent to their diagnosis, however, deposition transcripts do not bear this out. . . . The doctors stated that they only needed to know that Rock had twisted his ankle; they did not need to know the additional detail that Rock may have twisted the ankle while stepping through a rusted-out or defective step or by slipping in some grease in order to diagnose or treat Rock's injury. . . . [T]he district court was correct in ruling Rock's statements to his doctors as inadmissible under Federal Rule of Evidence 803(4). . . . [Affirmed.]

WARD v. STATE

50 N.E.3d 752 (Ind. 2016)

RUSH, Chief Justice.

Dee Ward was charged with battering J.M., his girlfriend. During treatment for her injuries, J.M. told a paramedic and a forensic nurse that Ward was her attacker. When J.M. failed to appear for depositions or to testify at trial, the State relied on her statements to the paramedic and the forensic nurse to implicate Ward, over Ward's objection that the evidence was "testimonial hearsay" that violated his federal and State confrontation rights.

We hold the statements are non-testimonial. Asking J.M. who attacked her was not aimed at obtaining a substitute for trial testimony — rather, it was a vital part of providing appropriate medical and psychological treatment and service referrals, as the applicable standard of care requires. Accordingly, J.M.'s hearsay statements were properly admitted into evidence. We therefore affirm Ward's convictions. . . .

As of April 2013, Ward and J.M. had been dating and living together off and on for about two years and had a child together. During that time, J.M. also sometimes lived with her mother and [stepfather. On April 10, 2013, after Ward dropped J.M. off at the house of her mother and stepfather, J.M.'s stepfather called 911 to report that J.M. had been beaten.]

At about 2:24 p.m., paramedic Linda Hodge–McKinney ("the Paramedic") received an "[a]ssault trauma" dispatch and arrived at the scene about three minutes later. The Paramedic found J.M. lying on a bed in a fetal position crying, with extensive bruising on her body. When the Paramedic asked J.M. to rate her pain "[o]n a scale of one to ten, with . . . ten being the most amount of pain you've ever been in," J.M. rated her pain a ten. A police officer who arrived shortly after the paramedics also observed "[m]assive bruising, basically all over her body especially her legs and buttocks, welts, dark blue and black bruises. Pretty severe." After the officer left the room, J.M. advised the Paramedic that her boyfriend "Dee" was the source of her injuries.

Concerned that J.M. may have suffered internal injuries, the Paramedic transported J.M. to a local hospital, administering intravenous pain medication along the way. At the emergency room, forensic nurse Julie Morrison ("the Forensic Nurse") treated J.M., observing that she was "obviously in a lot of discomfort" and "rolled up in a ball . . . in a near fetal position on one side, all hunched over, sort of in a protective sort of stance." When the Forensic Nurse asked what happened, J.M. stated that she had been "struck repeatedly with a belt," and that "it was her boyfriend Dee Ward" who beat her. Meanwhile, the Forensic Nurse oversaw J.M.'s safety and discharge planning, classifying J.M. as a "no information patient" to prevent people (specifically the attacker) from learning her whereabouts. Further examination and testing ruled out internal injuries, and J.M. was discharged to her parents' home later that evening with referrals to two domestic-violence support organizations, a recommendation for counseling, a prescription for pain medication, and instructions for minimizing the swelling. . . .

[I]n *Ohio v. Clark,* 576 U.S. ___ , 135 S.Ct. 2173 (2015), the United States Supreme Court . . . clarified that determining the "primary purpose" of statements made to non-law enforcement personnel — that is, whether it was intended to be available as a substitute for trial testimony in a later criminal prosecution — is highly fact-sensitive. That approach is consistent with *Perry* [*v. State*, 956 N.E.2d 41 (Ind. Ct. App. 2011),] and Indiana's other pre-*Clark* cases addressing Confrontation Clause questions about identification statements made during medical treatment. Those cases scrutinized identity statements in context to discern whether their primary purpose was testimonial, which is essentially the approach *Clark* prescribes. *Perry* recognized that "[s]tatements attributing fault or establishing a perpetrator's identity are typically inadmissible under the medical diagnosis [and treatment] exception" — but also recognized an exception to that general rule "in cases involving child abuse, sexual assault, and/or *domestic violence.*" 956 N.E.2d at 49 (emphasis added). In essence, *Perry* reasoned that because of the unique nature of those cases, identifying the attacker serves a primarily *medical,* not testimonial, purpose because a "physician generally must know who the abuser was in order to render proper treatment because the physician's treatment will necessarily differ when the abuser is a member of the victim's family or household." *Id.* (quoting *Nash v. State,* 754 N.E.2d 1021, 1025 (Ind.Ct.App.2001)).

Here, the record shows that when the Paramedic arrived on the scene, she encountered J.M. lying on a bed in a fetal position, crying, and in severe pain. Her body revealed extensive bruising. The Paramedic asked J.M. what happened to her, and she responded that she "was at her boyfriend's house and he made her stay the night and from about 3:00 in the morning to 6:00 in the morning he beat her with a belt and wouldn't let her leave." When questioned by the State on the purpose of asking J.M. what happened to her, the Paramedic responded: "For one thing, to find out why we were called out to the house, why were we there for her. She is lying on the bed whimpering, crying, so I need to know what happened and what she needs for us to do for her today." The State also inquired, "[i]s it important to determine who caused the injuries to the patient you are treating," to which the Paramedic responded, "[i]t is for us at that time. Because like I said before, I need to know if they are still there or if they are anywhere around to cause any more harm." Responding to the State's further inquiry, the Paramedic testified that J.M. said her boyfriend's name was Dee.

Considering the relevant circumstances, it does not appear to us that the primary purpose of the Paramedic's questioning of J.M. was to create an out-of-court substitute for trial testimony. Ward argues that the Paramedic was not responding to an ongoing emergency because he carried out his assault several hours earlier. But as [*Michigan v. Bryant,* 562 U.S. 344 (2011),] makes plain, "there may be *other* circumstances, aside from ongoing emergencies, when a statement is not procured with a primary purpose of creating an out-of-court substitute for trial testimony." Here, the Paramedic's priority was to treat an obviously battered victim who apparently was suffering in pain. The Paramedic never told J.M. that her answers might be used to arrest or punish her abuser; J.M. never hinted that she intended her statements for that purpose (and was likely in no condition to form such an intent, given the pain she was in); and the conversation was informal — a far cry from "the formalized station-house questioning in *Crawford* or the police interrogation and battery affidavit in *Hammon.*" *Clark,* 135 S.Ct. at 2181. In sum, J.M.'s statements to the Paramedic were non-testimonial and therefore unobjectionable on Confrontation Clause grounds.

We likewise find J.M.'s statements to the Forensic Nurse to be non-testimonial.... [A] forensic nurse's primary function is providing medical treatment, not gathering evidence. Medical scholarship confirms that identifying attackers is integral to the standard of care for "medical treatment" of domestic abuse victims. Doctors and nurses in various clinical settings — including emergency room, primary care, surgery, and mental health facilities — are instructed they "must be prepared to engage patients around the issue of I[ntimate] P[artner] V[iolence] and provide assessment *and* referral." Nancy Sugg, MD, MPH, *Intimate Partner Violence: Prevalence, Health Consequences, and Intervention,* 99 Med. Clin. N. Am. 629, 640 (2015) (emphasis added). Specifically, experts urge doctors and nurses to acknowledge the violence, assess patient safety, refer the victim for additional treatment or services, and document the injuries *and the abuser. Id.* Indeed, a "forensic nurse is a nurse who provides specialized care for patients who are victims and/or perpetrators of trauma (both intentional and unintentional). Forensic nurses are *nurses* first and foremost," even though they are also specially trained in injury identification, evaluation, and documentation. *Int'l Ass'n of Forensic Nurses,* (available at http://www.forensicnurses.org/?page=whatisfn) (last visited February 19, 2016).

By this definition, everything the Forensic Nurse did here served the primary purpose of medical treatment. When ambulance personnel alerted her of J.M.'s arrival, she examined J.M. in the emergency room. She informed J.M. she worked in conjunction with J.M.'s other doctors and nurses "to make sure she is taken care of medically and she didn't have any underlying injuries that we couldn't see immediately," and J.M. consented to the examination understanding that purpose. During the evaluation, the Forensic Nurse first took J.M.'s medical history in which J.M. . . . described how she sustained her injuries — including naming the attacker — and then she examined and documented J.M.'s injuries. Meanwhile, she oversaw J.M.'s safety and discharge planning, and classified J.M. as a "no information patient" to prevent people (specifically the attacker) from learning J.M.'s whereabouts. She then ensured J.M. would be discharged to a safe location (home with the mother, not the attacker). Finally, the Forensic Nurse recommended counseling and made the appropriate referrals to the Julian Center and Legacy House.

The Forensic Nurse's treatment of J.M. mirrored the treatment she administers to all violence victims she sees. She "always do[es] the same thing . . . ." She takes a medical history, asks how the injuries occurred, and performs a "head to toe" examination. She needs to know what and who caused the injury because that information affects treatment, including safety and discharge plans. She explained:

> Especially, again, victims of *any* type of violence, it would be really important to know if they knew who the perpetrator was. Because a large part of the forensic nurse[']s job is to collaborate with social work and the patient in order to ensure [a] safety plan for that person if they are well enough to be discharged.
>
> * * *
>
> Your resources and safety plan would be a lot different, for instance, if you are attacked by a stranger, an unknown person in a parking garage, let's say, downtown, versus somebody who might be a family member or someone you are living with. If there is a common child, if you share a child, because there might be visitation, custody issues. So it's critically important that [the forensic nurse] can find out who that person is.

Similarly, the Forensic Nurse stated hospital protocol required her to assess a patient's psychological or emotional injuries because "[i]t has to do a lot with their ability to care for themselves once they are discharged." She testified she and other forensic nurses (at her hospital and around the country) follow this process when treating patients like J.M., because it reflects the duty of care owed to all victims of violence. . . .

[P]atient safety is a "critical" part of the comprehensive standard of care for treating victims of domestic violence. Sugg, 99 Med. Clin. N. Am. Providers *must* issue a safety plan. *Id.* And that plan is not just the final instruction a patient receives; it is a process of "assessment" that begins "[b]efore the patient leaves the office," *id.*, with questions like "what happened?" and "who did this?" *See id.* Answering these questions determines what resources patients need from their doctors and nurses — "for instance, are they safe to go home or do they need to access a domestic violence shelter?" *Id.* (Recall that the Paramedic who first arrived on the scene also, consistent with that standard, specifically asked J.M. what she needed from them.) Likewise, proper documentation works in tandem with safety assessments and planning because it "helps coordinate care between multi-disciplinary providers." [*Id.*] Doctors and nurses are instructed to record the assailant's name and relationship to the victim if the victim divulges that information. *Id.*

. . . The standard of care for "medical treatment" of domestic abuse goes beyond physical injuries, and even beyond immediate outcomes like who takes a victim home or what medications a patient receives. Rather, it requires nurses and physicians to rely on information obtained from patients to triage their injuries — both mental and physical — and implement comprehensive treatment plans. Doctors and nurses *need* to know the identity of the perpetrator when treating a victim of domestic violence. *Perry*. And specifically here, the Forensic Nurse *needed* to know who beat J.M. in order to classify her status while in the hospital (no information patient), discharge her home to a safe place (home with her mother and not her abuser), and make proper post-discharge referrals (follow-up counseling and referrals to Julian Center and Legacy House) — all eminently reasonable measures to address J.M.'s risk. . . .

Ward emphasizes that the boilerplate consent forms [signed by J.M.] included an information-release provision, which permitted (but did not compel) the hospital to disclose J.M.'s information if requested by law enforcement. But . . . [t]hat secondary provision did not change the *primary* purpose of the exam and the information it gathered, from medical treatment to investigation. . . .

Considering their context, we deem J.M.'s statements to the Forensic Nurse identifying Ward as her attacker non-testimonial, not barred by the Confrontation Clause, and properly admitted under Evidence Rule 803(4). Of course, Evidence Rule 803(4) should not be abused by asserting a pretextual medical purpose as a backdoor for admitting what is really testimonial hearsay. But that is the very problem the "primary purpose" test is designed to solve — to discern, in context, whether the asserted purpose of the statement really *is* "primary," or merely pretext for an impermissible purpose. Faithfully applying the "primary purpose" test in context, as *Clark* and *Perry* prescribe, and as we have here, will therefore guard against those abuses. There is no need to confine our view of valid "medical purposes" to treatment of only physical injuries, or information exchanged in an introduction or language in a consent form. . . . Indeed, the standard of care *required* the Forensic Nurse to take reasonable measures to address J.M.'s risk. The trial court correctly recognized the legitimate primary medical purpose for asking J.M. to identify her attacker and properly admitted the Forensic Nurse's testimony. . . .

Accordingly, J.M.'s hearsay statements to the Paramedic and Forensic Nurse identifying Ward as her assailant were not testimonial, and were properly admitted into evidence. Ward's convictions are affirmed.

[Justice Rucker filed an opinion dissenting in part.]

PROBLEMS

3.42. A woman brings her infant daughter into the emergency room and tells the intake clerk, "My boyfriend burned her with a cigarette. He gets nasty when he's been drinking." Is all or part of this statement admissible against the boyfriend in a subsequent prosecution for battery?

3.43. Along with his wife, a miner sues his employer for causing his respiratory illness. Their lawyer hires a physician as an expert witness, and the miner tells the doctor, "My lungs started to hurt ten years ago, a month or so after I started working in the mine." The miner dies before trial. Is his statement to the doctor admissible to prove when the disease began to manifest itself?

6. Recorded Recollection

Suppose an eyewitness to an accident appears at trial as a witness but can no longer remember what happened. If the witness previously wrote down her recollections, modern evidence law follows Wigmore in distinguishing two different ways in which the record may be used. The doctrine of "past recollection recorded" allows the record, in certain cases, to be introduced into evidence — or, in federal court and in many states, read to the jury — to prove the truth of what it asserts, notwithstanding the hearsay rule. Past recollection recorded is therefore an exception to the hearsay rule. It is often confused with what Wigmore called "present recollection revived" and other writers have sometimes called "present recollection refreshed." This is a technique not for introducing a document, nor even for having it read to the jury, but rather for jogging the memory of a forgetful witness, and thereby allowing the witness to testify from "present recollection."

There is room for debate whether witnesses commonly distinguish as Wigmore did between having their memory refreshed and simply repeating what they previously wrote. But the rules of evidence and conventional trial practice assume that they do. Moreover, conventional practice allows *anything* to be used to revive the recollection of a forgetful witness, as long as it is first shown to opposing counsel — and subject, of course, to the judge's general authority to regulate trial procedures in the interests of fairness and efficiency.

Statements that fall within the exception for "recorded recollection" are admissible as evidence, not just available for use to refresh the witness's memory. But a traditional limitation on this exception, preserved in the Federal Rules of Evidence and most of its state analogs, allows the statement to be read to the jury but prohibits the jury from actually looking at it. It is debatable whether this limitation makes any sense; as you will see, the Massachusetts Supreme Judicial Court abandoned it more than half a century ago.

[F.R.E. 612, 803(5); C.E.C. §1237]

ADVISORY COMMITTEE NOTE TO F.R.E. 803(5)

A hearsay exception for recorded recollection is generally recognized and has been described as having "long been favored by the federal and practically all the state courts that have had occasion to decide the question." United States v. Kelly, 349 F.2d 720, 770 (2d Cir. 1965). . . . The guarantee of trustworthiness is found in the reliability inherent in a record made while events were still fresh in mind and accurately reflecting them.

The principal controversy attending the exception has centered, not upon the propriety of the exception itself, but upon the question whether a preliminary requirement of impaired memory on the part of the witness should be imposed. The authorities are divided. If regard be had only to the accuracy of the evidence, admittedly impairment of the memory of the witness adds nothing to it and should not be required. Nevertheless, the absence of the requirement, it is believed, would encourage the use of statements care-fully prepared for purposes of litigation under the supervision of attorneys, investigators, or claim adjusters. Hence the example includes a requirement that the witness not have "sufficient recollection to enable him to testify fully and accurately." To the same effect are California Evidence Code §1237 and New Jersey Rule 63(1)(b), and this has been the position of the federal courts. . . .

No attempt is made in the exception to spell out the method of estab-lishing the initial knowledge or the contemporaneity and accuracy of the record, leaving them to be dealt with as the circumstances of the particular case might indicate. Multiple person involvement in the process of observing and recording, as in Rathbun v. Brancatella, 93 N.J. L. 222, 107 A. 279 (1919), is entirely consistent with the exception.

Locating the exception at this place in the scheme of the rules is a matter of choice. There were two other possibilities. The first was to regard the state-ment as one of the group of prior statements of a testifying witness which are excluded entirely from the category of hearsay by Rule 801(d)(1). That category, however, requires that declarant be "subject to cross-examination," as to which the impaired memory aspect of the exception raises doubts. The other possibility was to include the exception among those covered by Rule 804. Since unavailability is required by that rule and lack of memory is listed as a species of unavailability by the definition of the term in Rule 804(a)(3), that treatment at first impression would seem appropriate. The fact is, how-ever, that the unavailability requirement of the exception is of a limited and peculiar nature. Accordingly, the exception is located at this point rather than in the context of a rule where unavailability is conceived of more broadly.

FISHER v. SWARTZ

130 N.E.2d 575 (Mass. 1955)

Spalding, Justice.

In this action of contract to recover for labor and materials alleged to have been furnished to the defendant, the plaintiff had a verdict. The case is here on the defendant's exception to a ruling on evidence.

The plaintiff testified that he furnished certain labor and materials in repairing a house owned by the defendant. While testifying he "refresh[ed] his recollection" from a carbon copy of an itemized statement of charges made for the labor and materials furnished by him.

The statement contained more than a hundred items. The original of this statement had been sent to the defendant. Following the use of the copy to aid his testimony, the plaintiff offered it in evidence and the defendant objected. . . . [T]he copy was admitted in evidence subject to the defendant's exception.

In support of the ruling the plaintiff argues that the statement contained business entries which were admissible under G.L. (Ter. Ed.) c. 233, §78. But there is lacking here the preliminary finding by the judge of the statutory prerequisites. . . . It is apparent from the record that no attempt was made to bring the statement within the statute and that counsel and the judge dealt with it on the basis of a memorandum which had aided the plaintiff while testifying. . . .

If the evidence is admissible it must be on other grounds. A writing may be used by a witness in different ways. He may use it to revive or stimulate a present recollection, or, having no present recollection even with the aid of the writing, he may use it merely as a record of his past knowledge. Professor Wigmore has classified these situations as "present recollection revived" and "past recollection recorded" and several courts in recent years have employed these designations. In order to decide whether the statement in question was admissible it becomes necessary to determine to which of these classifications it belongs, for the legal consequences are not the same. In a case of "present recollection revived" the witness, although he may use the writing to refresh his recollection, must testify to the fact as he remembers it and he may not read or show the writing to the jury. But in a case of "past recollection recorded" the judge in his discretion may permit a witness "to incorporate in his testimony a writing expressive of his past knowledge, and to read it and even to show it to the jury." Bendett v. Bendett, 315 Mass. 59, 64 [1943]. . . . While the record in the case at bar is not as clear as it might be, we think that it may fairly be inferred that the writing was a record of the witness' past recollection and was treated as such by counsel and the trial judge. . . .

The defendant does not argue that the statement was not a record of past recollection. His position in substance is that it is not admissible in any event, and he relies on Bendett v. Bendett, cited above. That that case sustains the defendant's contention cannot be gainsaid. There the plaintiff while testifying had used a diary kept in the usual course of business to "refresh his recollection." It is not clear from the opinion — and an inspection of the original papers furnishes no additional light — whether the memorandum revived a present memory or was a record of past recollection. The opinion dealt with the question on the basis that it might have been the latter. So treated, the court said that it saw "no reason for denying to the trial judge discretion to permit a witness to incorporate in his testimony a writing expressive of his past knowledge, and to read it and even to show it to the jury." But, as the court pointed out, the judge went further and admitted the writing as independent evidence and not as a part of the testimony of the plaintiff. This was held to be error. The court recognized that in some jurisdictions, "because of the slight practical difference between the incorporation of a writing in the testimony of a witness and the admission of the writing as evidence by itself, a written record of the past knowledge of a witness is held admissible in evidence." The court, nevertheless, was of opinion that "such a writing under some circumstances might have some inherent evidential weight independently of its adoption by the witness as the expression and embodiment of his testimony. In such a case, neither party would be entitled to have that weight thrown into the scale, on the merits of the case, unless the writing should be admissible on some other ground."

In view of the importance of this question in the trial of causes we are disposed to reconsider it. Further study of the question has convinced us that both reason and authority lead to the conclusion that the writing ought to be admissible as evidence. It is to be noted that in the Bendett case a majority of the court was of opinion that, although it was error to permit the memorandum to be put in evidence, the error, nevertheless, was harmless. The reason was that the witness had testified with respect to the items contained in the memorandum and had been cross-examined about them. "Thus," said the court, "the jury had been made familiar with everything material that was contained in the book. The admission of the book in evidence merely put before their eyes what they knew already. So far as appears there was nothing in the sight of the items in the book that was more convincing than the testimony of the plaintiff that they were the items in an account that he knew to be true. We do not see how the defendant was harmed." But that would be the case in most if not all situations where a memorandum of past recollection was put in evidence. Prior to its admission the witness would usually have read to the court or jury the contents of the memorandum, and its admission as evidence, since it would have added little or nothing, would generally be treated as harmless error. We prefer a less squeamish approach to the question. Rather than to say the admission of the writing is error, but error that does no harm, we think that it is better to say that there is no error at all.

This is the prevailing view elsewhere and is favored by distinguished scholars in the field of evidence. . . . Wigmore on Evidence (3d ed.) §754; McCormick on Evidence, §278. See Maguire, Evidence, Common Sense & Common Law, pages 37–39. See also . . . Model Code of Evidence, Rule 504. As the Supreme Court of Errors aptly said in a well-considered opinion, "It seems to us to be pressing the use of a legal fiction too far for a court to permit the statement made by such paper to be read as evidence, while holding that the law forbids the admission as evidence of the paper which is the original and only proof of the statement admitted." Curtis v. Bradley, 65 Conn. 99, 109 [1894]. Accordingly we are of opinion that the judge in the case at bar did not err in admitting the statement in question and that to the extent that the Bendett case is opposed to this view we decline to follow it. . . . Exceptions overruled.

UNITED STATES v. RICCARDI

174 F.2d 883 (3d Cir. 1949)

KALODNER, Circuit Judge.

The defendant was [convicted of] . . . wilfully, unlawfully and feloniously having transported or having caused to be transported in interstate commerce certain chattels of the value of $5,000 or more. . . . We are not here primarily concerned with the particular fraudulent representations which the defendant made. Rather we are called upon to decide the propriety of the method utilized at the trial to prove what chattels the defendant obtained and transported, and their value. In short, the principal question is whether the witnesses who testified to these essentials were properly permitted to refresh their memory. . . .

The chattels involved are numerous items of bric-a-brac, linens, silverware, and other household articles of quality and distinction. They were the property of Doris Farid es Sultaneh, and were kept in her home at Morristown,

New Jersey, from which the defendant is alleged to have transported them to Arizona in a truck and station wagon. The defendant did not deny receiving some of the lady's chattels, but did deny both the quantity and quality alleged....

To prove the specific chattels involved, the government relied on the testimony of Doris Farid; to prove their value, it relied on the testimony of an expert, one Leo Berlow.

Farid testified that as the chattels were being moved from the house, she made longhand notes, and that later she copied these notes on her typewriter. Only one of the original notes was produced, and became part of the evidence of the case, a search by Farid having failed to disclose the others. The government sought to have Farid testify with respect to the chattels by using the typewritten notes for the purpose of refreshing her recollection.[2]

Although the defendant's objection was overruled, the government, on the next day of the trial, submitted to Farid lists of chattels taken out of a copy of the indictment, but from which had been deleted such information as dates and values [footnote omitted]. With the aid of these lists, the witness testified that her recollection was refreshed[4] and that she presently recognized and could identify each item. She was then permitted to read the lists aloud, and testified that she knew that the items were loaded on the truck or station wagon, as the case was. The lists were neither offered nor received in evidence.

The expert, Berlow, testified that he had visited Doris Farid's home on numerous occasions in his professional capacity as dealer in antiques, bric-a-brac, etc.; that he was very familiar with the furnishings therein, having examined the household for the purpose of buying items from Farid or selling them for her on commission. He was shown the same lists which Farid had used to refresh her recollection, and with their aid testified that he could recall the items individually, with some exceptions; that he remembered them to the extent that he could not only describe the items, but in many instances could state where in the house he had seen them; and that he could give an opinion as to their value. This he was permitted to do.

---

2. At pages 114a–115a of Appellant's Appendix, the following appears:

"The Court: That isn't the question. When you look at that typewritten sheet, does that refresh your recollection as to the items therein mentioned?
"The Witness: It does.
"The Court: In what way?
"The Witness: Well, every item here — for instance: '2 Chinese vases octagonal shape Satsuma, light for mantel' I remember.
"The Court: You remember those items individually as packed?
"The Witness: Individually, each one.
"The Court: I will allow her to refresh her recollection, but I will expect you to produce the original notes."

4. For example, at page 140a of Appellant's Appendix:

"The Court: Well, Madam, as you look at that list does it refresh your recollection?
"The Witness: I lived with these things, your Honor, I know them.
"The Court: You lived with them yourself?
"The Witness: I did.
"The Court: So when you look at that paper, it does refresh your recollection?
"The Witness: Absolutely."

... It is [the defendant's] position that the lists should not have been used because they were not made by the witnesses at or shortly after the time of the transaction while the facts were fresh in memory. It is further contended that ... what Farid did, in fact, was to read off the lists as proof of the actual articles loaded on the vehicles.

The government, on the other hand, asserts that the witnesses gave their independent recollection, which is admissible, albeit refreshed, because it is the recollection and not the writing which is the evidence. It goes further, and urges that where the witness has an independent recollection, anything may be used to stimulate and vitalize that recollection with regard to source or origin.[5]

Refreshing the recollection of a witness is not an uncommon trial practice, but as a theory of evidentiary law its content and application are far from clear. ... An analysis as good and trustworthy as presently exists appears in Chapter XXVIII, 3 Wigmore on Evidence (3rd ed. 1940). Professor Wigmore separated, broadly, what he called "past recollection recorded" from "present recollection revived," attributing much of the confusion in the cases to a failure to make this distinction and to the use of the phrase "refreshing the recollection" for both classes of testimony. The primary difference between the two classifications is the ability of the witness to testify from present knowledge: where the witness' memory is revived, and he presently recollects the facts and swears to them, he is obviously in a different position from the witness who cannot directly state the facts from present memory and who must ask the court to accept a writing for the truth of its contents because he is willing to swear, for one reason or another, that its contents are true. ...

The difference between present recollection revived and past recollection recorded has a demonstrable effect upon the method of proof. In the instance of past recollection recorded, the witness, by hypothesis, has no present recollection of the matter contained in the writing. Whether the record is directly admitted into evidence, or indirectly by the permissive parroting of the witness, it is nevertheless a substitute for his memory and is offered for the truth of its contents. It assumes a distinct significance as an independent probative force, and is therefore ordinarily required to meet certain standards. ...

In the case of present recollection revived, the witness, by hypothesis, relates his present recollection, and under oath and subject to cross-examination asserts that it is true; his capacities for memory and perception may be attacked and tested; his determination to tell the truth investigated and revealed; protestations of lack of memory, which escape criticism and indeed constitute a refuge in the situation of past recollection recorded, merely undermine the probative worth of his testimony. It is in recognition of these factors that we find:

> "The law of contemporary writing or entry qualifying it as primary evidence has no application. The primary evidence here is not the writing. It was not

5. This is in paraphrase of Lord Ellenborough's statement in Henry v. Lee, 2 Chitty 124: "If upon looking at any document he can so far refresh his memory as to recollect a circumstance, it is sufficient; and it makes no difference that the memorandum is not written by himself, for it is not the memorandum that is the evidence but the recollection of the witness."

introduced in evidence. It was not offered. The primary evidence is the oral statement of the hostile witness. It is not so important when the statement was made or by whom if it serves the purpose to refresh the mind and unfold the truth." Hoffman v. United States, 9 Cir., 1937, 87 F.2d 410, 411.

"When a party uses an earlier statement of his own witness to refresh the witness' memory, the only evidence recognized as such is the testimony so refreshed. . . . Anything may in fact revive a memory; a song, a scent, a photograph, an allusion, even a past statement known to be false. When a witness declares that any of these has evoked a memory, the opposite party may show, either that it has not evoked what appears to the witness as a memory, or that, although it may so appear to him, the memory is a phantom and not a reliable record of its content. When the evoking stimulus is not itself an account of the relevant occasion, no question of its truth can arise; but when it is an account of that occasion, its falsity, if raised by the opposing party, will become a relevant issue if the witness has declared that the evoked memory accords with it. . . ." United States v. Rappy, 2 Cir., 1947, 157 F.2d 964, 967-968, certiorari denied 329 U.S. 806.

In the instant case, the learned trial judge determined that both Farid and the expert, Berlow, testified from present recollection. On the record, we cannot say that it was plainly not so. Both witnesses stated that they knew the chattels and could identify them. Farid, who testified that she was present and helped to pack them, said she could remember which were transported; Berlow said he could give an opinion of their value. On a number of occasions the trial judge investigated the foundations of their claim to present recollection and satisfied himself as to its bona fides. . . . [T]he trial judge immediately recognized that the items of property involved were so numerous that in the ordinary course of events no one would be expected to recite them without having learned a list by rote memory. On the other hand, the items were such that a person familiar with them reasonably could be expected to recognize them and tell what he knows. Under these circumstances, the District Judge might well have permitted the government, in lieu of the procedure followed, to ask Farid leading questions, directing her attention to specific items, and asking her whether she knew what happened to them. This is especially true of Berlow, who did not purport to have any knowledge of the movement of the articles. Clearly, it would have been pointless to ask him to give the value of every article he had ever seen in Farid's home. The same result could have been achieved legitimately without the use of the lists by orally directing his attention to any specific article previously identified by Farid and asking him whether he had seen it, presently remembered it, and could give an opinion as to its value. By the use of lists, nothing more or different was accomplished.

Moreover, we think the procedure followed lay within the discretion of the trial court, and that no prejudicial error ensued. . . . The defense had at its disposal the customary opportunities and all the necessary material to test the witness' recollection and other testimonial qualifications, including the single original longhand list which Farid located, the typewritten lists which she said were made at the time of the events involved, and the lists the prosecution used. It might very well have put Farid through severe cross-examination with respect to each chattel she identified on direct examination, but chose instead to attack the reliability of her memory by other means.

Accordingly, it is our conclusion that the learned trial judge did not abuse his discretion, either in determining that the witnesses testified from present recollection, or in permitting the use of the lists described herein. . . . [T]he judgment of the District Court will be affirmed.

"Perhaps *this* will refresh your memory."

PROBLEM

3.44. An eyewitness to a hit-and-run accident calls his wife 15 minutes later, tells her the license plate number of the car he saw leave the scene, and asks her to write it down. She does so. Under what circumstances will her note be admissible in a later prosecution of the driver? Under what circumstances may it be shown to the jury? Under what circumstances may it be used to refresh the recollection of the husband or the wife?

7. Business Records

The business records exception to the hearsay rule applies to more than simply "businesses" as that term is usually understood, but it finds its roots in common law decisions allowing litigants to prove commercial transactions through carefully maintained records rather than by requiring testimony from all of the employees involved. Historically, the exception has been defended by appeal both to the reliability of such records and to the practical necessities of litigation. As with other exceptions to the hearsay rule, opinions differ regarding whether the original rationales for the business records rule justify the exception in its current form.

[F.R.E. 803(6), 803(7); C.E.C. §§1270–1272]

a. Generally

ADVISORY COMMITTEE NOTES TO F.R.E. 803(6)

Exception (6) This represents an area which has received much attention from those seeking to improve the law of evidence. The Commonwealth Fund Act was the result of a study completed in 1927 by a distinguished committee under the chairmanship of Professor Morgan. With changes too minor to mention, it was adopted by Congress in 1936 as the rule for federal courts. 28 U.S.C. §1732. A number of states took similar action. . . . These reform efforts were largely within the context of business and commercial records, as the kind usually encountered, and concentrated considerable attention upon relaxing the requirement of producing as witnesses, or accounting for the nonproduction of, all participants in the process of gathering, transmitting, and recording information which the common law had evolved as a burdensome and crippling aspect of using records of this type. . . . The element of unusual reliability of business records is said variously to be supplied by systematic checking, by regularity and continuity which produce habits of precision, by actual experience of business in relying upon them, or by a duty to make an accurate record as part of a continuing job or occupation. . . .

STATE v. ACQUISTO

463 A.2d 122 (R.I. 1983)

WEISBERGER, Justice.

This case comes before us on the defendant's appeal from a judgment of conviction of first-degree sexual assault entered against him in the Superior Court. . . . The defendant presented evidence of alibi. Two of the alibi witnesses were defendant's mother, Mrs. Julia Griffin, and Mrs. Ann Callahan, both of whom were employed as stipendiary volunteers (senior companions) at the Institute of Mental Health (IMH) during the period in issue. . . . [They testified that they saw the defendant at the home he shared with his mother on the morning of September 27, 1979, when the assault took place, and] that they were home that morning since the employees of the IMH were on strike and therefore they were not able to go to work.

In rebuttal the state presented Mrs. Marie C. Judge who testified that she was the custodian of records for the Department of Elderly Affairs. Part of her duties included the handling of payroll records for senior companions. Mrs. Judge testified that she received payroll vouchers from the IMH which were signed by Mrs. Griffin and Mrs. Callahan. These vouchers were offered in evidence and tended to show that Mrs. Griffin and Mrs. Callahan worked during the morning of September 27. These vouchers further indicated that the strike at the IMH was not in progress on September 27 but had in fact occurred the prior week, September 17 through September 19. The defendant challenges the receipt of these records in evidence on the ground that they do not meet the common-law standards for introduction of business records. The defendant cites *Quint v. Pawtuxet Valley Bus Lines*, 114 R.I. 473, 481, 335 A.2d 328, 333 (1975), as setting forth the following common-law requirements for admissibility of business records:

> "The record maker and each human link in the chain of information, if living and competent, had to testify that the entry was made in the regular course of business in his handwriting or under his immediate supervision and each provider of information contained in the report had to testify. If any necessary witness such as the maker was deemed incompetent or was absent from the jurisdiction at trial time, other witnesses had to identify the record and explain how and by whom it was kept. *State v. Mace*, 6 R.I. 85 (1859)."

... The restriction of the common law in introduction of business records has been roundly criticized by Professor Wigmore in 5 Wigmore, *Evidence* §1530 at 451–52 (Chadbourn rev. 1974):

> "In such a case, it should be sufficient if the books were verified on the stand by a supervising officer who knew them to be the books of regular entries kept in that establishment; thus the production on the stand of a battalion of bookkeepers, salesmen, shipping clerks, teamsters, foremen, or other employees, should be dispensed with....
>
> "Such entries are dealt with in that way in the most important undertakings of mercantile and industrial life. They are the ultimate basis of calculation, investment, and general confidence in every business enterprise. Nor does the practical impossibility of obtaining constantly and permanently the verification of every employee affect the trust that is given to such books. It would seem that expedients which the entire commercial world recognizes as safe could be sanctioned, and not discredited, by courts of justice."

Similarly, in commenting upon the common-law requirement of authentication, Professor McCormick suggests that

> "[i]n light of present business practices, the common law requirement is clearly unreasonable. The complex nature of modern business organizations is such that all participants in the preparation of a record can most often not be identified or, if they can be pinpointed, could not reasonably be expected to have any helpful recollection concerning the specific transactions at issue. Moreover, production of the large numbers of participants that would be required would be a substantial burden on the offering party, a burden not likely to be justified by the benefits to be derived from requiring production of all participants." *McCormick's Handbook of the Law of Evidence* §312 at 729 (2d ed. Cleary 1972).

A most reasonable balance has been struck in the Federal Rules of Evidence dealing with the introduction of business records.... [W]e believe that the common-law requirement adds nothing to the reliability of the record to be introduced, given the business practices of the twentieth century. Therefore, we adopt the standards set forth in Federal Rule 803(6) for the introduction of business records as evidence in criminal cases....

Applying the standards set forth in Federal Rule 803(6), the foundation laid for introduction of these exhibits was adequate. Mrs. Judge was the custodian of the records. She was responsible for administering payroll. The claim for payment made by the two senior companions and approved by their supervisor was the type of information upon which her payroll records and authorization for payment were based. This is not unlike the circumstances described in 5 Wigmore, *supra*, at §1530, wherein the custodian of records makes entries on the basis of information given by others. The defendant further objects to the receiving of these payroll vouchers into evidence because they were prepared prior to the making up of the payroll. This circumstance does not constitute a violation of the standards set forth in Federal Rule 803(6). It is specifically provided that a memorandum in any form of acts, events, or conditions made "at or near the time by, or from information transmitted by, a person with knowledge," may be admitted into evidence. In the instant case Mrs. Judge testified that although the vouchers were made up in advance, she would be notified before the payroll was completed in the event that any information contained on the voucher should be changed. In this case no such change was transmitted. Consequently, the trial justice was not in error in admitting the payroll vouchers into evidence.... [T]he judgment of conviction is affirmed....

ADVISORY COMMITTEE NOTE TO THE 2000
AMENDMENT TO F.R.E. 803(6)

The amendment provides that the foundation requirements of Rule 803(6) can be satisfied under certain circumstances without the expense and inconvenience of producing time-consuming foundation witnesses. Under current law, courts have generally required foundation witnesses to testify. See, e.g., Tongil Co., Ltd. v. Hyundai Merchant Marine Corp., 968 F.2d 999 (9th Cir. 1992) (reversing a judgment based on business records where a qualified person filed an affidavit but did not testify). Protections are provided by the authentication requirements of Rule 902(11) for domestic records, Rule 902(12) for foreign records in civil cases, and 18 U.S.C. §3505 for foreign records in criminal cases.

b. Qualifying "Businesses"

REPORT OF THE HOUSE JUDICIARY COMMITTEE
H.R. Rep. No. 93-650 (1973)

Rule 803(6) as submitted by the Court permitted a record made "in the course of a regularly conducted activity" to be admissible in certain circumstances. The Committee believed there were insufficient guarantees of reliability in records made in the course of activities falling outside the scope of "business" activities as that term is broadly defined in 28 U.S.C. 1732. Moreover, the Committee concluded that the additional requirement of Section 1732 that it must have been the regular practice of a business to make the record is a necessary further assurance of its trustworthiness. The Committee accordingly amended the Rule to incorporate these limitations.

REPORT OF THE CONFERENCE COMMITTEE

Conf. Rep. No. 93-1597 (1974)

The House bill provides in subsection (6) that records of a regularly conducted "business" activity qualify for admission into evidence as an exception to the hearsay rule. "Business" is defined as including "business, profession, occupation and calling of every kind." The Senate amendment drops the requirement that the records be those of a "business" activity and eliminates the definition of "business." The Senate amendment provides that records are admissible if they are records of a regularly conducted "activity."

The Conference adopts the House provision that the records must be those of a regularly conducted "business" activity. The Conferees changed the definition of "business" contained in the House provision in order to make it clear that the records of institutions and associations like schools, churches and hospitals are admissible under this provision. The records of public schools and hospitals are also covered by Rule 803(8), which deals with public records and reports.

KEOGH v. COMMISSIONER OF INTERNAL REVENUE

713 F.2d 496 (9th Cir. 1983)

DUNIWAY, Circuit Judge:

In this case we review the tax court's finding of income tax deficiencies against a Las Vegas casino employee.... Appellant husband here, petitioner in the tax court, was employed at the Dunes Hotel & Country Club, in Las Vegas. He worked in the casino, where he dealt blackjack or ran "big wheel" or roulette games and was known as a 21 dealer. The 21 dealers earned regular wages paid semimonthly. In addition, 21 players sometimes gave them tips or "tokes" in the form of coins or casino chips.... The tax court found that during the years in question, 1969-1971, all 21 dealers at the Dunes pooled their tokes, and that the pool was divided equally once a day among all the dealers who had worked during that day's three shifts....

The Commissioner asserted that the Keoghs had underreported tip income in 1969, 1970, and 1971. He calculated Keogh's toke income through a statistical analysis based on entries in a diary kept by one John Whitlock, Jr., not a party to this action, who worked at the Dunes from March 4, 1967 to May 7, 1970. In the diary, the date of the month and the day of the week were listed on the left side of each page, and separate vertical columns were designated "gross," "net," "tax," and "tips." Beginning in January, 1968, there was an additional column designated "F. I. C. A.," and beginning in April, 1969, a further column designated "insurance." Wage entries were made in the notebook approximately every two weeks in amounts that were the same as those in the Dunes' payroll records for Whitlock. An entry of "off," "sick," "vac," or a dollar amount was made in the diary in the "tips" column for each day. . . . [I]t is undisputed that Whitlock had, as the tax court found, "a poor reputation for honesty and truthfulness," was dismissed by the Dunes for unsatisfactory work, and had been convicted, with his wife, of receiving stolen property. . . .

At trial before the tax court, the principal evidence was a photocopy of the Whitlock diary and testimony by Barbara Mikle, by then Whitlock's former wife. Whitlock, though subpoenaed by the Commissioner, failed to appear. . . .

The Whitlock diary, offered in evidence to prove the truth of its contents as they related to tokes received by Dunes 21 dealers, was hearsay and thus inadmissible unless excepted by one or more rules of evidence. F. R. Evid. 801, 802. . . . [W]e find the diary admissible under Rule 803(6). . . .

[The Keoghs argue] that Rule 803(6) does not apply to the diary because it was not a business record. They argue that the diary was Whitlock's personal record, not a record of the business enterprise involved, the Dunes. But Whitlock's diary, even though personal to him, shows every indication of being kept "in the course of" his own "business activity," "occupation, and calling." *See* 4 Weinstein's Evidence §803(6)[03] (1981 ed.) at 803-155: "[P]ersonal records kept for business reasons may be able to qualify. A housekeeper's records kept neatly and accurately for purposes of balancing bank statements, keeping strict budgets and preparing income tax returns could qualify under the statute."

The reliability usually found in records kept by business concerns may be established in personal business records if they are systematically checked and regularly and continually maintained. *See United States v. Hedman*, 7 Cir., 1980, 630 F.2d 1184, 1197-1198 (diary of payoffs by extortion victim); *United States v. McPartlin*, 7 Cir., 1979, 595 F.2d 1321, 1347-1350 (desk calendar-appointment diary, and cases there cited); Weinstein, *supra* (reliability determined from "testimony indicating that they were kept meticulously"); Advisory Committee Note to Rule 803(6). . . .

Here, Mikle testified that she saw Whitlock and only Whitlock make entries in the diary; that he usually made them after night shifts of work; that when he made no entries for three to four days, he would copy entries for those days from a record kept in his wallet; that he usually made no entries in the diary on his days off; and that she understood the diary to contain a record of tokes he received from his work as a dealer. . . .

[T]here is no evidence that Whitlock's motives in making the entries were suspect. The diary contained his own personal financial records; there is no reason put forward for him to have lied to himself. The reliability of the tip entries is corroborated by the fact that other entries corresponded with Dunes' payroll records, and that reliability is not tarnished by the fact that Whitlock, as the Keoghs are alleged to have done, reported to the government smaller amounts of tip income than he in fact received and recorded in the diary. Neither is Rule 803(6) made inapplicable by the fact that Mikle, not Whitlock, testified to lay the foundation for the diary. She testified adequately as to the regularity of the entries.

The Keoghs contend that the testimony of Whitlock as custodian of the diary was required because only he could speak to his reliance on the records kept there. But the record gives us no reason to believe that Whitlock did not rely on his personal financial diary; therefore, we do not find that the tax court abused its discretion in admitting it without Whitlock's personal testimony.... Affirmed.

UNITED STATES v. GIBSON

711 F.2d 871 (9th Cir. 1982) (sub nom. United States v. Foster)

ALARCON, Circuit Judge:

[Johnnie Gibson and several codefendants were convicted of heroin trafficking.] ... Over Gibson's objection, [cooperating prosecution witness Minyon] Logan's ledger was admitted into evidence under the business record exception of Fed. R. Evid. 803(6). The ledger, which contained records of drug transactions, implicated Gibson in the conspiracy. Gibson contends that the ledger was improperly admitted because the records were not kept in the course of regularly conducted business activity and because the entries were untrustworthy.

To be admissible as a business record under Rule 803(6), the record must have been kept in the "regular course" of a business activity.... Logan testified that she kept a record of most of her large drug transactions. She stated that it was her regular practice to enter into the ledger the number of balloons that went out on a particular day and how much money she took in. The transactions were recorded contemporaneously, and Logan relied on them. This evidence was sufficient to satisfy Rule 803(6).

The fact that the ledger was an incomplete record of Gibson's drug dealings and contained several blank pages and unrelated entries did not render the ledger inadmissible. The accuracy of the remaining pages was not altered simply because Logan did not record every heroin sale that occurred. Nor does the fact that the entries were made out of sequence destroy their accuracy. The entries were made at or near the time of the events described and they satisfied the regularity requirement. Their sequence was therefore irrelevant.

Gibson argues that the entries were nonetheless untrustworthy. However, because Logan had to rely on the entries, there would have been little reason for her to distort or falsify them.... All appellants' convictions on all counts are Affirmed.

c. Qualifying Records

PALMER V. HOFFMAN

318 U.S. 109 (1943)

Mr. Justice DOUGLAS delivered the opinion of the Court.

This case arose out of a grade crossing accident which occurred in Massachusetts.... The accident occurred on the night of December 25, 1940.

On December 27, 1940, the engineer of the train, who died before the trial, made a statement at a freight office of petitioners where he was interviewed by an assistant superintendent of the road and by a representative of the Massachusetts Public Utilities Commission. This statement was offered in evidence by petitioners under the Act of June 20, 1936, 49 Stat. 1561, 28 U.S.C. §695.[1] They offered to prove (in the language of the Act) that the statement was signed in the regular course of business, it being the regular course of such business to make such a statement. Respondent's objection to its introduction was sustained.

We agree with the majority view below that it was properly excluded. . . . [T]he fact that a company makes a business out of recording its employees' versions of their accidents does not put those statements in the class of records made "in the regular course" of the business within the meaning of the Act. If it did, then any law office in the land could follow the same course, since business as defined in the Act includes the professions. We would then have a real perversion of a rule designed to facilitate admission of records which experience has shown to be quite trustworthy. Any business by installing a regular system for recording and preserving its version of accidents for which it was potentially liable could qualify those reports under the Act. . . . The probability of trustworthiness of records because they were routine reflections of the day to day operations of a business would be forgotten as the basis of the rule. . . . [I]t is manifest that in this case those reports are not for the systematic conduct of the enterprise as a railroad business. Unlike payrolls, accounts receivable, accounts payable, bills of lading and the like these reports are calculated for use essentially in the court, not in the business. Their primary utility is in litigating, not in railroading. . . . Affirmed.

LEWIS v. BAKER

526 F.2d 470 (2d Cir. 1975)

WATERMAN, Circuit Judge:

Plaintiff, Clifford J. Lewis, Jr., brought this action . . . alleging he suffered a disabling injury while employed by the Penn Central Railroad. Judgment was entered in favor of defendants after a jury trial. Plaintiff appeals. . . .

On the date of his injury, October 26, 1969, plaintiff was employed as a freight brakeman or car dropper in the Penn Central railroad freight yard in Morrisville, Pennsylvania. . . . [He claimed he was injured when the handbrake on

---

1. "In any court of the United States and in any court established by Act of Congress, any writing or record, whether in the form of an entry in a book or otherwise, made as a memorandum or record of any act, transaction, occurrence, or event, shall be admissible as evidence of said act, transaction, occurrence, or event, if it shall appear that it was made in the regular course of any business, and that it was the regular course of such business to make such memorandum or record at the time of such act, transaction, occurrence, or event or within a reasonable time thereafter. All other circumstances of the making of such writing or record, including lack of personal knowledge by the entrant or maker, may be shown to affect its weight, but they shall not affect its admissibility. The term 'business' shall include business, profession, occupation, and calling of every kind."

a boxcar he was moving failed to hold.] At the trial, defendants sought to rebut plaintiff's allegations of a faulty brake with evidence that the brake had functioned properly immediately prior to the accident when the plaintiff tested it, and immediately after the accident when it was checked in connection with the preparation of an accident report. It was the defendants' contention that plaintiff improperly set, or forgot to set, a necessary brake handle....

In support of their interpretation of the events, defendants offered into evidence a "personal injury report" and an "inspection report." Frank Talbott, a trainmaster, testified that the personal injury report was signed by him and prepared under his supervision. The information had been provided to him by William F. Campbell, the night trainmaster. Talbott confirmed the authenticity of the record and testified that he was required to make out such reports of injuries as part of the regular course of business. At the trial David W. Halderman, an assistant general foreman for the defendants, identified the inspection report which had been prepared by Campbell and by Alfred Zuchero, a gang foreman. This report was based upon an inspection of the car Campbell and Zuchero had conducted less than four hours after the accident. Halderman testified that Zuchero was dead and that Campbell was employed by a railroad in Virginia. The latter was thus beyond the reach of subpoena. Halderman also confirmed that following every accident involving injury to an employee his office was required to complete inspection reports, and that such reports were regularly kept in the course of business. Over objection, the court admitted both reports into evidence ... under the Federal Business Records Act....[1]

Appellant argues ... the Supreme Court's decision in *Palmer v. Hoffman*, 318 U.S. 109 (1943), precludes their admission into evidence.... In *Palmer v. Hoffman*, the engineer preparing the report had been personally involved in the accident, and as Circuit Judge Frank stated in his opinion for the Court of Appeals, the engineer knew "at the time of making it that he [was] very likely, in a probable law suit relating to that accident, to be charged with wrongdoing as a participant in the accident, so that he [was] almost certain, when making the memorandum or report, to be sharply affected by a desire to exculpate himself and to relieve himself or his employer of liability." 129 F.2d 976, 991 (2d Cir. 1942) (italics omitted). Here there could have been no similar motivation on the part of Talbott, Campbell or Zuchero, for not one of them was involved in the accident, or could have possibly been the target of a

---

1. 28 U.S.C. §1732 provides, insofar as is applicable:

Record made in regular course of business ...

   (a) In any court of the United States and in any court established by Act of Congress, any writing or record, whether in the form of an entry in a book or otherwise, made as a memorandum or record of any act, transaction, occurrence, or event, shall be admissible as evidence of such act, transaction, occurrence, or event, if made in regular course of any business, and if it was the regular course of such business to make such memorandum or record at the time of such act, transaction, occurrence, or event or within a reasonable time thereafter.

   All other circumstances of the making of such writing or record, including lack of personal knowledge by the entrant or maker, may be shown to affect its weight, but such circumstances shall not affect its admissibility.

   The term "business," as used in this section, includes business, profession, occupation, and calling of every kind.

lawsuit by Lewis. . . . In the absence of a motive to fabricate, a motive so clearly spelled out in *Palmer v. Hoffman*, the holding in that case is not controlling to emasculate the Business Records Act. Therefore the trial court must look to those earmarks of reliability which otherwise establish the trustworthiness of the record. . . .

As we stated in *Taylor v. Baltimore & Ohio R.R. Co.*, [344 F.2d 281 (2d Cir. 1965),] "[i]t would ill become a court to say that the regular making of reports required by law is not in the regular course of business." In addition to their use by the railroad in making reports to the ICC, the reports here were undoubtedly of utility to the employer in ascertaining whether the equipment involved was defective so that future accidents might be prevented. These factors, we think, are sufficient indicia of trustworthiness to establish the admissibility of the reports into evidence under the Federal Business Records Act. . . . Affirmed.

ADVISORY COMMITTEE NOTE TO F.R.E. 803(6)

. . . Amplification of the kinds of activities producing admissible records has given rise to problems which conventional business records by their nature avoid. . . . Entries in the form of opinions were not encountered in traditional business records in view of the purely factual nature of the items recorded, but they are now commonly encountered with respect to medical diagnoses, prognoses, and test results, as well as occasionally in other areas. . . . [T]he rule specifically includes both diagnoses and opinions, in addition to acts, events, and conditions, as proper subjects of admissible entries.

Problems of the motivation of the informant have been a source of difficulty and disagreement. In Palmer v. Hoffman, 318 U.S. 109 (1943), exclusion of an accident report made by the since deceased engineer, offered by defendant railroad trustees in a grade crossing collision case, was upheld. The report was not "in the regular course of business," not a record of the systematic conduct of the business as a business, said the Court. The report was prepared for use in litigating, not railroading. While the opinion mentions the motivation of the engineer only obliquely, the emphasis on records of routine operations is significant only by virtue of impact on motivation to be accurate. Absence of routineness raises lack of motivation to be accurate. The opinion of the Court of Appeals had gone beyond mere lack of motive to be accurate: the engineer's statement was "dripping with motivations to misrepresent." Hoffman v. Palmer, 129 F.2d 976, 991 (2d Cir. 1942). The direct introduction of motivation is a disturbing factor, since absence of motive to misrepresent has not traditionally been a requirement of the rule; that records might be self-serving has not been a ground for exclusion. As Judge Clark said in his dissent, "I submit that there is hardly a grocer's account book which could not be excluded on that basis." A physician's evaluation report of a personal injury litigant would appear to be in the routine of his business. If the report is offered by the party at whose instance it was made, however, it has been held inadmissible, Yates v. Bair Transport, Inc., 249 F. Supp. 681 (S.D.N.Y. 1965), otherwise if offered by the opposite party, Korte v. New York, N.H. & H.R. Co., 191 F.2d 86 (2d Cir. 1951), cert. denied 342 U.S. 868.

The decisions hinge on motivation and which party is entitled to be concerned about it. Professor McCormick believed that the doctor's report or the accident report were sufficiently routine to justify admissibility. Yet hesitation must be experienced in admitting everything which is observed and recorded in the course of a regularly conducted activity. Efforts to set a limit are illustrated by Hartzog v. United States, 217 F.2d 706 (4th Cir. 1954), error to admit worksheets made by since deceased deputy collector in preparation for the instant income tax evasion prosecution, and United States v. Ware, 247 F.2d 698 (7th Cir. 1957), error to admit narcotics agents' records of purchases.... Some decisions have been satisfied as to motivation of an accident report if made pursuant to statutory duty, since the report was oriented in a direction other than the litigation which ensued. The formulation of specific terms which would assure satisfactory results in all cases is not possible. Consequently the rule proceeds from the base that records made in the course of a regularly conducted activity will be taken as admissible but subject to authority to exclude if "the sources of information or other circumstances indicate lack of trustworthiness."

Occasional decisions have reached for enhanced accuracy by requiring involvement as a participant in matters reported. . . . The rule includes no requirement of this nature. Wholly acceptable records may involve matters merely observed, e.g. the weather.

The form which the "record" may assume under the rule is described broadly as a "memorandum, report, record, or data compilation, in any form." The expression "data compilation" is used as broadly descriptive of any means of storing information other than the conventional words and figures in written or documentary form. It includes, but is by no means limited to, electronic computer storage....

d. Sources of Information

ADVISORY COMMITTEE NOTE TO F.R.E. 803(6)

. . . Sources of information presented no substantial problem with ordinary business records. All participants, including the observer or participant furnishing the information to be recorded, were acting routinely, under a duty of accuracy, with employer reliance on the result, or in short "in the regular course of business." If, however, the supplier of the information does not act in the regular course, an essential link is broken; the assurance of accuracy does not extend to the information itself, and the fact that it may be recorded with scrupulous accuracy is of no avail.[1] An illustration is the police report incorporating information obtained from a bystander: the officer qualifies as acting in the regular course but the informant does not. The leading case, *Johnson v. Lutz*, 253 N.Y. 124, 170 N.E. 517 (1930), held that a report thus prepared was inadmissible. Most of the authorities have agreed with the decision. The point is not dealt with specifically in the Commonwealth Fund Act, the Uniform Act, or Uniform Rule 63(13). However, Model Code Rule 514 contains the requirement "that it was the regular course of that business for one with personal knowledge ... to make such a memorandum or record or to transmit information thereof to be included in such a memorandum or record...." The rule follows this lead in requiring an informant with knowledge acting in the course of the regularly conducted activity....

WILSON v. ZAPATA OFF-SHORE CO.

939 F.2d 260 (5th Cir. 1991)

GARWOOD, Circuit Judge:

[Plaintiff Elizabeth Wilson appealed from adverse judgments in her suits against her former employer, Zapata Off-Shore Co., for sex discrimination and emotional distress.] Wilson left Zapata in October 1984 because she was experiencing emotional problems, which she claims were caused by a hostile work environment aboard the rig. She was admitted to Riverside Hospital in Jackson, Mississippi on October 16, 1984, where she was treated for anxiety-related disorders....

Wilson . . . challenges the district court's refusal to exclude portions of hospital records reporting a statement by Wilson's sister, Laird, to a social worker, who recorded that "informant reports that the patient is a habitual liar and has been all of her life." . . . Wilson is correct that the hospital record contains double hearsay. Double hearsay in the context of a business record exists when the record is prepared by an employee with information supplied by another person. If both the source and the recorder of the information, as well as every other participant in the chain producing the record, are acting in the regular course of business, the multiple hearsay is excused by Rule 803(6). *United States v. Baker*, 693 F.2d 183, 188 (D.C. Cir. 1982). However, if the source of the information is an outsider, as in the facts before us, Rule 803(6) does not, by itself, permit the admission of the business record. The outsider's statement must fall within another hearsay exception to be admissible because it does not have the presumption of accuracy that statements made during the regular course of business have. Further, Federal Rule of Evidence 805 requires that all levels of hearsay satisfy exception hearsay requirements before the statement is admissible.

Rule 803(6) provides a hearsay exception for records kept in the course of *any* regularly conducted business activity, which would include hospitals.... The second level of hearsay presents a closer question. The out-of-court statements by Laird were offered to prove the truth of the matter asserted, and thus were classic hearsay. Zapata argues that Laird's statements fall within Fed. R. Evid. 803(4), which excepts from the hearsay rule statements made for purposes of medical diagnosis or treatment. The test, when examining whether statements contained in medical records relating to a patient's condition are admissible hearsay, is whether such statements are of the type pertinent to a physician in providing treatment. Courts have construed Rule 803(4) to include statements made for psychiatric diagnosis. *See, e.g., Morgan v. Foretich*, 846 F.2d 941, 949 (4th Cir. 1988) (allowing statements made by child abuse victim to psychiatrist). Moreover, Rule 803(4) does not always require that the out-of-court statements refer to the condition of the declarant. McCormick, *McCormick on Evidence*, §292 at pp. 840–41 (1984). It is apparent that the treating psychiatrists in this case were concerned with learning about Wilson's background, lifestyle and history of psychiatric treatment. Further, it was obviously important for the psychiatrists to know whether Wilson was a credible informant. Statements by Wilson's sister, recorded two days after Wilson's admission to the hospital, could be appropriate and helpful background information for the psychiatrists to consider in the diagnosis and treatment of Wilson's complaints. The value of the statements, however, would appear to be somewhat compromised by their total generality and conclusory nature. . . .

We pretermit determination of whether admission of the records was error. Even [if] it were, we will not reverse if we find that the error was harmless. We conclude that it is highly probable that the admission of these medical reports did not affect Wilson's substantial rights. We note that Wilson's sister was called to testify and denied making the statements to the social worker. There was abundant other evidence casting serious doubt on Wilson's credibility, as well as directly contradicting her version of the crucial events on which she based her suit. . . . Affirmed.

e. Absence of Record

ADVISORY COMMITTEE NOTE TO F.R.E. 803(7)

Failure of a record to mention a matter which would ordinarily be mentioned is satisfactory evidence of its nonexistence. While probably not hearsay as defined in Rule 801, supra, decisions may be found which class the evidence not only as hearsay but also as not within any exception. In order to set the question at rest in favor of admissibility, it is specifically treated here.

UNITED STATES v. GENTRY

925 F.2d 186 (7th Cir. 1991)

EASTERBROOK, Circuit Judge.

[Defendant Kevin Gentry] told fellow employees — plus the security force of the mall where he worked — that he had bit into a pin when he ate M & M candy bought from a vending machine. One of Gentry's fellow employees found some metal embedded in the candy. Sheriff's deputies who investigated the report found Gentry's claim hard to believe and asked him to take a polygraph test. Gentry did; the examiner concluded that he was lying; after the examiner switched off the machine, Gentry confessed that he had put the pin in the candy and made the report to get attention. He was prosecuted for [making a false report of food tampering in violation of 18 U.S.C.] §1365(c)(1) and received a sentence of 12 months' imprisonment. . . .

Gentry . . . objects to testimony from an employee of the manufacturer that there were no other reports of pins in M & M candy. The testimony was relevant; it implies that the pin came from Gentry rather than the factory (or a tamperer other than Gentry). And Fed. R. Evid. 803(7) allows this use of business records to show the nonoccurrence of an event. . . . The conviction is affirmed. . . .

PROBLEMS

3.45. An author hurt in an automobile collision sues the other driver for negligence and seeks compensation for money she lost because her injuries prevented her from finishing a novel. She seeks to introduce copies of daily e-mail messages she sent to her brother before the accident, describing her progress on the novel. Do the messages qualify as business records?

3.46. Barry Bonds, a professional baseball player, testified before a federal grand jury in 2003 that he had never used performance-enhancing steroids. The government later indicted him for perjury and sought to prove its case at trial by introducing reports prepared by a blood and urine testing company, indicating that samples produced by Bonds were determined to contain steroids. The samples were provided to the laboratory by a personal trainer who worked for Bonds; the trainer apparently told the laboratory the samples had come from Bonds. The trainer refused to testify at trial, though, even after he was held in contempt. The trial judge then ruled that both the reports and the trainer's statements to the laboratory were inadmissible hearsay. Should the reports have been deemed admissible under the business records exception? (For the Ninth Circuit's answer, see *United States v. Bonds*, 608 F.3d 495 (9th Cir. 2010).)

8. Public Records

The public records exception of Federal Rule of Evidence 803(8) is narrower than the business records exception codified in Rule 803(6), and in fact consists of three separate exceptions. Federal courts have struggled with the wording of Rule 803(8), and with the problem of public records that fail to satisfy the requirements of that exception but fall within another exception. The latter problem arises particularly often in connection with the business records rule, because most, if not all, public agencies qualify as "businesses" for purposes of that exception.

In criminal cases, of course, public records introduced by the prosecution need to satisfy not only the statutory rules of evidence but also the Confrontation Clause. In three decisions the Supreme Court has explored the application of *Crawford v. Washington* to laboratory records of the kind often introduced against criminal defendants at trial. The first two of these cases, *Melendez-Diaz v. Massachusetts* and *Bullcoming v. New Mexico*, are excerpted in this section. The third case, *Williams v. Illinois*, appears in Chapter 9, where the special rules for expert testimony are explored.

There are two important questions the Supreme Court has not defini-tively resolved about applying the hearsay rule and the Confrontation Clause to public records. The first is whether there is a category of "ministerial" or "nonadversarial" records that are by definition non-testimonial and therefore exempt from the requirements of the Confrontation Clause; the second is whether public records that do not satisfy the public records exception in Rule 803(8) can be introduced under the business records exception in Rule 803(6). Lower courts have answered these questions in different ways. Three illustrative decisions are excerpted at the end of this section. (As we will see in Chapter 9, the Supreme Court addressed the admissibility of "nonadversarial" records under the Confrontation Clause in *Williams v. Illinois*, but the frac-tured set of opinions in that case failed to provide clear guidance.)

[F.R.E. 803(8)-803(10); C.E.C. §§1280, 1281, 1284]

ADVISORY COMMITTEE NOTE TO F.R.E. 803(8)

Public records are a recognized hearsay exception at common law and have been the subject of statutes without number. . . . Justification for the exception is the assumption that a public official will perform his duty prop-erly and the unlikelihood that he will remember details independently of the record. As to items (a) and (b), further support is found in the reliability fac-tors underlying records of regularly conducted activities generally. •

(a) Cases illustrating the admissibility of records of the office's or agen-cy's own activities are numerous. Chesapeake & Delaware Canal Co. v. United States, 250 U.S. 123 (1919), Treasury records of miscellaneous receipts and dis-bursements; Howard v. Perrin, 200 U.S. 71 (1906), General Land Office records; Ballew v. United States, 160 U.S 187 (1895), Pension Office records.

(b) Cases sustaining admissibility of records of matters observed are also numerous. United States v. Van Hook, 284 F.2d 489 (7th Cir. 1960), remanded for resentencing 365 U.S. 609, letter from induction officer to District Attorney, pursuant to army regulations, stating fact and circumstances of refusal to be inducted; T'Kach v. United States, 242 F.2d 937 (5th Cir. 1957), affidavit of White House personnel officer that search of records showed no employment of accused, charged with fraudulently representing himself as an envoy of the President; Minnehaha County v. Kelley, 150 F.2d 356 (8th Cir. 1945); Weather Bureau records of rainfall; United States v. Meyer, 113 F.2d 387 (7th Cir. 1940), cert. denied 311 U.S. 706, map prepared by government engineer from infor-mation furnished by men working under his supervision.

(c) The more controversial area of public records is that of the so-called "evaluative" report. The disagreement among the decisions has been due in part, no doubt, to the variety of situations encountered, as well as to differ-ences in principle. . . . Various kinds of evaluative reports are admissible under federal statutes. . . . While these statutory exceptions to the hearsay rule are left undisturbed, Rule 802, the willingness of Congress to recognize a substan-tial measure of admissibility for evaluative reports is a helpful guide.

Factors which may be of assistance in passing upon the admissibility of evaluative reports include: (1) the timeliness of the investigation, (2) the special skill or experience of the official, (3) whether a hearing was held and the level at which conducted, (4) possible motivation problems suggested by Palmer v. Hoffman, 318 U.S. 109 (1943). Others no doubt could be added.

The formulation of an approach which would give appropriate weight to all possible factors in every situation is an obvious impossibility. Hence the rule, as in Exception (6), assumes admissibility in the first instance but with ample provision for escape if sufficient negative factors are present. In one respect, however, the rule with respect to evaluative reports under item (c) is very specific: they are admissible only in civil cases and against the government in criminal cases in view of the almost certain collision with confrontation rights which would result from their use against the accused in a criminal case.

BEECH AIRCRAFT CORP. v. RAINEY

488 U.S. 153 (1988)

Justice BRENNAN delivered the opinion of the Court.

In this action we address a longstanding conflict among the Federal Courts of Appeals over whether Federal Rule of Evidence 803(8)(C), which provides an exception to the hearsay rule for public investigatory reports containing "factual findings," extends to conclusions and opinions contained in such reports. . . . This litigation stems from the crash of a Navy training aircraft at Middleton Field, Alabama, on July 13, 1982, which took the lives of both pilots on board, Lieutenant Commander Barbara Ann Rainey and Ensign Donald Bruce Knowlton. . . . The two pilots' surviving spouses brought a product liability suit against petitioners Beech Aircraft Corporation, the plane's manufacturer, and Beech Aerospace Services, which serviced the plane under contract with the Navy. The plaintiffs alleged that the crash had been caused by a loss of engine power, known as "rollback," due to some defect in the aircraft's fuel control system. The defendants, on the other hand, advanced the theory of pilot error, suggesting that the plane had stalled during [an] abrupt avoidance maneuver.

. . . One piece of evidence presented by the defense was an investigative report prepared by Lieutenant Commander William Morgan on order of the training squadron's commanding officer and pursuant to authority granted in the Manual of the Judge Advocate General. This "JAG Report," completed during the six weeks following the accident, was organized into sections labeled "finding of fact," "opinions," and "recommendations," and was supported by some 60 attachments. The "finding of fact" included statements like the following:

> "13. At approximately 1020, while turning crosswind without proper interval, 3E955 crashed, immediately caught fire and burned. . . .
>   "27. At the time of impact, the engine of 3E955 was operating but was operating at reduced power."

Among his "opinions" Lieutenant Commander Morgan stated, in paragraph 5, that due to the deaths of the two pilots and the destruction of the aircraft "it is almost impossible to determine exactly what happened to Navy 3E955 from the time it left the runway on its last touch and go until it impacted the ground." He nonetheless continued with a detailed reconstruction of a possible set of events, based on pilot error, that could have caused the accident. The next two paragraphs stated a caveat and a conclusion:

> "6. Although the above sequence of events is the most likely to have occurred, it does not change the possibility that a 'rollback' did occur.

> "7. The most probable cause of the accident was the pilots [*sic*] failure to maintain proper interval."

The trial judge initially determined, at a pretrial conference, that the JAG Report was sufficiently trustworthy to be admissible, but that it "would be admissible only on its factual findings and would not be admissible insofar as any opinions or conclusions are concerned." The day before trial, however, the court reversed itself and ruled, over the plaintiffs' objection, that certain of the conclusions would be admitted. Accordingly, the court admitted most of the report's "opinions," including the first sentence of paragraph 5 about the impossibility of determining exactly what happened, and paragraph 7, which opined about failure to maintain proper interval as "[t]he most probable cause of the accident." On the other hand, the remainder of paragraph 5 was barred as "nothing but a possible scenario," and paragraph 6, in which investigator Morgan refused to rule out rollback, was deleted as well.[3]

. . . Following a 2-week trial, the jury returned a verdict for petitioners. A panel of the Eleventh Circuit reversed and remanded for a new trial. . . . Considering itself bound by the Fifth Circuit precedent of *Smith v. Ithaca Corp.*, 612 F.2d 215 (1980), the panel agreed with Rainey's argument that Federal Rule of Evidence 803(8)(C), which excepts investigatory reports from the hearsay rule, did not encompass evaluative conclusions or opinions. Therefore, it held, the "conclusions" contained in the JAG Report should have been excluded. . . .

Federal Rule of Evidence 803 provides that certain types of hearsay statements are not made excludable by the hearsay rule, whether or not the declarant is available to testify. Rule 803(8) defines the "public records and reports" which are not excludable, as follows:

> "Records, reports, statements, or data compilations, in any form, of public offices or agencies, setting forth (A) the activities of the office or agency, or (B) matters observed pursuant to duty imposed by law as to which matters there was a duty to report, . . . or (C) in civil actions and proceedings and against the Government in criminal cases, factual findings resulting from an investigation made pursuant to authority granted by law, unless the sources of information or other circumstances indicate lack of trustworthiness."

Controversy over what "public records and reports" are made not excludable by Rule 803(8)(C) has divided the federal courts from the beginning. In the present litigation, the Court of Appeals followed the "narrow"

---

3. The record gives no indication why paragraph 6 was deleted. Neither at trial nor on appeal have respondents raised any objection to the deletion of paragraph 6.

interpretation of *Smith v. Ithaca, supra,* which held that the term "factual findings" did not encompass "opinions" or "conclusions." Courts of Appeals other than those of the Fifth and Eleventh Circuits, however, have generally adopted a broader interpretation. For example, the Court of Appeals for the Sixth Circuit, in *Baker v. Elcona Homes Corp.,* 588 F.2d 551 (1978), *cert. denied,* 441 U.S. 933 (1979), held that "factual findings admissible under Rule 803(8)(C) may be those which are made by the preparer of the report from disputed evidence...."[6] The other Courts of Appeals that have squarely confronted the issue have also adopted the broader interpretation. We agree and hold that factually based conclusions or opinions are not on that account excluded from the scope of Rule 803(8)(C).

... We begin with the language of the Rule itself. Proponents of the narrow view have generally relied heavily on a perceived dichotomy between "fact" and "opinion" in arguing for the limited scope of the phrase "factual findings." *Smith v. Ithaca Corp.* contrasted the term "factual findings" in Rule 803(8)(C) with the language of Rule 803(6) (records of regularly conducted activity), which expressly refers to "opinions" and "diagnoses." "Factual findings," the court opined, must be something other than opinions.

For several reasons, we do not agree. In the first place, it is not apparent that the term "factual findings" should be read to mean simply "facts" (as opposed to "opinions" or "conclusions"). A common definition of "finding of fact" is, for example, "[a] conclusion by way of reasonable inference from the evidence." Black's Law Dictionary 569 (5th ed. 1979). To say the least, the language of the Rule does not compel us to reject the interpretation that "factual findings" includes conclusions or opinions that flow from a factual investigation. Second, we note that, contrary to what is often assumed, the language of the Rule does not state that "factual findings" are admissible, but that "*reports* ... setting forth ... factual findings" (emphasis added) are admissible. On this reading, the language of the Rule does not create a distinction between "fact" and "opinion" contained in such reports.

Turning next to the legislative history of Rule 803(8)(C), we find no clear answer to the question of how the Rule's language should be interpreted. Indeed, in this litigation the legislative history may well be at the origin of the dispute. Rather than the more usual situation where a court must attempt to glean meaning from ambiguous comments of legislators who did not focus directly on the problem at hand, here the Committees in both Houses of Congress clearly recognized and expressed their opinions on the precise question at issue. Unfortunately, however, they took diametrically opposite positions. Moreover, the two Houses made no effort to reconcile their views, either through changes in the Rule's language or through a statement in the Report of the Conference Committee.

---

6. *Baker* involved a police officer's report on an automobile accident. While there was no direct witness as to the color of the traffic lights at the moment of the accident, the court held admissible the officer's conclusion on the basis of his investigations at the accident scene and an interview with one of the drivers that "apparently ... unit #2 ... entered the intersection against a red light."

The House Judiciary Committee, which dealt first with the proposed rules after they had been transmitted to Congress by this Court, included in its Report but one brief paragraph on Rule 803(8):

"The Committee approved Rule 803(8) without substantive change from the form in which it was submitted by the Court. The Committee intends that the phrase 'factual findings' be strictly construed and that evaluations or opinions contained in public reports shall not be admissible under this Rule." H.R. Rep. No. 93-650, p. 14 (1973).

The Senate Committee responded at somewhat greater length, but equally emphatically:

"The House Judiciary Committee report contained a statement of intent that 'the phrase "factual findings" in subdivision (c) be strictly construed and that evaluations or opinions contained in public reports shall not be admissible under this rule.' The committee takes strong exception to this limiting understanding of the application of the rule. We do not think it reflects an understanding of the intended operation of the rule as explained in the Advisory Committee notes to this subsection. . . . We think the restrictive interpretation of the House overlooks the fact that while the Advisory Committee assumes admissibility in the first instance of evaluative reports, they are not admissible if, as the rule states, 'the sources of information or other circumstances indicate lack of trustworthiness'. . . .

"The committee concludes that the language of the rule together with the explanation provided by the Advisory Committee furnish sufficient guidance on the admissibility of evaluative reports." S. Rep. No. 93-1277, p. 18 (1974).

Clearly this legislative history reveals a difference of view between the Senate and the House that affords no definitive guide to the congressional understanding. It seems clear however that the Senate understanding is more in accord with the wording of the Rule and with the comments of the Advisory Committee.[9]

The Advisory Committee's comments are notable, first, in that they contain no mention of any dichotomy between statements of "fact" and "opinions" or "conclusions." What was on the Committee's mind was simply whether what it called "evaluative reports" should be admissible. Illustrating the previous division among the courts on this subject, the Committee cited numerous cases in which the admissibility of such reports had been both sustained and denied. It also took note of various federal statutes that made certain kinds of evaluative reports admissible in evidence. What is striking about all of these examples is that these were reports that stated conclusions. *E.g., Moran v. Pittsburgh-Des Moines Steel Co.*, 183 F.2d 467, 472-473 (CA3 1950) (report of Bureau of Mines concerning the cause of a gas tank explosion admissible); *Franklin v. Skelly Oil Co.*, 141 F.2d 568, 571-572 (CA10 1944) (report of state fire marshal on the cause of a gas explosion inadmissible); 42 U.S.C. §269(b) (bill of health by appropriate official admissible as prima facie evidence of vessel's sanitary history and condition). The Committee's concern was clearly

---

9. As Congress did not amend the Advisory Committee's draft in any way that touches on the question before us, the Committee's commentary is particularly relevant in determining the meaning of the document Congress enacted.

whether reports of this kind should be admissible. Nowhere in its comments is there the slightest indication that it even considered the solution of admitting only "factual" statements from such reports. Rather, the Committee referred throughout to "reports," without any such differentiation regarding the statements they contained. What the Committee referred to in the Rule's language as "reports ... setting forth ... factual findings" is surely nothing more or less than what in its commentary it called "evaluative reports." Its solution as to their admissibility is clearly stated in the final paragraph of its report on this Rule. That solution consists of two principles: First, "the rule ... assumes admissibility in the first instance...." Second, it provides "ample provision for escape if sufficient negative factors are present."

That "provision for escape" is contained in the final clause of the Rule: evaluative reports are admissible "unless the sources of information or other circumstances indicate lack of trustworthiness." This trustworthiness inquiry — and not an arbitrary distinction between "fact" and "opinion" — was the Committee's primary safeguard against the admission of unreliable evidence, and it is important to note that it applies to all elements of the report. Thus, a trial judge has the discretion, and indeed the obligation, to exclude an entire report or portions thereof — whether narrow "factual" statements or broader "conclusions" — that she determines to be untrustworthy. Moreover, safeguards built into other portions of the Federal Rules, such as those dealing with relevance and prejudice, provide the court with additional means of scrutinizing and, where appropriate, excluding evaluative reports or portions of them. And of course it goes without saying that the admission of a report containing "conclusions" is subject to the ultimate safeguard — the opponent's right to present evidence tending to contradict or diminish the weight of those conclusions.

Our conclusion that neither the language of the Rule nor the intent of its framers calls for a distinction between "fact" and "opinion" is strengthened by the analytical difficulty of drawing such a line. It has frequently been remarked that the distinction between statements of fact and opinion is, at best, one of degree:

> "All statements in language are statements of opinion, i.e., statements of mental processes or perceptions. So-called 'statements of fact' are only more specific statements of opinion. What the judge means to say, when he asks the witness to state the facts, is: 'The nature of this case requires that you be more specific, if you can, in your description of what you saw.'" W. King & D. Pillinger, Opinion Evidence in Illinois 4 (1942) (footnote omitted), quoted in 3 J. Weinstein & M. Berger, Weinstein's Evidence §701[01], p. 701-6 (1988).

See also E. Cleary, McCormick on Evidence 27 (3d ed. 1984) ("There is no conceivable statement however specific, detailed and 'factual', that is not in some measure the product of inference and reflection as well as observation and memory"); R. Lempert & S. Saltzburg, A Modern Approach to Evidence 449 (2d ed. 1982) ("A factual finding, unless it is a simple report of something observed, is an opinion as to what more basic facts imply"). Thus, the traditional requirement that lay witnesses give statements of fact rather than opinion may be considered, "[l]ike the hearsay and original documents rules ... a 'best evidence' rule." McCormick, Opinion Evidence in Iowa, 19 Drake L. Rev. 245, 246 (1970).

In the present action, the trial court had no difficulty in admitting as a factual finding the statement in the JAG Report that "[a]t the time of impact, the engine of 3E955 was operating but was operating at reduced power." Surely this "factual finding" could also be characterized as an opinion, which the investigator presumably arrived at on the basis of clues contained in the airplane wreckage. Rather than requiring that we draw some inevitably arbitrary line between the various shades of fact/opinion that invariably will be present in investigatory reports, we believe the Rule instructs us — as its plain language states — to admit "reports . . . setting forth . . . factual findings." The Rule's limitations and safeguards lie elsewhere: First, the requirement that reports contain factual findings bars the admission of statements not based on factual investigation. Second, the trustworthiness provision requires the court to make a determination as to whether the report, or any portion thereof, is sufficiently trustworthy to be admitted.

A broad approach to admissibility under Rule 803(8)(C), as we have outlined it, is also consistent with the Federal Rules' general approach of relaxing the traditional barriers to "opinion" testimony. Rules 702–705 permit experts to testify in the form of an opinion, and without any exclusion of opinions on "ultimate issues." And Rule 701 permits even a lay witness to testify in the form of opinions or inferences drawn from her observations when testimony in that form will be helpful to the trier of fact. We see no reason to strain to reach an interpretation of Rule 803(8)(C) that is contrary to the liberal thrust of the Federal Rules.

We hold, therefore, that portions of investigatory reports otherwise admissible under Rule 803(8)(C) are not inadmissible merely because they state a conclusion or opinion. As long as the conclusion is based on a factual investigation and satisfies the Rule's trustworthiness requirement, it should be admissible along with other portions of the report.[13] As the trial judge in this action determined that certain of the JAG Report's conclusions were trustworthy, he rightly allowed them to be admitted into evidence. We therefore reverse the judgment of the Court of Appeals in respect of the Rule 803(8)(C) issue. . . .

MELENDEZ-DIAZ v. MASSACHUSETTS

557 U.S. 305 (2009)

Justice Scalia delivered the opinion of the Court.

The Massachusetts courts in this case admitted into evidence affidavits reporting the results of forensic analysis which showed that material seized by the police and connected to the defendant was cocaine. The question presented is whether those affidavits are "testimonial," rendering the affiants

---

13. We emphasize that the issue in this litigation is whether Rule 803(8)(C) recognizes any difference between statements of "fact" and "opinion." There is no question here of any distinction between "fact" and "law." We thus express no opinion on whether legal conclusions contained in an official report are admissible as "findings of fact" under Rule 803(8)(C).

"witnesses" subject to the defendant's right of confrontation under the Sixth Amendment....

At trial, the prosecution placed into evidence the bags seized from a codefendant and from the police cruiser [in which Melendez-Diaz and his two codefendants were transported to the police station following their arrests]. It also submitted three "certificates of analysis" showing the results of the forensic analysis performed on the seized substances. The certificates reported the weight of the seized bags and stated that the bags "[h]a[ve] been examined with the following results:The substance was found to contain: Cocaine." The certificates were sworn to before a notary public by analysts at the State Laboratory Institute of the Massachusetts Department of Public Health, as required under Massachusetts law.

Petitioner objected to the admission of the certificates, asserting that our Confrontation Clause decision in *Crawford v. Washington*, 541 U.S. 36 (2004), required the analysts to testify in person. The objection was overruled, and the certificates were admitted pursuant to state law as "prima facie evidence of the composition, quality, and the net weight of the narcotic ... analyzed." Mass. Gen. Laws, ch. 111, §13.

The jury found Melendez-Diaz guilty. He appealed, contending, among other things, that admission of the certificates violated his Sixth Amendment right to be confronted with the witnesses against him. The Appeals Court of Massachusetts rejected the claim, relying on the Massachusetts Supreme Judicial Court's decision in *Commonwealth v. Verde*, 444 Mass. 279 (2005), which held that the authors of certificates of forensic analysis are not subject to confrontation under the Sixth Amendment. The Supreme Judicial Court denied review....

There is little doubt that the documents at issue in this case fall within the "core class of testimonial statements." ... Our description of that category [in *Crawford*] mentions affidavits twice. ... The documents at issue here, while denominated by Massachusetts law "certificates," are quite plainly affidavits:"declaration[s] of facts written down and sworn to by the declarant before an officer authorized to administer oaths." Black's Law Dictionary 62 (8th ed. 2004). They are incontrovertibly a "'solemn declaration or affirmation made for the purpose of establishing or proving some fact.'" *Crawford, supra* (quoting 2 N.Webster,An American Dictionary of the English Language (1828)). The fact in question is that the substance found in the possession of Melendez-Diaz and his codefendants was, as the prosecution claimed, cocaine—the precise testimony the analysts would be expected to provide if called at trial. The "certificates" are functionally identical to live, in-court testimony, doing "precisely what a witness does on direct examination." *Davis v. Washington*, 547 U.S. 813 (2006) (emphasis deleted).

Here, moreover, not only were the affidavits "'made under circumstances which would lead an objective witness reasonably to believe that the statement would be available for use at a later trial,'" *Crawford, supra*, but under Massachusetts law the *sole purpose* of the affidavits was to provide "prima facie evidence of the composition, quality, and the net weight" of the analyzed substance. We can safely assume that the analysts were aware of the affidavits' evidentiary purpose, since that purpose — as stated in the relevant state-law provision — was reprinted on the affidavits themselves.

In short, under our decision in *Crawford* the analysts' affidavits were testimonial statements, and the analysts were "witnesses" for purposes of the Sixth Amendment. Absent a showing that the analysts were unavailable to testify at trial *and* that petitioner had a prior opportunity to cross-examine them, petitioner was entitled to "'be confronted with'" the analysts at trial. *Crawford, supra*. . . .

Respondent . . . argues that the analysts are not subject to confrontation because they are not "accusatory" witnesses, in that they do not directly accuse petitioner of wrongdoing; rather, their testimony is inculpatory only when taken together with other evidence linking petitioner to the contraband. This finds no support in the text of the Sixth Amendment or in our case law.

The Sixth Amendment guarantees a defendant the right "to be confronted with the witnesses *against him*." To the extent the analysts were witnesses (a question resolved above), they certainly provided testimony *against* petitioner, proving one fact necessary for his conviction — that the substance he possessed was cocaine. The contrast between the text of the Confrontation Clause and the text of the adjacent Compulsory Process Clause confirms this analysis. While the Confrontation Clause guarantees a defendant the right to be confronted with the witnesses "against him," the Compulsory Process Clause guarantees a defendant the right to call witnesses "in his favor." U.S. Const., Amdt. 6. The text of the Amendment contemplates two classes of witnesses — those against the defendant and those in his favor. The prosecution *must* produce the former;[3] the defendant *may* call the latter. Contrary to respondent's assertion, there is not a third category of witnesses, helpful to the prosecution, but somehow immune from confrontation. . . .

Respondent and the dissent argue that the analysts should not be subject to confrontation because they are not "conventional" (or "typical" or "ordinary") witnesses of the sort whose *ex parte* testimony was most notoriously used at the trial of Sir Walter Raleigh. It is true, as the Court recognized in *Crawford*, that *ex parte* examinations of the sort used at Raleigh's trial have "long been thought a paradigmatic confrontation violation." But the paradigmatic case identifies the core of the right to confrontation, not its limits. The right to confrontation was not invented in response to the use of the *ex parte* examinations in *Raleigh's Case*, 2 How. St. Tr. 1 (1603). That use provoked such an outcry precisely because it flouted the deeply rooted common-law tradition "of live testimony in court subject to adversarial testing." *Crawford, supra* (citing 3 W. Blackstone, Commentaries on the Laws of England 373-374 (1768)). . . .

Respondent claims that there is a difference, for Confrontation Clause purposes, between testimony recounting historical events, which is "prone to distortion or manipulation," and the testimony at issue here, which is the "resul[t] of neutral, scientific testing." Relatedly, respondent and the dissent argue that confrontation of forensic analysts would be of little value because "one would not reasonably expect a laboratory professional . . . to feel quite

---

3. The right to confrontation may, of course, be waived, including by failure to object to the offending evidence; and States may adopt procedural rules governing the exercise of such objections. . . . .

differently about the results of his scientific test by having to look at the defendant."

This argument is little more than an invitation to return to our overruled decision in *Roberts*, which held that evidence with "particularized guarantees of trustworthiness" was admissible notwithstanding the Confrontation Clause. What we said in *Crawford* in response to that argument remains true:

> "To be sure, the Clause's ultimate goal is to ensure reliability of evidence, but it is a procedural rather than a substantive guarantee. It commands, not that evidence be reliable, but that reliability be assessed in a particular manner: by testing in the crucible of cross-examination. . . . Dispensing with confrontation because testimony is obviously reliable is akin to dispensing with jury trial because a defendant is obviously guilty. This is not what the Sixth Amendment prescribes."

Respondent and the dissent may be right that there are other ways — and in some cases better ways — to challenge or verify the results of a forensic test. But the Constitution guarantees one way: confrontation. We do not have license to suspend the Confrontation Clause when a preferable trial strategy is available.

Nor is it evident that what respondent calls "neutral scientific testing" is as neutral or as reliable as respondent suggests. Forensic evidence is not uniquely immune from the risk of manipulation. According to a recent study conducted under the auspices of the National Academy of Sciences, "[t]he majority of [laboratories producing forensic evidence] are administered by law enforcement agencies, such as police departments, where the laboratory administrator reports to the head of the agency." And "[b]ecause forensic scientists often are driven in their work by a need to answer a particular question related to the issues of a particular case, they sometimes face pressure to sacrifice appropriate methodology for the sake of expediency." A forensic analyst responding to a request from a law enforcement official may feel pressure — or have an incentive — to alter the evidence in a manner favorable to the prosecution.

Confrontation is one means of assuring accurate forensic analysis. . . . Like the eyewitness who has fabricated his account to the police, the analyst who provides false results may, under oath in open court, reconsider his false testimony. And, of course, the prospect of confrontation will deter fraudulent analysis in the first place.

Confrontation is designed to weed out not only the fraudulent analyst, but the incompetent one as well. Serious deficiencies have been found in the forensic evidence used in criminal trials. One commentator asserts that "[t]he legal community now concedes, with varying degrees of urgency, that our system produces erroneous convictions based on discredited forensics." Metzger, Cheating the Constitution, 59 Vand. L.Rev. 475, 491 (2006). One study of cases in which exonerating evidence resulted in the overturning of criminal convictions concluded that invalid forensic testimony contributed to the convictions in 60% of the cases. Garrett & Neufeld, Invalid Forensic Science Testimony and Wrongful Convictions, 95 Va. L. Rev. 1, 14 (2009). And the National Academy Report concluded: "*The forensic science system, encompassing both research and practice, has serious problems that can only be addressed by a national commitment to overhaul the current structure that supports the forensic science community in this country."* Like expert witnesses generally, an analyst's lack of proper training or deficiency in judgment may be disclosed in cross-examination.

This case is illustrative. The affidavits submitted by the analysts contained only the bare-bones statement that "[t]he substance was found to contain: Cocaine." At the time of trial, petitioner did not know what tests the analysts performed, whether those tests were routine, and whether interpreting their results required the exercise of judgment or the use of skills that the analysts may not have possessed. While we still do not know the precise tests used by the analysts, we are told that the laboratories use "methodology recommended by the Scientific Working Group for the Analysis of Seized Drugs." At least some of that methodology requires the exercise of judgment and presents a risk of error that might be explored on cross-examination. See 2 P. Giannelli & E. Imwinkelried, Scientific Evidence §23.03[c], pp. 532–533, ch. 23A, p. 607 (4th ed. 2007) (identifying four "critical errors" that analysts may commit in interpreting the results of the commonly used gas chromatography/mass spectrometry analysis); Shellow, The Application of *Daubert* to the Identification of Drugs, 2 Shepard's Expert & Scientific Evidence Quarterly 593, 600 (1995) (noting that while spectrometers may be equipped with computerized matching systems, "forensic analysts in crime laboratories typically do not utilize this feature of the instrument, but rely exclusively on their subjective judgment").

The same is true of many of the other types of forensic evidence commonly used in criminal prosecutions. "[T]here is wide variability across forensic science disciplines with regard to techniques, methodologies, reliability, types and numbers of potential errors, research, general acceptability, and published material." National Academy Report. . . . Contrary to respondent's and the dissent's suggestion, there is little reason to believe that confrontation will be useless in testing analysts' honesty, proficiency, and methodology — the features that are commonly the focus in the cross-examination of experts.

Respondent argues that the analysts' affidavits are admissible without confrontation because they are "akin to the types of official and business records admissible at common law." But the affidavits do not qualify as traditional official or business records, and even if they did, their authors would be subject to confrontation nonetheless.

Documents kept in the regular course of business may ordinarily be admitted at trial despite their hearsay status. See Fed. Rule Evid. 803(6). But that is not the case if the regularly conducted business activity is the production of evidence for use at trial. Our decision in *Palmer v. Hoffman*, 318 U.S. 109, 63 S. Ct. 477, 87 L. Ed. 645 (1943), made that distinction clear. There we held that an accident report provided by an employee of a railroad company did not qualify as a business record because, although kept in the regular course of the railroad's operations, it was "calculated for use essentially in the court, not in the business."[7] The analysts' certificates — like police reports

_____

7. The early common-law cases likewise involve records prepared for the administration of an entity's affairs, and not for use in litigation. See, *e.g., King v. Rhodes*, 1 Leach 24, 168 Eng. Rep. 115 (1742) (admitting into evidence ship's muster-book); *King v. Martin*, 2 Camp. 100, 101, 170 Eng. Rep. 1094, 1095 (1809) (vestry book); *King v. Aickles*, 1 Leach 390, 391–392, 168 Eng. Rep. 297, 298 (1785) (prison logbook).

generated by law enforcement officials — do not qualify as business or public records for precisely the same reason. See Rule 803(8) (defining public records as "excluding, however, in criminal cases matters observed by police officers and other law enforcement personnel").

Respondent seeks to rebut this limitation by noting that at common law the results of a coroner's inquest were admissible without an opportunity for confrontation. But as we have previously noted, whatever the status of coroner's reports at common law in England, they were not accorded any special status in American practice. See *Crawford, Giles v. California* (BREYER, J., dissenting); Evidence-Official Records-Coroner's Inquest, 65 U. Pa. L. Rev. 290 (1917).

The dissent identifies a single class of evidence which, though prepared for use at trial, was traditionally admissible: a clerk's certificate authenticating an official record — or a copy thereof — for use as evidence. But a clerk's authority in that regard was narrowly circumscribed. He was permitted "to certify to the correctness of a copy of a record kept in his office," but had "no authority to furnish, as evidence for the trial of a lawsuit, his interpretation of what the record contains or shows, or to certify to its substance or effect." *State v. Wilson*, 141 La. 404, 409, 75 So. 95, 97 (1917). See also *State v. Champion*, 116 N.C. 987, 21 S.E. 700, 700-701 (1895); 5 J. Wigmore, Evidence §1678 (3d ed. 1940). . . . A clerk could by affidavit *authenticate* or provide a copy of an otherwise admissible record, but could not do what the analysts did here: *create* a record for the sole purpose of providing evidence against a defendant.

Far more probative here are those cases in which the prosecution sought to admit into evidence a clerk's certificate attesting to the fact that the clerk had searched for a particular relevant record and failed to find it. Like the testimony of the analysts in this case, the clerk's statement would serve as substantive evidence against the defendant whose guilt depended on the nonexistence of the record for which the clerk searched. Although the clerk's certificate would qualify as an official record under respondent's definition — it was prepared by a public officer in the regular course of his official duties — and although the clerk was certainly not a "conventional witness" under the dissent's approach, the clerk was nonetheless subject to confrontation. See *People v. Bromwich*, 200 N.Y. 385, 388-389, 93 N.E. 933, 934 (1911); *People v. Goodrode*, 132 Mich. 542, 547, 94 N.W. 14, 16 (1903); Wigmore, *supra*, §1678. . . .

Business and public records are generally admissible absent confrontation not because they qualify under an exception to the hearsay rules, but because — having been created for the administration of an entity's affairs and not for the purpose of establishing or proving some fact at trial — they are not testimonial. Whether or not they qualify as business or official records, the analysts' statements here — prepared specifically for use at petitioner's trial — were testimony against petitioner, and the analysts were subject to confrontation under the Sixth Amendment.

Respondent asserts that we should find no Confrontation Clause violation in this case because petitioner had the ability to subpoena the analysts. But that power — whether pursuant to state law or the Compulsory Process Clause — is no substitute for the right of confrontation. Unlike the Confrontation Clause, those provisions are of no use to the defendant when the witness is unavailable or simply refuses to appear. Converting the prosecution's duty under the Confrontation Clause into the defendant's privilege under state law or the Compulsory Process Clause shifts the consequences of adverse-witness no-shows from the State to the accused. More fundamentally, the Confrontation Clause imposes a burden on the prosecution to present its witnesses, not on the defendant to bring those adverse witnesses into court. Its value to the defendant is not replaced by a system in which the prosecution presents its evidence via *ex parte* affidavits and waits for the defendant to subpoena the affiants if he chooses.

Finally, respondent asks us to relax the requirements of the Confrontation Clause to accommodate the "'necessities of trial and the adversary process.'" It is not clear whence we would derive the authority to do so. The Confrontation Clause may make the prosecution of criminals more burdensome, but that is equally true of the right to trial by jury and the privilege against self-incrimination. The Confrontation Clause — like those other constitutional provisions — is binding, and we may not disregard it at our convenience.

We also doubt the accuracy of respondent's and the dissent's dire predictions. . . . Perhaps the best indication that the sky will not fall after today's decision is that it has not done so already. Many States have already adopted the constitutional rule we announce today, while many others permit the defendant to assert (or forfeit by silence) his Confrontation Clause right after receiving notice of the prosecution's intent to use a forensic analyst's report. Despite these widespread practices, there is no evidence that the criminal justice system has ground to a halt in the States that, one way or another, empower a defendant to insist upon the analyst's appearance at trial. Indeed, in Massachusetts itself, a defendant may subpoena the analyst to appear at trial, and yet there is no indication that obstructionist defendants are abusing the privilege. . . .

Defense attorneys and their clients will often stipulate to the nature of the substance in the ordinary drug case. It is unlikely that defense counsel will insist on live testimony whose effect will be merely to highlight rather than cast doubt upon the forensic analysis. Nor will defense attorneys want to antagonize the judge or jury by wasting their time with the appearance of a witness whose testimony defense counsel does not intend to rebut in any fashion. . . . Given these strategic considerations, and in light of the experience in those States that already provide the same or similar protections to defendants, there is little reason to believe that our decision today will commence the parade of horribles respondent and the dissent predict.

This case involves little more than the application of our holding in *Crawford v. Washington.* The Sixth Amendment does not permit the prosecution to prove its case via *ex parte* out-of-court affidavits, and the admission of such evidence against Melendez-Diaz was error.[14] We therefore reverse the judgment of the Appeals Court of Massachusetts and remand the case for further proceedings not inconsistent with this opinion.

[Justice Thomas filed a concurring opinion.]

---

14. We of course express no view as to whether the error was harmless. The Massachusetts Court of Appeals did not reach that question and we decline to address it in the first instance. . . .

Justice KENNEDY, with whom THE CHIEF JUSTICE, Justice BREYER, and Justice ALITO join, dissenting.

... The Court says that, before the results of a scientific test may be introduced into evidence, the defendant has the right to confront the "analyst." One must assume that this term, though it appears nowhere in the Confrontation Clause, nevertheless has some constitutional substance that now must be elaborated in future cases....

Consider how many people play a role in a routine test for the presence of illegal drugs. One person prepares a sample of the drug, places it in a testing machine, and retrieves the machine's printout—often, a graph showing the frequencies of radiation absorbed by the sample or the masses of the sample's molecular fragments. A second person interprets the graph the machine prints out—perhaps by comparing that printout with published, standardized graphs of known drugs. Meanwhile, a third person—perhaps an independent contractor—has calibrated the machine and, having done so, has certified that the machine is in good working order. Finally, a fourth person—perhaps the laboratory's director—certifies that his subordinates followed established procedures.

It is not at all evident which of these four persons is the analyst to be confronted under the rule the Court announces today. If all are witnesses who must appear for in-court confrontation, then the Court has, for all practical purposes, forbidden the use of scientific tests in criminal trials.... [R]equiring even one of these individuals to testify threatens to disrupt if not end many prosecutions where guilt is clear but a newly found formalism now holds sway....

The facts of this case illustrate the formalistic and pointless nature of the Court's reading of the Clause. Petitioner knew, well in advance of trial, that the Commonwealth would introduce the tests against him. The bags of cocaine were in court, available for him to test, and entered into evidence. Yet petitioner made no effort, before or during trial, to mount a defense against the analysts' results. Petitioner could have challenged the tests' reliability by seeking discovery concerning the testing methods used or the qualifications of the laboratory analysts. See Mass. Rule Crim. Proc. 14(a)(2) (2009). He did not do so. Petitioner could have sought to conduct his own test. See Rule 41. Again, he did not seek a test; indeed, he did not argue that the drug was not cocaine. Rather than dispute the authenticity of the samples tested or the accuracy of the tests performed, petitioner argued to the jury that the prosecution had not shown that he had possessed or dealt in the drugs.

Despite not having prepared a defense to the analysts' results, petitioner's counsel made what can only be described as a *pro forma* objection to admitting the results without in-court testimony, presumably from one particular analyst. Today the Court, by deciding that this objection should have been sustained, transforms the Confrontation Clause from a sensible procedural protection into a distortion of the criminal justice system....

One purpose of confrontation is to impress upon witnesses the gravity of their conduct. ... A further purpose is to alleviate the danger of one-sided interrogations by adversarial government officials who might distort a witness's testimony. The Clause guards against this danger by bringing the interrogation into the more neutral and public forum of the courtroom.... But neither purpose is served by the rule the Court announces today. It is not plausible that a laboratory analyst will retract his or her prior conclusion upon catching sight of the defendant the result condemns. After all, the analyst is far removed from the particular defendant and, indeed, claims no personal knowledge of the defendant's guilt. And an analyst performs hundreds if not thousands of tests each year and will not remember a particular test or the link it had to the defendant....

For the sake of these negligible benefits, the Court threatens to disrupt forensic investigations across the country and to put prosecutions nationwide at risk of dismissal based on erratic, all-too-frequent instances when a particular laboratory technician, now invested by the Court's new constitutional designation as the analyst, simply does not or cannot appear.... The Court's holding is a windfall to defendants, one that is unjustified by any demonstrated deficiency in trials, any well-understood historical requirement, or any established constitutional precedent....

The Court's fundamental mistake is to read the Confrontation Clause as referring to a kind of out-of-court statement — namely, a testimonial statement — that must be excluded from evidence. The Clause does not refer to kinds of statements. Nor does the Clause contain the word "testimonial." The text, instead, refers to kinds of persons, namely, to "witnesses against" the defendant. Laboratory analysts are not "witnesses against" the defendant as those words would have been understood at the framing....

Instead, the Clause refers to a conventional "witness" — meaning one who witnesses (that is, perceives) an event that gives him or her personal knowledge of some aspect of the defendant's guilt. Both *Crawford* and *Davis* concerned just this kind of ordinary witness — and nothing in the Confrontation Clause's text, history, or precedent justifies the Court's decision to expand those cases....

Though there is "virtually no evidence of what the drafters of the Confrontation Clause intended it to mean," *White v. Illinois*, 502 U.S. 346, 359 (1992) (THOMAS, J., concurring in part and concurring in judgment), it is certain the Framers did not contemplate that an analyst who conducts a scientific test far removed from the crime would be considered a "witnes[s] against" the defendant. The Framers were concerned with a typical witness — one who perceived an event that gave rise to a personal belief in some aspect of the defendant's guilt....

The infamous treason trial of Sir Walter Raleigh provides excellent examples of the kinds of witnesses to whom the Confrontation Clause refers. *Raleigh's Case*, 2 How. St. Tr. 1 (1603); see *Crawford* (Raleigh's trial informs our understanding of the Clause because it was, at the time of the framing, one of the "most notorious instances" of the abuse of witnesses' out-of-court statements). Raleigh's accusers claimed to have heard Raleigh speak treason, so they were witnesses in the conventional sense. We should limit the Confrontation Clause to witnesses like those in Raleigh's trial....

Though the Framers had no forensic scientists, they did use another kind of unconventional witness — the copyist. A copyist's work may be as essential to a criminal prosecution as the forensic analyst's. To convict a man of bigamy, for example, the State often requires his marriage records. But if the original records cannot be taken from the archive, the prosecution must rely on copies of those records, made for the purpose of introducing the copies into evidence at trial. In that case, the copyist's honesty and diligence are just as important as the analyst's here. If the copyist falsifies a copy, or even misspells a name or transposes a date, those flaws could lead the jury to convict. Because so much depends on his or her honesty and diligence, the copyist often prepares an affidavit certifying that the copy is true and accurate.

Such a certificate is beyond question a testimonial statement under the Court's definition: It is a formal out-of-court statement offered for the truth of two matters (the copyist's honesty and the copy's accuracy), and it is prepared for a criminal prosecution.

During the Framers' era copyists' affidavits were accepted without hesitation by American courts. See, *e.g., United States v. Percheman*, 7 Pet. 51, 85, 8 L. Ed. 604 (1833) (opinion for the Court by Marshall, C. J.); see also Advisory Committee's Note on Fed. Rule Evid. 902(4), 28 U.S.C. App., p. 390 ("The common law . . . recognized the procedure of authenticating copies of public records by certificate"); 5 J. Wigmore, Evidence §§1677, 1678 (J. Chadbourn rev. 1974). And courts admitted copyists' affidavits in criminal as well as civil trials. This demonstrates that the framing generation, in contrast to the Court today, did not consider the Confrontation Clause to require in-court confrontation of unconventional authors of testimonial statements. . . .

The modern trend in the state courts has been away from the Court's rule and toward the admission of scientific test results without testimony — perhaps because the States have recognized the increasing reliability of scientific testing. It appears that a mere six courts continue to interpret their States' hearsay laws to require analysts to testify. And, of course, where courts have grounded their decisions in state law, rather than the Constitution, the legislatures in those States have had, until now, the power to abrogate the courts' interpretation if the costs were shown to outweigh the benefits. Today the Court strips that authority from the States by carving the minority view into the constitutional text. . . .

Laboratory analysts who conduct routine scientific tests are not the kind of conventional witnesses to whom the Confrontation Clause refers. The judgment of the Appeals Court of Massachusetts should be affirmed.

BULLCOMING v. NEW MEXICO

564 U.S. 647 (2011)

JUSTICE GINSBURG delivered the opinion of the Court with respect to all but Part IV and footnote 6.*

. . . [P]etitioner Donald Bullcoming was arrested on charges of driving while intoxicated (DWI). Principal evidence against Bullcoming was a forensic laboratory report certifying that Bullcoming's blood alcohol concentration

---

* JUSTICE SOTOMAYOR and JUSTICE KAGAN join all but Part IV of this opinion. JUSTICE THOMAS joins all but Part IV and footnote 6.

was well above the threshold for aggravated DWI. At trial, the prosecution did not call as a witness the analyst who signed the certification. Instead, the State called another analyst who was familiar with the laboratory's testing procedures, but had neither participated in nor observed the test on Bullcoming's blood sample. . . . We hold that surrogate testimony of that order does not [satisfy the Confrontation Clause]. . . .

I

. . . Because Bullcoming refused to take a breath test, the police obtained a warrant authorizing a blood-alcohol analysis. Pursuant to the warrant, a sample of Bullcoming's blood was drawn at a local hospital. To determine Bullcoming's blood-alcohol concentration (BAC), the police sent the sample to the New Mexico Department of Health, Scientific Laboratory Division (SLD). In a standard SLD form titled "Report of Blood Alcohol Analysis," participants in the testing were identified, and the forensic analyst certified his finding.

SLD's report contained in the top block "information . . . filled in by [the] arresting officer." This information included the "reason [the] suspect [was] stopped" (the officer checked "Accident"), and the date ("8.14.05") and time ("18:25 PM") the blood sample was drawn. The arresting officer also affirmed that he had arrested Bullcoming and witnessed the blood draw. The next two blocks contained certifications by the nurse who drew Bullcoming's blood and the SLD intake employee who received the blood sample sent to the laboratory.

Following these segments, the report presented the "certificate of analyst," completed and signed by Curtis Caylor, the SLD forensic analyst assigned to test Bullcoming's blood sample [using gas chromatography]. Caylor recorded that the BAC in Bullcoming's sample was 0.21 grams per hundred milliliters, an inordinately high level. Caylor also affirmed that "[t]he seal of th[e] sample was received intact and broken in the laboratory," that "the statements in [the analyst's block of the report] are correct," and that he had "followed the procedures set out on the reverse of th[e] report." Those "procedures" instructed analysts, *inter alia*, to "retai[n] the sample container and the raw data from the analysis," and to "not[e] any circumstance or condition which might affect the integrity of the sample or otherwise affect the validity of the analysis." Finally, in a block headed "certificate of reviewer," the SLD examiner who reviewed Caylor's analysis certified that Caylor was qualified to conduct the BAC test, and that the "established procedure" for handling and analyzing Bullcoming's sample "ha[d] been followed.". . . . [1]

---

1. Gas chromatography is a widely used scientific method of quantitatively analyzing the constituents of a mixture. See generally H. McNair & J. Miller, Basic Gas Chromatography (2d ed. 2009) (hereinafter McNair). Under SLD's standard testing protocol, the analyst extracts two blood samples and inserts them into vials containing an "internal standard" — a chemical additive. The analyst then "cap[s] the [two] sample[s]," "crimp[s] them with an aluminum top," and places the vials into the gas chromatograph machine. Within a few hours, this device produces a printed graph — a chromatogram — along with calculations representing a software-generated interpretation of the data. See Brief for State of New Mexico Dept. of Health, SLD as *Amicus Curiae* 16-17.

Caylor's report that Bullcoming's BAC was 0.21 supported a prosecution for aggravated DWI, the threshold for which is a BAC of 0.16 grams per hundred milliliters. The State accordingly charged Bullcoming with this more serious crime....

On the day of trial, the State announced that it would not be calling SLD analyst Curtis Caylor as a witness because he had "very recently [been] put on unpaid leave" for a reason not revealed.... The State ... proposed to introduce Caylor's finding as a "business record" during the testimony of Gerasimos Razatos, an SLD scientist who had neither observed nor reviewed Caylor's analysis. Bullcoming's counsel opposed the State's proposal....[2] The trial court overruled the objection.... The jury convicted Bullcoming of aggravated DWI, and [the conviction was affirmed on appeal]....

II

... An analyst's certification prepared in connection with a criminal investigation or prosecution, the Court held [in *Melendez-Diaz v. Massachusetts*, 557 U.S. (2009)], is "testimonial," and therefore within the compass of the Confrontation Clause.[6] ... The New Mexico Supreme Court held surrogate testimony adequate to satisfy the Confrontation Clause in this case because analyst Caylor "simply transcribed the resul[t] generated by the gas chromatograph machine," presenting no interpretation and exercising no independent judgment. Bullcoming's "true 'accuser,'" the court said, was the machine, while testing analyst Caylor's role was that of "mere scrivener." Caylor's certification, however, reported more than a machine-generated number.

Although the State presented testimony that obtaining an accurate BAC measurement merely entails "look[ing] at the [gas chromatograph] machine and record[ing] the results," authoritative sources reveal that the matter is not so simple or certain. "In order to perform quantitative analyses satisfactorily and ... support the results under rigorous examination in court, the analyst must be aware of, and adhere to, good analytical practices and understand what is being done and why." Stafford, Chromatography, in Principles of Forensic Toxicology 92, 114 (B. Levine 2d ed. 2006). See also McNair 137 ("Errors that occur in any step can invalidate the best chromatographic analysis, so attention must be paid to all steps."); D. Bartell, M. McMurray, & A. ImObersteg, Attacking and Defending Drunk Driving Tests §16:80 (2d revision 2010) (stating that 93% of errors in laboratory tests for BAC levels are human errors that occur either before or after machines analyze samples). Even after the machine has produced its printed result, a review of the chromatogram may indicate that the test was not valid. See McNair 207–214.

Nor is the risk of human error so remote as to be negligible. *Amici* inform us, for example, that in neighboring Colorado, a single forensic laboratory produced at least 206 flawed blood-alcohol readings over a three-year span, prompting the dismissal of several criminal prosecutions. See Brief for National Association of Criminal Defense Lawyers et al. as *Amici Curiae* 32–33....

2. The State called as witnesses the arresting officer and the nurse who drew Bullcoming's blood. Bullcoming did not object to the State's failure to call the SLD intake employee or the reviewing analyst. "It is up to the prosecution," the Court observed in *Melendez-Diaz v. Massachusetts*, "to decide what steps in the chain of custody are so crucial as to require evidence; but what testimony *is* introduced must (if the defendant objects) be introduced live."

6. To rank as "testimonial," a statement must have a "primary purpose" of "establish[ing] or prov[ing] past events potentially relevant to later criminal prosecution." *Davis v. Washington*, 547 U.S. 813, 822 (2006)....

Caylor certified that he received Bullcoming's blood sample intact with the seal unbroken, that he checked to make sure that the forensic report number and the sample number "correspond[ed]," and that he performed on Bullcoming's sample a particular test, adhering to a precise protocol. He further represented, by leaving the "[r]emarks" section of the report blank, that no "circumstance or condition . . . affect[ed] the integrity of the sample or . . . the validity of the analysis."These representations, relating to past events and human actions not revealed in raw, machine-produced data, are meet for cross-examination.

The potential ramifications of the New Mexico Supreme Court's reasoning, furthermore, raise red flags. Most witnesses, after all, testify to their observations of factual conditions or events, *e.g.*, "the light was green,""the hour was noon." Such witnesses may record, on the spot, what they observed. Suppose a police report recorded an objective fact — Bullcoming's counsel posited the address above the front door of a house or the read-out of a radar gun. Could an officer other than the one who saw the number on the house or gun present the information in court — so long as that officer was equipped to testify about any technology the observing officer deployed and the police department's standard operating procedures? As our precedent makes plain, the answer is emphatically "No." . . .

The New Mexico Supreme Court stated that the number registered by the gas chromatograph machine called for no interpretation or exercise of independent judgment on Caylor's part. We have already explained that Caylor certified to more than a machine-generated number. In any event, the comparative reliability of an analyst's testimonial report drawn from machine-produced data does not overcome the Sixth Amendment bar. This Court settled in *Crawford* that the "obviou[s] reliab[ility]" of a testimonial statement does not dispense with the Confrontation Clause. . . .

Recognizing that admission of the blood-alcohol analysis depended on "live, in-court testimony [by] a qualified analyst," the New Mexico Supreme Court believed that Razatos could substitute for Caylor because Razatos "qualified as an expert witness with respect to the gas chromatograph machine and the SLD's laboratory procedures." But surrogate testimony of the kind Razatos was equipped to give could not convey what Caylor knew or observed about the events his certification concerned, *i.e.*, the particular test and testing process he employed. Nor could such surrogate testimony expose any lapses or lies on the certifying analyst's part. Significant here, Razatos had no knowledge of the reason why Caylor had been placed on unpaid leave. With Caylor on the stand, Bullcoming's counsel could have asked questions designed to reveal whether incompetence, evasiveness, or dishonesty accounted for Caylor's removal from his work station. Notable in this regard, the State never asserted that Caylor was "unavailable"; the prosecution conveyed only that Caylor was on uncompensated leave. Nor did the State assert that Razatos had any "independent opinion" concerning Bullcoming's BAC. . . .

More fundamentally, as this Court stressed in *Crawford*,"[t]he text of the Sixth Amendment does not suggest any open-ended exceptions from the confrontation requirement to be developed by the courts." Nor is it "the role of courts to extrapolate from the words of the [Confrontation Clause] to the values behind it, and then to enforce its guarantees only to the extent they serve (in the courts' views) those underlying values." *Giles* v. *California*, 554 U.S. 353, 375 (2008). Accordingly, the Clause does not tolerate dispensing with confrontation simply because the court believes that questioning one witness about another's testimonial statements provides a fair enough opportunity for cross-examination. . . . In short, when the State elected to introduce Caylor's certification, Caylor became a witness Bullcoming had the right to confront. . . .

III

. . . Distinguishing Bullcoming's case from *Melendez-Diaz*, where the analysts' findings were contained in certificates "sworn to before a notary public," the State emphasizes that the SLD report of Bullcoming's BAC was "unsworn." As the New Mexico Supreme Court recognized, "'the absence of [an] oath [i]s not dispositive' in determining if a statement is testimonial." Indeed, in *Crawford*, this Court rejected as untenable any construction of the Confrontation Clause that would render inadmissible only sworn *ex parte* affidavits, while leaving admission of formal, but unsworn statements "perfectly OK." . . .

In all material respects, the laboratory report in this case resembles those in *Melendez-Diaz*. Here, as in *Melendez-Diaz*, a law-enforcement officer provided seized evidence to a state laboratory required by law to assist in police investigations. Like the analysts in *Melendez-Diaz*, analyst Caylor tested the evidence and prepared a certificate concerning the result of his analysis. Like the *Melendez-Diaz* certificates, Caylor's certificate is "formalized" in a signed document, headed a "report." Noteworthy as well, the SLD report form contains a legend referring to municipal and magistrate courts' rules that provide for the admission of certified blood-alcohol analyses. . . . [T]he formalities attending the "report of blood alcohol analysis" are more than adequate to qualify Caylor's assertions as testimonial. . . .

IV

The State and its *amici* urge that unbending application of the Confrontation Clause to forensic evidence would impose an undue burden on the prosecution. This argument, also advanced in the dissent, largely repeats a refrain rehearsed and rejected in *Melendez-Diaz*. The constitutional requirement, we reiterate, "may not [be] disregard[ed] . . . at our convenience," and the predictions of dire consequences, we again observe, are dubious.

New Mexico law, it bears emphasis, requires the laboratory to preserve samples, which can be retested by other analysts, and neither party questions SLD's compliance with that requirement. Retesting "is almost always an option . . . in [DWI] cases," Brief for Public Defender Service for District of Columbia et al. as *Amici Curiae* 25 (hereinafter PDS brief), and the State had that option here: New Mexico could have avoided any Confrontation Clause problem by asking Razatos to retest the sample, and then testify to the results of his retest rather than to the results of a test he did not conduct or observe. . . .

Furthermore, notice-and-demand procedures, long in effect in many jurisdictions, can reduce burdens on forensic laboratories. Statutes governing these procedures typically "render . . . otherwise hearsay forensic reports admissible[,] while specifically preserving a defendant's right to demand that the prosecution call the author/analyst of [the] report." PDS Brief 9. . . .

Even before this Court's decision in *Crawford*, moreover, it was common prosecutorial practice to call the forensic analyst to testify. Prosecutors did so "to bolster the persuasive power of [the State's] case[,] . . . [even] when the defense would have preferred that the analyst did *not* testify." PDS Brief 8. . . .

Tellingly, in jurisdictions in which "it is the [acknowledged] job of . . . analysts to testify in court . . . about their test results," the sky has not fallen. PDS Brief 23. State and municipal laboratories "make operational and staffing decisions" to facilitate analysts' appearance at trial. *Ibid.* Prosecutors schedule trial dates to accommodate analysts' availability, and trial courts liberally grant continuances when unexpected conflicts arise. *Id.*, at 24–25. In rare cases in which the analyst is no longer employed by the laboratory at the time of trial, "the prosecution makes the effort to bring that analyst . . . to court." *Id.*, at 25. And, as is the practice in New Mexico, laboratories ordinarily retain additional samples, enabling them to run tests again when necessary.[10]

* * *

For the reasons stated, the judgment of the New Mexico Supreme Court is reversed, and the case is remanded for further proceedings not inconsistent with this opinion.[11]

JUSTICE SOTOMAYOR, concurring in part.

. . . Although this case is materially indistinguishable from the facts we considered in *Melendez-Diaz*, I highlight some of the factual circumstances that this case does *not* present. First, this is not a case in which the State suggested an alternate purpose, much less an alternate *primary* purpose, for the BAC report. For example, the State has not claimed that the report was necessary to provide Bullcoming with medical treatment. . . . Second, this is not a case in which the person testifying is a supervisor, reviewer, or someone else with a personal, albeit limited, connection to the scientific test at issue. . . . It would be a different case if, for example, a supervisor who observed an analyst conducting a test testified about the results or a report about such results. . . . Third, this is not a case in which an expert witness was asked for his independent opinion about underlying testimonial reports that were not themselves admitted into evidence. See Fed. Rule Evid. 703 (explaining that facts or data of a type upon which experts in the field would reasonably rely in forming an opinion need not be admissible in order for the expert's opinion based on the facts and data to be admitted). . . . We would face a different

---

10. The dissent refers, selectively, to experience in Los Angeles, but overlooks experience documented in Michigan. In that State, post-*Melendez-Diaz*, the increase in in-court analyst testimony has been slight. Compare PDS Brief 21 (in 2006, analysts provided testimony for only 0.7% of all tests), with Michigan State Police, Forensic Science Division, available at http://www .michigan.gov/msp/0,1607,7-123-1593_3800-15901—,00.html (in 2010, analysts provided testimony for approximately 1% of all tests).

11. As in *Melendez-Diaz*, we express no view on whether the Confrontation Clause error in this case was harmless. The New Mexico Supreme Court did not reach that question, and nothing in this opinion impedes a harmless-error inquiry on remand.

question if asked to determine the constitutionality of allowing an expert witness to discuss others' testimonial statements if the testimonial statements were not themselves admitted as evidence. Finally, this is not a case in which the State introduced only machine-generated results, such as a printout from a gas chromatograph.... Thus, we do not decide whether, as the New Mexico Supreme Court suggests, a State could introduce (assuming an adequate chain of custody foundation) raw data generated by a machine in conjunction with the testimony of an expert witness....

JUSTICE KENNEDY, with whom THE CHIEF JUSTICE, JUSTICE BREYER, and JUSTICE ALITO join, dissenting.

Whether or not one agrees with the reasoning and the result in *Melendez-Diaz*, the Court today takes the new and serious misstep of extending that holding to instances like this one. Here a knowledgeable representative of the laboratory was present to testify and to explain the lab's processes and the details of the report.... [and] the defense used the opportunity in cross-examination to highlight the absence [of other] laboratory employees. Under questioning by Bullcoming's attorney, Razatos acknowledged that his name did not appear on the report; that he did not receive the sample, perform the analysis, or complete the review; and that he did not know the reason for some personnel decisions. After weighing arguments from defense counsel concerning these admissions, and after considering the testimony of Mr. Razatos, who knew the laboratory's protocols and processes, the jury found no reasonable doubt as to the defendant's guilt.

In these circumstances, requiring the State to call the technician who filled out a form and recorded the results of a test is a hollow formality. The defense remains free to challenge any and all forensic evidence. It may call and examine the technician who performed a test. And it may call other expert witnesses to explain that tests are not always reliable or that the technician might have made a mistake. The jury can then decide whether to credit the test, as it did here. The States, furthermore, can assess the progress of scientific testing and enact or adopt statutes and rules to ensure that only reliable evidence is admitted....

Instead of freeing the Clause from reliance on hearsay doctrines, the Court has now linked the Clause with hearsay rules in their earliest, most rigid, and least refined formulations. See, *e.g.*, Mosteller, Remaking Confrontation Clause and Hearsay Doctrine Under the Challenge of Child Sexual Abuse Prosecutions, 1993 U. Ill. L.Rev. 691, 739-740, 742, 744-746; Gallanis, The Rise of Modern Evidence Law, 84 Iowa L. Rev. 499, 502-503, 514-515, 533-537 (1999). In cases like *Melendez-Diaz* and this one, the Court has tied the Confrontation Clause to 18th century hearsay rules unleavened by principles tending to make those rules more sensible. Sklansky, Hearsay's Last Hurrah, 2009 S. Ct. Rev. 1, 5-6, 36. As a result, the Court has taken the Clause far beyond its most important application, which is to forbid sworn, *ex parte*, out-of-court statements by unconfronted and available witnesses who observed the crime and do not appear at trial....

Today's opinion repeats an assertion from *Melendez-Diaz* that its decision will not "impose an undue burden on the prosecution." But evidence to the contrary already has begun to mount. See, *e.g.*, Brief for State of California et al. as *Amici Curiae* 7 (explaining that the 10 toxicologists for the Los Angeles Police Department spent 782 hours at 261 court appearances during a 1-year period); Brief for National District Attorneys Association et al. as *Amici Curiae* 23 (observing that each blood-alcohol analyst in California processes 3,220 cases per year on average). New and more rigorous empirical studies further detailing the unfortunate effects of *Melendez-Diaz* are sure to be forthcoming. . . .

UNITED STATES v. TORRALBA-MENDIA

784 F.3d 652 (9th Cir. 2015)

MURPHY, District Judge [sitting by designation]:

A jury convicted Miguel Torralba-Mendia of conspiring to smuggle undocumented immigrants into the United States. . . . During the trial, the government . . . introduced I–213 immigration forms, which were labeled a "Record of Deportable/Inadmissible Alien." The government introduced the forms to show that many of the passengers detained during the investigation were, in fact, deported. Torralba argues that the forms contained inadmissible hearsay. . . .

Under Rule 803(8), a record or statement of a public office is admissible as an exception to the hearsay rule if it sets out "a matter observed while under a legal duty to report, but not including, in a criminal case, a matter observed by law-enforcement personnel." Fed.R.Evid. 803(8)(A)(ii).

In *United States v. Lopez* we held the public records exception applied to a "Verification of Removal." 762 F.3d 852, 861 (9th Cir. 2014). The verification of removal contained the date, port, and manner of the alien's departure, as well as the alien's photograph, signature and fingerprint, and an officer's signature. We reasoned the officer had a legal duty to fill out the form, explaining that "[r]ecording and maintaining verifications that an individual has been deported falls under the rubric of responsibilities assigned to the Department of Homeland Security; therefore, completing the verification of removal form is appropriate to the function of the agency." Furthermore, we found the documents admissible notwithstanding the general prohibition against admitting records created by law enforcement. We reasoned the law enforcement prohibition's purpose was to "exclude observations made by officials at the scene of the crime or apprehension, because observations made in an adversarial setting are less reliable than observations made by public officials in other situations." The verification of removal, by contrast, was a "ministerial, objective observation" that merely "records the movement of aliens across the United States border," and was therefore "inherent[ly] reliab[le] because of the Government's need to keep accurate records of the movement of aliens."

The same principles apply here. The admitted record of a deportable alien contains the same information as a verification of removal: The alien's name, photograph, fingerprints, as well as the date, port and method of departure, and the officer's signature. The government redacted all other statements, including the officer's narration explaining how the alien was apprehended, and the alien's statements regarding his country of origin and address.

Furthermore, the record of a deportable alien, like a verification of removal, is part of an alien's A–File, filled out and kept by the Department of Homeland Security in its regular course of business. Finally, the admitted forms are a ministerial, objective observation detailing how the aliens were repatriated, and do not implicate the purposes animating the law enforcement exception. Other circuits addressing this issue have found I–213 forms admissible under Rule 803(8). *See United States v. Caraballo,* 595 F.3d 1214, 1226 (11th Cir. 2010); *Renteria-Gonzalez v. I.N.S.,* 322 F.3d 804, 817 n.16 (5th Cir. 2003)....

Torralba also contends the admission of the I–213 forms violated his confrontation rights.... The Supreme Court has explained that public records are normally non-testimonial because they are "created for the administration of an entity's affairs and not for the purpose of establishing or proving some fact at trial." *Melendez-Diaz v. Massachusetts,* 557 U.S. 305, 324 (2009). We have repeatedly held that immigration documents contained in an alien's A-file are non-testimonial because they are "not made in anticipation of litigation, and because [they are] simply a routine, objective cataloging of an unambiguous factual matter." *Lopez,* 762 F.3d at 860.... The same principles apply here. Nothing in the I–213 forms suggest the documents were completed in anticipation of litigation. Rather, the I–213 form "is routinely completed by Customs and Border Patrol agents in the course of their non-adversarial duties, not in the course of preparing for a criminal prosecution." *Caraballo,* 595 F.3d at 1226. As is evident from the form itself, the record of a deportable alien merely collects the alien's biographical information, gives the officer an opportunity to describe how the person was apprehended (which the government redacted), and states whether they were deported or voluntarily returned. Agents complete I–213 forms regardless of whether the government decides to prosecute anyone criminally.... As with other evidence in an alien's A-file, the documents are prepared for administrative purposes, not as evidence in a later trial. Accordingly, because the documents are not testimonial, their admission did not run afoul of the Confrontation Clause.... Affirmed.

STATE v. DAVIS

140 Haw. 252 (2017)

Opinion of the Court by POLLACK, J.

This case concerns the admissibility of [a machine operator's sworn statements] to prove that the Intoxilyzer used to test Raymond S. Davis's breath alcohol content was in proper working order. The State relied on these out-of-court statements in establishing the reliability of Davis's breath alcohol test results, which in turn served as a basis for his conviction for the offense of operating a vehicle under the influence of an intoxicant. [The trial court admitted the records under Rule 803(b)(8)(B) of the Hawai'i Rules of Evidence, which is modeled on the analogous federal rule. But the statement] that the "Intoxilyzer was operating accurately" ... [is an] interpretative conclusion ... and therefore does not constitute a "matter observed" [within the meaning of Rule 803(b)(8)(B)]....

The State also sought to admit [the statements] as business records under HRE Rule 803(b)(6). "Although ordinarily the proponent of hearsay is entitled to 'shop around' among the exceptions, the public records exception of [the Federal Rules of Evidence] preempts this subject matter [of business records] and forecloses access to business records admissibility." Addison M. Bowman, *Hawaii Rules of Evidence Manual* §803-3[6][F], at 8-41 (2016-2017 ed.). Thus, it is generally understood that records excluded by HRE Rule 803(b)(8) cannot be admitted through the "back door" as a business record under HRE Rule 803(b)(6). *See United States v. Weiland*, 420 F.3d 1062, 1074 (9th Cir. 2005) ("The government may not circumvent the specific requirements of [Federal] Rule [of Evidence] 803(8) by seeking to admit public records as business records under Rule 803(6). Nor may the government attempt to combine Rules 803(6) and 803(8) into a hybrid rule to excuse its failure to comply with either."); *United States v. Orellana-Blanco*, 294 F.3d 1143, 1149 (9th Cir. 2002) ("When public records are used against a defendant in a criminal prosecution, the public records exception is the exclusive applicable hearsay exception."); *United States v. Cain*, 615 F.2d 380, 382 (5th Cir. 1980) ("[S]tatements inadmissible as public agency reports under Rule 803(8) may not be received merely because they satisfy Rule 803(6) ... section (6) does not open a back door for evidence excluded by section (8)."). ... The State may not "circumvent the requirements" of HRE Rule 803(b)(8)(B) by seeking their admission under HRE Rule 803(b)(6). Bowman, *supra*, §803-3[6][F], at 8-41; *Weiland*, 420 F.3d at 1074 (indicating that the business records hearsay exception is not an avenue for admitting evidence that is inadmissible under the public records exception). Therefore [the statements] were not admissible as business records under HRE Rule 803(b)(6). ... [Reversed and remanded for new trial.]

UNITED STATES v. LUNDSTROM

880 F.3d 423 (8th Cir. 2018)

WOLLMAN, Circuit Judge.

[Defendant Gilbert Lundstrom ran a bank that federal regulators shut down for poor financial practices; Lundstrom was subsequently convicted of fraudulently concealing the bank's loan losses.] Lundstrom ... argues that the district court improperly admitted certain reports written by [employees of the federal Office of Thrift Supervision] as business records under Federal Rule of Evidence 803(6). ... Lundstrom asserts that the reports prepared by government agencies cannot be admitted as business records under Rule 803(6), given that the public records exception to the rule against hearsay — Rule 803(8)(A)(iii) — excludes "factual findings from a legally authorized" investigation when a report containing such findings is offered against a criminal defendant.

We have affirmed the admission of government reports under Rule 803(6) in criminal cases. In *United States v. Williams*, 720 F.3d 674, 698-99 (8th Cir. 2013), we concluded that law-enforcement fingerprint cards from a prior arrest were business records admissible under Rule 803(6) in a later drug-distribution and money-laundering prosecution. We reasoned that the fingerprint cards "were created as part of a routine booking procedure and not in anticipation of litigation, i.e., 'for the administration of an entity's affairs and not for the purpose of establishing or proving some fact at trial.'" *Id.* at 698 (quoting *Melendez-Diaz v. Massachusetts*, 557 U.S. 305, 324 (2009)). Thus, the cards were admissible as business records "because they were created 'in the regular course of business'" and not "'solely for an evidentiary purpose.'" *Id.* at 699 (quoting *Melendez-Diaz*, 557 U.S. at 321-22, and *Bullcoming v. New Mexico*, 564 U.S. 647, 664 (2011)). In *United States v. Voice*, 622 F.3d 870, 879 (8th Cir. 2010), we held that the defendant's sex-offender registration document was admissible as a business record under Rule 803(6) in a SORNA prosecution because the registration was maintained by the state's division of criminal investigation in [the] normal course of business and not in anticipation of litigation.

We conclude that the foregoing considerations likewise rendered admissible the OTS reports at issue here. OTS examiners supervise banks to ensure their soundness and compliance with financial laws and regulation; they do not conduct criminal investigations, collect evidence, or bring criminal charges. Accordingly, the OTS reports were admissible as business records under Rule 803(6) because the reports were created for the administration of the OTS's affairs and not for the purpose of establishing facts at trial.

Rule 803(8)(A)(iii) does not require the exclusion of the OTS Reports. Rule 803(8)(A)(iii) was intended to protect a criminal defendant's Confrontation Clause rights by ensuring that a police report could not be admitted unless its author testified. We believe that the rule should apply to reports prepared by law enforcement officials at the scene of a crime or in investigating a crime, and not to reports authored by other government agents regarding routine matters in nonadversarial settings. Even assuming that Rule 803(8)(A)(iii) applies here, however, the rule does not require the exclusion of the OTS reports because the authors testified and were subject to cross-examination. . . . The judgment is affirmed.

9. Former Testimony

Federal Rule of Evidence 804 collects several exceptions to the hearsay rule that traditionally have applied only when, for any of several specified reasons, the declarant is unavailable to testify in the trial in which his or her statements are offered as evidence. The first of these exceptions pertains to testimony previously given by the declarant in another trial or proceeding — including a deposition or earlier hearing in the same case. The precise circumstances in which Rule 804 allows the introduction of former testimony remains, in some respects, controversial.

One confusion should be avoided from the outset. The breadth of the former testimony exception depends in part on whether the proceeding in which the exception is invoked is criminal or civil. What matters is the nature of the *second* proceeding, not the nature of the proceeding in which the declarant originally testified. The exception can be invoked in a criminal case only if the criminal defendant was a party to the earlier proceeding, and had an opportunity and a "similar motive" to cross-examine the now unavailable declarant. Even if the rules themselves did not impose this restriction, the Confrontation Clause would, because whatever else counts as "testimonial" within the meaning of *Crawford v. Washington* and *Davis v. Washington*, actual testimony in an earlier proceeding plainly falls within that category.

[F.R.E. 804(a) & (b)(1); C.E.C. §§1290–1292]

ADVISORY COMMITTEE NOTE TO F.R.E. 804

. . . Rule 803, supra, is based upon the assumption that a hearsay statement falling within one of its exceptions possesses qualities which justify the conclusion that whether the declarant is available or unavailable is not a relevant factor in determining admissibility. The instant rule proceeds upon a different theory: hearsay which admittedly is not equal in quality to testimony of the declarant on the stand may nevertheless be admitted if the declarant is unavailable and if his statement meets a specified standard. The rule expresses preferences: testimony given on the stand in person is preferred over hearsay, and hearsay, if of the specified quality, is preferred over complete loss of the evidence of the declarant. The exceptions evolved at common law with respect to declarations of unavailable declarants furnish the basis for the exceptions enumerated in the proposal. . . .

Former testimony does not rely upon some set of circumstances to substitute for oath and cross-examination, since both oath and opportunity to cross-examine were present in fact. The only missing one of the ideal conditions for the giving of testimony is the presence of trier and opponent ("demeanor evidence"). This is lacking with all hearsay exceptions. Hence it may be argued that former testimony is the strongest hearsay and should be included under Rule 803, supra. However, opportunity to observe demeanor is what in a large measure confers depth and meaning upon oath and cross-examination. Thus in cases under Rule 803 demeanor lacks the significance which it possesses with respect to testimony. In any event, the tradition, founded in experience, uniformly favors production of the witness if he is available. The exception indicates continuation of the policy. This preference for the presence of the witness is apparent also in rules and statutes on the use of depositions, which deal with substantially the same problem. . . .

The common law did not limit the admissibility of former testimony to that given in an earlier trial of the same case, although it did require identity of issues as a means of insuring that the former handling of the witness was the equivalent of what would now be done if the opportunity were presented. Modern decisions reduce the requirement to "substantial" identity. Since identity of issues is significant only in that it bears on motive and interest in developing fully the testimony of the witness, expressing the matter in the latter terms is preferable. . . .

As a further assurance of fairness in thrusting upon a party the prior handling of the witness, the common law also insisted upon identity of parties, deviating only to the extent of allowing substitution of successors in a narrowly construed privity. Mutuality as an aspect of identity is now generally discredited, and the requirement of identity of the offering party disappears except as it might affect motive to develop the testimony. The question remains whether strict identity, or privity, should continue as a requirement with respect to the party against whom offered. The rule departs to the extent of allowing substitution of one with the right and opportunity to develop the testimony with similar motive and interest. This position is supported by modern decisions. . . .

ROGER C. PARK ET AL., EVIDENCE LAW: A STUDENT'S GUIDE TO THE LAW OF EVIDENCE AS APPLIED IN AMERICAN TRIALS

§17.02, at 612-13 (4th ed. 2018)

[A] typical instance of the operation of the former testimony exception arises when a case has been reversed on appeal and remanded for a new trial. If a witness at the first trial is unavailable for the second, then that witness' testimony is admissible under the exception. . . .

When the testimony is offered in the form of a transcript of the prior trial, there are two levels of hearsay. First, the transcript is the statement of the court reporter about what was said on the witness stand at the prior trial. The public records exception creates an exception for this statement. Many jurisdictions have statutes that provide specific exceptions for statements of court reporters. Second, the witness' testimony at the prior trial is also hearsay, at least under the federal definition. The present exception applies to allow it to be received.

Former testimony often comes into evidence through some route other than this exception. For example, former testimony can be used to impeach a witness with a prior inconsistent statement. . . . Rule 801(d)(1)(A) provides the basis for receiving the testimony. Similarly, former testimony of the opposing party is admissible against that party under Rule 801(d)(2) without the need for laying the foundation required by the exception for former testimony.

UNITED STATES v. BOLLIN

264 F.3d 391 (4th Cir. 2001)

CYNTHIA HOLCOMB HALL, Senior Circuit Judge.

[Defendant Gary Bollin was convicted of participating in an investment fraud scheme.] Bollin contends that the district court abused its discretion when it allowed the Government to present a redacted version of his grand jury testimony but refused to allow him to present the omitted portions under the rule of completeness or the former testimony exception to the hearsay rule. We find no abuse of discretion.

Federal Rule of Evidence 804(b)(1) provides an exception to the hearsay rule for the former testimony of a declarant where the declarant is unavailable as a witness.[16] A declarant is "unavailable" when the declarant "is exempted by ruling of the court on the ground of privilege from testifying concerning the subject matter of the declarant's statement." Bollin contends that he was "unavailable" because he had invoked his Fifth Amendment privilege against self-incrimination.

A criminal defendant who invokes his Fifth Amendment privilege makes himself unavailable to any other party. Rule 804(a) provides, however, that "[a] declarant is not unavailable as a witness if exemption, refusal, claim of lack of memory, inability, or absence is due to the procurement or wrongdoing of the proponent of a statement for the purpose of preventing the witness from attending or testifying." By invoking his Fifth Amendment privilege, Bollin made himself unavailable for the purpose of preventing his testimony, and he therefore cannot invoke the exception in Rule 804(b)(1). *Accord United States v. Peterson*, 100 F.3d 7, 13 (2d Cir. 1996) (holding that a defendant who exercises his privilege not to testify at a second trial of his case is not entitled to introduce the testimony he gave at the first trial); *United States v. Kimball*, 15 F.3d 54, 55-56 (5th Cir. 1994) (same).

Bollin identifies several portions of his grand jury testimony that he contends should have been admitted under [the "rule of completeness" codified in Federal Rule of Evidence 106]. We have reviewed Bollin's grand jury testimony as admitted and his unredacted grand jury testimony. Like the district court, we conclude that the omitted testimony was not necessary to avoid misleading the jury or otherwise place the admitted testimony in context. The fact that some of the omitted testimony arguably was exculpatory does not, without more, make it admissible under the rule of completeness.... Affirmed.

KIRK v. RAYMARK INDUSTRIES, INC.

61 F.3d 147 (3d Cir. 1995)

COWEN, Circuit Judge.

. . . Alfred Kirk ("decedent"), a retired painter, died on July 5, 1988 at the age of 65 from malignant asbestos-induced mesothelioma. Mrs. Sarah Kirk ("Kirk"), suing on behalf of herself and her deceased husband's estate, filed this diversity action against eight defendants, including Owens-Corning Fiberglas Corporation ("Owens-Corning"). Kirk alleged that her husband's mesothelioma was caused by exposure to dust from asbestos products during his employment at the New York Shipyard in Camden, New Jersey, during the late 1950's and early 1960's. . . .

During the liability phase of the trial, Owens-Corning offered the expert testimony of Dr. Harry Demopoulos to prove that the overwhelming majority of asbestos-induced mesotheliomas are caused by crocidolite asbestos fiber.

---

16. Bollin also argues that his grand jury statements are not hearsay. His statements to the grand jury were made out of court, and Bollin would introduce them to prove the truth of the matter asserted. They are hearsay. *See* Fed. R. Evid. 801(c). The statements were admissible by the Government as admissions under Rule 801(d)(2).

This testimony supported Owens-Corning's defense that its product, Kaylo, which did not contain crocidolite fiber, could not have caused the decedent's mesothelioma. Over Owens-Corning's objection, Kirk was permitted to read to the jury the prior trial testimony of Dr. Louis Burgher from an unrelated New Jersey State Court asbestos action in 1992. In that case, Dr. Burgher had been an expert witness for Owens-Corning and testified on cross-examination that it was possible for mesothelioma to be caused by chrysotile fibers contaminated with tremolite. Kirk was clearly attempting to discredit Owens-Corning's defense offered through Dr. Demopoulos by revealing to the jury that Owens-Corning's expert witness in a previous case voiced a different and contradictory opinion as to which asbestos fibers cause mesothelioma. . . .

Owens-Corning argues that the district court erred in allowing the jury to hear this evidence in light of the fact that it was hearsay. Although the record is at best vague as to what the district court's basis was for allowing such testimony, Kirk attempts to justify its admission under two distinct theories — either the testimony was not hearsay pursuant to Rule 801(d)(2)(C) of the Federal Rules of Evidence or it was hearsay, but subject to an exception pursuant to Rule 804(b)(1).[18]

Kirk first attempts to justify the district court's admission of the prior trial testimony of Dr. Burgher by arguing it is an admission by a party opponent since it is a statement by a person authorized by Owens-Corning to speak concerning mesothelioma and is thus not hearsay. *See* Fed. R. Evid. 801(d)(2)(C). . . . Because an expert witness is charged with the duty of giving *his or her* expert *opinion* regarding the matter before the court, we fail to comprehend how an expert witness, who is not an agent of the party who called him, can be authorized to make an admission for that party. . . . Accordingly, we find Dr. Burgher's prior trial testimony to be hearsay in the context of the present trial.

Because the testimony of Dr. Burgher is hearsay, we must next inquire whether it falls within any of the hearsay exceptions enumerated in the Federal Rules of Evidence. Kirk argues that Dr. Burgher's testimony falls within the former testimony hearsay exception of Rule 804(b)(1). . . . [I]t is the proponent of the statement offered under Rule 804 who bears the burden of proving the unavailability of the declarant. We can find nothing in the record that indicates any "reasonable means" employed by Kirk to procure the services of Dr. Burgher so that he might testify at trial. *See McCormick* [*on Evidence*] §253, at 134 [(4th ed. 1992)] (mere absence of the declarant, standing alone, does not establish unavailability); *see also Moore v. Mississippi Valley State University*, 871 F.2d 545, 552 (5th Cir. 1989) (deposition inadmissible in civil trial where no evidence to establish unavailability offered).

Kirk claims that Dr. Burgher, who is a resident of Nebraska, was beyond her ability to subpoena and was thus unavailable. However, Kirk made no independent attempt to contact Dr. Burgher, offer him his usual expert witness fee,

---

18. Alternatively, Kirk argues that assuming *arguendo* it was error to admit the testimony of Dr. Burgher, it was harmless error because the weight of the medical testimony of Kirk's other witnesses was overwhelming. In light of our decision to remand for a new trial because the jury was improperly constituted, we need not address whether any evidentiary errors may be harmless.

and request his attendance at trial. Because Dr. Burgher was never even as much as contacted, Kirk has failed to prove that she used "reasonable means" to enlist his services.... [Reversed.]

CLAY v. JOHNS-MANVILLE SALES CORP.

722 F.2d 1289 (6th Cir. 1984)

GEORGE CLIFTON EDWARDS, JR., Circuit Judge.

In these two cases plaintiffs John Ed Clay and Curtis Bailey, each joined by his wife, brought actions for damages against defendants Johns-Manville Sales Corporation and Raybestos-Manhattan, Inc., on the basis of products liability claims resulting from plaintiffs' exposure to asbestos containing products manufactured by the defendants. The cases were tried in the United States District Court for the Eastern District of Tennessee and ended in jury verdicts for the defendants.

Appellants urge that . . . the District Judge erred in excluding a deposition taken from a witness, Dr. Kenneth Wallace Smith, in *DeRocco v. Forty-eight Installation, Inc.*, No. 7880 (W.D. Pa. 1974). At the time of the *DeRocco* proceeding, Dr. Smith was 63 years of age and had acquired his knowledge about asbestos disease in the employment of the Johns-Manville Corporation, the largest asbestos manufacturer in the field. Serving Johns-Manville during a good portion of his 22 years of employment as the only full-time physician in the organization, Dr. Smith's deposition is peculiarly relevant to the extent of the knowledge possessed by manufacturers of the hazards of asbestos containing products during the years when appellants Clay and Bailey allege they were exposed to asbestos.

Dr. Smith had died before the trial of this case. The key question in relation to the admissibility of this evidence is posed by the language of Rule 804(b)(1) of the Federal Rules of Evidence, which [exempts from the hearsay rule, when the declarant is unavailable, testimony] "given as a witness at another hearing of the same or a different proceeding, or in a deposition taken in compliance with law in the course of the same or another proceeding, if the party against whom the testimony is now offered, or, in a civil action or proceeding, a predecessor in interest, had an opportunity and similar motive to develop the testimony by direct, cross, or redirect examination."

To ascertain the meaning of "predecessor in interest," an examination of legislative history is necessary. As originally proposed by the Supreme Court, Rule 804(b)(1) would have admitted prior testimony of an unavailable witness if the party against whom it is offered or a person "with a motive and interest" similar to him had an opportunity to examine that witness. The House of Representatives substituted the current "predecessor in interest" language. The House Committee on the Judiciary offered the following explanation for the alteration:

> The Committee considered that it is generally unfair to impose upon the party against whom the hearsay evidence is being offered responsibility for the manner in which the witness was previously handled by another party. The sole exception to this, in the Committee's view, is when a party's predecessor in interest in a civil action or proceeding had an opportunity and similar motive to

examine the witness. The Committee amended the Rule to reflect these policy determinations.

H.R. Rep. No. 650, [93d Cong., 1st Sess. 15 (1973)].

Although the Senate accepted the change proposed by the House, the Senate Committee on the Judiciary made the following observation about the import of the House actions: . . .

The House amended the rule to apply only to a party's predecessor in interest. Although the committee recognizes considerable merit to the rule submitted by the Supreme Court, a position which has been advocated by many scholars and judges, we have concluded that the difference between the two versions is not great and we accept the House amendment.

S. Rep. No. 1277, 93d Cong., 2d Sess. 28 (1974).

We join the Third Circuit in agreeing with the Senate Committee that the difference between the ultimate revision and the Rule, as originally proposed, is "not great." *Lloyd v. American Export Lines, Inc.*, 580 F.2d 1179, 1185 (3d Cir.), *cert. denied*, 439 U.S. 969 (1978). Accordingly, we adopt the position taken by the *Lloyd* court which it expressed in the following language:

While we do not endorse an extravagant interpretation of who or what constitutes a "predecessor in interest," we prefer one that is realistically generous over one that is formalistically grudging. We believe that what has been described as "the practical and expedient view" expresses the congressional intention: "if it appears that in the former suit a party having a like motive to cross-examine about the same matters as the present party would have, was accorded an adequate opportunity for such examination, the testimony may be received against the present party." Under these circumstances, the previous party having like motive to develop the testimony about the same material facts is, in the final analysis, a predecessor in interest to the present party.

See also Rule v. International Association of Bridge, Structural Ornamental Iron Workers, Local 396, 568 F.2d 558, 569 (8th Cir. 1977); Weinstein & Berger, *Evidence* §804(b)(1) [04] at 804-67 (1969) ("[C]ases decided since the enactment of Rule 804(b)(1) for the most part indicate a reluctance to interpret 'predecessor in interest' in its old, narrow, and substantive law sense, of privity"). *Contra In re IBM Peripheral EDP Devices Antitrust Litigation*, 444 F. Supp. 110 (N.D. Cal. 1978).

Our examination of the record submitted in this case satisfies us that defendants in the DeRocco case had a similar motive in confronting Dr. Smith's testimony, both in terms of appropriate objections and searching cross-examination, to that which Raybestos has in the current litigation. . . . [Reversed and remanded for retrial.]

VOLLAND-GOLAND v. CITY OF CHICAGO

89 F. Supp. 3d 983 (N.D. Ill. 2015)

SHADUR, Senior District Judge.

[Two Chicago police officers used pepper spray and physical force to arrest John Volland following a traffic stop. At Volland's criminal trial for assault and resisting arrest, Volland testified in his own defense, and the jury acquitted him. Volland then sued the officers and the city under 42 U.S.C. §1983 for violating his civil rights. Volland died of natural causes before the case came to trial, and Volland's sister, as executor of his estate, moved *in limine* to allow introduction of his testimony from the criminal trial.]

... Volland and defendants lock horns over the admissibility of Volland's prior testimony under Rule 804(b)(1). ... No one disputes that Volland is unavailable to testify, that his prior testimony was given at one of the enumerated proceedings (a criminal trial) or that the State had a full opportunity to cross-examine him during that proceeding. Instead the parties cross swords over two matters: whether the State can properly be considered a predecessor in interest to defendants (and especially to the Officers) and whether the State had a similar motive to develop Volland's testimony by cross-examination. ...

[E]very federal Court of Appeals to address the issue head-on has determined that the term "predecessor in interest" does not invoke the common law concept of privity but rather sets out a more forgiving standard (*see, e.g., Supermarket of Marlinton, Inc. v. Meadow Gold Dairies, Inc.*, 71 F.3d 119, 128 (4th Cir. 1995); *Clay v. Johns–Manville Sales Corp.*, 722 F.2d 1289, 1294–95 (6th Cir. 1983); *Lloyd v. Am. Export Lines, Inc.*, 580 F.2d 1179, 1185–87 (3d Cir. 1978) and other authorities cited in those cases). ... [T]he State's stake in Volland's criminal trial was entirely commensurate to defendants' current stake in this action. It should go without saying that state and local governments take very seriously indeed any alleged assaults on their police officers, and defendants never credibly argue that there were particular facts that made the State's interest in prosecuting Volland less than would be typical. ... [A]lthough the State's interest in securing a conviction of Volland and defendants' present interest in avoiding damages liability are different in kind, neither interest is clearly weightier than the other. And so when the State put Volland on trial and cross-examined him it had "the requisite stake in the proceeding" ([*United States v.*] *Feldman*, 761 F.2d [380, 387 (7th Cir. 1985)]) so as to be held a predecessor in interest of defendants for the purposes of Rule 804(b)(1).

With the predecessor-in-interest issue thus squared away, this opinion turns to the question whether the State had a "similar motive" to develop Volland's testimony through cross-examination. ... [D]efendants attempt to make much of the difference between the charges the State leveled against Volland (resisting a peace officer and battery) and the theories of relief Volland now advances in support of his claim against defendants (violations of the Fourth Amendment and conspiracy to commit such violations, as well as state law torts of battery and malicious prosecution), urging that each of those infractions involves a different set of elements that must be proved separately. As defendants would have it, the State had to show one set of facts (that Volland resisted and battered the Officers), while defendants now have to advance a different set of facts (that the Officers did not use unreasonable force or stop Volland without reasonable suspicion, for example). And that, say defendants, destroys any similarity of motive to develop Volland's testimony. ...

In fact ... both Volland's criminal trial and this civil action turn on the resolution of identical factual questions: what physical force (if any)

Volland used against the Officers, what physical force the Officers used against Volland, whether the latter force was reasonable under the circumstances and finally the order in which events unfolded.... [T]he State's cross-examination of Volland had objectives essentially identical to those in any examination that defendants hypothetically could conduct now if Volland were still alive.... Both this action and the criminal trial involve the same incident, and both the State's and defendants' success hinged or hinges on the ability to discredit Volland's account of what happened — globally as well as in every minute detail. That is more than enough for admissibility under Rule 804(b)(1).... [P]laintiff's motion to admit Volland's testimony from the prior criminal trial is granted....

GLEN WEISSENBERGER, THE FORMER TESTIMONY HEARSAY EXCEPTION: A STUDY IN RULEMAKING, JUDICIAL REVISIONISM, AND THE SEPARATION OF POWERS

67 N.C. L. Rev. 295, 316, 320 (1989)

[T]he House left the term "predecessor in interest" undefined. As a result, courts have been inconsistent in their interpretations of this language — at times to the point of ignoring it. Initial interpretations of language by commentators suggested that the "predecessor in interest" language denotes the "traditional rule," which at common law meant privity. As Professor Lilly explains:

> Although the phrase "predecessor in interest" (which the courts frequently use interchangeably with the phrase "persons in privity") has an exasperating inexactness about it, the expression generally refers to the predecessor from whom the present party received the right, title, interest or obligation that is at issue in the current litigation. For example, a decedent is a predecessor in interest to ("in privity with") both his personal representative and those, such as heirs and legatees, who take from him; so, too, is a grantor of property a predecessor to his grantee, as is a principal to his surety.

Professor Lilly's interpretation of "predecessor in interest" is consistent with the House committee's overriding policy emphasis on fairness in modifying the advisory committee's version of rule 804(b)(1), which contained no such limitation....

While numerous federal courts have followed the *Lloyd* reasoning ... judicial interpretations of rule 804(b)(1) have been far from uniform. Some courts have emphasized that Congress intended rule 804(b)(1) to be strictly construed because of fairness considerations. Other courts have not specifically focused on the legislative history of rule 804(b)(1) or expressly followed *Lloyd*, but have excluded prior testimony evidence on the basis of absence of the appropriate motive. Other courts have concluded that former testimony may be admitted when a substantial identity of issues existed in the two actions, coupled with a similar motive and meaningful opportunity to cross examine the witness....

UNITED STATES v. SALERNO

505 U.S. 317 (1992)

Justice THOMAS delivered the opinion of the Court.

Federal Rule of Evidence 804(b)(1) states an exception to the hearsay rule that allows a court, in certain instances, to admit the former testimony of an unavailable witness. We must decide in this case whether the Rule permits a criminal defendant to introduce the grand jury testimony of a witness who asserts the Fifth Amendment privilege at trial.

The seven respondents, Anthony Salerno, Vincent DiNapoli, Louis DiNapoli, Nicholas Auletta, Edward Halloran, Alvin O. Chattin, and Aniello Migliore, allegedly took part in the activities of a criminal organization known as the Genovese Family of La Cosa Nostra (Family) in New York City. In 1987, a federal grand jury in the Southern District of New York indicted the respondents and four others on the basis of these activities. The indictment charged the respondents with a variety of federal offenses, including 41 acts constituting a "pattern of illegal activity" in violation of the Racketeer Influenced and Corrupt Organizations Act (RICO), 18 U.S.C. §1962(b).

Sixteen of the alleged acts involved fraud in the New York construction industry in the 1980's. According to the indictment and evidence later admitted at trial, the Family used its influence over labor unions and its control over the supply of concrete to rig bidding on large construction projects in Manhattan. The Family purportedly allocated contracts for these projects among a so-called "Club" of six concrete companies in exchange for a share of the proceeds.

Much of the case concerned the affairs of the Cedar Park Concrete Construction Corporation (Cedar Park). Two of the owners of this firm, Frederick DeMatteis and Pasquale Bruno, testified before the grand jury under a grant of immunity. In response to questions by the United States, they repeatedly stated that neither they nor Cedar Park had participated in the Club. At trial, however, the United States attempted to show that Cedar Park, in fact, had belonged to the Club by calling two contractors who had taken part in the scheme and by presenting intercepted conversations among the respondents. The United States also introduced documents indicating that the Family had an ownership interest in Cedar Park.

To counter the United States' evidence, the respondents subpoenaed DeMatteis and Bruno as witnesses in the hope that they would provide the same exculpatory testimony that they had presented to the grand jury. When both witnesses invoked their Fifth Amendment privilege against self-incrimination and refused to testify, the respondents asked the District Court to admit the transcripts of their grand jury testimony. . . . The District Court refused. . . . It observed that Rule 804(b)(1) permits admission of former testimony against a party at trial only when that party had a "similar motive to develop the testimony by direct, cross, or redirect examination." The District Court held that the United States did not have this motive, stating that the "motive of a prosecutor in questioning a witness before the grand jury in the investigatory stages of a case is far different from the motive of a prosecutor in conducting the trial." A jury subsequently convicted the respondents of the RICO counts and other federal offenses.

The United States Court of Appeals for the Second Circuit reversed, holding that the District Court had erred in excluding DeMatteis' and Bruno's grand jury testimony. Although the Court of Appeals recognized that "the government may have had no motive . . . to impeach . . . Bruno or DeMatteis" before the grand jury, it concluded that "the government's motive in examining the witnesses . . . was irrelevant." The Court of Appeals decided that, in order to maintain "adversarial fairness" Rule 804(b)(1)'s similar motive element should "evaporat[e]" when the Government obtains immunized testimony in a grand jury proceeding from a witness who refuses to testify at trial. We granted certiorari, and now reverse and remand. . . .

When Congress enacted the prohibition against admission of hearsay in Rule 802, it placed 24 exceptions in Rule 803 and 5 additional exceptions in Rule 804. Congress thus presumably made a careful judgment as to what hearsay may come into evidence and what may not. To respect its determination, we must enforce the words that it enacted. The respondents, as a result, had no right to introduce DeMatteis' and Bruno's former testimony under Rule 804(b)(1) without showing a "similar motive." This Court cannot alter evidentiary rules merely because litigants might prefer different rules in a particular class of cases.

The respondents' argument for a different result takes several forms. They first assert that adversarial fairness requires us to infer that Rule 804(b)(1) contains implicit limitations. They observe, for example, that the Advisory Committee Note to Rule 804 makes clear that the former testimony exception applies only to statements made under oath or affirmation, even though the Rule does not state this restriction explicitly. The respondents maintain that we likewise may hold that Rule 804(b)(1) does not require a showing of similar motive in all instances.

The respondents' example does not persuade us to change our reading of Rule 804(b)(1). If the Rule applies only to sworn statements, it does so not because adversarial fairness implies a limitation, but simply because the word "testimony" refers only to statements made under oath or affirmation. See Black's Law Dictionary 1476 (6th ed. 1990). We see no way to interpret the text of Rule 804(b)(1) to mean that defendants sometimes do not have to show "similar motive."

The respondents also assert that courts often depart from the Rules of Evidence to prevent litigants from presenting only part of the truth. For example, citing *United States v. Miller*, 600 F.2d 498 (CA5 1979), the respondents maintain that, although parties may enjoy various testimonial privileges, they can forfeit these privileges by "opening the door" to certain subjects. . . . Even assuming that we should treat th e hearsay rule like the rules governing testimonial privileges, we would not conclude that a forfeiture occurred here. Parties may forfeit a privilege by exposing privileged evidence, but do not forfeit one merely by taking a position that the evidence might contradict. In *Miller*, for example, the court held that a litigant, "after giving the jury his version of a privileged communication, [could not] prevent the cross-examiner from utilizing *the communication itself* to get at the truth" (emphasis added). In this case, by contrast, the United States never presented to the jury any version of what DeMatteis and Bruno had said in the grand jury proceedings. Instead, it attempted to show Cedar Park's participation in the Club solely through other evidence available to the respondents. . . .

The respondents finally argue that adversarial fairness may prohibit suppression of exculpatory evidence produced in grand jury proceedings. They note that, when this Court required disclosure of a grand jury transcript in *Dennis v. United States*, 384 U.S. 855 (1966), it stated that "it is rarely justifiable for the prosecution to have exclusive access" to relevant facts. They allege that the United States nevertheless uses the following tactics to develop evidence in a one-sided manner: If a witness inculpates a defendant during the grand jury proceedings, the United States immunizes him and calls him at trial; however, if the witness exculpates the defendant, as Bruno and DeMatteis each did here, the United States refuses to immunize him and attempts to exclude the testimony as hearsay. The respondents assert that dispensing with the "similar motive" requirement would limit these tactics.

We again fail to see how we may create an exception to Rule 804(b)(1). The *Dennis* case, unlike this one, did not involve a question about the admissibility of evidence. Rather, it concerned only the need to disclose a transcript to the defendants. Moreover, in *Dennis*, we did not hold that adversarial fairness required the United States to make the grand jury transcript available. Instead, we ordered disclosure under the specific language of Federal Rule of Criminal Procedure 6(e). In this case, the language of Rule 804(b)(1) does not support the respondents. Indeed, the respondents specifically ask us to ignore it. Neither *Dennis* nor anything else that the respondents have cited provides us with this authority.

The question remains whether the United States had a "similar motive" in this case. The United States asserts that the District Court specifically found that it did not and that we should not review its factual determinations. It also argues that a prosecutor generally will not have the same motive to develop testimony in grand jury proceedings as he does at trial. A prosecutor, it explains, must maintain secrecy during the investigatory stages of the criminal process and therefore may not desire to confront grand jury witnesses with contradictory evidence. It further states that a prosecutor may not know, prior to indictment, which issues will have importance at trial and accordingly may fail to develop grand jury testimony effectively.

The respondents disagree with both of the United States' arguments. They characterize the District Court's ruling as one of law, rather than fact, because the District Court essentially ruled that a prosecutor's motives at trial always differ from his motives in grand jury proceedings. The respondents contend further that the grand jury transcripts in this case actually show that the United States thoroughly attempted to impeach DeMatteis and Bruno. They add that, despite the United States' stated concern about maintaining secrecy, the United States revealed to DeMatteis and Bruno the identity of the major witnesses who testified against them at trial.

The Court of Appeals, as noted, erroneously concluded that the respondents did not have to demonstrate a similar motive in this case to make use of Rule 804(b)(1). It therefore declined to consider fully the arguments now presented by the parties about whether the United States had such a motive. Rather than to address this issue here in the first instance, we think it prudent to remand the case for further consideration.

It is so ordered.

Justice BLACKMUN, concurring.

... Because "similar motive" does not mean "identical motive," the similar-motive inquiry, in my view, is inherently a *factual* inquiry, depending in part on the similarity of the underlying issues and on the context of the grand jury questioning. It cannot be that the prosecution either *always or never* has a similar motive for questioning a particular witness with respect to a particular issue before the grand jury as at trial. ... Because this case involves factual issues unusual in complexity and in number and because neither the District Court nor the Court of Appeals apparently engaged in the type of factual inquiry appropriate for resolution of the similar-motive inquiry, I join the majority in remanding the case for further consideration.

Justice STEVENS, dissenting.

... As the Court explains, the grand jury testimony of Bruno and DeMatteis was totally inconsistent with the Government's theory of the alleged RICO conspiracy to rig bids on large construction projects in Manhattan. ... It is therefore clear that before the grand jury the Government had precisely the same interest in establishing that Bruno's and DeMatteis' testimony was false as it had at trial. Thus, when the prosecutors doubted Bruno's and DeMatteis' veracity before the grand jury — as they most assuredly did — they unquestionably had an "opportunity and similar motive to develop the testimony by direct, cross, or redirect examination" within the meaning of Rule 804(b)(1). ...

[A party] might decide — for tactical reasons or otherwise — not to engage in a rigorous cross-examination, or even in any cross-examination at all. In such a case, however, I do not believe that it is accurate to say that the party lacked a similar motive to cross-examine the witness; instead, it is more accurate to say that the party had a similar motive to cross-examine the witness (*i.e.*, to undermine the false or misleading testimony) but chose not to act on that motive. Although the Rules of Evidence allow a party to make that choice about whether to engage in cross-examination, they also provide that she must accept the consequences of that decision — including the possibility that the testimony might be introduced against her in a subsequent proceeding. ...

I am therefore satisfied that the Government had an "opportunity and similar motive" to develop the grand jury testimony of witnesses Bruno and DeMatteis; consequently, the transcript of that testimony was admissible against the Government at respondents' trial under Rule 804(b)(1). For that reason, I would affirm the judgment of the Court of Appeals.

PROBLEMS

3.47. A newspaper reports that a local hospital illegally disposes of hazardous materials. The hospital sues for libel. At trial the newspaper elicits testimony from a janitorial employee of the hospital that the hospital director had him pour toxic waste into a storm drain. Under what circumstances, if any, will the transcript of this testimony be admissible in a subsequent criminal case against the hospital director for illegal dumping?

3.48. The manager of a gasoline station is prosecuted for illegally burying engine oil in a vacant field. A mechanic who works at the station testifies that, at the manager's direction, she buried engine oil in the field. The jury returns a verdict of not guilty. Under what circumstances, if any, may the mechanic's testimony be introduced in a subsequent civil suit for cleanup costs, brought by the city against the company that owns the gasoline station?

10. Dying Declarations

One of the oldest of the exceptions to the hearsay rule allows the introduction of certain "dying declarations." Like the business records doctrine, the exception for dying declarations has traditionally been justified on grounds both of reliability and practical necessity.

[F.R.E. 804(b)(2); C.E.C. §1242]

McCORMICK ON EVIDENCE

§309, at 2:507 (Kenneth S. Broun ed., 7th ed. 2013)

Of the doctrines that authorize the admission of special classes of hearsay, the doctrine relating to dying declarations is the most mystical in its theory and traditionally among the most arbitrary in its limitations. The notion of the special likelihood of truthfulness of deathbed statements was widespread long before the recognition of a general rule against hearsay in the early 1700s. Not surprisingly, nearly as soon as we find a hearsay rule, we also find an exception for dying declarations.[4]

SHEPARD v. UNITED STATES

290 U.S. 96 (1933)

Mr. Justice CARDOZO delivered the opinion of the Court.

[The defendant was convicted of the murder of his wife. At trial, the decedent's nurse testified that Mrs. Shepard told her on May 22, 1929, "Dr. Shepard

---

4. The classic statement of the basis of the rule was made by Chief Baron Eyre in Rex v. Woodcock, 1 Leach 500, 168 Eng. Rep. 352 (K.B. 1789):

Now the general principle on which this species of evidence is admitted is, that they are declarations made in extremity, when the party is at the point of death, and when every hope of this world is gone; when every motive to falsehood is silenced, and the mind is induced by the most powerful considerations to speak the truth; a situation so solemn, and so awful, is considered by the law as creating an obligation equal to that which is imposed by a positive oath administered in a Court of Justice. . . .

has poisoned me." Before making this statement, Mrs. Shepard allegedly asked the nurse to bring a bottle of whiskey from her room, identified it as liquor she drank just before collapsing, said it had smelled and tasted strange, and asked if it could be tested for poison. The nurse also testified that Mrs. Shepard "said she was not going to get well; she was going to die."]

... Upon the hearing in this court the government finds its main prop in the position that what was said by Mrs. Shepard was admissible as a dying declaration. This is manifestly the theory upon which it was offered and received. The prop, however, is a broken reed. To make out a dying declaration, the declarant must have spoken without hope of recovery and in the shadow of impending death. The record furnishes no proof of that indispensable condition. . . .

[The declarant's] illness began on May 20. She was found in a state of collapse, delirious, in pain, the pupils of her eyes dilated, and the retina suffused with blood. The conversation with the nurse occurred two days later. At that time her mind had cleared up, and her speech was rational and orderly. There was as yet no thought by any of her physicians that she was dangerously ill, still less that her case was hopeless. To all seeming she had greatly improved, and was moving forward to recovery. There had been no diagnosis of poison as the cause of her distress. Not till about a week afterwards was there a relapse, accompanied by an infection of the mouth, renewed congestion of the eyes, and later hemorrhages of the bowels. Death followed on June 15.

Nothing in the condition of the patient on May 22 gives fair support to the conclusion that hope had then been lost. She may have thought she was going to die and have said so to her nurse, but this was consistent with hope, which could not have been put aside without more to quench it. Indeed, a fortnight later, she said to one of her physicians, though her condition was then grave, "You will get me well, won't you?" Fear or even belief that illness will end in death will not avail of itself to make a dying declaration. There must be "a settled hopeless expectation" (Willes, J. in *Reg. v. Peel*, 2 F. & F. 21, 22) that death is near at hand, and what is said must have been spoken in the hush of its impending presence. *Mattox v. United States*, 146 U.S. 140, 151; *Carver v. United States*, 160 U.S. 553; *Id.*, 164 U.S. 694; *R. v. Perry*, (1909) 2 K.B. 697; *People v. Sarzano*, 212 N.Y. 231, 235, 106 N.E. 87; 3 Wigmore on Evidence, §§1440, 1441, 1442, collating the decisions. Despair of recovery may indeed be gathered from the circumstances if the facts support the inference. There is no unyielding ritual of words to be spoken by the dying. Despair may even be gathered, though the period of survival outruns the bounds of expectation. What is decisive is the state of mind. Even so, the state of mind must be exhibited in the evidence, and not left to conjecture. The patient must have spoken with the consciousness of a swift and certain doom.

What was said by this patient was not spoken in that mood. There was no warning to her in the circumstances that her words would be repeated and accepted as those of a dying wife, charging murder to her husband, and charging it deliberately and solemnly as a fact within her knowledge. To the focus of that responsibility her mind was never brought. She spoke as one ill, giving voice to the beliefs and perhaps the conjectures of the moment. The liquor was to be tested, to see whether her beliefs were sound. She did not speak as one dying, announcing to the survivors a definitive conviction, a legacy of knowledge on which the world might act when she had gone.

The petitioner insists that the form of the declaration exhibits other defects that call for its exclusion, apart from the objection that death was not imminent and that hope was still alive. Homicide may not be imputed to a defendant on the basis of mere suspicions, though they are the suspicions of the dying. To let the declaration in, the inference must be permissible that there was knowledge or the opportunity for knowledge as to the acts that are declared. Wigmore, §1445(2)... The form is not decisive, though it be that of a conclusion, a statement of the result with the antecedent steps omitted. Wigmore, §1447. "He murdered me," does not cease to be competent as a dying declaration because in the statement of the act there is also an appraisal of the crime. One does not hold the dying to the observance of all the niceties of speech to which conformity is exacted from a witness on the stand. What is decisive is something deeper and more fundamental than any difference of form. The declaration is kept out if the setting of the occasion satisfies the judge, or in reason ought to satisfy him, that the speaker is giving expression to suspicion or conjecture, and not to known facts. The difficulty is not so much in respect of the governing principle as in its application to varying and equivocal conditions. In this case, the ruling that there was a failure to make out the imminence of death and the abandonment of hope relieves us of the duty of determining whether it is a legitimate inference that there was the opportunity for knowledge. We leave that question open.... [Reversed.]

UNITED STATES v. SACASAS

381 F.2d 451 (2d Cir. 1967)

WATERMAN, Circuit Judge:

This is an appeal from a judgment of conviction [for bank robbery] entered in the United States District Court for the Southern District of New York after a three-day trial by jury.... On the day fixed for imposition of sentence appellant moved for a new trial based upon newly discovered evidence. The motion was denied; the purported evidence, if true, would not have been admissible. The ruling is appealed from, though appellant practically concedes it to have been correct. According to one Boyle, a fellow-inmate of the Federal House of Detention with Richard L. Mahan, who had been indicted with appellant, and who, there awaiting trial, died before trial, [Mahan] told Boyle ten minutes before Mahan finally lost consciousness, "If anything happens to me tell them that the Greek had nothing to do with the job." Appellant seeks to persuade that this hearsay evidence should be admissible under the "dying declaration" exception to the exclusion of hearsay. Of course the exception is inapplicable here — Mahan was not dying following a homicidal attack, and neither appellant, "the Greek," nor Mahan had been prosecuted for a homicide. 5 Wigmore, Evidence §§1432-1434 (2d ed. 1940). Conviction affirmed.

ADVISORY COMMITTEE NOTE TO F.R.E. 804(b)(2)

The exception is the familiar dying declaration of the common law, expanded somewhat beyond its traditionally narrow limits. While the original religious justification for the exception may have lost its conviction for some persons over the years, it can scarcely be doubted that powerful psychological pressures are present. See 5 Wigmore §1443 and the classic statement of Chief Baron Eyre in Rex v. Woodcock, 1 Leach 500, 502, 168 Eng. Rep. 352, 353 (K.B. 1789).

The common law required that the statement be that of the victim, offered in a prosecution for criminal homicide. Thus declarations by victims in prosecutions for other crimes, e.g. a declaration by a rape victim who dies in childbirth, and all declarations in civil cases were outside the scope of the exception. An occasional statute has removed these restrictions . . . or has expanded the area of offenses to include abortions. Kansas by decision extended the exception to civil cases. While the common law exception no doubt originated as a result of the exceptional need for the evidence in homicide cases, the theory of admissibility applies equally in civil cases and in prosecutions for crimes other than homicide. The same considerations suggest abandonment of the limitation to circumstances attending the event in question, yet when the statement deals with matters other than the supposed death, its influence is believed to be sufficiently attenuated to justify the limitation. Unavailability is not limited to death. See subdivision (a) of this rule. Any problem as to declarations phrased in terms of opinion is laid at rest by Rule 701, and continuation of a requirement of firsthand knowledge is assured by Rule 602.

REPORT OF THE HOUSE JUDICIARY COMMITTEE

H.R. Rep. No. 93-650, at 15 (1973)

[Rule 804] as submitted by the Court . . . proposed to expand the traditional scope of the dying declaration exception (i.e. a statement of the victim in a homicide case as to the cause or circumstances of his believed imminent death) to allow such statements in all criminal and civil cases. The Committee did not consider dying declarations as among the most reliable forms of hearsay. Consequently, it amended the provision to limit their admissibility in criminal cases to homicide prosecutions, where exceptional need for the evidence is present. This is existing law. At the same time, the Committee approved the expansion to civil actions and proceedings where the stakes do not involve possible imprisonment, although noting that this could lead to forum shopping in some instances.

DAVIS v. STATE

207 So.3d 142 (Fla. 2016)

PER CURIAM.

[Leon Davis, Jr., was convicted of murdering Yvonne Bustamonte and Juanita Luciano, and he was sentenced to death. Davis robbed the insurance agency where Bustamonte and Luciano worked, bound them with duct tape, poured gasoline on them, and lit the building on fire. Both victims managed to escape from the building but later died from their burns. Lt. Joe Elrod of the Lake Wales Police Department, who responded to the scene, talked to Bustamonte while she waited for a medical airlift.]

Before trial, Davis filed a motion to exclude Bustamante's statements [to Lt. Elrod], and the trial court held an extensive evidentiary hearing during which it received testimony from multiple witnesses. . . . Lt. Elrod testified that when he first approached Bustamante, he observed a badly burned woman [and] quickly surmised that Bustamonte would not survive her injuries. As a result, he began to ask Bustamante pointed questions for the purpose of obtaining her statement. . . . Bustamante explained that she and Luciano were working when Davis entered their office, demanded money from them, and tried to rob them. She said that when they did not give Davis the money that he wanted, he threw gasoline on them and set them on fire. Lt. Elrod asked her if she knew the perpetrator's identity. Bustamante told him, "yes, it was Leon Davis," and that he was a client of their insurance business. Bustamante appeared coherent and alert, and she spoke clearly in response to Lt. Elrod's questions.

Other witnesses at the evidentiary hearing also testified that they heard Bustamante describe the events at Headley and identify Davis. Additionally, medical personnel testified about Bustamante's grave physical condition, and eyewitness Fran Murray testified that Bustamante stated that she was going to die. Following the hearing, the trial court determined that Bustamante's statements were admissible as a dying declaration. Her statements were admitted at trial through the testimony of Lt. Elrod and other witnesses.

To date, the United States Supreme Court has not answered whether the dying declaration exception remains viable in light of *Crawford.* Yet, in dicta, the Supreme Court has provided some guidance on the matter. Notably, in *Crawford,* although the facts of that case did not involve a dying declaration, the Court observed that dying declarations have been the "one deviation" to the rule excluding testimonial hearsay in criminal cases:

> The one deviation we have found involves dying declarations. The existence of that exception as a general rule of criminal hearsay law cannot be disputed . . . . Although many dying declarations may not be testimonial, there is authority for admitting even those that clearly are . . . . We need not decide in this case whether the Sixth Amendment incorporates an exception for testimonial dying declarations. If this exception must be accepted on historical grounds, it is *sui generis.*

Crawford, 541 U.S. at 56 n.6 (internal citations omitted). Subsequently, in *Giles v. California,* 554 U.S. 353, 358 (2008), the Supreme Court stated: "We have previously acknowledged that two forms of testimonial statements were admitted at common law even though they were unconfronted. The first of these were declarations made by a speaker who was both on the brink of death and aware that he was dying." Courts that have confronted the post-*Crawford* viability of the dying declaration have generally interpreted these statements as strong suggestions by the United States Supreme Court that the dying declaration exception does not run afoul of the Sixth Amendment right of confrontation. . . .

Today . . . this Court joins the overwhelming majority view that the dying declaration exception remains viable post-*Crawford*. The unique nature and purpose of the dying declaration exception, observed in *Crawford* and *Giles,* justifies its continuing utility and validity as an exception to the rule against hearsay. . . . [T]he dying declaration exception recognizes the extraordinary nature of the dying person's ability to speak to the circumstances that placed her in that grave position, and quite possibly to identify the perpetrator and ensure that the one who commits murder is held accountable. . . . Davis . . . argues that dying declarations are inherently unreliable. He cites to *U.S. v. Mayhew,* 380 F.Supp.2d 961, 966 (S.D.Ohio 2005), where a federal district court expressly "reject[ed] the government's argument that dying declarations are an exception to the Confrontation Clause." The court stated that it "doubts the inherent reliability of such statements," and it noted the incentives that even a dying person might have to offer false dying statements. The court observed:

> For example, the declarant might have been in a revengeful state of mind which would color his dying statements. No longer subject to the fear of retaliation by his enemies, the declarant might falsely incriminate those persons whom he disliked. If the decedent had no religious belief or fear of punishment after death, the statements made while dying would seem to lose much of the trustworthiness traditionally attributed to them. In general, self-serving declarations would be particularly suspect, for the decedent could thereby exculpate himself from questionable association with the circumstances surrounding his death. The declarant's physical and mental state of mind at the moment of death may weaken the reliability of his statements.

Id. (quoting Note, *Affidavits, Depositions, and Prior Testimony,* 46 Iowa L.R. 356, 375-76 (1961)).

While not impossible, we do think it improbable that a dying person would use the fleeting moments of her earthly existence to, rather than place blame at the feet of her actual murderer, intentionally falsely incriminate someone else. After all, "[t]he admission of the [dying declaration] is justified upon the ground of necessity, and in view of the consideration that the certain expectation of almost immediate death will remove all temptation to falsehood and enforce as strict adherence to the truth as the obligation of an oath could impose." *Mattox v. U.S.,* 146 U.S. 140, 152 (1892). . . .

In light of our holding that *Crawford* did not abrogate the dying declaration exception in Florida, we now turn to whether Bustamante's statements to Lt. Elrod constituted a dying declaration. . . . In order for the dying declaration exception to apply, "the deceased must have known and 'appreciated his condition as being that of an approach to certain and immediate death,' although it is not necessary that the declarant 'make express utterances' that he would never recover." *Hayward v. State,* 24 So.3d [17, 30 (Fla. 2009)] (quoting *Henry v. State,* 613 So.2d 429, 431 (Fla.1992)). In determining whether to admit hearsay as a dying declaration, "'the court should satisfy itself, on the totality of the circumstances,' that the deceased knew he was dying." *Id.* at 30-31 (quoting *Henry,* 613 So.2d at 431). The "absence of all hope of recovery, and appreciation by the declarant of his speedy and inevitable death, are a preliminary foundation that must always be laid to make such declarations admissible." *Id.* at 31 (quoting *McRane v. State,* 142 Fla. 240, 194 So. 632, 636 (1940)). Based on the totality of the circumstances, the trial court did not err in admitting Bustamante's dying declaration.... [T]he trial court's conclusion was ably supported by testimony of multiple witnesses, who all revealed the dire circumstances that Bustamante faced after Davis set her body on fire.... Moreover, Bustamante clearly expressed her belief that she was not going to survive. Thus, we conclude that the trial court properly admitted Bustamante's statements as a dying declaration.... [W]e affirm Davis's convictions and sentences....

[Justices Canady and Polston concurred in the result. Justice Perry, joined by Justice Quince, filed an opinion concurring in part and dissenting in part.]

PROBLEM

3.49. Summoned to the scene of a shooting, Officer Rachel Raskin finds the victim, Eugene Engels, bleeding badly and gasping for breath. Engels tells Raskin that he was shot by Larry Libby, to prevent him from testifying about a shooting the previous week. Engels says, "I was with Mike Mallon when he shot Casey Carleton — that kid on Acorn Avenue. Libby is Mallon's cousin. They're like brothers. Libby thought I might snitch. I told him I wouldn't. He didn't trust me." Shortly after speaking with Raskin, Engels loses consciousness. Paramedics take him to the hospital, and he is placed on life support. He survives but does not regain consciousness. Five months later, Mallon is on trial for Carleton's murder. Engels is still on life support and still in a coma. Can the prosecutor call Raskin to testify about what Engels told her?

11. Declarations Against Interest

Unlike the admissions doctrine, the exception for declarations against interest applies to statements by anyone, not just statements made by or attributable to the party against whom they are introduced. But, again unlike the admissions doctrine, the present exception applies only to statements that are obviously contrary to the interest of the declarant — so contrary, in fact, that a "reasonable person" would make the statement only if it were true. The major controversies associated with this exception have concerned its application to declarations that appear to subject the declarant to criminal liability.

[F.R.E. 804(b)(3); C.E.C. §1230]

ADVISORY COMMITTEE NOTE TO F.R.E. 804(b)(3)

The circumstantial guaranty of reliability for declarations against interest is the assumption that persons do not make statements which are damaging to themselves unless satisfied for good reason that they are true. If the statement is that of a party, offered by his opponent, it comes in as an admission, Rule [801(d)(2)], and there is no occasion to inquire whether it is against interest, this not being a condition precedent to admissibility of admissions by opponents.

The common law required that the interest declared against be pecuniary or proprietary but within this limitation demonstrated striking ingenuity in discovering an against-interest aspect. The exception discards the common law limitation and expands to the full logical limit. One result is to remove doubt as to the admissibility of declarations tending to establish a tort liability against the declarant or to extinguish one which might be asserted by him, in accordance with the trend of the decisions in this country. Another is to allow statements tending to expose declarant to hatred, ridicule, or disgrace, the motivation here being considered to be as strong as when financial interests are at stake. And finally, exposure to criminal liability satisfies the against-interest requirement. The refusal of the common law to concede the adequacy of a penal interest was no doubt indefensible in logic, but one senses in the decisions a distrust of evidence of confessions by third persons offered to exculpate the accused arising from suspicions of fabrication either of the fact of the making of the confession or in its contents, enhanced in either instance by the required unavailability of the declarant. . . . The requirement of corroboration is included in the rule in order to effect an accommodation between these competing considerations. When the statement is offered by the accused by way of exculpation, the resulting situation is not adapted to control by rulings as to the weight of the evidence, and hence the provision is cast in terms of a requirement preliminary to admissibility. The requirement of corroboration should be construed in such a manner as to effectuate its purpose of circumventing fabrication.

Ordinarily the third-party confession is thought of in terms of exculpating the accused, but this is by no means always or necessarily the case: it may include statements implicating him, and under the general theory of declarations against interest they would be admissible as related statements. . . . Whether a statement is in fact against interest must be determined from the circumstances of each case. Thus a statement admitting guilt and implicating another person, made while in custody, may well be motivated by a desire to curry favor with the authorities and hence fail to qualify as against interest. . . . On the other hand, the same words spoken under different circumstances, e.g., to an acquaintance, would have no difficulty in qualifying. The rule does not purport to deal with questions of the right of confrontation.

REPORT OF THE HOUSE JUDICIARY COMMITTEE

H.R. Rep. No. 93-650, at 16 (1974)

The Court's Rule . . . proposed to expand the hearsay limitation from its present federal limitation to include statements subjecting the declarant to criminal liability and statements tending to make him an object of hatred, ridicule, or disgrace. The Committee eliminated the latter category from the subdivision as lacking sufficient guarantees of reliability. As for statements against penal interest, the Committee shared the view of the Court that some such statements do possess adequate assurances of reliability and should be admissible. It believed, however, as did the Court, that statements of this type tending to exculpate the accused are more suspect and so should have their admissibility conditioned upon some further provision insuring trustworthiness. The proposal in the Court Rule to add a requirement of simple corroboration was, however, deemed ineffective to accomplish this purpose since the accused's own testimony might suffice while not necessarily increasing the reliability of the hearsay statement. The Committee settled upon the language "unless corroborating circumstances clearly indicate the trustworthiness of the statement" as affording a proper standard and degree of discretion.

UNITED STATES v. DURAN SAMANIEGO

345 F.3d 1280 (11th Cir. 2003)

CARNES, Circuit Judge.

[Between 1972 and 1989, Roberto Duran Samaniego won four world boxing championships. He retired in 2002.] Duran claims that his championship belts were stolen from his house in Panama by his brother-in-law, Bolivar Iglesias, in September of 1993. . . . It is undisputed that Duran's championship belts ultimately came into the hands of Luis Gonzalez Baez, a Miami businessman, and that Baez attempted to sell the belts to undercover FBI agents (who had set up a sting operation) for $200,000. Baez was arrested, but he claimed that the belts had not been stolen. The government confiscated the belts and filed an interpleader action in federal district court to determine whether Duran or Baez is the rightful owner of the belts. The case was tried to a jury, which returned a verdict in favor of Duran. This is Baez's appeal from the judgment the district court entered in accordance with that verdict.

Baez's principal contention on appeal is that the district court should not have admitted testimony about a purported apology from Bolivar Iglesias. Over Baez's objection, the district court permitted a number of witnesses, including Duran and some of his family members, to testify that Iglesias apologized in their presence for stealing the belts. Baez contends that testimony is inadmissible hearsay. The district court allowed it on the theory that the out-of-court statement described an existing state of mind or emotion, and for that reason fit within the hearsay exception set out in Federal Rule of Evidence 803(3). . . . The question, as Baez's argument frames it, is whether Iglesias's apology falls within the exclusion from Rule 803(3) admissibility because it is a "statement of memory or belief to prove the fact remembered or believed."

An apology is evidence of a then-existing state of mind or emotion: remorse. Iglesias's apology is admissible to prove the truth of the matter asserted — that Iglesias felt remorse at the time he made the apologetic statement. That is not the problem. The problem is . . . that "the state-of-mind exception does not permit the witness to relate any of the declarant's statements as to why he held the particular state of mind, or what he might have believed that would have induced the state of mind." *United States v. Cohen*, 631 F.2d 1223, 1225 (5th Cir. 1980). . . . [T]he purpose of the exclusion from Rule 803(3) admissibility is "to narrowly limit those admissible statements to declarations of condition — 'I'm scared' — and not belief — 'I'm scared because [someone] threatened me.'" *Id.*

The testimony admitted in this case was not limited to the fact that Iglesias had expressed remorse, but also included the fact that he said he apologized for and asked forgiveness for having stolen the belts. The testimony most often came in response to questions from Duran's counsel about how the witness knew Iglesias had stolen the belts. What Iglesias said was offered to show not only that he was remorseful, but also that he had stolen the belts. Rule 803(3) expressly prohibits the use of a statement of then-existing state of mind in this way. That prohibition, the committee notes explain, is necessary "to avoid the virtual destruction of the hearsay rule which would otherwise result from allowing state of mind, provable by a hearsay statement, to serve as the basis for an inference of the happening of the event which produced the state of mind."

Our conclusion that Iglesias's apology was not properly admitted under Rule 803(3) does not end the matter. Although the district court admitted the statement under Rule 803(3), Duran offered the testimony concerning the apology as a statement against interest by a declarant unavailable at trial, which is admissible under Rule 804(b)(3). The district court did not reach that alternative ground for admissibility, but we do because we will not hold that the district court abused its discretion where it reached the correct result even if it did so for the wrong reason. The part of Iglesias's apology in which he admitted having stolen Duran's belts is a statement against interest, because it would "subject the declarant to civil or criminal liability" within the meaning of Rule 804(b)(3). For a statement against interest to be admissible under Rule 804, however, the declarant must have been unavailable at the time of the trial within the meaning of Rule 804(a).

Iglesias was not present at the trial, but that does not mean he was unavailable for Rule 804 purposes. Subsection (a) of that rule tells us a witness should be considered unavailable in five separate circumstances, only one of which is relevant in this case: The declarant is unavailable if he "is absent from the hearing and the proponent of a statement has been unable to procure the declarant's attendance (or in the case of a hearsay exception under subdivision (b)(2), (3), or (4), the declarant's attendance or testimony) by process or other reasonable means."

Duran could not procure Iglesias's attendance or testimony by process because Iglesias, a citizen of Panama, apparently was living in that country at the time of the trial, and "foreign nationals located outside the United States . . . are beyond the subpoena power of the district court." *United States v. Drogoul*, 1 F.3d 1546, 1553 (11th Cir. 1993). Duran did enlist the help of Iglesias's immediate family in an attempt to locate him and persuade him to return to the United States and testify. Iglesias's sister, who is Duran's wife, testified that she and her mother had tried to locate Iglesias on five different occasions, but finding him had proven impossible. Iglesias's mother testified that she had tried to contact him in order to get him to come back and testify but was unable to get Iglesias.

Using the efforts of Iglesias's sister and mother, as Duran did, is a reasonable means of attempting to locate Iglesias in Panama and persuade him to travel to the United States to testify. It follows that Duran did establish Iglesias was unavailable to testify under Rule 804(a)(5), so the out-of-court statement Iglesias made was admissible under Rule 804(b)(3) as a statement against interest. The district court did not abuse its discretion in admitting the statement, albeit on the wrong ground. . . . The judgment entered on the jury's verdict stands, and under it Roberto Duran is entitled to regain his championship belts.

UNITED STATES v. JACKSON

335 F.3d 170 (2d Cir. 2003)

McLaughlin, Circuit Judge.

. . . [A] jury found defendant Charles L. Jackson guilty of conspiring to import 5 kilograms or more of cocaine into the United States. . . . Jackson challenges his conviction on evidentiary grounds. He contends that the court abused its discretion in refusing to admit the entire plea allocution of co-conspirator Steve Brown. . . . Specifically, Jackson challenges the exclusion of Brown's statement that Brown never supervised Jackson. . . .

Under Rule 804(b)(1), an unavailable witness's testimony from a prior hearing or proceeding is not barred by the hearsay rule "if the party against whom the testimony is now offered . . . had an opportunity and similar motive to develop the testimony by direct, cross, or redirect examination." . . . Here, both sides concede that Brown was unavailable at Jackson's trial because he had properly invoked his Fifth Amendment right against self-incrimination. . . . [The issue] is whether the Government had an opportunity and similar motive to examine Brown at his plea allocution. . . . Under Fed. R. Crim. P. 11, the purpose of a plea proceeding is to ensure that the defendant's plea is knowing, voluntary, and grounded on a proper factual basis. . . . [A] plea proceeding is conducted solely by the district court judge who is primarily responsible for ensuring that the requirements of Rule 11 are satisfied. On the rare occasion where the prosecutor is permitted to address the defendant, the questions posed are usually formulaic and perfunctory. The Government's role at a plea proceeding is quite limited, and certainly does not include the opportunity to engage in the type of examination contemplated by Rule 804(b)(1). . . . Moreover, [w]e agree with the Third and Seventh Circuits that the Government does not have the same motive to examine the defendant at a plea hearing as it does at other proceedings. *See United States v. Lowell*, 649 F.2d 950, 965 (3d Cir. 1981); *United States v. Powell*, 894 F.2d 895, 901 (7th Cir. 1990). Here, the Government had no reason to cross-examine Brown at his plea allocution about his supervision over Jackson. That Brown's plea colloquy may have included misstatements or inaccuracies did not preclude it from providing an adequate factual basis for the plea. The district court, therefore, did not abuse its discretion in excluding Brown's plea allocution under Rule 804(b)(1).

Jackson's contention that Brown's plea allocution might be admissible under Rule 804(b)(3) is a stronger argument, but it too is ultimately without merit. Rule 804(b)(3) allows the admission of a hearsay statement by an unavailable witness if that statement "at the time of its making . . . so far tended to subject the declarant to civil or criminal liability . . . that a reasonable person in the declarant's position would not have made the statement unless believing it to be true." This exception rests on the notion that "reasonable people, even reasonable people who are not especially honest, tend not to make self-inculpatory statements unless they believe them to be true." *Williamson v. United States*, 512 U.S. 594, 599 (1994).

Rule 804(b)(3) further requires that, if the statement exposes the declarant (*i.e.*, Brown) to criminal liability and is offered to exculpate the accused (*i.e.*, Jackson), the proponent of the statements must identify "corroborating circumstances [that] clearly indicate the trustworthiness of the statement." *Id.* at 605. The purpose of this corroboration requirement is to "circumvent[] fabrication" by the declarant. *See* Fed. R. Evid. 804(b)(3) Advisory Committee Notes....

Although we have recognized that statements from a guilty plea allocution can be admitted under Rule 804(b)(3) ... their admission is strictly circumscribed by the Supreme Court's holding in *Williamson v. United States* ... that Rule 804(b)(3) "does not allow admission of non-self-inculpatory statements, even if they are made within a broader narrative that is generally self-inculpatory." ... [E]ach particular hearsay statement offered under Rule 804(b)(3) must be separately parsed and must, itself, be self-inculpatory....

[T]he statements by Brown that Jackson sought to introduce at trial were not themselves self-inculpatory as to Brown. They did not, therefore, satisfy *Williamson.* Brown's statements that he never supervised Jackson and never asked Jackson to go to Jamaica to smuggle drugs did not in any way inculpate Brown or expose him to criminal liability. Accordingly, the separate guarantee of trustworthiness required by Rule 804(b)(3) is non-existent as to these statements. If anything, these statements were probably exculpatory as to Brown as they minimized the number of people that he supervised during the conspiracy.

Moreover, even if Brown's statements could be construed as self-inculpatory, Jackson has failed to satisfy the corroboration requirement of Rule 804(b)(3).... [D]uring his plea allocution Brown made conflicting assertions about Jackson's role in the conspiracy. For example, Brown first asserted that Jackson was a person with whom he had arrangements to smuggle drugs into the country. At another point, however, Brown claimed that Jackson smuggled cocaine into the country only for Guthrie.... [And] Brown's own motives for making the statements exculpating Jackson were highly suspect. Because Brown was aware at the time of his plea that there was a possibility that he could be called upon to testify at Jackson's trial (he was on the Government's witness list), the district court sagely noted that Brown's apparent attempt to exculpate Jackson may well have been an effort to avoid testifying against one of his co-conspirators.

Accordingly, the district court did not abuse its discretion in failing to admit Brown's plea allocution statements under the Rule 804(b)(3) exception to the hearsay rule.... [Affirmed in relevant part.]

PROBLEMS

3.50. Dwight, charged with armed robbery of a bank, seeks to elicit testimony from Sarah that her husband told her, just before he died of injuries he suffered in an automobile accident, "I'm not going to make it. There's something you've got to make right. That stickup job they're putting on Dwight — it was me." Is Sarah's testimony admissible? Does it matter whether some of the money from the robbery was later found in her husband's car?

3.51. As part of its case against Dwight, the prosecution seeks to introduce testimony from Frank that, while Frank was on a fishing trip with Greg, Greg boasted of planning a bank robbery and having someone else carry it out. Frank will further testify that he asked Greg who carried out the robbery, and that Greg said it was Dwight. Greg cannot now be located. Is the testimony from Frank admissible? Does it matter whether a large cash deposit was made to Greg's bank account on the day after the robbery?

3.52. Uriah commits suicide and leaves a note explaining, "I can no longer live with the guilt. Wesley and I killed Vidor." Is Uriah's note admissible in a murder prosecution of Wesley? In a wrongful death lawsuit brought against Wesley and against Uriah's estate by Vidor's widow?

12. Forfeiture by Wrongdoing

Rule 804(b)(6) was added in 1997 to codify a common law exception aimed at preventing use of the hearsay rule by a party who purposely and wrongfully causes a declarant's unavailability.

[F.R.E. 804(b)(6); C.E.C. §§1231, 1350]

ADVISORY COMMITTEE NOTE TO 1997 AMENDMENT TO F.R.E. 804

... Rule 804(b)(6) has been added to provide that a party forfeits the right to object on hearsay grounds to the admission of a declarant's prior statement when the party's deliberate wrongdoing or acquiescence therein procured the unavailability of the declarant as a witness. This recognizes the need for a prophylactic rule to deal with abhorrent behavior "which strikes at the heart of the system of justice itself." *United States v. Mastrangelo*, 693 F.2d 269, 273 (2d Cir. 1982), cert. denied, 467 U.S. 1204 (1984). The wrong-doing need not consist of a criminal act. The rule applies to all parties, including the government.

Every circuit that has resolved the question has recognized the principle of forfeiture by misconduct, although the tests for determining whether there is a forfeiture have varied.... The usual Rule 104(a) preponderance of the evidence standard has been adopted in light of the behavior the new Rule 804(b)(6) seeks to discourage.

GILES v. CALIFORNIA

554 U.S. 353 (2008)

Justice SCALIA delivered the opinion of the Court....

[Dwayne Giles fatally shot his ex-girlfriend, Brenda Avie. A jury convicted him of murder, rejecting his claim of self-defense. Among the evidence at trial were] statements that Avie had made to a police officer responding to a domestic-violence report about three weeks before the shooting. Avie, who was crying when she spoke, told the officer that Giles had accused her of having an affair, and that after the two began to argue, Giles grabbed her by the shirt, lifted her off the floor, and began to choke her. According to Avie, when she broke free and fell to the floor, Giles punched her in the face and head, and after she broke free again, he opened a folding knife, held it about three feet away from her, and threatened to kill her if he found her cheating on him. Over Giles' objection, the trial court admitted these statements into evidence under a provision of California law that permits admission of out-of-court statements describing the infliction or threat of physical injury on a declarant when the declarant is unavailable to testify at trial and the prior statements are deemed trustworthy. Cal. Evid. Code Ann. §1370. . . .

The State does not dispute here, and we accept without deciding, that Avie's statements accusing Giles of assault were testimonial. But it maintains (as did the California Supreme Court) that the Sixth Amendment did not prohibit prosecutors from introducing the statements because an exception to the confrontation guarantee permits the use of a witness's unconfronted testimony if a judge finds, as the judge did in this case, that the defendant committed a wrongful act that rendered the witness unavailable to testify at trial. We held in *Crawford* that the Confrontation Clause is "most naturally read as a reference to the right of confrontation at common law, admitting only those exceptions established at the time of the founding."We therefore ask whether the theory of forfeiture by wrongdoing accepted by the California Supreme Court is a founding-era exception to the confrontation right.

We have previously acknowledged that two forms of testimonial statements were admitted at common law even though they were unconfronted. The first of these were declarations made by a speaker who was both on the brink of death and aware that he was dying. See, *e.g.*, *King* v. *Woodcock*, 168 Eng. Rep. 352, 353-354 (1789). . . . Avie did not make the unconfronted statements admitted at Giles' trial when she was dying, so her statements do not fall within this historic exception.

A second common-law doctrine, which we will refer to as forfeiture by wrongdoing, permitted the introduction of statements of a witness who was "detained" or "kept away" by the "means or procurement" of the defendant. . . . The terms used to define the scope of the forfeiture rule suggest that the exception applied only when the defendant engaged in conduct *designed* to prevent the witness from testifying. . . . We are aware of no case in which the exception was invoked although the defendant had not engaged in conduct designed to prevent a witness from testifying, such as offering a bribe. . . . In cases where the evidence suggested that the defendant had caused a person to be absent, but had not done so to prevent the person from testifying — as in the typical murder case involving accusatorial statements by the victim — the testimony was excluded unless it was confronted or fell within the dying-declaration exception. Prosecutors do not appear to have even *argued* that the judge could admit the unconfronted statements because the defendant committed the murder for which he was on trial.

Consider *King* v. *Woodcock*. William Woodcock was accused of killing his wife, Silvia, who had been beaten and left near death. A Magistrate took

Silvia Woodcock's account of the crime, under oath, and she died about 48 hours later. The judge stated that "[g]reat as a crime of this nature must always appear to be, yet the inquiry into it must proceed upon the rules of evidence." Aside from testimony given at trial in the presence of the prisoner, the judge said, there were "two other species which are admitted by law: The one is the dying declaration of a person who has received a fatal blow; the other is the examination of a prisoner, and the depositions of the witnesses who may be produced against him" taken under the Marian bail and committal statutes. Silvia Woodcock's statement could not be admitted pursuant to the Marian statutes because it was unconfronted — the defendant had not been brought before the examining Magistrate and "the prisoner therefore had no opportunity of contradicting the facts it contains." Thus, the statements were admissible only if the witness "apprehended that she was in such a state of mortality as would inevitably oblige her soon to answer before her Maker for the truth or falsehood of her assertions." Depending on the account one credits, the court either instructed the jury to consider the statements only if Woodcock was "in fact under the apprehension of death," 168 Eng. Rep., at 354, or determined for itself that Woodcock was "quietly resigned and submitting to her fate" and admitted her statements into evidence, 1 E. East, Pleas of the Crown 356 (1803). . . . Many other cases excluded victims' statements when there was insufficient evidence that the witness was aware he was about to die. . . .

The State and the dissent note that common-law authorities justified the wrongful-procurement rule by invoking the maxim that a defendant should not be permitted to benefit from his own wrong. See, *e.g.*, G. Gilbert, Law of Evidence 140-141 (1756) (if a witness was "detained and kept back from appearing by the means and procurement" testimony would be read because a defendant "shall never be admitted to shelter himself by such evil Practices on the Witness, that being to give him Advantage of his own Wrong"). But as the evidence amply shows, the "wrong" and the "evil Practices" to which these statements referred was conduct *designed* to prevent a witness from testifying. The absence of a forfeiture rule covering this sort of conduct would create an intolerable incentive for defendants to bribe, intimidate, or even kill witnesses against them. There is nothing mysterious about courts' refusal to carry the rationale further. The notion that judges may strip the defendant of a right that the Constitution deems essential to a fair trial, on the basis of a prior *judicial* assessment that the defendant is guilty as charged, does not sit well with the right to trial by jury. It is akin, one might say, to "dispensing with jury trial because a defendant is obviously guilty." *Crawford*, 541 U.S., at 62.

Not only was the State's proposed exception to the right of confrontation plainly not an "exceptio[n] established at the time of the founding," *id.*, at 54; it is not established in American jurisprudence *since* the founding. American courts never — prior to 1985 — invoked forfeiture outside the context of deliberate witness tampering. . . . In 1997, this Court approved a Federal Rule of Evidence, entitled "Forfeiture by wrongdoing," which applies only when the defendant "engaged or acquiesced in wrongdoing that was intended to, and did, procure the unavailability of the declarant as a witness." Fed. Rule of Evid. 804(b)(6). We have described this as a rule "which codifies the forfeiture doctrine." *Davis* v. *Washington*, 547 U.S. 813, 833 (2006). Every commentator we are aware of has concluded the requirement of intent "means that the exception applies only if the defendant has in mind the particular purpose of making the witness unavailable."[2] The commentators come out this way because the dissent's claim that knowledge is sufficient to show intent is emphatically *not* the modern view.

In sum, our interpretation of the common-law forfeiture rule is supported by (1) the most natural reading of the language used at common law; (2) the absence of common-law cases *admitting* prior statements on a forfeiture theory when the defendant had not engaged in conduct designed to prevent a witness from testifying; (3) the common law's uniform exclusion of unconfronted inculpatory testimony by murder victims (except testimony given with awareness of impending death) in the innumerable cases in which the defendant was on trial for killing the victim, but was not shown to have done so for the purpose of preventing testimony; (4) a subsequent history in which the dissent's broad forfeiture theory has not been applied. The first two and the last are highly persuasive; the third is in our view conclusive. . . .

The dissent closes by pointing out that a forfeiture rule which ignores *Crawford* would be particularly helpful to women in abusive relationships — or at least particularly helpful in punishing their abusers. Not as helpful as the dissent suggests, since only *testimonial* statements are excluded by the Confrontation Clause. Statements to friends and neighbors about abuse and intimidation, and statements to physicians in the course of receiving treatment would be excluded, if at all, only by hearsay rules, which are free to adopt the dissent's version of forfeiture by wrongdoing. In any event, we are puzzled by the dissent's decision to devote its peroration to domestic abuse cases. Is the suggestion that we should have one Confrontation Clause (the one the Framers adopted and *Crawford* described) for all other crimes, but a special, improvised, Confrontation Clause for those crimes that are frequently directed against women? Domestic violence is an intolerable offense that legislatures may choose to combat through many means — from increasing criminal penalties to adding resources for investigation and prosecution to funding awareness and prevention campaigns. But for that serious crime, as for others, abridging the constitutional rights of criminal defendants is not in the State's arsenal.

The domestic-violence context is, however, relevant for a separate reason. Acts of domestic violence often are intended to dissuade a victim from resorting to outside help, and include conduct designed to prevent testimony to police officers or cooperation in criminal prosecutions. Where such an abusive relationship culminates in murder, the evidence may support a finding that the crime expressed the intent to isolate the victim and to stop her from reporting abuse to the authorities or cooperating with a criminal prosecution — rendering her prior statements admissible under the forfeiture doctrine. Earlier abuse, or threats of abuse, intended to dissuade the victim from resorting to outside help would be highly relevant to this inquiry, as

---

2. Only a single state evidentiary code appears to contain a forfeiture rule broader than our holding in this case (and in *Crawford*) allow. . . . These rules cast more than a little doubt on the dissent's assertion that the historic forfeiture rule creates intolerable problems of proof. The lone forfeiture exception whose text reaches more broadly than the rule we adopt is an Oregon rule adopted in 2005. ›

would evidence of ongoing criminal proceedings at which the victim would have been expected to testify. . . .

The state courts in this case did not consider the intent of the defendant because they found that irrelevant to application of the forfeiture doctrine. This view of the law was error, but the court is free to consider evidence of the defendant's intent on remand. . . . The judgment of the California Supreme Court is vacated. . . .

Justice THOMAS, concurring.

I write separately to note that I adhere to my view that statements like those made by the victim in this case do not implicate the Confrontation Clause. . . . Nonetheless, in this case respondent does not argue that the contested evidence is nontestimonial, the court below noted "no dispute" on the issue, and it is outside the scope of the question presented. Because the Court's opinion accurately reflects our Confrontation Clause jurisprudence where the applicability of that Clause is not at issue, I join the Court in vacating the decision below.

Justice ALITO, concurring.

I join the Court's opinion, but I write separately to make clear that, like Justice THOMAS, I am not convinced that the out-of-court statement at issue here fell within the Confrontation Clause in the first place. . . .

Justice SOUTER, with whom Justice GINSBURG joins, concurring in [relevant] part.

. . . The historical record as revealed by the exchange simply does not focus on what should be required for forfeiture when the crime charged occurred in an abusive relationship or was its culminating act; today's understanding of domestic abuse had no apparent significance at the time of the Framing, and there is no early example of the forfeiture rule operating in that circumstance. Examining the early cases and commentary, however, reveals two things that count in favor of the Court's understanding of forfeiture when the evidence shows domestic abuse. The first is the substantial indication that the Sixth Amendment was meant to require some degree of intent to thwart the judicial process before thinking it reasonable to hold the confrontation right forfeited; otherwise the right would in practical terms boil down to a measure of reliable hearsay, a view rejected in *Crawford* v. *Washington*, 541 U.S. 36 (2004). The second is the absence from the early material of any reason to doubt that the element of intention would normally be satisfied by the intent inferred on the part of the domestic abuser in the classic abusive relationship, which is meant to isolate the victim from outside help, including the aid of law enforcement and the judicial process. If the evidence for admissibility shows a continuing relationship of this sort, it would make no sense to suggest that the oppressing defendant miraculously abandoned the dynamics of abuse the instant before he killed his victim, say in a fit of anger. The Court's conclusion . . . thus fits the rationale that equity requires and the historical record supports.

Justice BREYER, with whom Justice STEVENS and Justice KENNEDY join, dissenting.

. . . [A]n examination of the forfeiture rule's basic purposes and objectives indicates that the rule applies here. At the time of the founding, a leading treatise writer described the forfeiture rule as designed to assure that the prisoner "shall never be admitted to shelter himself by such evil Practices on the Witness, that being to give him Advantage of his own Wrong." [1 G. Gilbert, Law of Evidence 214–215 (1791).] . . . What more "evil practice" . . . than to murder the witness? And what greater evidentiary "advantage" could one derive from that wrong than thereby to prevent the witness from testifying, *e.g.*, preventing the witness from describing a history of physical abuse that is not consistent with the defendant's claim that he killed her in self-defense?

. . . [T]he defendant here knew that murdering his ex-girlfriend would keep her from testifying; and that knowledge is sufficient to show the *intent* that law ordinarily demands. . . . With a few criminal law exceptions not here relevant, the law holds an individual responsible for consequences known likely to follow just as if that individual had intended to achieve them. A defendant, in a criminal or a civil case, for example, cannot escape criminal or civil liability for murdering an airline passenger by claiming that his purpose in blowing up the airplane was to kill only a single passenger for her life insurance, not the others on the same flight. . . . [T]he law does not often turn matters of responsibility upon *motive*, rather than *intent*. And there is no reason to believe that application of the rule of forfeiture constitutes an exception to this general legal principle. . . . [T]o turn application of the forfeiture rule upon proof of the defendant's *purpose* (rather than *intent*), as the majority does, creates serious practical evidentiary problems . . . [and] cannot be squared with the exception's basically ethical objective. . . .

Each year, domestic violence results in more than 1,500 deaths and more than 2 million injuries; it accounts for a substantial portion of all homicides; it typically involves a history of repeated violence; and it is difficult to prove in court because the victim is generally reluctant or unable to testify. . . . Regardless of a defendant's purpose, threats, further violence, and ultimately murder, can stop victims from testifying. See [Lininger, Prosecuting Batterers After *Crawford*, 91 Va. L. Rev. 747, 769 (2005)] (citing finding that batterers threaten retaliatory violence in as many as half of all cases, and 30 percent of batterers assault their victims again during the prosecution). A *constitutional* evidentiary requirement that insists upon a showing of purpose (rather than simply intent or probabilistic knowledge) may permit the domestic partner who made the threats, caused the violence, or even murdered the victim to avoid conviction for earlier crimes by taking advantage of later ones. . . . [T]he Court . . . grants the defendant not fair treatment, but a windfall. I can find no history, no underlying purpose, no administrative consideration, and no constitutional principle that requires this result. Insofar as Justice SOUTER's [concurrence] in effect presumes "purpose" based on no more than evidence of a history of domestic violence, I agree with it. In all other respects, however, I must respectfully dissent.

13. Residual Exception

The residual or "catchall" exception to the federal hearsay rule allows the introduction of certain out-of-court statements that seem reliable and highly probative but are not admissible under other exceptions. The rule was amended in

2019 in an effort to broaden its coverage, but there is continuing disagreement about how much freedom courts should have to supplement the traditional hearsay exceptions on a case-by-case basis.

[F.R.E. 807]

ADVISORY COMMITTEE NOTE TO F.R.E. 807

The contents of Rule 803(24) and Rule 804(b)(5) have been combined and transferred to a new Rule 807. This was done to facilitate additions to Rules 803 and 804. No change in meaning is intended.

ADVISORY COMMITTEE NOTE TO 2019 AMENDMENT TO RULE 807

The amendment does not alter the case law prohibiting parties from proceeding directly to the residual exception, without considering the admissibility of the hearsay under Rules 803 and 804. A court is not required to make a finding that no other hearsay exception is applicable. But the opponent cannot seek admission under Rule 807 if it is apparent that the hearsay could be admitted under another exception.

The rule in its current form applies to hearsay "not specifically covered" by a Rule 803 or 804 exception. The amendment makes the rule applicable to hearsay "not admissible under" those exceptions. This clarifies that a court assessing guarantees of trustworthiness may consider whether the statement is a "near-miss" of one of the Rule 803 or 804 exceptions. If the court employs a "near-miss" analysis it should — in addition to evaluating all relevant guarantees of trustworthiness — take into account the reasons that the hearsay misses the admissibility requirements of the standard exception.

In deciding whether the statement is supported by sufficient guarantees of trustworthiness, the court should not consider the credibility of any witness who relates the declarant's hearsay statement in court. The credibility of an in-court witness does not present a hearsay question. To base admission or exclusion of a hearsay statement on the witness's credibility would usurp the jury's role of determining the credibility of testifying witnesses. The rule provides that the focus for trustworthiness is on circumstantial guarantees surrounding the making of the statement itself, as well as any independent evidence corroborating the statement. The credibility of the witness relating the statement is not a part of either enquiry.

Of course, even if the court finds sufficient guarantees of trustworthiness, the independent requirements of the Confrontation Clause must be satisfied if the hearsay statement is offered against a defendant in a criminal case.

The Committee decided to retain the requirement that the proponent must show that the hearsay statement is more probative than any other evidence that the proponent can reasonably obtain. This necessity requirement will continue to serve to prevent the residual exception from being used as a device to erode the categorical exceptions.

GLEN WEISSENBERGER & JAMES J. DUANE, FEDERAL RULES OF EVIDENCE

§807.1, at 746-747 (7th ed. 2011)

The legislative history of former Rules 803(24) and 804(b)(5) illustrates that the exceptions contained therein represented a compromise between the competing goals of allowing flexibility in the development of the hearsay system on one hand and ensuring some degree of certainty for trial preparation on the other. Although the Supreme Court approved the Advisory Committee's draft, the [House] Judiciary Committee deleted the residual exceptions from Rules 803 and 804 as "injecting too much uncertainty into the law of evidence and impairing the ability of practitioners to prepare for trial." The Committee believed that "if additional hearsay exceptions are to be created, they should be by amendments to the Rules, not on a case-by-case basis."

The Senate Judiciary Committee reinstated the residual exceptions, but added several restrictions to narrow their scope. While the Senate's draft was intended to provide room for growth in the hearsay rules, the Committee nevertheless cautioned that "[i]t is intended that the residual hearsay exceptions will be used very rarely, and only in exceptional circumstances." The Conference Committee approved the Senate's version of the Rules, but added a requirement that the proponent of the evidence offered under one of the residual exceptions must give his opponent sufficient notice before trial to enable him to prepare to meet the evidence. As enacted, Rules 803(24) and 804(b)(5) adopted the approach taken by some pre-Rules decisions that evaluated the trustworthiness of and need for a particular hearsay statement rather than the strict applicability of a specific exception. The residual exception now embodied in Rule 807 continues to allow courts to follow this approach to the admission of hearsay.

UNITED STATES v. SLATTEN

865 F.3d 767 (D.C. Cir. 2017)

PER CURIAM:

Nicholas Slatten [and three co-defendants] were contractors with Blackwater Worldwide Security, which in 2007 was providing security services to the United States State Department in Iraq. As a result of . . . shootings that injured or killed at least 31 Iraqi civilians [in Nisur Square, Baghdad]. . . Slatten was convicted of first-degree murder [and his co-defendants were convicted of manslaughter]. . . .

[Before trial] Slatten argued for severance because he sought to introduce exculpatory evidence — the co-defendant's admissions that he, not Slatten, initiated the Nisur Square attack by firing on [a] white Kia — evidence inadmissible in a joint trial with the co-defendant. The district court denied Slatten's motion to sever, finding the co-defendant's admissions constituted inadmissible hearsay. We disagree. Because the co-defendant's admissions were vital to Slatten's defense and possessed sufficient circumstantial guarantees of trustworthiness, we believe they were admissible under Federal Rule of Evidence 807. Accordingly, because the district court erroneously denied severance, we reverse Slatten's first-degree murder conviction . . . and remand his case for a new trial. . . .

[T]he government maintained that Slatten's shot was the match that ignited the Nisur Square firestorm—that Slatten intentionally opened fire on the white Kia because of an anti-Iraqi animus. . . . But in the hours and days following the Nissur Square attack, it was another member of [Slatten's] team—a co-defendant here—who said that he had fired the first shots at the white Kia. Just hours after the shooting, the co-defendant was interviewed and debriefed by State Department investigators operating in Baghdad. Before his interview, the investigators told the co-defendant that if he was "honest and truthful, that nothing would be used against [him], and that they were there to gather information not to be used in a criminal setting." During his first debriefing, the co-defendant told the investigators that he had "engaged and hit the driver" of the white Kia sedan. [The co-defendant made the same claim to investigators, under similar promises of immunity, twice in the following week, once in writing and once orally.]

. . . Although we agree with Slatten that, at their joint trial, his co-defendant qualified as "an unavailable witness" [for purposes of Rule 804(b)(3) of the Federal Rules of Evidence], and that his co-defendant's statements do possess indicia of trustworthiness, Slatten could not show that his co-defendant's statements were so inculpatory that a reasonable person in the latter's position would have made the statements only if he believed them to be true; his co-defendant's statements were immunized and, as a general matter, a self-defense claim is not "clearly" against a declarant's interest. . . . Accordingly, it was not an abuse of discretion to conclude, as the district court did, that the co-defendant's statements did not fit within Rule 804(b)(3)'s exception.

Rule 803(6) provides an exception to the hearsay rule for records that are, inter alia, "kept in the course of a regularly conducted activity of a business." Rule 803(6) does not support the admissibility of the co-defendant's statements because he himself was not acting in the regular course of business when he made his statements to State Department investigators. Having rejected Rule 804(b)(3)'s and Rule 803(6)'s applicability, we turn to Rule 807. . . .

The residual hearsay exception "was designed to encourage the progressive growth and development of federal evidentiary law by giving courts the flexibility to deal with new evidentiary situations which may not be pigeonholed elsewhere." *United States v. Mathis*, 559 F.2d 294, 299 (5th Cir. 1977). . . . That said, we also recognize that the residual hearsay exception is "extremely narrow and require[s] testimony to be 'very important and very reliable.'" *United States v. Washington*, 106 F.3d 983, 1001 (D.C. Cir. 1997) (per curiam); *accord* [*S.E.C. v First City Fin. Corp.*, 890 F.2d 1215, 1225 (D.C. Cir. 1989)] ("[T]he legislative history of the [residual hearsay] exception indicates that it should be applied sparingly."). Indeed, were Rule 807 to be liberally applied, the exception might read out the rule. . . . *See Akrabawi v. Carnes Co.*, 152 F.3d 688, 697 (7th Cir. 1998) ("We . . . narrowly constru[e] the residual provision to prevent it from becoming the exception that swallows the hearsay rule."). . . . Thus, only in the most "exceptional circumstances" does Rule 807 make admissible a statement that does not fall within one of Rule 803's or Rule 804's enumerated hearsay exceptions. *See [United States v. Kim*, 595 F.2d 755, 765-66 (D.C. Cir. 1979)]; *United States v. Phillips*, 219 F.3d 404, 419 & n.23 (5th Cir.

2000) ("The [residual hearsay] exception is to be used only rarely, in truly exceptional cases." . . .).

We believe this case presents one of those exceptional circumstances. . . . Several of the circumstances surrounding the co-defendant's declarations indicate their reliability and manifest that he was likely telling the truth at the time he made his statements. He was almost completely immunized when he made his statements — he faced no criminal liability (absent one exception discussed below) as a result of his providing the investigators his account of the Nisur Square attack. Immunity can indicate trustworthiness, particularly if the immunized statements do not cast blame or "divert attention" to another. More importantly, the one exception to the co-defendant's immunity may have been an even greater incentive encouraging his honesty; that is, he faced criminal liability under 18 U.S.C. § 1001 if he made a materially false statement to the investigators and he expressly acknowledged that he could be so prosecuted. . . . [In addition, the co-defendant's consistency in his multiple statements] supports [their] reliability . . . and, consequently, his veracity.

The record also contains [corroborating] evidence. . . . Iraqi Police Officer Ali Ghalaf Salman Mansur Al-Hamidi was "within feet" of the Blackwater convoy in Nisur Square on the day of the attack. Al-Hamidi testified that . . . from his proximity to the convoy, he was "100 percent certain" that a man in the co-defendant's precise position fired the first shots. Al-Hamidi's partner, Sarhan Dheyab Abdul Monem, also testified that, from his "very close" vantage point "about three to four meters away from [the] armored cars," he also witnessed the first shots coming from the co-defendant's precise position. . . . Blackwater convoy member Jeremy Krueger also provided corroboration, testifying that the first shots he heard in Nisur Square sounded like "5.56 rounds," the co-defendant's ammunition, not 7.62 rounds, Slatten's ammunition. . . .

After thorough review of the record, we are not aware of evidence "more probative on the point for" which Slatten seeks to admit his co-defendant's statements. . . . Finally, the record demonstrates that Slatten gave the government "reasonable notice of [his] intent to offer the statement[s]." . . .

. . . [B]ecause of the critical nature of the co-defendant's statements . . . [their] exclusion was] not harmless error. . . [Moreover the] district court recognized that the severance issue here largely hinged on the admissibility of the co-defendant's statements. . . . Because joinder of Slatten's and his co-defendant's trial rendered the latter's otherwise admissible statements . . . unavailable to Slatten, it was an abuse of discretion to deny Slatten's motion to sever. Accordingly, we reverse Slatten's [murder] conviction . . . and remand for a new trial. . . .

UNITED STATES v. BOYCE

742 F.3d 792 (7th Cir. 2014)

POSNER, Circuit Judge, concurring.

. . . I would like to see . . . Rule 807 ("Residual Exception") swallow much of Rules 801 through 806 and thus many of the exclusions from evidence, exceptions to the exclusions, and notes of the Advisory Committee. The "hearsay rule" is too complex, as well as being archaic. Trials would go better with a simpler rule, the core of which would be the proposition (essentially a simplification of Rule 807) that hearsay evidence should be admissible when it is reliable, when the jury can understand its strengths and limitations, and when it will materially enhance the likelihood of a correct outcome.

VICTOR GOLD, THE THREE COMMANDMENTS OF AMENDING THE FEDERAL RULES OF EVIDENCE

85 Fordham L. Rev. 1615, 1617, 1623-24 (2017)

In the more than forty years since the enactment of the Rules, courts have been cautious when considering evidence under the residual exception. But it is not accurate to say that the exception has been used "very rarely." The Advisory Committee's Reporter collected all reported cases in the past ten years in which a court reviewed a claim that hearsay was admissible under Rule 807. He informed the Advisory Committee that he found 114 cases in which the court seriously addressed a Rule 807 question and excluded the evidence. He also found seventy-one cases in which the hearsay was found admissible under Rule 807. While admitting that this data provides an imprecise picture of how the residual exception has been applied, the Reporter drew two conclusions: (1) the residual exception is being invoked with surprising frequency and (2) courts are excluding the proffered evidence more often than they are admitting it. . . .

While [expansion of] the residual exception may often make the exceptions in Rules 803 and 804 superfluous, the greatest impact would be on the rule against hearsay itself, Rule 802. . . . Of course, Rule 403 gives courts discretion to exclude otherwise admissible evidence in an appropriate case. However, no Rule establishes discretion to admit evidence that is otherwise inadmissible. This is because such a Rule runs counter to the very notion of codifying rules of admissibility. The Senate Judiciary Committee made this very point when considering the residual exception: "an overly broad residual hearsay exception could . . . vitiate the rationale behind codification of the rules."

14. Review

PROBLEMS

3.53. Pam falls down a stairway in a commercial building owned by Donald; she then sues Donald for damages. Pam alleges that the heel of her shoe got caught on a tear in the stairway carpet. Pam calls Sam, a tenant in the building, to testify that Tony, another tenant, said to Sam a week before the accident, "I saw the building manager this morning and told him he should fix that torn carpet." Is Sam's testimony admissible?

3.54. Dan is on trial for possession of methamphetamine. Will, a narcotics officer and expert dog handler, testifies that he was patrolling the train station with a dog trained to detect methamphetamine; that when Dan approached, the dog barked and pawed at Dan's briefcase in a manner that indicated the briefcase contained methamphetamine; and that Dan then ran outside and threw his briefcase into a river, from which it could not be recovered. Is any of this testimony barred by the hearsay rule?

3.55. Paul sues Deena for the wrongful death of Paul's wife, Lily, caused when Deena's car collided with Lily's. Deena calls a hospital nurse to testify that, two days before her death, Lily said, in great pain, "The accident was all my fault." Is the nurse's testimony admissible?

3.56. Darren's car collides with Pierre's, and Pierre sues for negligence. Pierre testifies that Elizabeth, Darren's passenger, made an excited utterance immediately after the accident, asserting that Darren had run a red light. Darren calls Fiona, a bystander, to testify that Elizabeth, who is now deceased, later told Fiona that in fact the light had been yellow. For what purposes, if any, is Fiona's testimony admissible?

3.57. Horatio is prosecuted for a bank robbery that took place on February 4 in California. His defense is that he was in Texas on that date. Horatio seeks to introduce a letter he wrote to his sister in January; the letter says that Horatio will see his sister in Houston, Texas, on February 4. Is the letter inadmissible hearsay?

3.58. The Sea Breeze Grill sues the C Breeze Bar-N-Grill for infringing its trade name. To prove that the names are likely to be confused, the plaintiff seeks to introduce daily logs it had its employees keep over a three-month period, describing telephone calls and comments from customers indicating confusion about the two names. Are the logs admissible?

3.59. Dwayne is on trial for criminal bankruptcy fraud. Dwayne's late sister, Suzanne, testified adversely to Dwayne in earlier civil bankruptcy proceedings involving similar issues. Dwayne's lawyers in the earlier case cross-examined Suzanne but made no serious effort to challenge her credibility. At the fraud trial, can the prosecution introduce a video recording of Suzanne's earlier testimony?

3.60. In a burglary trial, the prosecution calls as witnesses a married couple, Sean and Pat. They each testify that they looked out their front window and saw thieves break into the jewelry store across the street, grab merchandise, and then flee in a car. According to their further testimony, Pat called 911 while Sean grabbed a pair of binoculars and then read the license plate number to Pat, who relayed it to the 911 operator. Does the hearsay rule preclude introducing an audio recording of the 911 call to establish the license number of the car used by the burglars?

3.61. Phil sues his co-worker Dennis for injuries Phil claims he suffered when Dennis assaulted him during a melee in a crowded bar, but Dennis claims he was not the person who attacked Phil. Phil was treated for his injuries at Hamilton Hospital. To bolster his identification of Dennis as his attacker, Phil seeks to introduce a patient chart, identified and described by Hamilton Hospital's custodian of records. The chart contains an annotation made by the emergency room doctor who treated Phil, indicating that "patient says he was attacked by Dennis." Does the hearsay rule bar admission of the chart?

3.62. Claude is struck by a car while he is crossing the street at an intersection and later dies from his injuries while still in the hospital. Claude's estate sues the driver of the car, Quentin, for wrongful death. At trial, the estate calls a nurse to testify that, four days after the accident and three hours before Claude died, Claude told the nurse that the car that hit him had run a red light. To lay the foundation for introducing Claude's statement, the estate submits to the court an affidavit from a physician, indicating that she was on duty the day Claude died, and that Claude said several times that day that he knew he was about to die. Does the hearsay rule allow the court to consider the affidavit? Does it allow the introduction of the nurse's testimony?

3.63. Draco is being prosecuted for murder. At a preliminary hearing, which Draco attends with his lawyer, Draco's alleged accomplice, Edith, testifies for the prosecution. But when the prosecution later calls Edith to the stand at Draco's trial, Edith refuses to testify, and she persists in her refusal even after the judge orders her to testify. The prosecutors then offer into evidence a transcript of Edith's testimony at the preliminary hearing. Does the hearsay rule allow the transcript to be introduced?

3.64. Diego is on trial for the murder of Velma. Taking the stand in his own defense, Diego testifies that he shot Velma in self-defense after she came at him with a knife. In rebuttal, the prosecution seeks to introduce testimony from Velma's brother, Wes, that the night before her death Velma told Wes that she was deeply in love with Diego and would do anything for him. Does the hearsay rule bar this testimony?

3.65. Beck, an author, sues his publisher, Horton House, for unpaid royalties on digital sales of his book *Toucan Dance*. Beck files interrogatories asking Horton House how many digital copies of the book it has sold over the past five years. Horton House replies, through its lawyers, by referring Beck to a recent newspaper story indicating that "Horton House has reportedly sold 16,000 digital copies of Beck's book *Toucan Dance*." Will the hearsay rule allow Beck to introduce the newspaper article at trial to prove the number of digital copies of his book Horton House has sold?

3.66. Paolo sues Dmitri for injuries received in a traffic accident. Dmitri claims the accident was Paolo's fault, because it was dark and Paolo didn't have his lights on. Dmitri calls Wyatt, a bystander, to testify that Rachel, who was riding as a passenger in Paolo's car, told Wyatt at the scene of the accident that "we should have had our lights on." Is the testimony barred by the hearsay rule?

3.67. Dmitri seeks to elicit testimony from Wyatt, the bystander, that he was talking with another bystander, Xavier, just before the crash and that Xavier said, "That car doesn't have its lights on." Xavier cannot now be located. Is Wyatt's testimony admissible?

3.68. Dmitri calls another bystander who saw the accident, Zane. Dmitri expects Zane to testify that Paolo's car was traveling about 50 miles an hour. Instead, Zane testifies that Paolo's car was traveling about 15 or 20 miles an hour. Dmitri then calls a police officer to testify that when the officer arrived at the scene of the accident, Zane told the officer that Paolo's car was traveling about 50 miles an hour. For what purposes, if any, is the officer's testimony admissible?

3.69. Darcy is on trial for fatally stabbing Vidor in a bar fight; Vidor died from his wounds a week after the assault. Over a defense objection, the prosecution introduces testimony from Vidor's sister that an hour before Vidor died, he said, "Listen, this is important. I'm dying. Darcy is the one who stabbed me. I want you to tell him that I forgive him." Over a prosecution objection, the defense then introduces testimony from Vidor's friend, Fouad, that three days earlier, when Vidor thought he would survive, he told Fouad that he had been stabbed by Gavin, a business competitor. Was the judge right to overrule both objections?

3.70. Declan is on trial for bank robbery. Called as a prosecution witness, the bank teller is unable to identify Declan as the robber. The prosecutor then calls a police officer who testifies that the teller picked Declan out of a lineup shortly after the robbery and identified him as the robber. Is the officer's testimony admissible?

3.71. Delroy is on trial for murder and testifies that he shot the victim in self-defense. In rebuttal, the prosecutor calls the police officer who was dispatched to the scene of the shooting after Delroy called 911. The officer testifies that when he arrived at the scene, he asked Delroy what had happened, and Delroy said, "I was cleaning my gun and it went off accidentally." Is the officer's testimony admissible?

3.72. While crossing Wisconsin Avenue, Petra is hit by a car. The car speeds away before she can see it. Petra sues Dagwood, claiming that he was the driver. Testifying for Petra at trial, Officer Ontiveros testifies that shortly after the accident, a driver stopped him and reported a hit-and-run accident on Wisconsin Avenue and described the car involved as a "yellow convertible with out-of-state license plates." Other evidence in the case establishes that on the day of the accident Dagwood was driving a yellow convertible with out-of-state plates. Is the officer's testimony admissible?

3.73. Pemba sues Dabir for a back injury Pemba claims he received when he slipped on Dabir's driveway. Dabir claims the injury is the result of a fall Pemba took from a ladder three years earlier. Pemba calls Winnie, his longtime physician, to testify that Pemba came in for an examination after the driveway incident and told Winnie that up until he slipped on Dabir's driveway, he had been working full time, without pain or impaired mobility, in a job that involved lifting heavy boxes. Is Winnie's testimony admissible?

3.74. Wen is called as a witness in a contract case and asked if he attended a meeting with the defendant on November 19 of the previous year. Wen says he cannot recall. Leah, the attorney who called Wen, asks for permission to show him her handwritten notes of her pretrial interview with Wen, in which he described a meeting he attended with the defendant on November 19. Should the judge allow that?

3.75. Portia injures herself while shopping at Agora Groceries. She sues the store, alleging that she was knocked to the floor by a cart pushed by Elias, a stock clerk. Elias testifies that Portia fell near the cart but was not hit by it. Shortly after Portia's fall, Elias filled out an accident report form that Agora requires its employees to complete following any accident in the store. On the form, Elias said that Portia was singing to herself and twirling in the aisle, lost her balance, and then fell. Agora's lawyer offers the report into evidence. Is it admissible?

3.76. Pericles, a restaurateur, sues his competitor Deon for unfair competition, alleging that Deon has stolen Pericles's recipe for corn chowder. Over Deon's objection, may Pericles testify that he heard Deon's assistant manager, Erika, say that Deon had bribed one of Pericles's employees to give Deon the recipe?

3.77. Paloma sues her surgeon, Sagar, for medical malpractice. To prove that proper procedures were followed, Sagar seeks to introduce a hospital chart with notations describing Paloma's operation. The notations were made by a medical assistant who was not present during the surgery. He made the entries pursuant to standard hospital procedure, but he cannot remember which of the doctors and nurses who participated in the operation gave him the information that he entered on the chart. Are the medical assistant's entries inadmissible hearsay?

3.78. Two brothers, Jan and Karl, are prosecuted for breaking into and looting a bank vault. The morning after the break-in, bank employees discovered the following message spray-painted on the ceiling of the vault: "The Perfect Purloiner strikes!" The prosecution wishes to have Jan's former girlfriend testify that he used to talk about someday writing a novel about a thief who calls himself "the Perfect Purloiner." Is this testimony admissible against Jan? Against Karl?

D. Hearsay and Machine-Generated Proof

The rule against hearsay, in all American jurisdictions, applies only to assertions by humans. But what about information conveyed by machines, such as a thermometer reading, the "raw data" from the gas chromatograph referenced by Justice Sotomayor in her *Bullcoming* concurrence, or a medical diagnosis reported by a sophisticated artificial intelligence system? Should these conveyances of information be considered "assertions" covered by the hearsay rule? If not, how should the rules of evidence regulate machine output? And in criminal cases, should machines ever be considered "witnesses against" a criminal defendant for purposes of the Confrontation Clause? These questions have become more relevant in the past decade, as parties increasingly rely on machine-generated proof. Consider the material that follows.

PEOPLE v. LOPEZ
147 Cal.Rptr.3d 559 (Cal. 2012)

Kenard, J.

[Defendant Lopez was convicted of vehicular manslaughter while intoxicated. To prove intoxication, the prosecution relied on a nontestifying laboratory analyst's blood-alcohol report. Lopez argued that the entirety of the report was testimonial hearsay, the admission of which violated the Confrontation Clause.]

[P]ages 2 through 6 [of the report] consist entirely of data generated by a gas chromatography machine to measure calibrations, quality control, and the concentration of alcohol in a blood sample. Even though nontestifying analyst Peña's signature appears on the laboratory report's second page (the printout of the machine's calibrations) and the remaining pages bear the handwritten initials "JRP" (presumably Jorge Peña's initials), no statement by Peña, express or implied, appears on any of those pages.

Not yet considered by the United States Supreme Court is whether the prosecution's use at trial of a machine printout violates a defendant's right to confront and cross-examine the machine's operator when, as here, the printout contains no statement from the operator attesting to the validity of the data shown. We agree with those federal appellate courts that have upheld the use of such printouts. (*See* U.S. v. Moon (7th Cir. 2008) 512 F.3d 359, 362 ["the instruments' readouts are not 'statements,' so it does not matter whether they are 'testimonial'"]; U.S. v. Washington (4th Cir. 2007) 498 F.3d 225, 231 ["the raw data generated by the machines do not constitute 'statements,' and the machines are not 'declarants'"]; *see also Bullcoming, supra* (conc. opn. of Sotomayor, J.) [the prosecution's introduction only of "machine-generated results, such as a printout from a gas chromatograph," may not violate the defendant's confrontation right].) Because, unlike a person, a machine cannot be cross-examined, here the prosecution's introduction into evidence of the machine-generated printouts . . . of nontestifying analyst Peña's laboratory report did not implicate the Sixth Amendment's right to confrontation.

[The Court also concluded that the rest of the report was hearsay but nontestimonial, and affirmed Lopez's conviction.]

LIU, J., dissenting.

[A]s a result of ever more powerful technologies, our justice system has increasingly relied on ex parte computerized determinations of critical facts in criminal proceedings — determinations once made by human beings. A crime lab's reliance on gas chromatography may be a marked improvement over less accurate or more subjective methods of determining blood-alcohol levels. The allure of such technology is its infallibility, its precision, its incorruptibility. But I wonder if that allure should prompt us to remain alert to constitutional concerns, lest we gradually recreate through machines instead of magistrates the civil law mode of ex parte production of evidence that constituted the "principal evil at which the Confrontation Clause was directed."

ANDREA ROTH, MACHINE TESTIMONY

126 Yale L.J. 1972, 1976-83 (2017)

. . . [A]s machines extend their reach and expertise, to the point where competing expert systems have reached different "opinions" related to the same scientific evidence, a new sense of urgency surrounds basic questions about what machine conveyances are and what problems they pose for the law of evidence....

. . . [M]achine sources potentially suffer "black box" dangers that could lead a factfinder to draw the wrong inference from information conveyed by a machine source. A machine does not exhibit a character for dishonesty or suffer from memory loss. But a machine's programming, whether the result of human coding or machine learning, could cause it to utter a falsehood by design. A machine's output could be imprecise or ambiguous because of human error at the programming, input, or operation stage, or because of machine error due to degradation and environmental forces. And human and machine errors at any of these stages could also lead a machine to misanalyze an event. Just as the "hearsay dangers" are believed more likely to arise and remain undetected when the human source is not subject to the oath, physical confrontation, and cross-examination, black box dangers are more likely to arise and remain undetected when a machine utterance is the output of an "inscrutable black box."

Because human design, input, and operation are integral to a machine's credibility, some courts and scholars have reasoned that a human is the true "declarant" of any machine conveyance. But while a designer or operator might be partially epistemically or morally responsible for a machine's statements, the human is not the sole source of the claim . . . . Human experts often act as "mere scrivener[s]" on the witness stand, regurgitating the conveyances of machines. Their testimony might create a veneer of scrutiny when in fact the actual source of the information, the machine, remains largely unscrutinized.

. . . [T]he hearsay rule itself could not easily be modified to accommodate machines, given its focus on the oath, physical confrontation, and cross-examination . . . Instead, . . . [l]awmakers should . . . consider . . . front-end protocols [that] could include software testing, machine-learning performance evaluations, and variations of "adversarial design," in which competing perspectives are incorporated at the design stage into the variables and analytical assumptions of algorithms. Next, lawmakers should consider pretrial disclosure and access rules for machines, especially machine "experts." These rules might allow litigants to access machines before trial to test different parameters or inputs (much like posing hypotheticals to human experts). The rules might also require public access to programs for further testing or "tinkering"; disclosure of "source code," if necessary to meaningfully scrutinize the machine's claims; and the discovery of prior statements or "Jencks material" of machines, such as COBRA data for breath-testing machines....

For machines offering "expert" evidence . . . , [c]ourts . . . should treat software engineers as part of the relevant scientific community and determine reliability not only of the method, but also of the software implementing that method, based on industry standards. In some cases, courts would likely need to access proprietary source code to assess the code's ability to operationalize an otherwise reliable method.

Beyond the admissibility stage, an opponent should be allowed to impeach machines at trial, just as the opponent can impeach human witnesses and declarants even when a judge deems their assertions reliable. . . . Lawmakers might even impose live testimony requirements for human designers, inputters, or operators in certain cases where testimony is necessary to scrutinize the accuracy of inputs, as the United Kingdom has done in criminal cases. Courts could also give jury instructions for certain machines typically under- or overvalued by jurors, akin to those used for human declarants like accomplices. And they could impose corroboration requirements, akin to those imposed on accomplice testimony and confessions, for certain risky machines or machines whose results lie within a certain margin of error....

Finally, in criminal cases, machine sources of accusation — particularly proprietary software created for litigation — might be "witnesses against" a defendant under the Confrontation Clause. Accusatory machine output potentially implicates the central concerns underlying the Clause in three ways. First, if substituted for the testimony of witnesses otherwise subject to credibility testing, machine testimony allows the State to evade responsibility for accusations. Second, the State's ability to shape and shield testimony from scrutiny through proprietary black box algorithms is analogous to the ex parte affidavit practice that preoccupied the Framers. Third, machines are potentially unreliable when their processes are shrouded in a black box. While machines generally cannot be physically confronted, they can be impeached in other ways, and courts and scholars should revisit cases in which the Supreme Court appears to recognize implicitly that "confrontation" includes a right of meaningful impeachment.

EDWARD CHENG AND ALEX NUNN, BEYOND THE WITNESS: BRINGING A PROCESS PERSPECTIVE TO MODERN EVIDENCE LAW

97 Texas L. Rev. 1077, 1106-07, 1110-11 (2019)

What process-based evidence requires is a functional analog to being "called to the stand".... For a witness, taking the stand creates transparency: the factfinder and the public can see and scrutinize the witness. Taking the stand also exposes the witness to cross-examination. Process-based evidence is therefore in need of a procedural tool that will achieve those same results — a tool that will render process-based evidence more transparent and vulnerable to scrutiny.

Enhanced discovery is just such a tool. Conventionally, discovery conjures up images of banker's boxes or hard drives full of documents, and in some cases, that will precisely be what the opposing party needs to challenge process-based evidence. Discovery of calibration results, performance reviews, standard operating procedures, company policies, design documents, and the like all enable an opponent to scrutinize the process that created the process-based evidence and challenge its reliability.

But sometimes, "putting the process on the stand" requires more than conventional discovery.... Instead, an opponent may want access to the machine or process itself. If a mass spectrometer provides critical evidence in a case, the opponent may wish to test that machine using known samples. If a laboratory used a standard procedure to test for cocaine, then the opponent may wish to send blinded (but known) test samples to challenge the lab's accuracy.

. . . So how then can we recast Confrontation Clause jurisprudence to account for our new understanding of process-based evidence? . . . When it comes to process-based evidence, the functional accuser — the "witness[] against [the defendant]" — is the underlying process, not the various people who may have contributed to the process. And thus the right of Confrontation involves the defendant's ability to challenge the process, not a talking head on the witness stand.

E. HEARSAY AND DUE PROCESS

The Constitution places two significant constraints on hearsay law.

First, as we have seen, the Confrontation Clause of the Sixth Amendment, made applicable to the states through the Due Process Clause of the Fourteenth Amendment, prohibits the use of certain hearsay evidence against a criminal defendant. This prohibition may apply even to evidence that is otherwise admissible under the rules of evidence. Even when statements are rendered inadmissible by the hearsay rule, it can be important to know whether the Confrontation Clause also bars their introduction. For one thing, a constitutional violation, unlike a mere violation of the hearsay rule, will not be harmless unless the government can demonstrate beyond a reasonable doubt that it did not affect the verdict. More importantly, inadmissibility under the Confrontation Clause triggers the *Bruton* doctrine — the special prohibition the Supreme Court has crafted against relying on limiting instructions to cure the prejudice created in a joint trial when a confession by one defendant would violate the Confrontation Clause if introduced against the other defendant.

The second constitutional supplement to hearsay law, discussed below, stems from the Due Process Clauses of the Fifth and Fourteenth Amendments. The Supreme Court has held that due process can require the admission of some evidence *offered* by a criminal defendant, even if the hearsay rule (or other rules of evidence) would otherwise prohibit use of the statements. Few statements, though, appear to fall within this category.

CHAMBERS v. MISSISSIPPI

410 U.S. 284 (1973)

Mr. Justice POWELL delivered the opinion of the Court.

Petitioner, Leon Chambers, was tried by a jury in a Mississippi trial court and convicted of murdering a policeman. The jury assessed punishment at life imprisonment, and the Mississippi Supreme Court affirmed, one justice dissenting. . . . [T]he petition for certiorari was granted to consider whether petitioner's trial was conducted in accord with principles of due process under the Fourteenth Amendment. We conclude that it was not.

I

The events that led to petitioner's prosecution for murder occurred in the small town of Woodville in southern Mississippi. On Saturday evening, June 14, 1969, two Woodville policemen, James Forman and Aaron "Sonny" Liberty, entered a local bar and pool hall to execute a warrant for the arrest of a youth named C. C. Jackson. Jackson resisted and a hostile crowd of some 50 or 60 persons gathered. The officers' first attempt to handcuff Jackson was frustrated when 20 or 25 men in the crowd intervened and wrestled him free. Forman then radioed for assistance and Liberty removed his riot gun, a 12-gauge sawed-off shotgun, from the car. Three deputy sheriffs arrived shortly thereafter and the officers again attempted to make their arrest. Once more, the officers were attacked by the onlookers and during the commotion five or six pistol shots were fired. Forman was looking in a different direction when the shooting began, but immediately saw that Liberty had been shot several times in the back. Before Liberty died, he turned around and fired both barrels of his riot gun into an alley in the area from which the shots appeared to have come. The first shot was wild and high and scattered the crowd standing at the face of the alley. Liberty appeared, however, to take more deliberate aim before the second shot and hit one of the men in the crowd in the back of the head and neck as he ran down the alley. That man was Leon Chambers.

Officer Forman could not see from his vantage point who shot Liberty or whether Liberty's shots hit anyone. One of the deputy sheriffs testified at trial that he was standing several feet from Liberty and that he saw Chambers shoot him. Another deputy sheriff stated that, although he could not see whether Chambers had a gun in his hand, he did see Chambers 'break his arm down' shortly before the shots were fired. The officers who saw Chambers fall testified that they thought he was dead but they made no effort at that time either to examine him or to search for the murder weapon. Instead, they attended to Liberty, who was placed in the police car and taken to a hospital where he was declared dead on arrival. A subsequent autopsy showed that he had been hit with four bullets from a .22-caliber revolver.

Shortly after the shooting, three of Chambers' friends discovered that he was not yet dead. James Williams,[1] Berkley Turner, and Gable McDonald loaded him into a car and transported him to the same hospital. Later that night, when the county sheriff discovered that Chambers was still alive, a guard was placed outside his room. Chambers was subsequently charged with Liberty's murder. He pleaded not guilty and has asserted his innocence throughout.

The story of Leon Chambers is intertwined with the story of another man, Gable McDonald. McDonald, a lifelong resident of Woodville, was in the crowd on the evening of Liberty's death. Sometime shortly after that day, he left his wife in Woodville and moved to Louisiana and found a job at a sugar mill. In November of that same year, he returned to Woodville when his wife informed him that an acquaintance of his, known as Reverend Stokes, wanted

---

1. James Williams was indicted along with Chambers. The State, however, failed to introduce any evidence at trial implicating Williams in the shooting. At the conclusion of the State's case-in-chief, the trial court granted a directed verdict in his favor.

to see him. Stokes owned a gas station in Natchez, Mississippi, several miles north of Woodville, and upon his return McDonald went to see him. After talking to Stokes, McDonald agreed to make a statement to Chambers' attorneys, who maintained offices in Natchez. Two days later, he appeared at the attorneys' offices and gave a sworn confession that he shot Officer Liberty. He also stated that he had already told a friend of his, James Williams, that he shot Liberty. He said that he used his own pistol, a nine-shot .22-caliber revolver, which he had discarded shortly after the shooting. In response to questions from Chambers' attorneys, McDonald affirmed that his confession was voluntary and that no one had compelled him to come to them. Once the confession had been transcribed, signed, and witnessed, McDonald was turned over to the local police authorities and was placed in jail.

One month later, at a preliminary hearing, McDonald repudiated his prior sworn confession. He testified that Stokes had persuaded him to confess that he shot Liberty. He claimed that Stokes had promised that he would not go to jail and that he would share in the proceeds of a lawsuit that Chambers would bring against the town of Woodville. On examination by his own attorney and on cross-examination by the State, McDonald swore that he had not been at the scene when Liberty was shot but had been down the street drinking beer in a cafe with a friend, Berkley Turner. When he and Turner heard the shooting, he testified, they walked up the street and found Chambers lying in the alley. He, Turner, and Williams took Chambers to the hospital. McDonald further testified at the preliminary hearing that he did not know what had happened, that there was no discussion about the shooting either going to or coming back from the hospital, and that it was not until the next day that he learned that Chambers had been felled by a blast from Liberty's riot gun. In addition, McDonald stated that while he once owned a .22-caliber pistol he had lost it many months before the shooting and did not own or possess a weapon at that time. The local justice of the peace accepted McDonald's repudiation and released him from custody. The local authorities undertook no further investigation of his possible involvement.

Chambers' case came on for trial in October of the next year. At trial, he endeavored to develop two grounds of defense. He first attempted to show that he did not shoot Liberty. Only one officer testified that he actually saw Chambers fire the shots. Although three officers saw Liberty shoot Chambers and testified that they assumed he was shooting his attacker, none of them examined Chambers to see whether he was still alive or whether he possessed a gun. Indeed, no weapon was ever recovered from the scene and there was no proof that Chambers had ever owned a .22-caliber pistol. One witness testified that he was standing in the street near where Liberty was shot, that he was looking at Chambers when the shooting began, and that he was sure that Chambers did not fire the shots.

Petitioner's second defense was that Gable McDonald had shot Officer Liberty. He was only partially successful, however, in his efforts to bring before the jury the testimony supporting this defense. Sam Hardin, a lifelong friend of McDonald's, testified that he saw McDonald shoot Liberty. A second witness, one of Liberty's cousins, testified that he saw McDonald immediately after the shooting with a pistol in his hand. In addition to the testimony of these two witnesses, Chambers endeavored to show the jury that McDonald had repeatedly confessed to the crime. Chambers attempted to prove that McDonald had admitted responsibility for the murder on four separate occasions, once when he gave the sworn statement to Chambers' counsel and three other times prior to that occasion in private conversations with friends.

In large measure, he was thwarted in his attempt to present this portion of his defense by the strict application of certain Mississippi rules of evidence. Chambers asserts in this Court, as he did unsuccessfully in his motion for new trial and on appeal to the State Supreme Court, that the application of these evidentiary rules rendered his trial fundamentally unfair and deprived him of due process of law. It is necessary, therefore, to examine carefully the rulings made during the trial.

II

Chambers filed a pretrial motion requesting the court to order McDonald to appear.... The trial court granted the motion.... At trial, after the State failed to put McDonald on the stand, Chambers called McDonald, laid a predicate for the introduction of his sworn out-of-court confession, had it admitted into evidence, and read it to the jury. The State, upon cross-examination, elicited from McDonald the fact that he had repudiated his prior confession. McDonald further testified, as he had at the preliminary hearing, that he did not shoot Liberty, and that he confessed to the crime only on the promise of Reverend Stokes that he would not go to jail and would share in a sizable tort recovery from the town. He also retold his own story of his actions on the evening of the shooting, including his visit to the cafe down the street, his absence from the scene during the critical period, and his subsequent trip to the hospital with Chambers.

At the conclusion of the State's cross-examination, Chambers renewed his motion to examine McDonald as an adverse witness. The trial court denied the motion, stating:"He may be hostile, but he is not adverse in the sense of the word, so your request will be overruled." On appeal, the State Supreme Court upheld the trial court's ruling, finding that "McDonald's testimony was not adverse to appellant" because "[n]owhere did he point the finger at Chambers."

Defeated in his attempt to challenge directly McDonald's renunciation of his prior confession, Chambers sought to introduce the testimony of the three witnesses to whom McDonald had admitted that he shot the officer. The first of these, Sam Hardin, would have testified that, on the night of the shooting, he spent the late evening hours with McDonald at a friend's house after their return from the hospital and that, while driving McDonald home later that night, McDonald stated that he shot Liberty. The State objected to the admission of this testimony on the ground that it was hearsay. The trial court sustained the objection.[4]

---

4. Hardin's testimony, unlike the testimony of the other two men who stated that McDonald had confessed to them, was actually given in the jury's presence. After the State's objection to Hardin's account of McDonald's statement was sustained, the trial court ordered the jury to disregard it.

Berkley Turner, the friend with whom McDonald said he was drinking beer when the shooting occurred, was then called to testify. In the jury's presence, and without objection, he testified that he had not been in the cafe that Saturday and had not had any beers with McDonald. The jury was then excused. In the absence of the jury, Turner recounted his conversations with McDonald while they were riding with James Williams to take Chambers to the hospital. When asked whether McDonald said anything regarding the shooting of Liberty, Turner testified that McDonald told him that he "shot him." Turner further stated that one week later, when he met McDonald at a friend's house, McDonald reminded him of their prior conversation and urged Turner not to "mess him up." Petitioner argued to the court that, especially where there was other proof in the case that was corroborative of these out-of-court statements, Turner's testimony as to McDonald's self-incriminating remarks should have been admitted as an exception to the hearsay rule. Again, the trial court sustained the State's objection.

The third witness, Albert Carter, was McDonald's neighbor. They had been friends for about 25 years. Although Carter had not been in Woodville on the evening of the shooting, he stated that he learned about it the next morning from McDonald. That same day, he and McDonald walked out to a well near McDonald's house and there McDonald told him that he was the one who shot Officer Liberty. Carter testified that McDonald also told him that he had disposed of the .22-caliber revolver later that night. He further testified that several weeks after the shooting, he accompanied McDonald to Natchez where McDonald purchased another .22 pistol to replace the one he had discarded.[5] The jury was not allowed to hear Carter's testimony. Chambers urged that these statements were admissible, the State objected, and the court sustained the objection. On appeal, the State Supreme Court approved the lower court's exclusion of these witnesses' testimony on hearsay grounds.

In sum, then, this was Chambers' predicament. As a consequence of the combination of Mississippi's "party witness" or "voucher" rule and its hearsay rule, he was unable either to cross-examine McDonald or to present witnesses in his own behalf who would have discredited McDonald's repudiation and demonstrated his complicity. Chambers had, however, chipped away at the fringes of McDonald's story by introducing admissible testimony from other sources indicating that he had not been seen in the cafe where he said he was when the shooting started, that he had not been having beer with Turner, and that he possessed a .22 pistol at the time of the crime. But all that remained from McDonald's own testimony was a single written confession countered by an arguably acceptable renunciation. Chambers' defense was far less persuasive than it might have been had he been given an opportunity to subject McDonald's statements to cross-examination or had the other confessions been admitted.

---

5. A gun dealer from Natchez testified that McDonald had made two purchases. The witness' business records indicated that McDonald purchased a nine-shot .22-caliber revolver about a year prior to the murder. He purchased a different style .22 three weeks after Liberty's death.

III

The right of an accused in a criminal trial to due process is, in essence, the right to a fair opportunity to defend against the State's accusations. The rights to confront and cross-examine witnesses and to call witnesses in one's own behalf have long been recognized as essential to due process.... Both of these elements of a fair trial are implicated in the present case.

A

Chambers was denied an opportunity to subject McDonald's damning repudiation and alibi to cross-examination. He was not allowed to test the witness' recollection, to probe into the details of his alibi, or to "sift" his conscience so that the jury might judge for itself whether McDonald's testimony was worthy of belief. *Mattox v. United States*, 156 U.S. 237, 242-243 (1895). The right of cross-examination is more than a desirable rule of trial procedure. It is implicit in the constitutional right of confrontation, and helps assure the "accuracy of the truth-determining process." *Dutton v. Evans*, 400 U.S. 74, 89 (1970); *Bruton v. United States*, 391 U.S. 123, 135-37 (1968). It is, indeed, "an essential and fundamental requirement for the kind of fair trial which is this country's constitutional goal." *Pointer v. Texas*, 380 U.S. 400, 405 (1965). Of course, the right to confront and to cross-examine is not absolute and may, in appropriate cases, bow to accommodate other legitimate interests in the criminal trial process. But its denial or significant diminution calls into question the ultimate "integrity of the fact-finding process" and requires that the competing interest be closely examined. *Berger v. California*, 393 U.S. 314, 315 (1969).

In this case, petitioner's request to cross-examine McDonald was denied on the basis of a Mississippi common-law rule that a party may not impeach his own witness. The rule rests on the presumption — without regard to the circumstances of the particular case — that a party who calls a witness "vouches for his credibility." *Clark v. Lansford*, 191 So. 2d 123, 125 (Miss. 1966). Although the historical origins of the "voucher" rule are uncertain, it appears to be a remnant of primitive English trial practice in which "oath-takers" or "compurgators" were called to stand behind a particular party's position in any controversy. Their assertions were strictly partisan and, quite unlike witnesses in criminal trials today, their role bore little relation to the impartial ascertainment of the facts.[7]

Whatever validity the "voucher" rule may have once enjoyed, and apart from whatever usefulness it retains today in the civil trial process, it bears little present relationship to the realities of the criminal process.[8] It might have been logical for the early common law to require a party to vouch for the credibility of witnesses he brought before the jury to affirm his veracity.

---

7. 3A J. Wigmore, Evidence §896, pp. 658-660 (J. Chadbourn ed. 1970); C. McCormick, Evidence §38, pp. 75-78 (2d ed. 1972).

8. The "voucher" rule has been condemned as archaic, irrational, and potentially destructive of the truth-gathering process, C. McCormick, *supra*, n.7; E. Morgan, Basic Problems of Evidence 70-71 (1962); 3A J. Wigmore, *supra*, n.7, §898, p. 661.

Having selected them especially for that purpose, the party might reasonably be expected to stand firmly behind their testimony. But in modern criminal trials, defendants are rarely able to select their witnesses: they must take them where they find them. Moreover, as applied in this case, the "voucher" rule's[9] impact was doubly harmful to Chambers' efforts to develop his defense. Not only was he precluded from cross-examining McDonald, but, as the State conceded at oral argument, he was also restricted in the scope of his direct examination by the rule's corollary requirement that the party calling the witness is bound by anything he might say. He was, therefore, effectively prevented from exploring the circumstances of McDonald's three prior oral confessions and from challenging the renunciation of the written confession. . . .

The argument that McDonald's testimony was not "adverse" to, or "against," Chambers is not convincing. The State's proof at trial excluded the theory that more than one person participated in the shooting of Liberty. To the extent that McDonald's sworn confession tended to incriminate him, it tended also to exculpate Chambers. And, in the circumstances of this case, McDonald's retraction inculpated Chambers to the same extent that it exculpated McDonald. It can hardly be disputed that McDonald's testimony was in fact seriously adverse to Chambers. The availability of the right to confront and to cross-examine those who give damaging testimony against the accused has never been held to depend on whether the witness was initially put on the stand by the accused or by the State. We reject the notion that a right of such substance in the criminal process may be governed by that technicality or by any narrow and unrealistic definition of the word "against." The "voucher" rule, as applied in this case, plainly interfered with Chambers' right to defend against the State's charges.

B

We need not decide, however, whether this error alone would occasion reversal since Chambers' claimed denial of due process rests on the ultimate impact of that error when viewed in conjunction with the trial court's refusal to permit him to call other witnesses. The trial court refused to allow him to introduce the testimony of Hardin, Turner, and Carter. Each would have testified to the statements purportedly made by McDonald, on three separate occasions shortly after the crime, naming himself as the murderer. The State Supreme Court approved the exclusion of this evidence on the ground that it was hearsay.

The hearsay rule, which has long been recognized and respected by virtually every State, is based on experience and grounded in the notion that untrustworthy evidence should not be presented to the triers of fact. Out-of-court statements are traditionally excluded because they lack the conventional indicia of reliability: they are usually not made under oath or other circumstances that impress the speaker with the solemnity of his statements; the

---

9. The "voucher" rule has been rejected altogether by the newly proposed Federal Rules of Evidence, Rule 607, Rules of Evidence for United States Courts and Magistrates (approved Nov. 20, 1972, and transmitted to Congress to become effective July 1, 1973, unless the Congress otherwise determines).

declarant's word is not subject to cross-examination; and he is not available in order that his demeanor and credibility may be assessed by the jury. A number of exceptions have developed over the years to allow admission of hearsay statements made under circumstances that tend to assure reliability and thereby compensate for the absence of the oath and opportunity for cross-examination. Among the most prevalent of these exceptions is the one applicable to declarations against interest — an exception founded on the assumption that a person is unlikely to fabricate a statement against his own interest at the time it is made. Mississippi recognizes this exception but applies it only to declarations against pecuniary interest. It recognizes no such exception for declarations, like McDonald's in this case, that are against the penal interest of the declarant.

This materialistic limitation on the declaration-against-interest hearsay exception appears to be accepted by most States in their criminal trial processes, although a number of States have discarded it. Declarations against penal interest have also been excluded in federal courts under the authority of *Donnelly v. United States*, 228 U.S. 243, 272-273 (1913), although exclusion would not be required under the newly proposed Federal Rules of Evidence. Exclusion, where the limitation prevails, is usually premised on the view that admission would lead to the frequent presentation of perjured testimony to the jury. It is believed that confessions of criminal activity are often motivated by extraneous considerations and, therefore, are not as inherently reliable as statements against pecuniary or proprietary interest.

While that rationale has been the subject of considerable scholarly criticism, we need not decide in this case whether, under other circumstances, it might serve some valid state purpose by excluding untrustworthy testimony.

The hearsay statements involved in this case were originally made and subsequently offered at trial under circumstances that provided considerable assurance of their reliability. First, each of McDonald's confessions was made spontaneously to a close acquaintance shortly after the murder had occurred. Second, each one was corroborated by some other evidence in the case — McDonald's sworn confession, the testimony of an eyewitness to the shooting, the testimony that McDonald was seen with a gun immediately after the shooting, and proof of his prior ownership of a .22-caliber revolver and subsequent purchase of a new weapon. The sheer number of independent confessions provided additional corroboration for each. Third, whatever may be the parameters of the penal-interest rationale,[20] each confession here was in a very real sense self-incriminatory and unquestionably against interest. McDonald stood to benefit nothing by disclosing his role in the shooting to any of his three friends and he must have been aware of the possibility that disclosure would lead to criminal

---

20. The Mississippi case which refused to adopt a hearsay exception for declarations against penal interest concerned an out-of-court declarant who purportedly stated that he had committed the murder with which his brother had been charged. The Mississippi Supreme Court believed that the declarant might have been motivated by a desire to free his brother rather than by any compulsion of guilt. The Court also noted that the declarant had fled, was unavailable for cross-examination, and might well have known at the time he made the statement that he would not suffer for it. *Brown v. State*, 99 Miss. 719, 55 So. 961 (1911). There is, in the present case, no such basis for doubting McDonald's statements.

prosecution. Indeed, after telling Turner of his involvement, he subsequently urged Turner not to "mess him up." Finally, if there was any question about the truthfulness of the extrajudicial statements, McDonald was present in the courtroom and was under oath. He could have been cross-examined by the State, and his demeanor and responses weighed by the jury. The availability of McDonald significantly distinguishes this case from the prior Mississippi precedent, *Brown v. State, supra,* and from the *Donnelly*-type situation, since in both cases the declarant was unavailable at the time of trial.[21]

Few rights are more fundamental than that of an accused to present witnesses in his own defense. In the exercise of this right, the accused, as is required of the State, must comply with established rules of procedure and evidence designed to assure both fairness and reliability in the ascertainment of guilt and innocence. Although perhaps no rule of evidence has been more respected or more frequently applied in jury trials than that applicable to the exclusion of hearsay, exceptions tailored to allow the introduction of evidence which in fact is likely to be trustworthy have long existed. The testimony rejected by the trial court here bore persuasive assurances of trustworthiness and thus was well within the basic rationale of the exception for declarations against interest. That testimony also was critical to Chambers' defense. In these circumstances, where constitutional rights directly affecting the ascertainment of guilt are implicated, the hearsay rule may not be applied mechanistically to defeat the ends of justice.

We conclude that the exclusion of this critical evidence, coupled with the State's refusal to permit Chambers to cross-examine McDonald, denied him a trial in accord with traditional and fundamental standards of due process. In reaching this judgment, we establish no new principles of constitutional law. Nor does our holding signal any diminution in the respect traditionally accorded to the States in the establishment and implementation of their own criminal trial rules and procedures. Rather, we hold quite simply that under the facts and circumstances of this case the rulings of the trial court deprived Chambers of a fair trial. . . .

Reversed and remanded.

[Justice White filed a concurring opinion. Justice Rehnquist filed a dissenting opinion.]

21. McDonald's presence also deprives the State's argument for retention of the penal-interest rule of much of its force. In claiming that "[t]o change the rule would work a travesty on justice," the State posited the following hypothetical:

"If the rule were changed, A could be charged with the crime; B could tell C and D that he committed the crime; *B could go into hiding* and at A's trial C and D would testify as to B's admission of guilt; A could be acquitted and B would return to stand trial; B could then provide several witnesses to testify as to his whereabouts at the time of the crime. The testimony of those witnesses along with A's statement that he really committed the crime could result in B's acquittal. A would be barred from further prosecution because of the protection against double jeopardy. No one could be convicted of perjury as A did not testify at his first trial, B did not lie under oath, and C and D were truthful in their testimony." Brief for Respondent 7 n.3 (emphasis supplied).

Obviously, B's absence at trial is critical to the success of the justice-subverting ploy.

FORTINI v. MURPHY

257 F.3d 39 (1st Cir. 2001)

BOUDIN, Chief Judge.

This is an appeal by Robert Fortini from a federal district court order dismissing Fortini's petition for a writ of habeas corpus. Fortini is currently serving a life sentence, having been convicted in state court of second degree murder [for the shooting death of Ceasar Monterio. At trial, Fortini argued self-defense. The trial judge excluded evidence that the victim, Ceasar Monterio, assaulted four men on a basketball court shortly before his confrontation with Fortini. He argued in his habeas petition that this ruling violated *Chambers v. Mississippi*.]

Fortini's constitutional claim presents a difficult issue that cannot be said to be directly governed by existing Supreme Court precedent. . . . Although *Chambers* unquestionably remains "the law," *e.g., Crane v. Kentucky*, 476 U.S. 683, 690 (1986), the Court has rarely used it to overturn convictions and in recent years has made clear that it can be invoked only in extreme cases. Most recently, a majority of the Court said that a state law justification for exclusion will prevail unless it is "arbitrary or disproportionate" and "infringe[s] upon a weighty interest of the accused," *United States v. Scheffer*, 523 U.S. 303, 308 (1998). *See also Montana v. Egelhoff*, 518 U.S. 37, 53 (1996) (plurality opinion suggestion that any justification is sufficient to satisfy due process).

Inevitably, the lower federal courts have tended to "balance" incommensurate competing interests, taking account of the importance of the testimony to the defense, its inherent strength and reliability, and various kinds of countervailing reasons for excluding it offered by the state. Nevertheless, in cases less powerful than *Chambers*, a defendant whose proffer of evidence was rejected for any conventionally plausible reason or rule usually has an uphill struggle.

Admittedly, Fortini has a strong argument that the evidence in question should have been admitted under conventional evidence rules. . . . Although the evidence of the basketball court episode was certainly not relevant to *Fortini*'s state of mind (since he did not then know about the fight), it was relevant to Monterio's state of mind, making it more likely than it would be without the evidence that Monterio lunged at Fortini, as the latter claimed. . . . [I]t might look as if the basketball court incident was merely character evidence, tending to portray Monterio as a violent man. Such evidence is commonly excluded by courts because of its remoteness and tendency to prejudice the jury. Fed. R. Evid. 404. . . . But in a federal court, and so far as we can tell under Massachusetts law, the basketball court incident was so close in time to the shooting as to suggest that it might fall within the exceptions that admit (where pertinent) acts demonstrating state of mind and emotion of the actor, here Monterio. . . .

Even highly relevant evidence can be excluded if it is unduly prejudicial. The evidence in question was certainly prejudicial in the pertinent sense, that is, it invited the jury to acquit because it made Monterio out to be a violent and dangerous man of whom the world was well rid. But the state court did not exclude the evidence on grounds of undue prejudice and there is no certainty that it would have done so if it had appreciated the relevance of the evidence. Nor did the Appeals Court mention prejudice of this kind.

It might thus be argued that there was *no* valid justification invoked for excluding the evidence. The Appeals Court itself assumed *arguendo* that the evidence should not have been excluded. Although the [Supreme Judicial Court] has never squarely addressed the issue, it is hard for us to see why — assuming relevance — such bad acts would be categorically inadmissible where offered to show the state of mind of the victim rather than the state of mind of the defendant....

Yet not every *ad hoc* mistake in applying state evidence rules, even in a murder case, should be called a violation of due process; otherwise every significant state court error in excluding evidence offered by the defendant would be a basis for undoing the conviction. The few Supreme Court cases that actually undid convictions based on a *Chambers* analysis involved far more egregious situations; and the more recent decisions of the Court we have cited create serious doubts that the Court is interested in carrying the doctrine beyond egregious cases.

Chambers and *Crane* both involved highly probative evidence absolutely critical to the defense.... By contrast, in the present case the defendant offered direct testimony on the pertinent issue — whether Monterio lunged at him. The basketball court incident that was excluded is at best indirect evidence which does no more than add to existing proof that Monterio was in a mood to lunge....

[W]e conclude that the exclusion of evidence in question does not rise to the level of a *Chambers* violation. The evidence at best lies on the margin of a blurred line that divides character evidence, commonly but not always excluded, *cf.* Fed. R. Evid. 404, from state-of-mind evidence; the evidence at best does no more than increase somewhat the likelihood of a lunge, already the subject of Fortini's direct testimony; and the risk of unfair prejudice to the prosecution was real even if many courts would not have chosen to exclude the evidence on this ground.

It is very difficult to predict the evolution of *Chambers* because in over 30 years it has been used by the Supreme Court only a handful of times to overturn convictions; and the Supreme Court's standards are quite vague, although understandably so in a due process matter. Although this is a close case, exclusion of the evidence does not in our view add up to the kind of fundamental unfairness that warrants a federal court in finding a violation of due process. The exclusion in our view was error but it was not constitutional error.... [T]he judgment of the district court is affirmed....

CHARACTER EVIDENCE

"*Wait a minute. I thought I was on trial here—
not my vented spoonbill cap.*"

A. THE BASIC RULE AND ITS EXCEPTIONS

A longstanding principle of Anglo-American evidence law prohibits proving a person's character to support an inference that the person acted in conformity with his character on a particular occasion. The prosecutor in a murder case, for example, generally cannot rely on evidence that the defendant has a violent temper. The rule customarily is justified on the ground that "propensity" evidence of this sort, while probative, is likely to be unduly prejudicial.

Like the hearsay rule, the character-for-propensity evidence rule depends in its application on the purpose for which the challenged evidence is offered. Just as out-of-court statements are barred by the hearsay rule only if they are offered to prove the truth of what they assert, so evidence of a character trait is barred only if it is offered to prove conduct in conformity with the trait. Sometimes a party might offer character evidence for a non-propensity purpose, such as to prove in a child custody case that a party is a good or bad parent. In such circumstances, where character is "in issue" in the case, the ban on its use for propensity does not apply.

But unlike the hearsay rule, with its myriad exceptions, the character-for-propensity evidence rule (often, if misleadingly, referred to simply as the ban on "character evidence") has only three exceptions: one for the character of a criminal defendant, one for the character of the victim or alleged victim of a criminal offense, and one for the character of a witness. The first two exceptions generally must be first invoked by a criminal defendant; once the defendant chooses to open up the question of his or her character, or the character of the victim or alleged victim, the prosecution can follow suit.

Despite being simpler than the hearsay doctrine, the system of rules that has emerged for character evidence when offered for propensity is no less controversial. Wigmore praised the character-for-propensity ban as "a revolution in the theory of criminal trials, and . . . one of the peculiar features, of vast moment, which distinguishes the Anglo-American from the Continental System of Evidence." But more recent reviews are more mixed. Professor Richard Uviller complained a quarter-century ago that "today, character evidence most often appears either in burlesque of its function, or as a product of an arcane legalistic wordplay, or as a cruel and senseless shard of forgotten dogma." Many critics agree.

The following cases and excerpts address the rationale of the character-for-propensity evidence rule, its basic operation, and the exceptions for the character of a criminal defendant and the character of a victim or alleged victim. The third exception to the rule, concerning the character of a witness, authorizes a form of impeachment and rehabilitation. It is taken up in Chapter 7 of this book.

[F.R.E. 404(a); C.E.C. §§1101(a), 1102–1103]

PEOPLE v. ZACKOWITZ

172 N.E. 466 (N.Y. 1930)

Cardozo, C. J.

On November 10, 1929, shortly after midnight, the defendant in Kings county shot Frank Coppola and killed him without justification or excuse. A crime is admitted. What is doubtful is the degree only.

Four young men, of whom Coppola was one, were at work repairing an automobile in a Brooklyn street. A woman, the defendant's wife, walked by on the opposite side. One of the men spoke to her insultingly, or so at least she understood him. The defendant, who had dropped behind to buy a newspaper, came up to find his wife in tears. He was told she had been insulted, though she did not then repeat the words. Enraged, he stepped across the street and upbraided the offenders with words of coarse profanity. He informed them, so the survivors testify, that "if they did not get out of there in five minutes, he would come back and bump them all off." Rejoining his wife, he walked with her to their apartment house located close at hand. He was heated with liquor which he had been drinking at a dance. Within the apartment he induced her to tell him what the insulting words had been. A youth had asked her to lie with him, and had offered her $2. With rage aroused again, the defendant went back to the scene of the insult and found the four young men still working at the car. In a statement to the police, he said that he had armed himself at the apartment with a .25-caliber automatic pistol. In his testimony at the trial he said that this pistol had been in his pocket all the evening. Words and blows followed, and then a shot. The defendant kicked Coppola in the stomach. There is evidence that Coppola went for him with a wrench. The pistol came from the pocket, and from the pistol a single shot, which did its deadly work. The defendant walked away and at the corner met his wife who had followed him from the home. The two took a taxicab to Manhattan, where they spent the rest of the night at the dwelling of a friend.

On the way the defendant threw his pistol into the river. He was arrested on January 7, 1930, about two months following the crime.

At the trial the vital question was the defendant's state of mind at the moment of the homicide. Did he shoot with a deliberate and premeditated design to kill? Was he so inflamed by drink or by anger or by both combined that, though he knew the nature of his act, he was the prey to sudden impulse, the fury of the fleeting moment? If he went forth from his apartment with a preconceived design to kill, how is it that he failed to shoot at once? How to reconcile such a design with the drawing of the pistol later in the heat and rage of an affray? These and like questions the jurors were to ask themselves and answer before measuring the defendant's guilt. Answers consistent with guilt in its highest grade can reasonably be made. Even so, the line between impulse and deliberation is too narrow and elusive to make the answers wholly clear. The sphygmograph records with graphic certainty the fluctuations of the pulse. There is no instrument yet invented that records with equal certainty the fluctuations of the mind. At least, if such an instrument exists, it was not working at midnight in the Brooklyn street when Coppola and the defendant came together in a chance affray. With only the rough and ready tests supplied by their experience of life, the jurors were to look into the workings of another's mind, and discover its capacities and disabilities, its urges and inhibitions, in moments of intense excitement. Delicate enough and subtle is the inquiry, even in the most favorable conditions, with every warping influence excluded. There must be no blurring of the issues by evidence illegally admitted and carrying with it in its admission an appeal to prejudice and passion.

Evidence charged with that appeal was, we think, admitted here. Not only was it admitted, and this under objection and exception, but the changes were rung upon it by prosecutor and judge. Almost at the opening of the trial the people began the endeavor to load the defendant down with the burden of an evil character. He was to be put before the jury as a man of murderous disposition. To that end they were allowed to prove that at the time of the encounter and at that of his arrest he had in his apartment, kept there in a radio box, three pistols and a tear-gas gun. There was no claim that he had brought these weapons out at the time of the affray, no claim that with any of them he had discharged the fatal shot. He could not have done so, for they were all of different caliber. The end to be served by laying the weapons before the jury was something very different. The end was to bring persuasion that here was a man of vicious and dangerous propensities, who because of those propensities was more likely to kill with deliberate and premeditated design than a man of irreproachable life and amiable manners. Indeed, this is the very ground on which the introduction of the evidence is now explained and defended. The district attorney tells us in his brief that the possession of the weapons characterized the defendant as "a desperate type of criminal," a "person criminally inclined." . . . The weapons were not brought by the defendant to the scene of the encounter. They were left in his apartment where they were incapable of harm. In such circumstances, ownership of the weapons, if it has any relevance at all, has relevance only as indicating a general disposition to make use of them thereafter, and a general disposition to make use of them thereafter is without relevance except as indicating a "desperate type of criminal," a criminal affected with a murderous propensity.

. . . If a murderous propensity may be proved against a defendant as one of the tokens of his guilt, a rule of criminal evidence, long believed to be of fundamental importance for the protection of the innocent, must be first declared away. Fundamental hitherto has been the rule that character is never an issue in a criminal prosecution unless the defendant chooses to make it one. Wigmore, Evidence, vol. 1, §§55, 192. In a very real sense a defendant starts his life afresh when he stands before a jury, a prisoner at the bar. There has been a homicide in a public place. The killer admits the killing, but urges self-defense and sudden impulse. Inflexibly the law has set its face against the endeavor to fasten guilt upon him by proof of character or experience predisposing to an act of crime. The endeavor has been often made, but always it has failed. At times, when the issue has been self-defense, testimony has been admitted as to the murderous propensity of the deceased, the victim of the homicide, but never of such a propensity on the part of the killer. The principle back of the exclusion is one, not of logic, but of policy. There may be cogency in the argument that a quarrelsome defendant is more likely to start a quarrel than one of milder type, a man of dangerous mode of life more likely than a shy recluse. The law is not blind to this, but equally it is not blind to the peril to the innocent if character is accepted as probative of crime. "The natural and inevitable tendency of the tribunal — whether judge or jury — is to give excessive weight to the vicious record of crime thus exhibited, and either to allow it to bear too strongly on the present charge, or to take the proof of it as justifying a condemnation irrespective of guilt of the present charge." Wigmore, Evidence, vol. 1, §194, and cases cited.

A different question would be here if the pistols had been bought in expectation of this particular encounter. They would then have been admissible as evidence of preparation and design. A different question would be here if they were so connected with the crime as to identify the perpetrator, if he had dropped them, for example, at the scene of the affray. They would then have been admissible as tending to implicate the possessor (if identity was disputed), no matter what the opprobrium attached to his possession. Different, also, would be the question if the defendant had been shown to have gone forth from the apartment with all the weapons on his person. To be armed from head to foot at the very moment of an encounter may be a circumstance worthy to be considered, like acts of preparation generally, as a proof of preconceived design. There can be no such implication from the ownership of weapons which one leaves behind at home.

The endeavor was to generate an atmosphere of professional criminality. It was an endeavor the more unfair in that, apart from the suspicion attaching to the possession of these weapons, there is nothing to mark the defendant as a man of evil life. He was not in crime as a business. He did not shoot as a bandit shoots in the hope of wrongful gain. He was engaged in a decent calling, an optician regularly employed, without criminal record, or criminal associates. If his own testimony be true, he had gathered these weapons together as curios, a collection that interested and amused him. Perhaps his explanation of their ownership is false. There is nothing stronger than mere suspicion to guide us to an answer. Whether the explanation be false or true, he should not have been driven by the people to the necessity of offering it. Brought to answer a specific charge, and to defend himself against it, he was placed in a position where he had to defend himself against another, more general and sweeping. He was made to answer to the charge, pervasive and poisonous even if insidious and covert, that he was a man of murderous heart, of criminal disposition.

. . . The judgment of conviction should be reversed, and a new trial ordered.

CLEGHORN v. NEW YORK CENTRAL & HUDSON RIVER R.R. CO.

56 N.Y. 44 (1874)

CHURCH, Ch. J.

The accident was caused by the carelessness of the switchman, in neglecting to close the switch after the stock train had passed on to the side track, and in giving a false signal to the approaching passenger train, that the track was all right. . . . It is insisted that the court erred in admitting evidence of the intemperate habits of the switchman, and that the case of *Warner v. N.Y.C. R.R. Co.* (44 N.Y., 465) is a direct authority against it. That was a case of injury at a road crossing. It was proved that the flagman neglected to give the customary signal, and was intoxicated at the time. The Commission of Appeals held it error to show previous habits of intemperance known to the officers of the company, upon the ground that such evidence had no bearing upon the question of negligence at the time. In that view the decision was right. Previous intoxication would not tend to establish an omission to give the signal on the occasion of the accident. In this case it was sought to be proved, not only that Hartman was intoxicated at the time of the accident, but that he was a man of intemperate habits, which were known by the agent of the company, having the power to employ and discharge him and other subordinates, with a view of claiming exemplary damages. For this purpose the evidence was competent. It is unnecessary in this connection, to speak of the strength of the proof upon which a claim for exemplary damages was made in this case. It is sufficient to say that the evidence was competent upon the question of gross negligence on the part of the defendant in employing or continuing the employment of a subordinate known to be unfit for his position by reason of intoxication. [Judgment for plaintiff reversed on other grounds.]

BERRYHILL v. BERRYHILL

410 So. 2d 416 (Ala. 1982)

BEATTY, Justice.

. . . During the course of the custody proceeding, the petitioner asked the respondent if he had ever killed anyone. Although that question may be considered overbroad, we disagree with the conclusion by the Court of Civil Appeals that the relevancy of the question was not shown.

If character or reputation becomes a matter in issue in a civil suit, evidence with reference to such a party's reputation or character is admissible. . . . In a child custody proceeding, character is obviously in issue and "evidence touching the character, conduct, and reputation of the parties, or any other evidence tending to throw light on their fitness to be the custodian of the child, is admissible." *Milner v. Gatlin*, 143 Ga. 816, 85 S.E. 1045, 1047 (1915). . . . Thus, the question directed toward the respondent asking whether he had ever killed anyone would be relevant as an attempt to show a specific act of bad character bearing on the "fitness" of the respondent. . . . For these reasons the judgment of the Court of Civil Appeals is reversed. . . .

LARSON v. KLAPPRODT

231 N.W.2d 370 (S.D. 1975)
(sub nom. Walkon Carpet Corp. v. Klapprodt)

COLER, Justice.

. . . In his counterclaim defendant alleged that the plaintiff Larson had slandered him in telling certain persons that he both drank to excess and was sexually promiscuous. The trial court may properly have considered from the development of the evidence on that count and from other evidence in the record that the reputation of the defendant was not such, in its tarnished state, as to have been materially damaged by the slander of the plaintiff. Since damage to reputation was at least part of Klapprodt's claim, evidence of his reputation or past misdeeds was admissible both in establishing truth, *Tokmakian v. Fritz*, 1949, 75 R.I. 496, 67 A.2d 834, and in mitigating damages. *Kruglak v. Landre*, 1965, 23 A.D.2d 758, 258 N.Y.S.2d 550. The Restatement of Torts, Explanatory Notes §621, comment d, at 287 (Tent. Draft No. 20, 1974), supports this view. "In determining the amount of an award of general damages, the jury or other trier of fact may consider the character of the plaintiff and his general standing in the community as affecting the loss which he has sustained or will sustain." . . . Judgment is affirmed.

UNITED STATES v. BAEZ

761 Fed. Appx. 23 (2d Cir. 2019)

SUMMARY ORDER

Defendant-Appellant Atdilon Baez was tried and convicted of knowingly possessing a TEC-9 semi-automatic firearm after having been convicted of a felony, in violation of 18 U.S.C. §922(g)(1), and knowingly selling the TEC-9 to a convicted felon, in violation of 18 U.S.C. §922(d)(1). . . .

During pretrial proceedings, Baez indicated that he planned to raise at trial a defense of entrapment. To rebut this defense, the Government sought to introduce evidence showing Baez's predisposition to commit the charged offenses. . . . [T]he District Court admitted over Baez's objection certain evidence of Baez's statements, conduct, and prior convictions for weapons possession as proof of his predisposition to commit the charged offenses. Baez challenges these evidentiary rulings. . . .

"If a defendant presents credible evidence of government inducement, then the prosecutor must show predisposition beyond a reasonable doubt." *United States v. Bala*, 236 F.3d 87, 94 (2d Cir. 2000). [Accordingly, evidence of Baez's predisposition was not barred by the character evidence rule.] . . . We affirm the judgment of the District Court.

ADVISORY COMMITTEE NOTE TO F.R.E. 404(a)

Character questions arise in two fundamentally different ways. (1) Character may itself be an element of a crime, claim, or defense. A situation of this kind is commonly referred to as "character in issue." Illustrations are: the chastity of the victim under a statute specifying her chastity as an element of the crime of seduction, or the competency of the driver in an action for negligently entrusting a motor vehicle to an incompetent driver. No problem of the general relevancy of character evidence is involved, and the present rule therefore has no provision on the subject. . . . (2) Character evidence is susceptible of being used for the purpose of suggesting an inference that the person acted on the occasion in question consistently with his character. This use of character is often described as "circumstantial." Illustrations are: evidence of a violent disposition to prove that the person was the aggressor in an affray, or evidence of honesty in disproof of a charge of theft. . . .

In most jurisdictions today, the circumstantial use of character is rejected but with important exceptions: (1) an accused may introduce pertinent evidence of good character (often misleadingly described as "putting his character in issue"), in which event the prosecution may rebut with evidence of bad character; (2) an accused may introduce pertinent evidence of the character of the victim, as in support of a claim of self-defense to a charge of homicide or consent in a case of rape, and the prosecution may introduce similar evidence in rebuttal of the character evidence, or, in a homicide case, to rebut a claim that deceased was the first aggressor, however proved; and (3) the character of a witness may be gone into as bearing on his credibility. This pattern is incorporated in the rule. While its basis lies more in history and experience than in logic an underlying justification can fairly be found in terms of the relative presence and absence of prejudice in the various situations. In any event, the criminal rule is so deeply imbedded in our jurisprudence as to assume almost constitutional proportions and to override doubts of the basic relevancy of the evidence.

... The argument is made that circumstantial use of character ought to be allowed in civil cases to the same extent as in criminal cases, i.e. evidence of good (nonprejudicial) character would be admissible in the first instance, subject to rebuttal by evidence of bad character.... The difficulty with expanding the use of character evidence in civil cases is set forth by the California Law Revision Commission ... : "Character evidence is of slight probative value and may be very prejudicial. It tends to distract the trier of fact from the main question of what actually happened on the particular occasion. It subtly permits the trier of fact to reward the good man and to punish the bad man because of their respective characters despite what the evidence in the case shows actually happened."

McCORMICK ON EVIDENCE

§§191, 193, at 1:1060 n.2, 1072 (Kenneth S. Broun ed., 7th ed. 2013)

The difference in the [character evidence] rule as regards the prosecution and the defense has been characterized as an amelioration of the "brutal rigors" of the early criminal law. Maguire, Evidence — Common Sense and Common Law 204 (1947). But to say that the defendant deserves the benefit of all reasonable doubts and that good character may produce a reasonable doubt assumes what should be demonstrated — that the doubt is not the product of unfair prejudice.... Thus, one must consider whether a parade of character witnesses convinces most jurors that the defendant has led an exemplary life even when his past is not so unblemished and whether many defendants with checkered backgrounds will be in a position to produce such witnesses. Furthermore, to the extent that the ability to collect impressive character witnesses is concentrated among those accused of white collar rather than street crimes, one may question the fairness of an asymmetrical rule....

[When] the character of the *victim* is being proved ... [t]here is ... a risk of a different form of prejudice. Learning of the victim's bad character could lead the jury to think that the victim merely "got what he deserved" and to acquit for that reason. Nevertheless, at least in murder and perhaps in battery cases as well, when the identity of the first aggressor is really in doubt, the probative value of the evidence ordinarily justifies taking this risk.

JUSTIN SEVIER, LEGITIMIZING CHARACTER EVIDENCE

68 Emory L. Rev. 441, 445-47, 508 (2019)

It was only in the late nineteenth century that common law courts, responding to cultural changes inspired by egalitarian norms and Enlightenment thought, began to ban certain types of propensity evidence in determining a defendant's criminal or civil liability.... In barring propensity evidence at trial, common law courts subscribed to an outmoded theory of human behavior, whereby people ascribe others' acts almost entirely to their personality traits. Social psychology research suggests the opposite: the manner in which people form impressions of others is *interactional*, such that they evaluate behavior in light of a person's personality traits and in light of *situational* factors that induced the behavior....

[J]urors are attentive to propensity evidence at trial. They do not, however, weigh the evidence more heavily than other evidence presented at trial, and they carefully evaluate features of character evidence that increase or decrease its diagnosticity with respect to the defendant's legal liability. Moreover ... the public has less confidence in verdicts — and is less likely to *legitimize* those verdicts — if courts shield propensity evidence from legal fact finders.

[W]e should allow modern jurors to ... evaluate the relevant character evidence against the parties and decide how much (or how little) to credit it. The experimental data converge on the conclusion that jurors make reasonable judgments about the probative weight to attach to propensity evidence, and the public views the introduction of propensity evidence as consistent with notions of fair process. Thus, legitimizing the use of character evidence at trial will have beneficial effects not only for the perceived accuracy and fairness of American trial courts, but also for the public citizens who rely upon — and legitimize — the legal system.

PROBLEMS

4.1. A criminal defendant charged with heroin trafficking admits selling heroin to an undercover agent but claims to have been entrapped. Under federal law the defense of entrapment is unavailable to a defendant who was "predisposed" to commit the offense. The government seeks to call a rebuttal witness who will describe buying heroin from the defendant a month before the undercover purchase. Is the testimony barred by F.R.E. 404(a)?

4.2. A civil defendant, sued in federal court for wrongful death, claims he shot the victim in self-defense. In order to support his testimony that the victim attacked him, may the defendant introduce evidence that the victim had an explosive temper? In order to support his testimony that he reasonably feared for his life, may the defendant introduce evidence that the victim had a reputation for brutality?

4.3. A criminal defendant charged with murder testifies that he shot the victim only after the victim lunged at him with a knife. May the prosecution introduce evidence of the victim's peaceful character? May the prosecution introduce evidence of the defendant's violent character?

4.4. A criminal defendant charged with murder claims self-defense and introduces evidence that the victim was prone to violence. May the prosecution introduce evidence of the victim's peaceful character? May the prosecution introduce evidence of the defendant's violent character?

4.5. In an extortion prosecution, the government proves the defendant made vaguely menacing statements to the victim. In order to show that the defendant intended the statements as threats of physical harm, and that the statements put the victim in reasonable fear for his safety, may the government prove that the defendant has a well-known proclivity toward violence?

B. METHODS OF PROVING CHARACTER

The hearsay rule and its exceptions pay little attention to how an out-of-court statement is proved. All that matters, generally, is the nature of the statement itself and the purpose for which it is offered. The character evidence rule is different. When one of the three exceptions to the character evidence rule applies, it typically applies only to certain kinds of evidence of character — namely, testimony about a person's reputation, or a witness's own opinion about the person's character. What remains excluded, typically, is what many people would find the best proof of a person's character: evidence of how the person has actually acted on other occasions. The following materials discuss the rationale and operation of this counterintuitive rule.

[F.R.E. 405, 803(21); C.E.C. §§1102–1103, 1324]

MICHELSON v. UNITED STATES

335 U.S. 469 (1948)

Mr. Justice JACKSON delivered the opinion of the Court.

In 1947 petitioner Michelson was convicted of bribing a federal revenue agent. The Government proved a large payment by accused to the agent for the purpose of influencing his official action. The defendant, as a witness on his own behalf, admitted passing the money but claimed it was done in response to the agent's demands, threats, solicitations, and inducements that amounted to entrapment. It is enough for our purposes to say that determination of the issue turned on whether the jury should believe the agent or the accused.

... Defendant called five witnesses to prove that he enjoyed a good reputation. Two of them testified that their acquaintance with him extended over a period of about thirty years and the others said they had known him at least half that long. A typical examination in chief was as follows:

"*Q.*   Do you know the defendant Michelson? *A.* Yes.
"*Q.*   How long do you know Mr. Michelson? *A.* About 30 years.
"*Q.*   Do you know other people who know him? *A.* Yes.

"*Q.*   Have you had occasion to discuss his reputation for honesty and truthfulness and for being a law-abiding citizen? *A.* It is very good.

"*Q.*   You have talked to others? *A.* Yes.

"*Q.*   And what is his reputation? *A.* Very good."

These are representative of answers by three witnesses; two others replied, in substance, that they never had heard anything against Michelson.

... To four of these witnesses the prosecution also addressed the question the allowance of which, over defendant's objection, is claimed to be reversible error:

"Did you ever hear that on October 11th, 1920, the defendant, Solomon Michelson, was arrested for receiving stolen goods?"

None of the witnesses appears to have heard of this.

The trial court asked counsel for the prosecution, out of presence of the jury, "Is it a fact according to the best information in your possession that Michelson was arrested for receiving stolen goods?" Counsel replied that it was, and to support his good faith exhibited a paper record which defendant's counsel did not challenge.

The judge also on three occasions warned the jury, in terms that are not criticized, of the limited purpose for which this evidence was received.[3]

Defendant-petitioner challenges the right of the prosecution so to cross-examine his character witnesses. The Court of Appeals held that it was permissible. The opinion, however, points out that the practice has been severely criticized and invites us, in one respect, to change the rule [footnote omitted]. Serious and responsible criticism has been aimed, however, not alone at the detail now questioned by the Court of Appeals but at common-law doctrine on the whole subject of proof of reputation or character.[5]

3. In ruling on the objection when the question was first asked, the Court said: "... I instruct the jury that what is happening now is this: the defendant has called character witnesses, and the basis for the evidence given by those character witnesses is the reputation of the defendant in the community, and since the defendant tenders the issue of his reputation the prosecution may ask the witness if she has heard of various incidents in his career. I say to you that regardless of her answer you are not to assume that the incidents asked about actually took place. All that is happening is that this witness' standard of opinion of the reputation of the defendant is being tested. Is that clear?"

In overruling the second objection to the question the Court said: "Again I say to the jury there is no proof that Mr. Michelson was arrested for receiving stolen goods in 1920, there isn't any such proof. All this witness has been asked is whether he had heard of that. There is nothing before you on that issue. Now would you base your decision on the case fairly in spite of the fact that that question has been asked? You would? All right."

The charge included the following: "In connection with the character evidence in the case I permitted a question whether or not the witness knew that in 1920 this defendant had been arrested for receiving stolen goods. I tried to give you the instruction then that that question was permitted only to test the standards of character evidence that these character witnesses seemed to have. There isn't any proof in the case that could be produced before you legally within the rules of evidence that this defendant was arrested in 1920 for receiving stolen goods, and that fact you are not to hold against him; nor are you to assume what the consequences of that arrest were. You just drive it from your mind so far as he is concerned, and take it into consideration only in weighing the evidence of the character witnesses."

5. A judge of long trial and appellate experience has uttered a warning which, in the opinion of the writer, we might well have heeded in determining whether to grant certiorari here: "... evidence of good character is to be used like any other, once it gets before the jury,

It would not be possible to appraise the usefulness and propriety of this cross-examination without consideration of the unique practice concerning character testimony, of which such cross-examination is a minor part.

Courts that follow the common-law tradition almost unanimously have come to disallow resort by the prosecution to any kind of evidence of a defendant's evil character to establish a probability of his guilt. Not that the law invests the defendant with a presumption of good character, but it simply closes the whole matter of character, disposition and reputation on the prosecution's case-in-chief. The State may not show defendant's prior trouble with the law, specific criminal acts, or ill name among his neighbors, even though such facts might logically be persuasive that he is by propensity a probable perpetrator of the crime. The inquiry is not rejected because character is irrelevant; on the contrary, it is said to weigh too much with the jury and to so overpersuade them as to prejudge one with a bad general record and deny him a fair opportunity to defend against a particular charge. The overriding policy of excluding such evidence, despite its admitted probative value, is the practical experience that its disallowance tends to prevent confusion of issues, unfair surprise and undue prejudice.

But this line of inquiry firmly denied to the State is opened to the defendant because character is relevant in resolving probabilities of guilt. He may introduce affirmative testimony that the general estimate of his character is so favorable that the jury may infer that he would not be likely to commit the offense charged. This privilege is sometimes valuable to a defendant for this Court has held that such testimony alone, in some circumstances, may be enough to raise a reasonable doubt of guilt and that in the federal courts a jury in a proper case should be so instructed.

When the defendant elects to initiate a character inquiry, another anomalous rule comes into play. Not only is he permitted to call witnesses to testify from hearsay, but indeed such a witness is not allowed to base his testimony on anything but hearsay.... The witness may not testify about defendant's specific acts or courses of conduct or his possession of a particular disposition or of benign mental and moral traits; nor can he testify that his own acquaintance, observation, and knowledge of defendant leads to his own independent opinion that defendant possesses a good general or specific character, inconsistent with commission of acts charged. The witness is, however, allowed to summarize what he has heard in the community, although much of it may have been said by persons less qualified to judge than himself. The evidence which the law permits is not as to the personality of defendant but only as to the shadow his daily life has cast in his neighborhood. This has been well described in a different connection

and the less they are told about the grounds for its admission, or what they shall do with it, the more likely they are to use it sensibly. The subject seems to gather mist which discussion serves only to thicken, and which we can scarcely hope to dissipate by anything further we can add." L. Hand in *Nash v. United States*, 2 Cir., 54 F.2d 1006, 1007.

In opening its cyclopedic review of authorities from many jurisdictions, CORPUS JURIS SECUNDUM summarizes that the rules regulating proof of character "have been criticized as illogical, unscientific, and anomalous, explainable only as archaic survivals of compurgation or of states of legal development when the jury personally knew the facts on which their verdict was based." 32 C.J.S., Evidence, §433.

as "the slow growth of months and years, the resultant picture of forgotten incidents, passing events, habitual and daily conduct, presumably honest because disinterested, and safer to be trusted because prone to suspect. . . . It is for that reason that such general repute is permitted to be proven. It sums up a multitude of trivial details. It compacts into the brief phrase of a verdict the teaching of many incidents and the conduct of years. It is the average intelligence drawing its conclusion." Finch J., in *Badger v. Badger*, 88 N.Y. 546, 552, 42 Am. Rep. 263.

While courts have recognized logical grounds for criticism of this type of opinion-based-on-hearsay testimony, it is said to be justified by "overwhelming considerations of practical convenience" in avoiding innumerable collateral issues which, if it were attempted to prove character by direct testimony, would complicate and confuse the trial, distract the minds of jurymen and befog the chief issues in the litigation. *People v. Van Gaasbeck*, 189 N.Y. 408, 418, 82 N.E. 718.

. . . Thus the law extends helpful but illogical options to a defendant. Experience taught a necessity that they be counterweighted with equally illogical conditions to keep the advantage from becoming an unfair and unreasonable one. The price a defendant must pay for attempting to prove his good name is to throw open the entire subject which the law has kept closed for his benefit and to make himself vulnerable where the law otherwise shields him. The prosecution may pursue the inquiry with contradictory witnesses to show that damaging rumors, whether or not well-grounded, were afloat — for it is not the man that he is, but the name that he has which is put in issue.[16] Another hazard is that his own witness is subject to cross-examination as to the contents and extent of the hearsay on which he bases his conclusions, and he may be required to disclose rumors and reports that are current even if they do not affect his own conclusion. It may test the sufficiency of his knowledge by asking what stories were circulating concerning events, such as one's arrest, about which people normally comment and speculate. Thus, while the law gives defendant the option to show as a fact that his reputation reflects a life and habit incompatible with commission of the offense charged, it subjects his proof to tests of credibility designed to prevent him from profiting by a mere parade of partisans.

To thus digress from evidence as to the offense to hear a contest as to the standing of the accused, at its best opens a tricky line of inquiry as to a shapeless and elusive subject matter. At its worst it opens a veritable Pandora's box of irresponsible gossip, innuendo and smear. . . . Wide discretion is accompanied by heavy responsibility on trial courts to protect the practice from any misuse. The trial judge was scrupulous to so guard it in the case before us. He took pains to ascertain, out of presence of the jury, that the target of

---

16. A classic example in the books is a character witness in a trial for murder. She testified she grew up with defendant, knew his reputation for peace and quiet, and that it was good. On cross-examination she was asked if she had heard that the defendant had shot anybody and, if so, how many. She answered, "Three or four," and gave the names of two but could not recall the names of the others. She still insisted, however, that he was of "good character." The jury seems to have valued her information more highly than her judgment, and on appeal from conviction the cross-examination was held proper. *People v. Laudiero*, 192 N.Y. 304, 309, 85 N.E. 132.

the question was an actual event, which would probably result in some comment among acquaintances if not injury to defendant's reputation. He satisfied himself that counsel was not merely taking a random shot at a reputation imprudently exposed or asking a groundless question to waft an unwarranted innuendo into the jury box.... [The question permitted by the trial court] was proper cross-examination because reports of [Michelson's] arrest for receiving stolen goods, if admitted, would tend to weaken the assertion that he was known as an honest and law-abiding citizen.

. . . We do not overlook or minimize the consideration that "the jury almost surely cannot comprehend the Judge's limiting instructions," which disturbed the Court of Appeals. The refinements of the evidentiary rules on this subject are such that even lawyers and judges, after study and reflection, often are confused, and surely jurors in the hurried and unfamiliar movement of a trial must find them almost unintelligible. However, limiting instructions on this subject are no more difficult to comprehend or apply than those upon various other subjects.... [W]e think defendants in general and this defendant in particular have no valid complaint at the latitude which existing law allows to the prosecution to meet by cross-examination an issue voluntarily tendered by the defense.

. . . We concur in the general opinion of courts, textwriters and the profession that much of this law is archaic, paradoxical and full of compromises and compensations by which an irrational advantage to one side is offset by a poorly reasoned counter-privilege to the other. But somehow it has proved a workable even if clumsy system when moderated by discretionary controls in the hands of a wise and strong trial court. To pull one misshapen stone out of the grotesque structure is more likely simply to upset its present balance between adverse interests than to establish a rational edifice.... The judgment is affirmed.

[Justice Frankfurter filed a concurring opinion.]

Mr. Justice RUTLEDGE, with whom Mr. Justice MURPHY joins, dissenting.

. . . [I]n the guise of "testing the standards of the witness" when he speaks to reputation, the door has been thrown wide open to trying the defendant's whole life, both in general reputation and in specific incident. What is worse, this is without opportunity for the defendant to rebut either the fact or the innuendo for which the evidence is offered more generally than otherwise....

The very form of the question was itself notice of the fact to the jury. They well might assume, as men of common sense, that the court would not allow the question if the fact were only fiction. And why "on October 11th, 1920," rather than merely "in 1920" or "Have you ever heard of the defendant's being arrested, other than for the trademark violation?" Why also "for receiving stolen goods"? In my opinion the only answers to these questions are, not that the prosecution was "testing the witness' standard of opinion of reputation," but that it was telling the jury what it could not prove directly and what the petitioner had no chance to deny, namely, that he had been so arrested; and thereby either insinuating that he had been convicted of the crime or leaving to the jury to guess that this had been the outcome....

The mere fact of a single arrest twenty-seven years before trial, without further showing of criminal proceedings or their outcome, whether acquittal or conviction, seldom could have substantial bearing upon one's present general reputation; indeed it is not per se a derogatory fact. But it is put in generally, and I think was put in evidence in this case, not to call in question the witness' standard of opinion but, by the very question, to give room for play of the jury's unguarded conjecture and prejudice. This is neither fair play nor due process. It is a perversion of the criminal process as we know it. For it permits . . . trial of the accused not only for general bad conduct or reputation but also for conjecture, gossip, innuendo and insinuation. . . .

ADVISORY COMMITTEE NOTE TO F.R.E. 405

Of the three methods of proving character provided by the rule, evidence of specific instances of conduct is the most convincing. At the same time it possesses the greatest capacity to arouse prejudice, to confuse, to surprise, and to consume time. Consequently the rule confines the use of evidence of this kind to cases in which character is, in the strict sense, in issue and hence deserving of a searching inquiry. When character is used circumstantially and hence occupies a lesser status in the case, proof may be only by reputation and opinion. These latter methods are also available when character is in issue. This treatment is, with respect to specific instances of conduct and reputation, conventional contemporary common law doctrine. McCormick §153.

In recognizing opinion as a means of proving character, the rule departs from usual contemporary practice in favor of that of an earlier day. See 7 Wigmore §1986, pointing out that the earlier practice permitted opinion and arguing strongly for evidence based on personal knowledge and belief as contrasted with "the secondhand, irresponsible product of multiplied guesses and gossip which we term 'reputation'." It seems likely that the persistence of reputation evidence is due to its largely being opinion in disguise. Traditionally character has been regarded primarily in moral overtones of good and bad: chaste, peaceable, truthful, honest. Nevertheless, on occasion nonmoral considerations crop up, as in the case of the incompetent driver, and this seems bound to happen increasingly. If character is defined as the kind of person one is, then account must be taken of varying ways of arriving at the estimate. These may range from the opinion of the employer who has found the man honest to the opinion of the psychiatrist based upon examination and testing. No effective dividing line exists between character and mental capacity, and the latter traditionally has been provable by opinion.

According to the great majority of cases, on cross-examination inquiry is allowable as to whether the reputation witness has heard of particular instances of conduct pertinent to the trait in question. Michelson v. United States, 335 U.S. 469 (1948); Annot., 47 A.L.R.2d 1258. The theory is that, since the reputation witness relates what he has heard, the inquiry tends to shed light on the accuracy of his hearing and reporting. Accordingly, the opinion witness would be asked whether he knew, as well as whether he had heard. The fact is, of course, that these distinctions are of slight if any practical significance, and the second sentence of subdivision (a) eliminates them as a factor in formulating questions. This recognition of the propriety of inquiring into specific instances of conduct does not circumscribe inquiry otherwise into the bases of opinion and reputation testimony.

The express allowance of inquiry into specific instances of conduct on cross-examination in subdivision (a) and the express allowance of it as part of a case in chief when character is actually in issue in subdivision (b) contemplate that testimony of specific instances is not generally permissible on the direct examination of an ordinary opinion witness to character. . . .

ADVISORY COMMITTEE NOTE TO F.R.E. 803(21)

Exception (21) recognizes the traditional acceptance of reputation evidence as a means of proving human character. The exception deals only with the hearsay aspect of this kind of evidence. Limitations upon admissibility based on other grounds will be found in Rules 404, relevancy of character evidence generally, and 608, character of witness. The exception is in effect a recitation, in the context of hearsay, of Rule 405(a). . . .

GOVERNMENT OF THE VIRGIN ISLANDS v. ROLDAN

612 F.2d 775 (3d Cir. 1979)

GARTH, Circuit Judge.

This is an appeal from a conviction for murder in the first degree under V.I. Code tit. 14, §922(a)(1). . . . Testimony included that of Luz Maria Cruz, the wife of Roldan's nephew. Cruz was called by the Government. Defense counsel's cross-examination began as follows:

Q. Mrs. Cruz, I am a lawyer for Mr. Roldan, I am going to ask you a few questions. Now, have you known Mr. Roldan for two or three years?
A. Yes. I am married to my husband since 1961, ever since I know him.
Q. Do you ever see people other than Mr. Roldan going to his house?
A. No.
Q. Would you say that he is a lonely unsociable fellow?
A. He is a man that never bother anybody.

This line of questioning was not continued. . . .

On redirect examination, Cruz was asked the following questions by the Government:

Q. Mrs. Cruz, you are aware, are you not, that the Defendant was convicted previously of murder in the 1st degree?
MR. JOHNSON: (defense counsel) I object to the question and ask that it be stricken and the jury instructed to disregard.
THE COURT: I will overrule the objection on the grounds I previously stated.
A. (By the witness) Yes, I knew about that.
Q. (By Mr. Schwartz (Assistant U.S. Attorney)) You knew he was convicted of murder in the 1st degree?

A. Yes, sir, I have known of that.
Q. And you would still say he is a man who never bothers anyone?
A. Now, yes, I have to say that.

Roldan argues that it was error for the district court to have allowed the Government to inquire whether Cruz knew that Roldan had been convicted previously of first degree murder, since evidence of prior bad acts is generally inadmissible. . . . The district court determined that by asking the questions about Roldan's social habits, Roldan's counsel had put Roldan's character in issue. We agree. The last two questions which Roldan's counsel asked Cruz, are apparently directed toward establishing that Roldan had little contact with anyone and would therefore be unlikely to have reason to murder anyone. We do not think that Cruz' answer, "He is a man that never bother anybody," was a gratuitous, unsolicited remark; on the contrary, it was precisely the type of answer called for by defense counsel. The court's admission of the Government's impeachment testimony was thus proper.

Roldan objects further to the form of the impeachment questions, arguing that it was improper to use the phrases, "you are aware, are you not," and "[y]ou knew," rather than the form, "have you heard." . . . Even if Roldan has preserved this point for appeal, we find no error. Roldan's argument is predicated on *Michelson v. United States*, 335 U.S. 469, 482 (1948). . . . [T]the Advisory Committee Note to rule 405 implies that rule 405 overruled this aspect of *Michelson*. . . . There is thus no basis in the form of the impeachment questions for reversing Roldan's conviction. . . . We will therefore affirm the district court's March 16, 1979 judgment of sentence imposed upon Roldan.

UNITED STATES v. KRAPP

815 F.2d 1183 (8th Cir. 1987)

Ross, Circuit Judge.

Patricia E. Krapp appeals her conviction of three counts of making false record entries with intent to mislead, deceive or defraud the United States in violation of 18 U.S.C. §2073. . . . We affirm.

Krapp was the postmaster of the Pocahontas, Iowa post office from November 1983 to February 1986. An investigation by United States Postal Inspectors in January 1986 revealed a shortage of 100 coils of 22 cent stamps ($2200) at the Pocahontas post office. Krapp admitted to the inspectors that she had discovered the shortage in late November or early December 1985, but had failed to accurately reflect the shortage on certain postal forms and reports which she was required to fill out in connection with her duties as postmaster. Krapp stated that she did not report the shortage because she was investigating the incident and because she lacked expertise in filling out the postal forms. Krapp was charged with three counts of making false record entries with intent to defraud the United States.

At trial, Krapp presented a character witness who testified that Krapp had a reputation as "an honest, trustworthy person." On cross-examination the Assistant United States Attorney asked the witness "Are you aware that

Pat Krapp's husband with her knowledge omitted cash income that he had on his — on their tax returns?" Before the witness answered, Krapp's attorney objected to the question and moved for a mistrial on the basis that the question was improper. Although refusing to grant a mistrial, the trial court sustained the objection and admonished the jury to disregard the question. Krapp now argues that a mistrial should have been granted because the question was asked without good faith and served only to prejudice the jury.

... This court has previously recognized the possible prejudicial impact of "did you know" type impeachment questions if they have no basis in fact. *See Gross v. United States*, 394 F.2d. 216, 219 (8th Cir. 1968). *See also United States v. Nixon*, 777 F.2d 958, 970 (5th Cir. 1985). In *Gross*, we noted:

> The rule permitting the cross-examiner to ask the character witness whether he "has heard" of other particular crimes of accused involving the same trait is pregnant with possibilities of destructive prejudice. The mere asking by a respected official of such a question, however answered, may well suggest to the jury that the imputation is true.

Id. at 221 n.1 (quoting McCormick, Evidence (1954) §158, pp. 336, 337). Further, "[u]nless circumscribed by rules of fairness and grounded in demonstrated good faith on the part of the prosecution, the result could be most prejudicial to the defendant and make for a miscarriage of justice." *Id.* at 219 (citations omitted).

When asked by the trial judge outside the hearing of the jury what his good faith basis was for asking the question, the prosecutor stated that the notes of one of the postal inspectors reflected that Krapp had told the inspector that her husband received cash income which he did not report on their tax return. Further, the prosecutor had seen the tax returns and he believed them to be joint returns. Krapp replied that the postal inspector's notes concerned her 1985 tax return which the prosecutor knew had not been filed.

The trial court, in sustaining Krapp's objection, stated that he was not impugning any bad faith on the part of the prosecutor in asking the question, but found that the prejudicial effect of the question outweighed its probative value. We also make no determination as to whether the question was asked in good faith, although we find the issue to be a close one. Instead, we determine that even if the question were improper, when viewed in the context of the whole trial it was not so offensive as to warrant a mistrial. The question was asked only once, was unanswered, and the subject matter of the question was never brought up again before the jury. Further, the district court immediately admonished the jury to disregard the question. Also, from a review of the record we determine that there was substantial other evidence on which the jury could base Krapp's conviction such that the question did not have a substantial adverse impact on the verdict. Therefore, we find no abuse of discretion by the trial court in refusing to grant a mistrial.

However, we admonish the Assistant United States Attorney for asking Krapp's character witness about the Krapps' tax returns in front of the jury without first raising the matter with the trial judge. Before an attempt at impeachment of a character witness with "did you know" type questions such as this, the trial judge should have the opportunity, out of the hearing of the jury, to rule on the propriety of the questions. By failing to raise the matter first with the trial judge, the Assistant United States Attorney created the risk of mistrial after substantial time had been invested in the trial. . . .

UNITED STATES v. SETIEN

929 F.2d 610 (11th Cir. 1991) (sub nom. United States v. Camejo)

DYER, Senior Circuit Judge.

[Luis Setien and four other employees of Eastern Airlines were convicted of conspiracy to import cocaine.] Setien's witness Max Mermelstein made a proffer of his testimony outside the presence of the jury. He testified that during the period that Setien was accused of having been involved in the cocaine importation conspiracy, they met regularly as social friends. During that time, Mermelstein was involved as a high level importer and distributor of cocaine throughout the United States. He offered Setien the lure of easy money if he would quit his job as an Eastern Airlines baggage handler and just hang around Mermelstein while he conducted his narcotics business. Setien refused to involve himself in the narcotics business and repeatedly reminded Mermelstein of the damage he was doing to society. . . . The court ruled that the testimony was irrelevant under Rule 405(b) and was not admissible under Rule 404(b). We agree.

Evidence of good conduct is not admissible to negate criminal intent. *Michelson v. United States*, 335 U.S. 469, 477 (1948); *United States v. Russell*, 703 F.2d 1243, 1249 (11th Cir. 1983). Mermelstein's proffered testimony was merely an attempt to portray Setien as a good character through the use of prior "good acts." The trial judge properly exercised his discretion in excluding this testimony as inadmissible character evidence. . . . Affirmed.

UNITED STATES v. FORD

737 F.3d 1121 (7th Cir. 2013) (sub nom. United States v. White)

FLAUM, Circuit Judge.

[Felicia Ford and two codefendants were convicted of wire fraud in connection with a mortgage scam.] Ford took the stand at trial . . . [and] sought to testify that she had cooperated in an FBI investigation of an identity-theft scheme during the relevant period. . . . The court sustained the government's objection. It ruled that evidence of Ford's cooperation in the investigation of an entirely different fraud — a fraud in which she was not personally involved . . . — was unrelated and could confuse the jury.

On appeal, Ford argues that she should have been allowed to testify about her cooperation with the FBI as evidence of her law-abiding character under Rule 404(a)(2). . . . [S]he overlooks the fact that Rule 405 limits the form such evidence can take. Under 405(a), admissible character evidence may be introduced in the form of opinion or reputation testimony. Specific instances of the defendant's character, on the other hand, may only be introduced if that character "is an essential element of a charge, claim, or defense." Fed. R. Evid. 405(b). Ford's testimony about the time that she tipped off the FBI is evidence about a specific instance of her character. And Ford's law-abidingness, or lack thereof, is not an essential element of a wire fraud charge, nor a defense to it. We find no abuse of discretion in the district court's exclusion of this testimony. [Affirmed.]

McCORMICK ON EVIDENCE

§187, at 1:1021 (Kenneth S. Broun ed., 7th ed. 2013)

The phrase "character in issue" sometimes invites confusion. A defendant in a criminal case generally can bring in evidence of good character to show that he is not the type of person who would have committed [the] offense charged. Although courts sometimes speak loosely of this strategy as putting the defendant's character in issue, the defendant is using character solely as circumstantial evidence. When the defendant makes his character an issue in this manner, it merely means that the prosecution is allowed to bring forth certain kinds of rebuttal evidence of bad character. It does not justify evidence of specific acts, opinion, and reputation by either party. That freewheeling approach to character evidence is limited to the unusual situation in which an offense, claim, or defense for which character is an essential element is pled.

PROBLEMS

4.6. May a criminal defendant charged with tax evasion call his sister to testify that she thinks the defendant is thoroughly honest? May he call a neighbor to testify that he has a reputation as ethical and law-abiding? May he call a police officer to testify that the defendant turned in an expensive watch he found on the street? May the defendant himself testify about turning in the watch?

4.7. A criminal defendant charged with murder calls his minister, who testifies that the defendant is "gentle" and "wouldn't hurt anyone." Can the prosecution call a rebuttal witness who will testify that the defendant attacked him in a supermarket checkout line a year before the killing? Can the prosecutor ask the minister on cross-examination, "Are you aware that the defendant attacked someone in a supermarket checkout line?" Can the prosecutor ask the minister, "Have you heard that the defendant attacked someone in a supermarket checkout line?"

4.8. Henry Jumpertz was acquitted in 1859 of the murder of his mistress, Sophie Werner. Jumpertz claimed Werner had killed herself, and he "offered the testimony of witness suggesting that Sophie had suicidal tendencies and had earlier attempted suicide several times." *See* Jennifer L. Mnookin, *Scripting Expertise: The History of Handwriting Identification Evidence and the Judicial Construction of Reliability*, 87 Va. L. Rev. 1723, 1748-1751 (2001). Should this evidence have been admitted?

C. OTHER USES OF SPECIFIC CONDUCT

As we have seen, evidence of a defendant's character generally is inadmissible to prove his or her conduct in conformity with that character, unless the defendant chooses to place his or her character in controversy. And even if the defendant does choose to open that door, his or her character generally must be proved with opinion or reputation evidence, not with evidence of his or her conduct on other, specific occasions. Despite these rules, evidence of uncharged misconduct (typically offered by the prosecution) is routinely admitted in criminal cases. The evidence comes in on the theory that it is being used to prove something other than the defendant's character, so that the character evidence rule does not come into play at all. Despite (or perhaps because of) its widespread use and its explicit endorsement in modern evidence codes, this theory of admissibility remains highly controversial.

1. Permissible Purposes

[F.R.E. 404(b); C.E.C. §1101(b)]

UNITED STATES V. BEECHUM

582 F.2d 898 (5th Cir. 1978) (en banc)

TJOFLAT, Circuit Judge:

... A jury convicted Orange Jell Beechum, a substitute letter carrier for the United States Postal Service, of unlawfully possessing an 1890 silver dollar that he knew to be stolen from the mails, in violation of 18 U.S.C. §1708 (1976). To establish that Beechum intentionally and unlawfully possessed the silver dollar, the Government introduced into evidence two Sears, Roebuck & Co. credit cards found in Beechum's wallet when he was arrested. Neither card was issued to Beechum, and neither was signed. The Government also introduced evidence indicating that the cards had been mailed some ten months prior to Beechum's arrest to two different addresses on routes he had serviced.... We hold that the credit cards were properly admissible.

... [Rule 404(b)] follows the venerable principle that evidence of extrinsic offenses should not be admitted solely to demonstrate the defendant's bad character. Even though such evidence is relevant, because a man of bad character is more likely to commit a crime than one not, the principle prohibits such evidence because it is inherently prejudicial. *See, e.g., Michelson v. United States*, 335 U.S. 469, 475-76 (1948). Without an issue other than mere character to which the extrinsic offenses are relevant, the probative value of those offenses is deemed insufficient in all cases to outweigh the inherent prejudice. Where, however, the extrinsic offense evidence is relevant to an issue such as intent, it may well be that the evidence has probative force that is not substantially outweighed by its inherent prejudice. If this is so, the evidence may be admissible.

What the rule calls for is essentially a two-step test. First, it must be determined that the extrinsic offense evidence is relevant to an issue other than the defendant's character. Second, the evidence must possess probative value that is not substantially outweighed by its undue prejudice and must meet the other requirements of rule 403. . . . The task for the court in its ascertainment of probative value and unfair prejudice under rule 403 calls for a commonsense assessment of all the circumstances surrounding the extrinsic offense. As the Advisory Committee Notes to rule 404(b) state: "No mechanical solution is offered. The determination must be made whether the danger of undue prejudice outweighs the probative value of the evidence in view of the availability of other means of proof and other facts appropriate for making decision of this kind under Rule 403."

. . . [T]he credit card evidence is relevant to Beechum's intent with respect to the silver dollar. That Beechum possessed the credit cards with illicit intent diminishes the likelihood that at the same moment he intended to turn in the silver dollar. . . . We move now to the second step of the rule 404(b) analysis, the application of rule 403. . . . From the very inception of trial, it was clear that the crucial issue in the case would be Beechum's intent in possessing the silver dollar. He took the stand to proclaim that he intended to surrender the coin to his supervisor. The issue of intent was therefore clearly drawn, and the policies of justice that require a defendant to explain evidence that impugns his exculpatory testimony were in full force. . . . The credit card evidence bore directly on the plausibility of Beechum's story; justice called for its admission.

That the posture of this case demanded the admission of the credit card evidence is reinforced by the nature of the Government's proof on the issue of intent apart from that evidence. This proof consisted of the following. The Government called Cox, Beechum's supervisor, who testified that Beechum had had several opportunities to surrender the coin to him. Beechum denied this, and called two fellow employees who testified that Beechum had asked them if they had seen Cox. Absent the credit card evidence, the issue would have been decided wholly by the jury's assessment of the credibility of these witnesses. The Government, therefore, did not make out such a strong case of criminal intent that the credit card evidence would have been of little incremental probity. In fact, the credit card evidence may have been determinative.

. . . The probity of the credit card evidence in this case is augmented by the lack of temporal remoteness. Although Beechum may have obtained the cards as much as ten months prior to his arrest for the possession of the silver dollar, he kept the cards in his wallet where they would constantly remind him of the wrongfulness of their possession. In effect, Beechum's state of mind with respect to the credit cards continued through his arrest. He maintained contemporaneously the wrongful intent with respect to the cards and the intent as regards the coin. The force of the probity of this circumstance is illustrated by what Beechum would have had to convince the jury in order to avoid it. He would have been forced to argue that his state of mind was schizoid that he intended at the same time to relinquish the coin but to keep the cards. This situation does not differ significantly from one in which a thief is caught with a bag of loot, is charged with the larceny as to one of the items, but claims that he intended to return that item. Would any reasonable jury believe this story when it is established that he had stolen the rest of the loot?

The remaining considerations under rule 403 do not alter our conclusion as to the admissibility of the extrinsic offense evidence in this case. The extrinsic offense here is not of a heinous nature; it would hardly incite the jury to irrational decision by its force on human emotion. The credit card evidence was no more likely to confuse the issues, mislead the jury, cause undue delay, or waste time than any other type of extrinsic offense evidence. Since the need for the evidence in this case was great, it can hardly be said that the admission of the cards constituted "needless presentation of cumulative evidence."

It is significant that the court was careful to allay, as much as limiting instructions can, the undue prejudice engendered by the credit card evidence. It gave extensive instructions to the jury on the limited use of extrinsic offense evidence employed to prove unlawful intent.[23]

. . . [W]e conclude that the credit card evidence meets the requirements of rule 403. Therefore, the conditions imposed by the second step of the analysis under rule 404(b) have been met, and the extrinsic offense evidence in this case was properly admitted at trial. . . . Affirmed.

---

23. The Advisory Committee Notes to rule 403 require the judge to consider the effectiveness of a limiting instruction in reducing the prejudicial impact of evidence: "In reaching a decision whether to exclude on grounds of unfair prejudice, consideration should be given to the probable effectiveness or lack of effectiveness of a limiting instruction."

This is a context in which limiting instructions are of substantial efficacy, and we think the judge adequately admonished the jury to consider the credit card evidence solely on the issue of Beechum's intent. We reproduce below the instructions he gave.

> During the course of this trial certain evidence has been presented concerning an alleged transaction similar to that charged in the indictment, to wit, the possession by the Defendant of the two Sears credit cards, admitted in evidence as Government Exhibits 6 and 7.

> This evidence, if you choose to accept it, is admitted for the limited purpose of assisting you in determining the intent with which a defendant may have acted. In this regard, you are instructed that evidence of an alleged similar transaction may not be considered by the jury in determining whether an accused committed the acts or participated in the activity alleged in the indictment.

> Nor may evidence of such an alleged similar transaction of a like nature be considered for any other purpose whatever unless the jury first finds that the other evidence in the case, standing alone, establishes beyond a reasonable doubt that the accused participated in the activity alleged in the indictment.

> If the jury should find beyond a reasonable doubt from other evidence in the case that the accused participated in the activity alleged in the indictment, then the jury may consider evidence as to transactions of a like nature, in determining the state of mind or intent with which the accused did the act charged in the indictment.

> I want to instruct you very explicitly and unequivocally as to the very limited extent to which you may consider this evidence as to a similar offense.

> As I just instructed you, you may consider such evidence of another transaction of a like nature in determining the state of mind or intent with which the accused may have done the act charged in the indictment, but only if you first find that the other evidence standing alone establishes beyond a reasonable doubt that the defendant committed the act alleged in the indictment.

UNITED STATES v. BOYD

53 F.3d 631 (4th Cir. 1995)

HAMILTON, Circuit Judge.

Richard Edison Boyd appeals his conviction [for marijuana trafficking].... Boyd argues the district court abused its discretion in admitting ... testimony that Boyd personally used marijuana and cocaine. According to Boyd, such evidence was only admitted to show he had a bad character, and, therefore, must have committed the crimes of which he was charged. *See* Fed. R. Evid. 404(b) ("[E]vidence of other crimes, wrongs, or acts is not admissible to show action in conformity therewith."). We disagree.

... The government's theory was that Boyd participated in the charged conspiracies in order to support his personal drug use. *See United States v. Templeman*, 965 F.2d 617, 619 (8th Cir.) ("Evidence of [defendant's] personal use of cocaine indicates potential motives for his distribution of cocaine: to finance his own use of the drug and to insure himself of a ready supply."), *cert. denied*, 506 U.S. 980, 113 S. Ct. 482, 121 L. Ed. 2d 387 (1992).... [E]vidence of Boyd's personal marijuana and cocaine use would be admissible under Rule 404(b) as proof of his motive for participating in the charged conspiracies.

... Nor was its probative value substantially outweighed by its prejudicial effect. *See* Fed. R. Evid. 403. Of course, in one sense all incriminating evidence is inherently prejudicial. "The proper question under Rule 404(b), however, is whether such evidence has the potential to cause undue prejudice, and if so, whether the danger of such undue prejudice substantially outweighs its probative value." [*United States v. Mark*, 943 F.2d 444, 449 (4th Cir. 1991).] In this case, the balancing test undeniably weighs in favor of admitting the evidence, because the evidence of Boyd's personal use of marijuana and cocaine did not involve conduct any more sensational or disturbing than the crimes with which he was charged. [T]he jury heard and credited evidence that Boyd supplied hundreds of pounds of marijuana.... We conclude that Boyd's personal drug use was far less prejudicial than this evidence, the admission of which Boyd has not challenged on appeal. The evidence at issue was, therefore, admissible.... Affirmed.

UNITED STATES v. DeJOHN

638 F.2d 1048 (7th Cir. 1981)

HARLINGTON WOOD, JR., Circuit Judge.

Defendant John DeJohn appeals from a jury conviction on the charge of uttering and publishing two United States Treasury checks in violation of 18 U.S.C. §495. [The payees and defendant all lived at the same YMCA.] ... Defendant objects to testimony by a YMCA security guard who stated that he "arrested" the defendant when he found him behind a reception desk at the YMCA in violation of the establishment's rules. Defendant also objects to the testimony of a Chicago police officer that in the course of searching defendant at police headquarters on an occasion unrelated to the offense for which defendant was on trial, the officer found checks, one of them a Treasury check, made out to a payee named Michael Dore. The officer testified that defendant stated he had obtained the checks from a mailbox behind the reception desk at the YMCA and was holding them for safekeeping. Police were unable to locate the payee of the checks and no charges were filed against defendant as a result of the checks found in the search.

As applied to the defendant in a criminal case, Rule 404 prevents any effort to prove that the defendant acted in the criminal manner as charged by the introduction of evidence showing the defendant acted in a similar way at some other time not charged. As part (b) of the rule indicates, though, evidence of similar actions generally is admissible when introduced for purposes other than those which (under the rule) improperly show propensity to commit the crime. Here, the testimony of the security officer and the policeman was highly probative of the defendant's opportunity to gain access to the mailboxes and obtain the checks that he cashed at a later time knowing the checks to contain forged endorsements. This circumstantial evidence was properly admissible.

The issue of opportunity became material to the trial once defense counsel set forth the theory in opening argument that it was not their client who uttered the forged checks. Defendant's opportunity to gain access to the checks thus became a key issue. . . . Affirmed.

LEWIS v. UNITED STATES

771 F.2d 454 (10th Cir. 1985)

WILLIAM E. DOYLE, Circuit Judge.

Defendant Jermaine Lewis appeals his conviction for burglary of a post office, a violation of 18 U.S.C. §2115, and for destruction of government property, a violation of 18 U.S.C. §1361. . . . [D]efendant maintains that the district court erred in admitting into evidence testimony that defendant had participated in the burglary of a garage store earlier on the evening of the post office burglary. . . . Evidence of defendant's participation in a burglary several hours before the post office burglary with which defendant was charged falls squarely within Rule 404(b) as establishing defendant's plan and intent. The evidence was especially probative because defendant allegedly took from the store some equipment needed for the post office burglary. Therefore the district court did not abuse its discretion in admitting the evidence. . . . Affirmed.

UNITED STATES v. CROCKER

788 F.2d 802 (5th Cir. 1986)

CEREZO, District Judge.

Gerald James Crocker was convicted by a jury on one count of a two-count indictment for conspiring to commit bank theft, 18 U.S.C. Sections 371 and 2113(b), and was sentenced to three years imprisonment. . . . This particular conspiracy consisted of cashing counterfeit checks in various banks in the New England area from on or about January 1984 to May 3, 1984. . . . Besides obtaining and preparing checks, appellant's role was to drive a co-conspirator to the banks where the checks would be cashed and the proceeds split equally.

Crocker claims that the admission of evidence related to his 1977 arrest violated Fed. R. Evid. 404(b). . . . Defendant's "knowing" participation in the conspiracy was a crucial element which if not clearly established could have left the jury with the impression that defendant was merely driving his friend Gaeta to several New England banks. *Cf. United States v. Zeuli*, 725 F.2d 813–816 (1st Cir. 1984) ("In every conspiracy case . . . a not guilty plea renders the defendant's intent a material issue and imposes a difficult burden on the government.") The fact that defendant had been arrested before with co-conspirator Gaeta while in an automobile with counterfeit checks was highly probative of his knowledge that Gaeta's checks and his trips to the banks were for an illicit purpose. The district court did not abuse its discretion in admitting this evidence after balancing its probative value against its potential prejudice. . . . [Reversed on other grounds.]

UNITED STATES v. DOSSEY

558 F.2d 1336 (8th Cir. 1977)

HENLEY, Circuit Judge.

Debra Lynn Dossey appeals her conviction by a jury of armed bank robbery in violation of 18 U.S.C. §2113(d). We affirm.

On July 12, 1976 appellant was indicted for the robbery of the Capitol Branch of the First National Bank in Little Rock, Arkansas. At trial the teller at the bank testified that on February 27, 1976 she was approached by a young white female, who produced a pistol and demanded money. The teller complied with the demand and the robber fled. The teller described the robber as being a blond, about 22 or 23 years of age, weighing about 115 or 120 pounds, and being about 5′3″ tall. At the time of the robbery the robber was dressed in a blue plaid shirt and blue jeans and wore rose-colored, wire-framed glasses. The teller could not positively identify appellant as the robber, but testified that appellant "looks like" the robber.

Other testimony placed appellant and a companion, James Weaver, in Little Rock on the day of the robbery. The day after the robbery appellant and Weaver flew from Little Rock to Phoenix, Arizona.

. . . Ann Louise Jagow testified that she first met appellant in Phoenix, Arizona, in March, 1976. She testified that she had a conversation with appellant during which appellant admitted having done robberies in Little Rock. Appellant told Jagow that she was wearing a wig and her tinted glasses during one bank robbery, that she was armed, and that she made her escape by going over a brick wall and riding off with Weaver in her El Camino.

Miss Jagow further testified that she, along with appellant, Weaver and others planned and executed a bank robbery in Mesa, Arizona. She testified that appellant wore a blond wig and a blue T-shirt during the robbery, along with pinkish-tinted, wire-framed glasses. Finally, Miss Jagow testified that appellant had admitted committing bank robbery in Minnesota.

... We are of the opinion that the evidence of the Arizona robbery was admissible to prove identification of the person who robbed the Little Rock bank, an issue that was important due to the teller's inability positively to identify appellant. Miss Jagow testified that appellant, armed with a pistol, entered the Arizona bank alone, wearing a blond wig, a blue shirt and pinkish-tinted, wire-framed glasses. The similarity in modus operandi and disguise is great and the incidents were close in time. The substantial probative value of this evidence was not outweighed by the possibility of unfair prejudice and it was properly admitted.

It is questionable whether the district court should have admitted Miss Jagow's testimony about the Minnesota robberies. This testimony was of very limited probative value because its only connection with the Little Rock robbery was appellant's statement that she wore disguises in Minnesota. However, this testimony was limited to two brief answers and was not again referred to by the government. The district court also gave appropriate limiting instructions.[*] In these circumstances, we are convinced that the error, if any, was harmless beyond a reasonable doubt. ...

UNITED STATES v. WRIGHT

901 F.2d 68 (7th Cir. 1990)

POSNER, Circuit Judge.

A jury found Stanley Wright guilty of two counts of distributing cocaine and two of distributing it within a thousand feet of a school. 21 U.S.C. §§841(a)(1), 845a. The judge sentenced him to seven years in prison. The principal question raised by the appeal is whether the trial was contaminated by evidence of other criminal activity by Wright.

On two different days in May 1988, three plainclothes police officers bought a total of four bags of "crack" at $20 a bag from a man who sold it to the officers at curbside on a Chicago street a few blocks from Hyde Park, handing the bags through the window of the unmarked police car. The sales occurred in daylight, and from police photographs the officers identified the man as Stanley Wright. No arrest was made, however, and instead the police waited six

---

[*] ["Immediately after Jagow's testimony concerning the Arizona robbery, the trial court instructed the jury as follows: 'Now the Court has permitted in certain evidence that might suggest or indicate to the jury either other wrongs or other crimes in Arizona. Now you are not concerned with any other wrongs or crimes in Arizona, but the Court has admitted that only as it might bear upon the issue of identity of the people involved or person or persons involved in the robbery in Little Rock, Arkansas on February 27 and the modus operandi or the planning which might also go along with the question of identity. The jury may feel it is of no importance and disregard it entirely, but it has been admitted only because of its potential relevance on the issue of identity, plan and modus operandi and not for any other reason. You should not be concerned about whether there was any wrong or any other crime committed in Arizona.'" *United States v. Weaver*, 565 F.2d 129, 133–134 (8th Cir. 1977).]

months and then with court authorization placed a wiretap on Wright's telephone line in November 1988. The tap intercepted a conversation between Wright and an unidentified woman in which Wright bragged about being a drug dealer. At trial, over Wright's objection, the judge let the government play a tape recording of portions of the conversation to the jury. . . .

Wright did not admit in the recorded conversation making the sales — which had occurred six months earlier — that he is charged in this case with having made. He did admit committing other drug crimes. The admissibility of evidence of other crimes is governed by Rule 404(b) of the Federal Rules of Evidence, which provides that such evidence may not be used to prove a person's bad character or his propensity to commit crimes in conformity with that character, but may be used "for other purposes, such as proof of motive, opportunity, intent, preparation, plan, knowledge, or absence of mistake or accident." The judge admitted the conversation to establish identity and intent, and told the jury to limit their consideration of the conversation to those issues. There was, however, no issue of intent in this case — no question, for example, whether Wright knew what was in the packages that he sold the plainclothes officers. So the jury, if it obeyed the judge's instructions, could have used the recorded conversation only in connection with the issue of identity, that is, only to help decide whether Wright was the man who had sold the crack to the plainclothes officers.

By "identity," the district judge must have meant "guilt," and that is an impermissible equation. The intercepted telephone conversation may well show that Wright is more likely to be guilty of the crime with which he is charged than the average man on the street, who is not a drug dealer, but it does not in the least show that the man who had sold the plainclothes officers four bags of crack six months earlier was correctly identified as Stanley Wright. It would tend to show this if for example the conversation had indicated that Wright was at that time selling drugs on streets near where the transactions occurred, or if he had said something that only a party to those transactions would know. The conversation indicated neither of these things. . . .

The only relevance of the tape was to depict Wright as a drug dealer (and a brazen and boastful one at that), and, against this, the limiting instruction was not limiting at all. It told the jurors that they could consider the tape for what light it cast on the identity and intent of the man who had sold crack to the officers. The implication was that a drug dealer is more likely than someone who is not a drug dealer to sell drugs, even if at a different level of distribution from his accustomed one. No doubt this is true. "The inquiry [into previous criminal acts] is not rejected because character is irrelevant; on the contrary, it is said to weigh too much with the jury and to so overpersuade them as to prejudge one with a bad general record and deny him a fair opportunity to defend against a particular charge." *Michelson v. United States*, 335 U.S. 469, 475-76 (1948). The logic of the district court's ruling is that a drug defendant's prior drug convictions are admissible *per se*, even if they do not help to clear up a question of identification or establish a modus operandi or otherwise illuminate the particular conduct of which the defendant is accused, and even if he does not take the stand, which would lay him open to being impeached by his prior convictions. The use of evidence of other crimes to establish a propensity to commit the type of crime charged is the use of such evidence that Rule 404(b) forbids.

Some of that evidence has no probative value at all. If Wright were accused of a criminal violation of the securities laws, the fact that he may once have been found guilty of child molestation would not increase the probability that he was guilty of the securities offense. To exclude such evidence, however, Rule 404(b) is not necessary; irrelevant evidence of any kind is made inadmissible by Rules 402 and 403. The purpose of Rule 404(b) is to exclude a type of evidence — evidence that the defendant had previously engaged in a broadly similar criminal activity — which has some probative value but the admission of which would tend as a practical matter to deprive a person with a criminal record of the protection, in future prosecutions, of the government's burden of proving guilt beyond a reasonable doubt. As Justice Jackson pointed out in *Michelson*, a jury is not likely to insist on the government's satisfying so demanding a standard of proof if the defendant is a thoroughly bad sort who even if not clearly guilty of the crime with which he is charged is no doubt guilty of some similar crime or crimes for which he may never have been caught or, if caught, may not have been punished adequately.

. . . The government's back-up argument that the admission of the tape was, if error, a harmless one because the three officers positively identified Wright has no merit. Identification evidence is not infallible, and police officers are not disinterested witnesses. If the government's case were as airtight as the government now says it is, one wonders why it pressed so hard for the admission of the recorded conversation.

The judgment is reversed with instructions to grant the defendant a new trial.

UNITED STATES v. DAVIS

726 F.3d 434 (3d Cir. 2013)

SMITH, Circuit Judge.

Police arrested Terrell Davis after finding him in a Jeep with nearly a kilo of cocaine in the backseat. The arrest led to a conviction for possession with intent to distribute. As evidence that Davis recognized the cocaine in the Jeep, the government proved at trial that he had two prior convictions for possessing cocaine. Yet the government never proved that the cocaine from his past was similar in appearance, quantity, or form. We acknowledge that some of our cases admitting prior criminal acts under Federal Rule of Evidence 404(b) have been expansive. But our expansiveness is finite, and this case crosses the line. . . .

[The] District Court admitted the convictions as relevant to [knowledge]. . . . The government now argues on appeal that the evidence also was relevant to intent. Knowledge and intent are indeed proper purposes under . . . Rule 404(b). . . . But we have never held that a possession conviction is relevant to prove either knowledge or intent in a distribution trial, and rightly so.

Possession and distribution are different in ways that matter. . . . As to knowledge, one who possesses a drug might not recognize the same drug when prepared for distribution. The packaging or quantity might be different, and objects in greater quantities often have an appearance or smell of their own. . . . [T]he jury knew only that Davis had been twice convicted of possessing cocaine. The jury knew nothing of the packaging or quantity that led to those convictions, so it could not have known whether Davis's past helped him to recognize the nearly one kilogram of cocaine in the Jeep.

Then there is the problem that the cocaine from Davis's past might have been in a different form. Cocaine is consumable either as a powder or as one of several bases, most often crack. Neither form particularly resembles the other. As its name suggests, powder cocaine is a powder — specifically, a salt — that can be compressed or loose. On the other hand, crack cocaine is hard and waxy and often resembles small rocks or crystals. This distinction matters, and the jury did not know which form Davis had possessed back in 2007 and 2008. For all the jury knew, the cocaine could have been a dash of powder on a golden tray. It could have been hidden in the lining of a suitcase. Or it could have been crack cocaine — in crystal form, in liquid form, rolled up in paper, or stuffed in a syringe. In any of those instances, Davis's past would not have helped him to identify the compressed powder in the backseat.

Based on the bare-bones stipulation before it, the jury had no way of knowing whether Davis's experiences made him any more likely to recognize the cocaine in the backseat. The convictions simply were not probative of Davis's knowledge. . . . At best, the convictions had such limited probative value that they fail . . . the balancing requirement [of Rule 403]. . . . Either way, the convictions are inadmissible to prove Davis's knowledge.

The government nonetheless urges us to follow [*United States v. Lopez*, 340 F.3d 169 (3d Cir. 2003) and *United States v. Givan*, 320 F.3d 452 (3d Cir. 2003)]. In *Lopez*, we held that the defendant's participation in a cocaine-distribution conspiracy was admissible in a possession trial to prove knowledge of heroin, a different drug altogether. And in *Givan*, we held that the defendant's conviction for distributing cocaine was likewise admissible to prove knowledge and intent in a heroin-distribution trial. These cases are at the outer bounds of admissibility under Rule 404(b). At all events, the two cases are distinguishable because the defendants had been convicted of dealing cocaine, and drug dealers presumably have more knowledge of drugs in general. By contrast, a possession conviction does not imply a similar level of knowledge.

. . . Nor does a possession conviction imply an intent to distribute. Possession and distribution are distinct acts — far more people use drugs than sell them — and these acts have different purposes and risks. A prior conviction for possessing drugs by no means suggests that the defendant intends to distribute them in the future. . . .

In cases such as this, there is an ever-present danger that jurors will infer that the defendant's character made him more likely to sell the drugs in his possession. But that is precisely the type of inference that Rule 404(b) forbids. Any other conclusion would run the risk of unraveling the prior-acts rule. . . .

We join other circuits in declaring that a possession conviction is inadmissible to prove intent to distribute. The Sixth Circuit, for example, held that "possession of a small quantity of crack cocaine for personal use on one occasion . . . sheds no light on whether [the defendant] intended to distribute crack cocaine in his possession on another occasion nearly five months earlier."

United States v. Haywood, 280 F.3d 715, 721 (6th Cir. 2002). The Seventh and Ninth Circuits have suggested likewise. *See United States v. Santini,* 656 F.3d 1075, 1078 (9th Cir. 2011) (holding that prior convictions "for simple possession" were "not similar to the importation of marijuana and thus lack[] probative value"); . . . *United States v. Monzon,* 869 F.2d 338, 344 (7th Cir. 1989) (concluding that evidence of the defendant's prior marijuana possession was not probative of his intent to distribute cocaine); . . . *cf. Enriquez v. United States,* 314 F.2d 703, 717 (9th Cir. 1963) (concluding that a trial was unfair because the court had admitted evidence of marijuana possession to show intent to sell heroin). . . . Other circuits have reached the opposite result, but we are not persuaded. *See, e.g., United States v. Butler,* 102 F.3d 1191, 1196 (11th Cir. 1997); *United States v. Logan,* 121 F.3d 1172, 1178 (8th Cir. 1997); *United States v. Gadison,* 8 F.3d 186, 192 (5th Cir. 1993). We conclude that Davis's convictions should not have been before the jury — not as evidence of knowledge, not as evidence of intent. . . . [Reversed.]

UNITED STATES v. EKIYOR

89 F. Supp. 3d 928 (E.D. Mich. 2015)

GERALD E. ROSEN, Chief Judge.

Defendant Kemepaudor Ekiyor is charged . . . with one count of possession with intent to distribute cocaine . . . and one count of importation of cocaine. . . . These charges stem from allegations that as Defendant was traveling from Nigeria to his home in Ottawa, Canada with connections in Amsterdam and at the Detroit Metropolitan Airport, federal law enforcement agents at the Detroit airport discovered more than six kilograms of cocaine in a locked suitcase bearing a luggage tag with Defendant's name, with Defendant subsequently found to be in possession of a key that opened this locked suitcase.

Through the present motion . . . Defendant seeks to compel the Government to disclose information purportedly in the possession of the United States Drug Enforcement Administration and other federal agencies relating to the smuggling of drugs by baggage handlers. In Defendant's view, the Government's disclosure of this information is required under the authority of *Brady v. Maryland,* 373 U.S. 83 (1963). . . . The Government filed a response in opposition to this motion on February 25, 2015, observing that Defendant has been given the names and docket numbers of two recent cases in this District in which airport baggage handlers have been charged with drug smuggling activities, and arguing that any further disclosures sought in Defendant's motion would exceed the scope of the *Brady* materiality standard.

The Supreme Court's familiar ruling in *Brady* imposes upon the Government the duty to disclose "evidence favorable to an accused" that is "material either to guilt or to punishment." . . . Defendant does not suggest how the information he seeks might be admissible at his forthcoming trial or, at a minimum, might lead to the discovery of admissible evidence. To the contrary, the Court harbors serious doubts that the avenue Defendant proposes to explore will result in evidence that he may offer at trial for either substantive or impeachment purposes. . . . Evidence of the drug trafficking activities of a baggage handler in another case, if offered by Defendant here to suggest that a baggage handler likewise might have been responsible for the drugs found in his travel bag, would run afoul of the prohibition under Federal Rule of Evidence 404(b)(1) against the admission of "[e]vidence of a crime, wrong, or other act" to "prove a person's character in order to show that on a particular occasion the person acted in accordance with the character." . . .

More specifically, the information that Defendant seeks from the Government here, concerning the activities of baggage handlers in other cases, has been termed by the courts as "reverse 404(b)" evidence — that is, "evidence of a prior act by another [that] is offered as exculpatory evidence by the defendant, instead of being used by a prosecutor against a defendant." *United States v. Lucas,* 357 F.3d 599, 605 (6th Cir. 2004). Other circuits have adopted a more lenient standard for determining whether a defendant should be permitted to introduce reverse 404(b) evidence, noting that "the principal policy consideration underlying Rule 404(b)'s exclusionary rule is to protect the parties in an action, and in particular, criminal defendants, from the danger of unfair prejudice," and reasoning that this danger "does not exist" where "the *defendant* offers evidence of other crimes or bad acts of a third party exculpatorily." *See Lucas,* 357 F.3d at 612-14 (Rosen, D.J., concurring) (surveying the standards applied by other circuits in determining the admissibility of reverse 404(b) evidence, and advocating that the more lenient standard should be adopted in this Circuit). The Sixth Circuit, however, has held that "the standard analysis of Rule 404(b) evidence should generally apply," regardless of whether the Government seeks to introduce other acts evidence against a defendant or a defendant wishes to offer such evidence "with respect to an absent third party, not charged with any crime." *Lucas,* 357 F.3d at 606. Under the rule adopted by the Sixth Circuit, therefore, reverse 404(b) evidence of other acts by a third party is inadmissible if it is offered only to support a propensity inference — that is, to suggest that it is more likely that the third party conducted himself on another occasion in accordance with the character evidenced by the other act.

The Court fails to see how the information sought by Defendant could have any probative value at his trial apart from its use to support an impermissible propensity inference — namely, to suggest that because baggage handlers in other cases were accused or convicted of drug trafficking activities, it is more likely that a baggage handler is responsible in this case for the drug smuggling activity that the Government seeks to attribute to Defendant. Indeed, such a propensity inference would be particularly attenuated and inappropriate in this case, because absent evidence that the *same* baggage handler charged in another case also might have been in a position to plant drugs in Defendant's luggage without his knowledge, the materials sought by Defendant from other cases would tend to show only the propensity of an entire *class* of employees in the travel industry (baggage handlers) to engage in drug trafficking activities. If there is a theory of admissibility for such evidence, the Court is not aware of it, and Defendant certainly has not identified one. Thus, although this Court continues to believe that the broader use of reverse Rule 404(b) evidence approved in other circuits better reflects the policies underlying Rule 404(b), the baggage handler material sought in

Defendant's present motion would not be admissible even under this more generous standard.

Even assuming that Defendant could satisfy the Rule 404(b) criteria for admitting evidence of the crimes, wrongs, or other acts of baggage handlers, exclusion would nonetheless be called for under Fed. R.Evid. 403 if the probative value of this evidence would be "substantially outweigh[ed]" by the "risk of unfair prejudice, confusion of the issues, misleading the jury, or undue delay." In this case, Defendant's introduction of evidence of drug trafficking by baggage handlers would spawn a mini-trial to explore such matters as when and where these activities occurred, the precise nature of the activities, and whether these activities had any conceivable bearing on or relation to the events giving rise to the charges here, just so that the jury could meaningfully determine what weight, if any, to give to this evidence in assessing Defendant's guilt or innocence of the charged offenses. Given that the probative value of this baggage handler evidence would surely be modest, at best, and would rest on a number of tenuous inferences, the Court has no difficulty in concluding that this dubious probative value would be substantially outweighed by the risk of confusing the pertinent issues, misleading the jury, and unduly delaying the proceedings. . . . [Motion denied.]

ADVISORY COMMITTEE NOTE TO 1991 AMENDMENT TO F.R.E. 404

Rule 404(b) has emerged as one of the most cited Rules in the Rules of Evidence. And in many criminal cases evidence of an accused's extrinsic acts is viewed as an important asset in the prosecution's case against an accused. Although there are a few reported decisions on use of such evidence by the defense, *see, e.g., United States v. McClure*, 546 F.2d 670 (5th Cir. 1990) (acts of informant offered in entrapment defense), the overwhelming number of cases involve introduction of that evidence by the prosecution. The amendment to Rule 404(b) adds a pretrial notice requirement in criminal cases and is intended to reduce surprise and promote early resolution on the issue of admissibility. . . .

DANIEL J. CAPRA & LIESA L. RICHTER, CHARACTER ASSASSINATION: AMENDING FEDERAL RULE OF EVIDENCE 404(B) TO PROTECT CRIMINAL DEFENDANTS

118 Colum. L. Rev. 769, 831-32 (2018)

Rule 404(b) is the most litigated Federal Rule of Evidence, cropping up routinely in criminal cases, in which jury trials continue to be a mainstay. . . . It is an open secret that federal courts have traditionally played fast and loose with other-acts evidence, listing all proper purposes in justifying admissibility and allowing past misdeeds of criminal defendants to come before juries on a routine basis. The devastating effect of such other-acts evidence on juries is well-documented.

Recently, the Seventh, Third, and Fourth Circuits have issued opinions seeking to restore Rule 404(b) as a rule of *exclusion*. These opinions caution against use of any prior act that depends for its probative value upon inferences about a defendant's "propensity" to conduct him or herself in relevant ways. They have emphasized the importance of some "active" dispute launched by the defense to bring prior acts into play. Finally, these courts have worked to funnel all other-acts evidence through the Rule 404(b) gauntlet by eliminating or restricting significantly the doctrine of "inextricably intertwined" acts that may be admitted as part of proving the charged offense without application of Rule 404(b). All the while, several federal circuit courts continue to treat Rule 404(b) as a "rule of inclusion."

In order to resolve the conflict in the circuits over the proper handling of other-acts evidence in federal criminal cases, the time may be ripe for an amendment to Federal Rule of Evidence 404(b). . . . An amendment that could change the tune in the traditional approach to other-acts evidence, without cluttering Rule 404(b) with foreign terminology that invites costly litigation, would be a new balancing test that favors criminal defendants. Instead of relying on the standard Rule 403 balancing that admits other-acts evidence so long as its probative value isn't "substantially outweighed" by unfair prejudice, an amended rule could demand that the probative value of other-acts evidence admitted against a criminal defendant *outweigh* any potential for prejudice. By reversing the scale to favor exclusion, such an amendment could serve the important goals of the recent Seventh, Third, and Fourth Circuit precedent in a flexible manner consistent with the history and purpose of Rule 404(b).

PAUL F. ROTHSTEIN, INTELLECTUAL COHERENCE IN AN EVIDENCE CODE

28 Loy. L.A. L. Rev. 1259, 1260, 1265 (1995)

It is inescapable that the first sentence of Rule 404(b), the prohibitory sentence, is inconsistent with the second sentence, the permissive sentence, at least as those sentences are currently interpreted. The first sentence commands, in effect, "Thou shalt not use other crimes, wrongs, or acts to prove character in order to prove an act in conformity with that character." The second sentence, however, says, in effect, "Yes, but you may use those other crimes, wrongs, or acts in order to prove such facts as knowledge, intent, motive, identity, plan, or absence of mistake or accident." The standard interpretation of these two sentences is that evidence is excluded by the first sentence if it is offered on a "propensity" theory — that is, that the defendant's prior acts demonstrate a tendency to behave the same way in the future. But, under the second sentence, the evidence may be admissible if the relevance of the evidence does not depend on a propensity inference. This dichotomy does not hold up under closer examination. The first and second sentences cannot be construed consistently in light of their interpretation in case law. Both describe evidence offered on a propensity theory.

. . . [A] more promising way to produce intellectual coherence between the two sentences of Rule 404(b) . . . [is to assume that] the first sentence of

404(b) bans propensity, but only when it is the general and morally tinged propensity known as character. In other words, character, the word used and banned in the first sentence of the Rule, is not synonymous with "propensity." Instead, character is just one type of propensity — the amorphous, general, morally-tinged kind — that presents the specter of the several dangers the character rule worries about: that the propensity is too amorphous and general to lead to a solid inference of specific behavior; that the jury may not realize this; and that they might be induced to make prejudicial moral judgments of the person or relax the rigor of their scrutiny of the facts based on their willingness to punish for general or past "badness." The second sentence, the permissive sentence of Rule 404(b), licenses another kind of propensity. This is not character, which is excluded, but the more specific kind of propensity that may not be attended by the same dangers in the same degree. Finally, there is habit, governed by Rule 406, which licenses an even more specific and compelling kind of propensity. . . .

MIRKO BAGARIC & KUMAR AMARASEKARA, THE PREJUDICE AGAINST SIMILAR FACT EVIDENCE

5 Int'l J. Evid. & Proof 71, 93–95, 97–98 (2001)

[P]revious conduct is of little weight in predicting if a particular individual will commit a criminal offence. However, we suggest that previous conduct assumes considerable weight where it is *known* that a criminal act has been committed and the only fact in issue is by whom or whether the culprit had the requisite criminal intent. . . . Thereupon the issue is not whether the agent will re-offend. It is whether he or she is the perpetrator (or had the necessary guilty mind), given that the agent has demonstrated a behavioural capacity for committing that type of offence. In such circumstances, evidence of prior misconduct is highly relevant because fortunately the vast majority of us are not willing to rob banks or sexually abuse others under *any* circumstances. Evidence of prior similar misconduct places the accused in the small category of individuals who have a capacity for engaging in the relevant misconduct. . . .

To assume that similar fact evidence must inevitably prejudice the jury not only accords insufficient weight to the collective intelligence of such a body, but also discounts entirely the effect of defence counsel's cross-examination as well as the trial judge's caution. . . . [S]imilar fact evidence should be *prima facie* admissible as being relevant to the *mens rea* of the offence or the identity of the culprit. . . . [T]his would represent a considerable improvement on the present approach, which demonstrates an irrational prejudice against such evidence and substantially subverts the principal aim of the criminal trial process: to identify and punish those responsible for criminal offences.

2. Requisite Proof

Before introducing evidence of uncharged misconduct by the defendant, should the prosecution be required to prove to the court's satisfaction that the misconduct actually occurred? In *Huddleston v. United States*, excerpted below, the Supreme Court held that the Federal Rules of Evidence impose no such requirement. Instead, the court need only determine that a reasonable *juror* could find, based on all evidence in the case, that the uncharged misconduct actually occurred.

When reading *Huddleston*, ask yourself the following questions. Does it make sense to allow charged misconduct to be proven with evidence of uncharged misconduct that is itself contested? And what drives the Court's analysis in *Huddleston* — the language of the rules, the legislative history, or the Court's own sense of what will tend to make trials fair?

HUDDLESTON v. UNITED STATES

485 U.S. 681 (1988)

Chief Justice REHNQUIST delivered the opinion of the Court.

. . . This case presents the question whether [under Federal Rule of Evidence 404(b)] the district court must itself make a preliminary finding that the Government has proved the "other act" by a preponderance of the evidence before it submits the evidence to the jury. We hold that it need not do so.

Petitioner, Guy Rufus Huddleston, was charged with one count of selling stolen goods in interstate commerce, 18 U.S.C. §2315, and one count of possessing stolen property in interstate commerce, 18 U.S.C. §659. The two counts related to two portions of a shipment of stolen Memorex videocassette tapes that petitioner was alleged to have possessed and sold, knowing that they were stolen.

The evidence at trial showed that a trailer containing over 32,000 blank Memorex videocassette tapes with a manufacturing cost of $4.53 per tape was stolen from the Overnight Express yard in South Holland, Illinois, sometime between April 11 and 15, 1985. On April 17, 1985, petitioner contacted Karen Curry, the manager of the Magic Rent-to-Own in Ypsilanti, Michigan, seeking her assistance in selling a large number of blank Memorex videocassette tapes. After assuring Curry that the tapes were not stolen, he told her he wished to sell them in lots of at least 500 at $2.75 to $3 per tape. Curry subsequently arranged for the sale of a total of 5,000 tapes, which petitioner delivered to the various purchasers — who apparently believed the sales were legitimate.

There was no dispute that the tapes which petitioner sold were stolen; the only material issue at trial was whether petitioner knew they were stolen. The District Court allowed the Government to introduce evidence of "similar acts" under Rule 404(b), concluding that such evidence had "clear relevance as to [petitioner's knowledge]." The first piece of similar act evidence offered by the Government was the testimony of Paul Toney, a record store owner. He testified that in February 1985, petitioner offered to sell new 12" black and white televisions for $28 apiece. According to Toney, petitioner indicated that he could obtain several thousand of these televisions. Petitioner and Toney eventually traveled to the Magic Rent-to-Own, where Toney purchased 20 of the televisions. Several days later, Toney purchased 18 more televisions.

The second piece of similar act evidence was the testimony of Robert Nelson, an undercover FBI agent posing as a buyer for an appliance store. Nelson testified that in May 1985, petitioner offered to sell him a large quantity of Amana appliances — 28 refrigerators, 2 ranges, and 40 icemakers. Nelson agreed to pay $8,000 for the appliances. Petitioner was arrested shortly after he arrived at the parking lot where he and Nelson had agreed to transfer the appliances.'A truck containing the appliances was stopped a short distance from the parking lot, and Leroy Wesby, who was driving the truck, was also arrested. It was determined that the appliances had a value of approximately $20,000 and were part of a shipment that had been stolen.

Petitioner testified that the Memorex tapes, the televisions, and the appliances had all been provided by Leroy Wesby, who had represented that all of the merchandise was obtained legitimately. Petitioner stated that he had sold 6,500 Memorex tapes for Wesby on a commission basis. Petitioner maintained that all of the sales for Wesby had been on a commission basis and that he had no knowledge that any of the goods were stolen.

In closing, the prosecution explained that petitioner was not on trial for his dealings with the appliances or the televisions. The District Court instructed the jury that the similar acts evidence was to be used only to establish petitioner's knowledge, and not to prove his character. The jury convicted petitioner on the possession count only....

Before this Court, petitioner argues that the District Court erred in admitting Toney's testimony as to petitioner's sale of the televisions.... Petitioner acknowledges that this evidence was admitted for the proper purpose of showing his knowledge that the Memorex tapes were stolen. He asserts, however, that the evidence should not have been admitted because the Government failed to prove to the District Court that the televisions were in fact stolen.

Petitioner argues from the premise that evidence of similar acts has a grave potential for causing improper prejudice. For instance, the jury may choose to punish the defendant for the similar rather than the charged act, or the jury may infer that the defendant is an evil person inclined to violate the law. Because of this danger, petitioner maintains, the jury ought not to be exposed to similar act evidence until the trial court has heard the evidence and made a determination under Federal Rule of Evidence 104(a) that the defendant committed the similar act. Rule 104(a) provides that "[p]reliminary questions concerning the qualification of a person to be a witness, the existence of a privilege, or the admissibility of evidence shall be determined by the court, subject to the provisions of subdivision (b)."According to petitioner, the trial court must make this preliminary finding by at least a preponderance of the evidence.

We reject petitioner's position, for it is inconsistent with the structure of the Rules of Evidence and with the plain language of Rule 404(b). Article IV of the Rules of Evidence deals with the relevancy of evidence. Rules 401 and 402 establish the broad principle that relevant evidence — evidence that makes the existence of any fact at issue more or less probable — is admissible unless the Rules provide otherwise. Rule 403 allows the trial judge to exclude relevant evidence if, among other things, "its probative value is substantially outweighed by the danger of unfair prejudice." Rules 404 through 412 address specific types of evidence that have generated problems. Generally, these latter

Rules do not flatly prohibit the introduction of such evidence but instead limit the purpose for which it may be introduced. Rule 404(b), for example, protects against the introduction of extrinsic act evidence when that evidence is offered solely to prove character. The text contains no intimation, however, that any preliminary showing is necessary before such evidence may be introduced for a proper purpose. If offered for such a proper purpose, the evidence is subject only to general strictures limiting admissibility such as Rules 402 and 403.

Petitioner's reading of Rule 404(b) as mandating a preliminary finding by the trial court that the act in question occurred not only superimposes a level of judicial oversight that is nowhere apparent from the language of that provision, but it is simply inconsistent with the legislative history behind Rule 404(b). The Advisory Committee specifically declined to offer any "mechanical solution" to the admission of evidence under 404(b). Advisory Committee's Notes on Fed. Rule Evid. 404(b). Rather, the Committee indicated that the trial court should assess such evidence under the usual rules for admissibility: "The determination must be made whether the danger of undue prejudice outweighs the probative value of the evidence in view of the availability of other means of proof and other factors appropriate for making decisions of this kind under Rule 403." *Ibid*; see also S. Rep. No. 93-1277, p. 25 (1974) ("[I]t is anticipated that with respect to permissible uses for such evidence, the trial judge may exclude it only on the basis of those considerations set forth in Rule 403, i.e. prejudice, confusion or waste of time").

Petitioner's suggestion that a preliminary finding is necessary to protect the defendant from the potential for unfair prejudice is also belied by the Reports of the House of Representatives and the Senate. The House made clear that the version of Rule 404(b) which became law was intended to "plac[e] greater emphasis on admissibility than did the final Court version." H.R. Rep. No. 93-650, p. 7 (1973). The Senate echoed this theme: "[T]he use of the discretionary word 'may' with respect to the admissibility of evidence of crimes, wrongs, or other acts is not intended to confer any arbitrary discretion on the trial judge." S. Rep. No. 93-1277, supra, at 24. Thus, Congress was not nearly so concerned with the potential prejudicial effect of Rule 404(b) evidence as it was with ensuring that restrictions would not be placed on the admission of such evidence.

We conclude that a preliminary finding by the court that the Government has proved the act by a preponderance of the evidence is not called for under Rule 104(a). This is not to say, however, that the Government may parade past the jury a litany of potentially prejudicial similar acts that have been established or connected to the defendant only by unsubstantiated innuendo. Evidence is admissible under Rule 404(b) only if it is relevant. . . . In the Rule 404(b) context, similar act evidence is relevant only if the jury can reasonably conclude that the act occurred and that the defendant was the actor. *See United States v. Beechum*, 582 F.2d 898, 912-913 (CA5 1978) (en banc). In the instant case, the evidence that petitioner was selling the televisions was relevant under the Government's theory only if the jury could reasonably find that the televisions were stolen.

Such questions of relevance conditioned on a fact are dealt with under Federal Rule of Evidence 104(b). Rule 104(b) provides: "When the relevancy of evidence depends upon the fulfillment of a condition of fact, the court shall admit it upon, or subject to, the introduction of evidence sufficient to support a finding of the fulfillment of the condition." In determining whether the Government has introduced sufficient evidence to meet Rule 104(b), the trial court neither weighs credibility nor makes a finding that the Government has proved the conditional fact by a preponderance of the evidence. The court simply examines all the evidence in the case and decides whether the jury could reasonably find the conditional fact — here, that the televisions were stolen — by a preponderance of the evidence. The trial court has traditionally exercised the broadest sort of discretion in controlling the order of proof at trial, and we see nothing in the Rules of Evidence that would change this practice. Often the trial court may decide to allow the proponent to introduce evidence concerning a similar act, and at a later point in the trial assess whether sufficient evidence has been offered to permit the jury to make the requisite finding. If the proponent has failed to meet this minimal standard of proof, the trial court must instruct the jury to disregard the evidence.

We emphasize that in assessing the sufficiency of the evidence under Rule 104(b), the trial court must consider all evidence presented to the jury. "[I]ndividual pieces of evidence, insufficient in themselves to prove a point, may in cumulation prove it. The sum of an evidentiary presentation may well be greater than its constituent parts." *Bourjaily v. United States*, 483 U.S. 171, 179-180 (1987). In assessing whether the evidence was sufficient to support a finding that the televisions were stolen, the court here was required to consider not only the direct evidence on that point — the low price of the televisions, the large quantity offered for sale, and petitioner's inability to produce a bill of sale — but also the evidence concerning petitioner's involvement in the sales of other stolen merchandise obtained from Wesby, such as the Memorex tapes and the Amana appliances. Given this evidence, the jury reasonably could have concluded that the televisions were stolen, and the trial court therefore properly allowed the evidence to go to the jury.

We share petitioner's concern that unduly prejudicial evidence might be introduced under Rule 404(b). See *Michelson v. United States*, 335 U.S. 469, 475-476 (1948). We think, however, that the protection against such unfair prejudice emanates not from a requirement of a preliminary finding by the trial court, but rather from four other sources: first, from the requirement of Rule 404(b) that the evidence be offered for a proper purpose; second, from the relevancy requirement of Rule 402 — as enforced through Rule 104(b); third, from the assessment the trial court must make under Rule 403 to determine whether the probative value of the similar acts evidence is substantially outweighed by its potential for unfair prejudice; and fourth, from Federal Rule of Evidence 105, which provides that the trial court shall, upon request, instruct the jury that the similar acts evidence is to be considered only for the proper purpose for which it was admitted. . . . Affirmed.

PROBLEMS

4.9. On June 30, 1915, George Joseph Smith was convicted in London of murdering Bessie Mundy. Three years earlier Mundy had married Smith (who unbeknownst to her was already married), had executed a will leaving him all her property, and then had drowned in her bath. Smith claimed the drowning had been accidental, but at trial the prosecution proved that, following Mundy's death, two other women had died in their baths after going through marriage ceremonies with Smith and making out wills in his favor. The introduction of this evidence was the principal issue on appeal:

> Mr. Marshall Hall carried the appeal before [Lord Chief] Justice Darling and his brother judges on July 29, 1915. "All I say is 'not guilty',", he told the Court. "Until the prosecution has proved this death was not by accident they cannot proceed." He contended that the evidence of the other two deaths should never have been admitted, and that without it there was not a prima facie case to go to the jury.
>
> "Why, after all, can't lawyers act as sensible people?" demanded Mr. Justice Darling. That remark was typical of him. His practical common sense cut right through legal quibbles and got down to the true basis of true justice.
>
> "It would be difficult to believe," persisted counsel, "that the same number could come up on a roulette table five times in succession, but if it happened you would not be entitled to convict the croupier as a dishonest man."
>
> "If I saw it happen," observed the Lord Chief Justice, "and the same people were at the table all the time I should grow suspicious."
>
> After the three judges had consulted together for nearly half an hour the Lord Chief Justice delivered the judgment. The Court had decided that there was a prima facie case on the death of Bessie Mundy, without taking the other deaths into account at all. Therefore, they upheld Mr. Justice Scutton's decision to admit the evidence. . . . The appeal was dismissed. George Joseph Smith was executed without having confessed on August 13, 1915.

Dudley Barker, *Lord Darling's Famous Cases* 82 (1936); *see Rex v. Smith*, 11 Crim. App. 229, 84 K.B. 2153, [1914-1915] All E.R. 262 (1915).

Would the evidence of the other deaths be admissible under the Federal Rules of Evidence? What if without that evidence there was no prima facie case — i.e., what if the proof regarding Mundy's death, standing alone, would not allow a rational jury to find Smith guilty of murder?

4.10. A Nevada jury found Horace Tucker guilty of murdering Omar Evans, who was found shot to death on Tucker's couch in October 1963. Tucker claimed that he fell asleep and woke up to find Evans dead. At trial the prosecution proved that in 1957 another man, Earl Kaylor, had been found shot to death on Tucker's floor; on that occasion, too, Tucker claimed that he had been sleeping and awoke to find the corpse. Both times Tucker appeared to the police to have been drinking. The Nevada Supreme Court reversed Tucker's conviction, ruling that the trial judge should have excluded evidence of the 1957 death:

> There is nothing in this record to establish that Tucker killed Kaylor. Anonymous crimes can have no relevance in deciding whether the defendant committed the crime with which he is charged. Kaylor's assailant remains unknown. A fortiori, evidence of that crime cannot be received in the trial for the murder of Evans. . . . Here there was only conjecture and suspicion, aroused by the fact that Kaylor was found dead in Tucker's home. . . . [B]efore evidence of a collateral offense is admissible for any purpose, the prosecution must first establish by plain, clear and convincing evidence, that the defendant committed that offense. . . . Fundamental fairness demands this standard in order to preclude verdicts which might otherwise rest on false assumptions.

Tucker v. State, 412 P.2d 970, 972 (Nev. 1966). Would the result be the same under the Federal Rules of Evidence?

D. CHARACTER AND HABIT

Although evidence of character generally is *not* admissible to prove conduct in conformity with character on a particular occasion, evidence of habit *is* admissible to prove conduct in conformity with habit on a particular occasion. The habit rule gives rise to two mysteries: where the line is drawn between habit and character, and why the two are treated so differently.

[F.R.E. 406; C.E.C. §§1104–1105]

ADVISORY COMMITTEE NOTE TO F.R.E. 406

An oft-quoted paragraph, McCormick, §162, p. 340, describes habit in terms effectively contrasting it with character. "Character and habit are close akin. Character is a generalized description of one's disposition, or of one's disposition in respect to a general trait, such as honesty, temperance, or peacefulness. 'Habit,' in modern usage, both lay and psychological, is more specific. It describes one's regular response to a repeated specific situation. If we speak of character for care, we think of the person's tendency to act prudently in all the varying situations of life, in business, family life, in handling automobiles and in walking across the street. A habit, on the other hand, is the person's regular practice of meeting a particular kind of situation with a specific type of conduct, such as the habit of going down a particular stairway two stairs at a time, or of giving the hand-signal for a left turn, or of alighting from railway cars while they are moving. The doing of the habitual acts may become semi-automatic."

Equivalent behavior on the part of a group is designated "routine practice of an organization" in the rule.

Agreement is general that habit evidence is highly persuasive as proof of conduct on a particular occasion. Again quoting McCormick §162, p. 341: "Character may be thought of as the sum of one's habits though doubtless it is more than this. But unquestionably the uniformity of one's response to habit is far greater than the consistency with which one's conduct conforms to character or disposition. Even though character comes in only exceptionally as evidence of an act, surely any sensible man in investigating whether X did a particular act would be greatly helped in his inquiry by evidence as to whether he was in the habit of doing it."

When disagreement has appeared, its focus has been upon the question what constitutes habit, and the reason for this is readily apparent. The extent to which instances must be multiplied and consistency of behavior maintained in order to rise to the status of habit inevitably gives rise to differences of opinion. While adequacy of sampling and uniformity of response are key factors, precise standards for measuring their sufficiency for evidence purposes cannot be formulated.

The rule is consistent with prevailing views. Much evidence is excluded simply because of failure to achieve the status of habit. Thus, evidence of intemperate "habits" is generally excluded when offered as proof of drunkenness in accident cases, Annot., 46 A.L.R.2d 103, and evidence of other assaults is inadmissible to prove the instant one in a civil assault action, Annot., 66 A.L.R.2d 806. In Levin v. United States, 119 U.S. App. D.C. 156, 338 F.2d 265 (1964), testimony as to the religious "habits" of the accused, offered as tending to prove that he was at home observing the Sabbath rather than out obtaining money through larceny by trick, was held properly excluded: "It seems apparent to us that an individual's religious practices would not be the type of activities which would lend themselves to the characterization of 'invariable regularity.' [1 Wigmore 520.] Certainly the very volitional basis of the activity raises serious questions as to its invariable nature, and hence its probative value."

These rulings are not inconsistent with the trend towards admitting evidence of business transactions between one of the parties and a third person as tending to prove that he made the same bargain or proposal in the litigated situation. Nor are they inconsistent with such cases as Whittemore v. Lockheed Aircraft Corp., 65 Cal. App. 2d 737, 151 P.2d 670 (1944), upholding the admission of evidence that plaintiff's intestate had on four other occasions flown planes from defendant's factory for delivery to his employer airline, offered to prove that he was piloting rather than a guest on a plane which crashed and killed all on board while en route for delivery. . . .

REPORT OF THE HOUSE JUDICIARY COMMITTEE

Rule 406 as submitted to Congress contained a subdivision (b) providing that the method of proof of habit or routine practice could be "in the form of an opinion or by specific instances of conduct sufficient in number to warrant a finding that the habit existed or that the practice was routine." The Committee deleted this subdivision believing that that the method of proof of habit and routine practice should be left to the courts to deal with on a case-by-case basis. At the same time, the Committee does not intend that its action be construed as sanctioning a general authorization of opinion evidence in this area.

KORNBERG v. UNITED STATES

693 Fed. Appx. 542 (9th Cir. 2017)

MEMORANDUM

Plaintiff Melvin Kornberg appeals from the district court's judgment in favor of Defendant, the United States of America, following a bench trial. Plaintiff underwent a left-ear stapedectomy [at a Veterans Administration hospital] in an attempt to improve his hearing. Plaintiff's left chorda tympani nerve was damaged during procedure, leading to a partial loss of his sense of taste. Plaintiff claims that he was not given sufficient information about the risks of the stapedectomy to allow him to give informed consent to the operation. . . . [On appeal he] argues that the district court erred by admitting evidence of the regular practices and routines of two of the doctors who treated Plaintiff and of the medical center at which Plaintiff received treatment. The district court reasoned that the habit-and-routine evidence tended to show that the doctors and the medical center had provided sufficient information to Plaintiff. The court noted that it was considering the evidence "under [Rule] 406" of the Federal Rules of Evidence, which allows the admission of "[e]vidence of a person's habit or an organization's routine practice . . . to prove that on a particular occasion the person or organization acted in accordance with the habit or routine practice." Plaintiff did not object to the admission of this evidence at trial, so we review for plain error. We find no plain error. The doctors testified that it was their regular practice to go over the risks of surgery with patients at preoperative visits, and Plaintiff had such a visit with the doctors four days before his surgery. One of the doctors testified that she performed approximately 40 stapedectomies during her six years of residency, and that in each preoperative visit with a stapedectomy patient she "absolutely" went over the risk of damage to the chorda tympani nerve. The doctors' testimony concerning their typical practices was the type of testimony that can be admitted under Rule 406. . . . [Affirmed.]

ORTIZ v. CITY OF NEW YORK

No. 15CV2206(DLC) (S.D.N.Y. 2017)

COTE, United States District Judge.

The parties seek guidance in advance of this 42 U.S.C. §1983 trial on the extent to which medical records reflecting the plaintiff's hospitalization for intoxication will be admissible. It is undisputed that on June 1, 2014—the date of the incident at issue—the defendant police officers had the plaintiff taken by ambulance to a hospital and that the hospital recorded that the plaintiff was intoxicated, combative, and violent. The plaintiff asserts that he was not incapacitated by alcohol consumption on that day, and that the police had wrongfully assaulted and seized him. The defendants assert that the plaintiff was intoxicated and combative, and deny that they assaulted him.

The defendants have submitted the plaintiff's medical records for the date of the incident and two follow-up visits. They have also submitted medical records for one earlier date and three later dates which reflect treatment of the plaintiff for intoxication. . . . The defendants seek to admit the medical records to show the plaintiff's chronic alcohol abuse. They contend evidence of his alcohol abuse is relevant to the jury's evaluation not only of his conduct on June 1, 2014, when he interacted with the defendants, but also to his claim for damages, his credibility, and his ability to perceive and recall events. They assert as well that the records prior to June 1, 2014, are admissible as similar act evidence pursuant to Fed. R. Evid. 404(b) to demonstrate the plaintiff's knowledge of his dangerous conduct when intoxicated. They also contend that the entire set of records is admissible as habit evidence, to show that the plaintiff has a habit of drinking to the point that he is combative, incoherent and requires hospitalization....

The difference between character and habit evidence has been described as follows:

> The two are easily confused. People sometimes speak of a habit for care, a habit for promptness, or a habit of forgetfulness. They may say that an individual has a bad habit of stealing or lying. Evidence of these "habits" would be identical to the kind of evidence that is the target of the generalized rule against character evidence. Character is a generalized description of a person's disposition, or of the disposition in respect to a general trait, such as honesty, temperance or peacefulness, that usually is regarded as meriting approval or disapproval. Habit, in the present context, is more specific. It denotes one's regular response to a repeated situation. If we speak of a character for care, we think of the person's tendency to act prudently in all the varying situations of life — in business, at home, in handling automobiles and in walking across the street. A habit, on the other hand, is the person's regular practice of conduct. Thus, a person may be in the habit of bounding down a certain stairway two or three steps at a time, of patronizing a particular pub after each day's work, or of driving his automobile without a seatbelt. The doing of the habitual act may become semi-automatic, as with a driver who invariably signals before changing lanes.

1 McCormick On Evid. §195 (7th ed. 2013) (emphasis supplied). "Much evidence is excluded simply because of failure to achieve the status of habit. Thus, evidence of intemperate 'habits' is generally excluded when offered as proof of drunkenness in accident cases." Fed. R. Evid. 406 Advisory Committee's Note to 1972 Proposed Rules....

The Fifth Circuit has approved exclusion of evidence of four prior convictions for public intoxication over the course of three and one-half years when it is "clear that the [defendant] intended for the [plaintiff's] prior convictions to show that he was intoxicated on the night of the accident." *Reyes v. Missouri Pac. R. Co.*, 589 F.2d 791, 794 (5th Cir. 1979). On the other hand, the Eleventh Circuit approved use of anecdotal and reputation evidence of an employee's prior intoxication over the course of six years under Rule 406 to demonstrate a "uniform pattern of behavior" of carrying and consuming alcohol while on the job. *Loughan v. Firestone Tire & Rubber Co.*, 749 F.2d 1519, 1523 (11th Cir. 1985).

While discussions of the admissibility of evidence of alcohol abuse and alcoholism have existed mainly in the context of character and habit evidence, there is reason for courts to understand alcoholism outside these bounds. Today, alcoholism is considered as much a disease as a reflection of character or habit.... Viewed in this light, expert testimony regarding a witness's addiction to alcohol or medical records pertaining to a party's alcoholism may be admissible if the presence of the addiction is relevant to the issues at trial. For instance, in *Halvorsen v. Baird*, 146 F.3d 680 (9th Cir. 1998), the plaintiff disputed that he was intoxicated at the time of the events at issue. The Ninth Circuit held that a trial judge was "within his discretion in admitting" expert testimony that relied on information that the plaintiff had been admitted to a detox facility twice in the previous two years to support the point that a "typical characteristic of alcoholics is denial that they have been drinking when they plainly have."

. . . The June 1 and 2, 2014 medical records, and those records for the two follow-up treatments are largely admissible. Judgment is reserved on the admissibility of the remaining medical records.

THOMAS M. MENGLER, THE THEORY OF DISCRETION IN THE FEDERAL RULES OF EVIDENCE

74 Iowa L. Rev. 413, 417, 423–424 (1989)

Rule 406 . . . exemplifies well the drafters' conscious decision to provide trial courts with maneuvering room. . . . [A]t least regarding those rules designed to balance an item's probative value against its potentially harmful effects, the Federal Rules are misnamed. The drafters of the Federal Rules did not consider them as rigid rules to be mechanically applied, but rather as flexible principles for both trial and appellate courts.

The Committee's Note to Rule 406 contains two analytically distinct understandings of habit. The first understanding — described by some as the "psychological theory" — focuses on the nonvolitional or semiautomatic nature of a habit. The second understanding — which has been labeled the "probability theory" — focuses entirely on a person's regular response to a specific situation.

Regularity in responding to a specific situation is a requirement not only of the probability theory, but also of the psychological theory. In order for a response to be considered semiautomatic, it must uniformly follow a stimulus. But uniformity is just one aspect of the psychological theory. The other feature is that the individual's response must be unconsciously mechanical — Pavlovian. Thus, on this psychological theory, the routine practice of reading a novel before going to bed, while customary, could not be habitual because it is volitional. In contrast, the regular practice of turning the pages of the novel with one's left hand could be habitual because of its mechanical or automatic nature. . . .

[T]he Committee advanced two theories, not because of entrenched disagreement or indecision among Committee members, but from a deliberate design to build flexibility into the Federal Rules of Evidence. The Committee's primary reason for advancing two theories of habit was to promote trial court discretion. . . . The drafters, in effect, provided flexibility within the parameters of the Rule itself. For example, presented with evidence that a litigant regularly reads mystery novels before going to bed to prove the litigant was doing so on the night in question, a trial court either could exclude it under the psychological theory, since reading is volitional, or admit it under the probability theory, since the litigant's behavior was specific and sufficiently regular.

PROBLEM

4.11. Stan is being prosecuted for perjury. In her case in chief, the prosecutor seeks to introduce evidence from Stan's former employer that Stan "has a habit of telling lies whenever the truth seems inconvenient." Stan objects. Is the testimony admissible? Would the answer be different if the prosecutor sought to prove the habit by introducing specific examples of lies that Stan told his employer?

E. SEXUAL ASSAULT AND CHILD MOLESTATION

The character evidence rule and its exceptions used to take the same general shape in cases of sexual assault and child molestation as in other cases: The character of a criminal defendant was off-limits unless and until the defendant chose to make it admissible, and the defendant also had the option to make evidence of the victim's character admissible. But the rules no longer work this way in sex offense cases.

The first rules to change were those pertaining to evidence of the victim's character. "Rape shield statutes," adopted at the federal level and by most states in the 1970s, significantly curtail the ability of defendants in rape cases to offer evidence of the victim's character in an effort to prove consent on a particular occasion. These statutes responded to widespread perceptions that the admissibility of such evidence unduly harassed rape victims, discouraged victims from reporting rapes, and tended to be greatly overvalued by juries.

More recently, the Federal Rules of Evidence and some state codes have been amended to allow prosecutors and plaintiffs in cases of sexual assault and child molestation to offer evidence of the defendant's character in the case-in-chief, to prove propensity. Again, the amendments respond to perceived differences between cases of this kind and other cases. These new amendments remain highly controversial, for reasons that the readings below will make clear.

1. Character of the Victim

Evidence of the victim's character, and specifically a victim's chastity or lack thereof, used to be a staple of rape trials, in a way that was wholly unparalleled in other criminal prosecutions. As the older materials excerpted suggest, courts and commentators deemed such evidence highly probative on the question of consent, and sometimes admitted it even when consent was not at issue. These materials also suggest the reasons that evidence of a rape victim's sexual history was, and remains, so problematic. Juries — as well as judges and commentators — were apt to overvalue the evidence, treating it as more probative of consent than it actually was. What is more, the evidence was apt to be misused — treated as grounds for not worrying much about the rape, even if it did occur. Then, too, the admissibility of such evidence tended to transform rape trials into trials of victims, brutalizing them and powerfully discouraging other rape victims from coming forward.

Growing recognition of these problems eventually led, in the 1970s, to the widespread adoption of "rape shield statutes" in most states and at the federal level. The terms of these laws vary widely, but broadly speaking they ban the use of character evidence to prove the victim's consent. F.R.E. 412 is the federal version.

[F.R.E. 412; C.E.C. §§1103(c), 1106]

JOHN HENRY WIGMORE, A TREATISE ON THE ANGLO-AMERICAN SYSTEM OF EVIDENCE IN TRIALS AT COMMON LAW

§62, at 1:279–282 (2d ed. 1923)

The reasons of Auxiliary Policy which affect the use of a defendant's character by the prosecution are peculiar to that use, and do not affect the use of character *as against other persons* in a criminal case wherever it may be relevant.

One of those relevant uses is that of the character of a *rape-complainant* for chastity. The non-consent of the complainant is here a material element; and the character of the woman as to chastity is of considerable probative value in judging the likelihood of that consent: . . .

> 1856, Isham, J., in *State v. Johnson*, 28 Vt. 514: "In all cases of this character, the assent of the witness to the act is the material matter in issue, and on that question the defense generally rests on circumstantial testimony. In determining that question, which is purely a mental act, it is important to ascertain whether her consent would from her previous habits be the natural result of her mind, of whether it would be inconsistent with her previous life and repugnant to all her moral feelings. Such habits as are imputed to the witness by this inquiry have a tendency to show consent as the natural operation of her propensities, and rebut the inference or necessity of actual violence."
>
> 1895, Garoutte, J., in *People v. Johnson*, 106 Cal. 289: "This class of evidence is admissible for the purpose of tending to show the non-probability of resistance upon the part of the prosecutrix; for it is certainly more probable that a woman who has done these things voluntarily in the past would be much more likely to consent than one whose past reputation was without blemish, and whose general conduct could not truthfully be assailed. In other words, this class of evidence goes to the question of consent only."

The admissibility, on a *rape* charge, of the complainant's *character for chastity or unchastity* is generally conceded; and her *habits as a prostitute* are usually regarded as equivalent to a general trait of character. . . . The only difficulty in applying the principle is to distinguish between the use of Character, as bearing on consent, and the use of *specific acts of unchastity* as a means of evidencing the character itself. The latter kind of evidence being in many jurisdictions excluded, the woman's character as evidenced by reputation is alone admissible in those jurisdictions. . . .

GRAHAM v. STATE

67 S.W.2d 296 (Tex. Crim. App. 1933)

CHRISTIAN, J.

The offense is rape by force; the punishment, confinement in the penitentiary for fifty years. . . . [Appellant sought unsuccessfully to introduce testimony] that the general reputation of the prosecutrix for chastity was bad . . . [and] that prosecutrix habitually spent the night in her apartment with various men.

. . . Appellant having expressly declared that he did not have an act of intercourse with prosecutrix, there was no issue as to consent. Hence the general rule that, on the issue of consent, proof is admissible that prosecutrix' general reputation for chastity was bad, and that she had engaged in previous acts of intercourse with the accused, would have no application. . . . [But] it occurs to us that proof that prosecutrix bore the general reputation of being unchaste and had habitually engaged in acts of sexual intercourse with others was admissible as shedding light on the transaction. In its absence, it would appear that appellant's version of the transaction might be deemed incredible; whereas, if the jury had had such proof before them, the conclusion might have been reached that the condition of the prosecutrix resulted from a fight in which she was the aggressor. In other words, the jury might have concluded that she sought to bestow carnal favors, which were rejected, and that, as a result, a fight ensued in which she received the injuries described in the testimony. . . . The judgment is reversed, and the cause remanded.

REMARKS OF REP. ELIZABETH HOLTZMAN

124 Cong. Rec. H 11944 (Oct. 10, 1978)

[Representative Holtzman was the principal sponsor of H.R. 4727, which added Rule 412 to the Federal Rules of Evidence.]

Ms. HOLTZMAN. . . . Too often in this country victims of rape are humiliated and harassed when they report and prosecute the rape. Bullied and cross-examined about their prior sexual experiences, many find the trial almost as degrading as the rape itself. Since rape trials become inquisitions into the victim's morality, not trials of the defendant's innocence or guilt, it is not surprising that it is the least reported crime. It is estimated that as few as one in ten rapes is ever reported.

Mr. Speaker, over 30 States have taken some action to limit the vulnerability of rape victims to such humiliating cross-examination of their past sexual experiences and intimate personal histories. In federal courts, however, it is permissible still to subject rape victims to brutal cross-examination about their past sexual histories. H.R. 4727 would rectify this problem in Federal courts and I hope, also serve as a model to suggest to the remaining states that reform of existing rape laws is important to the equity of our criminal justice system. . . . It will protect women from both injustice and indignity.

ADVISORY COMMITTEE NOTE TO 1994 AMENDMENTS
TO F.R.E. 412

Rule 412 has been revised to diminish some of the confusion engendered by the original rule and to expand the protection afforded alleged victims of sexual misconduct. Rule 412 applies to both civil and criminal proceedings. The rule aims to safeguard the alleged victim against the invasion of privacy, potential embarrassment and sexual stereotyping that is associated with public disclosure of intimate sexual details and the infusion of sexual innuendo into the factfinding process. By affording victims protection in most instances, the rule also encourages victims of sexual misconduct to institute and to participate in legal proceedings against alleged offenders.

Rule 412 seeks to achieve these objectives by barring evidence relating to the alleged victim's sexual behavior or alleged sexual predisposition, whether offered as substantive evidence or for impeachment, except in designated circumstances in which the probative value of the evidence significantly outweighs possible harm to the victim.

The revised rule applies in all cases involving sexual misconduct without regard to whether the alleged victim or person accused is a party to the litigation. Rule 412 extends to "pattern" witnesses in both criminal and civil cases whose testimony about other instances of sexual misconduct by the person accused is otherwise admissible. When the case does not involve alleged sexual misconduct, evidence relating to a third-party witness' alleged sexual activities is not within the ambit of Rule 412. The witness will, however, be protected by other rules such as Rules 404 and 608, as well as Rule 403.

The terminology "alleged victim" is used because there will frequently be a factual dispute as to whether sexual misconduct occurred. It does not connote any requirement that the misconduct be alleged in the pleadings. Rule 412 does not, however, apply unless the person against whom the evidence is offered can reasonably be characterized as a "victim of alleged sexual misconduct." When this is not the case, as for instance in a defamation action involving statements concerning sexual misconduct in which the evidence is offered to show that the alleged defamatory statements were true or did not damage the plaintiff's reputation, neither Rule 404 nor this rule will operate to bar the evidence; Rules 401 and 403 will continue to control. Rule 412 will, however, apply in a Title VII action in which the plaintiff has alleged sexual harassment.

The reference to a person "accused" is also used in a non-technical sense. There is no requirement that there be a criminal charge pending against the person or even that the misconduct would constitute a criminal offense. Evidence offered to prove allegedly false prior claims by the victim is not barred by Rule 412. However, the evidence is subject to the requirements of Rule 404.

. . . Past sexual behavior connotes all activities that involve actual physical conduct, i.e. sexual intercourse or sexual contact. *See, e.g., United States v. Galloway*, 937 F.2d 542 (10th Cir. 1991), *cert. denied*, 113 S. Ct. 418 (1992) (use of contraceptives inadmissible since use implies sexual activity); *United States v. One Feather*, 702 F.2d 736 (8th Cir. 1983) (birth of an illegitimate child inadmissible); *State v. Carmichael*, 727 P.2d 918, 925 (Kan. 1986) (evidence of venereal disease inadmissible). In addition, the word "behavior" should be construed to include activities of the mind, such as fantasies or dreams. *See* 23C. Wright and K. Graham, Jr., Federal Practice and Procedure, §5384 at p. 548 (1980) ("While there may be some doubt under statutes that require 'conduct,' it would seem that the language of Rule 412 is broad enough to encompass the behavior of the mind.").

The rule has been amended to also exclude all other evidence relating to an alleged victim of sexual misconduct that is offered to prove a sexual predisposition. This amendment is designed to exclude evidence that does not directly refer to sexual activities or thoughts but that the proponent believes may have a sexual connotation for the factfinder. Admission of such evidence would contravene Rule 412's objectives of shielding the alleged victim from potential embarrassment and safeguarding the victim against stereotypical thinking. Consequently, unless the (b)(2) exception is satisfied, evidence such as that relating to the alleged victim's mode of dress, speech, or life-style will not be admissible.

. . . The reason for extending the rule to all criminal cases is obvious. The strong social policy of protecting a victim's privacy and encouraging victims to come forward to report criminal acts is not confined to cases that involve a charge of sexual assault. The need to protect the victim is equally great when a defendant is charged with kidnapping, and evidence is offered, either to prove motive or as background, that the defendant sexually assaulted the victim.

The reason for extending Rule 412 to civil cases is equally obvious. The need to protect alleged victims against invasions of privacy, potential embarrassment, and unwarranted sexual stereotyping, and the wish to encourage victims to come forward when they have been sexually molested do not disappear because the context has shifted from a criminal prosecution to a claim for damages or injunctive relief. There is a strong social policy in not only punishing those who engage in sexual misconduct, but in also providing relief to the victim. Thus, Rule 412 applies in any civil case in which a person claims to be the victim of sexual misconduct, such as actions for sexual battery or sexual harassment.

. . . Subdivision (b)(2) governs the admissibility of otherwise proscribed evidence in civil cases. It employs a balancing test rather than the specific exceptions stated in subdivision (b)(1) in recognition of the difficulty of foreseeing future developments in the law. Greater flexibility is needed to accommodate evolving causes of action such as claims for sexual harassment.

The balancing test requires the proponent of the evidence, whether plaintiff or defendant, to convince the court that the probative value of the proffered evidence "substantially outweighs the danger of harm to any victim and of unfair prejudice of any party." This test for admitting evidence offered to prove sexual behavior or sexual propensity in civil cases differs in three respects from the general rule governing admissibility set forth in Rule 403. First, it reverses that usual procedure spelled out in Rule 403 by shifting the burden to the proponent to demonstrate admissibility rather than making the opponent justify exclusion of the evidence. Second, the standard expressed in subdivision (b)(2) is more stringent than in the original rule; it raises the threshold for admission by requiring that the probative value of the evidence substantially outweigh the specified dangers. Finally, the Rule 412 test puts "harm to the victim" on the scale in addition to prejudice to the parties. . . .

OLDEN v. KENTUCKY

488 U.S. 227 (1988)

PER CURIAM.

Petitioner James Olden and his friend Charlie Ray Harris, both of whom are black, were indicted for kidnapping, rape, and forcible sodomy. The victim of the alleged crimes, Starla Matthews, a young white woman, gave the following account at trial: She and a friend, Regina Patton, had driven to Princeton, Kentucky, to exchange Christmas gifts with Bill Russell, petitioner's half brother. After meeting Russell at a local car wash and exchanging presents with him, Matthews and Patton stopped in J.R's, a "boot-legging joint" serving a predominantly black clientele, to use the restroom. Matthews consumed several glasses of beer. As the bar became more crowded, she became increasingly nervous because she and Patton were the only white people there. When Patton refused to leave, Matthews sat at a separate table, hoping to demonstrate to her friend that she was upset. As time passed, however, Matthews lost track of Patton and became somewhat intoxicated. When petitioner told her that Patton had departed and had been in a car accident, she left the bar with petitioner and Harris to find out what had happened. She was driven in Harris' car to another location, where, threatening her with a knife, petitioner raped and sodomized her. Harris assisted by holding her arms. Later, she was driven to a dump, where two other men joined the group. There, petitioner raped her once again. At her request, the men then dropped her off in the vicinity of Bill Russell's house.

On cross-examination, petitioner's counsel focused on a number of inconsistencies in Matthews' various accounts of the alleged crime. Matthews originally told the police that she had been raped by four men. Later, she claimed that she had been raped by only petitioner and Harris. At trial, she contended that petitioner was the sole rapist. Further, while Matthews testified at trial that petitioner had threatened her with a knife, she had not previously alleged that petitioner had been armed.

Russell, who also appeared as a State's witness, testified that on the evening in question he heard a noise outside his home and, when he went out to investigate, saw Matthews get out of Harris' car. Matthews immediately told Russell that she had just been raped by petitioner and Harris.

Petitioner and Harris asserted a defense of consent. According to their testimony, Matthews propositioned petitioner as he was about to leave the bar, and the two engaged in sexual acts behind the tavern. Afterwards, on Matthews' suggestion, Matthews, petitioner, and Harris left in Harris' car in search of cocaine. When they discovered that the seller was not at home, Matthews asked Harris to drive to a local dump so that she and petitioner could have sex once again. Harris complied. Later that evening, they picked up two other men, Richard Hickey and Chris Taylor, and drove to an establishment called The Alley. Harris, Taylor, and Hickey went in, leaving petitioner and Matthews in the car. When Hickey and Harris returned, the men gave Hickey a ride to a store and then dropped Matthews off, at her request, in the vicinity of Bill Russell's home.

Taylor and Hickey testified for the defense and corroborated the defendants' account of the evening. While both acknowledged that they joined the group later than the time when the alleged rape occurred, both testified that Matthews did not appear upset. Hickey further testified that Matthews had approached him earlier in the evening at J.R.'s and told him that she was looking for a black man with whom to have sex. An independent witness also appeared for the defense and testified that he had seen Matthews, Harris, and petitioner at a store called Big O's on the evening in question, that a policeman was in the store at the time, and that Matthews, who appeared alert, made no attempt to signal for assistance.

Although Matthews and Russell were both married to and living with other people at the time of the incident, they were apparently involved in an extramarital relationship. By the time of trial the two were living together, having separated from their respective spouses. Petitioner's theory of the case was that Matthews concocted the rape story to protect her relationship with Russell, who would have grown suspicious upon seeing her disembark from Harris' car. In order to demonstrate Matthew's motive to lie, it was crucial, petitioner contended, that he be allowed to introduce evidence of Matthew's and Russell's current cohabitation. Over petitioner's vehement objections, the trial court nonetheless granted the prosecutor's motion in limine to keep all evidence of Matthews' and Russell's living arrangement from the jury. Moreover, when the defense attempted to cross-examine Matthews about her living arrangements, after she had claimed during direct examination that she was living with her mother, the trial court sustained the prosecutor's objection.

Based on the evidence admitted at trial, the jury acquitted Harris of being either a principal or an accomplice to any of the charged offenses. Petitioner was likewise acquitted of kidnaping and rape. However, in a somewhat puzzling turn of events, the jury convicted petitioner alone of forcible sodomy. He was sentenced to 10 years' imprisonment.

Petitioner appealed, asserting, inter alia, that the trial court's refusal to allow him to impeach Matthews' testimony by introducing evidence supporting a motive to lie deprived him of his Sixth Amendment right to confront witnesses against him. The Kentucky Court of Appeals upheld the conviction. The court specifically held that evidence that Matthews and Russell were living together at the time of trial was not barred by the State's rape shield law. Moreover, it acknowledged that the evidence in question was relevant to petitioner's theory of the case. But it held, nonetheless, that the evidence was properly excluded as "its probative value [was] outweighed by its possibility for prejudice." By way of explanation, the court stated: "[T]here were the undisputed facts of race; Matthews was white and Russell was black. For the trial court to have admitted into evidence testimony that Matthews and Russell were living together at the time of the trial may have created extreme prejudice against Matthews." Judge Clayton, who dissented but did not address the evidentiary issue, would have reversed petitioner's conviction both because he believed the jury's verdicts were "manifestly inconsistent," and because he found Matthews' testimony too incredible to provide evidence sufficient to uphold the verdict.

The Kentucky Court of Appeals failed to accord proper weight to petitioner's Sixth Amendment right "to be confronted with the witnesses against him." That right, incorporated in the Fourteenth Amendment and therefore available in state proceedings, *Pointer v. Texas*, 380 U.S. 400 (1965), includes the right to conduct reasonable cross-examination. *Davis v. Alaska*, 415 U.S. 308, 315–316 (1974).

In *Davis v. Alaska*, we observed that, subject to "the broad discretion of a trial judge to preclude repetitive and unduly harassing interrogation ..., the cross-examiner has traditionally been allowed to impeach, i.e., discredit, the witness." We emphasized that "the exposure of a witness' motivation in testifying is a proper and important function of the constitutionally protected right of cross-examination." Recently, in *Delaware v. Van Arsdall*, 475 U.S. 673 (1986), we reaffirmed *Davis*, and held that "a criminal defendant states a violation of the Confrontation Clause by showing that he was prohibited from engaging in otherwise appropriate cross-examination designed to show a prototypical form of bias on the part of the witness, and thereby 'to expose to the jury the facts from which jurors ... could appropriately draw inferences relating to the reliability of the witness.'" 475 U.S., at 680, *quoting Davis, supra*, 415 U.S., at 318.

In the instant case, petitioner has consistently asserted that he and Matthews engaged in consensual sexual acts and that Matthews — out of fear of jeopardizing her relationship with Russell — lied when she told Russell she had been raped and has continued to lie since. It is plain to us that "[a] reasonable jury might have received a significantly different impression of [the witness'] credibility had [defense counsel] been permitted to pursue his proposed line of cross-examination." *Delaware v. Van Arsdall, supra*, 475 U.S., at 680.

The Kentucky Court of Appeals did not dispute, and indeed acknowledged, the relevance of the impeachment evidence. Nonetheless, without acknowledging the significance of, or even adverting to, petitioner's constitutional right to confrontation, the court held that petitioner's right to effective cross-examination was outweighed by the danger that revealing Matthews' interracial relationship would prejudice the jury against her. While a trial court may, of course, impose reasonable limits on defense counsel's inquiry into the potential bias of a prosecution witness, to take account of such factors as "harassment, prejudice, confusion of the issues, the witness' safety, or interrogation that [would be] repetitive or only marginally relevant," *Delaware v. Van Arsdall, supra*, at 679, the limitation here was beyond reason. Speculation as to the effect of jurors' racial biases cannot justify exclusion of cross-examination with such strong potential to demonstrate the falsity of Matthews' testimony.

In *Delaware v. Van Arsdall, supra*, we held that "the constitutionally improper denial of a defendant's opportunity to impeach a witness for bias, like other Confrontation Clause errors, is subject to *Chapman* [*v. California*, 386 U.S. 18 (1967)] harmless-error analysis." Thus we stated: "The correct inquiry is whether, assuming that the damaging potential of the cross-examination were fully realized, a reviewing court might nonetheless say that the error was harmless beyond a reasonable doubt. Whether such an error is harmless in a particular case depends upon a host of factors, all readily accessible to reviewing courts. These factors include the importance of the witness' testimony in the prosecution's case, whether the testimony was cumulative, the presence or absence of evidence corroborating or contradicting the testimony of the witness on material points, the extent of cross-examination otherwise permitted, and, of course, the overall strength of the prosecution's case."

Here, Matthews' testimony was central, indeed crucial, to the prosecution's case. Her story, which was directly contradicted by that of petitioner and Harris, was corroborated only by the largely derivative testimony of Russell, whose impartiality would also have been somewhat impugned by revelation of his relationship with Matthews. Finally, as demonstrated graphically by the jury's verdicts, which cannot be squared with the State's theory of the alleged crime, and by Judge Clayton's dissenting opinion below, the State's case against petitioner was far from overwhelming. In sum, considering the relevant *Van Arsdall* factors within the context of this case, we find it impossible to conclude "beyond a reasonable doubt" that the restriction on petitioner's right to confrontation was harmless.

The motion for leave to proceed in forma pauperis and the petition for certiorari are granted, the judgment of the Kentucky Court of Appeals is reversed, and the case is remanded for further proceedings not inconsistent with this opinion.

It is so ordered.

[Justice Marshall filed a dissenting opinion, objecting on procedural grounds to the Court's summary disposition of the case without oral argument.]

UNITED STATES v. WILLIS

826 F.3d 1265 (10th Cir. 2016)

McHugh, Circuit Judge.

Appellant Ivan Bennett Willis was charged with aggravated sexual abuse committed in Indian country. Mr. Willis admitted he had sex with a seventeen-year-old acquaintance, K.M., and that the events occurred in Indian country. But Mr. Willis maintained that K.M. consented to the encounter. Thus, the only issue at trial was whether Mr. Willis used force against K.M. After a two-day trial, the jury returned a guilty verdict. . . .

Throughout the summer and fall of 2013, K.M. lived with her cousin, Jamee Black, and Ms. Black's boyfriend, Wesley Bear. On the evening of [the alleged offense], K.M. was babysitting the couple's two children while Mr. Bear and Ms. Black were working. . . .

The district court . . . denied Mr. Willis's pretrial motion to admit evidence of K.M.'s sexual behavior. We review this determination for abuse of discretion. . . .

In sexual-offense cases, evidence of the victim's sexual behavior is generally inadmissible. Fed. R. Evid. 412(a). But an exception allows "evidence of specific instances of a victim's sexual behavior, if offered to prove that someone other than the defendant was the source of semen, injury, or other physical evidence." *Id.* R. 412(b)(1)(A). This exception applies "[w]here the prosecution has directly or indirectly asserted that the physical evidence originated with the accused." *Id.* R. 412 advisory committee's note to 1994 amendment.

Mr. Willis asserts the district court erred in excluding evidence that K.M. had sex with her boyfriend at the Bear/Black residence before her encounter with Mr. Willis. Specifically, Mr. Willis moved to introduce the report from K.M.'s sexual-assault examination, which showed that semen in K.M.'s underwear matched DNA samples from both Mr. Willis and K.M.'s boyfriend. According to Mr. Willis, this evidence established K.M.'s motive to lie: she did not want her boyfriend to know she had sex with Mr. Willis, and she did not want Mr. Bear and Ms. Black to know she had been having sex in their house while their children were present.

Mr. Willis's argument fails for several reasons. First, this is not a case where the government sought to prove the charges against Mr. Willis by showing that physical evidence originated exclusively with him. Consequently, Mr. Willis's reliance on our decision in *United States v. Begay*, 937 F.2d 515 (10th Cir. 1991), is misplaced. There, we reversed the defendant's conviction and remanded for a new trial because the district court had excluded evidence of past sexual assaults against the child-victim that was directly relevant to the source of physical evidence. We concluded the evidence should have been admitted to fully explain the victim's physical injuries and to support the defense theory that the injuries were caused by a previous assailant rather than by the defendant, who denied having any sexual contact with the victim. The same rationale does not apply here because Mr. Willis admits he had sex with K.M. . . . Evidence that K.M. had sex with another individual does not tend to make it more or less probable that K.M. consented to sex with Mr. Willis. Accordingly, that evidence was irrelevant to the only issue at trial. *See* Fed. R. Evid. 401(a). The district court therefore did not exceed its discretion in excluding it.

Moreover, Mr. Willis cannot show prejudice because he was able to present other evidence of K.M.'s potential motive to lie. On cross-examination, K.M. admitted that Mr. Bear and Ms. Black would have been disappointed if they learned she had consensual sex with Mr. Willis. And Ms. Black confirmed K.M.'s assumption, testifying she would be upset if she learned K.M. had engaged in consensual sex with Mr. Willis. Thus, Mr. Willis was able to introduce his defense theory to the jury even without the evidence of K.M.'s prior sexual behavior. Under these circumstances, even if the district court erred in excluding the evidence — and it did not — the error was harmless. . . . [Affirmed.]

UNITED STATES v. THOMPSON

178 F. Supp. 3d 86 (W.D.N.Y. 2016)

ARCADA, District Judge.

The Defendant has been charged in a four-count superseding indictment alleging violations of 18 U.S.C. §1591(a) (sex trafficking either of minors or by force, fraud, or coercion) and §1591(d) (obstruction or interference with enforcement of §1591). The Government alleges that the Defendant "operated a commercial sex business in the Western New York area" and that, as part of that business, he "recruited women" — including the three victims in this case — "to work as prostitutes under his direction and control." The Government further alleges that the Defendant "used physical and/or psychological coercion to force the victims to engage in commercial sex acts and to give him the money they earned." . . .

The Government has filed a motion *in limine* requesting . . . an order prohibiting the Defendant "from eliciting or presenting any evidence concerning [the] victims' sexual behavior, including prostitution, *prior to and subsequent to the time period*" at issue in the superseding indictment. . . . In a "criminal proceeding involving alleged sexual misconduct," Rule 412(a) prohibits evidence offered "to prove that a victim engaged in other sexual behavior," as well as evidence offered "to prove a victim's sexual predisposition." The Rule's purpose is straightforward: it is intended "to safeguard the alleged victim against the invasion of privacy, potential embarrassment and sexual stereotyping that is associated with public disclosure of intimate sexual details and the infusion of sexual innuendo into the factfinding process." 1994 Advisory Committee Note to Rule 412 (1994 ACN). . . .

Rule 412(a) prohibits the Defendant from introducing or eliciting evidence concerning the victims' sexual behavior (including prostitution) that occurred prior and subsequent to the time periods at issue in the superseding indictment. This is, without question, a case involving alleged "sexual misconduct." It is also a case in which Rule 412's purpose would be served by prohibiting evidence of the victims' "other sexual behavior." Finally, evidence of the victims' pre- and post-indictment sexual behavior would be evidence of "other sexual behavior"—that is, it would be evidence of the victims' "sexual behavior" *other than* the sexual behavior at issue in the superseding indictment. Rule 412(a) bars such evidence.

. . . The only exception relevant here is Rule 412(b)(1)(C), which allows a criminal defendant to introduce otherwise-inadmissible evidence of a victim's "other sexual behavior" if "exclusion would violate the defendant's constitutional rights." The Defendant identifies two constitutional rights that, in his view, would be violated by excluding such evidence: his Fifth Amendment right to present a defense, and his Sixth Amendment right under the Confrontation Clause. . . .

Among its protections, the Fifth Amendment's Due Process Clause guarantees "the right to present the defendant's version of the facts . . . to the jury so it may decide where the truth lies." *Washington v. Texas*, 388 U.S. 14, 19 (1967). It does not follow, however, that a criminal defendant has a right to offer evidence that is irrelevant to the Government's charges. . . .

The victims' pre- and post-indictment sexual behavior is irrelevant to, and therefore "does not provide a defense" for, what the Government must prove under §1591(a). *United States v. Elbert*, 561 F.3d 771, 777 (8th Cir. 2009). Put another way, whether the victims "engaged in acts of prostitution before or after their [alleged] encounters with [the Defendant] . . . would only prove *other* people may be guilty of similar offenses of recruiting, enticing, or causing these victims to engage in a commercial sex act." *Id.* at 777 (emphasis added). To be sure, the Defendant may introduce or elicit evidence concerning whether Victims 1 and 2 engaged in prostitution (during the time period at issue) of their own volition, and not as a result of "force, threats of force, fraud, coercion . . . or any combination of such means." §1591(a). But the Defendant may *not* attempt to show that Victims 1 and 2 voluntarily engaged in prostitution based on the fact that they allegedly engaged in prostitution before and after the events giving rise to this case. . . .

[Similarly], applying Rule 412(a) in this case does not violate the Defendant's Confrontation Clause rights. . . . "The Confrontation Clause guarantees a criminal defendant the right to cross-examine government witnesses at trial" by, among other means, testing "'the believability of a witness and the truth of his testimony.'" *United States v. Figueroa,* 548 F.3d 222, 227 (2d Cir.2008) (citing *Davis v. Alaska,* 415 U.S. 308, 316 (1974)). . . . [Nonetheless] courts "retain wide latitude insofar as the Confrontation Clause is concerned to impose reasonable limits on . . . cross-examination based on concerns about, among other things, harassment, prejudice, confusion of the issues, the witnesses' safety, or interrogation that is repetitive or only marginally relevant." *Delaware v. Van Arsdall,* 475 U.S. 673, 679 (1986).

One such "reasonable limit" is to prohibit the Defendant from cross-examining sex trafficking victims about acts of prostitution that are unrelated to the charges in the superseding indictment. This is for the simple reason, implicit in Rule 412, that the "unchastity of a victim has no relevance whatsoever to the victim's credibility as a witness." *Elbert,* 561 F.3d at 777. . . . Moreover, to the extent that prior acts of prostitution resulted in criminal convictions which might provide a basis for impeachment under Rule 609, Rule 412(a)'s prohibition trumps the Defendant's ability to impeach the victims with those convictions. . . . Further, even if Rule 412(a) did not prohibit the Defendant from impeaching the victims with prior prostitution-related convictions, the impeachment value of such evidence would be substantially outweighed by unfair prejudice and embarrassment to the victims. *See* Fed. R. Evid. 609(a)(1)(B). . . . A prior prostitution conviction . . . has relatively little impeachment value. On the other hand, in addition to possibly serving to harass or embarrass the victim, impeaching a victim in a prostitution case with the victim's prior prostitution conviction has the potential to unnecessarily confuse the jury by suggesting that, because prostitution is illegal, the victims' testimony is inherently suspect or that the defendant's alleged conduct is less culpable. . . . [Motion granted.]

POLO-CALDERON v. CORPORACION PUERTORRIQUEÑA DE SALUD

992 F. Supp. 2d 53 (D.P.R. 2014)

Besosa, District Judge.

[Plaintiff Jonathan Polo-Echevarria ("Polo") worked as a hospital clerk. He sued his employer and Polo's supervisor, Joaquin Rodriguez Benitez ("Rodriguez"), for sexual harassment; Polo's father was also a plaintiff. Polo claimed that Rodriguez sent him sexually themed text messages and invitations from anonymous accounts, and that when Polo discovered the sender was Rodriguez and filed a complaint, the result was Polo's dismissal.] Having elicited information [during discovery] from plaintiff [regarding his] sexuality and texting relationships with other known and unknown men, defendants seek to introduce that evidence at trial. . . .

The purpose of Rule 412 is to "prevent misuse of a complainant's sexual history in cases involving 'alleged sexual misconduct.'" *Rodriguez-Hernandez v. Miranda-Velez,* 132 F.3d 848, 856 (1st Cir. 1998). In order for defendants to admit evidence to prove the alleged victim's sexual behavior or sexual predisposition, they must demonstrate that "its probative value substantially outweighs the danger of harm to any victim and of unfair prejudice to any party." *Id.* Only if the alleged victim places his or her own reputation in controversy is that evidence admissible.

Defendants have not met their burden of establishing that the evidence's probative value "substantially outweighs" its prejudicial effect. They broadly claim that the evidence is of the "utmost relevance" to Polo's credibility, to the identity of the prpng@hotmail.com and "Siempre Atento" user, and to the issue of welcomeness pursuant to a Title VII hostile work environment sexual harassment claim. They argue that plaintiffs "by their own volition have placed in controversy Jonathan Polo's reputation" and that "all of Jonathan Polo's behavior, conduct, actions, and habits" are relevant to his state of mind, identity, presumptions, and conclusions. Defendants would have the Court believe that "[i]n this type of case[,] the person's private life ceases to be private at the time he claims that the text messages constituted sexual harassment."

The Court finds no defendable reason for allowing evidence at trial regarding Polo's private dating life — including his sexual preferences, family dynamics regarding his sexuality, dating history, and any relationships or communications with other men via text message or telephone that did not occur within the time periods in question. Nothing prevents defendants from presenting evidence of, and/or cross-examining plaintiff Polo about, the relationship in which Polo engaged with prpng@hotmail.com and "Siempre Atento," or the messages that the two exchanged. All of the examples defendants cite in their motion concern Polo's private sexual life outside of that relationship, however, and are "precisely the types of intrusive generalized questions about past, private, consensual sexual conduct that courts readily have found marginally (if at all) probative to sexual-harassment claims, highly prejudicial and likely to harm the plaintiff." *A.W. v. I.B. Corp.,* 224 F.R.D. 20, 26 (D. Me. 2004). Defendants hint that Polo's deposition excerpts somehow call into question Polo's moral character, paint him as a sexually promiscuous teenager, and suggest that Polo would not have been offended by the messages prpng@hotmail. com sent if someone to whom he was attracted had sent Polo the same thing. Their request to introduce that evidence at trial not only offends notions of justice but is unsupported in law, and the Court simply will not allow it. *See, e.g., Burns v. McGregor Elec. Indus.,* 989 F.2d 959, 963 (8th Cir. 1993) ("This rationale would allow a complete stranger to pursue sexual behavior at work that a female worker would accept from her husband or boyfriend. This standard would allow a male employee to kiss or fondle a female worker at the workplace. None of the plaintiff's conduct . . . was work related. [She] did not tell sexual stories or engage in sexual gestures at work. She did not initiate sexual talk or solicit sexual encounters with co-employees."); *Barta v. City & County of Honolulu,* 169 F.R.D. 132, 136 (1996) ("*The fact that the plaintiff may welcome sexual advances from certain individuals has absolutely no bearing on the emotional trauma she may feel from sexual harassment that is unwelcome. Past sexual conduct does not callous one to subsequent unwelcomed sexual advancements.*") (emphasis added). There is no evidence that Jonathan Polo's conduct was work-related, that he engaged in sexual activity at work, or that he solicited sexual encounters with co-workers while at CPS. That he may have welcomed sexual advances from other individuals who were altogether disconnected from his workplace in no way pertains to his sexual harassment claim against Rodriguez.

In short, the Court does not find the information defendants seek to admit relevant to Polo's credibility, to "Siempre Atento" and prpng@hotmail.com's identity, or even to "the gravamen of any sexual harassment claim [,] [which] is that the alleged sexual advances were 'unwelcome.'" *Meritor Sav. Bank, FSB v. Vinson,* 477 U.S. 57, 68 (1986). Indeed, to analyze plaintiff's sexual harassment claim, a jury will determine whether Polo welcomed the messages received from prpng@hotmail.com and "Siempre Atento" once he uncovered the true sender's identity. It has long been recognized, however, that a plaintiff's "private and consensual sexual activities do not constitute a waiver of his or her legal protections against unwelcome and unsolicited sexual harassment.["] *Winsor v. Hinckley Dodge, Inc.,* 79 F.3d 996, 1001 (10th Cir. 1996) (quoting *Katz v. Dole,* 709 F.2d 251, 254 n. 3 (4th Cir. 1983)); *see, also B.K.B. v. Maui Police Dep't,* 276 F.3d 1091, 1105 (9th Cir. 2002) ("Courts have held . . . that the probative value of evidence of a victim's sexual sophistication or private sexual behavior with regard to the welcomeness of harassing behavior in the workplace does not substantially outweigh the prejudice to her."); *Rodriguez-Hernandez,* 132 F.3d at 856 (upholding trial court's ruling that evidence concerning sexual-harassment plaintiff's moral character and promiscuity was inadmissible under Rule 412); *Burns,* 989 F.2d at 963 ("[T]he plaintiff's choice to pose for a nude magazine outside work hours is not material to the issue of whether plaintiff found her employer's work-related conduct offensive."); *EEOC v. Wal-Mart Stores,* 1999 WL 1032963, at *3, 1999 U.S. App. LEXIS 29858, *10–11 (10th Cir. 1999) (finding evidence of (1) plaintiff's sexual relationships with coworkers outside of work, and (2) plaintiff's employer's generalized suspicions about her relationships outside of work, to be irrelevant to her claims of harassment at work).

The Court simply finds no connection between the testimony that defendants seek to admit and the sexual harassment plaintiff Polo allegedly experienced from defendant Rodriguez. Accordingly, defendants' motion . . . is denied.

2.   Character of the Defendant

Rape shield statutes, as we have seen, are motivated in part by versions of the same concerns that have traditionally motivated the character evidence rule, particularly the danger that the jury will overvalue or misuse the evidence. In stark contrast, the federal rules regarding evidence of prior similar misconduct in sexual assault and child molestation cases, adopted in the 1990s, are motivated by a *rejection* of those concerns, at least in this special set of cases.

These rules were adopted in the face of strong and nearly universal condemnation by lawyers, scholars, and judges. The flavor of that opposition is suggested by some of the materials that follow. When reading these materials, ask yourself whether the rules are as bad as their critics make them out to be, and whether, in particular, it makes sense to criticize these rules — as many commentators have — for being excessively "political." Should politicians stay away from evidence law? It is worth recalling that F.R.E. 412, the rape shield statute, also originated through the political process. And if the rules are inconsistent with traditional thinking about character evidence, is this a reason to reject them or to rethink the older, more general rules about character evidence?

[F.R.E. 413–415; C.E.C. §§1108–1109]

REMARKS OF REP. SUSAN MOLINARI

140 Cong. Rec. H 8991-92 (Aug. 21, 1994)

[Rep. Molinari was the principal House sponsor of the legislation adding Rules 413-415 to the Federal Rules of Evidence.]

Ms. Molinari. Mr. Speaker, the revised conference bill contains a critical reform that I have long sought to protect the public from crimes of sexual violence — general rules of admissibility in sexual assault and child molestation cases for evidence that the defendant has committed offenses of the same type on other occasions. The enactment of this reform is first and foremost a triumph for the public — for the women who will not be raped and the children who will not be molested because we have strengthened the legal system's tools for bringing the perpetrators of these atrocious crimes to justice.

. . . We have agreed to a temporary deferral of the effective date of the new rules, pending a report by the Judicial Conference, in order to accommodate procedural objections raised by opponents of the reform. However, regardless of what the Judicial Conference may recommend, the new rules will take effect within at most 300 days of the enactment of this legislation, unless repealed or modified by subsequent legislation.

. . . The new rules will supersede in sex offense cases the restrictive aspects of Federal Rule of Evidence 404(b). In contrast to Rule 404(b)'s general prohibition of evidence of character or propensity, the new rules for sex offense cases authorize admission and consideration of evidence of an uncharged offense for its bearing "on any matter to which it is relevant." This includes the defendant's propensity to commit sexual assault or child molestation offenses, and assessment of the probability or improbability that the defendant has been falsely or mistakenly accused of such an offense.

In other respects, the general standards of the rules of evidence will continue to apply, including the restrictions on hearsay evidence and the court's authority under Evidence Rule 403 to exclude evidence whose probative value is substantially outweighed by its prejudicial effect. Also, the government (or the plaintiff in a civil case) will generally have to disclose to the defendant any evidence that is to be offered under the new rules at least 15 days before trial.

The proposed reform is critical to the protection of the public from rapists and child molesters, and is justified by the distinctive characteristics of the cases it will affect. In child molestation cases, for example, a history of similar acts tends to be exceptionally probative because it shows an unusual disposition of the defendant — a sexual or sadosexual interest in children — that simply does not exist in ordinary people. Moreover, such cases require reliance on child victims whose credibility can readily be attacked in the absence of substantial corroboration. In such cases, there is a compelling public interest in admitting all significant evidence that will illumine the credibility of the charge and any denial by the defense.

Similarly, adult-victim sexual assault cases are distinctive, and often turn on difficult credibility determinations. Alleged consent by the victim is rarely an issue in prosecutions for other violent crimes — the accused mugger does not claim that the victim freely handed over [his] wallet as a gift — but the defendant in a rape case often contends that the victim engaged in consensual sex and then falsely accused him. Knowledge that the defendant has committed rapes on other occasions is frequently critical in assessing the relative plausibility of these claims and accurately deciding cases that would otherwise become unresolvable swearing matches.

The practical effect of the new rules is to put evidence of uncharged offenses in sexual assault and child molestation cases on the same footing as other types of relevant evidence that are not subject to a special exclusionary rule. The presumption is in favor of admission. The underlying legislative judgment is that the evidence admissible pursuant to the proposed rules is typically relevant and probative, and that its probative value is normally not outweighed by any risk of prejudice or other adverse effects.

In line with this judgment, the rules do not impose arbitrary or artificial restrictions on the admissibility of evidence. Evidence of offenses for which the defendant has not previously been prosecuted or convicted will be admissible, as well as evidence of prior convictions. No time limit is imposed on the uncharged offenses for which evidence may be admitted; as a practical matter, evidence of other sex offenses by the defendant is often probative and properly admitted, notwithstanding very substantial lapses of time in relation to the charged offense or offenses. *See, e.g., United States v. Hadley,* 918 F.2d 848, 850-51 (9th Cir. 1990), *cert. dismissed,* 113 S. Ct. 486 (1992) (evidence of offenses occurring up to 15 years earlier admitted); *State v. Plymate,* 345 N.W.2d 327 (Neb. 1984) (evidence of defendant's commission of other child molestations more than 20 years earlier admitted).

Finally, the practical efficacy of these rules will depend on faithful execution by judges of the will of Congress in adopting this critical reform. To implement the legislative intent, the courts must liberally construe these rules to provide the basis for a fully informed decision of sexual assault and child molestation cases, including assessment of the defendant's propensities and questions of probability in light of the defendant's past conduct.

REPORT OF THE JUDICIAL CONFERENCE OF THE UNITED STATES ON THE ADMISSION OF CHARACTER EVIDENCE IN CERTAIN SEXUAL MISCONDUCT CASES

159 F.R.D. 51 (1995)

This report is transmitted to Congress in accordance with the Violent Crime Control and Law Enforcement Act of 1994, Pub. L. No. 103-322

(September 13, 1994). . . . Under the Act, new Rules 413, 414, and 415 would be added to the Federal Rule of Evidence. . . . [T]he Judicial Conference was provided 150 days within which to make and submit to Congress alternative recommendations. . . .

[T]he Judicial Conference's . . . Advisory Committee on Evidence Rules sent out a notice soliciting comments. . . . The notice was sent to the courts, including all federal judges, about 900 evidence law professors, 40 women's rights organizations, and 1,000 other individuals and interested organizations. . . . [The committee received back] 84 written comments, representing 112 individuals, 8 local and 8 national organizations. The overwhelming majority of the judges, lawyers, law professors, and legal organizations who responded opposed the new Evidence Rules 413, 414, and 415. . . . The [advisory] committee's report was unanimous except for a dissenting vote by the representative of the Department of Justice. The advisory committee believed that the concerns expressed by Congress and embodied in new Evidence Rules 413, 414, and 415 are already adequately addressed in the existing Federal Rules of Evidence. In particular, Evidence Rule 404(b) now allows the admission of evidence against a criminal defendant of the commission of prior crimes, wrongs, or acts for specified purposes, including to show intent, plan, motive, preparation, identity, knowledge, or absence of mistake or accident.

Furthermore, the new rules, which are not supported by empirical evidence, could diminish significantly the protections that have safeguarded persons accused in criminal cases and parties in civil cases against undue prejudice. These protections form a fundamental part of American jurisprudence and have evolved under long-standing rules and case law. A significant concern identified by the committee was the danger of convicting a criminal defendant for past, as opposed to charged, behavior or for being a bad person.

In addition, the advisory committee concluded that, because prior bad acts would be admissible even though not the subject of a conviction, minitrials within trials concerning those acts would result when a defendant seeks to rebut such evidence. . . .

The Advisory Committees on Criminal and Civil Rules unanimously, except for representatives of the Department of Justice, also opposed the new rules . . . After the advisory committees reported, the Standing Committee [on Rules of Practice and Procedure] unanimously, again except for the representative of the Department of Justice, agreed with the view of the advisory committees.

It is important to note the highly unusual unanimity of the members of the Standing and Advisory Committees, composed of over 40 judges, practicing lawyers, and academicians, in taking the view that Rules 413–415 are undesirable. Indeed, the only supporters of the Rules were representatives of the Department of Justice. . . .

The Judicial Conference concurs with the views of the Standing Committee and urges that Congress reconsider its policy determinations underlying Evidence Rules 413–415. In the alternative, . . . amendments to Evidence Rules 404 and 405 are recommended, in lieu of new Evidence Rules 413, 414, and 415.

STEPHEN A. SALTZBURG, MICHAEL M. MARTIN & DANIEL J. CAPRA, FEDERAL RULES OF EVIDENCE MANUAL

§413.01[1], at 2:413-2 to 413-3 (11th ed. 2015)

Congress passed [Rules 413, 414, and 415], as part of a general Crime Bill package, and bypassed the ordinary rulemaking process in doing so. As a compromise, Congress provided for the possibility of reconsideration should the Judicial Conference make a timely objection to the new rules. The Judicial Conference Advisory Committee on Evidence Rules, and subsequently the Standing Committee on Rules of Practice and Procedure and the Judicial Conference itself, concluded that the rule[s] embodied bad policy and recommended [their] reconsideration; Congress refused to do so.

As an alternative, the Advisory Committee drafted amendments to Rule 404 and 405 that would both "correct ambiguities and possible constitutional infirmities identified in new Evidence Rules 413, 414, and 415, and yet still effectuate Congressional intent." . . . Congress did not adopt any of these proposed changes, and so Rules 413–415, as originally enacted by Congress . . . became effective on July 9, 1995.

UNITED STATES v. LeCOMPTE

131 F.3d 767 (8th Cir. 1997)

ARNOLD, Chief Judge.

Before the trial of Leo LeCompte for the alleged sexual abuse of his wife's 11-year-old niece, "C.D.," under 18 U.S.C. §§2244(a)(1) and 2246(3) (1994), the defendant moved *in limine* to exclude evidence of prior uncharged sex offenses against another niece by marriage, "T.T." . . . In LeCompte's first trial, the government offered the evidence under Rule 404(b). It was not then able to offer the evidence under Rule 414 because of its failure to provide timely notice of the offer, as required by Rule 414. The District Court admitted the evidence, and the jury convicted LeCompte. On appeal, this Court held that the District Court's admission of the evidence under Rule 404(b) was improper, and reversed LeCompte's conviction. We now consider the admissibility of T.T.'s testimony in LeCompte's retrial, under Rule 414, the government having given timely notice the second time around.

On remand . . . [t]he District Court ruled that T.T.'s testimony was potentially admissible under Rule 414, but excluded by Rule 403. It noted that although the evidence's only relevance was as to LeCompte's propensity to commit child sexual abuse, Rule 414 expressly allowed its use on that basis. The Court then turned to a Rule 403 analysis of the evidence. As to the evidence's probative value, the Court recognized the similarities between C.D.'s and T.T.'s accounts: they were both young nieces of LeCompte at the time he molested them, he forced them both to touch him, he touched them both in similar places, and he exposed himself to both of them. The Court found that the evidence's probative value was limited, however, by several differences.

First, the acts allegedly committed against C.D. occurred with her siblings present, while the acts against T.T. occurred in isolation. Second, LeCompte had not played games with C.D. immediately before molesting her, as he had with T.T. Finally, the acts against C.D. and T.T. were separated by a period of eight years. The District Court concluded that the probative value of T.T.'s testimony was limited.

On the other hand, it found that the risk of unfair prejudice was high, reasoning that "T.T.'s testimony is obviously highly prejudicial evidence against defendant. . . . 'child sexual abuse deservedly carries a unique stigma in our society; such highly prejudicial evidence should therefore carry a very high degree of probative value if it is to be admitted.'" The Court therefore excluded the evidence under Rule 403. [The government took an interlocutory appeal pursuant to 18 U.S.C. §3731.]

. . . This Court has recognized that evidence otherwise admissible under Rule 414 may be excluded under Rule 403's balancing test. *United States v. Summer*, 119 F.3d 658, 661 (8th Cir. 1997). However, Rule 403 must be applied to allow Rule 414 its intended effect. . . . In light of the strong legislative judgment that evidence of prior sexual offenses should ordinarily be admissible, we think the District Court erred in its assessment that the probative value of T.T.'s testimony was substantially outweighed by the danger of unfair prejudice. The sexual offenses committed against T.T. were substantially similar to those allegedly committed against C.D. By comparison, the differences were small. In particular, the District Court itself acknowledged that the time lapse between incidents "may not be as significant as it appears at first glance, because defendant was imprisoned for a portion of the time between 1987 and 1995, which deprived defendant of the opportunity to abuse any children."

Moreover, the danger of unfair prejudice noted by the District Court was that presented by the "unique stigma" of child sexual abuse, on account of which LeCompte might be convicted not for the charged offense, but for his sexual abuse of T.T. This danger is one that all propensity evidence in such trials presents. It is for this reason that the evidence was previously excluded, and it is precisely such holdings that Congress intended to overrule. *Compare United States v. Fawbush*, 900 F.2d 150 (8th Cir. 1990) (prior acts of child sexual abuse inadmissible to show propensity under Rule 404(b)). . . . On balance, then, we hold that the motion *in limine* should not have been granted.

The order of the District Court is reversed, and the cause remanded for further proceedings not inconsistent with this opinion.

UNITED STATES v. MAJERONI

No. 2:13-cr-37-GZS (D. Me. 2013)

SINGAL, District Judge.

. . . Defendant Timothy Majeroni is charged with one count of Possession of Child Pornography in violation of 18 U.S.C. §§2252A(a)(5)(B) & 2256(8)(A). At the upcoming jury trial on this charge, the Government seeks to introduce evidence that Majeroni previously pled guilty and was sentenced on two counts of child pornography possession in this same court in 2001.... Defendant concedes that both his 2001 conviction and the pending charge fall within the ambit of "child molestation" as that term is defined in Federal Rule of Evidence 414(d)(2) and, thus, may be admitted under the plain language of Rule 414(a). However, he argues that the prior 2001 conviction should still be excluded pursuant Rule 403....

Rule 414 "reflects a congressional judgment to remove the propensity bar to admissibility of certain evidence" involving similar crimes of child molestation. *Martinez v. Cui*, 608 F.3d 54, 60 (1st Cir. 2010) (discussing Rule 415, a similar rule for civil cases involving sexual assault or child molestation); *see also United States v. Davis*, 624 F.3d 508, 512 (2d Cir. 2010) ("[T]he legislative sponsors of Rule 414 expected that convictions within its ambit would normally be admitted and that their prejudicial value would normally not be outweighed by the risk of prejudice."). As a result, the plain language of Rule 414 would appear to be incompatible with any exclusion of evidence pursuant to Rule 403. Nonetheless, the First Circuit has joined most other circuits in concluding that evidence that is relevant and admissible pursuant to Rules 413, 414 & 415 must still be subject to "Rule 403 scrutiny." *Martinez*, 608 F.3d at 60. Unlike other circuits, the First Circuit has not adopted or announced any special rules or factors courts should consider when a defendant seeks exclusion based on Rule 403 of evidence otherwise admissible under Rule 414.

[G]iven the similarity between the 2001 conviction and the current charge, the evidence is undoubtedly probative and highly prejudicial. However, the Court must "distinguish 'highly' prejudicial from 'unfairly' prejudicial." *Davis*, 624 F.3d at 512 (noting that "[t]he calibration necessary to distinguish 'highly' prejudicial from 'unfairly' prejudicial will often be difficult to determine"). Defendant proffers essentially two factors in support of finding an overwhelming danger of unfair prejudice: (1) the passage of more than a decade between the prior child pornography conviction and the present charge, and (2) the significant amount of other evidence available to the government to meet its burden of proof....

The Court disagrees with Defendant's suggestion that the passage of time between the prior conviction and the present charge gives rise to unfair prejudice. Notably, Rule 414 contains no time limit. Other courts have overruled Rule 403 objections for similar prior convictions when the convictions were up to twenty years old.... Ultimately, the age of Majeroni's prior child pornography conviction may result in the factfinder giving it less weight. However, the Court cannot say that the passage of less than twelve years between the prior conviction and the current charge makes admission of the prior conviction unduly prejudicial. In this case, this conclusion is bolstered by the significant similarity between the pending charge and the prior conviction, which indisputably involved possession of child pornography that could be viewed on a computer.

With respect to the Government's other available evidence, the Court agrees with the Government that the prior conviction is uniquely probative on the issue of Defendant's knowledge. Ultimately, the Government must prove that Defendant both knowingly possessed the laptop and that he knew there was child pornography on the laptop.... [T]he Court is satisfied that any risk of unfair prejudice associated with admitting the 2001 conviction is outweighed by the probative value of the prior conviction on both the knowledge element of the pending child pornography possession charge and Defendant's propensity to commit the charged offense. Additionally, a proper limiting instruction can ensure that the jury uses the prior conviction evidence for allowable purposes and thereby further limit the risk of unfair prejudice. . . .* [Motion to admit evidence granted.]

NOTE, SEARCHING FOR A BETTER CONSTITUTIONAL GUARANTOR FOR FRE 413-415: THE CONFLICT AMONG CIRCUITS IN APPLYING THE FRE 403 BALANCING TEST AND A NEW SOLUTION

2016 U. Ill. L. Rev. 1905, 1907

[T]here are conflicting views among the federal circuits regarding how to use the FRE 403 balancing test in the context of FRE 413-415 . . . Some courts argue that the FRE 403 balancing test should be applied lightly, and thus defer to Congress' decision about the special probative value of evidence of the defendant's prior sexual assaults or child molestation; for example, the Eighth Circuit adopts this approach. Some courts argue that the same standard should be used as in other contexts; for example, the First Circuit advocates this approach. Others promulgated special criteria in applying the FRE 403 balancing in this context; for example, the Seventh, Ninth, and Tenth Circuits adopted modified FRE 403 balancing tests.

TOM LININGER, EVIDENTIARY ISSUES IN FEDERAL PROSECUTIONS OF VIOLENCE AGAINST WOMEN

36 Ind. L. Rev. 687, 701-04 (2003)

California . . . pass[ed] a law in 1996 [now codified in Section 1109 of the California Evidence Code] that essentially waived the ban on propensity evidence in prosecutions of domestic violence . . . [I]ts sponsors were outraged by the exclusion of prior acts evidence in the murder trial of O.J. Simpson. The explicit purpose of [the law] was to strengthen the government's hand in prosecuting defendants accused of domestic violence . . .

---

* [The government proposed the following instruction in its brief: "You have heard evidence that the Defendant was convicted of possession of child pornography in the United States District Court for the District of Maine in 2001. You may consider this evidence on any matter to which you believe it is relevant. However, evidence of this prior offense on its own is not sufficient to prove the Defendant guilty of the crime charged in the Indictment. Bear in mind as you consider this evidence, at all times the government has the burden of proving beyond a reasonable doubt that the Defendant committed each of the elements of the offense charged in the Indictment. I remind you that the Defendant is not on trial for any act, conduct, or offense not charged in the Indictment." The government pointed out that in *United States v. Benally*, 500 F.3d 1085 (2007), the Tenth Circuit said a similar instruction had mitigated any bias resulting from the introduction of evidence of prior acts of sexual assault and child molestation under Rules 413 and 414.—Ed.]

Many commentators have criticized FRE 413 and FRE 414 on the following grounds, among others: 1) the prejudicial effect of propensity evidence in a criminal trial; 2) the theoretical inconsistency of these rules with FRE 404(b); 3) the lack of empirical evidence demonstrating a higher rate of recidivism among sex offenders and child molesters than among other offenders; and 4) the disproportionate effect of these rules on Native Americans. Whatever the merit of the approach embodied in FRE 413 and 414, some in Congress have already proposed that the approach be extended to all categories of violence against women, along the lines of California's model.

UNITED STATES v. CUNNINGHAM

103 F.3d 553 (7th Cir. 1996)

POSNER, Chief Judge.

. . ."Propensity" evidence and "motive" evidence need not overlap. They do not, for example, when past drug convictions are used to show that the defendant in a robbery case is an addict and his addiction is offered as the motive for the robbery. *See, e.g., People v. McConnell*, 335 N.W.2d 226, 230 (Mich. App. 1983); *cf. People v. Moreno*, 132 Cal. Rptr. 569 (1976) (man's theft of a woman's underwear). . . . They do overlap when the crime is motivated by a taste for engaging in that crime or a compulsion to engage in it (an "addiction"), rather than by a desire for pecuniary gain or for some other advantage to which the crime is instrumental in the sense that it would not be committed if the advantage could be obtained as easily by a lawful route. Sex crimes provide a particularly clear example. Most people do not have a taste for sexually molesting children. As between two suspected molesters, then, only one of whom has a history of such molestation, the history establishes a motive that enables the two suspects to be distinguished. In 1994, Rule 414 was added to the Federal Rules of Evidence to make evidence of prior acts of child molestation expressly admissible, without regard to Rule 404(b). But the principle that we are discussing is not limited to sex crimes. A "firebug" — one who commits arson not for insurance proceeds or revenge or to eliminate a competitor, but for the sheer joy of watching a fire — is, like the sex criminal, a person whose motive to commit the crime with which he is charged is revealed by his past commission of the same crime. No special rule analogous to Rules 413 through 415 is necessary to make the evidence of the earlier crime admissible, because 404(b) expressly allows evidence of prior wrongful acts to establish motive. . . .

OTHER FORBIDDEN INFERENCES

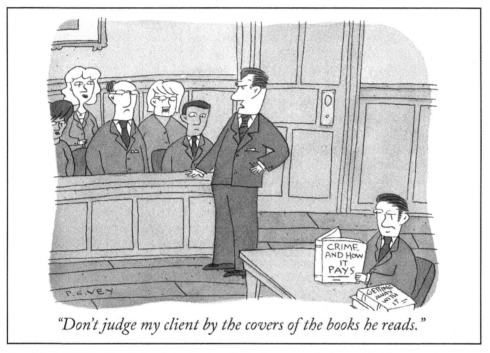

"Don't judge my client by the covers of the books he reads."

The hearsay rule and the character-for-propensity evidence rule share a similar structure: each forbids a certain kind of proof used for a certain kind of purpose. Neither rule operates when the proof in question is offered for some other purpose—when, that is to say, an out-of-court statement is introduced for some purpose other than proving the truth of what it asserts, or when evidence of a character trait is offered for some purpose other than proving action in conformity with the trait.

Several other, more minor rules of evidence law also have this structure. Evidence of subsequent remedial measures is typically inadmissible to prove fault. Settlement efforts generally cannot be proved to show the merit or weakness of a civil claim or criminal charge. Humanitarian payments typically are inadmissible to demonstrate liability. And the presence or absence of liability insurance generally cannot be proved to show fault or lack of fault.

Each of these rules is addressed in this chapter.

A. SUBSEQUENT REMEDIAL MEASURES

[F.R.E. 407; C.E.C. §1151]

ADVISORY COMMITTEE NOTE TO F.R.E. 407

The rule incorporates conventional doctrine which excludes evidence of subsequent remedial measures as proof of an admission of fault. The rule rests on two grounds. (1) The conduct is not in fact an admission, since the conduct is equally consistent with injury by mere accident or through contributory negligence. Or, as Baron Bramwell put it, the rule rejects the notion that "because the world gets wiser as it gets older, therefore it was foolish before." Hart v. Lancashire & Yorkshire Ry. Co., 21 L.T.R. N.S. 261, 263 (1869). Under a liberal theory of relevancy this ground alone would not support exclusion as the inference is still a possible one. (2) The other, and more impressive, ground for exclusion rests on a social policy of encouraging people to take, or at least not discouraging them from taking, steps in furtherance of added safety. The courts have applied this principle to exclude evidence of subsequent repairs, installation of safety devices, changes in company rules, and discharge of employees, and the language of the present rule is broad enough to encompass all of them.

The second sentence of the rule directs attention to the limitations of the rule. Exclusion is called for only when the evidence of subsequent remedial measures is offered as proof of negligence or culpable conduct. In effect it rejects the suggested inference that fault is admitted. Other purposes are, however, allowable, including ownership or control, existence of duty, and feasibility of precautionary measures, if controverted, and impeachment. Two recent federal cases are illustrative. Boeing Airplane Co. v. Brown, 291 F.2d 310 (9th Cir. 1961), an action against an airplane manufacturer for using an allegedly defectively designed alternator shaft which caused a plane crash, upheld the admission of evidence of subsequent design modification for the purpose of showing that design changes and safeguards were feasible. And Powers v. J.B. Michael & Co., 329 F.2d 674 (6th Cir. 1964), an action against a road contractor for negligent failure to put out warning signs, sustained the admission of evidence that defendant subsequently put out signs to show that the portion of the road in question was under defendant's control. The requirement that the other purpose be controverted calls for automatic exclusion unless a genuine issue be present and allows the opposing party to lay the groundwork for exclusion by making an admission. Otherwise the factors of undue prejudice, confusion of issues, misleading the jury, and waste of time remain for consideration under Rule 403.

CLAUSEN v. STORAGE TANK DEVELOPMENT CORP.

21 F.3d 1181 (1st Cir. 1994) (sub nom. Clausen v. Sea-3, Inc.)

LEVIN H. CAMPBELL, Senior Circuit Judge.

On February 6, 1989, Eric Clausen ("Clausen"), plaintiff-appellee, slipped, fell, and injured his back while working as a pile driver at a job site at a fuel terminal facility on the Piscataqua River, Portsmouth Harbor, Newington, New Hampshire. A Massachusetts resident, Clausen sued for negligence, under the diversity jurisdiction, in the United States District Court for the District of New Hampshire. Defendants were the owner of the facility, Storage Tank Development Corp. ("Storage Tank"), a New Hampshire corporation, and the occupier of the facility, Sea-3, Inc. ("Sea-3"), a Texas corporation. Defendants filed third-party complaints against Clausen's employer, Goudreau Construction Corp. ("Goudreau").

. . . Storage Tank owns docking facilities along the Piscataqua River in Newington, New Hampshire. These include a walkway-pier that first extends perpendicularly from the shore line into the water, and then turns ninety degrees to the left and extends upstream. A concrete mooring cell, referred to as Cell Three, is located in the water beyond the end of the walkway-pier. Cell Three, at the time of Clausen's injury, was connected to the end of the walkway-pier by the ramp upon which Clausen slipped and fell. . . .

Storage Tank complains of the allowance of evidence that, in 1992, Storage Tank, at Sea-3's request, replaced the ramp on which Clausen fell with a set of steps. . . . Because Storage Tank failed timely to object at trial to the admission of evidence of the subsequent alteration to the ramp in 1992, we review the district court's decision to allow such evidence only for plain error. . . . It is utterly clear that the district court's decision to permit the evidence of the changes made to the ramp in 1992, whether right or wrong, was not plain error.

Although Fed. R. Evid. 407 proscribes the admission of evidence of subsequent remedial measures to "prove negligence or culpable conduct," it allows such evidence . . . "when offered for another purpose, such as proving . . . control." The parties agree that control of the ramp area where Clausen's injury occurred was a material issue in this case. According to the appellant, one aspect of the control issue arose because both Storage Tank and Sea-3 asserted that Goudreau was in control of the work site and was, therefore, responsible for clearing and sanding the area where the plaintiff fell. Clausen points out that a second aspect of the control issue in this case, not alluded to by Storage Tank, involved whether Storage Tank, Sea-3, or both jointly, controlled the area where Clausen fell if Goudreau, at that time, did not control the ramp.

To be sure, Storage Tank argues that the evidence that it made changes to the ramp at the request of Sea-3 subsequent to Clausen's accident was inadmissible under the control exception to Fed. R. Evid. 407 because the evidence failed to satisfy the independent requirements of Fed. R. Evid. 403. Storage Tank maintains that, because the ramp was replaced in 1992, approximately three years after Clausen's fall, the evidence is not probative of whether Storage Tank or Sea-3 controlled the ramp, either separately or jointly, in 1989, particularly since, according to Storage Tank, the area had been exclusively occupied by Goudreau when Clausen's injury occurred. Whatever can be said for such arguments had Storage Tank preserved its right to argue the merits, they do not come close to demonstrating that it was plain error for the district court to believe that the evidence carried at least some probative weight as to who controlled the ramp in 1989.

Storage Tank also suggests that it was greatly prejudiced because the jury may have used the evidence of the ramp's replacement for an improper purpose. The judge, however, instructed the jury that "[e]vidence of the subsequent installation of stairs in 1992 is evidence relevant only on the issue of control. It is not to be considered evidence of liability or fault." According to the advisory committee's notes to Fed. R. Evid. 403, "[i]n reaching a decision whether to exclude on grounds of unfair prejudice, consideration should be given to the probable effectiveness or lack of effectiveness of a limiting instruction." Although limiting instructions may not always be effective, the inadequacy of the one in this situation is scarcely so patent as to support a finding of plain error. We do not readily assume that a jury disregards clear directions.... [Affirmed.]

IN RE ASBESTOS LITIGATION

995 F.2d 343 (2d Cir. 1993)

McLAUGHLIN, Circuit Judge.

John Crane-Houdaille, Inc. ("Crane") appeals from a personal injury and wrongful death judgment, jointly entered on July 31, 1992 by the United States District Courts for the Eastern and Southern Districts of New York (Charles P. Sifton, Judge), following a consolidated asbestos jury trial.... [The judgment was awarded to Anne McPadden, whose late husband, Martin McPadden, had worked with encapsulated asbestos valve packing manufactured by Crane.]

We find it necessary to focus on only one evidentiary error that seriously prejudiced the liability verdict. The district court erred in admitting evidence that Crane placed warnings on its asbestos product after decedent's last exposure. The warnings were subsequent remedial measures and, as such, inadmissible under Fed. R. Evid. 407....

In denying Crane's post-trial motion, the district court concluded that "plaintiff's use of the label evidence focused on the statement that no warning labels were placed on the products at the time of McPadden's exposure, not that the labels were placed on the products later because Crane recognized the danger." McPadden contends that this distinction salvages the evidence because Rule 407 permits the admission of subsequent warnings to prove feasibility. We are not persuaded.

"Feasibility" is not an open sesame whose mere invocation parts Rule 407 and ushers in evidence of subsequent repairs and remedies. To read it that casually will cause the exception to engulf the rule. Rule 407 states that a defendant must first contest the feasibility of a warning before the subsequent warning would become admissible. The record is clear that Crane at no point argued that it was unable to issue a warning. Instead, it vigorously denied that its product required a warning or was defective without a warning. Because our review of the record convinces us that feasibility was not a contested issue, it was error to permit McPadden to read into evidence ... deposition testimony concerning post-exposure warnings that were placed on the product more than 12 years after McPadden was last exposed to Crane's asbestos products.... [Reversed.]

DIEHL v. BLAW-KNOX

360 F.3d 426 (6th Cir. 2004)

SMITH, Circuit Judge.

. . . On May 24, 1999, Timothy Diehl was severely injured while working as a laborer on a road crew for IA Construction, Inc. ("IA"). On the day of the accident, the road crew was using a machine called a "road widener" to extend the shoulder of a road. Manufactured by Blaw-Knox in 1970, the road widener is used to deposit and spread material to one side of the roadway. The road widener is usually followed by laborers who must perform a number of tasks, including removing excess material that is inadvertently left on the paved portion of the roadway; removing stones that become lodged in the material; leveling off the material that has been spread; and straightening the outer edge of the deposited material. The laborers are then followed by a roller to press the material.

On the day of the accident, Mr. Diehl was working as one of the laborers behind the road widener. The road widener had come to a stop, and then began to move in reverse. Mr. Diehl, who was working within "a couple of feet" of the road widener, was not aware that the machine was reversing toward him. One of the exposed wheels struck Mr. Diehl's right ankle, trapping and crushing his lower leg.

[Mr. Diehl and his wife sued Blaw-Knox, alleging] that the road widener was defective in design for three reasons: (1) it lacked a bumper or any other enclosure of the rear wheels; (2) the back-up alarm was inaudible, particularly because it was placed on the front of the machine; and (3) it lacked proper warnings. The Diehls sought to introduce testimony by an IA mechanic that, shortly after the accident, the mechanic modified the road widener by (1) installing a rear bumper/guard that enclosed the rear tires; (2) relocating the back-up alarm to the rear of the machine; and (3) placing warning signs on the rear of the machine (the "IA redesign"). According to the mechanic's testimony, the IA redesign was done in response to the accident and for the purpose of preventing similar accidents. Significantly, IA is not a party to this lawsuit.

. . . The District Court . . . [ruled] that the IA redesign was a subsequent remedial measure inadmissible under Fed. R. Evid. 407. . . . Alternatively, the District Court excluded the evidence under Fed. R. Evid. 403, finding that evidence of remedial measures taken in 1999 would confuse the jury, whose focus was temporally limited to whether the product was safe in 1970. The jury returned a verdict for Blaw-Knox. . . .

"Rule 407 rests on the strong public policy of encouraging manufacturers to 'make improvements for greater safety.'" *Stecyk v. Bell Helicopter Textron, Inc.*, 295 F.3d 408, 412 (3d Cir. 2002) (quoting *Kelly Crown Equip. Co.*, 970 F.2d 1273, 1276 (3d Cir. 1992)); *see also* Fed. R. Evid. 407 advisory committee's note ("The other, and more impressive, ground for exclusion rests on a social policy of encouraging people to take, or at least not discouraging them from taking, steps in furtherance of added safety."). The Rule recognizes that manufacturers will be discouraged from improving the safety of their products if such changes can be introduced as evidence that their previous designs were defective.

This policy is not implicated where the evidence concerns remedial measures taken by an individual or entity that is not a party to the lawsuit. The admission of remedial measures by a non-party necessarily will not expose that non-party to liability, and therefore will not discourage the non-party from taking the remedial measures in the first place. It is noteworthy that each of the circuits to address this issue has concluded that Rule 407 does not apply to subsequent remedial measures taken by a non-party....

The able District Judge declined to follow these authorities, observing that the text of Rule 407 makes no exception for subsequent remedial measures taken by a non-party. This is true enough, but the Advisory Committee's notes to Rule 407 state that the rule "incorporates conventional doctrine which excludes evidence of subsequent remedial measures as proof of an admission of fault."... Prior to the enactment of Rule 407, conventional doctrine in this circuit was that the rule excluding evidence of repairs made after an accident was not applicable to repairs made by a non-party.... The Advisory Committee's reference to "an admission of fault" reinforces this limitation: it hardly makes sense to speak of a party's fault being "admitted" by someone other than the party. Furthermore, the Advisory Committee was well aware of the courts' consistent interpretation of the rule. The notes to the 1997 amendment of Rule 407 — making the rule applicable to products liability actions — cite with approval the First Circuit's opinion in *Raymond v. Raymond Corp.*[, 938 F.2d 1518 (1st Cir. 1991)]. The court in *Raymond* expressly ruled that "there is no rationale for excluding third party subsequent repairs under the Rule."

Because Rule 407 does not apply to evidence of subsequent remedial measures taken by a non-party, it was error for the District Court to exclude evidence of the IA redesign under that rule.

The District Court alternatively excluded evidence of the IA redesign under Fed. R. Evid. 403, which states that "[a]lthough relevant, evidence may be excluded if its probative value is substantially outweighed by the danger of unfair prejudice, confusion of the issues, or misleading the jury." A district court's explicit balancing analysis under Rule 403 should only be disturbed if it is irrational or arbitrary.

The court reasoned that the IA redesign would create a danger of unfair prejudice, confusion of the issues, and misleading of the jury, because "[t]he issue of a defect — as to whether or not there's a defect, requires a focus of the jury on the time of the manufacture of this machine in 1970, more than 30 years ago." Under Pennsylvania law, a product is defective if it "left the supplier's control *lacking any element necessary to make it safe for its intended use.*" *Lewis v. Coffing Hoist Div., Duff-Norton Co.*, 515 Pa. 334, 528 (1987); *accord Duchess v. Langston Corp.*, 564 Pa. 529 (2001) ("[O]ur jurisprudence requires that products are to be evaluated at the time of distribution when examining a claim of product defect."). "Since the employment of a subsequent remedial measure by definition occurs in a different time frame, the evidence is said to be of diminished relevance." *Duchess*. Still, the implementation of remedial measures to improve the safety of a product is consistent with an inference that the older product of a similar design was defective....

As a general matter, we appreciate the potential that subsequent design changes represent for distracting juries from the issue at hand — whether the product was defective when it left the manufacturer's hands.... As the Fifth Circuit put it in *Grenada Steel Industries, Inc. v. Alabama Oxygen Co.*:

> A priori judgments concerning why manufacturers do or do not alter their products, made by such dubious experts as judges, lawyers, and law professors, suffer from excessive reliance on logical deduction and surmise without the benefit of evidence of industry practice or economic factors. It seems to us, with no greater expertise than like-trained lawyers and judges, that changes in design or in manufacturing process might be made after an accident for a number of different reasons: simply to avoid another injury, as a sort of admission of error, because a better way has been discovered, or to implement an idea or plan conceived before the accident.

695 F.2d 883, 887–88 (5th Cir. 1983).... *Grenada Steel* is particularly instructive because that case also involved subsequent remedial measures taken by a non-party. Although the court in that case recognized that Rule 407 is inapplicable to non-party remedial measures, the evidence nevertheless implicated Rule 403 concerns:

> [W]e think the district court's exclusion of this evidence was proper because it lacked sufficient probative value and injected the dangers of confusion and misleading the jury.... Alternative designs may indicate that the product was unreasonably dangerous, but only if they were available at the time of manufacture. We fail to see how an alternative design, developed by another person years after the product in question was manufactured, is relevant to whether the product was reasonably safe at the time it was made.

Grenada Steel, 695 F.2d at 889.

The instant case, however, presents none of the risks discussed in *Grenada Steel*, or in other cases analyzing the potential for confusion in products liability cases. For one, the state of the art is not an issue in this case, *i.e.*, it is undisputed that the measures taken by IA — merely welding a bumper onto the rear of the road widener — were available to Blaw-Knox at the time of the manufacture. Accordingly, there is no temporal distinction for the jury to overlook between a feature reasonably necessary to make the road widener safe in 1999, and a feature reasonably necessary to make the road widener safe in 1970. *See generally Espeaignnette v. Gene Tierney Co., Inc.*, 43 F.3d 1, 7 (1st Cir. 1994) (holding that evidence of subsequent remedial measures taken by a non-party was not misleading or unfairly prejudicial on the issue of defect where evidence would not have introduced design choices not known or feasible at the time of manufacture).

Furthermore, we find no dispute in the record that the IA redesign was done in direct response to Mr. Diehl's accident and for the sole purpose of preventing such accidents. The IA mechanic that performed the redesign testified in deposition that the redesign was done to prevent the accident that befell Mr. Diehl. Because the purpose of the redesign was not contested, there was no danger that the jury would discount other plausible reasons for the redesign.

Despite the deference accorded to a trial court's Rule 403 balancing, we find no support in the record for the District Court's concerns that the IA redesign would confuse or mislead the jury. Because the evidence is probative of whether the road widener lacked a feature reasonably necessary to make the machine safe for its intended use, and because its relevance was not outweighed by other dangers, we find that the District Court abused its discretion by excluding evidence of the IA redesign. . . .

We . . . cannot say that it is highly probable that evidence of the IA redesign would not have affected the jury's conclusion that the 1970 design lacked a feature reasonably necessary to make the machine safe for its intended use.[5] Because we conclude that the exclusion of this evidence was not harmless error, we will reverse the judgment of the District Court and remand for a new trial.

B. SETTLEMENT EFFORTS

1. Civil Settlements

[F.R.E. 408; C.E.C. §§1152, 1154]

ADVISORY COMMITTEE NOTE TO F.R.E. 408

As a matter of general agreement, evidence of an offer to compromise a claim is not receivable in evidence as an admission of, as the case may be, the validity or invalidity of the claim. As with evidence of subsequent remedial measures, dealt with in Rule 407, exclusion may be based on two grounds. (1) The evidence is irrelevant, since the offer may be motivated by a desire for peace rather than from any concession of weakness of position. The validity of this position will vary as the amount of the offer varies in relation to the size of the claim and may also be influenced by other circumstances. (2) A more consistently impressive ground is promotion of the public policy favoring the compromise and settlement of disputes. McCormick §§76, 251. While the rule is ordinarily phrased in terms of offers of compromise, it is apparent that a similar attitude must be taken with respect to completed compromises when offered against a party thereto. This latter situation will not,

---

5. . . . [On remand] the District Court should [also] reconsider its exclusion of evidence that Blaw-Knox itself had redesigned the road widener to fully enclose the rear tires. . . . The Blaw-Knox redesign was done in 1983, 13 years after manufacture of the road widener and 16 years prior to the accident. Amended in 1997, Rule 407, by its terms, applies to remedial measures taken "after an injury or harm allegedly caused by an event." Fed. R. Evid. 407; *see also* Advisory Committee's notes to the 1997 amendment ("Evidence of measures taken by the defendant prior to the 'event' causing 'injury or harm' do not fall within the exclusionary scope of Rule 407 even if they occurred after the manufacture or design of the product."). . . . Because the Blaw-Knox redesign was done in 1983, 16 years prior to the accident, Rule 407 does not apply. Evidence of the Blaw-Knox redesign, of course, must still be analyzed under Rules 401 and 403.

of course, ordinarily occur except when a party to the present litigation has compromised with a third person. . . .

The practical value of the common law rule has been greatly diminished by its inapplicability to admissions of fact, even though made in the course of compromise negotiations, unless hypothetical, stated to be "without prejudice," or so connected with the offer as to be inseparable from it. McCormick §251, pp. 540-541. An inevitable effect is to inhibit freedom of communication with respect to compromise, even among lawyers. Another effect is the generation of controversy over whether a given statement falls within or without the protected area. These considerations account for the expansion of the rule herewith to include evidence of conduct or statements made in compromise negotiations, as well as the offer or completed compromise itself. . . .

The policy considerations which underlie the rule do not come into play when the effort is to induce a creditor to settle an admittedly due amount for a lesser sum. McCormick §251, p. 540. Hence the rule requires that the claim be disputed as to either validity or amount.

The final sentence of the rule serves to point out some limitations upon its applicability. Since the rule excludes only when the purpose is proving the validity or invalidity of the claim or its amount, an offer for another purpose is not within the rule. . . .

UNITED STATES v. DAVIS

596 F.3d 852 (D.C. Cir. 2010)

RANDOLPH, Senior Circuit Judge.

Terry Davis served as national treasurer of the Phi Beta Sigma fraternity. Accused of stealing from the fraternity, he was [convicted of theft and fraud, sentenced to 51 months in prison, and ordered] to pay $217,746.79 in restitution to the fraternity. . . .

[Davis's successor as national treasurer], Jimmy Hammock, testified that he asked Davis to produce the financial records Davis maintained on the fraternity's behalf. Davis provided some unused checks and financial reports but no cancelled checks or bank statements. Hammock also asked Davis why he had written fraternity checks payable to cash. Davis explained that he transferred the funds to the fraternity's payroll account.

Hammock testified about a second conversation with Davis regarding these checks. Hammock told Davis the fraternity had found $29,000 in checks made out to cash, none of which was deposited in the fraternity's bank account as Davis had claimed. Over an objection based on Rule 408 of the Federal Rules of Evidence, Hammock related the rest of the conversation: "Terry asked — he said 'Can we just split this $29,000.00 and make this situation just go away?' . . . I told him that [the] amount was in excess of a hundred thousand dollars. Terry's statement to me at that point was, 'I can't afford to pay that amount,' and then I told him — I said, 'Terry, if you want to do some — negotiate some kind of settlement, you need to talk to our legal counsel or our international president.'" . . .

Rule 408 . . . excludes evidence of settlement offers and negotiations when the evidence is "offered to prove liability for, invalidity of, or amount of a claim." . . . There can be no doubt that Davis offered to compromise a disputed claim. His offer was to split the $29,000 in checks to cash he thought the fraternity had discovered. . . . It is also clear that the government intended to introduce Davis's settlement offer in order to prove Davis's guilt, or in the words of Rule 408(a), his "liability." Offers to settle are excluded even if no settlement negotiations follow. Fed. R. Evid. 408(a)(1). . . . The Rule is meant to promote settlements. *See* Fed. R. Evid. 408 advisory committee's note (1974). If one party attempts to initiate negotiations with a settlement offer, the offer is excluded from evidence even if the counterparty responds: "I'm not negotiating with you." *See* Fed. R. Evid. 408 advisory committee's note (1972 proposed rule). It makes no sense to force the party who initiates negotiations to do so at his peril.

Rule 408 bars not only evidence of settlement offers, but also "statements made in compromise negotiations." Fed. R. Evid. 408(a)(2). Davis's other statements to Hammock during their second conversation were of that sort. Davis asked what it would take to "make this go away"; Hammock said pay back what you took; Davis countered with his offer to split the $29,000; Hammock countered that the missing funds totaled more than $100,000. That Hammock understood this give and take as a compromise negotiation is confirmed by his trial testimony . . . that he told Davis to talk to the fraternity's president or lawyer if he wanted to settle the matter. . . .

There is, as the government points out, a sentence in the 1972 advisory committee note to Rule 408 stating that an "effort to 'buy off' the prosecution or a prosecuting witness in a criminal case is not within the policy of the rule of exclusion." But . . . Davis was not charged with obstructing a criminal investigation or attempting to do so. We can say with some assurance that when he offered to split the difference on $29,000, he was not trying to bribe Hammock. All indications are that Davis was proposing to pay the money to the fraternity. It may be that an offer of settlement, excessive in amount, could be seen as an attempt to "buy off" a complaining party. But Davis's offer obviously was not of that sort, which is why Hammock rejected it out of hand.

The most important consideration is that the government did not introduce the Hammock-Davis conversation for the purpose of "proving an effort to obstruct a criminal investigation." Fed. R. Evid. 408(b). When asked at oral argument whether this was the government's purpose, counsel for the government candidly admitted it was not. She explained, as the prosecutor had argued to the jury, that the conversation revealed Davis's consciousness of guilt. But that is one of the prohibited purposes in Rule 408(a). Consciousness of guilt proves "liability" for a disputed claim under Rule 408(a).

We therefore hold that the district court abused its discretion in permitting Hammock to testify regarding Davis's offer of settlement and the statements that followed. . . . [Vacated and remanded.]

RAMADA DEVELOPMENT CO. v. RAUCH

644 F.2d 1097 (5th Cir. Unit B 1981)

TUTTLE, Circuit Judge.

On December 13, 1972, Martin Rauch signed a contract in which the Ramada Development Company agreed to design, furnish, and construct a 160-unit Ramada Inn Motor Hotel and Restaurant in Venice, Florida. . . . On January 31, 1975, approximately one year after Rauch occupied the motel and refused to make further payments to Ramada, Ramada brought this diversity action against Rauch for the balance due under the contract. . . . The defendant answered, denying liability and alleging a counterclaim against Ramada for failure to perform according to the contract and for negligence in planning and construction of the project. . . .

[T]he jury . . . gave a verdict that was basically favorable to Ramada. . . .

[Rauch challenges] the district court's exclusion of a document referred to as the Goldsmith Report. Goldsmith was an architect employed by Ramada in 1974 to study the defects that Rauch had alleged at that time. Rauch claims that he sought to introduce this report as "a part of his case in chief," because it confirmed the majority of the alleged defects. The district court heard testimony regarding the origins of the report and concluded that it was inadmissible under Federal Rule of Evidence 408 because the report was a tool used in an unsuccessful settlement attempt. Rauch contends that this ruling was in error because Rule 408 does not exclude all evidence presented in settlement attempts and there was the lack of any pre-trial understanding that the report could not be used in evidence. Rauch's claim of error is without merit.

Rule 408 . . . is designed to encourage settlements by fostering free and full discussion of the issues. The previous common law rule held that admissions of fact made in negotiations were admissible "unless hypothetical, stated to be 'without prejudice,' or so connected with the offer as to be inseparable from it." Advisory Committee Notes [to] Rule 408. After the House Committee rejected a proposed deviation from the common law rule, the Senate Committee [reverted to the Advisory Committee's proposal,] because

> The real impact of this [House] amendment however, is to deprive the rule of much of its salutary effect. The exception for factual admissions was believed by the Advisory Committee to hamper free communication between parties and thus to constitute an unjustifiable restraint upon efforts to negotiate settlements the encouragement of which is the purpose of the rule. Further, by protecting hypothetically phrased statements, it constituted a preference for the sophisticated, and a trap for the unwary.

S. Rep. No. 1277, 93d Cong., 2d Sess. (1974). The present rule fosters free discussion in connection with such negotiations and eliminates the need to determine whether the statement if not expressly qualified "falls within or without the protected area of compromise"; the question under the rule is "whether the statements or conduct were intended to be part of the negotiations toward compromise." 2 J. Weinstein & M. Berger, Weinstein's Evidence ¶408(03), at 408-20 to -21 (1980). The rule does not indicate that there must be a pre-trial understanding or agreement between the parties regarding the nature of the report. Indeed, Rauch's assertions in this regard would partially revive the common law rule that a party assert that his statement is made "without prejudice."

The Goldsmith Report, thus, appears to fit squarely within the exclusionary scope of rule 408. The only indication given by the parties of the report's origins is the testimony of Leonard Gilbert whose testimony can only be construed as supporting the position that Goldsmith was commissioned by Ramada to prepare a report that would function as a basis of settlement negotiations regarding the alleged defects in the motel. The report was to identify arguable defects that could then be discussed in monetary terms in the negotiations. The Goldsmith Report, as described by Mr. Gilbert, thus represents a collection of statements made in the course of an effort to compromise, and the district court properly held it inadmissible under the main provision of rule 408.

Rauch raises numerous reasons why the Goldsmith Report is admissible under the exceptions in rule 408. First, he argues that the report falls into the exception to rule 408 which holds that the rule "does not require the exclusion of any evidence otherwise discoverable merely because it is presented in the course of compromise negotiations." This sentence was intended to prevent one from being able to "immunize from admissibility documents otherwise discoverable merely by offering them in a compromise negotiation." S. Rep. No. 1277, 93d Cong., 2d Sess. (1974). Clearly such an exception does not cover the present case where the document, or statement, would not have existed but for the negotiations, hence the negotiations are not being used as a device to thwart discovery by making existing documents unreachable. Second, Rauch contends that the report was not only offered to prove the existence of defect but also to prove Ramada's notice of the alleged defects. Rule 408 "does not require exclusion when the evidence is offered for another purpose (other than proving the existence of defects)," but this provision, surely, was not intended to completely undercut the policy behind the rule. See 2 J. Weinstein & M. Berger, supra, ¶408(05), at 408-25 to -26 (court "should weigh the need for such evidence against the potentiality of discouraging future settlement negotiations"). This Court, in a pre-rules case, recognized that this exception, as codified in rule 408, must be balanced against the policy of encouraging settlements and the district court's judgment in this regard will be upset only for abuse of discretion. We cannot say that the district court abused its discretion; notice could be effectively proved by means less in conflict with the policy behind rule 408.[9] The exclusion of the Goldsmith Report under rule 408 must stand.... [Affirmed in relevant part.]

CARNEY v. AMERICAN UNIVERSITY

151 F.3d 1090 (D.C. Cir. 1998)

TATEL, Circuit Judge.

... A senior administrator at The American University since 1981, appellant Darion Carney became Director of Student Service in 1988, the highest ranking African American at the University. A year later, she became Acting

---

9. For example, the Court exhibits contain a series of letters dated in October, 1974 between counsel for both sides, referring to a list of complaints given to Goldsmith apparently at approximately the same time. These letters accompanied by the list which was not included in the exhibit could have proved this notice issue without prejudice to Ramada.

Dean of Students, serving in that capacity for two years while the University searched for a permanent Dean. She applied for the permanent position, but the University selected someone else. She then returned to her former position as Director of Student Services. Two years later, the University commenced "downsizing," a process which resulted in the elimination of Carney's position and her dismissal.

Soon after she lost her job, Carney informed the University by letter that she intended to sue. About the same time, a question arose as to whether she might be entitled to an additional three months' severance pay on top of her existing severance package. The University did not give her the extra three months' pay.

... Carney filed suit in the United States District Court for the District of Columbia, claiming that the University discriminated against her on the basis of her race when it did not select her for the Dean of Students position, and again when it eliminated her position. She also claimed that the University withheld extra severance pay in retaliation for exercising her civil rights. In defense, the University asserted that it had legitimate, nondiscriminatory reasons for not hiring her and for subsequently eliminating her position. With respect to her retaliation claim, the University argued first that it crafted Carney's severance package before it knew that she intended to sue, and second, that all evidence of linkage between the extra severance pay and her lawsuit is contained in inadmissible settlement correspondence.

The district court granted summary judgment for the University. [We affirm as to the discrimination claims but reverse and remand as to the claim of retaliation.]

Carney contends that the University withheld extra severance pay in retaliation for having signaled her intention to file suit. In a settlement letter from the University's lawyer dated December 12, 1994, responding to a letter from Carney's attorney, the University acknowledged that under certain interpretations of its personnel manuals, Carney might "arguably [be] entitl[ed] ... to an additional three months' pay." ... According to the University, the extra severance pay amounted to nothing more than a settlement offer.

Granting summary judgment for the University, the district court found that Carney failed to present evidence of causation, reasoning that the University crafted her initial severance package containing only seven months' severance pay before it knew that Carney intended to sue. The court also held that Rule 408 of the Federal Rules of Evidence prohibited Carney from relying on settlement correspondence to establish causation.

We disagree with the district court for two reasons. First, apart from the settlement letters, [Carney offered] evidence from which a jury could conclude that the University retaliated against Carney either by refusing to give her any extra pay or refusing even to consider it. ... Second, although settlement letters are inadmissible to prove liability or amount, they are admissible "when the evidence is offered for another purpose." Fed. R. Evid. 408. In particular, such correspondence can be used to establish an independent violation (here, retaliation) unrelated to the underlying claim which was the subject of the correspondence (race discrimination). *See Eisenberg v. University of N.M.*, 911 F.2d 1131, 1134 (10th Cir. 1991) (affidavit obtained in settlement negotiations admissible to impose Rule 11 liability); *Urico v. Parnell Oil Co.*,

708 F.2d 852, 854-55 (1st Cir. 1983) (evidence of settlement negotiations admissible to show interference with efforts to mitigate damages); *Resolution Trust Corp. v. Blasdell*, 154 F.R.D. 675, 681 (D. Ariz. 1993) (evidence of settlement negotiations admissible to prove retaliatory motive); *see also* 23 Charles Alan Wright & Kenneth W. Graham, Jr., Federal Practice and Procedure §5314, at 282 (1980) ("Rule 408 is [] inapplicable when the claim is based upon some wrong that was committed in the course of settlement discussions; e.g., libel, assault, breach of contract, unfair labor practice, and the like."). Carney offered the settlement correspondence not to prove that the University discriminated against her, but to show that the University committed an entirely separate wrong by conditioning her benefits on a waiver of her rights. The letters were therefore admissible. . . .

PRL USA HOLDINGS, INC. v. UNITED STATES POLO ASSOCIATION, INC.

520 F.3d 109 (2d Cir. 2008)

LEVAL, Circuit Judge.

This is an appeal by plaintiff PRL USA Holdings, Inc., holder of the Ralph Lauren trademarks for clothing, from the judgment of the United States District Court for the Southern District of New York, denying plaintiff's claims of trademark infringement. PRL has for many years used as a mark on Ralph Lauren clothing a famous logo showing in silhouette a mounted polo player with polo mallet raised. PRL brought this action against the United States Polo Association ("USPA") and its licensee, Jordache, Ltd., alleging that four logos used by the defendants on a clothing line, each showing a pair of mounted polo players — the so-called "double horsemen marks" — infringed the Ralph Lauren polo player logo. . . .

At trial, PRL presented evidence that consumers were likely to confuse all four double horsemen marks with Ralph Lauren's polo player symbol. The defendants presented contrary evidence and also attempted to prove the affirmative defense of estoppel by acquiescence by presenting evidence that PRL had affirmatively consented to the USPA's use of a version of the double horsemen mark.

PRL objected to this latter evidence of consent on the ground that it consisted of statements made in compromise negotiations, offered to prove the invalidity of its claims, and therefore should be excluded under Federal Rule of Evidence 408. The district court overruled PRL's objection and admitted the evidence.

Using a special verdict form, the jury . . . rejected the defendants' claim of estoppel by acquiescence. . . . [The jury further found that one of the defendants' double horsemen marks infringed PRL's trademarks, but that the other three did not.] The district court entered judgment accordingly. This appeal followed. . . .

[At trial, the] defendants offered the testimony of a former USPA employee, Merle Jenkins, and some corroborating evidence, that during the course of their settlement discussions, PRL gave the USPA consent to use a version of the double horsemen mark and implied that it was not "offensive" to PRL. PRL objected both before and during trial to all such evidence, citing Federal Rule of Evidence 408.

Under Rule 408 . . . evidence of "conduct or statements made in compromise negotiations" is "not admissible to prove liability for or invalidity of [a] claim or its amount." The Rule, however, explicitly provided an exception. It "does not require exclusion when the evidence is offered for another purpose." The district court ruled that the evidence was admissible to prove the defendants' assertion that PRL was estopped to claim infringement after it led the defendants to believe no claim of infringement would be brought, and the defendants spent millions in developing the marks in reliance on that assurance. . . .

[PRL argues that the evidence was barred by Rule 408 even if the evidence was] offered to prove an estoppel defense. The Rule provides that "conduct or statements made in compromise negotiations" are "not admissible to prove liability for or invalidity of [a] claim." Without doubt, the evidence was of "conduct [and] statements made in compromise negotiations." In addition, it was, in a sense, offered to demonstrate the "invalidity" of PRL's claim of trademark infringement. If the defendants' claim of estoppel would succeed, PRL's claim of infringement would fail. It follows, according to PRL's argument, that the evidence was offered for the prohibited purpose of proving the "invalidity" of its claim, and was thus prohibited by Rule 408.

The problem with PRL's clever argument is that it would deprive Rule 408's exception of all meaning. . . . All of the evidence a party offers at trial is intended to help establish its own position and defeat the adversary's position. In a sense, all evidence offered seeks either to "prove liability for or invalidity of [a] claim or its amount." If we accepted PRL's contention of the meaning of the Rule, there would be no evidence falling within the category whose exclusion is "not require[d]" because it is "offered for another purpose." The exception would be meaningless.

The exception clearly intends to exempt from the absolute prohibition of the Rule evidence focused on issues different from the elements of the primary claim in dispute. . . . [E]stoppel by acquiescence is an affirmative defense, which raises issues different from the elements of a claim of infringement. . . . A discussion between a trademark owner and a potential user of a similar mark in which the owner gives assurance that it will not sue for infringement may well be characterized as compromise negotiations. To construe Rule 408 as barring such evidence would substantially limit the opportunity of defendants to rely on the defense of estoppel, even when well substantiated. . . .

PRL argues further that the district court erred by refusing to give a limiting instruction it requested on the use of settlement evidence. The language of the requested instruction would have required the jury to ignore any evidence that it concluded was made in the context of settlement negotiations, regardless of whether the settlement evidence was received for a purpose authorized by Rule 408. The requested instruction was thus contrary to the plain language of Rule 408, and the district court did not err in refusing to give it. . . . PRL never requested an appropriate limiting instruction telling the jury for what purpose they could, and could not, consider the settlement evidence. We cannot tell whether PRL's failure to request an appropriate limiting instruction was strategic. Counsel often prefer not to propose a limiting instruction because the instruction may call the jury's attention to the harmful evidence. Nonetheless, whatever the reason for PRL's failure to request an appropriate limiting instruction, PRL cannot now complain of a lack of one. . . . We affirm the judgment of the district court.

2. Criminal Settlements

[F.R.E. 410; C.E.C. §1153]

ADVISORY COMMITTEE NOTE TO F.R.E. 410

Withdrawn pleas of guilty were held inadmissible in federal prosecutions in Kercheval v. United States, 274 U.S. 220 (1927). The Court pointed out that to admit the withdrawn plea would effectively set at naught the allowance of withdrawal and place the accused in a dilemma utterly inconsistent with the decision to award him a trial. The New York Court of Appeals, in People v. Spitaleri, 9 N.Y.2d 168, 212 N.Y.S.2d 53, 173 N.E.2d 35 (1961), re-examined and overturned its earlier decisions which had allowed admission. In addition to the reasons set forth in Kercheval, which was quoted at length, the court pointed out that the effect of admitting the plea was to compel defendant to take the stand by way of explanation and to open the way for the prosecution to call the lawyer who had represented him at the time of entering the plea. . . .

Pleas of *nolo contendere* are recognized by Rule 11 of the Rules of Criminal Procedure, although the law of numerous States is to the contrary. The present rule gives effect to the principal traditional characteristic of the *nolo* plea, i.e. avoiding the admission of guilt which is inherent in pleas of guilty. . . .

Exclusion of offers to plead guilty or *nolo* has as its purpose the promotion of disposition of criminal cases by compromise. As pointed out in McCormick §251, p. 543: "Effective criminal law administration in many localities would hardly be possible if a large proportion of the charges were not disposed of by such compromises." . . . As with compromise offers generally, Rule 408, free communication is needed, and security against having an offer of compromise or related statement admitted in evidence effectively encourages it.

Limiting the exclusionary rule to use against the accused is consistent with the purpose of the rule, since the possibility of use for or against other persons will not impair the effectiveness of withdrawing pleas or the freedom of discussion which the rule is designed to foster. . . .

UNITED STATES v. MEZZANATTO

513 U.S. 196 (1995)

Justice Thomas delivered the opinion of the Court.

Federal Rule of Evidence 410 and Federal Rule of Criminal Procedure 11(e)(6) provide that statements made in the course of plea discussions between a criminal defendant and a prosecutor are inadmissible against the defendant. The court below held that these exclusionary provisions may not be waived by the defendant. We granted certiorari to resolve a conflict among the Courts of Appeals, and we now reverse.

[Respondent Gary Mezzanatto was arrested after selling methamphetamine to an undercover agent.] On October 17, 1991, respondent and his attorney asked to meet with the prosecutor to discuss the possibility of cooperating with the Government. The prosecutor agreed to meet later that day. At the beginning of the meeting, the prosecutor informed respondent that he had no obligation to talk, but that if he wanted to cooperate he would have to be completely truthful. As a condition to proceeding with the discussion, the prosecutor indicated that respondent would have to agree that any statements he made during the meeting could be used to impeach any contradictory testimony he might give at trial if the case proceeded that far. Respondent conferred with his counsel and agreed to proceed under the prosecutor's terms.

Respondent then admitted knowing that the package he had attempted to sell to the undercover police officer contained methamphetamine, but insisted that he had dealt only in "ounce" quantities of methamphetamine prior to his arrest. Initially, respondent also claimed that he was acting merely as a broker for [another trafficker, Gordon Shuster,] and did not know that Shuster was manufacturing methamphetamine at his residence, but he later conceded that he knew about Shuster's laboratory. Respondent attempted to minimize his role in Shuster's operation by claiming that he had not visited Shuster's residence for at least a week before his arrest. At this point, the Government confronted respondent with surveillance evidence showing that his car was on Shuster's property the day before the arrest, and terminated the meeting on the basis of respondent's failure to provide completely truthful information.

Respondent eventually was tried on the methamphetamine charge and took the stand in his own defense. He maintained that he was not involved in methamphetamine trafficking and that he had thought Shuster used his home laboratory to manufacture plastic explosives for the CIA. He also denied knowing that the package he delivered to the undercover officer contained methamphetamine. Over defense counsel's objection, the prosecutor cross-examined respondent about the inconsistent statements he had made during the October 17 meeting. Respondent denied having made certain statements, and the prosecutor called one of the agents who had attended the meeting to recount the prior statements. The jury found respondent guilty, and the District Court sentenced him to 170 months in prison.

A panel of the Ninth Circuit reversed, over the dissent of Chief Judge Wallace. The Ninth Circuit held that respondent's agreement to allow admission of his plea statements for purposes of impeachment was unenforceable and that the District Court therefore erred in admitting the statements for that purpose....

Federal Rule of Evidence 410 and Federal Rule of Criminal Procedure 11(e)(6) (Rules or plea-statement Rules) are substantively identical. Rule 410 provides:

> "Except as otherwise provided in this rule, evidence of the following is not, in any civil or criminal proceeding, admissible against the defendant who . . . was a

participant in the plea discussions: . . . (4) any statement made in the course of plea discussions with an attorney for the prosecuting authority which do not result in a plea of guilty. . . ."

The Ninth Circuit noted that these Rules are subject to only two express exceptions, neither of which says anything about waiver, and thus concluded that Congress must have meant to preclude waiver agreements such as respondent's. In light of the "precision with which these rules are generally phrased," the Ninth Circuit declined to "write in a waiver in a waiverless rule."

The Ninth Circuit's analysis is directly contrary to the approach we have taken in the context of a broad array of constitutional and statutory provisions. Rather than deeming waiver presumptively unavailable absent some sort of express enabling clause, we instead have adhered to the opposite presumption. . . . The presumption of waivability has found specific application in the context of evidentiary rules. Absent some "overriding procedural consideration that prevents enforcement of the contract," courts have held that agreements to waive evidentiary rules are generally enforceable even over a party's subsequent objections. 21 C. Wright & K. Graham, Federal Practice and Procedure §5039, pp. 207–208 (1977) (hereinafter Wright & Graham). Courts have "liberally enforced" agreements to waive various exclusionary rules of evidence. Note, *Contracts to Alter the Rules of Evidence*, 46 Harv. L. Rev. 138, 139–140 (1933). Thus, at the time of the adoption of the Federal Rules of Evidence, agreements as to the admissibility of documentary evidence were routinely enforced and held to preclude subsequent objections as to authenticity. See, *e.g., Tupman Thurlow Co. v. S.S. Cap Castillo*, 490 F.2d 302, 309 (CA2 1974); *United States v. Wing*, 450 F.2d 806, 811 (CA9 1971). And although hearsay is inadmissible except under certain specific exceptions, we have held that agreements to waive hearsay objections are enforceable. See *Sac and Fox Indians of Miss. in Iowa v. Sac and Fox Indians of Miss. in Okl.*, 220 U.S. 481, 488–489 (1911); see also *United States v. Bonnett*, 877 F.2d 1450, 1458–1459 (CA10 1989) (party's stipulation to admissibility of document precluded hearsay objection at trial).

Indeed, evidentiary stipulations are a valuable and integral part of everyday trial practice. Prior to trial, parties often agree in writing to the admission of otherwise objectionable evidence, either in exchange for stipulations from opposing counsel or for other strategic purposes. Both the Federal Rules of Civil Procedure and the Federal Rules of Criminal Procedure appear to contemplate that the parties will enter into evidentiary agreements during a pretrial conference. See Fed. Rule Civ. Proc. 16(c)(3); Fed. Rule Crim. Proc. 17.1. During the course of trial, parties frequently decide to waive evidentiary objections, and such tactics are routinely honored by trial judges. See 21 Wright & Graham §5032, at 161 ("It is left to the parties, in the first instance, to decide whether or not the rules are to be enforced. . . . It is only in rare cases that the trial judge will . . . exclude evidence they are content to see admitted"); see also *United States v. Coonan*, 938 F.2d 1553, 1561 (CA2 1991) (criminal defendant not entitled "to evade the consequences of an unsuccessful tactical decision" made in welcoming admission of otherwise inadmissible evidence).

. . . There may be some evidentiary provisions that are so fundamental to the reliability of the factfinding process that they may never be waived without irreparably "discredit[ing] the federal courts." See 21 Wright & Graham §5039, at 207-208; see also *Wheat v. United States*, 486 U.S. 153, 162, 108 S. Ct. 1692, 1698-1699, 100 L. Ed. 2d 140 (1988) (court may decline a defendant's waiver of his right to conflict-free counsel); *United States v. Josefik*, 753 F.2d 585, 588 (CA7 1985) ("No doubt there are limits to waiver; if the parties stipulated to trial by 12 orangutans the defendant's conviction would be invalid notwithstanding his consent, because some minimum of civilized procedure is required by community feeling regardless of what the defendant wants or is willing to accept"). But enforcement of agreements like respondent's plainly will not have that effect. The admission of plea statements for impeachment purposes enhances the truth-seeking function of trials and will result in more accurate verdicts. . . . Under any view of the evidence, the defendant has made a false statement, either to the prosecutor during the plea discussion or to the jury at trial; making the jury aware of the inconsistency will tend to increase the reliability of the verdict without risking institutional harm to the federal courts.

. . . Respondent also contends that waiver is fundamentally inconsistent with the Rules' goal of encouraging voluntary settlement. . . . We need not decide whether and under what circumstances substantial "public policy" interests may permit the inference that Congress intended to override the presumption of waivability, for in this case there is no basis for concluding that waiver will interfere with the Rules' goal of encouraging plea bargaining. . . . [A]lthough the availability of waiver may discourage some defendants from negotiating, it is also true that prosecutors may be unwilling to proceed without it.

Prosecutors may be especially reluctant to negotiate without a waiver agreement during the early stages of a criminal investigation, when prosecutors are searching for leads and suspects may be willing to offer information in exchange for some form of immunity or leniency in sentencing. In this "cooperation" context, prosecutors face "painfully delicate" choices as to "whether to proceed and prosecute those suspects against whom the already produced evidence makes a case or whether to extend leniency or full immunity to some suspects in order to procure testimony against other, more dangerous suspects against whom existing evidence is flimsy or nonexistent." Hughes, *Agreements for Cooperation in Criminal Cases*, 45 Vand. L. Rev. 1, 15 (1992). Because prosecutors have limited resources and must be able to answer "sensitive questions about the credibility of the testimony" they receive before entering into any sort of cooperation agreement, *id.*, at 10, prosecutors may condition cooperation discussions on an agreement that the testimony provided may be used for impeachment purposes. If prosecutors were precluded from securing such agreements, they might well decline to enter into cooperation discussions in the first place and might never take this potential first step toward a plea bargain.

. . . Respondent asserts that there is a "gross disparity" in the relative bargaining power of the parties to a plea agreement and suggests that a waiver agreement is "inherently unfair and coercive." . . . The dilemma flagged by respondent is indistinguishable from any of a number of difficult choices that criminal defendants face every day. The plea bargaining process necessarily exerts pressure on defendants to plead guilty and to abandon a series of fundamental rights, but we have repeatedly held that the government "may encourage a guilty plea by offering substantial benefits in return for the plea." *Corbitt v. New Jersey*, 439 U.S. 212, 219 (1978). . . . The mere potential for abuse of prosecutorial bargaining power is an insufficient basis for foreclosing negotiation altogether. "Rather, tradition and experience justify our belief that the great majority of prosecutors will be faithful to their duty." *Newton v. Rumery*, 480 U.S. 386, 397 (1987) (plurality opinion). Thus, although some waiver agreements "may not be the product of an informed and voluntary decision," this possibility "does not justify invalidating all such agreements." *Newton*, 480 U.S. at 393 (majority opinion). Instead, the appropriate response to respondent's predictions of abuse is to permit case-by-case inquiries into whether waiver agreements are the product of fraud or coercion. We hold that absent some affirmative indication that the agreement was entered into unknowingly or involuntarily, an agreement to waive the exclusionary provisions of the plea-statement Rules is valid and enforceable. . . . Accordingly, the judgment of the Court of Appeals is reversed.

Justice GINSBURG, with whom JUSTICE O'CONNOR and Justice BREYER join, concurring.

The Court holds that a waiver allowing the Government to impeach with statements made during plea negotiations is compatible with Congress' intent to promote plea bargaining. It may be, however, that a waiver to use such statements in the case in chief would more severely undermine a defendant's incentive to negotiate, and thereby inhibit plea bargaining. As the Government has not sought such a waiver, we do not here explore this question.

Justice SOUTER, with whom Justice STEVENS joins, dissenting.

. . . Already, standard forms indicate that many federal prosecutors routinely require waiver of Rules 410 and 11(e)(6) rights before a prosecutor is willing to enter into plea discussions. . . . As the Government conceded during oral argument, defendants are generally in no position to challenge demands for these waivers, and the use of waiver provisions as contracts of adhesion has become accepted practice. Today's decision can only speed the heretofore illegitimate process by which the exception has been swallowing the Rules. . . .

It is true that many (if not all) of the waiver forms now employed go only to admissibility for impeachment. But although the erosion of the Rules has begun with this trickle, the majority's reasoning will provide no principled limit to it. The Rules draw no distinction between use of a statement for impeachment and use in the Government's case in chief. If objection can be waived for impeachment use, it can be waived for use as affirmative evidence, and if the Government can effectively demand waiver in the former instance, there is no reason to believe it will not do so just as successfully in the latter. When it does, there is nothing this Court will legitimately be able to do about it. The Court is construing a congressional Rule on the theory that Congress meant to permit its waiver. Once that point is passed, as it is today, there is no legitimate limit on admissibility of a defendant's plea negotiation statements beyond what the Constitution may independently impose or the traffic may bear. Just what the traffic may bear is an open question, but what cannot be denied is that the majority opinion sanctions a demand for waiver of such scope that a defendant who gives it will be unable even to acknowledge his desire to negotiate a guilty plea without furnishing admissible evidence against himself then and there. In such cases, the possibility of trial if no agreement is reached will be reduced to fantasy. The only defendant who will not damage himself by even the most restrained candor will be the one so desperate that he might as well walk into court and enter a naked guilty plea. It defies reason to think that Congress intended to invite such a result, when it adopted a Rule said to promote candid discussion in the interest of encouraging compromise.

UNITED STATES v. MERGEN

No. 06-CR-352 (E.D.N.Y. 2010)

GARAUFIS, District Judge.

[Defendant Volkan Mergen signed a cooperation agreement with the Government and, pursuant to that agreement, pled guilty to a reduced charge related to a residential arson. During the plea allocution, he admitted under oath that he had assisted in the arson. The cooperation deal later fell apart because the government concluded that Mergen lied during a debriefing session. The District Court allowed Mergen to withdraw his guilty plea.]

The Government seeks to introduce the statements Defendant made during his plea allocution. Though statements made in connection with a withdrawn or aborted plea would normally be inadmissible under Federal Rule of Evidence 410, the cooperation agreement under which Defendant entered his guilty plea specified that he would waive his rights to object to the use of such evidence in any prosecutions resulting from a breach of the agreement. Specifically, the Defendant waived "all claims under the United States Constitution, Rule 11(f) of the Federal Rules of Criminal Procedure, Rule 410 of the Federal Rules of Evidence, or any other federal statute or rule, that statements made by him on or after January 26, 2005, or any leads derived therefrom, should be suppressed."

. . . [A] defendant may agree to waive the protection of Rule 410, and courts will enforce such agreements unless there is "some affirmative indication that the agreement was entered into unknowingly or involuntarily." *United States v. Mezzanatto*, 513 U.S. 196, (1995). *Mezzanatto* involved a narrow waiver provision — one that only allowed plea negotiation statements to be used to impeach the defendant if he chose to testify at trial — but the Courts of Appeals have since allowed broader waivers. The Second Circuit upheld a waiver provision that permitted the government to introduce plea-related statements "to rebut contrary evidence or arguments presented by the defense," regardless of whether or not the defendant testifies. *United States v. Velez*, 354 F.3d 190, 196 (2d Cir.2004); see also *United States v. Hardwick*, 544 F.3d 565 (3d Cir.2008) (approving waiver for rebuttal purposes); *United States v. Rebbe*, 314 F.3d 402 (9th Cir.2002) (same); *United States v. Krilich*, 159 F.3d 1020 (7th Cir.1998) (same).

Although the Second Circuit has never confronted a waiver as broad as the one here — which allows the statements to be used for any purpose, not merely for rebuttal — there is no reason to believe that rebuttal-only waivers represent the outer limit of enforceable provisions . . . . Outside of the Second Circuit, other courts have examined waiver provisions containing no rebuttal limitation. Finding no "analytically coherent boundary between waivers for purposes of impeachment or rebuttal and waivers for the prosecution's case-in-chief," the Fifth Circuit upheld a limitless waiver provision like the one at issue in this case. *United States v. Sylvester*, 583 F.3d 285, 290-91 (5th Cir. 2009). The only other Courts of Appeals to confront such limitless waiver provisions, the Eighth Circuit and the D.C. Circuit, also held the provisions to be enforceable. See *United States v. Young*, 223 F.3d 905 (8th Cir. 2000); *United States v. Burch*, 156 F.3d 1315 (D.C. Cir. 1998). Indeed, Defendant points to no authority for limiting the reach of a knowing and voluntary waiver of rights under Rule 410. For these reasons, the court is convinced that the waiver in Defendant's cooperation agreement should be enforced according to its terms. Accordingly, Rule 410 poses no obstacle to the Government's use of Defendant's plea allocution statements as part of its case-in-chief . . . . SO ORDERED.

CHRISTOPHER B. MUELLER, "MAKE HIM AN OFFER HE CAN'T REFUSE" — *MEZZANATTO* WAIVERS AS LYNCHPIN OF PROSECUTORIAL OVERREACH

82 Mo. L. Rev. 1023, 1026, 1028, 1084 (2017)

Prosecutors had begun to get defendants to sign waivers before the decision in *Mezzanatto*, but that decision so strongly reinforced this technique that it quickly became commonplace in the federal system and spread to many states as well . . . . *Mezzanatto* . . . has reduced Rule 410 to a default provision — in federal courts, really a dead letter. . . . [C]ourts have . . . tended to enforce Mezzanatto waivers in all four of the situations in which they can operate — when bargaining fails to produce agreement, when agreement is reached but one side or the other withdraws, when courts do not accept pleas tendered pursuant to agreement, and when the defendant is allowed to withdraw a plea.

JOHN W. STRONG, CONSENSUAL MODIFICATIONS OF THE RULES OF EVIDENCE: THE LIMITS OF PARTY AUTONOMY IN AN ADVERSARY SYSTEM

80 Neb. L. Rev. 159, 159–164 (2001)

I start from the proposition, well known to all those trained in the Anglo-American legal tradition, that we have an adversary system, which is quite different from those employed in much of the non-English speaking world. The distinctiveness of the adversary system, as its name would suggest, lies in its allocation to the adversaries in the dispute the basic responsibility for discovering, marshalling, and presenting the facts of the case to the decision maker, either judge or jury, rather than assigning these tasks to a non-partisan official. Essentially two complementary justifications have been presented for this mode of proceeding. First, the adversary system is a sort of analog of laissez-faire economics, in the sense that as according to Adam Smith, individual pursuit of personal economic advantage will ultimately redound to the general public benefit. This places the burden of fact development and presentation upon those most interested in the result and will tend to ensure the fullest and ultimately most accurate depiction of the facts. A second justification sometimes asserted is that this allocation of responsibility is essentially fair, in the sense that those most immediately affected by judicial decisions should be given every reasonable opportunity to participate in the resolution process.

Consistent with these rationales, parties to litigation are, for the most part, given great latitude in the manner in which they choose to assert their rights in court. This autonomy is slightly less in criminal matters, where it is said that the state possesses a significant interest. But even here, the overriding interest in allowing self-determination will often prevail even to the extent of allowing the criminal defendant to make choices which would generally be thought to be undesirable and even foolish.

Not surprisingly, the rules of evidence, which are themselves part and parcel of the adversary system, generally also operate upon the principle of party responsibility. By that I mean it is usually the responsibility of the parties to see that the rules are applied. This responsibility is most clearly embodied in the so-called contemporaneous objection rule, which requires the party wishing to see a rule of evidence enforced to lodge an objection as soon as an impending violation of the rule is reasonably to be anticipated. Failure to make an objection will, in the great majority of instances, mean that the rule goes unenforced at trial. In addition, such a violation of the rule will provide no ground for claiming error on appeal. In other words, the usual result is that any rule not insisted upon by a party wishing to see it applied is waived.

And, of course, in addition to waiver, there are several other avenues by which the parties may forego enforcement of the usual rules. Foremost among these are pre-dispute contracts in which the parties specify what rules will apply in the event a dispute develops between them, and stipulations, which will sometimes constitute an agreed modification of the rules or represent mutual acceptance of a fact which otherwise would need to be established by ordinary evidentiary means. . . .

A seeming majority of courts have now retreated from the position, earlier common, that the parties are powerless to affect the rules by consensual agreement. . . . Today, though a contrariety of statements can still be found, the most common judicial formulation is that the parties are allowed wide discretion in determining what rules of evidence are to be enforced in a judicial proceeding, but may not by party agreement violate pubic policy. Beyond this very general statement, the decisions give only sketchy suggestions as to what the limitations of public policy may be.

C. MEDICAL PAYMENTS AND LIABILITY INSURANCE

[F.R.E. 409, 411; C.E.C. §1155]

ADVISORY COMMITTEE NOTE TO F.R.E. 409

The considerations underlying this rule parallel those underlying Rules 407 and 408, which deal respectively with subsequent remedial measures and offers of compromise. As stated in Annot., 20 A.L.R.2d 291, 293: "[G]enerally, evidence of payment of medical, hospital, or similar expenses of an injured party by the opposing party, is not admissible, the reason often given being that such payment or offer is usually made from humane impulses and not from an admission of liability, and that to hold otherwise would tend to discourage assistance to the injured person."

Contrary to Rule 408, dealing with offers of compromise, the present rule does not extend to conduct or statements not a part of the act of furnishing or offering or promising to pay. This difference in treatment arises from fundamental difference in nature. Communication is essential if compromises are to be effected, and consequently broad protection of statements is needed. This is not so in cases of payments or offers or promises to pay medical expenses, where factual statements may be expected to be incidental in nature....

ADVISORY COMMITTEE NOTE TO F.R.E. 411

The courts have with substantial unanimity rejected evidence of liability insurance for the purpose of proving fault, and absence of liability insurance as proof of lack of fault. At best the inference of fault from the fact of insurance coverage is a tenuous one, as is its converse. More important, no doubt, has been the feeling that knowledge of the presence of liability insurance would induce juries to decide cases on improper grounds. The rule is drafted in broad terms so as to include contributory negligence or other fault of a plaintiff as well as fault of a defendant. The second sentence points out the limits of the rule, using well established illustrations.

CHARTER v. CHLEBORAD

551 F.2d 246 (8th Cir. 1977)

PER CURIAM.

This is a diversity action to recover damages for alleged medical malpractice. In June of 1973, plaintiff was struck by a truck while working as a highway flagman. The accident caused extensive injuries to both of plaintiff's legs. Plaintiff was hospitalized and placed under the care of a general practitioner and defendant, a surgeon. Surgery was performed on both legs. As a result of severe complications plaintiff was transferred to another hospital where both legs were amputated above the knee. The trial of the matter resulted in a jury verdict for defendant and the district court denied plaintiff's motion for a new trial. . . .

[At trial p]laintiff offered the testimony of Dr. Joseph Lichtor, M.D., a Kansas City, Missouri orthopedic surgeon. . . . Dr. Lichtor testified that the cause of the complications and subsequent amputations was defendant's negligence. As a part of his rebuttal case, defendant offered the testimony of John J. Alder, an attorney from the Kansas City area. Mr. Alder testified that Dr. Lichtor's reputation for truth and veracity in the Kansas City area was bad. On cross-examination Mr. Alder testified that he did some defense work in medical malpractice cases. He also stated that some of his clients in those cases were insurance companies.

Plaintiff's counsel then asked him to name some of those companies and defendant objected to the relevancy of the matter. After a conference at the Bench the district court refused to allow further questioning on the subject of insurance. As plaintiff stated in his motion for a new trial, Mr. Alder was employed in part by the same liability carrier who represents defendant in this action.

It is well established that the existence of a liability insurance policy is not admissible to show one's negligence or other wrongful conduct. Fed. R. Evid. 411 (1975); C. McCormick, Evidence §201, at 479 (2d ed. 1972). This rule has its belief that such evidence is of questionable probative value or relevance and is often prejudicial. . . . Evidence of the existence of insurance may be offered for other purposes, however. . . .

In this case the fact that defendant's insurer employed Mr. Alder was clearly admissible to show possible bias of that witness. . . . plaintiff's claim rested for the most part on the credibility of his witness. When defendant undertook to impeach that witness plaintiff was entitled to attempt to show possible bias of Mr. Alder as surrebuttal. Considering the importance of expert testimony in this case we cannot conclude that the trial court's exclusionary ruling was mere harmless error. . . . Accordingly, the judgment of the district court is reversed and the action is remanded with directions to grant the plaintiff a new trial.

HIGGINS v. HICKS CO.

756 F.2d 681 (8th Cir. 1985)

FAGG, Circuit Judge.

This lawsuit is the result of two separate motorcycle accidents that occurred on a four-lane divided highway in South Dakota. The accidents occurred after sunset on a stretch of Interstate 90 that was under construction. The Hicks Company, under contract with the State of South Dakota, was resurfacing the interstate with asphalt. On the day of the accident, there was a 5.4 mile stretch of highway that had been resurfaced on the passing lane of eastbound I-90 but not on the driving lane. This left a 3–4 inch ridge over which a driver had to maneuver to move from the driving lane to the passing lane. Steven Martinez lost control of his motorcycle when moving from the driving lane to the passing lane and was fatally injured. Mallard Teal also lost control of his vehicle when changing lanes on this 5.4 mile stretch and claims damages as a result of the injuries he sustained.

Plaintiffs claim that The Hicks Company and the State of South Dakota were negligent in opening both eastbound lanes on I-90 at this 5.4 mile stretch without adequate warning signs. Defendants deny any negligence and claim Martinez and Teal were contributorily negligent in operating their motorcycles at a speed greater than was reasonable under the circumstances and in failing to keep a proper lookout. The jury returned a verdict favorable to The Hicks Company and the State of South Dakota.

[P]laintiffs contend that it was error for the district court to refuse to admit evidence that the State of South Dakota carries liability insurance. Plaintiffs contend that evidence of the state's liability insurance was admissible to eliminate any bias of the jurors as taxpayers of the State of South Dakota. We cannot agree.

Evidence of liability insurance may be admitted if relevant to an issue in the case or to prove bias or prejudice of a witness. Fed. R. Evid. 411. It is not admissible to prove negligence of the insured person. *Id.* The advisory committee note to Federal Rule 411 indicates that "knowledge of the presence or absence of liability insurance would induce juries to decide cases on improper grounds." We believe that evidence of the state's liability insurance was irrelevant to any issues in this case and that the evidence was properly excluded by the district court.... Affirmed.

CHARLES ALAN WRIGHT, KENNETH W. GRAHAM, JR. & VICTOR GOLD, FEDERAL PRACTICE AND PROCEDURE: EVIDENCE

23 §5362, at 428-37 (2d ed. 2018)

Evidence law scholars [have] been critical of the "archaic legal principle" upon which Rule 411 is based. Indeed, it is buried under an "avalanche of authoritative criticism." The mildest critic was Wigmore, who thought the common law rule "impracticable" because the benefits were so clearly outweighed by the costs of administering it. McCormick called the rule "a hollow shell" because of the many ways in which it could be evaded, while Morgan thought that enforcement of the rule led courts to "indulge in a lot of nonsense." An early critic saw the rule as a "coddling" of insurance companies, a view shared by a venerated torts scholar who referred to the "fantastic efforts which have been made by courts of the country to develop protection for indemnity insurers."

... [I]t is probably true that it is an "absurd hypothesis" that the existence of insurance will foster "a 'devil-may-care' attitude" on the part of the average driver. On the other hand, there are situations where evidence of liability insurance may be relevant to prove culpable conduct or lack thereof. For example, it does not seem implausible to suggest that the decision of whether to leave one's fireside to remove ice from the front walk on a winter day in South Dakota might be influenced by the presence or absence of personal liability to strangers who might fall. Similarly, assuming uninsured motorists are responsible for a disproportionate percentage of automobile accidents, driving without that protection may be probative of culpable conduct....

As for the countervailing factor of unfair prejudice a jury that wants to be told the amount of the defendant's insurance coverage because "we do not want to leave either party penniless" may have a better conception of justice than those who formulated the rule denying them this evidence.

... The need for a rule dealing with the admissibility of evidence of insurance arises because the insurance company is permitted to litigate disguised as its insured. Viewed from this perspective, the rule of evidence is not so much a doctrine of relevance as it is part of an arsenal of weapons that courts have developed to perpetuate the fiction that the insurance company is not a party though it controls the litigation and will pay the judgment.... Viewing the evidence rule from this broader perspective makes it seem even less defensible to the critics. The goal of the rule is seen as "impracticable" because the existence of insurance can be made known to the jury as early as voir dire examination. Moreover, at least in automobile litigation, modern jurors are likely to assume the existence of insurance, especially in jurisdictions where it is mandatory. The result is that the evidence rule is of little benefit to insurance companies but can work substantial prejudice to uninsured defendants. Finally, the attempt to enforce the rule puts the trial court on the horns of a dilemma. Rigorous enforcement is very expensive in terms of mistrials, the costs of adjudicating blame if that factor is relevant to reversal, and the waste of time spent trying to usher witnesses past the insurance company without their remarking its presence. If, on the other hand, the rule is loosely enforced it may give an unwarranted advantage to counsel who are sufficiently clever or unscrupulous enough to take advantage of such lax enforcement. In sum, if the goal is to prevent excessive verdicts against insurance companies, there are procedural devices — remittitur, for example — that are better suited to this purpose than a rule of evidence barring a party from proving what the jury already knows or suspects.

PROBLEMS

5.1. Following a traffic accident one driver says to the other, "I don't want to litigate this. I'll pay for the damage to your car, and I'll pay if you need to see a doctor." If the second driver later sues the first for negligence, is the first driver's statement admissible to prove fault?

5.2. An appliance repairer requires his customers to sign a contract providing that in any lawsuit brought against him, his lack of liability insurance will be admissible "without limitation." A clothes dryer he repairs catches fire and causes extensive damage to the customer's home. The customer sues the repairer for negligence. May the defendant introduce proof that he carries no liability insurance?

5.3. A bicycle company requires all its customers to sign a contract agreeing that in any lawsuit alleging a product defect, evidence that the defect was later remedied will be inadmissible for any purpose, including proof of feasibility. The brakes fail on a bicycle sold by the company, and the customer is injured. She sues alleging defective design. At trial the company claims the brakes could not feasibly have been made more reliable, and the customer seeks to counter that claim with evidence that, following her accident, the company changed the design of the brakes in a way that made them more reliable. Is the evidence admissible?

5.4. Dobbs and his passenger, Plunkett, are injured when the car Dobbs is driving collides with a truck owned and operated by Turpin Trucking Co. Plunkett sues Turpin for his personal injuries and calls Dobbs as a witness. On cross-examination, Turpin's lawyer asks Dobbs, "Isn't it true that you agreed to testify on Plunkett's behalf in this case as part of a settlement that Plunkett reached with your insurance carrier?" Should Plunkett's objection to this question be sustained?

TRIAL MECHANICS

"I'm going to ask the jury to hold its applause until all the
evidence has been introduced."

Evidence law leaves most questions regarding the mechanics of trial — the order of proof and the mode of examining witnesses — to the discretion of the trial judge. Nonetheless, several loose constraints are placed on that discretion, some by rule and others by tradition. This chapter addresses both kinds of constraints.

A. ORDER OF PROOF

A traditional rule of trial practice, codified in the Federal Rules of Evidence and its state counterparts, generally restricts cross-examination to the subjects

363

addressed in direct examination, and redirect examination to the subjects raised on cross-examination. But trial judges have broad discretion to depart from that rule, and from other traditional practices regarding the order of proof.

1. Generally

[F.R.E. 611(a) & (b); C.E.C. §§760–763, 765(a), 772–774]

ADVISORY COMMITTEE NOTE TO F.R.E. 611

Spelling out detailed rules to govern the mode and order of interrogating witnesses and presenting evidence is neither desirable nor feasible. The ultimate responsibility for the effective working of the adversary system rests with the judge. The rule sets forth the objectives which he should seek to attain. . . .

The tradition in the federal courts and in numerous state courts has been to limit the scope of cross-examination to matters testified to on direct, plus matters bearing upon the credibility of the witness. . . . [T]he matter is essentially one of the order of presentation and not one in which involvement at the appellate level is likely to prove fruitful. . . . The provision of the second sentence [of subsection (b)], that the judge may in the interests of justice limit inquiry into new matters on cross-examination, is designed for those situations in which the result otherwise would be confusion, complication, or protraction of the case, not as a matter of rule but as demonstrable in the actual development of the particular case. . . .

ROGER C. PARK ET AL., EVIDENCE LAW: A STUDENT'S GUIDE TO THE LAW OF EVIDENCE AS APPLIED IN AMERICAN TRIALS

§1.10, at 24 (4th ed. 2018)

As a general proposition, each subsequent layer of examination must stick to the issues raised in the previous questioning, or raise issues of credibility. The direct examiner's subsequent examinations of the witness are called redirect examinations and the cross-examiner's subsequent examinations of the witness are called re-cross examinations. The number of redirect and re-cross examinations that are necessary to present the full testimony to the jurors is entirely within the discretion of the trial judge.

The language of Rule 611(b) addresses only cross-examination, but the principle expressed in the Rule — that the subsequent examination is limited to the subject matter of the preceding examination — usually applies to both redirect examinations and re-cross examinations. The judge possesses vast discretion to promote the orderly presentation of evidence, and may allow the proponent on redirect to repair omissions in direct examination by allowing questions that go beyond the scope of the cross-examination.

STONE v. PEACOCK

968 F.2d 1163 (11th Cir. 1992)

PER CURIAM.

Plaintiff Calvin J. Stone lost a jury verdict ... in his suit against officers of the Georgia Department of Corrections claiming they terminated his employment in retaliation for his speaking out about the improper use of public property and funds. ... At the beginning of trial, the district court required Stone to testify first so that some chronology would be laid out at the beginning of the case. This initial testimony was not subject to cross-examination at that time. Stone's counsel protested the court's reordering of the witnesses. Federal Rules of Evidence Rule 611(a), however, gives courts reasonable control over the order and presentation of evidence. There may have been some error, but perhaps harmless in this case, if the court did not give Stone proper notice. The court's witness order requirement alone, however, is not reversible error absent some showing of harm. Although it does not appear that Stone has shown harm, we need not make this determination. If there is a retrial, the plaintiff will be on notice that he may be required by the court to testify at the beginning of the case. ... [Vacated and remanded in part on other grounds.]

ELGABRI v. LEKAS

964 F.2d 1255 (1st Cir. 1992)

STAHL, District Judge.

... Plaintiff-appellant Dr. Tarek H. Elgabri alleged various violations of state and federal antitrust laws, as well as a common law claim of tortious interference with prospective business relationships, against various doctors affiliated at four Rhode Island hospitals. The jury found for defendants on all counts. ...

Dr. Elgabri argues that his ability to call defendants during his case-in-chief was improperly limited by the trial court. He contends that he has an "unfettered right to call the adverse party on direct examination as part of his case-in-chief and to interrogate by leading questions without restrictions."

As part of his case-in-chief, Dr. Elgabri called defendant Dr. Lekas. After some examination of the witness, the court informed plaintiff during a recess that "it's unfair sometimes for a Plaintiff to prove his case through the mouth of the Defendant." Dr. Elgabri then continued his examination of Dr. Lekas.

After the day's testimony, the court decided to limit plaintiff's examination of defendants in his case-in-chief to subject matter that could not be obtained in any other fashion. The court suggested that plaintiff could prove the essential nature of a defendant's testimony in a proffer prior to the examination of each defendant. Defendants promised that they would take the stand as part of their case-in-chief and the court indicated that plaintiff would have ample opportunity to cross-examine them at that time. The court further indicated that no limits would be placed on the scope of cross-examination. Plaintiff thereafter made no further proffers and vigorously cross-examined the other defendants during their presentations. ...

We find that plaintiff did not have an "unfettered right" to call defendants during his case-in-chief. Rule 611(a) of the Federal Rules of Evidence [places the] . . . mode and order of questioning . . . in the trial court's discretion. We do not disturb decisions regarding courtroom management unless these decisions amount to an abuse of discretion that prejudices appellant's case. *Loinaz v. EG & G, Inc.*, 910 F.2d 1, 6 (1st Cir. 1990); *see also* 3 Jack B. Weinberg & Margaret A. Berger, *Weinstein's Evidence* 611[01] at 611–17 (1991) ("Once the judge exercises his power, his decision is virtually immune to attack and will be overturned only in the rare case where the appellate court finds a clear abuse of discretion that seriously damaged a party's right to a fair trial.").

Dr. Elgabri argues that Fed. R. Evid. 611(c), which allows for leading questions of adverse parties on direct examination, requires the court to allow direct examination of defendants in his case-in-chief. Rule 611(c) does not, however, impose such a requirement. Rather, Rule 611(c) only requires that the court allow a plaintiff who calls an adverse party on direct to use leading questions in his examination because the witness is presumed hostile. *See* Fed. R. Evid. 611(c), advisory committee's note; *see also* 3 *Weinstein's Evidence* 611[05] at 611-82 to 611-83.

In this case, the court reasonably held that plaintiff's examination of defendants should be limited in the described manner in order to make the presentation of evidence effective and to avoid needless consumption of time. Further, plaintiff does not argue that he failed to obtain evidence as a result of the district court's limiting of his presentation of his case; he only objects to the order of presentation. We therefore find no reversible error. . . .

UNITED STATES v. WILFORD

710 F.2d 439 (8th Cir. 1983)

LAY, Chief Judge.

[Wilford and three codefendants were convicted of extorting drivers at a waste treatment construction site in Cedar Rapids to join a Teamsters Union local.] . . . The defendants argue that a witness presented by the government during its rebuttal brought forward new facts not raised earlier, and that the defendants were entitled to present evidence on surrebuttal to counter the witness' testimony and to impeach his credibility. The trial court sustained the government's objection to surrebuttal by the defendants.

The witness, an investigator for the [National Labor Relations Board], testified as to his observation of events taking place at the Pittsburgh-Des Moines Steel Co. site. The government's stated purpose in offering the investigator's testimony was to show the similarity of the Pittsburgh-Des Moines incident to the incident for which the defendants were being tried. The defendants argue that they were entitled to present evidence in surrebuttal because the witness intimated that a violent act took place in connection with the stopping of a truck driven by a non-union driver, and because the defendants were entitled to show the investigator's bias against the Teamsters Union.

The decision whether to allow a party to present evidence in surrebuttal is committed to the sound discretion of the trial court. *United States v. Burgess*, 691 F.2d 1146, 1153 (4th Cir. 1982); *Kines v. Butterwoth*, 669 F.2d 6, 13 (1st Cir. 1981), *cert. denied*, 456 U.S. 980 (1982); *United States v. Greene*, 497 F.2d 1068, 1083 (7th Cir. 1974), *cert. denied*, 420 U.S. 909 (1975). In this case we find no abuse of discretion by the trial judge in his refusal to allow the defendants' surrebuttal. . . . [E]ven though a party is normally entitled to impeach the credibility of an opponent's key witness, in this case the investigator was not a key government witness, and in light of other evidence adduced at trial, his testimony regarding the similarity of the Pittsburgh-Des Moines incident to the incident for which the defendants were being tried was merely cumulative. Thus, it was not unfairly prejudicial for the trial court to refuse to allow the defendants to present evidence in surrebuttal. As the Seventh Circuit noted in *United States v. Greene*:

> When the point of completion of a trial has been reached, which was the situation here, the trial judge should be vested with substantial discretionary powers to bring the evidentiary phase to a close, or to put it another way, to curb the natural tendency of vigorous counsel to get in the final word.

We find no prejudicial error in the trial court's ruling. . . . [T]he defendants' convictions are affirmed.

UNITED STATES v. CARTER

910 F.2d 1524 (7th Cir. 1990)

CRABB, Chief District Judge.

Defendant Steven Carter was charged in a two-count indictment under 18 U.S.C. §2113(a) with robbing the Acme Continental Credit Union in [the CNA Insurance building in] Chicago on January 9, 1989 and again on January 20, 1989. The jury returned verdicts of guilty on both counts. . . .

Defendant argues that the trial court improperly allowed the government to exceed the scope of direct examination when it cross-examined Lashan Riggins.

The government did not call Riggins as a witness in its case in chief. Defendant called her as a defense witness. On cross-examination, the government exceeded the scope of direct examination by inquiring into the following subjects: (1) defendant's statement to her that he committed the robberies, made to her in the holding room at the police station after he confessed to the authorities; (2) her recollection of the clothing defendant wore when he left Indianapolis for Chicago on January 20, 1989; and (3) her recognition of the clothing discarded following the January 9 robbery as similar to clothing owned by defendant. Defendant objected to these questions at trial on the ground that they were prohibited by Fed. R. Evid. 611(b), but in each instance the trial court invoked its discretion under the rule to permit the questions.

The district court did not act improperly in so ruling. Although Fed. R. Evid. 611(b) limits cross-examination to the subject matter of direct examination, it grants the trial court discretion to "permit inquiry into additional matters as if on direct examination." A district court's evidentiary rulings are not subject to reversal unless the defendant can show a clear abuse of discretion. Moreover, because the management of cross-examination is peculiarly committed to the district court's discretion, "[t]he effect is to confine the matter largely to the trial level and to remove it from the area of profitable appellate review." *McCormick on Evidence*, §24 n.6 (3d ed. 1984).

Despite this deferential appellate standard, defendant argues that the court's decision to allow Riggins to be questioned on such matters constitutes an abuse of discretion because it enabled the government to present evidence that it chose not to offer in its case in chief and that would not have been proper rebuttal. Although defendant is correct in these assertions, he must show more than this to establish that the trial court abused its discretion. The testimony elicited challenged some of the alibis that defendant was presenting, such as his contention that he was not at the CNA building on January 9, 1989 and that he was misidentified as the robber on January 20, 1989. In light of the probative value of this evidence, the trial judge did not abuse his discretion by allowing the government to exceed the scope of Riggins's direct examination.... Affirmed.

2. Rule of Completeness

[F.R.E. 106; C.E.C. §356]

ADVISORY COMMITTEE NOTE TO F.R.E. 106

The rule is an expression of the rule of completeness.... The rule is based on two considerations. The first is the misleading impression created by taking matters out of context. The second is the inadequacy of repair work when delayed to a point later in the trial. The rule does not in any way circumscribe the right of the adversary to develop the matter on cross-examination or as part of his own case. For practical reasons, the rule is limited to writings and recorded statements and does not apply to conversations.

STEPHEN A. SALTZBURG, MICHAEL M. MARTIN & DANIEL J. CAPRA, FEDERAL RULES OF EVIDENCE MANUAL

§106.02[5], at 1:106-9 to 106-10 (10th ed. 2015)

Rule 106 is one of the rare examples of an evidence rule that permits one party to require another party to introduce more evidence than the latter desires to offer, or at least to have the latter party's case-in-chief interrupted while additional evidence is offered. Contrast Rule 106 with the typical approach to oral trial testimony. Questions asked on direct examination may produce a story that is shaded to the advantage of the party calling the witness. However, clarification does not occur until cross-examination. Thus, the Rule provides protection against initial offers of incomplete writings and recordings that is not provided against initial offers of incomplete testimony. The reason for limiting the Rule to writings and recordings, at least as to timing, was that a process of immediate interruption was thought to be unwieldy for witness testimony.

B. MODE OF QUESTIONING

Traditional Anglo-American trial practice allows leading questions on cross-examination but generally forbids them on direct examination. A "leading" question is a question phrased in such a way as to suggest the desired answer. There are long-standing exceptions to the general prohibition of leading questions on direct examination. The most important of these exceptions allows leading questions when necessary to develop the testimony — for example, when the witness's recollection needs refreshing, when the witness is a young child, or when the witness appears hostile or can be presumed to have sympathies aligned with the opposing party. Similarly, when cross-examination really amounts to direct examination — when, for example, one defendant cross-examines a friendly witness called by a codefendant — the traditional rule is that cross-examination must proceed without leading questions.

[F.R.E. 611(c); C.E.C. §§764, 767]

ADVISORY COMMITTEE NOTE TO F.R.E. 611

. . . The rule continues the traditional view that the suggestive powers of the leading question are as a general proposition undesirable. Within this tradition, however, numerous exceptions have achieved recognition: The witness who is hostile, unwilling, or biased; the child witness or the adult with communication problems; the witness whose recollection is exhausted; and undisputed preliminary matters. 3 Wigmore §§774-778. An almost total unwillingness to reverse for infractions has been manifested by appellate courts. The matter clearly falls within the area of control by the judge over the mode and order of interrogation and presentation and accordingly is phrased in words of suggestion rather than command.

The rule also conforms to tradition in making the use of leading questions on cross-examination a matter of right. The purpose of the qualification "ordinarily" is to furnish a basis for denying the use of leading questions when the cross-examination is cross-examination in form only and not in fact, as for example the "cross-examination" of a party by his own counsel after being called by the opponent (savoring more of re-direct) or of an insured defendant who proves to be friendly to the plaintiff.

The final sentence deals with categories of witnesses automatically regarded and treated as hostile. Rule 43(b) of the Federal Rules of Civil

Procedure has included only "an adverse party or an officer, director, or managing agent of a public or private corporation or of a partnership or association which is an adverse party." This limitation virtually to persons whose statements would stand as admissions is believed to be an unduly narrow concept of those who may safely be regarded as hostile without further demonstration. . . . The phrase of the rule, "witness identified with" an adverse party, is designed to enlarge the category of persons thus callable.

UNITED STATES v. NABORS

762 F.2d 642 (10th Cir. 1985)

SACHS, District Judge.

The defendant brothers, Charles Bruce Nabors and John Calvin Nabors, Jr., appeal from a final judgment entered in the district court after a jury verdict finding each of them guilty of bank robbery by means of a deadly weapon and conspiracy to commit bank robbery. . . . Key testimony connecting the defendants to the bank robbery was provided by twelve-year-old Tray Campbell, a nephew by marriage of John Nabors. . . . [Following the robbery, Tray discovered the defendants in the basement of his mother's home,] laughing and giggling about an amount of money that they had gotten. . . .

On direct examination of Tray Campbell, the Government's attorney asked the boy whether either of the defendants said anything immediately after they saw Tray for the first time in the . . . basement. The boy's initial reply was that John Nabors "turned around to his brother and said Tray's here." Counsel for John Nabors objected after the prosecutor continued this line of inquiry by asking, "Tray, exactly what did he say?" The trial court rejected the contention that the Government was asking improper leading questions and instead stated that "I think perhaps what he's doing is repeating what the witness has said essentially, and of course given the circumstances here which are quite obvious, the court is going to overrule the objection." The following inquiry then occurred:

> Q. (Prosecutor) Tray, have you told me before what they said?
> A. (Tray) Yes, sir.
> Q. And what did you tell me that John said?
> A. Can I say it?
> Q. Yes, you can say it.
> A. He said, he said, "Oh, shit, Tray's here."

Defendant characterizes this entire line of questioning as "an improper and extremely prejudicial method of interrogation of a child witness." We do not agree with this description. Although leading questions are not ordinarily permitted on direct examination except "as may be necessary to develop . . . testimony," (Federal Rule of Evidence 611(c)), the Notes of the Advisory Committee describe a long-recognized exception — "the child witness or the adult with communication problems." In this case the prosecutor did not suggest the language used, although he did press for a repetition of words previously used. Tray's hesitation in using a "naughty" word in a formal proceeding was understandable. The wording of that statement did tend to implicate the defendants in the bank robbery in that it indicated some alarm at being discovered; it was thus proper for the prosecutor to attempt to elicit its precise language. The trial court's ruling deserves deference because the court was in the best position to evaluate the emotional condition of the child witness and his hesitancy to testify. . . . [W]e affirm the judgments as to both defendants.

ELLIS v. CITY OF CHICAGO

667 F.2d 606 (7th Cir. 1981)

CUDAHY, Circuit Judge.

[Chicago Police Officer Frank Kusar entered plaintiffs' home based on a telephone tip and fatally shot plaintiffs' dog, allegedly after the dog lunged at him. Plaintiffs sued Kusar and the city for damages, claiming violation of their civil rights. The jury found for defendants, and plaintiffs appealed.]

. . . [P]laintiffs claim that the trial court erred in refusing to permit counsel for plaintiffs to use leading questions during his direct examinations of Officer Calandra and Sergeant Holub, police officers employed by the City of Chicago. Since 1975, the use of leading questions has been governed by Rule 611(c) of the Federal Rules of Evidence. This rule provides that while leading questions should not normally be used on direct examination, they may be employed "[W]hen a party calls a hostile witness, an adverse party, or a witness identified with an adverse party." Plaintiffs argue that the trial judge committed reversible error by refusing to recognize Officer Calandra and Sergeant Holub as witnesses identified with an adverse party for purposes of this Rule.

Before the adoption of Rule 611(c), the use of leading questions on direct examination required either a showing of actual hostility or a determination that the witness being examined was an adverse party, or an officer, director, or managing agent of such an adverse party. These limitations were designed to guard against the risk of improper suggestion inherent in examining friendly witnesses through the use of leading questions. The drafters of Rule 611(c), however, determined that these limitations represented "an unduly narrow concept of those who may safely be regarded as hostile without further demonstration." Fed. R. Evid. 611(c) (Advisory Committee Notes). The new rule was thus designed to enlarge the categories of witnesses automatically regarded as adverse, and therefore subject to interrogation by leading questions without further showing of actual hostility. *Id.*

We agree with plaintiffs that the district court should have permitted leading questions during plaintiffs' direct examinations of Officer Calandra and Sergeant Holub. These police officers were employees of defendant City of Chicago at all times during the litigation and were each present during portions of the incident which gave rise to this lawsuit. Moreover, the record indicates that both officers had worked closely with defendant Frank Kusar during the period of their employment. Officer Calandra and Sergeant Holub thus clearly qualified as "witness(es) identified with an adverse party" for purposes of Rule 611(c).

We do not believe, however, that this conclusion requires reversal of the judgment. In essence, Rule 611(c) codifies the traditional mode of dealing with leading questions. It acknowledges that they are generally undesirable on direct examination, that they are usually permissible on cross-examination, and that there are exceptions to both of these propositions. Although not explicitly stated, the rule is consistent with what has long been the law — that in the use of leading questions "much must be left to the sound discretion of the trial judge who sees the witness and can, therefore, determine in the interest of truth and justice whether the circumstances justify leading questions to be propounded to a witness by the party producing them." *St. Clair v. United States*, 154 U.S. 134 (1894). Such a decision will not be reversed absent a clear showing of prejudice to the complaining party.

Plaintiffs here have made no such showing of prejudice. Indeed, the record indicates that counsel for plaintiffs examined both Officer Calandra and Sergeant Holub at length without the use of leading questions and that neither witness was evasive or antagonistic. Moreover, defendants called Sergeant Holub as their own witness, thus permitting plaintiffs to ask leading questions on cross-examination. Finally, and most importantly, nowhere in their briefs do plaintiffs indicate what additional testimony they would have elicited had they been permitted to employ leading questions in their direct examinations of Officer Calandra and Sergeant Holub. Under these circumstances, any harm to plaintiffs from the district court's ruling is purely speculative. . . . Affirmed.

PROBLEMS

6.1. Two brothers, Dan and Doug, are charged with robbing a bank and are tried together. Dan calls their sister Wendy as a witness and elicits testimony that she went to the beach with both defendants on the day of the robbery. Following direct examination, Doug's lawyer cross-examines Wendy. He asks her, "The trip to the beach lasted all day, didn't it?" The prosecutor objects that "counsel is leading the witness." Should the objection be sustained? What if Doug were unrelated to Dan and Wendy?

6.2. Elaine, an eyewitness to a collision between a passenger car and a delivery van, tells a police officer who reports to the scene that the car entered the intersection first and then was struck by the van. The car driver later sues the van driver for negligence and calls Elaine as a witness. On direct examination, the plaintiff's counsel asks Elaine whether the car or the van entered the intersection first. Elaine says she cannot remember. Plaintiff's counsel then asks, "Do you remember talking to a police officer about the accident?" Elaine says she does. Plaintiff's counsel asks, "Do you remember telling the officer that the car entered the intersection first?" Defense counsel objects on grounds of hearsay and improper leading. How should the judge rule?

6.3. Suppose Elaine's memory does not fail her at trial; she testifies that the passenger car entered the intersection and then was struck by the van. On cross-examination, counsel for the van driver asks Elaine whether she is related by marriage to the plaintiff. Plaintiff's counsel objects that this is beyond the scope of direct examination. How should the judge rule?

C. SEQUESTERING WITNESSES

The practice of excluding witnesses from the courtroom until they testify — commonly known as "sequestering" witnesses or the "rule on witness"— is centuries old. A celebrated illustration both of the practice and of its traditional rationale appears in the Apocryphal story of Susanna and the Elders. Susanna is falsely accused of adultery and condemned to death. The prophet Daniel saves her by separately questioning the two elders who claim to have witnessed the liaison. Unable to coordinate their lies, they tell conflicting stories about where it occurred.

[F.R.E. 615; C.E.C. §777]

ADVISORY COMMITTEE NOTE TO F.R.E. 615

The efficacy of excluding or sequestering witnesses has long been recognized as a means of discouraging and exposing fabrication, inaccuracy, and collusion. 6 Wigmore §§1837–1838. The authority of the judge is admitted, the only question being whether the matter is committed to his discretion or one of right. The rule takes the latter position. No time is specified for making the request.

REPORT OF THE SENATE JUDICIARY COMMITTEE

S. Rep. No. 93-1277 (1974)

Many district courts permit government counsel to have an investigative agent at counsel table throughout the trial although the agent is or may be a witness. The practice is permitted as an exception to the rule of exclusion and compares with the situation defense counsel finds himself in — he always has the client with him to consult during the trial. The investigative agent's presence may be extremely important to government counsel, especially when the case is complex or involves some specialized subject matter. The agent, too, having lived with the case for a long time, may be able to assist in meeting trial surprises where the best-prepared counsel would otherwise have difficulty. Yet, it would not seem the Government could often meet the burden under rule 615 of showing that the agent's presence is essential. Furthermore, it could be dangerous to use the agent as a witness as early in the case as possible, so that he might then help counsel as a nonwitness, since the agent's testimony could be needed in rebuttal. Using another, nonwitness agent from the same investigative agency would not generally meet government counsel's needs.

This problem is solved if it is clear that investigative agents are within the group specified under the second exception made in the rule, for "an officer or employee of a party which is not a natural person designated as its representative by its attorney." It is our understanding that this was the intention of the House committee. It is certainly this committee's construction of the rule.

UNITED STATES v. MACHOR

879 F.2d 945 (1st Cir. 1989)

TORRUELLA, Circuit Judge.

After a joint jury trial, the four appellants . . . were convicted under 21 U.S.C. §841(a)(1) for aiding and abetting each other in the possession with intent to distribute cocaine. [They were arrested after trying to sell a kilogram of cocaine to an undercover agent and a confidential informant.] . . .

[Two of the appellants] argue that the trial court abused its discretion when it denied defendant's motion to exclude agent Rivera while the informant testified. In the alternative, Carrasco and Allen claim that the court abused its discretion by not ordering agent Rivera to testify before the informant.

Fed. R. Evid. 615 requires that the trial court sequester witnesses at the request of a party. There are several exceptions to this rule, however. The most common is that a party who is a natural person cannot be excluded from the courtroom. As an extension of this basic principle, Fed. R. Evid. 615(2) provides that, when a party is not a natural person, its designated representative is also exempted from the sequestration rule. It seems clear that a case agent representing the government is within this exception. . . .

Defendants maintain, however, that even after the promulgation of the new Federal Rules of Evidence, the court retained discretion to exclude a person who falls within the 615(2) exception. The courts are divided on this issue. Some cases support defendants' view that the trial court has discretion to exclude the government case agent. *United States v. Thomas*, 835 F.2d 219, 223 (9th Cir. 1987), *cert. denied*, 486 U.S. 1010 (1988); *United States v. Woody*, 588 F.2d 1212, 1213 (8th Cir. 1978), *cert. denied*, 440 U.S. 928 (1979).

The majority view, however, is that Fed. R. Evid. 615(2) has severely curtailed the discretion of the trial court to sequester the government's case agent. *See 3 Weinstein's Evidence*, §615[02], n. 8 and cases therein cited. The practical and policy concerns inherent in the promulgation of the rule support this view.[2] *See Senate Report [93-1277]*. Thus, we reject defendants' argument. . . . Appellants' convictions are affirmed.

D. QUESTIONING BY JUDGE

The Federal Rules of Evidence and most of their state counterparts expressly authorize trial judges to call their own witnesses and to interrogate witnesses called by the parties. But as the case excerpted below illustrates, judges risk reversal when they ask questions that seem to reveal their own assessment

---

2. We are not holding however, that the rule withdraws all discretion from the trial court to exclude a case agent in an exceptional case. Because this is not such a special circumstance, we need not decide the point.

of the evidence. The underlying idea is that jurors must be shielded from the views of judges, because they would defer improperly to those views. In particular, appellate courts expect trial judges to avoid revealing what they think about witnesses; otherwise, it is feared, we will sacrifice the principle that juries, not judges, should be assessing credibility.

Those expectations and assumptions are thoroughly ingrained in most practicing lawyers and judges. They explain not only why questioning by judges can be reversible error, but also why most states no longer permit judges to comment directly on the evidence, and why even judges who *are* permitted to comment on the evidence — such as those in federal court and in California state courts — risk reversal if their remarks are too pointed. Judges used to have far more freedom to comment on the evidence; they still have that freedom in the United Kingdom. We have grown accustomed to the view that fair trials require judges who keep their thoughts about witnesses largely to themselves, and that the only ones offering juries guidance about whom to believe should be the lawyers. When reading the materials below, ask yourself whether those assumptions are justified.

[F.R.E. 614; C.E.C. §775]

ADVISORY COMMITTEE NOTE TO F.R.E. 614

... While exercised more frequently in criminal than in civil cases, the authority of the judge to call witnesses is well established.... [T]he judge is not imprisoned within the case as made by the parties.

... The authority of the judge to question witnesses is also well established. The authority is, of course, abused when the judge abandons his proper role and assumes that of advocate, but the manner in which interrogation should be conducted and the proper extent of its exercise are not susceptible of formulation in a rule. The omission in no sense precludes courts of review from continuing to reverse for abuse.... The provision relating to objections is designed to relieve counsel of the embarrassment attendant upon objecting to questions by the judge in the presence of the jury, while at the same time assuring that objections are made in apt time to afford the opportunity to take possible corrective measures....

UNITED STATES v. TILGHMAN

134 F.3d 414 (D.C. Cir. 1998)

TATEL, Circuit Judge.

Convicted of lying in order to obtain disability benefits, appellant argues that the trial judge's repeated questioning of him prejudiced the jury and denied him a fair trial.... [We] reverse and remand for a new trial.

[Tilghman took disability leave from the government in 1983 and the next year incorporated Tilghman Enterprises Ltd. ("TEL"), which bid on federal agency contracts to investigate employment discrimination complaints. To receive disability payment he had to report his earnings each year on Department of Labor Form 1032. For every year but 1991, Tilghman reported no earnings.]

. . . Tilghman testified that he had no intention of defrauding the government. He told the jury that he honestly believed that he had no obligation to report his . . . investigative work on Form 1032 because TEL operated at a loss, because he never received any salary . . . and because a DOL employee told him over the telephone that he could earn up to $300 a month without reporting it.

During the first of Tilghman's two days on the stand, the district judge questioned him extensively in the presence of the jury. Defense counsel offered no objection. On the morning of the second day and before trial began, defense counsel moved for a mistrial, arguing that the judge's questioning influenced the jury and deprived Tilghman of a fair trial. The district judge denied the motion and continued to question Tilghman. Defense counsel objected to four questions and renewed his motion for mistrial at the close of the case. . . .

Rule 614(b) of the Federal Rules of Evidence expressly permits judges to question witnesses. Judges may do so repeatedly and aggressively to clear up confusion and manage trials or where "'testimony is inarticulately or reluctantly given.'" *United States v. Norris*, 873 F.2d 1519, 1525-26 (D.C. Cir. 1989) (upholding judge's participation in questioning defendant, although perhaps more extensive than it should have been, because it aimed at clarifying evidence) (quoting *United States v. Barbour*, 420 F.2d 1319, 1321 (D.C. Cir. 1969)).

District court authority to question witnesses and manage trials, however, has limits. Because juries, not judges, decide whether witnesses are telling the truth, and because judges wield enormous influence over juries, judges may not ask questions that signal their belief or disbelief of witnesses. *United States v. Wyatt*, 442 F.2d 858, 859-61 (D.C. Cir. 1971) (court's questioning of defendant and his alibi witnesses damaged defendant's credibility and therefore was reversible error). Because such questions can usurp the jury's factfinding function, cast the judge in the role of advocate, and "breach []the atmosphere of judicial evenhandedness that should pervade the courtroom," they can deprive defendants of fair trials. *Barbour*, 420 F.2d at 1321. Judges must therefore strive to preserve an appearance of impartiality and "'err on the side of [a]bstention from intervention.'" *Norris*, 873 F.2d at 1526. . . . We have reversed when judicial interrogation "may have damaged the appellant's credibility in the eyes of the jury" or "may have given the jury the impression that the judge doubted the defendant's credibility." *Wyatt*, 442 F.2d at 860, 861. We have sustained judicial questioning where the case was not "close" and the issues addressed by the judge were "peripheral to the main issues in the case." *United States v. Mangum*, 100 F.3d 164, 174 (D.C. Cir. 1996).

. . . [W]e need not decide whether the Day Two mistrial motion was sufficiently timely under Rule 614(c) to permit harmless error review of Day One questions. Counsel's objections were timely with respect to all Day Two questions; as the government concedes, moreover, when reviewing Day Two questions we must review the record as a whole, including Day One questions. . . .

. . . Central to his defense, Tilghman asserted that DOL employee Julio Mendez told him in a 1984 telephone call that he had no obligation to report earnings of up to $300 per month. While the prosecution questioned Tilghman about this claim [on Day Two], the following colloquy occurred:

> *THE COURT:*   You didn't put this on any form, did you?
>
> *DEFENDANT:*   Did I put it on a form? No sir; this was a telephone conversation.
>
> *THE COURT:*   Did this Julio Mendez put it on a form?
>
> *DEFENDANT:*   I don't know, sir.
>
> *THE COURT:*   We just have to take your word for it?
>
> *DEF. COUNSEL:*   Objection, Your Honor.
>
> *THE COURT:*   Overruled. Is that right?
>
> *DEFENDANT:*   I'm sworn to tell the truth, sir.
>
> *THE COURT:*   I know, but we have to take your word for it; is that right?
>
> *DEFENDANT:*   I don't know if he has any record of it or not.

Focusing on the absence of any evidence of this phone call, the prosecutor then questioned Tilghman for several transcript pages.

Earlier that same day, while Tilghman described for the jury his understanding of DOL Form 1032, the judge questioned him as follows:

> *THE COURT:*   You were an employee of Tilghman Enterprises?
>
> *DEFENDANT:*   That is correct, sir.
>
> *THE COURT:*   Doesn't that fit in the paragraph Employment other than self-Employment? Under this heading, you must report all employment.
>
> *DEFENDANT:*   For which you receive wages.
>
> *DEF. COUNSEL:*   Objection, Your Honor.
>
> *THE COURT:*   It goes on to say if you perform work for which you were not paid, you must show a rate of pay of what it would have cost. You didn't put that in any of them?
>
> *DEFENDANT:*   I felt that was not applicable, sir, because there was no way to compute those figures.
>
> *DEF. COUNSEL:*   Your Honor, if I may just renew my objection.
>
> *THE COURT:*   The objection is overruled.
>
> *PROSECUTOR:*   In other words, Mr. Tilghman, it is your belief that the Department of Labor had to specifically ask you, Okay, Mr. Tilghman, asterisks, we want to know about your corporation?
>
> *DEFENDANT:*   No. It was my belief that I had to answer carefully, accurately, and honestly; and I did so.

. . . [W]e think these questions "may have given the jury the impression that the judge doubted the defendant's credibility." *Wyatt*, 442 F.2d at 861. The judge's questions could have been particularly damaging because the indictment charged Tilghman with lying, making his credibility unusually critical to his defense. The jury could have interpreted the Mendez question — "[W]e have to take your word for it; is that right?" — as signaling that the judge considered Tilghman's oath irrelevant and his word suspect. Even the government conceded at oral argument that the judge should not have asked this question, calling it "unfortunate." From the second set of questions, the jury could have inferred that the judge accepted the government's theory of the case that Tilghman should have checked off the "self-employment" box on Form 1032.

Turning to Day One, the judge's questions reinforce our perception that the Day Two questions may have colored the jury's assessment of Tilghman's veracity. For example, as Tilghman explained to the jury how a bank officer had instructed him to fill out a loan application, the following exchange took place:

> THE COURT: You're an educated man, aren't you? You have a master's degree, and you did work for a doctorate. Is that right?
> DEFENDANT: That's correct, sir.
> THE COURT: Now, this is supposed to get a loan from the bank, and you put down as annual income $45,000 and expenditures $14,000. On the basis of that, they were going to give you a loan, right?
> DEFENDANT: I would assume so, yes.
> THE COURT: And those figures aren't accurate because the chairman of the board told you to put them in. . . .
> DEFENDANT: In essence, he did tell me what to put in.
> THE COURT: Do you think that any sane bank would give somebody a loan on figures that are totally made up? I mean, as an educated man who's been in business off and on, and government business, private business. Do you think [a] bank would give a loan to somebody on the basis of figures that are just made up by the chairman of the board?

Later on Day One, Tilghman described the bidding process for [employment discrimination] investigative contracts, stating that he and other investigators routinely lost money or broke even:

> THE COURT: Other people who [bid] in the same ball park with you, and they all must have lost money, too, is that right?
> DEFENDANT: I'm assuming so, sir, yes, sir, because [a] lot of them went out of business.
> THE COURT: I see. It's a peculiar business where everybody stays in for years and loses money all the time.
> DEFENDANT: All I can — the only thing I know to relate it to —
> THE COURT: Wouldn't you agree it's a peculiar business? . . .
> DEFENDANT: Not necessarily. I taught for years, and I could have made much more money doing something else.

A moment later, the judge interjected:

> THE COURT: Just a minute. Something occurred to me. You were not in the business of making money out of these contracts. You were perfectly content to lose money on these contracts.
> DEFENDANT: I was —
> THE COURT: You were a philanthropist; you wanted to help these people.
> DEFENDANT: No, I was hoping I could at least break even.

Like the questions on Day Two, these inquiries could have suggested to the jury that the judge disbelieved Tilghman. From the first set of questions, particularly the judge's reference to "any sane bank," the jury could have inferred that the judge thought Tilghman was lying about the basis of the loan. The judge's reference to philanthropy likewise could have suggested to the jury that he did not believe that Tilghman was losing money, as he testified. Having heard these Day One questions and the judge's Day Two challenge to Tilghman's honesty under oath, the jury could well have concluded that the judge considered Tilghman an untruthful witness. . . . Because the jury could reasonably have interpreted the judge's pointed comments as reflecting his personal disbelief of Tilghman, we cannot find that the government has "prove[n] beyond a reasonable doubt that [the judge's commentary] did not contribute to the verdict obtained." [*Chapman v. California*, 386 U.S. 18, 24 (1967).]

The government argues that because the judge also asked intrusive questions of government witnesses and badgered the prosecutor about her handling of exhibits, the jury could have perceived him as evenhanded. The record shows that the district judge did criticize the prosecution's case, implying, for example, that some government witnesses were unclear, confused, or inept. After questioning one government witness, the judge said to the prosecutor, "You better ask the questions. I don't know what she's talking about." To other witnesses he made such comments as: "You have never said just 'no' or 'yes.' You always go on and on and make a whole speech," 5/15 Tr. at 41, "Never mind, never mind. You are not helping me," and "Just answer the question. . . . We don't need an encyclopedia in response to every question." He also commented on the prosecution's evidence. When granting a defense objection, for example, he said: "I don't see any relevance whatever. I am surprised nobody has objected before," and during the prosecution's examination of a character witness he asked, "Are you finished with this line of questioning? . . . Or are you dredging up some more?" In addition, the judge criticized the prosecution's inefficient handling of exhibits. "I want to congratulate you," he said at one point, "[t]his is actually marked with a sticker."

. . . [W]e think the nature of the judge's treatment of the prosecution differed fundamentally from his questioning of Tilghman. Indeed, comparing the two illustrates the difference between appropriate, active, even aggressive judicial management and prejudicial judicial questioning. . . . It is one thing to criticize counsel about exhibits; it is quite another to question the defendant's credibility on the stand when the central issue is whether he is telling the truth. The judge's comments on the confusing quality of government testimony could not possibly undermine the prosecution's case in the same way that his questioning of Tilghman could have punctured the heart of the defense.

The government argues finally that the judge's instructions to the jury cured any improprieties. Having explained that the jury bears sole responsibility for determining the facts, the district judge instructed the jury as follows:

> And if I say anything about the facts, which normally I don't, you just disregard it because I don't have any responsibility, any obligation on the facts. It's entirely up to you. And if I say something, if I said something in the trial or say something in this closing charge about the facts, you just disregard it because you are [as] much judges on the facts as I am judge on the law. I hope you understand that. And that applies to anything I said in the course of the trial, the questions I may have asked or rulings I may have made, they're all not designed, and you should not take them as being my opinion on the facts because it's your opinion on the facts that counts.

This instruction was too little, too late. Although jury instructions can cure certain irregularities, at least under the plain error standard, we agree with the Second Circuit that where, as here, the trial judge asked questions, objected to by counsel, that could have influenced the jury's assessment of the defendant's veracity, such interference with jury fact-finding cannot be cured by standard jury instructions. *United States v. Filani*, 74 F.3d 378, 386 (2d Cir. 1996). We need not consider whether special instructions or other measures might cure such errors, for none was employed here. . . . [W]e reverse defendant's conviction and remand for a new trial. . . .

E. QUESTIONING BY JURORS

A slowly but steadily increasing number of judges, rebelling against the received wisdom that fairness requires jurors to listen passively throughout the trial, are experimenting with procedures that allow jurors to ask questions of witnesses. But they remain very much in the minority. Most judges, and most trial lawyers, remain deeply uncomfortable with the notion of jurors playing an active role in the trial, even in the most limited of ways. When reading the materials below, ask yourself what accounts for this discomfort, and whether it is justified.

UNITED STATES v. HERNANDEZ

176 F.3d 719 (3d Cir. 1999)

McKEE, Circuit Judge.

Julio Hernandez appeals his conviction for conspiring to obstruct interstate commerce by robbery . . . and receiving or possessing goods stolen from commerce. . . . This case arises from the highjacking of a tractor trailer truck containing 494 cases of cigarettes. . . .

We turn first to Hernandez' challenge to the District Court's practice of allowing jurors to participate in questioning witnesses during the course of the trial. The District Court allowed jurors to pose questions by handing the court written questions for the court's review. . . . [T]he court would then allow the attorneys to see the question so that counsel could make whatever objections they deemed appropriate, and the court could thus determine the admissibility and propriety of a question outside the hearing of the jury before asking the question.

One juror did submit a question in this manner. The juror asked: "[w]hat kind of rear doors are on the rear of the trailer?" However, the court did not ask the question of the witness. Rather, the court allowed the attorneys to decide what, if any, response each would make to the question.

The court then gave the following explanation to the jury:

> Let me just say with regard to questions that are presented by a witness,— by a juror, it well may be a particular witness who is on the stand at the time may not be the person to whom such a question would be addressed because he may not be a witness who may be in a position to answer the question.
>
> We appreciate having your questions because now the attorneys on both sides know what inquiries you would make and either they may address them through their closing arguments, or they know if they wish to bring any additional witnesses to address the question, that would be up to them.

... [Defendant's] challenge to the propriety of allowing juror questioning is an issue of first impression in this circuit.... Although we have not previously addressed this issue, several other courts of appeal have. Although those courts have consistently expressed concern over the dangers of the practice, they have refused to adopt a rule prohibiting juror questioning of witnesses during the course of a criminal trial. We take this opportunity to approve of the practice so long as it is done in a manner that insures the fairness of the proceedings, the primacy of the court's stewardship, and the rights of the accused.

... In *United States v. Bush*, [47 F.3d 511 (2d Cir. 1995),] jurors directly questioned witnesses, including the defendant. Defense counsel failed to object, and even engaged in a dialogue with the jurors. The practice of allowing such questioning was therefore reviewed for plain error. The court first noted that "[w]e have already held ... that direct questioning by jurors is a 'matter within the judge's discretion, like witness-questioning by the judge himself.'" The court noted that "[e]very circuit court that has addressed this issue agrees. State courts, moreover, have overwhelmingly placed juror questioning of witnesses within the trial judge's discretion, and indeed its common law roots are deeply entrenched." Nevertheless, the court expressed concern over this practice. "Although we reaffirm our earlier holding ... that juror questioning of witnesses lies within the trial judge's discretion, we strongly discourage its use." The court listed several dangers endemic to the practice including "turning jurors into advocates, compromising their neutrality," the "risk that jurors will ask prejudicial or otherwise improper questions," and counsel's inability to respond for fear of antagonizing, alienating, or embarrassing a juror. The court noted that

> [b]alancing the risk that a juror's question may be prejudicial against the benefit of issue-clarification will almost always lead trial courts to disallow juror questioning, in the absence of extraordinary or compelling circumstances.

However, the court affirmed the conviction because the challenged questioning had been "limited and controlled" and because the defendant could not demonstrate prejudice.

In *United States v. Sutton*, 970 F.2d 1001 (1st Cir. 1992), the court voiced similar concerns about allowing jurors to question witnesses even though the procedure used involved the court asking questions that the jurors had submitted in writing. Once again, the court allowed the practice though it was clearly troubled by it. "Although we think this practice may frequently court unnecessary trouble, we find no error in the circumstances of this case."

There, at the beginning of the trial, the trial court had informed the jurors that they could ask questions by handing written questions to the jury foreman who would then give them to the judge. "If your question even possibly could make any legal difference ... if it's relevant as the lawyers say, I'll ask it for you." On appeal, the court stated:

> Allowing jurors to pose questions during a criminal trial is a procedure fraught with perils. In most cases, the game will not be worth the candle. Nevertheless, we are fully committed to the principle that trial judges should be given wide latitude to manage trials. We are, moreover, supportive of reasoned efforts by the trial bench to improve the truth seeking attributes of the jury system. Consistent with this overall approach, and mindful that the practice ... may occasionally be advantageous, especially in complex cases and under carefully controlled conditions, we hold that allowing juror-inspired questions in a criminal case is not prejudicial per se, but is a matter committed to the sound discretion of the trial court.

Although the court allowed the practice, it was quick to discourage it. "We hasten to add that the practice, while not forbidden, should be employed sparingly and with great circumspection." The court also added to the list of concerns enunciated in *Bush*, though it acknowledged that the practice could further the search for truth by allowing jurors to clear up confusion. The court also recognized that allowing jurors to participate in questioning could enhance the attentiveness of jurors. Nevertheless, the court concluded "in most situations, the risks inherent in the practice will outweigh its utility."

In *United States v. Ajmal*, [67 F.3d 12, 14 (2d Cir. 1995),] the court did reverse a conviction based upon juror questioning of witnesses [including the defendant himself].... The trial judge there had taken precautions. He had required questions to be in writing, and the court, rather than the attorneys, asked the questions. In addition, the court only asked those questions that it believed were proper under the Federal Rules of Evidence. Nevertheless, the Court of Appeals held that the trial judge had abused his discretion.... [A]lthough the court was once again concerned with the practice of allowing juror questioning absent circumstances sufficient to justify the risk inherent in the procedure, the court ... based its reversal upon the trial court's encouragement of such questioning, and the frequency with which jurors had accepted the judge's invitation.

Here, the court received only one question from the jury. It was a fact question that was not even asked. We do not think that one fact question which is submitted to a judge in writing, but not even asked, can be labeled an abuse of discretion....

We agree that a trial judge who allows ... questioning [by jurors] in a given case should adopt a procedure to first screen the questions. However, we conclude that the danger of allowing jurors to ask questions orally far outweighs any perceived benefit of allowing juror questioning of witnesses. Thus, the judge should ask any juror-generated questions, and he or she should do so only after allowing attorneys to raise any objection out of the hearing of the jury.

The procedure utilized here is consistent with our admonitions and consistent with the sound exercise of judicial discretion. The court did not surrender its discretion as to whether to allow a given question to be asked, and the judge, not the attorneys (and certainly not the jurors), was to have asked any questions posed by a juror. This procedure is consistent with the holding of every court of appeals that has addressed this issue. We hold that the trial judge did not abuse her discretion.... [Reversed on other grounds.]

STATE v. FISHER

789 N.E.2d 222 (Ohio 2003)

MOYER, C.J.

Defendant-appellant, Michael A. Fisher, appeals from the judgment of the Tenth District Court of Appeals, which affirmed his conviction for felonious assault with a firearm specification....

Prior to the presentation of evidence, the trial court informed the jurors that they would be permitted to ask questions of the witnesses that testified at trial. The trial judge instructed the jurors to submit their questions in writing to the bailiff, whereupon the judge and the attorneys would review the questions in a sidebar conference. The trial judge would then determine whether the questions were admissible under the rules of evidence and would read the admissible questions aloud to the witnesses.

In accordance with the foregoing procedure, the jurors submitted 23 questions to six of the eight witnesses that testified at trial. The trial court disallowed five questions on evidentiary grounds and rephrased two questions for clarification. After reading a juror question, the trial court allowed the prosecution and defense counsel an opportunity to ask follow-up questions. Although defense counsel did not object to the particular questions that were read to the witnesses, counsel entered a continuing objection to the general practice of allowing jurors to submit questions....

Every federal circuit that has addressed the issue has concluded that the practice of allowing jurors to question witnesses is a matter within the discretion of the trial court. Several of the federal circuits, however, discourage the practice.... The vast majority of state courts have also concluded that juror questioning is a matter committed to the sound discretion of the trial court.... Nevertheless, several jurisdictions permit juror questioning only where procedural safeguards are employed. Other jurisdictions have relegated the procedure by which jurors submit questions to the discretion of the trial court.

Only five jurisdictions prohibit jurors from questioning witnesses.... Among these jurisdictions, however, Georgia, Mississippi, and Nebraska have concluded that such error may be either forfeited or harmless beyond a reasonable doubt.... [O]nly two states — Texas and Minnesota — have held that juror questioning is not subject to harmless error analysis....

The hallmark of the American trial is the pursuit of truth. Such truth — and, in the end, justice — is attainable only if counsel successfully communicates evidence to the jury. History has nonetheless relegated the jury to a passive role that dictates a one-way communication system — a system that, in its traditional form, is not amenable to resolving juror confusion. The practice of allowing jurors to question witnesses provides for two-way communication through which jurors can more effectively fulfill their fundamental role as factfinders.

In *United States v. Callahan*, 588 F.2d at 1086 [1979], the United States Court of Appeals for the Fifth Circuit articulated the paramount benefit of such communication: "There is nothing improper about the practice of allowing occasional questions from jurors to be asked of witnesses. If a juror is unclear as to a point in the proof, it makes good common sense to allow a question to be asked about it. If nothing else, the question should alert trial counsel that a particular factual issue may need more extensive development. Trials exist to develop truth. It may sometimes be that counsel are so familiar with a case that they fail to see problems that would naturally bother a juror who is presented with the facts for the first time."

Juror questioning not only enhances the ability of jurors to discern truth but also may provide counsel an opportunity to better comprehend jurors' thought processes and their perception of case weaknesses. Recognizing a similar advantage of juror questioning, the . . . Court of Appeals for the District of Columbia has observed: "Questions by jurors also may bring to the court's and counsel's attention *improper* concerns which can be promptly addressed with cautionary instructions, admonishing the juror who asked the question that the matter is not relevant to the case and should not be brought to the attention of other jurors or play any part in the inquiring juror's consideration of the case." *Yeager* [*v. Greene*, 502 A.2d 980, 998 (D.C. 1985)].

Furthermore, the practice of allowing jurors to question witnesses may increase juror attentiveness at trial. The D.C. Court of Appeals, acknowledging such a benefit, has observed that "there is reason to believe that permitting receivers of information, *e.g.*, jurors, to ask questions enhances not only their ability to understand what is being communicated, but results in their putting forth more effort to listen and to understand because they *know* they may ask questions. A concomitant benefit predictable from these effects might well be a reduced likelihood that the court will be required to intervene to question witnesses or elucidate issues that are clarified by juror questions." [*Id.* at 998-1000.]

Finally, empirical research suggests that jurors who are allowed to question witnesses are more satisfied with their service and more confident with their verdicts. As one Ohio jurist has noted, "Allowing jurors to ask questions makes jurors feel more like a part of the judiciary, and less like helpless outsiders trying to penetrate a sanctimonious institution. This type of change can only bring us closer to the ultimate goal of our legal system: justice." Valen, Jurors Asking Questions: Revolutionary or Evolutionary? (1993), 20 N. Ky. L. Rev. 423, 439.

Although we are cognizant of the potential benefits of juror questioning, we are also mindful of the concerns associated with the practice. Courts have identified four principal dangers inherent in juror questioning: (1) jurors may submit inadmissible questions, (2) counsel may refrain from objecting to improper questions for fear of offending jurors, (3) juror interruptions may disrupt courtroom decorum, and (4) such questioning may distort juror impartiality. The extent to which these dangers affect the trial process depends, in great part, upon the manner in which such questioning is conducted.

In the instant case, the procedural safeguards applied by the trial court operated to circumvent many of the foregoing dangers. These safeguards included (1) requiring the jurors to submit their questions in writing to the court, whereupon the judge could review and exclude improper questions, (2) providing counsel an opportunity to object at sidebar, thereby eliminating the danger that a juror would be affronted by an objection, and (3) specifying the precise time at which jurors should submit questions to prevent interference with attorney questioning and courtroom decorum.

The final concern associated with juror questioning lies in the potential distortion of the adversary system. Appellant argues that "by allowing jurors to question witnesses, the role of the jury is fundamentally changed" from neutral factfinder to partial advocate. Such an argument, however, rests on the erroneous premise that one must be passive to be impartial. To the contrary, [Ohio] Evid. R. 614(B) expressly authorizes the trial court — the factfinder in a bench trial — to "interrogate witnesses, in an impartial manner, whether called by itself or by a party." Consequently, the ability of a factfinder to question witnesses is not inconsistent with the duty of impartiality. . . .

The issue of whether juror questions are aimed at advocacy rather than clarification cannot be answered in the abstract, but instead requires courts to examine the nature of each question in the overall context of a trial. We conclude that the trial court is in the best position to render such a determination and, within its sound discretion, disallow improper juror questions. . . .

To minimize the danger of prejudice, however, trial courts that permit juror questioning should (1) require jurors to submit their questions to the court in writing, (2) ensure that jurors do not display or discuss a question with other jurors until the court reads the question to the witness, (3) provide counsel an opportunity to object to each question at sidebar or outside the presence of the jury, (4) instruct jurors that they should not draw adverse inferences from the court's refusal to allow certain questions, and (5) allow counsel to ask follow-up questions of the witnesses.

Our nation's profound commitment to trial by jury is founded on competing principles that, in one sense, foster the development of truth and, in another sense, stifle it. Such is the great paradox of the criminal justice system. To balance these principles in the assortment of cases with which a trial court is faced — dissimilar as one case is from another — appellate courts generally defer to the discretion of the trial court, rather than attempting to account for the infinite array of circumstances that may arise with a categorical rule. A less prudent approach would eviscerate that discretion at the first sign of abuse — or, worse yet, at the mere potential for it. . . .

[W]e hold that the decision to allow jurors to question witnesses is a matter within the discretion of the trial court and should not be disturbed on appeal absent an abuse of that discretion. The judgment of the court of appeals is affirmed.

UNITED STATES v. TAVARES

844 F.3d 46 (1st Cir. 2016)

TORRUELLA, Circuit Judge.

. . . Although we reverse based on more central issues [relating to the insufficiency of the evidence introduced by the prosecution], making the present issue moot, we must express our reservations about the extent and type of juror questions allowed by the trial judge in this case.

Whether to allow juror questions falls "to the sound discretion of the trial court." *United States v. Sutton*, 970 F.2d 1001, 1005 (1st Cir. 1992). But, as we have previously cautioned, jury questioning "should be reserved for exceptional situations, and should not become the routine, even in complex cases." *United States v. Cassiere*, 4 F.3d 1006, 1017 (1st Cir. 1993). Here, jurors submitted 281 questions, and the district court posed 180 of them to witnesses. That means that, over thirty-five days of testimony, eight questions were submitted and five questions asked per day on average. This volume of questions is far beyond anything approved of in this Circuit and suggests that the district court allowed juror questions to become routine rather than an exception.

Furthermore, the content of many of the questions jurors asked is troubling. Juror questions should serve the limited purpose of clarification, and they should be a "long-odds exception" reserved for the most critical points, *Sutton*, 970 F.2d at 1005. Here, though, the trial judge told the jurors that their questions should be guided by whether "the lawyer gets out what interests you from the witness." This invitation to go beyond seeking clarification led to questions (allowed over objection) . . . [that] elicited not just clarifications but gap-filling evidence. "[I]n a jury trial the primary finders of fact are the jurors. Their overriding responsibility is to stand between the accused and a potentially arbitrary or abusive Government that is in command of the criminal sanction." *United States v. Martin Linen Supply Co.*, 430 U.S. 564, 572 (1977). If a district court allows jurors to ask questions, it must ensure that the jurors do not turn into fact gatherers rather than factfinders by exceeding the bounds delineated in *Sutton* and *Cassiere*.

IMPEACHMENT AND
REHABILITATION

"Your witness"

A. INTRODUCTION

Impeachment and rehabilitation are ways in which evidence can be relevant. Evidence qualifies as impeachment if it is relevant because it suggests that a certain witness lacks credibility and therefore that his or her testimony should be disregarded. Evidence qualifies as rehabilitation if it is relevant because it rebuts impeachment evidence — i.e., because it suggests that a witness who has been impeached is in fact credible and should be believed. Impeachment and rehabilitation evidence is subject to all the rules of evidence examined elsewhere in this book, and also to some special restrictions, which are the subject of this chapter.

It is important not to confuse impeachment and rehabilitation with cross-examination and redirect examination. Much, perhaps most, impeachment goes on in cross-examination, and much, perhaps most, rehabilitation occurs in redirect examination. But cross-examination is often used for purposes other than impeachment, and redirect examination is often used for purposes other than rehabilitation. Lawyers often use cross-examination, for example, to elicit information that is helpful to their clients and that does not involve discrediting the witness; redirect examination is often used not to rehabilitate the witness, but to bring out additional facts known to the witness that are helpful to the party that called the witness. And just as cross-examination is not limited to impeachment and redirect examination is not limited to rehabilitation, so impeachment is not limited to cross-examination; parties can, and often do, impeach their own witnesses. Likewise, rehabilitation can occur outside of redirect examination.

As the materials below explain, there are special terms for distinguishing between, on the one hand, impeachment or rehabilitation that occurs "intrinsically" through the testimony of the witness being impeached or rehabilitated, and, on the other hand, impeachment or rehabilitation that occurs "extrinsically" through the use of other evidence — i.e., physical exhibits, or testimony from other witnesses. There are special terms, too, for distinguishing between different "modes" of impeachment — between, that is to say, different kinds of flaws (inconsistency, bias, a character for dishonesty, and the like) that can undermine the credibility of a witness. All of this terminology turns out to be important, because — as we will see later in this chapter — several of the special rules for impeachment and rehabilitation vary in their application depending on the manner and mode of attacking a witness's credibility.

[F.R.E. 607, 806; C.E.C. §§780, 785, 1202]

McCORMICK ON EVIDENCE

§33, at 1:205-06 (Kenneth S. Broun ed., 7th ed. 2013)

There are five main modes of attack upon a witness's credibility. The first, and probably most frequently employed, is proof of a prior inconsistent statement or "self contradiction," as it is sometimes imprecisely described. That technique consists of proof that the witness previously made statements inconsistent with his present testimony. The second is an attack showing that the witness is biased on account of emotional influences such as kinship for one party or hostility to another, or motives of pecuniary interest, whether legitimate or corrupt. The third is an attack on the witness's character, but lack of religious belief is not available as a basis of attack on credibility. The fourth is an attack showing a defect of the witness's capacity to observe, remember, or recount the matters testified about. The fifth is specific contradiction, that is, proof by other witnesses that material facts are not as testified to by the witness being impeached. Some of these attacks such as bias are not specifically or completely treated by the Federal or Revised Uniform Rules of Evidence, but nevertheless they are implicitly authorized by those rules. Article VI of the Federal Rules contains several provisions expressly regulating impeachment techniques such as proof of prior inconsistent statements, and the admissibility of other facts logically relevant to witness credibility is governed by the general analytic framework set out in Federal Rules 401–03.

The process of impeachment can proceed in two different stages. First, the facts discrediting the witness of his testimony may be elicited from the witness himself on cross-examination. A good faith basis for the inquiry is required. Certain modes of attack are limited to this stage; the shorthand expression is, "You must take his answer." When the mode of attack is limited in this manner, the cross-examiner is sometimes said to be restricted to "intrinsic" impeachment. Second, in other situations, the facts discrediting the witness may be proved by extrinsic evidence. For example, the plaintiff's witness to be impeached has already left the stand; and the impeaching defense attorney waits until her own case-in-chief and then proves the facts discrediting the testimony of the plaintiff's witness by a second witness or documentary evidence.

. . . In general, today there is less emphasis on impeachment of witnesses today than formerly. The courts now apply the elaborate, common law system of rules regulating impeachment less strictly. The system has been simplified by relying less on rules and more on judicial discretion. Again, Article VI of the Federal Rules contains only a handful of provisions expressly regulating impeachment techniques. In the case of all other impeachment techniques, a federal judge applies the general relevancy principles codified in Federal Rules 401 to 403.

B. CHARACTER FOR UNTRUTHFULNESS

The following materials address the special rules that govern impeachment for dishonesty — or, as the federal rules put it, "untruthfulness." This mode of impeachment is a variety of character evidence, because it involves proving the character of a person — in this case, a witness — in order to suggest that the person likely acted in conformity with his or her character on a particular occasion — in this case, that the witness has lied because it is his or her nature to lie. As we saw in Chapter 4, the character evidence rule generally prohibits this kind of proof. There is a traditional exception to the character evidence rule for evidence used to impeach a witness. But that exception, codified in F.R.E. 404(a)(3), carries with it some important limitations.

1. In General

[F.R.E. 608, 610; C.E.C. §§786–787, 789]

ADVISORY COMMITTEE NOTE TO F.R.E. 608

In Rule 404(a) the general position is taken that character evidence is not admissible for the purpose of proving that the person acted in conformity therewith, subject, however, to several exceptions, one of which is character evidence of a witness as bearing upon his credibility. The present rule develops that exception.

In accordance with the bulk of judicial authority, the inquiry is strictly limited to character for veracity, rather than allowing evidence as to character generally. The result is to sharpen relevancy, to reduce surprise, waste of time, and confusion, and to make the lot of the witness somewhat less unattractive.

The use of opinion and reputation evidence as means of proving the character of witnesses is consistent with Rule 405(a). While the modern practice has purported to exclude opinion, witnesses who testify to reputation seem in fact often to be giving their opinions, disguised somewhat misleadingly as reputation. And even under the modern practice, a common relaxation has allowed inquiry as to whether the witnesses would believe the principal witness under oath.

. . . In conformity with Rule 405, which forecloses use of evidence of specific incidents as proof in chief of character unless character is an issue in the case, the present rule generally bars evidence of specific instances of conduct of a witness for the purpose of attacking or supporting his credibility. . . . Conviction of crime as a technique of impeachment is treated in detail in Rule 609, and here is merely recognized as an exception to the general rule excluding evidence of specific incidents for impeachment purposes. Particular instances of conduct, though not the subject of criminal conviction, may be inquired into on cross-examination of the principal witness himself or of a witness who testifies concerning his character for truthfulness. Effective cross-examination demands that some allowance be made for going into matters of this kind, but the possibilities of abuse are substantial. Consequently safeguards are erected in the form of specific requirements that the instances inquired into be probative of truthfulness or its opposite and not remote in time. Also, the overriding protection of Rule 403 requires that probative value not be outweighed by danger of unfair prejudice, confusion of issues, or misleading the jury, and that of Rule 611 bars harassment and undue embarrassment. . . .

ADVISORY COMMITTEE NOTE TO F.R.E. 610

While the rule forecloses inquiry into the religious beliefs or opinions of a witness for the purpose of showing that his character for truthfulness is affected by their nature, an inquiry for the purpose of showing interest or bias because of them is not within the prohibition. Thus disclosure of affiliation with a church which is a party to the litigation would be allowable under the rule....

UNITED STATES v. LOLLAR

606 F.2d 587 (5th Cir. 1979)

JAMES C. HILL, Circuit Judge.

Howard Lollar appeals from his conviction for interstate transportation of stolen property valued in excess of $5,000, 18 U.S.C.A. §2314. The property was alleged to have been stolen by appellant and several of his employees from a warehouse in West Milford, New Jersey. We affirm.

After appellant testified at trial, the government recalled one of its witnesses and asked him whether he would believe appellant under oath. Defense counsel's objection was overruled, and the witness, a former employer, answered the question in the negative. Appellant now argues that it was error to allow the witness to offer his opinion on appellant's veracity.

Although a criminal defendant cannot be compelled to take the stand in his own defense, once he chooses to testify "he places his credibility in issue as does any other witness." *United States v. Jackson*, 588 F.2d 1046, 1055 (5th Cir. 1979). While the defendant's decision to testify does not open the door to attacks on his general character, it does free the government to offer evidence bearing on the defendant's believability as a witness. Historically, the most widely used method of impeaching a defendant's credibility was to call witnesses to testify that the defendant's reputation for truth and veracity was bad. The propriety of asking a more direct question, such as "would you believe this person under oath," caused a great deal of conflict among the courts and the commentators. Early cases in this Circuit adopted the position that such testimony could be used to impeach a witness' credibility. *See Miller v. United States*, 288 F. 816, 818 (5th Cir. 1923); *Held v. United States*, 260 F. 932, 933 (5th Cir. 1919). While this was the minority view among the courts, many commentators agreed that "the exclusion of opinion evidence was 'historically unsound.'" 3 Weinstein's Evidence ¶608 [04], at 608-20 (1978); *see* McCormick, Evidence §44, at 95 (1954); 7 Wigmore, Evidence §§1981-1986 (3d ed. 1940); Ladd, Techniques of Character Testimony, 24 Iowa L. Rev. 498, 509-13 (1939). This conflict was resolved in 1976 with the enactment of Rule 608(a) of the Federal Rules of Evidence....

> Witnesses may now be asked directly to state their opinion of the principal witness' character for truthfulness and they may answer for example, "I think X is a liar." The rule imposes no prerequisite conditioned upon long acquaintance or recent information about the witness; cross-examination can be expected to expose defects of lack of familiarity and to reveal reliance on isolated or irrelevant instances of misconduct or the existence of feelings of personal hostility towards the principal witness.

Weinstein's Evidence ¶608[04], at 608-20 (1978).

Accordingly, we hold that the district court was acting well within its discretion in overruling defense counsel's objection.... Affirmed.

GLAZE v. CHILDS

861 F.3d 724 (8th Cir. 2017)

COLLOTON, Circuit Judge.

Chariell Glaze, a former detainee at the Faulkner County Detention Center in Arkansas, sued Demontrel Childs, a former correctional officer at the Center. Glaze alleged that Childs violated Glaze's constitutional rights by failing to protect Glaze from a violent attack while he was detained. . . . Glaze's cellmate, Bradley Boyce, testified that he warned Childs that three inmates were planning to assault Glaze. According to Boyce, Childs responded that he would inform his lieutenant. Childs, however, denied that Boyce told him about the planned attack. The jury found in favor of Childs.

Glaze's appeal focuses on an evidentiary ruling of the district court. Before trial, the court granted Childs's motion *in limine* to exclude evidence that Childs resigned from the Center in lieu of accepting termination of his employment. Childs resigned after he was accused of passing a cigarette to an inmate in violation of institutional policy. . . .

Glaze contends that evidence about Childs's resignation was admissible under Rule 404(b). That rule precludes a litigant from introducing "[e]vidence of a crime, wrong, or other act . . . to prove a person's character in order to show that on a particular occasion the person acted in accordance with the character." But the court may allow evidence of prior bad acts "for another purpose, such as proving motive, opportunity, intent, preparation, plan, knowledge, identity, absence of mistake, or lack of accident." Glaze does not identify a permissible purpose for the resignation evidence under the rule; he asserts only that the evidence established Childs's "intentional disregard for standards of conduct." His argument seems to be that because Childs violated institutional policy on one occasion, he likely disregarded the alleged warning from Boyce on another. This is the type of propensity evidence that the rule prohibits. The district court thus did not abuse its discretion in ruling that the resignation evidence was inadmissible under Rule 404(b).

Glaze argues alternatively that the court should have allowed cross-examination about the resignation under Rule 608(b), because it was a specific instance of conduct that was probative of Childs's character for untruthfulness. The proffered evidence, however, did not involve deceit or fraud. There was no claim that Childs lied about passing cigarettes, only that he violated policy by doing so. The court thus properly declined to allow inquiry about the incident under Rule 608(b).

The judgment of the district court is affirmed.

UNITED STATES v. ROSA

891 F.2d 1063 (3d Cir. 1989)

STAPLETON, Circuit Judge.

[Joseph Rosa and 27 other defendants were charged with cocaine trafficking in a 113-count indictment. All but two of the defendants, Kostrick and Romano, pleaded guilty. Rosa testified for the government.]

Kostrick and Romano both contend that the district court improperly prohibited their cross-examination of Joseph Rosa ... regarding certain prior criminal conduct because Rosa had not been convicted for that conduct. This simply did not occur. The record reveals that the trial judge, in accordance with Federal Rules of Evidence 608 and 609, prohibited defendants' attorneys from questioning Rosa about criminal conduct for which he had not been convicted because that conduct was not probative of truthfulness or untruthfulness. The judge permitted defense counsel to question Rosa concerning his conspiratorial oath of loyalty to his crime family to the extent that it bore on truthfulness. Similarly, the trial judge correctly allowed cross-examination concerning a fraudulent insurance claim Rosa had filed, since fraud is one of the offenses that bears on a witness's credibility. The only subject on which the trial judge prohibited cross-examination was Rosa's alleged involvement in a bribe of public officials in connection with his insurance fraud. Bribery, however, is not the kind of conduct which bears on truthfulness or untruthfulness. Moreover, even if we regarded bribery as minimally probative of those matters, given the extensive examination permitted on the underlying fraud, we could not say that the trial judge abused his discretion in limiting cross-examination with respect to Rosa's alleged bribery. . . . The judgments with respect to Kostrick and Romano will be affirmed. . . .

UNITED STATES v. WHITE

972 F.2d 590 (5th Cir. 1992)

W. EUGENE DAVIS, Circuit Judge.

John Sennett White and John Michael Wilson appeal their convictions on charges of possession with intent to distribute cocaine and conspiracy to commit the same offense. . . . White and Wilson sought to invoke Rule 404(b), along with Rules 405(b) and 406, to introduce evidence of extrinsic offenses committed by Northcutt, the government's star witness. They proffered testimony by Northcutt's prior attorney that Northcutt had previously offered to fabricate testimony against an individual in exchange for government leniency in charges pending against him.

The defendants argue that Northcutt's testimony was admissible under Rule 404(b) to show Northcutt's intent to fabricate evidence in order to gain favorable consideration from the government in his own case. The district court, relying on Rule 608(b), ruled that the defendants could elicit the evidence of Northcutt's credibility only on cross-examination of Northcutt, not through an extrinsic source. We agree.

. . . [E]xcept for his credibility, Northcutt's intent was not an issue in the case. . . . This evidence could have served only one function: to demonstrate that Northcutt had a proclivity to lie and therefore was probably lying in this case. Rule 404(b) prohibits the use of extrinsic act evidence for this purpose. The use of evidence to attack a witness's credibility is subject to the limitations of Rule 608. Under that rule, specific instances of misconduct of a witness for that purpose can not be proved by extrinsic evidence. The trial court did not abuse its discretion by excluding the proffered testimony. . . . [Reversed in part on other grounds.]

UNITED STATES v. APONTE

31 F.3d 86 (2d Cir. 1994)

WINTER, Circuit Judge.

Michael Aponte appeals from a conviction and sentence entered by Judge Dominick L. DiCarlo, following a jury trial. The jury convicted Aponte of conspiracy to rob a United States Postal Service truck, in violation of 18 U.S.C. §371, and aiding and abetting the armed robbery of a Postal Service truck, in violation of 18 U.S.C. §§2, 2114. . . . [W]ith regard to the exclusion as hearsay of a sworn statement containing fabrications by government witness Gregory Quiles and of other documents giving false descriptions of "robbers" provided by Quiles, the district court may have applied the wrong evidentiary rule, but the statements were nevertheless properly excluded. Quiles' fabricated statement and false descriptions were not offered for the truth of the matter asserted and therefore were not hearsay. Fed. R. Evid. 801(c). Rather, the documents were offered to show Quiles' capacity for deception. However, the statements were excludable as extrinsic evidence of the character and conduct of Quiles. "Specific instances of the conduct of a witness, for the purpose of attacking or supporting the witness' credibility . . . may not be proved by extrinsic evidence." Fed. R. Evid. 608(b). . . . Affirmed.

PROBLEMS

7.1. If the defendant in a tax fraud prosecution testifies in her own defense, can the government ask her on cross-examination about a deceptive resume she sent to a prospective employer ten years ago? Under what circumstances, if any, can the government introduce the resume itself?

7.2. Suppose the defendant chooses not to testify but calls a character witness who testifies that he knows the defendant well and that she is "upright and extremely ethical." Can the government ask the witness whether he knows about the deceptive resume? Under what circumstances, if any, can the government introduce the resume itself?

7.3. In a prosecution of Gerald for bank robbery, Gerald's neighbor Max testifies that Gerald boasted of carrying out the robbery. Gerald later testifies he had nothing to do with the robbery, and he denies boasting about it. On cross-examination of Gerald, the prosecutor seeks to elicit that Gerald knew about, and did nothing to stop, a plan by Gerald's business associate Oscar to threaten to disclose that Max was sexually abused as a child if Max testified against Gerald. Defense counsel objects to this line of cross-examination. How should the judge rule?

7.4. Harry Potter is on trial at the Ministry of Magic for unauthorized use of magic by an underage sorcerer. Potter testifies he acted in self-defense. The chief defense witness, Albus Dumbledore, is asked whether Potter previously tried to cover up his use of magic on a different occasion by falsely claiming that the magic was performed by an elf. Dumbledore says the elf was in fact responsible for the magic and would admit it if called to court to testify. The court disallows the elf's testimony. Would that be the right result under the Federal Rules of Evidence? *See* J.K. Rowling, *Harry Potter and the Order of the Phoenix* 139–149 (2003).

2. Prior Criminal Convictions

The upshot of the general rules regarding impeachment for dishonesty is that a witness can be impeached with evidence that it is in his or her nature to be deceitful, but not by extrinsic evidence of specific acts of dishonesty. The ban on impeachment with extrinsic evidence of specific acts of deception is waived, though, for certain criminal convictions. Which criminal convictions? The answer given by common law courts was "felonies." But the modern, federal rule is more complicated.

a. Admissible and Inadmissible Convictions

[F.R.E. 609; C.E.C. §788]

UNITED STATES v. WONG

703 F.2d 65 (3d Cir. 1983)

Per Curiam.

This case presents the issue whether a district court has any discretion to exclude, as unduly prejudicial, evidence that a witness had previously been convicted of a crime involving dishonesty or false statement. The district court held that it had no discretion to weight the probative value of the prior conviction against its prejudicial effect. Agreeing with every other circuit to consider the matter, we affirm.

John Barry Wong was charged with seventeen counts of violation of the mail fraud statute, 18 U.S.C. §1341 (1976), and two counts of violation of the Racketeer Influenced and Corrupt Organizations statute, 18 U.S.C. §§1961–68 (1976 & Supp. V 1981). A jury found him guilty on all counts, and he was sentenced to seven years' imprisonment followed by five years' probation and ordered to make restitution of $100,000.

Wong had previously been convicted at least twice—a 1978 mail fraud conviction in a federal court in Pennsylvania and a 1981 Medicare fraud conviction in a federal court in Hawaii. At trial in this case, prior to putting his client on the stand, counsel for Wong moved to preclude use of these convictions for impeachment. The trial court stated that the probative value of the convictions did not outweigh their prejudicial effect. The trial court held, however, that since the two convictions were crimes involving dishonesty or false statement [so-called *crimen falsi*], under Fed. R. Evid. 609(a)(2) no balancing of prejudice against probative value was appropriate. Wong then took the stand; during his cross-examination the two convictions were introduced against him.

Wong now attacks as erroneous the legal conclusion of the trial judge that *crimen falsi* under Fed. R. Evid. 609(a)(2) are admissible as impeachment without reference to their prejudicial effect.

... Rule 609(a) differentiates on its face between convictions for crimes punishable by imprisonment of more than one year, which are admissible under 609(a)(1), and convictions for *crimen falsi*, which are admissible under 609(a)(2). The former may be admitted only if the trial court determines that their probative value outweighs their prejudicial effect. The latter simply "shall be admitted."

Wong suggests that the apparently mandatory admission of *crimen falsi* under Fed. R. Evid. 609(a)(2) is qualified by the general balancing test of Fed. R. Evid. 403. Wong asserts that the trial court therefore has the power to exclude *crimen falsi* convictions if it determines that their probative force is substantially outweighed by their prejudicial effect.

We disagree. As the First Circuit has recently noted, Rule 403 was not designed to override more specific rules; rather it was "designed as a guide for the handling of situations for which no specific rules have been formulated." *United States v. Kiendra*, 663 F.2d 349, 354 (1st Cir. 1981) (quoting Fed. R. Evid. 403 advisory committee note). Rule 609(a) is such a specific rule. It was the product of extensive Congressional attention and considerable legislative compromise, clearly reflecting a decision that judges were to have no discretion to exclude *crimen falsi*.

In an earlier draft, Rule 609 included a subsection, 609(a)(3), which would have allowed the court to exclude either convictions carrying an imprisonment of more than one year or *crimen falsi* convictions if it determined that their probative value was substantially outweighed by their prejudicial effect. Subsection (a)(3) was described as a particularized application of Rule 403.

Proposed section 609(a)(3) was severely criticized by Senator McClellan of Arkansas on the floor of the Senate. Thereafter, when the Supreme Court officially promulgated the Federal Rules of Evidence and transmitted them to the Congress, section 609(a)(3) had disappeared; at that point there was no reference in the section to any weighing by the trial judge of probative value against prejudicial effect.

Rule 609(a) then came under considerable scrutiny in Congress. Various ways of treating impeachment by conviction were proposed. The compromise that resulted in the final version of Rule 609(a) came in the Conference Committee and was described in the following terms by the Chairman of the Subcommittee on Criminal Justice of the House Judiciary Committee:

> The House version of the rule permitted the use of convictions for crimes of dishonesty or false statement. The Senate version permitted the use of convictions for any felony or for any crime of dishonesty or false statement....
>
> The conference rule strikes a middle ground between the two versions, but a ground as close or closer to the House version than to the Senate's. *The conference rule provides that evidence of a conviction of a crime involving dishonesty or false statement may always be used to impeach....* This constitutes no change from either the House or Senate version. The conference rule further provides that evidence of a prior felony conviction may be used for

impeachment but only if the court determines that the probative value of the conviction outweighs its prejudicial effect to the defendant.

120 Cong. Rec. 40,891 (1974) (Statement of Rep. Hungate presenting the Conference Report on H.R. 5463 to the House for final consideration) (emphasis added).

The Conference Report is likewise clear:

The admission of prior convictions involving dishonesty and false statement is not within the discretion of the Court. Such convictions are peculiarly probative of credibility and, under this rule, are always to be admitted.

H.R. Rep. No. 1597, 93d Cong., 2d. Sess. 9.

Thus the legislative history of Rule 609(a)(2) unambiguously demonstrates that a judge has no authority to prohibit the government's effort to impeach the credibility of a witness by questions concerning a prior *crimen falsi* conviction. In light of this clear Congressional judgment we hold that the general balancing test of Fed. R. Evid. 403 is not applicable to impeachment by *crimen falsi* convictions under Fed. R. Evid. 609(a)(2). The judgment of the district court will be affirmed.

UNITED STATES v. ESTRADA

430 F.3d 606 (2d Cir. 2005)

SOTOMAYOR, Circuit Judge.

[Defendant Felix DeJesus was convicted of narcotics trafficking.] At trial, the government called a number of cooperating witnesses. When defense counsel first proposed impeaching cooperator Jose Lugo with a burglary conviction, the district court judge explained his "general approach," stating that, for "a conviction that goes to credibility, conviction for fraud, that type of thing, then you can bring out the nature of the conviction. If it's simply a felony conviction, the fact of the conviction is I think what you bring out." The district court reasoned that "[t]he fact that it was burglary doesn't seem to have any independent relevance," and therefore limited cross examination on Lugo's burglary conviction to the fact of an unnamed felony conviction. Considering witness Ismael Padilla's larceny convictions, the district court judge indicated that whether larceny is *crimen falsi* depends on the underlying facts and permitted extended in camera questioning of the witness about his larceny convictions. At the conclusion of this examination, the district court judge stated that he had not "heard an argument for the probative value here unless it is a crime of falsity or deceit that [ ] goes to ... untruthfulness." The district court judge then indicated that, for crimes not bearing directly on veracity, "it's the fact and presumably the date, if you want to get it in, that goes to credibility, and the credibility of the witness is not further attacked if it's, you know, Crime A versus Crime B." He explained that he was not "aware of any judge in this district that lets in the nature of the conviction rather [than] simply the fact and the date."

The court then demonstrated the kind of questions defense counsel could pose: "In June 1992, you were convicted of a felony, right? And in

October 1993, you were convicted of another felony." The district court judge reiterated that his approach was "consistent with practice in this district." The district court applied the same analysis to cooperator William Rodriguez's felony drug convictions and his murder conviction, finding none of these convictions to bear on truthfulness. Finally, following extended *in camera* questioning of witness Joseph Butler, the district court found that Butler's robbery, escape, and manslaughter convictions did not "go to the question of truthfulness or veracity" and limited impeachment for each offense to the fact of an unnamed felony conviction and its date. . . .

The district court did not err . . . in determining that the circumstances of Padilla's larceny convictions did not involve falsity or deceit such as to fall within the ambit of Rule 609(a)(2). *See United States v. Hayes*, 553 F.2d 824, 827 (2d Cir. 1977) (noting that "crimes of force, such as armed robbery or assault, or crimes of stealth, such as burglary or petit larceny, do not come within" Rule 609(a)(2) (internal citations omitted)); *cf. United States v. Sellers*, 906 F.2d 597, 603 (11th Cir. 1990) ("[C]rimes such as theft, robbery, or shoplifting do not involve 'dishonesty or false statement' within the meaning of Rule 609(a)(2)."). While much successful crime involves some quantum of stealth, all such conduct does not, as a result, constitute crime of dishonesty or false statement for purposes of Rule 609(a)(2). *See Hayes*, 553 F.2d at 827 (stating that Congress limited the crimes covered by Rule 609(a)(2) because of the Rule's inflexibility and noting that a conviction that "involved nothing more than stealth" could not be introduced automatically under Rule 609(a) (2)); *cf. United States v. Brackeen*, 969 F.2d 827, 829-30 (9th Cir. 1992) (en banc) (distinguishing between the broad meaning of "dishonesty" as a lack of integrity or principles and its narrow meaning under Rule 609(a)(2) as a disposition to deceive). The district court thus did not abuse its discretion in treating Padilla's larceny convictions as Rule 609(a)(1) crimes rather than as *crimen falsi* automatically admissible under Rule 609(a)(2).

[However, the] district court misapplied Rule 609(a)(1) by limiting the scope of impeachment of the government's witnesses, as a matter of policy, to the fact and date of their felony convictions without permitting inquiry into the statutory names of the witnesses' offenses of conviction. . . . Both Rule 609(a)(1) and (a)(2) contemplate admitting "evidence" of a witness's convictions for impeachment purposes. . . . The overwhelming weight of authority supports this conclusion and suggests that, while it may be proper to limit . . . evidence of the underlying facts or details of a crime of which a witness was convicted, inquiry into the "essential facts" of the conviction, including the nature or statutory name of each offense, its date, and the sentence imposed is presumptively required by the Rule, subject [under Rule 609(a)(1)] to balancing under Rule 403. *See United States v. Howell*, 285 F.3d 1263, 1267-68 (10th Cir. 2002) (finding that evidence of the number and nature of felony offenses is ordinarily required under Rule 609(a)(1) because a witness's convictions bear to differing degrees on credibility depending on these characteristics); *United States v. Burston*, 159 F.3d 1328, 1335-36 (11th Cir. 1998) (holding that the probative value of prior felony convictions varies with their nature and number); *Campbell v. Greer*, 831 F.2d 700, 707 (7th Cir. 1987) (concluding in a civil case that the "crime must be named" because the jury cannot evaluate a witness's credibility "if all it is told is that the witness was convicted of a 'felony'"); 28 Charles Alan Wright & Victor James Gold, Federal Practice and Procedure: Evidence § 6134, at 224 (1993) (stating that the "mere fact" approach, under which only the fact of a felony conviction is admitted, is difficult "to justify with the language and structure of Rule 609"); 4 [Jack B. Weinstein & Margaret A. Berger, Weinstein's Federal Evidence] § 609.20[2] at 609-57 to 60 (stating that the impeaching party is usually limited to establishing the name of the offense, the date of conviction, and the sentence, and that it may be improper "to limit impeachment to the mere fact of a prior conviction, without allowing the impeaching party to specify the nature and number of offenses involved"). . . .

This interpretation of Rule 609 is consistent with both the Rule's structure and the insight that different felonies, even those that do not constitute *crimen falsi*, bear on credibility to varying degrees. . . . In conformity with Rule 403, unless the risk of unfair prejudice, confusion, or delay substantially outweighs the probative value of a felony conviction, it is the jury's function to assess the probative value of a witness's specific conviction or convictions as part of its overall evaluation of the witness's credibility. . . . Rule 609(a)(1) thus contemplates that district courts will admit evidence of the nature of a witness's prior felony convictions, including the statutory name of the offense, the date of conviction, and the sentence imposed, subject to Rule 403. . . .

Rule 609(a)(1) presumes that all felonies are at least somewhat probative of a witness's propensity to testify truthfully. *See United States v. Lipscomb*, 702 F.2d 1049, 1062 (D.C.Cir.1983) (en banc) (concluding that Congress believed that all felonies have some probative value on the issue of credibility). District courts under Rule 609(a)(1) are to consider the relative probative worth of a witness's specific offenses of conviction, however, in light of the factors listed under Rule 403, when determining whether to admit evidence of those convictions for impeachment purposes. . . .

[F]elonies not involving dishonesty or false statement such as to fall within the scope of Rule 609(a)(2) nonetheless bear on credibility to varying degrees. See 4 Weinstein & Berger § 609.05[3][b] at 609-39 ("Although Rule 609(a)(1) addresses convictions for crimes that do not involve dishonesty or false statement, some felonies are more related to veracity than are others."). We agree, therefore, with those of our sister circuits that have reasoned that all Rule 609(a)(1) felonies are not equally probative of credibility but that many are significantly probative of a witness's propensity for truthfulness. . . .

An influential case from the Court of Appeals for the District of Columbia that pre-dates the Federal Rules distinguished between crimes that reflect adversely on a person's integrity, and which therefore bear on honesty — such as those involving deceit, fraud, and theft — and acts of violence, "which may result from a short temper, a combative nature, extreme provocation, or other causes, [and] generally have little or no direct bearing on honesty and veracity." *Gordon v. United States*, 383 F.2d 936, 940 (D.C. Cir. 1967). The Gordon court thus stated a "rule of thumb" to be that "convictions which rest on dishonest conduct relate to credibility whereas those of violent or assaultive crimes generally do not." *Id.*; *see also* 28 Wright & Gold § 6134 at 233 ("[C]rimes of impulse or carelessness have little probative value since they say little about the propensity to engage in calculated law-breaking like perjury."); 4 Weinstein & Berger § 609.05[3][b] at 609-39 and 40 (noting that "crimes of violence generally have limited probative value concerning the witness's credibility" and that theft "crimes have greater impeachment value"). We find the distinction enunciated in *Gordon* to have substantial analytic value. While many felonies exemplifying untruthful behavior fall within the ambit of Rule 609(a)(2), many crimes that do not fit that provision are nonetheless quite probative of veracity.

This distinction between crimes falling outside Rule 609(a)(2) but nonetheless ranking high on the scale of probative worth on credibility, including, for example, theft and escape crimes, and those ranking low on that scale, including crimes of violence, appears in cases from numerous jurisdictions. . . . "Similarly high on the scale are crimes that involve evasions of responsibility or abuse of trust, a category that includes smuggling or failure to register or report when required, and at least sometimes drug importation and even sexual abuse of children in [the witness's] care." [Christopher B. Mueller & Laird C. Kirkpatrick, Evidence] § 6.31 at 563. Many drug crimes and crimes involving public morality, such as prostitution, may be less probative of veracity. *Id.* We hasten to add, however, that "crimes requiring planning or preparation bear more strongly on veracity than violence alone suggests because planning indicates deliberate and injurious violation of basic standards rather than impulse or anger, and usually it involves some element of deceiving the victim." *Id.* at 563-64; see also 28 Wright & Gold § 6134 at 233 ("[V]iolent crimes involving . . . premeditation are relatively higher in probative value because they suggest the witness is willing to break the law when it furthers his interests."). We also note that the gravity of an offense may bear on truthfulness, to the extent that more serious offenses indicate a stronger willingness to ignore the law. Mueller & Kirkpatrick § 6.31 at 564. *But see* 28 Wright & Gold § 6134 at 232-33 (noting that for "particularly depraved and offensive acts, such as wanton violence or sexual immorality, the jury is likely to draw the prejudicial inference that the witness is a bad person while at the same time the jury may derive little probative value from the conviction since these crimes say little about credibility" while acknowledging that particularly heinous crimes may be high in probative value insofar as they reflect a rejection of social mores).

In light of the foregoing, we agree with the observation, about an earlier iteration of Rule 609, that "[i]t is implausible that Congress believed that crimes falling on one side of the [Rule 609(a)] line are so probative of credibility that they should be admitted regardless of prejudice but that crimes falling just on the other side of the line may in some cases not be probative at all." *Lipscomb*, 702 F.2d at 1057. We find equally persuasive the point that "[m]ore likely, Congress anticipated that crimes of stealth (e.g., smuggling, burglary), while not quite crimes of 'dishonesty or false statement,' do reflect lack of credibility and should be admitted unless significantly prejudicial." *Id.* We thus find the gradations among Rule 609(a)(1) crimes, in terms of their bearing on truthfulness, to lie at the heart of the Rule 403 analysis that district courts must undertake when determining whether to admit for impeachment purposes evidence of a witness's convictions, including their statutory names, under Rule 609(a)(1). . . .

While the district court indicated that the fact of a witness's felony convictions was admissible under Rule 609(a)(1) "unless there is a 403 balancing problem," it obviated the need for such balancing by scrubbing the convictions of any factors that would be relevant to a Rule 403 analysis. . . . Thus, evidence of the witness Padilla's larceny convictions, for example, including the statutory name, date of conviction, and sentence imposed, perhaps should have been admitted under Rule 609(a)(1) if any of them were felonies. While not *crimen falsi* that are automatically admissible under Rule 609(a)(2), theft crimes, and other crimes involving stealth, nonetheless bear on a witness's propensity to testify truthfully. The district court may have been justified, by contrast, had it refused to permit the defendant to impeach government witnesses with crimes of violence, which may bear so marginally on honesty or veracity, depending on the circumstances of those crimes, as to justify exclusion under Rule 609(a)(1). . . .

Although the district court erroneously applied Rule 609(a)(1) . . . the . . . court court permitted DeJesus to present substantial evidence bearing on the prosecution witnesses' credibility . . . [and] the marginal impact of evidence relating to the cooperating witnesses' specific offenses of conviction could not have given a reasonable jury a significantly different impression. . . . Moreover, the government's case was strong enough to support DeJesus's conviction even apart from the testimony of . . . the witnesses whose prior felony convictions were admitted for impeachment purposes only as unnamed felonies. . . . The district court's evidentiary error was therefore harmless. [Affirmed.]

UNITED STATES v. AMAECHI

991 F.2d 374 (7th Cir. 1993)

CUMMINGS, Circuit Judge.

[Defendant Ihuoma Amaechi was convicted of narcotics trafficking based on evidence that he had taken delivery of a suitcase containing half a kilogram of heroin. Among the prosecution witnesses was Doreen Bennett, who had taken the suitcase to Amaechi.]

Defendant . . . suggests that the court erred in excluding evidence of Doreen Bennett's conviction for shoplifting. Bennett pleaded guilty on April 19, 1989 in Cook County Circuit Court to stealing less than $150, a misdemeanor, and was sentenced to a three-month term of supervision. Federal Rule of Evidence 609 allows evidence of a witness's prior conviction for impeachment if, among other things, the punishment could have exceeded one year (Bennett's did not), or if the crime involves dishonesty or false statement no matter how long the sentence. . . . Illinois law clearly contemplates that a sentence of supervision does not constitute a conviction for evidentiary purposes. *People v. Schuning*, 476 N.E.2d 423, 426 (Ill. 1985); *see also People v. Leeks*, 492 N.E.2d 920, 923 (Ill. 1986). Since Bennett's shoplifting did not result in a conviction, it may not be admitted to attack her credibility under Rule 609(a)(2).

The government also urges us to adopt the reasoning of nine circuits that shoplifting is not a crime of dishonesty unless committed in a fraudulent or deceitful manner. Shoplifting, of course, does involve dishonesty of a certain kind; the question is whether it involves the kind contemplated by Congress in drafting the Rules of Evidence — i.e., whether it indicates that a person may be more likely to commit perjury. The calculus underlying this realm of evidence law — that people who lie in other contexts are more likely to perjure themselves than people who steal — is empirically questionable on a number of levels. Some people who falsify forms, for example, would stop short of committing the crime of perjury, while many thieves may be incorrigible liars. Yet the drafters of the Rules of Evidence explicitly intended that Rule 609 be limited to crimes involving "some element of misrepresentation or other indication of a propensity to lie and excluding those crimes which, bad though they are, do not carry with them a tinge of falsification." [*United States v. Ortega*, 561 F.2d 803, 806 (9th Cir. 1977).] Having made the initial questionable assumption that some people are more given to perjury than others based on past conduct, we agree with nine other circuits that to include shoplifting as a crime of dishonesty would swallow the rule and allow any past crime to be admitted for impeachment purposes. Therefore, we hold that petty shoplifting does not in and of itself qualify as a crime of dishonesty under Rule 609. The district judge correctly prohibited Amaechi's counsel from impeaching Bennett with her shoplifting conviction. . . . [Defendant's conviction is affirmed.]

UNITED STATES v. SANDERS

964 F.2d 295 (4th Cir. 1992)

PHILLIPS, Circuit Judge.

Carlos Sanders appeals his convictions for assault with a dangerous weapon with intent to do bodily harm in violation of 18 U.S.C. §113(c), and for possession of contraband (a shank used in the assault) in violation of Virginia Code §53.1-203(4), as assimilated by 18 U.S.C. §13. . . . Sanders and Ricky Alston, both inmates at Lorton Reformatory, were indicted for . . . assaulting fellow inmate Bobby Jenkins with a shank on April 7, 1989.

Before trial, Sanders filed a motion *in limine* to exclude evidence of his prior convictions. Although the district court granted this motion in part by prohibiting the government from questioning Sanders about a stabbing for which he was acquitted and an armed robbery for which his conviction was reversed, the court declined to preclude the government from cross-examining Sanders about his prior assault and contraband possession convictions. The court ruled that the assault and contraband convictions were admissible under Federal Rules of Evidence 609(a) and 404(b).

After hearing the evidence, the jury acquitted Alston on the assault count and convicted Sanders of possession of a shank. The jury was unable to reach a verdict on the assault count against Sanders, however. . . . [In a subsequent retrial,] Sanders testified that he had acted in self-defense, claiming that Jenkins had attacked him first. The government cross-examined Sanders about his prior convictions as follows:

Q: You testified on direct that you are a convicted felon.
A: Yes, sir.

Q: And in fact you were convicted in 1988 for committing an assault in Lorton, weren't you?

A: Yes, sir.

Q: And you were also convicted of prisoner in possession of contraband at that time?

A: Yes, sir.

Q: You were convicted because you stabbed an inmate named Silas Horn (phonetic).

At this point, Sanders' counsel objected to any further questioning about the nature of the prior convictions and the district court sustained the objection. Trial was concluded in a half a day; the jury deliberated the rest of that day and into the next before returning a verdict of the lesser included offense of assault with a dangerous weapon with intent to do bodily harm. This appeal followed. Sanders challenges both his conviction of contraband possession on the first trial and of assault on the second.

. . . Sanders' convictions for assault and possession of contraband fall under 609(a)(1), and the district court therefore was required to balance the probative value of the evidence against its prejudicial effect in assessing its admissibility. Here, although evidence of the prior convictions may be thought somehow generally probative of Sanders' lack of credibility, they were extremely prejudicial since they involved the exact type of conduct for which Sanders was on trial.

We have recognized the prejudice that results from admitting evidence of a similar offense under Rule 609:

> Admission of evidence of a similar offense often does little to impeach the credibility of a testifying defendant while undoubtedly prejudicing him. The jury, despite limiting instructions, can hardly avoid drawing the inference that the past conviction suggests some probability that defendant committed the similar offense for which he is currently charged. The generally accepted view, therefore, is that evidence of similar offenses for impeachment purposes under Rule 609 should be admitted sparingly if at all.

United States v. Beahm, 664 F.2d 414, 418-19 (4th Cir. 1981) (footnote omitted). . . . It is unclear whether and how the district court may have sought to balance the probative value of this evidence against its prejudicial effect, since at the hearing on Sanders' motion *in limine* the district judge simply stated, "[t]hey [the government] are entitled to go into that [Sanders' prior convictions] both on the question of intent and impeachment." Even if the district court had explicitly conducted a balancing inquiry before admitting this evidence, we would find the evidence inadmissible under Rule 609(a) because of the high likelihood of prejudice that accompanies the admission of such similar prior convictions. As we stated in *Beahm*,

> [W]here as here the offense sought to be admitted against defendant had little bearing on his propensity to tell the truth, the district court should have recognized that the substantial likelihood of prejudice outweighed the minimal impeachment value of the evidence, and refused to admit the evidence, . . . or at the very least limited disclosure to the fact of conviction without revealing its nature.

... In the alternative, the district court held that Sanders' prior convictions were admissible under Rule 404(b) to show Sanders' intent to commit both crimes charged.... Since Sanders admitted the stabbing and claimed only that in doing so he acted in self-defense, the only factual issue in the case was whether that was the reason for the admitted act. The fact that Sanders had committed an assault on another prisoner and possessed contraband one year earlier had nothing to do with his reason for — his intent in — stabbing Jenkins. All that the evidence of the prior conviction of assault could possibly show was Sanders' propensity to commit assaults on other prisoners or his general propensity to commit violent crimes. The total lack of any probative value in the contraband possession conviction, except to show general criminal disposition, is even more stark. This is exactly the kind of propensity inference that Rule 404(b)'s built-in limitation was designed to prevent.... Because Sanders' prior convictions could only "prove the character of [Sanders] in order to show action and conformity therewith," we hold that the district court erred in admitting this evidence under Rule 404(b).

... The admission of Sanders' prior convictions was not harmless error as to his assault conviction. The assault prosecution turned essentially upon the jury's assessment of the relative credibility of Sanders and Jenkins, the direct protagonists, who gave widely conflicting versions of the stabbing. In such a situation, evidence having no possible basis except to show a propensity for violence on the part of the defendant obviously has the capacity to tip the balance in such a swearing contest.... We conclude, however, that the error in admitting the evidence of the prior convictions was harmless as to the possession count for which Sanders was convicted on his first trial. As opposed to the closeness of the case on the assault count — with the outcome depending upon the jury's assessment of conflicting testimony on Sanders' self-defense theory — the case on the possession count was not comparably close. As to that count, Sanders of course admitted possession of the shank used to stab Jenkins, he simply denied ownership, ascribing that to Jenkins. The evidence was not sufficiently strong in comparison to the Government's evidence that the shank was Sanders' to convince us that his conviction on that count was "substantially swayed" by the admission of this prior-conviction evidence.

We therefore affirm Sanders' conviction on the possession count, but reverse and remand for a new trial on the assault count....

UNITED STATES v. OAXACA

569 F.2d 518 (9th Cir. 1978)

DUNIWAY, Circuit Judge.

Oaxaca was charged in a one-count indictment alleging a single armed bank robbery. He was convicted after a jury trial.... At trial Oaxaca chose to testify in his own behalf. The prosecutor sought to impeach Oaxaca by introducing evidence that he had suffered two prior felony convictions. The defense attempted to bar any inquiry into the precise nature of the priors but the district judge, refusing to so limit the questioning, permitted the prosecutor to establish that Oaxaca had been convicted of burglary in 1967, and of bank robbery in 1972.

On appeal, Oaxaca acknowledges, as he must, that the district court had "wide discretion in deciding whether to exclude evidence of prior convictions as more prejudicial than probative of lack of credibility." *United States v. Prewitt*, 9 Cir., 1976, 534 F.2d 200, 201. While conceding that the court acted within its discretion in permitting inquiry into his criminal record generally, Oaxaca argues that evidence of the specific nature of his prior convictions was more prejudicial than probative and on this ground ought to have been excluded.

We find no abuse of discretion. The convictions were for crimes which reflected adversely on the defendant's honesty and integrity. As such they were relevant to the question of Oaxaca's credibility, which, in light of his alibi defense, was a key issue in the case.

The 1972 bank robbery conviction was not inadmissible per se, merely because the offense involved was identical to that for which Oaxaca was on trial. In *United States v. Wilson*, 9 Cir., 1976, 536 F.2d 883, we held that prior convictions for attempted robbery and receiving stolen property were properly admitted against a defendant charged with bank robbery, in light of their impeachment value. In *United States v. Hatcher*, 9 Cir., 1974, 496 F.2d 529, 530, we concluded that a defendant charged with violating the Dyer Act was properly impeached with evidence of three prior Dyer Act convictions, noting, "[t]he convictions were for theft which is more indicative of credibility than, say, convictions for crimes of violence." . . . Affirmed.

UNITED STATES v. HERNANDEZ

106 F.3d 737 (7th Cir. 1997)

RIPPLE, Circuit Judge.

Salvador Hernandez was convicted by a jury of conspiracy to kidnap in violation of 18 U.S.C. §1201(c) and of kidnaping in violation of 18 U.S.C. §1201(a). . . . [He] submits that the district court erred in admitting the evidence of a prior conviction for the possession of cocaine and marijuana. . . . [H]e points out that the prior conviction was for possession of cocaine and marijuana and that the current charges also were related to drugs because the ransom money was meant to pay back a drug deal. The admission of the similar prior conviction would suggest, he submits, his bad character or a willingness to commit this drug-related kidnaping. . . .

[W]e discern no abuse of discretion. At the outset, we note that the prior conviction occurred five years earlier and therefore was well within the time period of Rule 609. The district court ultimately determined that the evidence ought to be admitted because of its value in assessing the credibility of the defendant. The court was well aware that there was a similarity between the two crimes, a factor that requires caution on the part of the district court to avoid the possibility of the jury's inferring guilt on a ground not permissible under Rule 404(b). Nevertheless, the court acted within its discretion when it determined that, given the importance of the credibility issue in this case, evidence of the earlier conviction ought to be admitted. See *United States v. Causey*, 9 F.3d 1341, 1344-45 (7th Cir. 1993) (noting the danger of admitting evidence of similar crimes, but holding that a district court may nevertheless determine that the importance of the credibility determination requires admission of the previous conviction), *cert. denied*, 511 U.S. 1024 (1994). Finally, we note that the court's instruction cautioned the jury that the conviction was to be considered solely to assess the credibility of the defendant. . . . Affirmed.

RICHARD D. FRIEDMAN, CHARACTER IMPEACHMENT EVIDENCE: THE ASYMMETRIAL INTERACTION BETWEEN PERSONALITY AND SITUATION

43 Duke LJ. 816 (1994)

In my view, character impeachment evidence cannot substantially alter a rational juror's assessment of a criminal defendant's inclination to lie unless the juror follows a train of thought something like the following: "At first I thought it was very unlikely that, if Defoe committed robbery, he would be willing to lie about it. But now that I know he committed forgery a year before, that possibility seems substantially more likely." It seems plain, however, that it is highly improbable that a rational juror would follow such a train of thought. . . .

Character impeachment of criminal defendants should be eliminated, and all other character impeachment evidence, including proof of prior convictions, should be subject to a discretionary rule. In terms of the Federal Rules of Evidence, these changes could be accomplished quite simply. First, Rule 608, the discretionary rule that applies to all types of character impeachment evidence except for prior convictions, should be expanded to apply to that type of evidence as well but narrowed to exclude character impeachment of criminal defendants. Second, Rule 609, which now prescribes in substantial detail situations in which the trial court must, may, and may not admit evidence of prior convictions, should be eliminated. . . . We would no longer deal with the charade of evidence supposedly offered to prove that the accused is unworthy of belief but actually having little value in the circumstances to prove that proposition and really offered to show that the accused is a bad person with a propensity for criminal behavior. Nor would the prospect of such evidence scare the accused off the stand; not facing an overwhelming disincentive to testify, he would have an unobstructed opportunity to tell his side of the story under oath to a jury that could assess his testimony fully aware of his self-interest. . . .

ANNA ROBERTS, RECLAIMING THE IMPORTANCE OF THE DEFENDANT'S TESTIMONY: PRIOR CONVICTION IMPEACHMENT AND THE FIGHT AGAINST IMPLICIT STEREOTYPING

83 U. Chi. L. Rev. 835, 836-838 (2016)

A recent study of DNA exonerees revealed that, despite their factual innocence, 91 percent of those with prior convictions waived their right to testify at trial. The most common reason given by their counsel was the fear of the impact of impeachment by prior conviction. That fear was justified. First, in every case in which one of the exonerees with a criminal record did testify, the trial court permitted this type of impeachment; second, allowing the jury to learn of a defendant's criminal record increases the rate of conviction by as much as 27 percent. . . . .

The early case law emphasized that a paramount consideration in determining whether to permit prior conviction impeachment was whether the defendant would be chilled from testifying. Even if prior conviction evidence was probative of the defendant's credibility, and even if the probative value outweighed the prejudice, the risk that defendants might be deterred from testifying weighed heavily against permitting impeachment.

The case law that followed the enactment of the FRE ostensibly preserved these early themes. "The importance of the defendant's testimony" is one factor in the multifactor test that most circuits and many states use in conducting the probative/prejudicial balancing test that the relevant rule of evidence requires. Yet federal and state judges often ignore this factor or treat it as if it were of little worth. . . .

Research into implicit stereotyping and its amelioration shows why the collapse of the "importance of the defendant's testimony" factor is particularly significant. Implicit racial stereotyping constitutes one of the most significant, and intractable, threats to courtroom fairness. Those accused of crimes are disproportionately people of color, and people of color are frequently targets of implicit racial stereotyping. . . . [W]hen defendants are African American, unconscious associations are invoked between their race and concepts such as violence, weaponry, hostility, aggression, immorality, and — most damning of all — criminal guilt. And yet, . . . when fact finders hear from a member of a stereotyped group, and particularly when they hear information that individuates — or paints a unique picture of — that person, they are more likely to be able to form judgments about that individual that are based on the evidence rather than on stereotypes.

b. Preserving Claims of Error

LUCE v. UNITED STATES

469 U.S. 38 (1984)

Chief Justice Burger delivered the opinion of the Court.

. . . Petitioner was indicted on charges of conspiracy, and possession of cocaine with intent to distribute, in violation of 21 U.S.C. §§846 and 841(a)(1). During his trial in the United States District Court for the Western District of Tennessee, petitioner moved for a ruling to preclude the Government from using a 1974 state conviction to impeach him if he testified. There was no commitment by petitioner that he would testify if the motion were granted, nor did he make a proffer to the court as to what his testimony would be. In opposing the motion, the Government represented that the conviction was for a serious crime — possession of a controlled substance.

The District Court ruled that the prior conviction fell within the category of permissible impeachment evidence under Federal Rule of Evidence 609(a). The District Court noted, however, that the nature and scope of petitioner's trial testimony could affect the court's specific evidentiary rulings; for example, the court was prepared to hold that the prior conviction would be excluded if petitioner limited his testimony to explaining his attempt to flee from the arresting officers. However, if petitioner took the stand and denied any prior involvement with drugs, he could then be impeached by the 1974 conviction. Petitioner did not testify, and the jury returned guilty verdicts.

The United States Court of Appeals for the Sixth Circuit affirmed. . . . The Court of Appeals held that when the defendant does not testify, the court will not review the District Court's *in limine* ruling.

. . . Any possible harm flowing from a district court's *in limine* ruling permitting impeachment by a prior conviction is wholly speculative. The ruling is subject to change when the case unfolds, particularly if the actual testimony differs from what was contained in the defendant's proffer. Indeed even if nothing unexpected happens at trial, the district judge is free, in the exercise of sound judicial discretion, to alter a previous *in limine* ruling. On a record such as here, it would be a matter of conjecture whether the District Court would have allowed the Government to attack petitioner's credibility at trial by means of the prior conviction.

When the defendant does not testify, the reviewing court also has no way of knowing whether the Government would have sought to impeach with the prior conviction. If, for example, the Government's case is strong, and the defendant is subject to impeachment by other means, a prosecutor might elect not to use an arguably inadmissible prior conviction.

Because an accused's decision whether to testify "seldom turns on the resolution of one factor," *New Jersey v. Portash*, 440 U.S. 450, 467 (1979) (Blackmun, J., dissenting), a reviewing court cannot assume that the adverse ruling motivated a defendant's decision not to testify. In support of his motion a defendant might make a commitment to testify if his motion is granted; but such a commitment is virtually risk free because of the difficulty of enforcing it.

Even if these difficulties could be surmounted, the reviewing court would still face the question of harmless error. Were *in limine* rulings under Rule 609(a) reviewable on appeal, almost any error would result in the windfall of automatic reversal; the appellate court could not logically term "harmless" an error that presumptively kept the defendant from testifying. Requiring that a defendant testify in order to preserve Rule 609(a) claims will enable the reviewing court to determine the impact any erroneous impeachment may have had in light of the record as a whole; it will also tend to discourage making such motions solely to "plant" reversible error in the event of conviction.

. . . We hold that to raise and preserve for review the claim of improper impeachment with a prior conviction, a defendant must testify. Accordingly, the judgment of the Court of Appeals is affirmed. .

[Justice Brennan, joined by Justice Marshall, filed a concurring opinion. Justice Stevens took no part in the case.]

OHLER v. UNITED STATES

529 U.S. 753 (2000)

Chief Justice REHNQUIST delivered the opinion of the Court.

Petitioner, Maria Ohler, was arrested and charged with importation of marijuana and possession of marijuana with the intent to distribute. The District Court granted the Government's motion *in limine* seeking to admit evidence of her prior felony conviction as impeachment evidence under Federal Rule of Evidence 609(a)(1). Ohler testified at trial and admitted on direct examination that she had been convicted of possession of methamphetamine in 1993. The jury convicted her of both counts, and the Court of Appeals for the Ninth Circuit affirmed. We agree with the Court of Appeals that Ohler may not challenge the *in limine* ruling of the District Court on appeal.

. . . Generally, a party introducing evidence cannot complain on appeal that the evidence was erroneously admitted. *See* 1 J. Weinstein & M. Berger, Weinstein's Federal Evidence §103.14, 103–30 (2d ed. 2000). *Cf.* 1 J. Strong, McCormick on Evidence §55, p. 246 (5th ed. 1999) ("If a party who has objected to evidence of a certain fact himself produces evidence from his own witness of the same fact, he has waived his objection."). . . . Ohler argues that it would be unfair to apply such a waiver rule in this situation because it compels a defendant to forgo the tactical advantage of preemptively introducing the conviction in order to appeal the *in limine* ruling. She argues that if a defendant is forced to wait for evidence of the conviction to be introduced on cross-examination, the jury will believe that the defendant is less credible because she was trying to conceal the conviction. The Government disputes that the defendant is unduly disadvantaged by waiting for the prosecution to introduce the conviction on cross-examination. First, the Government argues that it is debatable whether jurors actually perceive a defendant to be more credible if she introduces a conviction herself. Second, even if jurors do consider the defendant more credible, the Government suggests that it is an unwarranted advantage because the jury does not realize that the defendant disclosed the conviction only after failing to persuade the court to exclude it.

Whatever the merits of these contentions, they tend to obscure the fact that both the Government and the defendant in a criminal trial must make choices as the trial progresses. For example, the defendant must decide whether or not to take the stand in her own behalf. If she has an innocent or mitigating explanation for evidence that might otherwise incriminate, acquittal may be more likely if she takes the stand. . . . But once the defendant testifies, she is subject to cross-examination, including impeachment by prior convictions, and the decision to take the stand may prove damaging instead of helpful. A defendant has a further choice to make if she decides to testify, notwithstanding a prior conviction. The defendant must choose whether to introduce the conviction on direct examination and remove the sting or to take her chances with the prosecutor's possible elicitation of the conviction on cross-examination.

The Government, too, in a case such as this, must make a choice. If the defendant testifies, it must choose whether or not to impeach her by use of her prior conviction. Here the trial judge had indicated he would allow its use, but the Government still had to consider whether its use might be deemed reversible error on appeal. This choice is often based on the Government's appraisal of the apparent effect of the defendant's testimony. If she has offered a plausible, innocent explanation of the evidence against her, it will be inclined to use the prior conviction; if not, it may decide not to risk possible reversal on appeal from its use. . . .

Petitioner's submission would deny to the Government its usual right to decide, after she testifies, whether or not to use her prior conviction against her. She seeks to short-circuit that decisional process by offering the conviction herself (and thereby removing the sting) and still preserve its admission as a claim of error on appeal.

But here petitioner runs into the position taken by the Court in a similar, but not identical, situation in *Luce v. United States*, 469 U.S. 38 (1984), that "[a]ny possible harm flowing from a district court's in limine ruling permitting impeachment by a prior conviction is wholly speculative." Only when the government exercises its option to elicit the testimony is an appellate court confronted with a case where, under the normal rules of trial, the defendant can claim the denial of a substantial right if in fact the district court's *in limine* ruling proved to be erroneous. In our view, there is nothing "unfair," as petitioner puts it, about putting petitioner to her choice in accordance with the normal rules of trial.

For these reasons, we conclude that a defendant who preemptively introduces evidence of a prior conviction on direct examination may not on appeal claim that the admission of such evidence was error. The judgment of the Court of Appeals for the Ninth Circuit is therefore affirmed.

[Justice Souter filed a dissenting opinion, joined by Justice Stevens, Justice Ginsburg, and Justice Breyer.]

PROBLEMS

7.5. A defendant prosecuted for felony tax fraud has previously been convicted of the same offense. If the defendant testifies, does the judge have discretion to exclude impeachment with the prior conviction?

7.6. A defendant prosecuted in federal court for embezzlement moves before trial to exclude evidence of his prior felony conviction in state court for shoplifting. The trial judge rules that the evidence is admissible as proof of intent and also, if the defendant testifies, for impeachment. Must the defendant testify in order to challenge this ruling on appeal?

C. PRIOR INCONSISTENT STATEMENTS

Just as there are special rules that govern impeachment for dishonesty, there are special rules that govern impeachment for inconsistency — that is to say, impeachment by showing the witness has told a different story in the past. But there are not as many rules on this subject as there used to be. In fact F.R.E. 613, which addresses impeachment with prior inconsistent statements, starts off by rejecting an old, common law restriction: the "rule in Queen's Case," which provided that before a prior, written statement could be used to impeach a witness, it had to be shown to the witness. F.R.E. 613 does preserve, though, a looser requirement that "extrinsic evidence" of a witness's prior inconsistent statement is admissible only if the witness is given a chance to explain or deny it, and the opposing party is given a chance to ask the witness about it.

It is easy to be confused about the relationship between this requirement and the hearsay rule. F.R.E. 613 and its state analogs set forth procedural prerequisites for the introduction of a prior inconsistent statement used to impeach a witness, but do not address the separate question of under what circumstances the prior inconsistent statement can be used not just for impeachment but also to prove the truth of the matter asserted. That question is addressed in Chapter 3 of this book.

[F.R.E. 613, 801(D)(1); C.E.C. §§769–770, 1235]

ADVISORY COMMITTEE NOTE TO F.R.E. 613

The Queen's Case, 2 Br. & B. 284, 129 Eng. Rep. 976 (1820), laid down the requirement that a cross-examiner, prior to questioning the witness about his own prior statement in writing, must first show it to the witness. Abolished by statute in the country of its origin, the requirement nevertheless gained currency in the United States. The rule abolishes this useless impediment to cross-examination. . . .

The familiar foundation requirement that an impeaching statement first be shown to the witness before it can be proved by extrinsic evidence is preserved but with some modifications. The traditional insistence that the witness be directed to the statement on cross-examination is relaxed in favor of simply providing the witness an opportunity to explain and the opposite party an opportunity to examine on the statement, with no specification of any particular time or sequence. Under this procedure, several collusive witnesses can be examined before disclosure of a joint prior inconsistent statement. . . . Also, dangers of oversight are reduced.

In order to allow for such eventualities as the witness becoming unavailable by the time the statement is discovered, a measure of discretion is conferred upon the judge. . . . Under principles of *expressio unius* the rule does not apply to impeachment by evidence of prior inconsistent conduct. The use of inconsistent statements to impeach a hearsay declaration is treated in Rule 806.

UNITED STATES v. LEBEL

622 F.2d 1054 (2d Cir. 1979) (sub nom. United States v. Praetorius)

KELLEHER, District Judge.

[Kenneth Lebel and several codefendants were convicted of conspiring to import heroin from Thailand into the United States.]

Lebel contends that the district court erred in disallowing evidence that witness Laws failed to identify him at the first trial. Laws had testified on direct examination at that trial that he met eight of the conspirators in Bangkok, and then identified them in the courtroom, with the exception of Lebel. He did, however, identify Lebel the following day. At the second trial, Lebel's counsel attempted to elicit this fact of non-identification of his client by examining Special Agent Yaniello, the D.E.A. case agent (who had been present at the first trial). The trial judge refused to allow the introduction of the non-identification testimony unless and until Laws was given a chance to explain or deny the statement on the witness stand. The judge relied upon F.R.E. Rule 613(b)....

Lebel's first contention is that the failure to identify was not a "statement" within the meaning of that term in the rule. The advisory committee note to the rule provides that the rule does not apply to evidence of prior inconsistent conduct. The only definition of "statement" to be found in the Federal Rules is the definition in Rule 801(a): "(a statement includes) nonverbal conduct of a person, if it is intended by him as an assertion." Under that definition, the identification or non-identification of persons in a courtroom can be termed a statement. Lebel's contention to the contrary is without merit.

Lebel, however, correctly points out that the trial judge was misinterpreting the rule in requiring that Laws be confronted with the "statement" immediately. The rule does not specify any particular order of calling witnesses, and so the defense should have been able to introduce the evidence during the examination of Agent Yaniello....

Having determined that it was error to refuse to admit the evidence, the next inquiry must be whether that error was harmless, or if a new trial is mandated. An error is harmless only if it did not influence the jury, or had but very slight effect. Here, it does not appear that the error committed requires reversal. First, it was impeachment testimony as to a collateral matter, Laws' credibility. Second, counsel for Lebel always had the opportunity of calling Laws to the witness stand and confronting him with the identification or non-identification; that was never done. Third, Laws was on the witness stand for two and one half days of cross-examination, and counsel did not inquire at that time about the failure to identify Lebel at the first trial. Under all these circumstances, we must conclude that the error was harmless.... The judgments of conviction are affirmed in all respects and as to each defendant.

UNITED STATES v. TRUMAN

688 F.3d 129 (2d Cir. 2012)

LOHIER, Circuit Judge.

A building partly owned by defendant Jeffrey Truman burned down.... The following month, police arrested twenty-year-old [Jeffrey] Truman, Jr., who confessed that he had burned the building at his father's direction.... Truman, Jr. pleaded guilty to third-degree arson pursuant to a cooperation agreement with the district attorney of Madison County and served a two-year term of imprisonment.

Truman was first tried in state court on arson, fraud, and related charges, with Truman, Jr. as the main witness against him. The charges were dismissed, however, when the State prosecutors proved unable to corroborate Truman, Jr.'s testimony, as required under New York law when an accomplice testifies for the prosecution. . . .

[Truman Jr. later entered into a cooperation agreement with federal authorities, and his father was indicted on federal charges of arson and fraud.] At Truman's federal trial, the Government called Truman, Jr. as a witness. . . . When the Government asked Truman, Jr. why he set the fire and about the content of his conversations with his father, he refused to answer. The District Court confirmed that Truman, Jr. would not answer and warned him that his refusal would constitute a breach of the cooperation agreement with the Government. He still refused, saying, "I can't," and, "I can't do this." In response, and over Truman's objection, the Government read portions of Truman, Jr.'s testimony from Truman's state court trial, in which Truman, Jr. confirmed that his father had asked him to start the fire. . . .

[The jury found Truman guilty but the trial judge granted a new trial, in part because the judge concluded in retrospect that] Truman, Jr.'s state court testimony was inadmissible hearsay. We disagree. . . . Truman, Jr. answered every question posed to him in cross-examination about his prior state court testimony, and therefore he was "subject to cross-examination" within the meaning of Rule 801(d)(1)(A). His prior testimony was also "inconsistent" with his refusal to answer questions about that testimony on direct examination at trial. In *United States v. Marchand,* we held that "if a witness has testified to . . . facts before a grand jury and forgets or denies them at trial, his grand jury testimony . . . falls squarely within Rule 801(d)(1)(A)." 564 F.2d 983, 999 (2d Cir. 1977). Our holding in *Marchand* naturally extends to a trial witness's refusal to answer questions posed and answered in prior sworn state court testimony. To the extent *Marchand* did not specifically address this issue, however, we now join all of our sister courts that have addressed the question in holding that where, as here, a witness who testifies under oath and is subject to cross-examination in a prior state court proceeding explicitly refuses to answer the same questions at trial, the refusal to answer is inconsistent with his prior testimony and the prior testimony is admissible under Rule 801(d)(1)(A). *See, e.g., United States v. Iglesias,* 535 F.3d 150, 159 (3d Cir. 2008) (refusal to testify with more than "one word admissions, evasive and rambling responses, and equivocations" inconsistent with "clear and straightforward" prior testimony); *United States v. Matlock,* 109 F.3d 1313, 1319 (8th Cir. 1997) (testimony that "attempted to minimize" defendant's role and that "was far less incriminating and therefore far less helpful to the government" inconsistent with prior testimony); *United States v. Williams,* 737 F.2d 594, 608 (7th Cir. 1984) ("limited, vague, and not inculpatory" testimony inconsistent with prior testimony). Our holding also coheres with a principal purpose of Rule 801(d)(1)(A), which is to protect against the "turncoat witness who changes his story on the stand and deprives the party calling him of evidence essential to his case." Fed. R. Evid. 801(d)(1)(A), Notes of Advisory Committee, 1972 Proposed Rules (quotation marks omitted). . . . [Reversed.]

UNITED STATES v. INCE

21 F.3d 576 (4th Cir. 1994)

MURNAGHAN, Circuit Judge.

Appellant Nigel D. Ince was convicted by a jury for assault with a dangerous weapon, with intent to do bodily harm. Because the United States' only apparent purpose for impeaching one of its own witnesses was to circumvent the hearsay rule and to expose the jury to otherwise inadmissible evidence of Ince's alleged confession, we reverse.

[Ince was arrested on suspicion of having fired a pistol at trucks leaving a concert on the grounds of Fort Belvoir, Virginia. Angela Neumann was with Ince at the time of his arrest.] As part of the investigation that followed, Military Policeman Roger D. Stevens interviewed and took a signed, unsworn statement from Neumann. She recounted that Ince had admitted to firing the shots, but said he no longer had the gun.

... At Ince's trial the Government called Neumann to the stand. When her memory supposedly failed her, the prosecution attempted to refresh her recollection with a copy of the signed statement that she had given Stevens on the night of the shooting. Even with her recollection refreshed, she testified that she could no longer recall the details of her conversation with Ince. Following Neumann's testimony, the Government excused her and called Stevens, who testified (over the objection of defense counsel) as to what Neumann had told him shortly after the shooting. The trial ended with a dead-locked jury.

At the second trial, the Government again called Neumann. She again acknowledged that she had given the military police a signed statement describing what Ince had told her immediately after the shooting. But she repeatedly testified that she could no longer recall the details of Ince's remarks, despite the prosecution's effort to refresh her recollection with a copy of the statement. . . . Over defense counsel's repeated objections, the Government again called MP Stevens to the stand, supposedly to impeach Neumann as to her memory loss. He testified that, within hours of the shooting, Neumann had told him that Ince had confessed to firing the gun. The Government also called two eyewitnesses who identified Ince as the gunman.

The defense's theory of the case was mistaken identity: Frank Kelly, not Nigel Ince, had fired the shots. . . . In an attempt to undermine the defense's theory of the case, the prosecution, in its closing argument, reminded the jurors that they had "heard testimony that Ms. Neumann made a statement to an MP [immediately following the shooting]. And she told [him] at that time that the defendant said, 'Frank didn't shoot the gun; I shot the gun.'"

The second time around, the jury convicted Ince. The district judge sentenced him to forty-one months in prison, plus two years of supervised release. . . . [T]he sole question presented on appeal is whether the admission of Stevens's testimony constituted reversible error.

Rule 607 of the Federal Rules of Evidence provides that "[t]he credibility of a witness may be attacked by any party, including the party calling the witness." One method of attacking the credibility of (i.e., impeaching) a witness is to show that he has previously made a statement that is inconsistent with his present testimony. Even if that prior inconsistent statement would otherwise be inadmissible as hearsay, it may be admissible for the limited purpose of impeaching the witness. At a criminal trial, however, there are limits on the Government's power to impeach its own witness by presenting his prior inconsistent statements. *See United States v. Morlang*, 531 F.2d 183 (4th Cir. 1975). In *Morlang*, we reversed the defendant's conviction for conspiracy to bribe and bribery because the Government had employed impeachment by prior inconsistent statement "as a mere subterfuge to get before the jury evidence not otherwise admissible."

At Morlang's trial the Government had called Fred Wilmoth, an original codefendant who had subsequently pleaded guilty, as its first witness despite the fact that his previous statements to the Government suggested he would be hostile. The real purpose for calling Wilmoth was apparently to elicit a denial that he had ever had a conversation with a fellow prisoner in which he had implicated Morlang. Having obtained the expected denial, the Government then called Raymond Crist, another prisoner, to impeach Wilmoth with the alleged prior inconsistent statement. As expected, Crist testified that his fellow inmate Wilmoth had made a conclusory statement from which one could only infer Morlang's guilt. As expected, the jury delivered a guilty verdict.

In reversing Morlang's conviction, Judge Widener explained that courts must not "permit the government, in the name of impeachment, to present testimony to the jury by indirection which would not otherwise be admissible. To permit the government in this case to supply testimony which was a naked conclusion as to Morlang's guilt in the name of impeachment," he explained, would be tantamount to convicting a defendant on the basis of hearsay:

> Foremost among [the notions of fairness upon which our system is based] is the principle that men should not be allowed to be convicted on the basis of unsworn testimony. . . .
>
> We must be mindful of the fact that prior unsworn statements of a witness are mere hearsay and are, as such, generally inadmissible as affirmative proof. The introduction of such testimony, even where limited to impeachment, necessarily increases the possibility that a defendant may be convicted on the basis of unsworn evidence, for despite proper instructions to the jury, it is often difficult for [jurors] to distinguish between impeachment and substantive evidence. . . . Thus, the danger of confusion which arises from the introduction of testimony under circumstances such as are presented here is so great as to upset the balance and [to] warrant continuation of the rule of exclusion.

Id.

. . . In the case at bar, MP Stevens testified that Ince had *admitted* to firing the gun — the critical element of the crime for which he was being tried. It is hard to imagine any piece of evidence that could have had a greater prejudicial impact than such a supposed naked confession of guilt. . . .

Given the likely prejudicial impact of Steven's testimony, the trial judge should have excluded it absent some extraordinary probative value. Because evidence of Neumann's prior inconsistent statement was admitted solely for purposes of impeachment, its probative value must be assessed solely in terms of its impeaching effect upon Neumann's testimony or overall credibility. Our review of the record below, however, shows that the probative value of Stevens's testimony *for impeachment purposes* was nil. Unlike the classic "turncoat" witness, Neumann certainly had not shocked the Government with her "loss of memory" at the second trial, as she had made it plain during the first trial that she would not readily testify to the alleged confession of her friend, Nigel Ince.

Furthermore, Neumann's actual in-court testimony did not affirmatively damage the Government's case; she merely refused to give testimony that the Government had hoped she would give. Thus, the prosecution had no need to attack her credibility. . . . She testified that, immediately after the shooting, as they left the scene of the crime but before the military police pulled them over, (1) Ince stated that Frank Kelly — the person whom Ince's lawyer identified at trial as the likely perpetrator of the crime — was *not* the person who had fired the gun, (2) Ince stated that "he didn't have [the gun] with him," and (3) Ince instructed Neumann to tell the military police that she knew nothing about the events of the evening. She presented no evidence affirming or denying Ince's alleged confession. Taken as a whole, then, Neumann's testimony probably *strengthened* the Government's case. Therefore, evidence attacking her credibility had no probative value *for impeachment purposes*.

Because Stevens's so-called "impeachment" testimony was both highly prejudicial and devoid of probative value as impeachment evidence, the trial judge should have recognized the Government's tactic for what it was — an attempt to circumvent the hearsay rule and to infect the jury with otherwise inadmissible evidence of Ince's alleged confession. Instead, the judge allowed Stevens's testimony to come before the jury in clear violation of *Morlang* and its progeny, notwithstanding defense counsel's proper and timely objections. . . . Accordingly, we reverse the conviction of Nigel D. Ince and remand the case for a new trial.

UNITED STATES v. WEBSTER

734 F.2d 1191 (7th Cir. 1984)

POSNER, Circuit Judge.

The defendant, Webster, was convicted of aiding and abetting the robbery of a federally insured bank and receiving stolen bank funds, was sentenced to nine years in prison, and appeals. Only one issue need be discussed. The government called the bank robber, King (who had pleaded guilty and been given a long prison term), as a witness against Webster. King gave testimony that if believed would have exculpated the defendant, whereupon the government introduced prior inconsistent statements that King had given the FBI inculpating Webster. Although the court instructed the jury that it could consider the statements only for purposes of impeachment, Webster argues that this was not good enough, that the government should not be allowed to get inadmissible evidence before the jury by calling a hostile witness and then using his out-of-court statements, which would otherwise be inadmissible hearsay, to impeach him.

Rule 607 of the Federal Rules of Evidence provides: "The credibility of a witness may be attacked by any party, including the party calling him." But it would be an abuse of the rule, in a criminal case, for the prosecution to call a witness that it knew would not give it useful evidence, just so it could introduce hearsay evidence against the defendant in the hope that the jury would miss the subtle distinction between impeachment and substantive evidence — or, if it didn't miss it, would ignore it. The purpose would not be to impeach the witness but to put in hearsay as substantive evidence against the defendant, which Rule 607 does not contemplate or authorize. We thus agree that "impeachment by prior inconsistent statement may not be permitted where employed as a mere subterfuge to get before the jury evidence not otherwise admissible." *United States v. Morlang*, 531 F.2d 183, 190 (4th Cir. 1975). Although *Morlang* was decided before the Federal Rules of Evidence became effective, the limitation that we have quoted on the prosecutor's rights under Rule 607 has been accepted in all circuits that have considered the issue.

But it is quite plain that there was no bad faith here. Before the prosecutor called King to the stand she asked the judge to allow her to examine him outside the presence of the jury, because she didn't know what he would say. The defendant's counsel objected and the voir dire was not held. We do not see how in these circumstances it can be thought that the prosecutor put King on the stand knowing he would give no useful evidence. If she had known that, she would not have offered to voir dire him, as the voir dire would have provided a foundation for defense counsel to object, under *Morlang*, to the admission of King's prior inconsistent statements. . . . The judgment of conviction is Affirmed.

PEOPLE v. FREEMAN

97 Cal. Rptr. 717 (Cal. Ct. App. 1971)

FRIEDMAN, Acting P.J.

[Defendant Norman Freeman was convicted of serving as the getaway driver in an armed robbery in which Foster served as a gunman. Freeman claimed at trial that he spent the morning of the robbery asleep at the home of his fiancée, Brenda Banks.] Claims of error arise from the testimony of Mrs. Anna Duckworth and Fred Knipp, a district attorney's investigator. Both were prosecution rebuttal witnesses, and both testified over defense objections. With reference to the Saturday morning in question, Mrs. Duckworth testified that about 7 a.m. she had gone to the nearby house of her daughter, Annette, girl friend of Foster. She testified that Foster was frequently at Annette's house but she did not know whether he was there on this particular morning. While Mrs. Duckworth was outside the house, a man came to the house. She heard her daughter greet the man with the words, "Hi, Norman." Several days later Knipp, the investigator, interviewed her. She admitted telling Knipp that her daughter had greeted a man by the name of Norman; denied telling Knipp that Foster had been in bed at Annette's house on the morning in question; denied telling Knipp that Norman twice came to the house that morning and, on the second occasion, had left the house in company with Foster; denied identifying the man as Norman Freeman.

Over objection the prosecutor called Knipp, who testified that he had interviewed Mrs. Duckworth, who told him that on the Saturday morning in question a man had twice come to the daughter's house, where Lee Foster was in bed; that on the second occasion Foster and the man had left the house together; that the man was Norman Freeman.

Without analysis and without citation of authority, defendant charges that Mrs. Duckworth's "Hi, Norman" testimony was hearsay. It was not hearsay, because not offered to prove the statement's truth or falsity but as evidence of the fact that the statement was made. Where the fact that a statement was made is relevant regardless of its truth or falsity, the statement is admissible. Thus Wigmore states: "Utterances serving to *identify* are admissible as any other circumstance of identification would be." Norman Freeman's presence at the home of Annette Duckworth (at a time when he said he was asleep at the home of his fiancée, Brenda Banks) was itself a relevant fact. The fact that the statement "Hi, Norman" was made tended to prove circumstantially that one Norman had come to the house of a person associated with Foster, the alleged associate of Norman Freeman in the armed robbery.

Defendant argues that the prosecution could not place Mrs. Duckworth on the stand, elicit her version of statements to Knipp as a device for getting in Knipp's inconsistent version of these statements, ostensibly as impeachment but really to prove the truth of the latter version. The argument is supported by *People v. Taylor*, 4 Cal. App. 2d 220, 223, a case antedating Evidence Code section 1235. Defendant does not cite or discuss section 1235.

Knipp's version of Mrs. Duckworth's statements was not admitted for the restricted purpose of impeaching Mrs. Duckworth, but as evidence of the statements' truth, that is, that Norman Freeman had twice been at the home of Annette Duckworth on the morning of the crime and had left in company with Foster (who had been identified by other evidence as defendant's crime partner). Had Mrs. Duckworth not previously denied her statements to Knipp, the latter's testimony would have been inadmissible hearsay. Manifestly the prosecutor did not elicit Mrs. Duckworth's version for its probative value but as a tool to unlock the evidentiary door to Knipp's conflicting version of Mrs. Duckworth's statements to him.

Evidence Code section 1235 declares: "Evidence of a statement made by a witness is not made inadmissible by the hearsay rule if the statement is inconsistent with his testimony at the hearing and is offered in compliance with Section 770." Section 1235 is designed to permit evidentiary use of a witness' inconsistent statement either to impeach him or as substantive evidence of the truth of the matters asserted. . . .

In some cases a witness' prior statement is offered by the opponent of the litigant who originally called him. More typically, a party calls a recanting, hostile witness as a prelude to the testimony of a subsequent witness who describes the conflicting declarations of the first. . . . The witness' recantation permits the inference that he has something to hide, and this inference provides the earlier version a measure of reliability.* The jury may choose which

---

* A parallel observation was voiced by the California Code Commission in its comments accompanying section 1235: ". . . The declarant is in court and may be examined and cross-examined in regard to his statements and their subject matter. In many cases, the inconsistent statement is more likely to be true than the testimony of the witness at the trial because it was made nearer in time to the matter to which it relates and is less likely to be influenced by the version to believe or reject both versions altogether. When a litigant intentionally brings in the declarant for the purpose of eliciting a predictably false version, he is not misusing section 1235 but utilizing it for the very purpose it is designed to fulfill — that is, to open the door to a second witness with a conceivably reliable indicator of the actual events. The technique conforms to the letter and spirit of section 1235, which supplies fact-finders with a formerly unavailable means for uncovering the truth.

The record here shows that both Mrs. Duckworth and Investigator Knipp first testified outside the jury's presence as part of a prosecution offer of proof. Later, over defense objections, both testified before the jury as rebuttal witnesses for the prosecution. In view of their *voir dire* testimony, both the prosecution and district attorney knew what to expect. After Mrs. Duckworth had finished testifying before the jury, she was excused with the consent of both counsel. Although she was not in court when Knipp gave his version of his interview with her, she could have been made available for further cross-examination had defense counsel so elected. Section 1235 permits the prior inconsistent statements if offered in compliance with section 770. The latter, in effect, requires either that the declarant be provided an opportunity to explain or deny the statement or that he be kept available for further testimony. The first of these conditions was satisfied. Under these circumstances the court correctly permitted Knipp to testify.

Judgment affirmed.

PROBLEMS

7.7. Would *People v. Freeman* come out differently in federal court?

7.8. Wendy testifies before a grand jury that her brother Dan told her he had set fire to a post office. At Dan's subsequent federal trial for arson, the prosecution calls Wendy as a witness, but she denies ever hearing her brother admit to setting the fire. The prosecutor asks her, "Didn't you testify before a grand jury that Dan told you he had set fire to a post office?" Wendy denies having so testified. After Wendy leaves the stand, may the government introduce a transcript of her grand jury testimony?

7.9. Suppose the jury in Dan's trial deadlocks and the judge declares a mistrial. In a subsequent retrial, the government again calls Wendy as a witness, and she again denies ever hearing her brother say that he set fire to a post office. May the prosecutor again ask Wendy about her contrary testimony before the grand jury?

7.10. Dana is charged with bank robbery. At trial she claims mistaken identity and testifies that on the afternoon of the robbery she was visiting her friend Alex. Alex has told the same story to government investigators, but they disbelieve him, partly because he was recently convicted of bank robbery in

---

controversy that gave rise to the litigation. The trier of fact has the declarant before it and can observe his demeanor and the nature of his testimony as he denies or tries to explain away the inconsistency. Hence, it is in as good a position to determine the truth or falsity of the prior statement as it is to determine the truth or falsity of the inconsistent testimony given in court."

an unrelated case. Dana does not call Alex as a witness. The government calls Alex to the stand in its rebuttal case, and he corroborates Dana's account. May the prosecutor now ask Alex about his conviction? What if the conviction were for perjury?

D. Bias and Incapacity

There are no special rules regarding impeachment for bias or incapacity, but each of these modes of impeachment can run afoul of other, more general rules of evidence.

Impeachment for bias consists of proving that a witness (or hearsay declarant) has a reason to lie or to slant his or her testimony. Examples include showing that an expert witness is being paid to testify, eliciting testimony that the witness is romantically involved with the party for whom he or she has testified, and — as in the Supreme Court decision excerpted below — demonstrating that the witness is in the same prison gang as the party for whom he or she has testified.

Impeachment for incapacity consists of demonstrating that the memory or perception of the witness is unreliable. The classic example is showing that the witness has bad eyesight, but incapacity can be mental as well as physical. A witness can be impeached, for example, by showing that he or she suffers from delusions. But evidence of mental incapacity is easily subject to abuse, and for that reason is often ruled inadmissible, as the materials below illustrate. The problem is that evidence of mental incapacity often can be used to cast aspersions on the character of the witness, and more particularly on aspects of character other than honesty — precisely the kind of character impeachment disallowed by F.R.E. 608. Vigilant courts take care not to allow such character impeachment in the guise of evidence of incapacity, and disallow incapacity evidence when the actual probative force of the evidence seems predominantly or exclusively to concern the defendant's character.

UNITED STATES v. ABEL

469 U.S. 45 (1984)

Justice REHNQUIST delivered the opinion of the Court.

. . . Respondent John Abel and two cohorts were indicted for robbing a savings and loan in Bellflower, Cal., in violation of 18 U.S.C. §§2113(a) and (d). The cohorts elected to plead guilty, but respondent went to trial. One of the cohorts, Kurt Ehle, agreed to testify against respondent and identify him as a participant in the robbery.

Respondent informed the District Court at a pretrial conference that he would seek to counter Ehle's testimony with that of Robert Mills. Mills was not a participant in the robbery but was friendly with respondent and with

Ehle, and had spent time with both in prison. Mills planned to testify that after the robbery Ehle had admitted to Mills that Ehle intended to implicate respondent falsely, in order to receive favorable treatment from the Government. The prosecutor in turn disclosed that he intended to discredit Mills' testimony by calling Ehle back to the stand and eliciting from Ehle the fact that respondent, Mills, and Ehle were all members of the "Aryan Brotherhood," a secret prison gang that required its members always to deny the existence of the organization and to commit perjury, theft, and murder on each member's behalf.

Defense counsel objected to Ehle's proffered rebuttal testimony as too prejudicial to respondent. After a lengthy discussion in chambers the District Court decided to permit the prosecutor to cross-examine Mills about the gang, and if Mills denied knowledge of the gang, to introduce Ehle's rebuttal testimony concerning the tenets of the gang and Mills' and respondent's membership in it. The District Court held that the probative value of Ehle's rebuttal testimony outweighed its prejudicial effect, but that respondent might be entitled to a limiting instruction if his counsel would submit one to the court.

At trial Ehle implicated respondent as a participant in the robbery. Mills, called by respondent, testified that Ehle told him in prison that Ehle planned to implicate respondent falsely. When the prosecutor sought to cross-examine Mills concerning membership in the prison gang, the District Court conferred again with counsel outside of the jury's presence, and ordered the prosecutor not to use the term "Aryan Brotherhood" because it was unduly prejudicial. Accordingly, the prosecutor asked Mills if he and respondent were members of a "secret type of prison organization" which had a creed requiring members to deny its existence and lie for each other. When Mills denied knowledge of such an organization the prosecutor recalled Ehle.

Ehle testified that respondent, Mills, and he were indeed members of a secret prison organization whose tenets required its members to deny its existence and "lie, cheat, steal [and] kill" to protect each other. The District Court sustained a defense objection to a question concerning the punishment for violating the organization's rules. Ehle then further described the organization and testified that "in view of the fact of how close Abel and Mills were" it would have been "suicide" for Ehle to have told Mills what Mills attributed to him. Respondent's counsel did not request a limiting instruction and none was given.

The jury convicted respondent. On his appeal a divided panel of the Court of Appeals reversed. . . . We hold that the evidence showing Mills' and respondent's membership in the prison gang was sufficiently probative of Mills' possible bias towards respondent to warrant its admission into evidence. Thus it was within the District Court's discretion to admit Ehle's testimony, and the Court of Appeals was wrong in concluding otherwise.

Both parties correctly assume, as did the District Court and the Court of Appeals, that the question is governed by the Federal Rules of Evidence. But the Rules do not by their terms deal with impeachment for "bias," although they do expressly treat impeachment by character evidence and conduct, Rule 608, by evidence of conviction of a crime, Rule 609, and by showing of religious beliefs or opinion, Rule 610. Neither party has suggested what significance we should attribute to this fact. Although we are nominally the promulgators of the Rules, and should in theory need only to consult our collective memories to analyze the situation properly, we are in truth merely a conduit when we deal with an undertaking as substantial as the preparation of the Federal Rules of Evidence. In the case of these Rules, too, it must be remembered that Congress extensively reviewed our submission, and considerably revised it.

Before the present Rules were promulgated, the admissibility of evidence in the federal courts was governed in part by statutes or Rules, and in part by case law. This Court had held in *Alford v. United States*, 282 U.S. 687 (1931), that a trial court must allow some cross-examination of a witness to show bias. This holding was in accord with the overwhelming weight of authority in the state courts as reflected in Wigmore's classic treatise on the law of evidence. *See id.* at 691, citing 3 J. Wigmore, Evidence §1368 (2d ed. 1923). Our decision in *Davis v. Alaska*, 415 U.S. 308 (1974), holds that the Confrontation Clause of the Sixth Amendment requires a defendant to have some opportunity to show bias on the part of a prosecution witness.

With this state of unanimity confronting the drafters of the Federal Rules of Evidence, we think it unlikely that they intended to scuttle entirely the evidentiary availability of cross-examination for bias. One commentator, recognizing the omission of any express treatment of impeachment for bias, prejudice, or corruption, observes that the Rules "clearly contemplate the use of the above-mentioned grounds of impeachment." E. Cleary, McCormick on Evidence §40, p. 85 (3d ed. 1984). Other commentators, without mentioning the omission, treat bias as a permissible and established basis of impeachment under the Rules. 3 D. Louisell & C. Mueller, Federal Evidence §341, p. 470 (1979); 3 J. Weinstein & M. Berger, Weinstein's Evidence §607[03] (1981).

We think this conclusion is obviously correct. Rule 401 defines as "relevant evidence" evidence having any tendency to make the existence of any fact that is of consequence to the determination of the action more probable or less probable than it would be without the evidence. Rule 402 provides that all relevant evidence is admissible, except as otherwise provided by the United States Constitution, by Act of Congress, or by applicable rule. A successful showing of bias on the part of a witness would have a tendency to make the facts to which he testified less probable in the eyes of the jury than it would be without such testimony.

The correctness of the conclusion that the Rules contemplate impeachment by showing of bias is confirmed by the references to bias in the Advisory Committee Notes to Rules 608 and 610, and by the provisions allowing any party to attack credibility in Rule 607, and allowing cross-examination on "matters affecting the credibility of the witness" in Rule 611(b). The Courts of Appeals have upheld use of extrinsic evidence to show bias both before and after the adoption of the Federal Rules of Evidence.

. . . Ehle's testimony about the prison gang certainly made the existence of Mills' bias towards respondent more probable. Thus it was relevant to support that inference. Bias is a term used in the "common law of evidence" to describe the relationship between a party and a witness which might lead the witness to slant, unconsciously or otherwise, his testimony in favor of or against a party. Bias may be induced by a witness' like, dislike, or fear of a party, or by the witness' self-interest. Proof of bias is almost always relevant because the jury, as finder of fact and weigher of credibility, has historically been entitled to assess all evidence which might bear on the accuracy and truth of a witness' testimony. The "common law of evidence" allowed the showing of bias by extrinsic evidence, while requiring the cross-examiner to "take the answer of the witness" with respect to less favored forms of impeachment.

. . . Respondent argues that even if the evidence of membership in the prison gang were relevant to show bias, the District Court erred in permitting a full description of the gang and its odious tenets. Respondent contends that the District Court abused its discretion under Federal Rule of Evidence 403, because the prejudicial effect of the contested evidence outweighed its probative value. In other words, testimony about the gang inflamed the jury against respondent, and the chance that he would be convicted by his mere association with the organization outweighed any probative value the testimony may have had on Mills' bias.

Respondent specifically contends that the District Court should not have permitted Ehle's precise description of the gang as a lying and murderous group. Respondent suggests that the District Court should have cut off the testimony after the prosecutor had elicited that Mills knew respondent and both may have belonged to an organization together. This argument ignores the fact that the *type* of organization in which a witness and a party share membership may be relevant to show bias. If the organization is a loosely knit group having nothing to do with the subject matter of the litigation, the inference of bias arising from common membership may be small or nonexistent. If the prosecutor had elicited that both respondent and Mills belonged to the Book of the Month Club, the jury probably would not have inferred bias even if the District Court had admitted the testimony. The attributes of the Aryan Brotherhood — a secret prison sect sworn to perjury and self-protection — bore directly not only on the *fact* of bias but also on the *source* and *strength* of Mills' bias. The tenets of this group showed that Mills had a powerful motive to slant his testimony towards respondent, or even commit perjury outright.

A district court is accorded a wide discretion in determining the admissibility of evidence under the Federal Rules. Assessing the probative value of common membership in any particular group, and weighing any factors counseling against admissibility is a matter first for the district court's sound judgment under Rules 401 and 403 and ultimately, if the evidence is admitted, for the trier of fact.

Before admitting Ehle's rebuttal testimony, the District Court gave heed to the extensive arguments of counsel, both in chambers and at the bench. In an attempt to avoid undue prejudice to respondent the court ordered that the name "Aryan Brotherhood" not be used. The court also offered to give a limiting instruction concerning the testimony, and it sustained defense objections to the prosecutor's questions concerning the punishment meted out to unfaithful members. These precautions did not prevent *all* prejudice to respondent from Ehle's testimony, but they did, in our opinion, ensure that the admission of this highly probative evidence did not *unduly* prejudice respondent. We hold there was no abuse of discretion under Rule 403 in admitting Ehle's testimony as to membership and tenets.

Respondent makes an additional argument based on Rule 608(b). That Rule allows a cross-examiner to impeach a witness by asking him about specific instances of past conduct, other than crimes covered by Rule 609, which are probative of his veracity or "character for truthfulness or untruthfulness." The Rule limits the inquiry to cross-examination of the witness, however, and prohibits the cross-examiner from introducing extrinsic evidence of the witness' past conduct.

Respondent claims that the prosecutor cross-examined Mills about the gang not to show bias but to offer Mills' membership in the gang as past conduct bearing on his veracity. This was error under Rule 608(b), respondent contends, because the mere fact of Mills' membership, without more, was not sufficiently probative of Mills' character for truthfulness. Respondent cites a second error under the same Rule, contending that Ehle's rebuttal testimony concerning the gang was extrinsic evidence offered to impugn Mills' veracity, and extrinsic evidence is barred by Rule 608(b).

... It seems clear to us that the proffered testimony with respect to Mills' membership in the Aryan Brotherhood sufficed to show potential bias in favor of respondent; because of the tenets of the organization described, it might also impeach his veracity directly. But there is no rule of evidence which provides that testimony admissible for one purpose and inadmissible for another purpose is thereby rendered inadmissible; quite the contrary is the case. It would be a strange rule of law which held that relevant, competent evidence which tended to show bias on the part of a witness was nonetheless inadmissible because it also tended to show that the witness was a liar.

We intimate no view as to whether the evidence of Mills' membership in an organization having the tenets ascribed to the Aryan Brotherhood would be a specific instance of Mills' conduct which could not be proved against him by extrinsic evidence except as otherwise provided in Rule 608(b). It was enough that such evidence could properly be found admissible to show bias.

The judgment of the Court of Appeals is

Reversed.

UNITED STATES v. SASSO

59 F.3d 341 (2d Cir. 1995)

KEARSE, Circuit Judge.

[Defendants Robert Sasso, Jr., and Anthony Armienti were convicted of trafficking in illegal firearms. Among the witnesses against them was Armienti's former girlfriend Kristine Kramer, who testified both to incriminating statements made by Armienti and to observations she made of both defendants.] At an in limine hearing outside the presence of the jury, it was revealed that in 1988, a truck that Kramer was driving accidentally struck and killed a fellow worker. Kramer testified that she became depressed and twice visited a psychiatrist for counseling. Shortly after these two visits, Kramer's family physician prescribed the antidepressant drug Prozac, which Kramer took "on and off" during the following year. Defendants sought permission to bring these facts out in the presence of the jury.... [The trial court denied the request.]

We see no abuse of discretion here. In light of the nature of Kramer's condition, i.e., a not-unpredictable depression resulting from her involvement in a specific catastrophic event, the fact that her depression was relatively recent did not necessarily suggest that condition had any probative value. Further, there was no indication that the accident in which she was involved in 1988 had put her in a delusional state or that any medications prescribed through 1990 or beginning in October 1992 would have affected her ability to perceive events or to understand what was said to her from July 1991, when she first met Armienti, until June 1992, when their intimate relationship ended. Indeed, there was no evidence that Kramer received or ingested any mood-altering drugs during the period in which she was involved with Armienti.

Chnapkova v. Koh, [985 F.2d 79, 81 (2d Cir. 1993),] on which defendants principally rely to support their contention that the evidence should have been admitted, is entirely distinguishable. In that case, the plaintiff claimed to have been disfigured in plastic surgery, and we held that it was an abuse of discretion for the trial court to exclude evidence that she believed, inter alia, that "'people were laughing at her'" and were talking about her "'on the T.V. & radio,'" 985 F.2d at 80 n.1 (quoting hospital records of the plaintiff's statements). That history of paranoid and delusional behavior indicated that the plaintiff suffered problems of perception, and her perceptions were directly related to the subject matter of the suit. Here, there was no indication that Kramer was delusional or paranoid, or had any difficulties in memory or perception. . . . The judgments of conviction are affirmed.

HENDERSON v. DETELLA

97 F.3d 942 (7th Cir. 1996)

ILANA DIAMOND ROVNER, Circuit Judge.

[An Illinois jury found Ladell Henderson guilty of murder and attempted murder, based in part on the testimony of Mona Chavez, who witnessed the murder and was the victim of the attempted murder. The trial judge refused to allow the defense to elicit testimony from an acquaintance of Chavez, Quintin Jones, that he had repeatedly seen her use drugs. The conviction was upheld on appeal, and Henderson's petition for federal habeas relief was rejected by the district court.]

Chavez's testimony was crucial to the state's case against Henderson. The use of narcotics can, obviously, affect the ability of a witness to perceive, to recall, and to recount the events she has observed. Whether Chavez may have been under the influence of narcotics at the time of the offense (or at some other pertinent time) was thus an appropriate subject of inquiry and impeachment.

But we agree that Henderson was not deprived of his right to confront the witnesses against him when the trial court barred the testimony of Quintin Jones. Had the proffer of Jones' testimony established that Chavez was using narcotics within the time frame of the events to which she testified, it might have been improper and prejudicial to Henderson to exclude the testimony. Instead, however, Jones was held up as a witness who would testify simply that he had known Chavez to use drugs on many occasions; we do not know when those occasions were in reference to the murder of Leonard and the attempted murder of Chavez. It is thus not at all clear that the testimony was probative of Chavez's ability to recognize and identify the individual who committed the offense. *See United States v. Robinson*, 956 F.2d 1388, 1398 (7th Cir.), *cert. denied*, 506 U.S. 1020 (1992) (testimony as to witness' drug use properly excluded where voir dire did not establish that it affected the witness' memory of relevant events). Absent a connection to Chavez's cognitive abilities, Jones' testimony would have served only to impeach her character, a purpose we have repeatedly deemed improper. Under these circumstances, we see no error, and certainly none rising to the level of a constitutional deprivation, in the decision to bar Jones from testifying on this topic.... The district court's decision to deny Henderson's petition for a writ of habeas corpus was therefore correct.

E. SPECIFIC CONTRADICTION

Like impeachment for incapacity or impeachment for bias, impeachment by specific contradiction is governed by no special provisions of the Federal Rules of Evidence or its state counterparts. There is a judge-made restriction on such impeachment, though, most commonly called the "collateral evidence rule." Sometimes it is referred to as the "specific contradiction rule."

The collateral evidence rule is confusing for reasons other than its varying names. The first problem is that it generally applies only to impeachment by specific contradiction, and the distinction between this mode of impeachment and others can be elusive. Impeachment by specific contradiction consists of demonstrating that some particular part of what a witness has testified to is false, and then suggesting that this gives the jury reason to disregard the remainder of the testimony. Sometimes this mode of impeachment is simply called "impeachment by contradiction." It is best to avoid that terminology, because it makes it easy to confuse this mode of impeachment with impeachment with prior inconsistent statements, which is sometimes referred to as "impeachment by self-contradiction."

The collateral evidence rule, in its most common formulation, bars extrinsic impeachment by specific contradiction on a "collateral matter." Here as elsewhere, "extrinsic" impeachment means impeachment through evidence other than testimony elicited from the witness being impeached. Because the collateral evidence rule applies only to extrinsic evidence, it does not restrict the ability of a party to impeach a witness by eliciting testimony on cross-examination contradicting part of the witness's earlier testimony.

The trickiest term in the collateral evidence rule is "collateral." Collateral in this context does not simply mean peripheral. It has a narrower, technical meaning. As the materials below explain, the classic test for a "collateral matter" under the collateral evidence rule asks whether the fact in question could be proven, i.e., is relevant, for any purpose *other* than contradicting the witness. A fact is collateral only if it fails this test. The materials below also explain the traditional rationale for the collateral evidence rule: to avoid the risk that the trial will be derailed by inquiry into side issues.

SIMMONS, INC. v. PINKERTON'S, INC.

762 F.2d 591 (7th Cir. 1985)

CUDAHY, Circuit Judge.

. . . Simmons, a manufacturer of residential and commercial bedding, owned a warehouse in Munster, Indiana, which it used as a regional distribution center for its products. In order to protect the warehouse, Simmons entered into a contract with defendant Pinkerton's, a national company providing investigative and security services, under which Pinkerton's agreed to provide uniformed guard protection for the warehouse 24 hours a day, 7 days a week. . . . [A fire broke out at the warehouse and caused extensive damage. The Indiana Fire Marshal's Office concluded the fire had been set as an "attention getter" by William Hayne, a Pinkerton employee assigned to guard the warehouse.] Simmons then brought this diversity action against Pinkerton's, and against the National Surety Corporation as surety for Pinkerton's. . . .

Pinkerton's . . . argues that the district court erred in admitting Hayne's testimony that he falsely told a Pinkerton's investigator that he had taken and passed a polygraph examination regarding the circumstances of the fire. After the fire, Pinkerton's asked Hayne to take a lie detector test in Chicago. He took the test, but apparently it was inconclusive for extraneous reasons. Hayne then agreed to take a second test in Indiana, but failed to make arrangements to do so. Nevertheless, Hayne later told a Pinkerton's investigator that he had taken the second test in Indiana and had passed it. At trial, over Pinkerton's objection, Simmons' attorney elicited from Hayne his admission that he had lied about this matter. . . .

Although "the rule in the Seventh Circuit is clear" that admission or exclusion of polygraph evidence is within the sound discretion of the trial judge, *United States v. Rumell*, 642 F.2d 213, 215 (7th Cir. 1981), for various reasons this discretion has most often been exercised in favor of exclusion, in this circuit, *See id.* at 215, as well as in others, *deVries v. St. Paul Fire and Marine Ins. Co.*, 716 F.2d 939, 945 n. 8 (1st Cir. 1983). Several circuits apparently exclude polygraph results entirely, *id.* Indeed, because of the perceived danger of prejudice, some courts also exclude evidence of a person's willingness or unwillingness to take a polygraph examination, *id.* at 944–45. For these reasons, Pinkerton's argues, it would have been error to admit the results of any polygraph that Hayne took as substantive evidence of the cause of the fire at the warehouse. The trial court did not admit Hayne's testimony as substantive evidence, however, but rather admitted it under Federal Rule of Evidence 608(b) to impeach Hayne's credibility through cross-examination about a specific instance of his conduct (his lie about the polygraph test) bearing on his character for truthfulness or untruthfulness. Pinkerton's contends that this was an improper basis for admission, because "a witness may not be impeached by contradiction as to collateral or irrelevant matters elicited on cross-examination," *United States v. Lambert*, 463 F.2d 552, 557 (7th

Cir. 1972). Since the test for whether a matter is collateral is "whether the party seeking to introduce it for purposes of contradiction would be entitled to prove it as part of his case," *id.*, and since Simmons presumably could not introduce evidence of the polygraph examination as a substantive part of its case, Pinkerton's concludes that the "collateral evidence rule" precludes Simmons from impeaching Hayne in any manner that included a reference to whether he took a polygraph test, or whether he passed such a test.

We disagree. Assuming, arguendo, that testimony relating to the polygraph exam was inadmissible as substantive evidence, Pinkerton's has failed to note distinctions between this case and the authority on which it relies which seem to make the collateral evidence rule completely inapplicable here. The rule apparently was developed in conjunction with a particular type of impeachment — impeachment by contradiction. Impeachment by contradiction simply involves presenting evidence that part or all of a witness' testimony is incorrect. Thus if an eyewitness to an auto accident testifies that the car that caused the accident was red, impeachment by contradiction relies on evidence that the car actually was yellow. The inference to be drawn is not that the witness was lying, but that the witness made a mistake of fact, and so perhaps her testimony may contain other errors and should be discounted accordingly.

Of course, a particular misstatement may or may not be probative of the witness' general accuracy, depending on the circumstances, and thus may or may not be worth the time it takes to establish it. For this reason the collateral evidence rule developed. In the above example, assuming the color of the car was not directly relevant to any substantive issue in the case (e.g., if the identity of the car were stipulated), it presumably would not be worth the fact finder's time to entertain a "mini-trial" on the issue of the car's color, simply to prove that the witness was mistaken as to this fact. Thus, while the accuracy of a witness' perception or memory can always be tested through traditional cross-examination techniques, the collateral evidence rule limits the extent to which the witness' testimony about non-essential matters may be contradicted by extrinsic proof. In short, if a matter is collateral (that is, if it could not be introduced into evidence as substantive proof) then it cannot be proven simply to contradict the witness' testimony for impeachment purposes. 3 J. Weinstein and M. Berger, Weinstein's Evidence ¶607[05], 607-61-607-72 (1984).

But the collateral evidence rule does not, as Pinkerton's contends, limit the scope of all types of impeachment by cross-examination to only those matters that could be proven as a substantive part of a case; rather it merely precludes extrinsic evidence of certain facts that would impeach by contradiction. Various types of impeachment are allowed, despite the recognition that the subject-matter of the impeachment could not be used substantively, precisely because a witness' credibility is always an important consideration. Impeachment by prior inconsistent statement is one example; another is the type of impeachment at issue here — an attack on a witness' character for truthfulness through cross-examination as to specific instances of the witness' previous conduct (which, of course, have not been the subject of his direct examination).

Federal Rule of Evidence 608(b), which governs this type of impeachment, is exactly tailored to strike the balance that the collateral evidence rule was designed to achieve with respect to impeachment by contradiction. Rule 608(b) allows cross-examination of a witness about specific instances of her past conduct, if probative of truthfulness or untruthfulness, but prohibits the proof of such conduct by extrinsic evidence. Thus, as with the collateral evidence rule, a relevant fact bearing on the witness' credibility — in this case, that he has lied in the past or acted in some other manner that casts doubt on veracity — may, in the discretion of the trial judge, be considered sufficiently important and probative to be elicited on cross-examination; yet, because of the dangers of confusion, prejudice, waste of time, and so on, that would be inherent if a "mini-trial" on the existence of that fact were allowed, extrinsic evidence of the matter is prohibited.[7]

Applying these principles to the testimony at issue here, it becomes obvious that the collateral evidence rule — in one sense now incorporated into Rule 608(b) — does not prohibit it. The testimony concerned an incident in which Hayne lied about having taken a polygraph examination. Whether or not Hayne took such a test or whether or not he passed may not have been admissible as substantive evidence. Nevertheless, in the discretion of the court, the "specific instance of conduct" in which he lied was, understandably, considered probative of his character for truthfulness or untruthfulness. Therefore, it was proper to allow Simmons to inquire about the incident while cross-examining Hayne. Of course, had Hayne denied the lie, the bar on the use of extrinsic evidence of specific instances of conduct to attack credibility in Rule 608(b) would have prohibited Simmons from proving the lie through the testimony of other witnesses. This sort of proof, however, was not offered. Clearly, the testimony carried some danger of prejudice, and just as clearly the trial court was obligated to balance this risk against the probative value of the testimony. The court did so, and we think it properly exercised its discretion in deciding that the testimony could be elicited under Rule 608(b).... For the foregoing reasons the judgment is Affirmed.

UNITED STATES v. COPELIN

996 F.2d 379 (D.C. Cir. 1993)

MIKVA, Chief Judge.

Warren Ricardo Copelin appeals his conviction on one count of unlawful distribution of cocaine.... Vanessa Moore, an undercover District of Columbia police officer, pre-recorded the serial numbers of three bills and used them to purchase two rocks of crack cocaine, totalling .144 gram, from a man she maintains was Mr. Copelin. The man who sold her the crack produced the drugs from a brown medicine bottle. After making the purchase, Officer Moore broadcast a radio lookout and description of the suspect, and, within

---

7. Indeed, even under the collateral evidence test, impeachment by contradiction of a witness' testimony generally would not be considered collateral — and thus would be allowed — where the impeaching matter indicates the witness' character for untruthfulness. See 3 J. Weinstein & M. Berger, Weinstein's Evidence ¶607[05], 607-65 (1984).

a few minutes, an arrest team stopped Mr. Copelin. Shortly thereafter, Officer Moore identified Mr. Copelin as the man who sold her drugs. When the arrest team officers searched Mr. Copelin, they found he possessed the pre-recorded currency. At the scene of the arrest, one of the officers found a brown medicine bottle containing 5.634 grams of cocaine base lying on the ground.

Mr. Copelin was charged with the unlawful distribution of crack cocaine, in connection with the two rocks he allegedly sold the officer, and with possession with intent to distribute in excess of five grams of crack cocaine, in connection with the drugs contained in the bottle. At trial, Mr. Copelin contended that he had not made the sale. He argued that Officer Moore was mistaking him for a man named David Bailey, with whom he was playing dice around the time of the sale. Mr. Copelin and his corroborating witnesses testified that they had seen Mr. Bailey repeatedly leave the dice game to engage in transactions. They further testified that money was rapidly changing hands during the game. . . .

Mr. Copelin's evidentiary claims concern a colloquy that occurred during the government's cross-examination of him at trial. The prosecutor asked him whether he knew that Mr. Bailey, the man Mr. Copelin contends actually made the sale, was in fact engaging in drug transactions during the dice game.

> Q: All right. And did you ever see him engage in a transaction where you knew it for sure?
> A: I would see money change hands, but other than seeing the actual drugs or anything, no, I haven't noticed.
> Q: You didn't see any actual drugs?
> A: No, sir.
> Q: Would you know what they looked like if you saw them?
> A: Yes. It's advertised on TV, too, sometimes in the commercials.
> Q: You see drugs advertised on TV?
> A: Yes, you know, on news or something like that.
> Q: And that's the only time you've ever seen drugs?
> A: Roughly, yes.
> Q: Roughly?
> A: Yes.

The prosecutor then requested a bench conference, during which he sought permission from the court to cross-examine Mr. Copelin as to his positive drug tests while he was on pretrial release.

> The defendant tested positive for cocaine on three separate occasions and I believe that provides a reasonable basis to assume that he has seen cocaine. . . . He's made a bald denial that he has ever seen cocaine aside from on TV right here on the stand. I believe that's false and as a result, I propose to cross-examine him on this, but I wanted to ask the Court about it in advance.

Over the objection of defense counsel, the trial judge, without explanation, permitted the prosecutor to proceed with this line of questioning.

> Q: Now, Mr. Copelin, isn't it true that as a condition of your release pending trial in this case, you were required to report to the Pretrial Services Administration for drug testing?
> A: Yes.

> *Q:* And isn't it true that you tested positive for cocaine on June 13th, 1991?
>
> *A:* Yes.
>
> *Q:* And you tested positive for cocaine on June 14th, 1991.
>
> *A:* Yes.
>
> *Q:* And you tested positive for cocaine on June 21st, 1991?
>
> *A:* I don't recall that one.
>
> *Q:* You don't recall that one?
>
> *A:* No, sir.
>
> *Q:* But despite having tested positive for cocaine on at least two occasions, you're telling the ladies and gentlemen of the jury that you have never seen cocaine except on television?
>
> *A:* It could be anywhere. I never seen it, never used it.

The government then went on to pursue other issues. . . . Mr. Copelin argues that the district court should not have allowed the government to question him as to the positive drug tests. As an initial matter, however, he concedes, as he must, that although "prior bad acts" evidence is not admissible to show a defendant's propensity to commit the crime at issue, there are circumstances under which a court may admit such evidence. Rule 404(b) of the Federal Rules of Evidence states:

> Evidence of other crimes, wrongs, or acts is not admissible to prove the character of a person in order to show action in conformity therewith. It may, however, be admissible for other purposes, such as proof of motive, opportunity, intent, preparation, plan, knowledge, identity, or absence of mistake or accident. . . .

Although it is not one of the listed permissible purposes, an attempt to impeach through contradiction a defendant acting as a witness is indisputably a legitimate reason to introduce evidence of other crimes or wrongs. . . . If "bad acts" evidence is offered for this reason, it is admissible unless "its probative value is substantially outweighed by the danger of unfair prejudice, confusion of the issues, or misleading the jury or by considerations of undue delay, waste of time, or needless presentation of cumulative evidence." Fed. R. Evid. 403.

Mr. Copelin . . . claims that the government's method of impeachment violated the ban on the use of extrinsic evidence to impeach by contradiction on collateral matters. It is true that this Circuit generally follows the rule that "a witness may not be impeached by extrinsic evidence (contradiction by another witness or evidence) on a collateral issue." *United States v. Tarantino*, 846 F.2d 1384, 1409 (D.C. Cir. 1988), *cert. denied*, 488 U.S. 840 (1988). . . . However, the rule disallowing the use of extrinsic evidence to impeach a witness as to a collateral matter is irrelevant to this case, because Mr. Copelin was impeached by his own statements on cross-examination, not by the testimony of another witness or by physical evidence. "[C]ases upholding a court's exclusion of *extrinsic* evidence offered to impeach a witness, on the ground of the issue's being 'collateral,' do not govern the scope of cross examination itself." *United States v. Stock*, 948 F.2d 1299, 1302 (D.C. Cir. 1991). . . .

When Mr. Copelin testified that he did not actually see David Bailey selling drugs, it was not entirely unnatural for the government to explore the basis for this response by inquiring whether Mr. Copelin had the ability to recognize drugs in the first place. . . . It may well be that the trial judge would have sustained timely objections by defense counsel to the prosecutor's questions concerning Mr. Copelin's ability to recognize drugs. Mr. Copelin's attorney did not issue any such objections, however, so in reviewing this aspect of the cross-examination, we are limited to correcting "plain errors." Fed. R. Crim. P. 52(b). The plain error exception to the contemporaneous objection requirement should be used sparingly, only for "particularly egregious errors," *United States v. Frady*, 456 U.S. 152, 163 (1982), that "seriously affect the fairness, integrity or public reputation of judicial proceedings." *United States v. Atkinson*, 297 U.S. 157, 160 (1936). The district court's failure to squelch the government's disputed line of questioning on its own initiative was certainly not plain error, if it was error at all.... [Reversed on other grounds.]

KEVIN C. McMUNIGAL & CALVIN WILLIAM SHARPE, REFORMING EXTRINSIC IMPEACHMENT

33 Conn. L. Rev. 363, 385–388 (2001)

No Federal Rule of Evidence explicitly addresses extrinsic contradiction of a witness by others. Federal courts dealing with this area of extrinsic impeachment often invoke the common law's collateral contradiction rule. Some federal courts, though, reject the collateral contradiction rule, using instead a case-by-case weighing approach under Rule 403. Federal courts also diverge on recognition of an exception to the collateral contradiction rule for statements by a witness made on direct rather than cross-examination.

The collateral contradiction rule . . . seems simple and clear: extrinsic evidence offered to contradict a witness on a collateral matter is automatically excluded. And the test most often used for distinguishing a collateral from a non-collateral matter, formulated by Wigmore, is easy to state: evidence is not collateral if the contradictory fact could have been shown for any purpose independent of the contradiction. The application of this definition, though, has resulted in "difficulty and dispute," and the boundary between collateral and noncollateral issues "is often indistinct when the collateral test is applied to the facts of a particular case." [4 Jack B. Weinstein & Margaret A. Berger, Weinstein's Federal Evidence, §607.06[3][a], at 607–676 (Joseph M. McLaughlin ed., 2d ed. 2000)] . . .

At its core, the collateral contradiction rule is based on categorical rejection of a particular theory of relevance to support admission of extrinsic contradiction evidence. . . . All contradiction evidence seeks to establish that a witness' testimony was inaccurate on some point. One theory of relevance which may be offered in support of contradiction evidence holds that the fact that the witness was inaccurate on one point, regardless of its subject, makes it more probable that he was inaccurate on other points critical to the case. . . . This relevance theory, sometimes described by the Latin phrase, *"falsus in uno, falsus in omnibus,"* draws a sort of propensity inference concerning inaccuracies in testimony. It seeks to build an inferential bridge from what may be an insignificant inaccuracy to some more significant inaccuracy in the witness' testimony. This transitive inaccuracy relevance theory is typically considered sufficient to support intrinsic impeachment evidence — the cross-examiner is allowed to ask the witness about possible inaccuracy on any point in her testimony subject to Rule 403. The central thrust of the collateral contradiction rule is a categorical rejection of the transitive inaccuracy relevance theory as adequate to support the admission of extrinsic evidence.

PROBLEMS

7.11 Abraham Lincoln's most famous performance as a trial lawyer came during his defense of William "Duff" Armstrong in 1858:

> Armstrong stood accused of the drunken murder of Preston Metzker in the vicinity of a camp meeting on an August night the previous year. Lincoln, as a friend of Armstrong's parents, volunteered to defend him, though he rarely took capital cases. The chief witness for the prosecution said the light of the moon at 10:00 p.m. enabled him to see the defendant strike the victim with "a slung shot" that killed him. Lincoln, in rebuttal, introduced in evidence an almanac showing there was very little moonlight at the hour in question; and this, it was said, secured Armstrong's acquittal. Newspapers publicized the story after Lincoln's nomination in 1860.
>
> Before long Democratic newspapers were claiming that the almanac Lincoln had introduced was for the wrong year. In 1872 Lamon's Life flatly asserted he had won the trial by trickery. An English law book, Ram on Facts, subsequently cited Lincoln's action in the case an instance of the commission of fraud. As a young attorney, Abram Bergen, who later became a judge in Kansas, had witnessed the trial in the Beardstown courtroom; he testified in 1898 that the correct almanac had been introduced, and moreover that the jury foreman later swore in an affidavit that he had personally verified the year of the almanac. Unfortunately, the almanac supposed to have been used had disappeared. But Boy Scouts later, and repeatedly, verified the dimness of the light at the same spot in the lunar period. The novelist Edward Eggleston, in 1887, offered a fictional treatment of the Armstrong case in The Graysons: A Story of Illinois. He moved the trial back twenty years and freely altered the facts while, of course, keeping Lincoln the hero. Toward the end of his life Armstrong told his own story. Lincoln had been right: there was no moon. "But it was light enough for everybody to see the fight. The fight took place in front of one of the bars, and each bar had two or three candles on it. I had no slungshot. . . . It was only a fist fight, and if I killed 'Pres' Metzker I killed him with my naked fist."

Merrill D. Peterson, *Lincoln in American Memory* 95 (1994);* *see also, e.g.,* Albert A. Woldman, *Lawyer Lincoln* 111-116 (1936).

Should the almanac have been excluded pursuant to the collateral evidence rule? Under the hearsay rule?

7.12. Suppose a truck collides with a motorcycle and the motorcyclist sues the truck driver. Ethan testifies that he saw the accident while waiting for a bus, and that the truck was speeding. Ethan previously told an insurance adjuster that he saw the accident while waiting to meet a friend — at least, so the adjuster recalls. When asked on cross-examination about his conversation with the adjuster, Ethan insists he told the adjuster he was waiting for a bus. In order to impeach Ethan, may the truck driver elicit testimony from the adjuster that Ethan said he saw the accident while waiting for a friend?

F. REHABILITATION

Rehabilitation is the opposite of impeachment. Impeachment is the introduction of evidence that suggests a witness's testimony lacks credibility. Rehabilitation is the introduction of evidence that suggests a witness's testimony in fact is worthy of belief. Just as there are five classic modes of impeachment — dishonesty, inconsistency, bias, incapacity, and specific contradiction — so one can describe five modes of rehabilitation — honesty, consistency, disinterest, capacity, and what might be called "specific corroboration." The Federal Rules of Evidence and their state counterparts contain special restrictions on only two of the possible modes of rehabilitation: "character for truthfulness" and prior consistent statements. But those special restrictions draw on and partially codify a general, common law rule against rehabilitating a witness before the witness has been impeached, a practice generally and pejoratively referred to as "bolstering." Courts tend to apply the general rule against bolstering — often justified as an application of balancing under F.R.E. 403 or C.E.C. 352 — to *all* forms of rehabilitation, not just to "character for truthfulness" and prior consistent statements. All rehabilitation, in other words, generally must follow impeachment. That is why it is called "rehabilitation."

When you read the materials that follow it is worth asking what justifies this general prohibition of bolstering. The traditional explanation, as you will see, is that bolstering drags out trials and invites the jury to take what a witness says on faith. But not everyone finds that explanation convincing.

1. In General

UNITED STATES v. LINDEMANN

85 F.3d 1232 (7th Cir. 1996)

CUMMINGS, Circuit Judge.

"Charisma," a show horse, died in its stall on the night of December 15, 1990. The insurance company that had issued a policy on Charisma's life concluded that the death was the result of natural causes and paid the $250,000 value of the policy. Subsequently, the Federal Bureau of Investigation uncovered an alleged conspiracy between Tommy Burns and Barney Ward to kill horses for pay, allowing the horses' owners to collect insurance proceeds. Burns gave the FBI information indicating that George Lindemann, Jr. ("Lindemann"), a partial owner of Charisma, had arranged the horse's death in order to gain the proceeds of its life insurance policy. Lindemann was tried and convicted of three counts of wire fraud in violation of 18 U.S.C. §1343. He appeals that conviction and we affirm.

... [Burns testified against Lindemann at trial, and Lindemann] challenges the admission of evidence regarding Burns' cooperation with the government on other cases. During Burns' cross-examination, Lindemann attacked the credibility of his testimony by suggesting that he would not have gotten a plea deal if he hadn't come up with the name of a "big fish" like Lindemann. Naturally, the government wanted to offer evidence to rebut Lindemann's assertion. Specifically, it wanted to explain to the jury that Lindemann's indictment and Burns' cooperation were the result of a much larger investigation involving the killing of 15 horses, including Charisma. Thus the government elicited from Burns the following testimony:

> Q: Now, Mr. Burns, when the federal agents came down to Florida after you were arrested for killing a horse, Streetwise, they asked you a lot of questions about your crimes; is that right?
>
> A: Yes, they did.
>
> Q: Were those agents focused on George Lindemann?
>
> A: No, they weren't. They basically focused on Helen Brach.
>
> Q: During the course of your cooperation, Mr. Burns, you cooperated against other wealthy people; isn't that right?
>
> A: Oh yeah.
>
> Q: And you've cooperated, have you not, Mr. Burns, with respect to other famous equestrians?
>
> A: Yes, I have....
>
> Q: Is George Lindemann a big part of your cooperation or a small part of your cooperation?
>
> A: They never treated him like he was a big part.
>
> Q: In fact, Mr. Burns, you told the government about many, many people that you killed horses for. To your knowledge, how many people did you discuss with the government, roughly?
>
> A: 30.
>
> Q: And how many of those people have pleaded guilty?
>
> A: 90 percent of them.

Immediately following this testimony, the court instructed the jury as follows:

> This testimony may be considered by you solely for the purpose of understanding the scope of Tom Burns' cooperation with the government. The fact that other subjects in the investigation may have pled guilty must not be considered by you to infer that the defendants are, therefore, guilty of the crimes with which they are charged.

... Lindemann argues that Burns' testimony was inadmissible because it was essentially "bolstering." "Bolstering" is the practice of offering evidence solely for the purpose of enhancing a witness's credibility before that credibility is attacked. Such evidence is inadmissible because it "has the potential for extending the length of trials enormously, . . . asks the jury to take the witness's testimony on faith, . . . and may . . . reduce the care with which jurors listen for inconsistencies and other signs of falsehood or inaccuracy." *United States v. LeFevour*, 798 F.2d 977, 983 (7th Cir. 1986). Once a witness's credibility has been attacked, however, the non-attacking party is permitted to admit evidence to "rehabilitate" the witness. *United States v. McKinney*, 954 F.2d 471, 478 (7th Cir. 1992), *certiorari denied*, 506 U.S. 1023 (1992).

Lindemann's suggestion that Burns falsely implicated him to obtain a plea deal was certainly an attack on the credibility of Burns' testimony. More specifically, it was an attempt to show that Burns had a bias. . . . Thus Lindemann was perfectly entitled to suggest his theory that Burns was lying about Lindemann in order to better the parameters of his plea deal. However, the direct consequence of the attack was that the government was entitled to introduce evidence to rehabilitate Burns on the issue.

The Federal Rules of Evidence specifically address the bolstering/rehabilitation aspect of only two of the five attack methods: Character for truthfulness and prior inconsistent statements.[8] The admissibility of evidence regarding a witness's bias, diminished capacity, and contradictions in his testimony is not specifically addressed by the Rules, and thus admissibility is limited only by the relevance standard of Rule 402. Therefore, because the attack at issue was on Burns' bias, and not on his character for truthfulness in general, Lindemann's contention that the limitations of Rule 608 should have applied is incorrect. . . .

[T]he admission of evidence regarding Burns' cooperation in other cases was relevant. The evidence specifically rebutted the allegation that Burns was biased out of self-interest in Lindemann's case: Burns' successful participation in numerous other cases meant that at the time he was negotiating over his plea deal, he had lots of information to use as bargaining chips. That fact was relevant under the standards of Fed. R. Evid. 402 because it made less probable the assertion that Burns was lying in Lindemann's case out of self-interest. Finally, the district court immediately warned the jury that it was not to infer Lindemann's guilt from the fact that other indicted individuals had pleaded guilty. Thus the evidence was used only to assess Burns' credibility, not as evidence of Lindemann's guilt.

In conclusion, because Lindemann attacked the credibility of Burns' testimony by asserting that Burns had a bias in Lindemann's case, the government was permitted to rebut that assertion by introducing evidence of its own. Furthermore, because that evidence was relevant according to Fed. R. Evid. 402, the district court's decision to admit it was not an abuse of discretion. . . . Affirmed.

---

8. Following the traditional rule against bolstering, Fed. R. Evid. 608 states that evidence of truthful character is admissible only after the character of the witness for truthfulness has been attacked. . . . Furthermore, Rule 608 provides specific limitations on the admissibility of rehabilitation evidence: Once a witness's character for truthfulness has been attacked, evidence is admissible "in the form of opinion or reputation" (608(a)) or non-extrinsic evidence elicited on cross-examination (608(b)). Fed. R. Evid. 801(d)(1)(B) contains the bolstering/rehabilitation rule by defining as nonhearsay only those prior consistent statements that are offered "to rebut an express or implied charge" against a witness of "recent fabrication or improper influence or motive."

2. Character for Truthfulness

[F.R.E. 608; C.E.C. §790]

ADVISORY COMMITTEE NOTE TO F.R.E. 608

... Character evidence in support of credibility is admissible under the rule only after the witness' character has first been attacked, as has been the case at common law. The enormous needless consumption of time which a contrary practice would entail justifies the limitation. Opinion or reputation that the witness is untruthful specifically qualifies as an attack under the rule, and evidence of misconduct, including conviction of crime, and of corruption also fall within this category. Evidence of bias or interest does not. McCormick §49; 4 Wigmore §§1106, 1107. Whether evidence in the form of contradiction is an attack upon the character of the witness must depend upon the circumstances. McCormick §49. Cf. 4 Wigmore §§1108, 1109. ...

BEARD v. MITCHELL
604 F.2d 485 (7th Cir. 1979)

Sprecher, Circuit Judge.

Plaintiff, Eloise Beard, appeals from a jury verdict finding the defendant, Roy Martin Mitchell, not [liable for] depriving her deceased brother of rights secured by the United States Constitution. ... On May 17, 1972, Jeff Beard was abducted and brutally murdered by Stanley Robinson, a Chicago police officer. An F.B.I. informant, William O'Neal accompanied Robinson on the night of the murder. Robinson was convicted of the crime in 1973. In 1975 plaintiff brought this suit against Roy Martin Mitchell, an F.B.I. agent who participated in the investigation of Robinson's activities. Plaintiff alleges that Mitchell's reckless conduct of the Robinson investigation resulted in the deprivation of Jeff Beard's constitutional rights, giving rise to a *Bivens* action for damages. The plaintiff contends that liability could be premised on Mitchell's reckless training and use of an informant, O'Neal, whose conduct allegedly caused Beard's death. Further plaintiff maintains that liability could be premised on Mitchell's failure to arrest Robinson prior to the murder or to take other preventive action. ...

The trial judge permitted Kocoras, the Assistant U.S. Attorney assigned to the Robinson case, to testify at trial that defendant Mitchell had a reputation for truthfulness. The plaintiff contends that this was an impermissible use of reputation evidence under Rule 608(a) of the Federal Rules of Evidence. The plaintiff concedes that she introduced prior inconsistent statements by Mitchell as a means of attacking his credibility but maintains that Rule 608 does not permit the admission of this type of evidence to counter impeachment accomplished by prior inconsistent statements.

Rule 608(a)(2) provides that "evidence of truthful character is admissible only after the character of the witness for truthfulness has been attacked by opinion or reputation evidence *or otherwise*." (Emphasis added.) The use of prior inconsistent statements may constitute an attack on truthfulness. The Supreme Court noted in *United States v. Hale*, 422 U.S. 171, 176 (1975) that "[a] basic rule of evidence provides that prior inconsistent statements may be used to impeach the credibility of a witness." Thus we can not conclude that the trial judge abused his discretion in allowing the testimony. . . . [Affirmed.]

UNITED STATES v. DANEHY

680 F.2d 1311 (11th Cir. 1982)

PER CURIAM

Thomas Danehy appeals his conviction under 18 U.S.C. §§2, 111, and 1114 for forcibly resisting, opposing, impeding, and interfering with Coast Guardsmen while they were engaged in the performance of their duties. [The government charged Danehy with trying to ram a Coast Guard boat with his fishing boat and then resisting Coast Guard officers who boarded his boat and arrested him. Danehy testified at trial and denied the allegations.]

Danehy claims that . . . he should have been allowed to introduce evidence of his reputation for truthfulness as his credibility had been attacked. We disagree.

We addressed precisely this issue in *United States v. Jackson*, 588 F.2d 1046, 1055 (5th Cir. 1979). There, as here, the "attack" on the defendant's credibility consisted of a vigorous cross-examination and the pointing out by the prosecutor of discrepancies between the defendant's testimony and that of other witnesses. This does not call into question the reputation of the defendant for truthfulness. The mere fact that a witness is contradicted by other evidence in a case does not constitute an attack upon his reputation for truth and veracity. *Kauz v. United States*, 188 F.2d 9 (5th Cir. 1951).

Danehy claims that under Rule 404 of the Federal Rules of Evidence an accused may always bring forth evidence of a pertinent character trait and that his reputation for truth is pertinent in the instant case. We reject this line of reasoning. Since Danehy is trying to offer evidence to bolster himself as a witness rather than to show a trait of character that is pertinent to the crime charged, it is Federal Rule of Evidence 608, not 404, that governs. Rule 608 specifically states that "evidence of truthful character is admissible only after the character of the witness for truthfulness has been attacked by opinion or reputation evidence or otherwise." Government counsel pointing out inconsistencies in testimony and arguing that the accused's testimony is not credible does not constitute an attack on the accused's reputation for truthfulness within the meaning of Rule 608. Thus, Danehy may not attempt to bolster his testimony by evidence as to his reputation for truthfulness. Therefore, the district court properly denied Danehy's request to call witnesses to testify to his reputation for truthfulness. . . . [Reversed on other grounds.]

UNITED STATES v. DRURY

396 F.3d 1303 (11th Cir. 2005)

MARCUS, Circuit Judge.

[Dr. Carl] Drury appeals his convictions for violating the federal murder-for-hire statute, 18 U.S.C. §1958, and for possessing a firearm in connection with a crime of violence, in violation of 18 U.S.C. §924(c). [Drury hired an undercover agent of the Bureau of Alcohol, Tobacco, and Firearms to kill his wife, and he provided the agent with a gun.] . . . Drury's basic defense at trial was that the whole murder-for-hire scheme was merely an ATF role-playing exercise. . . . Drury denied ever actually intending to have his wife killed. . . .

Drury . . . challenges the district court's exclusion of evidence of his truthful character. Drury claims that the government attacked his credibility at trial, entitling him to introduce rehabilitative evidence pursuant to Federal Rule of Evidence 608(a)(2). Rule 608(a)(2) provides that "evidence of truthful character is admissible only after the character of the witness for truthfulness has been attacked by opinion or reputation evidence or otherwise."

Drury does not suggest that the government presented any opinion or reputation evidence about his character, but argues that his character was "otherwise" attacked. He offers as the basis for this contention a series of scattered questions asked by the prosecutor during cross-examination of Drury. Among the examples of what Drury cites as the prosecution's "credibility-laden questions" are these: "Are you telling us that you told an arresting officer that you wanted to make a statement and he wouldn't let you?"; "Are you saying that he hushed you up?"; "Is that what you want this jury to believe?"; "You don't think the officer had any reason to think that you were trying to offer him a bribe?"; and "Is that what you are telling us?" Based on these and several other remarks of similar tenor, Drury sought to introduce testimony from six witnesses prepared to attest to his truthful character. . . .

An "attack" that consists only of "Government counsel pointing out inconsistencies in testimony and arguing that the accused's testimony is not credible does not constitute an attack on the accused's reputation for truthfulness within the meaning of Rule 608." *United States v. Daneby*, 680 F.2d 1311, 1314 (11th Cir. 1982). However, that is precisely the sort of "attack" Drury claims the prosecution to have launched during its cross-examination. Because such an attack is insufficient to authorize rehabilitation under Rule 608, we have little trouble concluding that the district court did not abuse its discretion in excluding Drury's proffered reputation-for-truthfulness testimony. . . . Affirmed.

UNITED STATES v. MURRAY

103 F.3d 310 (3d Cir. 1997)

ALITO, Circuit Judge.

Appellant Michael Murray was convicted following a jury trial of an intentional killing in furtherance of a continuing criminal enterprise ("CCE") in violation of 21 U.S.C. §848(e)(1)(A); conspiracy to distribute in excess of five kilograms of cocaine in violation of 21 U.S.C. §§846 and 841(a)(1); and distribution of and possession with intent to distribute cocaine in violation of 21 U.S.C. §841(a)(1). [Among the witnesses against Murray was a police informant named Richard Brown.] After Murray cross-examined Brown, the government called Lt. John Goshert, a Harrisburg police officer, to testify in support of Brown's reliability. Murray objected to Goshert's testimony on the ground that "the character of [Brown] for truthfulness" had not been "attacked by opinion or reputation evidence or otherwise," Fed. R. Evid. 608(a), and that even if it had, Lt. Goshert's testimony violated Fed. R. Evid. 608(b)'s proscription on proof of specific instances of conduct by extrinsic evidence. The court overruled Murray's objection.

. . . It is true that Murray did not present any opinion or reputation evidence to impeach Brown, but Murray's counsel performed an extended and vigorous cross-examination of Brown that exposed Brown's various illegal and sordid activities. Murray's counsel questioned Brown about his long-standing and heavy drug use, his acquaintance with many Harrisburg drug dealers, his apparent under-the-table tax-free compensation for his work as an informant, his convictions for drug possession and theft of services, his unlawful carrying of an unlicensed firearm, his concealment of his drug use from his friend and contact in the Harrisburg police department, and his prior inconsistent statements to the grand jury. In view of this questioning, the opinion or reputation testimony given by Lt. Goshert fell within the language of Rule 608(a)(2) permitting the introduction of such evidence to support a witness' credibility when his character for truthfulness has been "otherwise" attacked.

Murray's more persuasive argument is founded upon Rule 608(b)'s prohibition on proving specific instances of a witness' conduct by extrinsic evidence. Once Brown's character for truthfulness was attacked by Murray's counsel, the government was entitled to attempt to rehabilitate Brown by calling a witness to give opinion or reputation testimony as to Brown's character for truthfulness. But the government was not entitled to present "extrinsic evidence" of "specific instances" of Brown's conduct "for the purpose of . . . supporting [his] credibility." Fed. R. Evid. 608(b). Lt. Goshert's testimony was as follows:

> *Q:* Lieutenant Goshert, do you know an individual by the name of Richard Brown?
>
> *A:* Yes, I do.
>
> *Q:* Have you ever used Mr. Brown as a confidential informant?
>
> *A:* On numerous occasions, the Harrisburg Police has utilized him.
>
> *Q:* As a result pf [*sic*] your using Richard Brown as a confidential informant, have you made any cases?
>
> *A:* Yes, we have.
>
> *Q:* Do you have an idea of approximately how many?
>
> *A:* In excess of 65. 65, 66 something like that.
>
> *Q:* And search warrants, have you obtained search warrants based on his information?
>
> *A:* Yes, we have numerous times.
>
> *Q:* How long a period of time have you been dealing with Mr. Brown?

A: Since 1988.

Q: Based on your dealings with Mr. Brown and the cases you said that he has made, can you give us your opinion as to his reputation for being a reliable individual?

A: He is extremely reliable.

Q: In terms of the accuracy of the information?

A: Yes.

This testimony, in our view, included "extrinsic evidence" of Brown's character for truthfulness. *United States v. McNeill,* 887 F.2d 448, 453 (3d Cir. 1989) ("Extrinsic evidence is evidence offered through other witnesses rather than through cross-examination of the witness himself or herself."), *cert. denied,* 493 U.S. 1087 (1990). Murray argues that Lt. Goshert's quantification of the cases that Brown had "made" constituted evidence of "specific instances" of Brown's conduct and thus should have been excluded under Rule 608(b). The government contends that Lt. Goshert's testimony was proper as foundation for his opinion as to Brown's character for truthfulness. In support of the admission of Lt. Goshert's testimony in the district court, the government argued that "[t]here has got to be some basis for the jury to know how he can give that opinion as to his reputation. And by letting the jury know they have a close working relationship over a period of time and that they have been involved in all of these incidents, then there is a basis for him giving that opinion." We agree that Lt. Goshert's testimony that the Harrisburg police had used Brown as a confidential informant on "numerous occasions" since 1988 was necessary to establish that he had a basis on which to offer his opinion as to Brown's character for truthfulness. However, his testimony that Brown had "made" 65 or 66 cases was more specific than can be justified as necessary to establish a foundation.

United States v. Taylor, 900 F.2d 779 (4th Cir. 1990) presented a situation extremely similar to the instant case. In *Taylor* as in this case, the government's fortunes depended in large part on the credibility of an informant, and the government called a law enforcement officer to testify as to the informant's reliability. The officer testified that the informant "had acted as a buyer for the government on 15 to 18 drug buys," that he "had given reliable information in a particular case which resulted in the seller's conviction," and that "several others either pleaded guilty or were convicted as a result of [the informant's] testimony." The court held that it was error to admit evidence that the informant's testimony had resulted in convictions in other cases. Lt. Goshert's testimony was substantially identical, and we conclude that its admission contravened Rule 608(b).... [Reversed on these and other grounds.]

PROBLEMS

7.13. The plaintiff in a medical malpractice case calls a physician as an expert witness. The physician admits on cross-examination that she is being paid $5,000 for her testimony. Can the plaintiff now call a witness to testify that the physician is honest or has a reputation for honesty?

7.14. The prosecution in a shoplifting case calls a department store employee who testifies that she saw the defendant, while in a dressing room, cut price tags from clothing and stuff the clothing in her shopping bag. On cross-examination, defense counsel suggests that it would have been impossible for the witness to see what she claims to have seen through the slats of the dressing room door. Can the prosecution now call the employee's supervisor to testify that, in the supervisor's opinion, the employee would not lie under oath?

3. Prior Consistent Statements

[F.R.E. 801(D)(1), C.E.C. §§791, 1236]

TOME v. UNITED STATES

513 U.S. 150 (1995)

Justice KENNEDY delivered the opinion of the Court, except as to Part IIB.

Various Federal Courts of Appeals are divided over the evidence question presented by this case. At issue is the interpretation of a provision in the Federal Rules of Evidence bearing upon the admissibility of statements, made by a declarant who testifies as a witness, that are consistent with the testimony and are offered to rebut a charge of a "recent fabrication or improper influence or motive." Fed. Rule Evid. 801(d)(1)(B). The question is whether out-of-court consistent statements made after the alleged fabrication, or after the alleged improper influence or motive arose, are admissible under the Rule.

I

Petitioner Tome was charged in a one-count indictment with the felony of sexual abuse of a child, his own daughter, aged four at the time of the alleged crime. The case having arisen on the Navajo Indian Reservation, Tome was tried by a jury in the United States District Court for the District of New Mexico, where he was found guilty of violating 18 U.S.C. §§1153, 2241(c), and 2245(2)(A) and (B).

Tome and the child's mother had been divorced in 1988. A tribal court awarded joint custody of the daughter, A.T., to both parents, but Tome had primary physical custody. In 1989 the mother was unsuccessful in petitioning the tribal court for primary custody of A.T., but was awarded custody for the summer of 1990. Neither parent attended a further custody hearing in August 1990. On August 27, 1990, the mother contacted Colorado authorities with allegations that Tome had committed sexual abuse against A.T.

The prosecution's theory was that Tome committed sexual assaults upon the child while she was in his custody and that the crime was disclosed when the child was spending vacation time with her mother. The defense argued that the allegations were concocted so the child would not be returned to her father. At trial A.T., then 6 ½ years old, was the Government's first witness. For the most part, her direct testimony consisted of one- and two-word answers to a series of leading questions. Cross-examination took place over two trial days. The defense asked A.T. 348 questions. On the first day A.T. answered all the questions posed to her on general, background subjects.

The next day there was no testimony, and the prosecutor met with A.T. When cross-examination of A.T. resumed, she was questioned about those conversations but was reluctant to discuss them. Defense counsel then began questioning her about the allegations of abuse, and it appears she was reluctant at many points to answer. As the trial judge noted, however, some of the defense questions were imprecise or unclear. The judge expressed his concerns with the examination of A.T., observing there were lapses of as much as 40–55 seconds between some questions and the answers and that on the second day of examination the witness seemed to be losing concentration. The trial judge stated, "We have a very difficult situation here."

After A.T. testified, the Government produced six witnesses who testified about a total of seven statements made by A.T. describing the alleged sexual assaults: A.T.'s babysitter recited A.T.'s statement to her on August 22, 1990, that she did not want to return to her father because he "gets drunk and he thinks I'm his wife"; the babysitter related further details given by A.T. on August 27, 1990, while A.T.'s mother stood outside the room and listened after the mother had been unsuccessful in questioning A.T. herself; the mother recounted what she had heard A.T. tell the babysitter; a social worker recounted details A.T. told her on August 29, 1990, about the assaults; and three pediatricians, Drs. Kuper, Reich, and Spiegel, related A.T.'s statements to them describing how and where she had been touched by Tome. All but A.T.'s statement to Dr. Spiegel implicated Tome. (The physicians also testified that their clinical examinations of the child indicated that she had been subjected to vaginal penetrations. That part of the testimony is not at issue here.)

A.T.'s out-of-court statements, recounted by the six witnesses, were offered by the Government under Rule 801(d)(1)(B). The trial court admitted all of the statements over defense counsel's objection, accepting the Government's argument that they rebutted the implicit charge that A.T.'s testimony was motivated by a desire to live with her mother. The court also admitted A.T.'s August 22d statement to her babysitter under Rule 803(24), and the statements to Dr. Kuper (and apparently also to Dr. Reich) under Rule 803(4) (statements for purposes of medical diagnosis). The Government offered the testimony of the social worker under both Rules 801(d)(1)(B) and 803(24), but the record does not indicate whether the court ruled on the latter ground. No objection was made to Dr. Spiegel's testimony. Following trial, Tome was convicted and sentenced to 12 years' imprisonment.

On appeal, the Court of Appeals for the Tenth Circuit affirmed, adopting the Government's argument that all of A.T.'s out-of-court statements were admissible under Rule 801(d)(1)(B) even though they had been made after A.T.'s alleged motive to fabricate arose. The court reasoned that "the pre-motive requirement is a function of the relevancy rules, not the hearsay rules" and that as a "function of relevance, the pre-motive rule is clearly too broad ... because it is simply not true that an individual with a motive to lie always will do so. . . . Rather, the relevance of the prior consistent statement is more accurately determined by evaluating the strength of the motive to lie, the circumstances in which the statement is made, and the declarant's demonstrated propensity to lie." Applying this balancing test to A.T.'s first statement to her babysitter, the Court of Appeals determined that although A.T. might have had "some motive to lie, we do not believe that it is a particularly strong one." The court held that the District Judge had not abused his discretion in admitting A.T.'s out-of-court statements. It did not analyze the probative quality of A.T.'s six other out-of-court statements, nor did it reach the admissibility of the statements under any other rule of evidence.

We granted certiorari and now reverse.

II

The prevailing common-law rule for more than a century before adoption of the Federal Rules of Evidence was that a prior consistent statement introduced to rebut a charge of recent fabrication or improper influence or motive was admissible if the statement had been made before the alleged fabrication, influence, or motive came into being, but it was inadmissible if made afterwards. As Justice Story explained: "[W]here the testimony is assailed as a fabrication of a recent date, . . . in order to repel such imputation, proof of the *antecedent* declaration of the party may be admitted." *Ellicott v. Pearl*, 35 U.S. (10 Pet.) 412, 439 (1836) (emphasis added). See also *People v. Singer*, 300 N.Y. 120, 124-125, 89 N.E.2d 710, 712 (1949).

McCormick and Wigmore stated the rule in a more categorical manner: "[T]he applicable principle is that the prior consistent statement has no relevancy to refute the charge unless the consistent statement was made before the source of the bias, interest, influence or incapacity originated." E. Cleary, McCormick on Evidence §49, p. 105 (2d ed. 1972) (hereafter McCormick). See also 4 J. Wigmore, Evidence §1128, p. 268 (J. Chadbourn rev. 1972) (hereafter Wigmore) ("A consistent statement, at a *time prior* to the existence of a fact said to indicate bias...will effectively explain away the force of the impeaching evidence" (emphasis in original)). The question is whether Rule 801(d)(1) (B) embodies this temporal requirement. We hold that it does.

A

. . . Rule 801 defines prior consistent statements as nonhearsay only if they are offered to rebut a charge of "recent fabrication or improper influence or motive." Fed. Rule Evid. 801(d)(1)(B). Noting the "troublesome" logic of treating a witness' prior consistent statements as hearsay at all (because the declarant is present in court and subject to cross-examination), the Advisory Committee decided to treat those consistent statements, once the preconditions of the Rule were satisfied, as nonhearsay and admissible as substantive evidence, not just to rebut an attack on the witness' credibility. See Advisory Committee's Notes on Fed. Rule Evid. 801(d)(1). A consistent statement meeting the requirements of the Rule is thus placed in the same category as a declarant's inconsistent statement made under oath in another proceeding, or prior identification testimony, or admissions by a party opponent.

The Rules do not accord this weighty, nonhearsay status to all prior consistent statements. To the contrary, admissibility under the Rules is confined to those statements offered to rebut a charge of "recent fabrication or improper influence or motive," the same phrase used by the Advisory Committee in its description of the "traditiona[l]" common law of evidence, which was the background against which the Rules were drafted. Prior consistent statements may not be admitted to counter all forms of impeachment or to bolster the witness merely because she has been discredited. In the present context, the question is whether A.T.'s out-of-court statements rebutted the alleged link between her desire to be with her mother and her testimony, not whether they suggested that A.T.'s in-court testimony was true. The Rule speaks of a party rebutting an alleged motive, not bolstering the veracity of the story told.

This limitation is instructive, not only to establish the preconditions of admissibility but also to reinforce the significance of the requirement that the consistent statements must have been made before the alleged influence, or motive to fabricate, arose. That is to say, the forms of impeachment within the Rule's coverage are the ones in which the temporal requirement makes the most sense. Impeachment by charging that the testimony is a recent fabrication or results from an improper influence or motive is, as a general matter, capable of direct and forceful refutation through introduction of out-of-court consistent statements that predate the alleged fabrication, influence, or motive. A consistent statement that predates the motive is a square rebuttal of the charge that the testimony was contrived as a consequence of that motive. By contrast, prior consistent statements carry little rebuttal force when most other types of impeachment are involved. McCormick §49, p. 105 ("When the attack takes the form of impeachment of character, by showing misconduct, convictions or bad reputation, it is generally agreed that there is no color for sustaining by consistent statements. The defense does not meet the assault" (footnote omitted)); see also 4 Wigmore §1131, p. 293 ("The broad rule obtains in a few courts that consistent statements may be admitted *after* impeachment of any sort — in particular after any impeachment by *cross-examination*. But there is no reason for such a loose rule" (footnote omitted)).

There may arise instances when out-of-court statements that postdate the alleged fabrication have some probative force in rebutting a charge of fabrication or improper influence or motive, but those statements refute the charged fabrication in a less direct and forceful way. Evidence that a witness made consistent statements after the alleged motive to fabricate arose may suggest in some degree that the in-court testimony is truthful, and thus suggest in some degree that that testimony did not result from some improper influence; but if the drafters of Rule 801(d)(1)(B) intended to countenance rebuttal along that indirect inferential chain, the purpose of confining the types of impeachment that open the door to rebuttal by introducing consistent statements becomes unclear. If consistent statements are admissible without reference to the timeframe we find imbedded in the Rule, there appears no sound reason not to admit consistent statements to rebut other forms of impeachment as well. Whatever objections can be leveled against limiting the Rule to this designated form of impeachment and confining the rebuttal to those statements made before the fabrication or improper influence or motive arose, it is clear to us that the drafters of Rule 801(d)(1)(B) were relying upon the common-law temporal requirement.... The language of the Rule, in its concentration on rebutting charges of recent fabrication or improper influence or motive to the exclusion of other forms of impeachment, as well as in its use of wording that follows the language of the common-law cases, suggests that it was intended to carry over the common-law premotive rule.

B

Our conclusion that Rule 801(d)(1)(B) embodies the common-law premotive requirement is confirmed by an examination of the Advisory Committee's Notes to the Federal Rules of Evidence. We have relied on those well-considered Notes as a useful guide in ascertaining the meaning of the Rules. See, *e.g., Huddleston v. United States*, 485 U.S. 681, 688 (1988); *United States v. Owens*, 484 U.S. 554, 562 (1988). Where, as with Rule 801(d)(1)(B), "Congress did not amend the Advisory Committee's draft in any way . . . the Committee's commentary is particularly relevant in determining the meaning of the document Congress enacted." *Beech Aircraft Corp. v. Rainey*, 488 U.S. 153, 165–166, n.9 (1988). The Notes are also a respected source of scholarly commentary. Professor Cleary was a distinguished commentator on the law of evidence, and he and members of the Committee consulted and considered the views, criticisms, and suggestions of the academic community in preparing the Notes.

    The Notes disclose a purpose to adhere to the common law in the application of evidentiary principles, absent express provisions to the contrary. Where the Rules did depart from their common-law antecedents, in general the Committee said so. See, *e.g.,* Notes on Rule 804(b)(4) ("The general common law requirement that a declaration in this area must have been made *ante litem motam* has been dropped, as bearing more appropriately on weight than admissibility"); Rule 804(b)(2) ("The exception is the familiar dying declaration of the common law, expanded somewhat beyond its traditionally narrow limits"); Rule 804(b)(3) ("The exception discards the common law limitation and expands to the full logical limit"). The Notes give no indication, however, that Rule 801(d)(1)(B) abandoned the premotive requirement. The entire discussion of Rule 801(d)(1)(B) is limited to the following comment:

> "Prior consistent statements traditionally have been admissible to rebut charges of recent fabrication or improper influence or motive but not as substantive evidence. Under the rule they are substantive evidence. The prior statement is consistent with the testimony given on the stand, and, if the opposite party wishes to open the door for its admission in evidence, no sound reason is apparent why it should not be received generally."

Throughout their discussion of the Rules, the Advisory Committee's Notes rely on Wigmore and McCormick as authority for the common-law approach. In light of the categorical manner in which those authors state the premotive requirement, it is difficult to imagine that the drafters, who noted the new substantive use of prior consistent statements, would have remained silent if they intended to modify the premotive requirement. As we observed with respect to another provision of the Rules, "[w]ith this state of unanimity confronting the drafters of the Federal Rules of Evidence, we think it unlikely that they intended to scuttle entirely [the common law requirement]." *United States v. Abel*, 469 U.S. 45, 50 (1984). Here, we do not think the drafters of the Rule intended to scuttle the whole premotive requirement and rationale without so much as a whisper of explanation.

Observing that Edward Cleary was the Reporter of the Advisory Committee that drafted the Rules, the Court has relied upon his writings as persuasive authority on the meaning of the Rules. See *Daubert v. Merrell Dow Pharmaceuticals, Inc.*, 509 U.S. 579 (1993); *Abel, supra*, at 51–52. Cleary also was responsible for the 1972 revision of McCormick's treatise, which included an examination of the changes introduced by the proposed federal rules to the common-law practice of impeachment and rehabilitation. The discussion, which occurs only three paragraphs after the treatise's categorical description of the common-law premotive rule, also lacks any indication that the proposed rules were abandoning that temporal limitation. See McCormick §50, p. 107.

Our conclusion is bolstered by the Advisory Committee's stated "unwillingness to countenance the general use of prior prepared statements as substantive evidence." See Notes on Rule 801(d)(1). Rule 801(d), which "enumerates three situations in which the statement is excepted from the category of hearsay," *ibid.*, was expressly contrasted by the Committee with Uniform Rule of Evidence 63(1) (1953), "which allows *any* out-of-court statement of a declarant who is present at the trial and available for cross-examination." Notes on Rule 801(d)(1) (emphasis added). When a witness presents important testimony damaging to a party, the party will often counter with at least an implicit charge that the witness has been under some influence or motive to fabricate. If Rule 801 were read so that the charge opened the floodgates to any prior consistent statement that satisfied Rule 403, as the Tenth Circuit concluded, the distinction between rejected Uniform Rule 63(1) and Rule 801(d)(1)(B) would all but disappear.

That Rule 801(d)(1)(B) permits prior consistent statements to be used for substantive purposes after the statements are admitted to rebut the existence of an improper influence or motive makes it all the more important to observe the preconditions for admitting the evidence in the first place. The position taken by the Rules reflects a compromise between the views expressed by the "bulk of the case law . . . against allowing prior statements of witnesses to be used generally as substantive evidence" and the views of the majority of "writers . . . [who] ha[d] taken the opposite position." *Ibid.* That compromise was one that the Committee candidly admitted was a "judgment . . . more of experience than of logic." *Ibid.*

"A party contending that legislative action changed settled law has the burden of showing that the legislature intended such a change." *Green v. Bock Laundry Machine Co.*, 490 U.S. 504, 521 (1989) (applying that presumption in interpreting Federal Rule of Evidence 609). Nothing in the Advisory Committee's Notes suggests that it intended to alter the common-law premotive requirement.

C

The Government's final argument in favor of affirmance is that the common-law premotive rule advocated by petitioner is inconsistent with the Federal Rules' liberal approach to relevancy and with strong academic criticism, beginning in the 1940's, directed at the exclusion of out-of-court statements made by a declarant who is present in court and subject to cross-examination. This argument misconceives the design of the Rules' hearsay provisions.

Hearsay evidence is often relevant. . . . That certain out-of-court statements may be relevant does not dispose of the question whether they are admissible.

. . . To be sure, certain commentators in the years preceding the adoption of the Rules had been critical of the common-law approach to hearsay, particularly its categorical exclusion of out-of-court statements offered for substantive purposes. General criticism was directed to the exclusion of a declarant's out-of-court statements where the declarant testified at trial. As an alternative, they suggested moving away from the categorical exclusion of hearsay and toward a case-by-case balancing of the probative value of particular statements against their likely prejudicial effect. The Advisory Committee, however, was explicit in rejecting this balancing approach to hearsay:

"The Advisory Committee has rejected this approach to hearsay as involving too great a measure of judicial discretion, minimizing the predictability of rulings, [and] enhancing the difficulties of preparation for trial." Advisory Committee's Introduction to Article VIII.

. . . The statement-by-statement balancing approach advocated by the Government and adopted by the Tenth Circuit creates the precise dangers the Advisory Committee noted and sought to avoid: It involves considerable judicial discretion; it reduces predictability; and it enhances the difficulties of trial preparation because parties will have difficulty knowing in advance whether or not particular out-of-court statements will be admitted.

D

The case before us illustrates some of the important considerations supporting the Rule as we interpret it, especially in criminal cases. If the Rule were to permit the introduction of prior statements as substantive evidence to rebut every implicit charge that a witness' in-court testimony results from recent fabrication or improper influence or motive, the whole emphasis of the trial could shift to the out-of-court statements, not the in-court ones. The present case illustrates the point. In response to a rather weak charge that A.T.'s testimony was a fabrication created so the child could remain with her mother, the Government was permitted to present a parade of sympathetic and credible witnesses who did no more than recount A.T.'s detailed out-of-court statements to them. Although those statements might have been probative on the question whether the alleged conduct had occurred, they shed but minimal light on whether A.T. had the charged motive to fabricate. At closing argument before the jury, the Government placed great reliance on the prior statements for substantive purposes but did not once seek to use them to rebut the impact of the alleged motive.

We are aware that in some cases it may be difficult to ascertain when a particular fabrication, influence, or motive arose. Yet, as the Government concedes, a majority of common-law courts were performing this task for well over a century, and the Government has presented us with no evidence that those courts, or the judicial circuits that adhere to the rule today, have been unable to make the determination. Even under the Government's hypothesis, moreover, the thing to be rebutted must be identified, so the date of its origin cannot be that much more difficult to ascertain. By contrast, as the Advisory

Committee commented, the Government's approach, which would require the trial court to weigh all of the circumstances surrounding a statement that suggest its probativeness against the court's assessment of the strength of the alleged motive, would entail more of a burden, with no guidance to attorneys in preparing a case or to appellate courts in reviewing a judgment.

III

Courts must be sensitive to the difficulties attendant upon the prosecution of alleged child abusers. In almost all cases a youth is the prosecution's only eyewitness. But "[t]his Court cannot alter evidentiary rules merely because litigants might prefer different rules in a particular class of cases." *United States v. Salerno*, 505 U.S. 317, 322 (1992). When a party seeks to introduce out-of-court statements that contain strong circumstantial indicia of reliability, that are highly probative on the material questions at trial, and that are better than other evidence otherwise available, there is no need to distort the requirements of Rule 801(d)(1)(B). If its requirements are met, Rule 803(24) exists for that eventuality. We intimate no view, however, concerning the admissibility of any of A.T.'s out-of-court statements under that section, or any other evidentiary principle. These matters, and others, are for the Court of Appeals to decide in the first instance.

Our holding is confined to the requirements for admission under Rule 801(d)(1)(B). The Rule permits the introduction of a declarant's consistent out-of-court statements to rebut a charge of recent fabrication or improper influence or motive only when those statements were made before the charged recent fabrication or improper influence or motive. These conditions of admissibility were not established here.

The judgment of the Court of Appeals for the Tenth Circuit is reversed, and the case is remanded for further proceedings consistent with this opinion.

Justice SCALIA, concurring in part and concurring in the judgment.

I concur in the judgment of the Court, and join its opinion except for Part II-B. That Part, which is devoted entirely to a discussion of the Advisory Committee's Notes pertinent to Rule 801(d)(1)(B), gives effect to those Notes not only because they are "a respected source of scholarly commentary," but also because they display the "purpose" or "inten[t]" of the draftsmen.

I have previously acquiesced in, see, *e.g., Beech Aircraft Corp. v. Rainey*, 488 U.S. 153 (1988), and indeed myself engaged in, see *United States v. Owens*, 484 U.S. 554, 562 (1988), similar use of the Advisory Committee Notes. More mature consideration has persuaded me that is wrong. Having been prepared by a body of experts, the Notes are assuredly persuasive scholarly commentaries — ordinarily the most persuasive — concerning the meaning of the Rules. But they bear no special authoritativeness as the work of the draftsmen, any more than the views of Alexander Hamilton (a draftsman) bear more authority than the views of Thomas Jefferson (not a draftsman) with regard to the meaning of the Constitution. It is the words of the Rules that have been authoritatively adopted — by this Court, or by Congress if it makes a statutory change. See 28 U.S.C. §§2072, 2074 (1988 ed. and Supp. IV). In my view even the adopting Justices' thoughts, unpromulgated as Rules, have no authoritative (as opposed to persuasive) effect, any more than their thoughts regarding an opinion (reflected in exchanges of memoranda before the opinion issues) authoritatively demonstrate the meaning of that opinion. And the same for the thoughts of congressional draftsmen who prepare statutory amendments to the Rules. Like a judicial opinion and like a statute, the promulgated Rule says what it says, regardless of the intent of its drafters. The Notes are, to be sure, submitted to us and to the Members of Congress as the thoughts of the body initiating the recommendations, see §2073(d); but there is no certainty that either we or they read those thoughts, nor is there any procedure by which we formally endorse or disclaim them. That being so, the Notes cannot, by some power inherent in the draftsmen, change the meaning that the Rules would otherwise bear....

Justice BREYER, with whom THE CHIEF JUSTICE, Justice O'CONNOR, and Justice THOMAS join, dissenting.

The basic issue in this case concerns not hearsay, but relevance. As the majority points out, the common law permitted a lawyer to rehabilitate a witness (after a charge of improper motive) by pointing to the fact that the witness had said the same thing earlier — but only if the witness made the earlier statement before the motive to lie arose.... The majority believes that a hearsay-related rule, Federal Rule of Evidence 801(d)(1)(B), codifies this absolute timing requirement. I do not. Rule 801(d)(1)(B) has nothing to do with relevance. Rather, that Rule carves out a subset of prior consistent statements that were formerly admissible only to rehabilitate a witness (a nonhearsay use that relies upon the fact that the statement was made). It then says that members of that subset are "not hearsay." This means that, if such a statement is admissible for a particular rehabilitative purpose (to rebut a charge of recent fabrication or improper influence or motive), its proponent now may use it substantively, for a hearsay purpose (i.e., as evidence of its truth), as well.

... [O]ne can find a hearsay-related reason why the drafters might have decided to restrict the Rule to a particular category of prior consistent statements. Juries have trouble distinguishing between the rehabilitative and substantive use of the kind of prior consistent statements listed in Rule 801(d)(1)(B). Judges may give instructions limiting the use of such prior consistent statements to a rehabilitative purpose, but, in practice, juries nonetheless tend to consider them for their substantive value... It is possible that the Advisory Committee made them "nonhearsay" for that reason, i.e., as a concession "more of experience than of logic." Advisory Committee's Notes on Fed. Rule Evid. 801(d)(1)(B) (also noting that the witness is available for cross-examination in the courtroom in any event). If there was a reason why the drafters excluded from Rule 801(d)(1)(B)'s scope other kinds of prior consistent statements (used for rehabilitation), perhaps it was that the drafters concluded that those other statements caused jury confusion to a lesser degree. On this rationale, however, there is no basis for distinguishing between premotive and postmotive statements, for the confusion with respect to each would very likely be the same.

... I would read the Rule's plain words to mean exactly what they say: If a trial court properly admits a statement that is "consistent with the declarant's testimony" for the purpose of "rebut[ting] an express or implied charge ... of recent fabrication or improper influence or motive," then that statement is "not hearsay," and the jury may also consider it for the truth of what it says.

Assuming Rule 801(d)(1)(B) does not codify the absolute timing requirement, I must still answer the question whether, as a relevance matter, the common-law statement of the premotive rule stands as an absolute bar to a trial court's admission of a postmotive prior consistent statement for the purpose of rebutting a charge of recent fabrication or improper influence or motive.

. . . [T]here are sound reasons here for permitting an exception to the timing rule where circumstances warrant. For one thing, one can find examples where the timing rule's claim of "no relevancy" is simply untrue. A postmotive statement is relevant to rebut, for example, a charge of recent fabrication based on improper motive, say, when the speaker made the prior statement while affected by a far more powerful motive to tell the truth. A speaker might be moved to lie to help an acquaintance. But, suppose the circumstances also make clear to the speaker that only the truth will save his child's life. Or, suppose the postmotive statement was made spontaneously, or when the speaker's motive to lie was much weaker than it was at trial. In these and similar situations, special circumstances may indicate that the prior statement was made for some reason other than the alleged improper motivation; it may have been made not because of, but despite, the improper motivation. Hence, postmotive statements can, in appropriate circumstances, directly refute the charge of fabrication based on improper motive, not because they bolster in a general way the witness' trial testimony, but because the circumstances indicate that the statements are not causally connected to the alleged motive to lie.

. . . Trial judges may find it easier to administer an absolute rule. Yet, there is no indication in any of the cases that trial judges would, or do, find it particularly difficult to administer a more flexible rule in this context. And, there is something to be said for the greater authority that flexibility grants the trial judge to tie rulings on the admissibility of rehabilitative evidence more closely to the needs and circumstances of the particular case. Furthermore, the majority concedes that the premotive rule, while seemingly bright line, poses its own administrative difficulties.

This Court has acknowledged that the Federal Rules of Evidence worked a change in common-law relevancy rules in the direction of flexibility. See *Daubert v. Merrell Dow Pharmaceuticals, Inc.*, 509 U.S. 579 (1993). Article IV of the Federal Rules, which concerns relevance, liberalizes the rules for admission of relevant evidence. The Rules direct the trial judge generally to admit all evidence having "any tendency" to make the existence of a material fact "more probable or less probable than it would be without the evidence." Fed. Rules Evid. 401, 402. The judge may reject the evidence (assuming compliance with other rules) only if the probative value of the evidence is substantially outweighed by its tendency to prejudice a party or delay a trial. Rule 403. The codification, as a general matter, relies upon the trial judge's administration of Rules 401, 402, and 403 to keep the barely relevant, the time wasting, and the prejudicial from the jury. . . . Perhaps there are other circumstances in which categorical common-law rules serve the purposes of Rules 401, 402, and 403, and should, accordingly, remain absolute in the law. But, for the reasons stated above, this case, like *Daubert*, does not present such a circumstance. Thus, considered purely as a matter of relevancy law (and as though Rule 801(d)(1)(B) had not been written), I would conclude that the premotive rule did not survive the adoption of the Rules.

. . . Accordingly, I would hold that the Federal Rules authorize a district court to allow (where probative in respect to rehabilitation) the use of post-motive prior consistent statements to rebut a charge of recent fabrication or improper influence or motive (subject of course to, for example, Rule 403). Where such statements are admissible for this rehabilitative purpose, Rule 801(d)(1)(B), as stated above, makes them admissible as substantive evidence as well (provided, of course, that the Rule's other requirements, such as the witness' availability for cross-examination, are satisfied). In most cases, this approach will not yield a different result from a strict adherence to the pre-motive rule for, in most cases, postmotive statements will not be significantly probative. And, even in cases where the statement is admitted as significantly probative (in respect to rehabilitation), the effect of admission on the trial will be minimal because the prior consistent statements will (by their nature) do no more than repeat in-court testimony.

In this case, the Court of Appeals, applying an approach consistent with what I have described above, decided that A.T.'s prior consistent statements were probative on the question of whether her story as a witness reflected a motive to lie. There is no reason to reevaluate this factbound conclusion. Accordingly, I would affirm the judgment of the Court of Appeals.

ADVISORY COMMITTEE NOTE TO 2014 AMENDMENT TO F.R.E. 801

. . . Though the original Rule 801(d)(1)(B) provided for substantive use of certain prior consistent statements . . . [t]he Rule covered only those con-sistent statements that were offered to rebut charges of recent fabrication or improper motive or influence. The Rule did not, for example, provide for substantive admissibility of consistent statements that are probative to explain what otherwise appears to be an inconsistency in the witness's testimony. Nor did it cover consistent statements that would be probative to rebut a charge of faulty memory. Thus, the Rule left many prior consistent statements potentially admissible only for the limited purpose of rehabilitating a witness's credibility. The original Rule also led to some conflict in the cases; some courts distinguished between substantive and rehabilitative use for prior consistent statements, while others appeared to hold that prior consistent statements must be admissible under Rule 801(d)(1)(B) or not at all.

The amendment retains the requirement set forth in *Tome v. United States*, 513 U.S. 150 (1995): that under Rule 801(d)(1)(B), a consistent state-ment offered to rebut a charge of recent fabrication [or] improper influence or motive must have been made before the alleged fabrication or improper infer-ence or motive arose. The intent of the amendment is to extend substantive effect to consistent statements that rebut other attacks on a witness — such as the charges of inconsistency or faulty memory.

The amendment does not change the traditional and well-accepted limits on bringing prior consistent statements before the factfinder for credibility purposes. It does not allow impermissible bolstering of a witness.

As before, prior consistent statements under the amendment may be brought before the factfinder only if they properly rehabilitate a witness whose credibility has been attacked. As before, to be admissible for rehabilitation, a prior consistent statement must satisfy the strictures of Rule 403. As before, the trial court has ample discretion to exclude prior consistent statements that are cumulative accounts of an event. The amendment does not make any consistent statement admissible that was not admissible previously — the only difference is that prior consistent statements otherwise admissible for rehabilitation are now admissible substantively as well.

PROBLEM

7.15. In a bank robbery case, a teller who saw the robber testifies that he had a moustache. On cross-examination, the teller admits that two days after the robbery he told a police detective that the robber had no facial hair. The prosecution then calls the bank manager and seeks to have her testify that, several hours after the robbery, the teller told the bank manager that the robber had "a bushy moustache." Is this testimony admissible?

COMPETENCE

"At the time of the incident, I was employed in the Dunbar house as a pet."

A. IN GENERAL

The terms "competence" and "competency" are used in two different ways in evidence law. Sometimes — most often in older cases — the terms often are synonyms for "admissibility": Proof is "competent" if it should be allowed into evidence. Today the terms are used not to describe *evidence* but to describe *witnesses*: a witness is "competent" if he or she is allowed to testify. The subject of this chapter is competence in this modern sense.

Two or three centuries ago, many categories of potential witnesses were excluded as incompetent: children, felons, atheists, the mentally infirm, parties to the lawsuit, and so on. Most of these rules have now been abolished. The modern view is that practically anyone should be allowed to testify, and the jury should judge a witness's credibility for itself.

It is worth noting that this vote of confidence in the jury is highly specific. It is limited to the jury's ability to size up witnesses by listening to them, watching their demeanor, and assessing their performance under cross-examination. We do not have the same degree of confidence in the *general* ability of jurors to identify good and bad evidence; otherwise we would not keep all the complicated rules of evidence that are examined in the other chapters of this book. We could do with evidence law generally what we have done with the old rules of competence: junk them and instead rely on the jury to sort wheat from chaff. But we have not done that. We trust jurors to sort good *witnesses* from bad much more than we trust their general ability to sort good *evidence* from bad.

In part this is testament to the extraordinary faith our system places in *viva voce* evidence — faith, that is, that truth is best found by hearing from witnesses in open court. The old, restrictive rules of competence reflected a degree of fear concerning *vive voce* evidence, or at least a belief that hearing from certain witnesses was likely to impede rather than advance the search for truth. The modern, relaxed rules of competence are, in a sense, the flip side of the hearsay ban. The hearsay rule expresses our worries about how the jury will handle secondhand evidence; the relaxed rules of competence express our confidence in the jury's ability to handle firsthand evidence. In the words of one scholar, "the jury is the system's lie detector." George Fisher, *The Jury's Rise as Lie Detector*, 107 Yale L.J. 575, 708 (1997).

Our lenient rules with respect to competence are also a reminder that the rules of evidence are not written in a way that excludes, or shields jurors from, all evidence the drafters deem unreliable. Rather, the rules of exclusion — such as the rule against hearsay, the rule against character-for-propensity evidence, and the rule against unduly prejudicial evidence — target evidence the drafters think the jury will misuse or over- or under-value. Because the drafters have faith in the jury's ability to determine witness credibility, the rules of competence are accordingly liberal with respect to admissibility.

[F.R.E. 601; C.E.C. §700]

JAMES B. THAYER, SELECT CASES ON EVIDENCE AT THE COMMON LAW

1070 (1892)

Fortescue (De Laud. c. 26), who has the earliest account (about 1470) of witnesses testifying regularly to the jury, gives no information as to any ground for challenging them. But Coke, a century and a third later, makes certain qualifications of the assertion of the older judges, that "they had not seen witnesses challenged." He mentions as grounds of exclusion, legal infamy, being an "infidel," of non-sane memory, "not of discretion," a party interested, "or the like." And he says that "it hath been resolved by the justices [in 1612] that a wife cannot be produced either against or for her husband, *quia sunt duœ animœ in carne una*." He also points out that "he that challengeth a right in the thing in demand cannot be a witness."

Here are the outlines of the subsequent tests for the competency of witnesses. They were much refined upon, particularly the excluding ground of interest; and great inconveniences resulted. At last in the fourth and fifth decades of the present century, in England, nearly all objections to competency were abolished, or turned into matters of privilege. Similar changes, a little later, were widely made in this country.

ROSEN v. UNITED STATES

245 U.S. 467 (1918)

Mr. Justice CLARKE delivered the opinion of the court.

. . . Rosen and Wagner were indicted in the District Court of the United States for the Eastern District of New York with one Broder for conspiring to buy and receive certain checks and letters which had been stolen from "duly authorized depositories for mail matter of the United States," and which were known to the accused to have been so stolen. Broder pleaded guilty, and when he was afterwards called as a witness for the Government the objection was made that he was not competent to testify for the reason that, as was admitted by the Government, he had theretofore pleaded guilty to the crime of forgery in the second degree, in the Court of General Sessions, in the County and State of New York, had been sentenced to imprisonment, and had served his sentence. The objection was overruled and Broder was permitted to testify. This ruling was assigned as error in the Circuit Court of Appeals, where it was affirmed, and it is now assigned as error in this court. . . .

For the validity of the claim that Broder was disqualified as a witness by his sentence for the crime of forgery, the plaintiffs in error rely upon *United States v. Reid*, 12 How. 361, decided in 1852. In that case it was held that the competency of witnesses in criminal trials in United States courts must be determined by the rules of evidence which were in force in the respective States when the Judiciary Act of 1789 was passed, and the argument in this case is, that by the common law as it was administered in New York in 1789 a person found guilty of forgery and sentenced was thereby rendered incompetent as a witness until pardoned, and that, therefore, the objection to Broder should have been sustained.

While the decision in *United States v. Reid*, has not been specifically overruled, its authority must be regarded as seriously shaken by the decisions in *Logan v. United States*, 144 U.S. 263–301, and in *Benson v. United States*, 146 U.S. 325.

The Benson Case differed from the Reid Case only in that in the former the witness whose competency was objected to was called by the Government while in the latter he was called by the defendant. The testimony of the witness was admitted in the one case but it was rejected in the other, and both judgments were affirmed by this court — however forty years had intervened between the two trials. . . . In the almost twenty years which have elapsed since the decision of the Benson Case, the disposition of courts and of legislative bodies to remove disabilities from witnesses has continued, as that decision shows it had been going forward before, under dominance of the conviction of our time that the truth is more likely to be arrived at by hearing the testimony of all persons of competent understanding who may seem to have knowledge of the facts involved in a case, leaving the credit and weight of such testimony to be determined by the jury or by the court, rather than by rejecting witnesses as incompetent, with the result that this principle has come to be widely, almost universally, accepted in this country and in Great Britain.

Since the decision in the Benson Case we have significant evidence of the trend of congressional opinion upon this subject in the removal of the disability of witnesses convicted of perjury, Rev. Stats., §5392, by the enactment of the Federal Criminal Code in 1909 with this provision omitted and §5392 repealed. This is significant, because the disability to testify, of persons convicted of perjury, survived in some jurisdictions much longer than many of the other common-law disabilities, for the reason that the offense concerns directly the giving of testimony in a court of justice, and conviction of it was accepted as showing a greater disregard for the truth than it was thought should be implied from a conviction of other crime.

Satisfied as we are that the legislation and the very great weight of judicial authority which have developed in support of this modern rule, especially as applied to the competency of witnesses convicted of crime, proceed upon sound principle, we conclude that the dead hand of the common-law rule of 1789 should no longer be applied to such cases as we have here, and that the ruling of the lower courts on this first claim of error should be approved. . . .

It results that the judgments of the Circuit Court of Appeals must be Affirmed.

[Justices Van Devanter and McReynolds dissented.]

ADVISORY COMMITTEE NOTE TO F.R.E. 601

This general ground-clearing eliminates all grounds of incompetency not specifically recognized in the succeeding rules of this Article. Included among the grounds thus abolished are religious belief, conviction of crime, and connection with the litigation as a party or interested person or spouse of a party or interested person. With the exception of the so-called Dead Man's Acts, American jurisdictions generally have ceased to recognize these grounds.

The Dead Man's Acts are surviving traces of the common law disqualification of parties and interested persons. They exist in variety too great to convey conviction of their wisdom and effectiveness. These rules contain no provision of this kind. . . .

No mental or moral qualifications for testifying as a witness are specified. Standards of mental capacity have proved elusive in actual application. A leading commentator observes that few witnesses are disqualified on that ground. Weihofen, Testimonial Competence and Credibility, 34 Geo. Wash. L. Rev. 53 (1965). Discretion is regularly exercised in favor of allowing the testimony. A witness wholly without capacity is difficult to imagine. The question is one particularly suited to the jury as one of weight and credibility, subject to judicial authority to review the sufficiency of the evidence. 2 Wigmore §§501, 509. Standards of moral qualification in practice consist essentially of evaluating a person's truthfulness in terms of his own answers about it. Their principal utility is in affording an opportunity on voir dire examination to impress upon the witness his moral duty. This result may, however, be accomplished more directly, and without haggling in terms of legal standards, by the manner of administering the oath or affirmation under Rule 603.

Admissibility of religious belief as a ground of impeachment is treated in Rule 610. Conviction of crime as a ground of impeachment is the subject of Rule 609. Marital relationship is the basis for privilege under Rule 505. Interest in the outcome of litigation and mental capacity are, of course, highly relevant to credibility and require no special treatment to render them admissible along with other matters bearing upon the perception, memory, and narration of witnesses.

UNITED STATES v. LIGHTLY

677 F.2d 1027 (4th Cir. 1982)

ERVIN, Circuit Judge.

On December 19, 1979, Terrance McKinley, an inmate at Lorton Reformatory in northern Virginia, sustained serious stab wounds from an assault in his cell. Two of McKinley's fellow inmates, Randy Lightly and Clifton McDuffie, were investigated, but only Lightly was formally charged. McDuffie was not indicted by the grand jury because a court appointed psychiatrist found him incompetent to stand trial and criminally insane at the time of the offense. He is presently confined in a mental hospital.

On May 22, 1980, Lightly was convicted of assault with intent to commit murder, and sentenced to ten years' imprisonment to run consecutively with the sentence he already was serving. . . . The government's case included testimony from the victim, Terrance McKinley, inmates Harvey Boyd and Robert Thomas, and McKinley's treating physician, Dr. Lance Weaver, which indicated that McDuffie and Lightly cornered McKinley in his cell and repeatedly stabbed him with half pairs of scissors. Lightly received a severe cut on his hand in the assault. Lightly's account of the stabbing was that he was walking along cell block three when he saw McDuffie and McKinley fighting in McKinley's cell. Lightly said he went into the cell to stop the fight and while he was pulling McDuffie off of McKinley, McDuffie turned around and cut him. His testimony was corroborated by three other inmates.

The defense also attempted to have McDuffie testify. McDuffie would have testified that only he and not Lightly had assaulted McKinley. The court ruled McDuffie incompetent to testify because he had been found to be criminally insane and incompetent to stand trial, and was subject to halluci-nations.[1] We believe this was error and that Lightly is entitled to a new trial.

Every witness is presumed competent to testify, Fed. R. Evid. 601, unless it can be shown that the witness does not have personal knowledge of the matters about which he is to testify, that he does not have the capacity to recall, or that he does not understand the duty to testify truthfully. This rule applies to persons considered to be insane to the same extent that it applies to other persons. *United States v. Lopez*, 611 F.2d 44 (4th Cir. 1979); *Shuler v. Wainwright*, 491 F.2d 1213, 1223 (5th Cir. 1974). In this case, the testi-mony of McDuffie's treating physician indicated that McDuffie had a sufficient memory, that he understood the oath, and that he could communicate what he saw. The district judge chose not to conduct an in camera examination of McDuffie. On this record, it was clearly improper for the court to disqualify McDuffie from testifying. . . .

McDuffie's potential testimony would have substantially corroborated Lightly's testimony. His disqualification from testifying, therefore, cannot be considered harmless error. In finding Lightly entitled to a new trial on this ground, we decline to rule on the other issues he raised in this appeal. Reversed and Remanded.

B. PERSONAL KNOWLEDGE

Almost all restrictions on competence have now been eliminated. But not all. Among the few restrictions that remain is the rule requiring that a witness testify from personal knowledge. Even this rule is relaxed for witnesses testi-fying as experts — a topic taken up in the next chapter. For all other testifying witnesses, though, the personal knowledge requirement is yet another mani-festation of our system's faith in *viva voce* evidence. It works in conjunction with the hearsay rule to limit trial testimony, generally, to firsthand accounts.

Without the personal knowledge requirement for live testimony, the hearsay rule could be easily evaded. Instead of testifying, "I heard that Oliver was dealing cocaine out of his apartment," a witness could just say, "Oliver was dealing cocaine out of his apartment" — thereby avoiding reference to any out-of-court statements. Conversely, the personal knowledge requirement could do little work without the hearsay rule. A witness limited to recount-ing his or her firsthand experience could still testify, "Two months ago, here is what happened to me: I was told by some mutual friends that Oliver was dealing cocaine out of his apartment."

As you may recall from the chapter on hearsay, the personal knowledge requirement also applies to declarants whose out-of-court assertions are admitted under an exception to the rule against hearsay. While almost none of the hearsay exceptions in Rules 803 and 804 mention a personal knowl-edge requirement, courts have universally recognized that such a requirement

---

1. McDuffie believed that "Star Child" told him to kill McKinley because McKinley and Hodge, who apparently was a prison administrator, were going to kill him.

is implicit. The only exception is for statements of a party opponent, which are admissible for their truth regardless of whether the declarant had personal knowledge of what he or she is asserting. In that case, the reasoning goes, the party has the ability to take the witness stand and explain to the jury why the statement is not worthy of belief.

One problem raised by the personal knowledge requirement, explored in the materials below, is that deciding whether a witness has personal knowledge very often involves deciding whether to *believe* the witness. Suppose a witness claims to have seen the defendant fleeing the bank after it was robbed, but defense counsel suggests on cross-examination that the witness was too far away to see clearly — or, worse, was nowhere near the bank the day it was robbed. Does the judge need to resolve this matter in order to determine whether the witness is competent to testify? If the answer were yes, judges would in essence wind up deciding whether witnesses should be believed, the job our system generally entrusts to juries. So the personal knowledge of a witness is assessed under a sufficiency standard similar to that used to determine conditional relevance under Rule 104(b).

[F.R.E. 602; C.E.C. §702]

ADVISORY COMMITTEE NOTE TO F.R.E. 602

"... [T]he rule requiring that a witness who testifies to a fact which can be perceived by the senses must have had an opportunity to observe, and must have actually observed the fact" is a "most pervasive manifestation" of the common law insistence upon "the most reliable sources of information." McCormick §10, p. 19. These foundation requirements may, of course, be furnished by the testimony of the witness himself; hence personal knowledge is not an absolute but may consist of what the witness thinks he knows from personal perception. 2 Wigmore §650. It will be observed that the rule is in fact a specialized application of the provisions of Rule 104(b) on conditional relevancy.

This rule does not govern the situation of a witness who testifies to a hearsay statement as such, if he has personal knowledge of the making of the statement. Rules 801 and 805 would be applicable. This rule would, however, prevent him from testifying to the subject matter of the hearsay statement, as he has no personal knowledge of it.

The reference to Rule 703 is designed to avoid any question of conflict between the present rule and the provisions of that rule allowing an expert to express opinions based on facts of which he does not have personal knowledge.

UNITED STATES v. HICKEY

917 F.2d 901 (6th Cir. 1990)

MILBURN, Circuit Judge.

This case involves an appeal by Quinn Hickey from his jury conviction in a drug conspiracy case.... Hickey, along with eighteen co-defendants, was charged with numerous counts of conspiracy to distribute cocaine in violation of 21 U.S.C. §§841(a)(1) & 846, and use of a communication facility to facilitate a crime in violation of 21 U.S.C. §843(b). A jury trial commenced on September 8, 1988, and several of Hickey's co-defendants, including Bayron Moreno, were found guilty. However, the jury was unable to reach a verdict as to Hickey, and the court declared a mistrial as to him. Hickey was retried and found guilty on one of the conspiracy charges and two of the communications charges.

An investigation of drug trafficking in the Saginaw, Michigan, area soon centered on Jack Ventimiglia as his residence appeared to be the main terminal for considerable cocaine distribution. Ventimiglia was arrested and, pursuant to a plea agreement, testified for the government against several of his associates including Quinn Hickey.

Ventimiglia is a self-confessed cocaine addict, and his testimony at the trial was characterized by the district court as the words of a "loose cannon." In a lengthy cross-examination, defense counsel was able to expose Ventimiglia's cocaine addiction, his claimed lack of memory, his uncertainty as to details, and several inconsistencies in his testimony. In ruling on the defendant's motion for a judgment of acquittal, the district court stated that Ventimiglia's testimony alone would not support a guilty verdict; however, the district court denied the motion because the government had introduced, apart from Ventimiglia's testimony, "substantial circumstantial evidence that would tend to support the fact [that] Hickey was, in part, a seller."

. . . Hickey argues that the district court committed reversible error in allowing the jury to hear and consider the testimony of Ventimiglia. . . . After pointing out Ventimiglia's drug addiction and inconsistencies in Ventimiglia's testimony, Hickey argues that there was a "total lack of sufficient or supportive evidence to substantiate the findings that these witnesses had personal knowledge of the critical events in this prosecution upon which to base their testimony." This is not the first case in which we have faced an argument that the testimony of Jack Ventimiglia should be excluded. In *United States v. Moreno*, 899 F.2d 465 (6th Cir. 1990), we rejected an argument by Hickey's co-defendant in the first trial that inconsistencies in Ventimiglia's testimony, in light of his admitted drug addiction, showed that he was incompetent to testify.

In *Moreno* we relied upon *United States v. Ramirez*, 871 F.2d 582 (6th Cir.), *cert. denied*, 493 U.S. 841 (1989), a case which recognized that in some cases the ability of a witness might be so impaired that he cannot satisfy the personal knowledge requirement of Federal Rule of Evidence 602. . . . What we did not mention in *Ramirez* was the fact that the threshold of Rule 602 is low.

Rule 602 provides, in relevant part, that "[a] witness may not testify to a matter unless evidence is introduced sufficient to support a finding that the witness has personal knowledge of the matter." Testimony should not be excluded for lack of personal knowledge unless no reasonable juror could believe that the witness had the ability and opportunity to perceive the event that he testifies about. Weinstein, *Weinstein's Evidence* §602[02], at 602-8 to -11 (1988). . . . Despite the fact that Ventimiglia's testimony may have been, in large part, unbelievable to some and in spite of the possibility that his perception was sometimes impaired, a reasonable or rational juror could believe that Ventimiglia and the other prosecution witnesses perceived the course of events to which they testified. Accordingly, we hold that the district court did not abuse its discretion in permitting Ventimiglia's testimony or the testimony of the other prosecution witnesses. . . . [T]he judgment of conviction is Affirmed. . . .

C. Oath or Affirmation

Aside from personal knowledge, the only other general prerequisite for competence is that the witness swear an oath to tell the truth — or make some similar commitment to providing honest testimony. Within limits, courts are flexible about the precise form of the commitment.

One lingering controversy concerns whether the requirement that every witness take an oath or its equivalent includes a requirement that the witness understand and appreciate the oath. More specifically, there is controversy regarding whether children should be allowed to testify without some inquiry to determine whether they understand and appreciate what it means to promise to tell the truth.

Another question worth keeping in mind as you read the materials below: Given the general liberalization of rules of competence, and given the difficulties encountered in applying the oath requirement, why is that requirement retained at all?

[F.R.E. 603; C.E.C. §§701, 710]

UNITED STATES v. WARD

989 F.2d 1015 (9th Cir. 1993)

FLETCHER, Circuit Judge.

Wallace Ward appeals his conviction of three counts of attempt to evade income tax in violation of 26 U.S.C. §7201 and three counts of failure to file income taxes in violation of 26 U.S.C. §7203. . . . Ward is the president of I & O Publishing Company, a mail-order house and publisher located in Boulder City, Nevada. The prosecution presented evidence at trial that despite having substantial income, neither I & O nor Ward filed tax returns or paid income taxes for the years 1983, 1984 and 1985.

On March 29, 1990 a grand jury indicted Ward on three counts each of tax evasion and failure to file income tax returns. Ward chose to represent himself at trial. On July 9, 1990, Ward filed a "Motion to Challenge the Oath," which proposed an alternative oath that replaced the word "truth" with the phrase "fully integrated Honesty." The oath would read, "Do you affirm to speak with fully integrated Honesty, only with fully integrated Honesty and nothing but fully integrated Honesty?" For reasons we will not attempt to explain,

Ward believes that honesty is superior to truth. Magistrate Lawrence R. Leavitt ruled on August 2, 1990 that "the oath or affirmation which has been administered in courts of law throughout the United States to millions of witnesses for hundreds of years should not be required to give way to the defendant's idiosyncratic distinctions between truth and honesty." The district court overruled Ward's objections to the magistrate's order on August 28, 1990, and again on October 8, 1990. Ward pursued an interlocutory appeal on the issue, which was dismissed for lack of jurisdiction.

A three-day trial commenced on February 11, 1991. Ward made a lengthy opening statement and actively cross-examined government witnesses. At a sidebar during the second day of trial, Ward offered to take both the standard oath and his oath. The prosecutor was amenable to the compromise, but the district court refused to allow it. "This is an oath that has been used for a very long time," the district court said, "And I'm not going to establish a precedent where someone can come in and require the court to address that matter differently." At the close of the government's case on the third day of trial, Ward asked once again to testify under his oath. The judge again refused, saying "[T]he oath has been used for a very long time. . . . That's the oath that will be administered." Ward did not testify and presented no witnesses. The jury convicted Ward of all counts after an hour's deliberation.

. . . The court's interest in administering its precise form of oath must yield to Ward's First Amendment rights. To begin with, there is no constitutionally or statutorily required form of oath. Federal Rule of Evidence 603 requires only that a witness "declare that the witness will testify truthfully, by oath or affirmation administered in a form calculated to awaken the witness' conscience and impress the witness' mind with the duty to do so." The advisory committee notes to Rule 603 explain that "the rule is designed to afford the flexibility required in dealing with religious adults, atheists, conscientious objectors, mental defectives, and children. Affirmation is simply a solemn undertaking to tell the truth; no special verbal formula is required."

. . . Our cases have routinely held that it is reversible error for a district court to prevent a party from testifying solely on the basis of the party's religiously-based objections to the form of the oath. In *Gordon v. State of Idaho*, 778 F.2d 1397 (9th Cir. 1985), a plaintiff in a §1983 action professed religious objections to oath or affirmation, offering instead to say "I understand that I must tell the truth. I agree to testify under penalty of perjury." Using First Amendment analysis requiring that government use the "least restrictive means" to its ends when free exercise [of religion] is at stake, we held that it was an abuse of discretion for the district court to insist upon the standard oath and to dismiss plaintiff's case for failure to present evidence. Criminal trials additionally implicate the defendant's Fifth Amendment right to testify. . . . [*See, e.g.,*] *Moore v. United States*, 348 U.S. 966 (1955) (per curiam) (criminal defendant with religious objections to the word "solemnly" in the oath must be allowed to testify).

. . . While oaths including the familiar "truth, whole truth, and nothing but the truth" formulation date back at least to the seventeenth century, see 6 Wigmore, Evidence §1818(2) (Chadbourne rev. 1976), the principle that the form of the oath must be crafted in a way that is meaningful to the witness also predates our constitution. In *Omichund v. Barker*, 1 Atk. 22, 45 (1744),

Lord Chief Judge Willes wrote, "It would be absurd for [a non-Christian witness] to swear according to the Christian oath, which he does not believe; and therefore, out of necessity, he must be allowed to swear according to his own notion of an oath." See also *Atcheson v. Everitt*, 1 Cowp. 382, 389 (1776) (Mansfield, L.C.J.) ("[A]s the purpose of [the oath] is to bind his conscience, every man of every religion should be bound by that form which he himself thinks will bind his own conscience most").

This case has an odd twist in that the defendant offered to take the traditional "truth" oath, but only if he were permitted to also take his "fully integrated honesty" oath. In Ward's view, as best we can state it, only his oath expressed a commitment to the abstract purity of absolute "fully integrated honesty" that must be extracted from anyone before that person's word can be relied upon. The standard "truth" oath was so much surplusage — distasteful, wrong, but not necessarily a mortal sin to take.

His own oath superimposed on the traditional one would have taken nothing away from the commitment to tell the truth under penalties of perjury and, indeed, in the defendant's mind imposed upon him a higher duty. Under these circumstances the district court clearly abused its discretion in refusing the oath and preventing the defendant's testimony. We do not have a case where the witness offers to swear only to a cleverly worded oath that creates loopholes for falsehood or attempts to create a safe harbor for perjury as in *United States v. Fowler*, 605 F.2d 181, 185 (5th Cir. 1979), *cert. denied*, 445 U.S. 950 (1980), where the court properly refused testimony from a defendant who would not say so much as "I state that I will tell the truth in my testimony," and was willing to say only "I am a truthful man" or "I would not tell a lie to stay out of jail." Ward's "attempt[] to express a moral or ethical sense of right and wrong," [*Welsh v. United States*, 398 U.S. 333, 340 (1970)], coupled with the de rigueur fervor, brings his beliefs squarely within those safeguarded by the free exercise clause.

Ward also seeks to vindicate what he perceives to be his right to have all his witnesses sworn to his oath. This he cannot do. Ward has no standing to assert the First or Fifth Amendment rights of others. Ward also alleges numerous trial errors which we need not consider in light of our grant of a new trial.

Reversed and Remanded.

UNITED STATES v. ALLEN J.

127 F.3d 1292 (10th Cir. 1997)

BRORBY, Circuit Judge.

Allen J. appeals his adjudication of juvenile delinquency in the United States District Court for the District of New Mexico. In a non-jury trial held on September 11, 12, and 16, 1996, the district court adjudged Allen J. a juvenile delinquent pursuant to the Federal Juvenile Delinquency Act, 18 U.S.C. §5031, et seq., after finding he had committed Aggravated Sexual Abuse in violation of 18 U.S.C. §§2241(a), and 2246(2)(A) by knowingly using force to engage in a sex act with a juvenile. The case was in federal court because both Allen J. and the victim are Indians and because the incident took place within the Navajo Nation Indian Reservation in New Mexico. See 18 U.S.C. §3231. The district court placed Allen J. on probation until he reaches the age of twenty-one and required, among other things, completion of sex offender and substance abuse treatment at a youth facility.... The only issue Allen J. raises on appeal is whether the trial court erred in finding the victim competent to testify.

... Allen J. states the test for determining the competency of a child witness is found in *United States v. Spoonhunter*, 476 F.2d 1050 (10th Cir. 1973). In *Spoonhunter*, this Circuit applied the test for determining the competency of a child witness established by the Supreme Court in *Wheeler v. United States*, 159 U.S. 523 (1895). In that case, the Court held competency "depends on the capacity and intelligence of the child, [the child's] appreciation of the difference between truth and falsehood, as well as of [the child's] duty to tell the former." This determination was to be left primarily in the hands of the trial courts. The Court, however, warned trial courts to take care when excluding witnesses, in order to avoid "staying the hand of justice."

Both *Wheeler* and *Spoonhunter*, however, pre-date the enactment of Fed. R. Evid. 601 and 18 U.S.C. §3509.[2] For this reason, the *Wheeler* test this court has relied upon for years no longer completely states the applicable standard for determining the competency of a child witness, although it may inform any examinations taking place pursuant to 18 U.S.C. §3509(c) and may help explain the type of evidence necessary to demonstrate a compelling reason for such an examination.

... We agree with the district court's conclusion that the evidence offered by Allen J.... did not constitute a "compelling reason" to hold a §3509(c) competency examination. To counter the presumption favoring competency, Allen

---

2. Rule 601 was enacted in 1975, and §3509 was enacted in 1990. [18 U.S.C. §3509(c) reads in substance as follows: "(1) Nothing in this subsection shall be construed to abrogate rule 601 of the Federal Rules of Evidence. (2) A child is presumed to be competent. (3) A competency examination regarding a child witness may be conducted by the court only upon written motion and offer of proof of incompetency by a party. (4) A competency examination regarding a child may be conducted only if the court determines, on the record, that compelling reasons exist. A child's age alone is not a compelling reason. (5) The only persons who may be permitted to be present at a competency examination are the judge; the attorney for the Government; the attorney for the defendant; a court reporter; and persons whose presence, in the opinion of the court, is necessary to the welfare and wellbeing of the child, including the child's attorney, guardian ad litem, or adult attendant. (6) A competency examination regarding a child witness shall be conducted out of the sight and hearing of a jury. (7) Examination of a child related to competency shall normally be conducted by the court on the basis of questions submitted by the attorney for the Government and the attorney for the defendant including a party acting as an attorney pro se. The court may permit an attorney but not a party acting as an attorney pro se to examine a child directly on competency if the court is satisfied that the child will not suffer emotional trauma as a result of the examination. (8) The questions asked at the competency examination of a child shall be appropriate to the age and developmental level of the child, shall not be related to the issues at trial, and shall focus on determining the child's ability to understand and answer simple questions. (9) Psychological and psychiatric examinations to assess the competency of a child witness shall not be ordered without a showing of compelling need." For purposes of the statute, the term "child" is defined to include any person under the age of 18 "who is or is alleged to be" either "a victim of a crime of physical abuse, sexual abuse, or exploitation" or "a witness to a crime committed against another person." 18 U.S.C. §3509(a)(2)(A).]

J. asserted the victim suffers mild mental retardation, possibly due to Fetal Alcohol Syndrome, which caused her to repeat first grade. As the district court correctly pointed out, even if the victim only had the mental development of a much younger child, she would still be competent to testify. The evidence offered by Allen J. did not begin to show the victim had such severe problems she could not "understand and answer simple questions" 18 U.S.C. §3509(c)(8), or "underst[and] the difference between truth and falsehood, and the consequences of falsehood, and what was required by the oath," *Spoonhunter*, 476 F.2d at 1054.

When the victim was called to testify, the court asked her a series of questions seeking to confirm she understood the importance of the oath. These questions included: "Do you understand what it is to tell the truth?" and "Do you know the difference between the truth and a lie?" The victim did not respond to the judge's questioning. (The court then asked the prosecutor to try questioning the witness. The prosecutor began with simple questions ("[W]hat is your last name?", "How old are you?", and "Where do you live?"), which the victim answered. After about thirty questions along these lines, almost all of which the victim was able to answer correctly, the prosecutor shifted to questions relating to the difference between the truth and lies. Among other questions, the prosecutor asked the victim if she understood she had promised to tell the truth in court, to which the victim responded affirmatively. After this series of questions, which established the victim knew the difference between a truth and a lie, knew she was to tell the truth in court, and knew she would be punished if she told a lie, the court directed the prosecutor to proceed to the heart of her case.)[3] Defense counsel objected repeatedly throughout this process and throughout the remainder of the victim's testimony.

Allen J. essentially bases his appeal on several instances in the victim's testimony where she had difficulty answering questions. The victim did not respond to the trial judge's questioning. She gave wrong answers to some of counsel's questions (e.g., she said she was eleven, when she was thirteen), and she gave nonsensical answers to others (e.g., she answered "true" to the question "is it good or bad to tell a lie?"). In addition, she apparently paused for long periods of time before answering some questions.

Any inconsistencies in the victim's story or problems with her testimony, however, raise questions of credibility, not competence. . . . The credibility of a witness is a question to be determined by the trier of fact, not this court. . . . We find nothing in the record demonstrating the district court abused its discretion in permitting the victim in this case to testify. The decision of the district court is, therefore, Affirmed.

3. This initial questioning of the victim, during which the court satisfied itself the victim understood the need to be truthful in her statements, was not a competency examination pursuant to 18 U.S.C. §3509(c). Fed. R. Evid. 603 requires every witness to declare he or she will testify truthfully. In addition to confirming for the court the victim understood the oath, the initial questioning of the victim also served "to awaken the witness' conscience and impress the witness' mind with the duty to [testify truthfully]," as required by Rule 603. The type of questions asked by the prosecutor along this line, and the answers given by the victim, were comparable to examinations approved in *Spoonhunter*, 476 F.2d at 1054, and *Wheeler*, 159 U.S. at 524. For this reason, to the extent Allen J.'s argument may be construed to be an appeal based on Rule 603, we find the district court did not err and fully complied with the requirements of Rule 603.

VICTOR GOLD, DO THE FEDERAL RULES OF
EVIDENCE MATTER?

25 Loy. L.A. L. Rev. 909 (1992)

Some authorities have resurrected common law mental and moral competency requirements in the guise of interpreting Rules 602 and 603. Some courts read Rule 602 as imposing a mental capacity requirement, suggesting that witnesses lack personal knowledge unless they can comprehend their observations to an extent that makes their testimony trustworthy. Similarly, many courts establish a moral capacity requirement by concluding that the oath or affirmation requirement of Rule 603 cannot be satisfied unless the witness appreciates the nature of truth and the duty to tell the truth.

On its face, Rule 602 does not justify excluding testimony on the ground that a witness lacks the mental capacity to make testimony trustworthy. The Rule requires no more than that the trier of fact find there is evidence "sufficient to support a finding" that the witness has personal knowledge. This standard should be satisfied if a reasonable juror or judge could believe that the witness perceived the matters testified to. Based on the Rule's standard, it is up to the jury, not the judge, to decide if the witness is trustworthy. Rule 603 likewise imposes no moral capacity requirement. The Rule requires only that the witness perform the mechanical act of taking an oath or affirmation in a form calculated to awaken the witness's conscience and impress his or her mind with the legal duty to tell the truth. Nothing in the Rule suggests that the witness must in fact have his or her conscience awakened and mind so impressed. A member of the Advisory Committee reports that the Committee specifically considered and rejected imposition of any standard of moral qualification. Further, in his testimony before Congress in support of Rule 601, the Reporter for the Federal Rules made the point that the very presence of the oath or affirmation requirement in Rule 603 diminishes the need for competency evaluations of the sort conducted at common law. It is ironic then that Rule 603 has been turned into a vehicle for undermining Rule 601's general statement that every witness is competent.

PROBLEMS

8.1. The key prosecution witness in a criminal trial admits on cross-examination that he has been surreptitiously consuming opium throughout his testimony. The defense attorney asks the judge to strike the witness's testimony on grounds of competence. Should the request be granted?

8.2. The defendant in a civil case wishes to testify. He swears to tell "the truth and nothing but the truth," but will not swear or promise to tell "the whole truth." He explains that "no one ever knows the whole truth about anything." Defense counsel objects to the plaintiff's testimony on grounds of competence. How should the judge rule?

8.3. The defendant in an automobile accident case calls the plaintiff's five-year-old son, who was four at the time of the accident. The plaintiff claims her son is incompetent to testify, because his memory of the accident is too vague, because testifying about it would traumatize him, and because he does not understand what it means to swear or to promise to tell the truth. How should the judge respond?

D.   DEAD MAN STATUTES

Many states have so-called "dead man statutes," which bar parties to a lawsuit from testifying about certain transactions or incidents, if the other participant is now dead. The idea is to stop a litigant from taking advantage of the fact that the other person is no longer around to object. Dead man statutes are remnants of the much broader disqualification that used to apply to all parties, and they are unpopular with scholars, who tend to view them as relics of an older, less enlightened time. The drafters of the Federal Rules of Evidence chose not to include any such provision, but Congress added the second sentence of Rule 601 specifically to ensure that state dead man statutes would operate in any federal civil case governed by state substantive law.

REPORT OF THE HOUSE JUDICIARY COMMITTEE

H.R. Rep. No. 93-650 (1974)

Rule 601 as submitted to the Congress provided that "Every person is competent to be a witness except as otherwise provided in these rules." One effect of the Rule as proposed would have been to abolish age, mental capacity, and other grounds recognized in some State jurisdictions as making a person incompetent as a witness. The greatest controversy centered around the Rule's rendering inapplicable in the federal courts the so-called Dead Man's Statutes which exist in some States. Acknowledging that there is substantial disagreement as to the merit of Dead Man's Statutes, the Committee nevertheless believed that where such statutes have been enacted they represent State policy which should not be overturned in the absence of a compelling federal interest. The Committee therefore amended the Rule to make competency in civil actions determinable in accordance with State law with respect to elements of claims or defenses as to which State law supplies the rule of decision....

McCORMICK ON EVIDENCE

§65, at 1:432-36 (Kenneth S. Broun ed., 7th ed. 2013)

By far the most drastic common law incompetency rule was the doctrine excluding testimony by parties to the lawsuit and all persons having a direct pecuniary or proprietary interest in the outcome. In effect, this rule both imposed a disability on the party to testify in his own behalf and granted him a privilege not to be called as a witness against himself by the adversary. The disability had the specious justification of preventing self-interested perjury. The privilege lacked even that dubious rationale. It is almost unbelievable that the rule continued in force in England until the middle of the 19th century — and in this country for a few decades longer. In England, the reform was sweeping, and no shred of disqualification remains in civil cases.

In this country, however, the reformers were forced to accept a compromise. An objection was raised with respect to controversies over consensual transactions, such as contracts, or other events such as traffic accidents where one party died but the other survived. The thrust of the objection was that fraud might result if the surviving parties or interested persons could testify about the transaction or the event. The survivor could still testify although death had sealed the adverse party's lips. . . . Accordingly, statutes in numerous states still provide that the common law disqualification of parties and interested persons is abolished with a single exception. The exception was that they remain disqualified to testify concerning a transaction or communication with a person since deceased in a suit prosecuted or defended by the decedent's executor or administrator. . . . The practical consequence of these statutes comes into play when a survivor has rendered services, furnished goods, or lent money to a person whom he trusted without an independent, corroborating witness or admissible written evidence. The survivor is helpless if the other dies and the representative of his estate declines to pay. The survivor's mouth may even be closed in an action arising from a fatal automobile collision, or a suit on a note or account which the survivor paid in cash without obtaining a receipt. . . .

[M]ost commentators agree that the expedient of refusing to listen to the survivor is, in Bentham's words, "blind and brainless." In seeking to avoid injustice to one side, the statutory drafters ignored the equal possibility of creating injustice to the other. The survivor's temptation to fabricate a claim or defense is evident enough — so obvious indeed that any jury should realize that his story must be evaluated cautiously. In case of fraud, a searching cross-examination will often reveal discrepancies in the "tangled web" of deception. In any event, the survivor's disqualification is more likely to disadvantage the honest than the dishonest survivor. A litigant who would resort to perjury will hardly hesitate at suborning a third person, who would not be disqualified, to swear to the false story.

Legislators and courts are gradually coming to see the stupidity of the traditional survivors' evidence acts, and adopting liberalizing changes. A few states provide that the survivor may testify, but that his testimony is legally insufficient to support a judgment unless the testimony is corroborated by other evidence. Others authorize the trial judge to permit the survivor to testify when it appears that his testimony is necessary to prevent injustice. Both of these solutions have evident drawbacks which are avoided by a third type of statute. The third kind of statutory scheme sweeps away the disqualification entirely and allows the survivor to testify without restriction. However, the scheme evenhandedly minimizes the danger of injustice to the decedent's estate by admitting any relevant writings or oral statements by the decedent, both of which would ordinarily be excluded as hearsay.

ALABAMA CODE §12-21-163

In civil actions and proceedings, there must be no exclusion of any witness because he is a party or interested in the issue tried, except that no person having a pecuniary interest in the result of the action or proceeding shall be allowed to testify against the party to whom his interest is opposed as to any transaction with, or statement by, the deceased person whose estate is interested in the result of the action or proceeding or when such deceased person, at the time of such transaction or statement, acted in any representative or fiduciary relation whatsoever to the party against whom such testimony is sought to be introduced, unless called to testify thereto by the party to whom such interest is opposed or unless the testimony of such deceased person in relation to such transaction or statement is introduced in evidence by the party whose interest is opposed to that of the witness or has been taken and is on file in the case. No person who is an incompetent witness under this section shall make himself competent by transferring his interest to another.

CALIFORNIA EVIDENCE CODE §1261

(a) Evidence of a statement is not made inadmissible by the hearsay rule when offered in an action upon a claim or demand against the estate of the declarant if the statement was made upon the personal knowledge of the declarant at a time when the matter had been recently perceived by him and while his recollection was clear.

(b) Evidence of a statement is inadmissible under this section if the statement was made under circumstances such as to indicate its lack of trustworthiness.

E. COMPETENCE AND THE CONSTITUTION

The old, restrictive rules of competence are now greatly disfavored. The modern attitude finds expression not just in the widespread abandonment of those rules, but also in decisions finding lingering restrictions on competence constitutionally suspect when applied to witnesses called by a criminal defendant, and especially suspect when applied to testimony from the criminal defendant himself or herself.

ROCK v. ARKANSAS

483 U.S. 44 (1987)

Justice BLACKMUN delivered the opinion of the Court.

The issue presented in this case is whether Arkansas' evidentiary rule prohibiting the admission of hypnotically refreshed testimony violated petitioner's constitutional right to testify on her own behalf as a defendant in a criminal case.

Petitioner Vickie Lorene Rock was charged with manslaughter in the death of her husband, Frank Rock, on July 2, 1983. . . . When police arrived on the scene they found Frank on the floor with a bullet wound in his chest. . . . According to the testimony of one of the investigating officers, petitioner told him that "she stood up to leave the room and [her husband] grabbed her by the throat and choked her and threw her against the wall and . . . at that time she walked over and picked up the weapon and pointed it toward the floor and he hit her again and she shot him."

Because petitioner could not remember the precise details of the shooting, her attorney suggested that she submit to hypnosis in order to refresh her memory. Petitioner was hypnotized twice by Doctor Bettye Back, a licensed neuropsychologist with training in the field of hypnosis. Doctor Back interviewed petitioner for an hour prior to the first hypnosis session, taking notes on petitioner's general history and her recollections of the shooting. Both hypnosis sessions were recorded on tape. Petitioner did not relate any new information during either of the sessions, but, after the hypnosis, she was able to remember that at the time of the incident she had her thumb on the hammer of the gun, but had not held her finger on the trigger. She also recalled that the gun had discharged when her husband grabbed her arm during the scuffle. As a result of the details that petitioner was able to remember about the shooting, her counsel arranged for a gun expert to examine the handgun. . . . That inspection revealed that the gun was defective and prone to fire, when hit or dropped, without the trigger's being pulled.

When the prosecutor learned of the hypnosis sessions, he filed a motion to exclude petitioner's testimony. The trial judge held a pretrial hearing on the motion and concluded that no hypnotically refreshed testimony would be admitted. The court issued an order limiting petitioner's testimony to "matters remembered and stated to the examiner prior to being placed under hypnosis." At trial, petitioner introduced testimony by the gun expert, but the court limited petitioner's own description of the events on the day of the shooting to a reiteration of the sketchy information in Doctor Back's notes. The jury convicted petitioner on the manslaughter charge and she was sentenced to 10 years' imprisonment and a $10,000 fine.

On appeal, the Supreme Court of Arkansas rejected petitioner's claim that the limitations on her testimony violated her right to present her defense. The court concluded that "the dangers of admitting this kind of testimony outweigh whatever probative value it may have," and decided to follow the approach of States that have held hypnotically refreshed testimony of witnesses inadmissible *per se*. . . .

At this point in the development of our adversary system, it cannot be doubted that a defendant in a criminal case has the right to take the witness stand and to testify in his or her own defense. This, of course, is a change from the historic common-law view, which was that all parties to litigation, including criminal defendants, were disqualified from testifying because of their interest in the outcome of the trial. The principal rationale for this rule was the possible untrustworthiness of a party's testimony. Under the common law, the practice did develop of permitting criminal defendants to tell their side of the story, but they were limited to making an unsworn statement that could not be elicited through direct examination by counsel and was not subject to cross-examination.

[B]y the end of the second half of the 19th century, all States except Georgia had enacted statutes that declared criminal defendants competent to testify. Congress enacted a general competency statute in the Act of Mar. 16, 1878, and similar developments followed in other common-law countries. Thus, more than 25 years ago this Court was able to state:

> "In sum, decades ago the considered consensus of the English-speaking world came to be that there was no rational justification for prohibiting the sworn testimony of the accused, who above all others may be in a position to meet the prosecution's case." *Ferguson v. Georgia*, 365 U.S. [570,] 582 [(1961)].

The right to testify on one's own behalf at a criminal trial has sources in several provisions of the Constitution. It is one of the rights that "are essential to due process of law in a fair adversary process." *Faretta v. California*, 422 U.S. 806, 819 n.15 (1975). The necessary ingredients of the Fourteenth Amendment's guarantee that no one shall be deprived of liberty without due process of law include a right to be heard and to offer testimony. . . .

The right to testify is also found in the Compulsory Process Clause of the Sixth Amendment, which grants a defendant the right to call "witnesses in his favor," a right that is guaranteed in the criminal courts of the States by the Fourteenth Amendment. *Washington v. Texas*, 388 U.S. 14, 17–19 (1967). Logically included in the accused's right to call witnesses whose testimony is "material and favorable to his defense," *United States v. Valenzuela-Bernal*, 458 U.S. 858, 867 (1982), is a right to testify himself, should he decide it is in his favor to do so. In fact, the most important witness for the defense in many criminal cases is the defendant himself. There is no justification today for a rule that denies an accused the opportunity to offer his own testimony. Like the truthfulness of other witnesses, the defendant's veracity, which was the concern behind the original common-law rule, can be tested adequately by cross-examination. . . .

The opportunity to testify is also a necessary corollary to the Fifth Amendment's guarantee against compelled testimony. In *Harris v. New York*, 401 U.S. 222, 230 (1971), the Court stated: "Every criminal defendant is privileged to testify in his own defense, or to refuse to do so." . . .

The question now before the Court is whether a criminal defendant's right to testify may be restricted by a state rule that excludes her posthypnosis testimony. This is not the first time this Court has faced a constitutional challenge to a state rule, designed to ensure trustworthy evidence, that interfered with the ability of a defendant to offer testimony. In *Washington v. Texas*, 388 U.S. 14 (1967), the Court was confronted with a state statute that prevented persons charged as principals, accomplices, or accessories in the same crime from being introduced as witnesses for one another. The statute, like the original common-law prohibition on testimony by the accused, was grounded in a concern for the reliability of evidence presented by an interested party. . . .

As the Court recognized, the incompetency of a codefendant to testify had been rejected on nonconstitutional grounds in 1918, when the Court, refusing to be bound by "the dead hand of the common-law rule of 1789," stated:

> "'[T]he conviction of our time [is] that the truth is more likely to be arrived at by hearing the testimony of all persons of competent understanding who may seem to have knowledge of the facts involved in a case, leaving the credit and weight of such testimony to be determined by the jury or by the court....'" 388 U.S., at 22, quoting *Rosen v. United States*, 245 U.S. 467, 471 (1918).

The Court concluded that this reasoning was compelled by the Sixth Amendment's protections for the accused. In particular, the Court reasoned that the Sixth Amendment was designed in part "to make the testimony of a defendant's witnesses admissible on his behalf in court." 388 U.S., at 22.

With the rationale for the common-law incompetency rule thus rejected on constitutional grounds, the Court found that the mere presence of the witness in the courtroom was not enough to satisfy the Constitution's Compulsory Process Clause. By preventing the defendant from having the benefit of his accomplice's testimony, "the State *arbitrarily* denied him the right to put on the stand a witness who was physically and mentally capable of testifying to events that he had personally observed, and whose testimony would have been relevant and material to the defense." (Emphasis added.) *Id.* at 23.

Just as a State may not apply an arbitrary rule of competence to exclude a material defense witness from taking the stand, it also may not apply a rule of evidence that permits a witness to take the stand, but arbitrarily excludes material portions of his testimony. In *Chambers v. Mississippi*, 410 U.S. 284 (1973), the Court invalidated a State's hearsay rule on the ground that it abridged the defendant's right to "present witnesses in his own defense."...

Of course, the right to present relevant testimony is not without limitation.... But restrictions of a defendant's right to testify may not be arbitrary or disproportionate to the purposes they are designed to serve. In applying its evidentiary rules a State must evaluate whether the interests served by a rule justify the limitation imposed on the defendant's constitutional right to testify.

The Arkansas rule enunciated by the state courts does not allow a trial court to consider whether posthypnosis testimony may be admissible in a particular case; it is a *per se* rule prohibiting the admission at trial of any defendant's hypnotically refreshed testimony on the ground that such testimony is always unreliable. Thus, in Arkansas, an accused's testimony is limited to matters that he or she can prove were remembered *before* hypnosis. This rule operates to the detriment of any defendant who undergoes hypnosis, without regard to the reasons for it, the circumstances under which it took place, or any independent verification of the information it produced.

In this case, the application of that rule had a significant adverse effect on petitioner's ability to testify. It virtually prevented her from describing any of the events that occurred on the day of the shooting, despite corroboration of many of those events by other witnesses. Even more importantly, under the court's rule petitioner was not permitted to describe the actual shooting except in the words contained in Doctor Back's notes. The expert's description of the gun's tendency to misfire would have taken on greater significance if the jury had heard petitioner testify that she did not have her finger on the trigger and that the gun went off when her husband hit her arm.

In establishing its *per se* rule, the Arkansas Supreme Court simply followed the approach taken by a number of States that have decided that hypnotically enhanced testimony should be excluded at trial on the ground that it tends to be unreliable. Other States that have adopted an exclusionary rule, however, have done so for the testimony of *witnesses*, not for the testimony of a *defendant*. The Arkansas Supreme Court failed to perform the constitutional analysis that is necessary when a defendant's right to testify is at stake.

Although the Arkansas court concluded that any testimony that cannot be proved to be the product of prehypnosis memory is unreliable, many courts have eschewed a *per se* rule and permit the admission of hypnotically refreshed testimony. Hypnosis by trained physicians or psychologists has been recognized as a valid therapeutic technique since 1958, although there is no generally accepted theory to explain the phenomenon, or even a consensus on a single definition of hypnosis. See Council on Scientific Affairs, Scientific Status of Refreshing Recollection by the Use of Hypnosis, 253 J.A.M.A. 1918, 1918-1919 (1985) (Council Report). The use of hypnosis in criminal investigations, however, is controversial, and the current medical and legal view of its appropriate role is unsettled.

Responses of individuals to hypnosis vary greatly. The popular belief that hypnosis guarantees the accuracy of recall is as yet without established foundation and, in fact, hypnosis often has no effect at all on memory. The most common response to hypnosis, however, appears to be an increase in both correct and incorrect recollections. Three general characteristics of hypnosis may lead to the introduction of inaccurate memories: the subject becomes "suggestible" and may try to please the hypnotist with answers the subject thinks will be met with approval; the subject is likely to "confabulate," that is, to fill in details from the imagination in order to make an answer more coherent and complete; and, the subject experiences "memory hardening," which gives him great confidence in both true and false memories, making effective cross-examination more difficult. See generally M. Orne et al., Hypnotically Induced Testimony, in Eyewitness Testimony: Psychological Perspectives 171 (G. Wells & E. Loftus, eds., 1984); Diamond, Inherent Problems in the Use of Pretrial Hypnosis on a Prospective Witness, 68 Calif. L. Rev. 313, 333-342 (1980). Despite the unreliability that hypnosis concededly may introduce, however, the procedure has been credited as instrumental in obtaining investigative leads or identifications that were later confirmed by independent evidence. . . .

The inaccuracies the process introduces can be reduced, although perhaps not eliminated, by the use of procedural safeguards. One set of suggested guidelines calls for hypnosis to be performed only by a psychologist or psychiatrist with special training in its use and who is independent of the investigation. See Orne, The Use and Misuse of Hypnosis in Court, 27 Int'l J. Clinical and Experimental Hypnosis 311, 335-336 (1979). These procedures reduce the possibility that biases will be communicated to the hypersuggestive subject by the hypnotist. Suggestion will be less likely also if the hypnosis is conducted in a neutral setting with no one present but the hypnotist and the subject. Tape or video recording of all interrogations, before, during, and after hypnosis, can help reveal if leading questions were asked. Such guidelines do not guarantee the accuracy of the testimony, because they cannot control the subject's own motivations or any tendency to confabulate, but they do provide a means of controlling overt suggestions.

The more traditional means of assessing accuracy of testimony also remain applicable in the case of a previously hypnotized defendant. Certain information recalled as a result of hypnosis may be verified as highly accurate by corroborating evidence. Cross-examination, even in the face of a confident defendant, is an effective tool for revealing inconsistencies. Moreover, a jury can be educated to the risks of hypnosis through expert testimony and cautionary instructions. Indeed, it is probably to a defendant's advantage to establish carefully the extent of his memory prior to hypnosis, in order to minimize the decrease in credibility the procedure might introduce.

We are not now prepared to endorse without qualifications the use of hypnosis as an investigative tool; scientific understanding of the phenomenon and of the means to control the effects of hypnosis is still in its infancy. Arkansas, however, has not justified the exclusion of *all* of a defendant's testimony that the defendant is unable to prove to be the product of prehypnosis memory. A State's legitimate interest in barring unreliable evidence does not extend to *per se* exclusions that may be reliable in an individual case. Wholesale inadmissibility of a defendant's testimony is an arbitrary restriction on the right to testify in the absence of clear evidence by the State repudiating the validity of all posthypnosis recollections. The State would be well within its powers if it established guidelines to aid trial courts in the evaluation of posthypnosis testimony and it may be able to show that testimony in a particular case is so unreliable that exclusion is justified. But it has not shown that hypnotically enhanced testimony is always so untrustworthy and so immune to the traditional means of evaluating credibility that it should disable a defendant from presenting her version of the events for which she is on trial.

In this case, the defective condition of the gun corroborated the details petitioner remembered about the shooting. The tape recordings provided some means to evaluate the hypnosis and the trial judge concluded that Doctor Back did not suggest responses with leading questions. Those circumstances present an argument for admissibility of petitioner's testimony in this particular case, an argument that must be considered by the trial court. Arkansas' *per se* rule excluding all posthypnosis testimony infringes impermissibly on the right of a defendant to testify on his own behalf.

The judgment of the Supreme Court of Arkansas is vacated, and the case is remanded to that court for further proceedings not inconsistent with this opinion.

[Chief Justice Rehnquist filed a dissenting opinion.]

PROBLEM

8.4. Section 795(a) of the California Evidence Code provides as follows:

The testimony of a witness is not inadmissible in a criminal proceeding by reason of the fact that the witness has previously undergone hypnosis for the purpose of recalling events which are the subject of the witness' testimony, if all of the following conditions are met:

(1) The testimony is limited to those matters which the witness recalled and related prior to the hypnosis.
(2) The substance of the prehypnotic memory was preserved in written, audiotape, or videotape form prior to the hypnosis.
(3) The hypnosis was conducted in accordance with all of the following procedures:
    (A) A written record was made prior to hypnosis documenting the subject's description of the event, and information which was provided to the hypnotist concerning the subject matter of the hypnosis.
    (B) The subject gave informed consent to the hypnosis.
    (C) The hypnosis session, including the pre- and post-hypnosis interviews, was videotape recorded for subsequent review.
    (D) The hypnosis was performed by a licensed medical doctor, psychologist, licensed clinical social worker, or a licensed marriage, family and child counselor experienced in the use of hypnosis and independent of and not in the presence of law enforcement, the prosecution, or the defense.
(4) Prior to admission of the testimony, the court holds a hearing . . . at which the proponent of the evidence proves by clear and convincing evidence that the hypnosis did not so affect the witness as to render the witness' prehypnosis recollection unreliable or to substantially impair the ability to cross-examine the witness concerning the witness' prehypnosis recollection. . . .

The California courts have not applied §795(a) to the testimony of criminal defendants. *See People v. Aguilar*, 2667 Cal. Rptr. 879 (Cal. App. 1990). If so applied, would the statute be constitutional? Is the statute constitutional as applied to other witnesses called by criminal defendants?

F. JUDGES, JURORS, AND LAWYERS

Although almost everyone who is not a very young child is now competent to testify, three important categories of incompetence remain: judges, jurors, and lawyers generally may not testify in the cases in which they serve. The disqualification of judges as witnesses leads to little litigation and little controversy, as does the rule prohibiting a juror from testifying before the jury of which he or she is a member. But there is a good deal of controversy as well as frequent litigation about the ability of jurors to testify in a *post-trial* hearing to set aside the verdict because of irregularities involving the jury. And there is uncertainty about the status and proper contours of the so-called "advocate-witness" rule, which bars attorneys from appearing both as witnesses and attorneys in the same proceeding.

[F.R.E. 605, 606; C.E.C. §§703, 704, 1150]

ADVISORY COMMITTEE NOTE TO F.R.E. 605

In view of the mandate of 28 U.S.C. §455 that a judge disqualify himself in "any case in which he ... is or has been a material witness," the likelihood that the presiding judge in a federal court might be called to testify in the trial over which he is presiding is slight. Nevertheless the possibility is not totally eliminated.

The solution here presented is a broad rule of incompetency, rather than such alternatives as incompetency only as to material matters, leaving the matter to the discretion of the judge, or recognizing no incompetency. The choice is the result of inability to evolve satisfactory answers to questions which arise when the judge abandons the bench for the witness stand. Who rules on objections? Who compels him to answer? Can he rule impartially on the weight and admissibility of his own testimony? Can he be impeached or cross-examined effectively? Can he, in a jury trial, avoid conferring his seal of approval on one side in the eyes of the jury? Can he, in a bench trial, avoid an involvement destructive of impartiality? The rule of general incompetency has substantial support. See Report of the Special Committee on the Propriety of Judges Appearing as Witnesses, 36 A.B.A.J. 630 (1950); cases collected in Annot. 157 A.L.R. 311; McCormick §68, p. 147; Uniform Rule 42; California Evidence Code §703; Kansas Code of Civil Procedure §60-442; New Jersey Evidence Rule 42. Cf. 6 Wigmore §1909, which advocates leaving the matter to the discretion of the judge, and statutes to that effect collected in Annot. 157 A.L.R. 311.

The rule provides an "automatic" objection. To require an actual objection would confront the opponent with a choice between not objecting, with the result of allowing the testimony, and objecting, with the probable result of excluding the testimony but at the price of continuing the trial before a judge likely to feel that his integrity had been attacked by the objector.

ADVISORY COMMITTEE NOTE TO F.R.E. 606

Subdivision (a). The considerations which bear upon the permissibility of testimony by a juror in the trial in which he is sitting as juror bear an obvious similarity to those evoked when the judge is called as a witness. The judge is not, however in this instance so involved as to call for departure from usual principles requiring objection to be made; hence the only provision on objection is that opportunity be afforded for its making out of the presence of the jury.

Subdivision (b). Whether testimony, affidavits, or statements of jurors should be received for the purpose of invalidating or supporting a verdict or indictment, and if so, under what circumstances, has given rise to substantial differences of opinion. The familiar rubric that a juror may not impeach his own verdict, dating from Lord Mansfield's time, is a gross oversimplification. The values sought to be promoted by excluding the evidence include freedom of deliberation, stability and finality of verdicts, and protection of jurors against annoyance and embarrassment. McDonald v. Pless, 238 U.S. 264

(1915). On the other hand, simply putting verdicts beyond effective reach can only promote irregularity and injustice. The rule offers an accommodation between these competing considerations.

The mental operations and emotional reactions of jurors in arriving at a given result would, if allowed as a subject of inquiry, place every verdict at the mercy of jurors and invite tampering and harassment. The authorities are in virtually complete accord in excluding the evidence. As to matters other than mental operations and emotional reactions of jurors, substantial authority refuses to allow a juror to disclose irregularities which occur in the jury room, but allows his testimony as to irregularities occurring outside and allows outsiders to testify as to occurrences both inside and out. However, the door of the jury room is not necessarily a satisfactory dividing point, and the Supreme Court has refused to accept it for every situation. Mattox v. United States, 146 U.S. 140 (1892).

Under the federal decisions the central focus has been upon insulation of the manner in which the jury reached its verdict, and this protection extends to each of the components of deliberation, including arguments, statements, discussions, mental and emotional reactions, votes, and any other feature of the process. Thus testimony or affidavits of jurors have been held incompetent to show a compromise verdict, Hyde v. United States, 225 U.S. 347, 382 (1912); a quotient verdict, McDonald v. Pless, 238 U.S. 264 (1915); speculation as to insurance coverage, Holden v. Porter, 405 F.2d 878 (10th Cir. 1969); Farmers Coop. Elev. Ass'n v. Strand, 382 F.2d 224, 230 (8th Cir. 1967), cert. denied, 389 U.S. 1014; misinterpretation of instructions, Farmers Coop. Elev. Ass'n v. Strand, supra; mistake in returning verdict, United States v. Chereton, 309 F.2d 197 (6th Cir. 1962); interpretation of guilty plea by one defendant as implicating others, United States v. Crosby, 294 F.2d 928, 949 (2d Cir. 1961). The policy does not, however, foreclose testimony by jurors as to prejudicial extraneous information or influences injected into or brought to bear upon the deliberative process. Thus a juror is recognized as competent to testify to statements by the bailiff or the introduction of a prejudicial newspaper account into the jury room, Mattox v. United States, 146 U.S. 140 (1892). See also Parker v. Gladden, 385 U.S. 363 (1966).

This rule does not purport to specify the substantive grounds for setting aside verdicts for irregularity; it deals only with the competency of jurors to testify concerning those grounds. Allowing them to testify as to matters other than their own inner reactions involves no particular hazard to the values sought to be protected. The rule is based upon this conclusion. It makes no attempt to specify the substantive grounds for setting aside verdicts for irregularity. . . .

WARGER v. SHAUERS

574 U.S. 40 (2014)

Justice SOTOMAYOR delivered the opinion of the Court.

. . . Petitioner Gregory Warger was riding his motorcycle on a highway outside Rapid City, South Dakota, when a truck driven by respondent Randy

Shauers struck him from behind. . . . Warger sustained serious injuries that ultimately required the amputation of his left leg. Warger sued Shauers for negligence in Federal District Court. During jury selection . . . Warger's counsel asked whether any jurors would be unable to award damages for pain and suffering or for future medical expenses, or whether there was any juror who thought, "I don't think I could be a fair and impartial juror on this kind of case." Prospective juror Regina Whipple, who was later selected as the jury foreperson, answered no to each of these questions.

Trial commenced, and the jury ultimately returned a verdict in favor of Shauers. Shortly thereafter, one of the jurors contacted Warger's counsel to express concern over juror Whipple's conduct. The complaining juror subsequently signed an affidavit claiming that Whipple had spoken during deliberations about "a motor vehicle collision in which her daughter was at fault for the collision and a man died," and had "related that if her daughter had been sued, it would have ruined her life."

Relying on this affidavit, Warger moved for a new trial. He contended that Whipple had deliberately lied during *voir dire* about her impartiality and ability to award damages. Thus, he asserted, he had satisfied the requirements of *McDonough Power Equipment, Inc. v. Greenwood*, 464 U.S. 548 (1984), which holds that a party may "obtain a new trial" if he "demonstrate[s] that a juror failed to answer honestly a material question on *voir dire*, and . . . that a correct response would have provided a valid basis for a challenge for cause."

The District Court refused to grant a new trial, holding that the only evidence that supported Warger's motion, the complaining juror's affidavit, was barred by Federal Rule of Evidence 606(b). . . . The Eighth Circuit affirmed. We granted certiorari and now affirm. . . .

Rule 606(b) had its genesis in *Vaise v. Delaval*, 99 Eng. Rep. 944 (K.B.1785), in which Lord Mansfield held inadmissible an affidavit from two jurors claiming that the jury had decided the case through a game of chance. The rule soon took root in the United States, where it was viewed as both promoting the finality of verdicts and insulating the jury from outside influences.

Some versions of the rule were narrower than others. Under what was sometimes known as the "Iowa" approach, juror testimony regarding deliberations was excluded only to the extent that it related to matters that "'inhere[d]' in the verdict,'" which generally consisted of evidence of the jurors' subjective intentions and thought processes in reaching a verdict.[1] A number of courts adhering to the Iowa rule held that testimony regarding jury deliberations is admissible when used to challenge juror conduct during *voir dire*.

But other courts applied a broader version of the anti-impeachment rule. Under this version, sometimes called the "federal" approach, litigants were prohibited from using evidence of jury deliberations unless it was offered to

---

1. The Iowa rule derived from *Wright v. Illinois & Miss. Tel. Co.*, 20 Iowa 195 (1866), in which the Iowa Supreme Court held that a trial court considering a motion for a new trial should have accepted the affidavits of four jurors who claimed that their damages verdict had been determined by taking the average of the sums each juror thought proper (a "quotient" verdict). The *Wright* court reasoned that, unlike evidence of a juror's subjective intentions in reaching a verdict, whether the verdict had been obtained in this fashion was an "independent fact" and thus could and should be proved by any available evidence.

show that an "extraneous matter" had influenced the jury. The "great majority" of appellate courts applying this version of the rule held jury deliberations evidence inadmissible even if used to demonstrate dishonesty during *voir dire*. *Wilson v. Wiggins*, 54 Ariz. 240 (1939).

This Court occasionally employed language that might have suggested a preference for the Iowa rule. But to the extent that these decisions created any question as to which approach this Court followed, *McDonald v. Pless* [238 U.S. 264 (1915)] largely settled matters. There, we held that juror affidavits were not admissible to show that jurors had entered a "quotient" verdict, precisely the opposite of the result reached by the Iowa Supreme Court in its decision establishing the Iowa approach. In doing so, we observed that although decisions in a few States made admissible a "juror's affidavit as to an overt act of misconduct, which was capable of being controverted by other jurors," the argument in favor of that approach (*i.e.,* the Iowa rule) had not been generally accepted, because permitting such evidence "would open the door to the most pernicious arts and tampering with jurors."

Our subsequent decision in *Clark v. United States*, 289 U.S. 1 (1933), was consistent with our apparent rejection of the Iowa approach. In *Clark,* the Government had prosecuted for contempt a juror who, during *voir dire* in a prior case, had falsely denied knowing the defendant. We held that the prosecution could introduce evidence of what had occurred during deliberations in the prior case, rejecting the juror's argument that these communications were privileged. We were careful to explain, however, that nothing in our decision was "at variance with the rule . . . that the testimony of a juror is not admissible for the impeachment of his verdict." This was because the verdict in the original case was not at issue, and therefore "the rule against impeachment [was] wholly unrelated to the problem . . . before us." *Clark* thus clarified that the rule against jurors' impeaching their verdicts applies only in a proceeding actually impeaching that verdict — precisely the line Rule 606(b) draws when it refers to an "inquiry into the validity of a verdict."

In any event, these decisions predated Congress' enactment of Rule 606(b), and Congress was undoubtedly free to prescribe a broader version of the anti-impeachment rule than we had previously applied. The language of the Rule it adopted clearly reflects the federal approach: As enacted, Rule 606(b) prohibited the use of *any* evidence of juror deliberations, subject only to the express exceptions for extraneous information and outside influences.[2] For those who consider legislative history relevant, here it confirms that this choice of language was no accident. Congress rejected a prior version of the Rule that, in accordance with the Iowa approach, would have prohibited juror testimony only as to the "effect of anything upon . . . [any] juror's mind or emotions . . . or concerning his mental processes." Committee on Rules of Practice and Procedure of the Judicial Conference of the United States, Revised Draft of Proposed Rules of Evidence for the United States Courts and Magistrates, 51 F.R.D. 315, 387 (1971); see *Tanner v. United States*, 483 U.S. 107, 123-25 (1987) (detailing the legislative history of the Rule). Thus Congress "specifically understood, considered, and rejected a version of Rule 606(b)" that

---

2. The additional exception for mistakes made in entering the verdict on the verdict form was adopted in 2006. See 547 U.S. 1281, 1286.

would have likely permitted the introduction of evidence of deliberations to show dishonesty during *voir dire*. . . .

Warger . . . would restrict Rule 606(b)'s application to those claims of error for which a court must examine the manner in which the jury reached its verdict — claims, one might say, involving an inquiry into the jury's verdict. But the "inquiry" to which the Rule refers is one into the "*validity* of the verdict," not into the verdict itself. The Rule does not focus on the means by which deliberations evidence might be used to invalidate a verdict. It does not say "during an inquiry into jury deliberations," or prohibit the introduction of evidence of deliberations "for use in determining whether an asserted error affected the jury's verdict." It simply applies "[d]uring an inquiry into the validity of the verdict"— that is, during a *proceeding* in which the verdict may be rendered invalid. Whether or not a juror's alleged misconduct during *voir dire* had a direct effect on the jury's verdict, the motion for a new trial requires a court to determine whether the verdict can stand. . . .

Warger contends that excluding jury deliberations evidence tending to show that a juror lied during *voir dire* is unnecessary to fulfill Congress' apparent objectives of encouraging full and open debate in the jury room and preventing the harassment of former jurors. He observes that jurors remain free to, and may sometimes be forced to, disclose what happened in the jury room, and that ethical rules limit the ability of parties to harass jurors following trial. But these are arguments against Rule 606(b) generally, not arguments for the particular exception to the Rule that Warger seeks. Congress' enactment of Rule 606(b) was premised on the concerns that the use of deliberations evidence to challenge verdicts would represent a threat to both jurors and finality in those circumstances not covered by the Rule's express exceptions. Warger cannot escape the scope of the Rule Congress adopted simply by asserting that its concerns were misplaced.

Nor do we accept Warger's contention that we must adopt his interpretation of Rule 606(b) so as to avoid constitutional concerns. . . . [A]ny claim that Rule 606(b) is unconstitutional in circumstances such as these is foreclosed by our decision in *Tanner*. In *Tanner,* we concluded that Rule 606(b) precluded a criminal defendant from introducing evidence that multiple jurors had been intoxicated during trial, rejecting the contention that this exclusion violated the defendant's Sixth Amendment right to "'a tribunal both impartial and mentally competent to afford a hearing.'" We reasoned that the defendant's right to an unimpaired jury was sufficiently protected by *voir dire,* the observations of court and counsel during trial, and the potential use of "nonjuror evidence" of misconduct. Similarly here, a party's right to an impartial jury remains protected despite Rule 606(b)'s removal of one means of ensuring that jurors are unbiased. Even if jurors lie in *voir dire* in a way that conceals bias, juror impartiality is adequately assured by the parties' ability to bring to the court's attention any evidence of bias before the verdict is rendered, and to employ nonjuror evidence even after the verdict is rendered.[3]

---

3. There may be cases of juror bias so extreme that, almost by definition, the jury trial right has been abridged. If and when such a case arises, the Court can consider whether the usual safeguards are or are not sufficient to protect the integrity of the process. We need not consider the question, however, for those facts are not presented here.

We further hold, consonant with the Eighth Circuit, that the affidavit Warger sought to introduce was not admissible under Rule 606(b)(2)(A)'s exception for evidence as to whether "extraneous prejudicial information was improperly brought to the jury's attention."

Generally speaking, information is deemed "extraneous" if it derives from a source "external" to the jury. "External" matters include publicity and information related specifically to the case the jurors are meant to decide, while "internal" matters include the general body of experiences that jurors are understood to bring with them to the jury room. Here, the excluded affidavit falls on the "internal" side of the line: Whipple's daughter's accident may well have informed her general views about negligence liability for car crashes, but it did not provide either her or the rest of the jury with any specific knowledge regarding Shauers' collision with Warger. . . .

Warger . . . contends that because Whipple would have been disqualified from the jury had she disclosed her daughter's accident, *any* information she shared with the other jurors was extraneous. . . . Even if such a result were not precluded by Congress' apparent intent to adopt the restrictive federal approach, it is foreclosed by *Tanner,* which relied upon the doctrine that "treat[s] allegations of the physical or mental incompetence of a juror as 'internal' rather than 'external' matters." *Tanner* cited, in particular, cases holding that evidence of jurors' insanity, inability to understand English, and hearing impairments are all "internal" matters subject to exclusion under Rule 606(b). Were we to follow Warger's understanding of the "extraneous information" exception, all these cases, including *Tanner,* would have been wrongly decided: If the jurors were not able to serve on the jury in the first place, or should have been dismissed for their misconduct during the trial, then what they said or did during deliberations would necessarily be "extraneous" and admissible. *Tanner*'s implicit rejection of this view easily extends from the sort of juror incompetence considered in that case to the alleged bias considered here. . . .

PENA-RODRIGUEZ v. COLORADO

580 U.S. ___ (2017)

Justice KENNEDY delivered the opinion of the Court.

. . . In 2007, in the bathroom of a Colorado horse-racing facility, a man sexually assaulted two teenage sisters. The girls told their father and identified the man as an employee of the racetrack. The police located and arrested petitioner. Each girl separately identified petitioner as the man who had assaulted her.

The State charged petitioner with harassment, unlawful sexual contact, and attempted sexual assault on a child. Before the jury was empaneled, members of the venire were repeatedly asked whether they believed that they could be fair and impartial in the case. A written questionnaire asked if there was "anything about you that you feel would make it difficult for you to be a fair juror." The court repeated the question to the panel of prospective jurors and encouraged jurors to speak in private with the court if they had any concerns about their impartiality. Defense counsel likewise asked whether anyone felt that "this is simply not a good case" for them to be a fair juror. None of the empaneled jurors expressed any reservations based on racial or any other bias. And none asked to speak with the trial judge.

After a 3-day trial, the jury found petitioner guilty of unlawful sexual contact and harassment, but it failed to reach a verdict on the attempted sexual assault charge.... Following the discharge of the jury ... two jurors remained to speak with [defense] counsel in private. They stated that, during deliberations, another juror had expressed anti-Hispanic bias toward petitioner and petitioner's alibi witness. Petitioner's counsel reported this to the court and, with the court's supervision, obtained sworn affidavits from the two jurors.

The affidavits by the two jurors described a number of biased statements made by another juror, identified as Juror H. C. According to the two jurors, H. C. told the other jurors that he "believed the defendant was guilty because, in [H. C.'s] experience as an ex-law enforcement officer, Mexican men had a bravado that caused them to believe they could do whatever they wanted with women." The jurors reported that H. C. stated his belief that Mexican men are physically controlling of women because of their sense of entitlement, and further stated, "'I think he did it because he's Mexican and Mexican men take whatever they want.'" According to the jurors, H. C. further explained that, in his experience, "nine times out of ten Mexican men were guilty of being aggressive toward women and young girls." Finally, the jurors recounted that Juror H. C. said that he did not find petitioner's alibi witness credible because, among other things, the witness was "'an illegal.'" (In fact, the witness testified during trial that he was a legal resident of the United States.)

After reviewing the affidavits, the trial court acknowledged H. C.'s apparent bias. But the court denied petitioner's motion for a new trial, noting that "[t]he actual deliberations that occur among the jurors are protected from inquiry under [Colorado Rule of Evidence] 606(b)." Like its federal counterpart, Colorado's Rule 606(b) generally prohibits a juror from testifying as to any statement made during deliberations in a proceeding inquiring into the validity of the verdict. See Fed. Rule Evid. 606(b). The Colorado Rule reads as follows:

> "(b) Inquiry into validity of verdict or indictment. Upon an inquiry into the validity of a verdict or indictment, a juror may not testify as to any matter or statement occurring during the course of the jury's deliberations or to the effect of anything upon his or any other juror's mind or emotions as influencing him to assent to or dissent from the verdict or indictment or concerning his mental processes in connection therewith. But a juror may testify about (1) whether extraneous prejudicial information was improperly brought to the jurors' attention, (2) whether any outside influence was improperly brought to bear upon any juror, or (3) whether there was a mistake in entering the verdict onto the verdict form. A juror's affidavit or evidence of any statement by the juror may not be received on a matter about which the juror would be precluded from testifying."

Colo. Rule Evid. 606(b) (2016).

The verdict deemed final, petitioner was sentenced to two years' probation and was required to register as a sex offender. A divided panel of the

Colorado Court of Appeals affirmed petitioner's conviction [and the] Colorado Supreme Court affirmed by a vote of 4 to 3. . . . This Court granted certiorari to decide whether there is a constitutional exception to the no-impeachment rule for instances of racial bias. . . .

Some version of the no-impeachment rule is followed in every State and the District of Columbia. Variations make classification imprecise, but, as a general matter, it appears that 42 jurisdictions follow the Federal Rule, while 9 follow the Iowa Rule. Within both classifications there is a diversity of approaches. Nine jurisdictions that follow the Federal Rule have codified exceptions other than those listed in Federal Rule 606(b). At least 16 jurisdictions, 11 of which follow the Federal Rule, have recognized an exception to the no-impeachment bar under the circumstances the Court faces here: juror testimony that racial bias played a part in deliberations. According to the parties and *amici*, only one State other than Colorado has addressed this issue and declined to recognize an exception for racial bias.

The federal courts, for their part, are governed by Federal Rule 606(b), but their interpretations deserve further comment. Various Courts of Appeals have had occasion to consider a racial bias exception and have reached different conclusions. Three have held or suggested there is a constitutional exception for evidence of racial bias. See *United States* v. *Villar*, 586 F. 3d 76, 87–88 (CA1 2009) (holding the Constitution demands a racial-bias exception); *United States* v. *Henley*, 238 F. 3d 1111, 1119–1121 (CA9 2001) (finding persuasive arguments in favor of an exception but not deciding the issue); *Shillcutt* v. *Gagnon*, 827 F. 2d 1155, 1158–1160 (CA7 1987) (observing that in some cases fundamental fairness could require an exception). One Court of Appeals has declined to find an exception, reasoning that other safeguards inherent in the trial process suffice to protect defendants' constitutional interests. See *United States* v. *Benally*, 546 F. 3d 1230, 1240–1241 (CA10 2008). Another has suggested as much, holding in the habeas context that an exception for racial bias was not clearly established but indicating in dicta that no such exception exists. See *Williams* v. *Price*, 343 F. 3d 223, 237–239 (CA3 2003) (Alito, J.). And one Court of Appeals has held that evidence of racial bias is excluded by Rule 606(b), without addressing whether the Constitution may at times demand an exception. *See Martinez* v. *Food City, Inc.*, 658 F. 2d 369, 373–374 (CA5 1981). . . .

The recognition in *Warger* [*v. Shauers*, 574 U.S. 40 (2014),] that there may be extreme cases where the jury trial right requires an exception to the no-impeachment rule must be interpreted in context as a guarded, cautious statement. This caution is warranted to avoid formulating an exception that might undermine the jury dynamics and finality interests the no-impeachment rule seeks to protect. Today, however, the Court faces the question that . . . *Warger* left open. The Court must decide whether the Constitution requires an exception to the no-impeachment rule when a juror's statements indicate that racial animus was a significant motivating factor in his or her finding of guilt. . . .

It must become the heritage of our Nation to rise above racial classifications that are so inconsistent with our commitment to the equal dignity of all persons. This imperative to purge racial prejudice from the administration of justice was given new force and direction by the ratification of the Civil War Amendments.

"[T]he central purpose of the Fourteenth Amendment was to eliminate racial discrimination emanating from official sources in the States." *McLaughlin* v. *Florida*, 379 U.S. 184, 192 (1964). In the years before and after the ratification of the Fourteenth Amendment, it became clear that racial discrimination in the jury system posed a particular threat both to the promise of the Amendment and to the integrity of the jury trial. "Almost immediately after the Civil War, the South began a practice that would continue for many decades: All-white juries punished black defendants particularly harshly, while simultaneously refusing to punish violence by whites, including Ku Klux Klan members, against blacks and Republicans." Forman, Juries and Race in the Nineteenth Century, 113 Yale L. J. 895, 909-910 (2004). To take one example, just in the years 1865 and 1866, all-white juries in Texas decided a total of 500 prosecutions of white defendants charged with killing African-Americans. All 500 were acquitted. *Id.,* at 916. The stark and unapologetic nature of race-motivated outcomes challenged the American belief that "the jury was a bulwark of liberty," *id.,* at 909, and prompted Congress to pass legislation to integrate the jury system and to bar persons from eligibility for jury service if they had conspired to deny the civil rights of African-Americans, *id.,* at 920-930. Members of Congress stressed that the legislation was necessary to preserve the right to a fair trial and to guarantee the equal protection of the laws. *Ibid.*

The duty to confront racial animus in the justice system is not the legislature's alone. Time and again, this Court has been called upon to enforce the Constitution's guarantee against state-sponsored racial discrimination in the jury system. Beginning in 1880, the Court interpreted the Fourteenth Amendment to prohibit the exclusion of jurors on the basis of race. *Strauder v. West Virginia*, 100 U.S. 303-309 (1880). The Court has repeatedly struck down laws and practices that systematically exclude racial minorities from juries.... To guard against discrimination in jury selection, the Court has ruled that no litigant may exclude a prospective juror on the basis of race.... In an effort to ensure that individuals who sit on juries are free of racial bias, the Court has held that the Constitution at times demands that defendants be permitted to ask questions about racial bias during *voir dire*....

The unmistakable principle underlying these precedents is that discrimination on the basis of race, "odious in all aspects, is especially pernicious in the administration of justice." *Rose* v. *Mitchell*, 443 U.S. 545, 555 (1979). The jury is to be "a criminal defendant's fundamental 'protection of life and liberty against race or color prejudice.'" *McCleskey* v. *Kemp*, 481 U.S. 279, 310 (1987) (quoting *Strauder, supra,* at 309). Permitting racial prejudice in the jury system damages "both the fact and the perception" of the jury's role as "a vital check against the wrongful exercise of power by the State." *Powers* v. *Ohio*, 499 U.S. 400, 411 (1991)....

Racial bias of the kind alleged in this case differs in critical ways from the compromise verdict in *McDonald* [*v. Pless*, 238 U.S. 264 (1915)], the drug and alcohol abuse in *Tanner* [*v. United States*, 483 U.S. 107 (1987)], or the pro-defendant bias in *Warger*. The behavior in those cases is troubling and unacceptable, but each involved anomalous behavior from a single jury — or juror — gone off course. Jurors are presumed to follow their oath . . . and neither history nor common experience show that the jury system is rife with mischief of these or similar kinds. To attempt to rid the jury of every irregularity of this sort would be to expose it to unrelenting scrutiny. "It is not at all clear . . . that the jury system could survive such efforts to perfect it." *Tanner*, 483 U.S., at 120.

The same cannot be said about racial bias, a familiar and recurring evil that, if left unaddressed, would risk systemic injury to the administration of justice. This Court's decisions demonstrate that racial bias implicates unique historical, constitutional, and institutional concerns. An effort to address the most grave and serious statements of racial bias is not an effort to perfect the jury but to ensure that our legal system remains capable of coming ever closer to the promise of equal treatment under the law that is so central to a functioning democracy.

Racial bias is distinct in a pragmatic sense as well. In past cases this Court has relied on other safeguards to protect the right to an impartial jury. Some of those safeguards, to be sure, can disclose racial bias. *Voir dire* at the outset of trial, observation of juror demeanor and conduct during trial, juror reports before the verdict, and nonjuror evidence after trial are important mechanisms for discovering bias. Yet their operation may be compromised, or they may prove insufficient. For instance, this Court has noted the dilemma faced by trial court judges and counsel in deciding whether to explore potential racial bias at *voir dire*. . . . Generic questions about juror impartiality may not expose specific attitudes or biases that can poison jury deliberations. Yet more pointed questions "could well exacerbate whatever prejudice might exist without substantially aiding in exposing it." *Rosales-Lopez* [*v. United States*, 451 U.S. 182, 195 (1981)] (Rehnquist, J., concurring in result).

The stigma that attends racial bias may make it difficult for a juror to report inappropriate statements during the course of juror deliberations. It is one thing to accuse a fellow juror of having a personal experience that improperly influences her consideration of the case, as would have been required in *Warger*. It is quite another to call her a bigot.

The recognition that certain of the *Tanner* safeguards may be less effective in rooting out racial bias than other kinds of bias is not dispositive. All forms of improper bias pose challenges to the trial process. But there is a sound basis to treat racial bias with added precaution. A constitutional rule that racial bias in the justice system must be addressed — including, in some instances, after the verdict has been entered — is necessary to prevent a systemic loss of confidence in jury verdicts, a confidence that is a central premise of the Sixth Amendment trial right. . . .

For the reasons explained above, the Court now holds that where a juror makes a clear statement that indicates he or she relied on racial stereotypes or animus to convict a criminal defendant, the Sixth Amendment requires that the no-impeachment rule give way in order to permit the trial court to consider the evidence of the juror's statement and any resulting denial of the jury trial guarantee.

Not every offhand comment indicating racial bias or hostility will justify setting aside the no-impeachment bar to allow further judicial inquiry. For the inquiry to proceed, there must be a showing that one or more jurors made statements exhibiting overt racial bias that cast serious doubt on the fairness and impartiality of the jury's deliberations and resulting verdict. To qualify, the statement must tend to show that racial animus was a significant motivating factor in the juror's vote to convict. Whether that threshold showing has been satisfied is a matter committed to the substantial discretion of the trial court in light of all the circumstances, including the content and timing of the alleged statements and the reliability of the proffered evidence.

The practical mechanics of acquiring and presenting such evidence will no doubt be shaped and guided by state rules of professional ethics and local court rules, both of which often limit counsel's post-trial contact with jurors. . . . These limits seek to provide jurors some protection when they return to their daily affairs after the verdict has been entered. But while a juror can always tell counsel they do not wish to discuss the case, jurors in some instances may come forward of their own accord.

That is what happened here. In this case the alleged statements by a juror were egregious and unmistakable in their reliance on racial bias. Not only did juror H. C. deploy a dangerous racial stereotype to conclude petitioner was guilty and his alibi witness should not be believed, but he also encouraged other jurors to join him in convicting on that basis.

Petitioner's counsel did not seek out the two jurors' allegations of racial bias. Pursuant to Colorado's mandatory jury instruction, the trial court had set limits on juror contact and encouraged jurors to inform the court if anyone harassed them about their role in the case. Similar limits on juror contact can be found in other jurisdictions that recognize a racial-bias exception. *See, e.g.,* Fla. Standard Jury Instrs. in Crim. Cases No. 4.2 (West 2016) ("Although you are at liberty to speak with anyone about your deliberations, you are also at liberty to refuse to speak to anyone"); Mass. Office of Jury Comm'r, Trial Juror's Handbook (Dec. 2015) ("You are not required to speak with anyone once the trial is over. . . . If anyone tries to learn this confidential information from you, or if you feel harassed or embarrassed in any way, you should report it to the court . . . immediately"); N. J. Crim. Model Jury Charges, Non 2C Charges, Dismissal of Jury (2014) ("It will be up to each of you to decide whether to speak about your service as a juror").

With the understanding that they were under no obligation to speak out, the jurors approached petitioner's counsel, within a short time after the verdict, to relay their concerns about H. C.'s statements. A similar pattern is common in cases involving juror allegations of racial bias. *See, e.g., Villar,* 586 F. 3d, at 78 (juror e-mailed defense counsel within hours of the verdict); *Kittle* v. *United States,* 65 A. 3d 1144, 1147 (D. C. 2013) (juror wrote a letter to the judge the same day the court discharged the jury); *Benally,* 546 F. 3d, at 1231 (juror approached defense counsel the day after the jury announced its verdict). Pursuant to local court rules, petitioner's counsel then sought and received permission from the court to contact the two jurors and obtain affidavits limited to recounting the exact statements made by H. C. that exhibited racial bias.

While the trial court concluded that Colorado's Rule 606(b) did not permit it even to consider the resulting affidavits, the Court's holding today removes that bar. When jurors disclose an instance of racial bias as serious as the one involved in this case, the law must not wholly disregard its occurrence. . . .

As the preceding discussion makes clear, the Court relies on the experiences of the 17 jurisdictions that have recognized a racial-bias exception to the no-impeachment rule — some for over half a century — with no signs of an increase in juror harassment or a loss of juror willingness to engage in searching and candid deliberations.

The experience of these jurisdictions, and the experience of the courts going forward, will inform the proper exercise of trial judge discretion in these and related matters. This case does not ask, and the Court need not address, what procedures a trial court must follow when confronted with a motion for a new trial based on juror testimony of racial bias. . . . The Court also does not decide the appropriate standard for determining when evidence of racial bias is sufficient to require that the verdict be set aside and a new trial be granted. *Compare, e.g., Shillcutt*, 827 F. 2d, at 1159 (inquiring whether racial bias "pervaded the jury room"), *with, e.g., Henley*, 238 F. 3d, at 1120 ("One racist juror would be enough"). . . .

[B]latant racial prejudice is antithetical to the functioning of the jury system and must be confronted in egregious cases like this one despite the general bar of the no-impeachment rule. . . . The judgment of the Supreme Court of Colorado is reversed, and the case is remanded for further proceedings not inconsistent with this opinion.

[Justice Thomas filed a dissenting opinion. Justice Alito filed a dissenting opinion in which the Chief Justice and Justice Thomas joined.]

UNITED STATES v. EWING

979 F.2d 1234 (7th Cir. 1992)

COFFEY, Circuit Judge.

[Henry Lee Ewing was convicted of drug trafficking and sentenced to 15 months in prison. Police executing a search warrant at his home had found cocaine packaged in plastic bags, along with various other evidence of drug trafficking, including two composition notebooks with incriminating notations.]

Ewing maintains that the district court committed reversible error in not allowing his attorney, Renee E. Schooley, an assistant federal public defender, to testify about allegations that the Government tampered with the evidence used against him. Specifically, Ewing claims that the two composition notebooks found in his dining room did not have his name written on them when they were seized by the police during the search of his house. The two notebooks did have Ewing's name written on them when they were introduced at trial as evidence of his drug trafficking enterprise. Ewing's attorney was prepared to testify that six weeks before trial, when she and a paralegal from her office, Abigail Stottlar, examined the evidence gathered by the Alton police against Ewing and stored at the Alton police station, Ewing's name did not appear on either composition notebook.

Under the Illinois Rules of Professional Conduct, adopted by the United States District Court for the Southern District of Illinois as its own legal ethics code, a lawyer may not be both witness and counsel in the same case, except in exceptional circumstances. Rule 3.7 of the Illinois Rules provides, in pertinent part, that:

> "(a) A lawyer shall not accept or continue employment in contemplated or pending litigation if the lawyer knows or reasonably should know that the lawyer may be called as a witness on behalf of the client, except that the lawyer may undertake the employment and may testify: (1) if the testimony will relate to an uncontested matter; (2) if the testimony will relate to a matter of formality and the lawyer reasonably believes that no substantial evidence will be offered in opposition to the testimony; (3) if the testimony will relate to the nature and value of legal services rendered in the case by the lawyer or the firm to the client; or (4) as to any other matter, if refusal to accept or continue the employment would work substantial hardship on the client."*

"The advocate-witness rule, which articulates the professional impropriety of assuming the dual role of advocate and witness in a single proceeding, has deep roots in American law." *United States v. Johnston*, 690 F.2d 638, 642 (7th Cir. 1982) (en banc). "That counsel should avoid appearing both as advocate and witness except under special circumstances is beyond question." *United States v. Morris*, 714 F.2d 669, 671 (7th Cir. 1983).

> "The recognized rationales for forbidding counsel to appear as a witness are: . . . it eliminates the possibility that the attorney will not be a fully objective witness, . . . it reduces the risk that the trier of fact will confuse the roles of advocate and witness and erroneously grant testimonial weight to an attorney's arguments, . . . it reflects a broad concern that the administration of justice not only be fair, but also appear fair. . . ."

Id. "This rule, however, does not render an advocate incompetent as a witness, but merely *vests the trial court with discretion* to determine whether counsel may appear as a witness without withdrawing from the case." *Id.* (emphasis added). In *Johnston*, we considered whether a district court abused its discretion in refusing to allow a government prosecutor to testify at a pretrial suppression hearing. We concluded that allowing an advocate to testify "is a situation to be avoided if possible, but . . . will be permitted in extraordinary circumstances and for compelling reasons, usually where the evidence is not otherwise available." *See also United States v. Fogel*, 901 F.2d 23, 26 (4th Cir.), *cert. denied*, 498 U.S. 939 (1990) ("Courts have generally frowned on" allowing counsel to testify, but when "the testimony is important and no other witness would be able to supply it, then such testimony may be allowed.")

Our review of the instant record convinces us that the district court did not abuse its discretion in refusing to allow Ewing's counsel to testify about the alleged evidence tampering. Stottlar, the defense counsel's paralegal, testified before the jury that she and defense counsel examined the

---

* [*Cf.* ABA Model Rule of Professional Conduct 3.7: "(a) A lawyer shall not act as an advocate at a trial in which the lawyer is likely to be a necessary witness except where: (1) The testimony related to an uncontested issue; (2) the testimony related to the nature and value of legal services rendered in the case; or (3) disqualification of the lawyer would work substantial hardship on the client. (b) A lawyer may act as an advocate in a trial in which another lawyer in the lawyer's firm is likely to be called as a witness unless precluded from doing so by Rule 1.7 or Rule 1.9 [pertaining to conflicts of interest]." —Ed.]

evidence against Ewing at the Alton police station on August 30, 1991, six weeks before trial. Stottlar explained that she and defense counsel focused on the composition notebooks in their examination of the evidence because "[w]e were specifically looking to see if they had Henry Ewing's name on them at the time." Defense counsel then asked Stottlar, "[a]nd on August 30, 1991, did they [the composition notebooks] have Henry Ewing's name on them." "No," answered Stottlar. Immediately following the Government's brief cross examination of Stottlar, the district court gave the jury the following instruction:

> "Ladies and gentlemen, you have just heard the testimony of Abigail Stottlar regarding her trip to the Alton Police Department for the purpose of viewing physical evidence, some or all of which has been admitted in this case.
>
> "You have heard the testimony also that Renee Schooley, attorney for the defendant herein, accompanied Miss Stottlar and also examined the physical evidence.
>
> "For reasons that are of no concern to you, I have ruled that Renee Schooley cannot testify in this case."

Defense counsel requested this instruction to clear up any confusion the jurors might have had as to why she did not also testify about her examination of the evidence along with her paralegal. Immediately following this instruction, the defendant called a handwriting analyst, William H. Store, who testified that Henry Ewing did not write the words "Henry Ewing" which appeared on the front of the two composition notebooks introduced at trial.

As the district court observed, the defendant was able to place before the jury his evidence supporting the claim that his name was written on the composition notebooks after they had been seized by police. Stottlar's testimony provided Ewing's most powerful evidence that tampering had allegedly occurred. Schooley's testimony, although it would have served to corroborate Stottlar's story, would have been, as the district court noted, cumulative. Given the strong presumption against allowing counsel to testify as a witness, and the fact that the defendant was able to present Stottlar's critical eyewitness testimony, it was not an abuse of discretion for the district court to rule that Schooley's testimony would have been cumulative and thus that it would not be allowed.[4]

. . . Ewing's conviction and sentence are Affirmed.

---

4. One obvious solution to the problem would have been for Schooley to withdraw as defense counsel and then testify that Ewing's name was not on the composition notebooks when she examined them. The record on appeal contains no indication that defense counsel ever offered to withdraw from representation. In her brief and at oral argument, defense counsel asserted that she was prepared to withdraw from representation and have another attorney from the public defender's office replace her. She also claims that a potential replacement attorney was present in the district court's chambers when the matter was being discussed, and that the district court was aware of her willingness to withdraw. Schooley asserts that she did not make a formal offer to withdraw because the district court indicated that if she took the stand, the entire public defender's office would be disqualified from representing Ewing "which would mean that we would have to recess the trial for I don't know how long to make other arrangements. . . ."

PROBLEMS

8.5. Following her client's conviction, an attorney receives a letter from one of the jurors, admitting that the jury treated the deliberations "as a joke" and spent the entire time "singing camp songs." A courtroom deputy who sat outside the jury room tells the lawyer that throughout the deliberations he heard laughter and boisterous singing. In support of his motion for a new trial, the defendant seeks to introduce the letter and to have both the juror and the deputy testify. The prosecutor argues none of the evidence is admissible. How should the judge rule?

8.6. Because the prosecutor's office is on the same hallway as the jury room, the defense attorney suspects that the prosecutor may have heard the laughter and singing. She wishes to call him to the stand and examine him under oath. The prosecutor objects, citing the advocate-witness rule. How should the judge respond?

8.7. At the beginning of a civil trial, the judge instructs the jurors not to talk to anyone about the case while it is proceeding, including the lawyers. During the trial one of the jurors passes the plaintiff's attorney in the hallway and says, "You've got 'em running!" The attorney reports the remark to the judge and opposing counsel. May the judge question the juror under oath about the incident? May the judge question the juror under oath about the juror's continued ability to be fair and open-minded?

OPINIONS, EXPERTS, AND SCIENTIFIC EVIDENCE

"It is my considered opinion that drowning occurred due to a faulty room humidifier."

A. LAY OPINIONS

Many older cases allowed only expert witnesses to offer opinions and limited all other witnesses to testifying about "facts," not inferences or conclusions. All witnesses, moreover, were often barred from expressing opinions on the "ultimate issues" to be decided by the jury. Modern evidence law largely abandons these restrictions. Lay witnesses — i.e., witnesses who do not testify based on some special expertise — are free to offer opinions, even on ultimate issues. To be admissible, though, the opinions expressed by a lay witness must be helpful to the jury, and — critically — they must be based on the witness's own firsthand observations. Lay witnesses also cannot be experts in disguise; if a witness is indeed testifying based on special expertise, the party calling that witness must adhere to stricter admissibility requirements governing expert testimony and, under the rules of civil and criminal procedure, a variety of special disclosure obligations.

[F.R.E. 701, 704; C.E.C. §§800, 805]

ADVISORY COMMITTEE NOTE TO F.R.E. 701

. . . Witnesses often find difficulty in expressing themselves in language which is not that of an opinion or conclusion. While the courts have made concessions in certain recurring situations, necessity as a standard for permitting opinions and conclusions has proved too elusive and too unadaptable to particular situations for purposes of satisfactory judicial administration. McCormick §11. Moreover, the practical impossibility of determining by rule what is a "fact," demonstrated by a century of litigation of the question of what is a fact for purposes of pleading under the Field Code, extends into evidence also. 7 Wigmore §1919. The rule assumes that the natural characteristics of the adversary system will generally lead to an acceptable result, since the detailed account carries more conviction than the broad assertion, and a lawyer can be expected to display his witness to the best advantage. If he fails to do so, cross-examination and argument will point up the weakness. If, despite these considerations, attempts are made to introduce meaningless assertions which amount to little more than choosing up sides, exclusion for lack of helpfulness is called for by the rule.

ADVISORY COMMITTEE NOTE TO F.R.E. 704

. . . The older cases often contained strictures against allowing witnesses to express opinions upon ultimate issues, as a particular aspect of the rule against opinions. The rule was unduly restrictive, difficult of application, and generally served only to deprive the trier of fact of useful information. 7 Wigmore §§1920, 1921; McCormick §12. The basis usually assigned for the rule, to prevent the witness from "usurping the province of the jury," is aptly characterized as "empty rhetoric." 7 Wigmore §1920, p. 17. . . . Many modern decisions illustrate the trend to abandon the rule completely. . . .

Under Rules 701 and 702, opinions must be helpful to the trier of fact, and Rule 403 provides for exclusion of evidence which wastes time. These provisions afford ample assurances against the admission of opinions which would merely tell the jury what result to reach, somewhat in the manner of the oath-helpers of an earlier day. They also stand ready to exclude opinions phrased in terms of inadequately explored legal criteria. Thus the question, "Did T have capacity to make a will?" would be excluded, while the question, "Did T have sufficient mental capacity to know the nature and extent of his property and the natural objects of his bounty and to formulate a rational scheme of distribution?" would be allowed. McCormick §12.

GOVERNMENT OF THE VIRGIN ISLANDS v. KNIGHT

989 F.2d 619 (3d Cir. 1993)

COWEN, Circuit Judge.

While Henry Knight repeatedly struck Andreas Miller's head with a pistol, the gun discharged and killed Miller. . . . The jury found Knight guilty of voluntary manslaughter, possession of a firearm during the commission of a crime of violence, and possession of a firearm by a felon. . . . [T]he district court found Knight to be a habitual criminal and sentenced him to ten years imprisonment on all counts. . . .

Knight argues that it was reversible error to exclude an eyewitness' and an investigating officer's testimony that the firing of the gun was an accident. . . . Although we agree that the district court committed error by excluding the eyewitness' lay opinion, this error did not prejudice the defendant and therefore does not warrant a reversal of his conviction.

Federal Rule of Evidence 701 states:

> If the witness is not testifying as an expert, the witness' testimony in the form of opinions or inferences is limited to those opinions or inferences which are (a) rationally based on the perception of the witness and (b) helpful to a clear understanding of the witness' testimony or the determination of a fact in issue.

The requirement that a lay opinion be rationally based on the witness' perception requires that the witness have firsthand knowledge of the factual predicates that form the basis for the opinion. The district court properly excluded the investigating police officer's opinion because he did not observe the assault. In contrast, the eyewitness obviously had first-hand knowledge of the facts from which his opinion was formed.

Having met the firsthand knowledge requirement of Rule 701(a), the eyewitness' opinion was admissible if it would help the jury to resolve a disputed fact. The "modern trend favors admissibility of opinion testimony." . . . If circumstances can be presented with greater clarity by stating an opinion, then that opinion is helpful to the trier of fact. Allowing witnesses to state their opinions instead of describing all of their observations has the further benefit of leaving witnesses free to speak in ordinary language.

In this case, an eyewitness' testimony that Knight fired the gun accidentally would be helpful to the jury. The eyewitness described the circumstances that led to his opinion. It is difficult, however, to articulate all of the factors that lead one to conclude a person did not intend to fire a gun. Therefore, the witness' opinion that the gunshot was accidental would have permitted him to relate the facts with greater clarity, and hence would have aided the jury.

Based on an assessment of the witness' credibility, the jury then could attach an appropriate weight to this lay opinion.

Although the district court should not have excluded this opinion, the exclusion of the opinion was harmless error as it did not prejudice Knight. To find an error harmless, a court must be able to say that it is highly probable that the error did not contribute to the jury's judgment of conviction. *Government of the Virgin Islands v. Toto*, 529 F.2d 278, 284 (3d Cir. 1976). The eyewitness was permitted to describe fully the circumstances that led to his opinion — he stated that Knight never pointed the gun at the victim and never threatened to shoot the victim. Further, Knight himself testified that although he intended to assault Miller, the discharge of the gun was accidental, and defense counsel argued this theory to the jury. The jury could infer from these circumstances that the shooting was accidental.

The opinion of an unbiased eyewitness certainly may be viewed by a jury as more credible than the opinion of a criminal defendant. In this case, however, only a modicum of evidence was necessary to prove the accident theory of the defense because the prosecution barely disputed that the shooting was an accident. Indeed, the government all but conceded this point. During the government's closing argument, the prosecutor himself stated, "[The gunshot] may have been an accident. . . . [The beating] resulted in an unintentional, perhaps — probably unintentional and perhaps accidental discharge of that gun." Under these circumstances, the trial court's ruling could not have significantly prejudiced Knight and a reversal of the conviction is not warranted. . . .

ROBINSON v. BUMP

894 F.2d 758 (5th Cir. 1990)

DUHE, Circuit Judge.

This is a diversity negligence action brought by the estate and family of Willie Robinson against Willis Harris, MTD Products, and Henry Bump. The Robinsons appeal from a judgment denying relief against MTD and Bump.

MTD Products employed Henry Bump to operate an eighteen-wheel tractor-trailer rig. [After a car driven by Harris collided with the truck, Bump lost control and hit Robinson's car, killing Robinson and three other family members.] The jury found that Harris' negligence caused the accident but that Bump was not negligent. . . .

Battle, driver of the car following Bump, was called to testify for Bump and MTD. He testified that Bump was "in total control" of the truck until it was struck by the Harris vehicle. The appellants argue that this testimony constituted either a legal conclusion or an opinion on an ultimate issue. We review for abuse of discretion.

Rule 701 of the Federal Rules of Evidence permits a non-expert to testify in the form of an inference providing the inference is "rationally based on the perception of the witness" and "helpful to a clear understanding of the witness' testimony or the determination of a fact in issue." Under Rule 704 testimony in the form of an inference is "not objectionable because it embraces an ultimate issue to be decided by the trier of fact." . . .

While it is doubtful Battle was reciting anything more than his observations, the testimony was clearly admissible as an inference of a lay witness. Battle had every opportunity to observe the truck's movement, the movement of a truck is rationally connected to the control of its driver, and the testimony was helpful in allowing the jury to assess Bump's negligence. We find no abuse of discretion in allowing the testimony.... The judgment is Affirmed.

UNITED STATES v. HOUSTON

813 F.3d 282 (6th Cir. 2016)

ROGERS, Circuit Judge.

Rocky Houston appeals his conviction of being a felon in possession of a firearm in violation of 18 U.S.C. § 922(g)(1). At trial, the primary evidence against Houston was video footage of his possessing firearms at his and his brother's rural Tennessee farm.... [T]he district court denied Houston's pretrial motion to prohibit the Government from introducing lay opinion testimony of Special Agent Dobbs regarding the footage.... During his testimony, Dobbs identified for the jury when the recordings showed Houston, his brother, or firearms. Dobbs had become familiar with the brothers through conducting drive-bys and personally observing the brothers, as well as through studying the surveillance footage. Dobbs was also permitted to testify that one of the firearms in the video was a "Ruger Mini 14" because he gained personal familiarity with that type of firearm when a relative owned one....

Houston argues that Dobbs should not have been permitted to testify, because Dobbs did not observe the events firsthand. However, Federal Rule of Evidence 701 permits a lay witness to identify a defendant in a photograph when the witness is more likely than the jury to identify the individual....

Dobbs became familiar with Houston — including his typical dress and mannerisms — by observing him in person before Dobbs viewed the videos. Additionally, the video would occasionally "jump" and the images could be "grainy" when the zoom function was used. Accordingly ... the district court did not abuse its discretion. Similarly, the district court did not abuse its discretion when it permitted Dobbs to identify firearms in the video based on his general familiarity with firearms and the Ruger Mini 14 in particular. Just as Dobbs was more likely to be able to identify Houston in the poor quality videos due to his familiarity with Houston, Dobbs' general familiarity with firearms and the Ruger Mini 14 (which likely exceeded that of the average juror) also made him more likely to be able to identify firearms in the video. [Affirmed.]

ADVISORY COMMITTEE NOTE TO 2000 AMENDMENT TO F.R.E. 701

Rule 701 has been amended [by the addition of subsection (c)] to eliminate the risk that the reliability requirements set forth in Rule 702 will be evaded through the simple expedient of proffering an expert in lay witness clothing.... The amendment is not intended to affect the "prototypical example[s] of the type of evidence contemplated by the adoption of Rule 701 relat[ing] to the appearance of persons or things, identity, the manner of conduct, competency of a person, degrees of light or darkness, sound, size, weight, distance, and an endless number of items that cannot be described factually in words apart from inferences." *Asplundh Mfg. Div. v. Benton Harbor Eng'g*, 57 F.3d 1190, 1196 (3d Cir. 1995)....

The amendment incorporates the distinctions set forth in *State v. Brown*, 836 S.W.2d 530, 549 (1992), a case involving former Tennessee Rule of Evidence 701, a rule that precluded lay witness testimony based on "special knowledge." In *Brown*, the court declared that the distinction between lay and expert witness testimony is that lay testimony "results from a process of reasoning familiar in everyday life," while expert testimony "results from a process of reasoning which can be mastered only by specialists in the field." The court in *Brown* noted that a lay witness with experience could testify that a substance appeared to be blood, but that a witness would have to qualify as an expert before he could testify that bruising around the eyes is indicative of skull trauma. That is the kind of distinction made by the amendment to this Rule.

UNITED STATES v. AYALA-PIZARRO

407 F.3d 25 (1st Cir. 2005)

LYNCH, Circuit Judge.

Luis Daniel Ayala-Pizarro was convicted, after a four-day jury trial, of possession with intent to distribute 153 decks of heroin and of knowingly possessing a firearm in furtherance of a drug trafficking crime.... Ayala argues that the district court erred in permitting an arresting officer to cross the line from being a fact witness to being an expert witness when the officer testified about drug distribution points and how they operate as well as how heroin is normally packaged for distribution at these points....

Officer Mulero, one of the arresting officers, testified that he arrested Ayala at 2 p.m. on a Wednesday afternoon on Melilla Street in Loiza, Puerto Rico, near a house known to be a drug point. Officer Mulero and the other arresting officer ... observed Ayala and another man, Luis Vazquez Alvarez, at the right-hand corner of the house. Ayala and Vazquez did not see the officers, but the officers saw both men and that they were armed with firearms. Indeed, Ayala was trying to cock his gun, a Cobrai Model M11, nine millimeter caliber semiautomatic assault weapon, at the time. The officers then detained and arrested the two men. A search of Ayala turned up 153 aluminum-foil covered decks of heroin from his left pocket; his companion had $250. The officers arrested three other men standing nearby; each had a revolver. Experts determined that the heroin weighed 10.94 grams. An expert also testified that Ayala's gun was functioning and capable of firing in semiautomatic mode, and that its serial number was obliterated.

At trial, when the government asked Officer Mulero about his experience with drug points, as a lead-in to Mulero's testimony that Ayala was arrested at a known drug point, defense counsel objected, arguing that this was expert testimony and that because the government had not given notice of expert testimony from Mulero under Fed. R. Crim. P. 16(a)(1)(G), the witness could not so testify.[*]

At a subsequent bench conference, the government made a proffer that the witness would also testify that the particular packaging of the drugs seized showed they were packaged for distribution. Defense counsel countered that the testimony about the nature of the packaging was even more clearly expert testimony. The court ruled that the testimony that Melilla Street was a known drug point was permissible lay testimony. As to the packaging issue, the court ruled it needed to hear foundational evidence and allowed the testimony subject to a motion to strike.

Officer Mulero then testified as to how drug points work generally, stating:

> Basically one individual loads the drug while the other one collects the money, and then you have [men] who are armed and just waiting around in the event other gangs might come by and take action, and then you have others as vigilantes to see if the cops come.

Mulero testified about his experience with Melilla Street as a drug point. He also testified that he had made previous seizures of heroin at drug points, and that the heroin was typically packed in aluminum decks. Officer Mulero was then asked about the packaging of the drugs he seized from the defendant, and replied that the heroin was packaged "[i]n a shape or manner of a deck."...

On appeal, Ayala argues that he is entitled to a new trial because two parts of Mulero's testimony, first about how drug points operate and, second, about how heroin is packaged, could only be given by an expert and the government failed to give notice that Officer Mulero would testify as an expert....

We agree with the government that neither type of testimony was expert testimony at all, but was admissible as lay witness testimony under Fed. R. Evid. 701, even after the amendments to the two rules in December

---

[*] [Fed. R. Crim. P. 16(a)(1)(G) provides: "At the defendant's request, the government must give to the defendant a written summary of any testimony that the government intends to use under Rules 702, 703, or 705 of the Federal Rules of Evidence during its case-in-chief at trial. If the government requests discovery under subdivision (b)(1)(C)(ii) and the defendant complies, the government must, at the defendant's request, give to the defendant a written summary of testimony that the government intends to use under Rules 702, 703, or 705 of the Federal Rules of Evidence as evidence at trial on the issue of the defendant's mental condition. The summary provided under this subparagraph must describe the witness's opinions, the bases and reasons for those opinions, and the witness's qualifications."

Fed. R. Crim. P. 16(b)(1)(C) provides: "The defendant must, at the government's request, give to the government a written summary of any testimony that the defendant intends to use under Rules 702, 703, or 705 of the Federal Rules of Evidence as evidence at trial, if (i) the defendant requests disclosure under subdivision (a)(1)(G) and the government complies; or (ii) the defendant has given notice under Rule 12.2(b) of an intent to present expert testimony on the defendant's mental condition. This summary must describe the witness's opinions, the bases and reasons for those opinions, and the witness's qualifications." — ED.]

2000. The pre-amendment version of Rule 701 required lay opinion testimony to be "rationally based on the perception of the witness" and "helpful to a clear understanding of the witness' testimony or the determination of a fact in issue." In 2000, Rule 701 was amended to include the additional requirement that testimony admitted under the rule "not [be] based on scientific, technical, or other specialized knowledge within the scope of Rule 702." As the advisory committee's notes explain, this amendment was intended "to eliminate the risk that the reliability requirements set forth in Rule 702 will be evaded through the simple expedient of proffering an expert in lay witness clothing." . . .

We have noted that "[t]he line between expert testimony under Fed. R. Evid. 702 . . . and lay opinion testimony under Fed. R. Evid. 701 . . . is not easy to draw." *United States v. Colon Osorio*, 360 F.3d 48, 52–53 (1st Cir. 2004). Indeed, the same witness — for example, a law enforcement officer — may be qualified to "provide both lay and expert testimony in a single case." *See* Fed. R. Evid. 701, advisory committee's note (citing *United States v. Figueroa-Lopez*, 125 F.3d 1241, 1246 (9th Cir. 1997)). In this case, however, the testimony did not cross the line to become expert testimony.

As to the testimony about how drug points operate, Officer Mulero stated that he had investigated, patrolled, or made arrests at drug points on more than 100 occasions. His testimony stated what occurred at those drug points. This testimony was based on the requisite personal knowledge under Fed. R. Evid. 602 and also met the requirements of Fed. R. Evid. 701, because it was based on "particularized knowledge that the witness [had] by virtue of his . . . position" as a police officer assigned to patrol the neighborhood. Fed. R. Evid. 701, advisory committee's note.

Before the 2000 amendments, we had repeatedly noted that "the modern trend favors the admission of [lay] opinion testimony provided it is well founded on personal knowledge and susceptible to cross-examination." *See United States v. Vega-Figueroa*, 234 F.3d 744, 755 (1st Cir. 2000) (quoting *United States v. Paiva*, 892 F.2d 148, 157 (1st Cir. 1989)). While the 2000 amendments subject testimony falling within the scope of Rule 702 to heightened reliability requirements and rules governing pre-trial disclosure, Officer Mulero's testimony does not trigger these additional safeguards. It required no special expertise for Officer Mulero to conclude, based on his observations, that places which sell drugs are often protected by people with weapons. The defense could hardly be surprised by Mulero's testimony that Ayala was arrested at a drug point, nor was Ayala disabled from testing the reliability of Mulero's perceptions through cross-examination.

As to the packaging, the officer simply testified to his experience on prior drug arrests that the heroin seized at drug points was "basically packed in . . . aluminum decks," and that in this case the drugs were packaged "[i]n a shape or manner of a deck." The agent's testimony as to what he saw is not expert testimony. The jury was left to draw its own conclusions as to the contents and purpose of the decks, undoubtedly assisted by the fact that the 153 decks seized in this case, when tested, in fact contained heroin. . . .

The conviction is affirmed. . . .

UNITED STATES v. FREEMAN

730 F.3d 590 (6th Cir. 2013)

COLE, Circuit Judge.

Defendant-Appellant Marcus Freeman was convicted by a jury in the United States District Court for the Eastern District of Michigan of conspiracy to use interstate commerce facilities in the commission of murder for hire, 18 U.S.C. §1958. He received a sentence of life without parole. [The government alleged that Freeman's codefendant, Roy West, had paid Freeman to kill Leonard Day, after Day stole money, jewelry, a gun, and car keys from West.] Freeman now brings a direct appeal from that conviction, arguing that...the district court erred by permitting the Federal Bureau of Investigation agent in charge of the investigation to give lay testimony under Federal Rule of Evidence 701....

The government's primary evidence against Freeman consisted of 23,000 phone conversations between Freeman, West, . . . and other co-defendants. Seventy-seven of these calls were admitted as exhibits at trial, and portions of them were played for the jury. [Special Agent Scott Lucas] was called to testify regarding his personal impressions of the recorded conversations. [He] interpreted the conversations as they were played. His testimony ranged from voice and nickname identifications to substantive interpretations of the meaning of the various statements. Defense counsel objected near the beginning of this testimony: "I think this is outside of the scope of both the notice we received regarding this witness's expertise and his expertise. Both." While Agent Lucas had been qualified as an expert to testify to the meaning of specific code words and drug slang, both parties recognized that his testimony had moved outside the scope of his expert qualification. The prosecution responded: "Your honor, this is not expert testimony. This is based upon his personal knowledge of the investigation." The objection was overruled, and Agent Lucas continued to testify as a lay witness under Rule 701....

Throughout the recordings, Agent Lucas interpreted conversations between Freeman and his co-defendants to broadly illustrate the prosecution's theory of the case for the jury. At the end of one phone call between West and Freeman, for example, in which they discuss "the word on dude," Freeman says, "I told you I was chillin' over dude house." Freeman additionally says, presumably referring to Day's family, "[T]hey was talkin' about the dude, so he definitely phonin' in." Freeman ends the call by stating, "This shit should be any day now though fam for real. So I'm on it for sure 'cause I need that." Agent Lucas testified to the meaning of this call, including Freeman's final statement. Agent Lucas told the jury, "I believe he is referring to the fact that he needs the payment he expects from Roy West if he's successful in locating Leonard Day . . . for the purpose of recovering the jewelry and killing him." . . . Similar "interpretations" occurred throughout Agent Lucas's testimony. . . .

A witness may testify based on opinion, as opposed to testifying to facts of which he has direct knowledge, under two circumstances: as a lay person under Rule 701 or as an expert under Rule 702. "Such lay opinion testimony is permitted under Rule 701 because it has the effect of describing something that the jurors could not otherwise experience for themselves by drawing upon the witness's sensory and experiential observations that were made as a first-hand witness to a particular event." *United States v. Jayyousi*, 657 F3.d 1085, 1120 (11th Cir. 2011) (Barkett, J., concurring in part and dissenting in part)....

We conclude that here the prosecution did not establish a proper foundation for Agent Lucas's testimony under Rule 701. As several circuits have recognized, there is a risk when an agent "provides interpretations of recorded conversations based on his knowledge of the entire investigation ... that he [is] testifying based upon information not before the jury, including hearsay, or at the least, that the jury [c]ould think he ha[s] knowledge beyond what [is] before them...." [*United States v. Hampton*, 718 F.3d 978, 982-983 (D.C. Cir. 2013)]; *see also* [*United States v. Albertelli*, 687 F.3d 439, 447 (1st Cir. 2012)] (recognizing that an agent's "testimony may effectively smuggle in inadmissible evidence," that he may be "drawing inferences that counsel could do but with ... the imprimatur of testifying as a law enforcement officer," that he may "usurp the jury's function," and that he may be "doing nothing more than speculating").

Over the course of his testimony, Agent Lucas repeatedly substantiated his responses and inferences with generic information and references to the investigation as a whole. For example, he made statements such as "We learned over our wiretaps" and "We were able to determine that from some [of] the intercepted calls. . . ." He never specified *personal* experiences that led him to obtain his information but, instead, repeatedly relied on the general knowledge of the FBI and the investigation as a whole.... [T]he jury was left to trust that he had some information — information unknown to them — that made him better situated to interpret the words used in the calls than they were.... Agent Lucas failed to explain the basis of his interpretations — what experience he had that the jurors themselves did not have — and therefore failed to lay a foundation under 701.

Furthermore, . . . Agent Lucas's testimony . . . consisted of many opinions and conclusions the jury was well equipped to draw on their own. He effectively spoon-fed his interpretations of the phone calls and the government's theory of the case to the jury, interpreting even ordinary English language.... Take, for example, Agent Lucas's testimony as to [a] phone call [that took place shortly] after Day had been shot:

WEST: What's good?
FREEMAN: Everything good, man. Except for, you know . . . you know what I'm talkin' about . . . just that one little thing. We ain't get the bonus, dog. But, you know what I'm sayin', the situation is over with.

When asked what "situation" Freeman had referred to, Agent Lucas testified, "The situation discussed was regarding Leonard Day and his having stolen jewelry from Roy West, Roy West having put a hit on Leonard Day and Leonard Day ultimately being killed." . . . [I]t is not for an agent to divine what vague, plain English language means as Agent Lucas did repeatedly here. These types of conclusions are the province of a jury....

We can distinguish this case from out-of-circuit cases cited by the government. In those cases, the phone calls included cryptic language, and the testifier explained what personal knowledge he used in interpreting that language. For example, in [*United States v. Rollins*, 544 F.3d 820, 832 (7th Cir. 2008),] an agent testified based on thousands of calls that coconspirators devised code as they went along, using words with different meanings at different times. That agent opined about the meaning of otherwise nonsensical conversations involving, for example, "having drinks," the height of a "singer" in a "band," and "big shoes and little shoes." Here, however, Agent Lucas testified about not only code words but also common words used in common ways.

Moreover, we emphasize our concern that the jury may have been unduly persuaded by Agent Lucas's position as an FBI agent. An agent qualified as an expert may interpret coded drug language, as Agent Lucas did. And a lay witness who has personal knowledge of a particular drug or crime conspiracy may similarly testify to the meaning of coded language within his knowledge. But a case agent testifying as a lay witness may not explain to a jury what inferences to draw from recorded conversations involving ordinary language. At that point, his testimony is no longer evidence but becomes argument. Agent Lucas effectively told the jury that they were not as qualified as he to interpret the phone calls:

Q: You're just an everyday mope like everybody else, right?
A: In some respects, yes. But an everyday mope who has listened to approximately 23,000 Title III calls in this case.
Q: Right. But the Jury could listen to 23,000 phone calls . . . and reach a different personal conclusion, correct?
A: That's possible and it would not be based on 15 years of experience in the FBI.

Comments such as these "can convey the impression that evidence not presented to the jury, but known to the [prosecution], supports the charges against the defendant and thus jeopardize the defendant's right to be tried solely on the basis of the evidence presented to the jury." [*Hampton*, 718 F.3d at 983.] In such cases, the agent may receive unmerited credibility for his testimony when the jury suspects that he has investigative information they do not. An agent presented to a jury with an aura of expertise and authority increases the risk that the jury will be swayed improperly by the agent's testimony, rather than rely on its own interpretation of the evidence. We find enforcement of 701's criteria uniquely important under these circumstances. *See* [*id.*] at 981-82 ("Judicial scrutiny of a law-enforcement witness's purported basis for lay opinion is especially important because of the risk that the jury will defer to the officer's superior knowledge of the case and past experiences with similar crimes."). . . .

The government cursorily argues that, even if the district court abused its discretion by admitting Agent Lucas's testimony under Rule 701, the error was harmless because Agent Lucas could have been qualified as an expert under Rule 702 for the entire scope of his testimony. The government acknowledges that Agent Lucas's testimony exceeded the scope of its expert notice, *see* Fed. R. Crim. P. 16, but argues that "[c]ourts have found harmless error when a witness was unquestionably qualified to render expert testimony, even in the absence of . . . expert notices." . . . [But the] requirement that an opinion be "helpful to the jury" is the same under Rule 702(a) as under Rule 701(b). For the same reasons that many of Agent Lucas's opinions were not helpful to the jury as lay testimony under Rule 701(b), and therefore inadmissible, his opinions would not have been helpful as expert testimony under Rule 702(a).

Additionally, although Agent Lucas explicitly referred to his expertise and credentials, giving himself an aura of authority on the stand, it is not clear what expert methodology he relied on to form his opinions (outside of his expertise on street slang and drug terms, which had already been granted). Testimony under Rule 702 must be "the product of reliable principles and methods . . . reliably applied . . . to the facts of the case." Fed. R. Evid. 702. Here, Agent Lucas "provided virtually no methodology or guiding principles that would enable him to decode the wiretapped phone calls...." [*United States v. Johnson*, 617 F.3d 286, 294 (4th Cir. 2010)].... It is therefore unclear that the district court would have (or could have) allowed Agent Lucas to give his full testimony as an expert.... For the foregoing reasons, we vacate the conviction and remand for a new trial.

B. EXPERT TESTIMONY

Trial lawyers and trial judges have long felt that witnesses with specialized skills or knowledge can often offer helpful testimony even if they have no firsthand knowledge of the facts in a particular case. Therefore expert witnesses, unlike lay witnesses, are allowed to offer opinions based in whole or in part on information they have received secondhand, as long as the witness is sufficiently qualified to render an expert opinion, the information is of a kind typically relied upon by experts in the field, and the witness is truly drawing on some special skill or knowledge, as opposed to making judgments the jury could just as easily make itself.

During the past several decades, as more and more trials have involved scientific or technical issues, expert testimony has become increasingly common and increasingly important. It has also grown increasingly controversial. There is widespread concern that experts can be hired to say almost anything, and that juries are too easily bamboozled by charlatans. One solution might be for judges rather than parties to select expert witnesses. Judges in fact are authorized to appoint experts, but they rarely do — largely, perhaps, because the practice fits poorly with our system's general delegation of investigation and witness selection to the parties and their lawyers.

The Federal Rules of Evidence now try to prevent shoddy expert testimony in a different way: they require a trial judge to exclude expert testimony unless the judge concludes it is "reliable." This requirement codifies the holdings of three cases decided by the Supreme Court in the 1990s: *Daubert v. Merrell Dow Pharmaceuticals, Inc.*, 509 U.S. 579 (1993), *General Electric Co. v. Joiner*, 522 U.S. 136 (1997), and *Kumho Tire Co. v. Carmichael*, 526 U.S. 137 (1999). Each of these decisions is excerpted below, along with materials illustrating more traditional limitations on expert testimony.

[F.R.E. 702-706; C.E.C. §§801-804]

1. Permissible Subjects and Scope of Expert Testimony

ADVISORY COMMITTEE NOTE TO F.R.E. 702

An intelligent evaluation of facts is often difficult or impossible without the application of some scientific, technical, or other specialized knowledge. The most common source of this knowledge is the expert witness, although there are other techniques for supplying it.

Most of the literature assumes that experts testify only in the form of opinions. The assumption is logically unfounded. The rule accordingly recognizes that an expert on the stand may give a dissertation or exposition of scientific or other principles relevant to the case, leaving the trier of fact to apply them to the facts. Since much of the criticism of expert testimony has centered upon the hypothetical question, it seems wise to recognize that opinions are not indispensable and to encourage the use of expert testimony in non-opinion form when counsel believes the trier can itself draw the requisite inference. The use of opinions is not abolished by the rule, however. It will continue to be permissible for the experts to take the further step of suggesting the inference which should be drawn from applying the specialized knowledge to the facts. See Rules 703 to 705.

Whether the situation is a proper one for the use of expert testimony is to be determined on the basis of assisting the trier. "There is no more certain test for determining when experts may be used than the common sense inquiry whether the untrained layman would be qualified to determine intelligently and to the best possible degree the particular issue without enlightenment from those having a specialized understanding of the subject involved in the dispute." Ladd, Expert Testimony, 5 Vand. L. Rev. 414, 418 (1952). When opinions are excluded, it is because they are unhelpful and therefore superfluous and a waste of time. 7 Wigmore §1918.

The rule is broadly phrased. The fields of knowledge which may be drawn upon are not limited merely to the "scientific" and "technical" but extend to all "specialized" knowledge. Similarly, the expert is viewed, not in a narrow sense, but as a person qualified by "knowledge, skill, experience, training or education." Thus within the scope of the rule are not only experts in the strictest sense of the word, e.g., physicians, physicists, and architects, but also the large group sometimes called "skilled" witnesses, such as bankers or landowners testifying to land values.

HATCH v. STATE FARM FIRE & CASUALTY CO.

930 P. 2d 382 (Wyo. 1997)

THOMAS, Justice.

[State Farm Fire & Casualty Co. refused to pay for the damage caused by a fire in the Hatch family's house, because the company concluded that Frank Hatch had started the fire. Hatch was charged with arson, but the jury found him not guilty. The Hatches then sued State Farm for breaching its duty of good faith and fair dealing in resolving their policy claim, and for intentional infliction of emotional distress. A jury found for State Farm, and the Hatches appealed. The Supreme Court of Wyoming affirmed.]

... In the course of their case in chief, the Hatches offered the discovery deposition testimony of an expert witness, Carrol M. Cloyd (Cloyd), into evidence pursuant to Wyo. R. Civ. P. 32 because Cloyd had died before the trial. At the deposition, Cloyd had been qualified as an expert on insurance industry standards for good faith and fair dealing in the investigation and handling of insurance claims. . . . A major issue about Cloyd's testimony concerned questions he was asked about State Farm complying with the standard it had established by its advertising. According to the Hatches' theory, State Farm had engaged in an advertising campaign that features the slogan, "Like a good neighbor, State Farm is there." [The trial judge excluded] testimony from Cloyd as to whether, in his opinion, State Farm's actions complied with the standard expected of good faith and fair dealing and "a good neighbor." . . .

The questions and answers in Cloyd's deposition went beyond the industry standard for good faith and fair dealing in the investigation and handling of insurance claims. They purported to provide his opinion with respect to an extraneous and non-legal standard. The provision in Wyo. R. Evid. 702, concerning opinions of experts offering "specialized knowledge" that "will assist the trier of fact," does not justify such testimony. Cloyd's opinion, as to whether the advertising established a standard and on how a "good neighbor" would act, required no specialized knowledge, nor could it have assisted the jury in understanding the evidence or determining any of the facts in issue. It properly was excluded. His opinion as to how a "good neighbor" would act was beyond the realm of his expertise. . . .

MARTEN TRANSPORT LTD. v. PLATTFORM ADVERTISING, INC.

184 F. Supp. 3d 1006 (D. Kan. 2016)

Lungstrom, District Judge.

In this action, plaintiff Marten Transport, Ltd. ("Marten"), a trucking company, alleges that defendant PlattForm Advertising, Inc. ("PlattForm") used Marten's name and trademarks without authorization on websites on which PlattForm advertised truck driver jobs. The matter comes before the Court on PlattForm's motion to exclude expert testimony by Marten's expert[] . . . Richard Follis. . . .

Richard Follis is a consultant with experience in the transportation industry, including experience recruiting truck drivers. Mr. Follis's report contains opinions relating to the following: turnover of drivers in the trucking industry; costs of hiring drivers; lost revenues for empty trucks; a shortage of drivers in the industry; advertising by carriers for drivers, including online advertising; search engine optimization; and the relationship between a carrier and its advertising agency. . . .

PlattForm challenges two sets of opinions by Mr. Follis from his report. First, PlattForm takes issue with the opinions in a paragraph discussing the "importance of a carrier being able to capture every qualified driver possible" and various issues of concern to drivers and applicants. PlattForm argues that these opinions represent mere speculation without basis. These are the type of opinions, however, that Mr. Follis is qualified to render based on his expertise and long experience in the trucking industry. Thus, the Court rejects PlattForm's challenge to these opinions.

Second, PlattForm challenges Mr. Follis's opinions relating to search engine optimization (SEO). The section of Mr. Follis's report titled "Summary of Opinion" contains the following paragraphs:

> Advertising over the past 15 years has transformed dramatically. . . .With the advent of the web, portable computer, I phones [*sic*], etc., online recruiting is now and will continue to be the future of recruiting. . . . Consequently, truckload carriers are constantly looking for a better mousetrap to attract qualified class A drivers. Because of the new technology age this begins with a well thought out web page containing as many key words, pictures, and videos as possible. Key word examples are trucking, truck driver, driving jobs, class A drivers, one word description of routes, (local, dedicated, regional, OTR) etc. The next step is to get your website seen. This is where optimization comes in. Trying to optimize your web site on your own is very costly. However, if you subscribe to a pay per click provider or trucking websites you automatically increase theirs [sic] and your optimization.
>
> Search engines look for key words . . . . By subscribing to these trucking websites you increase your optimization due to a process called Algorithm. By being linked to a trucking web page the key words are more frequent due [*sic*] the trucking web page configuration as well as those other carrier web pages all being linked to the trucking web page. The more carriers and key words, the more viable the trucking web page is in the eyes of search engines such as Google and Yahoo. My experience is 10% to 12% of carriers [sic] hires come from trucking websites. Depending on frequency of updates and locations used, Craig's list can generate in the neighborhood of 25% of hires.

The section of the report titled "Conclusion" contains the following paragraphs:

> . . . Because Platform [*sic*] Advertising, Inc. placed advertising using Marten Transport, LTD. marks without a signed insertion order, it can only be for the purpose of increasing optimization for findingtruckingjobs.com and justtrucking jobs.com.
>
> Every carrier listed on their websites enhances optimization by increasing the key word menu, pictures, videos, which in turn raises their awareness with search engines such as Yahoo and Google. More awareness and better positioning on search engine pages equals better numbers to attract new clients. . . .

PlattForm argues that Mr. Follis is not qualified to give these SEO opinions and that the opinions are not supported by a reliable basis or methodology. The Court agrees.

Marten has not submitted a declaration or testimony from Mr. Follis (he was not deposed) or any other evidence in support of these opinions. Marten points to Mr. Follis's general experience in advertising for drivers. Such experience would make him qualified to render the opinions from the foregoing excerpts that do not directly relate to SEO. That would include the general use of key words in advertising for drivers, as that practice would fall within his experience. Such general experience in the industry, however, would not necessarily give a person the technical knowledge to understand and render an expert opinion concerning SEO, how it works, and how it could be affected in given circumstances — at least, not in the absence of evidence that the expert did obtain such expertise at some point in his career. Thus, Mr. Follis's experience does not provide the necessary support for his SEO opinions.

The Court's conclusion in this regard is bolstered by Mr. Follis's description of his assignment in the report. Mr. Follis states there that it was "understood" by him in rendering his opinions that PlattForm acted to increase its websites' SEO. That statement supports the conclusion that Mr. Follis did not reach that opinion on his own, based on his own expertise . . . .

For these reasons, PlattForm's motion to exclude is granted with respect to Mr. Follis's opinions concerning SEO . . . . The motion is otherwise denied.

REPORT OF THE SENATE JUDICIARY COMMITTEE ON RULE 704

S. Rep. No. 98-225 (1983)

The purpose of this amendment [adding §(b) to F.R.E. 704] is to eliminate the confusing spectacle of competing expert witnesses testifying to directly contradictory conclusions as to the ultimate legal issue to be found by the trier of fact. Under this proposal, expert psychiatric testimony would be limited to presenting and explaining their diagnoses, such as whether the defendant had a severe mental disease or defect and what the characteristics of such a disease or defect, if any, may have been. The basis for the limitation on expert testimony in insanity cases is ably stated by the American Psychiatric Association:

> . . . When . . . "ultimate issue" questions are formulated by the law and put to the expert witness who must then say "yea" or "nay," then the expert witness is required to make a leap in logic. He no longer addresses himself to medical concepts but instead must infer or intuit what is in fact unspeakable, namely, the probable relationship between medical concepts and legal or moral constructs such as free will. . . . Juries find themselves listening to conclusory and seemingly contradictory testimony that defendants are either "sane" or "insane" or that they do or do not meet the relevant legal test for insanity. This state of affairs does considerable injustice to psychiatry and, we believe, possibly to criminal defendants. . . . Psychiatrists, of course, must be permitted to testify fully about the defendant's diagnosis, mental state and motivation (in clinical and common sense terms) at the time of the alleged act so as to permit the jury or judge to reach the ultimate conclusion about which they and only they are expert. Determining whether a criminal defendant was legally insane is a matter for legal fact-finders, not for experts.

Moreover, the rationale for precluding ultimate opinion psychiatric testimony extends beyond the insanity defense to any ultimate mental state of the defendant that is relevant to the legal conclusion sought to be proved. The Committee has fashioned its Rule 704 provision to reach all such "ultimate" issues, e.g., premeditation in a homicide case, or lack of predisposition in entrapment.

2. Relating the Basis of an Expert Opinion to the Jury

Experts typically must rely on hearsay in rendering their opinions. For example, a forensic psychologist rendering a diagnosis might rely on statements made in textbooks read during his or her training; scientific studies; school records; and statements made to the psychologist by friends and family during interviews. Federal Rule 703 allows experts to rely on such evidence as a basis for their opinion, even if the evidence would otherwise be inadmissible, so long as it is of a type reasonably relied upon by those in the field.

But some criminal defendants have argued that a government expert's relating of the *testimonial* hearsay of other people to the jury, even if ostensibly for the non-hearsay purpose of explaining the basis of the expert's opinion, violates the Confrontation Clause if these other people do not also testify. The Supreme Court considered this issue in *Williams v. Illinois*, excerpted below. As you will see, the fractured opinions of the justices in *Williams* offer little guidance going forward. The opinion in *People v. Sanchez,* also excerpted below, shows how California has recently resolved the issue.

ADVISORY COMMITTEE NOTE TO F.R.E. 703

Facts or data upon which expert opinions are based may, under the rule, be derived from three possible sources. The first is the firsthand observation of the witness with opinions based thereon traditionally allowed. A treating physician affords an example.... The second source, presentation at the trial, also reflects existing practice. The technique may be the familiar hypothetical question or having the expert attend the trial and hear the testimony establishing the facts.... The third source contemplated by the rule consists of presentation of data to the expert outside of court and other than by his own perception. In this respect the rule is designed to broaden the basis for expert opinions beyond that current in many jurisdictions and to bring the judicial practice into line with the practice of the experts themselves when not in court. Thus a physician in his own practice bases his diagnosis on information from numerous sources and of considerable variety, including statements by patients and relatives, reports and opinions from nurses, technicians and other doctors, hospital records, and X-rays. Most of them are admissible in evidence, but only with the expenditure of substantial time in producing and examining various authenticating witnesses. The physician makes life-and-death decisions in reliance upon them. His validation, expertly performed and subject to cross-examination, ought to suffice for judicial purposes.

The rule also offers a more satisfactory basis for ruling upon the admissibility of public opinion poll evidence. Attention is directed to the validity of the techniques employed rather than to relatively fruitless inquiries whether hearsay is involved.

If it be feared that enlargement of permissible data may tend to break down the rules of exclusion unduly, notice should be taken that the rule requires that the facts or data "be of a type reasonably relied upon by experts in the particular field." The language would not warrant admitting in evidence the opinion of an "accidentologist" as to the point of impact in an automobile collision based on statements of bystanders since this requirement is not satisfied.

ADVISORY COMMITTEE NOTE TO 2000
AMENDMENT TO F.R.E. 703

Rule 703 has been amended to emphasize that when an expert reasonably relies on inadmissible information to form an opinion or inference, the underlying information is not admissible simply because the opinion or inference is admitted. . . . The amendment provides a presumption against disclosure to the jury of information used as the basis of an expert's opinion and not admissible for any substantive purpose, when that information is offered by the proponent of the expert. In a multi-party case, where one party proffers an expert whose testimony is also beneficial to other parties, each such party should be deemed a "proponent" within the meaning of the amendment.

WILLIAMS v. ILLINOIS

567 U.S. 50 (2012)

Justice ALITO announced the judgment of the Court and delivered an opinion, in which THE CHIEF JUSTICE, Justice KENNEDY, and Justice BREYER join.

In this case, we decide whether *Crawford v. Washington*, 541 U.S. 36 (2004), precludes an expert witness from testifying in a manner that has long been allowed under the law of evidence. Specifically, does *Crawford* bar an expert from expressing an opinion based on facts about a case that have been made known to the expert but about which the expert is not competent to testify? We also decide whether *Crawford* substantially impedes the ability of prosecutors to introduce DNA evidence and thus may effectively relegate the prosecution in some cases to reliance on older, less reliable forms of proof.

In petitioner's bench trial for rape, the prosecution called [Sandra Lambatos,] an expert who testified that a DNA profile produced by an outside laboratory, Cellmark, matched a profile produced by the state police lab using a sample of petitioner's blood. On direct examination, the expert testified that Cellmark was an accredited laboratory and that Cellmark provided the police with a DNA profile. The expert also explained the notations on documents admitted as business records, stating that, according to the records, vaginal swabs taken from the victim were sent to and received back from Cellmark. The expert made no other statement that was offered for the purpose of identifying the sample of biological material used in deriving the profile or for the purpose of establishing how Cellmark handled or tested the sample. Nor did the expert vouch for the accuracy of the profile that Cellmark produced. Nevertheless, petitioner contends that the expert's testimony violated the Confrontation Clause as interpreted in *Crawford*.

Petitioner's main argument is that the expert went astray when she referred to the DNA profile provided by Cellmark as having been produced from semen found on the victim's vaginal swabs. But both the Illinois Appellate Court and the Illinois Supreme Court found that this statement was not admitted for the truth of the matter asserted, and it is settled that the Confrontation Clause does not bar the admission of such statements. For more than 200 years, the law of evidence has permitted the sort of testimony that was given by the expert in this case. Under settled evidence law, an expert may express an opinion that is based on facts that the expert assumes, but does not know, to be true. It is then up to the party who calls the expert to introduce other evidence establishing the facts assumed by the expert. While it was once the practice for an expert who based an opinion on assumed facts to testify in the form of an answer to a hypothetical question, modern practice does not demand this formality and, in appropriate cases, permits an expert to explain the facts on which his or her opinion is based without testifying to the truth of those facts. See Fed. Rule Evid. 703. That is precisely what occurred in this case, and we should not lightly "swee[p] away an accepted rule governing the admission of scientific evidence." *Melendez-Diaz v. Massachusetts*, 557 U.S. 305, 330 (2009) (KENNEDY, J., dissenting).

We now conclude that this form of expert testimony does not violate the Confrontation Clause because that provision has no application to out-of-court statements that are not offered to prove the truth of the matter asserted. When an expert testifies for the prosecution in a criminal case, the defendant has the opportunity to cross-examine the expert about any statements that are offered for their truth. Out-of-court statements that are related by the expert solely for the purpose of explaining the assumptions on which that opinion rests are not offered for their truth and thus fall outside the scope of the Confrontation Clause. Applying this rule to the present case, we conclude that the expert's testimony did not violate the Sixth Amendment.

As a second, independent basis for our decision, we also conclude that even if the report produced by Cellmark had been admitted into evidence, there would have been no Confrontation Clause violation. The Cellmark report is very different from the sort of extrajudicial statements, such as affidavits, depositions, prior testimony, and confessions, that the Confrontation Clause was originally understood to reach. The report was produced before any suspect was identified. The report was sought not for the purpose of obtaining evidence to be used against petitioner, who was not even under suspicion at the time, but for the purpose of finding a rapist who was on the loose. And the profile that Cellmark provided was not inherently inculpatory. On the contrary, a DNA profile is evidence that tends to exculpate all but one of the more than 7 billion people in the world today. The use of DNA evidence to exonerate persons who have been wrongfully accused or convicted is well known. If DNA profiles could not be introduced without calling the technicians who participated in the preparation of the profile, economic pressures would encourage prosecutors to forgo DNA testing and rely instead on older forms of evidence, such as eyewitness identification, that are less reliable. The Confrontation Clause does not mandate such an undesirable development. This conclusion will not prejudice any defendant who really wishes to probe the reliability of the DNA testing done in a particular case because those who participated in the testing may always be subpoenaed by the defense and questioned at trial. . . .

[Justice BREYER filed a concurring opinion.]

Justice THOMAS, concurring in the judgment.

I agree with the plurality that the disclosure of Cellmark's out-of-court statements through the expert testimony of Sandra Lambatos did not violate the Confrontation Clause. I reach this conclusion, however, solely because Cellmark's statements lacked the requisite "formality and solemnity" to be considered "'testimonial'" for purposes of the Confrontation Clause. See *Michigan v. Bryant*, 562 U.S. 344 (2011) (Thomas, J., concurring in judgment).... I share the dissent's view of the plurality's flawed analysis....

Justice Kagan, with whom Justice Scalia, Justice Ginsburg, and Justice Sotomayor join, dissenting.

Some years ago, the State of California prosecuted a man named John Kocak for rape. At a preliminary hearing, the State presented testimony from an analyst at the Cellmark Diagnostics Laboratory — the same facility used to generate DNA evidence in this case. The analyst had extracted DNA from a bloody sweatshirt found at the crime scene and then compared it to two control samples — one from Kocak and one from the victim. The analyst's report identified a single match: As she explained on direct examination, the DNA found on the sweatshirt belonged to Kocak. But after undergoing cross-examination, the analyst realized she had made a mortifying error. She took the stand again, but this time to admit that the report listed the victim's control sample as coming from Kocak, and Kocak's as coming from the victim. So the DNA on the sweatshirt matched not Kocak, but the victim herself. See Tr. in No. SCD110465 (Super. Ct. San Diego Cty., Cal., Nov. 17, 1995), pp. 3-4 ("I'm a little hysterical right now, but I think ... the two names should be switched"). In trying Kocak, the State would have to look elsewhere for its evidence.

Our Constitution contains a mechanism for catching such errors — the Sixth Amendment's Confrontation Clause.... Under our Confrontation Clause precedents, this is an open-and-shut case. The State of Illinois prosecuted Sandy Williams for rape based in part on a DNA profile created in Cellmark's laboratory. Yet the State did not give Williams a chance to question the analyst who produced that evidence. Instead, the prosecution introduced the results of Cellmark's testing through an expert witness who had no idea how they were generated.... Lambatos's testimony is functionally identical to the "surrogate testimony" that New Mexico proffered in *Bullcoming*, which did nothing to cure the problem identified in *Melendez-Diaz* (which, for its part, straightforwardly applied our decision in *Crawford*)....

The plurality's primary argument to the contrary ... [is] that Lambatos's recitation of Cellmark's findings, when viewed through the prism of state evidence law, was not introduced to establish "the truth of any ... matter concerning [the] Cellmark" report. But ... when a witness, expert or otherwise, repeats an out-of-court statement as the basis for a conclusion ... the statement's utility is ... dependent on its truth. If the statement is true, then the conclusion based on it is probably true; if not, not. So to determine the validity of the witness's conclusion, the factfinder must assess the truth of the out-of-court statement on which it relies. That is why the principal modern treatise on evidence variously calls the idea that such "basis evidence" comes in not for its truth, but only to help the factfinder evaluate an expert's opinion "very weak," "factually implausible," "nonsense," and "sheer fiction." D. Kaye, D. Bernstein & J. Mnookin, The New Wigmore: Expert Evidence §4.10.1, pp. 196-197 (2d ed. 2011); *id.*, §4.11.6, at 24 (Supp.2012). "One can sympathize," notes that treatise, "with a court's desire to permit the disclosure of basis evidence that is quite probably reliable, such as a routine analysis of a drug, but to pretend that it is not being introduced for the truth of its contents strains credibility." *Id.,* §4.10.1, at 198 (2d ed. 2011); see also, *e.g., People v. Goldstein,* 6 N.Y.3d 119, 128 (2005) ("The distinction between a statement offered for its truth and a statement offered to shed light on an expert's opinion is not meaningful").... [A]dmission of the out-of-court statement in this context has no purpose separate from its truth; the factfinder can do nothing with it *except* assess its truth and so the credibility of the conclusion it serves to buttress....

[T]he plurality's second basis for denying Williams's right of confrontation also fails. The plurality can find no reason consistent with our precedents for treating the Cellmark report as nontestimonial. That is because the report is, in every conceivable respect, a statement meant to serve as evidence in a potential criminal trial. And that simple fact should be sufficient to resolve the question....

Justice THOMAS's unique method of defining testimonial statements fares no better.... Indeed, Justice Thomas's approach, if accepted, would turn the Confrontation Clause into a constitutional geegaw — nice for show, but of little value. The prosecution could avoid its demands by using the right kind of forms with the right kind of language.... And still worse: The new conventions, precisely by making out-of-court statements less "solem[n]" would also make them less reliable — and so turn the Confrontation Clause upside down.... It is not surprising that no other Member of the Court has adopted this position....

What comes out of four Justices' desire to limit *Melendez-Diaz* and *Bullcoming* in whatever way possible, combined with one Justice's one-justice view of those holdings, is — to be frank — who knows what. Those decisions apparently no longer mean all that they say....

PEOPLE v. SANCHEZ

204 Cal. Rptr. 3d 102 (2016)

CORRIGAN, Associate Justice.

[Appellant Marcos Sanchez was convicted of gun and drug charges, as well as "active participation" in the "Delhi" street gang, and engaging in a felony for the benefit of the gang. To establish that Sanchez was affiliated with the Delhi gang, the prosecutor called police detective David Stow as a "gang expert." In his testimony, Stow related the contents of several written "STEP notices" and "Field Identification" (FI) Cards stored in a statewide gang database. These notices each contained statements made by other police officers about their previous interactions with Sanchez, as well as incriminating statements allegedly made by Sanchez admitting to being associated with the gang. Sanchez argued that Stow's recounting of these out-of-court statements violated the rule against hearsay and the Confrontation Clause. The state argued that the statements were offered solely to show the basis of the expert's opinion, and not for their truth.]

In the context of a confrontation challenge to the admission of certain expert "basis" testimony, the high court addressed the not-for-the-truth rationale in *Williams v. Illinois* (2012) 567 U.S. 50.... Five justices, the four-member dissent and Justice Thomas writing separately, . . . called into question the continuing validity of relying on a not-for-the-truth analysis in the expert witness context.

We find persuasive the reasoning of a majority of justices in *Williams*. When an expert is not testifying in the form of a proper hypothetical question and no other evidence of the case-specific facts presented has [been] or will be admitted, there is no denying that such facts are being considered by the expert, and offered to the jury, as true. Indeed, the jury here was given a standard instruction that it "must decide whether information on which the expert relied was true and accurate." (CALCRIM No. 332 [Expert Witness Testimony].) . . .

. . . [W]hen the gang expert testified to case-specific facts based upon out-of-court statements and asserted those facts were true because he relied upon their truth in forming his opinion, he was reciting hearsay. Ordinarily, an improper admission of hearsay would constitute statutory error under the Evidence Code. Under *Crawford,* however, if that hearsay was testimonial and *Crawford*'s exceptions did not apply, defendant should have been given the opportunity to cross-examine the declarant or the evidence should have been excluded. Improper admission of such prosecution evidence would also be an error of federal constitutional magnitude.

. . . The Attorney General urges that excluding the content of testimonial hearsay would greatly hamper experts from giving opinions about gangs. The argument sweeps too broadly. Gang experts, like all others, can rely on background information accepted in their field of expertise under the traditional latitude given by the Evidence Code. They can rely on information within their personal knowledge, and they can give an opinion based on a hypothetical including case-specific facts that are properly proven. They may also rely on nontestimonial hearsay properly admitted under a statutory hearsay exception. What they cannot do is present, as facts, the content of testimonial hearsay statements. . . .

Any expert may still *rely* on hearsay in forming an opinion, and may tell the jury *in general terms* that he did so. . . . There is a distinction to be made between allowing an expert to describe the type or source of the matter relied upon as opposed to presenting, as fact, case-specific hearsay that does not otherwise fall under a statutory exception.

What an expert *cannot* do is relate as true case-specific facts asserted in hearsay statements, unless they are independently proven by competent evidence or are covered by a hearsay exception. It may be true that merely telling the jury the expert relied on additional kinds of information that the expert only generally describes may do less to bolster the weight of the opinion. The answer to this reality is twofold. First, the argument confirms that the proffered case-specific hearsay assertions *are* being offered for their truth. The expert is essentially telling the jury: "You should accept my opinion because it is reliable in light of these *facts* on which I rely." Second, in a criminal prosecution, while *Crawford* and its progeny may complicate some heretofore accepted evidentiary rules, they do so under the compulsion of a constitutional mandate as established by binding Supreme Court precedent.

In sum, we adopt the following rule: When any expert relates to the jury case-specific out-of-court statements, and treats the content of those statements as true and accurate to support the expert's opinion, the statements are hearsay. It cannot logically be maintained that the statements are not being admitted for their truth. If the case is one in which a prosecution expert seeks to relate *testimonial* hearsay, there is a confrontation clause violation unless (1) there is a showing of unavailability and (2) the defendant had a prior opportunity for cross-examination, or forfeited that right by wrongdoing.

[After concluding that the hearsay related by Stow was testimonial, the Court deemed the error harmful and reversed the trial court's findings on Sanchez's gang-related penalty enhancements.]

3. Court-Appointed Experts

[F.R.E. 706]

ADVISORY COMMITTEE NOTE TO F.R.E. 706

The practice of shopping for experts, the venality of some experts, and the reluctance of many reputable experts to involve themselves in litigation, have been matters of deep concern. Though the contention is made that court appointed experts acquire an aura of infallibility to which they are not entitled, the trend is increasingly to provide for their use. While experience indicates that actual appointment is a relatively infrequent occurrence, the assumption may be made that the availability of the procedure in itself decreases the need for resorting to it. The ever-present possibility that the judge may appoint an expert in a given case must inevitably exert a sobering effect on the expert witness of a party and upon the person utilizing his services.

LEBLANC v. PNS STORES, INC.

Civ. A. No 96-2764 (E.D. La. Oct. 21, 1996)

LIVAUDAIS, District Judge.

Defendant PNS Stores has filed this motion pursuant to Rule 706 of the Federal Rules of Evidence seeking a court-appointed physician.... This matter arises out of a slip and fall accident that took place at MacFrugal's Department Store on August 4, 1995.... [D]efendant wishes to have the Court appoint a physician of its choice to conduct an orthopedic and/or neurological examination of plaintiff....

[T]he enlistment of court-appointed experts pursuant to Federal Rule of Evidence 706 is not commonplace. See F.R.E. 706, Advisory Comm. Note; *In re Joint E. & S. Dists. Asbestos Litigation*, 830 F. Supp. 686 (E. & S. D.N.Y. 1993). In fact, "Rule 706 should be reserved for exceptional cases in which the ordinary adversary process does not suffice." *Id.* at 693....

It is the opinion of this Court that defendant has not demonstrated the necessity of appointing an independent physician. Defendant has been provided with the medical records of plaintiff since the filing of this motion. . . . Although Rule 706 is discretionary with the district court, it is appropriate only in rare circumstances and cannot be utilized as an alternative to communication and the adversary process. [Motion denied.]

JOHN SHEPARD WILEY, JR., TAMING PATENT: SIX STEPS FOR SURVIVING SCARY PATENT CASES

50 UCLA L. Rev. 1413, 1427–1428, 1437 (2002)

[T]he truly striking thing about the power to appoint expert witnesses is how rarely most judges use it. Federal Rule of Evidence 706 has been around since 1975. Its precursors are decades older. . . . [E]mpirical research shows, however, that only 20 percent of a 1988 sample of district judges had ever appointed a 706 expert. . . . This reluctance hardly stems from judicial affection for battling partisan experts. From the perspective of discovering truth, the presentations of adversarial experts have been problematic for a long time. The partisan expert witness has enormous potential as a weapon of pure advocacy. Excellent trial lawyers know this potential. They risk disadvantage and even defeat if they do not wring every drop of advocacy power from their retained experts. In the process, the search for truth can suffer. An expert witness can be the advocate's strongest ally. The expert can speak directly to judge and jury with a demeanor chosen for Walter Cronkite-like sincerity. The expert's motivation can be prompted by ample compensation and guaranteed through careful selection. For the advocate, finding and selecting experts can be a momentous event in the litigation process. Resume horsepower is useful, but better yet is a compelling personal communication style married to the proper attitude. What is the proper attitude? It can be a subtle thing, perhaps detected through give-and-take on casual and seemingly irrelevant issues during a private telephone call or a relaxed interview in a comfortable office. For the trial lawyer puzzling over whether to retain this expert, a core question is whether the expert will become a team player. At some deep level, will the expert come to embrace the cause of the client? Experts with the proper attitude willingly deploy their potentially awesome experience and intelligence in the advocate's service. The result is unlikely to involve lying or deception, if for no other reason than such conduct rarely survives cross-examination. The result is, however, likely to be highly partisan. And the highly partisan character of expert testimony can imperil the search for truth. When one trial lawyer tells a colleague in an unguarded moment that the lawyer is in the process of "shopping for an expert," we should reflect on how accurate this phrase truly is. As a result, there have been serious doubts about the adequacy of adversarial experts for a century or more.

Judges know about these problems with retained experts. Why then have they usually made so little use of court-appointed experts? . . . [T]here are two main reasons: Most judges have no personal experience with court experts, and the parties rarely, if ever, suggest the possibility. The lawyers have no interest in mentioning this alternative, because they are doing everything they can to control the litigation. The appointment of a court expert represents a dramatic loss of control. This stranger is unknown and is likely to be influential. He or she is not supposed to have the client's best interests at heart. This prospect is not just unattractive; it is positively threatening.

4. Special Reliability Requirements for Experts

[F.R.E. 702]

a. Introduction

For decades, observers of American trials have worried that it is too easy to find an expert to say almost anything, and that experts, no matter how foolish or partisan, come draped with a mantle of authority that gives their testimony tremendous and often unwarranted weight with jurors.

F.R.E. 706(a) illustrates one long-standing response to this problem: authorizing trial judges to appoint their own experts. But as we have seen, this authorization is rarely used. When Judge Livaudais wrote in the *Leblanc* decision, excerpted above, that court-appointed experts should not be used "as an alternative to . . . the adversary process," he voiced a discomfort that many if not most American trial judges probably share — a discomfort with factfinding under the control of the judge rather than the parties. American judges do not *want* to become European-style inquisitors. That is not the legal culture in which they have been raised, and it is not what they are used to.

So federal evidence law has taken a different approach to the problem of partisan or otherwise unreliable experts. Instead of trial judges recruiting their own experts, trial judges have been instructed to scrutinize the expert testimony offered by the parties to make sure that it is "reliable." This requirement was first imposed by the Supreme Court in a 1993 decision excerpted below, *Daubert v. Merrell Dow Pharmaceuticals, Inc.* In order to understand *Daubert*, it may help to have some background about the doctrine it displaced.

Before the 1920s, few if any courts applied a special reliability requirement to expert methods. Instead, so long as an expert was qualified and the testimony was relevant, courts left it to the jury to determine an expert method's reliability.

That changed with a 1923 decision by the D.C. Circuit Court of Appeals in *Frye v. United States*. James Alphonso Frye was accused of murder. His lawyer sought to introduce expert testimony that a crude, early predecessor of the modern polygraph had shown that Frye was telling the truth when he said he was innocent. Notably, the defense expert was a young psychologist named William Moulton Marston, who would later create the character of Wonder Woman (and her truth lasso). The machine used on Frye measured his blood pressure while he was asked questions about the murder. As the D.C. Circuit explained, "The theory seems to be that truth is spontaneous, and comes without conscious effort, while the utterance of a falsehood requires a conscious effort, which is reflected in the blood pressure." This business about truth coming naturally but fabrication taking effort should ring a bell: it is the same theory, more or less, that underlies the excited utterance and present sense impression exceptions to the hearsay rule. (And it turns out also to be pretty much the same theory underlying modern polygraphs.)

The D.C. Circuit disallowed Marston's testimony. In language that proved enormously influential, the court said that "while courts will go a long way in admitting expert testimony deduced from a well-recognized scientific principle or discovery, the thing from which the deduction is made must be sufficiently established to have gained general acceptance in the particular field in which it belongs."

This criterion — "general acceptance" — soon became the dominant test in American courtrooms for the admissibility of novel scientific evidence (the *Frye* "general acceptance" requirement does not apply to expert methods deemed either not scientific or not novel). *Frye* is still the test in many states today, including California and New York. But it has been displaced in federal courts, and in the courts of most states, by the very different standard the U.S. Supreme Court first announced in *Daubert*.

b. The Daubert Revolution

DAUBERT v. MERRELL DOW PHARMACEUTICALS, INC.

509 U.S. 579 (1993)

Justice BLACKMUN delivered the opinion of the Court.

. . . Petitioners Jason Daubert and Eric Schuller are minor children born with serious birth defects. They and their parents sued respondent in California state court, alleging that the birth defects had been caused by the mothers' ingestion of Bendectin, a prescription antinausea drug marketed by respondent. Respondent removed the suits to federal court on diversity grounds.

After extensive discovery, respondent moved for summary judgment, contending that Bendectin does not cause birth defects in humans and that petitioners would be unable to come forward with any admissible evidence that it does. In support of its motion, respondent submitted an affidavit of Steven H. Lamm, physician and epidemiologist, who is a well-credentialed expert on the risks from exposure to various chemical substances. Doctor Lamm stated that he had reviewed all the literature on Bendectin and human birth defects — more than 30 published studies involving over 130,000 patients. No study had found Bendectin to be a human teratogen (*i.e.*, a substance capable of causing malformations in fetuses). On the basis of this review, Doctor Lamm concluded that maternal use of Bendectin during the first trimester of pregnancy has not been shown to be a risk factor for human birth defects.

Petitioners did not (and do not) contest this characterization of the published record regarding Bendectin. Instead, they responded to respondent's motion with the testimony of eight experts of their own, each of whom also possessed impressive credentials. These experts had concluded that Bendectin can cause birth defects. Their conclusions were based upon "in vitro" (test tube) and "in vivo" (live) animal studies that found a link between Bendectin and malformations; pharmacological studies of the chemical structure of Bendectin that purported to show similarities between the structure of the drug and that of other substances known to cause birth defects; and the "reanalysis" of previously published epidemiological (human statistical) studies.

The District Court granted respondent's motion for summary judgment. The court stated that scientific evidence is admissible only if the principle upon which it is based is "'sufficiently established to have general acceptance in the field to which it belongs.'" The court concluded that petitioners' evidence did not meet this standard. Given the vast body of epidemiological data concerning Bendectin, the court held, expert opinion which is not based on epidemiological evidence is not admissible to establish causation. Thus, the animal-cell studies, live-animal studies, and chemical-structure analyses on which petitioners had relied could not raise by themselves a reasonably disputable jury issue regarding causation. Petitioners' epidemiological analyses, based as they were on recalculations of data in previously published studies that had found no causal link between the drug and birth defects, were ruled to be inadmissible because they had not been published or subjected to peer review.

The United States Court of Appeals for the Ninth Circuit affirmed. Citing *Frye v. United States*, 293 F. 1013, 1014 (1923), the court stated that expert opinion based on a scientific technique is inadmissible unless the technique is "generally accepted" as reliable in the relevant scientific community. The court declared that expert opinion based on a methodology that diverges "significantly from the procedures accepted by recognized authorities in the field . . . cannot be shown to be 'generally accepted as a reliable technique.'"

The court emphasized that other Courts of Appeals considering the risks of Bendectin had refused to admit reanalyses of epidemiological studies that had been neither published nor subjected to peer review. Those courts had found unpublished reanalyses "particularly problematic in light of the massive weight of the original published studies supporting [respondent's] position, all of which had undergone full scrutiny from the scientific community." Contending that reanalysis is generally accepted by the scientific community only when it is subjected to verification and scrutiny by others in the field, the Court of Appeals rejected petitioners' reanalyses as "unpublished, not subjected to the normal peer review process and generated solely for use in litigation." The court concluded that petitioners' evidence provided an insufficient foundation to allow admission of expert testimony that Bendectin caused their injuries and, accordingly, that petitioners could not satisfy their burden of proving causation at trial. . . .

In the 70 years since its formulation in the *Frye* case, the "general acceptance" test has been the dominant standard for determining the admissibility of novel scientific evidence at trial. Although under increasing attack of late, the rule continues to be followed by a majority of courts, including the Ninth Circuit.

The *Frye* test has its origin in a short and citation-free 1923 decision concerning the admissibility of evidence derived from a systolic blood pressure deception test, a crude precursor to the polygraph machine. In what has become a famous (perhaps infamous) passage, the then Court of Appeals for the District of Columbia described the device and its operation and declared:

"Just when a scientific principle or discovery crosses the line between the experimental and demonstrable stages is difficult to define. Somewhere in this twilight zone the evidential force of the principle must be recognized, and while courts will go a long way in admitting expert testimony deduced from a well-recognized scientific principle or discovery, *the thing from which the deduction is made must be sufficiently established to have gained general acceptance in the particular field in which it belongs.*" 293 F., at 1014 (emphasis added).

Because the deception test had "not yet gained such standing and scientific recognition among physiological and psychological authorities as would justify the courts in admitting expert testimony deduced from the discovery, development, and experiments thus far made," evidence of its results was ruled inadmissible. *Id.*

The merits of the *Frye* test have been much debated, and scholarship on its proper scope and application is legion. Petitioners' primary attack, however, is not on the content but on the continuing authority of the rule. They contend that the *Frye* test was superseded by the adoption of the Federal Rules of Evidence. We agree.

. . . [T]here is a specific Rule that speaks to the contested issue. Rule 702, governing expert testimony, provides:

"If scientific, technical, or other specialized knowledge will assist the trier of fact to understand the evidence or to determine a fact in issue, a witness qualified as an expert by knowledge, skill, experience, training, or education, may testify thereto in the form of an opinion or otherwise."

Nothing in the text of this Rule establishes "general acceptance" as an absolute prerequisite to admissibility. Nor does respondent present any clear indication that Rule 702 or the Rules as a whole were intended to incorporate a "general acceptance" standard. The drafting history makes no mention of *Frye*, and a rigid "general acceptance" requirement would be at odds with the "liberal thrust" of the Federal Rules and their "general approach of relaxing the traditional barriers to 'opinion' testimony." *Beech Aircraft Corp. v. Rainey*, 488 U.S. [153, 169 (1988)] (citing Rules 701 to 705). See also Weinstein, Rule 702 of the Federal Rules of Evidence is Sound; It Should Not Be Amended, 138 F.R.D. 631 (1991) ("The Rules were designed to depend primarily upon lawyer-adversaries and sensible triers of fact to evaluate conflicts"). Given the Rules' permissive backdrop and their inclusion of a specific rule on expert testimony that does not mention "'general acceptance,'" the assertion that the Rules somehow assimilated *Frye* is unconvincing. *Frye* made "general acceptance" the exclusive test for admitting expert scientific testimony. That austere standard, absent from, and incompatible with, the Federal Rules of Evidence, should not be applied in federal trials.

That the *Frye* test was displaced by the Rules of Evidence does not mean, however, that the Rules themselves place no limits on the admissibility of purportedly scientific evidence. Nor is the trial judge disabled from screening such evidence. To the contrary, under the Rules the trial judge must ensure that any and all scientific testimony or evidence admitted is not only relevant, but reliable.

The primary locus of this obligation is Rule 702, which clearly contemplates some degree of regulation of the subjects and theories about which an expert may testify. "*If scientific*, technical, or other specialized *knowledge will assist the trier of fact* to understand the evidence or to determine a fact in issue" an expert "may testify *thereto*." (Emphasis added.) The subject of an expert's testimony must be "scientific . . . knowledge."[2] The adjective "scientific" implies a grounding in the methods and procedures of science. Similarly, the word "knowledge" connotes more than subjective belief or unsupported speculation. The term "applies to any body of known facts or to any body of ideas inferred from such facts or accepted as truths on good grounds." Webster's Third New International Dictionary 1252 (1986). Of course, it would be unreasonable to conclude that the subject of scientific testimony must be "known" to a certainty; arguably, there are no certainties in science. See, *e.g.*, Brief for Nicolaas Bloembergen et al. as *Amici Curiae* 9 ("Indeed, scientists do not assert that they know what is immutably 'true'—they are committed to searching for new, temporary, theories to explain, as best they can, phenomena"); Brief for American Association for the Advancement of Science et al. as *Amici Curiae* 7-8 ("Science is not an encyclopedic body of knowledge about the universe. Instead, it represents a *process* for proposing and refining theoretical explanations about the world that are subject to further testing and refinement" (emphasis in original)). But, in order to qualify as "scientific knowledge," an inference or assertion must be derived by the scientific method. Proposed testimony must be supported by appropriate validation — *i.e.*, "good grounds," based on what is known. In short, the requirement that an expert's testimony pertain to "scientific knowledge" establishes a standard of evidentiary reliability.[3]

Rule 702 further requires that the evidence or testimony "assist the trier of fact to understand the evidence or to determine a fact in issue." This condition goes primarily to relevance. "Expert testimony which does not relate to any issue in the case is not relevant and, ergo, non-helpful." 3 Weinstein & Berger[, Weinstein's Evidence] §702[02], p. 702-18 [(1988)]. See also *United States v. Downing*, 753 F.2d 1224, 1242 (CA3 1985) ("An additional consideration under Rule 702 — and another aspect of relevancy — is whether expert testimony proffered in the case is sufficiently tied to the facts of the case that it will aid the jury in resolving a factual dispute"). The consideration has been aptly described by Judge Becker as one of "fit." *Ibid.* "Fit" is not always obvious, and scientific validity for one purpose is not necessarily scientific validity for other, unrelated purposes. The study of the phases of the moon, for example, may provide valid scientific "knowledge" about whether a certain night was dark, and if darkness is a fact in issue, the knowledge will assist the trier of fact. However (absent creditable grounds supporting such a link), evidence that the moon was full on a certain night will not assist the trier of fact in determining whether an individual was unusually likely to have behaved

---

2. Rule 702 also applies to "technical, or other specialized knowledge." Our discussion is limited to the scientific context because that is the nature of the expertise offered here.

3. We note that scientists typically distinguish between "validity" (does the principle support what it purports to show?) and "reliability" (does application of the principle produce consistent results?). . . . [O]ur reference here is to evidentiary reliability — that is, trustworthiness. . . . In a case involving scientific evidence, evidentiary reliability will be based upon scientific validity.

irrationally on that night. Rule 702's "helpfulness" standard requires a valid scientific connection to the pertinent inquiry as a precondition to admissibility.

That these requirements are embodied in Rule 702 is not surprising. Unlike an ordinary witness, see Rule 701, an expert is permitted wide latitude to offer opinions, including those that are not based on firsthand knowledge or observation. See Rules 702 and 703. Presumably, this relaxation of the usual requirement of firsthand knowledge — a rule which represents "a 'most pervasive manifestation' of the common law insistence upon 'the most reliable sources of information,'" Advisory Committee's Notes on Fed. Rule Evid. 602 (citation omitted) — is premised on an assumption that the expert's opinion will have a reliable basis in the knowledge and experience of his discipline.

Faced with a proffer of expert scientific testimony, then, the trial judge must determine at the outset, pursuant to Rule 104(a), whether the expert is proposing to testify to (1) scientific knowledge that (2) will assist the trier of fact to understand or determine a fact in issue.[4] This entails a preliminary assessment of whether the reasoning or methodology underlying the testimony is scientifically valid and of whether that reasoning or methodology properly can be applied to the facts in issue. We are confident that federal judges possess the capacity to undertake this review. Many factors will bear on the inquiry, and we do not presume to set out a definitive checklist or test. But some general observations are appropriate.

Ordinarily, a key question to be answered in determining whether a theory or technique is scientific knowledge that will assist the trier of fact will be whether it can be (and has been) tested. "Scientific methodology today is based on generating hypotheses and testing them to see if they can be falsified; indeed, this methodology is what distinguishes science from other fields of human inquiry." Green[, *Expert Witnesses and Sufficiency of the Evidence in Toxic Substances Litigation: The Legacy of* Agent Orange *and Bendectin Litigation*, 86 Nw. U. L. Rev. 643,] 645 [(1992)]. See also C. Hempel, Philosophy of Natural Science 49 (1966) ("[T]he statements constituting a scientific explanation must be capable of empirical test"); K. Popper, Conjectures and Refutations: The Growth of Scientific Knowledge 37 (5th ed. 1989) ("[T]he criterion of the scientific status of a theory is its falsifiability, or refutability, or testability")(emphasis deleted).

Another pertinent consideration is whether the theory or technique has been subjected to peer review and publication. Publication (which is but one element of peer review) is not a *sine qua non* of admissibility; it does not necessarily correlate with reliability, see S. Jasanoff, The Fifth Branch: Science Advisors as Policymakers 61–76 (1990), and in some instances well-grounded but innovative theories will not have been published, see Horrobin, *The Philosophical Basis of Peer Review and the Suppression of Innovation*, 263 JAMA 1438 (1990). Some propositions, moreover, are too particular, too new,

---

4. Although the *Frye* decision itself focused exclusively on "novel" scientific techniques, we do not read the requirements of Rule 702 to apply specially or exclusively to unconventional evidence. Of course, well-established propositions are less likely to be challenged than those that are novel, and they are more handily defended. Indeed, theories that are so firmly established as to have attained the status of scientific law, such as the laws of thermodynamics, properly are subject to judicial notice under Federal Rule of Evidence 201.

or of too limited interest to be published. But submission to the scrutiny of the scientific community is a component of "good science," in part because it increases the likelihood that substantive flaws in methodology will be detected. See J. Ziman, *Reliable Knowledge: An Exploration of the Grounds for Belief in Science* 130-133 (1978); Relman & Angell, How Good Is Peer Review?, 321 New Eng. J. Med. 827 (1989). The fact of publication (or lack thereof) in a peer reviewed journal thus will be a relevant, though not dispositive, consideration in assessing the scientific validity of a particular technique or methodology on which an opinion is premised.

Additionally, in the case of a particular scientific technique, the court ordinarily should consider the known or potential rate of error, see, *e.g., United States v. Smith*, 869 F.2d 348, 353-54 (CA7 1989) (surveying studies of the error rate of spectrographic voice identification technique), and the existence and maintenance of standards controlling the technique's operation, see *United States v. Williams*, 583 F.2d 1194, 1198 (CA2 1978) (noting professional organization's standard governing spectrographic analysis), cert. denied, 439 U.S. 1117 (1979).

Finally, "general acceptance" can yet have a bearing on the inquiry. A "reliability assessment does not require, although it does permit, explicit identification of a relevant scientific community and an express determination of a particular degree of acceptance within that community." *United States v. Downing*, 753 F.2d, at 1238. See also 3 Weinstein & Berger §702[03], pp. 702-41 to 702-42. Widespread acceptance can be an important factor in ruling particular evidence admissible, and "a known technique which has been able to attract only minimal support within the community," *Downing*, 753 F.2d, at 1238, may properly be viewed with skepticism.

The inquiry envisioned by Rule 702 is, we emphasize, a flexible one. Its overarching subject is the scientific validity and thus the evidentiary relevance and reliability — of the principles that underlie a proposed submission. The focus, of course, must be solely on principles and methodology, not on the conclusions that they generate.

Throughout, a judge assessing a proffer of expert scientific testimony under Rule 702 should also be mindful of other applicable rules. Rule 703 provides that expert opinions based on otherwise inadmissible hearsay are to be admitted only if the facts or data are "of a type reasonably relied upon by experts in the particular field in forming opinions or inferences upon the subject." Rule 706 allows the court at its discretion to procure the assistance of an expert of its own choosing. Finally, Rule 403 permits the exclusion of relevant evidence "if its probative value is substantially outweighed by the danger of unfair prejudice, confusion of the issues, or misleading the jury. . . ." Judge Weinstein has explained: "Expert evidence can be both powerful and quite misleading because of the difficulty in evaluating it. Because of this risk, the judge in weighing possible prejudice against probative force under Rule 403 of the present rules exercises more control over experts than over lay witnesses." Weinstein, 138 F.R.D., at 632.

We conclude by briefly addressing what appear to be two underlying concerns of the parties and *amici* in this case. Respondent expresses apprehension that abandonment of "general acceptance" as the exclusive requirement for admission will result in a "free-for-all" in which befuddled juries are confounded by absurd and irrational pseudoscientific assertions. In this regard respondent seems to us to be overly pessimistic about the capabilities of the jury and of the adversary system generally. Vigorous cross-examination, presentation of contrary evidence, and careful instruction on the burden of proof are the traditional and appropriate means of attacking shaky but admissible evidence. See *Rock v. Arkansas*, 483 U.S. 44, 61 (1987). Additionally, in the event the trial court concludes that the scintilla of evidence presented supporting a position is insufficient to allow a reasonable juror to conclude that the position more likely than not is true, the court remains free to direct a judgment, Fed. Rule Civ. Proc. 50(a), and likewise to grant summary judgment, Fed. Rule Civ. Proc. 56.... These conventional devices, rather than wholesale exclusion under an uncompromising "general acceptance" test, are the appropriate safeguards where the basis of scientific testimony meets the standards of Rule 702.

Petitioners and, to a greater extent, their *amici* exhibit a different concern. They suggest that recognition of a screening role for the judge that allows for the exclusion of "invalid" evidence will sanction a stifling and repressive scientific orthodoxy and will be inimical to the search for truth. See, *e.g.*, Brief for Ronald Bayer et al. as *Amici Curiae*. It is true that open debate is an essential part of both legal and scientific analyses. Yet there are important differences between the quest for truth in the courtroom and the quest for truth in the laboratory. Scientific conclusions are subject to perpetual revision. Law, on the other hand, must resolve disputes finally and quickly. The scientific project is advanced by broad and wide-ranging consideration of a multitude of hypotheses, for those that are incorrect will eventually be shown to be so, and that in itself is an advance. Conjectures that are probably wrong are of little use, however, in the project of reaching a quick, final, and binding legal judgment — often of great consequence — about a particular set of events in the past. We recognize that, in practice, a gatekeeping role for the judge, no matter how flexible, inevitably on occasion will prevent the jury from learning of authentic insights and innovations. That, nevertheless, is the balance that is struck by Rules of Evidence designed not for the exhaustive search for cosmic understanding but for the particularized resolution of legal disputes.

. . . [T]he judgment of the Court of Appeals is vacated, and the case is remanded for further proceedings consistent with this opinion.
[Chief Justice Rehnquist filed an opinion concurring in part and dissenting in part.]

GENERAL ELECTRIC CO. v. JOINER

522 U.S. 136 (1997)

Chief Justice Rehnquist delivered the opinion of the Court.

[While working as an electrician for the City of Thomasville, Georgia, respondent Robert Joiner came into frequent contact with fluids in the city's electrical transformers. Fluids in some of the transformers were later found to contain polychlorinated biphenyls (PCBs). After Joiner contracted lung cancer, he sued General Electric and Westinghouse Electric, the manufacturers of the transformers, and Monsanto, which had manufactured PCBs. The case was removed to federal court.]

The District Court ruled that there was a genuine issue of material fact as to whether Joiner had been exposed to PCB's. But it nevertheless granted summary judgment for petitioners because . . . the testimony of Joiner's experts had failed to show that there was a link between exposure to PCB's and small-cell lung cancer. The court believed that the testimony of respondent's experts to the contrary did not rise above "subjective belief or unsupported speculation." Their testimony was therefore inadmissible.

The Court of Appeals for the Eleventh Circuit reversed. It held that "[b]ecause the Federal Rules of Evidence governing expert testimony display a preference for admissibility, we apply a particularly stringent standard of review to the trial judge's exclusion of expert testimony." Applying that standard, the Court of Appeals held that the District Court had erred in excluding the testimony of Joiner's expert witnesses. The District Court had made two fundamental errors. First, it excluded the experts' testimony because it "drew different conclusions from the research than did each of the experts." The Court of Appeals opined that a district court should limit its role to determining the "legal reliability of proffered expert testimony, leaving the jury to decide the correctness of competing expert opinions." Second, the District Court had held that there was no genuine issue of material fact as to whether Joiner had been exposed to furans and dioxins. This was also incorrect, said the Court of Appeals, because testimony in the record supported the proposition that there had been such exposure. . . .

We have held that abuse of discretion is the proper standard of review of a district court's evidentiary rulings. Indeed, our cases on the subject go back as far as *Spring Co. v. Edgar*, 99 U.S. 645, 658 (1879), where we said that "[c]ases arise where it is very much a matter of discretion with the court whether to receive or exclude the evidence; but the appellate court will not reverse in such a case, unless the ruling is manifestly erroneous." The Court of Appeals suggested that *Daubert* somehow altered this general rule in the context of a district court's decision to exclude scientific evidence. But *Daubert* did not address the standard of appellate review for evidentiary rulings at all. . . .

[W]hile the Federal Rules of Evidence allow district courts to admit a somewhat broader range of scientific testimony than would have been admissible under *Frye*, they leave in place the "gatekeeper" role of the trial judge in screening such evidence. A court of appeals applying "abuse-of-discretion" review to such rulings may not categorically distinguish between rulings allowing expert testimony and rulings disallowing it. . . . On a motion for summary judgment, disputed issues of fact are resolved against the moving party — here, petitioners. But the question of admissibility of expert testimony is not such an issue of fact, and is reviewable under the abuse-of-discretion standard.

We hold that the Court of Appeals erred in its review of the exclusion of Joiner's experts' testimony. In applying an overly "stringent" review to that ruling, it failed to give the trial court the deference that is the hallmark of abuse-of-discretion review.

We believe that a proper application of the correct standard of review here indicates that the District Court did not abuse its discretion. Joiner's theory of liability was that his exposure to PCB's and their derivatives "promoted" his development of small-cell lung cancer. In support of that theory he proffered the deposition testimony of expert witnesses. Dr. Arnold Schecter testified that he believed it "more likely than not that Mr. Joiner's lung cancer was causally linked to cigarette smoking and PCB exposure." Dr. Daniel Teitelbaum testified that Joiner's "lung cancer was caused by or contributed to in a significant degree by the materials with which he worked."

Petitioners contended that the statements of Joiner's experts regarding causation were nothing more than speculation. Petitioners criticized the testimony of the experts in that it was "not supported by epidemiological studies . . . [and was] based exclusively on isolated studies of laboratory animals." Joiner responded by claiming that his experts had identified "relevant animal studies which support their opinions." He also directed the court's attention to four epidemiological studies on which his experts had relied.

The District Court agreed with petitioners that the animal studies on which respondent's experts relied did not support his contention that exposure to PCB's had contributed to his cancer. The studies involved infant mice that had developed cancer after being exposed to PCB's. The infant mice in the studies had had massive doses of PCB's injected directly into their peritoneums[5] or stomachs. Joiner was an adult human being whose alleged exposure to PCB's was far less than the exposure in the animal studies. The PCB's were injected into the mice in a highly concentrated form. The fluid with which Joiner had come into contact generally had a much smaller PCB concentration of between 0-to-500 parts per million. The cancer that these mice developed was alveologenic adenomas; Joiner had developed small-cell carcinomas. No study demonstrated that adult mice developed cancer after being exposed to PCB's. One of the experts admitted that no study had demonstrated that PCB's lead to cancer in any other species.

Respondent failed to reply to this criticism. Rather than explaining how and why the experts could have extrapolated their opinions from these seemingly far-removed animal studies, respondent chose "to proceed as if the only issue [was] whether animal studies can ever be a proper foundation for an expert's opinion." Of course, whether animal studies can ever be a proper foundation for an expert's opinion was not the issue. The issue was whether *these* experts' opinions were sufficiently supported by the animal studies on which they purported to rely. The studies were so dissimilar to the facts presented in this litigation that it was not an abuse of discretion for the District Court to have rejected the experts' reliance on them.

The District Court also concluded that the four epidemiological studies on which respondent relied were not a sufficient basis for the experts' opinions. The first such study involved workers at an Italian capacitor[6] plant who had been exposed to PCBs. Bertazzi, Riboldi, Pesatori, Radice, & Zocchetti,

---

5. The peritoneum is the lining of the abdominal cavity.
6. A capacitor is an electrical component that stores an electric charge.

Cancer Mortality of Capacitor Manufacturing Workers, 11 American Journal of Industrial Medicine 165 (1987). The authors noted that lung cancer deaths among ex-employees at the plant were higher than might have been expected, but concluded that "there were apparently no grounds for associating lung cancer deaths (although increased above expectations) and exposure in the plant." Given that Bertazzi et al. were unwilling to say that PCB exposure had caused cancer among the workers they examined, their study did not support the experts' conclusion that Joiner's exposure to PCB's caused his cancer.

The second study followed employees who had worked at Monsanto's PCB production plant. J. Zack & D. Musch, Mortality of PCB Workers at the Monsanto Plant in Sauget, Illinois (Dec. 14, 1979) (unpublished report). The authors of this study found that the incidence of lung cancer deaths among these workers was somewhat higher than would ordinarily be expected. The increase, however, was not statistically significant and the authors of the study did not suggest a link between the increase in lung cancer deaths and the exposure to PCB's.

The third and fourth studies were likewise of no help. The third involved workers at a Norwegian cable manufacturing company who had been exposed to mineral oil. Ronneberg, Andersen, & Skyberg, Mortality and Incidence of Cancer Among Oil-Exposed Workers in a Norwegian Cable Manufacturing Company, 45 British Journal of Industrial Medicine 595 (1988). A statistically significant increase in lung cancer deaths had been observed in these workers. The study, however, (1) made no mention of PCB's and (2) was expressly limited to the type of mineral oil involved in that study, and thus did not support these experts' opinions. The fourth and final study involved a PCB-exposed group in Japan that had seen a statistically significant increase in lung cancer deaths. Kuratsune, Nakamura, Ikeda, & Hirohata, Analysis of Deaths Seen Among Patients with Yusho — A Preliminary Report, 16 Chemosphere, Nos. 8/9, p. 2085 (1987). The subjects of this study, however, had been exposed to numerous potential carcinogens, including toxic rice oil that they had ingested.

Respondent points to *Daubert*'s language that the "focus, of course, must be solely on principles and methodology, not on the conclusions that they generate." He claims that because the District Court's disagreement was with the conclusion that the experts drew from the studies, the District Court committed legal error and was properly reversed by the Court of Appeals. But conclusions and methodology are not entirely distinct from one another. Trained experts commonly extrapolate from existing data. But nothing in either *Daubert* or the Federal Rules of Evidence requires a district court to admit opinion evidence that is connected to existing data only by the *ipse dixit* of the expert. A court may conclude that there is simply too great an analytical gap between the data and the opinion proffered. That is what the District Court did here, and we hold that it did not abuse its discretion in so doing. . . . We accordingly reverse the judgment of the Court of Appeals and remand this case for proceedings consistent with this opinion.

[Justice Breyer filed a concurring opinion. Justice Stevens filed an opinion concurring in part and dissenting in part.]

KUMHO TIRE COMPANY, LTD. v. CARMICHAEL

526 U.S. 137 (1999)

Justice BREYER delivered the opinion of the Court.

. . . On July 6, 1993, the right rear tire of a minivan driven by Patrick Carmichael blew out. In the accident that followed, one of the passengers died, and others were severely injured. In October 1993, the Carmichaels brought this diversity suit against the tire's maker and its distributor, whom we refer to collectively as Kumho Tire, claiming that the tire was defective. The plaintiffs rested their case in significant part upon deposition testimony provided by an expert in tire failure analysis, Dennis Carlson, Jr., who intended to testify in support of their conclusion.

Carlson's depositions relied upon certain features of tire technology that are not in dispute. A steel-belted radial tire like the Carmichaels' is made up of a "carcass" containing many layers of flexible cords, called "plies," along which (between the cords and the outer tread) are laid steel strips called "belts." Steel wire loops, called "beads," hold the cords together at the plies' bottom edges. An outer layer, called the "tread," encases the carcass, and the entire tire is bound together in rubber, through the application of heat and various chemicals. See generally, *e.g.*, J. Dixon, Tires, Suspension and Handling 68–72 (2d ed. 1996). The bead of the tire sits upon a "bead seat," which is part of the wheel assembly. That assembly contains a "rim flange," which extends over the bead and rests against the side of the tire. See M. Mavrigian, Performance Wheels & Tires 81, 83 (1998) (illustrations).

Carlson's testimony also accepted certain background facts about the tire in question. He assumed that before the blowout the tire had traveled far. (The tire was made in 1988 and had been installed some time before the Carmichaels bought the used minivan in March 1993; the Carmichaels had driven the van approximately 7,000 additional miles in the two months they had owned it.) Carlson noted that the tire's tread depth, which was 11/32 of an inch when new, had been worn down to depths that ranged from 3/32 of an inch along some parts of the tire, to nothing at all along others. He conceded that the tire tread had at least two punctures which had been inadequately repaired.

Despite the tire's age and history, Carlson concluded that a defect in its manufacture or design caused the blowout. He rested this conclusion in part upon three premises which, for present purposes, we must assume are not in dispute: First, a tire's carcass should stay bound to the inner side of the tread for a significant period of time after its tread depth has worn away. Second, the tread of the tire at issue had separated from its inner steel-belted carcass prior to the accident. Third, this "separation" caused the blowout.

Carlson's conclusion that a defect caused the separation, however, rested upon certain other propositions, several of which the defendants strongly dispute. First, Carlson said that if a separation is *not* caused by a certain kind of tire misuse called "overdeflection" (which consists of underinflating the tire or causing it to carry too much weight, thereby generating heat that can undo the chemical tread/carcass bond), then, ordinarily, its cause is a tire defect.

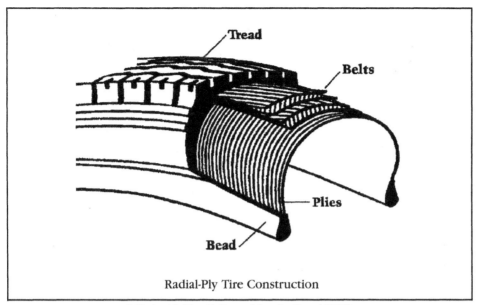

Radial-Ply Tire Construction

A. Markovich, How To Buy and Care For Tires 4 (1994).

Second, he said that if a tire has been subject to sufficient overdeflection to cause a separation, it should reveal certain physical symptoms. These symptoms include (a) tread wear on the tire's shoulder that is greater than the tread wear along the tire's center; (b) signs of a "bead groove," where the beads have been pushed too hard against the bead seat on the inside of the tire's rim; (c) sidewalls of the tire with physical signs of deterioration, such as discoloration; and/or (d) marks on the tire's rim flange. Third, Carlson said that where he does not find *at least two* of the four physical signs just mentioned (and presumably where there is no reason to suspect a less common cause of separation), he concludes that a manufacturing or design defect caused the separation.

Carlson added that he had inspected the tire in question. He conceded that the tire to a limited degree showed greater wear on the shoulder than in the center, some signs of "bead groove," some discoloration, a few marks on the rim flange, and inadequately filled puncture holes (which can also cause heat that might lead to separation). But, in each instance, he testified that the symptoms were not significant, and he explained why he believed that they did not reveal overdeflection. For example, the extra shoulder wear, he said, appeared primarily on one shoulder, whereas an overdeflected tire would reveal equally abnormal wear on both shoulders. Carlson concluded that the tire did not bear at least two of the four overdeflection symptoms, nor was there any less obvious cause of separation; and since neither overdeflection nor the punctures caused the blowout, a defect must have done so.

Kumho Tire moved the District Court to exclude Carlson's testimony on the ground that his methodology failed Rule 702's reliability requirement. The court agreed with Kumho that it should act as a *Daubert*-type reliability "gatekeeper," even though one might consider Carlson's testimony as "technical," rather than "scientific." The court then examined Carlson's methodology in light of the reliability-related factors that *Daubert* mentioned, such as a theory's testability, whether it "has been a subject of peer review or publication," the "known or potential rate of error," and the "degree of acceptance...within the relevant scientific community." The District Court found that all those factors argued against the reliability of Carlson's methods, and it granted the motion to exclude the testimony (as well as the defendants' accompanying motion for summary judgment).

The plaintiffs, arguing that the court's application of the *Daubert* factors was too "inflexible," asked for reconsideration. And the Court granted that motion. After reconsidering the matter, the court agreed with the plaintiffs that *Daubert* should be applied flexibly, that its four factors were simply illustrative, and that other factors could argue in favor of admissibility. It conceded that there may be widespread acceptance of a "visual-inspection method" for some relevant purposes. But the court found insufficient indications of the reliability of

> "the component of Carlson's tire failure analysis which most concerned the Court, namely, the methodology employed by the expert in analyzing the data obtained in the visual inspection, and the scientific basis, if any, for such an analysis."

It consequently affirmed its earlier order declaring Carlson's testimony inadmissible and granting the defendants' motion for summary judgment.

The Eleventh Circuit reversed.... It noted that "the Supreme Court in *Daubert* explicitly limited its holding to cover only the 'scientific context,'" adding that "a *Daubert* analysis" applies only where an expert relies "on the application of scientific principles," rather than "on skill- or experience-based observation." It concluded that Carlson's testimony, which it viewed as relying on experience, "falls outside the scope of *Daubert*," that "the district court erred as a matter of law by applying *Daubert* in this case"...

In *Daubert*, this Court held that Federal Rule of Evidence 702 imposes a special obligation upon a trial judge to "ensure that any and all scientific testimony ... is not only relevant, but reliable." The initial question before us is whether this basic gatekeeping obligation applies only to "scientific" testimony or to all expert testimony. We, like the parties, believe that it applies to all expert testimony.

For one thing, Rule 702 itself ... makes no relevant distinction between "scientific" knowledge and "technical" or "other specialized" knowledge. It makes clear that any such knowledge might become the subject of expert testimony. In *Daubert*, the Court specified that it is the Rule's word "knowledge," not the words (like "scientific") that modify that word, that "establishes a standard of evidentiary reliability." Hence, as a matter of language, the Rule applies its reliability standard to all "scientific," "technical," or "other specialized" matters within its scope. We concede that the Court in *Daubert* referred only to "scientific" knowledge. But as the Court there said, it referred to "scientific" testimony "because that [wa]s the nature of the expertise" at issue.

Neither is the evidentiary rationale that underlay the Court's basic *Daubert* "gatekeeping" determination limited to "scientific" knowledge. *Daubert* pointed out that Federal Rules 702 and 703 grant expert witnesses testimonial latitude unavailable to other witnesses on the "assumption that the expert's opinion will have a reliable basis in the knowledge and experience of his discipline." The Rules grant that latitude to all experts, not just to "scientific" ones.

Finally, it would prove difficult, if not impossible, for judges to administer evidentiary rules under which a gatekeeping obligation depended upon a distinction between "scientific" knowledge and "technical" or "other specialized" knowledge. There is no clear line that divides the one from the others. Disciplines such as engineering rest upon scientific knowledge. Pure scientific theory itself may depend for its development upon observation and properly engineered machinery. And conceptual efforts to distinguish the two are unlikely to produce clear legal lines capable of application in particular cases. Cf. Brief for National Academy of Engineering as *Amicus Curiae* 9 (scientist seeks to understand nature while the engineer seeks nature's modification); Brief for Rubber Manufacturers Association as *Amicus Curiae* 14-16 (engineering, as an "applied science," relies on "scientific reasoning and methodology"); Brief for John Allen et al. as *Amici Curiae* 6 (engineering relies upon "scientific knowledge and methods").

Neither is there a convincing need to make such distinctions. Experts of all kinds tie observations to conclusions through the use of what Judge Learned Hand called "general truths derived from . . . specialized experience." Hand, Historical and Practical Considerations Regarding Expert Testimony, 15 Harv. L. Rev. 40, 54 (1901). And whether the specific expert testimony focuses upon specialized observations, the specialized translation of those observations into theory, a specialized theory itself, or the application of such a theory in a particular case, the expert's testimony often will rest "upon an experience confessedly foreign in kind to [the jury's] own." *Ibid.* The trial judge's effort to assure that the specialized testimony is reliable and relevant can help the jury evaluate that foreign experience, whether the testimony reflects scientific, technical, or other specialized knowledge.

We conclude that *Daubert*'s general principles apply to the expert matters described in Rule 702. The Rule, in respect to all such matters, "establishes a standard of evidentiary reliability." . . .

The petitioners ask more specifically whether a trial judge determining the "admissibility of an engineering expert's testimony" *may* consider several more specific factors that *Daubert* said might "bear on" a judge's gate-keeping determination. . . . Emphasizing the word "may" in the question, we answer that question yes.

Engineering testimony rests upon scientific foundations, the reliability of which will be at issue in some cases. See, e.g., Brief for Stephen Bobo et al. as *Amici Curiae* 23 (stressing the scientific bases of engineering disciplines). In other cases, the relevant reliability concerns may focus upon personal knowledge or experience. As the Solicitor General points out, there are many different kinds of experts, and many different kinds of expertise. See Brief for United States as *Amicus Curiae* 18-19, and n.5 (citing cases involving experts in drug terms, handwriting analysis, criminal *modus operandi*, land valuation, agricultural practices, railroad procedures, attorney's fee valuation, and others). Our emphasis on the word "may" thus reflects *Daubert*'s description of the Rule 702 inquiry as "a flexible one." *Daubert* makes clear that the factors it mentions do *not* constitute a "definitive checklist or test." And *Daubert* adds that the gatekeeping inquiry must be "tied to the facts" of a particular "case." We agree with the Solicitor General that "[t]he factors identified in *Daubert* may or may not be pertinent in assessing reliability, depending on the nature of the issue, the expert's particular expertise, and the subject of his testimony." Brief for United States as *Amicus Curiae* 19. The conclusion, in our view, is that we can neither rule out, nor rule in, for all cases and for all time the applicability of the factors mentioned in *Daubert*, nor can we now do so for subsets of cases categorized by category of expert or by kind of evidence. Too much depends upon the particular circumstances of the particular case at issue. . . .

The trial court must have the same kind of latitude in deciding *how* to test an expert's reliability, and to decide whether or when special briefing or other proceedings are needed to investigate reliability, as it enjoys when it decides *whether or not* that expert's relevant testimony is reliable. Our opinion in *Joiner* makes clear that a court of appeals is to apply an abuse-of-discretion standard when it "review[s] a trial court's decision to admit or exclude expert testimony." That standard applies as much to the trial court's decisions about how to determine reliability as to its ultimate conclusion. Otherwise, the trial judge would lack the discretionary authority needed both to avoid unnecessary "reliability" proceedings in ordinary cases where the reliability of an expert's methods is properly taken for granted, and to require appropriate proceedings in the less usual or more complex cases where cause for questioning the expert's reliability arises. Indeed, the Rules seek to avoid "unjustifiable expense and delay" as part of their search for "truth" and the "jus[t] determin[ation]" of proceedings. Fed. Rule Evid. 102. Thus, whether *Daubert*'s specific factors are, or are not, reasonable measures of reliability in a particular case is a matter that the law grants the trial judge broad latitude to determine. And the Eleventh Circuit erred insofar as it held to the contrary.

We further explain the way in which a trial judge "may" consider *Daubert*'s factors by applying these considerations to the case at hand, a matter that has been briefed exhaustively by the parties and their 19 *amici.* The District Court did not doubt Carlson's qualifications, which included a master's degree in mechanical engineering, 10 years' work at Michelin America, Inc., and testimony as a tire failure consultant in other tort cases. Rather, it excluded the testimony because, despite those qualifications, it initially doubted, and then found unreliable, "the methodology employed by the expert in analyzing the data obtained in the visual inspection, and the scientific basis, if any, for such an analysis." . . .

[T]he transcripts of Carlson's depositions support both the trial court's initial uncertainty and its final conclusion. Those transcripts cast considerable doubt upon the reliability of both the explicit theory (about the need for two signs of abuse) and the implicit proposition (about the significance of visual inspection in this case). Among other things, the expert could not say whether the tire had traveled more than 10, or 20, or 30, or 40, or 50 thousand miles, adding that 6,000 miles was "about how far" he could "say with any certainty." The court could reasonably have wondered about the reliability of a method of visual and tactile inspection sufficiently precise to ascertain with some certainty the abuse-related significance of minute shoulder/center relative tread wear differences, but insufficiently precise to tell "with any certainty" from the tread wear whether a tire had traveled less than 10,000 or more than 50,000 miles. And these concerns might have been augmented by Carlson's repeated reliance on the "subjective[ness]" of his mode of analysis in response to questions seeking specific information regarding how he could differentiate between a tire that actually had been overdeflected and a tire that merely looked as though it had been. They would have been further augmented by the fact that Carlson said he had inspected the tire itself for the first time the morning of his first deposition, and then only for a few hours. (His initial conclusions were based on photographs.)

Moreover, prior to his first deposition, Carlson had issued a signed report in which he concluded that the tire had "not been . . . overloaded or underinflated," not because of the absence of "two of four" signs of abuse, but simply because "the rim flange impressions . . . were normal." That report also said that the "tread depth remaining was 3/32 inch," though the opposing expert's (apparently undisputed) measurements indicate that the tread depth taken at various positions around the tire actually ranged from .5/32 of an inch to 4/32 of an inch, with the tire apparently showing greater wear along *both* shoulders than along the center.

Further, in respect to one sign of abuse, bead grooving, the expert seemed to deny the sufficiency of his own simple visual-inspection methodology. He testified that most tires have some bead groove pattern, that where there is reason to suspect an abnormal bead groove he would ideally "look at a lot of [similar] tires" to know the grooving's significance, and that he had not looked at many tires similar to the one at issue.

Finally, the court, after looking for a defense of Carlson's methodology as applied in these circumstances, found no convincing defense. Rather, it found (1) that "none" of the *Daubert* factors, including that of "general acceptance" in the relevant expert community, indicated that Carlson's testimony was reliable; (2) that its own analysis "revealed no countervailing factors operating in favor of admissibility which could outweigh those identified in *Daubert*; and (3) that the "parties identified no such factors in their briefs." For these three reasons *taken together*, it concluded that Carlson's testimony was unreliable.

Respondents now argue to us, as they did to the District Court, that a method of tire failure analysis that employs a visual/tactile inspection is a reliable method, and they point both to its use by other experts and to Carlson's long experience working for Michelin as sufficient indication that that is so. But no one denies that an expert might draw a conclusion from a set of observations based on extensive and specialized experience. Nor does anyone deny that, as a general matter, tire abuse may often be identified by qualified experts through visual or tactile inspection of the tire. . . . [T]he question before the trial court was specific, not general. The trial court had to decide whether this particular expert had sufficient specialized knowledge to assist the jurors "in deciding the particular issues in the case." 4 J. McLaughlin. Weinstein's Federal Evidence §702.05[1], p. 702-33 (2d ed. 1998). . . .

The particular issue in this case concerned the use of Carlson's two-factor test and his related use of visual/tactile inspection to draw conclusions on the basis of what seemed small observational differences. We have found no indication in the record that other experts in the industry use Carlson's two-factor test or that tire experts such as Carlson normally make the very fine distinctions about, say, the symmetry of comparatively greater shoulder tread wear that were necessary, on Carlson's own theory, to support his conclusions. Nor, despite the prevalence of tire testing, does anyone refer to any articles or papers that validate Carlson's approach. Compare Bobo, Tire Flaws and Separations, in Mechanics of Pneumatic Tires 636-637 (S. Clark ed. 1981): C. Schnuth et al., Compression Grooving and Rim Flange Abrasion as Indicators of Over-Deflected Operating Conditions in Tires, presented to Rubber Division of the American Chemical Society, Oct. 21-24, 1997; J. Walter & R. Kiminecz, Bead Contact Pressure Measurements at the Tire-Rim Interface, presented to Society of Automotive Engineers, Feb. 24-28, 1975. Indeed, no one has argued that Carlson himself, were he still working for Michelin, would have concluded in a report to his employer that a similar tire was similarly defective on grounds identical to those upon which he rested his conclusion here. Of course, Carlson himself claimed that his method was accurate, but, as we pointed out in *Joiner*, "nothing in either *Daubert* or the Federal Rules of Evidence requires a district court to admit opinion evidence that is connected to existing data only by the *ipse dixit* of the expert."

. . . The District Court did not abuse its discretionary authority in this case. Hence, the judgment of the Court of Appeals is

Reversed.

[Justice SCALIA filed a concurring opinion. Justice STEVENS filed an opinion concurring in part and dissenting in part.]

c. The Current Legal Landscape

ADVISORY COMMITTEE NOTE TO 2000 AMENDMENT TO F.R.E. 702

Rule 702 has been amended in response to *Daubert v. Merrell Dow Pharmaceuticals, Inc.*, 509 U.S. 579 (1993), and to the many cases applying *Daubert*, including *Kumbo Tire Co. v. Carmichael*, 119 S. Ct. 1167 (1999). . . .

A review of the caselaw after *Daubert* shows that the rejection of expert testimony is the exception rather than the rule. *Daubert* did not work a "seachange over federal evidence law," and "the trial court's role as gatekeeper is not intended to serve as a replacement for the adversary system." *United States v. 14.38 Acres of Land Situated in Leflore County, Mississippi*, 80 F.3d 1074, 1078 (5th Cir. 1996). . . .

ELEANOR SWIFT, ONE HUNDRED YEARS OF EVIDENCE LAW REFORM: THAYER'S TRIUMPH

88 Cal. L. Rev. 2468, 2469, 2472-2473 (2000)

Taken together, *Joiner* and *Kumbo Tire* cordon off an area of judicial decision making at the trial court level that is exceedingly complex and difficult, and now appears to be practically immune from appellate review. It is difficult to imagine any choice of, or application of, *Daubert* factors that would be held to be erroneous.... Consistency and predictability in the trial court's method of making decisions about the reliability of expert testimony, and in the outcomes of those decisions, will be lost. Imagine the same expert offering the same type of scientific testimony, based upon the same sources of knowledge, in a series of cases. It will be possible under *Kumho Tire* for successive trial courts to select different *Daubert* factors, to apply them differently, and thus to reach different, inconsistent outcomes, admitting or excluding the same expertise. Under the abuse of discretion standard of review, appellate courts will uphold these inconsistent results. Indeed such inconsistency is inevitable under the opinion of the Court in *Kumho Tire*, which emphasizes that the Court will not refine *Daubert* into a categorical rule for application in "subsets of cases categorized by category of expert or by kind of evidence."

DAVID L. FAIGMAN, DAVID H. KAYE, MICHAEL J. SAKS & JOSEPH SANDERS, HOW GOOD IS GOOD ENOUGH? EXPERT EVIDENCE UNDER DAUBERT AND KUMHO

50 Case W. Res. L. Rev. 645, 656–657 (2000)

Despite some dicta in *Daubert* stating that the test embodied by Rule 702 is a more liberal one than *Frye*, when compared to the general acceptance test, the *Daubert* test requires more from some fields and less from others depending on the state of the knowledge being offered.... *Daubert* is more liberal when the expert evidence is solid, but on the cutting edge, and therefore not yet generally accepted. Presumably, this is the category Justice Blackmun had in mind when comparing the two tests. On the other hand, *Frye* is more liberal when what is offered is unsound expert evidence that nevertheless has become "generally accepted" in its field. This is the category that judges have encountered in numerous cases in the wake of *Daubert*, and found themselves puzzled about why a supposedly more liberal standard was leading them toward exclusion of evidence that long has been admitted without question.

The *Frye* test required faith to be placed in various fields and their practitioners, and inevitably made the courts more accepting of speculative, pseudo and sloppy science, but it had the appearance of being easier for judges to administer. *Daubert* requires that fields justify their claims, and this places a heavy cognitive burden on judges. The essential requirement of *Daubert* and its progeny is that to avoid exclusion, experts must offer the courts more than unsupported assertions; they must offer evidence about the basis of their asserted expertise sufficient to enable a judge to conclude that their expert testimony will provide dependable information to the factfinder.... We think all of this makes good sense. It should help insure that expert evidence will be more often informative than misleading.

RICHARD D. FRIEDMAN, "E" IS FOR ECLECTIC: MULTIPLE PERSPECTIVES ON EVIDENCE

87 Va. L. Rev. 2029, 2050–2052 (2001)

[I]n the realm of expert evidence as in that of hearsay, it is a mistake to make admissibility depend on a determination of reliability. . . . [W]e do not yet have any good basis for confidence that judges will do a significantly better job than juries in sorting out the wheat from the chaff . . . [so we] should not accept readily the premises that juries will tend to be led astray by bad expertise and that courts can help set them aright by filtering out bad expert evidence from good. . . .

[W]hen expert evidence is troublesome, the difficulty is likely to be not that the evidence is too unreliable to warrant admissibility, but that the plaintiff's case is, at least arguably, too weak as a matter of law to support a judgment. . . . This was true in each case in the Supreme Court's recent trilogy on expert evidence — *Daubert* itself . . .; *General Electric Co. v. Joiner* . . .; and *Kumho Tire Co. v. Carmichael*. . . . In each of these cases, the methods used by the experts were open to question — as is often so in cases involving expert testimony — and the conclusions they reached were dubious. But in none of them was the evidence worthless. . . . [T]he law of admissibility has been called on to carry weight that should be borne — if at all — by the law of sufficiency. . . . [I]f the court believes that control of the jury is necessary, it should exercise that control less by ruling the expert evidence inadmissible and more by ruling that, even given that evidence, the plaintiff does not have enough evidence to support a judgment.

BARBARA PFEFFER BILLAUER, DAUBERT DEBUNKED: A HISTORY OF LEGAL RETROGRESSION AND THE NEED TO REASSESS "SCIENTIFIC ADMISSIBILITY"

21 Suffolk J. Trial & App. Advoc. 1, 46–47 (2015–2016)

. . . [S]urveys report that judges feel unnerved by the gatekeeper role imposed by *Daubert*. [A common complaint about *Daubert* is that it] "forces judges to become amateur scientists, a role they are not well-prepared for and should not be asked to play." . . . [But it] may be that . . . a different educational approach . . . is necessary. . . . In a day or a week, there is no way even the most scientifically adept [judges] could learn the intricacies of genetics or artificial intelligence. What judges can be taught in a day is the meaning of "science." A weekend would suffice to teach the difference between validity and reliability — two distinct scientific concepts — mangled and comingled in . . . *Daubert*. What they can be taught in a week is some understanding of the scientific method and its limitations. These are general principles that apply to all scientific evidence, even cases not relying on science per se. As far as cases involving more sophisticated or interdisciplinary material such as epidemiological and toxic tort cases, which involve statistics, biostatistics, immunology, genetics, toxicology, obstetrics, and more, at least the basics should be introduced in law school as electives for students interested in pursuing these areas of law. Better cross-examination would better help judges, and better understanding of the basics helps everyone.

MARSH v. VALYOU

977 So. 2d 543 (Fla. 2007)

PER CURIAM.

After sustaining injuries in four separate car accidents between August 1995 and January 1998, the petitioner, Jill Marsh, filed a negligence action against a series of four defendants [including Robert Valyou and Avis Rent-A-Car]. She claimed the accidents caused fibromyalgia, which is a "syndrome of widespread pain, a decreased pain threshold, and characteristic symptoms including non-restorative sleep, fatigue, stiffness, mood disturbance, irritable syndrome, headache, paresthesias, and other, less common features." . . . Frederick Wolfe, et al., *The Fibromyalgia Syndrome: A Consensus Report on Fibromyalgia and Disability*, 23 J. Rheumatology 534, 534 (1996) [hereinafter *Consensus Report*].

Avis moved to preclude Marsh from presenting expert testimony that the accidents caused her fibromyalgia, arguing that the testimony did not meet the *Frye* standard for admissibility because the premise that trauma can cause fibromyalgia had not been generally accepted in the scientific community. The trial court held a *Frye* hearing and, after reviewing numerous documents related to fibromyalgia and hearing arguments of counsel, granted the motion. . . . Marsh then announced she had no claims apart from fibromyalgia [and a related syndrome], and the trial court entered summary judgment. Petitioner appealed. . . .

Despite the Supreme Court's decision in *Daubert*, we have since repeatedly reaffirmed our adherence to the *Frye* standard for admissibility of evidence. . . . Other states have adhered to *Frye* as well. *See, e.g.*, [Charles Alan Wright & Victor James Gold, *Federal Practice and Procedure* § 6266 (1997)] (noting that many states have adopted *Daubert*, but others have declined to do so); [David E. Bernstein & Jeffrey D. Jackson, *The Daubert Trilogy in the States*, 44 Jurimetrics 351, 356 (2004)] (noting that *Frye* "remains the rule in a significant minority of states"). . . .

Under *Frye*, "[t]he proponent of the evidence bears the burden of establishing by a preponderance of the evidence the general acceptance of the underlying scientific principles and methodology." *Castillo v. E.I. Du Pont Du Nemours & Co.*, 854 So. 2d 1264, 1268 (Fla. 2003). We review *Frye* issues de novo, with general acceptance considered as of the time of the appeal. *Id.* "By definition, the *Frye* standard *only applies* when an expert attempts to render an opinion that is based upon *new or novel scientific techniques.*" *U.S. Sugar Corp. v. Henson*, 823 So. 2d 104, 109 (Fla. 2002) (emphasis added). . . .

The expert medical causation testimony at issue here is not "new or novel." The American College of Rheumatology published classification criteria for fibromyalgia in 1990. *Consensus Report, supra*. . . . Marsh's experts based their diagnoses and opinions about the cause of her fibromyalgia on a review of her medical history, clinical physical examinations, their own experience, published research, and differential diagnosis. . . . Experts routinely form medical causation opinions based on their experience and training. . . . And there is always the possibility that two experts may reach dissimilar opinions based on their individual experience. However, a disagreement among experts does not transform an ordinary opinion on medical causation into a new or novel principle subject to *Frye*. . . . Because testimony causally linking trauma to fibromyalgia is based on the experts' experience and training, it is "pure opinion" admissible without having to satisfy *Frye*.

Marsh's experts did not base their opinions on new or novel scientific tests or procedures, and Respondents did not challenge the patient history, examination methods, clinical practices, or other methodologies upon which they did rely. . . . Instead, Respondents challenged the experts' *conclusions* that trauma caused Marsh's fibromyalgia. However, as we stated in *U.S. Sugar*, "[u]nder *Frye*, the inquiry must focus only on the general acceptance of the scientific principles and methodologies upon which an expert relies in rendering his or her opinion. Certainly the opinion of the testifying expert need not be generally accepted as well. . . . [O]nce the *Frye* test is satisfied through proof of general acceptance of the basis of an opinion, the expert's opinions are to be evaluated by the finder of fact and are properly assessed as a matter of weight, not admissibility." . . .

Trial courts must resist the temptation to usurp the jury's role in evaluating the credibility of experts and choosing between legitimate but conflicting scientific views. . . . A challenge to the conclusions of Marsh's experts as to causation, rather than the methods used to reach those conclusions, is a proper issue for the trier of fact. For these reasons, we hold that *Frye* does not apply to testimony of a causal link between trauma and fibromyalgia. . . .

[Moreover, even] if subject to *Frye*, testimony linking trauma to fibromyalgia satisfies it. The purpose of *Frye* is to ensure the reliability of expert testimony. . . . Numerous published articles and studies recognize an association between trauma and fibromyalgia. Respondents' own expert testified that he has seen situations where he thought trauma indirectly led to fibromyalgia. A lack of studies conclusively demonstrating a causal link between trauma and fibromyalgia and calls for further research do not preclude admission of the testimony. . . .

Frye does not require unanimity. While the precise etiology of fibromyalgia may not be fully understood, we hold that Marsh has sufficiently demonstrated the reliability of her experts' testimony, and the trial court erred in excluding it. . . . [Reversed.]

ANSTEAD, J., specially concurring.

. . . There are courts that have addressed the exact question of expert testimony linking physical trauma to fibromyalgia and found it admissible pursuant to the rule announced in *Daubert*. . . . I would hold that *Frye* has been superseded by the adoption of Florida's Evidence Code, and that under the relevancy standard contained in the code the expert opinion evidence in question was admissible. Hence, I concur in the majority's decision.

CANTERO, J., dissenting.

. . . I would hold that expert testimony causally linking trauma to fibromyalgia is subject to, and fails, the *Frye* test. . . . Whether trauma can ever cause fibromyalgia is a subject of much debate, and therefore the view that it can has not been generally accepted. I cannot agree with the majority that the jury should be left to sort out contentious and complex disputes about medical causation where experts in the relevant scientific community have been unable to agree. . . . [T]he majority decision turns the courtroom into a laboratory. . . . I respectfully dissent.

PROBLEM

9.1. In 2013, the Florida Evidence Code was amended to adopt the standards set forth in *Daubert, Joiner,* and *Kumho Tire*; the new provision roughly tracks the language of Federal Rule of Evidence 702. The legislative history makes clear that the Florida legislature intended to prohibit the kind of expert testimony the state Supreme Court found admissible in *Marsh v. Valyou.* As the concurring opinion in *Marsh* pointed out, though, there are cases in other jurisdictions finding testimony very similar to the evidence in *Marsh* admissible under the *Daubert* standard. Should the testimony at issue in *Marsh* be admissible in federal court? One commentator has suggested that "[t]he choice is not between easy *Frye* and difficult *Daubert*; it is between strict and lax scrutiny." Mike Redmayne, *Expert Evidence and Criminal Justice* 113 (2001). Is he right?

C. CURRENT CONTROVERSIES IN SCIENTIFIC EVIDENCE

> *Generally speaking. . . the more complex the scientific issues subject to proof, the more difficult it becomes to elucidate it through conventional partisan advocacy designed to win the day in the court. . . . [T]he scientization of proof is likely to exacerbate the presently minor frictions within traditional procedural arrangements. Their further deterioration should be considered likely on this ground alone.*
>
> Mirjan R. Damaška, *Evidence Law Adrift* (1997)

The following materials illustrate and discuss how the rules of evidence have been applied to several particularly controversial kinds of scientific proof: lie detection; expert testimony regarding human psychology; probabilistic evidence; DNA identification; "traditional" forensic sciences such as latent fingerprint analysis and arson investigations; and digital evidence.

1. Lie Detection

[C.E.C. §351.1]

UNITED STATES v. SCHEFFER

523 U.S. 303 (1998)

Justice THOMAS announced the judgment of the Court and delivered the opinion of the Court with respect to Parts I, II-A, and II-D....

This case presents the question whether Military Rule of Evidence 707, which makes polygraph evidence inadmissible in court-martial proceedings, unconstitutionally abridges the right of accused members of the military to present a defense. We hold that it does not.

I

In March 1992, respondent Edward Scheffer, an airman stationed at March Air Force Base in California, volunteered to work as an informant on drug investigations for the Air Force Office of Special Investigations (OSI). His OSI supervisors advised him that, from time to time during the course of his undercover work, they would ask him to submit to drug testing and polygraph examinations. In early April, one of the OSI agents supervising respondent requested that he submit to a urine test. Shortly after providing the urine sample, but before the results of the test were known, respondent agreed to take a polygraph test administered by an OSI examiner. In the opinion of the examiner, the test "indicated no deception" when respondent denied using drugs since joining the Air Force.

On April 30, respondent unaccountably failed to appear for work and could not be found on the base. He was absent without leave until May 13, when an Iowa state patrolman arrested him following a routine traffic stop and held him for return to the base. OSI agents later learned that respondent's urinalysis revealed the presence of methamphetamine.

Respondent was tried by general court-martial on charges of using methamphetamine, failing to go to his appointed place of duty, wrongfully absenting himself from the base for 13 days, and, with respect to an unrelated matter, uttering 17 insufficient funds checks. He testified at trial on his own behalf, relying upon an "innocent ingestion" theory and denying that he had knowingly used drugs while working for OSI. On cross-examination, the prosecution attempted to impeach respondent with inconsistencies between his trial testimony and earlier statements he had made to OSI.

Respondent sought to introduce the polygraph evidence in support of his testimony that he did not knowingly use drugs. The military judge denied the motion, relying on Military Rule of Evidence 707, which provides, in relevant part:

"(a) Notwithstanding any other provision of law, the results of a polygraph examination, the opinion of a polygraph examiner, or any reference to an offer to take, failure to take, or taking of a polygraph examination, shall not be admitted into evidence."

. . . Respondent was convicted on all counts and was sentenced to a bad-conduct discharge, confinement for 30 months, total forfeiture of all pay and allowances, and reduction to the lowest enlisted grade. The Air Force Court of Criminal Appeals affirmed in all material respects. . . .

By a 3-to-2 vote, the United States Court of Appeals for the Armed Forces reversed. Without pointing to any particular language in the Sixth Amendment, the Court of Appeals held that "[a] per se exclusion of polygraph evidence offered by an accused to rebut an attack on his credibility, . . . violates his Sixth Amendment right to present a defense." . . . We granted certiorari, and we now reverse.

II

A defendant's right to present relevant evidence is not unlimited, but rather is subject to reasonable restrictions. See *Taylor v. Illinois*, 484 U.S. 400, 410 (1988); *Rock v. Arkansas*, 483 U.S. 44, 55 (1987); *Chambers v. Mississippi*, 410 U.S. 284, 295 (1973). . . . [S]tate and federal rulemakers have broad latitude under the Constitution to establish rules excluding evidence from criminal trials. Such rules do not abridge an accused's right to present a defense so long as they are not "arbitrary" or "disproportionate to the purposes they are designed to serve." *Rock, supra*, at 56. . . .

A

State and federal governments unquestionably have a legitimate interest in ensuring that reliable evidence is presented to the trier of fact in a criminal trial. Indeed, the exclusion of unreliable evidence is a principal objective of many evidentiary rules. See, e.g., Fed. Rule Evid. 702; Fed. Rule Evid. 802; Fed. Rule Evid. 901; see also *Daubert v. Merrell Dow Pharmaceuticals, Inc.*, 509 U.S. 579, 589 (1993).

The contentions of respondent and the dissent notwithstanding, there is simply no consensus that polygraph evidence is reliable. To this day, the scientific community remains extremely polarized about the reliability of polygraph techniques. . . . Some studies have concluded that polygraph tests overall are accurate and reliable. . . . Others have found that polygraph tests assess truthfulness significantly less accurately — that scientific field studies suggest the accuracy rate of the "control question technique" polygraph is "little better than could be obtained by the toss of a coin," that is, 50 percent. . . .

This lack of scientific consensus is reflected in the disagreement among state and federal courts concerning both the admissibility and the reliability of polygraph evidence. Although some Federal Courts of Appeal have abandoned the per se rule excluding polygraph evidence, leaving its admission or exclusion to the discretion of district courts under *Daubert*, see, e.g., *United States v. Posado*, 57 F.3d 428, 434 (CA5 1995); *United States v. Cordoba*, 104 F.3d 225, 228 (CA9 1997), at least one Federal Circuit has recently reaffirmed its per se ban, see *United States v. Sanchez*, 118 F.3d 192, 197 (CA4 1997), and another recently noted that it has "not decided whether polygraphy has reached a sufficient state of reliability to be admissible." *United States v. Messina*, 131 F.3d 36, 42 (CA2 1997). Most States maintain per se rules excluding polygraph evidence. New Mexico is unique in making polygraph evidence generally admissible without the prior stipulation of the parties and without significant restriction. Whatever their approach, state and federal courts continue to express doubt about whether such evidence is reliable. . . .

The approach taken by the President in adopting Rule 707 — excluding polygraph evidence in all military trials — is a rational and proportional means of advancing the legitimate interest in barring unreliable evidence. Although the degree of reliability of polygraph evidence may depend upon a variety of identifiable factors, there is simply no way to know in a particular case whether a polygraph examiner's conclusion is accurate, because certain doubts and uncertainties plague even the best polygraph exams. Individual jurisdictions therefore may reasonably reach differing conclusions as to whether polygraph evidence should be admitted. We cannot say, then, that presented with such widespread uncertainty, the President acted arbitrarily or disproportionately in promulgating a per se rule excluding all polygraph evidence. . . .

B

It is equally clear that Rule 707 serves a second legitimate governmental interest: Preserving the court members' core function of making credibility determinations in criminal trials. A fundamental premise of our criminal trial system is that "the *jury* is the lie detector." *United States v. Barnard*, 490 F.2d 907, 912 (CA9 1973) (emphasis added), cert. denied, 416 U.S. 959 (1974). Determining the weight and credibility of witness testimony, therefore, has long been held to be the "part of every case [that] belongs to the jury, who are presumed to be fitted for it by their natural intelligence and their practical knowledge of men and the ways of men." *Aetna Life Ins. Co. v. Ward*, 140 U.S. 76, 88 (1891).

By its very nature, polygraph evidence may diminish the jury's role in making credibility determinations. . . . Unlike other expert witnesses who testify about factual matters outside the jurors' knowledge, such as the analysis of fingerprints, ballistics, or DNA found at a crime scene, a polygraph expert can supply the jury only with another opinion, in addition to its own, about whether the witness was telling the truth. Jurisdictions, in promulgating rules of evidence, may legitimately be concerned about the risk that juries will give excessive weight to the opinions of a polygrapher, clothed as they are in scientific expertise and at times offering, as in respondent's case, a conclusion about the ultimate issue in the trial. Such jurisdictions may legitimately determine that the aura of infallibility attending polygraph evidence can lead jurors to abandon their duty to assess credibility and guilt. Those jurisdictions may also take into account the fact that a judge cannot determine, when ruling on a motion to admit polygraph evidence, whether a particular polygraph expert is likely to influence the jury unduly. For these reasons, the President is within his constitutional prerogative to promulgate a *per se* rule that simply excludes all such evidence. . . .

D

. . . [T]he court members heard all the relevant details of the charged offense from the perspective of the accused, and the Rule did not preclude him from introducing any factual evidence. Rather, respondent was barred merely from introducing expert opinion testimony to bolster his own credibility. Moreover, in contrast to the rule at issue in *Rock*, Rule 707 did not prohibit respondent from testifying on his own behalf; he freely exercised his choice to convey his version of the facts to the court-martial members. We therefore cannot conclude that respondent's defense was significantly impaired by the exclusion of polygraph evidence. Rule 707 is thus constitutional under our precedents. . . . The judgment of the Court of Appeals is reversed.

Justice KENNEDY . . . concurring in part and concurring in the judgment. . . . The continuing, good-faith disagreement among experts and courts on the subject of polygraph reliability counsels against our invalidating a *per se* exclusion of polygraph results or of the fact an accused has taken or refused to take a polygraph examination. . . . Given the ongoing debate about polygraphs, I agree the rule of exclusion is not so arbitrary or disproportionate that it is unconstitutional. . . .

[I]t seems the principal opinion overreaches when it rests its holding on the additional ground that the jury's role in making credibility determinations is diminished when it hears polygraph evidence. I am in substantial agreement with Justice Stevens' observation that the argument demeans and mistakes the role and competence of jurors in deciding the factual question of guilt or innocence. In the last analysis the principal opinion says it is unwise to allow the jury to hear "a conclusion about the ultimate issue in the trial." I had thought this tired argument had long since been given its deserved repose as a categorical rule of exclusion. . . . The principal opinion is made less convincing by its contradicting the rationale of Rule 704 and the well considered reasons the Advisory Committee recited in support of its adoption.

Justice STEVENS, dissenting.

. . . The constitutional requirement that a blanket exclusion of potentially unreliable evidence must be proportionate to the purposes served by the rule obviously makes it necessary to evaluate the interests on both sides of the balance. Today the Court all but ignores the strength of the defendant's interest in having polygraph evidence admitted in certain cases. As the facts of this case illustrate, the Court is quite wrong in assuming that the impact of Rule 707 on respondent's defense was not significant because it did not preclude the introduction of any "factual evidence" or prevent him from conveying "his version of the facts to the court-martial members." Under such reasoning, a rule that excluded the testimony of alibi witnesses would not be significant as long as the defendant is free to testify himself. But given the defendant's strong interest in the outcome — an interest that was sufficient to make his testimony presumptively untrustworthy and therefore inadmissible at common law — his uncorroborated testimony is certain to be less persuasive than that of a third-party witness. A rule that bars him "from introducing expert opinion testimony to bolster his own credibility" unquestionably impairs any "meaningful opportunity to present a complete defense"; indeed, it is sure to be out-come-determinative in many cases. . . .

There are a host of studies that place the reliability of polygraph tests at 85% to 90%. While critics of the polygraph argue that accuracy is much lower, even the studies cited by the critics place polygraph accuracy at 70%.

Moreover, to the extent that the polygraph errs, studies have repeatedly shown that the polygraph is more likely to find innocent people guilty than vice versa. Thus, exculpatory polygraphs — like the one in this case — are likely to be more reliable than inculpatory ones.

Of course, within the broad category of lie detector evidence, there may be a wide variation in both the validity and the relevance of particular test results. Questions about the examiner's integrity, independence, choice of questions, or training in the detection of deliberate attempts to provoke misleading physiological responses may justify exclusion of specific evidence. But such questions are properly addressed in adversary proceedings; they fall far short of justifying a blanket exclusion of this type of expert testimony.

There is no legal requirement that expert testimony must satisfy a particular degree of reliability to be admissible. Expert testimony about a defendant's "future dangerousness" to determine his eligibility for the death penalty, even if wrong "most of the time," is routinely admitted. *Barefoot v. Estelle*, 463 U.S. 880, 898-901 (1983). Studies indicate that handwriting analysis, and even fingerprint identifications, may be less trustworthy than polygraph evidence in certain cases. And, of course, even highly dubious eyewitness testimony is, and should be, admitted and tested in the crucible of cross-examination. The Court's reliance on potential unreliability as a justification for a categorical rule of inadmissibility reveals that it is "overly pessimistic about the capabilities of the jury and of the adversary system generally. Vigorous cross-examination, presentation of contrary evidence, and careful instruction on the burden of proof are the traditional and appropriate means of attacking shaky but admissible evidence." *Daubert*, 509 U.S., at 596. . . .

There is, of course, some risk that some "juries will give excessive weight to the opinions of a polygrapher, clothed as they are in scientific expertise." In my judgment, however, it is much more likely that juries will be guided by the instructions of the trial judge concerning the credibility of expert as well as lay witnesses. . . . Common sense suggests that the testimony of disinterested third parties that is relevant to the jury's credibility determination will assist rather than impair the jury's deliberations. As with the reliance on the potential unreliability of this type of evidence, the reliance on a fear that the average jury is not able to assess the weight of this testimony reflects a distressing lack of confidence in the intelligence of the average American. . . .

The Government's concerns would unquestionably support the exclusion of polygraph evidence in particular cases, and may well be sufficient to support a narrower rule designed to respond to specific concerns. In my judgment, however, those concerns are plainly insufficient to support a categorical rule that prohibits the admission of polygraph evidence in all cases, no matter how reliable or probative the evidence may be. Accordingly, I respectfully dissent.

STATE v. SHARPE

435 P.3d 887 (Alaska 2019)

In each of the three underlying criminal cases in this consolidated appeal, the defendant sought to introduce expert testimony by a polygraph examiner that the defendant was truthful when he made exculpatory statements relating to the charges against him during a polygraph examination conducted using the "comparison question technique" (CQT). In two of the cases, the superior courts found that testimony based on a CQT polygraph examination satisfied the requirements for scientific evidence under *Daubert v. Merrell Dow Pharmaceuticals, Inc.*, and *State v. Coon* [974 P.2d 386 (Alaska 1999)]. In the third case, the superior court reached the opposite conclusion and found the evidence inadmissible.... [The tests in all three cases were administered by the same polygraph examiner, a psychologist named David Raskin.]

Under Alaska Evidence Rule 702(a), a qualified expert witness may testify to "scientific, technical, or other specialized knowledge" if that knowledge "will assist the trier of fact to understand the evidence or to determine a fact in issue."... In 1999 we adopted *Daubert* as the applicable admissibility standard for scientific expert testimony under the Alaska Rules of Evidence in *State v. Coon*....

In all polygraph examinations, whether the CQT or some other approach is used, the examinee is connected to a polygraph, an instrument that measures multiple physiological phenomena: pulse rate, blood pressure, respiration rate, and galvanic skin response in the hands and fingers.... The CQT exams administered in these cases are a form of specific-incident polygraph testing, as opposed to a polygraph examination for screening or background check purposes. Screening tests ask about a broad range of conduct, such as whether the examinee has ever committed a crime or used illegal drugs, but specific-incident tests, like the ones Dr. Raskin administered, focus on a particular crime, event, or other occurrence under investigation. The CQT examiner asks three types of questions: "neutral" or "irrelevant" questions ("Is your name Thomas?"), broad "control" or "comparison" questions ("During the first 35 years of your life, did you ever engage in a sexual act of which you should be ashamed?"), and specific "relevant" questions ("Did you ever touch G.B.'s breast?"). Each comparison question will ask about a broad category of past conduct, similar to but excluding the specific occurrence being investigated, and each question will be specifically designed to be ambiguous, broad, and vague but elicit a "No" answer. Because the comparison questions are broadly worded and address sensitive topics, the examinee is assumed to be deceptive or at least unsure of his answer. The underlying rationale of the CQT is that deceptive subjects will feel more threatened by the relevant questions and will view the comparison questions as less important; thus, deceptive subjects will have a stronger physiological reaction to the relevant questions. In contrast, truthful subjects are expected to feel more threatened by the comparison questions and will have a stronger physiological reaction than to the truthfully answered relevant questions. There are two reasons for this expectation: first, the sensitive topic of the comparison questions is assumed to generate a response; second, the examiner will have explained prior to the exam that the examinee's reactions to the comparison questions are important to the ultimate test result. Thus, the CQT is based on the premise that the relative magnitudes of the examinee's reactions to the relevant and comparison questions are indicative of his truthfulness or lack thereof when answering the relevant questions.

The examiner asks the examinee a list of prepared questions multiple times. For each relevant question, the examiner will compare the subject's reaction to his reaction to an adjacent comparison question. Each measured parameter is given a numerical score for each question pair, for example from -3 to +3, with a positive number indicating a stronger reaction to the comparison question and a negative number indicating a stronger reaction to the relevant question. The examiner totals the numerical scores: a high positive overall score is interpreted as indicating a truthful result; a high negative score is interpreted as indicating deception; a score close to zero, whether positive or negative, is considered inconclusive. . . .

The first question we must address is what standard of review the appellate court should apply to appeals from a *Daubert/Coon* determination made by the trial court. Our current standard, which the court of appeals urges us to reconsider, is the one laid out in *State v. Coon:* abuse of discretion. . . .

Although all federal circuits have adopted *Joiner*'s abuse of discretion standard for appellate review, a number of state courts have ruled to the contrary and adopted a stricter standard of review. For example, the New Mexico Supreme Court held . . . that the validity of a particular scientific theory is a form of "legislative fact" not specific to the circumstances of any particular case, and it therefore applies de novo review to such questions. Other states that have adopted a hybrid or de novo standard of review for *Daubert* determinations include Oklahoma, Washington, Kentucky, New Hampshire, West Virginia, and Oregon. In states that continue to apply the *Frye* standard of general acceptance, most apply de novo review on appeal.

The primary concern raised by jurisdictions applying abuse of discretion review . . . is the potential for inconsistent rulings in similarly situated cases. Our opinion in *Coon* dismissed this concern, finding it unlikely "that the inconsistency will be of such magnitude as to 'compromise the integrity of the judiciary in the eyes of the public.'" In light of the posture of the cases now before us, we may have been too optimistic. If two defendants offer similar scientific testimony and — after separate evidentiary hearings — one judge deems the testimony to be scientifically valid while another does not, that could be the result of differences between the particular cases and differences in the evidence presented at the hearings. But when the judge in the latter case relied on the evidentiary hearing from the first, and reached the opposite conclusion based on identical evidence, it is clear that the difference in outcome cannot be attributed to a difference in the amount or quality of the evidence.

That is essentially what happened in these cases. . . . This raises at least the appearance of arbitrariness, i.e., the appearance that the outcome of a *Daubert* determination in our courts depends more on which judge was assigned to the case than on the objective application of law to the evidence presented. Regardless of how accurate this appearance might be, it certainly has the potential to raise serious questions in the eyes of the public about the integrity of our judicial system, particularly when such inconsistencies occur in the context of serious criminal proceedings. . . .

For these reasons, we agree . . . with the dissent in *Coon* . . . that a more probing standard of review is warranted in an appeal from a *Daubert* determination. . . . Going forward, we will . . . apply our independent judgment to the question whether — based on the evidence presented and the scientific literature available — the technique or theory underlying the proposed expert testimony is sufficiently reliable to satisfy *Daubert* and *Coon*. . . .

Other jurisdictions that apply the *Daubert* test have ... rejected evidence based on the CQT method. For example ... the Connecticut Supreme Court adopted *Daubert* as the relevant standard for scientific evidence and upheld its traditional per se ban on admitting polygraph evidence. Jurisdictions that have adopted *Daubert* and maintain a per se exclusion of polygraph evidence include Idaho, West Virginia, Hawaii, Vermont, the District of Columbia, and the Court of Appeals for the Fourth Circuit. In *United States v. Scheffer* the Supreme Court held that a per se rule excluding polygraph evidence does not infringe on the constitutional rights of an accused to present evidence in his defense; implied in the Court's reasoning is the corollary conclusion that such a rule is also not inconsistent with *Daubert*. The superior court in [one of the cases under review] surveyed polygraph admissibility in "all 50 states and the federal circuits" at the time of the hearing and found that "30 jurisdictions still have a per se ban, 17 admit polygraph results based upon stipulation, and 12 leave the decision to the trial court's discretion on a case-by-case basis."

Of the jurisdictions that allow polygraph evidence based on the judge's discretion, New Mexico is a notable example. Unlike the Alaska Evidence Rules, the New Mexico Rules of Evidence (NMRE) specifically address polygraph examinations. Under NMRE 11-707, the opinion of a polygraph examiner "as to the truthfulness of a person's answers in a polygraph examination may be admitted" if a number of specific criteria regarding the examiner's qualifications and the test procedure are met.... [T]he New Mexico Supreme Court held that when the expert's qualification and the examination meet this rule's standards, "polygraph examination results are sufficiently reliable to be admitted" under the *Daubert* standard and NMRE 11-702 — New Mexico's equivalent to Alaska Evidence Rule 702.121 However, the court also concluded that NMRE 11-707 only makes polygraph evidence admissible subject to the discretion of the trial judge's balancing of probative value against unfair prejudice.

Both the Supreme Court in *Daubert* and our court in *Coon* explained that the listed factors should not be seen as a determinative checklist, but that the standard is a flexible one. Because the *Daubert* factors are a good starting point ... these factors will be discussed in turn here.

Empirical testing. ... For a CQT polygraph test to yield reliable inferences about deception, it must be the case that (1) deception on relevant and comparison questions produce different psychological states; (2) these psychological states produce measurably different physiological responses; (3) these physiological responses include the ones that the polygraph instrument measures; (4) these physiological responses are unlikely to arise from causes other than deception; (5) the scoring system captures the physiological differences relevant to deception; and (6) examiners accurately assign conclusions of deception or honesty to certain score values when they interpret scores. Many of these assumptions and hypotheses appear not to have been tested; even more important, some may not be readily testable.

In particular, CQT polygraph examinations are based on the theory that while a truthful person will respond more strongly to the comparison questions, a deceptive person will have a stronger reaction to the relevant questions. [William Iacono, a psychologist who testified in one of the cases under review,] criticized this as an unfounded assumption, arguing for example that a

truthful person might react strongly to the relevant questions due to the implications of a false accusation, while a guilty person outside of laboratory studies
might have a reduced reaction to the relevant questions due to the phenomenon of habituation. On those grounds, Dr. Iacono concluded that "the CQT
has . . . a weak theoretical foundation." He testified that this underlying theory
has not been properly tested, in part because laboratory studies cannot duplicate all of the considerations that might be relevant in the field — like habituation or a truthful examinee reacting to the relevant questions out of fear
of being falsely accused — and in part because field studies have difficulties
establishing the "ground truth" of whether an examined person was actually
lying. Determining ground truth presents practical problems that are difficult,
perhaps even impossible, to overcome, meaning that true accuracy rates may
not be empirically verifiable. Dr. Iacono testified that many field studies focus
on criminal cases and use confessions to determine ground truth, but noted
that this is problematic because whether or not a defendant passes or fails a
polygraph exam affects how likely he is to subsequently confess.

Several studies and surveys of polygraph research have reached similar conclusions. For example, a 2003 review of the scientific evidence on polygraphy
by the National Research Council concluded that "[p]olygraph research has not
developed and tested theories of the underlying factors that produce the observed
responses." Similarly, a more recent survey of academic literature concluded that
"[i]t appears unlikely that the proponents of the CQT will be able to reconcile
the theoretical flaws of their technique in the foreseeable future." Although there
have been numerous studies testing the practical applications of the comparison
question technique, our review of the record and the available academic literature reveals no studies actually testing the underlying psychological theories.
Ultimately, given the fact that certain assumptions of polygraph testing not only
are untested, but may be functionally *untestable*, we conclude that this factor
weighs decidedly against admitting polygraph testimony as scientific evidence.

Peer review. . . . Most of the studies cited by Dr. Raskin in support of the
technique are from the 1980s and 1990s, with some dated as far back as the
late 1970s; and although the superior court's *Daubert* hearing was conducted
in 2012, Dr. Raskin did not cite to any studies published more recently than
2003. Thus, although studies regarding CQT polygraphy have been published
in peer-reviewed journals, it does not appear that this has resulted in the kind
of refinement and development that makes publication and peer review relevant to a *Daubert* analysis. . . .

Acceptable error rate. . . . In the three cases currently before this court,
each defendant was said to have passed his polygraph test; the relevant question for the factfinder is whether, given this fact, the defendant was likely
truthful or whether the test was a false negative. To determine this likelihood,
more information is required; specifically, information about the base rate of
deceptive and truthful subjects.

The lack of a reliable base rate estimate was the underlying reason for
the Connecticut Supreme Court upholding its traditional per se ban on admitting polygraph evidence in *State v. Porter* [241 Conn. 57 (1997)]. Noting
"wide disagreement" about the accuracy rates for "a well run polygraph exam,"
the court decided that, even if the estimates of polygraph proponents were
accepted, the technique would still be "of questionable validity." The court

cited a field study by Dr. Raskin indicating a sensitivity of 87% and a specificity of 59%: "In other words, 13 percent of those who are in fact deceptive will be labeled as truthful . . . [and] 41 percent of subjects who are, in fact, truthful will be labeled as deceptive." The court further reasoned that, even if a test is accurate, its probative value as scientific evidence depends on its "predictive value" — the likelihood "that a person really is lying given that the polygraph labels the subject as deceptive" and the likelihood "that a subject really is truthful given that the polygraph labels the subject as not deceptive." This predictive value, the court explained, depends not only on the accuracy of the test but also "on the 'base rate' of deceptiveness among the people tested by the polygraph." Because the *Porter* court found a "complete absence of reliable data on base rates," it concluded that it had no possible way of assessing the test's probative value. With that in mind, the court concluded that even if polygraph evidence satisfies the *Daubert* standard, which it assumed without deciding, the probative value of such evidence is very low and substantially outweighed by its prejudicial effects.

As in *Porter*, the record before us is devoid of reliable data about the base rate of deceptiveness among polygraph examinees outside of lab tests; we also have not found such data in academic literature. Absent some reliable estimate of this base rate there is no way to estimate the reliability of polygraph results, and thus no way to determine whether any particular accuracy rate is acceptable. . . . Accordingly, this factor weighs against admitting polygraph evidence.

Standards for operation. . . . Standards do control some aspects of polygraph testing and many states also have statutes governing polygraph test administration, examinees' privacy rights, and licensing of examiners. To describe the standards for administration of polygraphs, Dr. Raskin pointed to New Mexico Evidence Rule 11-707 as providing "clear standards for tests to be offered as evidence" and described the rule as "a superior model for national standards." He also referenced standards adopted by national polygraph organizations and standards imposed by government agencies.

Rule 11-707 provides that a polygraph examiner's opinion testimony is admissible if the examiner is qualified, the scoring method used is "generally accepted as reliable by polygraph experts," the examiner was informed of relevant information regarding the examinee prior to the exam, two or more relevant questions were asked, three or more charts were taken, and the exam was recorded. However, what constitutes a "generally accepted" scoring method is not further defined. A "relevant question" is simply defined as "a clear and concise question which refers to specific objective facts directly related to the purpose of the examination and does not allow rationalization in the answer." . . . [Moreover,] Rule 11-707 is not a national standard. As . . . Dr. Raskin acknowledged, there is no one "controlling" industry standard and there may be great differences in "generally accepted principles."

It is clear that some aspects of the test lack standards, or at least consistent standards. Specifically, the formulation and ordering of questions, the conducting of the pretest interview, the choice of scoring system, and the evaluation of the examinee's demeanor leave much to the examiner's discretion. While the superior court's finding regarding CQT protocols was not clearly erroneous, we conclude that the lack of clear controlling standards for CQT administration weighs against its admissibility.

General acceptance. . . . Both Dr. Raskin and Dr. Iacono testified about a variety of surveys regarding the acceptance of polygraphy. Dr. Iacono also testified about a number of scientific publications that conclude polygraph examinations are unreliable. Based on a review of this evidence and literature, it appears that the parts of the scientific community who regularly utilize polygraphy have — perhaps unsurprisingly — widely accepted the technique, while the broader scientific community views the technique more skeptically. . . . Given the decades-long debate over the validity of polygraph evidence, the apparent lack of development in the technique as a response to that debate, and the apparently lackluster support for the technique outside the community of practicing polygraph examiners, we conclude that this factor also weighs against admitting polygraph evidence.

Other relevant factors. . . . Dr. Raskin, who testified at the *Daubert* hearing in favor of admitting polygraph evidence, is himself a practicing polygraph examiner and has financial ties to one manufacturer of polygraphs, earning royalties from the sale of polygraph machines he invented. Many of the studies cited as approving polygraph testing as scientifically valid were performed by Dr. Raskin or by other practicing examiners, and a number of the studies were published in polygraph industry publications. While we do not entirely discount this research and have examined it on its merits, we recognize that the polygraph industry has an obvious financial interest in confirming polygraph testing as valid and promoting its use and admissibility in court.

Conclusion. . . . In light of each of the factors discussed above, we conclude that on the evidence before us, CQT polygraph testing has not been shown to satisfy the standard for scientific evidence set forth in *Daubert* and *Coon. . . .* We . . . are unconvinced that the opinion of polygraph examiners amounts to "scientific, technical, or other specialized knowledge" that "will assist the trier of fact to understand the evidence or to determine a fact in issue," as required under Evidence Rule 702. Our opinion here does not mean that CQT polygraph testing will never be sufficiently reliable to pass muster as scientific evidence, but absent substantial evidence demonstrating that CQT polygraph testing produces reliable results based on sound, verifiable science, the results of CQT polygraph examinations cannot be admitted in evidence over objection. . . .

UNITED STATES v. SEMRAU

693 F.3d 510 (6th Cir. 2012)

Dr. Lorne Semrau appeals his conviction of three counts of healthcare fraud in violation of 18 U.S.C. § 1347. Among other issues, Dr. Semrau argues — on a matter of first impression in any jurisdiction — that results from a functional magnetic resonance imaging ("fMRI") lie detection test should have been admitted to prove the veracity of his denials of wrongdoing. . . .

[Defense expert] Dr. Steven J. Laken, Ph.D., is the President and CEO of Cephos Corporation . . . . Cephos holds a patent on a version of an fMRI-based lie detection method, which identifies Dr. Laken as its inventor. . . .

At the heart of Dr. Laken's lie detection method is fMRI imaging. An fMRI enables researchers to assess brain function "in a rapid, non-invasive manner with a high degree of both spatial and temporal accuracy." Henry T. Greely & July Illes, Neuroscience–Based Lie Detection: The Urgent Need for Regulation, 33 Am. J.L. & Med. 377, 379 (2007). When undergoing an fMRI scan, a subject lies down on a bed that slides into the center of a donut-shaped magnet core. . . . As the subject remains still, he or she is asked to perform a task while magnetic coils in the scanner receive electric current and the device gathers information about the subject's Blood Oxygen Level Dependent ("BOLD") response. By comparing the subject's BOLD response signals with the control state, small changes in signal intensity are detectable and can provide information about brain activity. . . .

Dr. Laken . . . conducted a series of laboratory studies to determine whether fMRI could be used to detect deception. Generally, these studies involved a test subject performing a task, such as "stealing" a ring or watch, and then scanning the subject while he or she answered questions about the task. The subjects were usually offered a modest monetary incentive if their lie was not detected. Dr. Laken agreed during cross-examination that he had only conducted studies on such "mock scenarios" and was not aware of any research in a "real-life setting" in which people are accused of "real crimes." He also testified that his studies examined only subjects between the ages of eighteen and fifty, although "we don't see any decreasing or increasing or any changes across accuracy rates in those individuals." Dr. Semrau was sixty-three years old at the time he underwent testing.

Based on these studies, as well as studies conducted by other researchers, Dr. Laken and his colleagues determined the regions of the brain most consistently activated by deception and claimed in several peer-reviewed articles that by analyzing a subject's brain activity, they were able to identify deception with a high level of accuracy. During direct examination at the *Daubert* hearing, Dr. Laken reported these studies found accuracy rates between eighty-six percent and ninety-seven percent. During cross-examination, however, Dr. Laken conceded that his 2009 "Mock Sabotage Crime" study produced an "unexpected" accuracy decrease to a rate of seventy-one percent. . . .

. . . Dr. Laken agreed that the test results do not indicate whether Dr. Semrau responded truthfully as to any specific question but rather show only whether he was generally truthful as to all of his answers collectively. . . . He also acknowledged that the scan results only show whether someone believes what he is saying at the time of the test rather than what his mental state was at the time of the events discussed, and that there is no research on the effect of a "long-term lie."

. . . The magistrate judge's [report], which was adopted by the district court, weighed several factors in Dr. Semrau's favor: "[T]he underlying theories behind fMRI-based lie detection are capable of being tested, and at least in the laboratory setting, have been subjected to some level of testing. It also appears that the theories have been subjected to some peer review and publication." . . . The Government . . . point[s] out that the bulk of the research supporting fMRI research has come from Dr. Laken himself.

The magistrate judge determined that Dr. Semrau could not satisfy the rate of error and controlling standards factor: "While it is unclear from the testimony what the error rates are or how valid they may be in the laboratory setting, there are no known error rates for fMRI-based lie detection outside the laboratory setting, i.e., in the 'real-world' or 'real-life' setting." . . . [F]ederal courts have long appreciated that certain kinds of analyses may have different rates of error depending on the setting because of the difficulties of simulating realistic conditions. . . .

The magistrate judge's [report] . . . also excluded Dr. Laken's testimony under Federal Rule of Evidence 403 . . . for three reasons. . . . First, the test was unilaterally obtained without the Government's knowledge, so the Government had no supervision of the testing and Dr. Semrau risked nothing because the results would never have been released had he failed. . . . Second, this court has held that the use of lie detection test results "solely to bolster a witness' credibility is 'highly prejudicial,' especially where credibility issues are central to the verdict." Sherlin, 67 F.3d at 1217 (quoting Barnier v. Szentmiklosi, 810 F.2d 594, 597 (6th Cir. 1987)); see also United States v. Scheffer, 523 U.S. 303, 313-14 (1998) ("[J]urisdictions may legitimately determine that the aura of infallibility attending polygraph evidence can lead jurors to abandon their duty to assess credibility and guilt."). Finally, a jury would not be assisted by hearing that Dr. Semrau's answers were truthful "overall" without learning which specific questions he answered truthfully or deceptively. . . .

We hold that the district court did not abuse its discretion in excluding the fMRI evidence pursuant to Rule 403 in light of (1) the questions surrounding the reliability of fMRI lie detection tests in general and as performed on Dr. Semrau, (2) the failure to give the prosecution an opportunity to participate in the testing, and (3) the test result's inability to corroborate Dr. Semrau's answers as to the particular offenses for which he was charged.

PROBLEM

9.2. California Evidence Code §351.1 provides that "the results of any polygraph examination, the opinion of a polygraph examiner, or any reference to an offer to take, failure to take or taking of a polygraph examination shall not be admitted into evidence in any criminal proceeding. . . unless all parties stipulate to the admission of such results." In 1994, Nicole Brown and her friend Ronald Goldman were stabbed to death. Brown's ex-husband, former football star O.J. Simpson, was charged with the murders. The prosecution sought to have Simpson's friend Ronald Shipp testify about remarks Simpson allegedly had made to Shipp the day after the murders. According to Shipp, Simpson had said that the police wanted him to take a lie detector test, but that Simpson was unsure whether to agree. Shipp said that Simpson had explained his reluctance by admitting, with a "kind of chuckle[]," that he "had a lot of dreams about killing her." The trial judge ruled that Shipp could recount what Simpson had said about his dreams, but that §351.1 required redaction of the reference to a lie detector test. Shipp then testified that Simpson had said "jokingly" that he had "had some dreams of killing her"; no mention was made of the request to take a lie detector test. At the conclusion of the trial, the judge instructed the jurors that they should disregard Shipp's testimony about Simpson's statement if they concluded "that the statement referred to subconscious thoughts while asleep," but should give the testimony "the weight to which you feel it is entitled" if they concluded that Simpson had made the statement and that "the statement referred to an expression of a desire or an expectation." *See* Gerald F. Uelmen, *The O.J. Files: Evidentiary Issues in a Tactical Context* 12-13, 20-21, 24-25 (1998). Did the judge handle this matter properly? (Simpson was acquitted of the murders but later found liable for the killings in a civil action for wrongful death.)

2. Social Science Evidence

STATE v. YOUNG

35 So.3d 1042 (La. 2010)

GUIDRY, J.

[Appellant Young was charged with first-degree murder and attempted murder for allegedly shooting two victims, one fatally, in a Baton Rouge parking lot during an attempted robbery. Through a confidential informant, police were led to suspect that Young was involved. Police also confirmed that Young owned a white car similar to a description given by bystanders of the assailant's car. One bystander identified Young as the assailant from a photographic array. Once police arrested Young, the surviving victim identified Young in a lineup procedure.] . . . After unsuccessful efforts to suppress eyewitness identifications of the defendant as the gunman, the defense gave notice of its intent to introduce expert testimony at trial on factors that might affect the reliability of the identifications. . . .

In [*State v.*] *Foret* [(1993)], this Court adopted the guidelines set forth by the United States Supreme Court in *Daubert* for determining the reliability of expert scientific testimony . . . .

The State argues that the "field of eyewitness identification psychology" has no known error rate, its findings are insufficiently quantifiable, and its theories are not falsifiable. It contends there has been no new jurisprudence or compelling scientific advances, since this Court's seminal decision in [*State v.*] *Stucke* [(1982)], to warrant reconsideration of this Court's ban on expert testimony regarding the validity of eyewitness identification. . . .

Conversely, the defense . . . claims emerging social science research in the field of eyewitness identification validates the reliability of the proposed testimony . . . . As evidence of the recognized field of study, the defense relies on the fact several jurisdictions that previously barred the admission of such testimony have changed their position on the issue. . . .

This Court is cognizant of the ongoing legal debate over the admissibility of expert psychological testimony on the validity of eyewitness identification. Generally, criminal defendants suggest jurors are ignorant of the alleged inadequacies of eyewitness testimony. Their proposed remedy is to allow qualified cognitive and memory experts to essentially educate jurors on the factors allegedly outside of the common experience that contribute to unreliability and inaccuracies in eyewitness testimony. These factors would include observations involving significant stress, weapon focus, cross-race identification,

identification based on time delays, and psychological phenomena, such as the feedback factor and unconscious transference, among others.

Unquestionably, eyewitness identifications can be imperfect. However, upon review, the touted advances in the social sciences regarding the validity of eyewitness identifications do not render obsolete the underlying premise for which such evidence was held to be inadmissible in *Stucke*. There is still a compelling concern that a potentially persuasive expert testifying as to the generalities of the inaccuracies and unreliability of eyewitness observations, that are already within a juror's common knowledge and experience, will greatly influence the jury more than the evidence presented at trial. . . . By merely being labeled as a specialist in eyewitness identifications, an expert has the broad ability to mislead a jury through the "education" process into believing a certain factor in an eyewitness identification makes that identification less reliable than it truly is. . . . Moreover, expert testimony on eyewitness identifications can be more prejudicial than probative because it focuses on the things that produce error without reference to those factors that improve the accuracy of identifications. The expert testimony presumes a misidentification, in the absence of presenting factors which support the validity of the identification. This fosters a disbelief of eyewitnesses by jurors.

This Court has long been reluctant to allow experts to offer opinions on the credibility of another witness for fear of the expert invading what is considered the exclusive province of the jury. Moreover, the concept of promoting battles of experts over whether the testimony of every witness is truthful and reliable is not desirable. These considerations are especially compelling in cases involving eyewitness identifications where any alleged deficiencies could easily be highlighted through effective cross-examination and artfully crafted jury instructions. . . .

With this in mind, we decline to overrule our decision in *Stucke* barring the admissibility of eyewitness identification testimony. We conclude the district court erred in finding the proposed testimony satisfied the standard for admission of expert testimony . . . .

District court judgment vacated; case remanded to the district court.

COMMONWEALTH v. WALKER

92 A.3d 766 (Pa. 2014)

TODD, J.

[Appellant was convicted of several counts of armed robbery and assault in connection with two incidents two weeks apart in Philadelphia in 2005. Both incidents involved men accosting college students early in the morning; the first involved a man brandishing a black handgun, and the second a silver handgun. In both incidents, several victims identified appellant as the robber after viewing photo arrays that included appellant and other men who closely resembled appellant. One of the victims in the second incident "immediately identified Appellant, viscerally reacting to his picture." The parties agreed that "[t]he sole evidence connecting Appellant to the robberies was eyewitness identification by the victims."]

Appellant filed a pre-trial motion in limine to present the expert testimony of Dr. Solomon Fulero regarding the fallibility of human memory, the science as to human recall, and scientific studies related to the reliability of eyewitness testimony generally. . . . [T]he court denied the motions . . ., relying upon Pennsylvania case law which holds that expert testimony concerning eyewitness identification is inadmissible. . . .

The recent advent of DNA testing has raised the profile of erroneous eyewitness identifications, and the resulting overturning of convictions based upon such testing has made the concern over the accuracy of eyewitness identification manifest. Further, . . . it is not an issue that impacts only the wrongfully accused; incorrectly identifying their attackers can be traumatizing for a victim, as well, due to the guilt of convicting an innocent person, and the resulting awareness that the criminal who perpetrated the crime remains at large. . . .

Since our decision in [*Commonwealth v. Spence* (1993)], 20 years of advances in scientific study have strongly suggested that eyewitnesses are apt to erroneously identify a person as the perpetrator of a crime when certain factors are present:

> [A] vast body of scientific research about human memory has emerged. That body of work casts doubt on some commonly held views relating to memory . . . Study after study revealed a troubling lack of reliability in eyewitness identifications. From social science research to the review of actual police line-ups, from laboratory experiments to DNA exonerations, the record proves that the possibility of mistaken identification is real. Indeed, it is now widely known that eyewitness misidentification is the leading cause of wrongful conviction across the country.

New Jersey v. Henderson, 208 N.J. 208, 27 A.3d 872, 877-78 (2011). *See also,* Wells and Smalarz, Eyewitness–Identification Evidence: Scientific Advances and the New Burden on Trial Judges, 48 Court Review 14 (2012) (noting vast amount of scientific literature regarding eyewitness identification research and summarizing general principles regarding mistaken identification). . . . The "extensive and comprehensive scientific research, as reflected in hundreds of peer reviewed studies and meta-analyses, convincingly demonstrates the fallibility of eyewitness identification testimony and pinpoints an array of variables that are most likely to lead to a mistaken identification." *Connecticut v. Guilbert,* 306 Conn. 218, 49 A.3d 705, 720 (2012); *see also,* Mark S. Brodin, Behavioral Science Evidence in the Age of *Daubert*: Reflections of a Skeptic, 73 U. Cin. L.Rev. 867, 889-90 (2005) ("Ironically, the form of social science evidence which is most solidly based in 'hard' empirical science has met with the most resistance in the courts. Expert testimony concerning the limitations and weaknesses of eyewitness identification is firmly rooted in experimental foundation, derived from decades of psychological research on human perception and memory as well as an impressive peer review literature."). . . .

As a direct result of this growing field of study, . . . there is a clear trend among state and federal courts permitting the admission of eyewitness expert testimony . . . .

The underpinnings of our current ban on expert testimony in the area of eyewitness reliability . . . is that the admission of such testimony will invade the province of the jury in making credibility determinations and provide an unwarranted appearance of authority on the subject of credibility.

Expert testimony on relevant psychological factors which may impact eyewitness identification, however, does not directly speak to whether a particular witness was untrustworthy, or even unreliable, as the expert is not rendering an opinion on whether a specific witness is accurate in his or her identification. Rather, such testimony teaches — it provides jurors with education by which they assess for themselves the witness's credibility. In light of demonstrated misconceptions that jurors and other lay persons may possess regarding the infallibility of eyewitness identification, and ideas contrary to "common sense," such as the [inverse] correlation between certainty and accuracy, use of expert testimony in appropriate cases will permit jurors to engage in the process of making credibility determinations with full awareness of limitations that eyewitness testimony may present. . . .

Moreover, our Rules of Evidence expressly contemplate just such a limited role for an expert, a role that does not impact credibility determinations. . . . The comment to Pa.R.E. 702 refers to the comments to Federal Rule of Evidence 702, which further explains, "[a]n intelligent evaluation of facts is often difficult or impossible without the application of some scientific, technical or other specialized knowledge[;] . . . The rule accordingly recognizes that an expert on the stand may give a dissertation or exposition of scientific or other principles relevant to the case, leaving the trier of fact to apply them to the facts." . . .

Our prior decisions . . . also offer that cross-examination coupled with closing arguments, is sufficient to convey the possibility of mistaken identification to the jury, and, thus, is a basis to categorically exclude expert testimony on eyewitness identification.

While cross-examination and advocacy in closing argument may be common methods to unearth falsehoods and challenge the veracity of a witness, it is less effective in educating the jury with respect to the fallibility of eyewitness identification. . . . This is especially true when cross-examining a neutral, credible, and confident witness before a jury, which may overestimate the veracity and reliability of eyewitness identification. *See generally* Jules Epstein, The Great Engine That Couldn't: Science, Mistaken Identity, and the Limits of Cross-Examination, 36 Stetson L.Rev. 727 (2007). Indeed, such information would not be within the permissible scope of cross-examination. . . .

Some further aspects of our limited decision to reject the *per se* ban on expert testimony regarding eyewitness identification require additional comment. As noted above, to be admissible under Pa.R.E. 702, proffered expert testimony must also address matters "beyond [the knowledge] possessed by the average layperson."

. . . [E]yewitness identification can be extremely powerful testimony; yet, its limits often are not understood by jurors. Studies have concluded that jurors misunderstand the accuracy of eyewitness identification. *See, e.g.,* Elizabeth F. Loftus et. al., Juror Understanding of Eyewitness Testimony: A Survey of 1000 Potential Jurors in the District of Columbia, 46 Jurimetrics J. 177 (2006); Handberg, Expert Testimony on Eyewitness Identification: A New Pair of Glasses for the Jury, 32 Am.Crim. L.Rev. 1013 (1995).

Case law reflects the same concerns. *See, e.g,* . . . *Newsome v. McCabe,* 319 F.3d 301, 305 (7th Cir. 2003) ("Jurors, however, tend to think that witnesses' memories are reliable (because jurors are confident of their own), and this gap between the actual error rate and the jurors' heavy reliance on eyewitness testimony sets the stage for erroneous convictions"); *United States v. Smithers,* 212 F.3d 306, 312 n.1, 316 (6th Cir.2000) ("Today, there is no question that many aspects of perception and memory are not within the common experience of most jurors, and in fact, many factors that affect memory are counterintuitive;" "Jurors tend to overestimate the accuracy of eyewitness identifications because they do not know the factors they should consider when analyzing this testimony.") . . . .

Factors at issue in this appeal — concerning weapons focus; the reduced reliability of identification in cross-racial identification cases; decreased accuracy in eyewitness identifications in high-stress/traumatic situations; the risk of mistaken identification when police investigators do not warn a witness, prior to viewing a photo array or line up, that the perpetrator may or may not be in the display; and the lack of correlation between witness statements of confidence and witness accuracy — all are topics which the average juror may know little about. . . .

Next, under Pa.R.E. 702, such testimony must "help the trier of fact to understand the evidence or determine a fact in issue." Pa.R.E. 702. . . . [I]n light of misconceptions that jurors and other lay persons may possess regarding the infallibility of eyewitness identification, use of expert testimony in appropriate cases would . . . assist the trier of fact . . . .

[The Court remanded the case for a *Frye* hearing to determine whether the defense expert's methodology was "generally accepted."]

STATE v. SALAZAR-MERCADO

325 P.3d 996 (Ariz. 2014)

Justice TIMMER, opinion of the Court.

The State indicted Martin Salazar-Mercado on multiple counts of child molestation and sexual conduct with a minor under age fifteen for abusing his cousin's daughter and step-son. Salazar-Mercado moved before trial to preclude the State from eliciting expert testimony from Dr. Wendy Dutton, a forensic interviewer who holds a Ph.D. in justice studies, about Child Sexual Abuse Accommodation Syndrome ("CSAAS"), which purportedly explains behaviors commonly exhibited by child sexual abuse victims. He primarily argued that Dutton's testimony would not satisfy amended Rule 702(d) [of the Arizona Rules of Evidence] because she was both a "cold" expert, meaning she would only educate the jury about CSAAS, and a "blind" expert, meaning she had no knowledge about the victims in this case and would not offer any opinions specific to them. The trial court denied the motion, and Dutton testified at trial, explaining generally how children perceive sexual abuse, describing behaviors involving disclosure of abuse, and relating circumstances in which children may make false allegations. The jury found Salazar–Mercado guilty on all but two counts, and the court imposed sentences, the most severe of which was life in prison with eligibility for release in thirty-five years. The court of appeals affirmed. . . .

We begin our analysis with the language of Rule 702:

A witness who is qualified as an expert by knowledge, skill, experience, training, or education may testify in the form of an opinion or otherwise if (a) the expert's scientific, technical, or other specialized knowledge will help the trier of fact to understand the evidence or to determine a fact in issue; (b) the testimony is based on sufficient facts or data; (c) the testimony is the product of reliable principles and methods; and (d) the expert has reliably applied the principles and methods to the facts of the case.

. . . This Court amended Rule 702 to conform to Federal Rule of Evidence 702, and the two rules are now identical. Consequently, the federal rule's background and its application by federal courts shed light on the meaning of Arizona's Rule 702(d). . . . The Advisory Committee Notes to the federal rule state that the original version of Federal Rule 702 permitted the admission of "cold" testimony: "The rule accordingly recognizes that an expert on the stand may give a dissertation or exposition of scientific or other principles relevant to the case, leaving the trier of fact to apply them to the facts." Fed. R. Evid. 702, Advisory Committee Notes, 1972 Proposed Rules; *see also United States v. Bighead*, 128 F.3d 1329, 1330-31 (9th Cir. 1997) (in child sexual abuse case, upholding admission of generalized, "cold" expert testimony about "general behavioral characteristics" of child victims, such as "delayed disclosure" and "script memory").

Federal Rule 702 was amended in 2000 to abandon the general-acceptance standard for admitting expert testimony established by *Frye v. United States*, 293 F. 1013 (D.C. Cir. 1923), in favor of the reliability-assessment framework announced in *Daubert v. Merrell Dow Pharmaceuticals, Inc.*, 509 U.S. 579 (1993), as clarified by *Kumho Tire Co. v. Carmichael*, 526 U.S. 137 (1999). The amended rule imposes a "gatekeeper" obligation on trial judges to admit only relevant and reliable expert testimony. But the amendment did not "alter the venerable practice" of permitting experts "to educate the factfinder about general principles, without ever attempting to apply these principles to the specific facts of the case." Fed. R. Evid. 702, Advisory Committee Notes, 2000 amend. It follows, therefore, that subsection (d) does not preclude this type of "cold" testimony. . . .

Courts applying Federal Rule 702 since 2000 have permitted experts to provide general, educative testimony. We are not aware of any case holding that Federal Rule 702(d) bars such testimony, nor does Salazar-Mercado cite any. . . . We hold that Rule 702(d) does not bar admission of "cold" expert testimony. A court may admit such testimony if it satisfies Rule 702(a)-(c).

Salazar-Mercado argues that Dutton's testimony was inadmissible because it did not satisfy Rule 702(a)-(c). Although Salazar-Mercado does not contest Dutton's qualifications, he challenges the helpfulness and reliability of her testimony. . . . Salazar-Mercado argues that because Dutton knew nothing about the events in this case and was prohibited by our decisions in *State v. Lindsey*, 149 Ariz. 472, 475 (1986), and *State v. Moran*, 151 Ariz. 378, 382-83 (1986), from opining on the veracity of the children's accusations or addressing hypothetical situations aligned with the facts of this case, her testimony did not "fit" the facts of this case, making it "unhelpful." *See* Rule 702(a). This argument essentially rephrases Salazar-Mercado's contention that Rule 702(d) bars "cold" testimony. We again reject it.

The children delayed reporting alleged sexual abuse by a relative and had trouble pinpointing when events occurred. One child victim changed her version of events between the time of reporting and trial. In other cases involving behaviors affecting a child victim's credibility, we have held that expert testimony about general behavior patterns of child sexual abuse victims may help the jury understand the evidence. The expert, however, cannot "go beyond the description of general principles of social or behavioral science" to offer opinions about "the accuracy, reliability or credibility of a particular witness in the case being tried . . . [or] of the type under consideration." *Lindsey,* 149 Ariz. at 474-75; *see also Moran,* 151 Ariz. at 382. Because Dutton's testimony might have helped the jury to understand possible reasons for the delayed and inconsistent reporting in this case, her testimony satisfied Rule 702(a). . . . The State . . . avowed that, in compliance with *Lindsey* and *Moran,* Dutton would not opine on the veracity of the victims in this case, and she did not do so at trial.

Because Salazar-Mercado failed to present any evidence raising questions about our prior decisions permitting CSAAS evidence and did not dispute that Dutton would stay within the *Lindsey/Moran* framework, the trial court did not abuse its discretion by finding that the State satisfied its burden of proving admissibility. Similarly, on this record, we are not persuaded to depart from our prior decisions permitting expert testimony that generally explains behavioral characteristics of child sexual abuse victims without offering opinions about the particular children in the case. . . .

We do not hold that CSAAS evidence or like evidence is always admissible. Based on a more complete record, a trial court may exercise its gatekeeping role to conclude that proffered expert testimony does not satisfy Rule 702 or that such testimony should be excluded under Rule 403. The court also should ensure that the expert remains within the bounds of proper expert testimony set by *Lindsey* and *Moran.* Any departure from these principles would supplant the jury's role.

. . . On the record before us, the trial court did not abuse its discretion by admitting Dutton's testimony. Consequently, we affirm Mercado's convictions and sentences. . . .

UNITED STATES v. LOPEZ

913 F.3d 807 (9th Cir. 2019)

BYBEE, J.

Defendant-Appellant Lashay Marie Lopez was convicted on three federal charges stemming from her purchase of a firearm through the use of false identification (ID). Because Lopez admitted to the offense conduct, the only issue before the jury was the affirmative defense of duress. Lopez claims that she purchased a handgun for Hector Karaca using her identical twin sister's ID in violation of her probation and federal law because Karaca threatened to harm Lopez and her family if she failed to acquire a gun for him.

In support of her duress defense, Lopez asked . . . to introduce expert testimony on Battered Woman Syndrome (BWS) and the effects of past abuse.

Lopez, who had been physically and sexually abused by her stepfather, contended that this evidence would "help provide context" to the jury regarding her fear of Karaca and why she did not seek help from the police. Lopez similarly asserted that the expert's description of the "characteristics of [a] domestic violence victim" would help explain her "counterintuitive" behavior regarding Karaca....

Lopez argues that [defense expert Dr. Cheryl] Karp's testimony supports two elements of the duress defense: (1) whether Lopez had a well-grounded fear that Karaca would harm her and her family if she refused to purchase a gun for him and (2) whether she had a reasonable opportunity to escape from him by calling the police. The government continues to counter that BWS evidence is incompatible with a duress defense because both aforementioned elements assess objective reasonableness.... BWS, the government argues, reflects only a defendant's "subjective vulnerability." [The Court discussed this argument at length and rejected it, concluding that BWS evidence was relevant to show both the objective reasonableness of Lopez's fear and her reasonable opportunity to escape.] ...

Although a defendant may testify to how her experiences shaped her perceptions, as the defendant was permitted to do in this case, this lay testimony is often insufficient to effectively mount a duress defense. "To effectively present the situation as perceived by the defendant, and the reasonableness of her fear," a defendant must often "overcome stereotyped impressions about women who remain in abusive relationships. It is appropriate that the jury be given a professional explanation of the battering syndrome and its effects on the woman through the use of expert testimony." [*People v. Humphrey*, 13 Cal. 4th 1073 (1996)]; *see also* [*United States v. Johnson*, 956 F.2d 894 (9th Cir. 1992)] ("Society often misinterprets the survival skills of battered women as signs of passivity and weakness coupled with an unwillingness to leave the violent relationship. A common misunderstanding is that the battered woman's responses are indicative of weak character." (citation omitted))....

Moreover, BWS testimony can provide juries an understanding of why victims of abuse sometimes make inconsistent statements or act in ways that appear counterintuitive to a layperson. For instance, in *Arcoren v. United States*, the key witness recanted at trial her prior grand jury testimony that her husband, the defendant, had raped her. 929 F.2d 1235, 1238 (8th Cir. 1991). The *government* then moved to introduce expert testimony on BWS. It argued, and the Eighth Circuit agreed, that such evidence would aid the jury in determining the defendant's credibility by providing the jury an explanation for the victim's change in testimony. Id. at 1239. "As the [expert] witness told the jury, [BWS] is a psychological condition, which leads a female victim of physical abuse to accept her beatings because she believes that she is responsible for them, and hopes that by accepting one more beating, the pattern will stop." Id. at 1240. The expert testimony thus "provided the jury with information that would help it to determine which" version of the victim's "testimony to credit." ...

We garner from the district court's series of oral rulings on the admissibility of Dr. Karp's testimony that the court perceived the question of admitting the BWS evidence as "close," but ultimately concluded that it was categorically irrelevant to Lopez's duress defense. In light of the foregoing discussion, this was an error of law, which constitutes an abuse of discretion. . . .

[Conviction vacated and case remanded for new trial.]

D. MICHAEL RISINGER, NAVIGATING EXPERT RELIABILITY: ARE CRIMINAL STANDARDS OF CERTAINTY BEING LEFT ON THE DOCK?

64 Alb. L. Rev. 99 (2000)

In its general meaning, all "syndrome" means is a group of symptoms or signs typical of an underlying cause or disease. In regard to physical illnesses with established causal agents, the concept of syndrome is uncontroversial. With regard to behavioral or psychological manifestations where the "cause" may commonly be constructed partly from the symptoms themselves, the notion of "syndrome" is more controversial. These problems are compounded by ethical restrictions on experimental research into behavioral syndromes, making most of the data utilized in their identification necessarily the product of inherently less reliable methodology. This is further complicated by the fact that many of those involved in both supplying the initial "data" and in analyzing it and constructing it into theories may wear two hats: researchers looking for empirically defensible constructs of reality, and therapists committed to helping their patients regardless of the objective reality of the patients' particular accounts. To this is sometimes added a third role, social policy advocate for the groups to which the patients are perceived to belong. It is not surprising that the result of all this is not always the most dependable science, especially in its forensic applications.

In a sense, any mental condition listed in any version of the [American Psychiatric Association's] Diagnostic and Statistical Manual is a "syndrome," and testimony concerning such syndromes has been part of the evidence proffered by criminal defendants on issues of insanity and diminished capacity since long before the first such manual. Nevertheless, the first asserted condition commonly associated with the modern controversy over "syndrome" evidence, "Rape Trauma Syndrome," surfaced in the psychological literature in 1974, in civil courtrooms in 1978, and criminal courtrooms in 1979. Then, spurred by the publication of Lenore Walker's influential, if empirically thin, 1979 book *The Battered Woman* (wherein was coined the phrase "battered woman syndrome"), and by the 1980 issuance of the DSM-III, which promoted the phenomenon of post traumatic stress effects to a full scale disorder, Battered Woman Syndrome and Post Traumatic Stress Disorder (PTSD) followed Rape Trauma Syndrome into the courtroom, trailed not long after by Child Sexual Abuse Accommodation Syndrome (CSAAS).

When used as defense-proffered evidence on insanity, diminished capacity or mens rea questions . . . these asserted "syndromes" seem to have been held to fairly low dependability standards, which was in keeping with the fairly lax foundational standards of the period. . . . [Syndrome evidence] has been generally received in most jurisdictions when so proffered by criminal defendants.

It was not long before prosecutors too found use for such testimony; however, not limited to state-of-mind issues, but bearing upon the brute fact issues of the happening of the crime or the identity of the perpetrator, and that presented a different set of jurisprudential problems. . . . [B]y the time of the decision in *Daubert*, certain general approaches to such prosecution evidence had already begun to work themselves out. A minority of jurisdictions allowed prosecutors to use some or all syndrome evidence pretty openly in very specific proof of the objective elements of the crime. In typical cases, the experts would interview the victim, evaluate their rendition and affect, then conclude that they demonstrated the syndrome and therefore had been the victim of battering, rape, or child molestation. The expert would generally not be allowed to explicitly say that the victim was truthful, or to identify the perpetrator of the crime, but the diagnostic finding not only provided evidence of the actus reus, but by implication corroborated the veracity, and to a lesser degree, the accuracy of the victim's rendition.

The majority of jurisdictions would not go so far. They have held that syndrome evidence was not admissible to prove the existence of the crime, but could be used in cases where there was a delay in reporting the crime, or some other detail of the victim's situation, which common assumptions might cause one to overvalue in discounting the victim's testimony. In those cases (and such conditions were commonly present) the expert would be allowed to explain the aspects of the syndrome that accounted for such a delay, and also normally to opine on whether the characteristics of the victim were consistent with the syndrome. And, beyond this, virtually every jurisdiction allowed expert testimony in such circumstances if the expert did not evaluate the individual victim, but testified as a clear and unambiguous educational expert summarizing what the expert claimed was known to science about the syndrome. Checking the available research to see if the empirical record supported such assertions was done haphazardly at best.

CHRISTOPHER SLOBOGIN, DOUBTS ABOUT *DAUBERT*: PSYCHIATRIC ANECDATA AS A CASE STUDY

57 Wash. & Lee. L. Rev. 919, 940-941 (2000)

Somewhat surprisingly, *Daubert* initially had little impact on the admissibility of behavioral science testimony in criminal cases. Despite the suspect reliability of such testimony, the proportion of cases in *Daubert* jurisdictions admitting expert evidence about such subjects as mental disorders, syndromes, intent, dangerousness, and child sex abuse victims either remained the same or actually increased in the first five years after that decision as compared to the five years prior to *Daubert*. Most courts . . . avoided taking a hard look at the scientific credentials of psychiatric opinion evidence, either by explicitly classifying it or by implicitly treating it as specialized knowledge, thus exempting it from *Daubert*'s threshold for "scientific" testimony.

After *Kumho* that tactic is no longer available, at least in federal court. *Daubert*'s reliability requirement now clearly applies to all expert testimony.

The question remains as to how courts should define reliability in the criminal context.

3. Probabilistic Evidence

a. A Probability Primer

Expert testimony purporting to apply the laws of probability has long been a source of particular concern and puzzlement, both for courts and for commentators. In one sense, of course, all proof is probabilistic; that is why Rule 401 of the Federal Rules of Evidence treats evidence as relevant as long as it tends to make some material fact "more probable or less probable" than it otherwise would be. But ordinarily the probabilities assessed in trials are left unquantified. When experts try to attach numbers to these probabilities, special difficulties arise.

The difficulties are not chiefly mathematical. In most cases the underlying mathematics is relatively uncomplicated, involving nothing more sophisticated than high-school algebra. The difficulties are philosophical: they pertain to how numerical probabilities should be understood, and for what purposes they may properly be employed. To understand those issues, and to follow the arguments that courts and commentators have made about them, it helps to be familiar with some basic concepts of mathematical probability.

Mathematicians and statisticians typically use the expression "$P(X)$" to stand for the probability of X, and the expression "$P(\sim X)$" to stand for the probability of the opposite — "not X." They define probabilities to run from zero to one: something that is impossible has a probability of zero, and something that is certain has a probability of one. And, by definition, $P(X)$ and $P(\sim X)$ add up to one, no matter what X is. So, for example, if we pick a playing card at random from a standard deck of 52 cards, and if X is "picking the jack of hearts," then:

$$P(X)=1/52$$

$$P(\sim X)=51/52$$

$$\text{and } P(X)+P(\sim X)=(1/52)+(51/52)=(52/52)=1$$

In everyday conversation, the terms "probability" and "odds" are often used interchangeably. But mathematicians and statisticians use the terms to refer to two different figures, albeit figures that each can be calculated from the other. When mathematicians and statisticians speak of the "odds" of something, they mean the probability of that thing, divided by the opposite probability. So, for example, the probability of the picking of the jack of hearts from a standard deck of 52 playing cards — what we have been calling "$P(X)$" — is 1/52. The *odds* of picking the jack of hearts can therefore be calculated as follows:

$$P(X) \div P(\sim X) = (1/52) \div (51/52) = 1/52$$

This may make intuitive sense if you read the fraction as "1 to 51." Since there is one card that is the jack of hearts and 51 cards that are not, the odds of picking the jack of hearts are 1 to 51. Similarly, if the probability of something (say, a coin landing heads up) is 1/2, then the odds are "1 to 1," or "even odds," which mathematically is 1/1, or 1.

A little bit more terminology: the expression "P(X|Y)" commonly refers to something called a "conditional probability"—in this case, the conditional probability of X given Y. If X is "picking the jack of hearts," and Y is "picking a jack," then P(X|Y) is the probability of picking the jack of hearts *if we know* that we have picked a jack. Since there are four jacks, and we have an equal chance of picking any of them, P(X|Y) in this example is 1/4. On the other hand, the conditional probability of Y given X—i.e., P(Y|X)—is one. If we know that we have picked the jack of hearts, then we necessarily know that we have picked a jack.

Sometimes knowing one thing tells us nothing about the probability of some other thing. Knowing that we have picked a jack from an ordinary deck of 52 playing cards, for example, tells us nothing about the suit of the card we have selected. We can express this mathematically. If Y is "picking a jack," and Z is "picking a heart," then:

$$P(Y \mid Z) = P(Y) = 1/13$$

and

$$P(Z \mid Y) = P(Z) = 1/4$$

When, as in this example, P(Y|Z) = P(Y), and P(Z|Y) = P(Z), mathematicians say that the probabilities of Y and Z are "independent."

Some important conclusions follow from all these definitions. First, independent probabilities can be multiplied together to calculate a so-called "joint probability"—i.e., the probability of two different things both happening. For example, the joint probability of picking a jack and picking a heart—i.e., the probability of picking the jack of hearts—can be calculated as follows:

$$P(X)=P(Y \text{ and } Z)=P(Y) \times P(Z)=(1/4) \times (1/13)=1/52$$

where, again, X is "picking the jack of hearts," Y is "picking a jack," and Z is "picking a heart." This is sometimes called the "product rule."

The product rule works, though, only if Y and Z are independent. We could stop Y and Z from being independent — we could make them "dependent"—by removing some cards from the deck. Suppose we remove the jack of clubs and the jack of spades, leaving only 50 cards — 13 of which are hearts, two of which are jacks, and one of which is the jack of hearts. Now P(Y), the probability of randomly picking a jack, is 2/50 rather than 1/13, and the P(Z), the probability of picking a heart, is 13/50 rather than 1/4. And P(Y and Z), the probability of picking the jack of hearts, is 1/50, or 0.02. But

$$P(Y) \times P(Z) = (2/50) \times (13/50) = 0.0104$$

and therefore

$$P(Y \text{ and } Z) \neq P(Y) \times P(Z)$$

There is a more general version of the product rule, though, that works even when the underlying probabilities are dependent rather than independent. Here it is:

$$P(Y \text{ and } Z) = P(Y) \times P(Z \mid Y)$$

In the case of our 50-card deck, $P(Z \mid Y)$ — the probability of picking a heart given that we have picked a jack — is 1/2, because there are only two jacks left in the deck, and one of them is the jack of hearts. So:

$$P(Y \text{ and } Z) = P(Y) \times P(Z \mid Y) = (2/50) \times (1/2) = 1/50$$

Because P(Y and Z) must be the same as P(Z and Y), we can also run the calculation the other way:

$$P(Y \text{ and } Z) = P(Z) \times P(Y \mid Z)$$

For the 50-card deck, $P(Y \mid Z)$ — the probability of picking a jack given that we have picked a heart — is 1/13, because all 13 hearts are left in the deck. So:

$$P(Y \text{ and } Z) = P(Z) \times P(Y \mid Z) = (13/50) \times (1/13) = 1/50$$

Remember, when probabilities are independent — as they are for picking a jack and picking a heart out of a standard, 52-card deck — $P(Z \mid Y) = P(Z)$ and $P(Y \mid Z) = P(Y)$. So when probabilities are independent, the more general version of the product rule reduces to the simpler version presented earlier:

$$P(Y \text{ and } Z) = P(Y) \times P(Z \mid Y) = P(Y) \times P(Z)$$

You may have noticed, perhaps with annoyance, that so far we have said nothing about what a probability *is* — all we have discussed is how they can be calculated. That is because mathematicians and statisticians have never been able to agree about what probabilities are. Mathematicians generally have contented themselves with describing how probabilities behave, whatever they actually represent. Among statisticians, on the other hand, there is a longstanding debate about what probability values mean. Some statisticians argue that a probability is simply a long-term frequency: the probability of picking the jack of hearts from a standard deck of playing cards is 1/52, they say, because if we repeat the experiment thousands of times, we will pick the jack of hearts roughly one out of every 52 times. Statisticians holding this view, sometimes called "frequentists," argue that the mathematical theory of probability, at least in its traditional form, cannot meaningfully be applied to probabilities of the sort typically at issue in a trial — e.g., the probability that a particular criminal defendant robbed a particular bank.

But other statisticians disagree. They argue that probabilities can be understood to represent subjective degrees of confidence. For statisticians of this school, sometimes called "subjectivists," it makes perfect sense to say, for example, "there is a 99% probability that the defendant robbed the bank." That simply means that we are as confident that the defendant robbed the bank as we would be of randomly drawing the jack of hearts from an imaginary deck of 100 cards, 99 of which are the jack of hearts.

Statisticians who take this view are sometimes also called "Bayesians," because they often make use of a formula called Bayes' Rule or Bayes' Theorem, after Thomas Bayes, an eighteenth-century English clergyman and statistician who focused attention on it. The formula, which can be derived from the basic rules of probability discussed above, is as follows:

$$[P(A \mid B) \div P(\sim A \mid B)] = [P(A) \div P(\sim A)] \times [P(B \mid A) \div P(B \mid \sim A)]$$

Notice that the first term on the right side of the equation — $[P(A) \div P(\sim A)]$ — simply represents the odds of A, as defined above. The term on the left side of the equation — $[P(A \mid B) \div P(\sim A \mid B)]$ — represents the "conditional odds" of A given B, i.e., what the odds of A become if we take B as a given. So the formula can be rewritten like this:

$$\text{odds}(A \mid B) = \text{odds}(A) \times [P(B \mid A) \div P(B \mid \sim A)]$$

If A is some fact being litigated — say, whether the defendant robbed the bank — and B is a piece of evidence — say, the robber was the same height as the defendant — then Bayes' Theorem provides, some statisticians believe, a method for updating the estimate of the probability of the litigated fact in light of the evidence. All we need to know, or at least be able to estimate, is what the probability of guilt would be *without* the evidence, and the ratio of two conditional probabilities: the probability that the height would match if the defendant were guilty (which presumably is one), and the probability that the height would match if the defendant were innocent (which will depend on how unusual the defendant's height is). All of this makes sense, though, only if it makes sense to quantify the probability of the defendant's guilt, and to combine that number mathematically with probabilities derived from long-term frequencies (like how often a man selected at random would be approximately 6 feet tall). Reverend Bayes thought it did, and so do many statisticians today — but many others do not.

b. "Trial by Mathematics"

PEOPLE v. COLLINS

438 P.2d 33 (Cal. 1968)

SULLIVAN, Justice.

We deal here with the novel question whether evidence of mathematical probability has been properly introduced and used by the prosecution in a criminal case. While we discern no inherent incompatibility between the disciplines of law and mathematics and intend no general disapproval or disparagement of the latter as an auxiliary in the fact-finding processes of the former, we cannot uphold the technique employed in the instant case.... Mathematics, a veritable sorcerer in our computerized society, while assisting the trier of fact in the search for truth, must not cast a spell over him. We conclude that on the record before us defendant should not have had his guilt determined by the odds and that he is entitled to a new trial. We reverse the judgment.

A jury found defendant Malcolm Ricardo Collins and his wife defendant Janet Louise Collins guilty of second degree robbery. Malcolm appeals from the judgment of conviction. Janet has not appealed.[17]

On June 18, 1964, about 11:30 a.m., Mrs. Juanita Brooks, who had been shopping, was walking home along an alley in the San Pedro area of the City of Los Angeles. She was pulling behind her a wicker basket carryall containing groceries and had her purse on top of the packages. She was using a cane. As she stooped down to pick up an empty carton, she was suddenly pushed to the ground by a person whom she neither saw nor heard approach. She was stunned by the fall and felt some pain. She managed to look up and saw a young woman running from the scene. According to Mrs. Brooks the latter appeared to weigh about 145 pounds, was wearing "something dark," and had hair "between a dark blond and a light blond," but lighter than the color of defendant Janet Collins' hair as it appeared at trial. Immediately after the incident, Mrs. Brooks discovered that her purse, containing between $35 and $40, was missing.

About the same time as the robbery, John Bass, who lived on the street at the end of the alley, was in front of his house watering his lawn. His attention was attracted by "a lot of crying and screaming" coming from the alley. As he looked in that direction, he saw a woman run out of the alley and enter a yellow automobile parked across the street from him. He was unable to give the make of the car. The car started off immediately and pulled wide around another parked vehicle so that in the narrow street it passed within six feet of Bass. The latter then saw that it was being driven by a male Negro, wearing a mustache and beard. At the trial Bass identified defendant as the driver of the yellow automobile. However, an attempt was made to impeach his identification by his admission that at the preliminary hearing he testified to an uncertain identification at the police lineup shortly after the attack on Mrs. Brooks, when defendant was beardless. . . .

At the seven-day trial the prosecution experienced some difficulty in establishing the identities of the perpetrators of the crime. The victim could not identify Janet and had never seen defendant. The identification by the witness Bass, who observed the girl run out of the alley and get into the automobile, was incomplete as to Janet and may have been weakened as to defendant. There was also evidence, introduced by the defense, that Janet had worn light-colored clothing on the day in question, but both the victim and Bass testified that the girl they observed had worn dark clothing.

In an apparent attempt to bolster the identifications, the prosecutor called an instructor of mathematics at a state college. Through this witness he sought to establish that, assuming the robbery was committed by a Caucasian woman with a blond ponytail who left the scene accompanied by a Negro with a beard and mustache, there was an overwhelming probability that the crime was committed by any couple answering such distinctive characteristics. The witness testified, in substance, to the "product rule," which states that the probability of the joint occurrence of a number of mutually independent events is equal to the product of the individual probabilities that each of the

---

events will occur.[18] Without presenting any statistical evidence whatsoever in support of the probabilities for the factors selected, the prosecutor then proceeded to have the witness assume probability factors for the various characteristics which he deemed to be shared by the guilty couple and all other couples answering to such distinctive characteristics.[19]

Applying the product rule to his own factors the prosecutor arrived at a probability that there was but one chance in 12 million that any couple possessed the distinctive characteristics of the defendants. Accordingly, under this theory, it was to be inferred that there could be but one chance in 12 million that defendants were innocent and that another equally distinctive couple actually committed the robbery. Expanding on what he had thus purported to suggest as a hypothesis, the prosecutor offered the completely unfounded and improper testimonial assertion that, in his opinion, the factors he had assigned were "conservative estimates" and that, in reality "the chances of anyone else besides these defendants being there, . . . having every similarity, . . . is somewhat like one in a billion."

Objections were timely made to the mathematician's testimony on the grounds that it was immaterial, that it invaded the province of the jury, and that it was based on unfounded assumptions. The objections were "temporarily overruled" and the evidence admitted subject to a motion to strike. When that motion was made at the conclusion of the direct examination, the court denied it, stating that the testimony had been received only for the "purpose of illustrating the mathematical probabilities of various matters, the possibilities for them occurring or re-occurring." . . .

As we shall explain, the prosecution's introduction and use of mathematical probability statistics injected two fundamental prejudicial errors into the case: (1) The testimony itself lacked an adequate foundation both in evidence and in statistical theory; and (2) the testimony and the manner in which the prosecution used it distracted the jury from its proper and requisite function of weighing the evidence on the issue of guilt, encouraged the jurors to rely upon an engaging but logically irrelevant expert demonstration, foreclosed the possibility of an effective defense by an attorney apparently unschooled in mathematical refinements, and placed the jurors and defense counsel at a disadvantage in sifting relevant fact from inapplicable theory.

18. In the example employed for illustrative purposes at the trial, the probability of rolling one die and coming up with a "2" is 1/6, that is, any one of the six faces of a die has one chance in six of landing face up on any particular roll. The probability of rolling two "2"s in succession is $1/6 \times 1/6$, or 1/36, that is, on only one occasion out of 36 double rolls (or the roll of two dice), will the selected number land face up on each roll or die.

19. Although the prosecutor insisted that the factors he used were only for illustrative purposes — to demonstrate how the probability of the occurrence of mutually independent factors affected the probability that they would occur together — he nevertheless attempted to use factors which he personally related to the distinctive characteristics of defendants. In his argument to the jury he invited the jurors to apply their own factors, and asked defense counsel to suggest what the latter would deem as reasonable. The prosecutor himself proposed the individual probabilities set out in the table below. Although the transcript of the examination of the mathematics instructor and the information volunteered by the prosecutor at that time create some uncertainty as to precisely which of the characteristics the prosecutor assigned to the individual probabilities, he restated in his argument to the jury that they should be as follows:

We initially consider the defects in the testimony itself. As we have indicated, the specific technique presented through the mathematician's testimony and advanced by the prosecutor to measure the probabilities in question suffered from two basic and pervasive defects — an inadequate evidentiary foundation and an inadequate proof of statistical independence. First, as to the foundation requirement, we find the record devoid of any evidence relating to any of the six individual probability factors used by the prosecutor and ascribed by him to the six characteristics as we have set them out in footnote 10, ante. To put it another way, the prosecution produced no evidence whatsoever showing, or from which it could be in any way inferred, that only one out of every ten cars which might have been at the scene of the robbery was partly yellow, that only one out of every four men who might have been there wore a mustache, that only one out of every ten girls who might have been there wore a ponytail, or that any of the other individual probability factors listed were even roughly accurate.[20]

The bare, inescapable fact is that the prosecution made no attempt to offer any such evidence. Instead, through leading questions having perfunctorily elicited from the witness the response that the latter could not assign a probability factor for the characteristics involved,[21] the prosecutor himself suggested what the various probabilities should be and these became the basis of the witness' testimony (see fn. 10, ante). It is a curious circumstance of this adventure in proof that the prosecutor not only made his own assertions of these factors in the hope that they were "conservative" but also in later argument to the jury invited the jurors to substitute their "estimates" should they wish to do so. We can hardly conceive of a more fatal gap in the prosecution's scheme of proof. A foundation for the admissibility of the witness' testimony

	Characteristic	*Individual Probability*
A.	Partly yellow automobile	1/10
B.	Man with mustache	1/4
C.	Girl with ponytail	1/10
D.	Girl with blond hair	1/3
E.	Negro man with beard	1/10
F.	Interracial couple in car	1/1000

In his brief on appeal defendant agrees that the foregoing appeared on a table presented in the trial court.

20. We seriously doubt that such evidence could ever be compiled since no statistician could possibly determine after the fact which cars, or which individuals, "might" have been present at the scene of the robbery; certainly there is no reason to suppose that the human and automotive populations of San Pedro, California, include all potential culprits — or, conversely, that all members of these populations are proper candidates for inclusion. Thus the sample from which the relevant probabilities would have to be derived is itself undeterminable. (See generally, Yaman, Statistics, An Introductory Analysis (1964), ch.I.)

21. The prosecutor asked the mathematics instructor: "Now, let me see if you can be of some help to us with some independent factors, and you have some paper you may use. Your specialty does not equip you, I suppose, to give us some probability of such things as a yellow car as contrasted with any other kind of car, does it? . . . I appreciate the fact that you can't assign a probability for a car being yellow as contrasted to some other car, can you? A. No, I couldn't."

was never even attempted to be laid, let alone established. His testimony was neither made to rest on his own testimonial knowledge nor presented by proper hypothetical questions based upon valid data in the record....

But, as we have indicated, there was another glaring defect in the prosecution's technique, namely an inadequate proof of the statistical independence of the six factors. No proof was presented that the characteristics selected were mutually independent, even though the witness himself acknowledged that such condition was essential to the proper application of the "product rule" or "multiplication rule." To the extent that the traits or characteristics were not mutually independent (e.g. Negroes with beards and men with mustaches obviously represent overlapping categories), the "product rule" would inevitably yield a wholly erroneous and exaggerated result even if all of the individual components had been determined with precision. (Siegel, Nonparametric Statistics for the Behavioral Sciences (1956) 19; see generally Harman, Modern Factor Analysis (1960).)

In the instant case, therefore, because of the aforementioned two defects — the inadequate evidentiary foundation and the inadequate proof of statistical independence — the technique employed by the prosecutor could only lead to wild conjecture without demonstrated relevancy to the issues presented. It acquired no redeeming quality from the prosecutor's statement that it was being used only "for illustrative purposes" since, as we shall point out, the prosecutor's subsequent utilization of the mathematical testimony was not confined within such limits.

We now turn to the second fundamental error caused by the probability testimony. Quite apart from our foregoing objections to the specific technique employed by the prosecution to estimate the probability in question, we think that the entire enterprise upon which the prosecution embarked, and which was directed to the objective of measuring the likelihood of a random couple possessing the characteristics allegedly distinguishing the robbers, was gravely misguided. At best, it might yield an estimate as to how infrequently bearded Negroes drive yellow cars in the company of blonde females with ponytails.

The prosecution's approach, however, could furnish the jury with absolutely no guidance on the crucial issue: *Of the admittedly few such couples, which one, if any, was guilty of committing this robbery?* Probability theory necessarily remains silent on that question, since no mathematical equation can prove beyond a reasonable doubt (1) that the guilty couple in fact possessed the characteristics described by the People's witnesses, or even (2) that only *one* couple possessing those distinctive characteristics could be found in the entire Los Angeles area.

As to the first inherent failing we observe that the prosecution's theory of probability rested on the assumption that the witnesses called by the People had conclusively established that the guilty couple possessed the precise characteristics relied upon by the prosecution. But no mathematical formula could ever establish beyond a reasonable doubt that the prosecution's witnesses correctly observed and accurately described the distinctive features which were employed to link defendants to the crime. Conceivably, for example, the guilty couple might have included a light-skinned Negress with bleached hair rather than a Caucasian blonde; or the driver of the car might have been wearing a false beard as a disguise; or the prosecution's witnesses might simply have been unreliable.[22]

The foregoing risks of error permeate the prosecution's circumstantial case. Traditionally, the jury weighs such risks in evaluating the credibility and probative value of trial testimony, but the likelihood of human error or of falsification obviously cannot be quantified; that likelihood must therefore be excluded from any effort to assign a number to the probability of guilt or innocence. Confronted with an equation which purports to yield a numerical index of probable guilt, few juries could resist the temptation to accord disproportionate weight to that index; only an exceptional juror, and indeed only a defense attorney schooled in mathematics, could successfully keep in mind the fact that the probability computed by the prosecution can represent, *at best*, the likelihood that a random couple would share the characteristics testified to by the People's witnesses — *not necessarily the characteristics of the actually guilty couple.*

As to the second inherent failing in the prosecution's approach, even assuming that the first failing could be discounted, the most a mathematical computation could ever yield would be a measure of the probability that a random couple would possess the distinctive features in question. In the present case, for example, the prosecution attempted to compute the probability that a random couple would include a bearded Negro, a blonde girl with a ponytail, and a partly yellow car; the prosecution urged that this probability was no more than one in 12 million. Even accepting this conclusion as arithmetically accurate, however, one still could not conclude that the Collinses were probably *the* guilty couple. . . .

Again, few defense attorneys, and certainly few jurors, could be expected to comprehend this basic flaw in the prosecution's analysis. Conceivably even the prosecutor erroneously believed that his equation established a high probability that no other bearded Negro in the Los Angeles area drove a yellow car accompanied by a ponytailed blonde. In any event, although his technique could demonstrate no such thing, he solemnly told the jury that he had supplied mathematical proof of guilt.

Sensing the novelty of that notion, the prosecutor told the jurors that the traditional idea of proof beyond a reasonable doubt represented "the most hackneyed, stereotyped, trite, misunderstood concept in criminal law." He sought to reconcile the jury to the risk that, under his "new math" approach to criminal jurisprudence, "on some rare occasion…an innocent person may be convicted." "Without taking that risk," the prosecution continued, "life would be intolerable . . . because . . . there would be immunity for the Collinses, for people who chose not to be employed to go down and push old ladies down and take their money and be immune because how could we ever be sure they are the ones who did it?"

In essence this argument of the prosecutor was calculated to persuade the jury to convict defendants whether or not they were convinced of their

---

22. In the instant case, for instance, the victim could not state whether the girl had a ponytail, although the victim observed the girl as she ran away. The witness Bass, on the other hand, was sure that the girl whom he saw had a ponytail. The demonstration engaged in by the prosecutor also leaves no room for the possibility, although perhaps a small one, that the girl whom the victim and the witness observed was, in fact, the same girl.

guilt to a moral certainty and beyond a reasonable doubt. Undoubtedly the jurors were unduly impressed by the mystique of the mathematical demonstration but were unable to assess its relevancy or value. Although we make no appraisal of the proper applications of mathematical techniques in the proof of facts, we have strong feelings that such applications, particularly in a criminal case, must be critically examined in view of the substantial unfairness to a defendant which may result from ill conceived techniques with which the trier of fact is not technically equipped to cope. We feel that the technique employed in the case before us falls into the latter category.

We conclude that the court erred in admitting over defendant's objection the evidence pertaining to the mathematical theory of probability and in denying defendant's motion to strike such evidence.... After an examination of the entire cause, including the evidence, we are of the opinion that it is reasonably probable that a result more favorable to defendant would have been reached in the absence of the above error. The judgment against defendant must therefore be reversed....

ROGER C. PARK, EVIDENCE SCHOLARSHIP, OLD AND NEW

75 Minn. L. Rev. 849, 855-856 (1991)

Among American law professors, scholarly interest in probability theory received its most significant boost from a celebrated case, *People v. Collins*, a 1968 decision of the California Supreme Court.... The *Collins* case inspired an article in the *Harvard Law Review* arguing that although *Collins* was correct on its facts, experts in other cases properly might use probability theory, in particular Bayes' Theorem, to aid the jury in making identification decisions.[23] The authors suggested a hypothetical case in which the defendant is accused of murdering his girlfriend. A partial palmprint was found on the knife that was used in the murder. It matches the defendant's palm. Yet the palmprint would also match the palm of one in a thousand people chosen at random, which means that in a metropolitan area hundreds of people would have the same palmprint characteristics. How is the jury to use that one in a thousand figure? Bayes' Theorem, which provides a way of determining how an evaluation of probability based upon initial evidence should be modified in light of additional evidence, could serve as a guide to the jury. If the trier of fact believed that the prior probability of defendant's guilt (before taking the palmprint into account) was 25%, Bayes' Theorem indicates that the trier should believe the posterior probability of guilt (after taking the palmprint into account) is 99.9%. The method often yields higher probabilities than intuition would yield. For example, if the prior probability is 25% and the frequency of the palmprint is one in a hundred, the posterior probability of guilt is 97%.

The proposition that the jury should be instructed about Bayes' Theorem attracted the attention of a talented and resourceful debater, Laurence Tribe,

---

23. Finkelstein & Fairley, *A Bayesian Approach to Identification Evidence*, 83 Harv. L. Rev. 489, 501-09 (1970).

then a young assistant professor at the Harvard Law School.[24] Tribe pointed out a host of problems. It would be difficult for jurors who are not familiar with formal probabilities to arrive at a consistent understanding of what they are supposed to do in formulating a prior probability. There is also a danger of the jury "dwarfing soft variables," that is, that the jury might overlook issues that cannot be quantified as it became mesmerized with those that could. Moreover, uncertainty about predicate facts can require the jury to make so many quantification decisions about so many issues that use of the theorem would be more confusing than helpful.

Although Tribe's view seems to have carried the day with regard to the use of Bayes' Theorem in instructing the jury, the debate did stimulate interest in Bayes' Theorem and probability theory. It has spawned a considerable body of scholarship that explores how probability theory might be used as a means of proof or as a way to help scholars model and evaluate trial processes.

UNITED STATES v. VEYSEY

334 F.3d 600 (7th Cir. 2003)

POSNER, Circuit Judge.

John Veysey appeals from his conviction, after a jury trial, and sentence of 110 years in prison for mail and wire fraud, arson, and the related offense of felony by fire. The facts are amazing, but we shall resist the temptation to recount them at length. In 1991 Veysey set fire to his house and inflated the claim that he then filed with his insurer. The insurer paid, and the house was rebuilt. The following year Veysey married a woman named Kemp, increased the insurance on the house, removed the valuable contents of the house, along with himself and his wife, and then cut the natural-gas line inside the house, causing the house to fill up with gas and explode spectacularly, utterly destroying it. He grossly exaggerated the value of the property allegedly lost in the explosion — some did not exist and some he had removed before the explosion. The insurance company (a different one) paid, and he used part of the proceeds to buy another house. The next year he tried to kill his wife by driving his van with her in it into a river. When that failed he killed her by poisoning her, and collected $200,000 in the proceeds of insurance policies on her life. He placed personal ads in newspapers, seeking to meet women. He became engaged to one of the women he met through his ads, named Donner, but broke his engagement after failing to procure a $1 million policy on her life. He then took up with a Ms. Beetle. This was in 1996 and the same year he burned down his house, again submitting an inflated estimate of the loss and receiving substantial proceeds from the insurance company (a different one, again). He then married Beetle, and they moved into a rented house. She insured her life for $500,000 with him as beneficiary. One night in 1998, after drugging her, he set fire to the house, hoping to kill both her and their

---

24. See Tribe, *Trial by Mathematics: Precision and Ritual in the Legal Process,* 84 Harv. L. Rev. 1329 (1971).

infant son, on whom he had also taken out a life insurance policy and who was in the house with her. They were rescued, and soon afterwards Veysey and Beetle divorced. The house was rebuilt and Veysey persuaded a woman named Hilkin to move in with him after she had accumulated some $700,000 in life insurance and named him as the primary beneficiary. He apparently intended to murder her, but he was arrested before his plans matured. There is more, but these are the highlights. . . .

[Veysey objects] to testimony by an actuary, Charles L. McClenahan, that the probability of four residential fires occurring by chance during the 106 months between April 1989 (when Veysey bought the first house that he is known to have set fire to) and January 1998 (when he set fire to his last house) was only one in 1.773 trillion; he described this as a conservative estimate. We can imagine two distinct grounds for Veysey's objection to the actuary's evidence. The first, which, though the stronger, Veysey's lawyer has not made — and in fact expressly disclaimed, when pressed, at argument — is that the calculation was based on implicit assumptions that are untenable.

A simplified version of what the actuary did is that he first determined the number of serious residential fires in the United States over the interval in which houses occupied by Veysey caught fire four times (with "serious" defined as a fire that caused a loss equal to or greater than 20 percent of the amount of fire insurance on the house, and so defined serious fires are 5.3 percent of all residential fires), then divided that number by the number of houses in the United States, and finally multiplied the resulting probability by itself four times. Suppose (we are using hypothetical figures for the sake of simplicity) the probability that a specific house would have caught fire during the 106-month interval were one in 1,000. Then, on the assumption of independence (an important qualification, discussed next), the probability that two specific houses would have caught fire during the interval would be one in a million (1/1,000 × 1/1,000), the probability that three specific houses would have caught fire would be one in a billion, and the probability that four would have caught fire would be one in a trillion.

This simplified calculation does modest violence to the actuary's method, as the mathematics of repeatable events is somewhat complex. When the actuary divided the number of fires by the number of houses, the result-ing quotient was not *really* the probability of a fire happening to a specific house, but an input into a formula designed to assess the probability of a repeated event, in this case a serious fire in a series of Veysey's dwellings. But as with our simple version, the actuary's actual computation assumed that the probabilities of each of a person's multiple fires are independent of each other — that the fact that you had a fire at one time or in one of your houses would not affect the probability that you would have a second fire in that house or a fire in your next house. The assumption was not defended by the actuary, and is unrealistic. . . . A fire in a house or in an apartment is likely to be the result, at least in part, of carelessness on the part of the occupant, implying that he is more likely to have another fire than a person who has never had a fire (though against this it can be argued that someone who has experienced a fire will be more careful to avoid a repetition — once burned is twice shy). Moreover, even if the assumption of independence were defensible, the actu-ary's calculation would be flawed by his failure to limit the reference group to residences comparable in design, materials, age, value, region, and other factors relevant to the likelihood of a fire in Veysey's residences.

But Veysey as we have said does not object to the actuary's methodology. His objection is that the actuary usurped the jury's function by testifying in effect that Veysey was guilty of the crimes with which he was charged *way* beyond a reasonable doubt, as the probability of his innocence was not 1 or 2 or 5 percent or whatever might be thought the implicit probability of innocence sufficient to prevent a finding of guilt beyond a reasonable doubt, but, if the actuary was believed, a mere .0000000000564 percent. Veysey's counsel goes so far as to argue that statistical evidence should never be admissible to establish an element of a crime. Fingerprint or DNA evidence is admissible, he acknowledges, but the jury must not be told what the probability is that such evidence actually establishes the proposition for which it is introduced, such as that the defendant's fingerprints were on the murder weapon.

In making this argument Veysey's counsel is gesturing toward an academic literature ... that argues that judges and jurors, because they lack knowledge of statistical theory, are both overawed and easily deceived by statistical evidence ... and toward decisions, such as *Smith v. Rapid Transit*, 317 Mass. 469 (1945), that refuse to permit a case to go to a jury on purely statistical evidence. In *Smith* the court held that it "was not enough" "that mathematically the chances somewhat favor the proposition that a bus of the defendant caused the accident."

Suppose, to consider a well-known hypothetical variant of *Smith*, that a person is hit by a bus, and it is known that 51 percent of the buses on the road where he was hit are owned by Bus Company *A* and 49 percent by Bus Company *B*. He sues *A* and asks for judgment on the basis of this statistic alone; he presents no other evidence. If the defendant also presents no evidence, should a jury be permitted to award judgment for the plaintiff? The law answers "no." But this is not because of doubt about the evidentiary value of statistical evidence. The true source of disquiet in the example, we believe, is the tacit assumption that the statistic concerning the ownership of the buses is the only evidence the plaintiff can obtain. If it is his only evidence, the inference to be drawn is not that there is a 51 percent probability that it was a bus owned by *A* that hit him but that he either investigated and discovered that it was actually a bus owned by *B* (which might be judgment-proof and so not worth suing), or that he has simply not bothered to conduct an investigation. In either event he should lose, in the first case obviously and in the second because a court should not be required to expend any of its scarce resources of time and effort on a case until the plaintiff has conducted a sufficient search to indicate that an expenditure of public resources is reasonably likely to yield a social benefit.

But if both bus companies had been determined to be negligent, so that the only issue was which had hit the plaintiff, then in many states the 51/49 ratio of *A*'s to *B*'s buses would be enough for a judgment against *A* — indeed against *A* and *B*. See *Sindell v. Abbott Laboratories*, 26 Cal. 3d 588 (1980); *Summers v. Tice*, 33 Cal. 2d 80 (1948); *Krist v. Eli Lilly & Co.*, 847 F.2d 293, 300 (7th Cir. 1990). Or if the ratio of buses owned by *A* to those owned by *B* were much higher than 51/49, the case against allowing "naked" statistical evidence to carry the plaintiff's burden of production on the issue of liability (rather than only causation) would be weakened. The law recognizes this not only in the obvious cases of fingerprint and DNA evidence, the admissibility of which depends on the improbability that two different people would have the same fingerprint or DNA signature, but also in the law's adoption of such presumptions as that a properly addressed, stamped, and mailed letter will reach the addressee. This is a purely statistical presumption because it is applied without regard to the particulars of the case beyond those required to satisfy the conditions of the presumption; and yet it can determine the outcome.

"All evidence is probabilistic — statistical evidence merely explicitly so," *Riordan v. Kempiners*, 831 F.2d 690, 698 (7th Cir. 1987) . . ., because nothing with which the law deals is metaphysically certain. Statistical evidence is merely probabilistic evidence coded in numbers rather than words. "Nothing about the nature of litigation in general, or the criminal process in particular, makes anathema of additional information, whether or not that knowledge has numbers attached. After all, even eyewitnesses are testifying only to probabilities (though they obscure the methods by which they generate those probabilities) — often rather lower probabilities than statistical work insists on." *Branion v. Gramly*, [855 F.2d 1256, 1264 (7th Cir. 1988)]. An eyewitness does not usurp the jury's function if he testifies that he is *positive* that he saw the defendant strike a match, and it would make no difference if he said that he is "99 percent" positive. The significant question would be the accuracy of the estimate. The actuary's one in 1.7 trillion estimate in this case probably was inaccurate, but not because it was a statistic. The issue of its accuracy has been waived, however, and in any event the error in its introduction was harmless; the other evidence against the defendant was overwhelming. . . . Affirmed.

IVEY v. COMMONWEALTH

486 S.W.3d 846 (Ky. 2016)

NOBLE, Justice.

The Appellant, Alfred Ivey, Jr., was convicted of two counts of rape of a minor. The crime resulted in a child, and a DNA paternity test was used as evidence against Ivey. On appeal, he alleges . . . that the trial court erred in allowing the expert to testify about the probability of paternity based on an improper statistical method . . . .

. . . [Ivey] does not challenge the DNA test itself, nor does he challenge all of the statistical conclusions that can be drawn from that test. Instead, he complains about the use of a 50% "prior probability" of paternity in calculating the final probability of paternity . . . . This Court previously upheld the use of that 50% figure in *Butcher v. Commonwealth*, 96 S.W.3d 3, 7 (Ky. 2002), concluding that it did not violate the presumption of innocence. Ivey claims that he was nevertheless entitled to a hearing under *Daubert v. Merrell Dow Pharmaceuticals, Inc.*, 509 U.S. 579 (1993), because no scientific method is forever beyond challenge, and that the method used by the expert was improper and unreliable. . . .

When it comes to the comparison, paternity testing is not the same as other kinds of DNA testing, such as that typically used for a criminal case in which a biological sample is compared to a defendant's to see if there is a match. This is because a child receives half its DNA from each parent. Thus, there will never be a complete match between the two DNA profiles, that of (putative) father and child. Instead, paternity testing looks at whether there is shared or common DNA. Using this comparison, an examiner first determines whether the putative father is excluded as a possible contributor to the child. If not, the examiner can then calculate a "paternity index, and [a] probability of paternity." *Butcher*, 96 S.W.3d at 6.

. . . [A] DNA examiner compares locations on the child's and putative father's DNA — frequently called loci. . . . In this case, fifteen loci were compared. Ivey was found not to be excluded because his DNA matched portions of the child's DNA at all fifteen loci.

The next step, if the putative father is not excluded, is to calculate the paternity index. . . . We have described the paternity index as follows:

> The paternity index is a value reflecting the likelihood that a tested man is the father of the child as opposed to an untested man of the same race. It is expressed as a number. If a paternity index can be assigned to a man, it means that he is that many more times likely to be the father than any other randomly selected male of his race. . . .

This description, however, is not completely accurate. The paternity index "does not measure the chance of defendant's paternity compared to that of a randomly selected man." D.H. Kaye, Plemel as a Primer on Proving Paternity, 24 Willamette L.Rev. 867, 877 (1988). That would be the "probability of paternity," *id.*, which is a different calculation, discussed below. Technically speaking, the paternity index is the ratio of "the probability of the alleged father transmitting the alleles and the probability of selecting these alleles at random from the gene pool." D.H. Kaye, The Probability of an Ultimate Issue: The Strange Cases of Paternity Testing, 75 Iowa L.Rev. 75, 89 (1989–1990). It has been described as a "likelihood ratio," that is, "a ratio of two conditional probabilities," but "is not itself a probability." 1 McCormick on Evidence § 211 n.17 (7th ed. 2013) "Unlike probabilities, which are bounded by 0 and 1, the likelihood ratio can exceed one. The larger the ratio, the more probative the evidence." *Id.* Thus, the paternity index is probative of paternity, but it does not actually tell us the probability the person tested is the father.

For example, in *Butcher*, the paternity index was 388/1 (or simply 388). We said that this meant the defendant was "388 times more likely to be the father of the child than a randomly selected male of the same race." 96 S.W.3d at 7. Again, this is not, strictly speaking, completely accurate. See 1 McCormick on Evidence § 211 n.18 (7th ed. 2013) (noting that *Butcher*'s formulation commits "the transposition fallacy" and is a "misinterpretation") . . . Instead, a paternity index of 388 "means that it is [388] times more likely that a union of [the defendant] and [the mother] would produce a child with the observed set of markers than would a union of [the mother] and a set of alleles picked at random from men of [the defendant's] race." Kaye, Plemel as a Primer, supra, at 874. Or to apply a simpler description by Professor Kaye, to *Butcher*'s facts: "Men of [the defendant's] phenotype, when crossed with the mother, would produce offspring with the child's phenotype [388] times as frequently as would randomly selected men." Kaye, The Probability of an Ultimate Issue, supra, at 91.

In Ivey's case, the paternity index was 11,900,000. (This likelihood ratio is substantially higher than that in *Butcher*, at least in part, because many more loci were compared.) Ivey's index is therefore that much more probative of paternity than the index in *Butcher*.

The third step is to calculate a probability of paternity . . . . This calculation uses Bayes' theorem, *Butcher*, 96 S.W.3d at 7, which "show[s] the effect of a new item of evidence on a previously established probability," 1 McCormick on Evidence § 211 (7th ed. 2013). "On its most basic level, the formula is nothing more than a mathematical way of representing how we incorporate new information into our reasoning." Michael I. Meyerson & William Meyerson, Significant Statistics: The Unwitting Policy Making of Mathematically Ignorant Judges, 37 Pepp. L.Rev. 771, 783 (2010). The new evidence in paternity testing is the result of the DNA test, specifically the paternity index. The established probability (of paternity), often referred to as a "prior probability," depends on other evidence, such as "access to the mother, fertility, and date of conception." *Butcher*, 96 S.W.3d at 7; . . . Applying Bayes' theorem to the prior probability results in what is called a posterior probability; in the context of paternity testing, the posterior probability is simply referred to as the probability of paternity. . . .

In theory, the prior probability could vary dramatically depending on the proof in a case. . . . For example, very strong, but not unassailable, proof of an alibi should result in a lower prior probability than proof showing that the defendant was present but simply denies having had sex with the victim. Similarly, evidence that a defendant had had a vasectomy — an effective but imperfect method of sterilization — would also result in a very low prior probability that he was the father.

"In the context of criminal cases, however, those using this formula to determine paternity typically insert a standard prior probability of .5 regardless of any other factors, which indicates a fifty percent chance that the alleged father actually had sexual intercourse with the mother." *Butcher*, 96 S.W.3d at 7. This again is somewhat of a misstatement. Rather than showing a 50% chance that the alleged putative father had intercourse with the mother, the 50% prior probability indicates a 50% probability, before the DNA test, that the alleged father is the biological father. This distinction is crucial because having intercourse does not guarantee a pregnancy, a fact acknowledged elsewhere in *Butcher*. In Ivey's case, using the 50% prior probability, his probability of paternity was calculated to be 99.9999%.

In *Butcher*, this Court specifically approved of the use of a 50% prior probability, over two dissents. The defendant in that case had claimed that use of that figure violated the presumption of innocence. . . .

Butcher, however, was not directly about whether the use of a 50% prior probability satisfies the reliability requirement of *Daubert*. . . . Nor did *Butcher* address the scholarly criticism now raised by Ivey or other criticism that has turned up in the Court's legal research. . . .

The statistics article Ivey presented claims that paternity testing "can lead to incorrect conclusions," where there is a problem with the "statistical assumptions," specifically in "assuming equal prior (pre-test) probabilities for an event in the face of ignorance concerning the actual probabilities." [citation omitted.] In other words, the authors claim that the use of the 50% prior probability is a logical error.

But the "error," to the extent it is one, appears to matter only under unrealistic conditions. . . . [I]f the prior probability was 0.001 (or 0.1%), which is a fairly low prior probability, the probability of paternity would be only .091, or 9.1%. *Id.* Or, to employ an example more germane to this case, as will become apparent shortly, if the prior probability was .01, or 1%, then the resulting probability of paternity would be only 50.25%.

But in this case, even with very low assumed prior probabilities, the probability of paternity exceeded 99.99%. . . .

. . . [I]n this case, the paternity index . . . resulted in such high probabilities of paternity with even very low prior probabilities, that Ivey's paternity is all but guaranteed. We cannot say that the method was unreliable in this case, even given the criticism . . . .

Those critical of using a 50% prior probability have a point. That number assumes that there is a prior probability at all that the defendant is the father, which may be inescapable since a 0% probability cannot be used. But, more importantly, that prior probability is fairly high (almost satisfying the civil burden of proof by itself). Despite our assertions in the past, it is not a truly neutral number. . . .

Thus, some commentators have suggested that jurors be presented with "a spectrum of prior and posterior probabilities." *Id.* at 881; see also 1 McCormick on Evidence § 211 (7th ed. 2013) ("[T]he expert could show the jury how the test results would affect not merely a prior probability of one-half, but a whole spectrum of prior probabilities."); David H. Kaye, DNA Evidence: Probability, Population Genetics, and the Courts, 7 Harv. J.L. & Tech. 101, 167 (1993-1994) (urging that an "expert present[] the jury with a table or graph showing how the posterior probability changes as a function of the prior probability"). . . .

We need not decide today whether such an approach is required. We note it only as one possible solution to the problem of the 50% prior probability. . . .

As . . . genetic testing becomes "more refined . . . the controversy over [probability of paternity] will wither." Kaye, The Probability of an Ultimate Issue, supra, at 88 n.64. This prophesy has not completely born[e] out, as questions are still being raised more than 25 years later. But as testing improves, we are convinced those questions are becoming of little consequence.

In the end, Ivey's complaints do not undermine the reliability of the evidence in this case. The evidence, therefore, was properly admissible. . . . [Affirmed.]

PROBLEM

9.3. A century before *People v. Collins*, the most famous mathematician in the United States, Benjamin Peirce, testified as an expert in *Robinson v. Mandell*, a federal diversity lawsuit over a disputed will. Sylvia Ann Howland died in 1865 with an estate worth more than $2 million. In a will dated 1863, Howland left roughly half her wealth to various individuals and institutions, and directed that the remainder be held in trust for the benefit of her niece, Hetty Robinson, with the principal distributed at Robinson's death to certain distant relatives. Robinson came forward with an earlier will leaving the entire estate to her and — on a second, separately signed page — invalidating all subsequent wills. The executor, Thomas Mandell, rejected the second page as a forgery. Robinson sued. Peirce and his son, the logician Charles Sanders Peirce, testified for the estate.

At his father's direction, Charles had compared 42 known signatures of Howland, superimposing two at a time and counting how many of the 30 downstrokes in each signature overlapped. He testified that, on average, six of the downstrokes — one out of five — matched up. But when the signature on the first page of the earlier will, which both sides agreed was genuine, was compared with the signature on the second page, which the estate suggested Robinson had simply traced, all 30 of the downstrokes coincided. Following his son to the stand, Benjamin Peirce testified that the probability that all 30 downstrokes would coincide in two signatures by Howland was $(1/5)^{30}$, or 1 divided by 2,666,000,000,000,000,000,000. "So vast improbability," he added, "is practically an impossibility. Such evanescent shadows of probability cannot belong to actual life. They are unimaginably less than those least things which the law cares not for." Accordingly, Peirce concluded, "the coincidence which has occurred here must have had its origin in an intention to produce it. It is utterly repugnant to sound reason to attribute this coincidence to any cause but design." *See* Louis Menand, *The Metaphysical Club* 163–176 (2001); Paul Meier & Sandy Zabell, *Benjamin Peirce and the Howland Will*, 75 J. Am. Stat. Ass'n 497 (1980); *The Howland Will Case*, 4 Am. L. Rev. 625 (1870). (Ultimately, the court ruled for the estate without reaching the allegations of forgery. No one other than Robinson had seen Howland sign the second page, and a federal "dead man" statute made parties to a suit over a will incompetent unless called by the other side or ordered by the court to testify. So there was a simple failure of proof. *See Robinson v. Mandell*, 20 F. Cas. 1027 (C.C.D. Mass. 1868) (No. 11,959).)

Would Benjamin Peirce's testimony be admissible today in federal court? He appears to have made an arithmetic error: $(1/5)^{30}$ is actually 1 divided by 9.313×10^{20}, not 1 divided by 2.666×10^{21}. Would the mistake affect the admissibility of his testimony?

4. DNA Identification

Forensic DNA testing has been relied upon by courts as evidence of identification for over 30 years. As you will see from the material excerpted below, many aspects of DNA typing are largely uncontroversial, such as comparisons between two DNA profiles, each from a single, high-quantity source of DNA (such as a cheek swab from a suspect and a large amount of blood or other biological material from a crime scene). Today, *Daubert* challenges to DNA-related expert testimony typically focus on more cutting-edge techniques, such as the presentation of match statistics in cases involving DNA database "cold hits"; testing of a very small amount of DNA ("low copy number" or "LCN" testing); interpretation of complex DNA mixtures with a large number of contributors; and the use of special software that automates DNA mixture interpretation and reports a computer-generated match statistic.

UNITED STATES v. DAVIS

602 F. Supp. 2d 658 (D. Md. 2009)

ROGER W. TITUS, District Judge.

[Defendant Earl Davis was charged in connection with the robbery and murder of an armored car employee who was shot by two gunmen when delivering deposits to a bank. The assailants tried to drive off in their Jeep Cherokee but were blocked by the driver of the armored car, so they car-jacked a bank customer and fled in her Pontiac Grand Am, which was later recovered.]

After the murder, officers from the Prince George's County Police Department responded to the crime scene and collected evidence. Numerous items were recovered, including a baseball cap worn by one of the shooters, two firearms, and steering wheel covers from the Jeep Cherokee and [the] Pontiac Grand Am. . . . These items were swabbed and analyzed for DNA. The DNA profiles of the major contributor to the DNA found in the ball cap and on the trigger and grip of the recovered firearms were entered into the local CODIS database. [CODIS refers to the Combined DNA Index System, which is a nationwide collection of databases containing DNA profiles from convicted offenders and crime scene evidence.] As a result of a search of the local database . . . there was a "hit" between the DNA recovered from the ball cap recovered at scene and the DNA of the Defendant. Law enforcement officers were notified of the match and advised to obtain a known sample from the Defendant. Pursuant to a search warrant, a DNA sample was taken from him and compared to the items recovered from the crime scene.

The DNA analysis was performed by the Prince George's County Serology/DNA Laboratory. The lab utilized a method of testing known as PCR/STR typing to analyze the DNA in this case. [The lab's conclusions included that Earl Davis was the source of DNA found on the baseball cap and the Grand Am steering wheel to "a reasonable degree of scientific certainty, in the absence of an identical twin"; that "[s]everal types in [the partial DNA profile obtained from a Glock handgun recovered from the crime scene] are consistent with the known profile of Earl Davis"; that DNA found on the Jeep Cherokee steering wheel was "consistent with the combined profiles" of Davis and another suspect; that "the major component of the profile [taken from the Grand Am steering wheel] matches the known profile of Earl Davis"; and that Earl Davis "cannot be excluded" as a "possible" contributor to the DNA mixture found on the Grand Am shifter. Davis challenged the admissibility of DNA test results and requested a *Daubert* hearing.]

I. FORENSIC DNA TESTING

. . . Each human body contains a large number of cells, each of which descends from successive divisions of the fertilized egg that was its origin. Virtually all non-reproductive cells in the body contain identical copies of a complex structure called deoxyribonucleic acid, or DNA. This structure represents the genetic code for that individual. The DNA is in the form of microscopic chromosomes, which are located in the nucleus of a cell. A chromosome is a thread of DNA surrounded by other materials, mainly protein. A fertilized egg contains 23 chromosomes, with one member of each pair being contributed by the mother and father, respectively. Each cell contains exact duplicates of the 46 cells from the fertilized parent cell. Therefore, each cell in the human body has the same DNA.

The structure of DNA consists of two strands, coiled in the form of a double helix, i.e., a twisted ladder. Each strand is composed of a string or a sequence of nucleotide bases held together by a sugar-phosphate backbone. To use the ladder metaphor, running between the sugar-phosphate strands (the side rails of the ladder) are billions of rungs, each of which is composed of two bases. There are only four possible types of bases — A, T, G, C, which represent adenine, thymine, guanine, and cytosine, respectively. The order in which the base pairs appear on the DNA ladder constitutes an individual's genetic code.

A gene is a particular DNA sequence located along a chromosome, ranging from a few thousand to tens of thousands of base pairs, that produces a specific product in the body. In other words, a gene is a site (a sequence of letters) on the DNA that encodes for a protein. A marker is a site on the DNA that does not code for proteins; the marker is also known as the locus (or location, plural "loci"). In essence, the specific base sequence on the gene acts as an encoded message to the body to produce certain amino acids, which ultimately combine to form a protein. The function of a given gene is determined by the order of bases in the gene. The position that gene occupies along the DNA thread is known as its locus.

Human beings share more biological similarities than differences. Thus, over 99% of human DNA does not vary from person to person. Each person's DNA, however, has certain regions where the rungs of the ladder will be different. These areas where loci are different are called "polymorphic" regions. The possible arrangements of base pairs that could occur in one of these polymorphic areas (i.e., the alternative forms of a gene that an individual could possess) are known as alleles. These alleles can result from differences in single base pairs, differences in multiple base pairs, or differences in the number of base pairs found in a given region. The individual genetic makeup described by the alleles is known as the genotype. In forensic analysis, the genotype for a group of analyzed loci is called the DNA profile. When a sample of DNA is typed, the lab examiner looks at predetermined polymorphic loci, identifies the alleles that make up the DNA sequence at those polymorphic loci, and then determines how likely it is for this sequence to appear in a given population.

In this case, the laboratory used a method of DNA typing known as PCR/STR typing. In PCR/STR typing, a process known as polymerase chain reaction, or PCR, is used to amplify targeted loci of the sample of DNA by replicating the process by which DNA duplicates itself naturally. Thus, the lab is able to produce a substantial number of specific, targeted segments of DNA which can then be typed and compared. Short Tandem Repeats, or STR's, are a group of loci which are used to type and compare the DNA. . . . A tandem repeat involves multiple copies of an identical DNA sequence arranged in direct succession in a particular region of a chromosome. An STR is a tandem repeat in which the core repeat units are just a few base pairs. Loci containing STR's are scattered throughout the chromosomes in enormous numbers. Such loci have a fairly large number of alleles and are usually capable of unique identification.

Once the amount of DNA is amplified by the PCR process, the analyst proceeds to identify fragments of different sizes by [measuring how quickly they migrate in an electric field,] a process known as electrophoresis.... [The primers used in PCR amplification] contain fluorescent tags, which become incorporated into the STR fragments.... During electrophoresis, the amplified fragments [pass through a gel, at the end of which they are struck by a laser, causing them to emit light]. By measuring the amount of time that it takes a particular fragment to reach the laser, the laboratory [determines] the size of the fragment and, therefore,... the number of sequence repeats. The faster a fragment moves ... the smaller it is....

The data generated are analyzed by an accompanying computer software program which ... detects the light being emitted and converts it into peaks of different sizes. The analyst then compares the configuration of these peaks against known reference standards in order to determine the number of alleles present at the target loci in a given sample. The signal must be of a certain strength, that is, the peak must be high enough to be interpreted before a laboratory will have enough confidence in the data to make an interpretation. In this case, the PCR process was used to amplify [the] thirteen STR loci ... [that] are the core DNA markers used in ... CODIS.

Once two DNA samples (i.e., the defendant's DNA and what was found on the evidence) are typed at a number of STR loci and are found to be sufficiently similar such that they could have originated from the same source, the analyst must determine the significance of the comparison. In other words, the analyst must determine how common or rare the particular DNA profile is based on population frequency data. The analyst does this by calculating the profile frequency, also called the random match probability. The profile frequency is simply the probability that an unrelated person chosen at random from the population would have the same DNA profile as the unknown sample.

The analyst will determine the statistical frequency of a particular DNA profile by multiplying the frequency of each of the alleles in the profile, and then correcting the result to account for inbreeding or substructuring[10] effects in the population. In other words, the statistical frequency of the DNA profile is calculated using a statistical concept known as the product rule....

[T]he PCR/STR analysis conducted in this case has been previously found reliable by other federal courts, and the highest court of Maryland, and ... no *Daubert* hearing is needed on that procedure....

---

10. Substructuring refers to the tendency toward decreasing genetic heterogeneity and allelic independence exhibited by ethnically homogeneous, non-randomly mating populations. In other words "a substructured population may be defined as one in which the probability of a random match between two of its members is greater than the likelihood of such a match between two members of the population at large." *See United States v. Chischilly*, 30 F.3d 1144, 1153 (9th Cir. 1994).

II. STATISTICAL SIGNIFICANCE OF THE COLD HIT MATCH

Defendant next moves to exclude the Government's DNA evidence based on the alleged lack of a reliable statistical interpretation of DNA evidence identified through a "cold hit" from a DNA database. . . . [In an affidavit,] Dr. Dan Krane, the defense expert, provided the following succinct explanation of the difference between what he described as "probable cause" hits and "cold hits":

> A "match" between the DNA profiles of two different samples means little without accompanying data on both the chance of coincidental matches and the possibility of false positives. Until recently, the DNA profiles that have been generated for forensic purposes have been almost exclusively those that could be characterized as "probable cause matches," in which DNA testing has been performed upon a reference sample taken from a suspect that has already been linked to a crime by direct or circumstantial evidence. A new category of DNA profile "matches" are becoming increasingly common however — those that are generated as a result of "cold hits" that result from the trawling of a large number of DNA profiles maintained in databases (usually those of previously convicted offenders). Since the primary difference between these kinds of matches is the manner in which a suspect is first identified, it is generally accepted that it is not possible to convert one type of case into the other (for instance, by simply retesting a reference sample once a "cold hit" has been identified). It is also generally accepted in the scientific community that the statistical significance of those two kinds of DNA profiles matches should be determined differently.

In most probable cause cases, the only statistical calculation presented along with DNA match evidence is one utilizing the "product rule." After profiling a specific number of loci on a strand of DNA, the analyst obtains, from published tables, the frequencies of variations in genetic material at each tested locus. The frequencies of all the tested loci are then multiplied together to obtain the frequency with which that particular profile is seen in various population groups. In probable cause cases, this number expresses two distinct concepts, though they happen to coincide: 1) the expected frequency, or rarity, of that particular DNA profile in the population; and 2) the chance that the suspect's DNA profile might coincidentally, but incorrectly, match the evidentiary profile (the "random match probability" or "RMP"). In probable cause cases, the product rule therefore indicates the rarity of the particular profile *and* answers the "coincidence question."

. . . However, because the search of the database increases the odds that a coincidental match will be found, the product rule calculation does *not* express the likelihood that a cold hit match is coincidental. What is not settled is the best way to calculate a similar "random match probability" for cold hit cases. An overwhelming number of scientific authorities agree that searching a large database of DNA profiles requires a novel statistical methodology to derive the significance of that type of match. . . .

There are at least three calculations that could potentially be presented along with evidence of a cold hit match to provide the appropriate context for the jury.

The first approach was proposed by the National Research Council in 1992. [National Research Council, *DNA Technology in Forensic Science* (1992).] This method corrects for ascertainment bias (the bias that exists when one searches for something rare in a set database) by using one set of loci to screen for and identify a suspect in a database, then using a different set of loci to confirm a match. Statistical analysis using the product rule would then be done on only the *second* set of loci. This result is generally agreed upon as reliable, though conservative, because it uses fewer loci in the calculation of the statistical significance of the match, resulting in "shorter odds" than if all loci were considered. This approach is considered valid, though not optimal, because there may be other valid methods that use more or all of the testable loci in determining the statistical significance of a match.

The National Research Council proposed another method just four years later. [National Research Council, *The Evaluation of Forensic DNA Evidence* (1996).] This approach calculates the odds of finding a match in a given database by multiplying the expected frequency of the profile (the rarity statistic, derived using the product rule) by the number of profiles in the database. This statistic has been called the "database match probability." This result would be the expected frequency of the profile in a sample the size of the database and thus the chance of randomly finding a match in a sample of that size. The database match probability has the most impact on the reliability of a cold hit match when few loci are tested because one is obviously more likely to find a coincidental match at seven or eight loci than at twelve or thirteen, and this likelihood only increases with the number of profiles compared. Arguably, this approach requires presentation to the fact-finder of *both* the rarity statistic *and* the database match probability.

The third method is known as either the Balding-Donnelly method (after the names of its two leading advocates), or the Bayesian method (named for the 19th-century inventor of the formula used). Instead of focusing on the probability of finding a match in a given database, this formula focuses on the elimination of other profiles during the search. Thus, the match becomes *more* significant with greater database sizes because the elimination of other known persons increases the chances that the identified suspect is actually the source of the sample DNA. Thus, a database match has a slightly *higher* probability of identifying the source of the evidentiary DNA than would be expected from the standard product rule calculation.

Each of the above methods for expressing the significance of a cold hit match has its advocates and detractors. Defendant argues that the absence of consensus as to the most "reliable" statistical methodology should preclude the Government from offering *any* DNA evidence in the case, or, at the very least, preclude use of "inappropriate likelihood ratios currently attached to sample BG1 (Jeep steering wheel cover)." This issue has not been addressed by a federal court, but has been resolved by the high courts of both California and the District of Columbia. *See People v. Nelson*, 43 Cal. 4th 1242 (2008); *United States v. Jenkins*, 887 A.2d 1013 (D.C. 2005). . . . [Applying *Frye* rather than *Daubert*, those] courts concluded that the issue . . . pertained to the *relevance* of the competing calculations, not to the *soundness* of the methodology:

> At the heart of this debate is a disagreement over the competing questions to be asked, not the methodologies used to answer those questions. The rarity statistic, the database match probability, and the Balding-Donnelly approach each answer unique and potentially relevant questions. More importantly, there is no controversy in the relevant scientific community as to the accuracy of

the various formulas. In other words, the math that underlies the calculations is not being questioned. Each approach to expressing significance of a cold hit DNA match accurately answers the question it seeks to address. The rarity statistic accurately expresses how rare a genetic profile is in a given society. Database match probability accurately expresses the probability of obtaining a cold hit from a search of a particular database. Balding-Donnelly accurately expresses the probability that the person identified through the cold hit is the actual source of the DNA in light of the fact that a known quantity of potential suspects was eliminated through the database search. These competing schools of thought do not question or challenge the validity of the computations and mathematics relied upon by the others. Instead, the arguments raised by each of the proponents simply state that their formulation is more probative, not more correct. Thus, the debate…is one of relevancy, not methodology[.]

Jenkins. The court then found that under its *Frye* test, there was no basis to exclude the DNA evidence.

Nelson followed *Jenkins*, also finding that cold hit statistics were an issue of relevancy, and that the RMP derived from the product rule was still relevant and admissible as an expression of *the rarity of the evidentiary profile.* However, the *Nelson* court further clarified that:

> The conclusion that statistics derived from the product rule are admissible in a cold hit case does not mean that they are the only statistics that are relevant and admissible. The database match probability statistic might also be admissible. As explained, it is unlikely the database match probability statistic would have been significant to the jury in this case given the size of even that number. But in a different case, if the database were large enough and the odds shorter than those here, the database match probability statistic might also be probative. Nothing we say prohibits its admission. . . .

This Court agrees with the *Jenkins* and *Nelson* decisions and concludes that there is no basis under *Daubert* or the Federal Rules of Evidence to exclude evidence of the DNA matches in this case. However, the Government shall only be permitted to present the product rule calculation as an expression of the rarity of the profile, but not as an expression of the random match probability, i.e., the answer to the "coincidence question." If the defense wishes to present statistical experts utilizing one or more of the above methods to argue that the match is deserving of less weight because it was obtained through a database search, it is free to do so. Ultimately, it shall be for the jury to decide the appropriate weight to assign to the forensic evidence.

III. MISCELLANEOUS ARGUMENTS

. . . The defense contends that the Court should hold a hearing under Rule 702 and *Daubert* to determine whether . . . all steps of the DNA typing methodology used in this case were correctly performed. The defense argues that PCR/STR DNA testing is a complicated and highly technical procedure that requires a series of distinct steps, and that each step is typically governed by multifaceted protocols. It says that *each step* is subject to independent review, and the third prong of Rule 702 requires that the Court be convinced that "the witness has applied the principles and methods reliably to the facts of the case."

The Government contends that these arguments essentially challenge the proficiency of the tester rather than the reliability of the test, so they go to the weight of the Government's evidence, not its reliability/admissibility. *See United States v. Beasley*, 102 F.3d 1440, 1448 (8th Cir. 1996); [*United States v.*] *Ewell*, 252 F. Supp. 2d 104, 114 (D.N.J. 2003); *United States v. Shea*, 957 F. Supp. 331 (D.N.H. 1997). The Court agrees, and therefore concludes that the defense's speculative assertions on this point do not require the exclusion of the evidence or a *Daubert* hearing under Rule 702. . . . [T]he Defendant makes few concrete allegations as to error or failure to follow protocol, but wants the Court to hold an evidentiary hearing to ascertain *if* certain procedures were followed. As the *Daubert* court stated, "vigorous cross examination, presentation of contrary evidence, and careful instruction on the burdens of proof are the traditional and appropriate means of attacking shaky, but admissible evidence." . . .

No statistical estimates were calculated for [the DNA collected from the Glock handgun and the Grand Am shifter]. However, the analysts concluded that Mr. Davis' DNA profile was "consistent" with "several" parts of the evidentiary profiles, and/or that Mr. Davis "cannot be excluded" as the source of the evidentiary samples. The Defendant challenges the admissibility of [these] opinions . . . without any supporting statistics whatsoever. . . .

The Court agrees with the numerous courts and authorities that have concluded that DNA evidence purporting to inculpate a defendant must be accompanied by some sort of explanation as to the significance of the consistency. Without such context, "the jury does not know what to make of the fact that the patterns match: the jury does not know whether the patterns are as common as pictures with two eyes, or as unique as the Mona Lisa." *United States v. Yee*, 134 F.R.D. 161, 181 (N.D. Ohio 1991). Therefore, the Court holds that evidence concerning these three samples will not be admitted unless the Government can provide reliable accompanying statistics explaining approximately how many persons in the general population would be "consistent" with this partial profile, and/or how many persons in the general population "cannot be excluded" based on the partial profile.

[However, the Court also concludes] — provided that the Government presents an appropriate statistical analysis for these samples — that the expert's opinions that the profiles are "consistent" or that the Defendant "cannot be excluded" are admissible. While this evidence is certainly deserving of less weight than a full-profile to full-profile match, the Court is convinced that the opinions here were the product of a reliable methodology. . . .

For two of the evidentiary samples, [the baseball cap and the Grand Am steering wheel], the analyst interpreting the results has opined that: "To a reasonable degree of scientific certainty, in the absence of an identical twin, Earl Davis is the source of this DNA." The defense requests that the Court preclude the Government from presenting these source attribution statements, and asks that the expert's testimony be limited to the presentation of a reliable statistical probability figure. It argues that such an opinion does not concern reliable "scientific, technical, or other specialized knowledge" within the meaning of Rule 702 and *Daubert*, and will not be helpful to the trier of fact because it is more prejudicial, misleading, and confusing than probative under Rule 403.

The Government's expert, [Meredith Kitey, the former DNA Laboratory Manager for the Prince George's County Police Department], states [in her affidavit] that since 2000, the FBI has routinely used source attribution statements to "simplify the 'match statement' for a jury when the statistical frequencies calculated for a sample are more than 100 times greater [than] the population of the United States." This equates to about 1 in 300 billion. She says that the use of source attribution statements is "a valid scientifically accepted opinion today."[*]

The defense submitted affidavits from three experts in an effort to refute Ms. Kitey's position on the use of source attribution statements. Dr. Dan Krane's affidavit argues that source attribution statements are inappropriate based on 13-locus STR profile matches absent definitive conclusions that (1) no relatives of the individual found to have a matching profile are reasonable alternative contributors of the evidentiary material; and (2) there were absolutely no errors in the testing and interpretation of the evidence samples. Further, Dr. Krane maintains that it is unreasonable to consider the possibility that the contributor of the evidence sample was not from a different population than those for which random match probability statistics have been generated. Dr. Sandy Zabell contends that the source attribution statement has no generally accepted meaning, and simply replaces scientifically-based RMP with a vague qualitative phrase. Dr. Laurence Mueller objects to source attribution statements primarily on the basis that they do not account for the possibility of laboratory error (i.e., false positives).

. . . [T]he defense urges the Court to find the source attribution statements unreliable for two reasons. First, coincidental matches between profiles of unrelated individuals found within the Arizona state and Prince George's County, Maryland databases — despite astronomical RMP calculations — cast doubt on the certainty with which the statements are made. In the prior proceedings in this case, a state court judge ordered the Maryland State Police CODIS director to search the Maryland DNA database against itself and determine the number of pairs of profiles that matched at 9 to 13 loci. On January 31, 2007, Maryland CODIS administrator Michelle Graves produced a declaration indicating that the search indicated 21 matches at 9 loci; 3 matches at 10 loci; 1 match at 11 loci; 4 matches at 12 loci; and 3 matches at 13 loci. A number of these matches were explained by the presence of identical twins or close relatives in the database, but several were between completely unrelated individuals. One individual in the Prince George's County database matched two other unrelated individuals at seven loci, an event that, according to the product rule, produced a RMP of 1 in 1 trillion. Dr. Mueller, upon reviewing this data, opined that the fact that coincidental matches were found in the Prince George's County database, containing less than ten thousand profiles, shows that statements or inferences of uniqueness can be fundamentally incorrect.

---

[*] [The court and the expert are both being a little sloppy here. Three-hundred billion is roughly a thousand times the size of the United States population, not a hundred times. "The FBI currently sets its source attribution threshold at around 1 in 280 billion, or about a thousand times the population of the United States." Andrea Roth, *Safety in Numbers? Deciding When DNA Alone Is Enough to Convict*, 85 N.Y.U. L. Rev. 1130, 1138-1139 (2010).— ED.]

Second, the Defendant argues that the FBI's use of source attribution statements is not generally accepted in the scientific community, and is at fact at odds with the practice of numerous other DNA laboratories both within and outside the United States. Highly respected laboratories such as the Connecticut State Crime Laboratory, the Orange County, California police laboratory, the Virginia and Michigan state crime labs, and several international common law jurisdictions reject the use of source attribution statements. Additionally, at least one federal district court has noted that, in most cases, "DNA evidence of a 'match' is only admitted with statistical evidence of the probability of a coincidental match, not as a definitive statement." *United States v. Green*, 405 F. Supp. 2d 104, 109 n.4 (D. Mass. 2005).

The defense states that to the best of its knowledge, this type of expert opinion evidence has never been admitted in a federal case over the objection of defense counsel. However, a nearly identical source attribution statement *was* recently found admissible by the highest court of Maryland in *Young v. State*, 388 Md. 99 (2005). . . . The Court of Appeals of Maryland first acknowledged that DNA evidence cannot be *conclusively* attributed to one person unless the entire DNA molecule is analyzed because unrelated individuals can have identical fragments at the targeted loci. However, it held that under "certain circumstances . . . new technologies result in infinitesimal random match probabilities that would be deemed conclusive by all but mathematicians and philosophers." The court then conducted a careful comparison of the evolving opinion in the scientific community concerning the use of source attribution statements (or, declarations of "uniqueness"), as shown by the difference between the conclusions reached [by the National Research Council in 1992 and 1996]. In 1992, the National Research Council "unambiguously presented accompanying statistical testimony as necessary and emphasized the inappropriateness of testifying to the uniqueness of the genotype." By 1996, however, the Council acknowledged that because scientific advances now permit the comparison of genetic markers at many more loci than previously possible,

> Opinion testimony about uniqueness would simplify the presentation of evidence by dispensing with specific estimates of population frequencies or probabilities. If the basis of an opinion were attacked on statistical grounds, however, or if frequency or probability estimates were admitted, this advantage would be lost. Nevertheless, *because the difference between a vanishingly small probability and an opinion of uniqueness is so slight, courts that decide on a criterion for uniqueness and determine that the criterion has been met may choose to allow the latter along with, or instead of, the former, when the scientific findings support such testimony.*

The *Young* court . . . concluded, however, that when thirteen STR loci are analyzed, as in the instant case, the random match probability for related individuals, even including siblings, is sufficiently low that the profile may be characterized as unique. Under those circumstances, then, there is no scientific basis for requiring statistical testimony to accompany an expert's opinion that two profiles "match," and the expert may contextualize his opinion with nothing more than a statement that to a reasonable degree of scientific certainty, the defendant is the "source" of the evidence. . . .

The Court finds the reasoning in *Young* very persuasive, and concludes that in this case — even though there is no bright-line point at which this result is mandated — the random match probability figures calculated for [the relevant] samples are sufficiently low so that the profile can be considered unique. Ms. Kitey's affidavit states that FBI policy only permits the use of source attribution statements when the random match probability is calculated as at least one hundred times the size of the entire population of the United States, or approximately 1 in 300 billion.* This Court finds that figure sufficiently infinitesimal that the Government's expert may opine, consistent with *Daubert* and Rule 702, that the Defendant is the source of these samples, and the report containing the challenged phrase is admissible.

This holding is not inconsistent with the Court's above conclusion ... that jurors require assistance contextualizing the significance of the "consistency" between the defendant's DNA profile and the evidentiary profile. This is usually accomplished by presenting a statistical estimate of the profile's regularity or rarity in a given population. The Court now simply builds upon that foundational principle by holding that when the random match probability becomes infinitesimally small, the profile is *so* rare that it may reasonably and rationally be considered unique. In these circumstances, where the random match probability between the two samples is less than 1 in 300 billion, the Court now holds that the appropriate context may be provided to the jury in the form of a source attribution statement.

The Court thus agrees with the holding in *Young* that there is no legal or scientific requirement that a source attribution statement (or opinion that a profile is "unique") must be explained or accompanied by the presentation of the random match probability figure or other statistical calculation. However, the Court does have broad discretion under the Federal Rules of Evidence, to ensure that evidence is presented in an effective and efficient manner. *See* Fed. R. Evid. 601(a) ("The court shall exercise reasonable control over the mode and order of interrogating witnesses and presenting evidence so as to (1) make the interrogation and presentation effective for the ascertainment of the truth [and] (2) avoid needless consumption of time."). In addition, under Rule 705, an "expert may testify in terms of opinion or inference and give reasons therefor without first testifying to the underlying facts or data, *unless the court requires otherwise.*" (Emphasis added.)

In light of the unique aspects of this case (i.e., the identification of the Defendant by a cold hit in a database and related questions of statistical significance), the Court believes this is a situation in which the Court should "require otherwise." The Court anticipates and expects that the Defendant will vigorously cross-examine the Government's expert on the statistical basis for her source attribution statement. Thus, in the interest of time and clarity, the Court will order that the Government, in its direct examination, *also* present the information that forms the basis for the conclusion that the Defendant is the source of the evidentiary DNA sample(s). The Defendant will then remain free to challenge the expert's conclusion through cross-examination regarding

---

* [See footnote * on page 588.— ED.]

such topics as differing statistical analyses, laboratory error rates, contamination, and any other and concerns he may have. . . .

The defense next contends that even if the Court finds the source attributions statements admissible under Rule 702, it should still preclude their admission under Rule 403. It argues that because of the "powerful and potentially misleading effect of expert evidence," the source attribution statements should be excluded because their probative value is substantially outweighed by their potential to confuse or mislead the jury.

The Court is mindful that "expert testimony may be assigned talismanic significance in the eyes of lay jurors, and, therefore, the district courts must take care to weigh the value of such evidence against its potential to mislead or confuse." [*United States v. Frazier*, 387 F.3d 1244 (11th Cir. 2004).] Some courts and commentators have worried that, particularly in cases where a large amount of statistical and scientific evidence will be presented, if the Government were permitted to present a source attribution statement as facially simple and definitive as "the defendant is the source of the DNA," jurors would "simply 'jump' to the bottom line . . . without giving any meaningful consideration to any dispute over the principles, which underlie the methodology used to generate" the expert's conclusion. *United States v. Porter*, 1991 WL 319015 (D.C. Sup. Ct. 1991), *vacated and remanded*, 618 A.2d 629 (D.C. 1992). According to this argument, a source attribution statement would effectively overwhelm a defendant's attempts to challenge the expert's findings, insofar as such challenges would have to delve into statistical matters that lack the same certainty and gravity with jurors, and that this problem cannot be overcome through cross-examination alone.

This argument might give the Court more pause if the Government in this case would be presenting naked source attribution statements. However, as the Court has directed that the Government also provide the statistical basis upon which the source attribution statements are made, the concern that jurors would simply latch onto the expert's conclusion without examining it with a critical eye is greatly mitigated. The Defendant *will* be able to adequately challenge the Government expert's findings and conclusions through cross examination. Therefore, the probative value of the source attribution statements is not substantially outweighed by the potential to confuse or mislead the jury, and the Court will not exclude the statements under Rule 403. . . .

For the foregoing reasons, Defendant's Motion To Exclude DNA Test Results and Request for *Daubert* Hearing will be denied. . . .

UNITED STATES v. McCLUSKEY

954 F.Supp.2d 1224 (D.N.M. 2013)

HERRERA, District Judge.

[Several codefendants, including Tracy Province, were charged with murder. The government conducted DNA testing on several swabs taken from the alleged murder weapon, a handgun, as well as the decedents' car. One item, 1B23B, a swab from the handgun's magazine, contained only a small amount ("low copy number" or "LCN") of DNA. The government's DNA analyst, Carrie

Zais Davis, testified that Province was, to a "reasonable degree of scientific certainty," the sole source of DNA on the magazine swab. The codefendants moved to exclude various aspects of Davis's testimony. The trial court denied these motions with respect to all aspects of Davis's testimony other than the LCN testing, which it discussed separately.]

The amount of DNA in Item 1B23B is 215 picograms (pg) — making this a Low Copy Number (LCN) result, according to the NMDPS [New Mexico Department of Public Safety] Lab's protocol. . . .

Defendant argues that Low Copy Number (LCN) DNA testing "is not considered generally reliable even in the forensic science community." . . .

. . . [T]he Court held an evidentiary hearing on the issue of admissibility under *Daubert* and Rule 702 of LCN testing results. . . . The Court heard testimony from three witnesses: Dr. William Watson and Carrie Zais Davis for the Government, and Dr. Dan Krane for Defendant. . . .

When there is too small a sample, the DNA testing (which would otherwise be reliable and yield results admissible under *Daubert* and Rule 702) may yield unreliable and non-reproducible results because of the significant increase in stochastic [random] effects. . . . LCN testing carries a greater potential for error due to difficulties in analysis and interpretation caused by four stochastic effects: allele drop-in, allele drop-out, stutter, and heterozygote peak height imbalance. John M. Butler, Fundamentals of Forensic DNA Typing 331 (2010)[1] . . . "Trying to generate a reliable STR profile with only a few cells from a biological sample is similar to looking for an object in the mud or trying to decipher the image in a fuzzy photograph." *Id*. Interpretation of LCN results is "not straightforward," and additional interpretive guidelines may be required. . . .

Laboratories may set an "empirically determined threshold (usually termed a 'stochastic threshold')" to establish a sample quantity which puts a sample "in the potential danger zone of unreliable results." John M. Butler, Advanced Topics in Forensic DNA Typing 339 (Academic Press 2011) . . . .

The Court recognizes that the NMDPS Lab's stochastic threshold is higher, at 250 pg, than the level defined as LCN by other labs and authorities. Other labs may get reliable results with lower quantities; procedures and results and stochastic thresholds vary from lab to lab. But what is important is that the NMDPS Lab has empirically determined that 250 pg is its own stochastic threshold; this means that the NMDPS Lab recognizes that, applying its own protocols and using its own instrumentation, it expects to see stochastic effects that may render the results unreliable when a sample under 250 pg is

---

1. [The Butler treatise cited by the court explains that under certain circumstances, genetic markers, called "alleles," might "drop in" or "drop out" from the computer graphs generated by the software used in developing DNA profiles. That is, a graph might contain a peak that is not a true genetic marker, or might omit a peak that is a true genetic marker. In addition, a graph might contain small "stutter" peaks that are not real genetic markers. A "heterozygote" is a person who has two different alleles at a genetic location (as compared to a "homozygote," who inherits the same genetic marker from both his or her mother and father at a particular genetic location). The court is accepting Butler's premise that with small quantities of DNA, interpretation becomes difficult because a person's two alleles at a particular genetic location might be different heights, making it appear that the peaks come from different contributors rather than the same contributor. — Ed.]

tested. The question before the Court is whether the Government has carried its burden of demonstrating, by a preponderance of the evidence, that the LCN testing by the NMDPS Lab in this case is nevertheless reliable.

The Government . . . show[ed] that a number of other laboratories around the world, and a few in this country, perform LCN testing. . . . But the . . . demonstration that LCN testing is done in other countries does not constitute any showing that those LCN results would meet the standard for admissibility under *Daubert* and Rule 702. . . . [O]ther laboratories use different procedures; even if it were shown that their LCN results were reliable, that would say nothing about whether the LCN results from the NMDPS Lab procedures are reliable. . . .

The Government cites one case from the Supreme Court of Queens County, New York, *People v. Megnath*, 898 N.Y.S.2d 408 (N.Y. Sup. Ct. 2010). . . . Defendant erroneously argues . . . that *Megnath* is not persuasive because it was decided under *Frye*; the case, however, would be more persuasive for admissibility under *Daubert*, since LCN testing was held to satisfy the more restrictive *Frye* test. But *Megnath* is not persuasive, for a number of reasons. First, the N.Y. OCME uses different procedures and interpretive methods than the NMDPS Lab; for instance, the N.Y. OCME increased the number of amplification cycles from 28 to 31. Second, the N.Y. OCME has done extensive internal validation of its LCN testing and has received certification and approval for it . . . . Third, the *Megnath* court held an evidentiary hearing and based its holding on the testimony and credibility of the witnesses presented in that court. Fourth, the *Megnath* court made the questionable findings that the *Frye* test only applies to novel scientific evidence and that LCN testing was "not a novel scientific technique" (despite changes in procedure and interpretive methods. . . . Fifth, the *Megnath* court did not account for the increase in stochastic effects in LCN testing, merely observing that stochastic effects may occur in any testing. . . .

The scientific literature cited by the parties does not give the Court a sound basis for decision. A number of leading authorities in the field take the position that LCN testing is not reliable. . . . See, e.g., Bruce Budowle, Low Copy Number Typing Still Lacks Robustness and Reliability, available at http://www.promega.com/resources/articles/profiles-in-dna/low-copy-numbertyping-still-lacks-robustness-and-reliability (2010) [Def's Ex. B8]. Although the Government cites some authorities as supporting the reliability of LCN testing, these authorities are discussing laboratories using different procedures and methods than the NMDPS Lab . . . .

. . . When asked by the Court to justify her conclusion that the profile was reliable, even though it was admittedly below the Lab's 250 pg stochastic threshold, and stochastic effects were in fact observed, Davis . . . blithely cited her experience: "So I guess, just based on my experience, I would say that this is a reliable profile." . . . Davis did not further justify or support her conclusion; she did not cite to any particular expertise with LCN testing, nor did she cite any specific testing or scientific literature.

When the Court asked whether there was a way to test her conclusion, Davis cited the statistics she had generated and said "the statistical weight on it, too, would give it more reliability." . . . On recross-examination, however, Davis retracted this statement, admitting that the statistical calculations had nothing to do with the reliability of the profile itself. . . .

The Court does not find credible Davis's testimony and conclusion on the reliability of the DNA profile for Item 1B23B. The Court is not persuaded by Davis's insistence that her experience — without citation to scientific studies, scientific literature, or any special training — justified her conclusion.... A court making a determination of reliability under *Daubert* and Rule 702 is justified in rejecting the "ipse dixit" of an expert. *Joiner*, 522 U.S. at 146. The Court concludes that this case, with respect to LCN testing, is like *Joiner* ... in which a reliable methodology is applied to a different area without sufficient justification, or in an unjustified extrapolation.....

Consideration of the *Daubert* factors leads the Court to conclude that the results of LCN testing by the NMDPS Lab are not reliable enough to meet the admittedly relaxed standard of *Daubert* and Rule 702....

PEOPLE v. PIKE

53 N.E.3d 147 (Ill. App. 2016)

Pucinski, Judge.

[Defendant was charged with armed robbery by firearm and several other offenses, and represented himself at trial. As part of its case, the government presented the testimony of a DNA analyst who conducted "Y-STR" DNA testing on a handgun associated with the robbery.]

Forensic scientist Katrina Gomez testified that she is employed by the Illinois State Police Forensic Science Center in Chicago. Gomez was accepted as an expert in forensic biology and DNA analysis without objection. Gomez was assigned to analyze the evidence collected in this case. Gomez was trained in short tandem repeat (STR) polymerase chain reaction (PCR) DNA testing and testified that the swabs did not contain sufficient DNA to develop a profile. Gomez then spoke with forensic scientist Lisa Fallara about the possibility of performing Y-chromosome STR (Y-STR) analysis on the DNA extract from the gun swabs. Gomez then sealed the items and forwarded them to Fallara for Y-STR testing.

. . . Fallara testified that Y-STR testing is generally accepted in the scientific community. Whereas traditional DNA testing looks at several areas of DNA along with several different chromosomes, Y-STR testing looks at several different locations only on the male Y chromosome; it is essentially male DNA testing. Fallara explained that Y chromosome DNA is passed down from the paternal line, so that a brother, father and father's father will all have the same Y-STR DNA profile. Fallara explained that Y-STR analysis is better suited for obtaining profiles from a limited amount of DNA....

. . . Fallara identified a low-level mixture of two Y-STR profiles on the DNA swabs from the 9-millimeter handgun at three locations, which was interpreted as a mixture of two males' DNA. Fallara was only able to do comparisons and statistics at one locus. When Fallara compared this profile with defendant's buccal swab DNA profile, she determined that defendant could not be excluded as a contributor. Fallara calculated a frequency estimating how rare the profile is in the general population, and testified that approximately 1 in 2 unrelated African-American males, 1 in 2 unrelated Caucasian males, and 1 in 2 unrelated Hispanic males cannot be excluded from having contributed to the mixture based on a 95% confidence limit for each population. Therefore, the profile was consistent with one in every two unrelated African–American, Caucasian, and Hispanic males. Defendant did not object to the admission of this evidence at trial and instead proceeded to cross-examine her.

On cross-examination by defendant, Fallara explained that defendant is included as a potential contributor to the mixture but that she could not identify defendant as the contributor. Fallara further explained her statistical calculation by stating, "I would say that every two randomly selected people, one out of those two could not be excluded." . . .

The major issue in this case is whether there was plain error in the admission of the DNA statistical probability expert testimony. . . . There was no objection at trial nor does defendant raise any *Frye* challenge . . . . Defendant's only plain error challenge to the probability calculation is relevance. Defendant argues that the trial court erred in admitting the DNA evidence because the "random match probability" of 50% rendered the evidence irrelevant and more prejudicial than probative. . . .

The fact that defendant could not be excluded and was included as a potential contributor . . . is indeed relevant. As the State argues, the fact that defendant was included as a potential contributor corroborates both of the victims' eyewitness identifications and tends to support the State's theory that defendant committed the crimes. . . .

But the statistic in this case was that 50% of the population also is included as potential contributors. Defendant cites to and echoes the same argument found in *People v. Harbold*, 124 Ill. App. 3d 363 (1984), where the defendant similarly argued that a blood typing statistical probability calculation of 1 in 500 was plain error because it was irrelevant and prejudicial. Back then, this court agreed and held the admission of this evidence was plain error because of the danger of the prosecutor's fallacy in misunderstanding the difference between random match probability and source probability and because the circumstantial evidence was factually close.

Of course, we have come a long way since 1984 with the development of DNA identification evidence and in our understanding of statistical probabilities. Since the holding in *Harbold*, courts in our State have recognized and repeatedly held that testimony regarding DNA statistical probabilities is generally accepted and admissible. . . .

But there are no reported decisions in our State that have addressed the issue of relevance where the DNA inclusion probability statistic admitted at trial is only 50%. There are federal decisions that have addressed this issue under a similar relevancy definition, and the weight of this authority is that such evidence should be excluded. . . .

We hold that the error in this case in admitting the 50% probability of inclusion statistic, though error, was not so serious as to constitute plain error, and thus defendant fails to satisfy the serious error prong to show plain error. The error was not of such magnitude as to deny defendant fair trial. In this case, Fallara clearly indicated that the 50% combined probability of inclusion referred to the percentage of the population that could have contributed to the mixed profile, clarified that defendant was included within this group, and also clearly testified that 50% of the population is also included in the group of potential contributors to the partial DNA profile off the gun. The expert in this case also clearly testified that she could not specifically identify defendant. This evidence was presented accurately and there could be no mistake that defendant in fact was only included as a potential contributor, along with 50% of the population, and in fact was not identified as "matching" the DNA. . . .

Affirmed.

PEOPLE v. WAKEFIELD

No. 107724 (N.Y. App. Aug. 15, 2019)

PRITZKER, Judge.

A caseworker from an organization that assists individuals with mental health issues, such as the victim, performed a welfare check at the victim's apartment after he failed to attend a scheduled appointment and could not be contacted. The victim was discovered dead in his apartment with a guitar amplifier cord wrapped around his neck. . . . An investigation ensued, during which several items owned by the victim, including a laptop, a PlayStation and an orange duffle bag, were discovered to be missing from his apartment. After a reward was offered for information about the victim's death, a friend of defendant came forth and advised law enforcement officials that defendant had admitted to him that he had killed the victim.

. . . Law enforcement collected a buccal swab from defendant to compare his DNA to that found at the crime scene. The data was eventually sent to Cybergenetics, a private company that used a software program called TrueAllele Casework System (hereinafter TrueAllele), for further testing. The DNA analysis by TrueAllele revealed, to a high degree of probability, that defendant's DNA was found on the amplifier cord, on parts of the victim's T-shirt and on the victim's forearm. Prior to trial, defendant moved to preclude admission of evidence derived from TrueAllele, or alternatively, for a hearing under *Frye*. . . .

At the *Frye* hearing, [TrueAllele creator Mark] Perlin explained that TrueAllele "automates the interpretation of the data signals that have already been generated by a laboratory." Perlin testified that DNA electropherograms are commonly analyzed by a person with some computer assistance. TrueAllele, however, takes the data that is entered and "proposes possibilities for what different genotypes can be." TrueAllele employs the Markov Chain Monte Carlo algorithm (hereinafter MCMC), which, according to Perlin, is "basically a way of solving integration problems" and "gives the probabilities of all the different possibilities, not just finding what might be a maximum possibility." Perlin also testified that TrueAllele is designed to have a certain degree of artificial intelligence to make additional inferences as more information becomes available. Perlin explained that, after objectively generating all genotype possibilities, TrueAllele answers the question of "how much more the suspect matches the evidence [than] a random person would," and the answer takes the form of a likelihood ratio.

The record reflects that articles evaluating TrueAllele have been published in six separate forensics journals. In addition, at the time of the *Frye* hearing, TrueAllele had undergone approximately 25 validation studies, some of which appeared in peer-reviewed publications. One peer-reviewed publication noted that, when a victim reference was available, "the computer was [4½] orders of magnitude more efficacious than human review on the same data" and that, when a victim reference was unavailable, "the average efficacy of the computer increased to six orders of magnitude." Another publication stated that, "[w]hile [TrueAllele] does find more matches and computes stronger statistics on average, it examines DNA evidence objectively without introducing bias that may favor the prosecution or defense," further noting that TrueAllele "maintains excellent specificity" and "calculates DNA match statistics with precision." The DNA Subcommittee of the New York State Forensic Science Commission offered a binding recommendation that TrueAllele be used by the State Police for its forensic casework. Approximately one month after the Subcommittee issued its recommendation, the full Commission approved TrueAllele for forensic casework. Perlin testified that TrueAllele was used to deconvolute the remains of victims from the September 11, 2001 World Trade Center attacks upon the request from the New York City Chief Medical Examiner's office. The National Institute of Standards and Technology, a division of the United States Department of Commerce, purchased TrueAllele, and its representatives have given presentations regarding TrueAllele's effectiveness. At the time of the *Frye* hearing, TrueAllele had also been used in various states and had been deemed admissible in Virginia, Pennsylvania and California....

Defendant also argues that his right to confront witnesses was violated by not having access to TrueAllele's source code. This argument raises legitimate and substantial questions concerning due process as impacted by cutting-edge science. Given the exponential growth of technologies such as artificial intelligence, to embrace the future we must assess, and perhaps reassess, the constitutional requirements of due process that arise where law and modern science collide (see e.g. Christian Chessman, A "Source" of Error: Computer Code, Criminal Defendants, and the Constitution, 105 Cal L Rev 179 [2017]; Katherine Kwong, The Algorithm Says You Did It: The Use of Black Box Algorithms to Analyze Complex DNA Evidence, 31 Harv JL & Tech 275 [2017]; Andrea Roth, Machine Testimony, 126 Yale LJ 1972 [2017]; Edward J. Imwinkelried, Computer Source Code: A Source of the Growing Controversy Over the Reliability of Automated Forensic Techniques, 66 DePaul L Rev 97 [2016]). Defendant's novel Confrontation Clause challenge, specifically, that the source code itself is an out-of-court declarant, raises these profound questions....

Before reaching the merits, a discussion of genetics and the relevant technology is necessary to understand the legal issues at play. Perlin, both at the *Frye* hearing and at trial, testified at length as to how TrueAllele computes the likelihood ratios. First, it is important to understand that the DNA extraction is not performed by TrueAllele. Here, the DNA extraction was done by a scientist at the State Police Forensic Investigations Center, and the raw data derived from the extraction was forwarded to Cybergenetics for additional testing. Perlin testified that there are two basic methodologies used in forensic DNA analysis. The first is a traditional approach and is undertaken through a process known as combined probability inclusion (hereinafter CPI), which involves, in relevant part, an analyst choosing which loci to report on and the application of thresholds to the data. These thresholds, which are often set by a manufacturer or laboratory, are intended to simplify the DNA for visual human review by eliminating consideration of possible artifacts and low template DNA so as to increase reporting confidence. The other method of DNA testing at issue is known as a probabilistic method, which can be either semi- or fully-continuous. According to Perlin, semi-continuous probabilistic systems still derive information from the alleles actually present and still apply certain thresholds, but these systems seek to make more use of the data available than that utilized in CPI. In contrast, fully-continuous probabilistic systems, such as TrueAllele, do not employ initial human analyst decision-making and, instead, consider all available data to look at more patterns. Thus, although CPI employs probabilities, it does not make use of all of the data produced, whereas TrueAllele considers all available data to look at more patterns.

To that end, TrueAllele utilizes the MCMC algorithm, which is used to solve high dimension calculus problems that would be impossible or impractical without a computer so as to identify all possibilities, not just the maximum possibility (see Ben Shaver, A Zero–Math Introduction to Markov Chain Monte Carlo Methods, Towards Data Science, available at https://towardsdatascience.com/a-zero-math-introduction-to-markov-chain-monte-carlo-methods-dcba889e0c50). MCMC is part of the public domain and, according to Perlin, is used in nearly every field of science. Perlin explained that the source code underlying TrueAllele is a "blueprint," or what provides TrueAllele with the instructions on how to execute the MCMC algorithm. More specifically, the human-written source code is turned into object code by an application, and the object code then executes the program. Perlin explained that TrueAllele utilizes approximately 170,000 lines of source code that have been developed, replaced and added to over the past 25 versions of the software. The software includes the user interface, which is the way TrueAllele interacts with a DNA database and furnishes its directions on solving the questions posed. The source code is protected as a trade secret and is only known by two individuals, one of whom is Perlin. Perlin also explained that TrueAllele is what is known as an "expert system," describing how, beyond the calculations made pursuant to the above mathematics, the program is designed to have a certain degree of artificial intelligence in order to make additional inferences as more information becomes available.

. . . [A]lthough Cybergenetics is independent from law enforcement, at the time the report was generated, Cybergenetics was "acting in the role of assisting the police and prosecutors in developing evidence for use at trial". . . . Accordingly, . . . [the] TrueAllele report is testimonial. . . .

Despite concluding that the TrueAllele report is testimonial, we do not find, given the particular facts of this case, that the source code, even through the medium of the computer, is a declarant. This is not to say that an artificial intelligence-type system could never be a declarant, nor is there little doubt that the report and likelihood ratios at issue were derived through distributed cognition between technology and humans (see Itiel E. Dror & Jennifer L. Mnookin, The Use of Technology in Human Expert Domains: Challenges and Risks Arising from the Use of Automated Fingerprint Identification Systems in Forensic Science, 9 Law, Probability & Risk 47, 48–49 [2010]). Indeed, similar to many expert reports, the testimonial aspects of the TrueAllele report are formulated through a synergy and distributed cognition continuum between human and machine (see Itiel E. Dror & Jennifer L. Mnookin, The Use of Technology in Human Expert Domains: Challenges and Risks Arising from the Use of Automated Fingerprint Identification Systems in Forensic Science, 9 Law, Probability & Risk at 48 [2010]), but this fact alone does not tip the scale so far as to transform the source code into a declarant.

As Perlin explained at the *Frye* hearing, there is human input when utilizing TrueAllele. Among other things, a human analyst tells the computer what to download and under what conditions to analyze the data, the analyst tells the computer what questions to ask when interpreting the data and the analyst downloads certain results from the computer, the analyst determines how many "runs," or cycles, of the data the system will complete and the analyst then makes comparisons to form the likelihood ratios. Also key to our analysis is that Perlin, the creator of TrueAllele and the individual who wrote the underlying source code, was present in court and testified, at length, as to genetic science, the TrueAllele program and the formulation of the TrueAllele report through the computer processors and algorithms, including the MCMC algorithm (compare *Melendez–Diaz v. Massachusetts*). Given the totality of the circumstances present here, we find that Perlin was the declarant in the epistemological, existential and legal sense rather than the sophisticated and highly automated tool powered by electronics and source code that he created. Accordingly, because Perlin testified at trial, we find that there was no Confrontation Clause violation as alleged by defendant because he had the opportunity to confront his true accuser. . . .

ERIN MURPHY, THE NEW FORENSICS: CRIMINAL JUSTICE, FALSE CERTAINTY, AND THE SECOND GENERATION OF SCIENTIFIC EVIDENCE

95 Cal. L. Rev. 721, 767–774 (2007)

Advocates of DNA typing . . . suggest that the rigors of DNA science will spare it from the embarrassments that plagued traditional forensic sciences. . . . [But] many of the characteristics that make second-generation [forensic] sciences [including not only DNA typing but also data mining, electronic location tracking, and biometric scanning] so appealing in fact places them at equal, if not greater, risk for error. . . .

[T]he technical complexity of second-generation techniques make[s] close and continuous judicial scrutiny of their methodological soundness less likely. Judges confronting sophisticated scientific evidence must invest greater intellectual and material resources to conduct a comprehensive examination of second-generation techniques. Even well-meaning judges may struggle to comprehend complicated scientific or mathematical principles, and the heightened likelihood of error may discourage a court from delving too deeply into such complicated scientific knowledge.

Judicial reluctance, however, only renders the initial hearings on a new technique more decisive, since few later judges will retread the treacherous path — especially if it is only to risk arriving at a result suspiciously contrary to that reached earlier. Yet at the initial stages, second-generation methodologies, with their requirements of mechanical sophistication and specialized technical knowledge, are even less likely to have withstood the scrutiny of an independent community of auditors. Indeed, the general rigor of second-generation sciences may also lend them an air of "mystic infallibility" that discourages critical inspection, and the existence of "real world" analogues, notwithstanding that the nonforensic applications in fact deploy meaningfully different methodologies, may bolster this sense. A judge who thinks that cell phones or GPS satellites or iris scans or DNA tests generally work in the world may be less inclined to question whether, when put to forensic purposes, the methodological underpinnings remain sound.

The high volume of second-generation cases only exacerbates this impulse. Resource constraints may ultimately persuade the "amateur scientists" of the bench, particularly those inclined to intellectual timidity with regard to sophisticated scientific techniques, to lean heavily upon the "lawlike" status of other courts' rulings rather than spend precious time deciphering a seemingly legitimate methodology. Of course, the more that forensic evidence is approved in cases in which the defendant admits guilt and the evidence goes unexamined, the more it affirms the belief that this kind of evidence is typically trustworthy and reliable.

But even an intellectually entrepreneurial judge willing to fully exercise her gatekeeper role under *Daubert* might not find much help from the adversarial parties.... [D]efense attorneys, like judges, may find themselves susceptible to the temptation simply to trust the integrity of the evidence, thus making the case seem insurmountable or "open-and-shut." Many lawyers will reasonably conclude that it requires too great an effort, and reaps too little a reward, to study such evidence in the hopes of uncovering a flawed methodological approach. And the more technically complex the evidentiary form, the more likely it becomes that even a well-meaning attorney may be incapable of comprehending the science regardless of the effort she expends. After all, not every attorney can be expected to master the methodological details of facial recognition software or DNA amplification and testing. Similarly, the seeming (or actual) impenetrability of the technique may discourage the attorney from conducting a thorough inspection for errors in its application....

[E]ven assuming a judge receptive to such a challenge, a defense attorney capable and well-resourced enough to pursue one, and an expert available for appointment, it remains unlikely that the expert could undertake the examination necessary to truly safeguard the integrity of the evidence. That is because the mechanical sophistication and technical complexity of this evidence all but forecloses independent research. The infrastructure necessary for true methodological testing is simply lacking. At the same time, the database-dependency of second-generation sciences, and the privacy and proprietary secrets concerns they raise, effectively prohibit access to the material necessary for independent research. Manufacturers of DNA typing kits, cell phone or search engine technologies, or biometric scanning software may bristle at disclosing broadly the technology underlying their particular techniques, even under a court "gag" order. Similarly, the relinquishment of data stored indiscriminately in databanks for exploratory purposes — whether iris patterns, DNA profiles, or cell records — understandably raises legitimate concerns about personal privacy. The database dependency of second-generation technologies also means that scrutiny of these techniques for case-specific errors in application itself requires access to large volumes of data, which may not be feasibly disclosed, or feasibly reviewed, in every case. . . .

[T]he very qualities that make second-generation technologies so desirable make it all the more likely they will never encounter adversarial scrutiny of any kind. And while this lack of scrutiny is troubling on its face, it becomes all the more troubling when considered in light of the very real possibility that, given the investigative power of these technologies, in many cases they may be the only actual evidence of the defendant's guilt.

ANDREA ROTH, SAFETY IN NUMBERS?: DECIDING WHEN DNA ALONE IS ENOUGH TO CONVICT

85 N.Y.U. L. Rev. 1130, 1140–1142, 1149–1151, 1158, 1185 (2010)

When national DNA databases were first developed in the 1990s, the number of cold hit prosecutions—those in which the suspect was identified through a database match—was relatively low. In the last decade, however, such cases have grown exponentially, [in part because] the databases are ever-expanding. . . . [S]tate and federal DNA databases have now grown to include not only convicted felons, but also misdemeanants, juveniles, and even arrestees. There are now over 7.8 million offender profiles in the FBI's Combined DNA Index System (CODIS), a group of federal and state databases that together have produced over 120,300 cold hits. . . .

The number of "pure cold hit" DNA cases is also expanding. In those cases, the entirety of the government's case — other than the prior interaction with legal authorities that placed the suspect in the database — consists of the DNA match and perhaps general evidence, such as the perpetrator's race or age, that limits the potential suspect population only to a small and quantifiable degree. . . . [S]everal pure cold hit suspects have been exonerated upon discovery by law enforcement that the cold hit was coincidental or the likely product of laboratory contamination or interpretive errors. . . .

A number of litigants have attempted to argue in pure cold hit cases that a DNA profile match alone, uncorroborated by other individualized evidence, is legally insufficient proof of guilt. . . . Appellate courts in the United States have uniformly rejected these sufficiency challenges. . . . [N]early all have relied on impressive-sounding RMPs — with denominators ranging from the millions to the quintillions — to conclusorily declare that the DNA evidence is sufficient because it shows beyond peradventure that the defendant is the source. . . . [N]one has discussed how high a source probability would have to be for an uncorroborated DNA profile match to be legally sufficient, nor explained why an RMP with a denominator in the millions is legally sufficient proof that the defendant is the source of the DNA when the relevant suspect population may well include millions of people, making another matching suspect likely. . . . [N]early every one has succumbed to the "fallacy of the transposed conditional," conflating the RMP with the source probability. . . . Yet [many] pure cold hit cases . . . involve RMPs with denominators in the sextillions — and thus astronomically high source probabilities regardless of the size of the suspect population. . . .

In ensuring fair trials in pure cold hit cases, courts will have to grapple with jurors' inability to understand statistics, and with the compounding concern that, because of DNA's near-mythical status in modern culture, some jurors may not understand that they can still acquit in the face of astronomically high source probabilities. Further challenges arise given the line between rational mistrust of certain futuristic evidence and fear-based nullification, on the one hand, and the line between being fully convinced and unduly mesmerized by scientific evidence, on the other.

JONATHAN J. KOEHLER, FORENSICS OR FAUXRENSICS? ASCERTAINING ACCURACY IN THE FORENSIC SCIENCES

49 Ariz. St. L.J. 1369, 1378-81 (2017)

The best chance for receiving guidance from the general scientific community on forensic error rates came from reports issued by the National Academy of Science (NAS) panels that addressed forensic science evidence. . . .

NRC [National Research Council] I was published in 1992 just a few years after DNA evidence first appeared in U.S. courtrooms. . . . NRC I . . . noted that DNA typing may be "vulnerable to error" and that "[l]aboratory error rates should be measured with appropriate proficiency tests and should play a role in the interpretation of results of forensic DNA typing." . . .

Unfortunately, NRC I did not clearly explain *why* it is important for a forensic technology that has high discriminatory power to measure and disclose its error rate. This task was left to a small group of statisticians, psychologists, legal scholars, and multi-disciplinary scholarswho echoed NRC I's calls for proficiency tests to identify DNA error rates. These scholars pointed out that the mathematics are such that the impact of the false positive error rate on the probative value of a highly discriminating technology such as DNA typing is larger than it is on less discriminating technologies. . . . Thus, even if a DNA analysis indicates that a DNA profile is so rare there is probably only one person on the planet who could be its source, the reliability of that reported match will ultimately turn on the overall risk of a false positive error (which includes sample switches, misrecordings, and related human errors), and not merely on the small risk that the match is coincidental. . . .

In 1993, at the behest of the FBI Director, the NAS convened a second group of scientists and scholars to take yet another look at forensic DNA evidence. NRC II, which was published in 1996, focused largely on statistical and population genetics matters. However, it also reviewed and rejected NRC I's call for proficiency tests to identify laboratory error rates. . . . NRC II also concluded that proficiency tests are not designed to measure error rates, that reliance on the results of such tests "is almost certain to yield wrong values" and unfair to the better laboratories.

Though NRC II's position on proficiency tests and error rates was quickly and forcefully criticized, few were listening to the critics. In the two decades since NRC II was published, *there have been virtually no blind proficiency tests designed to estimate case-relevant DNA match error rates.* Further, attempts to introduce error rate evidence at trial or to discuss the absence of good forensic error rate data through expert testimony generally fail.

5. Traditional Forensic Science

UNITED STATES v. HEBSHIE

754 F.Supp.2d 89 (D. Mass. 2010)

GERTNER, District Judge.

Petitioner James Hebshie ("Hebshie") was convicted of arson and mail fraud in June 2006 for an April 2001 fire in a commercial building in Taunton, Massachusetts. At the time of the fire, Hebshie was leasing space in the building for his convenience store, Main Street Lottery & News Store. He was sentenced to a mandatory fifteen years in prison, all the while proclaiming his innocence. After exhausting his appeals, Hebshie filed a petition for a writ of habeas corpus pursuant to 28 U.S.C. § 2255 based on the ineffective assistance of his trial counsel. His petition raises a number of grounds but its principal focus is the way counsel dealt with scientific testimony on arson.

The government had to prove that a crime had been committed at all — that the fire was intentionally set, rather than accidental — and that Hebshie was the perpetrator. To show arson, the government relied on two kinds of evidence — first, the "cause-and-origin" forensics expert who testified about where and how the fire started, and second, the testimony of the handler of an "accelerant-detection dog" and a laboratory technician to prove that it was incendiary in nature. To show that Hebshie was the perpetrator, the government demonstrated that Hebshie leased space in the building for his convenience store, that he owed roughly $5,000 to lottery authorities, that he was trying to sell the store, and that he sought to recover on an insurance policy. The arson evidence had substantial problems, as this decision shows; the evidence of Hebshie's motive to burn down his store was less than overwhelming....

By 2006, when Hebshie's trial took place, a number of articles in legal journals and cases cast a critical eye on the scientific reliability of arson evidence, methodologies, and techniques. Ordinarily competent counsel would have understood that men and women had been convicted, sentenced, perhaps even executed, on the basis of flawed arson evidence and taken appropriate steps to litigate the issues using all the tools available. But the case for relief is far stronger here than in the run-of-the-mill arson case; it does not depend upon that literature, those cases or even the drumbeat of concern about arson prosecutions. Hebshie's trial counsel had been specifically warned about deficiencies in this case by predecessor counsel and by the experts retained by them. Even more significant, when the Court pointedly inquired during the trial, not once, but three times, whether there would be a challenge to the arson expert testimony, the laboratory analysis, or the canine handler's testimony, even when the Court suggested it was willing to suspend the trial in order to conduct such a hearing, counsel declined.

Trial counsel never challenged the validity or reliability of the testimony of Sergeant David Domingos ("Domingos"), the government's "cause-and-origin" arson expert; John Drugan ("Drugan"), the laboratory technician; or Sergeant Douglas Lynch ("Lynch"), the accelerant-detection dog handler, either prior to or during the trial, much less called for any limitations on their testimony even when there were substantial grounds to do so. They never objected to testimony that went far beyond the science on which it was allegedly based. Not a single pretrial motion or proposed jury instruction was filed on expert issues at all. Nor did counsel object when the government fundamentally mis-characterized critical testimony from the canine handler in its closing. (In fact, Hebshie's counsel legitimized the government's experts when he addressed the jury; the testimony was "impressive," he said; he did not "quarrel" with it.) While one might imagine a strategic reason for not seeking a *Daubert* hearing under some circumstances, or for not objecting to certain testimony, abso-lutely no legitimate reason was argued here....

The most significant problems should have been abundantly clear — problems with the core evidence of arson, namely, the canine evidence and the laboratory analysis. Once Billy the dog sniffed a so-called accelerant in the left side of Hebshie's store, the area to which she had been led (the very area that Domingos concluded was where the fire started), government experts never checked other areas for "accelerants." They took no control or comparison samples from anywhere else, as the scientific method and arson investigation standards suggest. That single sample was then tested and found to be "light petroleum distillate." "Light petroleum distillate," however, is a cate-gory so broad that a host of entirely benign substances fit within it, especially in this case. Hebshie's store was a convenience store, after all; light petroleum distillate could be found in a number of the goods he offered for sale (lighter fluid or lighters, for example). In addition, it was a substance generated by the heat of the fire itself, a product of pyrolysis of other materials in the store (like carpet glue). In fact, the laboratory test was only probative of arson if one area tested positive while others did not, or if the test disclosed a chemical that would not normally be present at the scene. Nevertheless, the sample was never analyzed further....

Counsel's errors pretrial in dealing with the arson testimony, in any case, were compounded by their trial errors, especially with respect to Billy, the accelerant-detection dog. It is not an understatement to say that Lynch, the dog handler, was permitted to testify to an almost mystical account of Billy's powers and her unique olfactory capabilities. He presented unsubstantiated claims about the dog's accuracy. He was allowed to go on at great length about his emotional relationship with the dog and his entirely subjective abil-ity to interpret her face, what she thought, intended, and the "strength" of the alert she gave in this case....

Hebshie also argues counsel erred in connection with the cause-and-origin testimony.... A reasonable hypothesis, according to petitioner's experts, was that the fire began in the basement rather than in Hebshie's store, or that even if it had started there, that substances regularly found in a convenience store had accidentally ignited. Yet Domingos failed to preserve the scene in a way that enabled others, including defense experts — not to mention peer reviewers — to evaluate his conclusions. He failed to take photographs of the basement or even mention that he had been there in his investigation reports. In effect, few, if any, investigative materials involving places other than where Domingos concluded the fire had begun were collected before the building was razed to the ground and further investigation was impossible. And these failures were especially significant in the light of the challenges to Domingos' "interpretation" of the fire patterns raised at the habeas evidentiary hearing. . . .

In short, I find that due to counsel's failures, the very danger that *Daubert* and *Kumbo Tire* sought to avoid occurred: Questionable theorizing about arson, about Billy's mystical prowess, and the generic laboratory results, were presented as "science" to the jury, and as a result, Hebshie was convicted. Hebshie's § 2255 petition is GRANTED.

COMMONWEALTH v. GAMBORA

933 N.E.2d 50 (Mass. 2010)

BOTSFORD, J.

A jury convicted the defendant, Jesus Gambora, of murder. . . . [The victim, Jaya Desai, was killed during the robbery of a hotel that she and her family operated.] The defendant first challenges the admission of testimony from two expert witnesses, both State police detective lieutenants, identifying or "individualiz[ing]" two latent fingerprints found on a door pull at the crime scene to the defendant. His claim is that the evidence of fingerprint identification, and particularly evidence that a latent print could be "individualized" to a particular person, was inadmissible under *Daubert v. Merrell Dow Pharms., Inc.*, 509 U.S. 579 (1993), and *Commonwealth v. Lanigan*, 419 Mass. 15 (1994), because its underlying scientific or technical reliability had not been established, and indeed, has been shown to have no currently demonstrable scientific or technical basis.

The defendant filed a motion in limine before trial in which he sought to exclude all fingerprint evidence on the grounds that the Commonwealth could not demonstrate its reliability or scientific validity pursuant to *Daubert* and *Lanigan*. . . . The judge characterized the motion as a general challenge to the reliability of a fingerprint individualization method known as ACE-V, an acronym that stands for the four steps in the method's process: analysis, comparison, evaluation, and verification. The judge denied the motion without a hearing, ruling that the ACE-V methodology was "generally accepted within the . . . fingerprint-examiner community," and citing *Commonwealth v. Patterson*, 445 Mass. 626 (2005), a case in which this court concluded that "[c]onsistent with the decisions of other courts that have considered the issue since *Daubert*, . . . the underlying theory and process of latent fingerprint identification, and the ACE-V methodology in particular, are sufficiently reliable to admit expert opinion testimony regarding the matching of a latent impression with a full fingerprint."

At trial, Detective Lieutenant Drawec — who the defendant stipulated was a fingerprint examination and comparison expert — testified . . . that he "individualized" two of the latent prints [found on the hotel door pull] to the defendant's right index and middle fingers.... He then went over the specific points of comparison on which he had relied in making the individualizations. On cross-examination, defense counsel asked:

> Now when you testify and draw conclusions that there is an absolute certainty that there's a match, you never testify to statistics, to odds, or to probabilities when, for example, when a DNA [deoxyribonucleic acid] person makes a comparison they may say it's a one in one billion chance that it is that person, the odds are pretty great, but they say it's one in one billion.

> When you make an opinion, you don't talk in terms of probability, at all, you just say it is for sure, for certain, that's a print; correct?

Drawec answered, "That's correct." Defense counsel went on to question Drawec about errors that have been made in the field of fingerprint identification, and Drawec acknowledged that he was "aware of some errors being made."

Detective Lieutenant O'Hara then testified that he had "verified" Drawec's two individualizations by conducting his own comparison of the latent prints to the defendant's known prints....

In light of our decision in *Patterson* — a decision issued approximately three months before the trial in this case — the trial judge's denial of the defendant's motion in limine concerning the evidence, and his subsequent overruling of the defendant's objection to that evidence at trial, were to be expected. The defendant contends, however, that subsequent to the *Patterson* decision, a report published in 2009 by the National Research Council for the National Academy of Sciences (NAS) has called into more serious question the reliability of both the latent print identification theory and the ACE-V methodology. See National Research Council, Strengthening Forensic Science in the United States, A Path Forward 102-104, 136-145 (2009) (NAS Report)....

The NAS Report raises a number of questions about the reliability of certain aspects of the ACE-V methodology and expert testimony based on it. The report does not appear to question the underlying theory which grounds fingerprint identification evidence; as the report states, there is scientific evidence supporting the theory that fingerprints are unique to each person and do not change over a person's life. However, the NAS report adds, "[u]niqueness and persistence are necessary conditions for friction ridge identification [i.e., fingerprint identification] to be feasible, but those conditions do not... guarantee that prints from two different people are always sufficiently different that they cannot be confused, or that two impressions made by the same finger will also be sufficiently similar to be discerned as coming from the same source."

The NAS Report does not conclude that fingerprint evidence is so unreliable that courts should no longer admit it. The report does, however, stress the subjective nature of the judgments that must be made by the fingerprint examiner at every step of the ACE-V process, including an examiner's ultimate conclusion that a latent print is "individualized" to a specific, identified, known print. One result of the subjectivity, according to the report, is that "the outcome of a friction ridge analysis is not necessarily repeatable from examiner to examiner." The report also points to the related issue of unintentional examiner bias. The report summarizes its views of the ACE-V methodology as follows:

> "ACE-V provides a broadly stated framework for conducting friction ridge analyses. However, this framework is not specific enough to qualify as a validated method for this type of analysis. ACE-V does not guard against bias; it is too broad to ensure repeatability and transparency; and does not guarantee that two analysts following it will obtain the same results. For these reasons, merely following the steps of ACE-V does not imply that one is proceeding in a scientific manner or producing reliable results."

At the same time, the report notes that "[h]istorically, friction ridge analysis has served as a valuable tool, both to identify the guilty and to exclude the innocent." *Id.* Ultimately, the report focuses on the need to prevent overstatement of the accuracy of fingerprint comparisons,[14] and for additional research.

As this court did in *Patterson*, courts historically have found fingerprint identification evidence to be admissible. We recognize, however, that the issues highlighted in the NAS report are important, and deserve consideration. Nevertheless, we do not undertake such consideration in this case. The NAS Report accepts as "plausible" the proposition that "a careful comparison of two impressions can accurately discern whether or not they had a common source." NAS Report at 142. Our review of the trial testimony suggests that Lieutenant Drawec did conduct a careful comparison of the latent prints to the defendant's exemplars. Further, as indicated, one of the issues about which the NAS Report is most critical is the claim that a fingerprint examiner can state with absolute certainty that a particular latent print matches a known print, and that fingerprint comparisons conducted according to the ACE-V methodology are essentially error free. In the present case, neither fingerprint expert made such a claim, and the cross-examination by defense counsel emphasized the point. Even if we were to assume that it was error to permit Detective Lieutenant Drawec to testify that "individualization" of a latent print to a known print means that the prints came from the same source "to the exclusion of all others" and then to testify that he "individualized" two of the latent prints on the door pull to the defendant, the assumed error was

---

14. The NAS Report is critical of claims by those in the fingerprint examination community of absolute, essentially infallible certainty that a particular latent print belongs to a particular person:

> At present, fingerprint examiners typically testify in the language of absolute certainty. Both the conceptual foundations and the professional norms of latent fingerprinting prohibit experts from testifying to identification unless they believe themselves certain that they have made a correct match.... Given the general lack of validity testing for fingerprinting; the relative dearth of difficult proficiency tests; the lack of a statistically valid model of fingerprinting; and the lack of validated standards for declaring a match, such claims of absolute, certain confidence in identification are unjustified....

NAS Report at 142, quoting Mnookin, The Validity of Latent Fingerprint Identification: Confessions of a Fingerprinting Moderate, 7 Law, Probability & Risk 127, 139 (2008).

harmless in the circumstances of this case. . . . [because] the evidence linking the defendant to the crime was very strong.[22] . . . Judgments affirmed.

SPINA, J. (concurring, with whom IRELAND, J., joins).

. . . Drawec testified that the latent prints had been "individualized" to the defendant, and that this meant to the exclusion of all others, and that the prints *absolutely* belonged to the defendant. His testimony was not presented as his *opinion* that the prints belonged to the defendant. Rather, he indicated that by applying the ACE–V process, the prints were "individualized" to the defendant. By contrast, Detective Lieutenant Brian O'Hara properly testified that in his *opinion* they belonged to the defendant.

. . . Fingerprint experts should not be permitted to testify in the manner of Detective Lieutenant Drawec, because it is not opinion testimony. . . . No discipline, much less fingerprint analysis, has ever been shown to produce results that achieve absolute certainty. Although some courts have looked on fingerprint analysis as the gold standard of virtually all science, this view recently has been criticized by the 2009 report of the National Research Council.

While we normally leave the humbling of inflated opinions to cross-examination, there is a danger that the mystique of fingerprint identification, which has had a captivating hold on the criminal justice system and society at large for more than one hundred years, is such that cross-examination may not be enough to rectify the effect of a fingerprint expert's use of such terms as "individualized," "absolute," and "match" when testifying, as opposed to presenting the testimony as his or her "opinion" that the latent fingerprints are the defendant's.

While the "science" of fingerprint analysis may be valid, claims by its practitioners that the process can establish identity with absolute certainty are not. . . . Claims of absolute certainty are particularly irresponsible by a science based in large part on human judgment. In the context of a criminal trial, I would hold that, in the interest of maintaining the integrity of the fact-finding process, in the interests of justice and fair play, fingerprint experts be prohibited from expressing the results of their analysis as absolutely establishing identity, or individualizing fingerprints to a particular individual to the exclusion of all others. They should be confined to an expression of personal opinion that the latent print belongs to the defendant.

Trial counsel did exemplary work here in cross-examination. In addition, Detective Lieutenant O'Hara's proper *opinion* testimony at the verification

---

22. As our discussion of the NAS Report reflects, there is tension in the report between its assessments that, on the one hand, "it seems plausible that a careful comparison of two impressions can accurately discern whether or not they had a common source," but that, on the other, "merely following the steps of ACE-V does not imply that one is proceeding in a scientific manner or producing reliable results." We are not able to resolve that tension at this time, as the dialogue in the relevant community appears to be a continuing one, but nothing in this opinion should be read to suggest that the existence of the NAS Report alone will require the conduct of *Daubert-Lanigan* hearings as to the general reliability of expert opinions concerning fingerprint identifications. However, based on the NAS Report, we can say this much at the present time: Testimony to the effect that a latent print matches, or is "individualized" to, a known print, if it is to be offered, should be presented as an opinion, not a fact, and opinions expressing absolute certainty about, or the infallibility of, an "individualization" of a print should be avoided. . . .

stage of this ACE–V analysis, the defendant's own testimony, and other evidence identified by the court resulted in no prejudice to the defendant.

STATE v. McPHAUL

808 S.E.2d 294, 304-05 (N.C. 2017)

Calabria, Justice.

[Appellant McPhaul was charged with assault with intent to rob and murder a pizza delivery person, Tyler Lloyd. Lloyd was beaten with a baseball bat. The state called a fingerprint expert, Trudy Wood, to testify that McPhaul's known finger impressions "matched" latent fingerprints found on Lloyd's truck and on a food box seized during the search of the house from where the online pizza order was made. McPhaul filed a motion to exclude the testimony under *Daubert*.]

Wood testified that she uses the same examination technique as is commonly used in the field of latent print identification, and she employed this procedure while conducting her examination in this case. However, when Wood testified to her ultimate conclusions, she was unable to establish that she reliably applied the procedure to the facts of this case:

> [THE STATE:]   As to State's 35-A [and] Item 113, can you again demonstrate to the Jury the comparison between 35-A and 113?
>
> [WOOD:]   State's Exhibit 35-A is a latent print from the driver's door and it contains the left index finger of a fingerprint card bearing the name of [defendant].
>
> Q. And upon what is that conclusion based?
>
> A. My training and experience.
>
> Q. In looking at the individual minutia with those two fingerprints; is that correct?
>
> A. That's correct, the process I explained earlier. . . .
>
> [THE STATE:]   Item 109-A and 113, can you again demonstrate to the Jury what comparison those impressions are based on your examination?
>
> [WOOD:]   State's Exhibit 109-A from the Domino's chicken wing box, letter A, is identified as the right middle finger compared to the fingerprint card bearing the name of [defendant].
>
> Q. Is your conclusion, again, based upon the same procedure you described to the Jury?
>
> A. That's correct.
>
> Q. Looking for the striated minutia in that fingerprint and that latent print?
>
> A. That's correct.

Pursuant to [North Carolina Evidence] Rule 702(a)(3), this testimony is insufficient. To satisfy Rule 702's three-pronged reliability test, an expert witness must be able to explain not only the abstract methodology underlying the witness's opinion, but also that the witness reliably applied that methodology to the facts of the case. Wood previously testified that during an examination, she compares the pattern type and minutia points of the latent print and known impressions until she is satisfied that there are "sufficient characteristics and sequence of the similarities" to conclude that the prints match. However, Wood provided no such detail in testifying how she arrived at her actual conclusions *in this case*. Without further explanation for her conclusions, Wood implicitly asked the jury to accept her expert opinion that the prints matched. Since Wood failed to demonstrate that she "applied the principles and methods reliably to the facts of the case," as required by Rule 702(a)(3), we hold that the trial court abused its discretion by admitting this testimony.

. . . Defendant contends that absent Wood's testimony, there was a reasonable probability that the jury would have found him not guilty, because Lloyd could not identify defendant as his attacker, and the fingerprint testimony was the only evidence that tied defendant to the actual crime scene. We disagree.

The State presented abundant additional evidence to assist the jury, including: [police] seizure, during the lawful search of defendant's home, of items matching the description of Lloyd's stolen property; the aluminum bat discovered underneath an immediately adjacent residence; the close proximity between defendant's residence and the unsecured wireless network used to place the Domino's order; and the similarity between the descriptions of the suspects that Lloyd and the [confidential informant] independently provided to [police]. . . . In light of all of the evidence pointing to defendant's guilt, we conclude that he was not prejudiced by the erroneous admission of Wood's expert testimony. . . .

BRANDON GARRETT, THE RELIABLE
APPLICATION OF FINGERPRINT EVIDENCE

66 UCLA L. Rev. 64, 68 (2018)

. . . Nothing made error rates in fingerprinting more publicly salient than the error in the [2004] Brandon Mayfield case, in which a lawyer in Portland, Oregon was falsely accused of playing a role in the Madrid terrorist bombing based on erroneous fingerprint matches by multiple FBI analysts. An FBI expert had called it a "100 percent" certain match, but it was wrong, as Spanish authorities discovered. In response to the error, the Department of Justice made a series of recommendations for improved handling of latent fingerprint analysis. . . .

The Presidential Council of Advisors on Science and Technology (PCAST) 2016 report concluded that while "foundationally valid," fingerprint analysis should never be presented in court without evidence of its error rates and of the proficiency or reliability of not just the method, but the particular examiner using the method. The PCAST report noted that error rate studies had now been conducted on latent fingerprint analysis. In particular, two black box studies (referring to studies that independently test experts for errors using realistic materials) were conducted that were fairly methodologically sound and found nontrivial error rates: The false-positive error rate "could be as high as 1 error in 306 cases," based on an FBI study; or a rate of "1 error in 18 cases," based on a study by the Miami-Dade police laboratory. In the PCAST report, the focus was also placed more squarely on the individual expert: If the technique is a black box, and relies on the experience and training of a particular person, then how reliable is that person? Courts had typically not focused on that question. . . .

The *McPhaul* opinion does not provide a roadmap for judges to elicit a record which allows them to conclude whether an expert reliably applied a method to the facts of the case. Scientific sources, such as the PCAST report, do provide that guidance. Judges should demand full records concerning an expert's methods and what evidence they relied upon in their analysis, though that still would not entirely open up the black box. After all, what entitles the expert to conclude, after having observed visual similarities, that two prints are identified as coming from the same source to some degree of likelihood? Such a conclusion is difficult to verify, even where one knows in greater detail what the inputs were. That is why, in order to truly address the concerns raised both in *McPhaul* and the PCAST report, a judge should require that an expert disclose full documentation of every step in their examination process and qualify their conclusions.

NATIONAL DISTRICT ATTORNEY'S ASSOCIATION, NOVEMBER 16, 2016, LETTER TO WHITE HOUSE IN RESPONSE TO PCAST REPORT

Dear President Obama:

On behalf of the National District Attorneys Association (NDAA), the nation's largest prosecutor organization, . . . I write to you today regarding the Report to the President-Forensic Science in Criminal Courts: Ensuring Scientific Validity of Feature-Comparison Methods ("the Report"). The NDAA takes issue with, and has substantial concern about, the logic of the report and the manner in which it portrays several forensic disciplines. . . .

According to PCAST . . . scientific validity for subjective feature comparison methods can be established only through numerous, properly constructed, independent black box studies with a variety of samples from a diverse population of features. The report then posits that there is an insufficient number of these properly designed black box studies that comply with PCAST's unilaterally imposed criteria to establish the scientific validity of several of the disciplines discussed. . . .

By wrongly labeling the forensic feature comparison disciplines as belonging to the field of metrology, the report conveniently overlooks the ancient debate over precisely what constitutes "science." The answer to this question depends fundamentally upon which philosopher one finds most compelling and which definition one finds most persuasive. . . . Under many definitions, the feature comparison methods that are the subject of the report certainly incorporate aspects of science. These methods however, also independently constitute "technical" and "specialized knowledge" under Federal Rule of Evidence 702. Significantly, "technical" and "specialized knowledge" are not fields of knowledge for which *Daubert* requires scientific validity. . . .

PAUL GIANNELLI, FORENSIC SCIENCE:
DAUBERT'S FAILURE

68 Case W. Res. L. Rev. 869, 871-75 (2018)

Of the 329 exonerations based on DNA testing since 1989, more than one-quarter involved convictions based on "pattern" evidence — like hair samples, ballistics, tire tracks, and bite marks — testified to by so-called experts.... Why didn't the Supreme Court's "junk science" decision, *Daubert* ..., prevent or restrict the admissibility of testimony based on flawed forensic techniques? After all, *Daubert* was decided in 1993, twenty-five years ago....

Notwithstanding *Daubert's* promise, scholars soon discerned its uneven application in civil and criminal cases .... The title of a 2005 article summed up the state of the law — *"The (Near) Irrelevance of* Daubert *to Criminal Justice."* In short, in the criminal context, courts applied *Daubert*-lite....

... [T]he system's failure can be traced back to its inability to demand and properly evaluate foundational research — i.e., *Daubert's* first factor, empirical testing. Indeed, the justice system may be institutionally incapable of applying *Daubert* in criminal cases.

A different paradigm is needed, one that assigns an independent agency the responsibility of evaluating foundational research.... [T]his approach was recently recommended by the National Commission on Forensic Science and the President's Council of Advisors on Science and Technology ("PCAST"). Both recommended that the National Institute of Standards and Technology ("NIST") evaluate all forensic disciplines on a continuing basis, thereby injecting much needed scientific expertise into the criminal justice system.

JENNIFER L. MNOOKIN, THE UNCERTAIN
FUTURE OF FORENSIC SCIENCE

147 Daedalus 99, 107 (Fall 2018)

... [P]attern identification fields have faced modest, but not transformative, reform. Half full: the emergence of some credible research; the recognition by many practitioners that they are engaged in a probabilistic enterprise; substantial focus on these issues from two extremely prestigious, highly legitimate bodies of experts, NAS and PCAST; the creation of the NCFS [National Commission on Forensic Science] and a NIST [National Institute of Standards and Technology]-led effort that calls on the forensic science disciplines to identify standards and approaches in need of reform. Half empty: relevant research remains limited and many fields still lack adequate validation; though probabilistic in theory, trial testimony remains grounded on experience and subjective judgment; both judges and practitioners have largely resisted the conclusions of the NAS and PCAST reports; the NCFS no longer exists....

The future of forensic science remains uncertain, but our best chance for substantial ongoing improvements rests on the creation, or re-creation, of an entity akin to the NCFS. Simply put, we need some institutional structure, some body, separate from the courts, from adversarial advocates, and from practitioners themselves, a body that includes representatives from all these arena along with accomplished research scientists.

DAVID A. SKLANSKY & STEPHEN C. YEAZELL, COMPARATIVE LAW WITHOUT LEAVING HOME: WHAT CIVIL PROCEDURE CAN TEACH CRIMINAL PROCEDURE, AND VICE VERSA

94 Geo. L.J. 683, 728–731 (2006)

Ever since evidence law emerged as an integrated, systematic body of doctrine in the late 1800s and early 1900s, it has treated criminal and civil cases largely alike. . . . When efforts to codify evidence law began in earnest in the mid-twentieth century, the codifiers never proposed separate sets of rules for criminal and civil cases, and apparently never even considered doing so. . . . On the state level as well as the federal level, evidence law today is dominated by codes that apply to both civil and criminal cases. . . .

Of course there are exceptions to this general pattern of evidence rules spanning the civil-criminal divide. Some evidence rules apply only in criminal cases or only in civil cases. . . . [And not] all variations in evidence law across the criminal-civil divide are explicit. Judges are widely believed to apply the character evidence ban, for example, less strictly in civil cases than in criminal cases. . . . [But special evidence] rules for civil or criminal cases, whether express or unstated, are customarily viewed with skepticism. And that skepticism can be and has been a powerful force for reform.

The most striking recent example pertains to expert testimony. A decade ago the Supreme Court directed trial judges to begin screening expert testimony for "reliability," a mandate since codified in Federal Rule of Evidence 702. The new requirement was announced and elaborated by the Court in a series of civil cases, and it responded to concerns specifically focused on civil litigation — the widespread complaints about "junk science" in the courtroom. But the Court drew no distinction between civil and criminal cases. It would have been awkward to do so, because the Court justified the requirement of "reliability" as a gloss on the provisions of the Federal Rules of Evidence governing relevance and expert testimony, and those rules, like most other provisions of the Federal Rules of Evidence, themselves drew no distinction between civil and criminal cases. Nonetheless, lower courts, perhaps reading between the lines of the *United States Reports*, have assessed the "reliability" of expert testimony in civil cases much more rigorously than in criminal cases. Until quite recently, forensic science evidence — fingerprinting, ballistics, handwriting identification, hair analysis, bite mark identification, etc. — received something of a free pass, even when there was little or no proof of its reliability.

The double standard for the admissibility of expert testimony led some observers to grow skeptical of both the possibility and the wisdom of unified rules of evidence. But the resignation was unwarranted. The formal equivalence of treatment of expert testimony in civil and criminal trials is slowly and belatedly making itself felt in the courtroom. Forensic science evidence that has gone unquestioned for decades is suddenly under scrutiny. For example, several trial judges have excluded or significantly limited expert testimony by handwriting examiners — something that virtually never happened up until a few years ago. Even fingerprint examiners have come under pressure, from scholars if not yet from courts, to testify with more care and to qualify their claims of 100% accuracy. It is hard not to see this as an improvement. It is also hard to believe that it would have happened so rapidly were it not for the presumption, however loose, that rules of evidence announced in civil cases should also apply in criminal trials.

6. Digital Forensics

UNITED STATES v. PEMBROOK

119 F.Supp.3d 577 (E.D. Mich. 2015)

MICHELSON, District Judge.

On April 22, 2014, four men attempted to rob a jewelry store in Grand Rapids, Michigan, but, after one was shot by a store owner, they fled without merchandise. Later that same day, three men stole $1,500,000 in Rolex watches from a jewelry store in West Bloomfield, Michigan. . . . The Government believes Defendants are responsible for the robberies in part because of what it learned from data it obtained — without a warrant — from cellular-phone service providers. In particular, logs from the cell towers close by the two jewelry stores allegedly indicate that . . . [defendants] Calhoun, Briley, and Pembrook traveled together (at least roughly) from Philadelphia, Pennsylvania, to Wisconsin, to the location of the two robberies, and then back to Philadelphia.

Calhoun . . . seeks to exclude from trial the testimony of the Government's cell-site data expert [Christopher Hess]. . . .

Some background on how cellular towers communicate with cellular phones helps to understand how the Government used cell-site data to investigate the two jewelry-store robberies and the associated expert testimony the Government plans to elicit at trial.

For a cellular phone to receive a call, send a text message, or download a webpage, it must communicate with a cellular tower. . . . A cellular phone automatically searches for a signal from nearby towers and "[o]nce the phone locates a tower, it submits a unique identifier — its 'registration' information — to the tower so that any outgoing and incoming calls can be routed through the correct tower." *United States v. Powell*, 943 F. Supp.2d 759, 767 (E.D. Mich. 2013) (citing Timothy Stapleton, Note, The Electronic Communications Privacy Act and Cell Location Data, 73 Brook. L. Rev. 383, 387 (2007)). "Nearby" is a relative term: it can range from a block (maybe less) to a couple miles (maybe more) depending on the tower density in the area. . . . Further, although a cell phone often registers with its closest tower, "a variety of factors including physical obstructions and topography can determine which tower services a particular phone." *United States v. Evans*, 892 F. Supp. 2d 949, 952 (N.D.Ill.2012). . . .

Cellular service providers (e.g., Verizon Wireless) keep track of cell-phone communications with their towers . . .; courts refer to these logs as "cell-site data" or "cell-site location information" ("CSLI" for short) . . . . Although, a cell phone "regularly communicates with cell towers in its network" even in "idle" mode, *Evans*, 892 F.Supp.2d at 952, the Government avers that the cell-site data at issue in this case only corresponds to active cell-phone use, for example, receiving a call or sending a text . . . . Cell-site data might also include the "sector" of a tower to which the phone connected. For example, a tower's 360 degree coverage area might be partitioned into three 120 degree sectors. . . .

This cell-site data permits investigators to determine the location of a cell phone at a particular time. Assume cell-cite data show that, on June 1, 2015, a cell phone using the phone number (734) xxx–1234 initiated a call via a tower located at Liberty Street and 1st Street, in Ann Arbor, Michigan at 12:00 p.m. and terminated that call while connected with a tower located at Liberty and 5th Avenue at 12:04 p.m. With a map showing that Liberty runs east-west (with 1st Street intersecting Liberty west of 5th Avenue) and with information from the cellular-service provider that the (734) xxx–1234 account is John Smith's, this cell-site data indicates (but does not conclusively prove) that Smith's phone traveled east on Liberty (or a parallel street) in Ann Arbor just after noon on June 1, 2015. An examination of the sector information might allow further refinement of the phone's geographic location.

. . . Calhoun says that Hess' opinion is based on the "theory of granulization"— a theory untested by the scientific community. . . .

The basis for Calhoun's . . . argument, that Hess' testimony relies on an untested theory, is a single case: *United States v. Evans*, [*supra*]. There, the Government sought to rely upon the testimony of a cell-site expert to show that the criminal defendant, Antonio Evans, was in the area where a kidnapping took place. The court explained that the theory of granulization involved (1) identifying the cell tower, sector, and sector-coverage direction used by the phone during the relevant time period; (2) estimating "the range of each [sector's] coverage based on the proximity of the tower to other towers in the area," and (3) predicting "where the coverage area of one tower will overlap with the coverage area of another." Applying this theory to the facts at hand, the Government's expert intended to testify that Evans' cell-phone used two towers at the time of the kidnapping and that "[t]he building where the victim was held [fell] squarely within the coverage overlap of [those] two towers." The court found one significant problem was that the expert's coverage-overlap theory assumed that Evans' phone "used the towers closest to it at the time of the calls" without accounting for the possibility that Evans' [phone] might have connected to other towers because of signal obstruction or network traffic. "Second," the court reasoned, "the granulization theory remains wholly untested by the scientific community, while other methods of historical cell site analysis can be and have been tested by scientists." *Id*. "Given that multiple factors [could] affect the signal strength of a tower and that [the expert's] chosen methodology ha[d] received no scrutiny outside the law enforcement community," the court concluded that the Government had not carried its burden in establishing that the granulization method was reliable.

Hess' proposed testimony is not similar enough to that excluded in *Evans* to justify that result here. The Government explains that it "is not attempting to put a particular cell phone in [a] very specific location via Agent Hess' testimony"; instead, it "is attempting to show how the four phones in question originated in the Philadelphia, Pennsylvania [*sic*] on April 21, 2014, traveled in a similar pattern over the next few days, were in the Grand Rapids and West Bloomfield areas around the time of the robberies, and traveled back to Philadelphia on April 22-23, 2014." (Gov't Resp. to Mot. to Exclude at 10.) The Government "concedes" that cell-site data cannot place Defendants "in a precise location." (Id. at 11.) Thus, to the extent that Hess' testimony essentially consists of placing the four cell phones at issue in this case within a general geographic region, i.e., within a couple miles of a particular tower, the Court is not persuaded that Hess' testimony is based on the granulization theory or that *Evans* is on point.

As for testimony more akin to Hess'—that, because a log shows that a particular phone connected to a particular tower at a particular time, it can be inferred that a phone was within that tower's coverage area at that time—a number of courts have found such testimony to be based on reliable methods. . . . And to the extent that Hess has made assumptions about signal strength that call into question his estimate of where the phones were located at particular times, Defendants can test those assumptions on cross exam[ination]. . . .

As for Calhoun's argument that the Court cannot even tell if Hess' testimony is based on reliable methods because the Government's Rule 16 [discovery response] letter lacks sufficient disclosure, the Court mostly disagrees. . . .

It appears that Calhoun's real complaint . . . is that Hess did not disclose the "source" of certain assertions. . . . The following are among Hess' assertions that Calhoun complains of: even if the phone has a better signal to a tower different than the one providing service, "the phone will not randomly reselect to an adjacent tower unless the tower is on its 'neighbor list' which is controlled by the network service provider"; "[a]s the phone moves, it will choose a new serving cell based on signal strength and neighbor list"; a cell tower can be located anywhere; there are more towers in urban areas than in rural ones; and "[a] typical cell tower has THREE, 120° sectors." . . . Calhoun says that Hess has not disclosed "any source for these so-called 'principals.'" . . .

On this limited point the Court agrees with Calhoun. Although Federal Rule of Criminal Procedure 16 does not require detailed disclosure, . . . it does demand that the Government "describe . . . the bases and reasons for [its expert's] opinions," Fed. R. Crim. P. 16, and, according to the accompanying advisory committee note, that description "should cover not only written and oral reports, tests, reports, and investigations, but any information that might be recognized as a legitimate basis for an opinion under Federal Rule of Evidence 703," Fed. R. Crim. P. 16 advisory committee note (1993). Indeed, at oral argument, counsel for the Government indicated that they would explore whether more detailed information could be provided. Thus, the Court will order that the Government supplement its Rule 16 disclosure to explain the source of Hess' "Basic Princip[le]s Utilized in Record Analysis."

STATE v. PRATT

128 A.3d 883, 888-95 (Vt. 2015)

DOOLEY, Justice.

[Defendant Pratt was convicted of sexual abuse of his twelve-year-old niece. The primary evidence against Pratt at trial was a letter written by the niece detailing the abuse, eventually shared with her school principal; and information, recovered from his cell phone through software called Cellebrite, linking to pornographic websites, including one linking to a video involving a teenage girl.]

[D]efendant argues that the court erred in admitting the forensic expert's testimony regarding his use of the Cellebrite software for retrieving the contents of defendant's cell phone. Defendant's primary claim is that, while the forensic expert had a "general understanding of how the program works[,] . . . he did not have any understanding of the programming behind the software." Defendant also challenges the reliability of the testimony, arguing that the State was unable to satisfy . . . *Daubert*. . . . Specifically, defendant contends that the forensic expert's responses were "conclusory"; that he self-tested the program "using other software equally under scrutiny"; and that he read some periodicals about the program and is aware of its capabilities, but has no knowledge of its error rates and believes the program is reliable merely "because it [is] the most popular program used to examine cell phones and because he was told it was reliable."

. . . [S]everal other courts have taken a liberal approach in admitting testimony regarding computer software and other technical devices upon reliability foundations similar to that laid by the State here. Closely on point is *United States v. Chiaradio*, 684 F.3d 265 (1st Cir. 2012). In *Chiaradio* an FBI agent testified to his investigatory technique of using an enhanced peer-to-peer (EP2P) file sharing program to identify Internet Protocol addresses where child pornography has been downloaded. The defendant objected to the court's admission of the agent's testimony under Federal Rule of Evidence 702 because the EP2P technology was "too untested to form an adequate foundation" for the agent's testimony. In affirming the judgment of the trial court, the circuit court concluded:

> Although [the agent] was not a programmer, did not know the program's authors, and had never seen the source code, he had significant specialized experience with both EP2P and the manual re-creation of EP2P sessions. He testified that the program, with respect to identifying the source of particular files, had no error rate. He also demonstrated how the results of an EP2P investigation could be independently verified and made it clear that EP2P had never yielded a false positive.

Also on point is *Krause v. State*, 243 S.W.3d 95 (Tex. App. 2007). In *Krause* the court considered the qualifications of a forensic examiner using specialized software called I-Look to create an exact duplicate of the defendant's computer hard drive in order to search for evidence of child pornography. The forensic examiner testified that the hard drive was an exact copy because the "Hash value" — or "fingerprint" — of the copy matched that of the original. . . . With respect to the reliability of the software, the court stated:

Regarding the clarity with which the underlying scientific theory and technique can be explained to the court, [the expert] explained that he had used I-Look on computer files taken from [the defendant's] external hard drive and computers. I-Look indexed the files, and [the expert] was able to retrieve files containing child pornography from [the defendant's] hard drives. When [the expert] took a hard drive from a computer, he used a program like I-Look to automate the task of searching and finding the files on it. An image of the drive was taken; the files were copied, and I-Look validated the copy by a "Hash value," an algorithm that verifies the image. [The expert's] testimony established I-Look's reliability.

. . .

Forensic investigation increasingly requires the use of computer software or other technological devices for the extraction of data. While an investigator must have specialized knowledge in the use of the particular software or device, it is not required — nor is it practical — for an investigator to have expertise in or knowledge about the underlying programming, mathematical formulas, or other innerworkings of the software. . . .

As to the forensic expert's qualifications, he testified that he had over 800 hours of training in the forensic examination of computer hard drives, digital media, and cell phones and a week of specific training in Cellebrite with a company that specializes in training and assistance to law enforcement. He also testified that he has used the program to extract data from hundreds of phones since 2010. He conceded that someone in his position would not be able to speak about the underlying programming, stating, "[W]e're actually trained . . . to be very careful about how we talk about how the software and hardware works . . . we're not experts on that." He testified, however, that he read about the program, what it can do, what information it can reveal, and how he can search and sort through the data.

As to the reliability of the program, the forensic expert testified that "numerous agencies use the software" and that it is "the most popular hardware and software solution for examining cell phones." He testified that the program is routinely tested in the forensics community; the results are tested in his agency by defense experts and through peer review of data reports; and that because the program is commercially available, it is subject to testing. He also stated that he self-tests his extraction results by comparing the computerized results to the results of a manual examination to verify the data that has been extracted and that he compares the results of his extraction with results from other forensic programs that overlap with Cellebrite. He further stated that he has learned of the program's reliability in the forensic industry through his trainings, correspondence with colleagues, and email lists. He testified that, although the program's error rate never was expressly discussed in his training, the program's limitations were. . . .

Furthermore, any deficiencies in the program should be drawn out through the adversarial process. . . . Counsel for defendant had access to the cell phone and had the opportunity to have it scanned by his own computer experts. The trial court here properly exercised its discretion as gatekeeper; the software used by the forensic expert hardly can be characterized as "junk science." It is left to the fact finder to weigh its credibility. . . . *Affirmed.*

PRIVILEGES

"And, because a princess can't be forced to testify against her prince, they lived happily ever after."

A. IN GENERAL

Privilege rules differ from other rules of evidence in four important ways.

First, privileges are not just rules of admissibility. They govern not just whether particular evidence can be introduced at trial, but also whether disclosure of certain information can be compelled *before* trial. Indeed, the procedural context in which privileges most often are encountered is not an objection to the introduction of evidence at trial, but an objection to compelled disclosure, either through a grand jury subpoena or in the process of civil discovery.

Second, some evidentiary privileges—those that pertain to confidential communications with lawyers and certain other professionals—parallel rules of professional responsibility that impose duties of confidentiality. Usually the contours of the privilege and the duty of confidentiality coincide. But not always. The attorney-client privilege, in particular, is conceptually distinct from, and does not always coincide with, the duty of confidentiality you study in a course on professional responsibility.

Third, as the materials below explain, privileges differ from other rules of evidence in their purpose. Most other rules of evidence aim, at least in part, to improve the accuracy of factfinding. Privileges do not. In fact, it is widely acknowledged that privileges undermine the factfinding process and impair its accuracy. Privileges exist not because of their effect on factfinding but in spite of it. They are typically justified on the ground that they serve some goal outside the litigation process, most often the protection of some relationship that is thought to be socially beneficial and to require confidentiality.

Fourth and finally, privileges are not codified in the F.R.E., for reasons explained in the materials below. The sole provision of the F.R.E. that addresses privileges, Rule 501, directs federal courts to continue to develop and to apply a federal common law of privileges—except with respect to civil claims or defenses as to which state law provides the rule of decision. For those issues—typically (although not always) the claims and defenses raised in diversity cases—Rule 501 treats privileges the way that the second sentence of F.R.E. 601 treats competence: as, in effect, a matter of substance rather than procedure.

[F.R.E. 501; C.E.C. §911]

McCORMICK ON EVIDENCE

§72, at 1:465-67 (Kenneth S. Broun ed., 7th ed. 2013)

The overwhelming majority of all rules of evidence have as their ultimate justification some tendency to promote the objectives set forward by the conventional witness' oath, the presentation of "the truth, the whole truth, and nothing but the truth." Thus such prominent exclusionary rules as the hearsay rule, the opinion rule, the rule excluding bad character as evidence of crime, and the original documents (or "Best Evidence") rule, have as their common purpose the elucidation of the truth, a purpose that these rules seek to effect by operating to exclude evidence which is unreliable or which is calculated to prejudice or mislead.

By contrast the rules of privilege, of which the most familiar are the rule protecting against self-incrimination and those shielding the confidentiality of communications between husband and wife, attorney and client, and physician and patient, are not designed or intended to facilitate the fact-finding process or to safeguard its integrity. Their effect instead is clearly inhibitive; rather than facilitating the illumination of truth, they shut out the light. . . . Their warrant is the protection of interests and relationships which, rightly or wrongly, are regarded as of sufficient social importance to justify some sacrifice of availability of evidence relevant to the administration of justice.

CHRISTOPHER B. MUELLER & LAIRD C. KIRKPATRICK, EVIDENCE

§5.6, at 309-11 (5th ed. 2012)

As originally proposed, Article V of the Federal Rules of Evidence would have codified the law of privileges into 13 rules. Nine of those rules would have defined specific privileges covering required reports, lawyer-client and psychotherapist-patient communications, spousal testimony, communications to clergymen, political vote, trade secrets, secrets of state, and informant's identity. Another rule would have provided that only the privileges set forth in Article V or other act of Congress would be recognized in federal courts, thereby superseding the common law of privileges, and ignoring state privilege law. The three remaining rules would have addressed procedural incidents [of the] privileges such as waiver by voluntary disclosure, protection of privileged matter disclosed under court order, and the propriety of making adverse comments or suggesting adverse inferences based on a party's claim of privilege.

When Congress considered the proposed rules, Article V turned out to be particularly controversial for a number of reasons. First, it did not include some privileges, such as those covering communications between physician and patient, between spouses, and between journalists and sources, thereby arousing the opposition of many who supported those privileges. Second, proposed Rule 509 redefined the scope of the privileges covering state secrets [and] official information, and the latter was an exceedingly sensitive issue for Congress because the rules were being considered at the time of the Watergate scandal, in which an embattled President Nixon claimed a privilege with respect to conversations with his advisors relating to that affair. Third, the proposed privilege rules would have applied even in diversity cases and other cases where state law supplied the rule of decision, thereby overriding state privilege law.

Unable to resolve the controversies surrounding proposed Article V, Congress ultimately rejected the attempt to codify the federal law of privileges. . . . The legislative history makes clear that congressional rejection of proposed Article V was not to be construed as disapproval of the specific privileges contained therein. Congress intended to leave privilege law where it was, and not to freeze the evolution of the federal common law with respect to creation, modification, or repeal of specific privileges. Congress did, however, remove privileges from the general rulemaking power of the Supreme Court and adopted legislation providing that no formal rules of privilege promulgated by the Court could become effective until approved by Act of Congress. [28 U.S.C. §2074(b).]

B. ATTORNEY-CLIENT PRIVILEGE

[C.E.C. §§912, 950–962]

1. Introduction

It makes sense to start the study of privileges with the attorney-client privilege for several reasons. As the Supreme Court notes in the decision excerpted below, the attorney-client privilege is among the oldest privileges for confidential communications. It is the model, in many ways, for most other professional privileges. It is probably the most heavily litigated privilege. It may be the most zealously defended privilege, in part because, since most judges started out as lawyers, it hits close to home. Nonetheless, the privilege has always been controversial. Critics keep noting that it offers tremendous assistance to wrongdoers—and that it coincides suspiciously well with the professional interests of the bar. So before you get enmeshed in the intricacies of the privilege—its elements and its exceptions—it is worth considering the big picture. Why do we have an attorney-client privilege, and should we stick with it?

SWIDLER & BERLIN v. UNITED STATES

524 U.S. 399 (1998)

Chief Justice REHNQUIST delivered the opinion of the Court.

Petitioner, an attorney, made notes of an initial interview with a client shortly before the client's death. The Government, represented by the Office of Independent Counsel, now seeks his notes for use in a criminal investigation. We hold that the notes are protected by the attorney-client privilege.

This dispute arises out of an investigation conducted by the Office of the Independent Counsel into whether various individuals made false statements, obstructed justice, or committed other crimes during investigations of the 1993 dismissal of employees from the White House Travel Office. Vincent W. Foster, Jr., was Deputy White House Counsel when the firings occurred. In July, 1993, Foster met with petitioner James Hamilton, an attorney at petitioner Swidler & Berlin, to seek legal representation concerning possible congressional or other investigations of the firings. During a 2-hour meeting, Hamilton took three pages of handwritten notes. One of the first entries in the notes is the word "Privileged." Nine days later, Foster committed suicide.

In December 1995, a federal grand jury, at the request of the Independent Counsel, issued subpoenas to petitioners Hamilton and Swidler & Berlin for, inter alia, Hamilton's handwritten notes of his meeting with Foster. Petitioners filed a motion to quash, arguing that the notes were protected by the attorney-client privilege. [The district court granted the motion, but the Court of Appeals reversed.]

The attorney-client privilege is one of the oldest recognized privileges for confidential communications. *Upjohn Co. v. United States*, 449 U.S. 383, 389 (1981); *Hunt v. Blackburn*, 128 U.S. 464, 470 (1888). The privilege is intended to encourage "full and frank communication between attorneys and their clients and thereby promote broader public interests in the observance of law and the administration of justice." *Upjohn, supra*, at 389. The issue presented here is the scope of that privilege; more particularly, the extent to which the privilege survives the death of the client. Our interpretation of the privilege's scope is guided by "the principles of the common law ... as interpreted by the courts ... in the light of reason and experience." Fed. Rule Evid. 501; *Funk v. United States*, 290 U.S. 371 (1933).

The Independent Counsel argues that the attorney-client privilege should not prevent disclosure of confidential communications where the client has died and the information is relevant to a criminal proceeding. There is some authority for this position. One state appellate court, *Cohen v. Jenkintown Cab Co.*, 238 Pa. Super. 456, 357 A.2d 689 (1976), and the Court of Appeals below have held the privilege may be subject to posthumous exceptions in certain circumstances. . . .

But other than these two decisions, cases addressing the existence of the privilege after death — most involving the testamentary exception — uniformly presume the privilege survives, even if they do not so hold. . . . [The cases] view testamentary disclosure of communications as an exception to the privilege: "[T]he general rule with respect to confidential communications ... is that such communications are privileged during the testator's lifetime and, also, after the testator's death unless sought to be disclosed in litigation between the testator's heirs." [*United States v. Osborn*, 561 F.2d 1334, 1340 (CA9 1977).] The rationale for such disclosure is that it furthers the client's intent.[2]

. . . Commentators on the law also recognize that the general rule is that the attorney-client privilege continues after death. See, *e.g.*, 8 Wigmore, Evidence §2323 (McNaughton rev. 1961); Frankel, The Attorney-Client Privilege After the Death of the Client, 6 Geo. J. Legal Ethics 45, 78–79 (1992); 1 J. Strong, McCormick on Evidence §94, p. 348 (4th ed. 1992). Undoubtedly, as the Independent Counsel emphasizes, various commentators have criticized this rule, urging that the privilege should be abrogated after the client's death where extreme injustice would result, as long as disclosure would not seriously undermine the privilege by deterring client communication. See, *e.g.*, C. Mueller & L. Kirkpatrick, 2 Federal Evidence §199, at 380–381 (2d ed. 1994); Restatement (Third) of the Law Governing Lawyers §127, Comment d (Proposed Final Draft No. 1, Mar. 29, 1996). But even these critics clearly recognize that established law supports the continuation of the privilege and that a contrary rule would be a modification of the common law. See, *e.g.*, Mueller & Kirkpatrick, *supra*, at 379; Restatement of the Law Governing Lawyers, supra,

---

2. About half the States have codified the testamentary exception by providing that a personal representative of the deceased can waive the privilege when heirs or devisees claim through the deceased client (as opposed to parties claiming against the estate, for whom the privilege is not waived). . . .

§127, Comment c; 24 C. Wright & K. Graham, Federal Practice and Procedure §5498, p. 483 (1986).

Despite the scholarly criticism, we think there are weighty reasons that counsel in favor of posthumous application. Knowing that communications will remain confidential even after death encourages the client to communicate fully and frankly with counsel. While the fear of disclosure, and the consequent withholding of information from counsel, may be reduced if disclosure is limited to posthumous disclosure in a criminal context, it seems unreasonable to assume that it vanishes altogether. Clients may be concerned about reputation, civil liability, or possible harm to friends or family. Posthumous disclosure of such communications may be as feared as disclosure during the client's lifetime.

The Independent Counsel suggests, however, that his proposed exception would have little to no effect on the client's willingness to confide in his attorney. He reasons that only clients intending to perjure themselves will be chilled by a rule of disclosure after death, as opposed to truthful clients or those asserting their Fifth Amendment privilege. This is because for the latter group, communications disclosed by the attorney after the client's death purportedly will reveal only information that the client himself would have revealed if alive.

The Independent Counsel assumes, incorrectly we believe, that the privilege is analogous to the Fifth Amendment's protection against self-incrimination. But as suggested above, the privilege serves much broader purposes. Clients consult attorneys for a wide variety of reasons, only one of which involves possible criminal liability. Many attorneys act as counselors on personal and family matters, where, in the course of obtaining the desired advice, confidences about family members or financial problems must be revealed in order to assure sound legal advice. The same is true of owners of small businesses who may regularly consult their attorneys about a variety of problems arising in the course of the business. These confidences may not come close to any sort of admission of criminal wrongdoing, but nonetheless be matters which the client would not wish divulged.

The contention that the attorney is being required to disclose only what the client could have been required to disclose is at odds with the basis for the privilege even during the client's lifetime. In related cases, we have said that the loss of evidence admittedly caused by the privilege is justified in part by the fact that without the privilege, the client may not have made such communications in the first place. . . . This is true of disclosure before and after the client's death. Without assurance of the privilege's posthumous application, the client may very well not have made disclosures to his attorney at all, so the loss of evidence is more apparent than real. In the case at hand, it seems quite plausible that Foster, perhaps already contemplating suicide, may not have sought legal advice from Hamilton if he had not been assured the conversation was privileged.

The Independent Counsel additionally suggests that his proposed exception would have minimal impact if confined to criminal cases, or, as the Court of Appeals suggests, if it is limited to information of substantial importance to a particular criminal case.[3] However, there is no case authority for the proposition that the privilege applies differently in criminal and civil cases, and only one commentator ventures such a suggestion, see Mueller & Kirkpatrick, *supra*, at 380–381. In any event, a client may not know at the time he discloses information to his attorney whether it will later be relevant to a civil or a criminal matter, let alone whether it will be of substantial importance. Balancing ex post the importance of the information against client interests, even limited to criminal cases, introduces substantial uncertainty into the privilege's application. For just that reason, we have rejected use of a balancing test in defining the contours of the privilege. See *Upjohn*, 449 U.S., at 393 . . .

In a similar vein, the Independent Counsel argues that existing exceptions to the privilege, such as the crime-fraud exception and the testamentary exception, make the impact of one more exception marginal. However, these exceptions do not demonstrate that the impact of a posthumous exception would be insignificant, and there is little empirical evidence on this point.[4] The established exceptions are consistent with the purposes of the privilege, see *Glover*, 165 U.S., at 407–408; *United States v. Zolin*, 491 U.S. 554, 562–563 (1989), while a posthumous exception in criminal cases appears at odds with the goals of encouraging full and frank communication and of protecting the client's interests. A "no harm in one more exception" rationale could contribute to the general erosion of the privilege, without reference to common law principles or "reason and experience."

Finally, the Independent Counsel, relying on cases such as *United States v. Nixon*, 418 U.S. 683, 710 (1974), and *Branzburg v. Hayes*, 408 U.S. 665 (1972), urges that privileges be strictly construed because they are inconsistent with the paramount judicial goal of truth seeking. But both *Nixon* and *Branzburg* dealt with the creation of privileges not recognized by the common law, whereas here we deal with one of the oldest recognized privileges in

3. Petitioner, while opposing wholesale abrogation of the privilege in criminal cases, concedes that exceptional circumstances implicating a criminal defendant's constitutional rights might warrant breaching the privilege. We do not, however, need to reach this issue, since such exceptional circumstances clearly are not presented here.

4. Empirical evidence on the privilege is limited. Three studies do not reach firm conclusions on whether limiting the privilege would discourage full and frank communication. Alexander, The Corporate Attorney Client Privilege: A Study of the Participants, 63 St. John's L. Rev. 191 (1989); Zacharias, Rethinking Confidentiality, 74 Iowa L. Rev. 352 (1989); Comment, Functional Overlap Between the Lawyer and Other Professionals: Its Implications for the Privileged Communications Doctrine, 71 Yale L.J. 1226 (1962). These articles note that clients are often uninformed or mistaken about the privilege, but suggest that a substantial number of clients and attorneys think the privilege encourages candor. Two of the articles conclude that a substantial number of clients and attorneys think the privilege enhances open communication, Alexander, supra, at 244–246, 261, and that the absence of a privilege would be detrimental to such communication, Comment, 71 Yale L.J., supra, at 1236. The third article suggests instead that while the privilege is perceived as important to open communication, limited exceptions to the privilege might not discourage such communication, Zacharias, supra, at 382, 386. Similarly, relatively few court decisions discuss the impact of the privilege's application after death. This may reflect the general assumption that the privilege survives — if attorneys were required as a matter of practice to testify or provide notes in criminal proceedings, cases discussing that practice would surely exist.

the law. And we are asked, not simply to "construe" the privilege, but to narrow it, contrary to the weight of the existing body of caselaw.

It has been generally, if not universally, accepted, for well over a century, that the attorney-client privilege survives the death of the client in a case such as this. While the arguments against the survival of the privilege are by no means frivolous, they are based in large part on speculation—thoughtful speculation, but speculation nonetheless—as to whether posthumous termination of the privilege would diminish a client's willingness to confide in an attorney. In an area where empirical information would be useful, it is scant and inconclusive.

Rule 501's direction to look to "the principles of the common law as they may be interpreted by the courts of the United States in the light of reason and experience" does not mandate that a rule, once established, should endure for all time. But here the Independent Counsel has simply not made a sufficient showing to overturn the common law rule embodied in the prevailing caselaw. Interpreted in the light of reason and experience, that body of law requires that the attorney client privilege prevent disclosure of the notes at issue in this case. The judgment of the Court of Appeals is

Reversed.

[Justice O'Connor filed a dissenting opinion, joined by Justice Scalia and Justice Thomas.]

UNITED STATES v. JICARILLA APACHE NATION

564 U.S. 162 (2011)

Justice ALITO delivered the opinion of the Court.

... The Jicarilla Apache Nation (Tribe) occupies a 900,000–acre reservation in northern New Mexico that was established by Executive Order in 1887. The land contains timber, gravel, and oil and gas reserves, which are developed pursuant to statutes administered by the Department of the Interior. Proceeds derived from these natural resources are held by the United States in trust for the Tribe pursuant to the American Indian Trust Fund Management Reform Act of 1994, 108 Stat. 4239, and other statutes.

In 2002, the Tribe commenced a breach-of-trust action against the United States in the Court of Federal Claims (CFC) ... seek[ing] monetary damages for the Government's alleged mismanagement of funds held in trust for the Tribe. [During discovery, the government asserted the attorney-client privilege with regard to, *inter alia*,] (1) requests for legal advice relating to trust administration sent by personnel at the Department of the Interior to the Office of the Solicitor, which directs legal affairs for the Department, [and] (2) legal advice sent from the Solicitor's Office to personnel at the Interior and Treasury Departments. [The CFC ordered disclosure of almost all of these documents, and the Court of Appeals for the Federal Circuit denied the government's petition for mandamus. Both courts reasoned that the trust relationship between the Tribe and the government rendered the attorney-client privilege inapplicable.]

The Federal Rules of Evidence provide that evidentiary privileges "shall be governed by the principles of the common law ... in the light of reason and experience." Fed. Rule Evid. 501. The attorney-client privilege "is the oldest of the privileges for confidential communications known to the common law." *Upjohn Co. v. United States*, 449 U.S. 383, 389 (1981) (citing 8 J. Wigmore, Evidence §2290 (J. McNaughton rev. 1961)). Its aim is "to encourage full and frank communication between attorneys and their clients and thereby promote broader public interests in the observance of law and administration of justice." 449 U.S. at 389.

The objectives of the attorney-client privilege apply to governmental clients. "The privilege aids government entities and employees in obtaining legal advice founded on a complete and accurate factual picture." 1 Restatement (Third) of the Law Governing Lawyers §74, Comment *b*, pp. 573-574 (1998). Unless applicable law provides otherwise, the Government may invoke the attorney-client privilege in civil litigation to protect confidential communications between Government officials and Government attorneys. *Id.*, at 574 ("[G]overnmental agencies and employees enjoy the same privilege as nongovernmental counterparts"). The Tribe argues, however, that the common law also recognizes a fiduciary exception to the attorney-client privilege and that, by virtue of the trust relationship between the Government and the Tribe, documents that would otherwise be privileged must be disclosed....

English courts first developed the fiduciary exception as a principle of trust law in the 19th century. The rule was that when a trustee obtained legal advice to guide the administration of the trust, and not for the trustee's own defense in litigation, the beneficiaries were entitled to the production of documents related to that advice. The courts reasoned that the normal attorney-client privilege did not apply in this situation because the legal advice was sought for the beneficiaries' benefit and was obtained at the beneficiaries' expense by using trust funds to pay the attorney's fees.

The fiduciary exception quickly became an established feature of English common law, but it did not appear in this country until the following century. American courts seem first to have expressed skepticism. By the 1970's, however, American courts began to adopt the English common-law rule. See *Garner v. Wolfinbarger*, 430 F.2d 1093, 1103-1104 (C.A.5 1970) (allowing shareholders, upon a showing of "good cause," to discover legal advice given to corporate management).[3]

The leading American case on the fiduciary exception is *Riggs Nat. Bank of Washington, D.C. v. Zimmer*, 355 A.2d 709 (Del. Ch. 1976). In that

---

3. Today, "[c]ourts differ on whether the [attorney-client] privilege is available for communications between the trustee and counsel regarding the administration of the trust." A. Newman, G. Bogert & G. Bogert, Law of Trusts and Trustees §962, p. 68 (3d ed. 2010). Some state courts have altogether rejected the notion that the attorney-client privilege is subject to a fiduciary exception. See, *e.g., Huie v. DeShazo*, 922 S.W.2d 920, 924 (Tex. 1996) ("The attorney-client privilege serves the same important purpose in the trustee-attorney relationship as it does in other attorney-client relationships"); *Wells Fargo Bank v. Superior Ct.*, 22 Cal. 4th 201, 208-209 (2000) ("[T]he attorney for the trustee of a trust is not, by virtue of this relationship, also the attorney for the beneficiaries of the trust" (internal quotation marks omitted)). Neither party before this Court disputes the existence of a common-law fiduciary exception, however, so in deciding this case we assume such an exception exists.

case, the beneficiaries of a trust estate sought to compel the trustees to reimburse the estate for alleged breaches of trust. The beneficiaries moved to compel the trustees to produce a legal memorandum related to the administration of the trust that the trustees withheld on the basis of attorney-client privilege. The Delaware Chancery Court, observing that "American case law is practically nonexistent on the duty of a trustee in this context," looked to the English cases. Applying the common-law fiduciary exception, the court held that the memorandum was discoverable. It identified two reasons for applying the exception.

First, the court explained, . . . the beneficiaries were the "real clients" of the attorney who had advised the trustee on trust-related matters, and therefore the attorney-client privilege properly belonged to the beneficiaries rather than the trustees. . . . Second, the court concluded that the trustees' fiduciary duty to furnish trust-related information to the beneficiaries outweighed their interest in the attorney-client privilege. . . . Because more information helped the beneficiaries to police the trustees' management of the trust, disclosure was, in the court's judgment, "a weightier public policy than the preservation of confidential attorney-client communications."

. . . In order to apply the fiduciary exception in this case, the Court of Appeals analogized the Government to a private trustee. . . . The Government, of course, is not a private trustee. Though the relevant statutes denominate the relationship between the Government and the Indians a "trust," see, *e.g.*, 25 U.S.C. §162a, that trust is defined and governed by statutes rather than the common law. . . . As we have recognized in prior cases, Congress may style its relations with the Indians a "trust" without assuming all the fiduciary duties of a private trustee, creating a trust relationship that is "limited" or "bare" compared to a trust relationship between private parties at common law. . . .

In this case, the Tribe's claim arises from 25 U.S.C. §§161–162a and the American Indian Trust Fund Management Reform Act of 1994, §4001 *et seq.* These provisions define "the trust responsibilities of the United States" with respect to tribal funds. §162a(d). The Court of Appeals concluded that the trust relationship between the United States and the Indian tribes, outlined in these and other statutes, is "sufficiently similar to a private trust to justify applying the fiduciary exception." We disagree. . . . The two features justifying the fiduciary exception — the beneficiary's status as the "real client" and the trustee's common-law duty to disclose information about the trust — are notably absent in the trust relationship Congress has established between the United States and the Tribe.

[First,] the United States does not obtain legal advice as a "mere representative" of the Tribe; nor is the Tribe the "real client" for whom that advice is intended. . . . [T]he Government attorneys are paid out of congressional appropriations at no cost to the Tribe. . . . Courts look to the source of funds as a "strong indicator of precisely who the real clients were" and a "significant factor" in determining who ought to have access to the legal advice. *Riggs*, 355 A.2d at 712. We similarly find it significant that the attorneys were paid by the Government for advice regarding the Government's statutory obligations.

The payment structure confirms our view that the Government seeks legal advice in its sovereign capacity rather than as a conventional fiduciary of the Tribe. . . . The United States has a sovereign interest in the administration of Indian trusts distinct from the private interests of those who may benefit from its administration. . . . While one purpose of the Indian trust relationship is to benefit the tribes, the Government has its own independent interest in the implementation of federal Indian policy. For that reason, when the Government seeks legal advice related to the administration of tribal trusts, it establishes an attorney-client relationship related to its sovereign interest in the execution of federal law. In other words, the Government seeks legal advice in a "personal" rather than a fiduciary capacity. . . .

[Second, the United States] does not have the same common-law disclosure obligations as a private trustee. . . . The relevant statute in this case is 25 U.S.C. §162a(d), which delineates "trust responsibilities of the United States" that the Secretary of the Interior must discharge. The enumerated responsibilities include a provision identifying the Secretary's obligation to provide specific information to tribal account holders: The Secretary must "suppl[y] account holders with periodic statements of their account performance" and must make "available on a daily basis" the "balances of their account." §162a(d)(5). . . . Those provisions define the Government's disclosure obligation to the Tribe. . . . Reading the statute to incorporate the full duties of a private, common-law fiduciary would vitiate Congress' specification of narrowly defined disclosure obligations.

By law and regulation, moreover, the documents at issue in this case are classed "the property of the United States" while other records are "the property of the tribe." 25 CFR §115.1000 (2010). . . . Just as the source of the funds used to pay for legal advice is highly relevant in identifying the "real client" for purposes of the fiduciary exception, we consider ownership of the resulting records to be a significant factor in deciding who "ought to have access to the document." See *Riggs*, 355 A.2d, at 712. In this case, that privilege belongs to the United States. . . . [Reversed.]

[Justice Kagan recused herself. Justice Ginsburg filed a concurring opinion, in which Justice Breyer joined.]

Justice SOTOMAYOR, dissenting.

. . . [The attorney-client privilege] is a limited exception to the usual rules of evidence requiring full disclosure of relevant information. See 8 J. Wigmore, Evidence §2192, p. 64 (3d ed. 1940) (common law recognizes "fundamental maxim that the public . . . has a right to every man's evidence" and that "any exemptions which may exist are distinctly exceptional, being so many derogations from a positive general rule"). Because it "has the effect of withholding relevant information from the factfinder," courts construe the privilege narrowly. *Fisher v. United States*, 425 U.S. 391, 403 (1976). It applies "only where necessary to achieve its purpose," *ibid.*; "[w]here this purpose ends, so too does the protection of the privilege," *Wachtel v. Health Net, Inc.*, 482 F.3d 225, 231 (C.A.3 2007). . . .

In light of Federal Rule of Evidence 501 and the Government's role as a conventional fiduciary in managing Indian trust fund accounts, I would hold as a matter of federal common law that the fiduciary exception is applicable in the Indian trust context, and thus the Government may not rely on the attorney-client privilege to withhold communications related to trust management....

Given the history of governmental mismanagement of Indian trust funds, application of the fiduciary exception is, if anything, even more important in this context than in the private trustee context. The majority's refusal to apply the fiduciary exception in this case deprives the Nation—as well as the Indian tribes in the more than 90 cases currently pending in the federal courts involving claims of tribal trust mismanagement—of highly relevant information going directly to the merits of whether the Government properly fulfilled its fiduciary duties. Its holding only further exacerbates the concerns expressed by many about the lack of adequate oversight and accountability that has marked the Government's handling of Indian trust fund accounts for decades....

JEREMY BENTHAM, RATIONALE OF
JUDICIAL EVIDENCE
5:302-304 (1827)

English judges have taken care to exempt the professional members of the partnership from so unpleasant an obligation as that of rendering service to justice.... When, in consulting with a law adviser, attorney or advocate, a man has confessed his delinquency, or disclosed some fact which, if stated in court, might tend to operate in proof of it, such law adviser is not to be suffered to be examined as to any such point. The law adviser is neither to be compelled, nor so much as suffered, to betray the trust thus reposed in him. Not suffered? Why not? Oh, because to betray a trust is treachery; and an act of treachery is an immoral act.

An immoral sort of act, is that sort of act, the tendency of which is, in some way or other, to lessen the quantity of happiness in society. In what way does the supposed cause in question tend to the production of any such effect? The conviction and punishment of the defendant, he being guilty, is by the supposition an act the tendency of which, upon the whole, is beneficial to society....

But if such confidence, when reposed, is permitted to be violated, and if this be known (which, if such be the law, it will be), the consequence will be, that no such confidence will be reposed. Not reposed?—Well: and if it be not, wherein will consist the mischief? The man by the supposition is guilty; if not, by the supposition there is nothing to betray: let the law adviser say every thing he has heard, every thing he can have heard from his client, the client cannot have anything to fear from it. That it will often happen that in the case supposed no such confidence will be reposed, is natural enough: the first thing the attorney or advocate will say to his client, will be,—Remember that, whatever you say to me, I shall be obliged to tell, if asked about it. What, then will be the consequence? That a guilty person will not in general be able to derive quite so much assistance from his law adviser, in the way of concocting a false defence, as he may do at present.

WILLIAM H. SIMON, THE KAYE, SCHOLER AFFAIR: THE LAWYER'S DUTY OF CANDOR AND THE BAR'S TEMPTATIONS OF EVASION AND APOLOGY

23 Law & Soc. Inquiry 243 (1998)

For three years, lawyers from the New York firm of Kaye, Scholer, Fierman, Hays, & Handler devoted themselves to keeping the government off the back of Charles Keating while he engaged in financial and political exploits that eventuated in criminal convictions for Keating and several of his associates, billions of dollars in civil liability for Keating and a larger group of associates, formal criticism by the United States Senate of five of its members, and a loss to the federal banking insurance system estimated at $3.4 billion.... Succeeding Keating to ownership of the defunct Lincoln Savings & Loan, the banking agencies found themselves with access to records of confidential communications between the Keating crowd and the Kaye Scholer lawyers and, from this intimate vantage point, concluded that some of the lawyers' conduct went beyond the legitimate bounds of representation. The Office of Thrift Supervision (OTS) charged the lawyers with misconduct in a case the firm settled for $41 million and injunctive relief.

. . . The rationale for confidentiality with respect to ongoing or anticipated wrongful behavior is that it induces people to seek legal advice. But a person who intends to abide by the law in any event does not need this inducement. The key question is thus why it is important to induce people who think they might be inclined to violate the law to seek legal advice. Of course, such a person might learn something from the lawyer — say the size of the penalty — that would deter her from illegality. On the other hand, she might learn something that had the opposite effect. (Maybe the penalty will turn out to be lower than she expected.) So a key part of the bar's argument is that inducing people with a shaky commitment to law abidingness to seek legal advice is good because it gives their lawyers an opportunity to dissuade them from illegal conduct. The drafters of the Model Rules [of Professional Conduct] consider this practice so potent, they tell us, "Based upon experience, lawyers know that almost all clients follow the advice given, and the law is upheld (1983, Rule 1.6, comment, ¶3)."

Presumably the drafters were given pause by the chorus of ridicule with which many greeted OTS's suggestion that Kaye Scholer had a duty to exhort Lincoln's officers and directors to mend their ways. No one suggests that Kaye Scholer tried to dissuade the Lincoln people; the defense has been that it would have been transparently pointless for them to do so.... Lincoln thus appears to be an example of a case in which a rule abrogating confidentiality would not have had any bad effects. Very likely Keating would have refrained from seeking legal assistance. If OTS is right in suggesting Kaye Scholer exacerbated Lincoln's frauds, then it would have been a good thing for society if Keating had never retained the firm; even if OTS is wrong, there might not have been any social costs to depriving Keating of representation.

Of course, this is only one example. It is, however, a very large example, and one suspects one could find others among the aggressive S&L failures. Moreover, since the bar has yet to give us any specific examples of circumstances in which the confidentiality rule for ongoing and future acts provided positive social benefits, I'd say these cases were sufficient to shift the burden of going forward.

BENJAMIN H. BARTON, DO JUDGES SYSTEMATICALLY FAVOR THE INTERESTS OF THE LEGAL PROFESSION?

58 Ala. L. Rev. 453 (2008)

[M]any legal outcomes can be explained, and future cases predicted, by asking a very simple question: is there a plausible legal result in this case that will significantly affect the interests of the legal profession (positively or negatively)? If so, the case will be decided in the way that offers the best result for the legal profession. . . .

One of the oldest and most ingrained examples . . . is the [way in which] the attorney-client privilege has been accorded a unique and vaunted position among all professional privileges. . . . [T]he primacy of the attorney-client privilege — in comparison to other privileges like those accorded physicians, spouses, or clergy — cannot be justified solely jurisprudentially. Instead, the difference is most likely the inherent sympathy that judges have had for the importance of the attorney-client relationship. . . .

It is also worth noting what an exceptional product the attorney-client privilege allows lawyers to sell to clients. In conjunction with extremely tight professional confidentiality rules and norms, the attorney-client privilege offers clients protection for almost all disclosures. . . . If you are concerned at all about later confidentiality in court and need someone to talk to, you would be well advised to choose a lawyer.

2. Elements of the Privilege

Application of the attorney-client privilege typically requires four things: (a) a communication, (b) in confidence, (c) between a lawyer and client, (d) in the course of provision of professional legal services. In practice, analysis of the four elements often overlaps.

a. Communication

UNITED STATES v. KENDRICK

331 F.2d 110 (4th Cir. 1964)

PER CURIAM.

This is an appeal from the District Court's decision denying, after hearing, the petitioner's motion under 28 U.S.C.A. §2255 to vacate an illegal sentence on the grounds that the petitioner was incompetent to stand trial. . . . [In November 1960] he was tried and sentenced to seven years for three thefts from interstate commerce committed between July and September of that year. The substance of his allegations in the present action is . . . that at his trial in November of 1960 he was insane and suffering from amnesia; that as a result of his disabilities he was not competent to stand trial.

. . . We do not agree with the petitioner that the testimony of his trial counsel should have been excluded at the post-conviction hearing on the basis of the attorney-client privilege. . . . Communications made in confidence by a client to his attorney are protected by the attorney-client privilege. It is the substance of the communications which is protected, however, not the fact that there have been communications. Excluded from the privilege, also, are physical characteristics of the client, such as his complexion, his demeanor, his bearing, his sobriety and his dress. Such things are observable by anyone who talked with the client, and there is nothing, in the usual case, to suggest that the client intends his attorney's observations of such matters to be confidential. In short, the privilege protects only the client's confidences, not things which, at the time, are not intended to be held in the breast of the lawyer, even though the attorney-client relation provided the occasion for the lawyer's observation of them. *See generally* VIII Wigmore, Evidence (McNaughton Revision) §2306.

Here the attorney testified to just such nonconfidential matters. Petitioner, the attorney testified, was responsive, readily supplied the attorney with his version of the facts and the names of other people involved, was logical in his conversation and his reasoning, and appeared to know and understand everything that went on before and during the trial. No mention was made of the substance of any communication by client to attorney; the witness testified only about his client's cooperativeness and awareness.

All of the matters to which the attorney testified are objectively observable particularizations of the client's demeanor and attitude. Made at a time when neither client nor lawyer manifested any reason to suppose they were confidential, they were not within the privilege. . . . [Reversed on other grounds.]

TORNAY v. UNITED STATES

840 F.2d 1424 (9th Cir. 1988)

EUGENE A. WRIGHT, Circuit Judge.

. . . Stephen and Galene Tornay were the subject of an investigation by the Internal Revenue Service to determine their federal tax liability for tax years 1978 through 1983. The IRS sought to establish tax liability on a net worth, net expenditure basis. It issued summonses to three Oregon attorneys, whom the Tornays had retained in connection with a 1983 criminal conviction, for information regarding fees paid. When the attorneys complied with the summonses, the Tornays discharged them.

The Tornays also retained Seattle attorney Robert Wayne, their present counsel. [The IRS subsequently issued a summons to Wayne, seeking "information concerning the date, amount and form of legal fees paid to and trust funds deposited with Wayne by the Tornays during 1983."] Wayne failed to comply with the summons and continues to do so. The Tornays petitioned to quash....The Tornays insist that they will discharge Wayne if he is forced to comply with the summons. [The district court denied the petition, and the Tornays appealed.]

The purpose of the attorney-client privilege is to encourage full disclosure to attorneys so they are able to render effective legal assistance. 8 J. Wigmore, Evidence §§2291–92 (McNaughton rev. 1961). Because "the privilege has the effect of withholding relevant information from the factfinder, it applies only where necessary to achieve its purpose. Accordingly, it protects only those disclosures—necessary to obtain informed legal advice—which might not have been made absent the privilege." *Fisher v. United States*, 425 U.S. 391, 403 (1976).

We have said repeatedly, as the Tornays concede, that fee information generally is not privileged. Payment of fees is incidental to the attorney-client relationship, and does not usually involve disclosure of confidential communications arising from the professional relationship.

The Tornays argue that, in light of an exception to this rule, the privilege is applicable to information concerning fees paid to Wayne. The genesis of their argument is *Baird v. Koerner*, 279 F.2d 623 (9th Cir. 1960).

Baird involved several clients who directed their attorney to tender anonymously to the IRS delinquent tax payments and interest. The IRS issued a summons requiring counsel to identify his clients. We concluded that disclosure of the clients' identity was protected by the attorney-client privilege . . . because identifying the clients would be tantamount to conveying a privileged communication in which the clients disclosed their delinquent tax liabilities.

. . . *Baird* and its progeny do not apply here. The Tornays' identity was known to the IRS. The agency sought only the amount, date and form of the payments to Wayne. . . . The Tornays have not demonstrated the existence of exceptional circumstances that would make disclosure tantamount to revealing a confidential communication. . . .

. . . The Tornays argue that the privilege must be applied because the IRS summons has interfered with the attorney-client relationship. They say the primary reason for discharging their Oregon attorneys was their compliance with the IRS summonses. They presented two experienced defense lawyers who testified that: (1) a client is less forthcoming if he knows that his attorney might be called as a witness against him, and (2) a subpoena to a lawyer hinders the development of a defense because it distracts the lawyer.

We apply the attorney-client privilege only when necessary to effectuate its limited purpose of encouraging complete disclosure by the client. We are not persuaded that its purpose will be furthered by extending the privilege to information regarding fees paid by a client.

We do not believe that clients, knowing that their attorney may be compelled to testify about the amount, date, and form of fees paid, would be inhibited from disclosing fully information needed for effective legal representation. Nor do we accept a generalization that clients feel less free to disclose once it becomes apparent that their attorney's testimony may cause adverse results. The Tornays' voluntary discharge of their Oregon attorneys does not show that disclosure of fee information established a barrier to the free flow of information, nor does the possibility that an attorney may be required to expend time and resources to comply with a summons.

Some prospective clients, arguably, may decide not to retain counsel for legal services if they could be implicated by expenditures for those services. This is not, however, a sufficient justification to invoke the privilege. The privilege is not to immunize a client from liability stemming from expenditures for legal services. Its purpose is only to encourage persons who choose to be represented by counsel, despite the consequences of that choice, to confer candidly and openly with their attorney. The district court was correct in ruling that the attorney-client privilege was inapplicable. It did not abuse its discretion by denying the petition to quash. . . . The judgment is Affirmed.

b. In Confidence

UNITED STATES v. GANN

732 F.2d 714 (9th Cir. 1984)

ALARCON, Circuit Judge.

[Defendant Terry Gann was convicted of illegally possessing a sawed-off shotgun.] On April 28, 1982, the United States National Bank in Portland, Oregon was robbed of approximately $800 in currency and $18,000 in travelers' checks by Patrick Dussault. Dussault was observed fleeing in a yellow Mustang driven by Gann.

On May 19, 1982, warrants were issued for the search of Gann's home and of a 1972 green Vega automobile registered in his name. . . . After the agents found the bag containing the shotgun and shotgun ammunition in Gann's car, Detective Fantz of the Portland Police bureau decided to arrest him. Gann was in the house talking on the telephone in the presence of several law enforcement officers who were searching the house. One of the agents told Detective Fantz: "I think he is talking to his lawyer." Detective Fantz waited in the room in order to arrest Gann as soon as he got off the phone. Detective Fantz heard Gann state: "Looks like I'm going to have to go downtown," followed by the words "ex-con in possession, I guess." The government later introduced these statements to prove that Gann had knowledge of the shotgun and ammunition found in his vehicle. . . .

Because Gann knew, or should have known, that third parties were present, his attorney-client privilege claim must fail. The burden of proving that the privilege applies is upon the party asserting it. Here, Gann cannot show that his conversation with his attorney was made in confidence. The statement in question was made with the knowledge that he was surrounded by officers searching his residence. There is no evidence that Detective Fantz purposely positioned himself by the phone so that he could eavesdrop on a privileged communication. The evidence shows, instead, that the officer merely walked into the room and waited for Gann to complete his call.... The judgment is Affirmed.

UNITED STATES v. EVANS

113 F.3d 1457 (7th Cir. 1997)

CUMMINGS, Circuit Judge.

The trial of Jesse Evans, a Chicago alderman indicted on charges of racketeering (including acts of extortion, accepting bribes, and official misconduct), filing false tax returns, and obstruction of justice, is presently pending in the district court. This interlocutory appeal requires us to review an order of that court granting the government's pretrial motion *in limine* to admit certain testimony by attorney James Koch, which Evans asserts is protected by the attorney-client privilege....

In early January 1996, news reports revealed that Alderman Evans had been targeted in a federal corruption investigation of City officials.... After learning that his long-time friend and occasional client had been implicated in the investigation, attorney John Holden, who is also a Chicago police officer, contacted Evans and spoke with him about Evans' interviews with FBI agents. In the aftermath of this meeting, Holden arranged for and scheduled Evans to meet with three criminal defense attorneys so that Evans could explain his situation, seek legal advice, and decide which of the three attorneys, if any, to retain. On January 8, 1996, after scheduling an appointment on Evans' behalf with attorney James Koch, Holden took Evans to Koch's office where the three conferred....

The attorney-client privilege shields only those communications by a client to an attorney that were intended to be confidential. Thus as a general matter, the attorney-client privilege will not shield from disclosure statements made by a client to his or her attorney in the presence of a third party who is not an agent of either the client or attorney. See 8 Wigmore, Evidence §2311 ("One of the circumstances by which it is commonly apparent that the communication is not confidential is the *presence of a third person* who is not the agent of either client or attorney.")....

Evans attempts to avoid this general rule by arguing that Holden was present at the meeting with Evans and Koch in his capacity as Evans' attorney.... [T]he district judge recognized that resolution of this capacity issue turned on a credibility determination ... and she resolved the issue by crediting Koch's testimony. Koch expressly testified that Holden stated that he was present at the meeting *not* as an attorney, but as a personal friend of Evans and as a potential character witness....

... Evans is not aided by cases holding that the presence of a third party at an attorney-client consultation does not defeat the privilege where the third party's presence was needed to make the conference possible or to assist the attorney in rendering legal services. Beyond stating the general rule, Evans has failed to carry his burden of proving that Holden's presence was necessary to accomplish the objective of his consultation. Evans' only showing on this score lies in Holden's discredited testimony that he was present at the meeting in order to advise Evans as to the relative abilities of the several defense attorneys who were to be consulted. Giving effect to the district court's factual findings, we must conclude that Holden was present merely as a friend and potential character witness. This is plainly insufficient to establish the necessity of Holden's presence....

For the foregoing reasons, the district court's order granting the government's motion to admit Mr. Koch's testimony is affirmed.

UNITED STATES v. LAWLESS

709 F.2d 485 (7th Cir. 1983)

GRANT, Senior District Judge.

The Respondent-Appellee, J. Martin Lawless, an attorney in Peoria, Illinois, was retained by the co-executors of the estate to prepare the federal estate tax return of Edna E. Dieken, deceased. [The IRS sought by summons to obtain from Lawless all documents relating to or used in the preparation of the return. Lawless cited attorney-client privilege and refused to comply. After reviewing the disputed documents in camera, the district court ruled that two of them were privileged because "they were the type of information which I think the client is privileged to furnish to his attorney and not have the attorney disclose to the extent they were used in the preparation of the return." The government appealed.]

... When information is transmitted to an attorney with the intent that the information will be transmitted to a third party (in this case on a tax return), such information is not confidential. *Colton v. United States*, 306 F.2d 633, 638 (2d Cir. 1962), *cert. denied*, 371 U.S. 951 (1963).

The respondent argues that the information transmitted to him, as the attorney preparing the tax return, but which was not disclosed on the return, is protected by the privilege. If the client transmitted the information so that it might be used on the tax return, such a transmission destroys any expectation of confidentiality which might have otherwise existed.... Following the precedents of other Circuits ... this Court now finds that information transmitted for the purpose of preparation of a tax return, though transmitted to an attorney, is not privileged information.

The holding of the district court is reversed and the documents are returned to the district court for enforcement proceedings consistent with this opinion.

SMITHKLINE BEECHAM CORP. v. APOTEX CORP.

193 F.R.D. 530 (N.D. Ill. 2000)

BOBRICK, United States Magistrate Judge.

Before the court is the motion of defendants Apotex Corporation, Apotex Inc., and Torpharm, Inc. to compel the production of certain documents listed in the privilege log of plaintiffs Smithkline Beecham Corporation and Beecham Group, Inc. [Plaintiffs sued defendants for infringing plaintiffs' patent to an antidepressant drug.]

. . . [W]hen information is transmitted to an attorney with the intent that it be transmitted to a third party, the material is not privileged. *United States v. Lawless*, 709 F.2d 485, 487 (7th Cir. 1983). In the end, however, the question is: does the document in question reveal, directly or indirectly, the substance of a confidential attorney-client communication.

. . . Courts have struggled with the application of the attorney-client privilege to the practice of patent law. It was not until 1963, that the Supreme Court established that patent practice—advising clients as to patentability, drafting specifications and claims, preparation of arguments to establish patentability, etc.—was the practice of law. *Sperry v. Florida*, 373 U.S. 379 (1963). Since that time courts have either considered patent attorneys to be conduits of information between a client and the Patent Office, where the lack of expectation of confidentiality doomed the application of the privilege, *see, e.g. Jack Winter, Inc. v. Koratron Co.*, 50 F.R.D. 225, 228 (N.D. Cal. 1970), or have rejected the conduit theory, and held that nearly all communications between client and patent attorney are requests for legal advice in that they pertain to assessment of patentability, and preparation and prosecution of the patent application. *Knogo Corp. v. U.S.*, 213 U.S.P.Q. 936, 939-41 (1980). Courts have also attempted to draw a line between technical and legal information which, in the context of patent law, is not a line easily drawn. *See, e.g. In re Spaulding Sports Worldwide*, 203 F.3d 800, 806 n. 3 (Fed. Cir. 2000) (collecting cases). . . .

In *Spalding*, the Federal Circuit discussed the application of the privilege to materials that were substantially technical, but produced in a legal setting: "It is enough that the overall tenor of the document indicates that it is a request for legal advice or services. . . . [A]n attorney cannot evaluate patentability or prepare a competent patent application without knowing the prior art and obtaining the relevant technical information from the inventors." 203 F.3d at 806; *see also* [*McCook Metals L.L.C. v. Alcoa Inc.*, 192 F.R.D. 242, 254 (N.D. Ill. 2000)] (following Federal Circuit law with respect to materials unique to patent law). Accordingly, we find such documents, described as prepared in order to allow attorneys to assess patentability and sift information to prepare applications, to be immune from discovery under the attorney-client privilege. . . .

c. Between Attorney and Client

UNITED STATES v. KOVEL

296 F.2d 918 (2d Cir. 1961)

FRIENDLY, Circuit Judge.

. . . Kovel is a former Internal Revenue agent having accounting skills. Since 1943 he has been employed by Kamerman & Kamerman, a law firm specializing in tax law. A grand jury in the Southern District of New York was investigating alleged Federal income tax violations by Hopps, a client of the law firm; Kovel was subpoenaed to appear on September 6, 1961, a few days before the date, September 8, when the Government feared the statute of limitations might run. The law firm advised the Assistant United States Attorney that since Kovel was an employee under the direct supervision of the partners, Kovel could not disclose any communications by the client of the result of any work done for the client, unless the latter consented; the Assistant answered that the attorney-client privilege did not apply to one who was not an attorney.

. . . [Questioned before the grand jury about his communications with Hopps, Kovel declined to answer on the ground of privilege. His refusal was relayed to the district court.] The court held him in contempt, sentenced him to a year's imprisonment, ordered immediate commitment and denied bail. Later in the day, the grand jury having indicted, Kovel was released until September 12, at which time, without opposition from the Government, I granted bail pending determination of this appeal.

Here the parties continue to take generally the same positions as below — Kovel, that his status as an employee of a law firm automatically made all communications to him from clients privileged; the Government, that under no circumstances could there be privilege with respect to communications to an accountant. The New York County Lawyers' Association as amicus curiae has filed a brief generally supporting appellant's position.

Decision under what circumstances, if any, the attorney-client privilege may include a communication to a nonlawyer by the lawyer's client is the resultant of two conflicting forces. One is the general teaching that "The investigation of truth and the enforcement of testimonial duty demand the restriction, not the expansion, of these privileges," 8 Wigmore, Evidence (McNaughton Rev. 1961), §2192, p. 73. The other is the more particular lesson "That as, by reason of the complexity and difficulty of our law, litigation can only be properly conducted by professional men, it is absolutely necessary that a man . . . should have recourse to the assistance of professional lawyers, and . . . it is equally necessary . . . that he should be able to place unrestricted and unbounded confidence in the professional agent, and that the communications he so makes to him should be kept secret . . .," Jessel, M.R. in *Anderson v. Bank*, 2 Ch. D. 644, 649 (1876). Nothing in the policy of the privilege suggests that attorneys, simply by placing accountants, scientists or investigators on their payrolls and maintaining them in their offices, should be able to invest all communications by clients to such persons with a privilege the law has not seen fit to extend when the latter are operating under their own steam. On the other hand, in contrast to the Tudor times when the privilege was first recognized, see 8 Wigmore, Evidence, §2290, the complexities of modern existence prevent attorneys from effectively handling clients' affairs without the help of others; few lawyers could now practice without the assistance of secretaries, file clerks, telephone operators, messengers, clerks not yet admitted to the bar, and aides of other sorts. "The assistance of these agents being indispensable to his work and the communications of the client being often necessarily committed to them by the attorney or by the client himself, the privilege must include all the persons who act as the attorney's agents." 8 Wigmore, Evidence, §2301.

Indeed, the Government does not here dispute that the privilege covers communications to non-lawyer employees with "a menial or ministerial responsibility that involves relating communications to an attorney." We cannot regard the privilege as confined to "menial or ministerial" employees. Thus, we can see no significant difference between a case where the attorney sends a client speaking a foreign language to an interpreter to make a literal translation of the client's story; a second where the attorney, himself having some little knowledge of the foreign tongue, has a more knowledgeable non-lawyer employee in the room to help out; a third where someone to perform that same function has been brought along by the client; and a fourth where the attorney, ignorant of the foreign language, sends the client to a non-lawyer proficient in it, with instructions to interview the client on the attorney's behalf and then render his own summary of the situation, perhaps drawing on his own knowledge in the process, so that the attorney can give the client proper legal advice. All four cases meet every element of Wigmore's famous formulation, §2292, "(1) Where legal advice of any kind is sought (2) from professional legal adviser in his capacity as such, (3) the communications relating to that purpose, (4) made in confidence (5) by the client, (6) are at his instance permanently protected (7) from disclosure by himself or by the legal adviser, (8) except the protection be waived," save (7); literally, none of them is within (7) since the disclosure is not sought to be compelled from the client or the lawyer. Yet §2301 of Wigmore would clearly recognize the privilege in the first case and the Government goes along to that extent; §2301 would also recognize the privilege in the second case and §2311 in the third unless the circumstances negated confidentiality. We find no valid policy reason for a different result in the fourth case, and we do not read Wigmore as thinking there is. Laymen consulting lawyers should not be expected to anticipate niceties perceptible only to judges—and not even to all of them.

This analogy of the client speaking a foreign language is by no means irrelevant to the appeal at hand. Accounting concepts are a foreign language to some lawyers in almost all cases, and to almost all lawyers in some cases. Hence the presence of an accountant, whether hired by the lawyer or by the client, while the client is relating a complicated tax story to the lawyer, ought not destroy the privilege, any more than would that of the linguist in the second or third variations of the foreign language theme discussed above; the presence of the accountant is necessary, or at least highly useful, for the effective consultation between the client and the lawyer which the privilege is designed to permit. By the same token, if the lawyer has directed the client, either in the specific case or generally, to tell his story in the first instance to an accountant engaged by the lawyer, who is then to interpret it so that the lawyer may better give legal advice, communications by the client reasonably related to that purpose ought fall within the privilege; there can be no more virtue in requiring the lawyer to sit by while the client pursues these possibly tedious preliminary conversations with the accountant than in insisting on the lawyer's physical presence while the client dictates a statement to the lawyer's secretary or is interviewed by a clerk not yet admitted to practice. What is vital to the privilege is that the communication be made in confidence for the purpose of obtaining legal advice from the lawyer. If what is sought is not legal advice but only accounting service, as in *Olender v. United States,*

210 F.2d 795, 805–806 (9 Cir. 1954), or if the advice sought is the accountant's rather than the lawyer's, no privilege exists. We recognize this draws what may seem to some a rather arbitrary line between a case where the client communicates first to his own accountant (no privilege as to such communications, even though he later consults his lawyer on the same matter, *Gariepy v. United States*, 189 F.2d 459, 463 (6 Cir. 1951)), and others, where the client in the first instance consults a lawyer who retains an accountant as a listening post, or consults the lawyer with his own accountant present. But that is the inevitable consequence of having to reconcile the absence of a privilege for accountants and the effective operation of the privilege of client and lawyer under conditions where the lawyer needs outside help. We realize also that the line we have drawn will not be so easy to apply as the simpler positions urged on us by the parties—the district judges will scarcely be able to leave the decision of such cases to computers; but the distinction has to be made if the privilege is neither to be unduly expanded nor to become a trap.

. . . The judgment is vacated and the cause remanded for further proceedings consistent with this opinion.

UNITED STATES v. McPARTLIN

595 F.2d 1321 (7th Cir. 1979)

Tone, Circuit Judge.

The appellants were convicted, in a nine-week jury trial, of conspiring to violate the wire and travel fraud statutes and of substantive violations of those statutes.

The indictment charged that defendant Frederick B. Ingram, chairman of the board of the Louisiana-based Ingram Corporation, had paid defendant Robert F. McPartlin, an Illinois legislator, defendant Valentine Janicki, a trustee for the Metropolitan Sanitary District, and others more than $900,000 to secure for the Ingram Corporation a multi-million dollar sludge-hauling contract with the District. . . . William J. Benton, vice president of Ingram Corporation, was an unindicted co-conspirator who played a major role in the conspiracy and testified as a witness for the prosecution.

. . . Throughout the period covered by the indictment, Benton kept diaries, or appointment calendars, in which he made notes concerning meetings and telephone conversations, naming the persons involved and often recording the substance of the conversations. The Benton diaries figured prominently in the government's case, for they corroborated much of his testimony.

. . . An investigator acting for Frederick Ingram's counsel twice interviewed McPartlin with the consent of the latter's counsel for the purpose of determining whether there was a basis for challenging the truth of some of the diary entries. In the second of these interviews McPartlin made certain statements, which Ingram argues tend to support his defense. At trial, when Ingram offered evidence of these statements, McPartlin's counsel objected on the ground, inter alia, of the attorney-client privilege, and the court, after an in camera hearing, sustained the objection. . . .

McPartlin was entitled to the protection of the attorney-client privilege, because his statements were made in confidence to an attorney for a codefendant for a common purpose related to both defenses. They were made in connection with the project of attempting to discredit Benton, a project in which Ingram and McPartlin and their attorneys were jointly engaged for the benefit of both defendants. Ingram acknowledges that communications by a client to his own lawyer remain privileged when the lawyer subsequently shares them with co-defendants for purposes of a common defense. The common-defense rule, which is not as narrow as Ingram contends, has been recognized in cases spanning more than a century. Uninhibited communication among joint parties and their counsel about matters of common concern is often important to the protection of their interests. In criminal cases it can be necessary to a fair opportunity to defend. Therefore, waiver is not to be inferred from the disclosure in confidence to a co-party's attorney for a common purpose.

. . . Ingram argues that the co-defendants' defenses must be in all respects compatible if the joint-defense privilege is to be applicable. The cases do not establish such a limitation, and there is no reason to impose it. . . . The privilege protects pooling of information for any defense purpose common to the participating defendants. Cooperation between defendants in such circumstances is often not only in their own best interests but serves to expedite the trial or, as in the case at bar, the trial preparation.

Ingram also seems to argue that the communication was not privileged because it was made to an investigator rather than an attorney. The investigator was an agent for Ingram's attorney, however, so it is as if the communication was to the attorney himself. "It has never been questioned that the privilege protects communications to the attorney's . . . agents . . . for rendering his services." 8 Wigmore, Evidence §2301 at 583 (McNaughton rev. 1961); *cf. United States v. Kovel*, 296 F.2d 918, 921-922 (2d Cir. 1961) (client's communications to an accountant employed by his attorney).

Nor was it, as Ingram contends, fatal to the privilege that McPartlin made the statement, in effect, to Ingram's attorney rather than his own. When the Ingram and McPartlin camps decided to join in an attempt to discredit Benton, the attorney for each represented both for purposes of that joint effort. The relationship was no different than it would have been if during the trial the Ingram and McPartlin attorneys had decided that Ingram's attorney would cross-examine Benton on behalf of both, and during cross-examination McPartlin passed Ingram's attorney a note containing information for use in the cross-examination. The attorney who thus undertakes to serve his client's co-defendant for a limited purpose becomes the co-defendant's attorney for that purpose. [Affirmed.]

PASTERIS v. ROBILLARD

121 F.R.D. 18 (D. Mass. 1988)

JOYCE L. ALEXANDER, United States Magistrate.

[Marie and Stanley Pasteris sued Gary and Sharon Robillard for injuries Marie suffered when she fell down a flight of stairs at the Robillard's home.

The plaintiffs sought discovery of Gary Robillard's transcribed statement to his insurance company. The defendants objected on grounds of attorney-client privilege.]

. . . The attorney-client privilege protects certain communications between client and attorney. The privilege applies only if the person to whom the communication was made is a member of the bar of a court, or his subordinate, and in connection with this communication is acting as a lawyer. *United States v. United Shoe Machinery Corporation*, 89 F. Supp. 357, 358 (D. Mass. 1950). Absent this element, the privilege cannot be invoked. Defendants do not contend that Mr. Robillard's statement was made to an attorney. *United States v. Wilson*, 798 F.2d 509, 512–13 (1st Cir. 1986). Therefore, the statement, to merit protection, must have been given to a subordinate of an attorney who was acting as a lawyer when the statement was made.

Defendants state that Mr. Robillard's insurance policy requires his insurance company to defend him. Further, defendants aver that the insurance policy, running from defendants to the insurance company, requires that the insured cooperate with his insurer. Defendants conclude that the statement was given by Mr. Robillard to his insurer to assist the insurer, and the attorney it would retain to defend Mr. Robillard. Notwithstanding the insurance company's obligation to defend and Mr. Robillard's duty to cooperate, defendants do not advance facts showing that the person to whom the communication was made — presumably, i.e., an employee of the insurance company — was actually a subordinate of an attorney or that the individual taking the statement on behalf of the insurance company was acting as an attorney. Thus, defendants cannot invoke the attorney-client privilege. . . . So ordered.

UPJOHN CO. v. UNITED STATES

449 U.S. 383 (1981)

Justice REHNQUIST delivered the opinion of the Court.

. . . Petitioner Upjohn Co. manufactures and sells pharmaceuticals here and abroad. In January 1976 independent accountants conducting an audit of one of Upjohn's foreign subsidiaries discovered that the subsidiary made payments to or for the benefit of foreign government officials in order to secure government business. The accountants so informed petitioner, Mr. Gerard Thomas, Upjohn's Vice President, Secretary, and General Counsel. Thomas is a member of the Michigan and New York Bars, and has been Upjohn's General Counsel for 20 years. He consulted with outside counsel and R. T. Parfet, Jr., Upjohn's Chairman of the Board. It was decided that the company would conduct an internal investigation of what were termed "questionable payments." As part of this investigation the attorneys prepared a letter containing a questionnaire which was sent to "All Foreign General and Area Managers" over the Chairman's signature. The letter began by noting recent disclosures that several American companies made "possibly illegal" payments to foreign government officials and emphasized that the management needed full information concerning any such payments made by Upjohn. The letter indicated that the Chairman had asked Thomas, identified as "the company's General Counsel," "to conduct an investigation for the purpose of determining the nature and magnitude of any payments made by the Upjohn Company or any of its subsidiaries to any employee or official of a foreign government." The questionnaire sought detailed information concerning such payments. Managers were instructed to treat the investigation as "highly confidential" and not to discuss it with anyone other than Upjohn employees who might be helpful in providing the requested information. Responses were to be sent directly to Thomas. Thomas and outside counsel also interviewed the recipients of the questionnaire and some 33 other Upjohn officers or employees as part of the investigation.

On March 26, 1976, the company voluntarily submitted a preliminary report to the Securities and Exchange Commission on Form 8-k disclosing certain questionable payments. A copy of the report was simultaneously submitted to the Internal Revenue Service, which immediately began an investigation to determine the tax consequences of the payments. Special agents conducting the investigation were given lists by Upjohn of all those interviewed and all who had responded to the questionnaire. On November 23, 1976, the Service issued a summons pursuant to 26 U.S.C. §7602 demanding production of:

> "All files relative to the investigation conducted under the supervision of Gerard Thomas to identify payments to employees of foreign governments and any political contributions made by the Upjohn Company or any of its affiliates since January 1, 1971 and to determine whether any funds of the Upjohn Company had been improperly accounted for on the corporate books during the same period.
>
> "The records should include but not be limited to written questionnaires sent to managers of the Upjohn Company's foreign affiliates, and memorandums or notes of the interviews conducted in the United States and abroad with officers and employees of the Upjohn Company and its subsidiaries."

The company declined to produce the documents specified in the second paragraph on the grounds that they were protected from disclosure by the attorney-client privilege and constituted the work product of attorneys prepared in anticipation of litigation. On August 31, 1977, the United States filed a petition seeking enforcement of the summons under 26 U.S.C. §§7402(b) and 7604(a) in the United States District Court for the Western District of Michigan. That court adopted the recommendation of a Magistrate who concluded that the summons should be enforced. Petitioners appealed to the Court of Appeals for the Sixth Circuit which rejected the Magistrate's finding of a waiver of the attorney-client privilege, but agreed that the privilege did not apply "[t]o the extent that the communications were made by officers and agents not responsible for directing Upjohn's actions in response to legal advice . . . for the simple reason that the communications were not the 'client's.'" . . . In a concluding footnote the court stated that the work-product doctrine "is not applicable to administrative summonses issued under 26 U.S.C. §7602."

Federal Rule of Evidence 501 provides that "the privilege of a witness . . . shall be governed by the principles of the common law as they may be interpreted by the courts of the United States in light of reason and experience." The attorney-client privilege is the oldest of the privileges for confidential communications known to the common law. 8 J. Wigmore, Evidence

§2290 (McNaughton rev. 1961). Its purpose is to encourage full and frank communication between attorneys and their clients and thereby promote broader public interests in the observance of law and administration of justice. The privilege recognizes that sound legal advice or advocacy serves public ends and that such advice or advocacy depends upon the lawyer's being fully informed by the client. As we stated last Term in *Trammel v. United States*, 445 U.S. 40, 51 (1980): "The lawyer-client privilege rests on the need for the advocate and counselor to know all that relates to the client's reasons for seeking representation if the professional mission is to be carried out." And in *Fisher v. United States*, 425 U.S. 391, 403 (1976), we recognized the purpose of the privilege to be "to encourage clients to make full disclosure to their attorneys." This rationale for the privilege has long been recognized by the Court, see *Hunt v. Blackburn*, 128 U.S. 464, 470 (1888) (privilege "is founded upon the necessity, in the interest and administration of justice, of the aid of persons having knowledge of the law and skilled in its practice, which assistance can only be safely and readily availed of when free from the consequences or the apprehension of disclosure"). Admittedly complications in the application of the privilege arise when the client is a corporation, which in theory is an artificial creature of the law, and not an individual; but this Court has assumed that the privilege applies when the client is a corporation, *United States v. Louisville & Nashville R. Co.*, 236 U.S. 318, 336 (1915), and the Government does not contest the general proposition.

The Court of Appeals, however, considered the application of the privilege in the corporate context to present a "different problem," since the client was an inanimate entity and "only the senior management, guiding and integrating the several operations, . . . can be said to possess an identity analogous to the corporation as a whole." The first case to articulate the so-called "control group test" adopted by the court below, *Philadelphia v. Westinghouse Electric Corp.*, 210 F. Supp. 483, 485 (ED Pa.), *petition for mandamus and prohibition denied sub nom General Electric Co. v. Kirkpatrick*, 312 F.2d 742 (CA3 1962), *cert denied*, 372 U.S. 943 (1963), reflected a similar conceptual approach:

> "Keeping in mind that the question is, Is it the corporation which is seeking the lawyer's advice when the asserted privileged communication is made?, the most satisfactory solution, I think, is that if the employee making the communication, of whatever rank he may be, is in a position to control or even to take a substantial part in a decision about any action which the corporation may take upon the advice of the attorney, . . . then, in effect, *he is (or personifies) the corporation* when he makes his disclosure to the lawyer and the privilege would apply." (Emphasis supplied.)

Such a view, we think, overlooks the fact that the privilege exists to protect not only the giving of professional advice to those who can act on it but also the giving of information to the lawyer to enable him to give sound and informed advice. The first step in the resolution of any legal problem is ascertaining the factual background and sifting through the facts with an eye to the legally relevant. See ABA Code of Professional Responsibility, Ethical Consideration 4-1:

> "A lawyer should be fully informed of all the facts of the matter he is handling in order for his client to obtain the full advantage of our legal system. It is for the lawyer in the exercise of his independent professional judgment to separate

the relevant and important from the irrelevant and unimportant. The observance of the ethical obligation of a lawyer to hold inviolate the confidences and secrets of his client not only facilitates the full development of facts essential to proper representation of the client but also encourages laymen to seek early legal assistance."

See also *Hickman v. Taylor*, 329 U.S. 495, 511 (1947).

In the case of the individual client the provider of information and the person who acts on the lawyer's advice are one and the same. In the corporate context, however, it will frequently be employees beyond the control group as defined by the court below — "officers and agents ... responsible for directing [the company's] actions in response to legal advice" — who will possess the information needed by the corporation's lawyers. Middle-level — and indeed lower-level — employees can, by actions within the scope of their employment, embroil the corporation in serious legal difficulties, and it is only natural that these employees would have the relevant information needed by corporate counsel if he is adequately to advise the client with respect to such actual or potential difficulties....

The control group test adopted by the court below thus frustrates the very purpose of the privilege by discouraging the communication of relevant information by employees of the client to attorneys seeking to render legal advice to the client corporation. The attorney's advice will also frequently be more significant to noncontrol group members than to those who officially sanction the advice, and the control group test makes it more difficult to convey full and frank legal advice to the employees who will put into effect the client corporation's policy....

The narrow scope given the attorney-client privilege by the court below not only makes it difficult for corporate attorneys to formulate sound advice when their client is faced with a specific legal problem but also threatens to limit the valuable efforts of corporate counsel to ensure their client's compliance with the law. In light of the vast and complicated array of regulatory legislation confronting the modern corporation, corporations, unlike most individuals, "constantly go to lawyers to find out how to obey the law," Burnham, The Attorney-Client Privilege in the Corporate Arena, 24 Bus. Law. 901, 913 (1969), particularly since compliance with the law in this area is hardly an instinctive matter, see, e.g., *United States v. United States Gypsum Co.*, 438 U.S. 422, 440-441 (1978) ("the behavior proscribed by the [Sherman] Act is often difficult to distinguish from the gray zone of socially acceptable and economically justifiable business conduct"). The test adopted by the court below is difficult to apply in practice, though no abstractly formulated and unvarying "test" will necessarily enable courts to decide questions such as this with mathematical precision. But if the purpose of the attorney-client privilege is to be served, the attorney and client must be able to predict with some degree of certainty whether particular discussions will be protected. An uncertain privilege, or one which purports to be certain but results in widely varying applications by the courts, is little better than no privilege at all. The very terms of the test adopted by the court below suggest the unpredictability of its application. The test restricts the availability of the privilege to those officers who play a "substantial role" in deciding and directing a corporation's legal response.

Disparate decisions in cases applying this test illustrate its unpredictability. Compare, e.g., *Hogan v. Zletz*, 43 F.R.D. 308, 315–316 (ND Okla. 1967), *aff'd in part sub nom. Natta v. Hogan*, 392 F.2d 686 (CA10 1968) (control group includes managers and assistant managers of patent division and research and development department), with *Congoleum Industries, Inc. v. GAF Corp.*, 49 F.R.D. 82, 83–85 (ED Pa. 1969), *aff'd*, 478 F.2d 1398 (CA3 1973) (control group includes only division and corporate vice presidents, and not two directors of research and vice president for production and research).

The communications at issue were made by Upjohn employees[1] to counsel for Upjohn acting as such, at the direction of corporate superiors in order to secure legal advice from counsel. As the Magistrate found, "Mr. Thomas consulted with the Chairman of the Board and outside counsel and thereafter conducted a factual investigation to determine the nature and extent of the questionable payments *and to be in a position to give legal advice to the company with respect to the payments*." (Emphasis supplied.) Information, not available from upper-echelon management, was needed to supply a basis for legal advice concerning compliance with securities and tax laws, foreign laws, currency regulations, duties to shareholders, and potential litigation in each of these areas. The communications concerned matters within the scope of the employees' corporate duties, and the employees themselves were sufficiently aware that they were being questioned in order that the corporation could obtain legal advice. The questionnaire identified Thomas as "the company's General Counsel" and referred in its opening sentence to the possible illegality of payments such as the ones on which information was sought. A statement of policy accompanying the questionnaire clearly indicated the legal implications of the investigation. The policy statement was issued "in order that there be no uncertainty in the future as to the policy with respect to the practices which are the subject of this investigation." It began "Upjohn will comply with all laws and regulations," and stated that commissions or payments "will not be used as a subterfuge for bribes or illegal payments" and that all payments must be "proper and legal." Any future agreements with foreign distributors or agents were to be approved "by a company attorney" and any questions concerning the policy were to be referred "to the company's General Counsel." This statement was issued to Upjohn employees worldwide, so that even those interviewees not receiving a questionnaire were aware of the legal implications of the interviews. Pursuant to explicit instructions from the Chairman of the Board, the communications were considered "highly confidential" when made, and have been kept confidential by the company. Consistent with the underlying purposes of the attorney-client privilege, these communications must be protected against compelled disclosure.

The Court of Appeals declined to extend the attorney-client privilege beyond the limits of the control group test for fear that doing so would entail

---

1. Seven of the eighty-six employees interviewed by counsel had terminated their employment with Upjohn at the time of the interview. Petitioners argue that the privilege should nonetheless apply to communications by these former employees concerning activities during their period of employment. Neither the District Court nor the Court of Appeals had occasion to address this issue, and we decline to decide it without the benefit of treatment below.

severe burdens on discovery and create a broad "zone of silence" over corporate affairs. Application of the attorney-client privilege to communications such as those involved here, however, puts the adversary in no worse position than if the communications had never taken place. The privilege only protects disclosure of communications; it does not protect disclosure of the underlying facts by those who communicated with the attorney:

> "[T]he protection of the privilege extends only to *communications* and not to facts. A fact is one thing and a communication concerning that fact is an entirely different thing. The client cannot be compelled to answer the question, 'What did you say or write to the attorney?' but may not refuse to disclose any relevant fact within his knowledge merely because he incorporated a statement of such fact into his communication to his attorney." *Philadelphia v. Westinghouse Electric Corp.*, 205 F. Supp. 830, 831.

Here the Government was free to question the employees who communicated with Thomas and outside counsel. Upjohn has provided the IRS with a list of such employees, and the IRS has already interviewed some 25 of them. While it would probably be more convenient for the Government to secure the results of petitioner's internal investigation by simply subpoenaing the questionnaires and notes taken by petitioner's attorneys, such considerations of convenience do not overcome the policies served by the attorney-client privilege. As Justice Jackson noted in his concurring opinion in *Hickman v. Taylor*, 329 U.S., at 516: "Discovery was hardly intended to enable a learned profession to perform its functions . . . on wits borrowed from the adversary."

Needless to say, we decide only the case before us, and do not undertake to draft a set of rules which should govern challenges to investigatory subpoenas. Any such approach would violate the spirit of Federal Rule of Evidence 501. See S. Rep. No. 93-1277, p. 13 (1974) ("the recognition of a privilege based on a confidential relationship . . . should be determined on a case-by-case basis"). While such a "case-by-case" basis may to some slight extent undermine desirable certainty in the boundaries of the attorney-client privilege, it obeys the spirit of the Rules. At the same time we conclude that the narrow "control group test" sanctioned by the Court of Appeals, in this case cannot, consistent with "the principles of the common law as . . . interpreted . . . in the light of reason and experience," Fed. Rule Evid. 501, govern the development of the law in this area.

Our decision that the communications by Upjohn employees to counsel are covered by the attorney-client privilege disposes of the case so far as the responses to the questionnaires and any notes reflecting responses to interview questions are concerned. The summons reaches further, however, and Thomas has testified that his notes and memoranda of interviews go beyond recording responses to his questions. To the extent that the material subject to the summons is not protected by the attorney-client privilege as disclosing communications between an employee and counsel, we must reach the ruling by the Court of Appeals that the work-product doctrine does not apply to summonses issued under 26 U.S.C. §7602.

The Government concedes, wisely, that the Court of Appeals erred and that the work-product doctrine does apply to IRS summonses. This doctrine was announced by the Court over 30 years ago in *Hickman v. Taylor*, 329 U.S.

495 (1947). In that case the Court rejected "an attempt, without purported necessity or justification, to secure written statements, private memoranda and personal recollections prepared or formed by an adverse party's counsel in the course of his legal duties." The Court noted that "it is essential that a lawyer work with a certain degree of privacy" and reasoned that if discovery of the material sought were permitted

> "much of what is now put down in writing would remain unwritten. An attorney's thoughts, heretofore inviolate, would not be his own. Inefficiency, unfairness and sharp practices would inevitably develop in the giving of legal advice and in the preparation of cases for trial. The effect on the legal profession would be demoralizing. And the interests of the clients and the cause of justice would be poorly served."

The "strong public policy" underlying the work-product doctrine was reaffirmed recently in *United States v. Nobles*, 422 U.S. 225, 236–240 (1975), and has been substantially incorporated in Federal Rule of Civil Procedure 26(b)(3).[7] ... While conceding the applicability of the work-product doctrine, the Government asserts that it has made a sufficient showing of necessity to overcome its protections. The Magistrate apparently so found.

... It is clear that the Magistrate applied the wrong standard when he concluded that the Government had made a sufficient showing of necessity to overcome the protections of the work-product doctrine. The Magistrate applied the "substantial need" and "without undue hardship" standard articulated in the first part of Rule 26(b)(3). The notes and memoranda sought by the Government here, however, are work product based on oral statements. If they reveal communications, they are, in this case, protected by the attorney-client privilege. To the extent they do not reveal communications, they reveal the attorneys' mental processes in evaluating the communications. As Rule 26 and *Hickman* make clear, such work product cannot be disclosed simply on a showing of substantial need and inability to obtain the equivalent without undue hardship.

While we are not prepared at this juncture to say that such material is always protected by the work-product rule, we think a far stronger showing of necessity and unavailability by other means than was made by the Government or applied by the Magistrate in this case would be necessary to compel disclosure. Since the Court of Appeals thought that the work-product protection was never applicable in an enforcement proceeding such as this, and since the Magistrate whose recommendations the District Court adopted applied too lenient a standard of protection, we think the best procedure with

---

7. This provides, in pertinent part: "[A] party may obtain discovery of documents and tangible things otherwise discoverable under subdivision (b)(1) of this rule and prepared in anticipation of litigation or for trial by or for another party or by or for that other party's representative (including his attorney, consultant, surety, indemnitor, insurer, or agent) only upon a showing that the party seeking discovery has substantial need of the materials in the preparation of his case and that he is unable without undue hardship to obtain the substantial equivalent of the materials by other means. In ordering discovery of such materials when the required showing has been made, the court shall protect against disclosure of the mental impressions, conclusions, opinions, or legal theories of an attorney or other representative of a party concerning the litigation."

respect to this aspect of the case would be to reverse the judgment of the Court of Appeals for the Sixth Circuit and remand the case to it for such further proceedings in connection with the work-product claim as are consistent with this opinion.... It is so ordered.

[Chief Justice Burger filed an opinion concurring in part and concurring in the judgment.]

UNITED STATES v. RUEHLE

583 F.3d 600 (9th Cir. 2009)

TALLMAN, Circuit Judge.

[Defendant Ruehle was the Chief Financial Officer of Broadcom Corporation, which was investigated by the Securities and Exchange Commission and sued by several private parties in 2006 for alleged backdating of employee stock options. Broadcom hired the law firm Irell & Manella to investigate its practices in granting stock options, in part by interviewing Broadcom employees. In the course of this investigation, called the "Equity Review," Irell attorneys interviewed Ruehle on June 1, 2006, and he made incriminating statements. Irell forwarded these statements, along with other information, to the accounting firm Ernst & Young, which was conducting an independent audit of Broadcom. During a later criminal investigation of Ruehle, prosecutors interviewed the Irell attorneys, with Broadcom's authorization, about their conversations with Ruehle.]

On January 12, 2009, the government moved *ex parte* for a hearing to resolve whether the statements Ruehle made to Irell lawyers in June 2006 were privileged communications. Ruehle argued that he had an individual attorney-client relationship with Irell arising from the securities lawsuits, in which he was a named defendant. Beginning on February 23, 2009, the district court held a three-day evidentiary hearing at which Ruehle and Irell attorneys Heitz and Lefler testified.... Both Irell attorneys insisted that Irell's individual representation of Ruehle in relation to the civil securities lawsuits did not commence until after the June 1, 2006, interview. Among other things, the attorneys testified that they began the June 2006 meeting with a so-called *Upjohn* or corporate *Miranda* warning, which included notice that the Irell attorneys were acting as representatives of Broadcom—specifically, the Audit Committee—and that the privilege therefore rested only with the company. Ruehle, however, denied any recollection of receiving such cautionary warnings at the June 1, 2006, interview. Ruehle testified that at the time he spoke with Heitz and Lefler he believed Irell represented everyone named in the civil suits, including him, and that Heitz and Lefler were acting at least in part as his personal attorneys during the interview.

At the conclusion of the hearing, the district court rendered its oral ruling which strongly condemned the Irell attorneys' behavior with respect to the firm's handling of the Equity Review. The court then found that Ruehle "had a reasonable belief that Irell and Manella were his lawyers prior to the June 1, 2006 interrogation by Irell, and that he never gave informed written consent, either to the dual representation by Irell or the disclosure of privileged information to third parties, including Ernst & Young and the government." Based on this reasoning, the court ordered suppression. The district court subsequently issued a written order, which included an additional finding that Ruehle intended his statements to Heitz and Lefler to be confidential.... The court also referred Irell to the California State Bar for possible discipline in light of numerous perceived violations of state rules of professional conduct.

The government interlocutorily appealed the district court's suppression order and we consider it on an expedited basis.... [W]e hold that ... Ruehle's statements to the Irell attorneys were not "made in confidence" but rather for the purpose of disclosure to the outside auditors. That he might regret those statements after later learning of the subsequent corporate disclosure to law enforcement officials is not material to the privilege determination as of June 2006.

... The notion that Ruehle spoke with Irell attorneys Heitz and Lefler with the reasonable belief that his statements were confidential is unsupported by the record. Of particular significance is what was said in the meetings he attended prior to June 1, 2006, with Irell attorneys, company management, and the Audit Committee, as acknowledged in Ruehle's own testimony. He frankly admitted that he understood the fruits of Irell's searching inquiries would be disclosed to Ernst & Young in order to convince the independent auditors of the integrity of Broadcom's financial statements to the public, or to take appropriate accounting measures to rectify any misleading reports. We reject the district court's contrary finding ... [as] clearly erroneous....

Ruehle was no ordinary Broadcom employee. He served as the public company's CFO — the senior corporate executive charged with primary responsibility for Broadcom's financial affairs. This was a sophisticated corporate enterprise with billions of dollars in sales worldwide, aided by accountants, lawyers, and advisors entrusted with meeting a multitude of regulatory obligations. The duties undertaken by Ruehle broadly encompassed not only accurately and completely reporting the company's historical and current stock option granting practices, but also Broadcom's strict compliance with reporting and record keeping requirements imposed through the Securities Exchange Act of 1934 and the Sarbanes–Oxley Act of 2002, among many other federal and state rules and regulations. See, e.g., 15 U.S.C. §§ 7241, 7262(a). As the head of finance, Ruehle cannot now credibly claim ignorance of the general disclosure requirements imposed on a publicly traded company with respect to its outside auditors or the need to truthfully report corporate information to the SEC.

On appeal, Ruehle tries to minimize the damning evidence confirming his awareness that his interactions with Irell would not be held in confidence. He places much weight on the assertion that he only learned of the details of Irell's disclosures to Ernst & Young and the government in 2008 and that he was "shocked." ... [But the] salient point from a privilege perspective is that Ruehle readily admits his understanding that all factual information would be communicated to third parties .... Ruehle's subjective shock and surprise about the subsequent usage of the information ... is frankly of no consequence here.

In support of his case for invocation of the privilege, Ruehle also repeatedly points to attorney Heitz's testimony that he could not "split his mind" so as to distinguish between facts relevant to the Equity Review and those relevant to the defense of Ruehle in the pending civil securities litigation, because they both had at their core Broadcom's stock option granting practices. But his efforts to make gold from lead are met with failure. The implicit concession on Ruehle's part—that the information underlying the Equity Review and the lawsuits was largely inseparable, if not one and the same—is detrimental, not helpful, to his case. His admitted awareness that anything relating to the former would not be held in confidence but rather shared with at least one third party destroys the confidentiality essential to establishing the privilege as to both. . . .

Accordingly, we hold that Ruehle has failed to meet his burden of establishing the existence of an individual attorney-client privilege . . . . The district court's order suppressing the Irell evidence is reversed and the matter is remanded for trial.

d. To Facilitate Legal Service

HUGHES v. MEADE

453 S.W.2d 538 (Ky. 1970)

CLAY, Commissioner.

This is an original proceeding for a writ of prohibition against the Honorable N. Mitchell Meade, Judge of the Fayette Circuit Court. Petitioner, an attorney, seeks to restrain the respondent from enforcing a contempt ruling entered against him because of his refusal to answer a question as a witness in a criminal trial. Petitioner was not a party to, nor did he represent anyone as an attorney in such proceeding.

The proceeding in which he was called as a witness was the trial of one Williams on a criminal charge involving the theft of an IBM typewriter. Petitioner had participated in the return of an IBM typewriter to the Lexington Police Department. [He refused to disclose who had hired him to return it.] It is his contention that this information was a privileged communication under KRS 421.210(4), and the trial court improperly sought to compel him to disclose it. That subsection of the statute provides (insofar as pertinent): "No attorney shall testify concerning a *communication* made to him, *in his professional character*, by his client, or his advice thereon without the Client's consent. . . ." (Emphasis added.)

This statutory provision generally conforms to the common law policy and principle of attorney-client privilege (developed since 1800) and it is generally recognized in the United States. See 8 Wigmore, Evidence §2291 (McNaughton rev. 1961). This same author thus phrases the principle (page 554): "(1) Where legal advice of any kind is sought (2) from a professional legal adviser in his capacity as such, (3) the communications relating to that purpose, (4) made in confidence (5) by the client, (6) are at his instance permanently protected (7) from disclosure by himself or by the legal adviser, (8) except the protection be waived."

... In line with those limitations, it is generally held that the identity of a client is not a privileged communication. *United States v. Page* (C.A.2 1944), 144 F.2d 778, 782, *cert den.* 323 U.S. 752 (1944); *Behrens v. Hironimus* (C.A.4 1948), 170 F.2d 627, 628; *Colton v. United States* (C.A.2 1962), 306 F.2d 633, 637; *NLRB v. Harvey* (C.A.4 1965), 349 F.2d 900.... This general rule, however, like most others, is subject to exception under unusual circumstances. In the following cases the identity of the client was held within the scope of the privilege. *Ex parte McDonough*, 170 Cal. 230 (1915); *Baird v. Koerner* (C.A.9 1960), 279 F.2d 623; *In Re Kaplan*, 8 N.Y.2d 214 (1960); and *Tillotson v. Boughner* (C.A.7 1965), 350 F.2d 663.

In the above cases the attorney-client relationship was clearly established, and the acts performed were closely interrelated with the rendering of professional service. In *McDonough* the attorney had been employed by an undisclosed client to defend a criminal charge against another person. In *Baird* the attorney had turned over to the government a sum of money which some taxpayers, in consultation with the attorney, had determined was due and owing as unpaid income taxes. The court observed that the only reason for obtaining information concerning the clients' identities was for the purpose of prosecution. *Tillotson* involved facts similar to those in *Baird*. In *Kaplan* the attorney had been retained to pass on to a public investigating body certain information concerning certain apparent wrongdoing by municipal authorities. It was here observed that since the information had been given, the client's name deserved and needed protection.

As noted in the foregoing cases, the transactions about which information had been given constituted in essence the performance of a legal service. On the other hand, if the act in question fairly cannot be said to fall within the scope of professional employment, the privilege cannot be invoked. As said in 97 C.J.S. Witnesses §280, page 793:"Neither is there any privilege as to communications with reference to a matter in which the attorney acts, not in his professional capacity, but merely as an agent or attorney in fact, or in which the attorney acts merely as a depositary or as a trustee, particularly where he has instructions to deliver the instrument deposited to a third person, or abstracter of titles."

... Returning to the facts of this case, it is the opinion of the majority of the court that whether or not a bona fide attorney-client relationship existed between the petitioner and the undisclosed person, the principal transaction involved, i.e., the delivery of stolen property to the police department, was not an act in the professional capacity of petitioner nor was it the rendition of a legal service. He was acting as an agent or conduit for the delivery of property which was completely unrelated to legal representation. While repose of confidence in an attorney is something much to be desired, to use him as a shield to conceal transactions involving stolen property is beyond the scope of his professional duty and beyond the scope of the privilege.... The petition for a writ of prohibition is denied.

UNITED STATES v. DAVIS

636 F.2d 1028 (5th Cir. 1981)

WISDOM, Circuit Judge:

[Attorney Craig Davis appealed from a judgment enforcing an IRS summons requiring him to produce documents relating to the tax liability of his client.] The summons to Davis requests the workpapers he produced in the course of preparing Howard's tax returns and the tax records upon which they were based. Neither category of documents is privileged, because although preparation of tax returns by itself may require some knowledge of the law, it is primarily an accounting service. Communications relating to that service should therefore not be privileged, even though performed by a lawyer. *Olender v. United States*, 9 Cir. 1954, 210 F.2d 795, 805-06; *Canaday v. United States*, 8 Cir. 1966, 354 F.2d 849, 857. Some courts have suggested, to the contrary, that tax return preparation and tax advice is sufficiently "legal" in nature to trigger the privilege. *See Colton v. United States*, 2 Cir. 1962, 306 F.2d 633, 637, *cert. denied*, 1963, 371 U.S. 951. These services, however, are typically performed by accountants, and since there is no accountant-client privilege under federal law, there is no doubt that the papers summoned here would not be privileged if Howard had had a professional accountant prepare his returns. *Couch v. United States*, 1973, 409 U.S. 322, 335; *Falsone v. United States*, 5 Cir. 1953, 205 F.2d 734, *cert. denied*, 1953, 346 U.S. 864. It would make little sense to permit a taxpayer to invoke a privilege merely because he hires an attorney to perform the same task. The summons to Davis must therefore be enforced in its entirety. [Affirmed.]

WARTELL v. PURDUE UNIVERSITY

Cause No. 1:13-CV-99 RLM-APR (N.D. Ind. 2014)

Robert L. Miller, Jr., District Judge.

... Indiana University–Purdue University Fort Wayne Chancellor Michael Wartell asked for a waiver of the university's mandatory retirement age, and University President Frances Cordova declined the request. Dr. Wartell says Dr. Cordova then harassed and discriminated against him on the basis of sex and age, and Dr. Wartell filed an internal complaint against Dr. Cordova.... It seems that this sort of dispute between the president and chancellor aren't routine at Purdue, and Dr. Wartell expressed concern about the fairness of a process in which people who answer to the president would investigate and resolve his claim against the president. The board of trustees proposed a special one-time only method of addressing Dr. Wartell's complaint. Purdue Vice President Alysa Christmas Rollock proposed that method to Dr. Cordova and Dr. Wartell in a letter, and both agreed to it.... [Pursuant] to that procedure, Vice President Rollock engaged John C. Trimble, a prominent Indianapolis attorney, to serve as the investigator, to be paid by Purdue. Neither the president nor the chancellor objected to Mr. Trimble's selection. But it appears that Chancellor Wartell and Vice President Rollock might have differed in their understanding of the role Mr. Trimble was to play. Vice President Rollock retained Mr. Trimble as an attorney for Purdue. Chancellor Wartell didn't learn that Mr. Trimble had been retained in that capacity until much later.

Mr. Trimble set about the tasks outlined in the vice president's letter. He interviewed the president, the chancellor, and about twelve others. When he interviewed Dr. Wartell, Mr. Trimble didn't disclose that he was acting as Purdue's attorney . . . [Following the agreed-upon procedure,] Mr. Trimble prepared his report and submitted it to [a panel composed of three of the university's trustees, which was to make a final, binding decision in the case]. The panel found that no discrimination occurred, and sent its decision to the president, the chancellor, and Vice President Rollock.

. . . [Subsequently] Dr. Wartell filed suit in this court for sex discrimination, violation of due process, and breach of contract. Inevitably, Dr. Wartell filed a request for production of Mr. Trimble's report and associated documents, and Purdue refused to produce them because of the attorney-client and work-product privileges. Dr. Wartell moved to compel. . . . [Magistrate] Judge Rodovich ruled against Purdue with respect to the work-product doctrine, because the report and documents hadn't been prepared in anticipation of litigation; Purdue doesn't challenge that ruling.

Magistrate Judge Rodovich also rejected Purdue's attorney-client privilege claim. He . . . noted that Mr. Trimble was to perform investigative tasks a non-lawyer employee would perform in a less extraordinary case. Mr. Trimble interviewed people and wrote a recommendation to the three-trustee panel. No lawsuit was pending or imminent. Magistrate Judge Rodovich noted that Mr. Trimble didn't tell Chancellor Wartell that he was representing Purdue; an Indiana attorney generally must make such a disclosure when the organization he represents might have interests adverse to the officer with whom the lawyer is dealing. Ind. Prof. Cond. R. 1.13(f). Magistrate Judge Rodovich concluded that Purdue had "failed to meet its burden to show how Trimble's activities equated to legal advice." . . . Purdue filed a partial objection (Purdue doesn't challenge the magistrate judge's decision on the work-product privilege) to the order granting Dr. Wartell's motion to compel.

Federal law provides the rule of decision in this case, so federal common law, as interpreted in the federal courts in light of reason and experience, governs Purdue's privilege claim. Fed.R.Evid. 501. . . . Purdue contends that the magistrate judge erred as a matter of law by not following (or even discussing with respect to the attorney-client privilege) the court of appeals' decision in *Sandra T.E. v. South Berwyn Sch. Dist. 100,* 600 F.3d 612 (7th Cir. 2010). In *Sandra T.E.,* a law firm's investigative materials for a school were deemed privileged, Purdue argues, compelling a similar holding here. But this is a far different case than was *Sandra T.E.*

Sandra T.E. stemmed from criminal charges against a school teacher for molesting a number of elementary school students over a period of years. The School Board called in a law firm — Sidley Austin LLP — and sent letters to parents saying that Sidley Austin had been hired to conduct an investigation. Lawsuits were filed against the School Board for failing to protect the students, and the plaintiff parents moved to compel the School Board to produce the report of Sidley Austin's investigation and surrounding documents. . . . [T]he engagement letter between Sidley Austin and the Board ... [had] engaged the firm not merely to investigate, but also to evaluate the legal sufficiency of the Board's compliance procedures and to provide legal services to the Board in connection with the investigation. ... [Moreover, the court of appeals noted that during its] "confidential interviews with school-district employees, the attorneys provided so-called '*Upjohn* warnings' emphasizing that Sidley represented the School Board and not the employee and that the [Board] had control over whether the conversations remained privileged. ...

The magistrate judge noted that when Mr. Trimble interviewed Chancellor Wartell, Mr. Trimble didn't disclose any attorney-client relationship with Purdue. ... That Sidley Austin lawyers gave "*Upjohn* warnings" was evidence that they were acting as the school board's attorneys; that Mr. Trimble didn't do so was evidence that he was acting merely as an investigator, rather than as Purdue's attorney. ...

Sandra T.E. was very fact-specific: under those specific facts, the investigation was an essential part of the legal services and advice Sidley Austin was retained to provide to the school board. ... [Here, there] was no engagement letter in the record, nor any indication that the report to the three-trustee panel was labeled "Privileged and Confidential" or "Attorney–Client Communication". Instead, there was Vice President Rollock's letter indicating that an independent investigator would be appointed, with no hint that the "independent investigator" would be an attorney owing a fiduciary duty to Purdue, and Mr. Trimble's conduct of the interview with Chancellor Wartell, which was consistent with the role of an investigator rather than the role of an attorney for Purdue. ... Given the evidentiary materials before him, there was no clear error in Magistrate Rodovich's finding that, "The record does not reflect that Trimble was giving legal advice by conducting the investigation and report. Rather, he was conducting an internal investigation so that Purdue could determine how to respond prior to the prospect of litigation." Having found that Purdue wasn't seeking legal advice from Mr. Trimble, there was no clear error in the holding that the attorney-client privilege doesn't protect the communications between Mr. Trimble and Purdue.

For the foregoing reasons, the court ... OVERRULES the defendants' partial objection to the magistrate judge's grant of the plaintiff's motion to compel. ...

LUV N' CARE, LTD. v. WILLIAMS
INTELLECTUAL PROPERTY

Civil Action No. 18-MC-00212-WJM-KLM (D. Colo. 2019)

Entered by Magistrate Judge KRISTIN L. MIX

[Luv N' Care marketed a combined placemat and bowl for young children. So did another company, run by Lindsey Laurain. Luv N' Care entered into litigation in Louisiana with Laurain about which company had infringed the other's patents, and then filed a separate lawsuit in Colorado against

Williams Intellectual Property ("WIP"), a patent agent firm. The Colorado lawsuit sought documents from WIP relating to its work for Laurain. WIP claimed the documents were privileged.]

Federal Rule of Civil Procedure 26(b)(1) requires production of "any nonprivileged matter that is relevant to any party's claim or defense and proportional to the needs of the case." . . . The question of whether a patent-agent privilege exists is one of first impression in the Tenth Circuit. The privilege was first formally recognized by the Federal Circuit in *In re Queen's University at Kingston*, 820 F.3d 1287 (Fed. Cir. 2016); since *Queen's University*, every federal court that has been faced with the question of recognition of the patent-agent privilege has agreed with the Federal Circuit's determination. *See, e.g., Onyx Therapeutics, Inc. v. Cipla Ltd.*, No. 16-988-LPS, 2019 WL 668846 (D. Del. Feb. 15, 2019); . . . *but see In re Andrew Silver*, 500 S.W.3d 644, 646 (Tex. App. 2016) (declining to create independent patent-agent privilege, concluding that the Texas Constitution prohibited recognition of new privileges).

The patent-agent privilege recognized in *Queen's University* is rooted in the Supreme Court's ruling in *Sperry v. State of Florida ex rel. Florida Bar*, 373 U.S. 379, 383 (1963), which found that "the preparation and prosecution of patent applications for others constitutes the practice of law," even when conducted by non-attorney patent agents. Thus, in *Queen's University*, the Federal Circuit determined that the justification for the traditional attorney-client privilege based on the need for candor between an attorney and his or her client applied equally to patent agents and their clients.

However, the scope of the patent-agent privilege is narrow relative to the more broadly-applied attorney-client privilege. *Queen's University* recognized a privilege that is "coextensive" with the rights of patent agents to practice law before the U.S. Patent and Trademark Office ("USPTO"). Regulations promulgated by the USPTO [provide that "registration to practice before the Office in patent cases sanctions the performance of those services which are reasonably necessary and incident to the preparation and prosecution of patent applications or other proceeding before the Office involving a patent application or patent in which the practitioner is authorized to participate.]

Thus, the benefit of the patent-agent privilege is limited to those communications between a non-attorney patent agent and his or her client which are in furtherance of the execution of these functions. It follows that communications which are not "reasonably necessary and incident to the preparation and prosecution" of patent proceedings before the USPTO are not protected by the patent-agent privilege. For example, "communications with a patent agent who is offering an opinion on the validity of another party's patent in contemplation of litigation or for the sale or purchase of a patent, or on infringement, are not 'reasonably necessary and incident to the preparation and prosecution of patent applications,'" and thus are not protected by the privilege. *Queen's University*, 820 F.3d at 1301-02.

In *Onyx Therapeutics, Inc. v. Cipla Ltd.*, the United States District Court for the District of Delaware recognized the patent-agent privilege set forth in *Queen's University* but declined to extend it to communications from a group of scientists to a patent agent soliciting guidance in "understanding the patent landscape in order to direct their efforts" in pursuing patent prosecution in the future. The court there determined that such communications were "not 'reasonably necessary and incident to' the ultimate patent prosecution" and were thus not protected under the patent-agent privilege, even though such communications would be within the scope of the attorney-client privilege. . . .

[T]he Court assumes, without deciding, that the patent-agent privilege applies in the Tenth Circuit. . . . [E]very entry [in WIP's privilege log] purporting to assert the patent-agent privilege fails to meet the burden of showing that the privilege applies, as set out in *Queen's University*. For example, every communication involving Ben Williams, Ms. Laurain's patent agent, asserts that the entry is subject to the patent-agent privilege because of its subject matter: "Communications re: advice of patent agent and/or advice of patent agent + advice of counsel." However, merely soliciting advice of a patent agent does not satisfy the burden of showing that the privilege applies. Per *Queen's University*, the party asserting the privilege bears the burden of showing that the communications are "reasonably necessary and incident to the preparation and prosecution of patent applications or other proceeding before the [USPTO]." WIP's privilege log bears no mention of the preparation or prosecution of patent applications, and WIP has thus failed to satisfy the burden required by its assertion of privilege. . . .

PROBLEMS

10.1. Shortly after meeting with his lawyer on a separate matter, Dan is arrested for driving while intoxicated. At his trial, the prosecutor calls Dan's lawyer to the stand and asks her whether Dan appeared inebriated during their meeting. Dan objects on grounds of privilege. How should the judge rule?

10.2. Carolyn hires an accountant and tells him at their first meeting that she has not filed tax returns for the past five years because she could never find the time. She asks him whether he thinks she needs a lawyer, and he says yes. Are Carolyn's remarks to her accountant privileged?

10.3. The president of a chemical manufacturing company suspects that some of his employees are illegally disposing hazardous wastes. He hires a private detective firm to investigate. Are his conversations with the firm privileged? What about the conversations of his employees? Would the answers be different if he hired a law firm instead of a private detective firm? What if he hired a private detective firm, but the person he dealt with at the firm was a lawyer?

10.4. Craig wishes to become a U.S. citizen. Fred advertises his services as an "expert in immigration law." Craig hires Fred to help him complete the naturalization application. Contrary to Craig's belief, Fred is not a lawyer. Are Craig's confidential conversations with Fred privileged?

10.5. Colleen meets in her office with her lawyer. No one else is present, and they close the door. But their conversation is overheard by a window washer working outside the office immediately below Colleen's. Can Colleen prevent the window washer from testifying about what he heard?

10.6. From his desk at work, Collin sends his lawyer an e-mail message seeking legal advice. Collin's employer randomly monitors e-mail messages sent to and from Collin's workplace, in order to ensure the computer system is not misused. Collin was informed of the monitoring when he joined the company, but has forgotten about it. As it happens, Collin's employer does not read his message to his lawyer. Is the message privileged? Would the answer be different if the employer *did* read the message?

3. Waiver

Information protected by the attorney-client privilege, or any other privilege, loses its protection if the privilege is "waived." Waiver can be accomplished by any of a variety of actions inconsistent with a continuing intention to keep the protected communication confidential. The attorney-client privilege is held by the client, not the attorney, so in theory only the client can waive it. In practice, though, the privilege is often deemed waived because of actions by the attorney, on the ground that the attorney was acting as the agent of the client.

UNITED STATES v. BERNARD

877 F.2d 1463 (10th Cir. 1989)

Brorby, Circuit Judge.

Mr. Bernard appeals the judgment entered following his conviction of sixty-two criminal violations including [the making of illegal nominee loans.] . . . Two of these nominee loans were made to Mr. Treat. At trial, the government called Mr. Treat as a witness against the defendant. The gist of the testimony was that Mr. Treat had asked Mr. Bernard about the legality of making a nominee loan. Mr. Treat testified that Mr. Bernard told him that he (Mr. Bernard) had verified the legality of such a loan with an attorney, Mr. Tom Nally. . . . Later in the trial, the court ruled that Mr. Bernard waived his attorney-client privilege "in regard to the loans made by Bernard to Treat" and permitted the government to call Mr. Nally as a witness. Mr. Nally testified that Mr. Bernard was his client. He denied even discussing the question of the legality of nominee loans with his client.

. . . Mr. Bernard willingly sacrificed his attorney-client confidentiality and privilege by voluntarily disclosing the confidential communication to Mr. Treat. Any voluntary disclosure by the client is inconsistent with the attorney-client relationship and waives the privilege. Mr. Bernard did this in an effort to convince Mr. Treat that the proposed nominee loan was lawful and proper. Mr. Bernard, having revealed the purported conversation between himself and his counsel in an effort to induce Mr. Treat to engage in a nominee loan, cannot later claim the protection of the attorney-client privilege. . . . Affirmed.

TASBY v. UNITED STATES

504 F.2d 332 (8th Cir. 1974)

GIBSON, Chief Judge.

Johnnie Tasby appeals his jury conviction of making a false material declaration in violation of 18 U.S.C. §1623. He was sentenced to a term of three years' imprisonment to run consecutively to the term he is now serving. This prosecution arises from Tasby's testimony given under oath during two previous court proceedings. In the first proceeding Tasby was convicted of interstate kidnapping. This was affirmed on appeal. Subsequently, Tasby brought a petition for post-conviction relief pursuant to 28 U.S.C. 2255 which was denied after a hearing in the district court. This denial was affirmed on appeal.

At his original kidnapping trial Tasby testified in his own behalf. This occurred only after a record was made establishing through Tasby's own testimony that his attorney, Mr. Peek, had advised him not to take the stand, had explained to him the possible consequences of taking the stand, and that Tasby still wished to testify.

In the later §2255 proceeding Tasby claimed the ineffective assistance of counsel. In support of this claim Tasby testified that he did not wish to take the stand at the original trial. Further he stated that Mr. Peek had never advised him not to take the stand, alleging that he was coerced into taking the stand by Mr. Peek's statements that he would get 25 years to life if he did not testify. [Peek testified to the contrary at Tasby's trial for making a false material declaration.]

... We find no violation of the attorney-client privilege in the facts of this case. It has long been the law that a client may waive protection of the privilege, either expressly or impliedly. *Blackburn v. Crawfords*, 70 U.S. (3 Wall.) 175, 194 (1865). One of the circumstances which may support a conclusion of a waiver is an attack by the client upon his attorney's conduct which calls into question the substance of their communications. A client has a privilege to keep his conversations with his attorney confidential, but that privilege is waived when a client attacks his attorney's competence in giving legal advice, puts in issue that advice and ascribes a course of action to his attorney that raises the specter of ineffectiveness or incompetence. Here, the confidentiality of the attorney-client relationship was breached by Tasby. Surely a client is not free to make various allegations of misconduct and incompetence while the attorney's lips are sealed by invocation of the attorney-client privilege. Such an incongruous result would be inconsistent with the object and purpose of the attorney-client privilege and a patent perversion of the rule. When a client calls into public question the competence of his attorney, the privilege is waived. *Laughner v. United States*, 373 F.2d 326 (5th Cir. 1967); *Sherman v. United States*, 261 F. Supp. 522, 531 (D. Haw.), *aff'd* 383 F.2d 837 (9th Cir. 1966); *see Pruitt v. Peyton*, 243 F. Supp. 907 (E.D. Va. 1965); *United States v. Butler*, 167 F. Supp. 102 (E.D. Va. 1957), *aff'd* 260 F.2d 574 (4th Cir. 1958).

Tasby at the §2255 hearing attacked the representation of his attorney, thereby putting into question the substance of his communications with Tasby. We think this establishes Tasby's waiver of the privilege. In the present proceeding, Mr. Peek's testimony was relevant and material as to the truth or falsity of Tasby's prior declarations and the trial court was not in error in allowing Mr. Peek to testify. . . . Judgment of conviction affirmed.

HOLLINS v. POWELL

773 F.2d 191 (8th Cir. 1985)

Floyd R. Gibson, Senior Circuit Judge.

The defendants, the City of Wellston and Robert Powell, appeal from a judgment entered by the district judge upon a jury verdict finding them liable for violating the plaintiffs'—Margie Hollins', Mamie Wallace's, Annette McNeil's and Lloyd Brown's—constitutional rights. [Powell was the mayor of Wellston. The plaintiffs were city housing commissioners, appointed by Powell's predecessor. Powell questioned the legality of their appointments and named his own commissioners. When the plaintiffs nonetheless assembled for a regularly scheduled meeting and tried to conduct business, Powell had them arrested.]

Before trial, the plaintiffs sought to depose the City's attorney. The City filed a motion to quash the deposition, with an alternative request for a protective order, and the plaintiffs filed a motion to compel the deposition. The district court granted the plaintiffs' motion, noting that it appeared the City and Powell would raise advice of counsel as a defense, and held that the attorney-client privilege would be waived under those circumstances. The district court based its observations on the pleadings and the plaintiffs' assertions. Because the defendants had not yet raised advice of counsel as a defense, the court granted them seven days from entry of the order to inform the court whether the communications with the attorney would be part of the defense. The defendants failed to file a motion for reconsideration.

The City argues that because the district court erred by granting the motion to compel the deposition, it also erred in overruling the City's objection to the attorney's testimony at trial. We disagree. The district court properly granted the motion to compel and, although we do so for a different reason than did the district court, we hold that the defendants had waived the attorney-client privilege by the time the attorney was called as a witness.

Because the plaintiffs have sued the defendants for a violation of federal law, the federal law of privilege applies to this issue. Fed. R. Evid. 501. Initially, we note that the party who claims the benefit of the attorney-client privilege has the burden of establishing the right to invoke its protection. The defendants clearly failed to meet this burden as far as the deposition of the attorney is concerned. They adduced no evidence to support their assertion of the privilege. Thus, the district court did not err by granting the plaintiffs' motion to compel the deposition.

During the attorney's deposition, the City objected whenever it perceived that a question covered by the privilege was asked, and then instructed the attorney to answer the question. The plaintiffs argue that by proceeding in this manner the defendants waived the privilege. Under the circumstances of this case, the defendants preserved their right to claim the privilege at trial as to those questions to which they had objected. Had the defendants interrupted the deposition every time it objected to a question on the basis of privilege, and sought a protective order from the district court, they would have been violating the court's previous order. Thus, we reject the contention that the defendants waived the privilege during the deposition. Nonetheless, we hold that the defendants did waive the privilege during trial.

A client may waive the attorney-client privilege, and may do so either expressly or by implication. Waiver will be implied when a client has testified concerning portions of the attorney-client communication.

On plaintiffs' direct examination of him, Powell testified as to the substance of his conversations with the City's attorney, as well as to the substance of his conversations with his own attorney. This testimony occurred before the City's attorney was called as a witness. Because the City's attorney failed to object to the plaintiffs' relevant questions of Powell, it waived the attorney-client privilege. Thus, we need not determine whether the district court erred by relying on its pretrial order in overruling the City's objection to the attorney's testimony, for the privilege had been waived by that time. . . . [Judgment affirmed.]

IN RE VON BULOW

828 F.2d 94 (2d Cir. 1987)

CARDAMONE, Circuit Judge.

Petitioner Claus von Bulow seeks a writ of mandamus directing the United States District Court for the Southern District of New York (Walker, J.) to vacate its discovery order of February 12, 1987, granting plaintiff the right to discover certain conversations between petitioner and his attorneys. . . . On July 6, 1981 petitioner was indicted by a Newport County, Rhode Island, grand jury on two counts of assault with intent to murder for allegedly injecting his wife Martha von Bulow with insulin causing her to lapse into an irreversible coma. After a widely publicized jury trial, von Bulow was convicted on both counts on March 16, 1982. In April 1982 petitioner retained Harvard law professor Alan M. Dershowitz to represent him on appeal. In May 1982 von Bulow was sentenced to 30-years' imprisonment, but granted bail pending appeal. On April 27, 1984 the Rhode Island Supreme Court reversed both convictions, and upon retrial, he was acquitted on June 10, 1985.

Shortly after the acquittal, petitioner's wife, by her next friends, Alexander Auersperg and Annie Laurie Auersperg-Kneissal, Martha von Bulow's children from a prior marriage (plaintiff), commenced this civil action in federal court against petitioner alleging common law assault, negligence, fraud, and RICO violations. These claims arose out of the same facts and circumstances as the Rhode Island criminal prosecution.

In May 1986 Random House published a book entitled *Reversal of Fortune — Inside the von Bulow Case*, authored by attorney Dershowitz, which chronicles the events surrounding the first criminal trial, the successful appeal, and von Bulow's ultimate acquittal. After obtaining an advance copy of the book, plaintiff's counsel notified petitioner on April 23, 1986 that it would view publication as a waiver of the attorney-client privilege. Von Bulow's counsel responded that no waiver had occurred and that, accordingly, he would not act to stop the book's publication. After the book was released, von Bulow and attorney Dershowitz appeared on several television and radio shows to promote it.

Plaintiff then moved to compel discovery of certain discussions between petitioner and his attorneys based on the alleged waiver of the attorney-client privilege with respect to those communications related in the book. In order to avoid piecemeal rulings on each communication, counsel stipulated in July 1986 as to those controversial subjects appearing in *Reversal of Fortune*. On February 12, 1987 the United States District Court for the Southern District of New York (Walker, J.) found a waiver of the attorney-client privilege and ordered von Bulow and his attorneys to comply with discovery requested by plaintiff.

. . . By allowing publication of confidential communications in his attorney's book *Reversal of Fortune*, petitioner was held to have waived his attorney-client privilege. In reaching that conclusion, the district court considered the following facts. First, petitioner knew of, consented to, and actually encouraged attorney Dershowitz's plans to write a book providing an "insider look" into his case. Second, petitioner was warned before publication that such an act might trigger a waiver and, yet, took no active measures to preserve his confidences. Third, after publication, petitioner joined his attorney in enthusiastically promoting the book on television and radio shows. Based on these key facts, the district court determined that von Bulow had waived his attorney-client privilege.

Petitioner argues that this holding is erroneous because only the client — and not his attorney — may waive the privilege. Of course, the privilege belongs solely to the client and may only be waived by him. An attorney may not waive the privilege without his client's consent. Hence, absent a client's consent or waiver, the publication of confidential communications by an attorney does not constitute a relinquishment of the privilege by the client. *See, e.g., Schnell v. Schnall*, 550 F. Supp. 650, 653 (S.D.N.Y. 1982) (no waiver of attorney-client privilege where attorney testified at SEC hearing without presence or authorization of client). *See also Wigmore*, Evidence §2325, at 633 (McNaughton rev. ed. 1961) (attorney's voluntary disclosures remain privileged unless impliedly authorized by client).

A client may nonetheless by his actions impliedly waive the privilege or consent to disclosure. And an attorney may, in appropriate circumstances, possess "an implied authority to waive the privilege on behalf of his client." [*Drimmer v. Appleton*, 628 F. Supp. 1249, 1251 (S.D.N.Y. 1986)]; Wigmore, supra, §2325. Moreover, it is the client's responsibility to insure continued confidentiality of his communications. In *In re Horowitz*, 482 F.2d 72 (2d Cir.), *cert. denied*, 414 U.S. 867 (1973), Judge Friendly, speaking for the Court, warned: "[I]t is not asking too much to insist that if a client wishes to preserve the privilege under such circumstances, he must take some affirmative action to preserve confidentiality."

Applying these principles, it is quite clear that in finding that von Bulow waived his privilege the district court did not abuse its discretion. In light of petitioner's acquiescence in and encouragement of *Reversal of Fortune*'s publication, Judge Walker properly concluded that von Bulow consented to his attorney's disclosure of his confidences and effectively waived his attorney-client privilege. Our discussion now turns to examine the breadth of that waiver.

The district court held that plaintiffs were entitled to discover "the entire contents of all conversations from which Dershowitz published extracts in

Reversal of Fortune." The four relevant conversations between von Bulow and his attorneys were their initial one, and the ones regarding the bail hearing, appellate strategy, and von Bulow's decision to testify on his own behalf. Under that ruling, plaintiff is permitted to discover those parts of the four Identified conversations not made public in the book. Petitioner argues that the district court's holding improperly broadened the fairness doctrine to include extrajudicial disclosures and that, accordingly, the discovery order cannot stand. We agree.

. . . [T]he district judge based his decision on an extension of "[t]he principle that disclosure of a portion of a privileged conversation entitles an adversary to discovery of the matters discussed in the remainder of the conversation. . . ." The court reasoned that where reputation is at stake in a major case, it is tried today before the bar of public opinion, as well as in a courtroom. Judge Walker believed it unfair to permit a party to make use of privileged information as a sword with the public, and then as a shield in the courtroom. Thus, the trial judge found what is generally called a "waiver by implication," *see* Wigmore, supra, §2327, at 635, based on fairness considerations.

These considerations—which underlie "the fairness doctrine"—aim to prevent prejudice to a party and distortion of the judicial process that may be caused by the privilege-holder's selective disclosure during litigation of otherwise privileged information. Under the doctrine the client alone controls the privilege and may or may not choose to divulge his own secrets. But it has been established law for a hundred years that when the client waives the privilege by testifying about what transpired between her and her attorney, she cannot thereafter insist that the mouth of the attorney be shut. *Hunt v. Blackburn*, 128 U.S. 464, 470-71 (1888). From that has grown the rule that testimony as to part of a privileged communication, in fairness, requires production of the remainder. McCormick On Evidence §93, at 194-95 (2d ed. 1972).

Yet this rule protecting the party, the factfinder, and the judicial process from selectively disclosed and potentially misleading evidence does not come into play when, as here, the privilege-holder or his attorney has made extrajudicial disclosures, and those disclosures have not subsequently been placed at issue during litigation. In fact, the cases finding, as the district court did here, implied waivers on account of fairness involved material issues raised by a client's assertions during the course of a judicial proceeding. . . .

Applying the fairness doctrine, we hold therefore that the extrajudicial disclosure of an attorney-client communication—one not subsequently used by the client in a judicial proceeding to his adversary's prejudice—does not waive the privilege as to the undisclosed portions of the communication. Hence, though the district court correctly found a waiver by von Bulow as to the particular matters actually disclosed in the book, it was an abuse of discretion to broaden that waiver to include those portions of the four identified conversations which, because they were not published, remain secret. . . .

The district court next ruled that von Bulow's waiver extended to subject matter areas related to the published conversations with Dershowitz. This "subject matter waiver," which allows the attacking party to reach all privileged conversations regarding a particular subject once one privileged conversation on that topic has been disclosed, is simply another form of the waiver by implication rule discussed above. Like the "implied waiver," the subject matter waiver also rests on the fairness considerations at work in the context of litigation. *See Smith* [*v. Alyeska Pipeline Serv. Co.*, 538 F. Supp. 977, 979 (D. Del. 1982)] ("It would be unfair to allow a client to assert the attorney-client privilege and prevent disclosure of damaging communications while allowing the client to disclose other selected communications solely for self-serving purposes.")

For this reason, it too has been invoked most often where the privilege-holder has attempted to use the privilege as both "a sword" and "a Shield" or where the attacking party has been prejudiced at trial. . . . For example, in *Weil v. Investment/Indicators, Research & Management, Inc.*, 647 F.2d 18 (9th Cir. 1981), the Ninth Circuit held that the client had waived its attorney-client privilege "only as to communications about the matter actually disclosed" because the disclosure occurred early in the proceedings, was made to opposing counsel rather than to the court, and was not demonstrably prejudicial to the other party. Professor Wigmore's formulation of the subject matter waiver rule also contemplates the testimonial use of privileged information in the courtroom: "The client's offer of his own or the attorney's testimony as to a specific communication to the attorney is a waiver as to all other communications to the attorney on the same matter." Wigmore, supra, §2327, at 638.

But where, as here, disclosures of privileged information are made extrajudicially and without prejudice to the opposing party, there exists no reason in logic or equity to broaden the waiver beyond those matters actually revealed. Matters actually disclosed in public lose their privileged status because they obviously are no longer confidential. The cat is let out of the bag, so to speak. But related matters not so disclosed remain confidential. Although it is true that disclosures in the public arena may be "one-sided" or "misleading," so long as such disclosures are and remain extrajudicial, there is no legal prejudice that warrants a broad court-imposed subject matter waiver. The reason is that disclosures made in public rather than in court — even if selective — create no risk of legal prejudice until put at issue in the litigation by the privilege-holder. Therefore, insofar as the district court broadened petitioner's waiver to include related conversations on the same subject it was in error.

. . . [T]he petition for a writ of mandamus is granted and the district court is directed to vacate its discovery order of February 12, 1987.

CHRISTOPHER B. MUELLER & LAIRD C. KIRKPATRICK, EVIDENCE

§5.29, at 398 (5th ed. 2012)

There has been confusion in the cases whether inadvertent disclosure should be addressed as a problem of failed confidentiality or as a matter of waiver. The two issues are analytically distinct. The confidentiality requirement generally focuses on the intent of the communicator at the time the communication was made not to disclose the communication to persons who are outside the privilege. The client's subsequent conduct bears on confidentiality only to the extent that it provides circumstantial evidence of the client's intent at the time the communication was made.

Waiver focuses on whether the holder "voluntarily" disclosed or consented to disclosure of the privileged matter. Waiver occurs only after the making of a confidential communication — the privilege does not attach if the communication was not confidential. As a practical matter, similar standards have tended to evolve under both lines of analysis. If the holder did not take reasonable steps to protect against interception at the time the communication was made, the privilege is denied because of lack of confidentiality. If the holder (or the attorney acting as his agent) did not take reasonable steps to protect against subsequent disclosure, the privilege is lost on grounds of waiver.

4. Crime-Fraud Exception

Even when all the elements of the attorney-client privilege are satisfied and there is no basis for finding a waiver, the privilege has traditionally been limited by several exceptions. Among the most important is the "crime-fraud" exception, which applies when an attorney's services are obtained for purposes of furthering a future crime or fraud, regardless whether the attorney is aware of that purpose.

UNITED STATES v. ZOLIN

491 U.S. 554 (1989)

Justice BLACKMUN delivered the opinion of the Court.

This case arises out of the efforts of the Criminal Investigation Division of the Internal Revenue Service (IRS) to investigate the tax returns of L. Ron Hubbard, founder of the Church of Scientology (the Church), for the calendar years 1979 through 1983. . . . In the course of its investigation, the IRS sought access to 51 documents that had been filed with the Clerk of the Los Angeles County Superior Court in connection with a case entitled *Church of Scientology of California v. Armstrong*, No. C420 153. The *Armstrong* litigation involved, among other things, a charge by the Church that one of its former members, Gerald Armstrong, had obtained by unlawful means documentary materials relating to Church activities, including two tapes. Some of the documents sought by the IRS had been filed under seal.

The IRS, by its Special Agent Steven Petersell, served a summons upon the Clerk on October 24, 1984, pursuant to 26 U.S.C. §7603, demanding that he produce the 51 documents.[4] The tapes were among those listed. On November 21, IRS agents were permitted to inspect and copy some of the summoned materials, including the tapes.

---

4. The current Clerk of the Superior Court, Frank S. Zolin, is a named respondent in this case, but did not participate in briefing or argument before the Court of Appeals or before this Court. We use the term "respondents" to refer to Mary Sue Hubbard and the Church, the only active respondents in this Court.

On November 27, the Church and Mary Sue Hubbard, who had intervened in *Armstrong*, secured a temporary restraining order from the United States District Court for the Central District of California. The order required the IRS to file with the District Court all materials acquired on November 21 and all reproductions and notes related thereto, pending disposition of the intervenors' motion for a preliminary injunction to bar IRS use of these materials. By order dated December 10, the District Court returned to the IRS all materials except the tapes and the IRS' notes reflecting their contents.

On January 18, 1985, the IRS filed in the District Court a petition to enforce its summons.... Respondents asserted the [attorney-client] privilege as a bar to disclosure of the tapes. The IRS argued, among other things, however, that the tapes fell within the crime-fraud exception to the attorney-client privilege, and urged the District Court to listen to the tapes in the course of making its privilege determination. . . . After oral argument and an evidentiary hearing,. . . the District Court ruled that respondents had demonstrated that [the tapes] contain confidential attorney-client communications, that the privilege had not been waived, and that "[t]he 'fraud-crime' exception to the attorney-client privilege does not apply. The quoted excerpts tend to show or admit past fraud but there is no clear indication that future fraud or crime is being planned." On this basis, the court held that the Clerk "need not produce its copy of the tapes pursuant to the summons." The District Court denied the IRS' motion for reconsideration, rejecting the IRS' renewed request that the court listen to the tapes *in toto*. . . .

[The Court of Appeals agreed with respondents that] "the Government's evidence of crime or fraud must come from sources independent of the attorney-client communications recorded on the tapes" . . . On the basis of its review of the "independent evidence," the Court of Appeals affirmed the District Court's determination that the IRS had failed to establish the applicability of the crime-fraud exception.

. . . The attorney-client privilege must necessarily protect the confidences of wrongdoers, but the reason for that protection — the centrality of open client and attorney communication to the proper functioning of our adversary system of justice — "ceas[es] to operate at a certain point, namely, where the desired advice refers *not to prior wrongdoing*, but to *future wrongdoing*." 8 Wigmore, §2298, p. 573 (emphasis in original); see also *Clark v. United States*, 289 U.S. 1, 15 (1933). It is the purpose of the crime-fraud exception to the attorney-client privilege to assure that the "seal of secrecy," *ibid.*, between lawyer and client does not extend to communications "made for the purpose of getting advice for the commission of a fraud" or crime. *O'Rourke v. Darbishire*, [1920] A.C. 581, 604 (P.C.).

The District Court and the Court of Appeals found that the tapes at issue in this case recorded attorney-client communications and that the privilege had not been waived when the tapes were inadvertently given to Armstrong. 809 F.2d, at 1417 (noting that Armstrong had acquired the tapes from L. Ron Hubbard's personal secretary, who was under the mistaken impression that the tapes were blank). These findings are not at issue here. Thus, the remaining obstacle to respondents' successful assertion of the privilege is the Government's contention that the recorded attorney-client communications were made in furtherance of a future crime or fraud.

. . . We consider first the question whether a district court may ever honor the request of the party opposing the privilege to conduct an *in camera* review of allegedly privileged communications to determine whether those communications fall within the crime-fraud exception. We conclude that no express provision of the Federal Rules of Evidence bars such use of *in camera* review, and that it would be unwise to prohibit it in all instances as a matter of federal common law.

At first blush, two provisions of the Federal Rules of Evidence would appear to be relevant. Rule 104(a) provides: "Preliminary questions concerning the qualification of a person to be a witness, *the existence of a privilege*, or the admissibility of evidence shall be determined by the court. . . . In making its determination it is not bound by the rules of evidence *except those with respect to privileges*." (Emphasis added.) Rule 1101(c) provides: "The rule with respect to privileges applies at all stages of all actions, cases, and proceedings." Taken together, these Rules might be read to establish that in a summons-enforcement proceeding, attorney-client communications cannot be considered by the district court in making its crime-fraud ruling: to do otherwise, under this view, would be to make the crime-fraud determination without due regard to the existence of the privilege.

Even those scholars who support this reading of Rule 104(a) acknowledge that it leads to an absurd result.

> "Because the judge must honor claims of privilege made during his preliminary fact determinations, many exceptions to the rules of privilege will become 'dead letters,' since the preliminary facts that give rise to these exceptions can never be proved. For example, an exception to the attorney-client privilege provides that there is no privilege if the communication was made to enable anyone to commit a crime or fraud. There is virtually no way in which the exception can ever be proved, save by compelling disclosure of the contents of the communication; Rule 104(a) provides that this cannot be done." 21 C. Wright & K. Graham, Federal Practice & Procedure: Evidence §5055, p. 276 (1977) (footnote omitted).

We find this Draconian interpretation of Rule 104(a) inconsistent with the Rule's plain language. The Rule does not provide by its terms that all materials as to which a "clai[m] of privilege" is made must be excluded from consideration. In that critical respect, the language of Rule 104(a) is markedly different from the comparable California evidence rule, which provides that "the presiding officer may not require disclosure of information *claimed to be privileged* under this division in order to rule on the claim of privilege." Cal. Evid. Code Ann. §915(a) (West Supp. 1989) (emphasis added).[10] There is no reason to read Rule 104(a) as if its text were identical to that of the California rule. . . .

---

10. A good example of the effect of the California rule is provided by the record in this case. While the disputed matters were being briefed in Federal District Court, the State Superior Court held a hearing on a motion by Government attorneys seeking access to materials in the *Armstrong* case for ongoing litigation in Washington, D.C. The transcript of the hearing was made part of the record before the District Court in this case. Regarding the tapes, the Government argued to the Superior Court that the attorney-client conversations on the tapes reflect the planning or commission of a crime or fraud. That claim was supported by several declarations and other extrinsic evidence. The Government noted, however, that "the tape recordings themselves would...be the best evidence of exactly what was going on." The

Having determined that Rule 104(a) does not prohibit the *in camera* review sought by the IRS, we must address the question as a matter of the federal common law of privileges. See Rule 501. We conclude that a complete prohibition against opponents' use of *in camera* review to establish the applicability of the crime-fraud exception is inconsistent with the policies underlying the privilege.

We begin our analysis by recognizing that disclosure of allegedly privileged materials to the district court for purposes of determining the merits of a claim of privilege does not have the legal effect of terminating the privilege. Indeed, this Court has approved the practice of requiring parties who seek to avoid disclosure of documents to make the documents available for *in camera* inspection, see *Kerr v. United States District Court for Northern District of Cal.*, 426 U.S. 394, 404–405 (1976), and the practice is well established in the federal courts. Respondents do not dispute this point: they acknowledge that they would have been free to request *in camera* review to establish the fact that the tapes involved attorney-client communications, had they been unable to muster independent evidence to serve that purpose.

Once it is clear that *in camera* review does not destroy the privileged nature of the contested communications, the question of the propriety of that review turns on whether the policies underlying the privilege and its exceptions are better fostered by permitting such review or by prohibiting it. In our view, the costs of imposing an absolute bar to consideration of the communications *in camera* for purpose of establishing the crime-fraud exception are intolerably high.

"No matter how light the burden of proof which confronts the party claiming the exception, there are many blatant abuses of privilege which cannot be substantiated by extrinsic evidence. This is particularly true ... of ... situations in which an alleged illegal proposal is made in the context of a relationship which has an apparent legitimate end." Note, The Future Crime or Tort Exception to Communications Privileges, 77 Harv. L. Rev. 730, 737 (1964). A *per se* rule that the communications in question may never be considered creates, we feel, too great an impediment to the proper functioning of the adversary process....

We turn to the question whether *in camera* review at the behest of the party asserting the crime-fraud exception is *always* permissible, or, in contrast, whether the party seeking *in camera* review must make some threshold showing that such review is appropriate. In addressing this question, we attend to the detrimental effect, if any, of in camera review on the policies underlying the privilege and on the orderly administration of justice in our courts. We conclude that some such showing must be made.

Our endorsement of the practice of testing proponents' privilege claims through *in camera* review of the allegedly privileged documents has not been without reservation. This Court noted in *United States v. Reynolds*, 345 U.S. 1

---

intervenors stressed that, as a matter of California law, "you can't show the tapes are not privileged by the contents." The Superior Court acknowledged the premise that "you can't look at the conversation itself to make [the crime-fraud] determination," and concluded that the extrinsic evidence was not sufficient to make out a prima facie case that the crime-fraud exception applies.

(1953), a case which presented a delicate question concerning the disclosure of military secrets, that "examination of the evidence, even by the judge alone, in chambers" might in some cases "jeopardize the security which the privilege is meant to protect." Analogizing to claims of Fifth Amendment privilege, it observed more generally: "Too much judicial inquiry into the claim of privilege would force disclosure of the thing the privilege was meant to protect, while a complete abandonment of judicial control would lead to intolerable abuses."

The Court in *Reynolds* recognized that some compromise must be reached.... [I]t declined to "go so far as to say that the court may automatically require a complete disclosure to the judge before the claim of privilege will be accepted in any case." We think that much the same result is in order here.

A blanket rule allowing *in camera* review as a tool for determining the applicability of the crime-fraud exception, as *Reynolds* suggests, would place the policy of protecting open and legitimate disclosure between attorneys and clients at undue risk. There is also reason to be concerned about the possible due process implications of routine use of *in camera* proceedings. Finally, we cannot ignore the burdens *in camera* review places upon the district courts, which may well be required to evaluate large evidentiary records without open adversarial guidance by the parties.

There is no reason to permit opponents of the privilege to engage in groundless fishing expeditions, with the district courts as their unwitting (and perhaps unwilling) agents.... Indeed, the Government conceded at oral argument (albeit reluctantly) that a district court would be mistaken if it reviewed documents *in camera* solely because "the government beg[ged it]" to do so, "with no reason to suspect crime or fraud." We agree.

In fashioning a standard for determining when *in camera* review is appropriate, we begin with the observation that "*in camera* inspection . . . is a smaller intrusion upon the confidentiality of the attorney-client relationship than is public disclosure." Fried, Too High a Price for Truth: The Exception to the Attorney-Client Privilege for Contemplated Crimes and Frauds, 64 N.C. L. Rev. 443, 467 (1986). We therefore conclude that a lesser evidentiary showing is needed to trigger *in camera* review than is required ultimately to overcome the privilege. The threshold we set, in other words, need not be a stringent one.

We think that the following standard strikes the correct balance. Before engaging in *in camera* review to determine the applicability of the crime-fraud exception, "the judge should require a showing of a factual basis adequate to support a good faith belief by a reasonable person," *Caldwell v. District Court*, 644 P.2d 26, 33 (Colo. 1982), that *in camera* review of the materials may reveal evidence to establish the claim that the crime-fraud exception applies.

Once that showing is made, the decision whether to engage in *in camera* review rests in the sound discretion of the district court. The court should make that decision in light of the facts and circumstances of the particular case, including, among other things, the volume of materials the district court has been asked to review, the relative importance to the case of the alleged privileged information, and the likelihood that the evidence produced through *in camera* review, together with other available evidence then before the court, will establish that the crime-fraud exception does apply. The district court is also free to defer its *in camera* review if it concludes that additional evidence in support of the crime-fraud exception may be available that is *not* allegedly privileged, and that production of the additional evidence will not unduly disrupt or delay the proceedings.

    ... Because the Court of Appeals employed a rigid independent evidence requirement ... we vacate its judgment on this issue and remand the case for further proceedings consistent with this opinion. On remand, the Court of Appeals should consider whether the District Court's refusal to listen to the tapes *in toto* was justified by the manner in which the IRS presented and preserved its request for *in camera* review. In the event the Court of Appeals holds that the IRS' demand for review was properly preserved, the Court of Appeals should then determine, or remand the case to the District Court to determine in the first instance, whether the IRS has presented a sufficient evidentiary basis for *in camera* review, and whether, if so, it is appropriate for the District Court, in its discretion, to grant such review.

    It is so ordered.

C. SPOUSAL PRIVILEGES

There are two widely recognized spousal privileges. One is a privilege against disclosure of confidential spousal communications. It closely resembles the attorney-client privilege, except that it protects confidential communications between spouses during the course of a marriage, rather than confidential communications between an attorney and a client during the course of an attorney-client relationship. The second spousal privilege is the privilege against adverse spousal testimony. It is structured quite differently from the attorney-client privilege, and it was the subject of the Supreme Court decision reproduced below.

[C.E.C. §§970–987]

TRAMMEL v. UNITED STATES

445 U.S. 40 (1980)

Mr. Chief Justice BURGER delivered the opinion of the Court.

We granted certiorari to consider whether an accused may invoke the privilege against adverse spousal testimony so as to exclude the voluntary testimony of his wife. This calls for a re-examination of *Hawkins v. United States*, 358 U.S. 74 (1958).

I

On March 10, 1976, petitioner Otis Trammel was indicted with two others, Edwin Lee Roberts and Joseph Freeman, for importing heroin into the United

States from Thailand and the Philippine Islands and for conspiracy to import heroin in violation of 21 U.S.C. §§952(a), 962(a), and 963. The indictment also named six unindicted co-conspirators, including petitioner's wife Elizabeth Ann Trammel.

According to the indictment, petitioner and his wife flew from the Philippines to California in August 1975, carrying with them a quantity of heroin. Freeman and Roberts assisted them in its distribution. Elizabeth Trammel then traveled to Thailand where she purchased another supply of the drug. On November 3, 1975, with four ounces of heroin on her person, she boarded a plane for the United States. During a routine customs search in Hawaii, she was searched, the heroin was discovered, and she was arrested. After discussions with Drug Enforcement Administration agents, she agreed to cooperate with the Government.

Prior to trial on this indictment, petitioner moved to sever his case from that of Roberts and Freeman. He advised the court that the Government intended to call his wife as an adverse witness and asserted his claim to a privilege to prevent her from testifying against him. At a hearing on the motion, Mrs. Trammel was called as a Government witness under a grant of use immunity. She testified that she and petitioner were married in May 1975 and that they remained married.[1] She explained that her cooperation with the Government was based on assurances that she would be given lenient treatment.[2] She then described, in considerable detail, her role and that of her husband in the heroin distribution conspiracy.

After hearing this testimony, the District Court ruled that Mrs. Trammel could testify in support of the Government's case to any act she observed during the marriage and to any communication "made in the presence of a third person"; however, confidential communications between petitioner and his wife were held to be privileged and inadmissible. The motion to sever was denied.

At trial, Elizabeth Trammel testified within the limits of the court's pretrial ruling; her testimony, as the Government concedes, constituted virtually its entire case against petitioner. He was found guilty on both the substantive and conspiracy charges and sentenced to an indeterminate term of years pursuant to the Federal Youth Corrections Act, 18 U.S.C. §5010(b).

In the Court of Appeals petitioner's only claim of error was that the admission of the adverse testimony of his wife, over his objection, contravened this Court's teaching in *Hawkins v. United States, supra*, and therefore constituted reversible error. The Court of Appeals rejected this contention. It concluded that Hawkins did not prohibit "the voluntary testimony of a spouse who appears as an unindicted co-conspirator under grant of immunity from the Government in return for her testimony."

---

1. In response to the question whether divorce was contemplated, Mrs. Trammel testified that her husband had said that "I would go my way and he would go his."

2. The Government represents to the Court that Elizabeth Trammel has not been prosecuted for her role in the conspiracy.

II

The privilege claimed by petitioner has ancient roots. Writing in 1628, Lord Coke observed that "it hath beene resolved by the Justices that a wife cannot be produced either against or for her husband." 1 E. Coke, A Commentarie upon Littleton 6b (1628). See, generally, 8 J. Wigmore, Evidence §2227 (McNaughton rev. 1961). This spousal disqualification sprang from two canons of medieval jurisprudence: first, the rule that an accused was not permitted to testify in his own behalf because of his interest in the proceeding; second, the concept that husband and wife were one, and that since the woman had no recognized separate legal existence, the husband was that one. From those two now long-abandoned doctrines, it followed that what was inadmissible from the lips of the defendant-husband was also inadmissible from his wife.

Despite its medieval origins, this rule of spousal disqualification remained intact in most common-law jurisdictions well into the 19th century. See *id.*, §2333. It was applied by this Court in *Stein v. Bowman*, 13 Pet. 209, 220–223 (1839), in *Graves v. United States*, 150 U.S. 118 (1893), and again in *Jin Fuey Moy v. United States*, 254 U.S. 189, 195 (1920), where it was deemed so well established a proposition as to "hardly requir[e] mention." Indeed, it was not until 1933, in *Funk v. United States*, 290 U.S. 371, that this Court abolished the testimonial disqualification in the federal courts, so as to permit the spouse of a defendant to testify in the defendant's behalf. *Funk*, however, left undisturbed the rule that either spouse could prevent the other from giving adverse testimony. *Id.*, at 373. The rule thus evolved into one of privilege rather than one of absolute disqualification. See J. Maguire, Evidence, Common Sense and Common Law 78–92 (1947).

The modern justification for this privilege against adverse spousal testimony is its perceived role in fostering the harmony and sanctity of the marriage relationship. Notwithstanding this benign purpose, the rule was sharply criticized. Professor Wigmore termed it "the merest anachronism in legal theory and an indefensible obstruction to truth in practice." 8 Wigmore §2228, at 221. The Committee on Improvements in the Law of Evidence of the American Bar Association called for its abolition. 63 American Bar Association Reports 594–595 (1938). In its place, Wigmore and others suggested a privilege protecting only private marital communications, modeled on the privilege between priest and penitent, attorney and client, and physician and patient. See 8 Wigmore §2332 et seq.[5]

These criticisms influenced the American Law Institute, which, in its 1942 Model Code of Evidence advocated a privilege for marital confidences, but expressly rejected a rule vesting in the defendant the right to exclude all adverse testimony of his spouse. In 1953 the Uniform Rules of Evidence, drafted by the National Conference of Commissioners on Uniform State Laws,

---

5. This Court recognized just such a confidential marital communications privilege in *Wolfle v. United States*, 291 U.S. 7 (1934), and in *Blau v. United States*, 340 U.S. 332 (1951). In neither case, however, did the Court adopt the Wigmore view that the communications privilege be substituted in place of the privilege against adverse spousal testimony. The privilege as to confidential marital communications is not at issue in the instant case; accordingly, our holding today does not disturb *Wolfle* and *Blau*.

followed a similar course; it limited the privilege to confidential communications and "abolishe[d] the rule, still existing in some states, and largely a sentimental relic, of not requiring one spouse to testify against the other in a criminal action." Several state legislatures enacted similarly patterned provisions into law.

In *Hawkins v. United States*, 358 U.S. 74 (1958), this Court considered the continued vitality of the privilege against adverse spousal testimony in the federal courts. There the District Court had permitted petitioner's wife, over his objection, to testify against him. With one questioning concurring opinion, the Court held the wife's testimony inadmissible; it took note of the critical comments that the common-law rule had engendered but chose not to abandon it. Also rejected was the Government's suggestion that the Court modify the privilege by vesting it in the witness-spouse, with freedom to testify or not independent of the defendant's control. The Court viewed this proposed modification as antithetical to the widespread belief, evidenced in the rules then in effect in a majority of the States and in England, "that the law should not force or encourage testimony which might alienate husband and wife, or further inflame existing domestic differences."

Hawkins, then, left the federal privilege for adverse spousal testimony where it found it, continuing "a rule which bars the testimony of one spouse against the other unless both consent." Accord, *Wyatt v. United States*, 362 U.S. 525, 528 (1960).[7] However, in so doing, the Court made clear that its decision was not meant to "foreclose whatever changes in the rule may eventually be dictated by 'reason and experience.'"

III

A

The Federal Rules of Evidence acknowledge the authority of the federal courts to continue the evolutionary development of testimonial privileges in federal criminal trials "governed by the principles of the common law as they may be interpreted ... in the light of reason and experience." Fed. Rule Evid. 501. The general mandate of Rule 501 was substituted by the Congress for a set of privilege rules drafted by the Judicial Conference Advisory Committee on Rules of Evidence and approved by the Judicial Conference of the United States and by this Court. That proposal defined nine specific privileges, including a husband-wife privilege which would have codified the *Hawkins* rule and eliminated the privilege for confidential marital communications. In rejecting the proposed Rules and enacting Rule 501, Congress manifested an affirmative intention not to freeze

---

7. The decision in *Wyatt* recognized an exception to *Hawkins* for cases in which one spouse commits a crime against the other. This exception, placed on the ground of necessity, was a longstanding one at common law. See Lord Audley's Case, 123 Eng. Rep. 1140 (1631); 8 Wigmore §2239. It has been expanded since then to include crimes against the spouse's property, see *Herman v. United States*, 220 F.2d 219, 226 (CA4 1955), and in recent years crimes against children of either spouse, *United States v. Allery*, 526 F.2d 1362 (CA8 1975). Similar exceptions have been found to the confidential marital communications privilege. See 8 Wigmore §2338.

the law of privilege. Its purpose rather was to "provide the courts with the flexibility to develop rules of privilege on a case-by-case basis," 120 Cong. Rec. 40891 (1974) (statement of Rep. Hungate), and to leave the door open to change. See also S. Rep. No. 93-1277, p. 11 (1974); H.R. Rep. No. 93-650, p. 8 (1973).[8]

Although Rule 501 confirms the authority of the federal courts to reconsider the continued validity of the *Hawkins* rule, the long history of the privilege suggests that it ought not to be casually cast aside. That the privilege is one affecting marriage, home, and family relationships — already subject to much erosion in our day — also counsels caution. At the same time, we cannot escape the reality that the law on occasion adheres to doctrinal concepts long after the reasons which gave them birth have disappeared and after experience suggest the need for change. This was recognized in *Funk* where the Court "decline[d] to enforce . . . ancient rule[s] of the common law under conditions as they now exist." 290 U.S., at 382. For, as Mr. Justice Black admonished in another setting, "[w]hen precedent and precedent alone is all the argument that can be made to support a court-fashioned rule, it is time for the rule's creator to destroy it." *Francis v. Southern Pacific Co.*, 333 U.S. 445, 471 (1948) (dissenting opinion).

B

Since 1958, when *Hawkins* was decided, support for the privilege against adverse spousal testimony has been eroded further. Thirty-one jurisdictions, including Alaska and Hawaii, then allowed an accused a privilege to prevent adverse spousal testimony. 358 U.S., at 81, n.3 (STEWART, J., concurring). The number has now declined to 24.[9] In 1974, the National Conference on Uniform State Laws revised its Uniform Rules of Evidence, but again rejected the Hawkins rule in favor of a limited privilege for confidential communications. That proposed rule has been enacted in Arkansas, North Dakota, and Oklahoma — each of which in 1958 permitted an accused to exclude adverse spousal testimony.[10] The trend in state law toward divesting the accused of the

---

8. Petitioner's reliance on 28 U.S.C. §2076 for the proposition that this Court is without power to reconsider *Hawkins* is ill-founded. That provision limits this Court's statutory rulemaking authority by providing that rules "creating, abolishing, or modifying a privilege shall have no force or effect unless . . . approved by act of Congress." It was enacted principally to insure that state rules of privilege would apply in diversity jurisdiction cases unless Congress authorized otherwise. In Rule 501 Congress makes clear that §2076 was not intended to prevent the federal courts from developing testimonial privilege law in federal criminal cases on a case-by-case basis "in light of reason and experience"; indeed Congress encouraged such development.

9. Eight States provide that one spouse is incompetent to testify against the other in a criminal proceeding. . . . Sixteen States provide a privilege against adverse spousal testimony and vest the privilege in both spouses or in the defendant-spouse alone. . . . Nine States entitle the witness-spouse alone to assert a privilege against adverse spousal testimony. . . . The remaining 17 States have abolished the privilege in criminal cases. . . . In 1901, Congress enacted a rule of evidence for the District of Columbia that made husband and wife "competent but not compellable to testify for or against each other," except as to confidential communications. This provision, which vests the privilege against adverse spousal testimony in the witness-spouse, remains in effect. See 31 Stat. 1358, §§1068, 1069, recodified as D.C. Code §14-306 (1973).

10. In 1965, California took the privilege from the defendant-spouse and vested it in the witness-spouse, accepting a study commission recommendation that the "latter [was] more

privilege to bar adverse spousal testimony has special relevance because the laws of marriage and domestic relations are concerns traditionally reserved to the states. See *Sosna v. Iowa*, 419 U.S. 393, 404 (1975). Scholarly criticism of the Hawkins rule has also continued unabated.

C

Testimonial exclusionary rules and privileges contravene the fundamental principle that "'the public . . . has a right to every man's evidence.'" United States v. Bryan, 339 U.S. 323, 331 (1950). As such, they must be strictly construed and accepted "only to the very limited extent that permitting a refusal to testify or excluding relevant evidence has a public good transcending the normally predominant principle of utilizing all rational means for ascertaining truth." *Elkins v. United States*, 364 U.S. 206, 234 (1960) (Frankfurter, J., dissenting). Accord, *United States v. Nixon*, 418 U.S. 683, 709-710 (1974). Here we must decide whether the privilege against adverse spousal testimony promotes sufficiently important interests to outweigh the need for probative evidence in the administration of criminal justice.

It is essential to remember that the *Hawkins* privilege is not needed to protect information privately disclosed between husband and wife in the confidence of the marital relationship — once described by this Court as "the best solace of human existence." *Stein v. Bowman*, 13 Pet., at 223. Those confidences are privileged under the independent rule protecting confidential marital communications. *Blau v. United States*, 340 U.S. 332 (1951); see n.5, *supra*. The *Hawkins* privilege is invoked, not to exclude private marital communications, but rather to exclude evidence of criminal acts and of communications made in the presence of third persons.

No other testimonial privilege sweeps so broadly. The privileges between priest and penitent, attorney and client, and physician and patient limit protection to private communications. These privileges are rooted in the imperative need for confidence and trust. The priest-penitent privilege recognizes the human need to disclose to a spiritual counselor, in total and absolute confidence, what are believed to be flawed acts or thoughts and to receive priestly consolation and guidance in return. The lawyer-client privilege rests on the need for the advocate and counselor to know all that relates to the client's reasons for seeking representation if the professional mission is to be carried out. Similarly, the physician must know all that a patient can articulate in order to identify and to treat disease; barriers to full disclosure would impair diagnosis and treatment.

The *Hawkins* rule stands in marked contrast to these three privileges. Its protection is not limited to confidential communications; rather it permits an accused to exclude all adverse spousal testimony. As Jeremy Bentham

---

likely than the former to determine whether or not to claim the privilege on the basis of the probable effect on the marital relationship." See Cal. Evid. Code Ann. §§970-973 (West 1966 and Supp. 1979) and 1 California Law Revision Commission, Recommendation and Study Relating to the Marital "For and Against" Testimonial Privilege at F-5 (1956). Support for the common-law rule has also diminished in England. In 1972, a study group there proposed giving the privilege to the witness-spouse, on the ground that "if [the wife] is willing to give evidence . . . the law would be showing excessive concern for the preservation of marital harmony if it were to say that she must not do so." Criminal Law Revision Committee, Eleventh Report, Evidence (General) 93.

observed more than a century and a half ago, such a privilege goes far beyond making "every man's house his castle," and permits a person to convert his house into "a den of thieves." 5 Rationale of Judicial Evidence 340 (1827). It "secures, to every man, one safe and unquestionable and ever ready accomplice for every imaginable crime." *Id.*, at 338.

The ancient foundations for so sweeping a privilege have long since disappeared. Nowhere in the common-law world—indeed in any modern society—is a woman regarded as chattel or demeaned by denial of a separate legal identity and the dignity associated with recognition as a whole human being. Chip by chip, over the years those archaic notions have been cast aside so that "[n]o longer is the female destined solely for the home and the rearing of the family, and only the male for the marketplace and the world of ideas." *Stanton v. Stanton*, 421 U.S. 7, 14-15 (1975).

The contemporary justification for affording an accused such a privilege is also unpersuasive. When one spouse is willing to testify against the other in a criminal proceeding—whatever the motivation—their relationship is almost certainly in disrepair; there is probably little in the way of marital harmony for the privilege to preserve. In these circumstances, a rule of evidence that permits an accused to prevent adverse spousal testimony seems far more likely to frustrate justice than to foster family peace.[12] Indeed, there is reason to believe that vesting the privilege in the accused could actually undermine the marital relationship. For example, in a case such as this the Government is unlikely to offer a wife immunity and lenient treatment if it knows that her husband can prevent her from giving adverse testimony. If the Government is dissuaded from making such an offer, the privilege can have the untoward effect of permitting one spouse to escape justice at the expense of the other. It hardly seems conducive to the preservation of the marital relation to place a wife in jeopardy solely by virtue of her husband's control over her testimony.

IV

Our consideration of the foundations for the privilege and its history satisfy us that "reason and experience" no longer justify so sweeping a rule as that found acceptable by the Court in *Hawkins*. Accordingly, we conclude that the existing rule should be modified so that the witness-spouse alone has a privilege to refuse to testify adversely; the witness may be neither compelled to testify nor foreclosed from testifying. This modification—vesting the privilege in the witness-spouse—furthers the important public interest in marital harmony without unduly burdening legitimate law enforcement needs.

Here, petitioner's spouse chose to testify against him. That she did so after a grant of immunity and assurances of lenient treatment does not render her testimony involuntary. *Cf. Bordenkircher v. Hayes*, 434 U.S. 357 (1978).

---

12. It is argued that abolishing the privilege will permit the Government to come between husband and wife, pitting one against the other. That, too, misses the mark. Neither *Hawkins*, nor any other privilege, prevents the Government from enlisting one spouse to give information concerning the other or to aid in the other's apprehension. It is only the spouse's testimony in the courtroom that is prohibited.

Accordingly, the District Court and the Court of Appeals were correct in reject-ing petitioner's claim of privilege, and the judgment of the Court of Appeals is
   Affirmed.

   Mr. Justice STEWART, concurring in the judgment.

   Although agreeing with much of what the Court has to say, I cannot join an opinion that implies that "reason and experience" have worked a vast change since the *Hawkins* case was decided in 1958.... The fact of the matter is that the Court in this case simply accepts the very same arguments that the Court rejected when the Government first made them in the *Hawkins* case in 1958. I thought those arguments were valid then, and I think so now.

   The Court is correct when it says that "[t]he ancient foundations for so sweeping a privilege have long since disappeared." But those foundations had disappeared well before 1958; their disappearance certainly did not occur in the few years that have elapsed between the *Hawkins* decision and this one. To paraphrase what Mr. Justice Jackson once said in another context, there is reason to believe that today's opinion of the Court will be of greater interest to students of human psychology than to students of law.

PROBLEMS

   10.7. The prosecutor in a robbery case seeks to have the defendant's ex-wife testify that the defendant confessed his guilt to her while they were still married. The ex-wife is willing to testify, but the defendant objects. Is the testimony admissible?

   10.8. The prosecutor in a murder case seeks to have the defendant's wife testify that, the night of the victims' deaths, the defendant came home with a bloody shirt. The defendant and his wife were living together at the time but were not yet married. They married the following week. One month later, the defendant fled the country. He was captured and extradited 15 years later. The prosecution offers to prove that, while a fugitive, the defendant lived with a woman and did not communicate with his wife or provide her with financial support. The defendant's wife does not wish to testify against him. May she be compelled to do so?

D. OTHER PRIVILEGES

[C.E.C. §§990–1070]

McCORMICK ON EVIDENCE

§76.2, at 1:490-96 (Kenneth S. Broun ed., 7th ed. 2013)

   [A]ll states possess some form of husband-wife, and attorney-client priv-ilege. All afford some protection to certain government information. Most, though not all, allow at least a limited privilege to communications between physician and patient. In addition several other privileges are worthy of specific mention.

Though probably not recognized at common law, a privilege protecting confidential communications between clergymen and penitents has now been adopted in all 50 states. Wigmore's seemingly grudging acceptance of the privilege perhaps reflects the difficulty of justifying its existence on exclusively utilitarian grounds, since at least where penitential communications are required or encouraged by religious tenets, they are likely to continue to be made irrespective of the presence or absence of evidentiary privilege. A firmer ground appears available in the inherent offensiveness of the secular power attempting to coerce an act violative of religious conscience. Implementing a decent regard for religious convictions while at the same time avoiding making individual conscience the ultimate measure of testimonial obligation has proved to be attended by some difficulties. Early statutory forms of the privilege undertook to privilege only penitential communications "in the course of discipline enjoined by the church" to which the communicant belongs. This limitation, however, has been urged to be unduly, perhaps unconstitutionally, preferential to the Roman Catholic and a few other churches. The statutes have, accordingly, generally been broadened. Uniform Rule of Evidence 505, as promulgated in 1974, is typical in extending the privilege generally to "confidential communication[s] by a person to a clergyman in his professional character as spiritual advisor."

The states are split on the question of who can waive the clergyman penitent privilege. Some provide that the privilege belongs only to the communicant, others provide that it belongs to the clergy member and still others hold that it belongs to both.

One of the most persistently advocated privileges for many years . . . has been one shielding journalists from being testimonially required in court to divulge the identities of news sources. The rationale asserted for this privilege is analogous to that underlying the long-standing governmental informer's privilege* and is exclusively utilitarian in character. Thus, it is contended that the news sources essential to supply the public's need for information will be "dried up" if their identities are subject to compelled disclosure. Numerous attempts to have the privilege enacted by federal statute have failed, and it is

---

*. [See the discussion of the informant's privilege in United States v. Green, 670 F.2d 1148 (D.C. Cir. 1981): "One limitation on a defendant's right to cross-examine Government witnesses is the 'informer's privilege,' which allows the Government to refuse to disclose the identity of a person who has furnished information about criminal activities. . . . Long recognized at common law, the informer's privilege serves important individual and societal interests in protecting the anonymity of citizens who cooperate in law enforcement. The privilege protects the informer and his family from possible physical harm or from other potential undesirable consequences. Moreover, the availability of the privilege preserves the usefulness of those who have aided the police in law enforcement and may encourage other citizens to supply information concerning the commission of crimes." Nonetheless, "[t]he Supreme Court in . . . Roviaro v. United States, 353 U.S. 53 (1957) . . . held that at trial the informer's privilege is limited by 'the fundamental requirements of fairness. Where the disclosure of an informer's identity, or of the contents of his communication, is relevant and helpful to the defense of an accused, or is essential to a fair determination of a cause, the privilege must give way.'" Id. — ED.]

not one of those privileges that was incorporated into the Revised Uniform Rules of Evidence (1974). Moreover, the argument that a journalist's privilege is constitutionally to be implied from the First Amendment guarantee of a free press was seemingly rejected by the Supreme Court in Branzburg v. Hayes [408 U.S. 665 (1972)]. However, taking note that this rejection did not command an absolute majority of the Court, a substantial number of lower federal courts have undertaken to recognize a qualified journalist's privilege that may be penetrated by appropriate showings on the part of the party desiring the privileged information. Though occasionally referred to as a common law creation, despite *Branzburg*, the privilege has generally been said to derive from the First Amendment. Some form of privilege for journalists has been created by statute, [or] in a few cases by judicial decision, in a substantial number of states. A few state courts have also found the privilege to be implied by state constitutional provision. Unlike other professional privileges, it is generally conceived as belonging to the journalist, to be claimed or waived irrespective of the wishes of the news source.

Communications to accountants are privileged in perhaps a third of the states. . . . In recent years much attention has been bestowed upon the plight of the rape victim, and some sort of sexual assault victim-counselor privilege has been created by statute or court decision in a substantial number of states. . . . Even broader acceptance has been achieved by the principle that protection by evidentiary privilege is necessary for the deliberations of medical review committees.

There is occasional recognition of privilege for communications to confidential clerks, stenographers and other "employees" generally, school teachers, school counselors, participants in group psychotherapy, nurses, marriage counselors, private detectives, and social workers. A privilege for parent-minor child communications has been recommended but has received little judicial approval. Privileges for scientific researcher-subject and self-critical analysis have fared only somewhat better.

An attempt to obtain recognition of a federal privilege protecting against disclosure of confidential peer review materials of academic institutions has been rejected by the Supreme Court [in *University of Pennsylvania v. EEOC*, 493 U.S. 182 (1990)].

JAFFEE v. REDMOND

518 U.S. 1 (1996)

Justice STEVENS delivered the opinion of the Court.

After a traumatic incident in which she shot and killed a man, a police officer received extensive counseling from a licensed clinical social worker. The question we address is whether statements the officer made to her therapist during the counseling sessions are protected from compelled disclosure in a federal civil action brought by the family of the deceased. Stated otherwise, the question is whether it is appropriate for federal courts to recognize a "psychotherapist privilege" under Rule 501 of the Federal Rules of Evidence.

I

Petitioner is the administrator of the estate of Ricky Allen. Respondents are Mary Lu Redmond, a former police officer, and the Village of Hoffman Estates, Illinois, her employer during the time that she served on the police force. Petitioner commenced this action against respondents after Redmond shot and killed Allen while on patrol duty.

On June 27, 1991, Redmond was the first officer to respond to a "fight in progress" call at an apartment complex. As she arrived at the scene, two of Allen's sisters ran toward her squad car, waving their arms and shouting that there had been a stabbing in one of the apartments. Redmond testified at trial that she relayed this information to her dispatcher and requested an ambulance. She then exited her car and walked toward the apartment building. Before Redmond reached the building, several men ran out, one waving a pipe. When the men ignored her order to get on the ground, Redmond drew her service revolver. Two other men then burst out of the building, one, Ricky Allen, chasing the other. According to Redmond, Allen was brandishing a butcher knife and disregarded her repeated commands to drop the weapon. Redmond shot Allen when she believed he was about to stab the man he was chasing. Allen died at the scene. Redmond testified that before other officers arrived to provide support, "people came pouring out of the buildings," and a threatening confrontation between her and the crowd ensued.

Petitioner filed suit in Federal District Court alleging that Redmond had violated Allen's constitutional rights by using excessive force during the encounter at the apartment complex. The complaint sought damages under 42 U.S.C. §1983 and the Illinois wrongful death statute. At trial, petitioner presented testimony from members of Allen's family that conflicted with Redmond's version of the incident in several important respects. They testified, for example, that Redmond drew her gun before exiting her squad car and that Allen was unarmed when he emerged from the apartment building.

During pretrial discovery petitioner learned that after the shooting Redmond had participated in about 50 counseling sessions with Karen Beyer, a clinical social worker licensed by the State of Illinois and employed at that time by the Village of Hoffman Estates. Petitioner sought access to Beyer's notes concerning the sessions for use in cross-examining Redmond. Respondents vigorously resisted the discovery. They asserted that the contents of the conversations between Beyer and Redmond were protected against involuntary disclosure by a psychotherapist-patient privilege. The district judge rejected this argument. Neither Beyer nor Redmond, however, complied with his order to disclose the contents of Beyer's notes. At depositions and on the witness stand both either refused to answer certain questions or professed an inability to recall details of their conversations.

In his instructions at the end of the trial, the judge advised the jury that the refusal to turn over Beyer's notes had no "legal justification" and that the jury could therefore presume that the contents of the notes would have been unfavorable to respondents. The jury awarded petitioner $45,000 on the federal claim and $500,000 on her state-law claim.

The Court of Appeals for the Seventh Circuit reversed and remanded for a new trial. Addressing the issue for the first time, the court concluded that "reason and experience," the touchstones for acceptance of a privilege under Rule 501 of the Federal Rules of Evidence, compelled recognition of a psychotherapist-patient privilege.... The Court of Appeals qualified its recognition of the privilege by stating that it would not apply if "in the interests of justice, the evidentiary need for the disclosure of the contents of a patient's counseling sessions outweighs that patient's privacy interests." Balancing those conflicting interests, the court observed, on the one hand, that the evidentiary need for the contents of the confidential conversations was diminished in this case because there were numerous eyewitnesses to the shooting, and, on the other hand, that Officer Redmond's privacy interests were substantial. Based on this assessment, the court concluded that the trial court had erred by refusing to afford protection to the confidential communications between Redmond and Beyer.

The United States courts of appeals do not uniformly agree that the federal courts should recognize a psychotherapist privilege under Rule 501.... Because of the conflict among the courts of appeals and the importance of the question, we granted certiorari. We affirm.

II

Rule 501 of the Federal Rules of Evidence authorizes federal courts to define new privileges by interpreting "common law principles ... in the light of reason and experience."... The Rule thus did not freeze the law governing the privileges of witnesses in federal trials at a particular point in our history, but rather directed federal courts to "continue the evolutionary development of testimonial privileges." *Trammel v. United States*, 445 U.S. 40 (1980).

The common-law principles underlying the recognition of testimonial privileges can be stated simply. "'For more than three centuries it has now been recognized as a fundamental maxim that the public ... has a right to every man's evidence. When we come to examine the various claims of exemption, we start with the primary assumption that there is a general duty to give what testimony one is capable of giving, and that any exemptions which may exist are distinctly exceptional, being so many derogations from a positive general rule.'" *United States v. Bryan*, 339 U.S. 323 (1950) (quoting 8 J. Wigmore, Evidence §2192 (3d ed. 1940)). Exceptions from the general rule disfavoring testimonial privileges may be justified, however, by a "'public good transcending the normally predominant principle of utilizing all rational means for ascertaining the truth.'" *Trammel*, quoting *Elkins v. United States*, 364 U.S. 206 (1960) (Frankfurter, J., dissenting).

Guided by these principles, the question we address today is whether a privilege protecting confidential communications between a psychotherapist and her patient "promotes sufficiently important interests to outweigh the need for probative evidence...." *Trammel*. Both "reason and experience" persuade us that it does.

III

Like the spousal and attorney-client privileges, the psychotherapist-patient privilege is "rooted in the imperative need for confidence and trust." *Trammel*.

Treatment by a physician for physical ailments can often proceed successfully on the basis of a physical examination, objective information supplied by the patient, and the results of diagnostic tests. Effective psychotherapy, by contrast, depends upon an atmosphere of confidence and trust in which the patient is willing to make a frank and complete disclosure of facts, emotions, memories, and fears. Because of the sensitive nature of the problems for which individuals consult psychotherapists, disclosure of confidential communications made during counseling sessions may cause embarrassment or disgrace. For this reason, the mere possibility of disclosure may impede development of the confidential relationship necessary for successful treatment.[3] . . . By protecting confidential communications between a psychotherapist and her patient from involuntary disclosure, the proposed privilege thus serves important private interests.

Our cases make clear that an asserted privilege must also "serve public ends." *Upjohn Co. v. United States*, 449 U.S. 383 (1981). Thus, the purpose of the attorney-client privilege is to "encourage full and frank communication between attorneys and their clients and thereby promote broader public interests in the observance of law and administration of justice." *Ibid.* And the spousal privilege, as modified in *Trammel*, is justified because it "furthers the important public interest in marital harmony," *id.* The psychotherapist privilege serves the public interest by facilitating the provision of appropriate treatment for individuals suffering the effects of a mental or emotional problem. The mental health of our citizenry, no less than its physical health, is a public good of transcendent importance.[4]

In contrast to the significant public and private interests supporting recognition of the privilege, the likely evidentiary benefit that would result from the denial of the privilege is modest. If the privilege were rejected, confidential conversations between psychotherapists and their patients would surely be chilled, particularly when it is obvious that the circumstances that give rise to the need for treatment will probably result in litigation. Without a privilege, much of the desirable evidence to which litigants such as petitioner seek access—for example, admissions against interest by a party—is unlikely to come into being. This unspoken "evidence" will therefore serve no greater truth-seeking function than if it had been spoken and privileged.

That it is appropriate for the federal courts to recognize a psychotherapist privilege under Rule 501 is confirmed by the fact that all 50 States and the District of Columbia have enacted into law some form of psychotherapist privilege. We have previously observed that the policy decisions of the States bear on the question whether federal courts should recognize a new privilege or

---

3. See studies and authorities cited in the Brief for American Psychiatric Association et al. as Amici Curiae and the Brief for American Psychological Association as Amicus Curiae.

4. This case amply demonstrates the importance of allowing individuals to receive confidential counseling. Police officers engaged in the dangerous and difficult tasks associated with protecting the safety of our communities not only confront the risk of physical harm but also face stressful circumstances that may give rise to anxiety, depression, fear, or anger. The entire community may suffer if police officers are not able to receive effective counseling and treatment after traumatic incidents, either because trained officers leave the profession prematurely or because those in need of treatment remain on the job.

amend the coverage of an existing one. See *Trammel; United States v. Gillock*, 445 U.S. 360 (1980). Because state legislatures are fully aware of the need to protect the integrity of the factfinding functions of their courts, the existence of a consensus among the States indicates that "reason and experience" support recognition of the privilege. In addition, given the importance of the patient's understanding that her communications with her therapist will not be publicly disclosed, any State's promise of confidentiality would have little value if the patient were aware that the privilege would not be honored in a federal court. Denial of the federal privilege therefore would frustrate the purposes of the state legislation that was enacted to foster these confidential communications. . . .

The uniform judgment of the States is reinforced by the fact that a psychotherapist privilege was among the nine specific privileges recommended by the Advisory Committee in its proposed privilege rules. In *United States v. Gillock*, our holding that Rule 501 did not include a state legislative privilege relied, in part, on the fact that no such privilege was included in the Advisory Committee's draft. The reasoning in *Gillock* thus supports the opposite conclusion in this case. . . .

Because we agree with the judgment of the state legislatures and the Advisory Committee that a psychotherapist-patient privilege will serve a "public good transcending the normally predominant principle of utilizing all rational means for ascertaining truth," *Trammel*, we hold that confidential communications between a licensed psychotherapist and her patients in the course of diagnosis or treatment are protected from compelled disclosure under Rule 501 of the Federal Rules of Evidence.[5]

IV

All agree that a psychotherapist privilege covers confidential communications made to licensed psychiatrists and psychologists. We have no hesitation in concluding in this case that the federal privilege should also extend to confidential communications made to licensed social workers in the course of psychotherapy. The reasons for recognizing a privilege for treatment by psychiatrists and psychologists apply with equal force to treatment by a clinical social worker such as Karen Beyer. Today, social workers provide a significant amount of mental health treatment. See, e.g., U.S. Dept. of Health and Human Services, Center for Mental Health Services, Mental Health, United States, 1994; Brief for National Association of Social Workers et al. as Amici Curiae (citing authorities). Their clients often include the poor and those of modest means who could not afford the assistance of a psychiatrist or psychologist, *id.* (citing authorities), but whose counseling sessions serve the same public goals.[6] Perhaps in recognition of these circumstances, the vast majority of States explicitly extend a

---

5. Like other testimonial privileges, the patient may of course waive the protection.
6. The Judicial Conference Advisory Committee's proposed psychotherapist privilege defined psychotherapists as psychologists and medical doctors who provide mental health services. This limitation in the 1972 recommendation does not counsel against recognition of a privilege for social workers practicing psychotherapy. In the quarter-century since the

testimonial privilege to licensed social workers. We therefore agree with the Court of Appeals that "drawing a distinction between the counseling provided by costly psychotherapists and the counseling provided by more readily accessible social workers serves no discernible public purpose."

We part company with the Court of Appeals on a separate point. We reject the balancing component of the privilege implemented by that court and a small number of States. Making the promise of confidentiality contingent upon a trial judge's later evaluation of the relative importance of the patient's interest in privacy and the evidentiary need for disclosure would eviscerate the effectiveness of the privilege. As we explained in *Upjohn*, if the purpose of the privilege is to be served, the participants in the confidential conversation "must be able to predict with some degree of certainty whether particular discussions will be protected. An uncertain privilege, or one which purports to be certain but results in widely varying applications by the courts, is little better than no privilege at all."

These considerations are all that is necessary for decision of this case. A rule that authorizes the recognition of new privileges on a case-by-case basis makes it appropriate to define the details of new privileges in a like manner. Because this is the first case in which we have recognized a psychotherapist privilege, it is neither necessary nor feasible to delineate its full contours in a way that would "govern all conceivable future questions in this area." *Id.*[7] . . . The conversations between Officer Redmond and Karen Beyer and the notes taken during their counseling sessions are protected from compelled disclosure under Rule 501 of the Federal Rules of Evidence. The judgment of the Court of Appeals is affirmed.

Justice SCALIA, with whom THE CHIEF JUSTICE joins as to Part III, dissenting.

The Court has discussed at some length the benefit that will be purchased by creation of the evidentiary privilege in this case: the encouragement of psychoanalytic counseling. It has not mentioned the purchase price: occasional injustice. That is the cost of every rule which excludes reliable and probative evidence — or at least every one categorical enough to achieve its announced policy objective. In the case of some of these rules, such as the one excluding confessions that have not been properly "Mirandized," see *Miranda v. Arizona*, 384 U.S. 436 (1966), the victim of the injustice is always the impersonal State or the faceless "public at large." For the rule proposed here, the victim is more likely to be some individual who is prevented from proving a valid claim — or (worse still) prevented from establishing a valid defense. The latter is particularly unpalatable for those who love justice, because it causes

---

Committee adopted its recommendations, much has changed in the domains of social work and psychotherapy. See generally Brief for National Association of Social Workers et al. as Amici Curiae (and authorities cited). While only 12 States regulated social workers in 1972, all 50 do today. Over the same period, the relative portion of therapeutic services provided by social workers has increased substantially. See U.S. Dept. of Health and Human Services, Center for Mental Health Services, Mental Health, United States, 1994.

   7. Although it would be premature to speculate about most future developments in the federal psychotherapist privilege, we do not doubt that there are situations in which the privilege must give way, for example, if a serious threat of harm to the patient or to others can be averted only by means of a disclosure by the therapist.

the courts of law not merely to let stand a wrong, but to become themselves the instruments of wrong.

In the past, this Court has well understood that the particular value the courts are distinctively charged with preserving — justice — is severely harmed by contravention of "the fundamental principle that "'the public ... has a right to every man's evidence.'" *Trammel v. United States*, 445 U.S. 40, 50 (1980) (citation omitted). Testimonial privileges, it has said, "*are not lightly created nor expansively construed*, for they are in derogation of the search for truth." *United States v. Nixon*, 418 U.S. 683, 710 (1974) (emphasis added). Adherence to that principle has caused us, in the Rule 501 cases we have considered to date, to reject new privileges, see *University of Pennsylvania v. EEOC*, 493 U.S. 182 (1990) (privilege against disclosure of academic peer review materials); *United States v. Gillock*, 445 U.S. 360 (1980) (privilege against disclosure of "legislative acts" by member of state legislature), and even to construe narrowly the scope of existing privileges, see, e.g., *United States v. Zolin*, 491 U.S. 554, 568–570 (1989) (permitting in camera review of documents alleged to come within crime-fraud exception to attorney-client privilege); *Trammel*, supra (holding that voluntary testimony by spouse is not covered by husband-wife privilege). The Court today ignores this traditional judicial preference for the truth, and ends up creating a privilege that is new, vast, and ill defined. I respectfully dissent.

I

The case before us involves confidential communications made by a police officer to a state-licensed clinical social worker in the course of psychotherapeutic counseling. Before proceeding to a legal analysis of the case, I must observe that the Court makes its task deceptively simple by the manner in which it proceeds. It begins by characterizing the issue as "whether it is appropriate for federal courts to recognize a 'psychotherapist privilege,'" and devotes almost all of its opinion to that question. Having answered that question (to its satisfaction) in the affirmative, it then devotes less than a page of text to answering in the affirmative the small remaining question whether "the federal privilege should also extend to confidential communications made to licensed social workers in the course of psychotherapy."

Of course the prototypical evidentiary privilege analogous to the one asserted here — the lawyer-client privilege — is not identified by the broad area of advice giving practiced by the person to whom the privileged communication is given, but rather by the professional status of that person. Hence, it seems a long step from a lawyer-client privilege to a tax advisor-client or accountant-client privilege. But if one recharacterizes it as a "legal advisor" privilege, the extension seems like the most natural thing in the world. That is the illusion the Court has produced here: It first frames an overly general question ("Should there be a psychotherapist privilege?") that can be answered in the negative only by excluding from protection office consultations with professional psychiatrists (i.e., doctors) and clinical psychologists. And then, having answered that in the affirmative, it comes to the only question that the facts of this case present ("Should there be a social worker-client privilege with regard to psychotherapeutic counseling?") with the answer seemingly a foregone conclusion. At that point, to conclude against the privilege one must subscribe to the difficult proposition, "Yes, there is a psychotherapist privilege, but not if the psychotherapist is a social worker." . . .

II

To say that the Court devotes the bulk of its opinion to the much easier question of psychotherapist-patient privilege is not to say that its answer to that question is convincing. . . . Effective psychotherapy undoubtedly is beneficial to individuals with mental problems, and surely serves some larger social interest in maintaining a mentally stable society. But merely mentioning these values does not answer the critical question: are they of such importance, and is the contribution of psychotherapy to them so distinctive, and is the application of normal evidentiary rules so destructive to psychotherapy, as to justify making our federal courts occasional instruments of injustice? On that central question I find the Court's analysis insufficiently convincing to satisfy the high standard we have set for rules that "are in derogation of the search for truth." *United States v. Nixon*, 418 U.S. 683 (1974).

When is it, one must wonder, that the psychotherapist came to play such an indispensable role in the maintenance of the citizenry's mental health? For most of history, men and women have worked out their difficulties by talking to, *inter alios*, parents, siblings, best friends and bartenders — none of whom was awarded a privilege against testifying in court. Ask the average citizen: Would your mental health be more significantly impaired by preventing you from seeing a psychotherapist, or by preventing you from getting advice from your mom? I have little doubt what the answer would be. Yet there is no mother-child privilege.

How likely is it that a person will be deterred from seeking psychological counseling, or from being completely truthful in the course of such counseling, because of fear of later disclosure in litigation? And even more pertinent to today's decision, to what extent will the evidentiary privilege reduce that deterrent? The Court does not try to answer the first of these questions; and it cannot possibly have any notion of what the answer is to the second, since that depends entirely upon the scope of the privilege, which the Court amazingly finds it "neither necessary nor feasible to delineate." If, for example, the psychotherapist can give the patient no more assurance than "A court will not be able to make me disclose what you tell me, unless you tell me about a harmful act," I doubt whether there would be much benefit from the privilege at all. That is not a fanciful example, at least with respect to extension of the psychotherapist privilege to social workers. See Del. Code Ann., Tit. 24, §3913(2) (1987); Idaho Code §54-3213(2) (1994).

Even where it is certain that absence of the psychotherapist privilege will inhibit disclosure of the information, it is not clear to me that that is an unacceptable state of affairs. Let us assume the very worst in the circumstances of the present case: that to be truthful about what was troubling her, the police officer who sought counseling would have to confess that she shot without reason, and wounded an innocent man. If (again to assume the worst) such an act constituted the crime of negligent wounding under Illinois law, the officer would of course have the absolute right not to admit that she shot without reason in criminal court. But I see no reason why she should be enabled both not to admit it in criminal court (as a good citizen should), and to get the benefits of psychotherapy by admitting it to a therapist who cannot tell anyone else. And even less reason why she should be enabled to deny her guilt in the criminal trial — or in a civil trial for negligence — while yet obtaining the benefits of psychotherapy by confessing guilt to a social worker who cannot testify. It seems to me entirely fair to say that if she wishes the benefits of telling the truth she must also accept the adverse consequences. To be sure, in most cases the statements to the psychotherapist will be only marginally relevant, and one of the purposes of the privilege (though not one relied upon by the Court) may be simply to spare patients needless intrusion upon their privacy, and to spare psychotherapists needless expenditure of their time in deposition and trial. But surely this can be achieved by means short of excluding even evidence that is of the most direct and conclusive effect.

The Court confidently asserts that not much truth-finding capacity would be destroyed by the privilege anyway, since "without a privilege, much of the desirable evidence to which litigants such as petitioner seek access . . . is unlikely to come into being." If that is so, how come psychotherapy got to be a thriving practice before the "psychotherapist privilege" was invented? Were the patients paying money to lie to their analysts all those years? Of course the evidence-generating effect of the privilege (if any) depends entirely upon its scope, which the Court steadfastly declines to consider. And even if one assumes that scope to be the broadest possible, is it really true that most, or even many, of those who seek psychological counseling have the worry of litigation in the back of their minds? I doubt that, and the Court provides no evidence to support it.

The Court suggests one last policy justification: since psychotherapist privilege statutes exist in all the States, the failure to recognize a privilege in federal courts "would frustrate the purposes of the state legislation that was enacted to foster these confidential communications." This is a novel argument indeed. A sort of inverse pre-emption: the truth-seeking functions of federal courts must be adjusted so as not to conflict with the policies of the States. This reasoning cannot be squared with *Gillock*, which declined to recognize an evidentiary privilege for Tennessee legislators in federal prosecutions, even though the Tennessee Constitution guaranteed it in state criminal proceedings. Moreover, since, as I shall discuss, state policies regarding the psychotherapist privilege vary considerably from State to State, no uniform federal policy can possibly honor most of them. If furtherance of state policies is the name of the game, rules of privilege in federal courts should vary from State to State, a la *Erie*.

The Court's failure to put forward a convincing justification of its own could perhaps be excused if it were relying upon the unanimous conclusion of state courts in the reasoned development of their common law. It cannot do that, since no State has such a privilege apart from legislation. What it relies upon, instead, is "the fact that all 50 States and the District of Columbia have [1] enacted into law [2] some form of psychotherapist privilege." Let us consider both the verb and its object: The fact [1] that all 50 States have enacted this privilege argues not for, but against, our adopting the privilege judicially. At best it suggests that the matter has been found not to lend itself to judicial treatment — perhaps because the pros and cons of adopting the privilege, or of giving it one or another shape, are not that clear; or perhaps because the rapidly evolving uses of psychotherapy demand a flexibility that only legislation can provide. At worst it suggests that the privilege commends itself only to decisionmaking bodies in which reason is tempered, so to speak, by political pressure from organized interest groups (such as psychologists and social workers), and decisionmaking bodies that are not overwhelmingly concerned (as courts of law are and should be) with justice.

And the phrase [2] "some form of psychotherapist privilege" covers a multitude of difficulties. . . . To rest a newly announced federal common-law psychotherapist privilege, assertable from this day forward in all federal courts, upon "the States' unanimous judgment that some form of psychotherapist privilege is appropriate," is rather like announcing a new, immediately applicable, federal common law of torts, based upon the States' "unanimous judgment" that some form of tort law is appropriate. In the one case as in the other, the state laws vary to such a degree that the parties and lower federal judges confronted by the new "common law" have barely a clue as to what its content might be.

III

Turning from the general question that was not involved in this case to the specific one that is: The Court's conclusion that a social-worker psychotherapeutic privilege deserves recognition is even less persuasive. In approaching this question, the fact that five of the state legislatures that have seen fit to enact "some form" of psychotherapist privilege have elected not to extend any form of privilege to social workers, ought to give one pause. So should the fact that the Judicial Conference Advisory Committee was similarly discriminating in its conferral of the proposed Rule 504 privilege. . . .

A licensed psychiatrist or psychologist is an expert in psychotherapy — and that may suffice (though I think it not so clear that this Court should make the judgment) to justify the use of extraordinary means to encourage counseling with him, as opposed to counseling with one's rabbi, minister, family or friends. One must presume that a social worker does not bring this greatly heightened degree of skill to bear, which is alone a reason for not encouraging that consultation as generously. Does a social worker bring to bear at least a significantly heightened degree of skill — more than a minister or rabbi, for example? I have no idea, and neither does the Court. . . .

Another critical distinction between psychiatrists and psychologists, on the one hand, and social workers, on the other, is that the former professionals, in their consultations with patients, do nothing but psychotherapy. Social workers, on the other hand, interview people for a multitude of reasons. . . . Thus, in applying the "social worker" variant of the "psychotherapist" privilege, it will be necessary to determine whether the information provided to the social worker was provided to him in his capacity as a psychotherapist, or in his capacity as an administrator of social welfare, a community organizer, etc. Worse still, if the privilege is to have its desired effect (and is not to mislead the client), it will presumably be necessary for the social caseworker to advise, as the conversation with his welfare client proceeds, which portions are privileged and which are not. . . .

[A]lthough the Court is technically correct that "the vast majority of States explicitly extend a testimonial privilege to licensed social workers," that uniformity exists only at the most superficial level. No State has adopted the privilege without restriction; the nature of the restrictions varies enormously from jurisdiction to jurisdiction; and 10 States . . . effectively reject the privilege entirely. It is fair to say that there is scant national consensus even as to the propriety of a social-worker psychotherapist privilege, and none whatever as to its appropriate scope. In other words, the state laws to which the Court appeals for support demonstrate most convincingly that adoption of a social-worker psychotherapist privilege is a job for Congress. . . .

. . . In its consideration of this case, the Court was the beneficiary of no fewer than 14 amicus briefs supporting respondents, most of which came from such organizations as the American Psychiatric Association, the American Psychoanalytic Association, the American Association of State Social Work Boards, the Employee Assistance Professionals Association, Inc., the American Counseling Association, and the National Association of Social Workers. Not a single amicus brief was field in support of petitioner. That is no surprise. There is no self-interested organization out there devoted to pursuit of the truth in the federal courts. The expectation is, however, that this Court will have that interest prominently—indeed, primarily—in mind. Today we have failed that expectation, and that responsibility. It is no small matter to say that, in some cases, our federal courts will be the tools of injustice rather than unearth the truth where it is available to be found. The common law has identified a few instances where that is tolerable. Perhaps Congress may conclude that it is also tolerable for the purpose of encouraging psychotherapy by social workers. But that conclusion assuredly does not burst upon the mind with such clarity that a judgment in favor of suppressing the truth ought to be pronounced by this honorable Court. I respectfully dissent.

IN RE GRAND JURY

103 F.3d 1140 (3d Cir. 1997)

GARTH, Circuit Judge.

Three appeals presenting the same critical issue are before us. One appeal originated in the District Court of the Virgin Islands at docket number 95-7354. The other two appeals pertaining to the same Delaware defendant originated in the District Court of Delaware at docket numbers 96-7529 and 96-7530. We scheduled oral argument in all three appeals on the same day inasmuch as they raised the same question—should this court recognize a parent-child privilege? . . .

In the Virgin Islands case, the grand jury sitting in St. Croix subpoenaed the father of the target of the grand jury investigation as a witness. At the time of the alleged transactions, the [witness's] son was eighteen years old. . . . The father, a former FBI agent, lived with his wife and son in St. Croix. . . . [B]ased on his belief that the grand jury intended to question him about conversations that he had had with his son, the father moved to quash the subpoena, asserting that those conversations were privileged from disclosure under Fed. R. Evid. 501.

The father testified, at a hearing before the district court, that he and his son "ha[d] an excellent relationship, very close, very loving relationship." He further testified that if he were coerced into testifying against his son, "[their] relationship would dramatically change and the closeness that [they] have would end. . . ." The father further explained that the subpoena would impact negatively upon his relationship with his son:

> I will be living under a cloud in which if my son comes to me or talks to me, I've got to be very careful what he says, what I allow him to say. I would have to stop him and say, "you can't talk to me about that. You've got to talk to your attorney." It's no way for anybody to live in this country.

. . . [The district court denied] the father's motion to quash. On the same day, the district court granted the targeted son's motion to intervene and then stayed its order which denied the quashing of the father's subpoena pending any appeal. The court's memorandum opinion and order, although clearly sympathetic with the plight of the subpoenaed father, "regretfully decline[d] to recognize [a parent-child] privilege" because the Third Circuit had yet to address the issue and "every United States Court of Appeals that has confronted this question has declined to recognize the parent-child privilege."

In the Delaware case, a sixteen year old minor daughter was subpoenaed to testify before the grand jury, as part of an investigation into her father's participation in an alleged interstate kidnapping of a woman who had disappeared. . . . [The day before she was scheduled to testify,] a motion to quash subpoena was made by counsel for the daughter and her mother, as well as by separate counsel for the father. The motion sought to bar the testimony of the daughter claiming a parent-child privilege which would cover testimony and confidential communications. . . . [The district court denied the motion and ordered the daughter to testify.] She refused to testify and was found in contempt. The district court then stayed the imposition of sanctions during the pendency of these appeals. . . .

The central question in these appeals is one of first impression in this court: should we recognize a parent-child testimonial privilege? Appellants argue that recognition is necessary in order to advance important public policy interests such as the protection of strong and trusting parent-child relationships; the preservation of the family; safeguarding of privacy interests and protection from harmful government intrusion; and the promotion of healthy psychological development of children. These public policy arguments echo those advanced by academicians and other legal commentators in the myriad of law review articles discussing the parent-child testimonial privilege.

Although legal academicians appear to favor adoption of a parent-child testimonial privilege, no federal Court of Appeals and no state supreme court has recognized such a privilege. We too decline to recognize such a privilege. . . .

Federal Rule of Evidence 501 provides that "the privilege of a witness . . . shall be governed by the principles of the common law as they may be interpreted by the courts of the United States in the light of reason and experience." No such principle, interpretation, reason or experience has been drawn upon here.

It is true that Congress, in enacting Fed. R. Evid. 501, "manifested an affirmative intention not to freeze the law of privilege. Its purpose rather was to 'provide the courts with the flexibility to develop rules of privilege on a case-by-case basis,' and to leave the door open to change." *Trammel v. United States*, 445 U.S. 40, 47 (1980) (quoting 102 Cong. Rec. 40,891 (1974) (statement of Rep. William Hungate)). In doing so, however, we are admonished that privileges are generally disfavored; that "'the public ... has a right to every man's evidence'"; and that privileges are tolerable "only to the very limited extent that permitting a refusal to testify or excluding relevant evidence has a public good transcending the normally predominant principle of utilizing all rational means for ascertaining truth." [*Trammel*, 445 U.S. at 50].

In keeping with these principles, the Supreme Court has rarely expanded common-law testimonial privileges. Following the Supreme Court's teachings, other federal courts, including this court, have likewise declined to exercise their power under Rule 501 expansively. *See, e.g., United States v. Schoenheinz*, 548 F.2d 1389, 1390 (9th Cir. 1977) (declining to recognize an employer-stenographer privilege); *In re Grand Jury Impaneled on January 21, 1975*, 541 F.2d 373, 382 (3d Cir. 1976) (declining to recognize a required-reports privilege).

Neither the appellants nor the dissent has identified any principle of common law, and hence have proved no interpretation of such a principle. Nor has the dissent or the appellants discussed any common-law principle in light of reason and experience. Accordingly, no basis has been demonstrated for this court to adopt a parent-child privilege.

The Supreme Court's most recent pronouncement in the law of privileges, *Jaffee v. Redmond*, 116 S. Ct. 1923 (1996), which recognized a psychotherapist-patient privilege, supports the conclusion that a privilege should not, and cannot, be created here. . . . The *Jaffee* Court emphasized that a court, in determining whether a particular privilege "'promotes sufficiently important interests to outweigh the need for probative evidence,'" must be guided by "reason and experience." Specifically, the *Jaffee* Court instructed that a federal court should look to the "experience" of state courts: "[T]he policy decision of the States bear on the question [of] whether federal courts should recognize a new privilege or amend the coverage of an existing one."

Notably, in recognizing a psychotherapist-patient privilege, the Supreme Court relied on the fact that all fifty states had enacted some form of a psychotherapist privilege. The *Jaffee* Court explained that "it is appropriate to treat a consistent body of policy determinations by state legislatures as reflecting both 'reason' and 'experience.'" Here, by contrast, only four states have deemed it necessary to protect from disclosure, in any manner, confidential communications between children and their parents. . . . New York state courts have recognized a limited parent-child privilege, and Idaho and Minnesota have enacted limited statutory privileges protecting confidential communications by minors to their parents. In Massachusetts . . . minor children are statutorily disqualified from testifying against their parents in criminal proceedings. . . .

The policy determinations of these four states do not constitute a "consistent body of policy determinations by state[s]" supporting recognition of a parent-child privilege. Indeed, if anything, the fact that the over-whelming majority of states have chosen not to create a parent-child privilege supports the opposite conclusion: "reason and experience" dictate that federal courts should refuse to recognize a privilege rejected by the vast majority of jurisdictions.

The *Jaffee* Court also relied on the fact that the psychotherapist-patient privilege was among the nine specific privileges recommended by the Advisory Committee on Rules of Evidence in 1972. . . . [T]he parent-child privilege, like the state legislative privilege rejected in [*United States v. Gillock*, 445 U.S. 360 (1980)], was not among the enumerated privileges submitted by the Advisory Committee. Although this fact, in and of itself, is not dispositive with respect to the question as to whether this court should create a privilege, it strongly suggests that the Advisory Committee, like the majority of state legislatures, did not regard confidential parent-child communications sufficiently important to warrant "privilege" protection.

. . . In *In re Grand Jury Investigation*, 918 F.2d 374 (3d Cir. 1990) (Becker, J.), we adopted a clergy-communicant privilege. We did so, however, only after examining the state and federal precedents addressing the issue of a clergy-communicant privilege and after determining that these precedents, on balance, weighed in favor of recognizing such a privilege. . . . Moreover, like the *Jaffee* Court and perhaps in anticipation of *Jaffee*'s instructions, Judge Becker considered the "reason and experience" of the state legislatures and of the Advisory Committee. First, Judge Becker, writing for a unanimous panel, noted that "virtually every state has recognized some form of a clergy-communicant privilege." In addition, Judge Becker posited that "the proposed rules prove a useful reference point and offer guidance in defining the existence and scope of evidentiary privileges in the federal courts." . . . Judge Becker then concluded that "[t]he inclusion of the clergy-communicant privilege in the proposed rules, taken together with its uncontroversial nature, strongly suggests that [that] privilege is, in the words of the Supreme Court, 'indelibly ensconced' in the American common law." Judge Becker also provided a detailed exegesis of the historical development of the clergy-communicant privilege, stressing that common-law tradition, as reflected in practice and case law, supported recognition of such a privilege.

In contrast, the parent-child privilege sought to be recognized here is of relatively recent vintage, and is virtually no more than the product of legal academicians. Unlike, for example, the attorney-client privilege, which is "the oldest" common-law privilege, *see United States v. Zolin*, 491 U.S. 554, 562 (1989); *Upjohn Co. v. United States*, 449 U.S. 383, 389 (1981), the parent-child privilege lacks historical antecedents.

Furthermore, an analysis of the four Wigmore factors, which Judge Becker used to buttress this court's disposition in *In re Grand Jury Investigation*, does not support the creation of a privilege. Dean Wigmore's four-factor formula requires satisfaction of all four factors in order to establish a privilege:

(1) The communications must originate in a confidence that they will not be disclosed.

(2) This element of confidentiality must be essential to the full and satisfactory maintenance of the relation between the parties.

(3) The relation must be one which in the opinion of the community ought to be sedulously fostered.

(4) The injury that would inure to the relation by the disclosure of the communications must be greater than the benefit thereby gained for the correct disposal of litigation.

In re Grand Jury Investigation, 918 F.2d at 384 (quoting 8 John H. Wigmore, Evidence §2285 (J. McNaughton rev. ed. 1961)).

At least two of Wigmore's prerequisite conditions for creation of a federal common-law privilege are not met under the facts of these cases. We refer to the second and fourth elements of the Wigmore test.

First, confidentiality — in the form of a testimonial privilege — is not essential to a successful parent-child relationship, as required by the second factor. A privilege should be recognized only where such a privilege would be indispensable to the survival of the relationship that society deems should be fostered. For instance, because complete candor and full disclosure by the client is absolutely necessary in order for the attorney to function effectively, society recognizes an attorney-client privilege. Without a guarantee of secrecy, clients would be unwilling to reveal damaging information. As a corollary, clients would disclose negative information, which an attorney must know to prove effective representation, only if they were assured that such disclosures are privileged.

In contrast, it is not clear whether children would be more likely to discuss private matters with their parents if a parent-child privilege were recognized than if one were not. It is not likely that children, or even their parents, would typically be aware of the existence or non-existence of a testimonial privilege covering parent-child communications. On the other hand, professionals such as attorneys, doctors and members of the clergy would know of the privilege that attends their respective profession, and their clients, patients or parishioners would also be aware that their confidential conversations are protected from compelled disclosure.[8]

Moreover, even assuming arguendo that children and their parents generally are aware of whether or not their communications are protected from disclosure, it is not certain that the existence of a privilege enters into whatever thought processes are performed by children in deciding whether or not to confide in their parents. Indeed, the existence or nonexistence of a parent-child privilege is probably one of the least important considerations in any child's decision as to whether to reveal some indiscretion, legal or illegal, to a parent. Moreover, it is unlikely that any parent would choose to deter a child from

---

8. Notably, the Advisory Committee on the Rules of Evidence reached a similar conclusion with respect to a marital communications privilege. The Advisory Committee explained: "[Proposed Rule 505] recognizes no privilege for confidential communications [between spouses]. . . . [It cannot] be assumed that marital conduct will be affected by a privilege for confidential communications of whose existence the parties in all likelihood are unaware. The other communication privileges, by way of contrast, have as one party a professional person who can be expected to inform the other of the existence of the privilege."

revealing a confidence to the parent solely because a federal court has refused to recognize a privilege protecting such communications from disclosure.

Finally, the proposed parent-child privilege fails to satisfy the fourth condition of the Wigmore test. As explained above, any injury to the parent-child relationship resulting from non-recognition of such a privilege would be relatively insignificant. In contrast, the cost of recognizing such a privilege is substantial: the impairment of the truth-seeking function of the judicial system and the increased likelihood of injustice resulting from the concealment of relevant information. . . .

An even more compelling reason for rejecting a parent-child privilege stems from the fact that the parent-child relationship differs dramatically from other relationships. This is due to the unique duty owing to the child from the parent. A parent owes the duty to the child to nurture and guide the child. This duty is unusual because it inheres in the relationship and the relationship arises automatically at the child's birth.

If, for example, a fifteen year old unemancipated child informs her parent that she has committed a crime or has been using or distributing narcotics, and this disclosure has been made in confidence while the child is seeking guidance, it is evident to us that, regardless of whether the child consents or not, the parent must have the right to take such action as the parent deems appropriate in the interest of the child. That action could be commitment to a drug rehabilitation center or a report of the crime to the juvenile authorities. This is so because, in theory at least, juvenile proceedings are undertaken solely in the interest of the child. We would regard it intolerable in such a situation if the law intruded in the guise of a privilege, and silenced the parent because the child had a privilege to prevent disclosure.

This results in the analysis that any privilege, if recognized, must be dependent upon both the parent and child asserting it. However, in such a case, the privilege would disappear if the parent can waive it. It follows therefore that, if a child is able to communicate openly with a parent and seeks guidance from that parent, the entire basis for the privilege is destroyed if the child is required to recognize that confidence will be maintained only so long as the parent wants the conversation to be confidential. If, however, the parent can waive the privilege unilaterally, the goal of the privilege is destroyed. . . . [A]n effective parent-child privilege requires that the parent's lips be sealed, but such a sealing would be inexcusable in the parent-child relationship. No government should have that power.

. . . [In any event,] the legislature, not the judiciary, is institutionally better equipped to perform the balancing of the competing policy issues required in deciding whether the recognition of a parent-child privilege is in the best interests of society. Congress, through its legislative mechanisms, is also better suited for the task of defining the scope of any prospective privilege. Congress is able to consider, for example, society's moral, sociological, economic, religious and other values without being confined to the evidentiary record in any particular case. Thus, in determining whether a parent-child privilege should obtain, Congress can take into consideration a host of facts and factors which the judiciary may be unable to consider. These considerations are also relevant to determining whether the privilege, if it is to be recognized, should extend to adult children, adopted children or unemancipated minors.

Among additional factors that Congress could consider are other parameters of familial relationships. Does "parent" include step-parent or grandparent? Does "child" include an adopted child, or a step-child? Should the privilege extend to siblings? Furthermore, if another family member is present at the time of the relevant communication is the privilege automatically barred or destroyed?

. . . In short, if a new privilege is deemed worthy of recognition, the wiser course in our opinion is to leave the adoption of such a privilege to Congress. . . . Sympathy alone cannot justify the creation of a new and unprecedented privilege which does not meet the standards set by Congress, the Supreme Court and this court.

Accordingly, we will affirm [the district courts' orders].

MANSMANN, Circuit Judge, concurring and dissenting.

I write separately because I am convinced that the testimonial privilege issue raised by the Virgin Islands appeal is substantially different from that presented in the Delaware appeals and should be resolved in favor of the targeted son. The Virgin Islands appeal, which challenges the denial of a motion to quash a grand jury subpoena, requires that we confront an issue of first impression in our circuit: should we make available to a parent and child an evidentiary privilege which could be invoked to prevent compelling that parent to testify regarding confidential communications made to the parent by his child in the course of seeking parental advice and guidance? It appears that this precise question is one of first impression in the federal courts.

Because I conclude that the public good at issue, the protection of strong and trusting parent-child relationships, outweighs the government's interest in disclosure, I would exercise the authority granted to the federal courts by Congress under Rule 501 of the Federal Rules of Evidence and would recognize a limited privilege. Accordingly, I respectfully dissent. . . .

UNDER SEAL v. UNITED STATES

755 F.3d 213 (4th Cir. 2014)

THACKER, Circuit Judge.

[A 19-year-old man challenged a subpoena that required him to testify before a federal grand jury about the ownership of illegal firearms found in the house he shared with his parents; because the investigation targeted his father, he claimed that forcing him to testify would violate the parent-child privilege. The district court agreed and quashed the subpoena. The government appealed.]

No federal appellate court has recognized a parent-child privilege, and we decline to do so here. . . . "[R]eason and experience" do not warrant creation of the privilege in the face of substantial authority to the contrary. . . .[5] . . . Only

---

5. [N]ew privileges are perhaps most aptly created via the legislative process. In [an] ever-changing world, we should be "circumspect about creating new privileges based upon

a very small handful of federal district courts in this country have recognized the parent-child privilege. . . . In contrast, every federal appellate court that has considered adoption of the parent-child privilege — including our own — has rejected it. . . . [T]he district court erred in adopting the parent-child privilege and excusing [Appellee] from testifying before the grand jury. We reverse and remand.

MIRJAN R. DAMAŠKA, EVIDENCE LAW ADRIFT
12–13, 77–78 (1997)

Rules rejecting probative information for the sake of values unrelated to the pursuit of truth are clearly not limited to the world of Anglo-American justice. A piquant example is testimonial privileges: not only are they widespread on the Continent, but they often assume broader forms — much more encompassing than in the law of any common law country. Thus, in addition to refusing to answer self-incriminating questions, in many European jurisdictions witnesses can refuse to answer questions potentially capable of incriminating members of their family. Some countries go even further and dispense witnesses from the duty to answer any question likely to dishonor them or expose them to direct financial loss. Other countries grant parties in civil litigation a general dispensation from the duty to testify. Indeed, so expansive are some of these testimonial privileges that one wonders how the lawgivers' promises can be kept without seriously harming the interests of justice.

. . . The short answer is that Continental privileges are not invoked nearly so often as Anglo-American lawyers would expect. Prominent among the reasons is the paucity of contact between prospective witnesses and litigants' lawyers. . . . The pretrial collection of evidence is here primarily the job of the judge or some other official. Although counsel for the parties are not prohibited from conducting investigations, their contacts with prospective witnesses are disfavored. If revealed, these contacts are likely to diminish the credibility of the witness's testimony. Preparing witnesses for court is strongly disapproved and may in some countries come dangerously close to tampering with evidence. For all these reasons, lawyers conduct few factual investigations on their own, largely limiting themselves to conveying investigative leads to the official in charge of proof-taking.

---

perceived public policy considerations." *In re Grand Jury*, 103 F.3d 1104, 1154 (3d Cir. 1997). . . . Leaving this task to the legislative branch would also allow for the privilege to be more precisely defined. *See* [*id.*], 103 F.3d at 1157 ("If a new privilege were to be engraved in the concrete of our jurisprudence . . ., then it should be framed so that its contours are clear and unambiguous[.]"); *see also Upjohn Co. v. United States*, 449 U.S. 383, 393 (1981) ("An uncertain privilege, or one which purports to be certain but results in widely varying applications by the courts, is little better than no privilege at all.").

PHYSICAL EVIDENCE

"The proof was in the pudding, but the pudding was ruled inadmissible as evidence."

Most trial evidence takes the form of testimony from a witness. But most trials also involve at least some physical evidence—i.e., tangible exhibits such as documents, photographs, contraband, weapons, etc. Physical evidence is subject to many of the same rules as testimonial evidence. The documents generally are inadmissible if they contain hearsay; guns generally are inadmissible if they serve only to demonstrate the defendant's violent character. But physical evidence also may need to satisfy two more specialized rules.

First, all physical evidence must be *authenticated*. That is to say, the party offering the evidence must provide sufficient evidence to allow the factfinder to conclude that the evidence is genuine. As the materials in the first portion of this chapter explain, authentication is best understood as a specific application of a more general principle of evidence law: conditional relevance. Indeed, the rules follow the practice of trial lawyers in referring to the "authentication" not just of physical evidence, but also of certain *testimony* raising problems of conditional relevance — for example, testimony recounting conversations in which the opposing party is alleged to have participated.

Second, certain physical evidence — and certain forms of testimony — may be rendered inadmissible by the *best evidence rule*, which is the subject of the second part of this chapter. Unlike the requirement of authentication, which applies quite broadly, the best evidence rule has a narrow scope. In its modern formulation, the best evidence rule does *not* require, as a general matter, that a party introduce the best evidence available on any given point. Instead, it requires only that a party seeking to prove the content of a document introduce the original — and even that requirement has several significant exceptions.

Most physical evidence qualifies as what is sometimes called "real evidence": items that allegedly played some role in or were generated by the events in dispute. But lawyers often generate charts, photographs, diagrams, models, or video presentations specifically for trial, to clarify their case or to make it more vivid. "Demonstrative evidence" of this kind is usually thought subject to neither the requirement of authentication nor the best evidence rule. As the materials in the third and final part of this chapter demonstrate, demonstrative evidence is increasingly powerful and increasingly important, but courts and rulemakers remain unsure how to regulate it, or even whether to think of it as "evidence."

In discussing either "real" or "demonstrative" evidence, it is important to distinguish between introducing an exhibit and merely "marking" it. We touched on this in Chapter 1. The basic point is that a traditional, uncodified rule of trial practice requires any physical exhibit used during the trial to be marked. "Marking" means both physical labeling of the exhibit (usually with a sticker that says something like "Plaintiff's Exhibit 2" or "People's Exhibit 7B") and making it part of the formal record of the case (i.e., turning over custody of the exhibit to the court and keeping it with the documents and other materials available to reviewing courts). Exhibits must be marked even if they are never introduced into evidence but are used solely, for example, to refresh the recollection of a forgetful witness. But an exhibit that is merely marked cannot be relied upon by the jury in reaching a verdict. In order to serve this role, the marked exhibit must be introduced into evidence.

A. AUTHENTICATION

[F.R.E. 901–903; C.E.C. §§1400–1454]

ADVISORY COMMITTEE NOTE TO F.R.E. 901

Authentication and identification represent a special aspect of relevancy. Thus a telephone conversation may be irrelevant because on an unrelated topic or because the speaker is not identified. The latter aspect is the one here involved. Wigmore describes the need for authentication as "an inherent logical necessity."

This requirement of showing authenticity or identity falls in the category of relevancy dependent upon fulfillment of a condition of fact and is governed by the procedure set forth in Rule 104(b).

. . . The treatment of authentication and identification [in subdivision (b)] draws largely upon the experience embodied in the common law and in statutes to furnish illustrative applications of the general principle set forth in subdivision (a). The examples are not intended as an exclusive enumeration of allowable methods but are meant to guide and suggest, leaving room for growth and development in this area of the law. . . .

It should be observed that compliance with requirements of authentication or identification by no means assures admission of an item into evidence, as other bars, hearsay for example, may remain.

1. Authentication of Traditional Documents and Physical Objects

UNITED STATES v. LONG

857 F.2d 436 (8th Cir. 1988)

HEANEY, Circuit Judge.

Thaddeus Adonis Long and Edward Larry Jackson appeal from their convictions on a number of counts for their involvement in a check forging and bank fraud scheme. We affirm their convictions on all counts.

. . . At trial, Long called his fiancee, Mary Statten, as a witness. On direct examination, she briefly mentioned a contract Long signed prior to coming to Minnesota, which, according to her, led her and Long to believe he was participating in a legitimate business venture. The government did not object to her mentioning the contract. On cross-examination, the government questioned her quite extensively about the contract. She replied that the contract involved Thermo-Dynamics and that Jackson had hired Long for six months for $40,000 as a promoter. She indicated that Long had probably brought the contract with him to Minnesota. On re-direct examination, Statten identified an exhibit as the contract of employment. The government and Jackson objected to the exhibit as hearsay. The trial court sustained the objection.

At a side bar conference, Long's counsel argued that the exhibit was not being offered for its truth but rather to show Long's state of mind, as the best evidence of the agreement about which Statten testified on direct examination, or as a response to the government's cross-examination which implied that the contract was a recent fabrication. The trial court questioned whether the contract had been authenticated.

On appeal, the government only argues that the trial court did not abuse its discretion in excluding the contract because it had not been authenticated. To authenticate a document, the proponent need only prove a rational basis for the claim that the document is what the proponent asserts it to be.... This may be done with circumstantial evidence.

For the purpose of attempting to bolster Statten's testimony, we see no reason why the contract was insufficiently authenticated. The government contends that Statten was not a party or a signatory to the document or witness to its preparation. The question of authenticity here, however, is not whether the contract was an authentic contract between Jackson and Long but whether it reasonably could be the document which Statten claims she saw and read at the airport. The defense did not have to prove the contract's reliability and accuracy. This was a matter for the jury to determine after examining all the evidence.[2] Thus, the document was authenticated as the document which Statten claims she saw and read.

Any error which occurred, however, was harmless. The contract was introduced to bolster Statten's testimony that Long thought he was entering a legitimate business enterprise. Other evidence strongly indicated that Long had not unwittingly entered the fraud scheme. Long used various aliases and false forms of identification; he did nothing that could be construed as a legitimate business activity while in Minnesota; and the cash he withdrew from the bank was for his personal use. We, therefore, find no reversible error....

UNITED STATES v. CASTO

889 F.2d 562 (5th Cir. 1989)

CLARK, Chief Judge.

Diana Casto appeals her conviction in the United States District Court for the Western District of Texas on one count of conspiracy to possess with intent to distribute methamphetamine ... and two counts of aiding and abetting in the unlawful distribution of methamphetamine....

Casto contends that a break in the chain of custody pertinent to Government Exhibits Two, Three, Four, and Five, the packages of methamphetamine sold to the undercover agents by [codefendant Melinda] Gutierrez, should have rendered these exhibits inadmissible. Shortly after Officer Martinez seized the packages, they were sealed and sent to a Drug Enforcement Agency laboratory in Dallas, Texas. Over two months later the packages were tested by Frank Medina, a forensic chemist at the lab. Medina found that the packages contained methamphetamine. He then sent the packages back to Martinez, who held custody of them until trial. During the period between the arrival of the packages at the laboratory and Medina's testing, the packages

---

2. There is the danger that such documentary evidence may be given undue weight by a jury. As Weinstein and Berger observe, "[r]eal proof often has enormous apparent probative force because the lay trier may lose sight of the fact that its connection to a party may depend upon the credibility of an authenticating witness." J. Weinstein and M. Berger, Weinstein's Evidence, ¶901(a)[01], at 901-19 (1983). We believe, however, such a problem should be confronted under Rule 403, which states that relevant evidence may be excluded "if its probative value is substantially outweighed by the danger of unfair prejudice, confusion of the issues, or misleading the jury...."

were kept in a vault where a technician had placed them upon their arrival at the laboratory.

Martinez and Medina testified at trial as to their custody of the packages, but the technician did not testify. According to Casto the trial judge erred by disregarding this evidentiary flaw and allowing the packages into evidence. We disagree.

A trial judge is correct in allowing physical evidence to be presented to the jury as long as a reasonable jury could decide that the evidence is what the offering party claims it to be. Fed. R. Evid. 901. Any question as to the authenticity of the evidence is then properly decided by the jury. Thus, a break in the chain of custody affects only the weight and not the admissibility of the evidence. The trial court was correct to admit the packages of methamphetamine.... Affirmed.

UNITED STATES v. GRANT

967 F.2d 81 (2d Cir. 1992)

PER CURIAM.

Sharon Grant appeals from her conviction, following a jury trial, on charges of conspiracy to import heroin, importation of heroin, and possession of heroin with intent to distribute it in violation of 21 U.S.C. §§841(a)(1), 952(a), and 963.... Grant contends that the government failed to prove that the packages imported by [her traveling companion Gene] Kirven ... contained heroin. She points out that the government did not establish an airtight chain of custody over the packages from the time they were seized at the airport until the time they were tested in the laboratory by the government's chemist. Instead, the testimony and documents introduced at trial indicated that the packages were signed out of an airport vault on January 9, 1991 and not signed into the Drug Enforcement Agency's laboratory until January 23, 1991. There is nothing in the record to indicate what happened to the packages in the interim. From this lapse, Grant contends that there was insufficient evidence to establish that the laboratory tested the same substance that Kirven carried to the airport. Grant then argues that without the lab test, there was not sufficient evidence from which any reasonable jury could find that the packages contained heroin. We disagree.

We first note that this is not a typical "chain of custody" case. Chain of custody is usually an issue where a party attempts to introduce a piece of physical evidence.... In this case we need not determine whether the drugs were properly authenticated since the government did not offer the drugs themselves into evidence. Instead, the government presented the testimony of the chemist who analyzed the package. There is no need to authenticate the testimony of live witnesses.

This is not to say that the government's failure to establish a chain of custody is unimportant. In order to be admissible, the testimony of a live witness must be relevant, that is, must have a "tendency to make the existence of any fact that is of consequence to the determination of the action more probable or less probable than it would be without the evidence." Fed. R. Evid. 401. In order for the chemist's testimony to be relevant, there must be some likeli-hood that the substance tested by the chemist was the substance seized at the airport. The government's failure to establish a chain of custody from the moment the substance was seized to the time it was subjected to laboratory analysis makes this less likely, and thus casts some doubt on the admissibility of the chemist's testimony.

However, Grant did not object to the chemist's testimony at trial and does not assert here that the testimony should have been excluded. Even if Grant had pursued this argument, we doubt it would be successful, given the broad discretion afforded district courts in making relevancy determina-tions. . . . [W]e affirm her conviction and sentence in all respects.

2. Authentication of Digital Evidence

ADVISORY COMMITTEE NOTE TO 2017
AMENDMENTS TO F.R.E. 902

[Paragraph (13)] The amendment sets forth a procedure by which par-ties can authenticate certain electronic evidence other than through the testi-mony of a foundation witness. . . .

A certification under this Rule can establish only that the proffered item has satisfied the admissibility requirements for authenticity. The oppo-nent remains free to object to admissibility of the proffered item on other grounds—including hearsay, relevance, or in criminal cases the right to con-frontation. For example, assume that a plaintiff in a defamation case offers what purports to be a printout of a webpage on which a defamatory state-ment was made. Plaintiff offers a certification under this Rule in which a qualified person describes the process by which the webpage was retrieved. Even if that certification sufficiently establishes that the webpage is authentic, defendant remains free to object that the statement on the webpage was not placed there by defendant. Similarly, a certification authenticating a computer output, such as a spreadsheet, does not preclude an objection that the infor-mation produced is unreliable—the authentication establishes only that the output came from the computer.

A challenge to the authenticity of electronic evidence may require techni-cal information about the system or process at issue, including possibly retain-ing a forensic technical expert; such factors will affect whether the opponent has a fair opportunity to challenge the evidence given the notice provided. . . .

[Paragraph (14)] The amendment sets forth a procedure by which parties can authenticate data copied from an electronic device, storage medium, or an electronic file, other than through the testimony of a foundation witness. . . .

Today, data copied from electronic devices, storage media, and electronic files are ordinarily authenticated by "hash value." A hash value is a number that is often represented as a sequence of characters and is produced by an algo-rithm based upon the digital contents of a drive, medium, or file. If the hash values for the original and copy are different, then the copy is not identical to the original. If the hash values for the original and copy are the same, it is highly improbable that the original and copy are not identical. Thus, identical hash values for the original and copy reliably attest to the fact that they are exact duplicates. This amendment allows self-authentication by a certification of a qualified person that she checked the hash value of the proffered item and that it was identical to the original. The rule is flexible enough to allow certifications through processes other than comparison of hash value, including by other reliable means of identification provided by future technology.

A certification under this Rule can only establish that the proffered item is authentic. The opponent remains free to object to admissibility of the proffered item on other grounds—including hearsay, relevance, or in criminal cases the right to confrontation. For example, in a criminal case in which data copied from a hard drive is proffered, the defendant can still challenge hearsay found in the hard drive, and can still challenge whether the information on the hard drive was placed there by the defendant. . . .

UNITED STATES v. VAYNER

769 F.3d 125 (2d Cir. 2014)

Debra Ann Livingston, Circuit Judge.

Aliaksandr Zhyltsou was convicted after trial on a single count of the unlawful transfer of a false identification document. . . . [T]he government's principal evidence against Zhyltsou was the testimony of Vladyslav Timku, a Ukrainian citizen residing in Brooklyn who testified pursuant to a cooperation agreement and who had earlier pled guilty to conspiracy to commit wire fraud, aggravated identity theft, and impersonating a diplomat. Timku testified that he was a friend of Zhyltsou's and was familiar with Zhyltsou's work as a forger because he had previously paid Zhyltsou to create false diplomatic identification documents in a scheme to avoid taxes on the purchase and resale of luxury automobiles through a corporation called Martex International. Timku said that in the summer of 2009 he asked Zhyltsou to create a forged birth certificate that would reflect that Timku was the father of an invented infant daughter. Timku sought the birth certificate in an attempt to avoid compulsory military service in his native Ukraine, which permits a deferment of service for the parents of children under three years of age. According to Timku, Zhyltsou agreed to forge the birth certificate without charge, as a "favor," and began creating the fake birth certificate on a computer while the pair chatted in a Brooklyn Internet café. Timku testified that Zhyltsou sent the completed forgery to Timku via e-mail on August 27, 2009 from azmadeuz@gmail.com (the "Gmail address"), an e-mail address that Timku had often used to correspond with Zhyltsou. After receiving the document, Timku thanked Zhyltsou and then went on to use the fake document to receive the deferment from military service that he sought. The government introduced a copy of the e-mail, with the forged birth certificate as an attachment, which reflected that it was sent to Timku's e-mail address, "timkuvlad@yahoo.com," from azmadeuz @gmail.com.

The government presented several other witnesses who corroborated certain aspects of Timku's testimony—regarding the falsity of the birth certificate, the Ukrainian military deferment for parents of young children, and the path of the e-mail in question through servers in California. There was expert testimony to the effect that the e-mail originated in New York, but no evidence as to what computer it was sent from, or what IP addresses were linked to it. Thus, near the conclusion of the prosecution's case, only Timku's testimony directly connected Zhyltsou with the Gmail address that was used to transmit the fake birth certificate to Timku. Before the prosecution rested, however, the government indicated to the district court that it planned to call an unexpected final witness: Robert Cline, a Special Agent with the State Department's Diplomatic Security Service ("DSS"). The government said that it intended to introduce a printout of a web page that the government claimed to be Zhyltsou's profile on VK.com ("VK"), which Special Agent Cline described as "the Russian equivalent of Facebook." Zhyltsou objected, contending that the page had not been properly authenticated and was thus inadmissible under Federal Rule of Evidence 901. The district court overruled the defense objection, concluding that the VK page was "[Zhyltsou's] Facebook page. The information on there, I think it's fair to assume, is information which was provided by him." Moreover, the court ruled, "There's no question about the authenticity of th[e] document so far as it's coming off the Internet now."

During his testimony, Special Agent Cline identified the printout as being from "the Russian equivalent of Facebook." He noted to the jury that the page purported to be the profile of "Alexander Zhiltsov" (an alternate spelling of Zhyltsou's name), and that it contained a photograph of Zhyltsou. Importantly for the government's case, Special Agent Cline next pointed out that under the heading, "Contact Information," the profile listed "Azmadeuz" as "Zhiltsov's" address on Skype (a service that Special Agent Cline described as a "voice-over IP provider"). The web page also reflected that "Zhiltsov" worked at a company called "Martex International" and at an Internet café called "Cyber Heaven," which corresponded with Timku's earlier testimony that Zhyltsou and Timku had both worked for those entities. On cross-examination, Special Agent Cline admitted that he had only a "cursory familiarity" with VK, had never used the site except to view this single page, and did not know whether any identity verification was required in order for a user to create an account on the site. In its summation, the government argued that it had proven that Zhyltsou had produced the fake birth certificate and sent it to Timku using the Gmail address. In the final words of her summation, the Assistant United States Attorney ("AUSA") argued that proof of the connection between Zhyltsou and the Gmail address could be found on Zhyltsou's "own Russian Facebook page":

> It has the defendant's profile picture on it. You'll see that it confirms other facts that you've learned about the defendant. That he worked at Martex and at Cyber Heaven, for example. He told [a DSS agent] that he's from Belarus. This page says he's from Minsk, the capital of Belarus. And on that page, you'll see the name he uses on Skype which, like e-mail, is a way to correspond with people over the Internet.
>
> Azmadeuz. That [is] his online identity, ladies and gentlemen, for Skype and for [G]mail. That is [w]hat the defendant calls himself. Timku even told you that the defendant sometimes uses azmadeuz@yahoo.com. That [is] his own name

on the Internet. Timku didn't make it up for him. The defendant made it up for himself.

Aliaksandr Zhyltsou made a fake birth certificate and he sent it through e-mail. Those are the facts. The defendant is guilty. Find him so. Thank you.

After deliberating for approximately a day and a half, the jury found Zhyltsou guilty on the single charge contained in the indictment. Subsequently, the district court sentenced Zhyltsou principally to time served and one year of post-release supervision. . . .

[W]e conclude that the district court abused its discretion in admitting the VK web page, as it did so without proper authentication under Rule 901. The government did not provide a sufficient basis on which to conclude that the proffered printout was what the government claimed it to be — *Zhyltsou's* profile page — and there was thus insufficient evidence to authenticate the VK page and to permit its consideration by the jury.

In the district court, the government initially advanced the argument that it offered the evidence simply as a web page that existed on the Internet at the time of trial, not as evidence of Zhyltsou's own statements. The prosecution first represented to the district court that it was presenting the VK page only as "what [Special Agent Cline] is observing today on the Internet, just today," conceded that "the agent does not know who created it," and averred that Special Agent Cline would testify only that "he saw [the VK page] and this is what it says." Consistent with these representations, Special Agent Cline testified only that the page containing information related to Zhyltsou was presently accessible on the Internet and provided no extrinsic information showing that Zhyltsou was the page's author or otherwise tying the page to Zhyltsou.

At other times, however, the government repeatedly made a contrary argument to both the trial court and the jury, and insisted that the page belonged to and was authored by Zhyltsou. Nor is this surprising. The VK profile page was helpful to the government's case only if it belonged to Zhyltsou — if it was his profile page, created by him or someone acting on his behalf — and thus tended to establish that Zhyltsou used the moniker "Azmadeuz" on Skype and was likely also to have used it for the Gmail address from which the forged birth certificate was sent, just as Timku claimed. Moreover, the district court overruled Zhyltsou's hearsay objection and admitted a printout of the profile page, which stated that "Zhiltsov's" Skype username was "Azmadeuz," because it found that the page was created by Zhyltsou, and the statement therefore constituted a party admission. . . .

Rule 901 requires "evidence sufficient to support a finding that the item is what the proponent claims it is." It is uncontroverted that information *about* Zhyltsou appeared on the VK page: his name, photograph, and some details about his life consistent with Timku's testimony about him. But there was no evidence that Zhyltsou himself had created the page or was responsible for its contents. Had the government sought to introduce, for instance, a flyer found on the street that contained Zhyltsou's Skype address and was purportedly written or authorized by him, the district court surely would have required some evidence that the flyer did, in fact, emanate from Zhyltsou. Otherwise, how could the statements in the flyer be attributed to him? . . . And contrary to the government's argument, the mere fact that a page with Zhyltsou's name and photograph happened to exist on the Internet at the time of Special Agent Cline's testimony does not permit a reasonable conclusion that this page was created by the defendant or on his behalf.

It is true that the contents or "distinctive characteristics" of a document can sometimes alone provide circumstantial evidence sufficient for authentication. Fed. R. Evid. 901(b)(4). For example, a writing may be authenticated by evidence "that the contents of the writing were not a matter of common knowledge." [*United States v. Maldonado-Rivera*, 922 F.2d 934, 957 (2d Cir. 1990).] Here, however, all the information contained on the VK page allegedly tying the page to Zhyltsou was also known by Timku and likely others, some of whom may have had reasons to create a profile page falsely attributed to the defendant. Other than the page itself, moreover, no evidence in the record suggested that Zhyltsou even had a VK profile page, much less that the page in question was that page. Nor was there any evidence that identity verification is necessary to create such a page with VK, which might also have helped render more than speculative the conclusion that the page in question belonged to Zhyltsou.

We express no view on what kind of evidence *would* have been sufficient to authenticate the VK page and warrant its consideration by the jury. Evidence may be authenticated in many ways, and as with any piece of evidence whose authenticity is in question, the "type and quantum" of evidence necessary to authenticate a web page will always depend on context. [*United States v. Sliker*, 751 F.2d 477, 488 (2d Cir. 1984).] Given the purpose for which the web page in this case was introduced, however—to corroborate Timku's testimony that it was Zhyltsou who used the moniker "azmadeuz" for the Gmail address from which the forged birth certificate was sent—Rule 901 required that there be *some* basis beyond Timku's own testimony on which a reasonable juror could conclude that the page in question was not just any Internet page, but in fact *Zhyltsou's* profile. No such showing was made and the evidence should therefore have been excluded. . . .

It was, of course, vital to the government's case to prove that it was in fact Zhyltsou who used the Gmail address to send the fake birth certificate to Timku. This was the only point truly in contention at trial. Further, the prosecution's case on this point was far from overwhelming: with the limited exception of the circumstantial evidence that the Gmail account was closed shortly after Zhyltsou encountered federal agents, the *only* evidence that connected Zhyltsou to the emailed birth certificate, other than the VK page, was Timku's testimony.

The jury may well have been reluctant to rely on Timku's testimony alone. Pursuant to his cooperation agreement, Timku pled guilty to three felonies—aggravated identity theft, impersonating a diplomat, and conspiracy to commit wire fraud—each of which involved deceit. Timku's business operation, which he said he carried on with Zhyltsou's help, involved using fake identification papers and shell companies to commit tax fraud in the course of exporting luxury vehicles for sale in Ukraine and Russia. Timku admitted that he had destroyed evidence and fled the country after federal agents questioned him concerning this scheme. He also testified that he paid a United States citizen to enter into a sham marriage with him and opened a joint bank account in their names with the intention of deceiving immigration authorities into thinking that the marriage was genuine. All this likely undermined Timku's credibility, and may even have led the jury to believe that Timku could have used his expertise in fabricating identities and documents to create false evidence to substantiate his testimony against Zhyltsou. . . .

As a result, the printout of the VK profile was by no means cumulative, but played an important role in the government's case, which the AUSA augmented by highlighting the evidence in her summation. . . . Because the wrongly admitted evidence was "the sort of evidence that might well sway a jury" confronted with a case otherwise turning solely on the word of a single witness whose credibility was weak, [*United States v. Kaplan,* 490 F.3d 110, 123 (2d Cir. 2007)]; we conclude that the district court's error was not harmless and requires vacatur.

UNITED STATES v. BROWNE

834 F.3d 403 (3d Cir. 2016)

Krause, Circuit Judge.

. . . Appellant Tony Jefferson Browne was convicted of child pornography and sexual offenses with minors based in part on records of "chats" exchanged over Facebook and now contests his conviction on the ground that these records were not properly authenticated with evidence of his authorship. . . . Under the Facebook account name "Billy Button," Browne began exchanging messages with 18-year-old Nicole Dalmida in November 2011. They met in person a few months later and then exchanged sexually explicit photographs of themselves through Facebook chats. Browne then threatened to publish Dalmida's photos online unless Dalmida engaged in oral sex and promised to delete the photos only if she provided him the password to her Facebook account.

Using Dalmida's account, Browne made contact with four of Dalmida's "Facebook friends," all minors—T.P. (12 years old), A.M. (15 years old), J.B. (15 years old) and J.S. (17 years old)—and solicited explicit photos from them by a variety of means. Once he had the minors' photos, he repeated the pattern he had established with Dalmida, threatening all of them with the public exposure of their images unless they agreed to engage in various sexual acts and sent additional explicit photos of themselves to his Button Facebook account or to his phone number ("the 998 number"). He arranged to meet with three of the minors and sexually assaulted one.

On receiving information from the Virgin Islands Police Department, agents from the Department of Homeland Security (DHS) interviewed Dalmida and three of the minors. In June 2013, DHS arrested Browne and executed a search warrant on his residence. Among the items seized was a cell phone that matched the 998 number and from which text messages and photos of the minors were recovered. During questioning and at trial, Browne admitted the 998 number and phone belonged to him. DHS executed a search warrant on the Button Facebook account, which Browne also admitted belonged to him, and Facebook provided five sets of chats and a certificate of authenticity executed by its records custodian.

At trial, over defense counsel's objections, the District Court admitted the five Facebook chat logs and certificate of authenticity into evidence. Four of the chats involved communications between the Billy Button account and, respectively, Dalmida, J.B., J.S. and T.P. The fifth chat did not involve Button's account and took place between Dalmida and J.B., on the subject of Browne's sexual assault of J.B. The certificate stated, in accordance with Rule 902(11) of the Federal Rules of Evidence, that the records that Facebook had produced for the named accounts met the business records requirements of Rule 803(6)(A)-(C). Tracking the language of Rule 803(6), the custodian certified that the records "were made and kept by the automated systems of Facebook in the course of regularly conducted activity as a regular practice of Facebook . . . [and] were made at or near the time the information was transmitted by the Facebook user." . . .

Browne argues that the Facebook records were not properly authenticated because the Government failed to establish that he was the person who authored the communications. More specifically, Browne contends that no witness identified the Facebook chat logs on the stand; nothing in the contents of the messages was uniquely known to Browne; and Browne was not the only individual with access to the Button account or the 998 number. The Government, for its part, argues . . . that it authenticated the Facebook chat logs by way of Rule 902, under which extrinsic evidence is not required for certain documents that bear sufficient indicia of reliability as to be "self-authenticating." Specifically, the Government relies on Rule 902(11), which provides that "records of a regularly conducted activity" that fall into the hearsay exception under Rule 803(6)—more commonly known as the "business records exception"—may be authenticated by way of a certificate from the records custodian, as long as the proponent of the evidence gives the adverse party reasonable notice and makes the record and certificate available for inspection in advance of trial. . . .

[T]he relevance of the Facebook records hinges on the fact of authorship. To authenticate the messages, the Government was therefore required to introduce enough evidence such that the jury could reasonably find, by a preponderance of the evidence, that Browne and the victims authored the Facebook messages at issue. The records custodian here, however, attested only that the communications took place as alleged between the named Facebook accounts. Thus, accepting the Government's contention that it fulfilled its authentication obligation simply by submitting such an attestation would amount to holding that social media evidence need not be subjected to a "relevance" assessment prior to admission. Our sister Circuits have rejected this proposition in both the digital and non-digital contexts, as do we. *See United States v. Vayner*, 769 F.3d 125, 132 (2d Cir. 2014) (holding that a social media profile page was not properly authenticated where the government offered evidence only that the webpage existed and not that it belonged to the defendant). . . .

The Government's theory of self-authentication also fails for a second reason: it is predicated on a misunderstanding of the business records exception itself. Rule 803(6) is designed to capture records that are likely accurate and reliable in content, as demonstrated by the trustworthiness of the underlying sources of information and the process by which and purposes for which that information is recorded.... Facebook does not purport to verify or rely on the substantive contents of the communications in the course of its business. At most, the records custodian employed by the social media platform can attest to the accuracy of only certain aspects of the communications exchanged over that platform, that is, confirmation that the depicted communications took place between certain Facebook accounts, on particular dates, or at particular times. This is no more sufficient to confirm the accuracy or reliability of the contents of the Facebook chats than a postal receipt would be to attest to the accuracy or reliability of the contents of the enclosed mailed letter....

If the Government here had sought to authenticate only the timestamps on the Facebook chats, the fact that the chats took place between particular Facebook accounts, and similarly technical information verified by Facebook "in the course of a regularly conducted activity," the records might be more readily analogized to bank records or phone records conventionally authenticated and admitted under Rules 902(11) and 803(6).... We need not address the tenability of this narrow proposition here, however, as the Government's interest lies in establishing the admissibility of the chat logs in full. It suffices for us to conclude that, considered in their entirety, the Facebook records are not business records under Rule 803(6) and thus cannot be authenticated by way of Rule 902(11). In fact, the Government's position would mean that all electronic information whose storage or transmission could be verified by a third-party service provider would be exempt from the hearsay rules — a novel proposition indeed, and one we are unwilling to espouse.

Our conclusion that the Facebook chat logs were not properly authenticated under Rule 902(11) does not end our inquiry, for we may consider whether the Government has presented sufficient extrinsic evidence to authenticate the chat logs under Rule 901(a).... Conventionally, authorship may be established for authentication purposes by way of a wide range of extrinsic evidence. *See* Fed. R. Evid. 901(b). In *United States v. McGlory*, 968 F.2d 309 (3d Cir. 1992), for example, we rejected a defendant's challenge to the authentication of notes that he had allegedly handwritten because, despite being unable to fully establish authorship through a handwriting expert, the prosecution had provided "sufficient evidence from which the jury could find that [the defendant] authored the notes." The notes had been seized from the trash outside the defendant's known residences; some of the notes were torn from a notebook found inside his residences; some notes were found in the same garbage bag as other identifying information; and certain notes were written on note paper from hotels where the defendant stayed during the alleged conspiracy....

[I]t is no less proper to consider a wide range of evidence for the authentication of social media records than it is for more traditional documentary evidence.... [W]e conclude the Government provided more than adequate extrinsic evidence to support that the disputed Facebook records reflected online conversations that took place between Browne, Dalmida, and three of the four minors, such that "the jury could reasonably find" the authenticity of the records "by a preponderance of the evidence." [*United States v. Bergrin*, 682 F.3d 261 (3d Cir. 2012).]

First, although the four witnesses who participated in the Facebook chats at issue — Dalmida and three of the minors — did not directly identify the records at trial, each offered detailed testimony about the exchanges that she had over Facebook. This testimony was consistent with the content of the four chat logs that the Government introduced into evidence. Dalmida and two of the minors whose chat logs are at issue further testified that after conversing with the Button Facebook account or the 998 number that they received through communications with Button, they met in person with Button — whom they were able to identify in open court as Browne. . . .

Second, as reflected in the trial testimony of both Browne and Special Agent Blyden, Browne made significant concessions that served to link him to the Facebook conversations. Most notably, Browne testified that he owned the "Billy Button" Facebook account on which the search warrant had been executed and that he knew and had conversed on Facebook with Dalmida and two of the minors. . . . Browne also testified that he owned the phone that was seized from his residence — the same phone from which DHS recovered certain images that the victims identified on the stand as those they sent in response to commands from either the Button or Dalmida Facebook account or the 998 number. . . . And Browne admitted that he owned a second phone with the 344 number, which is significant because, although Browne attempted to distance himself from the incriminating phone with the 998 number with the unsupported contention that he loaned it to other individuals at various points in the relevant time period, one of the challenged Facebook conversations shows that "Button" also provided the 344 number to minor J.S. on two occasions while trying to elicit sexual acts and photos. In addition, in Browne's post-arrest statements, which were introduced at trial, he provided the passwords to the Button Facebook account and to the phone with the 998 number and admitted to exchanging nude photos with Dalmida, paying J.S. for nude photos, going to J.B.'s home, and knowing a third minor, T.P., whom he referenced by Facebook account name.

Third . . . the personal information that Browne confirmed on the stand was consistent with the personal details that "Button" interspersed throughout his Facebook conversations with Dalmida and three of the minors. For example, Browne testified that his address was 2031 Estate Lovenlund, that he was a plumber, and that he had a fiancée. The Facebook messages sent by "Button" are, in turn, replete with references to the fact that the sender was located or resided at Lovenlund. "Button" also stated to one minor, "I'm a plumber." The chats reflect that somewhere on his Facebook profile, Button represented himself as being engaged. And in one of the disputed Facebook chats, Button informed a minor that his name was "Tony . . . Browne."

Lastly, the Government not only provided ample evidence linking Browne to the Button Facebook account but also supported the accuracy of the chat logs by obtaining them directly from Facebook and introducing a certificate attesting to their maintenance by the company's automated systems. To the extent that certified records straight from the third-party service provider are less likely to be subject to manipulation or inadvertent distortion than, for instance, printouts of website screenshots, the method by which the Government procured the records in this case constitutes yet more circumstantial evidence that the records are what the Government claims.

In short, this is not a case where the records proponent has put forth tenuous evidence attributing to an individual social media or online activity that very well could have been conducted or fabricated by a third party. *See, e.g., Vayner*, 769 F.3d at 131; *see also Smith v. State*, 136 So.3d 424, 433 (Miss. 2014) (holding that name and photo on Facebook printout were not sufficient to link communication to alleged author).... Far from it. This record reflects abundant evidence linking Browne and the testifying victims to the chats conducted through the Button Facebook account and reflected in the logs procured from Facebook. The Facebook records were thus duly authenticated.

Browne makes much of the fact that the Government failed to ask the testifying witnesses point-blank to identify the disputed Facebook chats. As we explained, however, in *McQueeney v. Wilmington Trust Co.*, 779 F.2d 916 (3d Cir. 1985), where we reversed the district court's determination that certain records could not be admitted into evidence unless they were introduced by a testifying witness, circumstantial evidence can suffice to authenticate a document.... Although a witness with personal knowledge may authenticate a document by testifying that the document is what the evidence proponent claims it to be, this is merely one possible means of authentication and not, as Browne would have it, an exclusive requirement. *See* Fed. R. Evid. 901(b)(1).... Browne's authentication challenge collapses under the veritable mountain of evidence linking Browne to Billy Button and the incriminating chats....

Evidence that is properly authenticated may nonetheless be inadmissible hearsay if it contains out-of-court statements, written or oral, that are offered for the truth of the matter asserted and do not fall under any exception enumerated under Federal Rule of Evidence 802. Here, the Government offered more than sufficient evidence to authenticate four of the five Facebook records as chats that Browne himself participated in by way of the Button account, and these four records were properly admitted as admissions by a party opponent under Rule 801(d)(2)(A). Not so for the fifth.

We agree with Browne that the single chat in which Browne did not participate and which took place between Dalmida and J.B. regarding Button's "almost rape[]" of J.B. was inadmissible hearsay. Notwithstanding the other reasons the Government may have sought to admit it, the record functioned at least in part to prove the truth of the matter asserted, that is, that Browne sexually assaulted J.B. and subsequently threatened her with video evidence of the assault....

Although we conclude that the District Court erred in admitting this chat log, we do not perceive grounds for reversal.... We are confident there was no prejudice here.... [T]he Government set forth abundant evidence that not only served to tie Browne and the victims to the chat logs but also supported Browne's guilt on all of the counts for which he was convicted irrespective of those records. Indeed, the two individuals who made the hearsay statements reflected in the fifth chat log, Dalmida and J.B., testified at length to the very details included in that Facebook chat log. Because there was overwhelming, properly admitted evidence supporting Browne's conviction on every count, and the sole improperly admitted Facebook record was "at most, duplicative of [the witnesses'] admissible testimony," *United States v. Kapp*, 781 F.2d 1008, 1014 (3d Cir. 1986), the erroneous admission was harmless and

Browne's convictions must be sustained. . . . [W]e will affirm the judgment of the District Court.

UNITED STATES v. BERTRAM

259 F.Supp.3d 638 (E.D. Ky. 2017)

Van Tatenhove, District Judge.

[Five doctors who ran a laboratory were convicted of health care fraud. The government's evidence at trial included alleged e-mail exchanges among the defendants, as well as some between the defendants and an employee who dealt with billing.]

This case presents a recurring evidentiary concern in an age of advancing technology. Simply put, may emails be authenticated under the Federal Rules of Evidence by someone other than the sender or recipient? . . .

Despite the prevalence of email communication in this day and age, case law in the Sixth Circuit regarding how Rule 901 relates to the authentication of emails is sparse. A number of other courts, however, have suggested the key factor in the Rule 901(b) list when it comes to email authentication is Rule 901(b)(4). That provision explains that records may be authenticated by the introduction of testimony regarding their unique characteristics: i.e., the "appearance, contents, substance, internal patterns, or other distinctive characteristics of the item, taken together with all the circumstances." Fed. R. Evid. 901(b)(4). In fact, Rule 901(b)(4) is "one of the most frequently used to authenticate email and other electronic records." Lorraine v. Markel Am. Ins. Co., 241 F.R.D. 534, 546 (D. Md. 2007).

For example, the Eleventh Circuit found a number of emails to be properly authenticated under Rule 901(b)(4) in *United States v. Siddiqui*, 235 F.3d 1318 (11th Cir. 2000). In *Siddiqui*, the Government sought to introduce emails purportedly from Siddiqui, the defendant, through the individuals who received those emails. Siddiqui objected, but the Eleventh Circuit noted the emails' contents, patterns, and distinctive characteristics satisfied the authentication requirements in Rule 901(b)(4). For example, the emails bore an email address which included a portion of Siddiqui's name as well as the university at which he was employed. The emails referred to the author as "Mo," a nickname the Government witnesses could attribute to Siddiqui. Further, the content of the emails bolstered the idea that defendant Siddiqui was, in fact, the sender, because the content included information about which Siddiqui would know and because the Government witnesses could testify to related phone conversations with Siddiqui about the email content.

The same rationale has been employed by other courts ruling on the authenticity of both emails and text messages. For example, the D.C. Circuit Court found emails to be properly authenticated under Rule 901(b)(4) where the email addresses at issue contained the name of the person connected to the address; where the names of the senders or recipients of the emails were frequently included in either the email content or signature blocks; and where the email content involved "discussions of various identifiable matters." *United States v. Safavian*, 435 F.Supp.2d 36 (D.D.C. 2006). . . . *See also United*

States v. Kilpatrick, No. 10-20403 (E.D. Mich. Aug. 7, 2012) (noting the text messages in question had "distinctive characteristics" under Rule 901(b)(4) such as distinct auto-signatures, nicknames, unique PIN numbers, and distinctive language patterns).

These cases stand in contrast with two cases submitted by the Defendants, where emails were properly found unauthenticated under various Rules of Evidence, including Rule 901(b)(4). For instance, in *Jimena v. UBS AG Bank, Inc.*, an Eastern District of California court excluded emails one party sought to introduce through the email recipient. *See* No. 1:07-cv-00367 (E.D. Cal. June 27, 2011). The court noted that there was no evidence the recipient actually knew the purported sender or had prior communication with the sender. Also, there were no unique characteristics linking the received emails to the purported sender. Similarly, in *In re Second Chance Body Armor, Inc.*, the Western District of Michigan Bankruptcy Court excluded emails because they were "neither self-authenticating, authenticated by a witness with knowledge, nor authenticated through any other permissible means." *See* 434 B.R. 502, 505 (Bankr. W.D. Mich. 2010). In that case, one party attempted to authenticate certain emails through a witness with no personal knowledge of the conversation, who had never seen the email before, and who was not present at a meeting described in the contents of the email....

... [T]he weight of the case law suggests [that] ... the key consideration in email authentication is not simply whether the witness on the stand was a sender or recipient of the email, but whether the testifying witness can speak to the email's unique characteristics, contents, and appearance. After all, Federal Rule of Evidence 901 establishes a seemingly low bar for authenticating or identifying evidence in the first instance, and the characteristics set out in Rule 901(b)(4) are particularly useful in demonstrating that an email is, in fact, what it purports to be....

... [T]he Defendants objected to the Government's attempt to introduce emails between Defendants Bryan Wood and Brian Walters through [employee Kris] Kaiser, because Kaiser was not copied on those emails and presumably had never seen them before.... Despite Kaiser's lack of personal participation in the communication, she could speak to [its] authenticity ...

For example, Ms. Kaiser could verify the email addresses of both Defendants as the addresses used by those men based on her prior communication with them. The email addresses themselves contained some identifying information, which Ms. Kaiser was able to explain to the jury. The email address used by Brian Walters, "brian@premierintegrity.com", contains his first name and his workplace. And the email addressed used by Bryan Wood, "kyerdoc11kids@yahoo.com", makes reference to his professional work as an Emergency Medicine physician and the fact that he has eleven children. Further, the emails from Dr. Wood contain an auto-signature, "Bryan S Wood MD", and those emails were also signed "bw." Kaiser testified that she knew Dr. Wood typically signed his emails with those lowercase initials. Surely these are the kinds of "contents, substance, internal patterns, or other distinctive characteristics" contemplated under Federal Rule of Evidence 901(b)(4).

The Court notes that neither of those two Defendants ever actually alleged the emails were not authentic. The Defendants did not claim to have never seen or received the emails, and they did not attempt to argue that someone else (an administrative assistant, for example) had been using their email addresses. . . .

. . . [T]he Court has little doubt that the emails are exactly what they purport to be, and this remains true regardless of whether the authenticating witness was a sender or recipient. . . .

STATE v. BROWN

818 S.E.2d 735, 737-93 (S.C. 2018)

KITTREDGE, Justice.

A Zaxby's restaurant in Goose Creek, South Carolina, was robbed by two males . . . on Christmas Eve. During the robbery, a Zaxby's employee was shot by one of the robbers. As a result of law enforcement's investigation—including a traced scent trail, DNA evidence found on a ski mask and gun, an executed search warrant, and a tip that Petitioner [Brown] confessed to committing the crime with Christopher Wilson—Petitioner and Wilson were arrested and charged with robbery . . . . [D]uring the course of their investigation, law enforcement discovered that Wilson was wearing a GPS ankle monitor at the time of the robbery. Wilson's GPS records reflected that he was at Zaxby's during the robbery. Wilson pled guilty prior to Petitioner's trial.

At Petitioner's trial, . . . the State presented Agent Steward Powell's testimony to authenticate the GPS records. . . .:

Q.   And what does [your job duty involving GPS monitoring] entail?
A.   There is a GPS monitor affixed to the ankle of the offender, and their movements are tracked wherever they go.
Q.   How do they work? . . .
A.   The State has a GOC, general operations center, in Columbia. These offenders are tracked, 24 hours a day, seven days a week so they're always monitored. Us field agents . . . can log on to our computers and see in realtime where these offenders are.
Q.   Is that information recorded? . . .
A.   It's recorded by a third party vendor [Omni Link] that supplied the software and the hardware, the actual ankle monitor, for the system.
Q.   Is that information accurate?
A.   It is very accurate. We use it in court all the time.

. . . We hold that the GPS records were not properly authenticated. We do not doubt that Agent Powell was a proper witness and likely able to lay the necessary foundation. But in terms of establishing the accuracy of the GPS records, Agent Powell simply observed the GPS records are accurate because "[w]e use it in court all the time." Such a response provides no assistance in assessing the accuracy of the GPS records. . . .

. . . The State's argument that authentication was fulfilled through other means fails to appreciate the nature of GPS records and that these records are generated and result from, at least in part, the process or system used by a machine.

As recognized by the Fourth Circuit Court of Appeals,"Any concerns about the reliability of such machine-generated information is addressed through the process of authentication. . . ." *United States v. Washington*, 498 F.3d 225, 231 (4th Cir. 2007)."When information provided by machines is mainly a product of 'mechanical measurement or manipulation of data by well-accepted scientific or mathematical techniques,'" then "a foundation must be established for the information through authentication, which Federal Rule of Evidence 901(b)(9) allows such proof to be authenticated by evidence 'describing [the] process or system used to produce [the] result' and showing it 'produces an accurate result.'"

Other persuasive authority supports this approach. *See, e.g.*, Subdivision (b)(9)—Process or System, 31 Fed. Prac. & Proc. Evid. §7114 (1st ed. Apr. 2018) (stating "Rule 901(b)(9) governs the authentication of data produced by a machine purporting to measure or detect something, such as a radar gun, a breathalyzer, a global positioning system device, and the like"); *see also* Rule 902(13), FRE (allowing "[a] record generated by an electronic process or system that produces an accurate result" to be certified). Thus, we hold that the State needed to present "[e]vidence describing [the] process or system used to produce" the GPS records and "showing that the process or system produces an accurate result" in accordance with Rule 901(b)(9), SCRE, to authenticate Wilson's GPS records in this case. . . .

One jurisdiction, North Carolina, appears to use the same or similar vendor as the one used in this case—Omni Link—and has found an officer's testimony sufficient to authenticate GPS records. In *State v. Jackson*, 229 N.C.App. 644, 748 S.E.2d 50 (2013), an individual, wearing an electronic monitoring device, was accused of sexually assaulting a victim. At trial, the State introduced evidence from the defendant's electronic monitoring device in order to place the defendant at the scene of the assault. On appeal, the court evaluated whether the GPS tracking evidence was properly authenticated. The court stated, "Regarding the specific electronic monitoring device worn by defendant, [a trained sergeant] identified the device as the Omni–Link 210." The sergeant "described the different components of the device" and "testified about how the device operates using a combination of GPS signals and cell phone triangulations to track the location of the electronic monitoring device at least every four minutes." In addition, he explained how the "tracking data is then uploaded from the device to a secured server where it is stored" and "that the device primarily uses GPS signals, which are very accurate, usually within four to ten meters." He also testified that he "never had any issue with the accuracy of the data." Moreover, the court noted that the sergeant "described how he retrieved the data for defendant's electronic monitoring device for [the specific dates at issue] and produced the event log entered into evidence." . . .

After reviewing various authorities, we require that a witness should have experience with the electronic monitoring system used and provide testimony describing the monitoring system, the process of generating or obtaining the records, and how this process has produced accurate results for the particular device or data at issue. As noted, the witness need not be an expert. However, even under the minimally burdensome test we set forth, Agent Powell failed to properly authenticate the accuracy of the GPS records. Thus, it was error for the trial court to admit this evidence because the GPS records were not properly authenticated.

Despite this error, we hold that the error was harmless beyond a reasonable doubt due to the overwhelming evidence of guilt presented against Petitioner.... *Affirmed in result.*

PROBLEMS

11.1. Julia sues Samantha for injuries Julia suffered when her car was hit by Samantha's. Julia's lawyer wants to show the jury a photograph taken of Julia after the accident, to demonstrate the extent of her injuries. Does the photograph need to be authenticated? If so, how could that requirement be satisfied?

11.2. Clyde sues his torts professor, Harold, for slander, alleging that Harold said falsely during one of his lectures that Clyde had bribed his way into law school. Clyde's lawyer seeks to introduce an audiotape of the lecture. Does the tape need to be authenticated? If so, how could that requirement be satisfied?

11.3. A defendant in a robbery case seeks to buttress his alibi defense by introducing data from his "Fitbit" device, purportedly showing that at the time of the robbery, 11:13 P.M., the defendant was in a cycle of "deep sleep." Does the Fitbit data have to be authenticated? If so, how could that requirement be satisfied?

11.4. Priya sues Dennis for intentional infliction of emotional distress after allegedly receiving several disturbing text messages from what she claims to know to be Dennis' mobile phone number. The messages were sent to her through an "ephemeral app" called "Snapchat," in which messages permanently disappear shortly after they are sent. Priya took a screenshot on her iPhone of several of the messages, and wants to introduce them into evidence at trial. How might Priya lay a foundation for admission of the screenshots?

11.5. Pasiano is being prosecuted for unlawful reentry into the United States, after having been arrested by United States border patrol agents near the U.S.-Mexico border. His defense is that he was actually arrested in Mexico, not the United States. In order to prove he was arrested in the United States, the government calls the arresting border patrol agent, who testifies that she inputted the coordinates of the arrest location into a handheld GPS device. The government now seeks to introduce into evidence a Google Earth satellite image, with a "digital tack" placed on the image by Google software to correspond to the inputted GPS coordinates. The "digital tack," according to Google Earth's imaging data, is on the United States side of the border. Does the image have to be authenticated? If so, how could that requirement be satisfied?

B. THE BEST EVIDENCE RULE

Students studying for the bar exam are sometimes taught a rule of thumb: on a multiple-choice question, the best evidence rule is always the wrong answer. This is at best an exaggeration (the bar examiners are too tricky for any rule like this to work reliably), but it captures an important truth. Despite its grand name, the best evidence rule does very little work today.

There was a time when the best evidence rule meant what its name suggests: only the best evidence available on a particular question was admissible. As you will see, some judges and scholars still think that principle deserves to be followed. But prevailing law has made the best evidence rule a shadow of its former self. The rule is defined today to apply only in a narrow category of cases, and it is further hemmed in by a series of sweeping exceptions.

[F.R.E. 1001–1008; C.E.C. §§250–260, 1520–1523]

1. Scope and Purpose

JOHN H. LANGBEIN, HISTORICAL FOUNDATIONS OF THE LAW OF EVIDENCE: A VIEW FROM THE RYDER SOURCES

96 Colum. L. Rev. 1168 (1996)

… Written sometime before the author's death in 1726, Geoffrey Gilbert's treatise on *The Law of Evidence* was not published until 1754 … [but] became the most influential eighteenth-century book on evidence, going through seven editions in the hands of revisers. Although prefaced with some analytic discussion, Gilbert's book was essentially an abridgment—a law-finder that collected precedents, mostly from published yearbooks and law reports, but also from the juristic literature, including Coke, Hale, and Hawkins.

Gilbert arranged his treatise on the distinction between written and unwritten evidence, but written evidence occupied virtually all the book. As Twining has observed, "Gilbert tried to subsume all the rules of evidence under a single principle, the 'best evidence rule,'" a notion that is oriented to documentary authenticity. Among the topics concerning written evidence that Gilbert reviews are record versus nonrecord evidence, statutes, sealed versus unsealed instruments, proving copies when originals are lost, proving prior verdicts, proving chancery proceedings and depositions, evidencing wills, and the receipt of manorial court rolls. He continues with the complex rules governing proof of deeds, then bills of exchange and negotiable instruments.

The later eighteenth-century writers on evidence, Bathurst and Buller, followed Gilbert's emphasis on the best evidence rule as the organizing principle of the law of evidence. As late as 1806, a North Carolina court still proclaimed the view: "There is but one decided rule in relation to evidence, and that is, that the law requires the best evidence."

MEYERS v. UNITED STATES

171 F.2d 800 (D.C. Cir. 1949)

WILBUR K. MILLER, Circuit Judge.

Bleriot H. Lamarre and the appellant, Bennett E. Meyers, were jointly indicted for violating the District of Columbia statute which denounces perjury and subornation thereof. Three counts of the indictment charged Lamarre with as many separate perjuries in his testimony before a subcommittee of a committee of the United States Senate constituted to investigate the national defense program, and three more counts accused Meyers of suborning the perjuries of his codefendant.

Lamarre pleaded guilty to all three charges when he was arraigned on December 19, 1947, a few days after the return of the indictment. Meyers entered a plea of not guilty and was tried before a jury in the District Court of the United States for the District of Columbia.... Having been found guilty under each of the three counts against him, he appeals.

[Meyers was an army officer and the founder of Aviation Electric Corporation, which became a subcontractor on government work. Lamarre was the company's president.] In order to ascertain what connection, if any, the appellant had with Aviation Electric, the subcommittee subpoenaed Lamarre, who testified on Saturday, October 4, and Monday, October 6, in 1947. That testimony brought about the indictment which was the genesis of the case now before us.

... William P. Rogers, chief counsel to the senatorial committee, who had examined Lamarre before the subcommittee and consequently had heard all the testimony given by him before that body, was permitted to testify as to what Lamarre had sworn to the subcommittee. Later in the trial the government introduced in evidence a stenographic transcript of Lamarre's testimony at the senatorial hearing.

In his brief here the appellant characterizes this as a "bizarre procedure" but does not assign as error the reception of Rogers' testimony. The dissenting opinion, however, asserts it was reversible error to allow Rogers to testify at all as to what Lamarre had said to the subcommittee, on the theory that the transcript itself was the best evidence of Lamarre's testimony before the subcommittee.

That theory is, in our view, based upon a misconception of the best evidence rule. As applied generally in federal courts, the rule is limited to cases where the contents of a writing are to be proved. Here there was no attempt to prove the contents of a writing; the issue was what Lamarre had said, not what the transcript contained. The transcript made from shorthand notes of his testimony was, to be sure, evidence of what he had said, but it was not the only admissible evidence concerning it. Rogers' testimony was equally competent, and was admissible whether given before or after the transcript was received in evidence. Statements alleged to be perjurious may be proved by any person who heard them, as well as by a reporter who recorded them in shorthand.

A somewhat similar situation was presented in *Herzig v. Swift & Co.*, 146 F.2d 444, decided by the United States Court of Appeals for the Second Circuit in 1945. In that case the trial court had excluded oral testimony concerning the earnings of a partnership on the ground that the books of account were the best evidence. After pointing out the real nature and scope of the best evidence rule,[12] the court said, "... Here there was no attempt to prove

---

12. In doing so the court quoted with approval the following statement from McKelvey, Evidence, 604, 5th Ed., 1944: "In its modern application, the best evidence rule amounts to little more than the requirement that the contents of a writing must be proved by the introduction of the writing itself, unless its absence be satisfactorily accounted for." See also 4 Wigmore, Evidence, §§1174, 1177-1182, 3d Ed., 1940.

the contents of a writing; the issue was the earnings of a partnership, which for convenience were recorded in books of account after the relevant facts occurred. Generally, this differentiation has been adopted by the courts. On the precise question of admitting oral testimony to prove matters that are contained in books of account, the courts have divided, some holding the oral testimony admissible, others excluding it. The federal courts have generally adopted the rationale limiting the 'best evidence rule' to cases where the contents of the writing are to be proved. We hold, therefore, that the district judge erred in excluding the oral testimony as to the earnings of the partnership."

... As we have pointed out, there was no issue as to the contents of the transcript, and the government was not attempting to prove what it contained; the issue was what Lamarre actually had said. Rogers was not asked what the transcript contained but what Lamarre's testimony had been.... Since we perceive no prejudicial error in appellant's trial, the judgment entered pursuant to the jury's verdict will not be disturbed.

Affirmed.

PRETTYMAN, Circuit Judge (dissenting).

... I realize that there is a line of authority that (absent or incompetent the original witness) a bystander who hears testimony or other conversation may testify as to what was said, even though there be a stenographic report. And there is a line of cases which holds that a stenographic transcript is not the best evidence of what was said. There is also a legal cliche that the best evidence rule applies only to documentary evidence. The trial judge in this case was confronted with that authority, and a trial court is probably not the place to inaugurate a new line of authority. But I do not know why an appellate court should perpetuate a rule clearly outmoded by scientific development. I know that courts are reluctant to do so. I recognize the view that such matters should be left to Congress. But rules of evidence were originally judge-made and are an essential part of the judicial function. I knew of no reason why the judicial branch of Government should abdicate to the legislative branch so important a part of its responsibility.

I am of opinion, and quite ready to hold, that the rules of evidence reflected by the cases to which I have just referred are outmoded and at variance with known fact, and that the courts ought to establish a new and correct rule. The rationale of the so-called "best evidence rule" requires that a party having available evidence which is relatively certain may not submit evidence which is far less certain. The law is concerned with the true fact, and with that alone; its procedures are directed to that objective, and to that alone. It should permit no procedure the sole use of which is to obscure and confuse that which is otherwise plain and certain.

... The doctrine that stenographic notes are not the best evidence of testimony was established when stenography was not an accurate science.... But we have before us no such situation. Stenographic reporting has become highly developed, and official stenographic reports are relied upon in many of the most important affairs of life.... In the present instance, at least, no one has disputed the correctness of the transcript.

... Given both (1) an accurate stenographic transcription of a witness' testimony during a two-day hearing and (2) the recollection of one of the complainants as to the substance of that testimony, is the latter admissible as evidence in a trial of the witness for perjury? I think not. To say that it is, is to apply a meaningless formula and ignore crystal clear actualities. The transcript is, as a matter of simple, indisputable fact, the best evidence. The principle and not the rote of the law ought to be applied. . . .

ADVISORY COMMITTEE NOTES TO F.R.E. 1001–1002

In an earlier day, when discovery and other related procedures were strictly limited, the misleading[ly] named "best evidence rule" afforded substantial guarantees against inaccuracies and fraud by its insistence upon production or original documents. The great enlargement of the scope of discovery and related procedures in recent times has measurably reduced the need for the rule. Nevertheless important areas of usefulness persist: discovery of documents outside the jurisdiction may require substantial outlay of time and money; the unanticipated document may not practically be discoverable; criminal cases have built-in limitations on discovery. . . .

The rule [set forth in F.R.E. 1002] is the familiar one requiring production of the original of a document to prove its contents, expanded to include writings, recordings, and photographs, as defined in Rule 1001(1) and (2), supra.

Application of the rule requires a resolution of the question whether contents are sought to be proved. Thus an event may be proved by nondocumentary evidence, even though a written record of it was made. If, however, the event is sought to be proved by the written record, the rule applies. For example, payment may be proved without producing the written receipt which was given. Earnings may be proved without producing books of account in which they are entered. McCormick §198; 4 Wigmore §1245. Nor does the rule apply to testimony that books or records have been examined and found not to contain any reference to a designated matter.

The assumption should not be made that the rule will come into operation on every occasion when use is made of a photograph in evidence. On the contrary, the rule will seldom apply to ordinary photographs. In most instances a party wishes to introduce the item and the question raised is the propriety of receiving it in evidence. Cases in which an offer is made of the testimony of a witness as to what he saw in a photograph or motion picture, without producing the same, are most unusual. The usual course is for a witness on the stand to identify the photograph or motion picture as a correct representation of events which he saw or of a scene with which he is familiar. In fact he adopts the picture as his testimony, or, in common parlance, uses the picture to illustrate his testimony. Under these circumstances, no effort is made to prove the contents of the picture, and the rule is inapplicable.

On occasion, however, situations arise in which contents are sought to be proved. Copyright, defamation, and invasion of privacy by photograph or motion picture falls in this category. Similarly as to situations in which the picture is offered as having independent probative value, e.g. automatic photograph of bank robber. . . . The most commonly encountered of this latter group is of course, the X-ray, with substantial authority calling for production of the original.

It should be noted, however, that Rule 703, supra, allows an expert to give an opinion based on matters not in evidence, and the present rule must be read as being limited accordingly in its application. Hospital records which may be admitted as business records under Rule 803(6) commonly contain reports interpreting X rays by the staff radiologist, who qualifies as an expert, and these reports need not be excluded from the records by the instant rule.

The reference to Acts of Congress is made in view of such statutory provisions as 26 U.S.C. §7513, photographic reproductions of tax returns and documents, made by authority of the Secretary of the Treasury, treated as originals, and 44 U.S.C. §399(a), photographic copies in National Archives treated as originals.

UNITED STATES v. GONZALES-BENITEZ

537 F.2d 1051 (9th Cir. 1976)

KENNEDY, Circuit Judge.

Aida Gonzales-Benitez and Ambrosio Hernandez-Coronel were convicted for importing and distributing heroin. . . . Appellants contend the trial court erred in permitting testimony that related their conversations with the informers during a certain meeting in a motel room in Arizona. They claim that since the conversations were recorded on tapes, the tapes themselves, and not testimony of one of the participants, were the "best evidence" of the conversations. We are puzzled that this argument should be advanced so seriously and would not consider it if attorneys for both appellants had not argued the point so strenuously both in their briefs and in the court below. Certainly the trial court was correct in dismissing the objection out of hand.

The appellants simply misconstrue the purpose and effect of the best evidence rule. The rule does not set up an order of preferred admissibility, which must be followed to prove any fact. It is, rather, a rule applicable only when one seeks to prove the contents of documents or recordings. Fed. R. Evid. 1002. Thus, if the ultimate inquiry had been to discover what sounds were embodied on the tapes in question, the tapes themselves would have been the "best evidence."

However, the content of the tapes was not in itself a factual issue relevant to the case. The inquiry concerned the content of the conversations. The tape recordings, if intelligible,[2] would have been admissible as evidence of those conversations. But testimony by the participants was equally admissible and was sufficient to establish what was said. . . .

Affirmed.

2. We note that the reason the tapes were not introduced here was that the recording quality was so poor that the court translator was unable to understand and translate them.

DALE A. NANCE, THE BEST EVIDENCE PRINCIPLE

73 Iowa L. Rev. 227, 227–229, 295 (1988)

[T]here exists, even today, a principle of evidence law that a party should present to the tribunal the best evidence reasonably available on a litigated factual issue. This principle is not absolute, and in particular circumstances other considerations may override it or excuse its nonsatisfaction. Nevertheless, it is a general principle that manifests itself in a wide variety of concrete rules governing the trial process. In fact, it provides an organizing principle within the law of evidence. Consequently, it is improper for a court to reason from the premise, explicit or implicit, that there is no such principle. Unfortunately, such a premise has been widely professed by modern commentators and is regularly employed by the courts.

The case of *United States v. Gonzales-Benitez* illustrates the problem.... The point is not that the appellants in that case should have prevailed, but simply that the court's treatment of their argument was inadequate. The court should have considered whether the trial court had and abused a discretion to deny admission of the testimony pursuant to a general best evidence principle. At the very least, the court should have justified its implicit assumption that the phrase "best evidence" could only refer, in the context of this case, to the original document rule.

... [P]utting aside the rules, such as those governing privileges, which are said to serve extrinsic social policies, the remaining evidentiary rules are more plausibly attributable to the epistemic concerns of a tribunal encountering the adversarial presentation of evidence than to judicial concerns about the irrational behavior of weak-minded lay jurors.... This view understands at least a significant number of the rules of evidence as designed to protect the tribunal as a truth-finding, and thereby dispute-resolving, forum by imposing educative restraints and disciplinary sanctions upon litigants who would otherwise deprive the tribunal of the best, reasonably available evidence on a given issue. Although these measures may or may not be maximally conducive to the ascertainment of truth in the instant case, it is contemplated and hoped that their imposition will contribute in the long run not only to accurate fact-finding but also to a deserved public respect for the legal system.

... [F]airness to litigants requires that determinations of the use of the coercive power of the state be made on the best reasonably available evidence. Respect for the tribunal demands that it not be placed in the position of making such determinations upon evidence of lesser quality. In the final analysis, it must also be said that truth has intrinsic value, knowledge is a common good, and the presentation of the best reasonably available evidence is a crucial part of the participation in that good by persons who utilize the judicial system.... In any event, and this is most important, it seems impossible to understand fully the present system without reference to that principle. Certainly, then, appeals to it cannot reasonably be dismissed as no more than the invocation of a mistaken or outmoded idea.

2. Exceptions

ADVISORY COMMITTEE NOTES TO F.R.E. 1003–1008

When the only concern is with getting the words or other contents before the court with accuracy and precision, then a counterpart serves equally as well as the original, if the counterpart is the product of a method which insures accuracy and genuineness. . . . Therefore, if no genuine issue exists as to authenticity and no other reason exists for requiring the original, a duplicate is admissible under [F.R.E. 1003]. . . .

Basically the rule requiring the production of the original as proof of contents has developed as a rule of preference: if failure to produce the original is satisfactorily explained, secondary evidence is admissible. [F.R.E. 1004] specifies the circumstances under which production of the original is excused.

The rule recognizes no "degrees" of secondary evidence. While strict logic might call for extending the principle of preference beyond simply preferring the original, the formulation of a hierarchy of preferences and a procedure for making it effective is believed to involve unwarranted complexities. Most, if not all, that would be accomplished by an extended scheme of preferences will, in any event, be achieved through the normal motivation of a party to present the most convincing evidence possible and the arguments and procedures available to his opponent if he does not. . . .

Public records call for somewhat different treatment. Removing them from their usual place of keeping would be attended by serious inconvenience to the public and to the custodian. As a consequence judicial decisions and statutes commonly hold that no explanation need be given for failure to produce the original of a public record. McCormick §204; 4 Wigmore §§1215–1228. This blanket dispensation from producing or accounting for the original would open the door to the introduction of every kind of secondary evidence of contents of public records were it not for the preference given certified or compared copies. Recognition of degrees of secondary evidence in this situation is an appropriate *quid pro quo* for not applying the requirement of producing the original. . . .

Most preliminary questions of fact in connection with applying the rule preferring the original as evidence of contents are for the judge, under the general principles announced in Rule 104, *supra*. Thus, the question whether the loss of the originals has been established, or of the fulfillment of other conditions specified in Rule 1004 . . . is for the judge. However, questions may arise which go beyond the mere administration of the rule preferring the original and into the merits of the controversy. For example, plaintiff offers secondary evidence of the contents of an alleged contract, after first introducing evidence of loss of the original, and defendant counters with evidence that no such contract was ever executed. If the judge decides that the contract was never executed and excludes the secondary evidence, the case is at an end without ever going to the jury on a central issue. The latter portion [F.R.E. 1008] is designed to insure treatment of these situations as raising jury questions. The decision is not one for uncontrolled discretion of the jury but is subject to the control exercised generally by the judge over jury determinations. See Rule 104(b), *supra*.

UNITED STATES v. STOCKTON

968 F.2d 715 (8th Cir. 1992)

McMILLAN, Circuit Judge.

Gary Wayne Badley and William D. Stockton . . . appeal from final judgments entered in the United States District Court for the Western District of Missouri, upon jury verdicts, finding them guilty of involvement in a conspiracy to manufacture methamphetamine. . . .

During a search of [codefendant Terry] Appleby's residence in Thayer, Kansas, photographs were taken of "miscellaneous papers" and these photographs were introduced at trial (Exhibits 74-H and 74-I). According to Stockton, the government provided no reason why the originals could not be produced, and, therefore, the district court's admission of the photographs violated the Best Evidence Rule.

. . . We hold that the Best Evidence Rule does apply in this situation, but that the photographs were properly admitted as duplicates under Fed. R. Evid. 1003. While the government is correct that the Best Evidence Rule does not usually apply to photographs, this case is one of "those relatively rare instances in which [the photographs'] contents are sought to be proved." John W. Strong et al., *McCormick on Evidence* §232, at 65 (4th ed. 1992).[7] During the government's case-in-chief, Harley Sparks, a special agent with the DEA, testified to the contents of the photographs and specifically read from the photographs. Therefore, the contents of the photographs were at issue in this case.

These photographs are not the original documents and therefore violate Fed. R. Evid. 1002. But the analysis does not end there because Fed. R. Evid. 1003 allows duplicates to be introduced in the same manner as originals "unless (1) a genuine question is raised as to the authenticity of the original or (2) in the circumstances it would be unfair to admit the duplicate in lieu of the original." This rule allows photocopies or carbon copies to be introduced in lieu of the original documents unless there is a genuine challenge to the authenticity of the document. We see no distinction between a photocopy and the photographs used in this case. Photographs of notes were taken by DEA agents during a lawful search and one of the agents testified to contents of the photographs. No question was raised below as to the authenticity of the photographs so that exception is not at issue in this case. We hold,

---

7. The government argues that the Best Evidence Rule does not apply to photographs because they are demonstrative evidence. For example, in *United States v. Alexander*, 415 F.2d 1352, 1357 (7th Cir. 1969), *cert. denied*, 397 U.S. 1014 (1970), the Best Evidence Rule did not apply to a photograph of stolen mail because "[t]he photograph was introduced to show the quantity of mail seized at the time of arrest and not for the purpose of demonstrating anything about the contents of the particular letters." The photographs introduced in the present case were introduced to prove the contents of the writings which they represented, and, therefore, the Best Evidence Rule is applicable.

therefore, that the district court did not abuse its discretion in admitting the photographs which were admissible as duplicates in lieu of the original documents pursuant to Fed. R. Evid. 1003.

. . . Accordingly, we affirm the judgments of the district court.

UNITED STATES v. STANDING SOLDIER

538 F.2d 196 (8th Cir. 1976)

WEBSTER, Circuit Judge.

Victor Standing Solider appeals his conviction of assault with intent to kill. . . . [Following Standing Soldier's arrest, he signed a written statement of his involvement. Later his jailer gave Captain Gerald Hill of the Bureau of Indian Affairs Police] a note allegedly written by the appellant, stating that he wanted to talk. Apparently, the note was lost by tribal or federal authorities, but Captain Hill produced a typewritten copy at trial from which he testified. . . . The District Court permitted testimony concerning the note after Captain Hill testified that he had compared the signature on the note with that of appellant on the signed statement he had made and found them to be the same. . . .

Captain Hill . . . testified that he had attempted to locate the original note by contacting the criminal investigator and the FBI, but had been unable to find it, although he thought that it probably did still exist. . . . Fed. R. Evid. 1004(1) provides that the "original is not required, and other evidence of the contents of a writing . . . is admissible if . . . [a]ll originals are lost or have been destroyed, unless the proponent lost or destroyed them in bad faith." There being no evidence of bad faith on the part of the government and the original having been lost, the District Court properly permitted Captain Hill's oral testimony concerning the note. . . . The Federal Rules of Evidence recognize no "degrees" of secondary evidence and thus there was no requirement that the copy be introduced in preference to the oral testimony. See Fed. R. Evid. 1000, Notes of Advisory Committee. . . . The judgment of conviction is accordingly affirmed.

SEILER v. LUCASFILM, LTD.

808 F.2d 1316 (9th Cir. 1987)

FARRIS, Circuit Judge.

Lee Seiler, a graphic artist and creator of science fiction creatures, alleged copyright infringement by George Lucas and others who created and produced the science fiction movie "The Empire Strikes Back." . . . Seiler contends that he created and published in 1976 and 1977 science fiction creatures called Garthian Striders. In 1980, George Lucas released The Empire Strikes Back, a motion picture that contains a battle sequence depicting giant machines called Imperial Walkers. In 1981 Seiler obtained a copyright on his

Striders, depositing with the Copyright Office "reconstructions" of the originals as they had appeared in 1976 and 1977.

Seiler contends that Lucas' Walkers were copied from Seiler's Striders which were allegedly published in 1976 and 1977. Lucas responds that Seiler did not obtain his copyright until one year after the release of The Empire Strikes Back and that Seiler can produce no documents that antedate The Empire Strikes Back.

Because Seiler proposed to exhibit his Striders in a blow-up comparison to Lucas' Walkers at opening statement, the district judge held an evidentiary hearing on the admissibility of the "reconstructions" of Seiler's Striders. Applying the "best evidence rule," Fed. R. Evid. 1001–1008, the district court found at the end of a seven-day hearing that Seiler lost or destroyed the originals in bad faith under Rule 1004(1) and that consequently no secondary evidence, such as the post-Empire Strikes Back reconstructions, was admissible. In its opinion the court found specifically that Seiler testified falsely, purposefully destroyed or withheld in bad faith the originals, and fabricated and misrepresented the nature of his reconstructions. The district court granted summary judgment to Lucas after the evidentiary hearing. . . .

The best evidence rule embodied in Rules 1001–1008 represented a codification of longstanding common law doctrine. Dating back to 1700, the rule requires not, as its common name implies, the best evidence in every case but rather the production of an original document instead of a copy. Many commentators refer to the rule not as the best evidence rule but as the original document rule.

Rule 1002 states: "To prove the content of a writing, recording, or photograph, the original writing, recording, or photograph is required, except as otherwise provided in these rules or by Act of Congress." Writings and recordings are defined in Rule 1001 as "letters, words, or numbers, or their equivalent, set down by handwriting, typewriting, printing, photostating, photographing, magnetic impulse, mechanical or electronic recording, or other form of data compilation."

The Advisory Committee Note supplies the following gloss:

> Traditionally the rule requiring the original centered upon accumulations of data and expressions affecting legal relations set forth in words and figures. This meant that the rule was one essentially related to writings. Present day techniques have expanded methods of storing data, yet the essential form which the information ultimately assumes for usable purposes is words and figures. Hence the considerations underlying the rule dictate its expansion to include computers, photographic systems, and other modern developments.

Some treatises, whose approach seems more historical than rigorously analytic, opine without support from any cases that the rule is limited to words and figures. 5 Weinstein's Evidence (1983), ¶1001(1)[01] at 1001–11; 5 Louisell & Mueller, §550 at 285.

We hold that Seiler's drawings were "writings" within the meaning of Rule 1001(1); they consist not of "letters, words, or numbers" but of "their equivalent." To hold otherwise would frustrate the policies underlying the rule and introduce undesirable inconsistencies into the application of the rule.

In the days before liberal rules of discovery and modern techniques of electronic copying, the rule guarded against incomplete or fraudulent proof.

By requiring the possessor of the original to produce it, the rule prevented the introduction of altered copies and the withholding of originals. The purpose of the rule was thus long thought to be one of fraud prevention, but Wigmore pointed out that the rule operated even in cases where fraud was not at issue, such as where secondary evidence is not admitted even though its proponent acts in utmost good faith. Wigmore also noted that if prevention of fraud were the foundation of the rule, it should apply to objects as well as writings, which it does not. 4 Wigmore, Evidence §1180 (Chadbourn rev. 1972).

The modern justification for the rule has expanded from prevention of fraud to a recognition that writings occupy a central position in the law. When the contents of a writing are at issue, oral testimony as to the terms of the writing is subject to a greater risk of error than oral testimony as to events or other situations. The human memory is not often capable of reciting the precise terms of a writing, and when the terms are in dispute only the writing itself, or a true copy, provides reliable evidence. . . . [T]he importance of the precise terms of writings in the world of legal relations, the fallibility of the human memory as reliable evidence of the terms, and the hazards of inaccurate or incomplete duplication are the concerns addressed by the best evidence rule. . . .

Viewing the dispute in the context of the concerns underlying the best evidence rule, we conclude that the rule applies. McCormick summarizes the rule as follows:

> In proving the terms of a writing, where the terms are material, the original writing must be produced unless it is shown to be unavailable for some reason other than the serious fault of the proponent.

McCormick on Evidence §230, at 704. The contents of Seiler's work are at issue. There can be no proof of "substantial similarity" and thus of copyright infringement unless Seiler's works are juxtaposed with Lucas' and their contents compared. Since the contents are material and must be proved, Seiler must either produce the original or show that it is unavailable through no fault of his own. Rule 1004(1). This he could not do.

The facts of this case implicate the very concerns that justify the best evidence rule. Seiler alleges infringement by The Empire Strikes Back, but he can produce no documentary evidence of any originals existing before the release of the movie. His secondary evidence does not consist of true copies or exact duplicates but of "reconstructions" made after The Empire Strikes Back. In short, Seiler claims that the movie infringed his originals, yet he has no proof of those originals.

The dangers of fraud in this situation are clear. The rule would ensure that proof of the infringement claim consists of the works alleged to be infringed. Otherwise, "reconstructions" which might have no resemblance to the purported original would suffice as proof for infringement of the original. Furthermore, application of the rule here defers to the rule's special concern for the contents of writings. Seiler's claim depends on the content of the originals, and the rule would exclude reconstituted proof of the originals' content. Under the circumstances here, no "reconstruction" can substitute for the original.

Seiler argues that the best evidence rule does not apply to his work, in that it is artwork rather than "writings, recordings, or photographs." He contends that the rule both historically and currently embraces only words or numbers. Neither party has cited us to cases which discuss the applicability of the rule to drawings.

To recognize Seiler's works as writings does not, as Seiler argues, run counter to the rule's preoccupation with the centrality of the written word in the world of legal relations. Just as a contract objectively manifests the subjective intent of the makers, so Seiler's drawings are objective manifestations of the creative mind. The copyright laws give legal protection to the objective manifestations of an artist's ideas, just as the law of contract protects through its multifarious principles the meeting of minds evidenced in the contract. Comparing Seiler's drawings with Lucas' drawings is no different in principle than evaluating a contract and the intent behind it. Seiler's "reconstructions" are "writings" that affect legal relations; their copyrightability attests to that.

A creative literary work, which is artwork, and a photograph whose contents are sought to be proved, as in copyright, defamation, or invasion of privacy, are both covered by the best evidence rule. See McCormick, §232 at 706 n.9; Advisory Committee's Note to Rule 1002; 5 Louisell & Mueller, §550 at 285 n.27. We would be inconsistent to apply the rule to artwork which is literary or photographic but not to artwork of other forms. Furthermore, blueprints, engineering drawings, architectural designs may all lack words or numbers yet still be capable of copyright and susceptible to fraudulent alteration. In short, Seiler's argument would have us restrict the definitions of Rule 1001(1) to "words" and "numbers" but ignore "or their equivalent." We will not do so in the circumstances of this case.

Our holding is also supported by the policy served by the best evidence rule in protecting against faulty memory. Seiler's reconstructions were made four to seven years after the alleged originals; his memory as to specifications and dimensions may have dimmed significantly. Furthermore, reconstructions made after the release of The Empire Strikes Back may be tainted, even if unintentionally, by exposure to the movie. Our holding guards against these problems....

As we hold that the district court correctly concluded that the best evidence rule applies to Seiler's drawings, Seiler was required to produce his original drawings unless excused by the exceptions set forth in Rule 1004. The pertinent subsection is 1004(1), which provides:

> The original is not required, and other evidence of the contents of a writing, recording, or photograph is admissible if — (1) Originals lost or destroyed. All originals are lost or have been destroyed, unless the proponent lost or destroyed them in bad faith....

In the instant case,... the trial judge found that the reconstructions were inadmissible under the best evidence rule as the originals were lost or destroyed in bad faith. This finding is amply supported by the record.

Seiler argues on appeal that regardless of Rule 1004(1), Rule 1008 requires a trial because a key issue would be whether the reconstructions correctly reflect the content of the originals. Rule 1008 provides:

> When the admissibility of other evidence of contents of writings, recordings, or photographs under these rules depends upon the fulfillment of a condition of fact, the question whether the condition has been fulfilled is ordinarily for the

court to determine in accordance with the provisions of rule 104. However, when an issue is raised (a) whether the asserted writing ever existed, or (b) whether another writing, recording, or photograph produced at the trial is the original, or (c) whether other evidence of contents correctly reflects the contents, the issue is for the trier of facts to determine as in the case of other issues of fact.

Seiler's position confuses admissibility of the reconstructions with the weight, if any, the trier of fact should give them, after the judge has ruled that they are admissible. Rule 1008 states, in essence, that when the admissibility of evidence other than the original depends upon the fulfillment of a condition of fact, the trial judge generally makes the determination of that condition of fact. The notes of the Advisory Committee are consistent with this interpretation in stating: "Most preliminary questions of fact in connection with applying the rule preferring the original as evidence of contents are for the judge . . . thus the question of . . . fulfillment of other conditions specified in Rule 1004 . . . is for the judge." In the instant case, the condition of fact which Seiler needed to prove was that the originals were not lost or destroyed in bad faith. Had he been able to prove this, his reconstructions would have been admissible and then their accuracy would have been a question for the jury. In sum, since admissibility of the reconstructions was dependent upon a finding that the originals were not lost or destroyed in bad faith, the trial judge properly held the hearing to determine their admissibility. . . .

Affirmed.

PROBLEMS

11.6. Farmington Fuel Co. sues one of its customers, Cindy, for ten oil deliveries that Cindy denies were ever made. At trial, Farmington Fuel calls its office manager, Marjorie, to testify (a) that the company's employees always record each delivery in duplicate, giving one copy to the customer and placing one copy in the company's files; (b) that Marjorie keeps custody of those files; and (c) that she examined the files and found records of the ten deliveries. Is Marjorie's testimony admissible?

11.7. Law enforcement officers spotted Vincent Bennett's boat in U.S. waters near the Mexican border, sailing north, away from the border. They boarded the boat and eventually discovered 1,500 pounds of marijuana hidden inside it. Bennett was convicted of importing marijuana into the United States, based in part on testimony from one of the officers that he found a global positioning device on the boat, which included a "backtrack" feature indicating where the device (and presumably the boat) had been. The officer testified that when he activated the backtrack feature, the device plotted the boat's journey earlier that day from Mexican territorial waters several miles south of the U.S. border. At trial and again on appeal, Bennett challenged this testimony on grounds of hearsay and best evidence. Should either of these objections have been sustained? (The Ninth Circuit gave its answer in *United States v. Bennett*, 363 F.3d 947, 953-954 (2004).)

11.8. In *United States v. Workinger*, 90 F.3d 1409 (1996), the Ninth Circuit affirmed the defendant's conviction for tax evasion, and rejected his hearsay, authentication, and best evidence objections to a transcript of a sworn statement he had given years earlier to his former wife's attorney. "Although no court reporter was present, Workinger affirmed that he would tell the truth and the conversation was tape-recorded." The attorney, apparently following his standard practice, erased the tape after having it transcribed. The government called the secretary who transcribed the tape; she testified that she had listened to it "over and over" to make sure the transcript was accurate. The government also called the lawyer who took the statement; he testified that "to the best of his recollection" the transcript accurately reflected what the defendant had said.

All members of the appellate panel agreed that the trial court was right to admit the transcript, but they disagreed about why. The majority rejected the hearsay objection on the ground that "Workinger's statements in the transcript were admissions of a party-opponent," and therefore were not hearsay under Fed. R. Evid. 801(d)(2)(A). They further reasoned that the testimony from the attorney and the secretary "certainly met the minimum requirements for authentication." The panel did find the best evidence rule applicable to the case, because the content of the tape was at issue:

> It is true that, ultimately, the transcript of the tape was intended to reflect the content of the conversation that took place. But, more proximately, it was intended to reflect the content of the tape itself. When Johnson's secretary was given the tape and told to transcribe it, what she did was prepare a document which purported to indicate what she heard on the tape. But if somebody wanted to know the content of that tape, it itself *was* the best evidence of that.

Nonetheless the court concluded that the transcript was admissible under Fed. R. Evid. 1004(1), because the tape was unavailable through no fault of the government.

A concurring opinion argued that the best evidence rule was entirely inapplicable, because "the government did not seek, by introducing the transcript, to prove the content of the tapes but to prove what was said at the deposition itself." The concurrence reasoned that the transcript

> was admissible not because it accurately reflected the tape, but because . . . the attorney for the defendant's ex-wife, testified that it accurately reflected *the deposition*. Without this testimony from someone who was present, I'm not at all sure the transcript would have been admissible since, as the majority notes, the transcriber was not present when the testimony was given and thus could not authenticate the transcript as an accurate reflection of what was said at the deposition.

Who had the better of this argument?

C. DEMONSTRATIVE EVIDENCE

There is little law to learn with regard to demonstrative evidence. The *absence* of specific rules about demonstrative proof is, in fact, one of the three key things to understand about this topic. The other two are the continuing conceptual confusion about demonstrative evidence and the rapid increase in the prevalence and sophistication of this kind of proof.

The material below explores different types of demonstrative evidence, and courts' difficulty in determining whether to treat it as substantive evidence or simply as illustrative tools to help explain other evidence. Traditional forms of demonstrative evidence are considered first, followed by materials addressing demonstrative evidence in the modern, digital courtroom.

1. Traditional Demonstrative Evidence

McCORMICK ON EVIDENCE
§§212, 214 (Kenneth S. Broun ed., 7th ed. 2013)

Some types of evidence . . . are offered on the theory that the trier of fact obtains information relevant to a fact of consequence just from perceiving them, irrespective of whether any witness testifies to what he or she also perceives. Some common examples are a weapon allegedly used in the crime charged, a day-in-the-life film of a personal injury plaintiff, or a computer-generated simulation of the alleged cause of a collision. Such items are "substantive" evidence, with independent probative value for proving a fact of consequence in the case. By contrast, other types are offered on the relevance theory that they only "illustrate" the facts or opinions testified to by a witness. They are relevant if they aid the trier in understanding the witness's testimony, which itself makes a fact of consequence more or less probable. Examples include duplicates of objects involved in the events underlying the litigation, drawings, diagrams and models. The term "demonstrative aid" . . . identif[ies] . . . types of evidence whose relevance is illustrative, rather than substantive. Some courts refer to these aids as "pedagogic aids" or "devices." . . .

When a demonstrative aid is presented, its foundation differs considerably from the requirements for authenticating real evidence. It is not an object that itself was specifically connected to the parties or played a part in the events underlying the litigation. Its source and how it was created may be of no significance whatsoever. Instead, the theory justifying its admission is that the item is a fair and accurate representation of relevant testimony or documentary evidence otherwise admitted in the case. . . . Whether the admission of a particular demonstrative aid will in fact be helpful, or will instead tend to confuse or mislead the trier, is a matter within the sound discretion of the trial court . . .

JENNIFER L. MNOOKIN, THE IMAGE OF TRUTH: PHOTOGRAPHIC EVIDENCE AND THE POWER OF ANALOGY
10 Yale J.L. & Human. 1, 5, 43-44, 64-65, 70 (1998)

In the 1850s and before, legal evidence usually consisted of words — spoken testimony, written depositions, contracts, deeds, and the like. Those few

images present in court were often those that had received explicit legal
sanction, such as county-approved maps and surveys in land dispute cases,
or drawings and diagrams in patent cases. When unofficial drawings were
used, they were not thought to be evidence. Only with the advent of photography were these broader kinds of visual representations conceptualized as
evidence, their evidentiary value deemed significant enough to be fought over,
their improper inclusion or exclusion deemed worthy grounds for appeal.
Indeed, by the end of the century, the use of visual evidence had blossomed,
and images of many sorts, from photographs to diagrams to three-dimensional
models, were frequently used in an effort to persuade the jury. Visual representation, not limited to photography, had become a significant persuasive
technique in the courtroom. Now, an attorney or witness could not only
locate evidence, but could create it himself. He could represent his side of the
story with an elaborate visual image prepared especially for the lawsuit. These
forms of visual evidence were especially persuasive because jurors and judges
could see the evidence for themselves. To put it crudely, judicial response to
the photograph brought into existence that category of proof we now know
as "demonstrative evidence."

. . . [T]he prevailing judicial approach to the photograph was to align
it, by analogy, with maps, models, and diagrams. All of these were viewed as
constructed visual aids that a witness could use to illustrate his testimony.
These visual representations were viewed not as independent evidence but as
illustrative evidence that could aid a witness in communicating his point. The
justification for allowing such representations at all was that some matters
were more easily explained visually than orally; therefore, witnesses should
be allowed to use images whenever the use would clarify their points. . . . In
other words, a photograph, map, model, or diagram could be used as evidence
as long as an attesting witness proclaimed it a correct representation. The
visual aid was evidence in the sense that it was the witness's own description in visual rather than oral form. The visual representation itself, however,
was not to serve as proof that the witness's description was accurate, nor as
independent or corroborative evidence. It was merely the witness's testimony
rendered visually.

. . . And yet, despite this doctrinal declaration, it proved impossible for the
photograph not to be understood as evidence. The photograph was conceptually viewed as evidence almost from the moment of its invention—it was "a
witness on whose testimony the most certain conclusions may be confidently
founded." The sheer force of doctrine alone could not keep the photograph
secure in a box labeled "illustration"; the strong realist conception could not
simply be left behind at the courthouse door. A major consequence of linking
photographs to models, maps, and diagrams was that all of these forms of representation began to acquire the sheen of evidence.

. . . Demonstrative evidence has continued to hover awkwardly on the
boundary between illustration and proof. In their analysis of the topic, Robert
Brain and Daniel Broderick described the tremendous conceptual confusion
that still besets "demonstrative evidence," pointing out that "there is not even
a settled definition of the term." Some commentators define demonstrative
evidence to include all evidence that consists of "things" rather than testimony,
"all phenomena which can convey a relevant firsthand sense impression to

the trier of fact." Others limit its definition to those displays "principally used to illustrate or explain other testimonial, documentary, or real proof . . . a visual (or other sensory) aid." Some definitions deem it substantive, independent evidence, while others insist it serves merely the secondary, derivative purpose of illustration.

BAUGH v. CUPRUM S.A. DE C.V.

730 F.3d 701 (7th Cir. 2013)

HAMILTON, Circuit Judge.

. . . Plaintiff John Baugh suffered a severe brain injury when the Cuprum ladder he was using to clean his gutters buckled and collapsed. Baugh's wife Sharon brought this suit on his behalf against Cuprum S.A. de C.V. alleging defective design and negligence. There were no eyewitnesses to the incident. As a result of the injury, Mr. Baugh could not testify about what happened.

On December 21, 2010, about three months before trial, Cuprum informed plaintiff's counsel that it intended to use an exemplar of the actual ladder at trial. The exemplar ladder was new but had been built to the exact specifications of the ladder Mr. Baugh had been using. In a pretrial conference on February 1, 2011, the exemplar ladder was marked as an exhibit "for Demonstrative Purposes." Plaintiff objected to any use of the new exemplar ladder. Discovery had closed two years earlier, and the ladder had not been included in Cuprum's expert disclosures.

In response to the objection, Cuprum explained, "it's simply demonstrative exhibits that we'll use during the direct examination of [Cuprum's expert]. . . . And these exhibits are demonstrative. They are not substantive evidence. They are not to be admitted for substantive evidence. It's just simply to demonstrate and help the jury understand his testimony." The district judge determined that since the ladder was being offered only as a demonstrative exhibit, plaintiff's objections to untimely disclosure were irrelevant: "[T]he fact that it wasn't disclosed in connection with the experts' reports isn't by itself problematic to me if what we are talking about is demonstrative." The court thus permitted the ladder to be displayed and used in the courtroom during trial testimony by Cuprum's expert.

Cuprum used the exemplar ladder during trial to argue that, contrary to the design defect theory offered by plaintiff's expert, the ladder would not collapse under a normal load with all four legs on the ground. Cuprum's expert presented testimony and video in which he tested the strength and stability of the ladder. The video also showed him performing other tests that included jumping on the ladder as if it were a pogo stick and tipping the ladder in different positions.

The jury began its first day of deliberations around noon. As a demonstrative exhibit, of course, the ladder was not sent to the jury for use in deliberations. After about two hours, though, the jury sent a note to the judge asking to see the exemplar ladder. . . . plaintiff's counsel objected on the basis that the ladder "was introduced for—or brought into the courtroom for demonstrative purposes. . . . It was not offered into evidence by either side." . . . The judge sent the following note to the jury: "Dear Jurors: The exemplar ladder is a demonstrative exhibit. It was not admitted in evidence. You may, if you wish, step into the courtroom to look at the exemplar ladder, but we will not be sending it into the jury room during your deliberations." After receiving the note, however, the jury seemed to have lost interest in the ladder and did not actually look at it that day.

The second day, though, the jury renewed its request. . . . [After hearing further argument, the] court . . . permitted the jury to enter the courtroom by themselves and to look at the ladder. Approximately twenty minutes later, the jury sent a note asking if they could step on the ladder. Plaintiff's counsel again objected. . . . The district court reserved ruling until the following day. . . .

Ultimately, on the third day of deliberation, the court allowed the ladder to go into the jury room itself with a note: "Pursuant to your request, I am allowing the exemplar ladder to be taken into the jury room. You may fully examine the ladder. Under no circumstances are you to endeavor to reconstruct the occurrence." The letter and exemplar ladder were delivered to the jury room at approximately 10:09 a.m. At 1:48 p.m., the jury returned a verdict in favor of Cuprum. . . .

"Generally, it is within the trial court's discretion to determine which exhibits are provided to the jury during deliberations; we review this decision only for a clear abuse of discretion." *Deicher v. City of Evansville*, 545 F.3d 537, 542 (7th Cir. 2008). . . . Demonstrative exhibits that are *not* admitted into evidence pose quite different issues. The general rule is that materials not admitted into evidence simply should not be sent to the jury for use in its deliberations. *Bankcard America, Inc. v. Universal Bancard Systems, Inc.,* 203 F.3d 477, 483 (7th Cir. 2000) (sending three unadmitted documents to jury was "sloppy" and an error, but harmless); *Artis v. Hitachi Zosen Clearing, Inc.,* 967 F.2d 1132, 1142-43 (7th Cir. 1992) (error to send unadmitted damages summary to jury room for deliberations, but also harmless); see also *United States v. Holton,* 116 F.3d 1536, 1542 (D.C. Cir. 1997) ("To protect jury deliberations from improper influence, we ordinarily restrict the jury's access only to exhibits that have been accepted into evidence. . . ."). . . .

The term "demonstrative" has been used in different ways. . . . In its broadest and least helpful use, the term "demonstrative" is used to describe any physical evidence. See, *e.g., Finley v. Marathon Oil Co.,* 75 F.3d 1225, 1231 (7th Cir. 1996) (using "demonstrative evidence" as synonym for physical exhibits). . . . As Professors Wright and Miller lament, the term, "demonstrative" has grown "to engulf all the prior categories used to cover the use of objects as evidence. . . . As a result, courts sometimes get hopelessly confused in their analysis." 22 Charles Alan Wright & Arthur R. Miller, Federal Practice and Procedure §5172 (2d ed.). . . .

As the term was used in the district court and is used in this opinion, labeling an exhibit "demonstrative" signifies that the exhibit is not itself evidence — the exhibit is instead a persuasive, pedagogical tool created and used by a party as part of the adversarial process to persuade the jury. Robert D. Brain & Daniel J. Broderick, *The Derivative Relevance of Demonstrative Evidence: Charting Its Proper Evidentiary Status,* 25 U.C. Davis L. Rev. 957, 961 (1992) ("Demonstrative proof has only a secondary or derivative function at trial: it serves only to explain or clarify other previously introduced, relevant substantive evidence."). These pedagogical devices are used to aid the jury in its understanding of the evidence that has already been admitted. . . .

When the term is used this way, demonstrative exhibits are meant to "illustrate or clarify a party's position," and . . . are not properly considered evidence. *United States v. Milkiewicz*, 470 F.3d 390, 396-98 (1st Cir. 2006).[1] They instead aim to clarify, color, or "organize or aid the jury's examination of testimony or documents which are themselves admitted into evidence" to persuade the jury to see the evidence in a certain light favorable to the advocate's client. *United States v. Bray*, 139 F.3d 1104, 1111-12 (6th Cir. 1998) . . .[2]

. . . With this understanding of the term, the common phrase "demonstrative evidence" becomes a bit of an oxymoron. We will not try to police the use of the phrase, but there is value to using the term more narrowly and carefully, as it was used in the district court in this case, so that it does not apply to an exhibit that is properly admitted as substantive evidence through the Federal Rules of Evidence.[3]

Demonstrative exhibits that are not admitted into evidence should not go to the jury during deliberation, at least not without consent of all parties. We would not allow a lawyer to accompany the jury into the deliberation room to help the jurors best view and understand the evidence in the light most favorable to her client. The same goes for objects or documents used only as demonstrative exhibits during trial. . . .

In this case, the exemplar ladder was used during trial by the defense expert witness to illustrate his oral testimony. That is a classic and proper use of a demonstrative exhibit, and such use is properly left to the sound discretion of the judge presiding over the trial. See generally Fed. R. Evid. 611(a). The district court repeatedly recognized the distinction between demonstrative exhibits and substantive evidence during trial and after deliberations began. Yet the court eventually decided to cross this boundary by permitting the demonstrative exhibit to be treated as if it were substantive evidence and allowing the jury to see, touch, and manipulate it during deliberations. . . . [T]he district court believed it had discretion to send the demonstrative exhibit, in the narrow meaning that both the district court and we have used here, to the jury for deliberations.

---

1. The term "demonstrative" does not appear in the text of the Federal Rules of Evidence, nor does it appear in a single state evidence code. . . . This absence makes sense. When the term is used as it was used in this case by the court and counsel, demonstrative exhibits are not evidence at all.

2. Nothing in this opinion should be understood to call into question our cases permitting juries to consider transcripts of recorded conversations during deliberation.

3. The term "demonstrative" does appear once in the 1972 advisory committee's note to Federal Rule of Evidence 611(a), which gives trial judges the power to control the "mode" of testimony. . . . The relevant part of the advisory committee's note said: "Item (1) restates in broad terms the power and obligation of the judge as developed under common law principles. It covers such concerns as . . . the use of demonstrative evidence . . . and the many other questions arising during the course of a trial which can be solved only by the judge's common sense and fairness in view of the particular circumstances." The advisory committee's note used the term "demonstrative" in the broad sense of the term to refer to items actually admitted into evidence, which may present a variety of issues for trial management. Those issues are of course left to the trial judge's discretion.

That belief may have been based on prior opinions that used the broader meaning of the term "demonstrative" to apply to all sorts of physical evidence that has been admitted into evidence, rather than the narrower, more precise meaning used by the district court and in this opinion. We said recently that we "review the district court's decision to send demonstratives to the jury room for abuse of discretion," and that this discretion is properly exercised when decisions to send the "demonstratives" are applied evenhandedly to both parties. *United States v. Natale,* 719 F.3d 719, 743-44 (7th Cir. 2013), citing *United States v. Salerno,* 108 F.3d 730, 742 (7th Cir. 1997). In both *Natale* and *Salerno,* however, the term "demonstrative" was being used in the broader sense. In both cases we were referring to exhibits that had actually been admitted into evidence. Neither case approved sending the jury exhibits that were not in evidence . . . which would have run contrary to . . . long-standing practice. . . .

We acknowledge that the Tenth Circuit authorized a similar departure from the usual practice in *United States v. Downen,* 496 F.2d 314 (10th Cir. 1974), when it affirmed convictions in a fairly complex interstate vehicle theft case in which a government chart that organized the different stolen vehicles, dates, and counts of the indictment was allowed to go to the jury during deliberations. The chart itself had never been offered or admitted into evidence. The trial court gave detailed instructions to the effect that the chart was not evidence but contained only the government's theory of the case. Although the use of the chart might have been justified on quite narrow grounds, or perhaps found harmless, the Tenth Circuit explained its decision to affirm in sweeping language:

> [W]e hold that the submission of papers, documents or articles, whether or not admitted in evidence, to the jury for view during trial or jury deliberations, accompanied by careful cautionary instructions as to their use and limited significance, is within the discretion accorded the Trial Court in order that it may guide and assist the jury in understanding and judging the factual controversy.

. . . The Fifth Circuit followed *Downen* in *Big John, B.V. v. Indian Head Grain Co.,* 718 F.2d 143, 148-49 (5th Cir. 1983), when it affirmed a verdict reached after the jury was allowed to use a damages chart that had not been admitted into evidence.

We view both *Downen* and *Big John* as cases that departed from long-standing practice in this and other circuits and the learned treatises cited above, and as having done so with only the most tenuous support. In any event, we are aware of no case authorizing what happened here, where the district court overruled objections to an exhibit on the ground that it would be used only for demonstrative purposes and then, during jury deliberations, reversed course and treated the exhibit as if it had been admitted into evidence.[4]

The district court repeatedly made clear to both parties that the exemplar ladder was being offered and used only as a demonstrative exhibit. Even if

---

4. Since *Big John,* the Fifth Circuit appears to have followed the majority practice that we adhere to in this case. See *United States v. Harms,* 442 F.3d 367, 375 (5th Cir. 2006) (stating that demonstrative exhibits not admitted into evidence "should not go to the jury room absent consent of the parties"), quoting *United States v. Taylor,* 210 F.3d 311, 315 (5th Cir. 2000). . . .

the defendant might have been able to have the ladder admitted as substantive evidence (a question we do not decide), both parties were entitled to notice of that possibility and the opportunity to raise objections. The decision to allow the ladder to go to the jury room during deliberations after it had been treated during trial as a demonstrative exhibit, and not as evidence, was therefore an abuse of discretion. . . .

[I]n effect, plaintiff's counsel was lulled unintentionally into what turned out to be a false complacency that the ladder was not being offered as evidence, yet during jury deliberations, it was converted into a substantive piece of evidence that the jury could see, touch, handle, step on, and otherwise manipulate. Plaintiff never had an opportunity to plan for, mitigate, or rebut the effects of the ladder's introduction into jury deliberations and was prejudiced by his inability to respond to the ladder as substantive evidence. . . .

The jury deliberations spanned three days, and the jury reached a verdict shortly after it had the opportunity to examine, step on, and manipulate the exemplar ladder, going well beyond the exposure they had to the ladder when it was used as a demonstrative exhibit during the trial. The error may well have been decisive; we cannot say it was harmless. . . . We therefore Reverse the judgment and Remand the case to the district court for a new trial.

STATE v. COULTER

67 S.W.3d 3 (Tenn. Crim. App. 2001)

OGLE, Judge.

[Appellant Coulter was convicted of first-degree murder in the shooting death of his estranged wife. His defense at trial was that the killing was an impulsive act, rather than the result of premeditation. The state's evidence of premeditation included the testimony of a firearms expert, Special Agent Carman, who explained that a person would have to apply a significant amount of pressure — twelve pounds — to the trigger for the gun to fire "double action," meaning without the hammer first having been cocked.]

. . . Following Carman's testimony and in the presence of the jury, the prosecutor inquired of the trial court:

> Judge, I would like for the members of the jury to stand down and each one to pull the trigger of that gun so that they can find out for themselves how easy or difficult it is.

Still in the jury's presence, defense counsel responded that "[t]here's no sense in them coming down and pulling the trigger on this." Specifically, he observed that the weapon was an exhibit, and the jury members would have an opportunity to pull the trigger during their deliberations. In turn, the prosecutor explained to the court:

> Judge, I'd just like to make sure that they did. I think it's important. [The appellant] said something about I walked in there and then there was a pop and then there was another pop in part of his statement. It sounds like that this gun just kind of went off by itself.

Upon receiving this explanation, the court overruled the appellant's objection. . . .

. . . The principal issue at trial was whether or not the appellant possessed the requisite mental state of intent and premeditation . . . [A]ppellant's audio taped account of the murder indicated that the appellant could not recall consciously exerting pressure on the trigger of his revolver; rather, he simply heard the revolver discharge. In light of the appellant's account, the State needed to eliminate any reasonable doubt stemming from a possibility that the weapon accidentally discharged or otherwise discharged without the appellant's "conscious objective or desire." . . . Therefore, the amount of pressure required to pull the trigger of the revolver, particularly in the double action mode, was relevant, and permitting each member of the jury to pull the trigger undoubtedly assisted him or her in understanding Special Agent Carman's testimony. Indeed, one court has observed that

> [d]emonstrating the working of machinery is an accepted part of evidence. . . . "In general, when a question arises whether at a certain machine, house, field, mine, or other thing, a certain act can be done under given conditions of time, strength, skill, or achievement, one way [to obtain the answer] is to speculate about it, and another way is to try it; and it is a crude error to suppose that the law of evidence here prefers speculation to experience, abhors actual experiment, and delights in guesswork."

Bowlin v. State, 823 P.2d 676, 678 (Alaska Ct. App. 1991) (alteration in original).

. . . In light of the relevance of the demonstration, we believe that the trial court acted within its discretion in determining that a courtroom demonstration was an "efficient use of judicial resources." Neil P. Cohen et al., Tennessee Law of Evidence §403.6, at 154 (Michie ed., 3d ed. 1995). This issue is without merit.

UNITED STATES v. WEEKS

919 F.2d 248 (5th Cir. 1990)

EDITH H. JONES, Circuit Judge.

Defendant-appellant Danny Michael Weeks was convicted after a jury trial of two counts of kidnapping, two counts of interstate transportation of a stolen vehicle, and one count each of carrying a firearm during a crime of violence and possessing a firearm as a convicted felon. . . . We affirm. . . .

Weeks . . . contends that the district court erred in allowing the government to display a firearm to the jury even though it was not connected to Weeks. We agree with the government that the court did not abuse its discretion in permitting the display. Two of the six crimes charged in the indictment involved a firearm. Although the revolver was not the actual firearm used by the defendant, it belonged to a government firearms expert and was identified by kidnap victim Mayeaux as looking similar to the weapon that Weeks took from the trunk of her car and used during the offenses. The court did not admit the firearm into evidence—which would have allowed the jury to examine it during deliberations—but allowed it to be displayed for "demonstrative purposes only." Finally, the court instructed the jury that the revolver they had seen was merely a model similar to the one used in the crime. Weeks also claims that the government displayed the weapon in an inflammatory manner that unfairly prejudiced him. At trial, defense counsel objected because the prosecutor "clicked [the gun] and tried it again, emphasizing the use of it. It inflames the jury panel. I would object to him trying to point the gun and play with the handle, and he clicks it so it's that much more intimidating." The prosecutor disputed this characterization, stating that "[t]he gun's chamber was open. The barrel was open, Your Honor. As I walked toward the witness, the barrel closed." The court responded: "Next time keep it closed." From the cold record, we are unable to determine what actually happened, but the district court evidently accepted the government's version. The firearm display does not constitute reversible error. . . .

UNITED STATES v. HUMPHREY

279 F.3d 372 (6th Cir. 2002)

Moore, Circuit Judge.

Defendant-Appellant Cheryl Ann Humphrey ("Humphrey") appeals her jury conviction and sentence for one count of embezzling bank funds, in violation of 18 U.S.C. §656, and five counts of making false entries in bank records with the intent to defraud, in violation of 18 U.S.C. §1005. . . . From 1975 to 1996, Humphrey was employed as a bank and vault teller for Hamilton Bank, later known as SunTrust Bank ("Bank"), of Johnson City, Tennessee. . . .

Humphrey claims that the district court abused its discretion in admitting 107 coin bags as demonstrative evidence. At trial, the Government introduced as Government Exhibit 6a a vault cash form dated May 21, 1996, and verified by Humphrey that showed an inventory of $214,167.45 in loose coin. The Government also introduced a videotape dated May 21, 1996, that showed the area inside the Bank's vault where loose coin was stored. The purpose of the demonstrative evidence was to show the jury what 107 coin bags would look like and to establish that the vault did not contain that many coin bags. Six of the 107 bags were filled with coins; the remainder were stuffed with styrofoam peanuts to the approximate size of the bags filled with coins.

Defense counsel objected to the demonstration, arguing that the evidence was prejudicial because the bags filled with styrofoam were bigger than those filled with coins. The district court thought otherwise. After hearing from an expert witness who stated that the bags filled with styrofoam were representative of and "about the same size" in volume as the bags filled with coins, the district court admitted the exhibit, noting that defense counsel could raise this issue on cross-examination. Defense counsel proceeded to do so. Witnesses for the Government later testified that they did not see that much loose coin in the Bank's vault on May 21, 1996, or on any other day.

Under Federal Rule of Evidence 403, evidence that is relevant "may be excluded if its probative value is substantially outweighed by the danger of unfair prejudice." In admitting the coin bags into evidence, the district court did not expressly weigh their probative value against the danger of unfair prejudice, but it did recognize that the Government wanted the jury to see what the bags would look like in the Bank's vault. Reviewing this evidentiary decision, we are not persuaded that the district court abused its discretion. . . . [Convictions affirmed.]

ROLAND v. LANGLOIS

945 F.2d 956 (7th Cir. 1991)

Harlington Wood, Jr., Circuit Judge.

[Seeking damages for injuries he suffered when a carnival ride hit him in the head, Douglas Roland and his wife sued the operator of the ride and the carnival company. Following a judgment for defendants, the Rolands appealed.]

. . . [T]he district court admitted a life-size model [of a portion of the fence surrounding the ride,] offered by the defendants. . . . The district court has wide discretion in these matters . . . and we can find no abuse of that discretion on this record. . . . [T]he plaintiffs' principal complaint is that the model was not completely accurate. There is no requirement that demonstrative evidence be completely accurate, however, and the evidence was admitted only on the express condition that the jury be alerted to the perceived inaccuracies. Having reviewed the record in this case, moreover, and having struggled to familiarize ourselves with the scene of the accident, we agree with the district court that the benefits from the use of a life-size model were not substantially outweighed by the danger of unfair prejudice. *See* Fed. R. Evid. 403. . . . Affirmed.

UNITED STATES v. WOOD

943 F.2d 1048 (9th Cir. 1991)

O'scannlain, Circuit Judge.

Wood appeals his conviction for tax evasion. . . . Wood urges that the district court erred in admitting into evidence a summary chart prepared by the government's expert, while excluding from evidence a summary chart prepared by the defense expert.

Bob Marcinek, an agent with the Internal Revenue Service, testified as an expert on behalf of the government. Marcinek testified as to his opinion of Wood's tax liability, which he summarized in two charts. The government moved to admit the charts into evidence; the motion was granted without objection.

The defense offered its own expert, Larry Richter, to testify about Wood's tax liability. During the course of his testimony, Richter filled in a chart outlining his version of the correct tax calculations. Thereafter, Wood moved to admit the chart into evidence. The government objected, claiming that the chart was a "misapplication of the law." The district court sustained the government's objection. However, the court permitted Wood to use the chart during closing arguments, so long as the figures concerning business loss deductions were masked.

"When considering the admissibility of exhibits of this nature, it is critical to distinguish between charts or summaries *as evidence* and charts or summaries *as pedagogical devices*." *Pierce v. Ramsey Winch Co.*, 753 F.2d 416, 431 (5th Cir. 1985). Charts and summaries as evidence are governed by Federal Rule of Evidence 1006, which permits the introduction of charts, summaries, or calculations "of voluminous writings, recordings, or photographs which cannot conveniently be examined in court." In contrast, charts or summaries of testimony or documents already admitted into evidence are merely pedagogical devices, and are not evidence themselves. *See Pierce*, 753 F.2d at 431; *see also United States v. Poschwatta*, 829 F.2d 1477, 1481 (9th Cir. 1987) (describing such summary charts as "testimonial aids"), *cert. denied*, 484 U.S. 1064 (1988).

We have long held that such pedagogical devices should be used only as a testimonial aid, and should not be admitted into evidence or otherwise be used by the jury during deliberations. *See United States v. Soulard*, 730 F.2d 1292, 1300 (9th Cir. 1984). . . . *But see Poschwatta*, 829 F.2d at 1481 (concluding that "[a]lthough the better practice may have been for the court to allow the charts to be used as testimonial aids only," court did not abuse its discretion in admitting charts into evidence). Thus, the district court's refusal to admit Richter's charts into evidence, standing alone, was not error. . . . Nonetheless, we agree with Wood that the disparate treatment between the government's summary charts and that of the defendant warrants explanation. Such explanation is readily apparent from the record. In *Soulard*, we explained that "[t]he trial court . . . should carefully examine the summary charts to determine that everything contained in them is supported by the proof." Richter offered only one reason for his calculation of Wood's "gains or losses": that Wood operated a trade or business, and thus, he was eligible for a business loss deduction. . . . [T]his analysis is incomplete; Wood was not entitled to a business loss deduction unless the property loss was held by Wood "primarily for sale to customers in the ordinary course of his trade or business." I.R.C. §1221(1). Richter presented no evidence that Wood had customers. Thus, the chart was not supported by the proof. The district court did not err in masking the unsupported portion or in declining to admit the chart into evidence. . . . Affirmed.

BANNISTER v. TOWN OF NOBLE, OKLAHOMA

812 F.2d 1265 (10th Cir. 1987)

TACHA, Circuit Judge.

In this appeal we review a jury verdict for Bannister, a Texas resident, in a diversity suit alleging negligence against the Town of Noble, Oklahoma, for personal injuries arising out of a one-car accident which occurred in Oklahoma. . . . Noble contends that the district court abused its discretion by admitting into evidence three videotapes. The district court viewed the videotapes before admitting them into evidence.

The first videotape Noble challenges is a "Day in the Life" film. Such films purport to show how an injury has affected the daily routine of its victim. Typical "Day in the Life" films show the victim in a variety of everyday situations, including getting around the home, eating meals, and interacting with family members. These films are prepared solely to be used as evidence in litigation concerning the injury. Such evidence is often desired because "films illustrate, better than words, the impact the injury had had on the plaintiff's life." *Grimes v. Employers Mut. Liab. Ins. Co.*, 73 F.R.D. 607, 610 (D. Alaska 1977). Noble argues that Bannister's "Day in the Life" videotape was unduly prejudicial within the meaning of Fed. R. Evid. 403 and thus inadmissible. . . .

We have held that "the prejudicial effect of a videotape is to be decided on a case by case basis." *Durflinger v. Artiles*, 727 F.2d 888, 894 (10th Cir. 1984). . . . In the present case, the district court examined the film and concluded that it accurately portrayed the daily routine of the plaintiff and that it was not unduly prejudicial. We have reviewed the film as well. The film shows Bannister getting around school, getting into his car, pumping gasoline for his car, and performing several different tasks in his home. Although there are a couple of scenes that show Bannister conducting activities that he would be unlikely to do frequently, the film as a whole demonstrates Bannister's adaptation to his injury. We hold that the district court did not abuse its discretion in admitting the film depicting a "Day in the Life" of Clifford Bannister.

Noble next argues that the district court abused its discretion in admitting into evidence a videotape which shows a car like the one involved in the accident approaching an inclined ramp, becoming airborne, and landing. The film shows the jump three times, each time from a different angle. Bannister offered the videotape not as a reenactment, but as a demonstration showing the trajectory of this type of car with this type of suspension system. Noble argues that the film is not a demonstration but an attempted recreation of the accident and that there are substantial dissimilarities between the film event and the actual accident; thus, the film should have been excluded as unduly prejudicial.

We have approved the admission of filmed evidence "not meant to depict the actual event of the accident but rather to show mechanical principles" upon a showing that "the experiments were conducted under conditions that were at least similar to those which existed at the time of the accident." *Brandt v. French*, 638 F.2d 209, 212 (10th Cir. 1981). But "[d]emonstrations of experiments used to merely illustrate the principles in forming expert opinion do not require strict adherence to the facts." *Id.* "[W]hen experiments do not simulate the actual events at issue, the jury should be instructed that the evidence is admitted for a limited purpose or purposes." *Robinson v. Audi NSU Auto Union Aktiengesellschaft*, 739 F.2d 1481, 1484 (10th Cir. 1984). . . .

In the present case, Bannister offered the videotape not as a recreation but as a demonstration of certain principles. The district court viewed the film and then admitted it for this limited purpose. The district court instructed the jury that

[T]he film is not being introduced for the purpose of attempting to recreate the accident involved in this case. The Plaintiff does not contend that the film reenacts the accident. . . . The film is introduced only to demonstrate certain physical principles. . . . You're instructed not to consider this film as a reenactment of the accident.

We find no abuse of discretion.

Noble also argues that the district court erred when it allowed Bannister to show a videotape to the jury during closing argument. The videotape was edited to show portions of the "Day in the Life" tape, the demonstration tape, and a portion of a taped deposition of one of Bannister's doctors. We first note that the district court has a great deal of discretion in controlling arguments of counsel. Furthermore, a judgment should not be set aside unless it is clear that the closing argument has unduly aroused the sympathy of the jury thereby influencing the verdict. All of the videotapes used to make the closing argument tape had been properly admitted into evidence during the course of the trial. In addition, the district court viewed the videotape prior to allowing it to be shown to the jury. We have also reviewed the tape. We find that the district court did not abuse its discretion.... Affirmed.

2. The Digital Courtroom

VERIZON DIRECTORIES CORP. v. YELLOW BOOK USA, INC.

331 F.Supp.2d 136 (E.D.N.Y. 2004)

WEINSTEIN, Senior District Judge.

Verizon Directories Corporation has sued Yellow Book USA, Inc., alleging that the defendant has used false or misleading representations in advertising and in sales and marketing communications. The current phase of the litigation is a bench trial to determine preliminary injunctive relief, permanent injunctive relief and liability (damages issues, if any, to be put off for later jury determination).

The parties have presented almost all exhibits in computer-generated formats as well as by hard copy. They were dubious about the admissibility of the many pedagogical devices (often called "demonstratives") used in the trial. For the reasons stated below, the court finds that the scores of pedagogical devices used at trial, except for those stricken for error or lack of utility, are admitted into evidence.

... The applicable literature identifies four overlapping main categories of computer generated exhibits: static images, animations, simulations, and computer models. Presentations are frequently in a "power point" format with the attorney calling up data and images as needed from huge files.

The first category "consists of static images that are simply projected onto a large screen or computer panel or onto individual monitors by a computer display system." [Fred Galves, *Where the Not-So-Wild Things Are: Computers in the Courtroom, the Federal Rules of Evidence, and the Need for Institutional Reform and More Judicial Acceptance,* 13 Harv. J. Law & Tech. 161, 177 (2000).] These representations are common in courtrooms. They include tables, graphs, maps and diagrams.

Animations are, in their simplest terms, moving pictures. The computer allows otherwise static images to be "shown in rapid succession to create the [illusion] of motion." [Lori G. Baer & Christopher A. Riley, *Technology in the Courtroom: Computerized Exhibits and How to Present Them,* 66 Def. Couns. J. 176, 177 (1999).] The graphics are often crude or oversimplified. Animations are not intended "to recreate or simulate an event." Timothy W. Cerniglia, *Computer-Generated Exhibits—Demonstrative, Substantive or Pedagogical—Their Place in Evidence,* 18 Am. J. Trial Advoc. 1, 5 (1994).

The third category is "simulations" or "recreations." Computer functions allow the user to simulate actual events—or, more properly, the opinion of the creator as to the nature of the events. Most simulations are detailed and realistic. The recreated computer image of the event can be manipulated. It can be portrayed from different angles or from the viewpoints of different witnesses. A common use involves the recreation of accidents. *See, e.g., Datskow v. Teledyne Continental Motors,* 826 F.Supp. 677, 685–86 (W.D.N.Y. 1993) (noting that defendant objected to the "use of a videotaped computer-generated animation which illustrated . . . theory of where the fire began inside the engine and how it spread.").

The fourth category, computer models, are "nothing more than a compilation of mathematical formulae and expressions that are integrated into a sophisticated computer program or series of programs." Cerniglia, *supra,* at 6. An expert witness may test multiple hypotheses with the model and form opinions based on the results, producing graphics explicating the results.

A fifth category should be admitted. It is "enhanced images," occupying the space between static images and animations. For the most part, an enhanced image is static, but the attorney or witness may manipulate the image through, for example, highlighting, enlarging particular areas, and utilizing side-by-side split screen presentations or video-taped depositions with printed commentary or transcripts moving below in tandem with the image and audio of the deponent. Different colors can be used to emphasize particular elements of the presentation or to show which parts of a deposition are being presented by one side or the other. The parties may highlight selected text, enlarge graphics, modify images, or enlist other special effects to illuminate a relevant point. *See, e.g.,* Galves, *supra,* at 177 ("The computer technology here, therefore, simply makes those functions easier, quicker, and more legible and understandable.").

A sixth category, easel writings and diagrams created by an expert or attorney during the trial and in the presence of the trier, is old-hat. The technique is now improved by almost instantaneous computer creation of printed versions that can be projected onto the screen and converted to hard copy for the trier's notebook.

Computer-generated exhibits in this trial are predominantly of the "enhanced images" type. The judge, witness, court reporter, and lawyers have computer monitors at their respective stations. There is a large screen in the courtroom. The particular documents relied on by a witness or lawyer are displayed on the personal monitors and projected onto the large screen as appropriate. Nearly every static image of a document is enhanced by highlighting in color the portion of the text believed by counsel to be telling, and by enlarging the selected text in a superimposed box.

Relevant video deposition testimony is shown on the monitors and large screen. The image of the deposition is supplemented by subtitles. Questions by plaintiff—and the concomitant responses are displayed in red-colored text. Defendant's questions and responses are shown in blue-colored text. Documents and other data may be simultaneously shown on split screens. The portions of depositions relied upon and counter designations are broken up into "themes," explained by what amount to mini-summations.

The parties use graphics to complement testimony, showing graphs, numerical collections of raw and analyzed data from surveys, pie and bar charts, and cartoonish images of persons, stacks of books or other objects, and "thought bubbles." Although rudimentary, the images are effective in clarifying sometimes dense expert testimony, statistical surveys and theories. They also utilize easel writings and diagrams. When showing the television commercials at issue, images may be "freeze-framed." The information is projected onto the large screen in the courtroom and individual monitors from the party-operated computers or overhead projector. . . .

Tens of thousands of "bates-numbered" pages that are part of comprehensive collection of documents may be called up by the computer as needed. "Bates" labeling is commonly used to assign numbers to pages identified during pretrial or at trial. The term comes from the name of a brand of number stamping machine. Internal indexes and other controls of documents in litigation often use these identifying numbers. The numbers are now often automatically affixed during electronic rapid scanning by litigation support software and services providers. . . .

The parties provided the court with large numbers of notebooks containing traditional documents, witness lists, and identifying data in conjunction with the techniques already discussed, and pedagogicals. Were this a jury trial, including some of this information in individual juror notebooks with pictures and identifying data for witnesses would be appropriate. . . . It should be noted that while the present phase of the case is a bench trial, should the court decide there is liability, the damages phase will be tried before a jury. It would seem sensible to allow a jury determining damages, if this event should come to pass, to be assisted by the same pedagogical devices the court relied upon in determining liability.

. . . Pedagogical devices or demonstratives have long been recognized in the form of summaries, charts and other aids used by parties "to organize or aid the jury's examination of testimony or documents which are themselves admitted into evidence." *See* 6 Margaret A. Berger et al., Federal Evidence, §1006.04 [2] (Joseph McLauglin, ed. 2000). It is a common view among courts that such pedagogical devices "are not evidence themselves, but are used merely to aid the jury in its understanding of the evidence that has already been admitted." *United States v. Janati*, 374 F.3d 263, 273 (4th Cir. 2004) (citations omitted); *see also Gomez v. Great Lakes Steel Div. Nat'l Steel Corp.*, 803 F.2d 250, 257 (6th Cir. 1986). The use of such material in court is typically governed by Rule 611(a) of the Federal Rules of Evidence. *See* Fed.R.Evid. 611(a) ("The court shall exercise reasonable control over the mode and order of . . . presenting evidence so as to (1) make the . . . presentation effective for the ascertainment of truth. . . ."); *Janati*, 374 F.3d at 273 ("But displaying such charts is always under the supervision of the district court under Rule 611(a), and in the end they are not admitted as evidence."). . . .

Courts have generally declined to treat pedagogical devices as evidence. *See* Berger, *supra,* at §1006.08[4] ("Pedagogical-device summaries are used to summarize evidence, but they are not evidence themselves."). Although courts employ different terms for the aids, most circuits have generally excluded the devices from evidence. *See, e.g., United States v. Sawyer,* 85 F.3d 713, 740 (1st Cir. 1996); *United States v. Bradley,* 869 F.2d 121, 123 (2d Cir. 1989); *United States v. Pelullo,* 964 F.2d 193, 205 (3d Cir. 1992); *Janati,* 374 F.3d at 273; *Gomez,* 803 F.2d at 257; *United States v. Wood,* 943 F.2d 1048, 1053 (9th Cir. 1991).

In contrast to other decisions of the Court of Appeals for the Ninth Circuit, one panel of that court has seemingly sanctioned the admission of pedagogical devices under an abuse of discretion standard. *See United States v. Poschwatta,* 829 F.2d 1477, 1481 (9th Cir. 1987) ("Although the better practice may have been for the court to allow the charts to be used as *testimonial aids only,* the district court did not abuse its discretion. . . . The figures in the government chart already were admitted into evidence and the defendant did not challenge the figures. Defendant also had a full opportunity to cross-examine the witness. The charts arguably contributed to the clarity of the presentation to the jury and were a reasonable method of presenting evidence.") (citations omitted) (emphasis added). The Court of Appeals for the Sixth Circuit, in dicta, has recognized instances in which the admission of pedagogical devices is appropriate:

> We note in passing that in appropriate circumstances not only may such pedagogical device summaries be used as illustrative aids in the presentation of the evidence, but they may also be admitted into evidence even though not within the specific scope of Rule 1006. Such circumstances might be instances in which such pedagogical device is so accurate and reliable a summary illustration or extrapolation of testimonial or other evidence in the case as to reliably assist the factfinder in understanding the evidence, although not within the specific requirements of Rule 1006.

See United States v. Bray, 139 F.3d 1104, 1111-12 (6th Cir. 1998).

Pedagogical devices are often unfavorably compared to summaries admitted under Rule 1006. *See* Fed.R.Evid. 1006; The Evidence Project: Proposed Revisions to the Federal Rules of Evidence, 171 F.R.D. 330, 677 (Thomas C. Goldstein, ed. 1997) ("[S]ome courts . . . allowed summaries to be used only as nonevidentiary pedagogical devices."). Summaries, unlike Rule 611(a) aids, are admissible as proxies for voluminous records "which cannot be examined in court." Fed.R.Evid. 1006. Exclusion of pedagogical devices is grounded in the idea that such aids "are more akin to argument than evidence since [they] organize[] the jury's examination of testimony and documents already admitted in evidence." *Bray,* 139 F.3d at 1111. Nevertheless, the distinction between Rule 1006 summaries and Rule 611(a) pedagogical devices is often ignored by courts, and many admitted summaries actually restate previously admitted evidence. One commentator found that in one hundred percent of a sample of health care fraud cases the courts allowed pedagogical tools into evidence. *See* Pamela H. Bucy, *The Poor Fit of Traditional Evidentiary Doctrine and Sophisticated Crime: An Empirical Analysis of Health Care Fraud Prosecutions,* 62 Ford. L.Rev. 383, 416-17 (1994). The evidence treatises caution that pedagogical devices should be used only in conjunction with proper limiting instructions, "that jury aids . . . are not evidence-in-chief but are only the proponent's organization of the evidence presented." Berger, *supra,* at §1006.08[4].

. . . The purpose of a trial is to reveal the relevant real-world facts and to draw inferences leading to proof or disproof of operative elements of a cause of action; it is essentially a teaching learning process. *See, e.g., Tehan v. Shott,* 382 U.S. 406, 416 (1966) ("The basic purpose of a trial is the determination of truth. . . ."). As the eminent professors Jerome Michael and Mortimer Adler put the matter:

> In its logical aspect the trial of an issue of fact can be viewed as a process of teaching: By their proof and disproof of the contradictory propositions of which the issue is constituted, the litigants impart to the jury the knowledge which it needs in order to resolve the issue. . . . The process which, from the point of view of jurors, is a passive affair of learning or inference and, from the point of view of litigants, an active affair of teaching or proof, is a single process.

Jerome Michael & Mortimer J. Adler, *Real Proof: 1,* 5 Vand. L.Rev. 344, 344-46 (1952).

Forensic courtroom teaching is expected to be grounded in the real world. Evidence of that world is produced, and from that evidence, using hypotheses, generally based on knowledge the trier brings to the case, opinions are formed. They are based upon rational syllogisms, leading to conclusions about statements of fact that are material propositions (sometimes called operative facts) defined by the law. *See* John H. Mansfield, Norman Abrams & Margaret A. Berger, et al., Cases and Materials on Evidence 11-15 (9th ed.1997). . . .

The claim in this case is relatively simple: false or misleading advertising was used by defendant to harm the plaintiff. The methods of proof, however, involve complicated statistical data and expert testimony. This intricacy of proof is increasingly typical of federal trials. . . . Jurors can be authorized to take notes, but if the evidence and case are too complicated, their on-the-run jottings will do them little good in their jury room reasoning; ultimately, it is the trier's ability to think clearly in integrating evidence and arguments and in drawing rational conclusions that is the essence of our system of trials. *Cf. United States v. Casamento,* 887 F.2d 1141, 1151 (2d Cir.1989) ("This court has long approved the use of charts in complex trials, and has allowed the jury to have the charts in the jury room during its deliberations, so long as the judge properly instructs the jury that it is not to consider the charts as evidence.") (citations omitted).

The revolution in communicating that has occurred and is still occurring may sometimes be distracting, but it can strengthen the ability of courts to seek truth. Technology in litigation has changed enormously since the adoption of the Federal Rules of Evidence in 1975. . . . In any complex case, computer-generated presentations are the norm rather than the exception. . . . Subject to Rule 403, with somewhat more stringent control in jury trials, pedagogical aids should generally be admitted as evidence. They can be helpful to the court's understanding of the complex and voluminous amount of evidence presented, as in this case. The court is not as susceptible to the confusion the admission of such evidence might induce in juries. But this evidence should also be admitted as evidence in jury trials if it satisfies the requisites of Rules 402 and 403 of the Federal Rules of Evidence. . . . The district court's normal discretion can be utilized to mitigate situations in which parties have vastly different resources, creating an uneven technological playing field. In the instant case, both parties have the financial wherewithal to present comparable computer-generated evidence. The suggestion that trials are turning into legal smoke and mirror laser shows, lacking real substance, has no merit where the court exercises appropriate control.

In light of ever-changing technology, wide ownership of personal computers, expanding use of the internet, and personal digital assistant devices, among other electronic innovations, the lay person is increasingly immune to confusion by the encroachment of technology into heretofore primitive communication zones such as the jury room. *See, e.g., Datskow v. Teledyne Continental Motors,* 826 F.Supp. 677, 685 (W.D.N.Y. 1993) ("Jurors, exposed as they are to television, the movies, and picture magazines, are fairly sophisticated. With proper instruction, the danger of their overvaluing such proof is slight.") (quoting 1 J. Margaret A. Berger et al., Federal Evidence ¶ 403[5] at 403–88 (1992 ed.) (footnotes omitted)).

The day may soon come when jurors routinely have individual computers or computer monitors in the jury room. Most testimony in federal trials is already recorded electronically. . . . Modern juries take notes, have notebooks containing key evidence, and can ask questions through the court. . . . They need not be treated as illiterates as under the old English practice. . . . Increased flexibility in the use of educational devices will probably result in courtroom findings more consonant with truth and law. Whether designated as "pedagogical devices" or "demonstratives," this material may be admitted as evidence when it is accurate, reliable and will "assist the factfinder in understanding the evidence." *Bray,* 139 F.3d at 1112. Present highly professional and skilled counsel agree. They have stipulated to admit in evidence each of the nonstricken excellent pedagogical devices used in the trial.

. . . All pedagogical devices that the court has seen or heard are admitted as evidence, except where the court has ruled some such evidence unsatisfactory in conception or execution, and it has been stricken. The devices clarified relevant evidence and issues and are accurate and reliable. Their probative value is not "substantially outweighed by the danger of unfair prejudice or confusion of the issues, . . . or by considerations of undue delay, waste of time, or needless presentation of cumulative evidence." Fed. R. Evid. 403.

STATE v. DENTON

768 N.W.2d 250 (Wis. App. 2009)

NEUBAUER, J.

[Jeremy Denton and his codefendant were convicted of attempted kidnapping, attempted false imprisonment, and attempted robbery. The victim, Judy Giovannoni, testified that she was jogging along a highway when the defendants tried to force her into a car at gunpoint; she flagged down a second vehicle, driven by Dennis Hohisel, who let her into his vehicle and called 911. Hohisel, Giovannoni, and another passenger in Hohisel's car, Leah Biever, then followed the first car until they found it abandoned in a ditch.]

The defendants contend that the trial court erred in admitting a computer-generated animation introduced by the State to illustrate the testimony of the State's witnesses.[1]

... On the morning of the second and final day of trial, the State disclosed its intent to introduce a computer-generated animation to assist the jury in determining "who was where [and] when." The defendants objected.... After viewing the animation, the trial court commented:

> [T]he demonstration the Court has just now seen certainly is sophisticated. It ... doesn't rise to the level of video games, but it certainly is a sophisticated diagram.... I think that the defense is obviously wounded by this because it's pretty sophisticated and quite convincing.... Obviously it is prejudicial to the defense because it's quite clear how ... Giovannoni's testimony is illustrated but it is not unfair.

The animation was presented by Officer Anthony Ambach, who ... had not personally observed the scene, although he was familiar with the general area. The animation, which was based on "people's memories," was presented to the jury to "assist the jury in understanding directions, what people did, that sort of thing." Ambach, who was sequestered during the trial, based the animation upon his review of officers' reports and out-of-court discussions with Giovannoni, Hohisel, and Biever. He acknowledged that he had no personal knowledge of what was depicted in the animation.... While the trial court correctly determined that a party may use computer-generated animations to clarify a witness's testimony, the trial court erred in admitting the computer-generated animation as it was presented in this case.

---

1. The use of computer-generated animations as demonstrative aids at trial is a relatively recent development in the law. At the postconviction hearing, the district attorney in this case testified that this was the first time he had ever used a computer-generated animation at trial. However, the use of animations is recognized and described as follows in 2 KENNETH S. BROUN, MCCORMICK ON EVIDENCE §214 (6th ed. 2006):

> *Animations.* Computer-generated animations present a series of static images which the computer can show in rapid succession. This creates the illusion of motion, like a cartoon. Many simple animations are offered to illustrate the factual testimony of a witness. For example, an animated CGE [computer-generated exhibit] might portray the simple motion of a person walking; or, the images can move in rotation to show an object from different perspectives; gradual enlargement can show an object or scene from different distances. These simple animations are not used for the purpose of recreating or simulating an event. The authenticating testimony from a witness would establish that the animated CGE is a fair and accurate representation of what the witness is trying to describe, and admission of the animation would be within the discretion of the trial judge...

To the extent that CGEs represent simply a new type of illustrative evidence, their admissibility is controlled by the basic principles applied to all demonstrative aids. *Id.*, §218.

Computer-generated simulations and models, on the other hand, are not just illustrative evidence as they re-create disputed events. *Id.* Their creation requires the use of scientific data, principles and methods to formulate a computer-generated conclusion about the events at issue. *Id.* The conclusion is then sought to be introduced directly through the CGE or to be used by an expert to form an opinion. *Id.*

Demonstrative computer-generated animation should be introduced in conjunction with the witness's testimony it seeks to clarify — just as any diagram or photo intended to clarify a lay witness's testimony would be introduced. *See* [*Anderson v. State*, 223 N.W.2d 879 (Wis. 1974)] ("Demonstrative evidence, whether a model, a chart, a photograph . . . is used simply to lend clarity and interest to oral testimony [and] is merely incorporated by reference into a witness' testimony.") . . . Here, the State effectively presented its version of the substantive facts about what happened in animated form — during the evidentiary phase of the trial. Because Ambach was neither expert nor lay witness, and the video animation was not testified to as being either a fair and accurate representation or illustrative of any one witness's testimony, it had little probative value as a demonstrative exhibit, presented a very real danger of confusing and misleading the jury, and was unduly prejudicial to the defendants.

Far from being an exhibit which merely illustrated a lay witness's testimony or an expert's opinion, this exhibit was nothing more than a collage of information — bits and pieces from each of the State's witnesses when, mixed together, effectively represented the police officer's own version of what occurred at the time and place in question. But the animator was not an eyewitness to the crime. His assessment about how the crime actually unfolded was just that, his collage, his assessment. By bringing this nonevidentiary perspective of the evidence to life by means of the computer-generated animation, and advising the jury that this was a representation of what happened, the jury was invited to view the collage as fact. A pasting of differing and sometimes conflicting facts from a mixture of witnesses, in an order that made most sense to the State, thus became the final, conclusive historical factual presentation of the crime. This is why it was unduly prejudicial. The animation superceded the sifting and winnowing that a jury normally does when fact witnesses describe the same event in varying and sometimes contradictory ways. . . .

Given the absence of pretrial notice, lack of probative value, and the risk of prejudice and confusion about the role both of Ambach and the purpose of the animation, we simply cannot conclude that there is no reasonable possibility that the animation contributed to the conviction [and therefore that the error is harmless]. . . . Judgments and orders reversed. . . .

HON. HERBERT B. DIXON, JR., #AI, #VR, AND #IOT ARE COMING TO A COURTROOM NEAR YOU!

55 Judges' Journal 37, 38-39 (2016)

Imagine during one of your future trials that jurors in your courtroom are provided with virtual reality headsets, which allow them to view the accident site or crime scene digitally and walk around or be guided through a 3D world to examine vital details of the scene.

How can such an evidentiary presentation be accomplished? A system is being developed whereby investigators use a robot system inspired by NASA's Curiosity Mars rover using 3D imaging and panoramic videography equipment to record virtual reality video of the scene. The captured 360° immersive video and photographs of the scene would allow recreation of a VR experience with video and pictures of the original scene from every angle. Admissibility of this evidence would require a showing that the VR simulation fairly and accurately depicts what it represents. If a judge permits presentation of the evidence after its accuracy is established, jurors receiving the evidence could turn their heads and view various aspects of the scene by looking up, down, and around, and zooming in and out.

Unlike an animation or edited video initially created to demonstrate one party's point of view, the purpose of this type of evidence would be to gather data and objectively preserve the scene without staging or tampering. Even further, this approach would allow investigators to revisit scenes as they existed during the initial forensic examination and give jurors a vivid rendition of the site as it existed when the events occurred.

Also, if the site examiners used capabilities provided by Google's Project Tango during their examination of the scene, that would eliminate the need for sketches of the scene by capturing and highlighting the precise distance between objects and the relative position of all visible evidence as it existed upon arrival of the investigators.

JENNIFER MNOOKIN, REPEAT PLAY EVIDENCE: JACK WEINSTEIN, "PEDAGOGICAL DEVICES," TECHNOLOGY, AND EVIDENCE

64 DePaul L. Rev. 571, 577-79, 585-89 (2015)

... What if, in order to be admissible as evidence, simulations and animations had to be produced in such a way that the key assumptions and inputs could be modified for use by the opposing party, and the simulation rerun or the animation reproduced with the altered inputs? For some kinds of simulation packages, like premade accident-reconstruction software, it may be technologically reasonably straightforward to permit the opposing party to make modifications to certain predefined inputs. In other instances, it may, I grant, be far more complex to build a simulation in a way that permits ongoing modification of the key variables, and with animations as well, the feasibility of easily modifying the assumptions built into the depiction may vary. In addition, deciding precisely which variables need to be modifiable, and to what extent, could well raise its own practical challenges. But the key idea is that courts should have the power to require simulations (and perhaps animations too) to be modifiable along key axes as a precondition for admissibility. This would permit the opposing party to be able to reveal directly to the factfinder the power of specific assumptions in generating what is shown, and would go a considerable ways toward ameliorating the difficulties raised by resource disparities, at least for this specific kind of evidence.

In a particular car accident, for example, there may be no disagreement about road conditions or the weather, but conflicting admissible claims about the speed of a vehicle at the moment of impact. If one party depicts the accident by introducing an animation based on its evidence about the speed, the question becomes how would the animation visibly change if the assumption about the vehicle's speed were altered. Testing the assumptions of the animation or the simulation to see how robust it is, by permitting the opposing party to replace given assumptions with alternative ones (all of which must, of course, for both sides, be reasonable inferences from admissible evidence) is, conceptually, akin to a form of cross-examination of the simulation itself. To be sure, we do not normally imagine that machine-generated evidence requires cross-examination, but it may be time to begin thinking in those terms. . . .

Clearly, there are numerous questions—technological, legal, and conceptual—that would need to be addressed to make repeat play simulations genuinely workable. The point, for the moment, is not to argue strongly that repeat play simulations are a practicable or complete solution to the problems of resource differentials, potentially undue persuasive power, or the hidden assumptions that may be buried within computer-generated visual evidence. It may well be that all of these questions about repeat play animation and simulation could be satisfactorily addressed—or perhaps not. The broader point is that as visual evidence gains in significance, we need to think about how to innovate our courtroom procedures in ways that can match the technological innovations being introduced by savvy parties.

MAUREEN HOWARD & JEFFERY BARNUM, BRINGING DEMONSTRATIVE EVIDENCE IN FROM THE COLD: THE ACADEMY'S ROLE IN DEVELOPING MODEL RULES

88 Temple L. Rev. 513, 533, 548-49 (2016)

. . . Having left judges to their own devices to create court-specific discretionary guidelines for demonstrative evidence, professors have solidified the resulting confusion by teaching the next generation that demonstrative evidence lives outside the rules of evidence. In the classroom, in textbooks, and at continuing legal education seminars, those reared to accept the standardless status quo pass that acceptance to the next generation. . . .

While we do not have a set of Model Rules to propose at this time, the discussion going forward should include, at a minimum, the topics of terminology and juror use during deliberations. More specifically, the following items should be addressed in any model rule:

Clarifying terminology. Should visual aids bear different labels depending on whether they are employed during opening statement, during the presentation of evidence, or during closing argument? Perhaps jettisoning the terms "illustrative evidence" and "demonstrative evidence" entirely in favor of a new lexicon would be valuable . . . . Perhaps items used during opening statements could be labeled "preview aids." Items used during witness examinations could be called "nonverbal testimony" (if they are adopted by the witness as his testimony and merely communicate the content of that testimony to the jurors nonverbally) or "testimonial aids" otherwise. Items used during closing arguments might be called "argument aids."

Clarifying what goes to the jury deliberation room. Current practice is built largely on the general premise that admitted exhibits are delivered to jurors for review during deliberations. Should this continue to be the rule? It made immense sense that early practice was to deliver admitted exhibits to the jurors and not testimony. After all, two hundred years ago, there were far fewer exhibits admitted than is the case today in a large commercial lawsuit. As such, those exhibits would have been quite easy to deliver to the jurors, and easy for the jurors to review. Conversely, recordation and retrieval of oral testimony was much more involved and cumbersome. Considering there is no more value in a written letter admitted into evidence than the testimony of its author as to the underlying facts contained therein, the mere logistical difficulty in delivering these separate pieces of evidence seems to have been the driver for differentiating between exhibits and testimony. Now that many courts have the capability of recording testimony and producing an easy-to-access DVD (replete with an index), the logistical challenges are all but obviated. This is particularly true in cases with hundreds or thousands of admitted exhibits.

BURDENS, PRESUMPTIONS, AND JUDICIAL NOTICE

"*Not guilty, because puppies do these things.*"

A. BURDENS AND PRESUMPTIONS IN CIVIL CASES

The rules regarding presumptions, like the rules regarding relevance, continue to be influenced strongly by the thinking of James Bradley Thayer, who taught and wrote about evidence law at the beginning of the twentieth century. Surveying nineteenth-century evidence cases, Thayer noticed that judges often talked about facts being "presumed" but did not make clear what they meant. It seemed obvious that a presumption was a kind of legal relationship between two facts: the fact giving rise to the presumption ("the basic fact") and the fact being presumed ("the presumed fact"). But what exactly was the relationship?

Thayer thought the answer required distinguishing between two kinds of burdens borne by one party or the other in every lawsuit: the burden of persuasion and the burden of production. The burden of persuasion is the burden to satisfy the trier of fact, typically the jury, that a particular proposition has been demonstrated to a particular level of certainty. The principal burden of persuasion in a criminal trial, for example, requires the prosecution to prove the elements of the offense "beyond a reasonable doubt." Similarly, the burden of persuasion with regard to elements of a civil claim typically rests with the plaintiff. Instead of "beyond a reasonable doubt," though, the standard of proof required in a civil case is typically "preponderance of the evidence." In certain classes of civil cases involving particularly high stakes — e.g., civil commitment, or proceedings to set aside election results — an intermediate standard of "clear and convincing evidence" is applied.

Ordinarily, the burden of persuasion carries with it a more basic burden to produce some evidence. If a party has the burden to persuade the jury that a given fact is true, it typically also has the burden to produce some evidence of that fact. Otherwise the adverse party will be entitled to a directed verdict or to a dismissal of charges. Thayer distinguished this "burden of production" from the ultimate burden of persuasion, and he thought that presumptions should be understood to shift the first but not the second. For example, judges often said that a properly mailed letter is presumed to have been received. Thayer thought the presumption should operate only if there is no evidence the letter was not received. Once any such evidence is presented, Thayer argued that the presumption should drop out of the case and have no further effect.

This seemed silly to a later scholar, Edmund Morgan. He argued that presumptions should shift both the burden of production *and* the burden of proof. He thought, for example, that juries should be instructed to assume that any letter that had been properly mailed had been received, unless they were affirmatively convinced by the evidence that the letter had *not* been received.

Many current controversies regarding presumptions boil down to disagreements between followers of Thayer and followers of Morgan. But the boiling down can be hard to do. Morgan himself said that "[e]very writer of sufficient intelligence to appreciate the difficulties of the subject-matter has approached the topic of presumptions with a sense of hopelessness and left it with a feeling of despair." Surveying this body of doctrine in 1941, no less a lawyer than Judge Learned Hand declared with exasperation that courts "have mixed it up until nobody can tell what on earth it means." Whether things have improved since then is debatable. The law of presumptions today has few fans.

[F.R.E. 301, 302; C.E.C. §§110, 115, 500, 550, 600–670]

IN RE YODER CO.

758 F.2d 1114 (6th Cir. 1985)

CORNELIA G. KENNEDY, Circuit Judge.

In this Chapter 11 proceeding the Bankruptcy Court affirmed by the District Court, held that Mark S. Bratton's products liability claim for the loss of four fingers was barred for failure to timely file a proof of claim. Bratton contends that his claim should not be barred because he did not receive notice of the latest date for filing proofs of claim.

In 1981, Yoder filed a petition requesting relief under Chapter 11 of the Bankruptcy Code. At that time Bratton's products liability suit against Yoder was pending in a Michigan state court. Bratton's claim was listed as a "contingent, unliquidated and disputed" claim in the amended schedule of assets and liabilities filed by Yoder. The Bankruptcy Court issued an order setting July 13, 1981 as the last date for creditors to file proofs of claim against Yoder (the "bar date").

Bratton filed a proof of claim on March 15, 1982, about eight months after the bar date. Yoder applied to the Bankruptcy Court for an order expunging certain products liability claims, including Bratton's. Following a hearing on Yoder's application, at which Bratton was represented, the Bankruptcy Court found that Bratton had been sent sufficient notice of the bar date and that Bratton's failure to file timely proof of claim was not due to excusable neglect. Bratton's claim was therefore barred. The District Court affirmed, and Bratton appeals.

... Bratton's address on the amended schedule of assets and liabilities, the list which Yoder's employee testified was used to prepare the labels [for mailing notices of the bar date], was that of his attorney, A.T. Ornstein. Ornstein testified that he had not received notice of the bar date. Attorneys for two other listed products liability claimants also represented that they and their clients had not received notices of the bar date.

The Bankruptcy Court made a factual finding that notice of the bar date had been sent to Ornstein. The Court did not discuss its reasons for this finding or explain how it weighed the evidence, although the evidence concerning mailing was far from undisputed. . . . We do not need to decide whether the finding that notice was mailed was clearly erroneous, however, because we hold that the Bankruptcy Court abused its discretion in holding that Bratton did not file a late proof of claim as a result of excusable neglect. This holding was based on the closely related finding that Bratton's attorney received the notice, which we hold to be clearly erroneous.

Rule 906(b) of the Rules of Bankruptcy Procedure provides that a time period may be extended if failure to act in time "was the result of excusable neglect." . . . [N]onreceipt of notice would clearly constitute excusable neglect. The Bankruptcy Court's determination that no excusable neglect existed was based entirely on its finding that notice was received at Bratton's attorney's law firm. We thus turn to the question of whether this finding of receipt was clearly erroneous.

The Bankruptcy Court relied mainly on a presumption of receipt that it held arose from evidence that the notice was properly mailed. The common law has long recognized a presumption that an item properly mailed was received by the addressee. *Hagner v. United States*, 285 U.S. 427 (1932). The presumption arises upon proof that the item was properly addressed, had sufficient postage, and was deposited in the mail. *Simpson v. Jefferson Standard Life Insurance Co.*, 465 F.2d 1320, 1323 (6th Cir. 1972). For purposes of this discussion, we will assume that the presumption of receipt did arise.

The District Court held that the presumption had not been rebutted, reasoning that "testimony amounting to a mere denial that a properly mailed notice was not received is insufficient to rebut the presumption of receipt."[5] This statement is inconsistent with prior decisions of this Circuit. In *McKentry v. Secretary of HHS*, 655 F.2d 721 (6th Cir. 1981), the plaintiff and her attorney both filed affidavits that they had not received a notice of reconsideration from the Department of HHS. This Court held that this would have been sufficient evidence of nonreceipt to rebut the presumption of mailing, had it arisen. In *Baldwin v. Fidelity Phoenix Fire Insurance Co.*, 260 F.2d 951, 953 (6th Cir. 1958), there was evidence that a notice had been sent to an insurance company and to one of its agents. The agent testified that he had not received the notice. This Court held that the evidence was sufficient to support the jury's finding that notice was not received by the insurance company or the agent. These decisions are in consonance with the general proposition that a presumption is rebutted "upon the introduction of evidence which would support a finding of the nonexistence of the presumed fact." 10 Moore's Federal Practice ¶301.04[2] (2d ed.). Testimony of non-receipt, standing alone, would be sufficient to support a finding of non-receipt; such testimony is therefore sufficient to rebut the presumption of receipt.

The next question is whether the presumption, once rebutted, retains any effect.[7] The Bankruptcy Court found that it was "entitled to presume that notice has been received once a proper mailing is made, even though the intended recipient testifies that the notice never really came." The Bankruptcy Court reasoned as follows:

> According to the note of the Advisory Committee on Proposed Rules, Federal Rule 301 rejects the so-called "bursting bubble" theory, under which a presumption vanishes upon the introduction of evidence that negates the existence of the presumed fact. According to the Federal Rule, when evidence is put forth negating the fact that the presumption tends to support, the presumption still continues and is evidence to be weighed and considered with all of the other evidence in the case.

Federal Rule of Evidence 301 provides in part:

> [A] presumption imposes on the party against whom it is directed the burden of going forward with evidence to rebut or meet the presumption, but does not shift to such party the burden of proof in the sense of the risk of nonpersuasion, which remains throughout the trial upon the party on whom it was originally cast. A brief review of the history of this rule will aid in evaluating the Bankruptcy Court's reasoning. Before adoption of the Federal Rules of

---

5. To support the proposition that testimony of non-receipt does not rebut the presumption of receipt, the District Court relied on *In re Majors*, 19 B.R. 275 (Bankr. M.D. Tenn. 1982); *In re Torres*, 15 B.R. 794 (Bankr. E.D.N.Y. 1981); and *In re Heyward*, 15 B.R. 629 (Bankr. E.D.N.Y. 1981). These decisions are inconsistent with the common law views of presumptions and the law of this Circuit.

7. The fact sought to be established by the presumption is an element of a claim or defense to be determined under federal bankruptcy law, not state law. Federal law is therefore determinative of the effect of the presumption. Cf. Fed. R. Evid. 302.

Evidence there were two major theories concerning the effect of a presumption once rebuttal evidence is admitted. Under the Thayer or "bursting bubble" theory a presumption vanishes entirely once rebutted, and the question must be decided as any ordinary question of fact.[8] Under a later theory, proposed by Morgan, a presumption shifts the burden of proving the nonexistence of the presumed fact to the opposing party.

The version of Rule 301 that was proposed by the Advisory Committee, accepted by the Supreme Court, and submitted to Congress adopted the Morgan view.[10] That rule, however, was not enacted by Congress. The Advisory Committee notes, on which the Bankruptcy Court relied, that reject the "bursting bubble" theory pertain to the proposed rule, which was not enacted, and are thus of little help in interpreting the final rule.

The House of Representatives adopted a rule espousing an intermediate view, which would allow a rebutted presumption to be considered evidence of the fact presumed.[11] The Senate criticized the House rule on the ground that it made no sense to call a presumption evidence, and adopted the present language of Rule 301, which was adopted by the Conference Committee and enacted into law.

Most commentators have concluded that Rule 301 as enacted embodies the Thayer or "bursting bubble" approach. *See, e.g.*, 10 Moore's Federal Practice ¶301.04[4.-1] (2d ed.); 1 Weinstein's Evidence 301-12; IX Wigmore on Evidence §2493h (Chadbourn rev. 1981). *Contra* 21 C. Wright & K. Graham, Federal Practice and Procedure §§5121, 5122, 5126.[13]

8. The facts giving rise to the presumption often give rise to an inference that remains and may still be considered by the factfinder. See IX Wigmore on Evidence §2491 (Chadbourn rev. 1981) ("[T]he legal consequence [of the presumption] being removed, the inference, as a matter of reasoning, may still remain. . . .").

10. The text of the proposed rule was as follows: "In all cases not otherwise provided for by Act of Congress or by these rules a presumption imposes on the party against whom it is directed the burden of proving that the nonexistence of the presumed fact is more probable than its existence."

11. The House version of the rule was as follows: "In all civil actions and proceedings not otherwise provided for by Act of Congress or by these rules, a presumption imposes on the party against whom it is directed the burden of going forward with the evidence, and, even though met with contradicting evidence, a presumption is sufficient evidence of the fact presumed, to be considered by the trier of the facts."

13. Professors Wright and Graham interpret Rule 301 as providing that a rebutted presumption still suffices to carry the issue to the jury, which should be instructed that it may infer the presumed fact. 21 C. Wright & K. Graham, Federal Practice and Procedure §5122 at p. 572. This interpretation differs from the bursting bubble theory only in the effect given an "illogical" presumption, i.e., one where the facts giving rise to the presumption do not logically give rise to an inference that the presumed fact exists. See id. §5126 at pp. 609-1, 609 n.22. According to Wright and Graham, once an illogical presumption was rebutted the presumption would still have the effect of requiring that the question be sent to the jury with instructions that it may infer the presumed fact. Under the bursting bubble theory a rebutted illogical presumption would have no effect and the only evidence on the question would be the rebuttal evidence, which would be conclusive. However, in the case of a "logical" presumption, such as the presumption of receipt involved here, the jury would be allowed to consider the inference naturally drawn from the facts establishing the presumption whether or not the presumption is given any effect after rebuttal. Wright and Graham's interpretation would therefore have no effect on the present case.

Wright and Graham's conclusion that Rule 301 rejects the bursting bubble theory is based primarily on the Conference Committee's statement that: "If the adverse party does offer evidence contradicting the presumed fact, the court cannot instruct the jury that it may

At least two other circuit courts have expressly agreed. *Reeves v. General Foods Corp.*, 682 F.2d 515, 522 n. 10 (5th Cir. 1982); *Legille v. Dann*, 544 F.2d 1, 6-7 (D.C. Cir. 1976). The Thayer view is consistent with the language of Rule 301, which provides only that a presumption shifts "the burden of going forward with evidence to rebut or meet the presumption." Accordingly, we hold that a presumption under Rule 301 has no probative effect once rebutted. The Bankruptcy Court therefore erred in considering the presumption as evidence of receipt.

The only other evidence of receipt expressly considered by the Bankruptcy Court was that "Mr. Bratton's law firm did receive and respond to the notice setting debtor's objection to his claim for hearing." However, there was no evidence that the notices of the hearing were sent to the same addresses as were the notices of the bar date, which were sent more than a year earlier. The testimony was that no copy of the address labels made up for the bar date notices was kept, so a copy of those labels could not have been used to mail the later notices of the hearing on debtor's objections to claims. That Bratton received notice of the hearing is therefore not evidence that he received notice of the bar date.

The Bankruptcy Court erred in relying upon the presumption and notice of the hearing to establish receipt. Had it properly considered all the evidence it would have had to find that Bratton had not received notice. . . . The evidence other than Ornstein's testimony that he did not receive the notice is at best neutral. If the Bankruptcy Court had considered all the evidence without relying on a presumption and still found that notice was received, it would have been clearly erroneous. Non-receipt is sufficient ground for excusable neglect, and it is clear from the lower court opinions that had those courts found non-receipt the claim would have been allowed.

Accordingly, the judgment of the District Court is reversed and the case remanded for reversal of the Bankruptcy Court order expunging Bratton's claim.

LAW REVISION COMMISSION COMMENT TO CALIFORNIA EVIDENCE CODE §601

For several decades, courts and legal scholars have wrangled over the purpose and function of presumptions. The view espoused by Professors

---

presume the existence of the presumed fact from proof of the basic facts. *The court may, however, instruct the jury that it may infer the existence of the presumed fact from proof of the basic facts.* Id. §5121 n.27 (emphasis added). The emphasized portion of this quotation is not inconsistent with the bursting bubble theory. Nothing in the legislative history indicates that Congress was concerned with the distinction between "logical" and "illogical" presumptions. The statement that the jury may be instructed to consider an inference is most naturally read as permitting such an instruction when called for by the existence of a logical inference. An "inference" not based on logic is not an inference at all, but a presumption. Jurors would have no way to decide how much weight to give an "inference" drawn from a fact that their own logic tells them has no relevance to the question to be decided. The sentence immediately preceding the emphasized portion of the Conference Committee's report clearly indicates that the jury should not be allowed to apply a presumption once rebutted.

Thayer and Wigmore, accepted by most courts, and adopted by the American Law Institute's Model Code of Evidence, is that a presumption is a preliminary assumption of fact that disappears from the case upon the introduction of evidence sufficient to sustain a finding of the nonexistence of the presumed fact. In Professor Thayer's view, a presumption merely reflects the judicial determination that the same conclusionary fact exists so frequently when the preliminary fact exists that, once the preliminary fact is established, proof of the conclusionary fact may be dispensed with unless there is actually some contrary evidence:

> Many facts and groups of facts often recur, and when a body of men with a continuous tradition has carried on for some length of time this process of reasoning upon facts that often repeat themselves, they cut short the process and lay down a rule. To such facts they affix, by a general declaration, the character and operation which common experience has assigned to them. [Thayer, Preliminary Treatise on Evidence 326 (1898).]

Professors Morgan and McCormick argue that a presumption should shift the burden of proof to the adverse party. Morgan, Some Problems of Proof 81 (1956); McCormick, Evidence §317 at 671-672 (1954). They believe that presumptions are created for reasons of policy and argue that, if the policy underlying a presumption is of sufficient weight to require a finding of the presumed fact when there is no contrary evidence, it should be of sufficient weight to require a finding when the mind of the trier of fact is in equilibrium, and, *a fortiori*, it should be of sufficient weight to require a finding if the trier of fact does not believe the contrary evidence.

The classification of presumptions in the Evidence Code is based on a third view suggested by Professor Bohlen in 1920. Bohlen, The Effect of Rebuttable Presumptions of Law Upon the Burden of Proof, 68 U. Pa. L. Rev. 307 (1920). Underlying the presumptions provisions of the Evidence Code is the conclusion that the Thayer view is correct as to some presumptions, but that the Morgan view is right as to others. The fact is that presumptions are created for a variety of reasons, and no single theory or rationale of presumptions can deal adequately with all of them. Hence, the Evidence Code classifies all rebuttable presumptions as either (1) presumptions affecting the burden of producing evidence (essentially Thayer presumptions), or (2) presumptions affecting the burden of proof (essentially Morgan presumptions)....

CHRISTOPHER B. MUELLER & LAIRD C. KIRKPATRICK, EVIDENCE

§3.4, at 115-116 (5th ed. 2012)

Many terms are used to describe presumptions, and some are redundant or conflicting or have shifting meanings....

Conclusive or Irrebuttable Presumption. Substantive law sometimes borrows the language of presumptions. Under the Coal Mine Health and Safety Act of 1969, for example, a miner shown by X-ray or other clinical evidence to have pneumoconiosis (black lung disease) is "irrebuttably presumed" to be totally disabled, and the presumption "operates conclusively to establish entitlement to benefits." [*See* 30 U.S.C. §921] Under a California statute, it was irrebuttably presumed that a husband was the father of a child born to his wife during marriage (absent proof that they did not cohabit or that he was impotent), and the presumption still cannot be rebutted by ordinary evidence (testimony denying intercourse or evidence that the wife had intercourse with another). [*See* Cal. Evid. Code §621 (requiring finding of paternity unless blood tests indicate otherwise).] These rules are really not presumptions but substantive principles expressed in the language of presumptions.

Mandatory Presumption or Presumption of Law. Generally these terms refer to the true presumption. . . . A presumption controls decision if unopposed, so in jury-tried cases an instruction is in order and in bench trials the judge has no option but to find the presumed fact. "Mandatory" is redundant, and "presumption" by itself conveys the intended meaning.

Permissive Presumption, Inference, Presumption of Fact. These terms usually refer to conclusions that are permitted but not required. "Inference" is a better word to describe what is happening here. . . . Inference instructions amount to judicial comment on the evidence, almost nudging or inviting the jury to draw a conclusion. . . .

PROBLEMS

12.1. Section 641 of the California Evidence Code, classified as a Thayer presumption, provides that "[a] letter correctly addressed and properly mailed is presumed to have been received in the ordinary course of mail." Suppose a California tenant slips in the hallway of her apartment building and breaks her collarbone. She files a diversity suit against her out-of-state landlord for medical costs and lost wages. To prove negligence, the tenant testifies that three weeks before the accident she mailed the landlord a correctly addressed, properly stamped letter complaining that the hallway was slippery. The landlord testifies he never received the letter. The tenant asks the judge to instruct the jury that, if they conclude that her letter was correctly addressed and properly mailed, they must find that it was received in the ordinary course of the mail. Should the judge give the instruction?

12.2. Section 667 of the California Evidence Code, classified as a Morgan presumption, provides that "[a] person not heard from in five years is presumed to be dead." Suppose a testator in California leaves his house to his son, Saul, for the duration of Saul's life, but provides that on Saul's death the property will go to the State of California. Six years later the state sues Saul's wife, who is living in the house, for possession. The state introduces evidence that no one has heard from Saul for the past five years. The defendant testifies that she received a telephone call from Saul eight months ago. What instruction, if any, should the judge give the jury regarding the presumption?

12.3. Section 636 of the California Evidence Code, classified as a Thayer presumption, provides that "[t]he payment of earlier rent or installments is presumed from a receipt for later rent or installments." Suppose a California construction company buys a bulldozer from an out-of-state vendor. The bulldozer repeatedly breaks down, and five years after the purchase the construction company brings a federal diversity action against the vendor, alleging breach of warranty. The plaintiff introduces the purchase contract, which calls for payment in four annual installments, and a receipt for payment of the fourth installment. The defendant claims in its pleadings that the first three installments were never paid, but introduces no evidence to this effect and does not challenge the authenticity of the receipt. Is the plaintiff entitled to a directed verdict on the question of its payments for the bulldozer?

B. Burdens and Presumptions in Criminal Cases

The rules regarding burdens and presumptions in criminal cases can be even more puzzling than the parallel rules for civil cases. This is partly because of confusing terminology — distinguishing, for example, between "mandatory" and "permissive" presumptions. As the treatise excerpt at the end of the previous section explained, *all* true presumptions — including both Thayer presumptions and Morgan presumptions — are "mandatory" in the sense used by the Supreme Court.

The operation of presumptions in criminal cases is also complicated by the constitutional requirement that the prosecution shoulder the burden of proving guilt "beyond a reasonable doubt." As you will see, the Supreme Court has construed this requirement to prohibit shifting the burden of persuasion to a criminal defendant with regard to any element of the offense. But, as the following cases also demonstrate, the Court has found it difficult to reach agreement regarding the proper reach of that prohibition.

PATTERSON v. NEW YORK

432 U.S. 197 (1977)

Mr. Justice WHITE delivered the opinion of the Court.

. . . After a brief and unstable marriage, the appellant, Gordon Patterson, Jr., became estranged from his wife, Roberta. Roberta resumed an association with John Northrup, a neighbor to whom she had been engaged prior to her marriage to appellant. On December 27, 1970, Patterson borrowed a rifle from an acquaintance and went to the residence of his father-in-law. There, he observed his wife through a window in a state of semiundress in the presence of John Northrup. He entered the house and killed Northrup by shooting him twice in the head.

Patterson was charged with second-degree murder. In New York there are two elements of this crime: (1) "intent to cause the death of another person"; and (2) "caus[ing] the death of such person or of a third person." N.Y. Penal Law §125.25 (McKinney 1975). Malice aforethought is not an element of the crime. In addition, the State permits a person accused of murder to raise an affirmative defense that he "acted under the influence of extreme emotional disturbance for which there was a reasonable explanation or excuse."

New York also recognizes the crime of manslaughter. A person is guilty of manslaughter if he intentionally kills another person "under circumstances which do not constitute murder because he acts under the influence of extreme emotional disturbance." Appellant confessed before trial to killing Northrup, but at trial he raised the defense of extreme emotional disturbance.

The jury was instructed as to the elements of the crime of murder. Focusing on the element of intent, the trial court charged:

> "Before you, considering all of the evidence, can convict this defendant or any-one of murder, you must believe and decide that the People have established beyond a reasonable doubt that he intended, in firing the gun, to kill either the victim himself or some other human being....
>
> "Always remember that you must not expect or require the defendant to prove to your satisfaction that his acts were done without the intent to kill. Whatever proof he may have attempted, however far he may have gone in an effort to convince you of his innocence or guiltlessness, he is not obliged, he is not obligated to prove anything. It is always the People's burden to prove his guilt, and to prove that he intended to kill in this instance beyond a reasonable doubt."

The jury was further instructed, consistently with New York law, that the defendant had the burden of proving his affirmative defense by a preponderance of the evidence. The jury was told that if it found beyond a reasonable doubt that appellant had intentionally killed Northrup but that appellant had demonstrated by a preponderance of the evidence that he had acted under the influence of extreme emotional disturbance, it had to find appellant guilty of manslaughter instead of murder.

The jury found appellant guilty of murder. Judgment was entered on the verdict, and the Appellate Division affirmed. While appeal to the New York Court of Appeals was pending, this Court decided *Mullaney v. Wilbur*, 421 U.S. 684 (1975), in which the Court declared Maine's murder statute unconstitutional. Under the Maine statute, a person accused of murder could rebut the statutory presumption that he committed the offense with "malice afore-thought" by proving that he acted in the heat of passion on sudden provocation. The Court held that this scheme improperly shifted the burden of persuasion from the prosecutor to the defendant and was therefore a violation of due process. In the Court of Appeals appellant urged that New York's murder statute is functionally equivalent to the one struck down in Mullaney and that therefore his conviction should be reversed.

The Court of Appeals rejected appellant's argument, holding that the New York murder statute is consistent with due process. The Court distinguished Mullaney on the ground that the New York statute involved no shifting of the burden to the defendant to disprove any fact essential to the offense charged since the New York affirmative defense of extreme emotional disturbance bears no direct relationship to any element of murder.... We AFFIRM.

... [I]t is normally "within the power of the State to regulate procedures under which its laws are carried out, including the burden of producing evidence and the burden of persuasion," and its decision in this regard is not subject to proscription under the Due Process Clause unless "it offends some principle of justice so rooted in the traditions and conscience of our people as to be ranked as fundamental." *Speiser v. Randall*, 357 U.S. 513, 523 (1958); *Leland v. Oregon*, 343 U.S. 790, 798 (1952); *Snyder v. Massachusetts*, 291 U.S. 97, 105 (1934).

In determining whether New York's allocation to the defendant of proving the mitigating circumstances of severe emotional disturbance is consistent with due process, it is therefore relevant to note that this defense is a considerably expanded version of the common-law defense of heat of passion on sudden provocation and that at common law the burden of proving the latter, as well as other affirmative defenses indeed, "all . . . circumstances of justification, excuse or alleviation" rested on the defendant. 4 W. Blackstone, Commentaries *201; M. Foster, Crown Law 255 (1762); *Mullaney v. Wilbur*. This was the rule when the Fifth Amendment was adopted, and it was the American rule when the Fourteenth Amendment was ratified. *Commonwealth v. York*, 50 Mass. 93 (1845).

In 1895 the common-law view was abandoned with respect to the insanity defense in federal prosecutions. *Davis v. United States*, 160 U.S. 469 (1895). This ruling had wide impact on the practice in the federal courts with respect to the burden of proving various affirmative defenses, and the prosecution in a majority of jurisdictions in this country sooner or later came to shoulder the burden of proving the sanity of the accused and of disproving the facts constituting other affirmative defenses, including provocation. *Davis* was not a constitutional ruling, however, as *Leland v. Oregon* made clear.

At issue in *Leland v. Oregon* was the constitutionality under the Due Process Clause of the Oregon rule that the defense on insanity must be proved by the defendant beyond a reasonable doubt. Noting that *Davis* "obviously establish[ed] no constitutional doctrine," the Court refused to strike down the Oregon scheme, saying that the burden of proving all elements of the crime beyond reasonable doubt, including the elements of premeditation and deliberation, was placed on the State under Oregon procedures and remained there throughout the trial. To convict, the jury was required to find each element of the crime beyond a reasonable doubt, based on all the evidence, including the evidence going to the issue of insanity. Only then was the jury "to consider separately the issue of legal sanity per se. . . ." This practice did not offend the Due Process Clause even though among the 20 States then placing the burden of proving his insanity on the defendant, Oregon was alone in requiring him to convince the jury beyond a reasonable doubt.

In 1970, the Court declared that the Due Process Clause "protects the accused against conviction except upon proof beyond a reasonable doubt of every fact necessary to constitute the crime with which he is charged." *In re Winship*, 397 U.S. 358, 364 (1970). Five years later, in *Mullaney v. Wilbur*, 421 U.S. 684, 95 S. Ct. 1881, 44 L. Ed. 2d 508 (1975), the Court further announced that under the Maine law of homicide, the burden could not constitutionally be placed on the defendant of proving by a preponderance of the evidence that the killing had occurred in the heat of passion on sudden provocation. The Chief Justice and Mr. Justice Rehnquist, concurring, expressed their understanding that the *Mullaney* decision did not call into question the ruling in *Leland v. Oregon* with respect to the proof of insanity.

Subsequently, the Court confirmed that it remained constitutional to burden the defendant with proving his insanity defense when it dismissed, as not raising a substantial federal question, a case in which the appellant specifically challenged the continuing validity of *Leland v. Oregon*. This occurred in *Rivera v. Delaware*, 429 U.S. 877 (1976), an appeal from a Delaware conviction which, in reliance on *Leland*, had been affirmed by the Delaware Supreme Court over the claim that the Delaware statute was unconstitutional because it burdened the defendant with proving his affirmative defense of insanity by a preponderance of the evidence. The claim in this Court was that *Leland* had been overruled by *Winship* and *Mullaney*. We dismissed the appeal as not presenting a substantial federal question.

We cannot conclude that Patterson's conviction under the New York law deprived him of due process of law. The crime of murder is defined by the statute, which represents a recent revision of the state criminal code, as causing the death of another person with intent to do so. The death, the intent to kill, and causation are the facts that the State is required to prove beyond a reasonable doubt if a person is to be convicted of murder. No further facts are either presumed or inferred in order to constitute the crime. The statute does provide an affirmative defense that the defendant acted under the influence of extreme emotional disturbance for which there was a reasonable explanation which, if proved by a preponderance of the evidence, would reduce the crime to manslaughter, an offense defined in a separate section of the statute. It is plain enough that if the intentional killing is shown, the State intends to deal with the defendant as a murderer unless he demonstrates the mitigating circumstances.

Here, the jury was instructed in accordance with the statute, and the guilty verdict confirms that the State successfully carried its burden of proving the facts of the crime beyond a reasonable doubt. Nothing in the evidence, including any evidence that might have been offered with respect to Patterson's mental state at the time of the crime, raised a reasonable doubt about his guilt as a murderer; and clearly the evidence failed to convince the jury that Patterson's affirmative defense had been made out. It seems to us that the State satisfied the mandate of *Winship* that it prove beyond a reasonable doubt "every fact necessary to constitute the crime with which [Patterson was] charged."

In convicting Patterson under its murder statute, New York did no more than *Leland* and *Rivera* permitted it to do without violating the Due Process Clause. Under those cases, once the facts constituting a crime are established beyond a reasonable doubt, based on all the evidence including the evidence of the defendant's mental state, the State may refuse to sustain the affirmative defense of insanity unless demonstrated by a preponderance of the evidence.

The New York law on extreme emotional disturbance follows this pattern. This affirmative defense, which the Court of Appeals described as permitting "the defendant to show that his actions were caused by a mental infirmity not arising to the level of insanity, and that he is less culpable for having committed them," does not serve to negative any facts of the crime which the State is to prove in order to convict of murder. It constitutes a separate issue on which the defendant is required to carry the burden of persuasion; and unless we are to overturn *Leland* and *Rivera*, New York has not violated the Due Process Clause, and Patterson's conviction must be sustained.

We are unwilling to reconsider *Leland* and *Rivera*. But even if we were to hold that a State must prove sanity to convict once that fact is put in issue, it would not necessarily follow that a State must prove beyond a reasonable doubt every fact, the existence or nonexistence of which it is willing to recognize as an exculpatory or mitigating circumstance affecting the degree of culpability or the severity of the punishment. Here in revising its criminal code, New York provided the affirmative defense of extreme emotional disturbance, a substantially expanded version of the older heat-of-passion concept; but it was willing to do so only if the facts making out the defense were established by the defendant with sufficient certainty. The State was itself unwilling to undertake to establish the absence of those facts beyond a reasonable doubt, perhaps fearing that proof would be too difficult and that too many persons deserving treatment as murderers would escape that punishment if the evidence need merely raise a reasonable doubt about the defendant's emotional state. It has been said that the new criminal code of New York contains some 25 affirmative defenses which exculpate or mitigate but which must be established by the defendant to be operative.[10]

The Due Process Clause, as we see it, does not put New York to the choice of abandoning those defenses or undertaking to disprove their existence in order to convict of a crime which otherwise is within its constitutional powers to sanction by substantial punishment.

. . . It is said that the common-law rule permits a State to punish one as a murderer when it is as likely as not that he acted in the heat of passion or under severe emotional distress and when, if he did, he is guilty only of manslaughter. But this has always been the case in those jurisdictions adhering to the traditional rule. It is also very likely true that fewer convictions of murder would occur if New York were required to negative the affirmative defense at issue here. But in each instance of a murder conviction under the present law New York will have proved beyond a reasonable doubt that the defendant has intentionally killed another person, an act which it is not disputed the State may constitutionally criminalize and punish. If the State nevertheless chooses to recognize a factor that mitigates the degree of criminality or punishment, we think the State may assure itself that the fact has been established with

---

10. The State of New York is not alone in this result: "Since the Model Penal Code was completed in 1962, some 22 states have codified and reformed their criminal laws. At least 12 of these jurisdictions have used the concept of an 'affirmative defense' and have defined that phrase to require that the defendant prove the existence of an 'affirmative defense' by a preponderance of the evidence. Additionally, at least six proposed state codes and each of the four successive versions of a revised federal code use the same procedural device. Finally, many jurisdictions that do not generally employ this concept of 'affirmative defense' nevertheless shift the burden of proof to the defendant on particular issues." Low & Jeffries, DICTA: Constitutionalizing the Criminal Law?, 29 Va. Law Weekly, No. 18, p. 1 (1977) (footnotes omitted).

Even so, the trend over the years appears to have been to require the prosecution to disprove affirmative defenses beyond a reasonable doubt. See W. LaFave & A. Scott, Criminal Law §8, p. 50 (1972); C. McCormick, Evidence §341, pp. 800-802 (2d ed. 1972). The split among the various jurisdictions varies for any given defense. Thus, 22 jurisdictions place the burden of proving the affirmative defense of insanity on the defendant, while 28 jurisdictions place the burden of disproving insanity on the prosecution. Note, Constitutional Limitations on Allocating the Burden of Proof of Insanity to the Defendant in Murder Cases, 56 B.U. L. Rev. 499, 503-505 (1976).

reasonably certainty. To recognize at all a mitigating circumstance does not require the State to prove its nonexistence in each case in which the fact is put in issue, if in its judgment this would be too cumbersome, too expensive, and too inaccurate.[11]

. . . This view may seem to permit state legislatures to reallocate burdens of proof by labeling as affirmative defenses at least some elements of the crimes now defined in their statutes. But there are obviously constitutional limits beyond which the States may not go in this regard. "[I]t is not within the province of a legislature to declare an individual guilty or presumptively guilty of a crime." *McFarland v. American Sugar Rfg. Co.*, 241 U.S. 79, 86 (1916). The legislature cannot "validly command that the finding of an indictment, or mere proof of the identity of the accused, should create a presumption of the existence of all the facts essential to guilt." *Tot v. United States*, 319 U.S. 463, 469 (1943). . . .

Mullaney . . . held that a State must prove every ingredient of an offense beyond a reasonable doubt, and that it may not shift the burden of proof to the defendant by presuming that ingredient upon proof of the other elements of the offense. . . . Such shifting of the burden of persuasion with respect to a fact which the State deems so important that it must be either proved or presumed is impermissible under the Due Process Clause.

. . . [A] killing became murder in Maine when it resulted from a deliberate, cruel act committed by one person against another, "suddenly without any, or without a considerable provocation." Premeditation was not within the definition of murder; but malice, in the sense of the absence of provocation, was part of the definition of that crime. Yet malice, i.e., lack of provocation, was presumed and could be rebutted by the defendant only by proving by a preponderance of the evidence that he acted with heat of passion upon sudden provocation. In *Mullaney* we held that however traditional this mode of proceeding might have been, it is contrary to the Due Process Clause as construed in *Winship*.

As we have explained, nothing was presumed or implied against Patterson; and his conviction is not invalid under any of our prior cases. The judgment of the New York Court of Appeals is

Affirmed.

Mr. Justice POWELL, with whom Mr. Justice BRENNAN and Mr. Justice MARSHALL join, dissenting.

---

11. The drafters of the Model Penal Code would, as a matter of policy, place the burden of proving the nonexistence of most affirmative defenses, including the defense involved in this case, on the prosecution once the defendant has come forward with some evidence that the defense is present. The drafters recognize the need for flexibility, however, and would, in "some exceptional situations," place the burden of persuasion on the accused.

"Characteristically these are situations where the defense does not obtain at all under existing law and the Code seeks to introduce a mitigation. Resistance to the mitigation, based upon the prosecution's difficulty in obtaining evidence, ought to be lowered if the burden of persuasion is imposed on the defendant. Where that difficulty appears genuine and there is something to be said against allowing the defense at all, we consider it defensible to shift the burden in this way." ALI Model Penal Code §1.13, Comment, p. 113 (Tent. Draft No. 4, 1955).

Other writers have recognized the need for flexibility in allocating the burden of proof in order to enhance the potential for liberal legislative reforms. . . .

... The test the Court today establishes allows a legislature to shift, virtually at will, the burden of persuasion with respect to any factor in a criminal case, so long as it is careful not to mention the nonexistence of that factor in the statutory language that defines the crime. The sole requirement is that any references to the factor be confined to those sections that provide for an affirmative defense.... What *Winship* and *Mullaney* had sought to teach about the limits a free society places on its procedures to safeguard the liberty of its citizens becomes a rather simplistic lesson in statutory draftsmanship. Nothing in the Court's opinion prevents a legislature from applying this new learning to many of the classical elements of the crimes it punishes. It would be preferable, if the Court has found reason to reject the rationale of *Winship* and *Mullaney*, simply and straightforwardly to overrule those precedents....

COUNTY COURT OF ULSTER COUNTY v. ALLEN

442 U.S. 140 (1979)

Mr. Justice STEVENS delivered the opinion of the Court.

A New York statute provides that, with certain exceptions, the presence of a firearm in an automobile is presumptive evidence of its illegal possession by all persons then occupying the vehicle.... Four persons, three adult males (respondents) and a 16-year-old girl (Jane Doe, who is not a respondent here), were jointly tried on charges that they possessed two loaded handguns, a loaded machinegun, and over a pound of heroin found in a Chevrolet in which they were riding when it was stopped for speeding on the New York Thruway shortly after noon on March 28, 1973. The two large-caliber handguns, which together with their ammunition weighed approximately six pounds, were seen through the window of the car by the investigating police officer. They were positioned crosswise in an open handbag on either the front floor or the front seat of the car on the passenger side where Jane Doe was sitting. Jane Doe admitted that the handbag was hers. The machinegun and the heroin were discovered in the trunk after the police pried it open. The car had been borrowed from the driver's brother earlier that day; the key to the trunk could not be found in the car or on the person of any of its occupants, although there was testimony that two of the occupants had placed something in the trunk before embarking in the borrowed car. The jury convicted all four of possession of the handguns and acquitted them of possession of the contents of the trunk.

Counsel for all four defendants objected to the introduction into evidence of the two handguns, the machinegun, and the drugs, arguing that the State had not adequately demonstrated a connection between their clients and the contraband. The trial court overruled the objection, relying on the presumption of possession created by the New York statute. Because that presumption does not apply if a weapon is found "upon the person" of one of the occupants of the car, the three male defendants also moved to dismiss the charges relating to the handguns on the ground that the guns were found on the person of Jane Doe. Respondents made this motion both at the close of the prosecution's case and at the close of all evidence. The trial judge twice

denied it, concluding that the applicability of the "upon the person" exception
was a question of fact for the jury.

At the close of the trial, the judge instructed the jurors that they were
entitled to infer possession from the defendants' presence in the car. He did
not make any reference to the "upon the person" exception in his explanation of the statutory presumption, nor did any of the defendants object
to this omission or request alternative or additional instructions on the
subject.

. . . [Following affirmance of their convictions, the defendants] filed a
petition for a writ of habeas corpus in the United States District Court for the
Southern District of New York contending that they were denied due process
of law by the application of the statutory presumption of possession. The
District Court issued the writ, holding that . . . the mere presence of two guns
in a woman's handbag in a car could not reasonably give rise to the inference
that they were in the possession of three other persons in the car.

The Court of Appeals for the Second Circuit affirmed, . . . [concluding]
that the statute is unconstitutional on its face because the "presumption obviously sweeps within its compass (1) many occupants who may not know they
are riding with a gun (which may be out of their sight), and (2) many who may
be aware of the presence of the gun but not permitted access to it." . . .

Inferences and presumptions are a staple of our adversary system of fact-
finding. It is often necessary for the trier of fact to determine the existence
of an element of the crime — that is, an "ultimate" or "elemental" fact — from
the existence of one or more "evidentiary" or "basic" facts. The value of these
evidentiary devices, and their validity under the Due Process Clause, vary
from case to case, however, depending on the strength of the connection
between the particular basic and elemental facts involved and on the degree
to which the device curtails the factfinder's freedom to assess the evidence
independently. Nonetheless, in criminal cases, the ultimate test of any device's
constitutional validity in a given case remains constant: the device must not
undermine the factfinder's responsibility at trial, based on evidence adduced
by the State, to find the ultimate facts beyond a reasonable doubt. *See In re
Winship*, 397 U.S. 358, 364; *Mullaney v. Wilbur*, 421 U.S. [684], 702-703 n.31.

The most common evidentiary device is the entirely permissive inference
or presumption, which allows — but does not require — the trier of fact to infer
the elemental fact from proof by the prosecutor of the basic one and which
places no burden of any kind on the defendant. In that situation the basic fact
may constitute prima facie evidence of the elemental fact. . . . Because this
permissive presumption leaves the trier of fact free to credit or reject the inference and does not shift the burden of proof, it affects the application of the
"beyond a reasonable doubt" standard only if, under the facts of the case, there
is no rational way the trier could make the connection permitted by the inference. For only in that situation is there any risk that an explanation of the permissible inference to a jury, or its use by a jury, has caused the presumptively
rational factfinder to make an erroneous factual determination.

A mandatory presumption is a far more troublesome evidentiary device.
For it may affect not only the strength of the "no reasonable doubt" burden but
also the placement of that burden; it tells the trier that he or they must find
the elemental fact upon proof of the basic fact, at least unless the defendant

has come forward with some evidence to rebut the presumed connection between the two facts.[16]

In this situation, the Court has generally examined the presumption on its face to determine the extent to which the basic and elemental facts coincide. To the extent that the trier of fact is forced to abide by the presumption, and may not reject it based on an independent evaluation of the particular facts presented by the State, the analysis of the presumption's constitutional validity is logically divorced from those facts and based on the presumption's accuracy in the run of cases.[17]

It is for this reason that the Court has held it irrelevant in analyzing a mandatory presumption, but not in analyzing a purely permissive one, that there is ample evidence in the record other than the presumption to support a conviction.

Without determining whether the presumption in this case was mandatory, the Court of Appeals analyzed it on its face as if it were. In fact, it was

16. This class of more or less mandatory presumptions can be subdivided into two parts: presumptions that merely shift the burden of production to the defendant, following the satisfaction of which the ultimate burden of persuasion returns to the prosecution; and presumptions that entirely shift the burden of proof to the defendant. The mandatory presumptions examined by our cases have almost uniformly fit into the former subclass, in that they never totally removed the ultimate burden of proof beyond a reasonable doubt from the prosecution.

To the extent that a presumption imposes an extremely low burden of production — e.g., being satisfied by "any" evidence — it may well be that its impact is no greater than that of a permissive inference, and it may be proper to analyze it as such. *See generally Mullaney v. Wilbur*, 421 U.S. 684, 703 n.31.

In deciding what type of inference or presumption is involved in a case, the jury instructions will generally be controlling, although their interpretation may require recourse to the statute involved and the cases decided under it. . . .

17. [T]his point is illustrated by *Leary v. United States*[, 395 U.S. 6 (1969)]. In that case, Dr. Timothy Leary, a professor at Harvard University, was stopped by customs inspectors in Laredo, Tex., as he was returning from the Mexican side of the international border. Marihuana seeds and a silver snuffbox filled with semirefined marihuana and three partially smoked marihuana cigarettes were discovered in his car. He was convicted of having knowingly transported marihuana which he knew had been illegally imported into this country in violation of 21 U.S.C. §176a (1964 ed.). That statute included a mandatory presumption: "possession shall be deemed sufficient evidence to authorize conviction [for importation] unless the defendant explains his possession to the satisfaction of the jury." Leary admitted possession of the marihuana and claimed that he had carried it from New York to Mexico and then back.

Mr. Justice Harlan for the Court noted that under one theory of the case, the jury could have found direct proof of all of the necessary elements of the offense without recourse to the presumption. But he deemed that insufficient reason to affirm the conviction because under another theory the jury might have found knowledge of importation on the basis of either direct evidence or the presumption, and there was accordingly no certainty that the jury had not relied on the presumption. The Court therefore found it necessary to test the presumption against the Due Process Clause. Its analysis was facial. Despite the fact that the defendant was well educated and had recently traveled to a country that is a major exporter of marihuana to this country, the Court found the presumption of knowledge of importation from possession irrational. It did so, not because Dr. Leary was unlikely to know the source of the marihuana, but instead because "a majority of possessors" were unlikely to have such knowledge. Because the jury had been instructed to rely on the presumption even if it did not believe the Government's direct evidence of knowledge of importation (unless, of course, the defendant met his burden of "satisfying" the jury to the contrary), the Court reversed the conviction.

not. . . . The trial judge's instructions make it clear that the presumption was merely a part of the prosecution's case,[19] that it gave rise to a permissive inference available only in certain circumstances, rather than a mandatory conclusion of possession, and that it could be ignored by the jury even if there was no affirmative proof offered by defendants in rebuttal.[20]

The judge explained that possession could be actual or constructive, but that constructive possession could not exist without the intent and ability to exercise control or dominion over the weapons.[21] He also carefully instructed the jury that there is a mandatory presumption of innocence in favor of the defendants that controls unless it, as the exclusive trier of fact, is satisfied beyond a reasonable doubt that the defendants possessed the handguns in the manner described by the judge.[22]

19. "It is your duty to consider all the testimony in this case, to weigh it carefully and to test the credit to be given to a witness by his apparent intention to speak the truth and by the accuracy of his memory to reconcile, if possible, conflicting statements as to material facts and in such ways to try and get at the truth and to reach a verdict upon the evidence." Tr. 739-740.

"To establish the unlawful possession of the weapons, again the people relied upon the presumption and, in addition thereto, the testimony of Anderson and Lemmons who testified in their case in chief." *Id.*, at 744.

"Accordingly, you would be warranted in returning a verdict of guilt against the defendants or defendant if you find the defendants or defendant was in possession of a machine gun and the other weapons and that the fact of possession was proven to you by the People beyond a reasonable doubt, and an element of such proof is the reasonable presumption of illegal possession of a machine gun or the presumption of illegal possession of firearms, as I have just before explained to you." *Id.*, at 746.

20. "Our Penal Law also provides that the presence in an automobile of any machine gun or of any handgun or firearm which is loaded is presumptive evidence of their unlawful possession.

"In other words, these presumptions or this latter presumption upon proof of the presence of the machine gun and the hand weapons, you may infer and draw a conclusion that such prohibited weapon was possessed by each of the defendants who occupied the automobile at the time when such instruments were found. The presumption or presumptions is effective only so long as there is no substantial evidence contradicting the conclusion flowing from the presumption, and the presumption is said to disappear when such contradictory evidence is adduced." *Id.*, at 743.

"The presumption or presumptions which I discussed with the jury relative to the drugs or weapons in this case need not be rebutted by affirmative proof or affirmative evidence but may be rebutted by any evidence or lack of evidence in the case." *Id.*, at 760.

21. "As so defined, possession means actual physical possession, just as having the drugs or weapons in one's hand, in one's home or other place under one's exclusive control, or constructive possession which may exist without personal dominion over the drugs or weapons but with the intent and ability to retain such control or dominion." *Id.*, at 742.

22. "[Y]ou are the exclusive judges of all the questions of fact in this case. That means that you are the sole judges as to the weight to be given to the evidence and to the weight and probative value to be given to the testimony of each particular witness and to the credibility of any witness." *Id.*, at 730.

"Under our law, every defendant in a criminal trial starts the trial with the presumption in his favor that he is innocent, and this presumption follows him throughout the entire trial and remains with him until such time as you, by your verdict, find him or her guilty beyond a reasonable doubt or innocent of the charge. If you find him or her not guilty, then, of course, this presumption ripens into an established fact. On the other hand, if you find him or her guilty, then this presumption has been overcome and is destroyed." *Id.*, at 734.

"Now, in order to find any of the defendants guilty of the unlawful possession of the weapons, the machine gun, the .45 and the .38, you must be satisfied beyond a reasonable doubt that the defendants possessed the machine gun and the .45 and the .38, possessed it as I defined it to you before." *Id.*, at 745.

In short, the instructions plainly directed the jury to consider all the circumstances tending to support or contradict the inference that all four occupants of the car had possession of the two loaded handguns and to decide the matter for itself without regard to how much evidence the defendants introduced. . . .

As applied to the facts of this case, the presumption of possession is entirely rational. Notwithstanding the Court of Appeals' analysis, respondents were not "hitchhikers or other casual passengers," and the guns were neither "a few inches in length" nor "out of [respondents'] sight." The argument against possession by any of the respondents was predicated solely on the fact that the guns were in Jane Doe's pocketbook. But several circumstances — which, not surprisingly, her counsel repeatedly emphasized in his questions and his argument — made it highly improbable that she was the sole custodian of those weapons.

Even if it was reasonable to conclude that she had placed the guns in her purse before the car was stopped by police, the facts strongly suggest that Jane Doe was not the only person able to exercise dominion over them. The two guns were too large to be concealed in her handbag. The bag was consequently open, and part of one of the guns was in plain view, within easy access of the driver of the car and even, perhaps, of the other two respondents who were riding in the rear seat.

Moreover, it is highly improbable that the loaded guns belonged to Jane Doe or that she was solely responsible for their being in her purse. As a 16-year-old girl in the company of three adult men she was the least likely of the four to be carrying one, let alone two, heavy handguns. It is far more probable that she relied on the pocketknife found in her brassiere for any necessary self-protection. Under these circumstances, it was not unreasonable for her counsel to argue and for the jury to infer that when the car was halted for speeding, the other passengers in the car anticipated the risk of a search and attempted to conceal their weapons in a pocketbook in the front seat. The inference is surely more likely than the notion that these weapons were the sole property of the 16-year-old girl.

Under these circumstances, the jury would have been entirely reasonable in rejecting the suggestion — which, incidentally, defense counsel did not even advance in their closing arguments to the jury — that the handguns were in the sole possession of Jane Doe. Assuming that the jury did reject it, the case is tantamount to one in which the guns were lying on the floor or the seat of the car in the plain view of the three other occupants of the automobile. In such a case, it is surely rational to infer that each of the respondents was fully aware of the presence of the guns and had both the ability and the intent to exercise dominion and control over the weapons. The application of the statutory presumption in this case therefore comports with the standard laid down in *Tot v. United States*, 319 U.S. [463, 467 (1943)], and restated in *Leary v. United States*, 395 U.S. [6, 36 (1969)]. For there is a "rational connection" between the basic facts that the prosecution proved and the ultimate fact presumed, and the latter is "more likely than not to flow from" the former. . . .

The judgment is reversed. . . .

[Chief Justice Burger filed a concurring opinion. Justice Powell filed a dissenting opinion, joined by Justice Brennan, Justice Stewart, and Justice Marshall.]

SANDSTROM v. MONTANA

442 U.S. 510 (1979)

Mr. Justice BRENNAN delivered the opinion of the Court.

The question presented is whether, in a case in which intent is an element of the crime charged, the jury instruction, "the law presumes that a person intends the ordinary consequences of his voluntary acts," violates the Fourteenth Amendment's requirement that the State prove every element of a criminal offense beyond a reasonable doubt.

On November 22, 1976, 18-year-old David Sandstrom confessed to the slaying of Annie Jessen. Based upon the confession and corroborating evidence, petitioner was charged on December 2 with "deliberate homicide," Mont. Code Ann. §45-5-102 (1978), in that he "purposely or knowingly caused the death of Annie Jessen." At trial, Sandstrom's attorney informed the jury that, although his client admitted killing Jessen, he did not do so "purposely or knowingly," and was therefore not guilty of "deliberate homicide" but of a lesser crime. The basic support for this contention was the testimony of two court-appointed mental health experts, each of whom described for the jury petitioner's mental state at the time of the incident. Sandstrom's attorney argued that this testimony demonstrated that petitioner, due to a personality disorder aggravated by alcohol consumption, did not kill Annie Jessen "purposely or knowingly."

The prosecution requested the trial judge to instruct the jury that "[t]he law presumes that a person intends the ordinary consequences of his voluntary acts." Petitioner's counsel objected, arguing that "the instruction has the effect of shifting the burden of proof on the issue of" purpose or knowledge to the defense, and that "that is impermissible under the Federal Constitution, due process of law." ... The instruction was delivered, the jury found petitioner guilty of deliberate homicide, and petitioner was sentenced to 100 years in prison.

Sandstrom appealed to the Supreme Court of Montana, again contending that the instruction shifted to the defendant the burden of disproving an element of the crime charged, in violation of *Mullaney v. Wilbur*, [421 U.S. 684 (1975),] *In re Winship*, 397 U.S. 358 (1980), and *Patterson v. New York*, 432 U.S. 197 (1977). The Montana court conceded that these cases did prohibit shifting the burden of proof to the defendant by means of a presumption, but held that the cases "do not prohibit allocation of *some* burden of proof to a defendant under certain circumstances." Since in the court's view, "[d]efendant's sole burden ... was to produce *some* evidence that he did not intend the ordinary consequences of his voluntary acts, not to disprove that he acted 'purposely' or 'knowingly,' ... the instruction does not violate due process standards as defined by the United States or Montana Constitution. ..." ... We reverse.

The threshold inquiry in ascertaining the constitutional analysis applicable to this kind of jury instruction is to determine the nature of the presumption it describes. See *Ulster County Court v. Allen*, 442 U.S. 140 (1979). That determination requires careful attention to the words actually spoken to the jury, see *id.*, for whether a defendant has been accorded his constitutional rights depends upon the way in which a reasonable juror could have interpreted the instruction.

Respondent argues, first, that the instruction merely described a permissive inference — that is, it allowed but did not require the jury to draw conclusions about defendant's intent from his actions — and that such inferences are constitutional. These arguments need not detain us long, for even respondent admits that "it's possible" that the jury believed they were required to apply the presumption. Sandstrom's jurors were told that "[t]he law presumes that a person intends the ordinary consequences of his voluntary acts." They were not told that they had a choice, or that they might infer that conclusion; they were told only that the law presumed it. It is clear that a reasonable juror could easily have viewed such an instruction as mandatory.

In the alternative, respondent urges that, even if viewed as a mandatory presumption rather than as a permissive inference, the presumption did not conclusively establish intent but rather could be rebutted. On this view, the instruction required the jury, if satisfied as to the facts which trigger the presumption, to find intent *unless* the defendant offered evidence to the contrary. Moreover, according to the State, all the defendant had to do to rebut the presumption was produce "some" contrary evidence; he did not have to "prove" that he lacked the required mental state. Thus, "[a]t most, it placed a *burden of production* on the petitioner," but "did not shift to petitioner the *burden of persuasion* with respect to any element of the offense. . . ." Again, respondent contends that presumptions with this limited effect pass constitutional muster.

We need not review respondent's constitutional argument on this point either, however, for we reject this characterization of the presumption as well. Respondent concedes there is a "risk" that the jury, once having found petitioner's act voluntary, would interpret the instruction as automatically directing a finding of intent. Moreover, the State also concedes that numerous courts "have differed as to the effect of the presumption when given as a jury instruction without further explanation as to its use by the jury," and that some have found it to shift more than the burden of production, and even to have conclusive effect. Nonetheless, the State contends that the only authoritative reading of the effect of the presumption resides in the Supreme Court of Montana. And the State argues that by holding that "[d]efendant's sole burden under instruction No. 5 was to produce *some* evidence that he did not intend the ordinary consequences of his voluntary acts, not to disprove that he acted 'purposely' or 'knowingly,'" (emphasis added), the Montana Supreme Court decisively established that the presumption at most affected only the burden of going forward with evidence of intent — that is, the burden of production.[5]

The Supreme Court of Montana is, of course, the final authority on the legal weight to be given a presumption under Montana law, but it is not the

---

5. For purposes of argument, we accept respondent's definition of the production burden when applied to a defendant in a criminal case. We note, however, that the burden is often described quite differently when it rests upon the prosecution. See United States v. Vuitch, 402 U.S. 62, 72 n.7 (1971) ("evidence from which a jury could find a defendant guilty beyond a reasonable doubt"); C. McCormick, Evidence §338, p. 790, and n.33 (2d ed. 1972), p. 101, and n.34.1 (Supp. 1978). We also note that the effect of a failure to meet the production burden is significantly different for the defendant and prosecution. When the prosecution fails to meet it, a directed verdict in favor of the defense results. Such a consequence is not possible upon a defendant's failure, however, as verdicts may not be directed against defendants in criminal cases.

final authority on the interpretation which a jury could have given the instruction. If Montana intended its presumption to have only the effect described by its Supreme Court, then we are convinced that a reasonable juror could well have been misled by the instruction given, and could have believed that the presumption was not limited to requiring the defendant to satisfy only a burden of production. Petitioner's jury was told that "*[t]he law presumes* that a person intends the ordinary consequences of his voluntary acts." They were not told that the presumption could be rebutted, as the Montana Supreme Court held, by the defendant's simple presentation of "some" evidence; nor even that it could be rebutted at all. Given the common definition of "presume" as "to suppose to be true without proof," Webster's New Collegiate Dictionary 911 (1974), and given the lack of qualifying instructions as to the legal effect of the presumption, we cannot discount the possibility that the jury may have interpreted the instruction in either of two more stringent ways.

First, a reasonable jury could well have interpreted the presumption as "conclusive," that is, not technically as a presumption at all, but rather as an irrebuttable direction by the court to find intent once convinced of the facts triggering the presumption. Alternatively, the jury may have interpreted the instruction as a direction to find intent upon proof of the defendant's voluntary actions (and their "ordinary" consequences), unless *the defendant* proved the contrary by some quantum of proof which may well have been considerably greater than "some" evidence — thus effectively shifting the burden of persuasion on the element of intent. . . . [A]lthough the Montana Supreme Court held to the contrary in this case, Montana's own Rules of Evidence expressly state that the presumption at issue here may be overcome only "by a preponderance of evidence contrary to the presumption." Montana Rule of Evidence 301(b)(2). Such a requirement shifts not only the burden of production, but also the ultimate burden of persuasion on the issue of intent.

We do not reject the possibility that some jurors may have interpreted the challenged instruction as permissive, or, if mandatory, as requiring only that the defendant come forward with "some" evidence in rebuttal. However, the fact that a reasonable juror could have given the presumption conclusive or persuasion-shifting effect means that we cannot discount the possibility that Sandstrom's jurors actually did proceed upon one or the other of these latter interpretations. And that means that unless these kinds of presumptions are constitutional, the instruction cannot be adjudged valid.[8] It is the line of cases urged by petitioner, and exemplified by *In re Winship*, 397 U.S. 358 (1970), that provides the appropriate mode of constitutional analysis for these kinds of presumptions.

In *Winship*, this Court stated: "Lest there remain any doubt about the constitutional stature of the reasonable-doubt standard, we explicitly hold that the Due Process Clause protects the accused against conviction except upon proof beyond a reasonable doubt *of every fact* necessary to constitute the crime with which he is charged" (emphasis added). Accord, *Patterson v. New York*, 432 U.S., at 210. The petitioner here was charged with and

---

8. Given our ultimate result in this case, we do not need to consider what kind of constitutional analysis would be appropriate for other kinds of presumptions.

convicted of deliberate homicide, committed purposely or knowingly, under Mont. Code Ann. §45-5-102(a) (1978). It is clear that under Montana law, whether the crime was committed purposely or knowingly is a fact necessary to constitute the crime of deliberate homicide. Indeed, it was the lone element of the offense at issue in Sandstrom's trial, as he confessed to causing the death of the victim, told the jury that knowledge and purpose were the only questions he was controverting, and introduced evidence solely on those points. Moreover, it is conceded that proof of defendant's "intent" would be sufficient to establish this element. Thus, the question before this Court is whether the challenged jury instruction had the effect of relieving the State of the burden of proof enunciated in *Winship* on the critical question of petitioner's state of mind. We conclude that under either of the two possible interpretations of the instruction set out above, precisely that effect would result, and that the instruction therefore represents constitutional error.... Accordingly, the judgment of the Supreme Court of Montana is reversed, and the case is REMANDED for further proceedings not inconsistent with this opinion.

[Justice Rehnquist filed a concurring opinion, joined by Chief Justice Burger.]

STATE v. HARRISON

914 N.W.2d 178 (Iowa 2018)

ZAGER, Justice.

[Defendant Harrison, a sixteen year old tried as an adult, was convicted of first-degree felony murder arising from an incident in which he and a juvenile companion, Collins, robbed a marijuana dealer, McHenry, and Collins fatally shot McHenry. Harrison argued on appeal that Iowa's felony murder statute, which defines first-degree murder as including killings committed during the course of and in furtherance of a felony, violated the rule of *Sandstrom v. Montana* by creating a conclusive presumption that the killing was committed "willfully, deliberately, and with premeditation."]

The felony-murder rule aims to deter people from committing those felonies the legislature has deemed inherently dangerous to the life of others.... To promote deterrence, the rule transforms those felonies "into first-degree murder if a person is killed in the course of the felony, even though the felon had no specific intent or premeditation otherwise necessary to elevate the killing of another into first-degree murder."...

In contrast to first-degree murder ..., which requires a showing that the defendant "willfully, deliberately, and with premeditation kills another person," first-degree murder under the felony-murder rule only requires a showing that the defendant acted with the specific intent to commit the predicate felony that led to the killing.... This difference between the intent required for premeditated murder and felony murder has produced confusion and a lack of conformity in the way our court and other courts have explained the felony-murder rule in the past. For example, Harrison notes that our court previously stated in *State v. Heemstra*, that the elements of premeditated murder under section 707.2(1) — namely that the murder was committed "willfully, deliberately, and with premeditation" — "are presumed to exist if the State proves participation in the underlying forcible felony" for a charge of felony murder. 721 N.W.2d 549, 554 (Iowa 2006) (quoting Iowa Code § 707.2(1) (2001)). Harrison capitalizes on this language in his argument that the felony-murder rule creates a conclusive presumption that the defendant committed the killing with malice aforethought in violation of the Due Process Clauses of the Iowa and United States Constitutions. . . .

The felony-murder rule does not create a conclusive presumption that the defendant committed the murder "willfully, deliberately, and with premeditation," because these are not elements of first-degree felony murder in Iowa. . . . The substantive statutory definition of first-degree felony murder in Iowa does not include these elements since the state is only required to show the specific intent to commit the predicate felony rather than show the defendant acted with premeditation and deliberation to commit murder. . . . This is a substantive rule of law in Iowa and not simply an evidentiary shortcut to find malice or a presumption that malice existed on the part of the defendant. Consequently, whether the defendant acted "willfully, deliberately, and with premeditation" is wholly irrelevant when the defendant is charged with felony murder, regardless of the dicta Harrison cites from *Heemstra*. "In that event the 'conclusive presumption' is no more than a procedural fiction that masks a substantive reality, to wit, that as a matter of law malice is not an element of felony murder." *People v. Dillon*, 668 P.2d 697, 717 (1983) (*en banc*). . . Our ruling is supported by a number of other states, which have likewise considered and rejected claims that the felony-murder rule violates due process because it creates an unconstitutional presumption that the defendant committed the killing with malice aforethought. . . . *Affirmed.*

PROBLEMS

12.4. A federal statute passed in 1984 purports to impose on criminal defendants "the burden of proving the defense of insanity by clear and convincing evidence." 18 U.S.C. §17(b). Is this statute constitutional?

12.5. In January 1980, police in Santa Cruz, California, executed a search warrant at a second-hand store called Betty Boop's Junque Shop and found a variety of stolen property. The proprietors of the store were prosecuted for receiving stolen property. The elements of the offense are receiving property that has been stolen, and knowing the stolen nature of the property at the time of receiving it. The trial judge instructed the jury on the elements of the offense, the presumption of innocence, and the definition of reasonable doubt.

Relying on a statutory presumption, the judge also instructed the jury that if it found (1) that the defendants were dealers in second-hand merchandise, (2) that they had bought or received property under circumstances that should have prompted a reasonable inquiry regarding whether the seller had a legal right to sell it, and (3) that they had failed to make such an inquiry, "then you shall presume that defendants bought or received such property knowing it to have been stolen unless from all the evidence you have reasonable doubt that defendants knew the property was stolen."

When the jury asked about the presumption, the judge responded as follows: "There are two kinds of presumptions. One is a conclusive presumption that if you have the presumption, that's it, you don't go any further. This isn't that kind of presumption. It's what's called a rebuttable presumption, because you have the presumption, presume to know that the property was stolen, but they can go forward and raise a reasonable doubt that they actually knew that. So you still do have that question. Basically, it boils down to are you satisfied that they acquired the property or retained the property knowing it was stolen, or do you have a reasonable doubt."

Did these instructions violate the federal Constitution? (The California Supreme Court gave its answer in *People v. Roeder*, 189 Cal. Rptr. 501 (1983).)

C. Judicial Notice

Like presumptions, judicial notice is a topic that seems straightforward enough until one tries to set down some rules about it. Everyone agrees that there are some facts that should not have to be proved, because they cannot reasonably be disputed — like the fact that December 5, 1999, was a Sunday. And no one wants judges or jurors to ignore everything they know about the world from their experiences outside the courtroom. The difficult questions are, first, where to draw the lines and, second, how much of the line-drawing can usefully be accomplished through rules of general application.

Judicial notice should be distinguished from two other mechanisms for establishing facts without evidence. The first of these mechanisms is sometimes called "jury notice"; the Advisory Committee Note excerpted below refers to it as reliance on "non-evidence facts." The idea is that there are certain facts that do not need to be proved because they are part of the background understanding of the world that the trier of fact brings to the case. The example the Advisory Committee gives is the usual meaning and connotations of the word "car" — i.e., the fact that when people say "car," they usually mean an automobile, the fact that most automobiles have internal combustion engines and pneumatic tires, and so on. Other examples might be the fact that sadness sometimes makes people cry or the fact that apples grow on trees.

The second common mechanism for establishing facts without evidence and without judicial notice is a stipulation. A long-standing feature of our litigation system allows the parties to agree to certain facts and have the jury instructed to take them as proven, without introducing any evidence. This is another aspect of the extensive control that parties exert over factfinding in our system. We saw it in operation in *Old Chief v. United States*, excerpted in Chapter 2.

Much of the work you might think has to be done by judicial notice is really done by these other two mechanisms. This means that there is a role for judicial notice only with respect to facts about which the parties do *not* stipulate, and which do *not* represent such common knowledge that we can assume the jury knows them without being told. This might lead you to wonder why we even need a doctrine of judicial notice. After all, if facts are not so obvious that all jurors know them, and they are not matters about which the parties agree, why not just require proof? This is a good question, and it is worth keeping in mind as you read the cases and commentary excerpted below.

One other point is worth noting at the outset. Rule 201 of the Federal Rules of Evidence, which addresses judicial notice, leans heavily on a distinction between "adjudicative facts" and "legislative facts." Rule 201 regulates judicial notice of the former but not of the latter. In practice, however, the two categories of facts are often difficult to tell apart, and courts do not always even try — partly because, as you will see, the restrictions that F.R.E. 201 imposes on judicial notice of adjudicative facts are in many ways very similar to the restrictions that courts impose, as a matter of federal common law, on judicial notice of legislative facts. (The major exception is the wishy-washy jury instruction that Rule 201 tells trial judges to use when they deliver judicial notice of any fact in a criminal case.)

Whether the distinction between adjudicative and legislative facts assists sensible thinking about judicial notice remains an open question. Some states, like California, ignore the distinction entirely in their own evidence codes.

[F.R.E. 201; C.E.C. §§450–460]

ADVISORY COMMITTEE NOTE TO F.R.E. 201

This is the only evidence rule on the subject of judicial notice. It deals only with judicial notice of "adjudicative" facts. No rule deals with judicial notice of "legislative" facts....

Adjudicative facts are simply the facts of the particular case. Legislative facts, on the other hand, are those which have relevance to legal reasoning and the lawmaking process, whether in the formulation of a legal principle or ruling by a judge or court or in the enactment of a legislative body. The terminology was coined by Professor Kenneth Davis in his article An Approach to Problems of Evidence in the Administrative Process, 55 Harv. L. Rev. 364, 404–407 (1942)....

The usual method of establishing adjudicative facts is through the introduction of evidence, ordinarily consisting of the testimony of witnesses. If particular facts are outside the area of reasonable controversy, this process is dispensed with as unnecessary. A high degree of indisputability is the essential prerequisite.

Legislative facts are quite different. As Professor Davis says:

"My opinion is that judge-made law would stop growing if judges, in thinking about questions of law and policy, were forbidden to take into account the facts they believe, as distinguished from facts which are 'clearly...within the domain of the indisputable.' Facts most needed in thinking about difficult problems of law and policy have a way of being outside the domain of the clearly indisputable." A System of Judicial Notice Based on Fairness and Convenience, supra, at 82.

An illustration is Hawkins v. United States, 358 U.S. 74 (1958), in which the Court refused to discard the common law rule that one spouse could not testify against the other, saying, "Adverse testimony given in criminal proceedings would, we think, be likely to destroy almost any marriage." This conclusion has a large intermixture of fact, but the factual aspect is scarcely "indisputable." . . .

Professor Morgan gave the following description of the methodology of determining domestic law:

"In determining the content or applicability of a rule of domestic law, the judge is unrestricted in his investigation and conclusion. He may reject the propositions of either party or of both parties. He may consult the sources of pertinent data to which they refer, or he may refuse to do so. He may make an independent search for persuasive data or rest content with what he has or what the parties present. . . . [T]he parties do no more than to assist; they control no part of the process." Morgan, Judicial Notice, 57 Harv. L. Rev. 269, 270-271 (1944).

This is the view which should govern judicial access to legislative facts. It renders inappropriate any limitation in the form of indisputability, any formal requirements of notice other than those already inherent in affording opportunity to hear and be heard and exchanging briefs, and any requirement of formal findings at any level. . . .

Similar considerations govern the judicial use of non-adjudicative facts in ways other than formulating laws and rules. Thayer described them as a part of the judicial reasoning process.

"In conducting a process of judicial reasoning, as of other reasoning, not a step can be taken without assuming something which has not been proved; and the capacity to do this with competent judgment and efficiency, is imputed to judges and juries as part of their necessary mental outfit." Thayer, Preliminary Treatise on Evidence 279-280 (1898).

As Professor Davis points out, A System of Judicial Notice Based on Fairness and Convenience, in Perspectives of Law 69, 73 (1964), every case involves the use of hundreds or thousands of non-evidence facts. When a witness in an automobile accident case says "car," everyone, judge and jury included, furnishes, from non-evidence sources within himself, the supplementing information that the "car" is an automobile, not a railroad car, that it is self-propelled, probably by an internal combustion engine, that it may be assumed to have four wheels with pneumatic rubber tires, and so on. The judicial process cannot construct every case from scratch, like Descartes creating a world based on the postulate *Cogito, ergo sum*. These items could not possibly be introduced into evidence, and no one suggests that they be. Nor are they appropriate subjects for any formalized treatment of judicial notice of facts.

Another aspect of what Thayer had in mind is the use of non-evidence facts to appraise or assess the adjudicative facts of the case. Pairs of cases from two jurisdictions illustrate this use and also the difference between non-evidence facts thus used and adjudicative facts. In People v. Strook, 347 Ill. 460, 179 N.E. 821 (1932), venue in Cook County had been held not established by testimony that the crime was committed at 7956 South Chicago Avenue, since judicial notice would not be taken that the address was in Chicago. However, the same court subsequently ruled that venue in Cook County was established by testimony that a crime occurred at 8900 South Anthony Avenue, since notice would be taken of the common practice of omitting the name of the city when speaking of local addresses, and the witness was testifying in Chicago. People v. Pride, 16 Ill. 2d 82, 156 N.E.2d 551 (1951). And in Hughes v. Vestal, 264 N.C. 500, 142 S.E.2d 361 (1965), the Supreme Court of North Carolina disapproved the trial judge's admission in evidence of a state-published table of automobile stopping distances on the basis of judicial notice, though the court itself had referred to the same table in an earlier case in a "rhetorical and illustrative" way in determining that the defendant could not have stopped her car in time to avoid striking a child who suddenly appeared in the highway and that a nonsuit was properly granted. Ennis v. Dupree, 262 N.C. 224, 136 S.E.2d 702 (1964). It is apparent that this use of non-evidence facts in evaluating the adjudicative facts of the case is not an appropriate subject for a formalized judicial notice treatment.

In view of these considerations, the regulation of judicial notice of facts by the present rule extends only to adjudicative facts.

What, then, are "adjudicative" facts? Davis refers to them as those "which relate to the parties," or more fully:

> "When a court or an agency finds facts concerning the immediate parties — who did what, where, when, how, and with what motive or intent — the court or agency is performing an adjudicative function, and the facts are conveniently called adjudicative facts. . . .
>
> "Stated in other terms, the adjudicative facts are those to which the law is applied in the process of adjudication. They are the facts that normally go to the jury in a jury case. They relate to the parties, their activities, their properties, their businesses." 2 Administrative Law Treatise 353.

With respect to judicial notice of adjudicative facts, the tradition has been one of caution in requiring that the matter be beyond reasonable controversy. This tradition of circumspection appears to be soundly based, and no reason to depart from it is apparent. As Professor Davis says:

> "The reason we use trial-type procedure, I think, is that we make the practical judgment, on the basis of experience, that taking evidence, subject to cross-examination and rebuttal, is the best way to resolve controversies involving disputes of adjudicative facts, that is, facts pertaining to the parties. The reason we require a determination on the record is that we think fair procedure in resolving disputes of adjudicative facts calls for giving each party a chance to meet in the appropriate fashion the facts that come to the tribunal's attention, and the appropriate fashion for meeting disputed adjudicative facts includes rebuttal evidence, cross-examination, usually confrontation, and argument (either written or oral or both). The key to a fair trial is opportunity to use the appropriate weapons (rebuttal evidence, cross-examination, and argument) to meet adverse materials that come to the tribunal's attention." A System of Judicial Notice Based on Fairness and Convenience, in Perspectives of Law 69, 93 (1964).

The rule proceeds upon the theory that these considerations call for dispensing with traditional methods of proof only in clear cases. . . . In accord with the usual view, judicial notice may be taken at any stage of the proceedings, whether in the trial court or on appeal. . . .

UNITED STATES v. GOULD

536 F.2d 216 (8th Cir. 1976)

GIBSON, Chief Judge.

Defendants, Charles Gould and Joseph Carey, were convicted of conspiring to import . . . and actually importing . . . cocaine from Colombia, South America, into the United States in violation of the Controlled Substances Import and Export Act. 21 U.S.C. §951 et seq. (1970). [The statute prohibits the importation of "any controlled substance in schedule I or II."]

. . . The evidence persuasively showed that defendants and David Miller enlisted the cooperation of Miller's sister, Barbara Kenworthy, who agreed to travel to Colombia with defendants and smuggle the cocaine into the United States by placing it inside two pairs of hollowed-out platform shoes. . . . The success of the importation scheme was foiled when, upon Ms. Kenworthy's arrival to the Miami airport from Colombia, a customs agent insisted upon X-raying the cocaine-laden shoes. Approximately two pounds of cocaine were discovered and seized by customs officials. . . .

Defendants do not challenge the sufficiency of the evidence but contend that the District Court erred in . . . improperly taking judicial notice and instructing the jury that cocaine hydrochloride is a schedule II controlled substance. . . . Schedule II controlled substances, for the purpose of the Controlled Substances Import and Export Act, [include, *inter alia*,] . . . "Coca leaves and any salt, compound, derivative, or preparation of coca leaves, and any salt, compound, derivative, or preparation thereof which is chemically equivalent or identical with any of these substances, except that the substances shall not include decocainized coca leaves or extraction of coca leaves, which extractions do not contain cocaine or ecgonine." 21 U.S.C. §812 (1970); *see* 21 C.F.R. §1308.12 (1975).

At trial, two expert witnesses for the Government testified as to the composition of the powdered substance removed from Ms. Kenworthy's platform shoes at the Miami airport. One expert testified that the substance was comprised of approximately 60 percent cocaine hydrochloride. The other witness stated that the white powder consisted of 53 percent cocaine.[3] There was no direct evidence to indicate that cocaine hydrochloride is a derivative of coca leaves. In its instructions to the jury, the District Court stated: "If you find the substance was cocaine hydrochloride, you are instructed that cocaine hydrochloride is a schedule II controlled substance under the laws of the United States."

Our inquiry . . . is twofold. We must first determine whether it was error for the District Court to take judicial notice of the fact that cocaine hydrochloride is a schedule II controlled substance. Secondly, if we conclude that it was permissible to judicially notice this fact, we must then determine whether the District Court erred in instructing the jury that it must accept this fact as conclusive.

The first aspect of this inquiry merits little discussion. . . . It is apparent that courts may take judicial notice of any fact which is "capable of such instant and unquestionable demonstration, if desired, that no party would think of imposing a falsity on the tribunal in the face of an intelligent adversary." IX J. Wigmore, Evidence §2571, at 548 (1940). The fact that cocaine hydrochloride is derived from coca leaves is, if not common knowledge, at

---

3. It is not significant that one expert witness testified that the substance contained cocaine hydrochloride and the other testified that it was comprised in part of cocaine. The fact that cocaine hydrochloride contains cocaine is common knowledge. *United States v. Sims*, 529 F.2d 10, 11 (8th Cir. 1976).

least a matter which is capable of certain, easily accessible and indisputably accurate verification. *See* Webster's Third New International Dictionary 434 (1961). Therefore, it was proper for the District Court to judicially notice this fact. Our conclusion on this matter is amply supported by the weight of judicial authority. . . .

Our second inquiry involves the propriety of the District Court's instruction to the jurors that this judicially noticed fact must be accepted as conclusive by them. Defendants, relying upon Fed. R. Ev. 201(g), urge that the jury should have been instructed that it could discretionarily accept or reject this fact. . . .[4]

It is clear that the reach of rule 201 extends only to adjudicative, not legislative, facts. Fed. R. Ev. 201(a). Consequently, the viability of defendants' argument is dependent upon our characterization of the fact judicially noticed by the District Court as adjudicative, thus invoking the provisions of rule 201(g). In undertaking this analysis, we note at the outset that rule 201 is not all encompassing. "Rule 201 . . . was deliberately drafted to cover only a small fraction of material usually subsumed under the concept of 'judicial notice.'" 1 J. Weinstein, Evidence ¶201(01) (1975).

The precise line of demarcation between adjudicative facts and legislative Facts is not always easily identified. Adjudicative facts have been described as . . . "facts concerning the immediate parties who did what, where, when, how, and with what motive or intent the court. . . . Stated in other Terms, the adjudicative facts are those to which the law is applied in the process Of adjudication. They are the facts that normally go to the jury in a jury Case. They relate to the parties, their activities, their properties, their businesses." 2 K. Davis, Administrative Law Treatise §15.03, at 353 (1958).

Legislative facts, on the other hand, do not relate specifically to the activities or characteristics of the litigants. A court generally relies upon legislative Facts when it purports to develop a particular law or policy and thus Considers material wholly unrelated to the activities of the parties. . . . 2 K. Davis, Administrative Law Treatise, *supra* at §15.03. Legislative facts are established Truths, facts or pronouncements that do not change from case to Case but apply universally, while adjudicative facts are those developed in a Particular case.

Applying these general definitions, we think it is clear that the District Court in the present case was judicially noticing a legislative fact rather than an adjudicative fact. . . . The fact that cocaine hydrochloride is a derivative of coca leaves is a universal fact that is unrelated to the activities of the parties to this litigation. . . . [Accordingly,] rule 201(g) is inapplicable. The District

---

4. In the proposed federal Rules of Evidence, forwarded by the Supreme Court of the United States to Congress on February 5, 1973, rule 201(g) did not draw this distinction between civil and criminal cases. The proposed rule 201(g) provided that "[t]he judge shall instruct the jury to accept as established any facts judicially noticed." Congress disagreed with this unqualified rule requiring mandatory instructions in all cases. It was feared that requiring the jury to accept a judicially noticed adjudicative fact in a criminal case might infringe upon the defendants' Sixth Amendment right to a trial by jury. H. Rep. No. 93-650, 93d Cong., 1st Sess. 6–7 (1973), reprinted in 4 U.S. Code Cong. & Admin. News pp. 7075, 7080 (1974). Consequently, Congress adopted the present text of rule 201(g) which requires a mandatory instruction in civil cases but a discretionary instruction in criminal cases.

Court was not obligated to inform the jury that it could disregard the judicially noticed fact. In fact, to do so would be preposterous, thus permitting juries to make conflicting findings on what constitutes controlled substances under federal law. . . . The judgment of conviction is affirmed.

UNITED STATES v. LEWIS

833 F.2d 1380 (9th Cir. 1987)

ALARCON, Circuit Judge.

The government appeals from the district court's order suppressing a Confession on motion of defendant Jerri C. Lewis in this bank robbery prosecution. . . . [Lewis argued her confession] was involuntary because she was a "heroin addict suffering from the effects of drug withdrawal [and] was questioned in her hospital bed hours after she had awakened from a general anesthetic administered during surgery."

[In rejecting the prosecutor's claim that the confession was voluntary,] the court then made the following comment:

> Well, you see, I can't go with you on that. One of the reasons why, and I am frank to say, I am influenced by personal experience. I mean, I represent to you that I have never been a heroin addict and I have never experienced what it is like to come out from under heroin, but I have come out from under an anesthetic. And people have told me that — and I seem to be perfectly all right — and people have told me that I said the most incredible things during the few first six hours or so after I came out of a general anesthetic. And I have had the same experience related by other people.
>
> You are not accountable for what you do or say for quite a number of hours after you come out of a general anesthetic. So I cannot find that a person who is both withdrawing from heroin and coming out from under a general anesthetic and is under arrest and confronted by FBI agents is in a position to make a voluntary and knowing statement at that time.

. . . We begin our discussion of the applicable law with the statement of an obvious principle. The trial judge in this matter was not a competent witness to Lewis' condition. "The judge presiding at the trial may not testify in that trial as a witness. No objection need be made in order to preserve the point." Fed. R. Evid. 605.

. . . Lewis contends for the first time on appeal that the trial judge properly relied on his personal experience based on the court's power to take judicial notice of adjudicative facts under Rule 201 of the Federal Rules of Evidence. This argument is unpersuasive.

A trial judge is prohibited from relying on his personal experience to support the taking of judicial notice. "It is therefore plainly accepted that the judge is not to use from the bench, under the guise of judicial knowledge, that which he knows *only as an individual* observer outside of court." 9 J. Wigmore, Evidence in Trials at Common Law §2569, at 723 (J. Chadbourn rev. 1981) (emphasis in original).

In relying on his "personal knowledge" the trial judge did not advise the parties he was taking judicial notice of Lewis' condition at the time she spoke to the agents on October 21, 1986. Furthermore, the trial judge did not rely on facts "generally known within the territorial jurisdiction of the trial court or . . . capable of accurate and ready determination by resort to sources whose accuracy cannot reasonably be questioned." Fed. R. Evid. 201(b). Instead, he looked solely to his own reaction to an anesthetic. The record is silent concerning the nature of his illness, the surgical procedure performed upon the trial judge, the type and amount of anesthetic administered to him, or its general effect on a patient. Announcement on the record of the fact that a court is taking judicial notice is necessary to accord a party the "opportunity to be heard as to the propriety of taking judicial notice and the tenor of the matter noticed." Fed. R. Evid. 201(e).

Lewis relies on *Bey v. Bolger*, 540 F. Supp. 910 (E.D. Pa. 1982) for the proposition that "[c]ourts have also taken judicial notice of commonly known health facts." In *Bey*, the district court took judicial notice in a written memorandum setting forth the basis for its ruling in cross motions for partial summary judgment that a person suffering hypertension is susceptible to stroke, heart attack or other physical ailment. Thus, in *Bey*, the parties were given an opportunity to ask the court to reconsider the propriety of taking judicial notice of the effect of hypertension. Furthermore, the trial judge in *Bey* did not indicate to the parties that he was relying on his personal experience with hypertension.

The trial judge's reliance in the instant matter on facts known to him from his personal experience denied the government the opportunity to test the basis for the court's opinion concerning the effect of an anesthetic on a person's freedom of choice through the usual methods that assure trustworthiness in our adversarial system of justice. The prosecutor was denied the opportunity to contrast the nature of the illness or injury suffered by the judge with Lewis' abscessed shoulder, the amount of anesthesia administered to each, or the actual statements made by the judge which others characterized as "incredible" with the responses made by the defendant in this matter. . . . Reversed and Remanded.

CARLEY v. WHEELED COACH

991 F.2d 1117 (3d Cir. 1993)

COWEN, Circuit Judge.

Plaintiff Mary Carley appeals the grant of summary judgment dismissing her claim for personal injuries caused by an alleged design defect in an ambulance manufactured by defendant Wheeled Coach Industries, Inc. ("Wheeled Coach"). . . . [Carley, an emergency medical technician, was injured when the ambulance rolled over. Wheeled Coach contended that it was immune from liability because the ambulance had been manufactured pursuant to a contract with the United States General Services Administration, and the GSA knew as much about any design problems as the company.] The district court took judicial notice "of the fact that the government conducts numerous crashworthiness tests, and the well known rollover problems of vehicles having a high center of gravity." The court [therefore] concluded that . . . Wheeled Coach could not have been more aware than the government of the ambulance's tendency to rollover. We disagree. . . . The facts judicially noticed by the district court are not beyond reasonable dispute and therefore do not satisfy Rule 201(b).

The government may perform various tests on vehicles, but the quantity and nature of those tests are not matters of common knowledge, nor are they readily provable through a source whose accuracy cannot reasonably be questioned. Likewise, the district court could not have determined, beyond reasonable dispute, that the rollover propensities of vehicles with high centers of gravity are well known. Most people probably know little, if anything, about how high centers of gravity cause vehicular accidents. The facts judicially noticed by the district court are not the kind of readily ascertainable facts that satisfy Rule 201(b). *See, e.g., Policeman's Benevolent Ass'n v. Washington Twp.*, 850 F.2d 133, 137 (3d Cir. 1988) (court of appeals took judicial notice of township's police regulations), *cert. denied*, 490 U.S. 1004, 109 S. Ct. 1637, 104 L. Ed. 2d 153 (1989); *Government of the Virgin Islands v. Testamark*, 528 F.2d 742, 743 (3d Cir. 1976) (no error to take judicial notice of court records indicating defendant's prior conviction). *But see Town Sound & Custom Tops, Inc. v. Chrysler Motors Corp.*, 959 F.2d 468, 494-95 n.40 (3d Cir.) (court could not take judicial notice that standardizing of autosound systems was prevalent in the automotive industry), *cert. denied*, 506 U.S. 868 (1992).

Aside from the judicially noticed facts, there is no evidence on record showing that Wheeled Coach warned the GSA about dangers in its ambulance that were known to Wheeled Coach but not to the GSA. . . . We therefore will reverse the grant of summary judgment and remand the case to the district court. . . .

UNITED STATES v. BOWERS

660 F.2d 527 (5th Cir. 1981)

PER CURIAM.

Pok Sin Bowers was convicted, following a jury trial in the district court, for cruelty to a child in violation of the Georgia child abuse statute, Ga. Code Ann. §26-2801(b) (1980), as it applies to a federal reservation through the Assimilative Crimes Act, 18 U.S.C. §13 (1976). . . . Appellant asserts that the court committed reversible error in taking judicial notice that "Fort Benning, Georgia, is on land which is property of the United States and is under the jurisdiction of [the] United States." The alleged vice in this instruction is the court's failure to inform the jurors that they were not bound to accept the noticed fact. Appellant cites Fed. R. Evid. 201(g). . . .

Rule 201 "governs only judicial notice of adjudicative facts," and not legislative facts. Consequently, appellant's argument turns on the characterization of the fact judicially noticed. The Eighth Circuit has observed that

> Legislative facts are established truths, facts or pronouncements that do not change from case to case but apply universally, while adjudicative facts are those developed in a particular case.

United States v. Gould, 536 F.2d 216, 220 (8th Cir. 1976). The fact that Fort Benning is under federal jurisdiction is a well established fact appropriate for judicial notice. Unlike an adjudicative fact, this fact does not change from case to case but, instead, remains fixed. Consequently, the court committed no error in failing to instruct the jury it could disregard the judicially noticed fact. . . . Affirmed.

UNITED STATES v. BELLO

194 F.3d 18 (1st Cir. 1999)

Lipez, Circuit Judge.

Jesus Bello appeals his conviction and sentence for assaulting a fellow prisoner in the Metropolitan Detention Center in Guaynabo, Puerto Rico ("MDC-Guaynabo") in violation of 18 U.S.C. §113(a)(6). Bello claims that the court erred in taking judicial notice of the jurisdictional element of the offense, namely, that MDC-Guaynabo was within the territorial jurisdiction of the United States.

. . . By its terms, Rule 201 applies only to adjudicative facts, and the parties and the court assumed that the jurisdictional element at issue here involved an adjudicative rather than a legislative fact. They assumed correctly. Whether a fact is adjudicative or legislative depends not on the nature of the fact — e.g., who owns the land — but rather on the use made of it (*i.e.*, whether it is a fact germane to what happened in the case or a fact useful in formulating common law policy or interpreting a statute) and the same fact can play either role depending on context. *See* Fed. R. Evid. 201, Advisory Committee's note ("Adjudicative facts are simply the facts of the particular case. Legislative facts, on the other hand, are those which have relevance to legal reasoning and the lawmaking process. . . ."). Where the prison sits is an element of the offense and unquestionably an adjudicative fact,[4] and we review the trial court's decision to take judicial notice under Rule 201 for abuse of discretion.

. . . [J]udicial notice was proper pursuant to Rule 201(b)(2), based on "sources whose accuracy cannot reasonably be questioned." Indeed, "[g]eography has long been peculiarly susceptible to judicial notice for the obvious reason that geographic locations are facts which are not generally controversial and thus it is within the general definition contained in Fed. R. Evid.

---

4. Some other Courts of Appeals have held that Rule 201 is not applicable to judicial notice that a place is within the "special maritime and territorial jurisdiction of the United States," finding this to be a "legislative fact" beyond the scope of Rule 201. *See United States v. Hernandez-Fundora*, 58 F.3d 802, 811 (2d Cir. 1995); *United States v. Bowers*, 660 F.2d 527, 531 (5th Cir. 1981); *see also* II Kenneth Culp Davis & Richard J. Pierce, *Administrative Law Treatise*, §10.6, at 155 (3d. ed. 1994) ["Whether 123 C Street is inside or outside the city is a question about 123 C Street, not about a party. The question whether X lives in the city is a question of adjudicative fact, but, even though X lives at 123 C Street, the fact that that address is within the city is not an adjudicative fact."]. *But see* Wright & Graham, *Federal Practice & Procedure* §5103 n.16 (1999 Supp.) ("One court has resolved the problem by a dubious holding that the fact that Fort Benning is under the jurisdiction of the United States is a legislative fact," citing *Bowers*).

201(b). . . ." *United States v. Piggie*, 622 F.2d 486, 488 (10th Cir. 1980). . . . The government submitted to the court official government maps, letters from Army officials, and various legislative acts of Puerto Rico, all tending to show that MDC-Guaynabo was within the jurisdiction of the United States. . . .

The instruction offered by the court was as follows:

> Even though no evidence has been introduced about it in your presence, I believe that the fact that the Metropolitan Detention Center is within a land reserved for the use of the United States and under its exclusive jurisdiction . . . is of such common knowledge and can be so accurately and readily determined from the Metropolitan Detention Center officials that it cannot reasonably be disputed. You may, therefore, reasonably treat this fact as proven even though no evidence has been presented on this point before you.

As with any fact presented in the case, however, the final decision whether or not to accept it is for you to make and you are not required to agree with me.

This instruction . . . complied entirely with the dictates of the rule. . . .[10]

. . . Affirmed.

ALLSTAR MARKETING GROUP, LLC v. UNITED STATES

211 F. Supp. 3d 1319 (Ct. Int'l Trade 2017)

BARNETT, District Judge.

Plaintiff Allstar Marketing Group, LLC contests the denial of protest number 2809-11-100237 1 challenging U.S. Customs and Border Protection's liquidation of the subject import, a polyester fleece knit article referred to as a "Snuggie®," under subheading 6114.30.30 of the Harmonized Tariff Schedule of the United States ("HTSUS"), as "Other garments, knitted or crocheted: Of man-made fibers: Other," dutiable at 14.9 percent *ad valorem*. . . . Plaintiff contends that Customs should have classified the subject imports under subheading 6301.40.00, HTSUS, as "Blankets," dutiable at 8.5 percent *ad valorem*, or alternatively, under subheading 6307.90.98, HTSUS, as "Other made up articles," dutiable at 7 percent *ad valorem*.

There is no genuine issue of material fact regarding the properties of the subject import that would preclude summary judgment. . . . Retail packaging and television advertising describe the Snuggie® as a blanket with sleeves. . . . The Snuggie® is sold in the "bedding, housewares, general merchandise, 'impulse buy,' or 'as-seen-on-TV' departments of retail stores," never in the wearing apparel department.[11] . . . [T]he court grants Plaintiff's motion for summary judgment.

---

10. It . . . remains unsettled whether 201(g)'s non-conclusive standard, permitting a jury to disregard judicial notice in a criminal case, is constitutionally compelled. "With the exception of Nevada, all of the states with modern codes make judicial notice binding on the jury in all cases, criminal as well as civil." 21 Wright & Graham, *Federal Practice & Procedure* §5111 n.17, at 533. . . .

11. Defendant avers that "[p]eople have worn the Snuggie® during pub crawls" [and submits copies of black and white photographs in support]. Plaintiff disputes Defendant's

JEFFREY BELLIN & ANDREW GUTHRIE FERGUSON, TRIAL BY GOOGLE: JUDICIAL NOTICE IN THE INFORMATION AGE

108 N.W. L. Rev. 1137, 1159-68, 1174, 1181 (2014)

Courts often take judicial notice of [public information of government websites] with little discussion (or apparent recognition) of potential objections to doing so. . . . [T]he Court of Federal Claims took judicial notice of the symptoms of an unusual medical condition, as reflected in an online publication by the National Institutes of Health. . . .

. . . A district court in Texas took judicial notice of "the appraised fair-market value of the property" at issue in the litigation as "published on [the] Harris County Appraisal District's website." . . . [The district court for the Northern District of Ohio dismissed a claim against Wells Fargo because the statute underlying the claim did not apply to "national banks," and the court, after reviewing a list on the "Office of the Comptroller of the Currency's website," took judicial notice that Wells Fargo is, in fact, a "national bank." Courts have taken judicial notice of demographic information published online by the Census Bureau, such as "the racial breakdown for the Memphis metropolitan area population." . . . Perhaps the most inventive example of judicial notice to date comes from a court that, after noting the tracking number of an employment discrimination plaintiff's right-to-sue letter, "went to the United States Postal Service's website and entered the tracking number, which revealed [the date] that the right-to-sue letter was delivered." The court then deemed the plaintiff's suit untimely because it was filed more than ninety days after the letter was received (according to the Internet).

Courts are also taking judicial notice of information contained on non-governmental websites. Courts take judicial notice of medical information published on sites like the MayoClinic website, stock prices reflected in Yahoo! Finance, facts contained in news reports found on websites of CNN, BBC, and Yahoo!, and information contained in online flight schedules. . . .

Corporate websites containing pertinent information are another common source of information that is judicially noticed. A court took judicial notice of corporate relationships between insurance companies involved in the litigation before it, as delineated on one of their websites. . . . In a parole

---

assertion, and contends the photographs are not suitable subjects for judicial notice. Defendant contends "the photographs meet the standard for judicial notice because the information is 'generally known'" on the basis of "[a] quick internet search." Judicial notice of an adjudicative fact is appropriate when the fact in question is not subject to reasonable dispute because it "is generally known within the trial court's territorial jurisdiction," or "can be accurately and readily determined from sources whose accuracy cannot reasonably be questioned." Fed. R. Evid. 201(b); see also 28 U.S.C. § 2641(a)(2012) ("the Federal Rules of Evidence shall apply to all civil actions in the Court of International Trade"). The photographs are inappropriate subjects for judicial notice. Whether the persons appearing in the photographs are actually wearing the Snuggie® at issue here is "subject to reasonable dispute." *See* Fed. R. Evid. 201(b). Defendant provides no support for the accuracy of the ostensive source, "SnuggiePubCrawls.com." Moreover, mere fact of publication on a website does not make it "generally known." Thus, the court declines to consider the photographs.

revocation proceeding, a trial court "did a Google search" to confirm the suspicion that many variants of yellow hats are available for sale (the parole revocation was based on a bank robbery by a person wearing a yellow hat). Another court visited Facebook to take judicial notice of the steps necessary to sign in for a Facebook account. . . .

For judges who anticipate avoiding the pitfalls of online judicial notice by ignoring the concept, it is worth noting that the judicial reports include a prominent opinion reversing a trial court for refusing to take judicial notice of Internet sources. In *O'Toole v. Northrop Grumman Corp.*, [499 F.3d 1218 (10th Cir. 2007),] the Tenth Circuit reversed a district court's ruling with respect to damages because "the district court abused its discretion by failing to take judicial notice of the actual earnings history provided by Northrop Grumman on the [I]nternet." . . .

. . . Courts often rely on Google Maps to establish the distance between two geographic points (e.g., a defendant's location and the scene of the crime) referenced in the litigation. . . . Courts also take judicial notice of the estimates of driving (or walking) times provided by the website. In at least one case, a court appeared to rely on information that could only be obtained through Google Street View, which provides street level photographs of various locations.

By taking judicial notice, courts (and litigators) skip over thorny evidentiary questions such as: are the maps accurate (or in authentication terms, do they reflect what they purport to show) and what hearsay exception allows the court to consider out-of-court statements by Google as to relative locations, driving distances, and so on, for the truth of the matter asserted. Further, judicial notice allows the parties to introduce information procured from the Internet without the expense and delay of subpoenaing Google employees. . . .

Opposite Google Maps on the spectrum of online sources accepted by courts is Wikipedia. "Citing Wikipedia is as controversial as it is common." [*Fire Ins. Exch. v. Oltmanns*, 285 P.3d 802, 807 (Utah Ct. App. 2012) (Voros, J., concurring).] Wikipedia is a user-generated online encyclopedia, which means that, with limited exceptions, anyone can edit its entries. Though courts often cite Wikipedia to support their reasoning, they have generally declined requests to take judicial notice of facts found within its entries. Although written analysis is sparse, courts may be concluding that Wikipedia is not a "source[] whose accuracy cannot reasonably be questioned." . . .

Several factors make the prospect of more widespread and rational judicial notice of online sources attractive. Most obviously, the exercise can bring reliable information into the decision-making process, leading to more accurate determinations. In addition, online information is available to everyone and easy to access. Counsel need not worry about whether the Internet will cooperate, assert a Fifth Amendment privilege, or slant its story when approached by one party or the other to litigation. . . . An overburdened, under-motivated, resource-strapped public defender can review, and seek judicial notice of, the same websites as the most high-powered, well-funded white-collar defender. Finally, by removing unnecessary evidentiary obstacles, judicial notice preserves court time and resources, while also decreasing the burden on witnesses who might otherwise have to testify on uncontroversial points, such as the authenticity of a printout from Google Maps or the owner of the website, "www.mcdonalds.com."

Another consideration is that jurors already have independent access to online information. There is, consequently, no guarantee that courts can shut off access to the Internet even if they want to. Jurors confused about the geography where an incident took place, the weather on the date in question, or the chemical properties of a substance will be sorely tempted to look it up themselves. The temptation has always existed for jurors to do independent research, but the ease with which they can do so has changed dramatically. Judges warn jurors not to visit the crime scene, and jurors (mostly) comply. But will they visit the crime scene remotely via Google Maps? It may be better to funnel this curiosity through an open, transparent and (more likely) accurate process of judicial notice, than to leave it unregulated and in the shadows. . . .

. . . [C]ourts should examine at least three attributes of the online source: (1) knowledge of the subject matter, (2) independence from relevant bias, and (3) incentive to ensure accuracy. . . . A candid assessment of these three factors, however, will result in numerous determinations that reputable Internet sources come within Rule 201's scope and can, thus, help fact-finders resolve disputes in courtrooms across the country. . . .

In addition to these findings, courts should also preserve a copy of the source material or memorialize it in some way. A printout of the source, including the time and date of the viewing, should be made part of the record. In this way, the source material will be preserved for appeal. This type of transparency, preservation of the source, and judicial findings justifying reliance on the source will produce an accurate and reviewable record of judicial notice rulings as the practice evolves with Internet sources. . . .

PROBLEMS

12.6. Suppose a calendar manufacturer sues a rival for patent infringement, based in part on the fact that the rival's calendar, like the one the plaintiff has recently patented, is secured to the wall by a punched hole at the top. The defendant asks the court to take judicial notice of the fact that calendars have had this feature for many years, and the plaintiff objects. How should the court rule?

12.7. Suppose a spectator at a minor league baseball game gets hit by a line drive and sues the ballpark for negligence, alleging failure to post adequate warnings. The ballpark asks the judge to take judicial notice of the fact that the hazard of being hit by a ball at a professional baseball game is well known, and the plaintiff objects. How should the judge rule?

12.8. Suppose a criminal defendant moves to suppress evidence found during a patdown search and alleges the police lacked reason to suspect he was armed. The government proves the police had reason to suspect the defendant was selling cocaine and asks the judge to take judicial notice of the fact that drug dealers often carry weapons. The defendant objects. How should the judge rule?

12.9. In a prosecution for robbery of a federally insured bank, suppose the government asks the judge to instruct the jury that Bank of America — a branch of which the defendant is alleged to have robbed — is federally insured. The defendant objects. What instruction, if any, should the judge give? What if the defendant is alleged to have robbed a branch of Coast Federal Bank, and the government asks the court to take judicial notice of the fact that federal law requires any bank with "Federal" in its name to be federally insured?

12.10. The plaintiff in a copyright infringement case asks the court to take judicial notice of the contents of a previous version of the defendant's website, which is retrievable through the "Wayback Machine," a well-known and heavily utilized service operated by the nonprofit organization Internet Archive. Is judicial notice appropriate? If not, how could the material obtained from the Wayback Machine be authenticated and introduced into evidence?

12.11. For purposes of determining the admissibility of DNA identification evidence, can a court take judicial notice of the general reliability of the particular technology employed, without holding an evidentiary hearing? (Some courts have said yes.)

TABLE OF CASES

Principal cases are indicated by italics.

TABLE OF RULES, STATUTES, AND CONSTITUTIONAL PROVISIONS

Index